A HISTORY OF WORLD SOCIETIES

FOURTH EDITION

A History of World Societies

❋ *Volume I*
To 1715

John P. McKay

University of Illinois at
Urbana-Champaign

Bennett D. Hill

Georgetown University

John Buckler

University of Illinois at
Urbana-Champaign

HOUGHTON MIFFLIN COMPANY

Boston   Toronto
Geneva, Illinois   Palo Alto
Princeton, New Jersey

Senior Sponsoring Editor: Patricia A. Coryell
Senior Associate Editor: Jeffrey Greene
Manufacturing Manager: Florence Cadran
Marketing Manager: Clint Crockett

Credits: Pp. 17 and 23: From S. N. Kramer, *The Sumerians* (Chicago: University of Chicago Press, 1964), p. 238. Copyright University of Chicago Press. Reprinted by permission. p. 23: J. B. Pritchard, ed., *Ancient Near Eastern Texts*, Third edition. Copyright 1969 by Princeton University Press. Reprinted by permission of Princeton University Press. P. 72: Rigveda 10.90, translated by A. D. Baham, in *The Wonder That Was India* (New York: Grove Press, 1959). Reprinted by permission of Sidgwick & Jackson, London. P. 74: Juan Mascaro, trans., *The Upanishads* (London: Penguin Classics, 1965), pp. 117–118. Copyright Juan Mascaro, 1965. Reproduced by permission of Penguin Books Ltd. P. 75: *The Mahabharata*, J. A. B. van Buitenen, trans. Copyright 1973 by University of Chicago Press. Reprinted by permission. P. 99: D. C. Lau, trans. from *Book I of Tao Te Ching* by Lao Tzu (London: Penguin Classics, 1963), pp. 59, 75, and 82. Copyright D. C. Lau, 1963. Reproduced by permission of Penguin Books Ltd. P. 125: W. Barnstone, *Sappho*, Doubleday, 1965. Frag. 24, p. 22. Reprinted by permission of the author. P. 126: Reprinted by permission of the publishers and the Loeb Classical Library from J. M. Edmonds: *Greek Elegy and Iambius,* I. 70, frag. 10., Cambridge, Mass.: Harvard University Press, 1931. P. 256: From *The Muslim Discovery of Europe* by Bernard Lewis. Copyright 1983 by Bernard Lewis. Reprinted by permission of W. W. Norton & Company, Inc.

Cover image: *The Empress Theodora and her Court,* San Vitale, Ravenna, Italy. Art Resource, NY

Printed in the U.S.A.
Library of Congress Catalog Card Number: 95–77000
ISBN Student Text: 0-395-75378-3
ISBN Examination Copy: 0-395-76589-7
456789-VH-99   98

❈ ABOUT THE AUTHORS

John P. McKay Born in St. Louis, Missouri, John P. McKay received his B.A. from Wesleyan University (1961), his M.A. from the Fletcher School of Law and Diplomacy (1962), and his Ph.D. from the University of California, Berkeley (1968). He began teaching history at the University of Illinois in 1966 and became a professor there in 1976. John won the Herbert Baxter Adams Prize for his book *Pioneers for Profit: Foreign Entrepreneurship and Russian Industrialization, 1885–1913* (1970). He has also written *Tramways and Trolleys: The Rise of Urban Mass Transit in Europe* (1976) and has translated Jules Michelet's *The People* (1973). His research has been supported by fellowships from the Ford Foundation, the Guggenheim Foundation, the National Endowment for the Humanities, and IREX. His articles and reviews have appeared in numerous journals, including *The American Historical Review, Business History Review, The Journal of Economic History,* and *Slavic Review*. He edits *Industrial Development and the Social Fabric: An International Series of Historical Monographs.*

Bennett D. Hill A native of Philadelphia, Bennett D. Hill earned an A.B. at Princeton (1956) and advanced degrees from Harvard (A.M., 1958) and Princeton (Ph.D., 1963). He taught history at the University of Illinois at Urbana, where he was department chairman from 1978 to 1981. He has published *English Cistercian Monasteries and Their Patrons in the Twelfth Century* (1968) and *Church and State in the Middle Ages* (1970); and articles in *Analecta Cisterciensia, The New Catholic Encyclopaedia, The American Benedictine Review,* and *The Dictionary of the Middle Ages*. His reviews have

appeared in *The American Historical Review, Speculum, The Historian, The Catholic Historical Review,* and *Library Journal*. He has been a fellow of the American Council of Learned Societies and has served on committees for the National Endowment for the Humanities. Now a Benedictine monk of St. Anselm's Abbey, Washington, D.C., he is also a Visiting Professor at Georgetown University.

John Buckler Born in Louisville, Kentucky, John Buckler received his B.A. (*summa cum laude*) from the University of Louisville in 1967. Harvard University awarded him the Ph.D. in 1973. From 1984 to 1986 he was an Alexander von Humboldt Fellow at the Institut für Alte Geschichte, University of Munich. He has lectured at the Fondation Hardt at the University of Geneva, and has participated in numerous international conferences. He is currently the professor of Greek history at the University of Illinois. In 1980 Harvard University Press published his *The Theban Hegemony, 371–362 B.C.* He has also published *Philip II and the Sacred War* (Leiden 1989), and co-edited *BOIOTIKA: Vorträge vom 5. International Böotien-Kolloquium* (Munich 1989). He has assisted the National Endowment for the Humanities, and reviews articles for journals in the United States and Europe. He has published substantially on Plutarch in *Aufstieg und Niedergang der römischen Welt* (Berlin, New York. 1992). His articles have appeared in journals both here and abroad, including the *American Journal of History, Classical Philology, Rheinisches Museum für Philologie, Classical Quarterly, Wiener Studien, Symbolae Osloenses,* and many others.

Contents in Brief

❖ ❖ ❖ ❖ ❖ ❖ ❖ ❖

Contents

Maps

❖ ❖ ❖ ❖ ❖ ❖ ❖ ❖ ❖

Timelines/Genealogies

The comparative timeline, *A History of World Societies: A Brief Overview,* begins on page 594.

Listening to the Past

❋ ❋ ❋ ❋ ❋ ❋ ❋ ❋ ❋

Preface

A History of World Societies has grown out of our desire to infuse new life into the study of world civilization. We know full well that historians are using imaginative questions and innovative research to open up vast new areas of historical interest and knowledge. We recognize that these advances have dramatically affected economic, intellectual, and, especially, social history, and that new research and fresh interpretations are revitalizing the study of traditional, mainstream political, diplomatic, and religious developments. Despite history's vitality as a discipline, however, it seems to us that both the broad public and the intelligentsia have been losing interest in the past.

It is our conviction, based on considerable experience in introducing large numbers of students to the broad sweep of civilization, that a book reflecting current trends can excite readers and inspire a renewed interest in history and the human experience. Our strategy has been twofold.

First, we have made social history the core element of our work. We not only incorporate recent research by social historians but also seek to re-create the life of ordinary people in appealing human terms. A strong social element seems especially appropriate in a world history, for identification with ordinary people of the past allows today's reader to reach an empathetic understanding of different cultures and civilizations. At the same time we have been mindful of the need to give great economic, political, intellectual, and cultural developments the attention they deserve. We want to give individual students and instructors a balanced, integrated perspective so that they can pursue on their own or in the classroom those themes and questions that they find particularly exciting and significant.

Second, we have made every effort to strike an effective global balance. We are acutely aware of the great drama of our times—the passing of the era of Western dominance and the simultaneous rise of Asian and African peoples in world affairs. Increasingly, the whole world interacts, and to understand that interaction and what it means for today's citizens, we must study the whole world's history. Thus we have adopted a comprehensive yet manageable global perspective. We study all geographical areas and the world's main civilizations, conscious of their separate identities and unique contributions. We also stress the links between civilizations, for it is these links that have been transforming multicentered world history into the complex interactive process of different continents, peoples, and cultures that we see today.

CHANGES IN THE FOURTH EDITION

In preparing the fourth edition, we worked hard to keep *A History of World Societies* up-to-date and to strengthen our distinctive yet balanced approach. Six goals shaped our plan for this new edition.

More Concise Treatment of Western History

To achieve the optimal length, we shortened the text by approximately 10 percent overall. We accomplished this reduction primarily through cuts in Western-oriented material while adding important new information to our non-Western coverage. Thus the proportion of non-Western material has grown, but the overall length of the book has decreased. For this edition, two chapters on Rome were combined into one (Chapter 7), three chapters on medieval Europe were combined into two (Chapters 12 and 13), and three chapters on nineteenth-century Europe were combined into two (Chapters 25 and 26).

Updated Approach to Social History

In a thorough revision of our coverage of social developments we give greater attention to cultural and intellectual life and somewhat less to quantitative and demographic aspects. Increased emphasis on culture and attitudes invigorates our social history core and accurately reflects current scholarship and changing interests within the historical profession. Accordingly, this edition has expanded discussions of religious life, including the spread of Buddhism in ancient India (Chapter 3); popular religion in Mesopotamia (Chapter 1), in classical Greece (Chapter 5), in Aztec and Inca society (Chapter 14), and in revolutionary France (Chapter 23); the evolution of Jewish religion (Chapter 2), of Eastern monasticism (Chapter 8), and of Calvin's Geneva (Chapter 15); and the resurgence of Christianity (Chapter 31) and of Islam (Chapter 34) in the twentieth century.

Consistently greater attention to popular culture includes new sections on the experiences of Jews under Islam and Christianity (Chapter 9); on the cult of the royal mummies in Inca society (Chapter 14); on troubadour poets and recreation in the Middle Ages (Chapters 12 and 13); on community values in eighteenth-century Europe (Chapter 19); on Chinese attitudes toward wealth and consumption (Chapter 22); and on the counterculture in the 1960s (Chapter 33). New material on health and health care features recent research on medieval European practices and early hospitals (Chapter 12), on eighteenth-century practitioners in Europe (Chapter 19) and the Ottoman Empire (Chapter 21), and on declining birthrates in Asia and Latin America (Chapter 36).

Interactions between cultures are also highlighted: the relations between Egyptians and Nubians (Chapter 1), pagans and Christians (Chapter 7), Muslims and Jews (Chapter 9), European educated elites and popular classes (Chapters 18 and 19), Europeans and Africans in the slave trade (Chapter 20), Chinese and foreigners in the eighteenth century (Chapter 22), and rich and poor nations since 1945 (Chapter 36).

We also carefully revised sections on the life of the people to set social developments consistently in their broad historical context.

Incorporation of Recent Scholarship

We carefully revised every chapter to reflect recent scholarship. Because we are committed to a balanced approach, we once again incorporated important new findings on political, economic, and intellectual developments. Revisions of this nature include material on the Babylonian Captivity (Chapter 2), the spread of Buddhism in India (Chapter 3), living patterns in neolithic China (Chapter 4), democratic ideology in Athens and the political background of Plato and Aristotle's thought (Chapter 5), and Roman commerce and frontier relations between Romans and Germans (Chapter 7). Similar revisions in Chapter 8 through 17 incorporate new material on Islamic education in world perspective (Chapter 9), African geography (Chapter 10), the origins of European feudalism (Chapter 12), the Aztec practice of human sacrifice (Chapter 14), the political uses of pornography in early modern Europe (Chapter 15), and Louis XIV's relations with the nobility (Chapter 17).

There is important new material reflecting recent scholarship on the cultural impact of the Enlightenment (Chapters 18 and 19); the Swahili states and transatlantic slave trade (Chapter 20); the institutions of the Mughal state under Akbar (Chapter 21); Chinese foreign policy under the Qing (Chapter 22); banks in continental industrialization and the early labor movement (Chapter 24); the role of class conflict in nineteenth-century domestic politics, imperialism, and the origins of World War I (Chapters 26, 27, and 29); educational reforms and political culture in republican France (Chapter 26); the idea of race in the United States (Chapter 28); Nietzsche and his influence (Chapter 31); the Nazi state and the origins of Italian fascism (Chapter 32); and the growing diversity of life in the Third World (Chapter 35). Recent developments in Europe and the Western Hemisphere (Chapter 33) and in Asia and Africa, especially in China and South Africa (Chapter 34), are examined from an updated post–cold war perspective.

In short, recent research keeps the broad sweep of our history fresh and up-to-date.

Integrated Treatment of Women and Gender

We broadened our treatment of women's history and gender issues and integrated it into the main narrative rather than reserving it for separate sections. This approach reflects current scholarly thinking. Our updated discussion of Hellenistic women is integrated in the central narrative (Chapter 5). Gender roles and attitudes toward divorce are considered in the context of early Islam (Chapter 9). New material on European women in agriculture and commerce during the Middle Ages (Chapters 12 and 13), on gender roles in Aztec society (Chapter 14) and in early European arts and letters (Chapter 16), on women in the Ottoman Empire (Chapter 21), and on Japanese women in agriculture and family relations (Chapter 22) are appropriately positioned. Elite women and peasant women in village communities are reconsidered in the context of the Enlightenment (Chapters 18 and 19) and the French Revolution (Chapter 23). Women in twentieth-century European dictatorships are compared systematically (Chapter 32), and the place of women in Third World economic development and population growth is stressed (Chapter 35).

New "Problems of Historical Interpretation"

The addition of more "problems of historical interpretation" in the third edition was well received, so we increased their number in the fourth. We believe that the problematic element helps students develop the critical-thinking skills that are among the most precious benefits of studying history. New examples of this more open-ended, interpretive approach include the debate over the origins of Rome (Chapter 7), the impact of the Renaissance on the lives of ordinary and elite women (Chapter 15), the motives and legacy of Christopher Columbus (Chapter 16), popular reading habits in eighteenth-century Europe and their significance (Chapter 19), the question of racial identity in the United States and how it developed (Chapter 28), European social tensions and the origins of World War I (Chapter 29), the nature of twentieth-century dictatorships (Chapter 32), the validity of *Third World* as an analytical concept (Chapter 35), and prospects for the United Nations and world government (Chapter 36).

Revised Full-Color Art and Map Programs

Because the past can speak in pictures as well as in words, artwork remains an integral part of our book, and the illustrative component of our work was carefully revised. We added many new illustrations—our art program includes nearly two hundred color reproductions—letting great art and important events come alive. As in earlier editions, all illustrations were carefully selected to complement the text, and all carry captions that enhance their value. The use of full color throughout this edition clarifies the maps and graphs and enriches the textual material. The maps and their captions have been updated.

DISTINCTIVE FEATURES

Distinctive features, both new and revised, guide the reader in the process of historical understanding. Many of these features also show how historians sift through and evaluate evidence. Our goal is to suggest how historians actually work and think. We want the reader to think critically and to realize that history is neither a list of cut-and-dried facts nor a senseless jumble of conflicting opinions.

New Primary-Source Chapter Feature

One of our goals is to show how historians sift through and evaluate evidence—to suggest how historians actually work and think. We want to encourage students to think critically and to realize that history is neither a list of cut-and-dried facts nor a senseless jumble of conflicting opinions. To help students come to this realization, at the end of each chapter in the fourth edition we added a two-page passage from a primary source. This important new feature, entitled "Listening to the Past," extends and illuminates a major historical issue considered in the chapter. For example, in Chapter 3, a selection from the *Mahabharta* tells an ancient Indian creation story; and in Chapter 6, a selection from *Plutarch's Lives* recounts the sacrifice of a famous queen for her people. Chapter 12 presents a mind-opening Arab account of the First Crusade, and the German traveler Olearius provides a fascinating and influential picture of the Russian state and society in Chapter 17. A report on discussions with Africans concerning the abolition of the slave trade is found in Chapter 20, and a Jesuit priest's report on a trip to the Mughal court of Akbar is featured in Chapter

21. Writer Stephan Zweig probes the sexuality of young men and women in nineteenth-century Vienna in Chapter 26, and a reporter witnesses the bloody climax to Gandhi's civil disobedience in Chapter 30. A Jewish doctor who survived Auschwitz describes the horror of the Nazi death camps in Chapter 32, and poor rural women in today's Third World tell their stories in Chapter 35.

Each "Listening to the Past" section opens with a problem-setting introduction and closes with "Questions for Analysis" that invite students to evaluate the evidence as historians would. Drawn from writings addressing a variety of social, cultural, political, and intellectual issues, these sources promote active involvement and critical interpretation. Selected for their interest and importance and carefully fitted into their historical context, these sources do indeed allow students to listen to the past and to observe how history has been shaped by individual men and women, some of them great aristocrats, others ordinary folk.

Improved Chapter Features

Distinctive features from earlier editions have been retained but improved. To help guide students toward historical understanding, we again pose specific questions at the beginning of each chapter. These questions are answered in the course of each chapter, and each chapter ends with a concise summary. We re-examined and revised the questions and summaries to maximize their usefulness.

Once again in the narrative itself we quote extensively from a wide variety of primary sources, demonstrating in our use of these quotations how historians evaluate evidence. Thus the examination of primary sources is not only highlighted in the "Listening to the Past" material but is an integral part of the narrative as well. We believe that such extensive quotation from primary sources will help students learn to interpret and think critically.

Each chapter again contains an annotated listing of suggestions for further reading. Brief descriptions of each work will help readers know where to turn to continue thinking and learning about specific topics. These bibliographies have been revised and updated.

Revised Timelines

The chapter timelines that appeared in earlier editions are substantially improved, and the comparative timelines that were dispersed throughout the third edition have been brought together in an appendix at the end of the book. Comprehensive and easy to locate, this useful timeline will allow students to compare simultaneous political, economic, social, cultural, intellectual, and scientific developments over the centuries.

Flexible Format

World history courses differ widely in chronological structure from one campus to another. To accommodate the various divisions of historical time into intervals that fit a two-quarter, three-quarter, or two-semester period, *A History of World Societies* is published in three versions that embrace the complete work:

- One-volume hardcover edition: *A History of World Societies*
- Two-volume paperback edition: *A History of World Societies*, Volume 1, *To 1715* (Chapters 1–17), and Volume 2, *Since 1500* (Chapters 16–36)
- Three-volume paperback edition: *A History of World Societies*, Volume A, *From Antiquity Through the Middle Ages* (Chapters 1–14), Volume B, *From 1100 Through the French Revolution* (Chapters 13–23), and Volume C, *From the French Revolution to the Present* (Chapters 23–36)

Overlapping chapters in the two-volume and three-volume editions facilitate matching the appropriate volume with the opening and closing dates of a specific course.

ANCILLARIES

Our learning and teaching ancillaries enhance the usefulness of the textbook:

- *Study Guide*
- *Computerized Study Guide*
- *Instructor's Resource Manual*
- *Test Items*
- *Computerized Test Items*
- *Map Transparencies*

The excellent *Study Guide* has been thoroughly revised by Professor James Schmiechen of Central Michigan University. Professor Schmiechen has been a tower of strength ever since he critiqued our initial prospectus, and he has continued to give us many valuable suggestions as well as his warmly appreciated support. His *Study Guide* contains learning objectives, chapter summaries, chapter outlines, review questions, extensive multiple-choice exercises, self-check lists of important concepts and events, and a variety of study aids and suggestions. The fourth edition also retains the study-review exercises on the interpretation of visual sources and major political ideas as well as suggested issues for discussion and essay, chronology reviews, and sections on studying effectively. The sections on studying take the student through reading and studying activities like underlining, summarizing, identifying main points, classifying information according to sequence, and making historical comparisons. To enable both students and instructors to use the *Study Guide* with the greatest possible flexibility, the guide is available in two volumes, with considerable overlapping of chapters. Instructors and students who use only Volumes A and B of the textbook have all the pertinent study materials in a single volume: *Study Guide,* Volume 1 (Chapters 1–23). Those who use only Volumes B and C of the textbook also have all the necessary materials in one volume: *Study Guide*, Volume 2 (Chapters 13–36). The multiple-choice sections of the *Study Guide* are available in a *Computerized Study Guide*, a tutorial version that tells students not only which response is correct but also why each of the other choices is wrong; it also provides the number of the textbook page where each question is discussed. These "rejoinders" to the multiple-choice questions also appear in printed form at the end of the *Study Guide*. The *Computerized Study Guide* is available for IBM® computers.

The *Instructor's Resource Manual*, prepared by John Marshall Carter, contains instructional objectives, annotated chapter outlines, suggestions for lectures and discussion, paper and class activity topics, primary-source exercises, map activities, and lists of audio-visual resources. The accompanying *Test Items*, by Professor Charles Crouch of Georgia Southern University, offer identification, multiple-choice, map, and essay questions for a total of approximately 2,000 test items. These test items are available to adopters in both IBM® and Macintosh versions, both of which include editing capabilities.

In addition, a set of full-color *Map Transparencies* of all the maps in the textbook is available on adoption.

Acknowledgments

It is a pleasure to thank the many instructors who have read and critiqued the manuscript through its development.

Eva Baham
Southern University

Lester Bilsky
University of Arkansas, Little Rock

Kenneth Capalbo
Quincy University

Donald Clark
Trinity University

Frank Coppa
St. John's University

Francis Danquah
Southern University

Gloria-Thomas Emeagwali
Central Connecticut State University

Fuabeh Fonge
North Carolina Agricultural and Technical State University

Bruce Garver
University of Nebraska, Omaha

Ruth Hertzberg
Shippensburg University

Ahmed Ibriham
University of South Carolina

Michelle Scott James
MiraCosta College

Delmarie Klobe
Kapiolani Community College

David Kopf
University of Minnesota

Jim Norris
University of Arkansas, Monticello

Evelyn Rawski
University of Pittsburgh

Edward Reynolds
University of California, San Diego

Leila el-Tawil Sarieddine
Southern University

Cynthia Talbott
University of Northern Arizona

Colonel Steven Wager
United States Military Academy, West Point

Mary Watrous
Washington State University

Colonel James Scott Wheeler
United States Military Academy, West Point

Barbara Woods
South Carolina State University

It is also a pleasure to thank our editors at Houghton Mifflin for their effort and support over many years. To Elizabeth Welch, Senior Basic Book Editor, we owe a special debt of gratitude and admiration. To Jean Woy, Editor-in-Chief for History and Political Science, to Sean Wakely, Senior Sponsoring Editor, and to Jeff Greene, Senior Associate Editor, we express our sincere appreciation. And we thank most warmly Jan Fitter, Leslie Anderson Olney, and Carole Frohlich for their contributions in development, production, and art and photo research.

Many of our colleagues at the University of Illinois continued to provide information and stimulation for our book, often without even knowing it. N. Frederick Nash, Rare Book Librarian, made many helpful suggestions for illustrations, and the World Heritage Museum at the university allowed us complete access to its sizable holdings. James Dengate supplied information on objects from the museum's collection, and Caroline Buckler took many excellent photographs of the museum's objects. Such wide-ranging expertise was a great asset for which we are very appreciative. Bennett Hill wishes to express his sincere appreciation to Ramón de la Fuente for his patience, encouragement, and research assistance in the preparation of the fourth edition.

Each of us has benefited from the generous criticism of his co-authors, although each of us assumes responsibility for what he has written. John Buckler is the author of Chapters 1–7 and 11; Bennett Hill continues the narrative in Chapters 8–10, 12–16, 20–22, and 28; and John McKay is the author of Chapters 17–19, 23–27, and 29–36. Finally, we continue to welcome the many comments and suggestions that have come from our readers, for they have helped us greatly in this ongoing endeavor.

J.P.M.   B.D.H.   J.B.

A HISTORY OF WORLD SOCIETIES

1

Origins

A group of votive statuettes from the Abu Temple, Square Temple of the god Abu, Tell Asmar, 2700–2600 B.C. *(Source: Courtesy of The Oriental Institute of the University of Chicago, Victor J. Boswell, photographer)*

Before the dawn of history, bands of people across the earth gradually developed numerous cultures, each unique in some ways while at the same time having features in common. Especially important to the history of the world are events that took place in the ancient Near East (Mesopotamia, Anatolia, and Egypt), India, and China, where human beings abandoned the life of roaming and hunting to settle in stable agricultural communities. From these communities grew cities and civilizations—societies that invented concepts and techniques now integral to contemporary life. Fundamental is the independent development of writing by the Sumerians in Mesopotamia and by the Chinese, an invention that enabled knowledge to be preserved and facilitated the spread and accumulation of learning, lore, literature, and science. Mathematics, astronomy, and architecture were all innovations of ancient civilizations. So, too, were the first law codes and religious concepts, which still permeate daily life across the globe.

- How did nomadic hunters become urban dwellers?
- What geographical factors influenced this change?
- How do geographical factors explain both the elements common to different cultures and the features that differentiate them?

These questions sound the themes of the first four chapters. Chapters 1 and 2 look at how ancient Near Eastern civilizations helped to shape modern Western society. Chapters 3 and 4 explore the responses of the peoples of ancient India and China to these same questions.

✤ WHAT IS HISTORY AND WHY?

History is an effort to reconstruct the past to discover what people thought and did and how their beliefs and actions continue to influence human life. In order to appreciate the past fully, we must put it into perspective so that we can understand the factors that have helped to shape us as individuals, the society in which we live, and the nature of other peoples' societies. Why else should we study societies so separated from ours through time, distance, and culture as classical Greece, medieval India, early Japan, and modern Russia and Africa?

The matter of perspective is important. In a perfect world all human experience would be equally valuable for its own sake, even if it had little or no impact on the mainstream of history. Yet the evidence on which historians depend for their understanding of the past is far from perfect. Some peoples have left so few traces of themselves that they cannot be understood even in their own right, much less in connection with others. Such peoples are historical enigmas, best left to specialists while other historians examine the principal currents of human development. Historical perspective demands that most attention be devoted to peoples who are best known in their own context.

Historians begin to reconstruct the past by posing questions about it. How and why did cities emerge? How did the political system of a particular society evolve? How did people create an economic system to sustain a complex society? What were a society's religious beliefs, and how did they influence daily life? Historians ask such questions to guide their research and focus their approach to the past.

To answer such questions, historians examine *primary sources,* firsthand accounts of people who lived through the events—men and women who were in the best position to know what happened. Thus historians most commonly rely on the written record of human experience because, no matter how extensive the physical remains of a civilization may be, much of its history will remain a mystery if it has not left records that we can read. Until we are able to decipher the written texts left by the ancient civilization of Minoan Crete, for example, we can draw only vague conclusions about its history.

Of course, the historian's responsibility is to examine all of the evidence, not only written texts but nonverbal evidence. Examined properly, nonverbal sources provide a glimpse of the world as contemporaries saw it. Especially in conjunction with written documents, art can be a valuable and striking means of understanding the past. Similarly, archaeology has proved a valuable avenue to the past, whether an excavation uncovers an ancient Indian city, a medieval temple, or a modern factory building. Things as dissimilar as beautiful paintings and ordinary machines tell historians much about the ways in which people have lived and worked.

When studying written sources—the basic activity in historical research—historians assess the validity and perspective of each account. They try to determine whether sources are honest and accurate, generally by comparing and contrasting the testimony of several different observers. They criticize sources both externally, to attempt to uncover forgeries and errors, and internally, to find an author's motives for writing, inconsistencies within a document, biases, and even cases of outright lying. Some contemporary written accounts, especially from ancient and medieval periods, have been lost; they are known to posterity only because individuals who read the originals incorporated the information into their own writings. These *secondary sources* preserve much history that otherwise would have been lost. Thus historians analyze the viewpoints and accuracy of such derivative writings very carefully. For the modern period historians have a vast supply of primary sources—contemporary accounts of events, memoirs, personal letters, economic statistics, and government reports—all of them useful for understanding the past.

Once historians have pieced together what happened and have determined the facts, they interpret what they have found. Understanding of the past does not necessarily come easily. Unlike the exact physical sciences, history cannot reproduce experiments under controlled conditions, because no two historical events are precisely alike. A historian cannot put people into test tubes. Men, women, and children—the most complex organisms on this planet—are not as predictable as atoms or hydrocarbons.

To complicate matters further, for many epochs only the broad outlines are known, so interpretation is especially difficult. Historians know, for example, that the Hittite Empire collapsed at the height of its power, but interpretations of the causes of the collapse are still speculative. At the other end of the spectrum, some developments are so vast and complex that historians must master mountains of data before they can even begin to venture an interpretation. Events as diverse as the end of the western Roman Empire, the causes of the French Revolution, and the rise of communism in China are very complicated because so many people brought so many different forces to bear for so many different reasons. One simple explanation for such developments will never satisfy everyone, and this fact itself testifies to the complexity of human life.

Still another matter stands in the way of an accurate understanding of the past. Interpretations of the past sometimes change because people's points of view change. The values and attitudes of one generation may not be shared by another. Despite such differences in interpretation, the effort to examine and understand the past can give historians a perspective that is valuable in the present. By analyzing and interpreting evidence, historians come to understand not only the past but the relationship of the past to life today.

Social history, an important subject of this book, is itself an example of historians' reappraisal of the meaning of the past. For centuries historians took the basic facts, details, and activities of life for granted. Obviously, people lived in certain types of houses, ate certain foods that they either raised or bought, and reared families. These matters seemed so ordinary that few serious historians gave them much thought. Yet within our generation a growing number of scholars have demonstrated that the ways in which men, women, and children have lived are as worthy of study as the reigns of monarchs, the careers of great political figures, and the outcomes of big battles.

The topics of history and human societies lead to the question "What is civilization?" *Civilization* is easier to describe than to define. The word comes from the Latin adjective *civilis,* which means "pertaining to, or formed by, a citizen." Citizens willingly and mutually bind themselves in political, economic, and social organizations in which individuals merge themselves, their energies, and their interests in a larger community. In the course of time, *civilization* has come to embrace not only a people's social and political organization but also its particular shared way of thinking and believing, its art, and other facets of its culture—the complex whole that sets one people apart from other peoples who have different shared values and practices.

One way to understand this idea is to observe the origins and development of major civilizations, analyzing similarities and differences among them. At a fundamental level, the similarities are greater than the differences. Almost all peoples share some values, even though they may live far apart, speak different languages, and have different religions and political and social systems. By studying these shared cultural values, which stretch through time and across distance, we can see how the various events of the past have left their impression on the present and how the present may influence the future.

A word about culture is in order. *Culture* is normally defined as a particular type or stage of the intellectual, moral, artistic, and communal practices of a civilization. All people on this planet confront elemental challenges such as how to feed and shelter themselves (the economic aspect of culture) and how to govern their lives in harmony with others (the political and social aspects of culture). Cultures everywhere have felt the need to transmit to future generations what they have learned. Sometimes the content of the transmission is intellectual—for example, the preservation of astronomical information. Sometimes it is religious—for example, beliefs about the relation of the gods to humanity. Appreciation of life and the surrounding world has moved all peoples to create their own forms of art and music. Historians not only note the common themes to be found among various cultures but also study cultural differences. The study of history is the examination of how various peoples confronted and responded to the circumstances of their lives, what their responses had in common with the responses of others, and how their responses remained individual over time and across the planet earth.

THE FIRST HUMAN BEINGS

On December 27, 1831, young Charles Darwin stepped aboard the H.M.S. *Beagle* to begin a voyage to South America and the Pacific Ocean. In the course of that five-year voyage, he became convinced that species of animals and human beings had evolved from lower forms. At first Darwin was reluctant to publicize his theories because they ran counter to the biblical account of creation, which claimed that God had made Adam in one day. Finally, however, in 1859 he published *On the Origin of Species*. In 1871 he followed it with *The Descent of Man,* in which he argued that human beings and apes are descended from a common ancestor. Even before Darwin had proclaimed his theories, evidence to support them had come to light. In 1856 the fossilized bones of an early form of human

Paleolithic Cave Painting   All Paleolithic peoples relied on hunting for their survival. This scene, painted on the wall of a cave in southern France, depicts the animals normally hunted by the group of which the artist was a member. Paleolithic peoples may have hoped that by drawing these animals they would gain power over them. (*Source: Douglas Mazonowicz/Gallery of Prehistoric Art*)

were discovered in the Neander Valley of Germany. This "Neanderthal man," named after the place of his discovery, was physically more primitive than modern man (*Homo sapiens,* or thinking man). But he was clearly a human being and not an ape. Neanderthal man offered proof of Darwin's theory that *Homo sapiens* had evolved from less-developed forms.

Ideas of human evolution have changed dramatically, particularly in the past few years. Generations of paleoanthropologists—fossil hunters—have sought the "missing link." Ever since Darwin published his theories of evolution, scholars have tried to find the one fossil that would establish the point from which human beings and apes went their own different evolutionary ways. As recently as October 1994 scholars in Ethiopia found remains of a new species of hominid—a humanlike primate, showing both apelike and human skeletal features. The finders proudly suggested the discovery of the missing link, without being able to associate their hominid directly with other anthropological remains. But other recent discoveries have caused other scholars to question the very concept of the missing link and its implications. Fossil remains in China and Southeast Asia suggest that evolution was more complicated than paleoanthropologists previously thought and even that human beings may not have originated in Africa. In the light of the latest findings, paleoanthropologists must reinterpret their data; they must rethink everything that they have discovered.

The fossil record, extensive but incomplete, suggests that thousands of missing links may have existed, no one of them more important than any other. Given the small numbers of these primates and the extent of the globe, there is an almost infinitesimal chance of finding a skeleton that can be considered the missing link between other primates and human beings. A number of years ago Loren Eiseley, a noted American anthropologist, offered the wisest and humblest observation: "The human interminglings of hundreds of thousands of years of prehistory are not to be clarified by a single generation of archaeologists."[1]

Despite the enormous uncertainty surrounding human development, a reasonably clear picture can be drawn of two important early periods: the Paleolithic (Old Stone) Age and the Neolithic (New Stone) Age. The immensely long Paleolithic Age, which lasted from about 400,000 to 7000 B.C., takes its scholarly name from the crude stone tools the earliest hunters chipped from flint and obsidian, a black volcanic rock. During the much shorter Neolithic Age, which lasted from about 7000 to 3000 B.C., human beings began using new types of stone tools and, more important, pursuing agriculture.*

THE PALEOLITHIC AGE

Paleolithic peoples hunted a huge variety of animals, ranging from elephants in Spain to deer in China. The hunters were thoroughly familiar with the habits and migratory patterns of the animals on which they relied. But success in the hunt also depended on the quality and effectiveness of the hunters' social organization. Paleolithic hunters were organized—they hunted in groups. They used their knowledge of the animal world and their power of thinking to plan how to down their prey. Paleolithic peoples also nourished themselves by gathering nuts, berries, and seeds. Just as they knew the habits of animals, so they had vast knowledge of the plant kingdom. Some Paleolithic peoples even knew how to plant wild seeds to supplement their food supply. Thus they relied on every part of the environment for survival.

The basic social unit of Paleolithic societies was probably the family, and family bonds were no doubt stronger and more extensive than those of families in modern, urban, and industrialized societies. It is likely that the bonds of kinship were strong not just within the nuclear family of father, mother, and children but throughout the extended family of uncles, aunts, cousins, nephews, and nieces. People in nomadic societies typically depend on the extended family for cooperative work and mutual protection. The ties of kinship probably also extended beyond the family to the tribe. A tribe was a group of families led by a patriarch, a dominant male who governed the group. Tribe members considered themselves descendants of a common ancestor. Most tribes probably consisted of from thirty to fifty people.

---

*We follow the traditional practice in the West of expressing historical dates in relation to the birth of Jesus Christ. Dates before his birth are labeled B.C. (for *Before Christ*), and dates after his birth are labeled A.D. (*Anno Domini,* Latin for "in the year of the Lord"). A widely used alternative system refers to these dates as B.C.E. (Before the Common Era) and C.E. (Common Era).

 **Return of the Iceman**   This scene captures the discovery of a Neolithic herdsman who was trapped in the ice about fifty-three hundred years ago. The discovery was made by chance in September 1991. In an ancient accident, the man was sealed in ice with all of his tools, thus providing modern scholars with a unique view of the past. The discovery is so important that scientists have not yet done an autopsy on the corpse. *(Source: Paul Hanny/Liaison)*

As in the hunt, so too in other aspects of life—group members had to cooperate to survive. The adult males normally hunted abroad and between hunts made stone weapons. The women's realm was primarily the camp, but women too ranged through the neighborhood gathering nuts, grains, and fruits to supplement the group's diet. The women's primary responsibility was the bearing of children, who were essential to the continuation of the group. Women also had to care for the children, especially the infants. Part of women's work, too, was tending the fire, which served for warmth, cooking, and protection against wild animals.

Some of the most striking accomplishments of Paleolithic peoples were intellectual. They used reason to govern their actions. Thought and language permitted the lore and experience of the old to be passed on to the young. An invisible world also opened up to *Homo sapiens.* They developed the custom of burying their dead and leaving offerings with the body, perhaps in the belief that somehow life continued after death.

Paleolithic peoples produced the first art. They decorated cave walls with lifelike paintings of animals and scenes of the hunt. Located deep in the caves, some of these paintings still survive. Paleolithic peoples also began to fashion clay models of pregnant women and of animals. The statuettes of pregnant women seem to express a wish for fertile women to have babies and thus ensure the group's survival. The wall paintings and clay statuettes of Paleolithic peoples represent the earliest yearnings of human beings to control their environment.

THE NEOLITHIC AGE

Hunting is at best a precarious way of life, even when the diet is supplemented with seeds and fruits. Paleolithic tribes either moved with the herds and adapted themselves to new circumstances or perished. Several long ice ages—periods when glaciers covered vast parts of Europe—

subjected the small bands of Paleolithic hunters to extreme hardship.

Not long after the last ice age, around 7000 B.C., some hunters and gatherers began to rely chiefly on agriculture for their sustenance. Others continued the old pastoral and nomadic ways. Indeed, agriculture evolved over the course of time. Neolithic peoples had long known how to grow crops. The real transformation of human life occurred only when large numbers of people began to rely primarily and permanently on the grain they grew and the animals they domesticated. Agriculture made possible a more stable and secure life.

Neolithic peoples were responsible for many fundamental inventions and innovations that the modern world takes for granted. First, obviously, is systematic agriculture as the primary source of food. Neolithic peoples developed the primary economic activity of the entire ancient world and the basis of all modern life. With the settled routine of Neolithic farmers came the evolution of towns and eventually cities. Neolithic farmers usually raised more food than they could consume, and their surpluses gave rise to larger, healthier populations. Population growth in turn increased reliance on settled farming, for only systematic agriculture could sustain the growing numbers of people. Since surpluses of food could be bartered for other commodities, the Neolithic era also witnessed the beginnings of the large-scale exchange of goods. In time the increasing complexity of Neolithic societies led to the development of writing, prompted by the need to keep records and later by the urge to chronicle experiences, learning, and beliefs.

The transition to settled life had a profound impact on the family. The shared needs and pressures that encourage extended-family ties are less prominent in settled than in nomadic societies. Bonds to the extended family weakened. In towns and cities, the nuclear family was more dependent on its immediate neighbors than on kinfolk.

Nevertheless, the nomadic way of life and the family relationships it nurtured continued to flourish alongside settled agriculture. Dramatic evidence of this fact came to light on September 19, 1991, when a hiker in the Tyrolean Alps in Italy discovered the frozen body of a Neolithic herdsman. The corpse is the oldest found intact, and its preservation results from the man having been covered for some fifty-three hundred years by glacial ice. Although the discoverers did irreparable

damage to the site, enough remains to give a unique impression of European nomadic life and a surprising glimpse of its sophistication. The "Iceman," as he is now called, was found equipped with the implements of everyday life. Among them are advanced bows and arrows that prove a remarkable knowledge of ballistics. A number of tools, some of bone, wood, and even copper, show that European people were making the transition from the Neolithic Age to the time when they relied primarily on metals for their tools. Dental evidence suggests that the Iceman's diet consisted of milled grain. These findings strongly suggest that the Iceman was a hunter and gatherer but also that he and his society depended on tilled grain as a vital part of their diet. The Iceman proves that nomadic and pastoral life could and did coincide peacefully with the emerging agricultural settlements. Often farmers and nomads bartered with one another, each group trading its surpluses for those of the other. Although nomadic peoples continued to exist throughout the Neolithic period and into modern times, the future belonged to the Neolithic farmers and their descendants. The development of systematic agriculture may not have been revolutionary, but the changes that it ushered in certainly were.

Until recently, scholars thought that agriculture originated in the ancient Near East and gradually spread elsewhere. Contemporary work, however, points to a more complex pattern of development. For unknown reasons people in various parts of the world all seem to have begun domesticating plants and animals at roughly the same time, around 7000 B.C. Four main points of origin have been identified: (1) In the Near East, people in places as far apart as Tepe Yahya in modern Iran, Jarmo in modern Iraq, Jericho in Palestine, and Hacilar in modern Turkey (Map 1.1) raised wheat, barley, peas, and lentils. They also kept herds of sheep, pigs, and possibly goats. (2) In western Africa, Neolithic farmers domesticated many plants, including millet, sorghum, and yams. (3) In northeastern China, peoples of the Yangshao culture developed techniques of field agriculture, animal husbandry, potterymaking, and bronze metallurgy. (4) In Central and South America, Neolithic peoples domesticated a host of plants, among them corn, beans, and squash.

Once people began to rely on farming for their livelihood, they settled in permanent villages and built houses. The location of the village was cru-

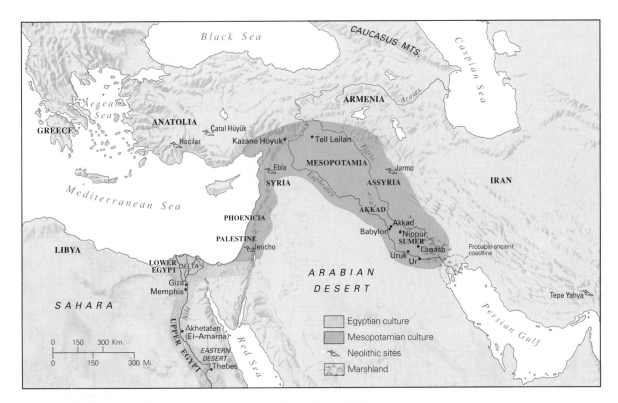

❋ **MAP 1.1 Spread of Cultures in the Ancient Near East**   This map illustrates the spread of Mesopotamian and Egyptian culture through a semicircular stretch of land often called the Fertile Crescent. From this area, knowledge and use of agriculture spread throughout the western part of Asia.

cial. Early farmers chose places where the water supply was constant and adequate for their crops and flocks. At first, villages were small, consisting of a few households. But by about 7000 B.C., as the population expanded and prospered, villages usually were transformed into walled towns. The fortifications were so large that they could have been raised only by a large labor force. They indicate that towns were developing social and political organization as well as growing in size and wealth. The fortifications, constructed by the whole community, would have been impossible without central planning.

One of the major effects of the advent of agriculture and settled life was a dramatic increase in population. The number and size of the towns prove that Neolithic society was expanding. Early farmers found that agriculture provided a larger and much more dependable food supply than hunting and gathering. No longer did the long winter months bring the threat of starvation.

Farmers learned to store the surplus for the winter. Because the farming community was better fed than ever before, it was also more resistant to diseases that kill people suffering from malnutrition. Thus Neolithic farmers were healthier and longer-lived than their predecessors.

The surplus of food had two other momentous consequences. First, grain became an article of commerce. The farming community traded surplus grain for items it could not produce itself. The community thus obtained raw materials such as precious gems and metals. Early towns in the region now known as Mesopotamia (see Map 1.1) imported copper from the north, and eventually copper replaced stone for tools and weapons. Trade also brought Neolithic communities into touch with one another, making possible the spread of ideas and techniques.

Second, agricultural surplus made possible the division of labor. It freed some members of the community from the necessity of raising food.

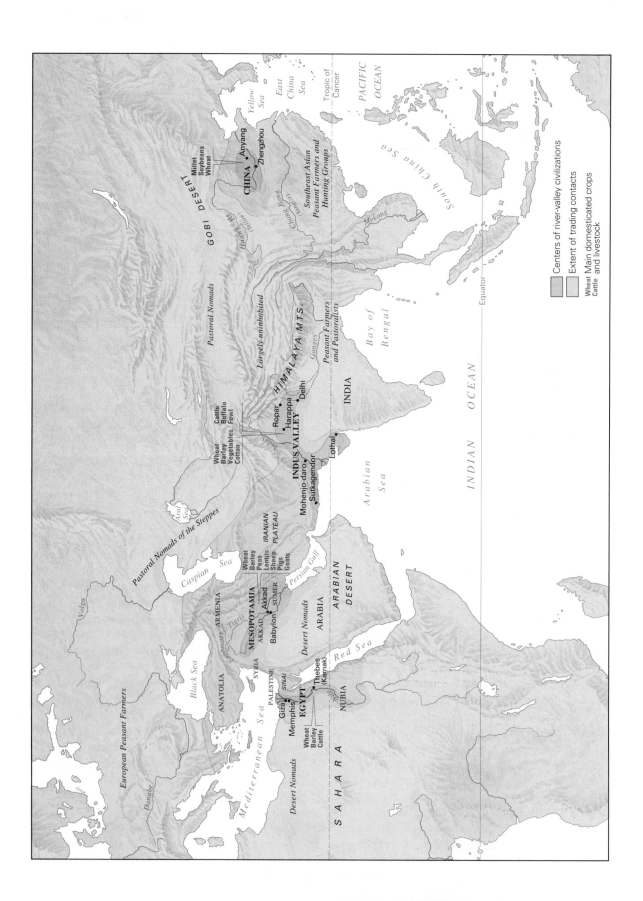

PACIFIC
OCEAN

East
China
Sea

Yellow
Sea

Tropic of
Cancer

GOBI DESERT

Millet
Soybeans
Wheat

Anyang
CHINA
Zhengzhou

Huang He (Yellow)

Chang Jiang (Yangtze)

Southeast Asian
Peasant Farmers and
Hunting Groups

Mekong

South China Sea

Pastoral Nomads

Largely uninhabited

HIMALAYA MTS.

Ganges

Peasant Farmers
and Pastoralists

Cattle
Buffalo
Fowl

Delhi

Ropar
Harappa

INDUS VALLEY

INDIA

Bay of
Bengal

Wheat
Barley
Vegetables
Cotton

Indus

Mohenjo-daro
Sutkagendor

Lothal

Aral
Sea

Pastoral Nomads of the Steppes

IRANIAN
PLATEAU

Wheat
Barley
Peas
Lentils
Sheep
Pigs
Goats

Arabian
Sea

INDIAN   OCEAN

Volga

Caspian
Sea

ARMENIA

Tigris

Euphrates

MESOPOTAMIA

AKKAD   Akkad

Babylon   SUMER

Persian Gulf

Equator

Black Sea

ANATOLIA

SYRIA

PALESTINE

SINAI

Desert Nomads

ARABIA

ARABIAN
DESERT

Red Sea

European Peasant Farmers

Danube

Mediterranean Sea

Giza
Memphis   EGYPT

Thebes
(Karnak)

NUBIA

Wheat
Barley
Cattle

Desert Nomads

SAHARA

Centers of river-valley civilizations

Extent of trading contacts

Wheat Main domesticated crops
Cattle and livestock

Some artisans and craftsmen devoted their attention to making the new stone tools that farming demanded—hoes and sickles for working in the fields and mortars and pestles for grinding grain. Other artisans began to shape clay into pottery vessels, which were used to store grain, wine, and oil and served as kitchen utensils. Still others wove baskets and cloth. People who could specialize in particular crafts produced more and better goods than any single farmer could.

Until recently it was impossible to say much about these goods. But in April 1985 archaeologists announced the discovery near the Dead Sea in modern Israel of a unique deposit of Neolithic artifacts. Buried in a cave were fragments of the earliest cloth yet found, the oldest painted mask, remains of woven baskets and boxes, and jewelry. The textiles are surprisingly elaborate, some woven in eleven intricate designs. These artifacts give eloquent testimony to the sophistication and artistry of Neolithic craftsmanship.

Prosperity and stable conditions nurtured other innovations and discoveries. Neolithic farmers improved their tools and agricultural techniques. They domesticated bigger, stronger animals, such as the bull and the horse, to work for them, and they invented tools such as the plow, which came into use by 3000 B.C. By then the wheel had been invented, and farmers devised ways of hitching bulls and horses to wagons. Neolithic farmers could raise more food more easily, because animals and machines were doing more of the work.

In arid regions such as Mesopotamia and Egypt, farmers learned to irrigate their land and later to drain it to prevent the buildup of salt in the soil. Water diverted from rivers opened new land to cultivation and deposited layers of rich mud, which increased the fertility of the soil. Thus the rivers, together with the manure of domesticated animals, kept replenishing the land. One result was a further increase in population and wealth. Irrigation, especially on a large scale, demanded group effort. The entire community had to plan which land to irrigate and how to lay out the canals. Then everyone had to help dig the canals. The demands of irrigation thus underscored the need for strong central authority within the community. Successful irrigation projects in turn strengthened such central authority by proving it effective and beneficial. Thus corporate spirit and governments to which individuals were subordinate—the makings of urban life—began to evolve.

The development of systematic agriculture was a fundamental turning point in the history of civilization. Farming gave rise to stable, settled societies, which enjoyed considerable prosperity. Settled circumstances and a certain amount of leisure made the accumulation and spread of knowledge easier. Sustained farming prepared the way for urban life.

❖ RIVERS, RESOURCES, AND CIVILIZATIONS

The development of systematic agriculture made possible a huge leap in human development, a leap that took place in several different parts of the world at roughly the same time (Map 1.2). In the ancient Near East, India, and China, Neolithic farmers created the conditions that permitted the evolution of urban civilization.

Certain geographical features were common to these early civilizations. The most important were the mighty river valleys in which they developed. The Egyptians relied on the Nile, the Mesopotamians on the Euphrates and the Tigris. The Indus nourished ancient Indian civilizations, and the great Yellow River in China made the birth of Chinese civilizations possible. Thus those four ancient civilizations could depend on a steady source of water, which also brought nutrients to the soil and fish as a source of food. Except for the violent Tigris and Yellow, the rivers also served as an easy means of communication. It was safer and simpler to use the Nile as a highway than to travel across the deserts surrounding Egypt. Likewise the Indus offered the fastest, most convenient path through the jungle. Communication facilitated the exchange of ideas while breaking down the barriers of isolation. The size and fertility of the broad valleys provided the food, wealth, and population, necessary ingredients to the development of large, sophisticated social structures.

❖ **MAP 1.2 River-Valley Civilizations** Although systematic agriculture developed in four great river valleys, variations in geography and climate meant that different crops were grown and societies emerged in distinct but similar ways.

Although great rivers were a common feature of these civilizations, soil and climate differed, and these differences left a significant imprint on human development. The rich mud carried by the Nile allowed abundant crops of wheat, and the dry desert air facilitated the preservation of surpluses of grain. The Indus flows through rich subtropical land well suited to growing a large variety of crops, but the humid climate quickly brought rot. Different climates meant that the rivers nurtured different crops and required different methods of agriculture. Geography and the means by which people turned it to their uses, then, influenced the way in which societies evolved.

In addition, the rivers themselves are different, demanding differences in the ways they were used. In Egypt and China, the peoples employed irrigation to bring water to arid land, enabling them to cultivate more fields. That was true in Mesopotamia too, but the farmers there also relied on irrigation to drain land to reclaim it for cultivation. In India farmers protected themselves against the floodwaters of the Indus while taking advantage of the rich mud that the river deposited. Whatever the differences, the rivers challenged early peoples to work together to make the best use of their geographical gifts, whether to divert water to new soil, to draw water from uncultivated fields, or to prevent water from destroying land already being farmed.

As the river-valley societies in the ancient Near East, India, and China outgrew their Neolithic past, they were forced to diversify their activities and abilities. New, centrally organized forms of government were required on a regular, permanent basis to coordinate massive irrigation projects, to administer the land, to govern the people, and to defend the people in time of war. Specialization in government and defense was part of a larger division of labor. Some members of society abandoned the plow to master the technology of metalworking. Others devoted themselves to the study of mathematics and architecture to meet the building needs of society. In the firm belief that they belonged to a world inhabited by gods, some people tried to explain the origin and workings of these higher beings, both to honor them and to teach their mysteries to others so that the divine and human could live in harmony. In the process they preserved traditions not only about their beliefs but also about their own lives—traditions that linked them to the past and helped them shape the future.

Knowledge became too valuable to lose and too complicated to be mastered easily. Whatever their specialization, people increasingly found it necessary to preserve knowledge and experience in a permanent form. To meet this need, they invented writing. They extended the experience of humanity beyond the individual's lifetime to future generations and created the foundations of an intellectual continuity that defied both time and death.

North and South America, Europe, sub-Saharan Africa, and Southeast Asia can all boast of many rivers. Yet only the peoples of Central America and the Incas of Peru in South America established civilizations comparable to those in the Near East, India, and China, though many centuries after the rise of the river-valley civilizations. Thus it seems clear that factors other than rivers were essential to the development of civilization. Climate may have been a limiting factor in places such as equatorial Africa and Southeast Asia. But why did nothing similar to Egyptian, Mesopotamian, Indian, and Chinese advances occur in areas of North America and Europe where the climate is relatively mild? The answer is that tools in those areas were primitive and totally inadequate. Instead of plowing the soil, early farmers not living in the river valleys of the Near East, India, or China mainly used hoes and digging-sticks. Lacking work animals, they relied on their own labor, not on animal power, to sow, harvest, and process grain. The crop yields that they worked so hard to get were so small that they could not expect sizable surpluses. The lack of food surpluses in turn made it hard for them to develop specialization of labor, to expand population, to build cities, and to accumulate knowledge in a durable form. Furthermore, areas such as parts of sub-Saharan Africa and the Caribbean are so naturally rich in readily available natural food resources that people did not have to toil for a living. Seldom did peoples in such areas develop sophisticated urban cultures.

Thus something more than geography, natural resources, climate, sustained agriculture, and population is needed to constitute a civilization. The significance of urban life to the growth of civilization cannot be overestimated. By banding together and observing common laws and values of life, people could pool their resources. Some people were farmers or craftsmen, and others were magis-

SIGNIFICANT EVENTS IN MESOPOTAMIAN HISTORY

PERIOD	EVENT
ca **3000** B.C.	Sumerians become prevalent in southern Mesopotamia
ca **2600** B.C.	Spread of Mesopotamian culture to northern Mesopotamia
ca **2331** B.C.	Sargon captures Sumer and creates a new capital, the city of Akkad
ca **1792** B.C.	Hammurabi wins control of Mesopotamia; Babylon the new capital of Mesopotamia
ca **1595** B.C.	Hittites and Kassites destroy Hammurabi's dynasty

trates or priests, but all cooperated to sustain and protect the community. Urban life provided the wealth, security, and stability to create civilization in its many forms.

Among the river-valley societies, nowhere can these abstractions be better seen than in the urban culture that flowered in the demanding environment of Mesopotamia, the first of the four societies to attain a level of development that can reasonably be called a civilization.

✵ MESOPOTAMIAN CIVILIZATION

An area roughly equivalent to modern Iraq, Mesopotamia drew its life from the Euphrates and Tigris rivers. Both have their headwaters in the mountains of Armenia in modern Turkey. Both are fed by numerous tributaries, and the entire river system drains a vast mountainous region. Overland routes in Mesopotamia usually followed the Euphrates because the banks of the Tigris are frequently steep and difficult. North of the ancient city of Babylon the land levels out into a barren expanse. The desert continues south of Babylon and still farther south gives way to a 6,000-square-mile region of marshes, lagoons, mud flats, and reed banks. At last, in the extreme south, the Euphrates and the Tigris unite and empty into the Persian Gulf (see Map 1.2).

This area became the home of many folk and the land of the first cities. The region around Akkad, near modern Baghdad, was occupied by bands of nomads related to one another by Semitic languages—languages that include Hebrew and Arabic. Into the south came the Sumerians, farmers and city builders who probably migrated from the east. By 3000 B.C. they had established a number of cities in the southernmost part of Mesopotamia, which became known as Sumer. As the Sumerians pushed north, they came into contact with the Semites, who readily adopted Sumerian culture and turned to urban life. The Sumerians soon changed the face of the land and made Mesopotamia the source of values and techniques that fundamentally influenced the societies of their immediate neighbors in both the West and the East (see Map 1.2).

In the context of world history, the capitalized terms "Western" and "Eastern" and "West" and "East" are *Eurocentric*—they describe events and culture from the viewpoint of European experience and values. This usage dates back to the ancient Greeks, who contrasted their life in "the West" with the lives of their non-Greek neighbors in the "East"—that is, in Africa and western Asia. Peoples in Asia and Africa would probably have dismissed the notion, and no one today uses the categories "West" and "East" to indicate the superiority of one set of historical developments to the other. Despite their flaws, the terms have come into

❄ **Aerial View of Ur** This photograph gives a good idea of the size and complexity of Ur, one of the most powerful cities in Mesopotamia. In the lower right-hand corner stands the massive ziggurat of Umammu. *(Source: Georg Gerster/Comstock)*

general use as a useful though artificial way to distinguish historical developments in Europe and the Americas from those in Asia.

Another expression already used in these pages, "the ancient Near East," also requires some explanation. It refers to a specific area of western Asia and northeastern Africa. In the north the ancient Near East included the western part of modern Turkey, extending south through the area now called the "Middle East" to Egypt in Africa. The major justification for this term is historical, not geographical. Although various peoples in this area developed their own civilizations to some extent independently, they did not develop in complete isolation but formed a well-defined unit.

Environment and Mesopotamian Culture

From the outset, geography had a profound effect on the evolution of Mesopotamian civilization. In this region agriculture is possible only with irrigation and good drainage. Consequently, the Sumerians and later the Akkadians built cities along the Tigris and Euphrates and their branches. Some major cities, such as Ur and Uruk, took root on tributaries of the Euphrates; others, notably Lagash, were built on tributaries of the Tigris (see Map 1.1). The rivers supplied fish, a major element of the city dwellers' diet. The rivers also provided reeds and clay for building materials. Since this entire area lacks stone, mud brick became the primary building block of Mesopotamian architecture.

Although the rivers sustained life, they also destroyed it by frequent floods that ravaged entire cities. Moreover, they restrained political development by making Sumer a geographical maze. Among the rivers, streams, and irrigation canals stretched open desert or swamp where nomadic tribes roamed. Communication among the isolated cities was difficult and at times dangerous. Thus each Sumerian city became a state, independent of the others and protective of its independence. Any city that tried to unify the country was resisted by the other cities. As a result, the political history of Sumer is one of almost constant warfare. Although Sumer was eventually unified, unification came late and was always tenuous.

The Invention of Writing and the First Schools

The origins of writing probably go back to the ninth millennium B.C., when Near Eastern peoples used clay tokens as counters for record keeping. By the fourth millennium people had realized that drawing pictures of the tokens on clay was simpler than making tokens. This breakthrough in turn suggested that more information could be conveyed by adding pictures of still other objects. The result was a complex system of pictographs in which each sign pictured an object. These pictographs were the forerunners of a Sumerian form of writing known as *cuneiform,* from the Latin term for "wedge-shaped," used to describe the strokes of the stylus.

How did this pictographic system work, and how did it evolve into cuneiform writing? At first, a scribe who wanted to indicate a star just drew a picture of it (line A of Figure 1.1) on a wet clay tablet, which became rock-hard when baked. Anyone looking at the picture knew what it meant and thought of the word for star. This system had serious limitations, for it could not represent abstract ideas or combinations of ideas. For instance, how could it depict a slave woman?

The solution to that problem appeared when the scribe discovered that signs could be combined to express meaning. To refer to a slave woman, the scribe used the sign for woman (line B) and the sign for mountain (line C)—literally, "mountain

Meaning	Pictograph	Ideogram	Phonetic sign
A Star			
B Woman			
C Mountain			
D Slave woman			
E Water In			

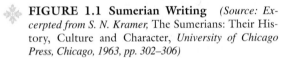

✳ **FIGURE 1.1 Sumerian Writing** *(Source: Excerpted from S. N. Kramer,* The Sumerians: Their History, Culture and Character, *University of Chicago Press, Chicago, 1963, pp. 302–306)*

woman" (line D). Because the Sumerians regularly obtained their slave women from the mountains, this combination of signs was easily understandable.

The next step was to simplify the system. Instead of drawing pictures, the scribe made conventionalized signs that were generally understood to represent ideas. Thus the signs became *ideograms:* they symbolized ideas. The sign for star could also be used to indicate heaven, sky, or even god.

The real breakthrough came when the scribe learned to use signs to represent sounds. For instance, the scribe drew two parallel wavy lines to indicate the word *a* or "water" (line E). Besides water, the word *a* in Sumerian also meant "in." The word *in* expresses a relationship that is very difficult to represent pictorially. Instead of trying to invent a sign to mean "in," some clever scribe used the sign for water because the two words sounded alike. This phonetic use of signs made possible the combining of signs to convey abstract ideas.

The Sumerian system of writing was so complicated that only professional scribes mastered it, and even they had to study it for many years. One graduate of a scribal school had few fond memories of the joy of learning:

My headmaster read my tablet, said:
"There is something missing," caned me.

. . . .

The fellow in charge of silence said:
"Why did you talk without permission," caned me.
The fellow in charge of the assembly said:
"Why did you stand at ease without permission,"
  caned me.[2]

The Sumerian system of schooling set the educational standards for Mesopotamian culture, and the Akkadians and later the Babylonians adopted its practices and techniques. Mesopotamian education always had a practical side because of the economic and administrative importance of scribes. Most scribes took administrative positions in the temple or palace, where they kept records of business transactions, accounts, and inventories. But scribal schools did not limit their curriculum to business affairs. They were also centers of culture and scholarship. Topics of study included mathematics, botany, and linguistics. Advanced students copied and studied the classics of Sumerian literature. Talented students and learned scribes wrote compositions of their own. As a result, many literary, mathematical, and religious texts survive today, giving a full picture of Mesopotamian intellectual and spiritual life.

Mesopotamian Thought and Religion

The Mesopotamians made significant and sophisticated advances in mathematics using a numerical system based on units of sixty, ten, and six. They developed the concept of place value—that the value of a number depends on where it stands in relation to other numbers. Mesopotamian mathematical texts are of two kinds: tables and problems. Scribes compiled tables of squares and square roots, cubes and cube roots, and reciprocals. They wrote texts of problems dealing not only with equations and pure mathematics but also with concrete matters such as how to plan irrigation ditches. The building of cities, palaces, temples, and canals demanded practical knowledge of geometry and trigonometry.

Mesopotamian medicine was a combination of magic, prescriptions, and surgery. Mesopotamians believed that demons and evil spirits caused sickness and that magic spells could drive them out.

Or, alternatively, they believed that a physician could force a demon out by giving the patient a foul-tasting prescription. As medical knowledge grew, some prescriptions were found to work and thus were true medicines. Physicians relied heavily on plants, animals, and minerals for recipes, often mixing them with beer to cover their unpleasant taste. Surgeons practiced a dangerous occupation, and the penalties for failure were severe. One section of Hammurabi's law code (see page 21) decreed: "If a physician performed a major operation on a seignior with a bronze lancet and has caused the seignior's death, or he opened up the eye-socket . . . and has destroyed the . . . eye, they shall cut off his hand."[3] No wonder that one medical text warned physicians to avoid a dying person.

Mesopotamian thought had its profoundest impact on theology and religion. The Sumerians originated many beliefs, and the Akkadians and Babylonians added to them. Although the Mesopotamians thought that many gods ran the world, they did not consider all gods and goddesses equal. Some deities had very important jobs, taking care of music, law, sex, and victory. Others had lesser tasks, overseeing leatherworking and basket weaving.

Divine society was a hierarchy. According to the Sumerians the air-god Enlil was king of the gods and laid down the rules by which the universe was run. Enki, the god of wisdom, put Enlil's plans into effect. The Babylonians believed that the gods elected Marduk as their king and that he assigned the lesser gods various duties. Once the gods received their tasks, they carried them out forever.

The Mesopotamians considered natural catastrophes to be the work of the gods. At times the Sumerians described their chief god, Enlil, as "the raging flood which has no rival." The gods, they believed, even used nature to punish the Mesopotamians. According to the myth of the Deluge, which gave rise to the biblical story of Noah, the god Enki warned Ziusudra, the Sumerian Noah:

A flood will sweep over the cult-centers;
To destroy the seed of mankind . . .
Is the decision, the word of the assembly of the gods.[4]

The Mesopotamians did not worship their deities because they believed their gods were benevolent. Human beings were too insignificant to pass judgment on the conduct of the gods, and the gods were too superior to honor human morals. Rather, the Mesopotamians worshiped the gods because they believed their gods were mighty. Likewise, it was not the place of men and women to understand the gods. The Sumerian equivalent to the biblical Job once complained to his god:

The man of deceit has conspired against me,
And you, my god, do not thwart him,
You carry off my understanding.[5]

The motives of the gods were not always clear. In times of affliction one could only pray and offer sacrifices to appease them.

The Mesopotamians had many myths to account for the creation of the universe. According to one Sumerian myth (echoed in Genesis, the first book of the Bible), only the primeval sea existed at first. The sea produced heaven and earth, which were united. Heaven and earth gave birth to Enlil, who separated them and made possible the creation of the other gods. Babylonian beliefs were similar. In the beginning was the primeval sea, the goddess Tiamat, who gave birth to the gods. When Tiamat tried to destroy the gods, Marduk, the chief god of the Babylonians, proceeded to kill her and divide her body and thus created the sky and earth. These myths are the earliest known attempts to answer the question "How did it all begin?" The Mesopotamians obviously thought about these matters, as they thought about the gods, in human terms. They never organized their beliefs into a philosophy, but their myths offered understandable explanations of natural phenomena. The myths were emotionally satisfying, and that was their greatest appeal.

Mesopotamian myths also explained the origin of human beings. In one myth the gods decided to make their lives easier by creating servants in their own image. Nammu, the goddess of the watery deep, brought the matter to Enki. After some thought, Enki instructed Nammu and the others:

Mix the heart of the clay that is over the abyss.
The good and princely fashioners will thicken the
  clay.
You, do you bring the limbs into existence.[6]

In Mesopotamian myth, as in Genesis, men and women were made in the divine image but without godlike powers.

Stele of Naramsin   Naramsin, the grandson of Sargon, was one of the greatest of the Akkadian kings. The topmost figure on this stele, or commemorative tablet, he displays his power by defeating his enemies in battle. Naramsin's horned crown suggests that he considered himself divine. *(Source: Louvre © Photo R.M.N.)*

One of the Mesopotamians' oldest deities was Inanna, a complicated goddess who represented the passions of love and war. Although she could be kind, she could also be harsh. She took many forms, one of the most important being mother-earth, who gave birth to everything in the world.

Inanna was worshiped by the Semites as Ishtar, and her cult lasted into Roman times.

In addition to myths, the Sumerians produced the first epic poem, the *Epic of Gilgamesh,* which evolved as a reworking of at least five earlier myths (see Listening to the Past). An epic poem is a narration of the achievements, labors, and sometimes the failures of heroes and embodies a people's or a nation's conception of its own past. Historians use epic poems to learn about various aspects of a society. The Sumerian epic recounts the wanderings of Gilgamesh—the semihistorical king of Uruk—and his companion Enkidu, their fatal meeting with the goddess Ishtar, after which Enkidu dies, and Gilgamesh's subsequent search for eternal life. Although Gilgamesh finds a miraculous plant that gives immortality to anyone who eats it, a great snake steals it from him. Despite this loss, Gilgamesh visits the lower world to bring Enkidu back to life, thereby learning of life after death. The *Epic of Gilgamesh* is not only an excellent piece of literature but also an intellectual triumph. It shows the Sumerians grappling with such enduring questions as life and death, humankind and deity, and immortality.

Sumerian Society

Their harsh environment fostered a grim, even pessimistic, spirit among the Mesopotamians. The Sumerians sought to please and calm the gods, especially the patron deity of the city. Encouraged and directed by the traditional priesthood, which was dedicated to understanding the ways of the gods, the people erected shrines in the center of each city and built their houses around them. The best way to honor the gods was to make the shrine as grand and as impressive as possible, for gods who had a splendid temple might think twice about sending floods to destroy the city.

Sumerian society was a complex arrangement of freedom and dependence, and its members were divided into four categories: nobles, free clients of the nobility, commoners, and slaves. The nobility consisted of the king and his family, the chief priests, and high palace officials. Generally, the king, at first elected by the citizenry, rose to power as a war leader. He established a regular army, trained it, and led it into battle. The might of the king and the frequency of warfare quickly made

him the supreme figure in the city, and kingship soon became hereditary. The symbol of royal status was the palace, which rivaled the temple in grandeur.

The king and the lesser nobility held extensive tracts of land that, like the estates of the temple, were worked by slaves and clients. Clients were free men and women who were dependent on the nobility. In return for their labor, the clients received small plots of land to work for themselves. Although this arrangement assured the clients of a livelihood, the land they worked remained the possession of the nobility or the temple. Thus the nobility not only controlled most—and probably the best—land but also commanded the obedience of a huge segment of society. They were the dominant force in Mesopotamian society.

Commoners were free citizens. They were independent of the nobility, but they could not rival the nobility in social status and political power. Commoners belonged to large patriarchal families that owned land in their own right. Commoners could sell their land if the family approved, but even the king could not legally take their land without their approval. Commoners had a voice in the political affairs of the city and full protection under the law.

Slavery has been a fact of life throughout history. Some Sumerian slaves were foreigners and prisoners of war. Some were criminals who had lost their freedom as punishment for their crimes. Still others served as slaves to repay debts. These were relatively fortunate because the law required that they be freed after three years. All slaves were subject to whatever treatment their owners might mete out. They could be beaten and even branded. Yet they were not considered dumb beasts. They could borrow money and received at least some legal protection. They engaged in trade and made profits. Indeed, many slaves bought their freedom.

❧ THE SPREAD OF MESOPOTAMIAN CULTURE

The Sumerians established the basic social, economic, and intellectual patterns of Mesopotamia, but the Semites played a large part in spreading Sumerian culture far beyond the boundaries of Mesopotamia. The interaction of the Sumerians and Semites, in fact, gives one of the very first glimpses of a phenomenon that can still be seen today. History provides abundant evidence of peoples of different origins coming together, usually on the borders of an established culture. The result is usually cultural change outweighing any hostility, for each side learns from the other. The outcome in these instances is the evolution of a new culture that consists of two or more old parts. Although the older culture almost invariably looks on the newcomers as inferior, the new just as invariably contributes something valuable to the old. So it was in 2331 B.C. The Semitic chieftain Sargon conquered Sumer and created a new empire. The symbol of his triumph was a new capital, the city of Akkad. Sargon, the first "world conqueror," led his armies to the Mediterranean Sea. Although his empire lasted only a few generations, it spread Mesopotamian culture throughout the Fertile Crescent, the belt of rich farmland that extends from Mesopotamia in the east up through Syria in the north and down to Egypt in the west (see Map 1.1).

Sargon's impact and the extent of Mesopotamian influence even at this early period have been dramatically revealed at Ebla in modern Syria. In 1964 archaeologists there unearthed a once-flourishing Semitic civilization that had assimilated political, intellectual, and artistic aspects of Mesopotamian culture. In 1975 the excavators uncovered thousands of clay tablets that proved that the people of Ebla had learned the art of writing from the Mesopotamians. Eblaite artists borrowed heavily from Mesopotamian art but developed their own style, which in turn influenced Mesopotamian artists. The Eblaites transmitted the heritage of Mesopotamia to other Semitic centers in Syria.

Further evidence of these developments came to light in November 1993, when American and Turkish archaeologists reported evidence of Sumerian influences far removed from Mesopotamia. At Tell Leilan in northern Syria and at Kazam Hoyuk in southern Turkey, researchers found proof of large urban centers that shared Sumerian culture as early as ca 2600 B.C. Finds included evidence of widespread literacy, a functioning bureaucracy, and links with Ebla and Mesopotamia. These discoveries also point to another conclusion. These frontier cities came under Sumerian influence not by conquest but because they found Mesopotamian culture attractive and useful. In this process, a universal culture developed in the ancient Near East, a culture basically Mesopotamian but fertilized by the traditions, genius, and ways of many other peoples.

The question to answer is why Mesopotamian culture had such an immediate and wide appeal. In the first place it was successful and enjoyed the prestige of its success. Newcomers wanted to find a respectable place in this old and venerated culture. It also provided an easy means of communication among people on a broad scale. The Eblaites could efficiently deal with the Mesopotamians and others who embraced this culture in ways that all could understand. Culture ignores borders. Despite local variations, so much common ground existed that similar political and economic institutions, exchange of ideas and religious beliefs, methods of writing, and a shared etiquette served as links among all who embraced Mesopotamian culture.

The Triumph of Babylon

Although the empire of Sargon was extensive, it was short-lived. The Akkadians, too, failed to solve the problems posed by Mesopotamia's geography and population pattern. Most scholars have attributed the fall of the Akkadian empire to internal problems and external invasions. Yet dramatic discoveries announced in August 1993 suggest strongly that climate also played a role in the demise of Akkadian power. Archaeologists have found evidence of a long, harsh drought, perhaps lasting as long as three hundred years, that struck the northern regions of the empire. The areas most severely affected were in modern Iraq, Syria, and parts of southern Turkey. Abandonment of the northern cities led to a stream of refugees to the south, overtaxing the economic resources of the cities there and straining their social and political structures. Cuneiform tablets mention this migration. The turmoil that resulted from this large influx of peoples may have contributed to the fighting that consumed the Akkadian empire.

It was left to the Babylonians to unite Mesopotamia politically and culturally. The Babylonians were Amorites, a Semitic people who had migrated from Arabia and settled on the site of Babylon along the middle Euphrates, where that river runs close to the Tigris. Babylon enjoyed an excellent geographical position and was ideally suited to be the capital of Mesopotamia. It dominated trade on the Tigris and Euphrates rivers: all commerce to and from Sumer and Akkad had to pass by its walls. It also looked beyond Mesopotamia. Babylonian merchants followed the Tigris north to Assyria and Anatolia. The Euphrates led merchants to Syria, Palestine, and the Mediterranean. The city grew great because of its commercial importance and soundly based power.

Sumerian Ram   In the art of many Near Eastern cultures, animals were symbols of fertility, linked to the gods. This ram standing behind a thorn bush represents a deity who has taken the form of an animal. *(Source: Courtesy of the Trustees of the British Museum)*

Babylon was also fortunate to have a farseeing and able king, Hammurabi (r. 1792–1750 B.C.). Hammurabi set out to do three things: make Babylon secure, unify Mesopotamia, and win for the Babylonians a place in Mesopotamian civilization. The first two he accomplished by conquering Assyria in the north and Sumer and Akkad in the south. Then he turned to his third goal.

Politically, Hammurabi joined in his kingship the Semitic concept of the tribal chieftain and the Sumerian idea of urban kingship. Culturally, he encouraged the spread of myths that explained how Marduk, the god of Babylon, had been elected king of the gods by the other Mesopotamian deities. Hammurabi's success in making Marduk the god of all Mesopotamians made Babylon the religious center of Mesopotamia. Through Hammurabi's genius the Babylonians made their own contribution to Mesopotamian culture—a culture vibrant enough to maintain its identity while assimilating new influences. Hammurabi's conquests and the activity of Babylonian merchants spread this enriched culture north to Anatolia and west to Syria and Palestine.

Life Under Hammurabi

One of Hammurabi's most memorable accomplishments was the proclamation of a law code that offers a wealth of information about daily life in Mesopotamia. Hammurabi's was not the first law code in Mesopotamia; indeed, the earliest goes back to about 2100 B.C. Like earlier lawgivers, Hammurabi proclaimed that he issued his laws on divine authority "to establish law and justice in the language of the land, thereby promoting the welfare of the people." Hammurabi's code inflicted such penalties as mutilation, whipping, and burning. Despite its severity, a spirit of justice and a sense of responsibility pervade the code. Hammurabi genuinely felt that his duty was to govern the Mesopotamians as righteously as possible. He tried to regulate the relations of his people so that they could live together in harmony.

The Code of Hammurabi has two striking characteristics. First, the law differed according to the social status of the offender. Aristocrats were not punished as harshly as commoners, nor commoners as harshly as slaves. Second, the code demanded that the punishment fit the crime. It called for "an eye for an eye, and a tooth for a tooth," at least among equals. However, an aristocrat who destroyed the eye of a commoner or slave could pay a fine instead of losing his own eye. Otherwise, as long as criminal and victim shared the same social status, the victim could demand exact vengeance.

Hammurabi's code began with legal procedure. There were no public prosecutors or district attorneys, so individuals brought their own complaints before the court. Each side had to produce written documents or witnesses to support its case. In cases of murder, the accuser had to prove the defendant guilty; any accuser who failed to do so was put to death. This strict law was designed to prevent people from lodging groundless charges. The Mesopotamians were very worried about witchcraft and sorcery. Anyone accused of witchcraft, even if the charges were not proved, underwent an ordeal by water. The gods themselves would decide the case. The defendant was thrown into the Euphrates, which was considered the instrument of the gods. A defendant who sank was guilty; a defendant who floated was innocent. (In medieval Europe and colonial America, accused witches also underwent ordeals by water, but they were considered innocent only if they sank.) Another procedural regulation covered the conduct of judges. Once a judge had rendered a verdict, he could not change it. Any judge who did so was fined heavily and deposed. In short, the code tried to guarantee a fair trial and a just verdict.

Consumer protection is not a modern idea; it goes back to Hammurabi's day. Merchants and businessmen had to guarantee the quality of their goods and services. A boatbuilder who did sloppy work had to repair the boat at his own expense. A boatman who lost the owner's boat or sank someone else's boat had to replace it and its cargo. Housebuilders guaranteed their work with their lives. If careless work resulted in the collapse of a house and the death of its inhabitants, the builder was put to death. A merchant who tried to increase the interest rate on a loan forfeited the entire amount. Hammurabi's laws tried to ensure that consumers got what they paid for and paid a just price.

Crime was a feature of Mesopotamian urban life just as it is in modern cities. Burglary was a serious problem, hard to control. Because houses were built of mud brick, it was easy for an intruder to dig through the walls. Hammurabi's punishment

Law Code of Hammurabi   Hammurabi ordered his code to be inscribed on a stone pillar and set up in public. At the top of the pillar Hammurabi is depicted receiving the scepter of authority from the god Shamash. (*Source: Hirmer Verlag München*)

for burglary matched the crime. A burglar caught in the act was put to death on the spot, and his body was walled into the breach that he had made. The penalty for looting was also grim: anyone caught looting a burning house was thrown into the fire.

Mesopotamian taverns were notorious haunts of criminals. Tavernkeepers were expected to keep order and arrest anyone overheard planning a crime. Taverns were normally run by women, and they also served as houses of prostitution. Prostitution was disreputable but neither illegal nor regulated by law. Despite their social stigma, taverns were popular places, for Mesopotamians were fond of beer and wine. Tavernkeepers made a nice profit, but if they were caught increasing their profits by watering drinks, they were drowned.

Because farming was essential to Mesopotamian life, Hammurabi's code dealt extensively with agriculture. Tenant farming was widespread. Tenants rented land on a yearly basis, paying a proportion of their crops as rent. Unless the land was carefully cultivated, it quickly reverted to wasteland. Thus tenants faced severe penalties for neglecting the land or not working it at all. Since irrigation was essential to grow crops, tenants had to keep the canals and ditches in good repair. Otherwise the land would be subject to floods and farmers to crippling losses. Anyone whose neglect of the canals resulted in damaged crops had to bear all the expense of the lost crops. If a tenant could not pay the costs of the damaged crops, he would then be sold into slavery.

The oxen that farmers used for plowing and threshing grain were ordinarily allowed to roam the streets. If an ox gored a passerby, its owner had to pad its horns, tie it up, or bear the responsibility for future damages. Sheep raising was very lucrative because textile production was a major Mesopotamian industry (Mesopotamian cloth was famous throughout the Near East). The shepherd was a hired man with considerable responsibility. He was expected to protect the flock from wild animals, which were a standing problem, and to keep the sheep out of the crops. This strict regulation of agriculture paid rich dividends. The Mesopotamians often enjoyed bumper crops of grain, which fostered a large and thriving population.

Hammurabi gave careful attention to marriage and the family. As elsewhere in the Near East, marriage had aspects of a business agreement. The prospective groom and the father of the future bride arranged everything. The man offered the father a bridal gift, usually money. If the man and his bridal gift were acceptable, the father provided his daughter with a dowry. After marriage the dowry belonged to the woman (although the husband normally administered it) and was a means of protecting her rights and status. Once the two men agreed on financial matters, they drew up a contract; no marriage was considered legal without

one. Either party could break off the marriage, but not without paying a stiff penalty. Fathers often contracted marriages while their children were still young. The girl either continued to live in her father's house until she reached maturity or went to live in the house of her father-in-law. During this time she was legally considered a wife. Once she and her husband came of age, they set up their own house.

The wife was expected to be rigorously faithful. The penalty for adultery was death. According to Hammurabi's code: "If the wife of a man has been caught while lying with another man, they shall bind them and throw them into the water."[7] The husband had the power to spare his wife by obtaining a pardon for her from the king. He could, however, accuse his wife of adultery even if he had not caught her in the act. In such a case she could try to clear herself before the city council, which investigated the charge. If she was found innocent, she could take her dowry and leave her husband. If a woman decided to take the direct approach and kill her husband, she was impaled.

The husband had virtually absolute power over his household. He could even sell his wife and children into slavery to pay debts. Sons did not lightly oppose their fathers, and any son who struck his father could have his hand cut off. A father was free to adopt children and include them in his will. Artisans sometimes adopted children to teach them the family trade. Although the father's power was great, he could not disinherit a son without just cause. Cases of disinheritance became matters for the city to decide, and the code ordered the courts to forgive a son for his first offense. Only if a son wronged his father a second time could he be disinherited.

Hammurabi's code restricted married women from commercial pursuits. Financial documents, however, prove that many women engaged in business without hindrance. Some carried on the family business. Others became wealthy landowners in their own right.

Law codes, preoccupied as they are with the problems of society, provide a bleak view of things. Other Mesopotamian documents give a happier glimpse of life. Although the code dealt with marriage in hard-fisted fashion, a Mesopotamian poem tells of two people meeting secretly in the city. Their parting is delightfully modern:

Come now, set me free, I must go home,
Kuli-Enlil . . . set me free, I must go home.
What can I say to deceive my mother?[8]

Countless wills and testaments show that husbands habitually left their estates to their wives, who in turn willed the property to their children. All this suggests happy family life.

Mesopotamians found their lives lightened by holidays and religious festivals. Traveling merchants brought news of the outside world and swapped marvelous tales. Despite their pessimism the Mesopotamians enjoyed a vibrant and creative culture, a culture that left its mark on the entire Near East.

EGYPT, THE LAND OF THE PHARAOHS (3100–1200 B.C.)

The Greek historian and traveler Herodotus in the fifth century B.C. called Egypt the "gift of the Nile." No other single geographical factor had such a fundamental, profound impact on the shaping of Egyptian life, society, and history as the Nile (Map 1.3). Unlike the rivers in Mesopotamia, it rarely brought death and destruction. The Nile was primarily a creative force. The Egyptians never feared the relatively tame Nile in the way the Mesopotamians feared the Tigris. Instead they sang its praises:

Hail to thee, O Nile, that issues from the earth and
*   comes to keep Egypt alive! . . .*
He that waters the meadows which Re created,
He that makes to drink the desert . . .
He who makes barley and brings emmer [wheat] into
*   being . . .*
He who brings grass into being for the cattle . . .
He who makes every beloved tree to grow . . .
O Nile, verdant art thou, who makest man and cattle
*   to live.*[9]

Dedication to the Sumerian Goddess Inanna
This alabaster and gold votive figurine dates to ca 2850 B.C. and is typical of many other figures dedicated to the gods. This one was found in the excavation of a temple of the goddess Inanna at Nippur. (*Source: Iraqi National Museum, Baghdad*)

To the Egyptians, the Nile was the supreme fertilizer and renewer of the land. Each September the Nile floods its valley, transforming it into a huge area of marsh or lagoon. By the end of November the water retreats, leaving behind a thin covering of fertile mud ready to be planted with crops.

The annual flood made the growing of abundant crops almost effortless, especially in southern Egypt. Herodotus, used to the rigors of Greek agriculture, was amazed by the ease with which the Egyptians raised crops:

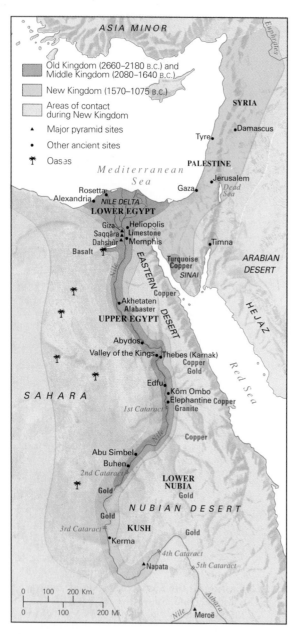

MAP 1.3 Ancient Egypt Geography and natural resources provided Egypt with centuries of peace and abundance.

pigs into it. When the pigs trample down the seed, he waits for the harvest. Then when the pigs thresh the grain, he gets his crop.[10]

The extraordinary fertility of the Nile Valley made it easy to produce an annual agricultural surplus, which in turn sustained a growing and prosperous population.

Whereas the Tigris and Euphrates and their tributaries carved up Mesopotamia into isolated areas, the Nile unified Egypt. The river was the region's principal highway, promoting easy communication throughout the valley. As individual bands of settlers moved into the Nile Valley, they created stable agricultural communities. By about 3100 B.C. there were some forty of these communities in constant contact with one another. This contact, encouraged and facilitated by the Nile, virtually ensured the early political unification of Egypt.

Egypt was fortunate because it was nearly self-sufficient. Besides the fertility of its soil, Egypt possessed enormous quantities of stone, which served as the raw material of architecture and sculpture. Abundant clay was available for pottery, as was gold for jewelry and ornaments. The raw materials that Egypt lacked were close at hand. The Egyptians could obtain copper from Sinai and timber from Lebanon. They had little cause to look to the outside world for their essential needs, which helps to explain the insular quality of Egyptian life.

Geography further encouraged isolation by closing Egypt off from the outside world (see Map 1.3). Yet Egypt was not completely sealed off. As early as 3250 B.C., Mesopotamian influences, notably architectural techniques and materials and perhaps even writing, made themselves felt in Egyptian life. Still later, from 1680 to 1580 B.C., northern Egypt was ruled by foreign invaders, the Hyksos. Infrequent though they were, such periods of foreign influence fertilized Egyptian culture without changing it in any fundamental way.

The God-King of Egypt

The geographical unity of Egypt quickly gave rise to political unification of the country under the authority of a king whom the Egyptians called *pharaoh*. The details of this process have been lost. Although some scholars have recently suggested

For indeed without trouble they obtain crops from the land more easily than all other men. . . . They do not labor to dig furrows with the plough or hoe or do the work which other men do to raise grain. But when the river by itself inundates the fields and the water recedes, then each man, having sown his field, sends

that the origins of Egyptian kingship can be found in Nubia, to the south of Egypt, the evidence is against the idea. First, the concept of kingship is an early and virtually worldwide political notion. Second, the Nubian artifacts so far found can be dated only by Egyptian archaeological finds. That suggests that the Nubians borrowed and adapted some of the symbols of the pharaoh and other aspects of Egyptian culture. What little is known of Nubian kingship indicates typical rule of a single region, in this case much of it mountainous. In contrast, Egyptian kingship is intimately connected with the Nile Valley. The pharaoh was the king of both Upper and Lower Egypt, a geographical situation that did not exist in Nubia.

Most probably, as was the case with the Mesopotamians and the Eblaites, the Egyptians and Nubians enjoyed a long period of mostly peaceful relations during which each learned from the other. Such exchanges of ideas involve the adaptation of certain aspects of culture to fit new, particular, and local circumstances. This situation is precisely what one routinely finds on frontiers. In these cases, all parties bring new ideas and customs together. As a result, they all assimilate what they desire and reject what they find unnecessary. Although the Nubian concept of kingship did not apply to Egyptian geographical conditions, the cultural bonds between the two peoples became so strong that they remained even after the Roman conquest of Egypt centuries later.

The Egyptians themselves told of a great king, Menes, who united Egypt into a single kingdom around 3100 B.C. Thereafter the Egyptians divided their history into *dynasties,* or families of kings. For modern historical purposes, however, it is more useful to divide Egyptian history into periods (see page 29). The political unification of Egypt ushered in the period now known as the Old Kingdom, an era remarkable for prosperity, artistic flowering, and the evolution of religious beliefs.

In religion, the Egyptians developed complex, often contradictory, ideas about an afterlife. These beliefs were all rooted in the environment. The climate of Egypt is so stable that change is cyclical and dependable: the heat of summer bakes the land, and in the fall the Nile always floods and replenishes it. The dry air preserves much that would decay in other climates. Thus there is an air of permanence about Egypt; the past is never far from the present.

This cyclical rhythm permeated Egyptian religious beliefs. According to the Egyptians, Osiris, a fertility god associated with the Nile, died each year, and each year his wife Isis brought him back to life. Osiris eventually became king of the dead, weighing human beings' hearts to determine whether they had lived justly enough to deserve everlasting life. Osiris's care of the dead was shared by Anubis, the jackal-headed god who annually helped Isis resuscitate Osiris. Anubis was the god of mummification, so essential to Egyptian funerary rites.

The focal point of religious and political life in the Old Kingdom was the pharaoh, who commanded the wealth, resources, and people of all Egypt. The pharaoh's power was such that the Egyptians considered him to be the falcon-god Horus in human form. The link between the pharaoh and the god Horus was doubly important. In Egyptian religion Horus was the son of Osiris (king of the dead), which meant that the pharaoh, a living god on earth, became one with Osiris after death. The pharaoh was not simply the mediator between the gods and the Egyptian people. He was the power that achieved the integration between gods and humans, between nature and society, that ensured peace and prosperity for the land of the Nile. The pharaoh was thus a guarantee to his people, a pledge that the gods of Egypt (unlike those of Mesopotamia) cared for their people.

The king's surroundings had to be worthy of a god. Only a magnificent palace was suitable for his home; in fact, the word *pharaoh* means "great house." The king's tomb also had to reflect his might and exalted status. To this day the great pyramids at Giza near Cairo bear silent but magnificent testimony to the god-kings of Egypt. The pharaoh's ability to command the resources and labor necessary to build a huge pyramid amply demonstrates that the god-king was an absolute ruler.

The Pharaoh's People

Because the common folk stood at the bottom of the social and economic scale, they were always at the mercy of grasping officials. The arrival of the tax collector was never a happy occasion. One Egyptian scribe described the worst consequences of such a visit:

❋   **Narmer Palette**   This ceremonial object celebrates the deeds of Narmer, but it also illustrates several of the attributes of the pharaoh in general. At the top left, the conquering pharaoh views the decapitated corpse of an unknown enemy, showing his duty to defend Egypt by defeating its enemies. This same theme recurs on the right where the pharaoh—also represented by the falcon, symbol of Horus—is about to kill a captive. *(Source: Jean Vertut)*

And now the scribe lands on the river-bank and is about to register the harvest-tax. The janitors carry staves and the Nubians rods of palm, and they say, Hand over the corn, though there is none. The cultivator is beaten all over, he is bound and thrown into a well, soused and dipped head downwards. His wife has been bound in his presence and his children are in fetters.[11]

That was an extreme situation. Nonetheless, taxes might amount to 20 percent of the harvest, and tax collection could be brutal.

Egyptian society seems to have been a curious mixture of freedom and constraint. Slavery did not become widespread until the New Kingdom. There was neither a caste system nor a color bar, and humble people could rise to the highest positions if they possessed talent. Most ordinary folk, however, were probably little more than serfs who could not easily leave the land of their own free will. Peasants were also subject to forced labor, including work on the pyramids and canals. Young men were drafted into the pharaoh's army, which served both as a fighting force and as a labor corps.

The vision of thousands of people straining to build the pyramids and countless artists adorning the pharaoh's tomb brings to the modern mind a distasteful picture of oriental despotism. Indeed, the Egyptian view of life and society is alien to people raised on Western concepts of individual freedom and human rights. To ancient Egyptians the pharaoh embodied justice and order—harmony among human beings, nature, and the divine. If the pharaoh was weak or allowed anyone to challenge his unique position, he opened the way to chaos. Twice in Egyptian history the pharaoh failed to maintain rigid centralization. During those two eras, known as the First and Second Intermediate periods, Egypt was exposed to civil war and invasion. But the monarchy survived, and in each period a strong pharaoh arose to crush the rebels or expel the invaders and restore order.

The Hyksos in Egypt (1640–1570 B.C.)

While Egyptian civilization flourished behind its bulwark of sand and sea, momentous changes were taking place in the ancient Near East, changes that would leave their mark even on rich, insular Egypt. These changes involved enormous and remarkable movements, especially of peoples who spoke Semitic languages.

The original home of the Semites was perhaps the Arabian peninsula. Some tribes moved into northern Mesopotamia, others into Syria and Palestine, and still others into Egypt. Shortly after 1800 B.C. people whom the Egyptians called *Hyksos,* which means "Rulers of the Uplands," began to settle in the Nile Delta. Many scholars have sought the origins of the Hyksos. Available evidence indicates that they entered Egypt from the areas of modern Israel and Lebanon. Yet that is only a partial explanation, for the movements of the Hyksos were part of a larger pattern of migration during this period. The history of Mesopotamia records many such wanderings of people in search of better homes for themselves. Such nomads normally settled in and accommodated themselves with the native cultures. The process was mutually beneficial: each group had something to give and to learn from the other. So it was in Egypt, although Egyptian tradition, as later

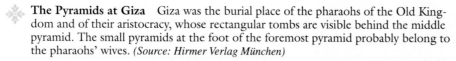

The Pyramids at Giza   Giza was the burial place of the pharaohs of the Old Kingdom and of their aristocracy, whose rectangular tombs are visible behind the middle pyramid. The small pyramids at the foot of the foremost pyramid probably belong to the pharaohs' wives. *(Source: Hirmer Verlag München)*

Hippopotamus Hunt This wall painting depicts the success of two men in a small boat who have killed a hippopotamus, seen in the lower right-hand corner. Behind the hippopotamus swims a crocodile hoping for a snack. *(Source: Egyptian Museum SMPK, Berlin/Bildarchiv Preussischer Kulturbesitz)*

recorded by the priest Manetho in the third century B.C., depicted the coming of the Hyksos as a brutal invasion:

In the reign of Toutimaios—I do not know why—the wind of god blew against us. Unexpectedly from the regions of the east men of obscure race, looking forward confidently to victory, invaded our land, and without a battle easily seized it all by sheer force. Having subdued those in authority in the land, they then barbarously burned our cities and razed to the ground the temples of the gods. They fell upon all the natives in an entirely hateful fashion, slaughtering them and leading both their children and wives into slavery. At last they made one of their people king, whose name was Salitis. This man resided at Memphis, leaving in Upper and Lower Egypt tax collectors and garrisons in strategic places.[12]

Although the Egyptians portrayed the Hyksos as a conquering horde, they were probably no more than nomads looking for good land. Their entry into the Nile Delta was probably gradual and generally peaceful. The Hyksos introduced new ideas and techniques into Egyptian life. They brought with them the method of making bronze and casting it into tools and weapons that became standard in Egypt. They thereby brought Egypt fully into the Bronze Age culture of the Mediterranean world, a culture in which the production and use of bronze implements became basic to society. Bronze tools made farming more efficient than ever before because they were sharper and more durable than the copper tools they replaced. The Hyksos's use of bronze armor and weapons, as well as horse-drawn chariots and the composite bow (made of laminated wood and horn and far more powerful than the simple wooden bow), revolutionized Egyptian warfare. But however much the Egyptians learned from the Hyksos, Egyptian culture eventually absorbed the newcomers. The Hyksos came to worship Egyptian gods and modeled their monarchy on the pharaonic system.

The New Kingdom: Revival and Empire (1570–1200 B.C.)

Politically, Egypt was only in eclipse during the Hyksos period. The Egyptian sun shone again when a remarkable line of kings, the pharaohs of the Eighteenth Dynasty, arose to challenge the Hyksos. The pharaoh Ahmose (1558–1533 B.C.) pushed the Hyksos out of the Nile Delta. Thutmose I (1512–1500 B.C.) subdued Nubia in the south, and Thutmose III (1490–1436 B.C.) conquered Palestine and Syria. These warrior-pharaohs

PERIODS OF EGYPTIAN HISTORY

PERIOD	DATES	SIGNIFICANT EVENTS
Archaic	3100–2660 B.C.	Unification of Egypt
Old Kingdom	2660–2180 B.C.	Construction of the pyramids
First Intermediate	2180–2080 B.C.	Political chaos
Middle Kingdom	2080–1640 B.C.	Recovery and political stability
Second Intermediate	1640–1570 B.C.	Hyksos "invasion"
New Kingdom	1570–1075 B.C.	Creation of an Egyptian empire Akhenaten's religious policy

inaugurated the New Kingdom—a period in Egyptian history characterized by enormous wealth and conscious imperialism. During this period and probably for the first time, widespread slavery became a feature of Egyptian life. The pharaoh's armies returned home leading hordes of slaves, who constituted a new labor force for imperial building projects.

The kings of the Eighteenth Dynasty created the first Egyptian empire. Egyptian religion and customs flourished in Nubia, making a huge impact on African culture there and in neighboring areas. The warrior-kings celebrated their success with monuments on a scale unparalleled since the pharaohs of the Old Kingdom had built the pyramids. Even today the colossal granite statues of these pharaohs and the rich tomb objects of Tutankhamen ("King Tut") testify to the might and splendor of the New Kingdom.

One of the most extraordinary of this unusual line of kings was Akhenaten (r. 1367–1350 B.C.), a pharaoh more concerned with religion than with conquest. Nefertiti, his wife and queen, encouraged his religious bent. Akhenaten's religion was often unpopular among the people and the traditional priesthood, and its practice declined in the later years of his reign. After his death, it was condemned and denounced; consequently, not much is known about it. Most historians, however, agree that Akhenaten and Nefertiti were *monotheists*— that is, believers in one universal god, the sun-god

Aton, whom they worshiped. They considered all other Egyptian gods and goddesses frauds and declined to worship them. Yet their belief suffered from an obvious inconsistency. Because the pharaoh himself was considered to be a god, Akhenaten's monotheism somewhat illogically embraced two divine beings. What Akhenaten meant by monotheism was that Aton was the only real god among the traditional Egyptian deities.

Akhenaten's monotheism, imposed from above, failed to find a place among the people. His god had no connection with the past of the Egyptian people, who trusted the old gods and felt comfortable praying to them. The Egyptians had long worshiped a host of gods, chief among whom was Amon-Re, whom they worshiped as king of the gods. Many Egyptians were sincerely devoted to their traditional gods, who they thought had preserved Egypt and would grant them life after death.

To such genuine religious sentiments were added the motives of the traditional priesthood. Many priests were scandalized by Akhenaten's brand of monotheism, and many were concerned about their own welfare. By deposing the old gods, Akhenaten destroyed the priests' livelihood and their reason for existence. Out of pure self-interest, the established priesthood opposed Akhenaten, and their opposition drove the pharaoh to intolerance and persecution. With a vengeance he tried to root out the old gods and their rituals.

To celebrate his break with the past, Akhenaten built a new capital, Akhetaten, present-day El-Amarna (see Map 1.3). There Aton was honored with an immense temple and proper worship. Worship of Aton focused on truth (as Akhenaten defined it) and a desire for the natural. The pharaoh and his queen demanded that the truth be carried

Akhenaten and Aton This relief shows the pharaoh and his family giving offerings to Aton, who is represented as the sun. It also demonstrates a new realism in Egyptian art. *(Source: Egyptian Museum, Cairo)*

over into art. Unlike Old Kingdom painting and sculpture, which blended the actual and the abstract, the art of this period became relentlessly realistic. Sculptors molded exact likenesses of Akhenaten, despite his ugly features and misshapen body. Artists portrayed the pharaoh in intimate family scenes, playing with his infant daughter or expressing affection to members of his family. On one relief Akhenaten appears gnawing a cutlet of meat; on another he lolls in a chair. Akhenaten was being portrayed as a mortal man, not as the divine pharaoh of Egypt.

Average Egyptians were no doubt distressed and disheartened when their familiar gods were outlawed, for those were the gods who they believed had made Egypt powerful and unique. The fanaticism and persecution that accompanied the new monotheism were in complete defiance of the Egyptian tradition of tolerant *polytheism*—the worship of several gods. Thus when Akhenaten died, his religion died with him.

 ## THE HITTITE EMPIRE

At about the time the Hyksos entered the Nile Delta, the Hittites, who had long been settled in Anatolia (modern Turkey), became a major power in that region and began to expand eastward (Map 1.4). The Hittites were an Indo-European people. The term *Indo-European* refers to a large family of languages that includes English, most of the languages of modern Europe, Greek, Latin, Persian, and Sanskrit, the sacred tongue of ancient India. During the eighteenth and nineteenth centuries, European scholars learned that peoples who spoke related languages had spread as far west as Ireland and as far east as central Asia. In the twentieth century, linguists deciphered the language of the Hittites and the Linear B script of Mycenaean Greece. When both languages proved to be Indo-European, scholars were able to form a clearer picture of these vast movements. Archaeologists were able to date the migrations roughly and put them into their historical context.

Despite the efforts of many scholars, the original home of the Indo-Europeans remains to be identified. Judging primarily from the spread of the lan-

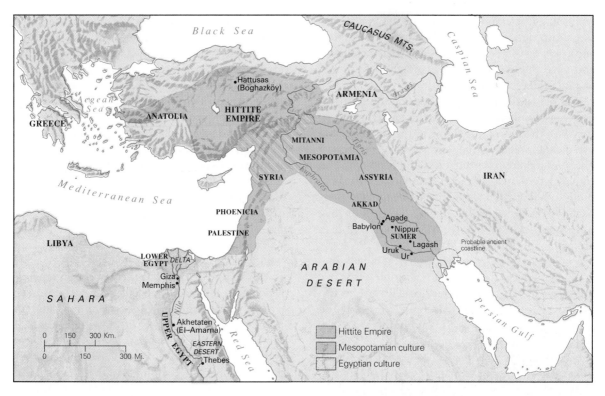

MAP 1.4 Balance of Power in the Near East   This map shows the regions controlled by the Hittites and Egyptians at the height of their power. The striped area represents the part of Mesopotamia conquered by the Hittites during their expansion eastward.

guages, linguists have suggested that the migrations started from the steppes region north of the Black and Caspian seas. Although two great waves began around 2000 B.C. and 1200 B.C., these migrations on the whole followed a sporadic and gradual progression. The Celtic-speaking Gauls, for example, did not move into the area of present-day France, Belgium, and Germany until the seventh century B.C., long after most Indo-Europeans had found new homes.

Around 2000 B.C. Indo-Europeans were on the move on a massive scale. Peoples speaking the ancestor of Latin pushed into Italy, and Greek-speaking Mycenaeans settled in Greece. The Hittites came into prominence in Anatolia, and other folk thrust into Iran, India, and central Asia. At first the waves of Indo-Europeans and other peoples disrupted already existing states, but in time the newcomers settled down.

The Rise of the Hittites

Until recently, scholars thought that as part of these vast movements the Hittites entered Anatolia only around 1800 B.C. Current archaeological work and new documents, however, prove that the Hittites had settled there at least as early as 2700 B.C. Nor did they overrun the country in a sweeping invasion, burning, looting, and destroying. Their arrival and diffusion seem to have been rather peaceful, accompanied by intermarriage and alliance with the natives. So well did the Hittites integrate themselves into the local culture of central Anatolia that they even adopted the worship of several native deities.

Their mastery of iron technology set the Hittites apart. Although it is not yet known whether the Hittites were first to discover the possibilities of iron and the ways to use it, they mastered iron technology before anyone else in the Near East. Their knowledge permitted them to craft weapons and tools far superior to those of their neighbors and gave them a decided advantage in both war and commerce.

The rise of the Hittites to prominence in Anatolia is reasonably clear. During the nineteenth century B.C. the native kingdoms in the area engaged in suicidal warfare that left most of Anatolia's once-flourishing towns in ashes and rubble. In this climate of exhaustion the Hittite king Hattusilis I built a hill citadel at Hattusas (modern Boghazköy), from which he led his Hittites against neighboring kingdoms (see Map 1.4). Hattusilis's grandson and successor, Mursilis I (ca 1595 B.C.), extended the Hittite conquests as far as Babylon. With help from the Kassites, a people who had newly settled along the upper reaches of the Euphrates River, Mursilis captured the city and snuffed out the dynasty of Hammurabi. While the Hittites carried off Babylonian loot, the Kassites took control of the territory. Upon his return home, the victorious Mursilis was assassinated by members of his own family, an act that plunged the kingdom into confusion and opened the door to foreign invasion. Mursilis's career is representative of the success and weakness of the Hittites. They were extremely vulnerable to attack by vigilant and tenacious enemies. But once they were united behind a strong king, the Hittites were a power to be reckoned with.

Hittite Society

The geography of central Anatolia encouraged the rise of self-contained agricultural communities. Each was probably originally ruled by a petty king, but under the Hittites a group of local officials known as the Elders handled community affairs. Besides the farming population, Hittite society included a well-defined group of artisans who fashioned pottery, cloth, leather goods, and metal tools. Documents also report that traveling merchants peddled goods and gossip, reminding individual communities that they were part of a larger world. Like many other societies, ancient and modern, the Hittites held slaves, who nonetheless enjoyed certain rights under the law.

At the top of Hittite society was the aristocracy, among whom the relatives of the king constituted a privileged group. The king's relations were a mighty and often unruly group who served as the chief royal administrators. Hittite nobles often revolted against the king, a tendency that weakened central authority and left Hittite society open to outside attack. Below the nobles stood the warriors, who enjoyed the right to meet in their own assembly, the *pankus*. The pankus met to hear the will of the king but could not vote on policy. It was, however, a court of law with the authority to punish criminals.

Above the aristocracy stood the king and queen. The king was the supreme commander of the army, chief judge, and supreme priest. He carried on all diplomatic dealings with foreign powers and in times of war he personally led the Hittite army into the field. The queen held a strong, independent position. She had important religious duties to perform, and some Hittite queens engaged in diplomatic correspondence with foreign queens.

Like many other newcomers to the ancient Near East, the Hittites readily assimilated the cultures that they found. They soon fell under the powerful spell of the more advanced Mesopotamian culture. They adopted the cuneiform script for their own language. Hittite kings published law codes, just as Hammurabi had done, and their royal correspondence followed Mesopotamian forms. The Hittites delighted in Mesopotamian myths, legends, epics, and art. To the credit of the Hittites, they used these Mesopotamian borrowings to create something of their own.

The Era of Hittite Greatness (ca 1475–ca 1200 B.C.)

Like the Egyptians of the New Kingdom, the Hittites eventually produced an energetic and capable line of kings. Those kings restored order and rebuilt Hittite power by controlling the aristocracy, securing central Anatolia, and regaining Syria. Around 1300 B.C. the Hittites stopped the Egyptian army of Rameses II at the battle of Kadesh in Syria. Having fought each other to a standstill, the Hittites and Egyptians first made peace, then an alliance. Alliance was followed by friendship, and friendship by active cooperation. The two greatest powers of the early Near East tried to make war between themselves impossible.

 **Hittite Sphinx Gate**   Little praise can be heaped on Hittite art. This sphinx was a symbol of divine protection of the city of Alaca Hüyük. In much of the Near East the placement of ferocious-looking animals at the city gates to ward off evil was common. (*Source: Antonello Perissinotto, Padua*)

They next included the Babylonians in their diplomacy. All three empires developed an official etiquette in which they treated one another as "brothers." They made alliances for offensive and defensive protection and swore to uphold one another's authority. These contacts facilitated the exchange of ideas throughout the Near East. Furthermore, the Hittites passed much knowledge and lore from the Near East to the newly arrived Greeks in Europe (see Chapter 5). The details of Hittite contact with the Greeks are unknown, but enough literary themes and physical objects exist to prove the connection.

THE FALL OF EMPIRES (CA 1200 B.C.)

Like the Hittite kings, Rameses II (ca 1290–1224 B.C.) used the peace after the battle of Kadesh to promote the prosperity of his own kingdom. Free from the expense and waste of warfare, he concentrated the income from the natural wealth and the foreign trade of Egypt on internal affairs. In the age-old tradition of the pharaohs, he began new building projects that brought both employment to his subjects and grandeur to Egypt. From Nubia to the delta of the Nile he bedecked his kingdom with grand, new monuments. Once again, Egypt was wealthy and secure within its natural boundaries. In many ways, he was the last great pharaoh of Egypt.

This stable and generally peaceful situation endured until the late thirteenth century B.C., when invaders destroyed both the Hittite and the Egyptian empires. The most famous of these marauders, called "Sea Peoples" by the Egyptians, remain one of the puzzles of ancient history. Despite much new work, modern archaeology is still unable to identify the Sea Peoples satisfactorily. The reason for this uncertainty is that the Sea Peoples were a collection of peoples who went their own, individual ways after their attacks on the Hittites and Egyptians. It is known, however, that their incursions were part of a larger movement of peoples. Although there is serious doubt about whether the Sea Peoples alone overthrew the Hittites, they did deal both the Hittites and the Egyptians a hard blow, making the Hittites vulnerable to overland invasion from the north and driving the Egyptians back to the Nile Delta. The Hittites fell under the external blows, but the Egyptians, shaken and battered, retreated to the delta and held on.

SUMMARY

During the long span of years covered by this chapter, human beings made astonishing strides, advancing from primitive hunters to become builders of sophisticated civilizations. Four great rivers provided the natural conditions necessary to sustain settled life. Yet because the rivers presented different problems to different peoples, developments across the globe were not identical. By mastering the plant and animal worlds, human beings prospered dramatically. With their basic bodily needs more than satisfied, they realized even greater achievements, including more complex social groupings, metal technology, and long-distance trade. The intellectual achievements of these centuries were equally impressive. Ancient Near Eastern peoples created advanced mathematics, monumental architecture, and engaging literature. Although the societies of the Near East suffered stunning blows in the thirteenth century B.C., more persisted than perished. The great

achievements of Mesopotamia and Egypt survived to enhance the lives of those who came after.

NOTES

1. L. Eiseley, *The Unexpected Universe* (New York: Harcourt Brace Jovanovich, 1969), p. 102.
2. Quoted in S. N. Kramer, *The Sumerians,* (Chicago: University of Chicago Press, 1964), p. 238.
3. J. B. Pritchard, ed., *Ancient Near Eastern Texts,* 3d ed. (Princeton, N.J.: Princeton University Press, 1969), p. 175. Hereafter called *ANET.*
4. *ANET,* p. 44.
5. *ANET,* p. 590.
6. Kramer, *The Sumerians,* p. 150.
7. *ANET,* p. 171.
8. Kramer, *The Sumerians,* p. 251.
9. *ANET,* p. 372.
10. Herodotus, *The Histories* 2.14. Translated by John Buckler.
11. Quoted in A. H. Gardiner, "Ramesside Texts Relating to the Taxation and Transport of Corn," *Journal of Egyptian Archaeology* 27 (1941): 19–20.
12. Manetho, *History of Egypt,* frag. 42.75–77. Translated by John Buckler.

SUGGESTED READING

Those interested in the tangled and incomplete story of human evolution will be rewarded by a good deal of new work, much of it difficult. C. E. Oxnard, *Fossils, Teeth and Sex* (1987), concludes that the search for the "missing link" is the wrong approach because the question is ultimately impossible to answer. I. Rouse, *Migrations in Prehistory* (1989), studies population movements using information from cultural remains. A broad study about women's role in these events comes from M. Ehrenberg, *Women in Prehistory* (1989).

Some very illuminating general studies of Near Eastern developments have recently reached print. H. W. F. Saggs, *Civilization Before Greece and Rome* (1989), provides a fresh analysis of the period that incorporates archaeological and literary evidence to discuss the many achievements of ancient Eastern societies. Similar in nature is A. B. Knapp, *The History and Culture of Ancient Western Asia and Egypt* (1988), a good synthesis by an able scholar. H. J. Nissen examines a broad range of subjects in *The Early History of the Ancient Near East* (1988), which covers the period from 9000 to 2000 B.C., and in *Archaic Bookkeeping* (1993), which discusses the development of early writing and its use in the administration of the ancient economy. Most welcome is the publication of D. Schmandt-Besserat's two-volume work on the origins of writing: *Before Writing;* volume 1 (1992) explores the development of cuneiform writing, and volume 2 (1992) provides the actual evidence. There is nothing to match it on the topic.

H. Crawford, *Sumer and the Sumerians* (1991), gives a fresh appraisal of the Sumerians and poses some intriguing questions. In a very ambitious and thoughtful book, G. Algaze, *The Uruk World System* (1993), examines how the early Mesopotamians expanded their civilization. Older but still valuable is H. W. F. Saggs, *Everyday Life in Babylonia and Assyria* (1965), which offers a delightful glimpse of Mesopotamian life. G. Pettinato, the excavator of Ebla, gives the most thorough description of the site and its importance in *Ebla* (1991).

N. Grimal, *A History of Ancient Egypt* (1992), provides the most recent reassessment of Egyptian history. A bit older but still useful is C. G. Kemp, *Ancient Egypt: Anatomy of a Civilization* (1988), a comprehensive study of Egyptian society. A. Blackman, *Gods, Priests and Men* (1993), is a series of studies in the religion of pharaonic Egypt. B. S. Lesko, *The Remarkable Women of Ancient Egypt,* 2d ed. (1987), is a brief survey of aristocratic and ordinary women that concludes that Egyptian women led freer lives than women of the Greco-Roman period. G.

Robins, *Women in Ancient Egypt* (1993), which is richly illustrated, adds visual information to the literary sources. W. L. Moran, *The Amarna Letters* (1992), has translated the Egyptian documents that are so important to the understanding of events in the New Kingdom. Moran also includes a commentary that explains the significance of the documents. D. B. Redford, *Akenaten: The Heretic King* (1984), puts Akhenaten into his historical context, both political and religious. The title of L. Manniche, *Sexual Life in Ancient Egypt* (1987), aptly describes the book's subject. M. Lichtheim, *Ancient Egyptian Literature,* 3 vols. (1975–1980), is a selection of readings covering the most important periods of Egyptian history.

O. R. Gurney, *The Hittites,* 2d ed. (1954), is still a fine introduction by an eminent scholar. Good also is J. G. MacQueen, *The Hittites and Their Contemporaries in Asia Minor,* 2d ed. (1986). J. P. Mallory, *In Search of the Indo-Europeans* (1989), uses language, archaeology, and myth to study the Indo-Europeans. The 1960s were prolific years for archaeology in Turkey. A brief survey by one of the masters of the field is J. Mellaart, *The Archaeology of Modern Turkey* (1978), which also tests a great number of widely held historical interpretations. The Sea Peoples have been recently studied by T. and M. Dothan, *People of the Sea* (1992), who concentrate their work on the Philistines.

A truly excellent study of ancient religions, from Sumer to the late Roman Empire, is M. Eliade, ed., *Religions of Antiquity* (1989).

PAST

A Quest for Immortality

The human desire to escape the grip of death, to achieve immortality, is one of the oldest wishes of all peoples. The Sumerian Epic of Gilgamesh *is the earliest recorded treatment of this topic. The oldest elements of the epic go back at least to the third millennium B.C. According to tradition, Gilgamesh was a king of Uruk whom the Sumerians, Babylonians, and Assyrians considered a hero-king and a god. In the story Gilgamesh and his friend Enkidu set out to attain immortality and join the ranks of the gods. They attempt to do so by performing wondrous feats against fearsome agents of the gods, who are determined to thwart them.*

During their quest Enkidu dies. Gilgamesh, more determined than ever to become immortal, begins seeking anyone who might tell him how to do so. His journey involves the effort not only to escape from death but also to reach an understanding of the meaning of life.

The passage begins with Enkidu speaking of a dream that foretells his own death.

Listen, my friend [Gilgamesh], this is the dream I dreamed last night. The heavens roared, and earth rumbled back an answer; between them I stood before an awful being, the sombre-faced man-bird; he had directed on me his purpose. His was a vampire face, his foot was a lion's foot, his hand was an eagle's talon. He fell on me and his claws were in my hair, he held me fast and I smothered; then he transformed me so that my arms became wings covered with feathers. He turned his stare towards me, and he led me away to the palace of Irkalla, the Queen of Darkness [the goddess of the underworld; in other words, an agent of death], to the house from which none who enters ever returns, down the road from which there is no coming back.

At this point Enkidu dies, whereupon Gilgamesh sets off on his quest for the secret of immortality. During his travels he meets with Siduri, the wise and good-natured goddess of wine, who gives him the following advice.

Gilgamesh, where are you hurrying to? You will never find that life for which you are looking. When the gods created man they allotted to him death, but life they retained in their own keeping. As for you, Gilgamesh, fill your belly with good things; day and night, night and day, dance and be merry, feast and rejoice. Let your clothes be fresh, bathe yourself in water, cherish the little child that holds your hand, and make your wife happy in your embrace; for this too is the lot of man.

Ignoring Siduri's advice, Gilgamesh continues his journey, until he finds Utnapishtim. Meeting Utnapishtim is especially important because, like Gilgamesh, he was once a mortal but the gods so favored him that they put him in an eternal paradise. Gilgamesh puts to Utnapishtim the question that is the reason for his quest.

Oh, father Utnapishtim, you who have entered the assembly of the gods, I wish to question you concerning the living and the dead, how shall I find the life for which I am searching?

Utnapishtim said "There is no permanence. Do we build a house to stand forever, do we seal a contract to hold for all time? Do brothers divide an inheritance to keep forever, does the flood-time of rivers endure? . . . What is there between the master and the servant when both have fulfilled their doom? When the Anunnaki [the gods of the underworld], the judges, come together, and Mammetun [the goddess of fate] the mother of destinies, together they decree the fates of men. Life and death they allot but the day of death they do not disclose.

Then Gilgamesh said to Utnapishtim the Faraway, "I look at you now, Utnapishtim, and your appearance is no different from mine; there is nothing strange in your features. I thought I should find you like a hero prepared for battle, but you lie here taking your ease on your back. Tell me truly, how was it that you came to enter the company of the gods and to possess everlasting life?" Utnapishtim said to Gilgamesh, "I shall reveal to you a mystery, I shall tell you a secret of the gods."

Utnapishtim then tells Gilgamesh of a time when the great god Enlil had become angered with the Sumerians and encouraged the other gods to wipe out humanity. The god Ea, however, warned Utnapishtim about the gods' decision to send a great flood to destroy the Sumerians. He commanded Utnapishtim to build a boat big enough to hold his family, various artisans, and all animals in order to survive the flood that was to come. Although Enlil was infuriated by the Sumerians' survival, Ea rebuked him. Then Enlil relented and blessed Utnapishtim with eternal paradise. After telling the story, Utnapishtim foretells Gilgamesh's fate.

Utnapishtim said, ". . . The destiny was fulfilled which the father of the gods, Enlil of the mountain, had decreed for Gilgamesh: In nether-earth the darkness will show him a light: of mankind, all that are known, none will leave a monument for generations to compare with his. The heroes, the wise men, like the new moon have their waxing and waning. Men will say, Who has ever ruled with might and power like his? As in the dark month, the month of shadows, so without him there is no light. O Gilgamesh, this was the meaning of your dream [of immortality]. You were given the kingship, such was your destiny, everlasting life was not your destiny. Because of this do not be sad at heart, do not be grieved or oppressed; he [Enlil] has given you power to bind and to loose, to be the darkness and the light of mankind. He has given unexampled supremacy over the people, victory in battle from which no fugitive re-

⚜ Gilgamesh, from the decorative panel of a lyre unearthed at Ur. (*Source: The University Museum, University of Pennsylvania*)

turns, in forays and assaults from which there is no going back. But do not abuse this power, deal justly with your servants in the palace, deal justly before the face of the Sun."

Questions for Analysis

1. What does *The Epic of Gilgamesh* reveal about Sumerian attitudes toward the gods and human beings?

2. At the end of his quest, did Gilgamesh achieve immortality? If so, what was the nature of that immortality?

3. What does the epic tell us about Sumerian views of the nature of human life? Where do human beings fit into the cosmic world?

Source: *The Epic of Gilgamesh,* translated by N. K. Sanders. Copyright © 1972 by Penguin Books, Ltd.

2

Small Kingdoms and Mighty Empires in the East

Reconstruction of the "Ishtar Gate," Babylon, early sixth century B.C. In the Berlin Museum. *(Source: Staatlich e Museen zu Berlin)*

The migratory invasions that brought down the Hittites and stunned the Egyptians in the late thirteenth century B.C. ushered in an era of confusion and weakness. Although much was lost in the chaos, the old cultures of the ancient Near East survived to nurture new societies. In the absence of powerful empires, the Phoenicians, Syrians, Hebrews, and many other peoples carved out small independent kingdoms. During this period Hebrew culture and religion evolved under the influence of urbanism, kings, and prophets.

In the ninth century B.C. this jumble of small states gave way to an empire that for the first time embraced the entire Near East. Yet the very ferocity of the Assyrian Empire led to its downfall only two hundred years later. In 550 B.C. the Persians and Medes, who had migrated into Iran, created a vast empire stretching from Anatolia in the west to the Indus Valley in the east. For over two hundred years the Persians gave the ancient Near East peace and stability.

- How did Egypt, its political greatness behind it, pass on its cultural heritage to its African neighbors?
- How did the Hebrew state and Hebrew religious thought evolve, and what was daily life like in Hebrew society?
- What enabled the Assyrians to overrun their neighbors, and how did their cruelty finally cause their undoing?
- How did Iranian nomads create the Persian Empire?

In this chapter we seek answers to these questions.

MIGRATIONS

The massive migrations of peoples during this period were merely one aspect of the movement of human populations that has been ongoing since the Paleolithic Age. Just as Indo-European and Semitic-speaking peoples sought new land around 1200 B.C., so in the nineteenth and twentieth centuries peoples from Europe and Asia came to North America seeking new opportunities for a more prosperous life. In antiquity, however, the picture is especially complex, and the reasons for movement are varied and unclear. The Hyksos moved into Egypt looking for new land (see pages 27–28). The later onslaught of the Sea Peoples on Egypt seems more like random raids than migrations even though many of the Sea Peoples established permanent homes elsewhere in the Mediterranean (pages 33–34). The Hebrews left Egypt to escape a harsh government (pages 40–41). In short, one major reason for migrations is the poverty of the environment, sometimes combined with overpopulation, which forces people to seek better land. Another is the reaction to vast movements of people. Weaker folk push ahead of the newcomers seeking new homes elsewhere and, as they move, create for others the same problems and challenges that they themselves had confronted. Still other migrants simply try to escape cruel or oppressive governments. In many instances more than one of these factors lie behind the migrations. Each case must be studied individually.

The effects of migrations are as varied as the reasons for them. Some newcomers, like the Hyksos and the Hittites, who came peaceably, draw important lessons from the established peoples whom they encounter, and they contribute something of their own to the cultural environment, which is thereby enriched for both the new arrivals and the native inhabitants. Other migrations result in the obliteration of the native population. As a result, some peoples are known today only by name. No one has yet studied this vast historical phenomenon on its own massive scale, but it can be safely said that the outcome of many of the migrations that occurred around the thirteenth century B.C. was a combination of destruction and fertilization.

EGYPT, A SHATTERED KINGDOM

The invasions of the Sea Peoples brought the great days of Egyptian power to an end. One scribe left behind a somber portrait of Egypt stunned and leaderless:

The land of Egypt was abandoned and every man was a law to himself. During many years there was no leader who could speak for others. Central government lapsed, small officials and headmen took over the whole land. Any man, great or small, might kill his neighbor. In the distress and vacuum that followed . . .

men banded together to plunder one another. They treated the gods no better than men, and cut off the temple revenues.[1]

Egyptians suffered a four-hundred-year period of political fragmentation, a new dark age known to Egyptian specialists as the Third Intermediate Period (eleventh to seventh centuries B.C.). The decline of Egypt was especially sharp in foreign affairs. Whereas the pharaohs of the Eighteenth Dynasty had held sway as far abroad as Syria, their weak successors found it unsafe to venture far from home. In the wake of the Sea Peoples, numerous small kingdoms sprang up in the Near East. Each was fiercely protective of its own independence. To those kingdoms Egypt was a memory, and foreign princes often greeted Egyptian officials with suspicion or even contempt. In the days of Egypt's greatness, petty kings would never have dared to treat Egyptian officials in such a humiliating fashion.

Disrupted at home and powerless abroad, Egypt fell prey to invasion by its African neighbors. Libyans from North Africa filtered into the Nile Delta, where they established independent dynasties. Indeed, from 950 to 730 B.C. northern Egypt was ruled by Libyan pharaohs. The Libyans built cities, and for the first time a sturdy urban life grew up in the delta. Although the coming of the Libyans changed the face of the delta, the Libyans genuinely admired Egyptian culture and eagerly adopted Egypt's religion and way of life.

In southern Egypt, meanwhile, the energetic Africans of Nubia extended their authority northward throughout the Nile Valley. Nubian influence in these years, though pervasive, was not destructive. Since the imperial days of the Eighteenth Dynasty (see pages 29–30), the Nubians, too, had adopted many features of Egyptian culture. Now Nubian kings and aristocrats embraced Egyptian culture wholesale. The thought of destroying the heritage of the pharaohs would have struck them as stupid and barbaric. Thus the Nubians and the Libyans repeated an old phenomenon: new peoples conquered old centers of political and military power and were assimilated into the older culture.

The reunification of Egypt occurred late and unexpectedly. With Egypt distracted and disorganized by foreign invasions, an independent African state, the kingdom of Kush, grew up in modern Sudan with its capital at Nepata. Like the Libyans, the Kushites worshiped Egyptian gods and used

Egyptian hieroglyphs. In the eighth century B.C. their king Piankhy swept through the entire Nile Valley from Nepata in the south to the delta in the north. United once again, Egypt enjoyed a brief period of peace during which Egyptians continued to assimilate their conquerors. In the kingdom of Kush, Egyptian methods of administration and bookkeeping, arts and crafts, and economic practices became common, especially among the aristocracy. Nonetheless, reunification of the realm did not lead to a new Egyptian empire. In the centuries between the fall of the New Kingdom and the recovery of Egypt, several small but vigorous kingdoms had taken root and grown to maturity in the ancient Near East. By 700 B.C. Egypt was once again a strong kingdom but no longer a mighty empire.

Yet Egypt's legacy to its African neighbors remained vibrant and rich. By trading and exploring southward along the coast of the Red Sea, the Egyptians introduced their goods and ideas as far south as the land of Punt, probably a region on the Somali coast. Egypt was the primary civilizing force in Nubia, which became another version of the pharaoh's realm, complete with royal pyramids and Egyptian deities. Egyptian religion penetrated as far south as Ethiopia. Just as Mesopotamian culture enjoyed wide appeal throughout the Near East, so Egyptian culture had a massive impact on northeastern Africa. Nor was Egyptian influence limited to Africa. Through earlier military, economic, and diplomatic contacts with Palestine and Syria, Egyptian ideas and beliefs later found their way to Europe.

✦ THE CHILDREN OF ISRAEL

The fall of the Hittite Empire and Egypt's collapse created in the western Near East a vacuum of power that allowed for the rise of numerous small states. No longer crushed between the Hittites in the north and the Egyptians in the south, various peoples—some of them newcomers—created homes and petty kingdoms in Syria, Phoenicia, and Palestine. After the Sea Peoples had raided Egypt, a branch of them, known in the Bible as Philistines, settled along the coast of Palestine (Map 2.1). Establishing themselves in five cities somewhat inland from the sea, the Philistines set about farming and raising flocks.

Another sturdy new culture was that of the Phoenicians, a Semitic-speaking people who had long inhabited several cities along the coast of modern Lebanon. They had lived under the shadow of the Hittites and Egyptians, but in this period the Phoenicians enjoyed full independence. Unlike the Philistine newcomers, who turned from seafaring to farming, the Phoenicians took to the sea and became outstanding merchants and explorers. In trading ventures they sailed as far west as modern Tunisia, where in 813 B.C. they founded the city of Carthage, which would one day struggle with Rome for domination of the western Mediterranean. Phoenician culture was urban, based on the prosperous commercial centers of Tyre, Sidon, and Byblos.

The Phoenicians' overwhelming cultural achievement was the development of an alphabet: they, unlike other literate peoples, used one letter to designate one sound, a system that vastly simplified writing and reading. The Greeks modified this alphabet and then used it to write their own language. The Phoenicians made another significant contribution by spreading the technical knowledge of ironworking. The Hittites were the first people in the Near East to smelt iron, but the Phoenicians passed the complex technique west to the Greeks and south to the Africans. Once in Africa, the technology spread farther south, though gradually. Most of West Africa had acquired the process by 250 B.C., and sub-Saharan Africa produced steel by A.D. 500.

South of Phoenicia arose another small kingdom, the land of the ancient Jews or Hebrews. It is difficult to say precisely who the Hebrews were and what brought them to this area because virtually the only source for much of their history is the Bible, which is essentially a religious document. Even though it contains much historical material, it also contains many Hebrew myths and legends. Moreover, it was compiled at different times; the earliest parts date to between about 950 and 800 B.C.

Earlier Mesopotamian and Egyptian sources refer to people called "Hapiru," which seems to mean homeless, independent nomads. According to Hebrew tradition, the followers of Abraham migrated from Mesopotamia, but Egyptian documents record Hapiru already in Syria and Palestine in the second millennium B.C. The Hebrews were probably a part of them. Together with other seminomadic peoples they probably migrated into the

MAP 2.1 Small Kingdoms in the Near East
This map illustrates the political fragmentation of the Near East after the great wave of invasions that occurred during the thirteenth century B.C.

Nile Delta seeking good land. According to the Bible the Egyptians enslaved them. One group, however, under the leadership of Moses, perhaps a semimythical figure, left Egypt in what the Hebrews remembered as the Exodus. From Egypt they wandered in the Sinai Peninsula until they settled in Palestine in the thirteenth century B.C. Their arrival was by no means peaceful. In a series of vicious wars and savage slaughters they suffered defeats and setbacks but slowly won a place and gradually spread their power northward. Archaeology testifies that the thirteenth century B.C. in Palestine was a time of warfare and disruption. It also shows that the situation in Palestine was far more complicated than the Bible suggests.

In Palestine the Hebrews encountered the Philistines; the Amorites, relatives of Hammurabi's

Standing Sphinx The sphinx was both a decorative and protective figure in ancient art and society. This ivory is a splendid illustration of the sphinx itself—part human, part bird, and part lion. This sphinx also displays the richness of Phoenician art at this period. *(Source: Iraqi National Museum, Baghdad)*

Babylonians; and the Semitic-speaking Canaanites. Despite the numerous wars, contact between the Hebrews and their new neighbors was not always hostile. The Hebrews freely mingled with the Canaanites, and some went so far as to worship Baal, an ancient Semitic fertility god represented as a golden calf. Archaeological research supports the biblical account of these developments. In 1990 an expedition sponsored by Harvard University discovered a statue of a golden calf in its excavations of Ashkelon in modern Israel. Despite the anger expressed in the Bible over Hebrew worship of Baal, there is nothing surprising about the phenomenon. Once again, newcomers adapted themselves to the culture of an older, well-established people.

The greatest danger to the Hebrews came from the Philistines, whose superior technology and military organization at first made them invincible. In Saul (ca 1000 B.C.), a farmer of the tribe of Benjamin, the Hebrews found a champion and a spirited leader. Saul was the Hebrews' first secular king (see Listening to the Past). According to the biblical account, Saul carried the war to the Philistines, often without success. Yet in the meantime he established a monarchy over the twelve Hebrew tribes. Thus, under the peril of the Philistines, the Hebrews evolved from scattered, independent units into a centralized political organization in which the king directed the energies of the people. From this period derives the name *Israelites* for these erstwhile nomads.

Saul's work was carried on by David of Bethlehem, who in his youth had followed Saul into battle against the Philistines. Through courage and cunning, David pushed back the Philistines and waged war against his other neighbors. To give his kingdom a capital, he captured the city of Jerusalem, which he enlarged, fortified, and made the religious and political center of his realm. David's military successes won the Hebrews unprecedented security, and his forty-year reign was a period of vitality and political consolidation.

David's son Solomon (ca 965–925 B.C.) applied his energies to creating a nation out of a collection of tribes ruled by a king. He divided the kingdom, for purposes of effective administration, into twelve territorial districts cutting across the old tribal borders. To bring his kingdom up to the level of its more sophisticated neighbors, he set about a building program to make Israel a respectable Near Eastern state. Work was begun on a magnificent temple in Jerusalem, on cities, palaces, fortresses, and roads. Solomon worked to bring Israel into the commercial mainstream of the world around it and kept up good relations with Phoenician cities to the north. To finance all of the construction and other activities that he initiated, Solomon imposed taxes far greater than any levied before, much to the displeasure of his subjects.

Solomon dedicated the temple in grand style and made it the home of the Ark of the Covenant, the cherished chest that contained the holiest of Hebrew religious articles. The temple in Jerusalem was intended to be the religious heart of the kingdom and the symbol of Hebrew unity. It also became the stronghold of the priesthood, for a legion of priests was needed to conduct religious sacrifices, ceremonies, and prayers. Yet Solomon's efforts were hampered by strife. In the eyes of some people, he was too ready to unite other religions with the worship of the Hebrew god Yahweh, and the financial demands of his building program and his use of forced labor for building projects further fanned popular resentment. However, Solomon turned a rude kingdom into a state with broad commercial horizons and greater knowledge of the outside world. At his death, the Hebrew kingdom broke into two political sections (see Map 2.1). The northern half became Israel, with its capital at Samaria. The southern half was Judah, and Solomon's city of Jerusalem remained its center. With political division went a religious rift: Israel, the northern kingdom, established rival sanctuaries for gods other than Yahweh.

War soon broke out between Israel and Judah, as recorded in the Bible. Unexpected and independent evidence of this warfare came to light in August 1993 when an Israeli archaeologist found an inscription that refers to the "House of David," the royal line of Israel. The stone celebrates an Israelite victory from the early ninth century B.C. This discovery is the first mention of King David's royal family outside the Bible and helps to confirm the biblical account of the fighting between the two kingdoms.

Eventually, the northern kingdom of Israel was wiped out by the Assyrians, but the southern kingdom of Judah survived numerous calamities until the Babylonians crushed it in 587 B.C. The survivors were sent into exile in Babylonia, a period commonly known as the Babylonian Captivity. From 587 B.C. until 538 B.C., men known as prophets kept Yahweh's religion alive in the midst of far older Babylonian religious practices. They predicted that Yahweh would permit their return to their homeland if they remained true only to him. In 538 B.C. the Persians under their king Cyrus the Great permitted some forty thousand exiles to return to Jerusalem. During and especially after the Babylonian Captivity the exiles redefined their beliefs and practices and thus established what they believed was the law of Yahweh. Those who lived by these precepts can be called *Jews*.

The Evolution of Jewish Religion

While evolving politically from fierce nomads to urban dwellers, the Hebrews were also evolving spiritual ideas that still permeate contemporary

Nomadic Semitic Tribe   This Egyptian fresco captures the essentials of nomadic life. These Semites have captured a gazelle and an ibex. The four men behind the leaders hold their weapons, a bow and spears, which they used for both hunting and defense. Bringing up the rear is a domesticated burro. *(Source: Erich Lessing/Art Resource, NY)*

The Golden Calf According to the Hebrew Bible, Moses descended from Mount Sinai, where he had received the Ten Commandments, and found the Hebrews worshiping a golden calf, which was against Yahweh's laws. In July 1990 an American archaeological team found this model of a gilded calf inside a pot. The figurine dates to about 1550 B.C. and proves the existence of the cult represented by the calf in Palestine. *(Source: Courtesy of the Leon Levy expedition to Ashkelon/Carl Andrews)*

societies. Their chief literary product, the Old Testament or Hebrew Bible, has fundamentally influenced both Christianity and Islam and still exerts a compelling force on the modern world.

Fundamental to an understanding of Jewish religion is the concept of the *Covenant,* a formal agreement between Yahweh and the Hebrew people. According to the Bible, the god Yahweh (later called Jehovah by Christians) appeared to Moses on Mount Sinai. There Yahweh made a covenant with the Hebrews that was in fact a contract: if the Hebrews worshiped Yahweh as their only god, he would consider them his chosen people and pro-

tect them from their enemies. The Hebrews believed that Yahweh had led them out of bondage in Egypt and had helped them conquer their new land, the promised land. In return, the Hebrews worshiped Yahweh and Yahweh alone. They also obeyed Yahweh's Ten Commandments, an ethical code of conduct revealed to them by Moses. The Covenant was a powerful force in Hebrew life. The Old Testament records one occasion when the entire nation formally reaffirmed it:

And the king [of the Jews] stood by a pillar, and made a covenant before the lord, to walk after the lord, and to keep his commandments and his testimonies and his statutes with all their heart and all their soul, to perform the words of this covenant that were written in this book [Deuteronomy]. And all the people stood to the covenant.[2]

Yahweh was unique because he was a lone god. Unlike the gods of Mesopotamia and Egypt, Yahweh was not the son of another god, nor did he have a divine wife or family. Initially anthropomorphic, Yahweh gradually lost human form and became totally spiritual. Although Yahweh could assume human form, he was not to be depicted in any form. The Hebrews considered graven images—statues and other physical representations—idolatrous.

At first Yahweh was probably viewed as no more than the god of the Hebrews and sometimes faced competition from Baal and other gods in Palestine. Enlil, Marduk, Amon-Re, and the others sufficed for foreigners, but not for the Hebrews. In time, however, the Hebrews came to regard Yahweh as the only god. This was the beginning of true monotheism. Unlike Akhenaten's brand of monotheism (see pages 29–30), Hebrew monotheism was not an unpopular religion imposed by the ruler. It was the religion of a whole people, deeply felt and cherished. Some might fall away from Yahweh's worship, and various holy men had to exhort the Hebrews to honor the Covenant, but on the whole the people clung to Yahweh.

The Hebrews did not consider it their duty to spread a belief in the one god. They rarely proselytized, as Christians later did. As the chosen people, their chief duty was to maintain the worship of Yahweh as he demanded. That worship was embodied in the Ten Commandments, which forbade the Hebrews to steal, murder, lie, or commit adultery.

✳ **Aerial View of Hazor**   This sweeping scene illustrates the strength and the economic basis of a Jewish citadel. At the left is the fortified upper city, and in the background is the agricultural land that sustained it. *(Source: Zev Radovan, Jerusalem)*

From the Ten Commandments evolved Hebrew law, a code of law and custom originating with Moses and built on by priests and prophets. The earliest part of this code, the Torah or Mosaic law, was often as harsh as Hammurabi's code, which had a powerful impact on it. Later tradition, largely the work of prophets who lived from the eleventh to the fifth centuries B.C., was more humanitarian. The work of the prophet Jeremiah (ca 626 B.C.) exemplifies this gentler spirit.

Jeremiah's emphasis is on mercy and justice, on avoiding wrongdoing to others because it is displeasing to Yahweh. These precepts replaced the old law's demand for "an eye for an eye." Jeremiah's message is thus representative of a subtle and positive shift in Hebrew thinking. Jeremiah proclaimed that the god of anger was also the god of forgiveness: "Return, thou backsliding Israel, saith the lord; and I will not cause mine anger to fall upon you; for I am merciful, saith the lord, and I will not keep anger forever."[3] Although Yahweh would punish wrongdoing, he would not destroy those who repented. One generation might be punished for its misdeeds, but Yahweh's mercy was a promise of hope for future generations.

The uniqueness of this phenomenon can be seen by comparing the essence of Hebrew monotheism with the religious outlook of the Mesopotamians. Whereas the Mesopotamians considered their gods capricious, the Hebrews knew what Yahweh expected. The Hebrews believed that their god would protect them and make them prosper if they obeyed his commandments. The Mesopotamians thought human beings insignificant compared to the gods, so insignificant that the gods might even be indifferent to them. The Hebrews, too, considered themselves puny in comparison to Yahweh. Yet they were Yahweh's chosen people, whom he had promised never to abandon. Finally, though the Mesopotamians believed that the gods generally preferred good to evil, their religion did not demand ethical conduct. The Hebrews could please their god only by living up to high moral standards as well as worshiping him.

Many parts of the Old Testament show obvious debts to Mesopotamian culture. Nonetheless, to the Hebrews goes the credit for developing a religion so emotionally satisfying and ethically grand that it not only flourished but also profoundly influenced Christianity and Islam.

Daily Life in Israel

Historians generally know far more about the daily life of the aristocracy and the wealthy in ancient societies than about the conditions of the common people. Jewish society is an exception simply because the Bible, which lays down laws for all Jews, has much to say about peasants and princes alike. Comparisons with the social conditions of Israel's ancient neighbors and modern anthropological work among Palestinian Arabs shed additional light on biblical practices. Thus the life of the common people in ancient Israel is better known than, for instance, the lives of ordinary Romans or ancient Chinese.

The nomadic Hebrews first entered Palestine as tribes, numerous families who thought of themselves as all related to one another. At first, good farmland, pastureland, and water spots were held in common by the tribe. Common use of land was—and still is—characteristic of nomadic peoples. But as formerly nomadic peoples turned increasingly to settled agriculture, communal use of land gave way to family ownership. So it was with the ancient Hebrews. Slowly the shift from nomad to farmer affected far more than just how people fed themselves. Family relationships reflected evolving circumstances. With the transition to settled agriculture, the tribe gradually became less important than the extended family. With the advent of village life and finally full-blown urban life, the extended family in turn gave way to the nuclear family.

For women, the evolution of Jewish society led to less freedom of action, especially in religious life. At first women served as priestesses in festivals and religious cults. Some were considered prophetesses of Yahweh, although they never conducted his official rituals. In the course of time, however, the worship of Yahweh became more male oriented and male dominated. Increasingly, Yahweh became the god of holiness, and to worship him people had to be pure in mind and body. Women were seen as ritually impure because of menstruation and childbirth. Because of these "impurities," women began to play a much reduced role in religion. Even when they did participate in religious rites, they were segregated from men. For the most part, women were confined to the home and the care of the family.

Marriage was one of the most important and joyous events in Hebrew family life. The typical marriage in ancient Israel was monogamous, and a virtuous wife was revered and honored. Perhaps the finest and most fervent song of praise to the good wife comes from the book of Proverbs in the Bible:

Who can find a virtuous woman? for her price is far above rubies. . . . Strength and honour are her clothing; and she shall rejoice in time to come. She openeth her mouth with wisdom; and in her tongue is the law of kindness. She looketh well to the ways of her household, and eateth not the bread of idleness. Her children arise up, and call her blessed; her husband also, and he praiseth her. . . . Favour is deceitful, and beauty is vain: but a woman that feareth the lord, she shall be praised.[4]

The commandment "Honor thy father and thy mother" was fundamental to the Mosaic law. The wife was a pillar of the family, and her work and wisdom were respected and treasured.

Betrothal and marriage were serious matters in ancient Israel. As in Mesopotamia, they were left largely in parents' hands. Boys and girls were often married quite early, and the parents naturally made the arrangements. Rarely were the prospective bride and groom consulted. Marriages were often contracted within the extended family commonly among first cousins—a custom still found among Palestinian Arabs today. Although early Jewish custom permitted marriage with foreigners, the fear of alien religions eventually led to restrictions against mixed marriages.

The father of the groom offered a bridal gift to the bride's father. This custom, the marriage price, also existed among the Mesopotamians and still survives among modern Palestinian Arabs. The gift was ordinarily money, the amount depending on the social status and wealth of the two families. In other instances, the groom could work off the marriage price by performing manual labor. At the time of the wedding the man gave his bride and her family wedding presents; unlike Mesopotamian custom, the bride's father did not provide her with a dowry. A dowry is meant to protect the position of the wife, and the lack of it in Israel made it easier for the husband to divorce his wife without financial loss.

As in Mesopotamia, marriage was a legal contract, not a religious ceremony. At marriage a woman left her own family and joined the family and clan of her husband. The occasion when the bride joined her husband's household was festive. The groom wore a crown and his best clothes. Accompanied by his friends, also dressed in their finest and carrying musical instruments, the bridegroom walked to the bride's house, where she awaited him in her richest clothes, jewels, and a veil, which she removed only later when the couple was alone. The bride's friends joined the group, and together they all marched in procession to the groom's house, their way marked by music and songs honoring the newlyweds. Though the wedding feast might last for days, the couple consummated their marriage on the first night. The next day the blood-stained linen was displayed to prove the bride's virginity.

The right to initiate a divorce was available only to the husband. Even adultery by the husband was not necessarily grounds for divorce, although Jewish law, like the Code of Hammurabi, punished a wife's adultery with death. Jewish custom generally frowned on divorce, and the typical man and woman entered into marriage fully expecting to spend the rest of their lives together.

The newly married couple was expected to begin a family at once. Children, according to the book of Psalms, "are an heritage of the lord: and the fruit of the womb is his reward."[5] The desire for children to perpetuate the family was so strong that if a man died before he could sire a son, his brother was legally obliged to marry the widow. The son born of the brother was thereafter considered the offspring and heir of the dead man. If the brother refused, the widow had her revenge by denouncing him to the elders and publicly spitting in his face.

Sons were especially desired because they maintained the family bloodline and kept the ancestral property within the family. The first-born son had special rights, honor, and responsibilities. At his father's death he became the head of the household and received a larger inheritance than did his younger brothers. Daughters were less valued because they would eventually marry and leave the family. Yet in Jewish society, unlike other cultures, infanticide was illegal; Yahweh had forbidden it.

As in most other societies, in ancient Israel the early education of children was in the mother's hands. She taught her children right from wrong and gave them their first instruction in the moral values of society. As boys grew older, they received more education from their fathers in religion and the history of their people. Many children were taught to read and write, and the head of each family was probably able to write. Fathers also taught sons the family craft or trade. Boys soon learned that inattention could be painful, for Jewish custom advised fathers to be strict: "He that spareth his rod hateth his son: but he that loveth him chasteneth him betimes."[6]

Most children grew to adulthood in the context of farm life, whose demands and rhythm changed little over time. Young people began with light tasks. Girls traditionally tended flocks of sheep and drew water from the well for household use. At the well, which was a popular meeting spot, girls could meet other young people and travelers passing through the country with camel caravans. After the harvest, young girls followed behind the reapers to glean the fields. Even this work was governed by law and custom. Once the girls had gone through the fields, they were not to return, for Yahweh had declared that anything left behind belonged to the needy.

Boys also tended flocks, especially in wild areas. Like the young David, they practiced marksmanship with slings and entertained themselves with music. They shared light work such as harvesting grapes and beating the limbs of olive trees to shake the fruit loose. Only when they grew to full strength did they perform the hard work of harrowing, plowing, and harvesting.

The land was precious to the family, not simply because it provided a living but also because it was a link to the past. Ironically, the success of the first Hebrew kings endangered the future of many family farms. With peace, more settled conditions, and increasing prosperity, some Jews began to amass large holdings by buying out the poor and struggling farmers. Far from discouraging this development, the kings created their own huge estates. In many cases slaves, both Jewish and foreign, worked these large farms and estates shoulder to shoulder with paid free men. In still later times, rich landowners rented plots of land to poor free families; the landowners provided the renters with seed and livestock and normally took half of the yield as rent.

The development of urban life among the Jews created new economic opportunities, especially in crafts and trades. People specialized in certain occupations, such as milling flour, baking bread, making pottery, weaving, and carpentry. All these crafts were family trades. Sons worked with their father, daughters with their mother. If the business prospered, the family might be assisted by a few paid workers or slaves. The practitioners of a craft usually lived in a particular street or section of the town, a custom still prevalent in the Middle East.

Commerce and trade developed later than crafts. In the time of Solomon, foreign trade was the king's domain. Aided by the Phoenicians, Solomon built a fleet to trade with Red Sea ports. He also participated in the overland caravan trade. Otherwise, trade with neighboring countries was handled by foreigners, usually Phoenicians. Jews dealt mainly in local trade, and in most instances craftsmen and farmers sold directly to their customers. Many of Israel's wise men disapproved of commerce and considered it unseemly and immoral to profit from the work of others.

These social and economic developments also left their mark on daily life by prompting the compilation of two significant works, the Torah and the Talmud. The Torah is basically the Mosaic law, or the first five books of the Bible. The Talmud is a later work, begun during the Babylonian Captivity and completed by the end of the sixth century B.C. The Talmud records civil and ceremonial law and Jewish legend.

The dietary rules of the Jews provide an excellent example of both the relationship between the Torah and the Talmud and their effect on ordinary life and culture. According to the Torah, people were not to eat meat that they found in the field. This very sensible prohibition protected them from eating dangerous food. Yet some rules also were needed for meat in the city. The solution, set forth in the Talmud, was a set of regulations for the proper way to conduct ritual slaughter. Some of the rules were very burdensome. The ritual defined the knife to be used in the slaughter and the way in which it was to be used. Accompanying these precise acts were prayers to be given when the animal's throat was cut. So too with the Torah's prohibition against cooking a young goat in its mother's milk. The Talmud's interpretation of this Mosaic law went to such lengths that milk and meat could not be eaten at the same table and different bowls had to be used to serve them. Even different towels had to be used to cleanse them. What began as simple and sensible dietary rules became a complicated ritual, one that many Orthodox Jews follow today.

Between the eclipse of the Hittites and Egyptians and the rise of the Assyrians, the Hebrews moved from nomadism to urban life and full participation in the mainstream of ancient Near Eastern culture. Developing their unique religion and customs, they drew from the practices of other peoples and contributed to the lives of their neighbors.

ASSYRIA, THE MILITARY MONARCHY

Small kingdoms like those of the Phoenicians and the Hebrews could exist only in the absence of a major power. The beginning of the ninth century B.C. saw the rise of such a power: the Assyrians of northern Mesopotamia, whose chief capital was at Nineveh on the Tigris River. The Assyrians were a Semitic-speaking people heavily influenced, like so many other peoples of the Near East, by the Mesopotamian culture of Babylon to the south. They were also one of the most warlike peoples in history, largely because throughout their history they were threatened by neighboring folk. Living in an open, exposed land, the Assyrians experienced frequent and devastating attacks by the wild, war-loving tribes to their north and east and by the Babylonians to the south. The constant threat to survival experienced by the Assyrians promoted political cohesion and military might. Yet they were also a mercantile people who had long pursued commerce both with the Babylonians in the south and other peoples in the north.

The Power of Assyria

For over two hundred years the Assyrians labored to dominate the Near East. Year after relentless year, Assyrian armies hammered at the peoples of the west. These ominous events inaugurated two turbulent centuries marked by Assyrian military campaigns, constant efforts by Syria and the two Jewish kingdoms to maintain or recover their independence, and eventual Assyrian conquest of Babylonia and northern Egypt. In addition, periodic political instability occurred in Assyria itself, which prompted stirrings of freedom throughout the Near East.

By means of almost constant warfare the kings Tiglath-pileser III (r. 774–727 B.C.) and Sargon II (r. 721–705 B.C.) carved out an empire that stretched from east and north of the Tigris River to central Egypt (Map 2.2). Revolt against the Assyrians inevitably promised the rebels bloody battles, prolonged sieges accompanied by starvation, plague, and sometimes even cannibalism, and finally surrender followed by systematic torture and slaughter.

Though atrocity and terrorism struck unspeakable fear into Assyria's subjects, Assyria's success was actually due to sophisticated, farsighted, and effective military organization. By Sargon's time the Assyrians had invented the mightiest military machine the ancient Near East had ever seen. The mainstay of the Assyrian army, the soldier who ordinarily decided the outcome of battles, was the infantryman armed with spear and sword and protected by helmet and armor. The Assyrian army also featured archers, some on foot, others on horseback, still others in chariots. Some infantry archers wore heavy armor. These soldiers served as a primitive field artillery, whose job was to sweep the enemy's walls of defenders so that others could storm the defenses. Slingers also served as artillery in pitched battles. For mobility on the battlefield, the Assyrians organized a corps of chariots.

Assyrian military genius was remarkable for the development of a wide variety of siege machinery and techniques, including excavation to undermine city walls and battering rams to knock down walls and gates. Never before in the Near East had anyone applied such technical knowledge to warfare. The Assyrians even invented the concept of a corps of engineers, who bridged rivers with pontoons or provided soldiers with inflatable skins for swimming. Furthermore, the Assyrians knew how to coordinate their efforts, both in open battle and

Siege of a City Art here serves to glorify horror. The Assyrian king Tiglath-pileser III launches an assault on a fortified city. The impaled bodies shown at the center demonstrate the cruelty of Assyrian warfare. Also noticeable are the various weapons and means of attack used against the city. *(Source: Courtesy of the Trustees of the British Museum)*

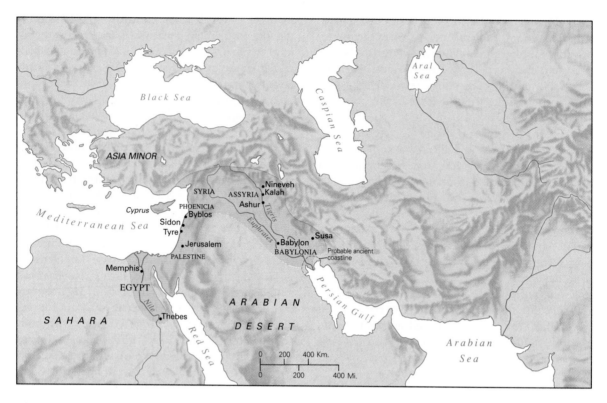

MAP 2.2 The Assyrian Empire   The Assyrian Empire at its height (ca 650 B.C.) included almost all of the old centers of power in the ancient Near East. As comparison with Map 2.3 shows, however, its size was far smaller than that of the later Persian Empire.

in siege warfare. King Sennacherib's account of his siege of Jerusalem in 701 B.C. is a vivid portrait of the Assyrian war machine in action:

As to Hezekiah, the Jew, he did not submit to my yoke, I laid siege to 46 of his strong cities, walled forts and to the countless small villages in their vicinity, and conquered them by means of well-stamped earth-ramps, and battering rams brought thus near to the walls combined with the attack by foot soldiers, using mines, breaches as well as sapper work. . . . Hezekiah himself, whom the terror-inspiring splendor of my lordship had overwhelmed and whose irregular and elite troops which he had brought into Jerusalem, his royal residence, in order to strengthen it, had deserted him, did send me, later, to Nineveh, my lordly city, together with 30 talents of gold . . . and all kinds of valuable treasures.[7]

Hezekiah and Jerusalem shared the fate of many a rebellious king and capital and were indeed lucky

to escape severe reprisals. The Assyrians were too powerful and well organized and far too tenacious to be turned back by isolated strongholds, no matter how well situated or defended.

Assyrian Rule and Culture

The Assyrians knew not only how to win battles but also how to use their victories. As early as the reign of Tiglath-pileser III, the Assyrian kings began to organize their conquered territories into an empire. The lands closest to Assyria became provinces governed by Assyrian officials. Kingdoms beyond the provinces were not annexed but became dependent states that followed Assyria's lead. The Assyrian king chose their rulers either by regulating the succession of native kings or by supporting native kings who appealed to him. Against more distant states the Assyrian kings waged frequent war in order to conquer them outright or make the dependent states secure.

In the seventh century B.C. Assyrian power seemed secure. Yet the downfall of Assyria was swift and complete. Babylon finally won its independence in 626 B.C. and joined forces with the newly aggressive Medes, an Indo-European-speaking folk from Iran. Together the Babylonians and the Medes destroyed the Assyrian Empire in 612 B.C., paving the way for the rise of the Persians. The Hebrew prophet Nahum spoke for many when he asked: "Nineveh is laid waste: who will bemoan her?"[8] Their cities destroyed and their power shattered, the Assyrians disappeared from history, remembered only as a cruel people of the Old Testament who oppressed the Hebrews. The glory of their empire was forgotten.

Yet modern archaeology has brought the Assyrians out of obscurity. In 1839 the intrepid English archaeologist and traveler A. H. Layard began to excavate Nineveh, then a mound of debris beside the Tigris. His findings electrified the world. Layard's workers unearthed masterpieces, including monumental sculpted figures—huge, winged bulls, human-headed lions, and sphinxes—as well as brilliantly sculpted friezes. Equally valuable were numerous Assyrian cuneiform documents, which ranged from royal accounts of mighty military campaigns to simple letters by common people.

Among the most renowned of Layard's finds were the Assyrian palace reliefs, whose number has been increased by the discoveries of twentieth-century archaeologists. Assyrian kings delighted in scenes of war, which their artists depicted in graphic detail. By the time of Ashurbanipal (r. 668–633 B.C.), Assyrian artists had hit on the idea of portraying a series of episodes—in fact, a visual narrative of events that had actually taken place. Scene followed scene in a continuous frieze, so that the viewer could follow the progress of a military campaign from the time the army marched out until the enemy was conquered. So, too, with another theme of the palace reliefs, the lion hunt. Hunting lions was probably a royal sport, although some scholars have suggested a magical significance, arguing that the hunting scenes depict the

Royal Lion Hunt   This relief from the palace of Ashurbanipal at Nineveh shows the king fighting a lion and is a typical representation of the energy and artistic brilliance of Assyrian sculptors. The lion hunt was a favorite theme of Assyrian palace reliefs. *(Source: Courtesy of the Trustees of the British Museum)*

king as the protector of his people, the one who wards off evil.

Assyrian art, like much of Egyptian art, was realistic, but the warmth and humor of Egyptian scenes are absent from Assyrian reliefs. Stark and often brutal in subject matter, Assyrian realism is well represented by the illustration reproduced on page 51, which portrays the climax of the royal lion hunt. The king, mounted on horseback, has already fired arrows into two lions, who nonetheless are still full of fight. The king thrusts his spear into another lion, which has begun its spring. The artistic rendering of the figures is exciting, anatomically correct, and in proper proportion and perspective. The whole composition conveys both action and tension. Assyrian art fared better than Assyrian military power. The techniques of Assyrian artists influenced the Persians, who adapted them to gentler scenes.

In fact, many Assyrian innovations, military and political as well as artistic, were taken over wholesale by the Persians. Although the memory of Assyria was hateful throughout the Near East, the fruits of Assyrian organizational genius helped enable the Persians to bring peace and stability to the same regions where Assyrian armies had spread terror.

 Persian Warrior This statuette, about fifteen inches in height, of a Persian soldier is elaborate in its portrayal of the warrior's arms and armor. The writing on the base identifies this warrior as the guardian god of a town. *(Source: Teheran Museum, Iran)*

 ## THE EMPIRE OF THE PERSIAN KINGS

Like the Hittites before them, the Iranians were Indo-Europeans from central Europe and southern Russia. They migrated into the land that now bears their name, the area between the Caspian Sea and the Persian Gulf. Like the Hittites, they then fell under the spell of the more sophisticated cultures of their Mesopotamian neighbors. But the Iranians went on to create one of the greatest empires of antiquity, one that encompassed scores of peoples and cultures. The Persians, the most important of the Iranian peoples, had a farsighted conception of empire. Though as conquerors they willingly used force to accomplish their ends, they normally preferred to depend on diplomacy and toleration to rule.

The Land of Mountains and Plateau

Persia—the modern country of Iran—stretches from the Caspian Sea in the north to the Persian Gulf in the south (Map 2.3). Between the Tigris-Euphrates Valley in the west and the Indus Valley in the east rises an immense plateau surrounded on all sides by lofty mountains that cut off the interior from the sea.

The central plateau is very high, a landscape of broad plains, scattered oases, and two vast deserts. The high mountains, which catch the moisture coming from the sea, generate ample rainfall for the plateau. This semitropical area is fertile, in marked contrast to the aridity of most of Iran. The mountains surrounding the central plateau are dot-

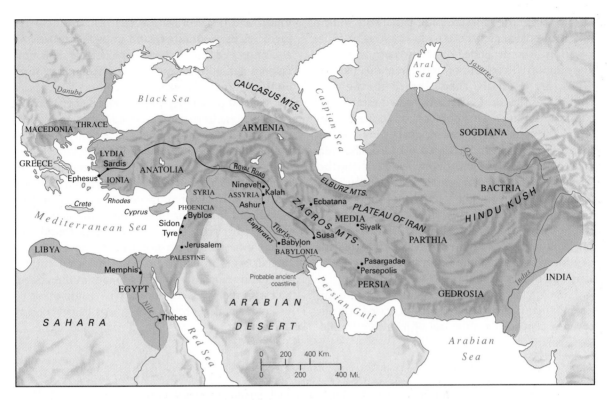

MAP 2.3 The Persian Empire   By 513 B.C. the Persian Empire included more of the ancient Near East than had the Assyrian Empire, and it extended as far east as western India. With the rise of the Medes and Persians, the balance of power in the Near East shifted east of Mesopotamia for the first time.

ted with numerous oases, often very fertile. From time immemorial they have served as havens for small groups of people. At the center of the plateau lies an enormous depression—a region devoid of water and vegetation, so glowing hot in summer that it is virtually impossible to cross. This depression forms two distinct grim and burning salt deserts, perhaps the most desolate spots on earth. These two deserts form a barrier between East and West.

Iran's geographical position and topography explain its traditional role as the highway between East and West. Throughout history nomadic peoples migrating from the broad steppes of Russia and central Asia have streamed into Iran. Confronting the uncrossable salt deserts, most have turned either eastward or westward, moving on until they reached the advanced and wealthy urban centers of Mesopotamia and India. When cities emerged along the natural lines of East-West communication, Iran became the area where nomads

met urban dwellers, a meeting ground of unique significance for the civilizations of both East and West.

The Coming of the Medes and Persians

The Iranians entered this land around 1000 B.C. They were part of the vast movement of Indo-European-speaking peoples whose wanderings led them in many successive waves into Europe, the Near East, and India (see page 30). These Iranians were nomads who migrated with their flocks and herds. Like their kinsmen the Aryans, who moved into India (see page 53), they were horse breeders, and the horse gave them a decisive military advantage over the native prehistoric peoples of Iran. The Iranians rode into battle in horse-drawn chariots or on horseback and easily swept the natives. Because the influx of Iranians went on for centuries, cultural interchange between victorious newcomers and conquered natives was ongoing.

The Iranians initially created a patchwork of tiny kingdoms. The chieftain or petty king was basically a warlord who depended on fellow warriors for aid and support. This band of noble warriors, like the Greek heroes of the *Iliad,* formed the fighting strength of the army. The king owned estates that supported him and his nobles. For additional income the king levied taxes, which were paid in kind and not in cash. He also demanded labor services from the peasants. Below the king and his warrior nobles were free people who held land and others who owned nothing. Artisans produced the various goods needed to keep society running. At the bottom of the social scale were slaves—probably both natives and newcomers. To them fell the drudgery of hard labor and household service to king and nobles.

This early period saw some significant economic developments. The use of iron increased. By the seventh century B.C., the use of iron farm imple-ments had become widespread. The results were increases in productivity and in overall prosperity and improved standards of living. At the same time Iranian agriculture saw the development of small estates. Farmers worked small plots of land, and the general prosperity of the period gave rise to a sturdy peasantry, who enjoyed greater freedom than the freedom experienced by their peers in Egypt and Mesopotamia.

Iran had considerable mineral wealth, and its iron, copper, and lapis lazuli attracted Assyrian raiding parties. Even more important, mineral wealth and Iranian horse breeding stimulated brisk trade with the outside world. Kings found that merchants, who were not usually Iranians, produced large profits to help fill the royal coffers. Overland trade also put the Iranians in direct contact with their western and eastern neighbors.

Gradually two groups of Iranians began coalescing into larger units. The Persians had settled in

Tomb of Cyrus   Despite his greatness, Cyrus retained a sense of perspective. His tomb, though monumental in size, is rather simple and unostentatious. Greek writers reported that it bore the following epitaph: "O man, I am Cyrus the son of Cambyses. I established the Persian Empire and was king of Asia. Do not begrudge me my memorial." *(Source: The Oriental Institute, University of Chicago)*

Persis, the modern region of Fars, in southern Iran. Their kinsmen the Medes occupied Media, the modern area of Hamadan in the north; the Medes' capital was at Ecbatana. The Medes were vulnerable to attack by nomads from the north, but their greatest threat was the frequent raids by the Assyrian army. Even though distracted by grave pressures from their neighbors, the Medes united under one king around 710 B.C. and extended their control over the Persians in the south. In 612 B.C. the Medes were strong enough to join the Babylonians in overthrowing the Assyrian Empire. With the rise of the Medes, the balance of power in the area for the first time shifted east of Mesopotamia.

The Creation of the Persian Empire

In 550 B.C. Cyrus the Great (r. 559–530 B.C.), king of the Persians and one of the most remarkable statesmen of antiquity, threw off the yoke of the Medes by conquering them and turning their country into his first *satrapy,* or province. In the space of a single lifetime, Cyrus created one of the greatest empires of antiquity. Two characteristics lifted Cyrus above the common level of warrior kings. First, he thought of Iran, not just Persia and Media, as a state. His concept has survived a long, complex, often turbulent history to play its part in the contemporary world. Second, Cyrus held an enlightened view of empire. Many of the civilizations and cultures that fell to his armies were, he realized, far older, more advanced, and more sophisticated than his. Free of the narrow-minded snobbery of the Egyptians, the religious exclusiveness of the Hebrews, and the calculated cruelty of the Assyrians, Cyrus gave his subject peoples and their cultures respect, toleration, and protection. Conquered peoples continued to enjoy their institutions, religion, language, and way of life under the Persians.

The Persian Empire, which Cyrus created, became a political organization sheltering many different civilizations. To rule such a vast area and so many diverse peoples demanded talent, intelligence, sensitivity, and a cosmopolitan view of the world. These qualities Cyrus and many of his successors possessed in abundance. Though the Persians were sometimes harsh, especially toward those who rebelled against them, they were for the most part enlightened rulers. Consequently, they

gave the ancient Near East over two hundred years of peace, prosperity, and security.

With Iran united, Cyrus looked at the broader world. He set out to achieve two goals. First, he wanted to win control of the west and thus of the terminal ports of the great trade routes that crossed Iran and Anatolia. Second, he strove to secure eastern Iran from the pressure of nomadic invaders. In 550 B.C. neither goal was easy to accomplish. To the northwest was the young kingdom of Lydia in Anatolia, whose king Croesus was proverbial for his wealth. To the west was Babylonia, enjoying a new period of power now that the Assyrian Empire had been crushed. To the southwest was Egypt, still weak but sheltered behind its bulwark of sand and sea. To the east ranged tough, mobile nomads, capable of massive and destructive incursions deep into Iranian territory.

Cyrus turned first to Croesus's Lydian kingdom, which fell to him around 546 B.C., along with the Greek cities along the coast of Anatolia. Cyrus thus gained important ports that looked out to the Mediterranean world. In addition, for the first time the Persians came into direct contact with the Greeks, a people with whom their later history was to be intimately connected (see page 129).

From Lydia, Cyrus next marched to the far eastern corners of Iran. In a brilliant campaign he conquered the regions of Parthia and Bactria. All of Iran was now Persian, from Mesopotamia in the west to the western slopes of the Hindu Kush in the east. In 540 B.C. Cyrus moved against Babylonia, now isolated from outside help. When Persian soldiers marched quietly into Babylon the next year, the Babylonians welcomed Cyrus as a liberator. He won the hearts of the Babylonians with humane treatment, toleration of their religion, and support of their efforts to refurbish their capital.

Cyrus was equally generous toward the Jews. He allowed them to return to Palestine, from which they had been deported by the Babylonians. He protected them, gave them back the sacred items they used in worship, and rebuilt the temple of Yahweh in Jerusalem. The Old Testament sings the praises of Cyrus, whom the Jews considered the shepherd of Yahweh, the lord's anointed. Rarely have conquered peoples shown such gratitude to their conquerors. Cyrus's benevolent policy created a Persian Empire in which the cultures and religions of its members were respected and honored. Seldom have conquerors been as wise, sensitive, and farsighted as Cyrus and his Persians.

✳ **Darius the Great and Ahura Mazda** In this rock carving, Darius, king of the Persians, in the presence of the god Ahuramazda and with his blessing, triumphs over lesser and sometimes rebellious kings. The scene asserts the divine approval of Darius's right to rule. *(Source: Robert Harding Picture Library)*

Thus Spake Zarathustra

Iranian religion was originally simple and primitive. Ahuramazda, the chief god, was the creator and benefactor of all living creatures. Yet, unlike Yahweh, he was not a lone god. The Iranians were polytheistic. Mithra the sun-god, whose cult later spread throughout the Roman Empire, saw to justice and redemption. Other Iranian deities personified the natural elements: moon, earth, water, and wind. As in ancient India, fire was a particularly important god. The sacred fire consumed the blood sacrifices that the early Iranians offered to all of their deities.

Early Iranian religion was close to nature and unencumbered by ponderous theological beliefs. A priestly class, the Magi, developed among the Medes to officiate at sacrifices, chant prayers to the gods, and tend the sacred flame. A description of this early worship comes from the German historian Eduard Meyer:

Iranian religion knew neither divine images nor temples. On a hilltop one called upon god and his manifestations—sun and moon, earth and fire, water and wind—and erected altars with their eternal fire. But in other appropriate places one could, without further preparation, pray to the deity and bring him his offerings, with the assistance of the Magi.[9]

In time the Iranians built fire temples for these sacrifices. As late as the nineteenth century, fire was still worshiped in Baku, a major city on the Russian-Iranian border.

Around 600 B.C. the religious thinking of Zarathustra—Zoroaster, as he is better known—breathed new meaning into Iranian religion. So little is known of Zoroaster that even the date of his birth is unknown, but it cannot be earlier than around 1100 B.C. The most reliable information about Zoroaster comes from the *Zend Avesta,* a collection of hymns and poems, the earliest part of which treats Zoroaster and primitive Persian religion.

Zoroaster preached a novel concept of divinity and human life. Life, he taught, is a constant battleground for two opposing forces, good and evil: Ahuramazda, who embodies good and truth, is opposed by Ahriman, a hateful spirit who stands for evil and falsehood. Ahuramazda and Ahriman are locked together in a cosmic battle for the human race. But, according to Zoroaster, people are not mere pawns in this struggle. Each person has to choose which side to join—whether to lead a life of good behavior and truthful dealings with others or one of wickedness and lies.

Zoroaster emphasized the individual's responsibility in this decision. He taught that people possess the free will to decide between Ahuramazda

ANCIENT NEAR EAST

ca 1700 B.C.	Covenant formed between Yahweh and the Hebrews. Emergence of Hebrew monotheism
ca 1570–ca 1075 B.C.	New Kingdom in Egypt
ca 1475–ca 1200 B.C.	Rise and fall of the Hittite Empire
13th century B.C.	Moses leads Exodus of the Hebrews from Egypt into Palestine
ca 1100–700 B.C.	Founding of numerous small kingdoms, including those of the Phoenicians, Syrians, Philistines, and Hebrews
ca 1000 B.C.	Saul establishes monarchy over Hebrews, under threat of Philistines Persians and Medes enter central plateau of Persia
10th century B.C.	David captures Jerusalem, which becomes religious and political center of Judah. Solomon inherits the throne and further unites Hebrew kingdom
925 B.C.	Solomon dies. Hebrew kingdom us divided politically into Israel and Judah
ca 900–612 B.C.	Rise and fall of the Assyrian Empire
813 B.C.	Phoenicians found Carthage
774–705 B.C.	Assyrian kings, Tiglath-pileser III and Sargon II conquer Palestine, Syria, Anatolia, Israel, Judha, and Egypt
ca 710 B.C.	Medes unite under one king and conquer Persians
626 B.C.	Babylonia wins independence from Assyria
612 B.C.	Babylonians and Medes destroy Assyrian capital of Nineveh
ca 600 B.C.	Zoroaster revitalizes Persian religion
550 B.C.	Cyrus the Great conquers Medes, founds Persian Empire
546 B.C.	Cyrus defeats Croesus, wins Lydia
540 B.C.	Persian soldiers under Cyrus enter Babylon
525 B.C.	Cambyses, Cyrus's heir to the throne, conquers Egypt
521–464 B.C.	Darius I and Xerxes complete Persian conquest of ancient East, an area stretching from Anatolia in the west to the Indus Valley in the east Persian attempts to invade Greece unsuccessful

and Ahriman and must rely on their own conscience to guide them. Their decisions are crucial, Zoroaster warned, for there will be a time of reckoning. He promised that Ahuramazda will eventually triumph over evil and lies and that at death each person will stand before the tribunal of good, where Ahuramazda, like the Egyptian god Osiris, will judge whether the dead lived righteously. In short, Zoroaster taught the concept of a Last Judgment at which Ahuramazda will decide each person's eternal fate.

In Zoroaster's thought the Last Judgment was linked to the notion of a divine kingdom after death for those who had been good and truthful.

They would accompany Ahuramazda to what Zoroaster called the "House of Song" and the "Abode of Good Thought," where they would dwell with Ahuramazda forever. Liars and the wicked, denied this blessed immortality, would be condemned to eternal pain, darkness, and punishment. Thus Zoroaster preached a Last Judgment that led to a heaven or a hell.

Though tradition has it that Zoroaster's teachings originally met with opposition and coldness, his thought converted Darius (r. 521–486 B.C.), one of the most energetic men ever to sit on the Persian throne. The Persian royal family adopted Zoroastrianism but did not try to impose it on others. Under the protection of the Persian kings, Zoroastrianism swept through Iran, winning converts and sinking roots that sustained healthy growth for centuries. Zoroastrianism survived the fall of the Persian Empire to influence religious thought in the age of Jesus and to make a vital contribution to Manicheanism, a theology that was to spread through the Byzantine Empire and pose a significant challenge to Christianity. A handful of the faithful still follow the teachings of Zoroaster, whose vision of divinity and human life has transcended the centuries.

Persia's World Empire

Cyrus's successors rounded out the Persian conquest of the ancient Near East. In 525 B.C. Cyrus's son Cambyses (r. 530–522 B.C.) subdued Egypt. Darius (r. 521–486 B.C.) and his son Xerxes (r. 486–464 B.C.) invaded Greece but were fought to a standstill and forced to retreat (see pages 129–130). The Persians never won a permanent foothold in Europe, but Darius carried Persian arms into India. Around 513 B.C. western India became the Persian satrapy of Hindu Kush, which included the valley of the Indus River. Thus within thirty-seven years the Persians transformed themselves from a subject people to the rulers of an empire that included Anatolia, Egypt, Mesopotamia, Iran, and western India. They created an empire encom-

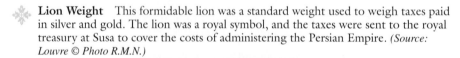

Lion Weight   This formidable lion was a standard weight used to weigh taxes paid in silver and gold. The lion was a royal symbol, and the taxes were sent to the royal treasury at Susa to cover the costs of administering the Persian Empire. *(Source: Louvre © Photo R.M.N.)*

The Royal Palace at Persepolis   Darius began and Xerxes finished building a grand palace worthy of the glory of the Persian Empire. Pictured here is the monumental audience hall, where the king dealt with ministers of state and foreign envoys. (*Source: George Holton/Photo Researchers*)

passing all of the oldest, most honored kingdoms and peoples of the ancient Near East, which never before had been united in one such vast political organization (see Map 2.3).

The Persians knew how to use the peace they had won on the battlefield. The sheer size of the empire made it impossible for one man to rule it effectively. So they divided the empire into some twenty huge satrapies measuring hundreds of square miles, many of them kingdoms in themselves. Each satrapy had a *satrap,* or governor, drawn from the Median and Persian nobility and often a relative of the king. The governor was directly responsible to the king. An army officer, also responsible to the king, commanded the military forces stationed in the satrapy. Still another official collected the taxes. Moreover, the king sent out royal inspectors to watch the satraps and other officials.

Effective rule of the empire demanded good communication. To meet this need, the Persians established a network of roads. The main highway, known as the Royal Road, spanned some 1,677 miles from the coast of western Asia to western Iran (see Map 2.3). The distance was broken into 111 post stations, each equipped with fresh horses for the king's messengers. Other roads branched out to link all parts of the empire from the coast of western Asia to the valley of the Indus River. This system of communication enabled the Persian king to keep in touch with his subjects and officials. He was able to rule efficiently, keep his ministers in line, and protect the rights of the peoples under his control.

How effective Persian rule could be, even in small matters, is apparent in a letter from King Darius to the satrap of Ionia, the Greek region of Anatolia. The satrap had transplanted Syrian fruit trees in his province, an experiment Darius praised. Yet the governor had also infringed on the rights granted to the sanctuary of the Greek god Apollo, an act that provoked the king to anger:

The King of Kings, Darius the son of Hystaspes says this to Gadatas, his slave [satrap]. I learn that you are not obeying my command in every particular. Because you are tilling my land, transplanting fruit trees from across the Euphrates [Syria] to Asia Minor, I praise your project, and there will be laid up for you great favor in the king's house. But because you mar my dispositions towards the gods, I shall give you, unless you change your ways, proof of my anger when wronged. For you exacted payment from the sacred gardeners of the temple of Apollo, and you ordered them to dig up secular land, failing to understand the attitude of my forefathers towards the god, who told the Persians the truth.[10]

This document alone suggests the efficiency of Persian rule and the compassion of Persian kings. Conquered peoples, left free to enjoy their traditional ways of life, found in the Persian king a capable protector. No wonder many Near Eastern peoples were, like the Jews, grateful for the long period of peace they enjoyed as the subjects of the Persian Empire.

SUMMARY

During the centuries following the Sea Peoples' invasions, Egypt was overrun by its African neighbors, and its long and rich traditions and culture, its firmly established religion, and its administrative techniques became the heritage of these conquerors. The defeat of Egypt also led to conditions that allowed the Hebrews to create their own state. A series of strong leaders fighting hard wars won the Hebrews independence and security. In this atmosphere Hebrew religion evolved and flourished, thanks to priests, prophets, and common piety among the people.

The Assyrians made the Near East tremble in terror of their armies. Their cruelty raised powerful enemies against them. Most important were the Iranians, who created the Persian Empire. Military and, particularly, political abilities gave the Persians the tools they needed to govern a host of different peoples. For over two hundred years Persian kings offered their subjects enlightened rule. The Persians gave the ancient Near East a period of peace and stability in which peoples enjoyed their native traditions and lived in concord with their neighbors.

Meanwhile, to the east the Indians and Chinese were confronting many of the problems that the peoples farther west were solving. The direction of developments in India and China differed from that in the Near East, largely but not entirely because of geography. The results, however, were essentially the same: sophisticated civilizations based on systematic agriculture and complex social structures, cultures, and religions.

NOTES

1. James H. Breasted, *Ancient Records of Egypt,* vol. 4 (Chicago: University of Chicago Press, 1907), para. 398.
2. 2 Kings 23:3.
3. Jeremiah 3:12.
4. Proverbs 31:10, 25–30.
5. Psalms 128:3.
6. Proverbs 13:24.
7. J. B. Pritchard, ed., *Ancient Near Eastern Texts,* 3d ed. (Princeton, N.J.: Princeton University Press, 1969), p. 288.
8. Nahum 3:7.
9. E. Meyer, *Geschichte des Altertums,* 7th ed., vol. 4, pt. 1 (Darmstadt: Wissenschaftliche Buchgesellschaft, 1975), pp. 114–115. Translated by John Buckler.
10. R. Meiggs and D. M. Lewis, *A Selection of Greek Historical Inscriptions* (Oxford: Clarendon Press, 1969), no. 12.

SUGGESTED READING

Although late Egyptian history is still largely a specialist's field, K. A. Kitchen, *The Third Intermediate Period in Egypt* (1973), is a sturdy synthesis of the period from 1100 to 650 B.C. Valuable, too, is M. L. Bierbrier's monograph, *Late New Kingdom in Egypt, c. 1300–664 B.C.* (1975). D. B. Redford, *Egypt, Canaan, and Israel in Ancient Times* (1992), is an excellent study of relations among the three states. G. Herm,

The Phoenicians (1975), treats Phoenician seafaring and commercial enterprises.

The Jews have been one of the best-studied people in the ancient world, so many good treatments of Jewish history and society are available. E. Anati, *Palestine Before the Hebrews* (1962), though dated, still provides a sound historical treatment of life in Palestine from human origins to the conquest of Canaan. More recent is G. Alon, *The Jews in Their Land* (1989), which covers the Talmudic age. H. Shanks, ed., *The Rise of Ancient Israel* (1991), is a collection of papers that treat numerous aspects of the period. R. Tappy, *The Archaeology of Israelite Samaria* (1993), studies the archaeological remains of the period. S. Niditch, *War in the Hebrew Bible* (1992), addresses the ethics of violence in the Bible. A general introduction to the Bible is B. M. Mezter and M. D. Coogan, eds., *The Oxford Companion to the Bible* (1993). H. W. Attridge, ed., *Of Scribes and Scrolls* (1990), gives a fascinating study of the Hebrew Bible and of Christian origins. Turning to politics, M. Smith, *Palestinian Parties and Politics That Shaped the Old Testament,* 2d ed. (1987), takes a practical look at events. G. W. Ahlstrom, *Royal Administration and National Religion in Ancient Palestine* (1982), treats secular and religious aspects of Hebrew history. W. D. Davis et al., *The Cambridge History of Judaism,* vol. 1 (1984), begins an important new synthesis with work on Judaism in the Persian period. R. Hachlili, *Ancient Jewish Art and Archaeology in the Land of Israel* (1988), attempts to trace the development and meaning of Jewish art in its archaeological context.

The Assyrians, despite their achievements, have not attracted the scholarly attention that other Near Eastern peoples have. Even though woefully outdated, A. T. Olmstead, *History of Assyria* (1928), has the merit of being soundly based in the original sources. H. W. F. Saggs, *Everyday Life in Babylonia and Assyria,* rev. ed. (1987), offers a general and well-illustrated survey of Mesopotamian history from 3000 to 300 B.C. Those who appreciate the vitality of Assyrian art should start with the masterful work of R. D. Barnett and W. Forman, *Assyrian Palace Reliefs,* 2d ed. (1970), an exemplary combination of fine photographs and learned but not difficult discussion.

Several new works on ancient Iran have lately appeared. A comprehensive survey of Persian history is given by one of the leading scholars in the field, R. N. Frye, *History of Ancient Iran* (1984). I. Gershevitch, ed., *The Cambridge History of Iran,* vol. 2 (1985), provides a full account of ancient Persian history, but many of the chapters are already out-of-date. E. Herzfeld, *Iran in the Ancient East* (1987), puts Persian history in a broad context. Most welcome is M. A. Dandamaev, *A Political History of the Achaemenid Empire* (1989), which discusses in depth the history of the Persians and the organization of their empire. M. Boyce, a leading scholar in the field, provides a sound and readable treatment of the essence of Zoroastrianism in her *Zoroastrianism* (1979).

LISTENING TO THE
PAST

The Covenant Between Yahweh and the Hebrews

This passage from the Hebrew Bible addresses two themes important to the Hebrews: the meaning of kingship and the nature of the Covenant between the Hebrews and Yahweh (here referred to as "the Lord"). The Hebrew Bible tells a great deal about the people who created it. From the following passage we may discern what the Hebrews thought about their own past and religion.

The background of the selection is a political crisis that has some archaeological support. The war with the Philistines put a huge strain on Hebrew society, and new and effective political and military leadership was needed to meet the situation. The elders of the tribes of Israel had previously chosen judges to lead the community only in times of crisis. The Hebrew people now demanded that a secular kingship be established, even though their Covenant declared their god Yahweh to be their king. Samuel, the last of the judges, with Yahweh's approval, anointed Saul as the first Hebrew king. In this excerpt Samuel confronts the Hebrews, reminding them of their obligation to honor the Covenant.

Then said Samuel to the people, Come, and let us go to Gilgal, and renew the kingdom there. And all the people went to Gilgal; and there they made Saul king before the Lord in Gilgal; and there they sacrificed sacrifices of peace offerings before the Lord; and there Saul and all the men of Israel rejoiced greatly.

And Samuel said unto all Israel, Behold, I have hearkened unto your voice in all that you said to me, and have made a king over you. And now, behold, the king walks before you; and I am old and gray-headed; and, behold, my sons are with you: and I have walked before you from my childhood until this day. Behold, here I am: witness against me before the Lord, and before his anointed: whose ox have I taken? or whose ass have I taken? or

whom have I defrauded? whom have I oppressed? or of whose hand have I received any bribe to blind my eyes with it? and I will restore it to you.

And they said, You have not defrauded us, nor oppressed us, neither have you taken anything from any man's hand.

And he said to them, the Lord is witness against you, and his anointed is witness this day, that you have not found anything in my hand. And they answered, he is witness.

At this point Samuel reminds the Hebrews that Yahweh has always been faithful to them, and he lists a number of times in history in which the Hebrews violated their Covenant. Then Samuel gives them stern advice, capped by a threat about any future disobedience.

Now therefore behold the king whom you have chosen, and whom you have desired! and, behold, the Lord has set a king over you. If you will fear the Lord, and serve him, and obey his voice, and not rebel against the commandment of the Lord, then shall both you and also the king who reigns over you continue following the Lord your God: But if you will not obey the voice of the Lord, but rebel against the commandment of the Lord, then shall the hand of the Lord be against you, as it was against your fathers.

Now therefore stand and see this great thing, which the Lord will do before your eyes. Is it not wheat harvest today? I will call to the Lord, and he shall send thunder and rain; that you may perceive and see that your wickedness is great, which you have done in the sight of the Lord, in asking you a king.

So Samuel called to the Lord; and the Lord sent thunder and rain that day: and all the people greatly feared the Lord and Samuel. And all the people said to Samuel, pray for your servants to the Lord your God, so that we will not die: for we have added to all of our sins this evil, to ask us for a king.

And Samuel said to the people, Fear not: you have done all this wickedness; yet turn not aside from following the Lord, but serve the Lord with all your heart; And do not turn aside; for then should you go after vain things, which cannot profit nor deliver; for they are vain. For the Lord will not forsake his people for his great name's sake: because it pleases the Lord to make you his people. Moreover, as for me, God forbid that I should sin against the Lord in ceasing to pray for you: but I will teach you the good and the right way: Only fear the Lord, and serve him in truth with all your heart: for consider how great things he has done for you. But if you shall still act wickedly, you will be consumed, both you and your king.

Questions for Analysis

1. How did Samuel explain his anointment of a king?

2. What was Samuel's attitude toward kingship?

3. What were the duties of the Hebrews toward Yahweh?

4. Might those duties conflict with those toward the secular king? If so, in what ways, and how might the Hebrews avoid the conflict?

Source: Abridged and adapted from 1 Samuel 11:15, 12:1–5, 16–25, *The Holy Bible.* Copyright © 1974 The Gideons International.

Ark of the Covenant, depicted in a relief from Capernaum Synagogue, second century A.D. *(Source: Ancient Art & Architecture Collection)*

Ancient India to ca A.D. 200

The North Gate is one of four ornately carved gates guarding the Buddhist memorial shrine at Sanchi, Madhya Pradesh. Satavahana, 2nd century B.C. *(Source: Jean-Louis Nou)*

While the peoples of the ancient Near East were spreading their cultures and grappling with the political administration of large tracts of land, people in India were wrestling with similar problems—taming the land, settling it, improving agricultural techniques, building cities and urban cultures, and asking basic questions about social organization and the nature of human life.

Like the civilizations of Mesopotamia and Egypt, the earliest Indian civilization centered on a great river, the Indus. Like the people of the ancient Near East, the people of ancient India confronted challenging climate and topography. They suffered monsoons; they faced jungle in some areas and desert in others. The fertile but undeveloped and underpopulated territory offered Neolithic pioneers and their descendants either prosperity or extinction, depending on how well they met the varied demands of the land. As in the ancient Near East, so too in India agriculture promoted an increase in population, and the needs of metal technology encouraged wider contacts.

- How did the ancient Indians respond to the problems that ancient Near Eastern peoples were confronting?
- How did they meet the challenge of the land itself?
- What role did religion play in Indian life?
- What kind of social and political organization developed in India?
- What intellectual and religious values did this society generate?

These questions are the central concerns of this chapter.

❉ THE LAND AND ITS FIRST TAMERS (CA 2500–1500 B.C.)

The subcontinent of India, a landmass as large as western Europe, juts southward into the warm waters of the Indian Ocean. India is a land of contrasts. Some regions are among the wettest on earth; others are dry and even arid desert and scrub land. High mountain ranges in the north drop off to the low river valleys of the Indus and Ganges.

Three regions of India are of overriding geographical significance: (1) the ring of mountains in the north that separates India from its neighbors, (2) the great river valleys of the Indus and Ganges and their tributaries, and (3) the southern peninsula, especially the narrow coastal plains and the large Deccan Plateau (Map 3.1). The lower reaches of the Himalaya Mountains—the northern geographical boundary of the subcontinent—are covered by some of India's densest forests, sustained by heavy rainfall. Immediately to the south the land drops away to the fertile river valleys of the Indus and Ganges. On these lowland plains, which stretch all the way across the subcontinent, agriculture has traditionally flourished. Furthermore, the flat terrain enabled invaders to sweep across and beyond the northern Indian plain, once they passed the area of Delhi. South of these valleys rise the Vindhya Mountains and the dry, hilly Deccan Plateau. Only along the coasts do the hills give way to narrow plains. In short, geography divides India into many subregions, some of them huge, fertile, and capable of sustaining large and vigorous populations.

The Himalayas, which in many places exceed 25,000 feet in height, protected ancient India from wandering peoples in search of new lands to settle. Throughout much of antiquity the Indian Ocean served to keep out invaders while fostering maritime trade with both the Near East and China and Southeast Asia. Only in the northwest—the area between modern Afghanistan and Pakistan—was India accessible to outsiders. This region, penetrated by the Khyber Pass, has traditionally been the highway of invaders—a highway whose other terminus was the flourishing cultures of the ancient Near East. Thus geography segregated India, but it also made possible contact with the ideas, practices, and technology of the earliest civilizations.

The Himalayas shield the subcontinent from the northern cold. They also hold in the monsoon rains that sweep northward from the Indian Ocean each summer. The monsoons and the melting snows of the Himalayas in the north provide India with most of its water. In some areas the resulting moistness and humidity created vast tracts of jungle and swamp. The Ganges, for example, was a particularly forbidding region, and only gradually did settlers move there from the tamer west. Much of India, however, is subtropical and dry. In

65

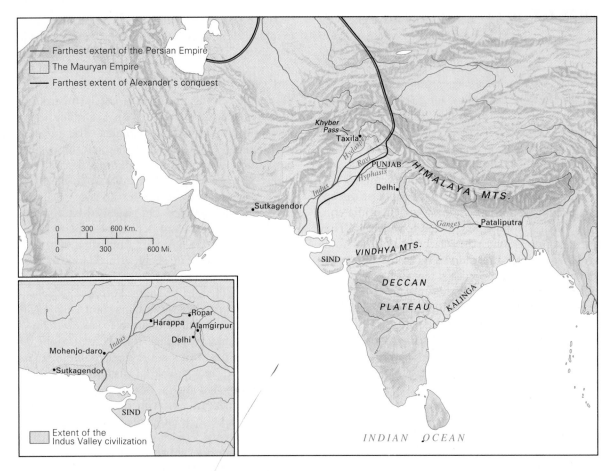

❀   **MAP 3.1 The Development of India from ca 2500 to ca 250 B.C.**   This map shows the development of India from the days of the Indus Valley civilization to the reign of Ashoka. Although northwestern India fell to foreign conquerors such as the Persians and Alexander the Great, most of India was unscathed by these incursions. Ashoka created the first real Indian empire.

general, the monsoon area of southwestern India experiences the heaviest rainfall; the driest region is the northeast. Geography and climate, and especially good water resources, combined to make the Punjab and the valley of the Indus River—now in Pakistan—the most attractive regions for India's first settlers.

The story of the first civilization in India, known as the Indus civilization, is one of the most dramatic in the entire ancient world. In 1921 archaeologists discovered astonishing evidence of a thriving and sophisticated urban culture dating to about 2500 B.C. About the tantalizing problem of the origin of the Indus civilization, the eminent English archaeologist Sir Mortimer Wheeler has commented:

By the middle of the 3rd millennium, something very important was happening in the Indus valley, and happening probably at great speed. Who the first leaders were who led their people, however hesitantly, down to the wide and jungle-ridden plain we shall never know, nor why they ventured; but they were bold men, pioneers in the fullest sense, no mere ejects from the highland zone. Some, perhaps many of them, led forlorn hopes and perished. . . . Seemingly the attempted colonization of the valley continued intermittently, failure succeeding failure, until at last a leader, more determined and far-sighted and fortunate than the rest, won through.[1]

This dramatic description of the earliest development of social life in India still possesses merit, but recent discoveries have clarified matters greatly. Wheeler was wrong, when he said that "we shall never know" about the earliest years of Indian life. Contemporary archaeologists and scholars have constructed a more complex interpretation of these events. They have found evidence of a gradual evolution of society from the Neolithic period to the Indus civilization. Scattered settlements consisted of people who made buildings of mudbrick. By at least 5000 B.C., these people had begun to raise crops of barley and wheat and to domesticate cattle, sheep, and goats. They basically laid the foundations of village and later urban life.

They created a thriving and sophisticated urban culture. Like the Mesopotamian city, the Indian city was surrounded by extensive farmland, which fed its inhabitants. These pioneers also developed a script, which is still undeciphered. As early as the reign of Sargon of Akkad in the third millennium B.C., trade between India and Mesopotamia carried goods and ideas between the two cultures, probably by way of the Persian Gulf.

The Indus civilization extended over fully 1.25 million square kilometers in the Indus Valley. Its two best-known cities were Mohenjo-daro in southern Pakistan and Harappa some four hundred miles to the north in the Punjab. Other sites have since been found in southern Pakistan, at Sutkagendor in the west, as far east as Alamgirpur near modern Delhi, and as far north as Ropar (see Map 3.1). Numerous sites are still being excavated, and a full portrait of this vast civilization will have to await archaeologists' findings. It is already clear, however, that the Indus civilization was marked by a striking uniformity of culture and, simultaneously, by regional variation.

Some important new linguistic work suggests that other peoples were also filtering into India from western Asia while the Indus civilization was flourishing. The Dravidians, who are usually considered natives of central and southern India, probably moved through the Indus Valley at about this time. The situation is far from clear because of the many movements of peoples in the subcontinent during these early years. There is, however, nothing to suggest that the Dravidians came as waves of invaders. For all that anyone knows today, they could have been newcomers who adopted various aspects of the Indus civilization, or they could have been an indigenous people who devised their own particular culture, sometimes borrowing heavily from the Harappan culture. Archaeology

Figurine from Mohenjo-daro   Part of the legacy of the Indus civilization is its artistic creations, such as this figurine of a bearded man. The composition is at once bold and sophisticated. Yet even glimpses such as this give little clue to the origins of the creators of the Indus civilization. (*Source: National Museum, Karachi*)

can tell us a great deal about how people lived, but it cannot always tell us how even major developments came about. In short, the movement of ancient peoples into India was a far more complex process than anyone imagined even a few years ago. Only future work in a variety of fields can clarify this immense phenomenon.

Mohenjo-daro and Harappa are currently the best-understood keys to the Indus civilization. Both cities were huge, over three miles in circumference, and housed large populations. Built of fired mud brick, Mohenjo-daro and Harappa were largely unfortified, although both were defended by great citadels that towered 40 or 50 feet above the surrounding plain. Both cities were logically planned from the outset, not merely villages that grew and sprawled haphazardly. In both, blocks of houses were laid out on a grid plan, centuries before the Greeks used this method of urban design. Streets were straight and varied from 9 to 34 feet in width. The houses of both cities were substantial, many two stories tall, some perhaps three, their brick exteriors unadorned. The focal point of the Indus houses was a central open courtyard onto which the rooms opened.

Perhaps the most surprising aspect of the elaborate planning of these cities is their complex system of drainage, well preserved at Mohenjo-daro. Each house had a bathroom with a drain connected to municipal drains located under the major streets. These brick-built channels, which carried off refuse, had openings to allow clearing of blockages.

Both cities also contained numerous large structures, which excavators think were public buildings. One of the most important is the state granary, a large storehouse for the community's grain. Moreover, a set of tenement buildings next to a series of round working-floors near the granary at Harappa suggests that the central government dominated the storage and processing of the city's cereal crops. The citadel at Mohenjo-daro further testifies to the power of the city's rulers: here stood monumental buildings, including a marketplace or place of assembly, a palace, and a huge bath featur-

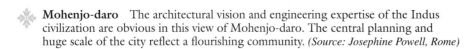

Mohenjo-daro   The architectural vision and engineering expertise of the Indus civilization are obvious in this view of Mohenjo-daro. The central planning and huge scale of the city reflect a flourishing community. *(Source: Josephine Powell, Rome)*

Bronze Chariot This bronze figure from Mohenjo-daro is an excellent example of early Indian bronze work. But it poses a problem. The vehicle itself is too slender to be a cart, as usually stated, but is well suited to be a chariot for war. *(Source: National Museum, New Delhi)*

ing a pool some 39 feet by 23 feet and 8 feet deep. The Great Bath, like later Roman baths, was an intricate structure with spacious dressing rooms for the bathers. Because the Great Bath at Mohenjo-daro resembles the ritual purification pools of later Indian society, some scholars have speculated that power was in the hands of a priest-king and that the Great Bath played a role in the religious rituals of the city. But little is yet known about the religious life of Mohenjo-daro and Harappa or about their government. Nonetheless, the power and authority of the government, whether secular or religious, are apparent in the intelligent central planning of these cities.

The prosperity of the Indus civilization depended on constant and intensive cultivation of the rich river valley. The Indus, like the Nile, provided farmers with fertile alluvial soil enriched by annual floods. Farmers built earth embankments to hold the floodwaters. The results of this labor were abundant crops of wheat, barley, vegetables, and cotton. The Indus people also domesticated cattle, buffalo, fowl, and possibly pigs and asses. Their efforts led to a high standard of living and to the surpluses that they traded with Mesopotamia. They were also in contact with neighbors closer to home, trading with the peoples of southern India for gold and with the ancient Afghans for silver.

Despite tantalizing glimpses of a serene and stable society, the intellectual and religious life of the Indus people is largely unknown. Fertility was a major concern to them, as it is to most agricultural people: they apparently worshiped a mother-goddess who looked after the welfare of the community. Some later Indian religious beliefs may have originated in this period. One of the most engaging of the early Indian deities—who is depicted at Mohenjo-daro with his customary three faces, surrounded by wild animals—closely resembles Siva, a major Hindu god. The Indus people's great fondness for animals is apparent in the popularity of terra-cotta animal figurines. Their attitude prefigures the deep respect for the animal world that Indians have traditionally felt. Indeed, they give the impression of having been a people in tune with the world around them, a world they understood and enjoyed. The Indus people maintained their equilibrium with nature for hundreds of years, spreading their culture throughout the valley and enjoying a tranquil development.

Yet this civilization, which appeared in history so suddenly, perished just as mysteriously. After years of prosperity, Mohenjo-daro and Harappa suffered a long decline, perhaps as a result of deforestation, a change in climate, and their huge demands on the land. The first excavators of Mohenjo-daro found some skeletons of men, women, and children, many with ax or sword wounds, scattered across the ground. Contemporary archaeologists, however, point out that too few skeletons at Mohenjo-daro showed signs of violence to indicate wholesale slaughter. Others suggest that the population may have fallen prey to diseases such as malaria. What is not disputed is that many of the Indus people lived on, though disrupted and scattered. With them they carried the accomplishments and values of their culture, which became an important element in the development of later Indian civilization. In fact, the rich religious life of the people proved more important than politics because it was the shared and enduring cultural heritage of the land. Kings came and went; the gods remained, thus religion was the glue that held Indian society together.

THE ASCENDANCY OF THE ARYANS (CA 1500–500 B.C.)

The Aryans, an Indo-European people who entered India from the northwest, may not have reached India until many years after the fall of the Indus civilization. Nevertheless, the Aryans, like the Hittites and later the Greeks, formed part of the widespread migrations that transformed the face of much of the ancient world, an event that forever changed the face of India. The Aryans were part of the enormous movement of Indo-Europeans described in Chapter 1 (see page 3). Their arrival was a turning point in Indian history. Nomadic wanderers, the Aryans came in search of land; the Indus Valley, with its rich plains and predictable climate, lured them on. There they met the native Dravidians, with whom they at first fought. Later the two peoples forged the basis of subsequent Indian society.

Most knowledge of the early Aryans comes from the Rigveda, the oldest and most sacred of the Hindu scriptures. The Rigveda is not a history but a collection of hymns in praise of the Aryan gods. Even so, the hymns contain some historical information that sheds light on the Aryans and on native Indians. The Rigveda and other Vedas, which were also sacred writings, are crucial to understanding the social evolution of India during this period, sometimes called the Dark Ages of India.

The Rigveda portrays the Aryans as a group of battle-loving pastoral tribes, a heroic folk at war with one another and with the native population of India. Their use of horses and bronze weapons in warfare gave them superiority over the natives. At the head of the Aryan tribe was its chief, or *raja,* who led his followers in battle and ruled them in peacetime. Next to the chief was the priest, entrusted with sacrifices to the gods and the knowledge of sacred rituals. In time, as Aryan society (also known as Vedic society) laid increasing emphasis on proper performance of the religious rituals, priests evolved into a distinct class possessing precise knowledge of the complex rituals and of the invocations and formulas that accompanied them. The warrior nobility rode to battle in chariots and perhaps on horseback and expressed its will in assemblies. The commoners supported society by tending herds and, increasingly as conditions settled, working the land. To the non-Aryans fell the drudgery of menial tasks. It is difficult to define precisely their social status. Though probably not slaves at this point, they were certainly dependents of the Aryans, and worked for them in return for support and protection. Women held a more favorable position in this period than in later times: they were not yet given in child-marriage, and widows had the right to remarry.

Gradually the Aryans pushed farther eastward into the valley of the Ganges River, a land of thick jungle populated by tribes. The jungle was as stubborn an enemy as its inhabitants, and clearing it presented a tremendous challenge. For the next six hundred years, the Aryans migrated eastward, finally founding the important city of Delhi. During this time the Aryans and their Indian predecessors blended their cultures, each influencing the other. The resulting synthesis constituted an entirely new Indian society.

The Shaping of Indian Society

Because the push into the jungle demanded an especially large and tightly organized political entity, tribes merged under strong rulers whose power grew increasingly absolute. As rulers claimed sovereignty over specific territory, political rule shifted from tribal chieftainship to kingship. The priests, or *Brahmans,* supported the growth of royal power in return for royal confirmation of their own religious rights, power, and status. The Brahmans also served a political function as advisers to the kings. In the face of this royal-priestly alliance, the old tribal assemblies of warriors withered away.

Development of the newly won territory led to further changes. Cleared land under cultivation needed constant work to keep it from reverting to jungle. The typical response to this challenge was the village. In this period India evolved into the land of villages it still is today. Even the later growth of cities did not eclipse the village as the hallmark of Indian society. Yet villages did not conform to a single social pattern. In the south the typical village consisted of groups of families who considered themselves related to one another, but as always there were exceptions, as when some villagers married outside their own village and outside the family. Each family was a large patriarchal joint or extended family composed of several nuclear families who lived and worked together. In the north, by contrast, marriage outside the village was more common, and families' kinship ties extended over wider areas than in the south. What all Indian villages had in common was a tradition of mutual cooperation born of common interests and obligations. The close-knit society of the village has consistently been a stabilizing element in Indian history. Yet as self-sufficient as it was, the village was far from isolated. It was connected with other villages both socially and economically, and formed the basic component in the various kingdoms of which it was a part. Unfortunately for the villagers, their primary contact with the ruling raja was paying him taxes. Yet in turn they could hope for a stable government and protection from invaders.

Social contact between Aryans and natives led to the development of the complicated system of social organization known as the caste system. A *caste* is a hereditary class of social equals who share the same religion, pursue a specific trade or occupation, and avoid extensive social intercourse with members of other castes. Initially this system had two goals: to distinguish Aryans from non-Aryans and to mark birth or descent. The caste system was fluid at first and allowed for a surprising amount of social mobility. Even in the early days of conquest the Aryans mixed with the conquered population, and that slow mingling eventually resulted in the Indian society that emerged into the full light of history. The blending was intellectual and religious as well as social. Only as conditions stabilized over the years did the system become strict and the number of castes grow.

To further complicate matters there was a system of *jati,* large joint family groups that became

Bronze Sword   A striking example of the quality of Aryan arms is this bronze sword, with its rib in the middle of the blade for strength. Native Indians lacked comparable weapons. *(Source: Courtesy of the Trustees of the British Museum)*

incorporated into society. Although the origin of the *jati* is uncertain, they became members of a specific caste, whose function was essentially economic. In effect, they specialized in specific trades, and even enjoyed governance by a ruling council of elders. In time some families branched out into trades not entirely related to the traditional trades of their families. The result was the broadening of the economic and the social importance of the *jati.* Eventually, the castes were subdivided into hundreds and even thousands of *jati.* Although this system may seem hopelessly confusing to others, it actually led to social stability. People know where they stood in society, and the *jati* also provided the opportunity for some social mobility within the caste.

By about 500 B.C. four main groups of Indian society—the priests *(Brahman),* the warriors *(Kshatriya),* the peasants *(Vaishya),* and the serfs *(Shudra)* —were evolving. Indians themselves ascribed this stratification to the gods, as the Rigveda testifies:

When they divided the [primeval] Man
  into how many parts did they divide him?
What was his mouth, what were his arms,
  what were his thighs and his feet called?
The Brahman was his mouth, of his
  arms was made the warrior.
His thighs became the Vaishya, of
  his feet the Shudra was born.[2]

According to this division of duties, the priests conducted religious sacrifices and treasured the religious lore. The warriors protected society from external attack and maintained law and order within it, and the peasants grew the food and paid the taxes. The serfs, who were originally the property of the tribe, served the others by performing hard labor. Those without places in this tidy social division—that is, those who entered it later than the others or who had lost their caste status through violations of ritual—were *outcastes*. That simply meant that they belonged to no caste. In time, some of these people became "untouchables," because they were "impure." They were so scorned because they earned their livings by performing such undesirable jobs as slaughtering animals and dressing skins. Although their work was economically valuable, it was considered unworthy and socially polluting.

Slavery was also a feature of social life, as it was elsewhere in antiquity. The scanty evidence available suggests that slavery in Aryan society resembled Mesopotamian slavery. In India there was no caste of slaves, although in practice most slaves would have come from the lower castes, which were economically disadvantaged. In the Aryan period, slaves were often people captured in battle, but these captives could be ransomed by their families. Still later, slavery was less connected with warfare; it was more of an economic and social institution. At birth, slave children automatically became the slaves of their parents' masters. Indian slaves

could be bought, used as collateral, or even given away. As in ancient Mesopotamia, a free man might sell himself and his family into slavery because he could not pay his debts. And, as in Hammurabi's Mesopotamia, he could, if clever, hard working, or fortunate, buy his and his family's way out of slavery.

Slaves in India performed tasks similar to those of slaves in other societies. Like Joseph in ancient Egypt, a man might serve as a royal counselor, having more actual authority than many a free man. Otherwise slaves served in their masters' fields, mines, or houses. Whatever their economic function, socially they were members of their master's household. Indian masters were required to perform the customary duties necessary for the welfare of the soul of a deceased slave. Indian law forbade a master from abandoning slaves in their old age; it also recommended manumission of slaves as an act of piety. Nonetheless, in Indian literature there is ample evidence of the abuse of slaves; and as in other societies—both ancient and modern—it is sometimes impossible to determine to what extent laws and social injunctions were actually put into practice.

Early Indian Religion

In religion and intellectual life, a momentous revolution was occurring in Indian society. The Aryan gods represented natural phenomena. Some of them were great brawling figures, like Agni, the god of fire; Indra, wielder of the thunderbolt and god of war; and Rudra, the divine archer who spread disaster and disease by firing his arrows at people. Others were shadowy figures, like Dyaus, the father of the gods, who appears in Greek as Zeus and in Latin as Jupiter. Varuna, the god of order in the universe, was a hard god, quick to punish those who sinned and thus upset the balance of nature. Ushas, the goddess of dawn, was a refreshingly gentle deity who welcomed the birds, gave delight to human beings, and kept off evil spirits. Although the Aryan gods had their duties, they differed from the Greek deities and Mesopotamian gods in that they rarely had distinctive personalities or extensive mythologies. All the Aryan gods enjoyed sacrifices, however, and ritual was an essential ingredient in early Aryan religion. Gradually, under the priestly monopoly of the Brahmans, correct sacrifice and proper ritual became so important that most Brahmans believed a

❀ **Ascetic Instructing Pupils**   All major branches of Indian intellectual thought, whether philosophical or religious, insisted on the proper education of students. Here an ascetic explains the tenets of his beliefs to a younger generation. *(Source: Indian Museum, Calcutta/Dinodia Picture Agency)*

properly performed ritual would force a god to grant a worshiper's wish. These beliefs became known as Brahmanism.

Religion became sterile and unsatisfying to many, even among the priestly class. In search of a faith richer and more mystical, some Brahmans retreated to the forests to seek a personal road to the gods. Through *asceticism*—severe self-discipline and self-denial—and meditation on the traditional teachings of the Vedas, these pioneers breathed new life into the old rituals. They concluded that disciplined meditation on the ritual sacrifice could produce the same results as the physical ritual it-

self. Thus they reinterpreted the ritual sacrifices as symbolic gestures with mystical meanings. Slowly Indian religion was changing from primitive worship to a way of thought that nourished human needs and eased human fears.

Two cardinal doctrines prevailed: *samsara,* the transmigration of souls by a continual process of rebirth, and *karma,* the tally of good and bad deeds that determined the status of an individual's next life. Good deeds led to better future lives; evil deeds, to worse future lives, even to reincarnation as an animal. Two methods of escape from continual reincarnation were possible: extreme asceticism and *yoga,* or intense meditation. Either method, if pursued successfully, allowed the individual to be absorbed into a timeless and changeless state. Thus gradually arose the concept of a wheel of life that included human beings, animals, and even gods.

To most people, especially those on the low end of the economic and social scale, these concepts were attractive. All existence, no matter how harsh and bitter, could be progress to better things. By living righteously and doing good deeds, people could improve their lot in the next life. Yet there was another side to these ideas: the wheel of life could be seen as a treadmill, giving rise to a yearning for release from the relentless cycle of birth and death. Hence the new concepts created tension in religious thought.

The solution to this baffling problem appears in the Upanishads, a collection of sacred texts created by ascetics who opened up new vistas in religious speculation. The authors of the Upanishads fostered the concept of *moksha,* or release from the wheel of life. All people, they taught, have in themselves an eternal truth and reality called *atman,* which corresponds to an identical but greater all-encompassing reality called *Brahman.* These mystics and ascetics claimed that life in the world is actually an illusion, and the only way to escape it and the wheel of life is to realize that reality is unchanging. By studying the Vedas, by penance, and by meditation, one could join one's individual self with the universal reality. This profound and subtle teaching they summed up in one sentence: "Thou art That." What does this sentence mean? The Chandogya Upanishad tells the story of a father explaining it to his son:

"Believe me, my son, an invisible and subtle essence is the Spirit of the whole universe. That is Reality. That is Atman. THOU ART THAT."

"Explain more to me, father," said Svetaketu.

"So be it, my son.

"Place this salt in water and come to me tomorrow morning."

Svetaketu did as he was commanded, and in the morning his father said to him: "Bring me the salt you put into the water last night."

Svetaketu looked into the water, but could not find it, for it had dissolved.

His father then said: "Taste the water from this side. How is it?"

"It is salt."

"Taste it from the middle. How is it?"

"It is salt."

"Taste it from that side. How is it?"

"It is salt."

"Look for the salt again and come again to me."

The son did so, saying: "I cannot see the salt. I only see water."

His father then said: "In the same way, O my son, you cannot see the Spirit. But in truth he is here.

"An invisible and subtle essence is the Spirit of the whole universe. That is Reality. That is Truth. THOU ART THAT."[3]

Providing a transcendent means to escape the problems presented by the wheel of life, these revolutionary ideas appealed to those who were dissatisfied with the old Brahman religion of sacrifice, and they even won the support of the Brahman and kings. The thought of the Upanishads gave Brahman a high status to which the poor and lowly could aspire in future life; consequently the Brahman greeted these concepts, and those who taught them, with tolerance and understanding. They made a place for them in traditional religious practice. The rulers of Indian society had excellent practical reasons to encourage the new trends. The doctrines of samsara and karma encouraged the poor and oppressed to labor peacefully and dutifully. The revolutionary new doctrines actually promoted stability in social and political life.

By about 500 B.C., all these trends—political, social, and religious—had led to a society, shaped by conqueror and conquered, in which all had a place. Urban life flourished alongside a vigorous village life, both sustained by agriculture. Gone were the warrior chieftains, their place taken by hereditary kings who ruled large territorial states with the support of a hereditary priestly class. Many of India's basic values already had taken shape at this early date.

 INDIA'S SPIRITUAL FLOWERING

India's spiritual growth came into full bloom in the sixth and fifth centuries B.C. This period of stunning moral and philosophical thought gave rise to three of the world's greatest religions: Hinduism, Jainism, and Buddhism. The evolution of these sects is complex and somewhat obscure. Hinduism is the most direct descendant of the old Vedic religion. Jainism and Buddhism shared that heritage but reacted against it and against Hinduism. Jainism and Buddhism originated as schools of moral philosophy, preoccupied with the nature of ultimate reality and with ethical conduct.

Hinduism

Hinduism may be the world's oldest flourishing religion. It is certainly one of the world's largest faiths, with millions of adherents in India and other Asian countries, the West Indies, and South Africa. It is also a complex of social customs, doctrines, and beliefs.

Although influenced by Jainism and Buddhism, Hinduism was most firmly rooted in traditional Indian religion. The bedrock of Hinduism is the belief that the Vedas are sacred revelations and that a specific caste system is implicitly prescribed in them. Thus Hinduism is both a collection of religious beliefs and a sacred division of society.

Religiously and philosophically, Hinduism is diverse. It assumes that there are innumerable legitimate ways of worshiping the supreme principle of life. Consequently it readily incorporates new sects, doctrines, beliefs, rites, and deities. The numerous Hindu gods are all considered aspects of Brahma, the supreme and undefinable principle of life. According to Hinduism, Brahma suffuses all things and at the same time transcends all things. The various deities are considered specific manifestations of Brahma. Each of them helps people to reach Brahma by means of rituals.

Hinduism is a guide to life, whose goal is to reach Brahma. There are four steps in this search, progressing from study of the Vedas in youth to complete asceticism in old age. In their quest for Brahma, people are to observe *dharma,* a moral law nearly as complex as Hinduism itself. Dharma stipulates the legitimate pursuits of Hindus: material gain, so long as it is honestly and honorably achieved; pleasure and love, for the perpetuation of the family; and moksha, release from the wheel of life and unity with Brahma. The society that a scrupulous observance of dharma could create is depicted in the *Mahabharata,* a long epic poem in which the law is personified as King Dharma (see Listening to the Past):

All the people, relying on King Dharma, lived happily like souls that rely on their own bodies that are favored with auspicious marks and deeds. The bull of the Bharatas cultivated Law, Profit, and Pleasure alike, like a family man honoring three kinsmen alike to himself. To Law, Profit, and Pleasure, now incarnated on earth in equal proportions, the king himself appeared as the fourth. In this overlord of men the Vedas found a superb student, the great sacrifices a performer, the four classes a pure guardian. Luck had found her place, wisdom its apex, all Law its kinsman with this lord of the earth.[4]

In short, Hinduism spells out the goals of life and how to attain them.

After the third century B.C., Hinduism began to emphasize the roles and personalities of powerful gods—especially Brahma, the creator; Siva, the cosmic dancer who both creates and destroys; and Vishnu, the preserver and sustainer of creation. Since these gods are personal manifestations of Brahma, Brahma can be known through them. Thus people could reach Brahma by devotion to personal gods. From this emphasis on a god-force in all life came a tradition of nonviolence to all living creatures.

India's best-loved sacred hymn, the Bhagavad Gita, is a spiritual guide to the most serious problem facing a Hindu—how to live in the world and yet honor dharma and thus achieve release. The heart of the Bhagavad Gita is the spiritual conflict confronting Arjuna, a human hero about to ride into battle against his own kinsmen. As he surveys the battlefield, struggling with the grim notion of killing his relatives, Arjuna voices his doubts to his charioteer, none other than the god Krishna himself. When at last Arjuna refuses to spill his family's blood, Krishna instructs him, as he has instructed generations of Hindus, on the true meaning of Hinduism:

Interwoven in his creation, the Spirit Brahma is beyond destruction. No one can bring to an end the Spirit which is everlasting. For beyond time he dwells in these bodies, though these bodies have an end in their time; but he remains immeasurable, immortal. Therefore, great warrior, carry on thy fight. If any man thinks he slays, and if another thinks he is slain, neither knows the ways of truth. The Eternal in man cannot kill; the Eternal in man cannot die. He is never born, and he never dies. He is in Eternity: he is for evermore. Never born and eternal, beyond times gone or to come, he does not die when the body dies. When a man knows him as never-born, everlasting, never-changing, beyond all destruction, how can that man kill a man, or cause another to kill?[5]

Krishna then clarifies the relation between human reality and the eternal spirit. He explains compassionately to Arjuna the duty to act—to live in the world and carry out his duties as a warrior. Indeed, the Bhagavad Gita urges the necessity of action, which is essential for the welfare of the world. Arjuna has the warrior's duty to wage war in compliance with his dharma. Only those who live

Siva One of the three most important Vedic gods, Siva represented both destruction and procreation. Here Siva, mounted on a bull and carrying a spear, attacks the demon Andhaka. Siva is seen as a fierce and bloodthirsty warrior. *(Source: C. M. Dixon/Photo Resources)*

within the divine law without complaint will be released from karma. One person's dharma may be different from another's, but both must follow their own dharma.

The intimate relation between Hindu religion and the social structure of Indian life merits special attention. They are inseparable parts of a unity that forms the core of Indian civilization. The caste system on the social and economic side forms one part of the equation, and Hinduism on the religious side forms the other. Religion justifies the caste system, and that social system in turn stands as visible proof of the validity of religious teaching. The stability of the village, absolutely basic to Indian civilization, is proof of the strength of this social and religious bond, which allows each village to be almost a complete universe in itself.

Early in India's history Hinduism provided a complex and sophisticated philosophy of life and a religion of enormous emotional appeal. Hinduism also inspired and preserved, in Sanskrit and the major regional languages of India, the vast literature that is India's priceless literary heritage.

Jainism

The founder and most influential thinker of Jainism, Vardhamana Mahavira (ca 540–468 B.C.), the son of an aristocrat, accepted the doctrines of karma and rebirth but developed the animistic philosophy that human beings, animals, plants, and even inanimate objects and natural phenomena all have living souls. Mahavira taught that the universe and everything in it are composed of souls, usually mixed with matter. These souls, though infinite in number, are finite in nature, having definite limits. Souls float or sink, according to Mahavira, depending on the amount of matter with which they are mixed. The only way for any soul to reach eternal happiness is to rid itself of all matter so that it can float to the top of the universe.

Mahavira's followers, known as Jains, believed that people could achieve eternal bliss only by living lives of asceticism and avoiding evil thoughts and actions. The Jains considered all life too sacred to be destroyed. Yet if everything in the world possesses a soul, how can one live without destroying other life? The rigorously logical answer is that one cannot. Strictly speaking, the Jains could adhere to their beliefs only by starving to death. But instead of going to this extreme, the Jains created a hierarchy of life, with human beings at the apex, fol-

Kali Ma The consort of Siva, Kali Ma represented both destructive and procreative powers, as he did. Here she assumes her role as the mother-goddess, but her necklace of skulls reminds viewers of her ferocity. *(Source: C. M. Dixon/Photo Resources)*

lowed by animals, plants, and inanimate objects. A Jain who wished to do the least possible violence to life became a vegetarian.

Nonviolence became a cardinal principle of Jainism and soon took root throughout Indian society. Although Jainism never took hold as widely as Hinduism and Buddhism, it has been an influential strand in Indian thought, and numbers several million adherents in India today. The Jains can claim, perhaps untruly, credit for one of the most practical innovations in Indian history, the creation

Praying Men Around a Stupa The stupa was a domed building erected as a Buddhist shrine. In this picture a group of holy men surround the stupa in prayer and reverence. *(Source: Eliot Elisofon Collection, Harry Ransom Humanities Center, University of Texas, Austin)*

of the Brahman alphabet. Because of the various dialects of the people, a simplified method of writing was needed to unite the kingdom. According to tradition, an aristocratic Jain woman invented an alphabet that made communication easier throughout the subcontinent.

Siddhartha Gautama and Buddhism

Siddhartha Gautama (ca 563–483 B.C.), better known as the Buddha, meaning the "Enlightened One," lived at the time when Jainism and Hinduism were evolving. The Buddha, like Mahavira, also became dissatisfied with settled life and abandoned it for a wandering, ascetic existence. The Buddha was so distressed by human suffering that he abandoned his family's Hindu beliefs in a quest

for a more universal, ultimate enlightenment. He tried techniques of extreme asceticism, including fasting, but found that they led nowhere. Only through meditation did he achieve the universal enlightenment in which he comprehended everything, including how the world of samsara actually worked.

Followers later believed that the Buddha taught them only what was necessary but that he had seen much more. According to this view, what he considered necessary were the "Four Noble Truths" contained in his first sermon: (1) pain and suffering, frustration, and anxiety are ugly but inescapable parts of human life; (2) suffering and anxiety are caused by the human weaknesses of greed, selfishness, and egoism; (3) people can understand these weaknesses and triumph over them;

and (4) this triumph is made possible by following a simple code of conduct, which the Buddha called the "Eightfold Path."

First, the Buddha explained, people have to understand the evils they are suffering. Ultimate release can be achieved only if one has a clear view of the pain and misery of one's life. Second, one has to decide firmly to free oneself from suffering. Third, one can do so by means of what the Buddha called "right conduct" and fourth by "right speech," a way of living in which one practices the virtues of love and compassion, joy, and serenity in daily life. The fifth step on the Eightfold Path is to choose "right livelihood," a means of earning a living that does not interfere with the attainment of ultimate enlightenment. The sixth step is "right endeavor," the conscious effort to eliminate distracting and harmful desires. People can most readily see the worthlessness of desires, according to the Buddha, by recognizing that everything and everyone in the world will pass away. Nothing is permanent. The seventh step is "right awareness," constant contemplation of one's deeds and words, giving full thought to their importance and whether they lead to enlightenment. "Right contemplation" is the last step expected of travelers on the Eightfold Path. This step entails deep meditation on the impermanence of everything in the world.

With the attainment of the eighth step, the traveler achieves *nirvana*, a state of happiness gained by the extinction of self and desires and the release from the effects of karma. Thus the Buddha propounded his own version of karma and how it worked. Though rooted in Hinduism, Buddhism set off on a road of its own, a road that eventually led out of India.

The Buddha also taught that if people understand that everything changes with time, they will neither cling to their egos nor worry about what they believe to be their eternal souls. To Buddhists a human being is a collection of parts, physical and mental. As long as the parts remain combined, that combination can be called "I." When that combination changes, as at death, the various parts remain in existence, ready to become the building blocks of different combinations. According to Buddhist teaching, life is passed from person to person as a flame is passed from candle to candle.

Buddhism placed little emphasis on gods. The gods might help people out of difficulties like illness, but they are not judges who reign beyond the grave or help achieve enlightenment. Nevertheless, the Buddha did conceive of a spiritual state of reality beyond the physical that can be called *nirvana*, which is basically a Hindu concept. In Indian thought *nirvana* is complicated and seen in several ways. For instance, among the Hindus it meant the reunion of the individual with Bramha. Among the Buddhists it meant that people who faithfully followed the Buddha's precepts could escape their mortal life with its tribulations and become united with the cosmic world. In short, the Buddha pointed the way for individuals to merge with the universe. As he told his followers: "There is an unborn, an unoriginated, an unmade, an uncompounded; were there not . . . there would be no escape from the world of the born, the originated, the made and the compounded."[6] This unborn and unmade power had nothing to do with the journey to nirvana. That was entirely up to the individual.

The success of Buddhism largely resulted from the Buddha's teaching that everyone, noble and peasant, educated and ignorant, male and female, could follow the Eightfold Path. Moreover, the Buddha was extraordinarily undogmatic. Convinced that each person must achieve enlightenment alone, he emphasized that the Path was important only because it led the traveler to enlightenment, not for its own sake. He compared it to a raft, essential to cross a river but useless once on the far shore. He warned his followers not to let dogma stand in the way of the journey. Buddhism differed from Hinduism by its willingness to accept anyone who wished to join, and in effect it tacitly rejected the caste system.

Like Mahavira, the Buddha formed a circle of disciples. He continually reminded the *Sangha*—an order of Buddhist monks—that each person must reach ultimate fulfillment by individual effort, but he also recognized the value of a group of people striving for the same goal. Buddhism also established an order of nuns that gave women the opportunity to seek for "truth" as men had traditionally done.

After the Buddha's death, the Sangha met to decide exactly what Buddhist doctrine was and to smooth out differences of interpretation. The result was the split of Buddhism into two great branches: the *Theravada* (or *Hinayana*, Way of the Elders, or Lesser Vehicle) and the *Mahayana* (or Larger Vehicle). The Theravada branch, which found its greatest popularity in Southeast Asia,

INDIA TO CA A.D. 200   ✤

ca 2500–1500 B.C.	Indus civilization
ca 1500–500 B.C.	Arrival of the Aryans and development of Vedic society
6th–5th centuries B.C.	Development of Hinduism, Jainism, and Buddhism
ca 513 B.C.	Persian conquest of northwestern India and the Indus Valley
326 B.C.	Alexander the Great conquers northwestern India and the Indus Valley
322–298 B.C.	Reign of Chandragupta
ca 269–232 B.C.	Reign of Ashoka
ca 261 B.C.	Ashoka conquers Kalinga, leading to spread of Buddhism in India
ca 183–145 B.C.	Greek Invasion of India
ca 140 B.C.	First Chinese ambassadors to India
1st century A.D.	Shaka and Kushan invasions of India
A.D. 25–3rd century	Kushan rule in northwestern India
ca A.D. 78	Kushan emperor Kanishka promotes Buddhism

from Sri Lanka to Kampuchea (modern Cambodia), asserted that its tenets rested on the authentic teachings of Buddha—in short, that it represented the oldest and purest form of Buddhism. By ca 20 B.C. the monks of the Theravada branch had met to write down what they considered the authentic teachings of the Buddha and Buddhist tradition. Theravada Buddhism is called the Lesser Vehicle because of its conservative and strict doctrines. Followers believed that the individual is saved only through a rigorous monastic life. These distinctions are solely doctrinal in that the followers of the Buddha defined what they thought Buddhism ought to mean. In that respect, they created divisions of varying interpretations of Buddhism similar to those of later Christians and Muslims, who made similar distinctions in their interpretation of the teachings of Jesus and Mohammed.

Mahayana Buddhism, far more liberal than the Theravada branch, believed that Buddhism was a vast system capable of saving many living things. It also held that the teachings of Buddha were fluid and would evolve over time in different cultures and climates. Mahayana Buddhism emphasized the compassionate side of the Buddha's message. It was known as the Larger Vehicle because it maintained that there were many ways to salvation. Mahayana Buddhism stressed the possibility of other buddhas yet to come and taught that all buddhas follow a path open to everyone in the world. Mahayana held that the Buddha in his previous lives had been a *bodhisattva*—a wise being, a buddha-in-becoming. Bodhisattvas have achieved enlightenment but decline the reward of nirvana to help others. Later Mahayana Buddhism created a huge pantheon of heavenly buddhas and bodhisattvas to whom people could pray for help toward enlightenment.

Mahayana Buddhism eventually won the hearts and minds of the Chinese, Japanese, Koreans, and Vietnamese. Yet not until the dramatic conversion of the Indian king Ashoka, some two centuries after the death of the Buddha, did Buddhist teachings spread much beyond India. Indian merchants, not missionaries, were crucial to the spread of Buddhism. They carried Buddhist beliefs along

The Great Buddha   This figure of Buddha sits grandly and serenely in a cave in Jung-Kang. Here the portrayal of Buddha is typical of Theravada Buddhism, in which individuals sought their salvation alone through asceticism, meditation, and monasticism. *(Source: Werner Forman/Art Resource, NY)*

with their wares far beyond India into Sri Lanka, parts of southeast Asia, and China, Korea, and Japan.

INDIA AND THE WEST (CA 513–298 B.C.)

Between the arrival of the Aryans and the rise of Hinduism, India enjoyed freedom from outside interference. In the late sixth century B.C., however, western India was swept up in events that were changing the face of the ancient Near East. During this period the Persians were creating an empire that stretched from the western coast of Anatolia to the Indus River (see page 58–59). India became

involved in these events when the Persian emperor Darius conquered the Indus Valley about 513 B.C.

Persian control did not reach eastward beyond the banks of the Indus. Even so, as part of the Persian Empire, western India enjoyed immediate contact not only with the old cultures of Egypt and Mesopotamia but also with the young and vital culture of the Greeks. What effects did contact with Persia and the lands farther west have on India?

Culturally the Persian conquest resembled the Hyksos period in Egypt (see page 27) in that it was a fertilizing event, introducing new ideas, techniques, and materials into India. As members of the vast Persian Empire, Indians learned administrative techniques—how to rule large tracts of land

and huge numbers of people. From the Persians the Indians learned the technique of minting silver coins, and they adopted the Persian monetary standard to facilitate trade with other parts of the empire. Even states in the Ganges Valley, which were never part of the empire, adopted the use of coinage. Another innovation was the introduction of the Aramaic language and script, the official language of the Persian Empire. Indians adapted the Aramaic script to their needs and their languages and were able to keep records and publish proclamations just as the Persians did.

Likewise, India participated in the larger economic world created by the Persians. Trade increased dramatically with other regions under Persian rule. Once again hardy merchants took the sea route to the West, as had their predecessors in the Indus civilization. Caravan cities grew in number and wealth as overland trade thrived in the peace brought about by Persian rule. In short, the arrival of the Persians drew India into the mainstream of sophisticated urban, commercial, and political life in the ancient world.

Into this world stormed Alexander the Great, who led his Macedonian and Greek troops through the Khyber Pass into the Indus Valley in 326 B.C. (see pages 149–150). What he found in India is most readily apparent in Taxila, a major center of trade in the Punjab (see Map 3.1). The Greeks described Taxila as "a city great and prosperous, the biggest of those between the Indus River and the Hydaspes [the modern Jhelum River]—a region not inferior to Egypt in size, with especially good pastures and rich in fine fruits."[7] Modern archaeology has proved the Greeks' praise excessive: despite its prosperity and importance as a seat of Hindu learning, Taxila was an unassuming town, a poor town when compared with the cities of the Near East.

From Taxila, Alexander marched to the mouth of the Indus River before turning west and leaving India forever. A riot of bloodshed and destruction, Alexander's invasion facilitated the rise of the first kingdom to embrace all of India.

The Mauryan Empire (ca 322–232 B.C.)

Alexander disrupted the political map of western India and died without organizing his conquests, leaving the area in confusion. Chandragupta, the ruler of a small state in the Ganges Valley, took ad-

vantage of this situation by defeating his enemies piecemeal until, by 322 B.C., he had made himself sole master of India. In 304 B.C. he defeated the forces of Seleucus, a general of Alexander the Great who founded the Seleucid monarchy. In the wake of this battle, Seleucus surrendered the easternmost provinces of his monarchy and concluded a treaty of alliance with Chandragupta. Hence Chandragupta not only defeated one of the mightiest of Alexander's lieutenants but also entered the world of Hellenistic politics (see Chapter 6).

The real heir to Alexander's conquest, Chadragupta created the great Mauryan Empire, which stretched from the Punjab and Himalayas in the north almost to the tip of the subcontinent, from modern Afghanistan in the west to Bengal in the east. In the administration of his empire, Chandragupta adopted the Persian practice of dividing the area into provinces. Each province was assigned a governor, most of whom were drawn from Chandragupta's own family. The smallest unit in this system was typically the village, the mainstay of Indian life. From his capital at Pataliputra, in the valley of the Ganges, the king sent agents to the provinces to oversee the workings of government and to keep him informed of conditions in his realm. Chandragupta also enjoyed the able assistance of his great minister Kautilya, who wrote a practical treatise on statecraft. For the first time in Indian history, one man governed most of the subcontinent, exercising control through delegated power.

With stunning effectiveness Chandragupta applied the lessons learned from Persian rule. He established a complex bureaucracy to see to the operation of the state and a bureaucratic taxation system that financed public services. He also built a regular army, complete with departments for everything from naval matters to the collection of supplies. He exercised tight control, to some degree repressing the people in order to retain power.

Megasthenes, a Greek ambassador of King Seleucus, left a lively description of life at Chandragupta's court. Like many other monarchs, Chandragupta feared treachery, especially assassination, and took elaborate precautions against intrigue. According to Megasthenes:

Attendance on the king's person is the duty of women, who indeed are bought from their fathers. Outside the gates of the palace stand the bodyguards and the rest of the soldiers. . . . Nor does the king sleep during the day, and at night he is forced at various hours to change his bed because of those plotting against him. Of his non-military departures from the palace one is to the courts, in which he passes the day hearing cases to the end, even if the hour arrives for attendance on his person. . . . When he leaves to hunt, he is thickly surrounded by a circle of women, and on the outside by spear-carrying bodyguards. The road is fenced off with ropes, and to anyone who passes within the ropes as far as the women death is the penalty.[8]

Those measures worked: after resigning the kingship, according to the tradition of the Jains, Chandragupta died the peaceful death of a Jain ascetic in 298 B.C. He left behind a kingdom organized to maintain order and defend India from invasion. India enjoyed economic prosperity and communication with its neighbors. At a time when many of the major cultures of the world were in direct touch with one another, the Indians, who had created much from their own experience and had learned much from others, could proudly make their own contributions in both cultural and material spheres.

The Reign of Ashoka (ca 269–232 B.C.)

The years after Chandragupta's death in 298 B.C. were an epoch of political greatness, thanks largely to Ashoka, one of India's most remarkable figures. The grandson of Chandragupta, Ashoka extended the Mauryan Empire to its farthest limits. The era of Ashoka was enormously important in the religious and intellectual history of the world. A man in search of spiritual solace, Ashoka embraced Buddhism and helped to establish it as an important religion. Buddhism would take deep and lasting root throughout much of the East, but not in India itself.

As a young prince, Ashoka served as governor of two important provinces, both seats of Buddhism—at this time still solely an Indian religion—and both commercially wealthy. While governor, Ashoka met and married Devi, a woman of the merchant class who would later end her life spreading Buddhism to Sri Lanka. In religion Ashoka was deeply influenced by Brahmanism and Jainism, which pointed him toward a broad religious outlook.

At the death of his father about 274 B.C., Ashoka rebelled against his older brother, the rightful king, and after four years of fighting succeeded in his bloody bid for the throne. Crowned king of India, Ashoka ruled intelligently and energetically. He was equally serious about his pleasures, especially those of the banquet hall and harem. In short, Ashoka in the early years of his reign was an efficient and contented king whose days were divided between business and pleasure.

The change that occurred in the ninth year of his reign affected not just Ashoka and his subjects but the subsequent history of India and the rest of

Lion Capital of Ashoka This lion capital from a column of Ashoka handsomely represents the emperor's political power. It also illustrates significant Near Eastern and Greek influences on the Indian art of this period. *(Source: Raghubir Singh)*

the world. In that year Ashoka conquered Kalinga, the modern state of Orissa on the east coast of India; in a grim and savage campaign, Ashoka reduced Kalinga by wholesale slaughter. As Ashoka himself admitted, "In that (conquest) one hundred and fifty thousand were killed (or maimed) and many times that number died."[9] Yet instead of exulting like a conqueror, Ashoka was consumed with remorse and revulsion at the horror of war. On the battlefield of Kalinga, the conquering hero looked for a new meaning in life; the carnage of Kalinga gave birth to a new Ashoka. The king embraced Buddhism and used the machinery of his empire to spread Buddhist teachings throughout India.

Ashoka's remarkable crisis of conscience has been the subject of considerable debate, much like the later conversion to Christianity of the Roman emperor Constantine. No one will ever know the content of Ashoka's mind, but the practical results of his conversion led to a more humane governance of India. Ashoka emphasized compassion, nonviolence, and adherence to dharma. He may have perceived dharma as a kind of civic virtue, a universal ethical model capable of uniting the diverse peoples of his extensive empire. Ashoka erected inscriptions to inform the people of his policy. In one edict, he spoke to his people like a father:

Whatever good I have done has indeed been accomplished for the progress and welfare of the world. By these shall grow virtues namely: proper support of mother and father, regard for preceptors and elders, proper treatment of Brahmans and ascetics, of the poor and the destitute, slaves and servants.[10]

Ashoka's new outlook can be seen as a form of *paternalism,* well-meaning government that provides for the people's welfare without granting them much responsibility or freedom. He appointed new officials to oversee the moral welfare of the realm and made sure that local officials administered humanely.

Ashoka felt the need to protect his new religion and keep it pure. Warning Buddhist monks that he would not tolerate *schism*—divisions based on differences of opinion about doctrine or ritual—he threw his support to religious orthodoxy. At the same time, Ashoka honored India's other religions. Hinduism and Jainism were revered and respected, and the emperor even built shrines for their worshipers.

Despite his devotion to Buddhism, Ashoka never neglected his duties as emperor. He tightened the central government of the empire and kept a close check on local officials. He also built roads and rest spots to improve communication within the realm. Ashoka himself described this work:

On the highways Banyan trees have been planted so that they may afford shade to men and animals; mango-groves have been planted; watering-places have been established for the benefit of animals and men.[11]

These measures also facilitated the march of armies and the armed enforcement of Ashoka's authority. Ashoka's efforts were eminently successful: never before his reign and not again until the modern period did so much of India enjoy peace, prosperity, and humane rule.

India and Its Invaders (ca 250 B.C.–A.D. 200)

Ashoka's reign was the high point of ancient India's political history. His successors remained on the throne until about 185 B.C.; thereafter India was subject to repeated foreign invasions, confined principally to the northwest, that constantly changed the political map of the country. Invaders held northwestern India, and petty Indian kings ruled small realms in the rest of India. For many years the history of India was a tale of relentless war between invaders and Indians and among native Indian kings as well. The energy consumed by these internal wars prevented the Indians from driving out the invaders, from bringing peace and prosperity to the land. Still, even though each wave of newcomers left its mark on the cultural heritage of India, Indian civilization triumphed, changing the invaders as well as being fertilized by them.

The Kushans, whose authority in India lasted until the third century A.D., were particularly significant because their empire encompassed much of central Asia as well as northwestern India. The Kushans put India in closer contact with its eastern neighbors. The Kushan invaders were assimilated into Indian society as Kshatriyas, of higher status than native Vaisya, Shudra, outcastes, and untouchables, and once again a backward nomadic people fell under the spell of a more sophisticated civilization.

The Kushans played a valuable role by giving northwest India a long period in which to absorb the newcomers and adapt the cultural innovations introduced by the various invaders. Kushans and Indians alike absorbed Greek ideas. Greek culture made its greatest impression on Indian art. Greek artists and sculptors working in India adorned Buddhist shrines, modeling the earliest representation of Buddha on Hellenistic statues of Apollo, and they were the leading force behind the Gandhara school of art in India. Only the form, however, was Greek; the content was purely Buddhist. In short, India owes a modest cultural debt to Hellenism. Just as Ashoka's Buddhist missionaries made no impression on the Greek world, so Hellenism gave India some fresh ideas but had no lasting impact on the essence of Indian life. Only Buddhism, which addressed itself to all human beings rather than to any particular culture, was at all significant as a meeting ground for the Greeks, Indians, and Kushans. Otherwise, the outlooks and values of Greek and Indian cultures were too different and too tenacious for one to assimilate the essence of the other.

From the perspective of history, the most significant and lasting gift of these years was the spread of Buddhism to China. India's invaders embraced Buddhism enthusiastically and protected the Buddhist order. They preferred the teachings of the Mahayana sect, more compassionate and flexible than its rival Theravada branch. In the course of their commercial dealings, they carried Mahayana Buddhism across inner Asia to China, transforming it from a purely Indian sect into an international religion.

Kushan Girl This young woman, splendidly bedecked with jewelry, is carrying a platter of food, presumably for a feast. Indian art of this period is justly noted for its realism and its portrayal of ordinary events. *(Source: Courtesy, Archaeological Museum, Mathura)*

SUMMARY

By roughly 250 B.C. India had developed a highly accomplished urban civilization sustained by systematic agriculture. Many of the fundamental ideals, beliefs, customs, and religious practices that would leave their mark on succeeding generations had already taken shape. These early years of Indian history were especially rich in religion. Not only did the Indians form several different views of the nature of life and visions of an afterlife, but they also made a fundamental impact on life in China by the spread of Buddhism. Hinduism, both religious and social in nature, was for the Indians themselves perhaps the most important development of this period, an ancient heritage that is still a vital factor in Indian life.

NOTES

1. M. Wheeler, *Early India and Pakistan to Ashoka* (London: Thames and Hudson, 1959), pp. 106–107.
2. Rigveda 10.90, translated by A. L. Basham, in *The Wonder That Was India* (New York: Grove Press, 1954), p. 241.
3. J. Mascaro, trans., *The Upanishads* (London: Penguin Books, 1965), pp. 117–118.
4. J. A. B. van Buitenen, trans., *The Mahabharata,* vol. 1, *The Book of the Beginning* (Chicago: University of Chicago Press, 1973), 214.1–7.
5. J. Mascaro, trans., *The Bhagavad Gita* (London: Penguin Books, 1962), 2.17–21.
6. Quoted in N. W. Ross, *Three Ways of Asian Wisdom* (New York: Simon and Schuster, 1966), p. 94.
7. Arrian, *Anabasis* 5.8.2; Plutarch, *Alexander* 59.1. Translated by John Buckler.
8. Strabo, 15.1.55. Translated by John Buckler.
9. Quoted in B. G. Gokhale, *Asoka Maurya* (New York: Twayne Publishers, 1966), p. 157.
10. Pillar Edict 7, quoted ibid., p. 169.
11. Quoted ibid., pp. 168–169.

SUGGESTED READING

Much splendid work has been done on the geographical background of ancient Indian society. Two fine works are B. L. C. Johnson, *South Asia: Selective Studies of the Essential Geography of India, Pakistan, and Ceylon* (1969), and, for the ecological history of India, M. Gadgil and R. Guha, *This Fissured Land* (1993). A masterpiece in its own right is J. Schwartzberg, ed., *An Historical Atlas of South Asia* (1978), the epitome of what a historical atlas should be. Its contents range well into contemporary times.

General histories of India are too numerous to list, with the exception of A. L. Basham, *The Wonder That Was India* (1959), one of the monuments of the field and a good introduction to nearly every aspect of ancient Indian history. Solid too are R. Thapar, *Ancient Indian Social History* (1978), and R. B. Inden, *Imagining India* (1990), a difficult work that controversially covers all essential aspects of Indian life. Both are highly recommended. Especially rewarding are Z. Liu, *Ancient India and Ancient China* (1988); S. F. Mahmud, *A Concise History of Indo-Pakistan,* 2d ed. (1988); and H. Scharff, *The State in Indian Tradition* (1989), which covers the period from the Aryans to the Muslims.

Work on the Indus civilization continues at a rapid pace. A very good survey of the topic is H. Kulke and D. Rothermund, *A History of India* (1990), as is N. N. Bhattacharya, *Ancient Indian History and Civilization* (1988), which focuses on India before A.D. 1000. See also G. L. Possehl, ed., *Harappan Civilization: A Contemporary Perspective* (1982), which combines excavation reports and analysis of material. Possehl's *Ancient Cities of the Indus* (1979) reprints articles by a number of scholars, thus providing a variety of perspectives on early Indus developments. Trade between the Indus and Mesopotamian civilizations is treated in E. C. L. During Caspers, "Sumer, Coastal Arabia and the Indus Valley in Protoliterate and Early Dynastic Eras," *Journal of Economic and Social History of the Orient* 22 (1979): 121–135. See also G. L. Possehl and M. H. Ravel, *Harappan Civilization and Rojdi* (1989), which uses the newest archaeological findings to explore the Harappan civilization. D. K. Chakrabarti, *The Early Use of Iron in India* (1992), uses archaeological evidence to prove that the ancient Indians used iron far earlier than previously thought.

For the arrival of the Aryans and subsequent developments, see R. Thapar, *From Lineage to State* (1990), which examines the historical kingdoms of the mid-first millenium B.C., N. R. Banerjee, *The Iron Age in India* (1965), and C. Chakraborty, *Common Life in the Rig-veda and Atharvaveda* (1977), which treat the period from different points of view. More difficult but rewarding is F. Southworth, "Lexical Evidence for Early Contacts Between Indo-Aryan and Dravidian," in M. M. Deshpande and P. E. Hook, eds., *Aryan and Non-Aryan in India* (1979), pp. 191–234; the book contains a number of other stimulating articles on the period.

Early Indian religion is a complex subject, but a series of books provides a good introduction to the topic. P. S. Jaini, *The Jaina Path of Purification* (1979), and T. Hopkins, *Hindu Religious Tradition* (1971), cover two of the major religions, to which should be added K. K. Klostermaier, *A Survey of Hinduism* (1989), and K. H. Potter, *Guide to Indian Philosophy* (1988).

Buddhism is such a popular topic that the bibliography is virtually endless. H. Akira, *A History of Indian Buddhism* (1990), treats the early history of the Buddha and his followers. Also enlightening is W. Rahula, *What the Buddha Taught* (1971), which sheds light on the Theravada tradition, and R. Robinson and W. Johnson, *The Buddhist Religion,* 3d ed. (1982), which is more comprehensive. Still unsurpassed for its discussion of the relations between Buddhism and Hinduism is the grand work of C. N. Eliot, *Hinduism and Buddhism,* 3 vols. (reprinted 1954), which traces the evolution of theistic ideas in both religions. C. Humphreys has written extensively about Buddhism. The student may wish to consult his *Buddhism* (1962), *Exploring Buddhism* (1975), or *The Wisdom of*

Buddhism (new ed., 1979). More recent is D. Fox, *The Heart of Buddhist Wisdom* (1985).

A stimulating and far-reaching discussion of intellectual developments in India is R. Thapar, "Ethics, Religion, and Social Protest in the First Millennium B.C. in North India," *Daedalus* 104 (Spring 1975): 119–132. Good translations of Indian literature discussed in the chapter are listed in the Notes.

Among the numerous works describing India's relations with the Persian Empire and Alexander the Great are several titles cited in Suggested Reading for Chapters 2 and 6. P. H. L. Eggermont, *Alexander's Campaigns in Sind and Baluchistan* (1975), focuses solely on Alexander's activities in India, as does E. Badian in I. Gershevitch, ed., *The Cambridge History of Iran* (1985). A. J. Dani, *The Historic City of Taxila* (1988), uses anthropological and historic evidence to study this important city and its influence. S. Jones, *Afghanistan* (1992), gives the most recent general history of the area.

Chandragupta's reign is treated in R. K. Mookerji, *Chandragupta Maurya and His Times,* rev. ed. (1966). J. C. Heesterman, "Kautilya and the Ancient Indian State," *Wiener Zeitschrift* 15 (1971): 5–22, analyzes the work and thought of Chandragupta's great minister of state.

The kingdom of Ashoka has attracted much attention. In addition to Gokhale's book cited in the Notes, R. Thapar's excellent *Asoka and the Decline of the Mauryas* (1961) is still an indispensable work on the subject. B. S. Miller, *The Power of Art* (1992), discusses the impact of patronage on art—on those who subsidized works and on those who created them —and the pervasiveness of patronage throughout southern India.

For the Greek invasions, see W. W. Tarn, *The Greeks in Bactria and India* (1951), a difficult book but still valuable. A. K. Narain's more recent treatment, *The Indo-Greeks* (1967), is equally valuable and a bit more readable. For contact between the Hellenistic world and India, see J. W. Sedlar, *India and the Greek World* (1980), which approaches the problem of cultural transmission between the two civilizations. C. Drekmeier, *Kingship and Community in Early India* (1968), takes a broader approach to early developments.

LISTENING TO THE
PAST

An Account of the Gods and the Creation of the World

Indian religious concepts were very complicated. Poets and priests explained early ideas in a vast poem, the Mahabharata, *written in Sanskrit. The work included epics, theology, ethical and metaphysical doctrine; it also included legends and literary romances. The core of the* Mahabharata *is similar to Homer's* Iliad *in that it treats a political and military clash of epic proportions. In short, it describes the struggle between five heroic brothers, the Pandavas, and their one hundred cousins for the rule of the land. The section presented below has nothing to do with this mighty conflict. Instead it explains the origin of the universe and of human life within it. It also deals with the nature and significance of Brahman.*

The seers said:

Tell us that ancient Lore that was related by the eminent sage Dvaipāyana, which the Gods and brahmin seers honored when they heard it! That divine language of the sublime Histories, in all the varieties of words and books, the sacred Account of the Bhāratas, that language of complex word and meaning, ruled by refinement and reinforced by all sciences, which Vaiśaṃpāyana, at Dvaipāyana's bidding, repeated truthfully to the satisfaction of King Janamejaya at the king's sacrifice. We wish to hear that Grand Collection, now joined to the Collections of the Four Vedas, which Vyāsa the miracle-monger compiled, replete with the Law and dispelling all danger of evil!

The Bard said:

I bow to the Primeval Person the Lord, widely invoked and lauded, who is the True, the One-Syllabled Brahman, manifest and unmanifest, everlasting, at once the existent and the nonexistent, Creator of things high and low. I bow to him who is the Ancient One, supreme, imperishable, blissful and blessing, the most desirable Viṣṇu, faultless and resplendent, who is Kṛṣṇa Hṛṣīkeśa, the preceptor of all creatures, those that move and those that move not; the God Hari.

I shall speak the entire thought of that great seer and saint who is venerated in all the world, Vyāsa of limitless brilliance. Poets have told it before, poets are telling it now, other poets shall tell this history on earth in the future. It is indeed a great storehouse of knowledge, rooted in the three worlds, which the twiceborn retain in all its parts and summaries. Fine words adorn it, and usages human and divine; many meters scan it; it is the delight of the learned.

When all this was without light and unillumined, and on all its sides covered by darkness, there arose one large Egg, the inexhaustible seed of all creatures. They say that this was the great divine cause, in the beginning of the Eon; and that on which it rests is revealed as the true Light, the everlasting Brahman. Wondrous it was and beyond imagining, in perfect balance in all its parts, this unmanifest subtle cause that is that which is and that which is not.

From it was born the Grandfather, the Sole Lord Prajāpati, who is known as Brahmā, as the Preceptor of the Gods, as Sthāṇu, Manu, Ka, and Parameṣṭhin. From him sprang Dakṣa, son of Pracetas, and thence the seven sons of Dakṣa, and from them came forth the twenty-one Lords of Creation. And the Person of immeasurable soul, the One whom the seers know as the universe; and the Viśve Devas, and the Ādityas as well as the Vasus and the two Aśvins. Yakṣas, Sādhyas, Piśācas, Guhyakas, and the Ancestors were born from it, and the wise and impeccable Seers. So also the many royal seers, endowed with every virtue. Water, Heaven and Earth, Wind, Atmosphere, and Space, the year, the seasons, the months, the fortnights, and days and nights in turn, and whatever else, has all come forth as witnessed by the world. Whatever is found to exist, moving and unmoving, it is all again thrown together, all this world, when the destruction of the Eon has struck. Just as with the change of the season all the various signs of the season appear, so also these beings at the beginning of each Eon. Thus, without beginning and without end, rolls the wheel of existence around in this world, causing origin and destruction, beginningless and endless.

There are thirty-three thousand, thirty-three hundred, and thirty-three Gods—this is the summing-up of creation.

The great Sun is the son of the sky and the soul of the eye, the Resplendent One who is also Savitar, Ṛcīka, Arka, Āśāvaha, the Bringer-of-Hope, and Ravi. Of all the sons of the Sun Vivasvant, the last one was Mahya, who had a son that shone like a God, who is hence known as Subhrāj—the Well-Shining One. Subhrāj had three sons of much fame who had abundant offspring, Daśajyoti, Śatajyoti, and the self-possessed Sahasrajyoti. The great-spirited Daśajyoti had ten thousands sons, Śatajyoti ten times that number, and Sahasrajyoti again ten times that. From them arose the lineage of the Kurus, those of the Yadus and of Bhararta, the lines of Yayāti and Ikṣvāku and of the royal seers in general—many dynasties arose and creations of creatures in their abundant varieties.

All are abodes of being. And there is a triple mystery—Veda, Yoga, and science—Law, Profit, and Pleasure. The seer saw the manifold sciences of Law, Profit, and Pleasure, and the rule that emerged for the conduct of worldly affairs. And the ancient histories with their commentaries, and the various revelations—*everything has been entered here,* and this describes this Book.

Brahmā, the Creator, is seated on a lotus connected to the navel of the reclining Vishnu, the cohesive force of the universe. *(Source: C.L. Bharany, New Delhi. Courtesy, Thames and Hudson)*

Questions for Analysis

1. How does the vision of the creation of the world in this text compare with that found in the first book of the Hebrew Bible?

2. What does the *Mahabharata* tell of the connection between human life and the nature of the universe?

3. Does the poem offer the prospect for ordinary people to understand cosmic and human realities?

Source: *The Mahabharata,* trans. J. A. B. van Buitenen. Copyright © 1973 by University of Chicago Press. Reprinted by permission.

4

The Rise and Growth of China to ca A.D. 200

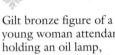

Gilt bronze figure of a young woman attendant holding an oil lamp, which consists of twelve component parts. From the tomb of Princess Dou Wan at Mancheng, Hebei province, 2nd century B.C. *(Source: The Cultural Relics Bureau and The Metropolitan Museum of Art)*

Ancient China provides another example of an early people confronting a formidable geographical challenge in order first to survive and then to build a complex and sophisticated civilization. The Chinese had inhabited eastern Asia from at least the Neolithic period. Like the Egyptians, they prospered along a great river. But the Yellow River was hardly the gentle Nile. It needed to be tamed before it would sustain life, and taming it called for group effort on a massive scale. The success of the Chinese in meeting this challenge is reflected in the flowering of Chinese culture, in the overall political stability of the area, and in the prosperity of China's people. As in Mesopotamia, Egypt, and India, so in China there were wars, and dynasty followed dynasty, but political disruption never crippled Chinese cultural evolution. Moreover, the Chinese were remarkably successful in governing a huge population settled over a vast area. Their success resulted in political and social stability seldom, if ever, found elsewhere in the ancient world.

- How did the early Chinese confront the geographical factors of climate, soil, and land?
- What did their response share with the solutions of ancient Near Eastern and Indian peoples to these same problems, and how did it differ?
- What form did Chinese success take in the shaping of society?

These are the questions addressed in this chapter.

❖ THE LAND AND ITS CHALLENGE

Geography had left India an opening to the northwest and thus to the civilizations of the ancient Near East. In contrast, both terrain and distance made China's links to the broader world tenuous (Map 4.1). Between India and China towered the ice-clad and forbidding peaks of the Himalayas and the Pamirs, and beyond lay the vast expanses of Tibet and Chinese Turkestan. Geography isolated China in other directions as well. To the north stretched the Gobi Desert, some 500,000 square miles of desolate waste, and the Mongolian Plateau. To the south rose mountains covered with forests and tracts of jungle. China's main avenue to the major civilizations of the outside world was a threadlike corridor to the northwest, through the vastness of central Asia, past India, and ultimately to Mesopotamia. Though isolated, China was not sealed off completely from other seats of civilization.

China encompasses two immense river basins: those of the Yellow River in the north and the Yangtze in the south. Both rivers rise in the mountains of Tibet and flow eastward across China (see Map 4.1). The Yellow River carries tons of loess, a fine, light-colored dust whose color gives the river its name. Loess is exceptionally fertile and easy to cultivate, and this basin was the site of China's earliest agricultural civilization in the Neolithic Age (see page 7). Yet like the Tigris in Mesopotamia, the Yellow River can be a rampaging torrent, bringing disastrous floods and changing course unpredictably. The Yellow River was frequently called China's Sorrow, because of its flooding. Only in the sixth century B.C. was it somewhat tamed with dikes, which eventually allowed China's great northern plain to nurture a huge population.

The Yangtze river valley was also farmed from Neolithic times, but there is no convincing reason to think that the peoples could be called "Chinese" in the way that modern peoples define "Chinese." As in the West, so also in China various newcomers entered the area, first establishing their own individual cultures before coming together later to make a generally recognized Chinese culture.

The basins of the Yellow and Yangtze rivers are separated in the west by mountains, which give way to hills and finally disappear altogether in the flat country near the coast. The two basins are quite distinct, however, when it comes to farming. Dry farming of wheat and millet characterizes the Yellow River basin in the north; irrigated rice agriculture predominates in the warmer and wetter basin of the Yangtze. In the extreme south is the valley of the Xi, or West, River, an area of mild climate and fertile soil that would later form the southern boundary of China. Except for the river valleys, China is largely mountainous or semidesert land; people could thrive only in certain areas within this enormous expanse of land. Geography thus helped to ensure that human development in China would cling to the mighty river systems.

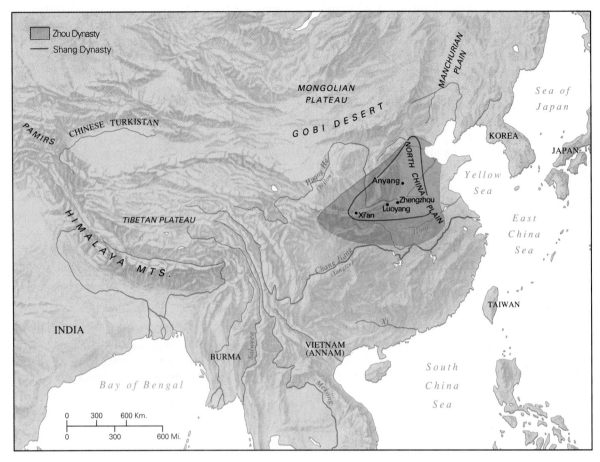

MAP 4.1   China Under the Shang and Zhou Dynasties, 1523–221 B.C.   The heartland of Chinese development is illustrated by this map, which shows the importance of the Yellow River in early Chinese life. Under the Zhou, Chinese authority reached the Yangtze River.

THE SHANG DYNASTY (CA 1523–1027 B.C.)

At about the time the Aryans were transforming Indian life, the kings of the Shang Dynasty rose to power in northern China. Unlike the Aryans, the Shang were natives, very closely linked to indigenous Neolithic peoples. Chinese Neolithic farmers had long ago settled into a life of sustained agriculture and animal domestication. Asia scholars dispute the nature and degree of outside influence on early Chinese development, but most agree that ancient Chinese culture was largely a native growth. China did not suffer massive foreign invasion. Archaeology has recently proved that Neolithic cultures also flourished in Manchuria, along the southeastern coast, and through the Yangtze Valley. To this relatively self-contained society, the Shang gave a long period of rule. Once considered legendary rather than historical, the Shang Dynasty has been verified from its own written records and the work of modern archaeologists.

Social Organization

The excavations at the modern cities of Anyang, the Shang capital, and Zhengzhou (Chengchou), perhaps the oldest city in China, have shed surprisingly bright light on the Shang kings and the society they ruled. Social divisions among the Shang were apparently simple but sharp: a ruling class of aristocrats, headed by a king and an incipient bureaucracy, directed the work and lives of everyone else. Warfare was a constant feature of Shang life, and the nobles were the warriors of Shang, those who enforced Shang rule. The Shang kings ruled northern China as a kind of family patrimony. The kings and the aristocracy owned slaves, many of whom had been captured in war. They also controlled the peasants, who served as semifree serfs.

The common people—serfs and slaves—performed all the economic functions of society. Most were farmers, whose way of life was basically Neolithic. Even in this remote period, however, Shang farmers knew how to cultivate the silkworm. Silken threads were woven into fine cloth, and under later emperors silk became China's prime export. Nonetheless, Shang farmers worked their fields with Neolithic tools and methods. Their homes too were Neolithic in construction. Each family dug in the ground a pit that served as the living area. Often they dug an entrance passage. The central feature of the house was the hearth, which was dug out of the floor of the pit. The family thatched the roof with reeds and clay, making a conical hutlike house. Although they helped create the wealth of Shang, peasant farmers enjoyed little of it themselves.

Other commoners were artisans. Dependent on the nobles, they manufactured the weapons, ritual vessels, jewelry, and other items demanded by the aristocracy. Shang craftsmen worked in stone, bone, and bronze but are best known for their bronze work. These early Chinese artists created some of the world's most splendid bronze pieces. Among the Shang, bronze was considered a noble metal, fit for weapons and ceremonial vessels but much too precious to be made into tools.

At the top of Shang society lived the king and his nobles, mighty figures elevated far above the common people. They lived in large houses built on huge platforms of pounded earth. The architecture of these houses set a pattern for house building that has flourished into modern times. The king and nobles enjoyed the magnificent bronze work of the artisans and carried bronze weapons into battle. Even after death, the king and his relatives had crucial social roles to play. The living worshiped and entreated them to intercede with the great gods, especially Shangoi, the supreme god, to protect the lives and future hopes of their descendants. At first only the king and his family were worthy of such honors, but this custom was an early form of ancestor worship, which seems to

✳ **Ritual Vessel** This Shang bronze vessel excellently demonstrates the sophistication and technical mastery of early Chinese artists. The usual interpretation of the piece is that the tiger is protecting the man who is the head of his clan. Or the tiger may be having breakfast. *(Source: Michael Holford)*

have originated in Neolithic times. Whatever its origins, ancestor worship was an abiding element of Chinese religious belief.

Origins of Chinese Writing

Writing developed considerably later in China than in Sumer or India. The origins of Chinese writing appear to be deeply rooted in Shang religion. The kings of Shang were high priests and frequently wanted to ask questions of the gods. Their medium was oracle bones—generally the shoulder

 Zhou Ritual Vessel   This bronze vessel is ample proof that Zhou bronzesmiths could rival their Shang predecessors. The bronze work is complicated and the fanciful animal shape delightful. *(Source: Robert Harding Picture Library)*

bones of oxen or the bottom shells of tortoises—on which they wrote their questions. Originally pictographic, the signs used by the Shang contained phonetic values. Even so, the Shang and their successors created thousands of signs. The result was a very complex system. But despite this complexity, mastery of even a few signs (like mastery of a few signs of Sumerian cuneiform) enabled people to keep records. Fluent literacy demanded dedication, time, leisure, and thus wealth.

This system of writing proved popular and enduring. Later, when the script was simplified and standardized, it could be written and understood readily by literate Chinese who spoke different dialects. Since many Chinese dialects were mutually unintelligible, the standardization of the written language, once achieved, proved to be indispensable for political, social, and cultural stability for centuries to come. The script spread throughout China and eventually to Korea and Japan, where it was adapted to local needs. Both the Koreans and

the Japanese adopted their own variations of the Chinese pronunciation of the signs. In effect, both read the signs and adapted them to their own spoken languages.

Literary mastery required such an effort and was so politically important and socially valuable that education and scholarship were revered. The literate elite was essential to the king and deeply respected by the peasants. Literacy made possible a bureaucracy capable of keeping records and conducting correspondence with commanders and governors far from the palace. Hence literacy became the ally of royal rule, facilitating communication with and effective control over the realm. Literacy also preserved the learning, lore, and experience of early Chinese society, a precious historical heritage for future ages.

✤ THE TRIUMPH OF THE ZHOU (CA 1027–221 B.C.)

Some Shang oracle bones mention the king of Zhou (Chou), a small realm in the basin of the Wei River, a tributary of the Yellow River on the western frontier of the Shang domains. The Zhou were an agricultural people who had emigrated into the region, perhaps from the northwest. They were also culturally sophisticated masters of bronze and of horse-drawn chariots. In the eleventh century B.C. the Zhou king, a dependent of the Shang, became increasingly rebellious and ultimately overturned the Shang Dynasty.

The Rule of the Zhou

When the Zhou overthrew the Shang, they led China into the historical period. They extended Chinese rule beyond the boundaries of the Shang, and they grappled with the problems of governing the newly won territory. Because their contact with the Shang resulted in their adoption of much of Shang culture, the political victory of the Zhou caused no cultural break. Nevertheless, the Zhou made significant social and cultural strides. They succeeded in giving China a long period in which to consolidate these advances.

To justify their conquest ideologically, the Zhou founders declared that the last Shang king had forfeited his right to rule because of his excesses and incompetence. They asserted that Heaven itself had transferred its mandate to rule China from the Shang house to its worthier rivals, the Zhou. This justification later served as the basis of the broader concept of the Mandate of Heaven (see page 105).

The victorious Zhou confronted the formidable challenge of governing enormous areas of land. Communication within the realm was poor, and one king could not administer it all effectively. Moreover, the original Zhou capital was near Sian in western China, too remote for efficient rule of the new domain. The Zhou solved these problems by building a second capital at Loyang in the North China Plain (see Map 4.1) and by creating a loosely governed state.

The king of the Zhou gave huge tracts of land to members of the royal family and to others who had demonstrated their talent and loyalty. At the outset, the newly appointed lords received their authority from the king. In a formal ceremony the king handed the new lord a lump of earth, symbolizing the king's gift of land. The lord pledged loyalty to the king and usually promised to send him military forces if he requested them. A written record was made of the grant and of the new lord's obligations and rights—an unprecedented secular use of writing. The Zhou king was also the supreme religious leader of the land; he interceded with the gods for the welfare of Chinese society.

Shang Oracle Bone   On one side of the bone the Shang diviner wrote his questions to the gods. In this case, the message related to a hunt. On the other side of the bone the diviner applied a hot point. When the cracks in the bone led to the writing, the interpreter read the gods' message. Most questions dealt with the harvest, weather, travel, and hunting. *(Source: Lowell Georgia/Photo Researchers)*

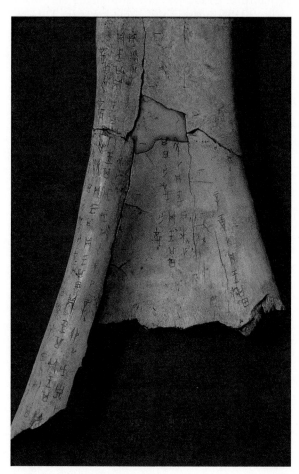
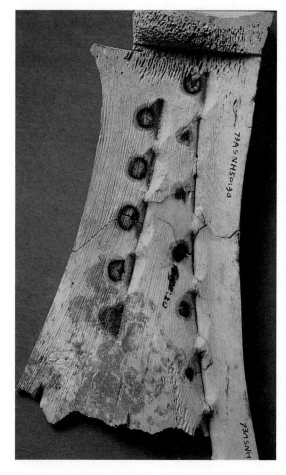

At first the Zhou kings exercised strong control over their political dependencies. Gradually, the power of the lords grew as the prosperity of their holdings increased. The dependencies of the Zhou were actually small islands of settlement scattered all over northern China, separated by wide tracts of undeveloped land. Over several centuries the growing populations of these settlements cleared new land, and eventually permanent cities arose. Once small and vulnerable, these settlements began to coalesce into compact regional states and then to fight among themselves over borders and territories. In this conflict the states in the interior of China were eclipsed by those on the borders, which took advantage of their geographical position to expand. The expansion spread Chinese culture ever wider. While conquering new territory, the lords of the border states were also absolute rulers in their own right. Around them developed a hereditary class of aristocratic ministers of state, warriors, administrators, and tax collectors. China was gradually becoming a land of numerous independent kingdoms.

Along with the growing independence of the lords went a decline in the power and stature of the Zhou kings. The lords used their troops to realize their own ambitions and stopped sending forces to the kings, disregarding their political obligations. In 771 B.C. a Zhou king was defeated and killed by rebel lords. After that the Zhou abandoned their western capital and made Loyang, the eastern capital, their permanent seat.

During the period known as the Era of the Warring States (402–221 B.C.), the entire political organization of the Zhou Dynasty disintegrated. The Zhou kings became little more than figureheads. The dreary cycle of warfare finally ended in 221 B.C., when the ruler of Qin (Ch'in), who had forced the abdication of the last Zhou king in 256 B.C., conquered all the other states.

Social Change and Cultural Advancement in the Zhou Period

The political events of the Zhou period were to have a lasting impact on Chinese society. As the older interior states declined, the aristocracies of these states lost their wealth. Educated, literate, and talented people were forced to seek their fortunes far from home. And the border states, dependent as they were on military and adminis-trative efficiency, needed capable people to keep the wheels of government turning. The upshot was that impoverished aristocrats gravitated to the border states, where their much-needed talents opened the door to careers as ministers and officials. Merit, not birth, made the difference. This period saw the origins of a trained and able civil service, a group that saw to the daily workings of government and, later, gave a warm reception to the great philosophies of the Zhou period. The rise of Chinese philosophy was largely a response to the political turmoil and warfare that wracked the country, which helps to explain its secular orientation.

Despite the long years of warfare and slaughter, the Zhou period could boast of some remarkable cultural achievements. Around the walled garrisons that the Zhou established to hold down the Shang people, cities grew up, some with huge populations. The roads and canals built to import food and goods to the city dwellers stimulated trade and agriculture. Trade was also stimulated and made easier by the invention of coined money. The significance of these cities is almost incalculable. They were places where people could find the seat of government, meaning that they could visit the palaces of those who governed them. People could also visit major religious shrines and large markets. The centralization of society also led to a more efficient economic exchange between the country and the city, and as usual an easier way for the government to levy and collect taxes.

A surge in technology during the Zhou period permanently altered warfare, agriculture, and ultimately urban life. Under the Zhou, craftsmen and artisans discovered the use of iron and rapidly developed its uses. Zhou metalsmiths produced both wrought and cast iron—a remarkable achievement not matched in Europe until the fourteenth century. Zhou craftsmen turned out an imposing number of weapons, especially dagger-axes and swords.

In agriculture the Chinese under the Zhou Dynasty replaced the Neolithic stone and bone tools of the Shang with iron. Plows with iron shares broke the ground easily. Iron sickles, knives, and spades made the raising and harvesting of crops easier and far more efficient than ever before. By increasing productivity, metal technology gave Zhou farmers the tools to support a thriving urban culture.

❖ THE BIRTH OF CHINESE PHILOSOPHY

The Zhou period was an era of intellectual creativity. Many thoughtful and literate people turned their minds to the basic question of how people could live the happiest and most productive lives in the most efficiently run society. Chinese thinkers were more secular than religious in their outlook. While Indian mystics were creating a complex socioreligious system, the Chinese were exploring philosophies of political development. Fascinated by political, social, and economic problems, they sought universal rules for human conduct. This period gave rise to three branches of thought—Confucianism, Daoism, and Legalism—that along with the popular belief represented by *I Ching* left an indelible stamp on the history of China.

Confucianism

Of the three schools of thought, Confucianism has had the most profound impact on China. The historical Kung Fuci (551–479 B.C.)—better known in the West as Confucius—was primarily a teacher and did not put his thoughts into writing. His fame comes largely from his students, who collected his sayings in a book called the *Analects*.

Confucius's family was aristocratic but poor, and the young man had few immediate prospects of success. His family had him educated so that he could take his place in the civil service, yet he achieved fame not as a minister of state but as a teacher. Confucius taught the sons of nobles but yearned to advise lords. Setting out with a small band of students, he sought employment from the lords of the emerging regional states in northeastern China. He served intermittently as a minor official and continued to spread his ideas. At last Confucius returned home to die among his students, considering himself a failure because he had never held high office.

Confucius's thought centered on the duties and proper behavior of the individual within society. He was far more interested in orderly and stable human relationships than in theology or religious matters. For all his fame, Confucius was not so much an original thinker as a brilliant synthesizer of old ideas. He taught that there is a universal law that even the sun, moon, and stars follow and that human beings too should live according to this law. Confucius considered the family the basic unit of society. Within the family, male was superior to female, age to youth. Thus husband was obeyed by wife, father by son, elder brother by younger. The eldest male was the head of the family. This order was to be respected even when those in authority were wrong:

The Master said, In serving his father and mother a man may gently remonstrate with them. But if he sees that he has failed to change their opinion, he should resume an attitude of deference and not thwart them; he may feel discouraged, but not resentful.[1]

Order in the family was the essential building block of order in society at large.

A man of moderation, Confucius was an earnest advocate of gentlemanly conduct. Only such conduct, which involved a virtuous and ethical life, could bring about peaceful social relations and well-run government. The Confucian gentleman was a man of integrity, education, and culture, a man schooled in proper etiquette. Asked to evaluate Zi-chan, a minister of the Zheng state, Confucius discussed the virtues of a "gentleman":

In him were to be found four of the virtues that belong to the Way of the true gentleman. In his private conduct he was courteous, in serving his master he was punctilious, in providing for the needs of the people he gave them even more than their due; in exacting service from the people, he was just.[2]

The way in which a gentleman disciplined himself is apparent in the conduct of Master Tseng, the most important of Confucius's followers:

Master Tseng said, Every day I examine myself on these three points: in acting on behalf of others, have I always been loyal to their interests? In intercourse with my friends, have I always been true to my word? Have I failed to repeat the precepts that have been handed down to me?[3]

Confucius pointed out that aristocratic birth did not automatically make a man a gentleman. Men of humble birth could reach this exalted level through education and self-discipline. Confucius did not advocate social equality, but his teachings minimized the importance of class distinctions and opened the way for intelligent and talented people

Daoist Painting One of the finest aspects of Daoism was its appreciation of nature and the feeling that people should find their place in it. This painting vividly illustrates the peacefulness, grace, and charm that Daoists believed people can experience by being in harmony with nature. *(Source: National Palace Museum, Taipei, Taiwan, Republic of China)*

to rise in the social scale. The Confucian gentleman was made, not born.

This gentleman found his calling as a civil servant: he advised the ruler wisely, administered the kingdom intelligently, and dealt with the people humanely. Confucianism urged good government, emphasizing the duty of a good ruler to rule his people wisely and with compassion. Confucius commented on the qualities of a good ruler:

A country of a thousand war-chariots cannot be administered unless the ruler attends strictly to business, punctually observes his promises, is economical in expenditure, shows affection towards his subjects in general, and uses the labour of the peasantry only at the proper times of year.[4]

Confucianism was a vital ingredient in the evolution of an effective civil service. As a social movement, Confucianism was a distinct and specially recruited community whose membership was ideally restricted to learned and talented people who embraced high standards of ethical awareness and conduct. Confucianism offered those in authority a body of expertise on the creation and consolidation of a well-ordered, sound, and powerful state. That expertise, like medical knowledge, demanded to be taken on its own innate merits and was thus offered in the form of advice and persuasion; it could not legitimately be imposed by violence. Neither revolutionaries nor toadies, Confucian scholar-bureaucrats opposed bad government by upholding in nonviolent ways the best ideals of statecraft. The Confucian ideal proved so powerful that it continued to shape Chinese society.

Daoism

The later Zhou period was a time of philosophical ferment. Many others besides Confucius were grappling with the problems of humanity, society, and the universal. Especially significant were the Daoists (often written as Daoists), followers of a school of thought traditionally ascribed to Lao Zi (Lao-tzu). Little is known about Lao Zi's life; he is supposed to have lived in the sixth century B.C., but his very existence has been questioned. The book attributed to him, *Dao De Ching (Book of the Way and Its Power),* is probably the work of several people and dates only from the fourth century B.C. (see Listening to the Past).

Where Confucian political thought was practical and humanistic, Daoism argued that political authority cannot bestow peace and order if it restricts itself to the rules and customs of society. The only effective social control stems, according to Lao Zi, from adherence to the ultimate nature of reality. The only way to achieve this end, Lao Zi taught, is to follow Dao, or the Way of Nature. *Dao De Ching* portrays the Way as the creative force of nature:

There is a thing confusedly formed,
Born before heaven and earth.
Silent and void
It stands alone and does not change,
Goes round and does not weary.
It is capable of being the mother of the world.
I know not its name
So I style it "the way."[5]

According to Daoists, people could be happy only if they abandoned the world and reverted to nature, living simply and alone. Those who followed the Way had no further need of human society. If the philosophy of Daoism had ever been carried to its logical extreme, Daoism would have created a world of hermits.

Daoism treated the problems of government in a dramatically different way from Confucianism. In essence, the Daoists were convinced that government could do most for people by doing as little as possible. *Dao De Ching* boldly declares that people are better-off left to themselves:

Exterminate the sage, discard the wise,
And the people will benefit a hundredfold;
Exterminate benevolence, discard rectitude,
And the people will again be filial;
Exterminate ingenuity, discard profit,
And there will be no more thieves and bandits.[6]

Lao Zi argued that public works and services, from road building to law courts, led to higher taxes, which in turn led to unhappiness and even popular resistance. The fewer laws and rules, the better, Daoists urged. The Daoists also spelled out how, if there had to be a government at all, the people should be ruled:

Therefore in governing the people, the sage
empties their minds but fills their bellies,

weakens their wills but strengthens their
bones. He always keeps them innocent of
knowledge and free from desire, and ensures
that the clever never dare to act.[7]

The people are to be well treated, according to the Daoists, but they will be happiest if they remain uneducated and materially satisfied.

Daoism was most popular among the rulers and ministers who actually governed Chinese society. It gave them a safety valve in a rough-and-tumble world, a way of coping with the extreme pressures they faced. If a ruler suffered defeat or a minister fell out of favor, he could always resign himself to his misfortune by attributing it to the chaos of the world. In this respect Daoism became a philosophy of consolation—but only for a chosen few. The elite often adopted Daoism for consolation and Confucianism for serious everyday affairs.

Legalism

More pragmatic than Confucianism was Legalism, the collective name later given to a number of distinct but related schools of practical political theory that flourished during the late Zhou period. Among the founders of Legalism were Han Fei Zi (d. 233 B.C.) and Li Su (Li Ssu) (d. 208 B.C.). Both were former Confucians who had been heavily influenced by Daoism. Both were pragmatic realists who thought that the state should possess as much power as possible and extend it relentlessly. Their ideal state was authoritarian: the sensible ruler, in their view, should root out all intellectual dissent or resistance and all competing political ideas. Since human nature is evil, according to the Legalists, the ruler must keep the people disciplined and even suppressed if they are rebellious. The people should be well treated but need not be educated. The ruler should appropriate their labor to feed his armies and their wealth to fill his coffers. No frivolity is to be tolerated: people are to work and produce; they should not waste their time on the study of history, philosophy, and other unproductive pursuits. Rather than refute Confucian political ideas, Legalism repressed or dismissed them, as many twentieth-century ideologies have done to conflicting ideas. Nonetheless, Legalism was realistic and offered Chinese rulers practical solutions to the problems of governing large populations over great distances.

Legalism was at first influential in practical affairs. Both Han Fei Zi and Li Zi were high officials, in a position to put Legalist theories into practice. Though Legalism offered an effective, if harsh, solution to the problems confronting Zhou society, it was ultimately too narrow to compete successfully as an independent school with Confucianism and Daoism.

I Ching and Yin and Yang

Chinese thought was not entirely tied to philosophical schools or outlooks. It remained greatly influenced, especially at the popular level, by a belief that individuals were integral parts of a cosmic whole that they could understand. One aspect of this attitude was the belief that people could learn profound truths and receive dependable guidance to successful lives through interpretations of oracles. I Ching (The Book of Changes) also served this purpose. I Ching directs readers in how to lead an ethical life and how to live in harmony with the universe. It is thus more ethical than philosophical, yet its philosophical content and importance should not be denied.

The I Ching is essentially a book of oracles, and readers used its contents by reading the result of randomly tossed coins. When people wanted answers to questions troubling them, they read the results of the throw of the coins and consulted the appropriate oracle. For instance, for those seeking to understand the continuous flow of life, the appropriate oracle was the following:

Creativity is a constant—flowing through our lives and our world; the very essence of all things. It is one moment built upon its predecessor, the continuous flow of existence. From this, the cosmic example, one must model his inner self, aspiring to consistency in his moments of cosmic unity. It is in this construct of persistent contact and identification with the ceaseless power of heaven that the goal is realized.[8]

For those who wanted to be in harmony with this flow, the best oracle was this:

If one is to be in touch with the cosmic flow, he must develop a consciousness that will permit communication. Through the wide gate of his spirit's awareness, the sage receives the earth-intended force and humbly puts it to use for all men. Through this attitude of serving, he builds cooperation so that men may learn to work together in the shaping of their destinies.[9]

These two examples are enough to demonstrate that the I Ching uses ethics, philosophy, and plain common sense to enable people to live a happy, moral life. The I Ching did not demand acceptance of any particular philosophical or political doctrine; it simply provided sound advice.

Another attempt to understand the relationship between cosmic forces and human life led to the concept of Yin and Yang. Han thinkers developed the idea that these two elementary powers governed a constant cosmic process. Yang represents the strong, radiant, dry, and manly; Yin represents the weak, dark, moist, and womanly. They constantly work together to bring about a changing but predictable relation of power in the world, a power that is related to the four seasons. Yang becomes strong in spring and comes to fullest strength in summer, only to decline in autumn and still further in winter. Yin reigns supreme in autumn and winter. Together they represent the natural rhythms of the year, those of birth, growth, and death. Both are essential to the process of life, for they are in essence dual. Yin and Yang are not opponents like good and evil. Rather they are complementary. Neither can exist alone.

The concept of Yin and Yang attempted to put the observable facts of human life into an intelligible form. It accounts for the changes in the seasons, their natures, their fruits, the climates of each, and the place of human beings in this natural and eternal cycle. Unlike Hindu religion, which held out the opportunity to escape from the burdens of life, Yin and Yang helped people to think of themselves as a legitimate part of a natural order and not necessarily as an alien or unfortunate part. Both I Ching and Yin and Yang gave people an understandable way of orienting themselves in the world.

THE AGE OF EMPIRE

The leader of the state of Qin (Ch'in) who deposed the last Zhou king in 256 B.C. had within thirty-five years made himself sole ruler of China, taking the title Qin Shi Huangdi (Ch'in Shih Huang Ti), or First Emperor (r. 256–210 B.C.).

✦ **Army of the First Emperor**   When the grave of the First Emperor was recently discovered, an army of ceramic soldiers came to light. Six thousand statues, armed with spears, swords, bows, and crossbows, were found intact in a huge pit, here seen still in excavation. The statues give a vivid idea of the army that unified China. *(Source: George Holton/Photo Researchers, Inc.)*

Thus began the Qin Dynasty. Although the Qin Dynasty lasted only some fifteen years, the work of its emperors endured for centuries. Indeed, the Western name for China is derived from the Qin. The First Emperor unified China under a central government, and the Han Dynasty, which replaced the Qin, maintained this unity for centuries. Under the emperors of the Qin and Han, China flourished economically, culturally, and socially.

The Qin and Unification of China

The ancient Chinese historian Sima Qian (Szu-ma Ch'ien) left this vivid description of the victory of the First Emperor:

With its superior strength Ch'in [Qin] pressed the crumbling forces of its rivals, pursued those who had fled in defeat, and overwhelmed and slaughtered the army of a million until their shields floated upon a river of blood. Following up the advantages of its victory, Ch'in gained mastery over the empire and divided up its mountains and rivers. The powerful states begged to submit to its sovereignty and the weaker ones paid homage at its court.[10]

The Qin extended their sway as far south as modern Hong Kong and the South China Sea, introducing Chinese influence into vast new areas. With this hard-won victory came political unity, which the First Emperor was determined to maintain.

The First Emperor considered a highly centralized state necessary to ensure a united China. He and his prime minister, Li Su, a founder of Legalism, embarked on an imaginative, sweeping, and rigorous program of centralization that touched the lives of nearly everyone in China. At the head of the state stood the emperor, an autocrat possessing absolute power. His first act was to cripple the nobility. The First Emperor ordered the nobles to leave their lands and appear at his court. Aristocratic families all across China were torn from their estates and transported to Xianyang (Hsien-yang), the capital of Qin, where they built new homes around the court. The emperor took over their estates and organized China into a system of large provinces subdivided into smaller districts, each governed by three principal officials.

The emperor controlled the provinces by appointing governors and lesser administrators, as well as other officials to keep watch on them. These officers were not drawn from the old aristocracy; they owed their power and position entirely to the favor of the emperor. Unlike the old aristocracy, they could not claim hereditary rights to their positions. The governors kept order in the provinces, enforcing laws and collecting taxes. One of their most important and least popular duties was to draft men for the army and for work on huge building projects.

In the interest of harnessing the enormous human resources of his people, the First Emperor ordered a census of the entire population. Census information helped the imperial bureaucracy to plan its activities—to estimate the costs of public works, the tax revenues needed to pay for them, and the labor force available for military service and building projects.

A highly centralized empire needs good communications. But communication over an area as vast as China presented huge challenges. The emperor met them in several ways. First there was the problem of language itself. During the Zhou period, each state often spoke its own distinct dialect, which contained words borrowed from other dialects. Written language also varied from dialect to dialect; some people used signs that were unintelligible to others. These variations in language made central administration difficult. To solve this problem, the First Emperor and his ministers standardized the written script.

The First Emperor also standardized the weights, measures, and coinage of the realm. The old coinages of conquered states were abolished, and the Qin established its own traditional coinage as the imperial currency. This coinage and system of weights and measures made it much easier for the central government to collect taxes. The emperor also standardized the axle lengths of carts. Most Chinese roads at the time were nothing more than deep tracks cut by the wheels of carts. Uniform axle lengths meant that all carts could use the same ruts, making travel and communication quicker and more convenient.

The First Emperor initiated land reforms that gave peasant farmers greater rights. He furthered irrigation projects and encouraged land reclamation to bring more soil under cultivation. These efforts, together with the widespread use of iron tools, increased agricultural production and fostered prosperity. The emperor also promoted the weaving of textiles, especially silk, which remained the aristocrat of Chinese fabrics. Thanks to the new road system, trade increased. Merchants became important figures, although their social status remained low. The growth of trade stimulated the growth of towns, and the broadened economy enlarged the tax base for the government.

Foreign Danger and Internal Unrest

While the First Emperor was working to bring China unity and prosperity, he faced constant peril on the northern border. For years the Chinese had pushed northward, driving out the nomadic Huns, who in later centuries would carry death, destruction, and terror to the decaying Roman Empire. Chinese encroachment endangered the very survival of the Huns. Each of their scattered tribes was led by its own chieftain. The Huns, on horseback and armed with swords and bows, struck back in quick and repeated raids, plundering prosperous towns and farms, then disappearing into the vastness of the north. The success of the Huns was not always temporary. One chieftain conquered numerous Chinese tribes in the north, thereby creating a Hunnish empire on the Chinese frontier.

Since Chinese expansion in the north had all along met stiff opposition, the northern states had built long walls for self-protection as early as the fourth century B.C. The First Emperor ordered these various stretches of wall to be linked together in one great wall, extending from the sea some fourteen hundred miles to the west (Map 4.2). The number of laborers who worked on the wall

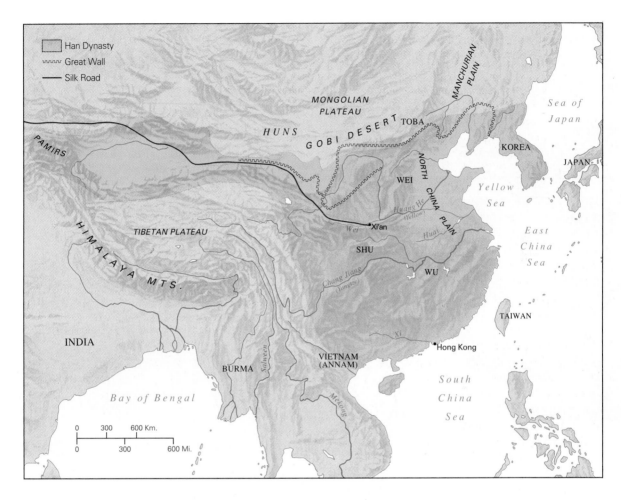

Han Dynasty
Great Wall
Silk Road

MAP 4.2 China Under the Han Dynasty, 206 B.C.–A.D. 220 The glory of the Han Dynasty is evident from this map. The Han pushed the frontiers into central and southeastern Asia and ruled over far more territory than any previous dynasty.

and the sheer amount of construction material needed are stunning tribute to the First Emperor's power. The Great Wall of China is probably humanity's most immense ancient creation. The Great Wall and the huge numbers of troops guarding the frontier gave the north a period of peace.

Despite their achievements the Qin were unpopular rulers. The First Emperor was primarily interested in his own wealth and power and did not tolerate opposition. A Legalist, he distrusted Confucian scholars and reportedly had some 460 of them buried alive. He tried without success to destroy Confucian literature and China's ancient literary heritage by a massive campaign of book burning. He enforced the tenets of Legalism vigorously and ruthlessly in an effort to wipe out any

system of thought that might challenge his autocratic position. The Qin demanded obedience, not intelligence.

The Qin took advantage of the new prosperity to levy heavy taxes, especially on the peasants. Taxation, forced labor on the Great Wall and on other projects, and military service mercilessly disrupted many peasant households. While the men were away, their families worked long, dreary hours to feed themselves and meet the staggering burden of taxes.

The oppressiveness of the Qin bred fierce hatred among the people. One person described the First Emperor as a monster who "had the heart of a tiger and a wolf. He killed men as though he thought he could never finish, he punished men as

❋ **Great Wall of China**   The size and sheer awesomeness of the Great Wall comes through strikingly in this print. Over hill and through valley the Great Wall spanned some 3,000 miles of northern China. *(Tony Stone Images/Chicago Inc.)*

though he were afraid he would never get around to them all."[11] The death of the First Emperor in 210 B.C. sparked massive revolts. Huge bands of peasants took up arms against the new emperor. In the ensuing struggle for power, Liu Bang (Liu Pang), a peasant and petty official of the Qin, defeated his opponents and in 206 B.C. established the Han Dynasty.

The Glory of the Han Dynasty (206 B.C.–A.D. 220)

The Han Dynasty marked the beginning of China's early imperial age. The dynasty also gave the Chinese their own name: they have traditionally called themselves "men of Han." Liu Bang, the victorious rebel, was no revolutionary. He re-

tained the main features of Qin administration and made no social reforms, but the extreme political centralization of the Qin was relaxed. At least in theory, the Han Empire had an autocratic emperor aided by an educated but nonaristocratic bureaucracy. The basis of the empire, as always, was China's vigorous and hard-working peasants.

Under capable emperors like Liu Bang (r. 206–195 B.C.) and his immediate successors, China recovered from the oppression and turmoil of the Qin period. Unable to conquer the Huns, who were renewing their threats on the northern border, the Chinese first tried to buy them off with lavish presents and stirred up internal trouble among Hun chieftains. In 133 B.C., however, Emperor Han Wudi (Han Wu Ti) went on the attack. In fourteen years of fighting, the Han drove the

Huns still farther north. Chinese armies advanced into western Turkestan, where they opened up direct relations with the subcontinent of India. Equally impressive were the Han emperors' gains in the east. Chinese armies conquered western Korea, where they took over trade with Japan. The Han also extended their rule to the southeastern coast of China, and by 111 B.C. the emperor Han Wudi had conquered northern Vietnam (see Map 4.2).

Han military successes resulted in a dramatic increase in trade with the outside world. After Wudi conquered northern Vietnam, Chinese and foreign merchants moved in and set up trading stations under the supervision of Chinese officials. Southern China and northern Vietnam became meeting grounds for different cultures. The people of northern Vietnam accepted Chinese culture, and regions not far to the south were falling under the influence of Indian culture carried there by Indian merchants. Indeed, an independent state, called Funan by the Chinese, arose in modern southern Vietnam and Cambodia among Malayan people who adopted many aspects of Indian culture.

Under the Han emperors Chinese merchants opened a new route from southwestern China by way of the rivers of Vietnam and Burma to ports on the Bay of Bengal. A Later Han emperor sent an ambassador direct to the West (see page 204). Trade between China and its neighbors, together with the political and social stability of Han rule, gave China an unparalleled time of peace and prosperity.

Han Confucianism and Intellectual Revolt

Confucianism made a comeback during the Han Dynasty, but it was a changed Confucianism. Although many Confucian texts had fed the First Emperor's bonfires, some dedicated scholars had hidden their books, and others had memorized whole books: one ninety-year-old man was able to recite two books virtually in their entirety. These heroic efforts saved much of China's ancient literature and Confucian thought, yet extensive textual corruption introduced non-Confucian elements into traditional Confucian texts.

While trying to reconstruct the past, the new Confucianism was influenced by other schools of thought, even by the hated Legalism. Strengthened by these influences, Confucianism again took hold. Its hold was so strong that Confucianism endured as the intellectual and cultural basis in China until the present.

During the Han era, Confucian scholars pondering China's past put into systematic form a concept that went back to the Zhou. They elaborated the related theories of the *dynastic cycle* and the *Mandate of Heaven*. The link between the cycle and the mandate was divine approval of the performance of a dynasty. Rule of China was the gift of Heaven, which was considered a deity. With Heaven's blessing the duty of the emperor and his successors was to expand the borders, if possible, or at least to foster prosperity and maintain order for noble and peasant alike, with as little interference as possible in the lives of the people. Once emperors failed in their duty, whether through weakness or corruption, conditions deteriorated, and the empire was left prey to foreign invasion and internal unrest. At that point, Confucian scholars argued, the dynastic cycle came full circle. By failing to maintain the Mandate of Heaven, the last emperor of the dynasty lost his authority to the first man who could restore order and prosperity. That man succeeded because Heaven transferred the mandate to him. Dynasties waxed and waned according to how well they served the requirements of Heaven.

According to Han Confucianism, the emperor was the intermediary between his subjects and Heaven. He served this function by performing all the sacred rites to the deities correctly and scrupulously and by watching for signs that Heaven was displeased. Confucianism explained history by looking to the virtues and vices of individuals, especially emperors and dynasties. Confucian historians saw history not as progressive but as cyclical, as repetitions of the same kinds of events.

Yet the Confucians did not have the field of political thought solely to themselves. Huang Lao Daoism made a considerable impact on Chinese thinking. Owing to the recent discovery of manuscripts from a tomb, we now have a better understanding of this influential political philosophy. Huang Lao held rulers to strict codes of duty and conduct. It expected rulers to serve the people and to keep to a minimum their own material possessions and governmental expenditures. Rulers were obliged to obey the law, not only in public affairs but also in their personal conduct with other individuals. They were to use the army only in just causes or on other appropriate occasions, such as the defense of the people from foreign invasion. They must follow the way (or *dao*), which encompassed law, ethical principles, and forms and names. They must respect the natural order of the world, which included the forces of yin and yang and the cycle of the seasons. Huang Lao drafted a blueprint for efficient and humane conduct and administration of public affairs.

In this climate of thought, the study of history flourished. Generations of Chinese scholars devoted their efforts to studying particular dynasties and events and individual rulers, ministers, and generals. The Chinese, like the Greeks, conceived of history as broader and more complex than the mere chronicling of events. Indeed, during the Han Dynasty China produced one of its finest historians, Sima Qian (Szu-ma Ch'ien) (ca 145–86 B.C.). Like the Greek Thucydides, he believed fervently in visiting the sites where history was made, examining artifacts, and questioning people about events. Sima was also interested in China's geographical variations, local customs, and local history. As an official of the emperor, he had access to important people and documents and to the imperial library. Having decided to write a history of China down to his own time, Sima set about interviewing eyewitnesses and those who had shaped events. He also reviewed official documents and written records. The result, ten years in the making, was his classic *Records of the Grand Historian,* a massive work of literary and historical genius.

Nor did Sima's work die with him. The Ban (Pan), a remarkably creative family, took up his study of the Han. Among the most eminent of them was Ban Zhao (Pan Chao), China's first woman historian and scholar. Ban Zhao also wrote poems and essays, notably *Lessons for Women* on the education of women. Taking up Sima Jian history, the Ban family wrote the first history of a Chinese dynasty. Thereafter, official court historians wrote the history of every dynasty. Like their Greek and Roman counterparts, Chinese historians considered recent and current history important in their investigations.

Han intellectual pursuits were not limited to history. In medicine, the Han period produced its own Hippocrates, Jing Jhi, a practicing physician whose *Treatise on Fevers* became a standard work in Chinese medicine. Chinese surgeons grappled with the problem of reducing the pain of surgery, and the Han physician Hua Duo developed a drug that, mixed with wine, would render a patient unconscious.

The career of Zhang Heng (A.D. 78–139), the great mathematician, was strikingly similar to that of the Hellenistic philosopher Eratosthenes. Both delved deeply into astronomy and concluded that the world is round, not flat as many of their contemporaries assumed. Not content to speculate, Zhang Heng built models to test his theories. He even designed a seismograph capable of discerning the direction in which an earthquake was taking place, though not its severity. The brilliance of Han intellectual activity shone in its breadth and achievements.

Daily Life During the Han Dynasty

Because the people who chronicled events in Han China were an elite writing for other elites, more is known about the upper levels of society than about the lower levels. The lives of the common people were taken for granted or considered too vulgar to write about. But even though a complete portrayal is beyond reach, it is possible to sketch the outlines of daily life in Han China.

The peasant farmer was the backbone of Han society. Agriculture was considered an important and honorable activity that distinguished the civilized Chinese from their barbaric and nomadic neighbors. Small households of farmers worked the land and generated most of the revenue of the empire. The Chinese peasant family was probably small, four or five people, frequently including a grandparent. Both women and men performed hard manual labor in the fields. Men were typically required to spend time each year in the service of the emperor; and while they were away, their wives ran the farm. Farmers' existence was tenuous, for floods, drought, and unduly harsh taxes could wipe them out. When severely oppressed by harsh, inefficient, and sometimes corrupt government, the peasants revolted, turned to a life of begging or banditry, or put themselves under the protection of powerful landlords. Thus the Han emperors were rightly proud of the peace and security of their reigns, which spared Chinese farmers the worst evils.

The staple grain under cultivation varied with the soil and climate. In the warm and wet south, rice was the traditional crop. In the north, farmers raised millet and wheat wherever possible or barley on land too poor for wheat. Farmers also grew hemp, which was woven into coarse clothing for the common people. Some fortunate farmers had groves of timber or bamboo to supplement their crops; or they grew mulberry trees, the leaves of which nourish silkworms, or groves of lac trees, from which came a resin used on decorative lacquer ware. Wherever possible, farmers grew fruit and nut trees. Farmers near cities found ready profit growing vegetables and ginger and other spices for city folk. Tea and sugar cane were raised in southern China but were still luxury items during the Han period.

Land use became systematic and effective under the Han, probably as a result of experience and of innovations recommended by Chao Kuo, a Han minister. Chao Kuo introduced a systematic ridge-and-furrow system of planting that yielded fairly regular harvests and facilitated crop rotation. To maintain the fertility of the soil, farmers treated their land with manure and crushed bones. The in-

tensive character of Chinese agriculture meant that very little land was available for pasturage. Unlike his Indian counterpart, the Chinese farmer seldom raised cattle, horses, or donkeys. Dogs, pigs, and chickens were the typical domestic farm animals. The lack of draft animals meant that most farm work was done by hand and foot.

Farmers used a variety of tools, but the most important was the plow. The earliest wooden plow was a simple tool, more often pulled by humans than by animals. The new and more effective plow introduced during the Han period was fitted with two plowshares and guided by a pair of handles and was typically pulled by a pair of oxen. Farmers used fans to blow the chaff from kernels of grain, and they used either mortar and pestle or hand mills to grind grain into flour. The Chinese also developed an elaborate system using long hammers to mill grain and pound earth. Eventually, the hammers were driven by waterpower. Irrigation water was pumped into the fields with devices

 Han Workers This series of sculptures depict ordinary people and their animals routinely carrying out the basic economic functions of Chinese society. One figure carries a basket, while another leads an ox. These sculptures illustrate the simplicity and hardship of daily life. *(Source: J. L. Klinger, Heidelberg)*

ranging from a simple pole with an attached bucket and counterweight to a sophisticated machine worked by foot.

The agricultural year began in mid-February with the breaking up of heavy soil and manuring of the fields. February was also the beginning of the new year, a time of celebration and an important religious festival. This was the time to sow and transplant seedlings. During the second and third months of the year, farmers practiced their archery to defend themselves against the bandits who infested the countryside; as a further precaution, they repaired the gates and locks of their houses. The fifth month was the time to cut the hay; the sixth, to hoe the fields. Meanwhile, the women of the family nurtured silkworms and made silk cloth,

which they would later dye, and they wove the hemp into coarse cloth. With the harvest, processing, and storage of the crop, farmers were ready for winter and the coming year.

City life was varied and hectic compared with the regularity of farming. The wealthiest urbanites lived in splendid houses of two or more stories, surrounded by walls and containing at least one courtyard. These large homes had such features as storage rooms and rooms for animals in the courtyard. The rooms or outhouses used for grain storage were built on stilts to protect against rats and moisture, which could cause rot or mildew.

The house itself was usually four-sided, with the door in one wall. The floors of the poor were covered with animal skins and mats of woven grass;

A Han Manor   An excellent representation of a rural manor house, this clay model displays a courtyard, gatehouse, and watchtower—in effect, a small fort. *(Source: Cultural Relics Publishing House, Beijing)*

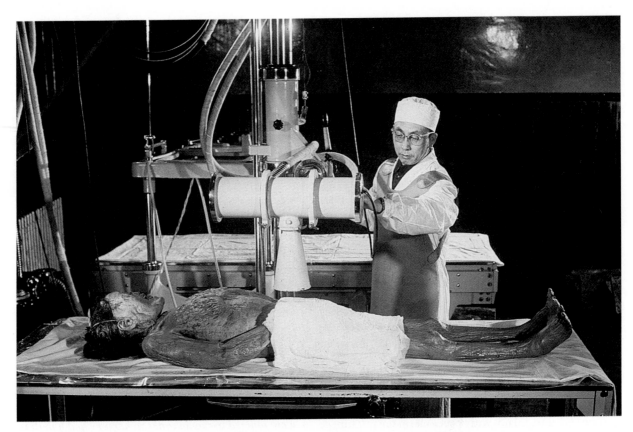

Corpse of Lady Xin   Although this may seem no way in which to treat a lady, the scientist and many other experts from across China convened to examine the corpse of Lady Xin, who died some twenty-one hundred years ago. The autopsy revealed that just before her death she had consumed 130 musk-melon seeds. *(Source: China Pictorial, Beijing)*

those of the rich, with finely embroidered cushions and wool rugs. The bedrooms of wealthy homes were furnished with wooden beds, embroidered draperies, and beautiful screens for privacy. Fine furniture of expensive wood and beautifully lacquered bowls graced the houses of the wealthy.

Wealthy urban dwellers loved costly clothes, and everyone who could afford to do so bought fine and brightly colored silks. The wealthy also spent money on furs, usually fox and squirrel and sometimes badger. Expensive shoes lined with silk and decorated with leather became extremely popular. Wealthy women wore jewelry of jade and other precious and semiprecious stones, as well as gold earrings and finger rings. The urban poor probably had easier and somewhat cheaper access to silk garments than did their rural neighbors, but their clothing was primarily made of coarse hemp cloth.

The diet of city folk, like their clothing, could be rich and varied. Owing to general prosperity, people during the Han period began to eat meat more frequently. Demand increased dramatically for wild game and young animals and fish, which were seasoned with leeks, ginger, and herbs. No longer was rice wine, like meat, a luxury for festival days. It began to be consumed avidly, and wealthy Chinese began to age vintages for twenty or thirty years. The Chinese were especially fond of pork, and roast pig was one of the most popular gourmet dishes. The Chinese also enjoyed liver and dog meat. Wood and pottery utensils were standard features of common households, but rich people relegated wood and pottery to the kitchen and dined on dishes decorated with gold and silver.

People with money and taste patronized music. The rich often maintained private musical troupes generally playing bells, drums, and pipes. Flutes and stringed instruments were also popular. People of more common taste flocked to puppet shows and performances of jugglers and acrobats. Magic shows dazzled the impressionable, and cockfighting appealed to bloody tastes. Gambling was popular but considered decidedly vulgar. Archaeologists have found several board games.

As gangs of bandits infested the countryside, so crime plagued the cities. Officials were open to corruption and sometimes connived with criminals and gangs of thugs who had the support of wealthy and powerful families. At times the situation got so far out of hand that private armies roamed the streets, wearing armor and carrying knives and preying on the weak and helpless. Poor people who lacked influence suffered outrages and violence with no hope of justice or retribution.

Silk was in great demand all over the known world during the Han period, and caravans transported bales of it westward. Another distinctive Chinese product was the lacquer ware. Han craftsmen developed lacquer work to a fine art. Because lacquer creates a hard surface that withstands wear, it was ideal for cups, dishes, toilet articles, and even parts of carriages. Such works of art were only for the rich; poor people contented themselves with plain lacquer ware at best. Some of the most splendid examples of lacquer work are elaborately carved and inlaid with precious metals. Chinese craftsmen loved geometric designs. The accuracy of some of their work suggests that they used mechanical tools.

Perhaps the most momentous product of Han imagination was the invention of paper, which the Chinese traditionally date to A.D. 105. Scribes had previously written on strips of bamboo and wood. Fine books for the wealthy were written on silk rolls. Cai Lun, to whom the Chinese attribute the invention of paper, worked the fibers of rags, hemp, bark, and other scraps into sheets of paper. Though far less durable than wood, paper was far cheaper than silk and became a convenient means of conveying the written word. By the fifth century, paper was in common use, preparing the way for the invention of printing.

Han craftsmen continued the Chinese tradition of excellent metallurgy. By the beginning of the first century A.D., China had about fifty state-run ironworking factories. These factories smelted iron ore into ingots before turning it over to the craftsmen who worked it into tools and other articles. Their products demonstrate a sophisticated knowledge of metals. Han workmen turned out iron plowshares, agricultural tools with wooden handles, and weapons and armor. Han metalsmiths

were mass-producing superb crossbows long before the crossbow was dreamed of in Europe.

Iron was replacing bronze in tools, but bronzeworkers still turned out a host of goods. Bronze was prized for jewelry, mirrors, dishes, and spoons. Bronze was also used for minting coins and for precision tools such as carpenters' rules and adjustable wrenches. Surviving bronze gear-and-cog wheels bear eloquent testimony to the sophistication of Han machinery.

Distribution of the products of Han craftsmen was in the hands of merchants, whom Chinese aristocrats, like ancient Hebrew wise men, considered necessary but lowly. In the Chinese scale of values, agriculture was honorable because farmers worked to win the gifts that nature bestowed. Merchants, however, thrived on the toil of others, and the art of winning profits was considered ungentlemanly and not quite legitimate. The first Han emperor took action to put merchants in their place, as the great historian Sima relates:

After peace had been restored to the empire, Liu Pang issued an order forbidding merchants to wear silk or ride in carriages, and increased the taxes that they were obliged to pay in order to hamper and humiliate them.[12]

Yet the emperors and ministers of Han China realized that merchants had become indispensable. One outcome of this ambiguity was the conclusion that merchants ought to be regulated. Another was an early form of limited socialism—state monopolies on essential commodities like iron and salt, which made for price stability.

Retail merchants set up shop in stalls in the markets, grouped together according to their wares. All the butchers, for example, congregated in one part of the market, each trying to outsell the others. Nearly everything could be found in the markets, from food to horses and cattle, from ox carts and metal hardware to fine silks. The markets were also the haunts of entertainers and fortunetellers. The imperial government stationed officials in the markets to police the selling of goods and to levy taxes on the merchants. In markets public execution of criminals served as an example and a warning to would-be criminals and political agitators in the crowd.

The transportation of goods in bulk was still difficult and expensive. Roads were primitive, but the Han developed several sturdy and effective types of

CHINA TO CA A.D. 400

ca 1523–ca 1027 B.C.	Shang Dynasty and invention of writing
ca 1027–221 B.C.	Zhou Dynasty
551–479 B.C.	Confucius and rise of Confucianism
4th century B.C.	Lao Zi and development of Daoism
ca 250–208 B.C.	Han Fei Zi and Li Su and development of Legalism
221–210 B.C.	Establishment of the Qin Dynasty and unification of China Construction of the Great Wall Destruction of Confucian literature
206 B.C.–A.D. 220	Establishment of the Han Dynasty
111 B.C.	Chinese expansion to the South China Sea and Vietnam
A.D. 221–280	Three Kingdoms era
4th–5th centuries	Barbarian invasions

carts and wagons, and a new harness for horses came into widespread use. Earlier harnesses had fitted around the horse's neck, choking the animal when it pulled a load. The new harness fitted around the horse's chest and over its back, enabling it to pull heavier loads with less effort. This efficient horse collar finally reached medieval Europe in the eighth century A.D., a product of Asian technology that influenced the history of the West.

Because of the difficulty of overland travel, the Chinese relied heavily on water transport. Since the major rivers of China run from east to west, canals were cut between the rivers to make north-south traffic possible. Bulk foodstuffs and goods could be transported fairly cheaply and swiftly on river boats, which also provided reasonably comfortable living quarters for crew and passengers. Maintenance of canals and dikes was expensive and made huge demands on the labor force, but these waterways allowed China to establish a flexible and effective network of communication.

The Fall of Han China

The Han Empire was an imposing political edifice. Eventually, however, wars on the frontiers and the emperors' enormous building projects put an intolerable strain on society. The emperors drew so heavily on the peasants as soldiers and as workers that agricultural production declined severely. Great landlords saw their chance to expand their holdings and to shift the burden of taxation onto the already hard-pressed peasantry. Ground down by ambitious emperors and unscrupulous landowners, many peasants lost their land and sold their children, farm animals, and tools to the landowners, ending as tenants, hired laborers, or outlaws.

The emperor Wang Mang (r. A.D. 9–23), who was a usurper, attempted to reverse these trends. He tried to re-establish a state monopoly on grain so that private speculators could not exploit famines and shortages to make huge profits. He set about redistributing land to the peasants and wanted to abolish slavery. Unfortunately, Wang Mang's commendable efforts did little to improve conditions, and he was killed in a peasant uprising. Han Kuang Wu in turn defeated the rebels and established the later Han Empire in A.D. 25.

After a century of peace, the later Han emperors found themselves facing the same problems that Wang Mang had tried to solve. Once again great landlords took over peasants' land and burdened them with heavy taxes. Disorder, intrigue, and assassination at court distracted the government. A murderous rivalry developed between the old scholar-officials, who had traditionally administered political affairs, and the palace eunuchs, men usually of lowly origin who wielded huge influence from their lair among the women of the imperial harem. Turmoil and palace revolt meant that the great landlords were left unhindered. Once again the peasants staged massive uprisings. When the imperial armies were dispatched to put down the unrest, the victorious generals used their forces to carve out petty kingdoms for themselves. The palace eunuchs revolted against the emperor and his scholar-officials, and the Han Empire collapsed in general turmoil.

In the years that followed, known as the Three Kingdoms Era (A.D. 221–280), the empire was broken into three separate kingdoms. These kingdoms conformed to the natural geographical divisions of the land: the kingdom of Wei held the north; Shu, the upper Yangtze River Valley; and Wu, the lower Yangtze River Valley (see Map 4.2). Throughout this period, China experienced further disorder and barbarian trouble.

The difficulties with barbarians increased in later years, with catastrophic invasions from the north. Most significant were the conquests by the nomadic Toba from Mongolia, who created their own northern dynasty. Early in the fifth century the Toba assumed control of northern China, making the Great Wall their northern boundary. They extended their sway into central Asia and stopped further barbarian invasions of China. Southern China, which remained under Chinese rule, actually benefited from these invasions: thousands of Chinese, among them many scholar-officials, fled to the south, where they devoted their energies and talents to developing southern China economically and culturally.

Barbarian invasions caused China distress and disruption, but the Toba and other nomads quickly came under the spell of Chinese culture linguistically, politically, and economically. The Toba emperor ordered the Toba nobility to speak Chinese at his court and to dress and act like the Chinese elite. The Toba adopted Chinese agricultural techniques and the bureaucratic method of administering the empire. China's political system was so excellently suited to the land and its people

that no barbarian invader could have done without it. That system encompassed not just a bureaucracy fully dependent on the Chinese language, but the culture, religion, and outlook of Chinese society. In that respect, China absorbed its invaders more successfully than India had done.

SUMMARY

Chinese mastery of the land led to the harnessing of China's resources. A vital aspect of this triumph was the development of a systematic method of agriculture capable of sustaining a huge population. Prosperity and growth in population allowed the Chinese to shape their lives as never before. One result was a vibrant and sophisticated intellectual life. Whereas Indian society was largely permeated by religion, Chinese thought was for the most part secular in orientation. Although China sometimes experienced internal disorder and the threat of invasion, political upheaval never destroyed China's cultural heritage. By the end of the Han Dynasty, writing, Confucianism, and the complex political organization of a huge region had left an enduring mark on the Chinese people.

NOTES

1. A. Waley, trans., *The Analects of Confucius* (London: George Allen and Unwin, 1938), 4.18.
2. Ibid., 5.15.
3. Ibid., 1.4.
4. Ibid., 1.5.
5. D. C. Lau, trans., *Lao Tzu, Tao Te Ching* (London: Penguin Books, 1963), 1.25.56.
6. Ibid., 1.19.43.
7. Ibid., 1.3.9.
8. Anonymous, *Change* (Virginia Beach: A.R.E. Press, 1971), p. 1.
9. Ibid., p. 2.
10. B. Watson, trans., *Records of the Grand Historian of China Translated from the Shih chi of Ssu-ma Ch'ien* (New York: Columbia University Press, 1961), 1.31.
11. Ibid., 1.53.
12. Ibid., 2.79.

SUGGESTED READING

In general, see H. T. Zurndorfer, *China Bibliography* (1995), a splendid research guide to reference works about past and present China, which is as remarkably broad as it is deep. E. L. Shaughnessy, *Sources of Eastern Zhou History* (1991), treats the development of bronze technology. M. Loewe, *The Pride That Was China* (1990), is a good general survey by a major scholar who draws heavily on archaeological material. R. S. Dawson, ed., *The Legacy of China* (1990), is a synthesis of all important aspects of early Chinese life, similar to that of P. S. Ropp, ed., *Heritage of China* (1990), which is strong on comparisons between Chinese and Western developments. W. C. Liu, *An Introduction to Chinese Literature* (1991), is an ample survey of all genres of literature, extending to modern times. A lively and charming introduction to daily life in China is *Shih Ching,* more easily accessible in A. Waley, trans., *The Book of Songs* (1960). See also Z. R. Liu, *Ancient India and Ancient China* (1988). Other solid general treatments of East Asia include C. Schirokauer, *A Brief History of Chinese and Japanese Civilizations,* 2d ed. (1989), and J. K. Fairbank, E. O. Reischauer, and A. Craig, *East Asia: Tradition and Transformation,* rev. ed. (1989).

For the development of the Chinese language, see Ho Ping-ti, *The Cradle of the East* (1975). A lively and readable account of early life and the origins of writing, told primarily from an archaeological standpoint, is J. Hay, *Ancient China* (1973). More technical are K. Chang, *The Archaeology of Ancient China,* 4th ed. (1986), and *Food in Chinese Culture* (1977), an edited volume containing historical and anthropological material. H. G. Creel, one of the foremost scholars of early Chinese thought, in *The Origins of Statecraft in China* (1970), argues forcefully that early Zhou emperors maintained firm control over their political dependencies in the first centuries of their dynasty.

A fascinating starting point for the study of early Chinese thought is D. Bodde, *Chinese Thought, Society, and Science* (1991), which ranges widely across those aspects of culture and thought that bore on the development of science. A. C. Graham, *Studies in Chinese Philosophy and Philosophical Literature* (1990), is a sensible, broad treatment of all branches of philosophical thought. Much has been written on Confucius and the Confucian tradition. A. Waley's translation of the *Analects of Confucius* (1938) is an eminently readable version of the work attributed to Confucius.

For a good general approach, see F. W. Mote, *Intellectual Foundations of China,* 2nd ed., (1989). The complexities of Daoism are lucidly set out by H. G. Creel, *What Is Taoism?* (1970), which discusses the differences between purposive and contemplative Daoism. One of the most significant of the contemplative Daoists was Zhuang Zi (Chuang-tzu), whose career is studied by A. C. Graham, *Chuang-tzu: The Seven Inner Chapters* (1981). H. G. Creel provides a sound introduction to Legalism in *Shen Pu-hai* (1974), which demonstrates that, far from being monolithic, Legalism consisted of a number of schools of practical political theory. On the careers of Han Fei Zi and Li Su, see D. Bodde, *China's First Unifier* (1938).

The political and military success of the Qin is the subject of D. Bodde, *China's First Unifier: A Study of the Ch'in Dynasty as Seen in the Life of Li Ssu (280?–208 B.C.)* (1958). P. Nancarrow, *Early China and the Wall* (1978), discusses the importance of the Great Wall of China to early Chinese society. A good account of Qin road building is J. Needham, *Science and Civilization in China,* vol. 4, part 3 (1970).

The Han Dynasty has been amply treated by a master scholar, H. H. Dubs, whose *History of the Former Han Dynasty,* 3 vols. (1938–1955), is comprehensive. The turmoil of Confucianism in this period is ably treated in a series of studies, among them E. Balazs, *Chinese Civilization and Bureaucracy* (1964); H. Welch and A. Seidel, eds., *Facets of Taoism* (1979), which ranges more broadly than its title might suggest; and especially C. Chang, *The Development of Neo-Confucian Thought* (1957), a solid discussion of Han Confucianism. B. Watson has provided two good studies of Ssu-ma Ch'ien (Sima Qian) and his historical work: *Records of the Grand Historian of China* (1961) and *Ssu-ma Ch'ien: Grand Historian of China* (1958). China's most important woman scholar is the subject of N. L. Swann, *Pan Chao: Foremost Woman Scholar of China* (1950). K. Frifelt and P. Sorensen, eds., *South Asian Archaeology* (1988), contains a number of papers devoted to South Asia and its broader connections.

M. Loewe, *Everyday Life in Early Imperial China* (1968), paints a vibrant picture of ordinary life during the Han period, a portrayal that attempts to include all segments of Han society. W. Zhongshu, *Han Civilization* (1982), excellently treats many aspects of material life under the Han, including architecture, agriculture, manufacture, and burial. Last, B. Hinsch, *Passions of the Cut Sleeve* (1990), is the only book in English that treats homosexuality in China.

The Daoist Approach to Administering the Empire

The principal writing of the Daoists, the Dao De Jing *is one of the most widespread of Chinese political and philosophical documents. It is a handbook on how to govern the empire. The author or authors take the existence of the empire for granted; they do not account for how it came into being or speculate about its ultimate purpose. The* Dao De Jing *focuses on how to maintain the smooth and peaceful functioning of the machinery of empire. Its advice is both practical and ethical. It also insists on the merits of political and social security. Above all, the work is a cry for stability and how to maintain it. It served as a practical guide for public administrators, giving them precepts about how best to carry out their duties.*

LXII

The way is the refuge for the myriad creatures.
It is that by which the good man protects,
And that by which the bad is protected.
Beautiful words when offered will win high
   rank in return;
Beautiful deeds can raise a man above others.
Even if a man is not good, why should he be
abandoned?
Hence when the emperor is set up and the
three ducal ministers are appointed, he who
makes a present of the way without stirring
from his seat is preferable to one who offers
presents of jade disks followed by a team of
four horses. Why was this way valued of old?
Was it not said that by means of it one got
what one wanted and escaped the consequences when one transgressed?
Therefore it is valued by the empire.

LXIII

Do that which consists in taking no action;
pursue that which is not meddlesome; savour
that which has no flavour.

Make the small big and few many; do good
to him who has done you an injury.
Lay plans for the accomplishment of the difficult before it becomes difficult; make something big by starting with it when small.
Difficult things in the world must needs have
their beginnings in the easy; big things must
needs have their beginnings in the small.
Therefore it is because the sage never attempts to be great that he succeeds in becoming great.
One who makes promises rashly rarely keeps
good faith; one who is in the habit of considering things easy meets with frequent difficulties.
Therefore even the sage treats some things as
difficult. That is why in the end no difficulties
can get the better of him.

LXIV

It is easy to maintain a situation while it is still
   secure;
It is easy to deal with a situation before symptoms develop;
It is easy to break a thing when it is yet brittle;
It is easy to dissolve a thing when it is yet
   minute.
Deal with a thing while it is still nothing;
Keep a thing in order before disorder sets in.
A tree that can fill the span of a man's arms
Grows from a downy tip;
A terrace nine storeys high
Rises from hodfuls of earth;
A journey of a thousand miles
Starts from beneath one's feet.
Whoever does anything to it will ruin it; whoever lays hold of it will lose it.
Therefore the sage, because he does nothing,
never ruins anything; and, because he does
not lay hold of anything, loses nothing.
In their enterprises the people

Always ruin them when on the verge of
   success.
Be as careful at the end as at the beginning
And there will be no ruined enterprises.
Therefore the sage desires not to desire
And does not value goods which are hard to
   come by;
Learns to be without learning
And makes good the mistakes of the
   multitude
In order to help the myriad creatures to be
   natural and to refrain from daring to act.

LXV

Of old those excelled in the pursuit of the
way did not use it to enlighten the people but
to hoodwink them. The reason why the peo-
ple are difficult to govern is that they are too
clever.
Hence to rule a state by cleverness
Will be to the detriment of the state;
Not to rule a state by cleverness
Will be a boon to the state.
These two are models.
Always to know the models
Is known as mysterious virtue.
Mysterious virtue is profound and
   far-reaching,
But when things turn back it turns back with
   them.
Only then is complete conformity realized.

The philoshoper Lao-tzû holds his scroll
of the 'Tao-te-ching.' (Source: National
Palace Museum, Taipei, Taiwan, Republic of
China)

Questions for Analysis

1. According to the Daoists, what is the primary function of the mandarin scholar-
   official?

2. How is he instructed to perform his official
   duties?

3. Is he in any way expected to reform the imperial system, or should he aim to carry out
   customary duties?

Source: Lao Tzu, Tao Te Ching, trans. D. C. Lau.
Copyright 1963 by Penguin Books. Reprinted by permission.

5

The Legacy of Greece

Bronze statue of Poseidon (Zeus?), fifth century B.C. *(Source: Ancient Art & Architecture Collection)*

The rocky peninsula of Greece was the home of the civilization that fundamentally shaped European civilization and ultimately influenced the rest of the world. The Greeks were the first to explore questions that continue to concern thinkers to this day. Going beyond mythmaking and religion, the Greeks strove to understand, in logical, rational terms, both the universe and the position of men and women in it. The result was the birth of philosophy and science—subjects that were far more important to most Greek thinkers than religion. The Greeks speculated on human beings and society and created the very concept of politics.

The history of the Greeks is divided into two broad periods: the Hellenic period (the subject of this chapter), roughly the time between the arrival of the Greeks (approximately 2000 B.C.) and the victory over Greece in 338 B.C. by Philip of Macedon; and the Hellenistic period (the subject of Chapter 6), the age beginning with the remarkable reign of Philip's son, Alexander the Great (336–323 B.C.) and ending with the Roman conquest of the Hellenistic East (200–148 B.C.).

- What geographical factors helped to mold the evolution of the city-state?
- How did the impact of the Minoans and Mycenaeans lead to the concept of a heroic past?
- How did the Greeks develop basic and enduring political forms, forms as different as democracy and tyranny?
- What did the Greek intellectual triumph entail, and what were its effects?
- How and why did the Greeks eventually fail?

These questions signal the themes of this chapter.

HELLAS: THE LAND

Hellas, as the ancient Greeks called their land, encompassed the Aegean Sea and its islands as well as the Greek peninsula (Map 5.1). The Greek peninsula itself, stretching in the direction of Egypt and the Near East, is an extension of the Balkan system of mountains. Perhaps the best and most eloquent description of Greece comes from the eminent German historian K. J. Beloch:

Greece is an alpine land, which rises from the waters of the Mediterranean Sea, scenically probably the most beautiful region in southern Europe. The noble contours of the mountains, the bare, rocky slopes, the dusty green of the conifer forests, the white cover of snow that envelops the higher summits for the greatest part of the year, added to which is the profound blue surface of the sea below, and above everything the diffused brightness of the southern sun; this gives a total picture, the charm of which impresses itself unforgettably on the soul of the observer.[1]

The rivers of Greece are never more than creeks, and most of them go dry in the summer. Greece is, however, a land blessed with good harbors. The islands of the Aegean serve as steppingstones between the peninsula and Asia Minor.

Despite the beauty of the region, geography acted as an enormously divisive force in Greek life. The mountains of Greece dominate the landscape, cutting the land into many small pockets and isolating areas of habitation. Innumerable small peninsulas open to the sea. The geographical fragmentation of Greece encouraged political fragmentation. Furthermore, communications were extraordinarily poor. Rocky tracks—usually nothing more than a pair of ruts cut into the rock to accommodate wheels—were far more common than roads. These conditions discouraged the growth of great empires.

THE MINOANS AND MYCENAEANS (CA 1650–CA 1100 B.C.)

Neither historians, archaeologists, nor linguists can confidently establish when Greek-speaking peoples made the Balkan peninsula of Greece their homeland. All that can now safely be said is that they, like the Hittites, Persians, and Aryans, were still another wave of Indo-Europeans who were expanding throughout Europe and Asia during much of antiquity. By about 1650 B.C. Greeks had established themselves at the great city of Mycenae in the Peloponnesus and elsewhere in Greece. Quite probably the Greeks merged with the natives of small farming communities, and from that union emerged the society that modern scholars call Mycenaean, after Mycenae, the most important site of this new Greek-speaking culture.

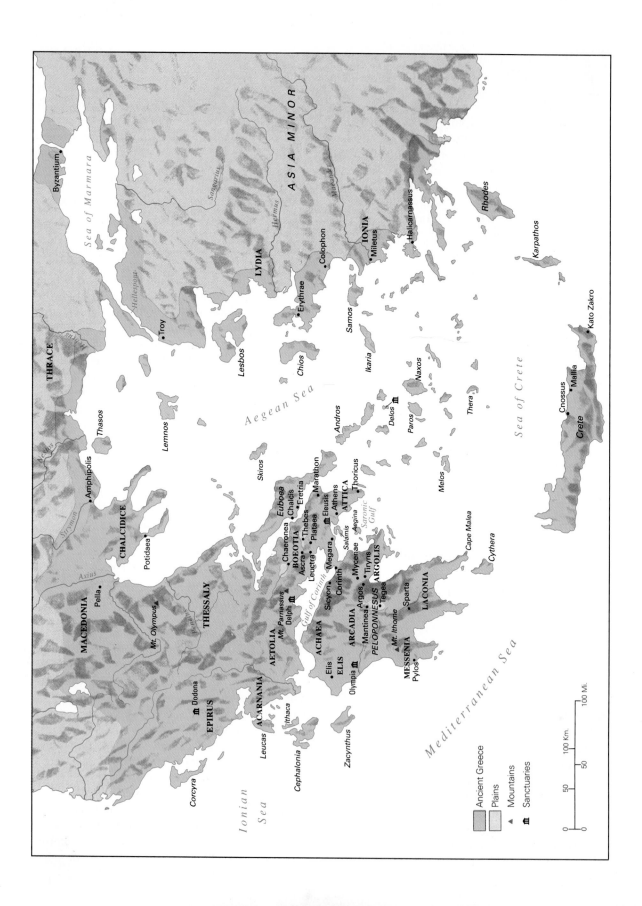

Minoan Naval Scene This fresco discovered at Thera probably depicts the homecoming of a Minoan fleet of warships. Though later Greeks thought that the Minoans had ruled the sea, fleets such as the one pictured here probably protected Minoan maritime interests and suppressed piracy. Despite its military nature, the scene displays the general air of festivity characteristic of Minoan art. *(Source: National Archaeological Museum, Archaeological Receipts Fund)*

Of this epoch the ancient Greeks themselves remembered almost nothing. The *Iliad* and the *Odyssey,* Homer's magnificent epic poems (eighth century B.C.), retain some dim memory of this period but very little that is authentic. One of the sterling achievements of modern archaeology is the discovery of this lost past. In the nineteenth century Heinrich Schliemann, a German businessman, fell in love with the *Iliad* and decided to find the sites it mentioned. He excavated Troy in modern Turkey, Mycenae, and several other sites in Greece to discover the lost past of the Greek people. At the turn of this century, the English archaeologist

MAP 5.1 Ancient Greece In antiquity the home of the Greeks included the islands of the Aegean Sea and the western shore of Asia Minor as well as the Greek peninsula itself.

Sir Arthur Evans uncovered the remains of an entirely unknown civilization at Cnossus in Crete, and he gave it the name Minoan after the mythical Cretan king Minos. Scholars since then have further illuminated this long-lost era, and despite many uncertainties a reasonably clear picture of the Minoans and Mycenaeans has begun to emerge.

By about 1650 B.C. the island of Crete was the home of the flourishing and vibrant Minoan culture. The Minoans had occupied Crete from at least the Neolithic period. They had also developed a script, now called Linear A, to express their language in writing. Because Linear A is yet undeciphered, however, only archaeology and art offer clues to Minoan life. The symbol of Minoan culture was the palace. Around 1650 B.C. Crete was dotted with palaces, such as those at Mallia on the northern coast and Kato Zakro on the eastern tip of the island. Towering above all others in importance was the palace at Cnossus.

Few specifics are known about Minoan society except that at its head stood a king and his nobles, who governed the lives and toil of Crete's farmers, sailors, shepherds, and artisans. The implements of the Minoans, like those of the Mycenaeans, were bronze, so archaeologists have named this period the Bronze Age. Minoan society was wealthy and, to judge from the absence of fortifications on the island, peaceful. Enthusiastic sailors and merchants, the Minoans traded with Egypt and the cities of the area known today as the Middle East, or Levant. They also established trading posts throughout the Aegean Sea, which brought them into contact with the Mycenaeans on the Greek peninsula.

By about 1650 B.C. Greek-speakers were firmly settled at Mycenae, which became a major city and trading center. Later, other Mycenaean palaces and cities developed at Thebes, Athens, Tiryns, and Pylos. As in Crete, the political unit was the kingdom. The king and his warrior aristocracy stood at the top of society. The seat and symbol of the king's power and wealth was his palace, which was also the economic center of the kingdom. Palace scribes kept records in Greek with a script (now known as Linear B) that was derived from Minoan Linear A. The scribes kept account of taxes and drew up inventories of the king's possessions. Little is known of the king's subjects except that they were the artisans, traders, and farmers of Mycenaean society. The Mycenaean economy was marked by an extensive division of labor, tightly controlled from the palace. At the bottom of the social scale were the slaves, who were normally owned by the king and aristocrats but who also worked for ordinary craftsmen.

Contacts between the Minoans and Mycenaeans were originally peaceful, and Minoan culture flooded the Greek mainland. But around 1450 B.C. the Mycenaeans attacked Crete, destroying many Minoan palaces and taking possession of the grand palace at Cnossus. For about the next fifty years the Mycenaeans ruled much of the island until a further wave of violence left Cnossus in ashes. These events are more disputed than understood. Archaeologists cannot determine whether the Mycenaeans at Cnossus were attacked by other Mycenaeans or whether the conquered Minoans rose in revolt.

Whatever the answer, the Mycenaean kingdoms and their culture in Greece benefited from the fall of Cnossus and the collapse of its trade. Mycenaean commerce quickly expanded throughout the Aegean, reaching as far abroad as Anatolia, Cyprus, and Egypt. Prosperity, however, did not bring peace, and between 1300 and 1000 B.C. kingdom after kingdom suffered attack and destruction.

Later Greeks accused the Dorians, who spoke a particular dialect of Greek, of overthrowing the Mycenaean kingdoms. Yet some modern linguists argue that the Dorians dwelt in Greece during the Mycenaean period. Archaeologists generally conclude that the Dorians, if not already present, could have entered Greece only long after the era of destruction. In fact, the legends preserved by later Greeks told of grim wars between Mycenaean kingdoms and of the fall of great royal families. Apparently Mycenaean Greece destroyed itself in a long series of internecine wars, a pattern that later Greeks would repeat.

The fall of the Mycenaean kingdoms ushered in a period of such poverty, disruption, and backwardness that historians usually call it the Dark Age of Greece (ca 1100–800 B.C.). Even literacy, which was not widespread in any case, was a casualty of the chaos. Yet this period was a time of widespread movements of Greek-speaking peoples. Some Greeks sailed to Crete, where they established new communities. A great wave of Greeks spread eastward through the Aegean to the coast of Asia Minor. These immigrations turned the Aegean into a Greek lake. The people who stayed behind gradually rebuilt Greek society. They thus provided an element of continuity, a link between the Mycenaean period and the Greek culture that emerged from the Dark Age.

❖ HOMER, HESIOD, AND THE HEROIC PAST (1100–800 B.C.)

The Greeks, unlike the Hebrews, had no sacred book that chronicled their past. Instead they had the *Iliad* and the *Odyssey* to describe a time when gods still walked the earth. And they learned the origin and descent of the gods from the *Theogony,* an epic poem by Hesiod (ca 700 B.C.). Instead of authentic history the poems of Homer and Hesiod offered the Greeks an ideal past, a largely legendary Heroic Age. These poems contains scraps of information about the Bronze Age, much about the early Dark Age, and some about the poets' own era. Chronologically, the Heroic Age falls mainly in the period between the collapse of the Mycenaean world and the rebirth of literacy.

The *Iliad* recounts an expedition of Mycenaeans, whom Homer called "Achaeans," to besiege the city of Troy in Asia Minor. The heart of the *Iliad,* however, concerns the quarrel between Agamemnon, the king of Mycenae, and Achilles, the tragic hero of the poem, and how their anger and pride brought suffering to the Achaeans. The *Odyssey,* probably composed later than the *Iliad,* narrates the adventures of Odysseus, one of the Achaean heroes who fought at Troy, during his voyage home from the fighting.

The splendor of these poems does not lie in their plots, although the *Odyssey* is a marvelous adventure story. Rather, both poems portray engaging but often flawed characters who are larger than life and yet typically human. Homer was also strikingly successful in depicting the great gods, who generally sit on Mount Olympus and watch the fighting at Troy like spectators at a baseball game, although they sometimes participate in the action. Homer's deities are reminiscent of Mesopotamian gods and goddesses. Hardly a decorous lot, the Olympians are raucous, petty, deceitful, and splendid. In short, they are human.

Homer at times portrayed the gods in a serious vein, but he never treated them in a systematic fashion, as did Hesiod, who lived somewhat later than Homer. Hesiod's epic poem, the *Theogony,* traces the descent of Zeus. Hesiod was influenced by Mesopotamian myths, which the Hittites had adopted and spread to the Aegean. Like the Hebrews, however, Hesiod envisaged his cosmogony—his account of the way the universe developed—in moral terms. Cronus, the son of Earth and Heaven, like the Mesopotamian Enlil, separated the two and became king of the gods. Zeus, the son of Cronus, defeated his evil father and took his place as king of the gods. He then sired Lawfulness, Right, Peace, and other powers of light and beauty. Thus, in Hesiod's conception, Zeus was the god of righteousness, who loved justice and hated wrongdoing.

In another epic poem, *Works and Days,* Hesiod wrote of his own time and his own village of Ascra in Boeotia, a scenic place set between beautiful mountains and fertile plains. In his will, Hesiod's father had divided his lands between Hesiod and his brother, Perses. Perses bribed the aristocratic authorities to give him the larger part of the inheritance and then squandered his wealth. Undaunted by the injustice of the powerful, Hesiod thundered back:

Bribe-devouring lords, make straight your decisions,
Forget entirely crooked judgments.
He who causes evil to another harms himself.
Evil designs are most evil to the plotter.[2]

Hesiod did not receive justice from the political authorities of the day, but he fully expected divine vindication. Hesiod spoke of Zeus as Jeremiah had spoken of Yahweh, warning that Zeus would see that justice was done and injustice punished. He cautioned his readers that Zeus was angered by those who committed adultery, harmed orphans, and offended the aged.

 ## THE POLIS

After the upheavals that ended the Mycenaean period and the slow recovery of prosperity during the Dark Age, the Greeks developed their basic political and institutional unit, the *polis,* or city-state. Only three city-states were able to muster the resources of an entire region behind them (see Map 5.1): Sparta, which dominated the regions of Laconia and Messenia; Athens, which united the large peninsula of Attica under its rule; and Thebes, which in several periods marshaled the resources of the fertile region of Boeotia. Otherwise, the political pattern of ancient Greece was one of many small city-states, few of which were much stronger or richer than their neighbors.

Physically the term *polis* designated a city or town and its surrounding countryside. The people of a typical polis lived in a compact group of houses within a city. The city's water supply came from public fountains and cisterns. By the fifth century B.C. the city was generally surrounded by a wall. The city contained a point, usually elevated, called the *acropolis,* and a public square or marketplace, the *agora*. On the acropolis, which in the early period was a place of refuge, stood the temples, altars, public monuments, and various dedications to the gods of the polis. The agora was originally the place where the warrior assembly met,

The Polis of Argos This view, taken from the east of modern Argos, remarkably illustrates the structure of an ancient polis. Atop the hill in the background are the remains of the ancient acropolis. At its foot to the right are foundations of ancient public and private buildings. In the foreground are modern houses, situated where ancient homes were located. *(Source: John Buckler)*

but it became the political center of the polis. In the agora were porticoes, shops, and public buildings and courts.

The unsettled territory of the polis—arable land, pastureland, and wasteland—was typically its source of wealth. Farmers left the city each morning to work their fields or tend their flocks of sheep and goats, and they returned at night. On the wasteland men often quarried stone or mined for precious metals. Thus the polis was the scene of both urban and agrarian life.

The size of the polis varied according to geographical circumstances. Population figures for Greece are mostly guesswork, because most city-states were too small to need a census. But regardless of its size or wealth, the polis was fundamental to Greek life. The intimacy of the polis was an important factor. The smallness of the polis enabled Greeks to see how the individual fitted into the overall system—how the human parts made up the social whole. These simple facts go far to explain why the Greek polis was fundamentally different from the great empires of Persia and China. The Greeks knew their leaders and elected them to limited terms of office. They were unlike the subjects of the Mauryan Empire or the Han Dynasty, who might spend their entire lives without ever seeing their emperors. One result of these factors is the absence in Greek politics of a divine emperor. Another is the lack of an extensive imperial bureaucracy and a standing army. The ancient Greeks were their own magistrates, administrators, and soldiers.

Instead of a standing army, the average polis relied on its own citizens for protection. Very rich citizens often served as cavalry. However, the heavily armed infantry was the backbone of the army. The foot soldiers, or *hoplites,* provided their own equipment and were basically amateurs. When in battle, they stood in several dense lines, in which cohesion and order became as valuable as courage.

The polis could be governed in any of several ways. In a *monarchy,* a term derived from the Greek for "the rule of one man," a king represented the community, reigning according to law and respecting the rights of the citizens. Or the *aristocracy* could govern the state. Or the running of the polis could be the duty and prerogative of an *oligarchy,* which literally means "the rule of a few"—in this case a small group of wealthy citizens, not necessarily of aristocratic birth. Or the polis could be governed as a *democracy,* through the rule of the people, a concept that in Greece meant that all citizens, regardless of birth or wealth, administered the workings of government. How a polis was governed depended on who had the upper hand. When the wealthy held power, they usually instituted oligarchies; when the people could break the hold of the rich, they established democracies. Still another form of Greek government was *tyranny,* rule by a tyrant, a man who had seized power by extralegal means, generally by using his wealth to gain a political following that could topple the existing government.

Because the bonds that held the polis together were so intimate, Greeks were extremely reluctant to allow foreigners to share fully in its life. An alien, even someone Greek by birth, could almost never expect to be made a citizen. Nor could women play a political role. Women participated in the civic cults and served as priestesses, but the polis had no room for them in state affairs. This exclusiveness doomed the polis to a limited horizon.

Although each polis was jealous of its independence, some Greeks banded together to create leagues of city-states. Here was the birth of Greek federalism, a political system in which several states formed a central government while remaining independent in their internal affairs. United in a league, a confederation of city-states was far stronger than any of the individual members and better able to withstand external attack.

The passionate individualism of the polis proved to be another serious weakness. The citizens of each polis were determined to remain free and autonomous. Rarely were the Greeks willing to unite in larger political bodies. The political result in Greece, as in Sumer, was almost constant warfare.

The polis could dominate, but unlike Rome it could not incorporate.

 ## THE LYRIC AGE (800–500 B.C.)

The maturation of the polis coincided with one of the most vibrant periods of Greek history, an era of extraordinary expansion geographically, artistically, and politically. Greeks ventured as far east as the Black Sea and as far west as Spain (Map 5.2). With the rebirth of literacy, this period also witnessed a tremendous literary flowering as poets broke away from the heroic tradition and wrote about their own lives. Politically these were the years when Sparta and Athens—the two poles of the Greek experience—rose to prominence.

Overseas Expansion

Between 1100 and 800 B.C. the Greeks not only recovered from the breakdown of the Mycenaean world but also grew in wealth and numbers. This new prosperity brought with it new problems. Greece is a small and not especially fertile country. The increase in population meant that many men and their families had very little land or none at all. Land hunger and the resulting social and political tensions drove many Greeks to seek new homes outside Greece.

The Mediterranean offered an escape valve, for the Greeks were always a seafaring people. To them the sea was a highway, not a barrier. Through their commercial ventures they had long been familiar with the rich areas of the western Mediterranean. Moreover, the geography of the Mediterranean basin favored colonization. The land and climate of the Mediterranean region are remarkably uniform. Greeks could travel to new areas, whether to Cyprus in the east or to Malta in the west, and establish the kind of settlement they had known in Greece.

From about 750 to 550 B.C. Greeks from the mainland and from Asia Minor poured onto the coasts of the northern Aegean, the Ionian Sea, and the Black Sea and into North Africa, Sicily, southern Italy, southern France, and Spain (see Map 5.2). Just as the migrations of the Dark Age had

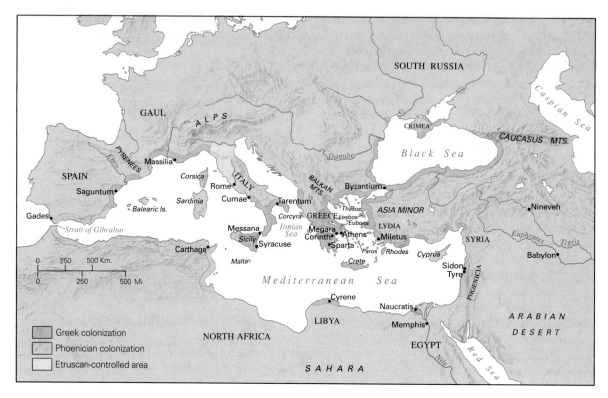

MAP 5.2 Colonization of the Mediterranean   Though both the Greeks and the Phoenicians colonized the Mediterranean basin at roughly the same time, the Greeks spread over a far greater area.

Lyric Poets

One man can in many ways stand as the symbol of the vital and robust era of colonization. Archilochus, born on the island of Paros, was himself a colonist. He was also a poet of genius, the first of the lyric poets who left an indelible mark on this age. Unlike the epic poets, who portrayed the deeds of heroes, Archilochus sang of himself. He knew the sea, the dangers of sailing, and the price that the sea often exacted. He spoke of one shipwreck in grim terms and even treated the god of the sea with irony: "Of fifty men gentle Poseidon left one, Koiranos, to be saved from shipwreck."

Together with others from Paros he took part in the colonization of Thasos in the northern Aegean. He described the island in less-than-glowing terms: "Like the spine of an ass it stands, crowned to the brim with a wild forest." His opinion of his fellow colonists was hardly kinder: "So the misery of all Greece came together in Thasos." Yet at Thasos he fell in love with a woman named Neoboule. They did not marry because her father opposed the match. In revenge, Archilochus seduced Neoboule's younger sister, railed at the entire family, and left Thasos to live the life of a mercenary.

His hired lance took him to Euboea, and he left a striking picture of the fighting there:

Not many bows will be strung, nor slings be slung
When Ares begins battle in the plain.
There will be the mournful work of the sword:
For in this kind of battle are the spear-famed
Lords of Euboea experienced.[3]

Archilochus exemplifies the energy, restlessness, self-reliance, and sense of adventure that characterize this epoch. People like Archilochus broke old familiar ties, faced homelessness and danger and built new homes for themselves. They made the Mediterranean Greek.

Individualism set a new tone in Greek literature. For the first time in Western civilization, men and women began to write of their own experiences. Their poetry reflected their belief that they had something precious to say about themselves. To them poetry did not belong only to the gods or to the great heroes on the plain of Troy. One of the most unforgettable of these writers is the poet Sappho.

Unlike Archilochus, Sappho neither braved the wilds nor pushed into the unknown, yet she was no less individual than he. Sappho was born in the seventh century B.C. on the island of Lesbos. Her marriage produced a daughter, to whom she wrote some of her poems. Sappho's poetry is personal and intense. She delighted in her surroundings, which were those of aristocratic women, and she celebrated the little things around her. Hers was a world of natural beauty, sacred groves, religious festivals, wedding celebrations, and noble companions. Sappho fondly remembered walks with a woman friend:

There was neither a hill nor a sanctuary
Nor a stream of running water
Which we failed to visit;
Nor when spring began any grove
Filled with the noise of nightingales.[4]

Sappho is best known for erotic poetry, for she expressed her love frankly and without same. She was bisexual, and much of her poetry dealt with her homosexual love affairs. In one of her poems she remembered the words of her lover:

Greek Influence Abroad   This gold comb is a remarkable combination of Greek and Eastern details. The art is almost purely Greek. The mounted horseman is clothed with largely Greek armor, but he attacks an Eastern enemy. The horseman's companion is also Eastern. This splendid piece testifies to the exchange of artistic motifs and styles in the eastern Mediterranean basin. *(Source: Hermitage, Leningrad)*

✿ **Mosaic Portrait of Sappho** The Greek letters in the upper left corner identify this idealized portrait as that of Sappho. The mosaic, which was found at Sparta, dates to the late Roman Empire and testifies to Sappho's popularity in antiquity. *(Source: Caroline Buckler)*

Sappho, if you don't come out,
Surely I will no longer love you.
O come to us and free your lovely
Strength from your bed.
Lifting off your Chian robe,
Bathe in the waters like a
Pure lily beside a spring.[5]

In antiquity Sappho's name became linked with female homosexual love. Today the English word *lesbian* is derived from Sappho's island home. The Greeks accepted bisexuality—that men and women could enjoy both homosexual and heterosexual lovemaking. Homosexual relationships normally carried no social stigma.

In their poetry Archilochus and Sappho reveal two sides of Greek life in this period. Archilochus exemplifies the energy and adventure of the age; Sappho expresses the intensely personal side of life. The link connecting the two poets is their individualism, their faith in themselves, and their desire to reach out to other men and women in order to share their experiences, thoughts, and wisdom.

The Growth of Sparta

During the Lyric Age the Spartans expanded the boundaries of their polis and made it the leading power in Greece. Like other Greeks, the Spartans faced the problems of overpopulation and land hunger. Unlike other Greeks, the Spartans solved these problems by conquest, not by colonization. To gain more land, the Spartans set out in about 735 B.C. to conquer Messenia, a rich, fertile region in the southwestern Peloponnesus. This conflict, the First Messenian War, lasted for twenty years and ended in a Spartan triumph. The Spartans appropriated Messenian land and turned the Messenians into *helots,* or state serfs.

In about 650 B.C., Spartan exploitation and oppression of the Messenian helots led to a helot revolt so massive and stubborn that it became known as the Second Messenian War. The Spartan poet Tyrtaeus, a contemporary of these events, vividly portrayed the ferocity of the fighting:

For it is a shameful thing indeed
When with the foremost fighters
An elder falling in front of the young men
Lies outstretched,
Having white hair and grey beard,
Breathing forth his stout soul in the dust,
Holding in his hands his genitals
stained with blood.[6]

Confronted with such horrors, Spartan enthusiasm for the war waned. Finally, after some thirty years of fighting, the Spartans put down the revolt. Nevertheless, the political and social strain it caused led to a transformation of the Spartan polis. After the victory the non-nobles, who had done much of the fighting, demanded rights equal to those of the nobility. Their agitation disrupted society until the aristocrats agreed to remodel the state.

Although the Spartans later claimed that the changes brought about by this compromise were the work of Lycurgus, a legendary, semidivine lawgiver, they were really the work of the entire Spartan people. The Lycurgan regimen, as these reforms were called, established an oligarchy of citizens who were all considered legally equal. Sparta was ruled by two kings, assisted by a council of twenty-eight nobles. The civil executive power was in the hands of five *ephors,* overseers elected from and by all the people.

The Hoplite Phalanx When the Greeks adopted heavy armor, weapons, and shields, their lack of mobility forced them to fight in several dense lines, each behind the other. To help the hoplites maintain their pace during the attack, a flute player here plays a marching tune. *(Source: Villa Giulia Museum/Scala/Art Resource, NY)*

To provide for their economic needs, the Spartans divided the land of Messenia among all citizens. Helots worked the land, raised the crops, provided the Spartans with their living, and occasionally served in the army. The Spartans kept the helots in line with systematic terrorism, hoping to beat them down and keep them quiet. Spartan citizens were supposed to devote their time exclusively to military training.

In the Lycurgan system every citizen owed primary allegiance to Sparta. Suppression of the individual together with emphasis on military prowess led to a barracks state. Family life itself was sacrificed to the polis. Once Spartan boys reached the age of twelve, they were enrolled in separate companies with other boys of their age. They slept outdoors on reed mats and underwent rugged physical and military training until age twenty-four, when they became front-line soldiers. For the rest of their lives, Spartan men kept themselves prepared for combat, and the older men were expected to be models of endurance, frugality, and sturdiness to the younger men. In battle Spartans were supposed to stand and die rather than retreat. An anecdote about one Spartan mother sums up Spartan military values. As her son was setting off to battle, the mother handed him his shield and advised him to come back either victorious, carrying the shield, or dead, being carried on it.

Similar rigorous requirements applied to Spartan women, who may have been unique in all of Greek society. They were prohibited from wearing jewelry or ornate clothes. They exercised strenuously in the belief that hard physical training promoted the birth of healthy children. Yet they were hardly oppressed. They enjoyed a more active and open public life than most other Greek women, even though they could neither vote nor hold office.

They were far more emancipated than many other Greek women, in part because Spartan society felt that mothers and wives had to be as hardy as their sons and husbands. Sparta was not a place for weaklings, male or female. Spartan women saw it as their privilege to be the wives and mothers of victorious warriors, and on several occasions their own courage became legendary. They had a reputation for independent spirit and self-assertion. Their position stemmed from their genuine patriotism, but also from their title to much Spartan land. For all of these reasons, they shared with Spartan men a footing that most other Greek women lacked in their own societies.

In addition to emphasizing military values for both sexes, the Lycurgan regimen had another purpose as well: it served to instill in society the civic virtues of dedication to the state and a code of moral conduct. These aspects of the Spartan system were generally admired throughout the Greek world.

The Evolution of Athens

Like Sparta, Athens faced pressing social and economic problems during the Lyric Age, but the Athenian response was far different from that of the Spartans. Instead of creating an oligarchy, the Athenians extended to all citizens the right and duty of governing the polis. Indeed, the Athenian democracy was one of the most thoroughgoing in Greece.

In 621 B.C. Draco, an Athenian aristocrat, published the first law code of the Athenian polis. Although his code was thought harsh, it embodied the idea that the law belonged to the citizens. Nevertheless, by the early sixth century B.C. social and economic conditions had led to an explosive situation. The aristocracy governed Athens oppressively. The aristocrats owned the best land, met in an assembly to govern the polis, and interpreted the law. Noble landowners were forcing small farmers into economic dependence. Many families, unable to repay loans from their wealthy neighbors, were sold into slavery; others were exiled and their land was pledged to the rich.

In many other city-states conditions like those in Athens led to the rise of tyrants. One person who recognized these problems clearly was Solon, an aristocrat and poet and a man opposed to tyrants.

He was also the one man in Athens who enjoyed the respect of both aristocrats and peasants. Like Hesiod, Solon used his poetry to condemn the aristocrats for their greed and dishonesty. He recited his poems in the Athenian agora, where everyone could hear his relentless call for justice and fairness. Around 594 B.C. the nobles elected him *archon,* chief magistrate of the Athenian polis, and gave him extraordinary power to reform the state.

Solon immediately freed all people enslaved for debt, recalled all exiles, canceled all debts on land, and made enslavement for debt illegal. He also divided society into four legal groups on the basis of wealth. In the most influential group were the wealthiest citizens, but even the poorest and least powerful group enjoyed certain rights. Solon allowed them into the old aristocratic assembly, where they could take part in the election of magistrates. His work done, Solon insisted that all swear to uphold his reforms. Then, because many were clamoring for him to become tyrant, he left Athens.

Solon's reforms solved some immediate problems but did not bring peace to Athens. Some aristocrats attempted to make themselves tyrants, while others banded together to oppose them. In 546 B.C. Pisistratus, an exiled aristocrat, returned to Athens, defeated his opponents, and became tyrant. Pisistratus reduced the power of the aristocracy while supporting the common people. Under his rule Athens prospered, and his building program began to transform the city into one of the splendors of Greece.

Athenian acceptance of tyranny did not long outlive Pisistratus, for his son Hippias ruled harshly, committing excesses that led to his overthrow. After a brief period of turmoil between factions of the nobility, Cleisthenes, a wealthy and prominent aristocrat, emerged triumphant in 508 B.C., largely because he won the support of the people. Cleisthenes created the Athenian democracy with the full knowledge and approval of the Athenian people. He reorganized the state completely but presented every innovation to the assembly for discussion and ratification. All Athenian citizens had a voice in Cleisthenes' work.

Cleisthenes created the *deme,* a local unit, to serve as the basis of his political system. Citizenship was tightly linked to the deme, for each deme kept the roll of those within its jurisdiction who were admitted to citizenship. Cleisthenes grouped all the demes into ten tribes, which thus formed the link between the demes and the central government. The central government included an assembly of all citizens and a new council of five hundred members.

The democracy functioned on the idea that all full citizens, the *demos,* were sovereign. Yet not all citizens could take time from work to participate in government. Therefore, they delegated their power to other citizens by creating various offices to run the democracy. The most prestigious of them was the board of ten archons, who were charged with handling legal and military matters. Legislation was in the hands of two bodies, the *boule,* or council, composed of five hundred members, and the *ecclesia,* the assembly of all citizens. The boule was perhaps the major institution of the democracy. By supervising the various committees of government and proposing bills to the assembly, it guided Athenian political life and held the democracy together. The ecclesia, however, had the final word. Open to all male citizens over eighteen years of age, this assembly could accept, amend, or reject bills put before it. Every member could express his opinion on any subject on the agenda. A simple majority vote was needed to pass or reject a bill.

Athenian democracy was to prove an inspiring model. It demonstrated that a large group of people, not just a few, could efficiently run the affairs of state. By heeding the opinions, suggestions, and wisdom of all its citizens, the polis enjoyed the maximum amount of good counsel. Athenian democracy, however, must not be thought of in modern terms. In Athens democracy was a form of government in which in theory poor men as well as rich enjoyed political power and responsibility. In practice, though, most important offices were held by aristocrats. Furthermore, Athenian democracy denied political rights to many people, including women and slaves. Unlike modern democracies, Athenian democracy did not mean that citizens would vote for others who would then run the state. Instead, every citizen was expected to be able to perform the duties of most magistrates. In Athens citizens voted and served. The people were the government. It is this union of the individual and the state—the view that the state exists for the

good of the citizen, whose duty it is to serve it well—that has made Athenian democracy so compelling a model.

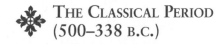

THE CLASSICAL PERIOD (500–338 B.C.)

In the years from 500 to 338 B.C. Greek civilization reached its highest peak in politics, thought, and art. In this period the Greeks beat back the armies of the Persian Empire. Then, turning their spears against one another, they destroyed their own political system in a century of warfare. Some thoughtful Greeks felt prompted to record and analyze these momentous events; the result was the creation of history. This era also saw the flowering of philosophy, as Greek thinkers began to ponder the nature and meaning of the universe and human experience. The Greeks also invented drama, and Greek architects reached the zenith of their art. Because Greek intellectual and artistic efforts attained their fullest and finest expression in these years, this age is called the Classical period.

The Deadly Conflicts (499–404 B.C.)

One of the hallmarks of the Classical period was warfare. In 499 B.C. the Greeks of Asia Minor, with the feeble help of Athens, rebelled against the Persian Empire. In 490 B.C. the Persians struck back at Athens but were beaten off at the Battle of Marathon, a small plain in Attica (Map 5.3). In 480 B.C. the Persian king Xerxes retaliated with a mighty invasion force. Facing this emergency, many of the Greeks united to resist the invaders. The Spartans provided the overall leadership and commanded the Greek armies. The Athenians, led by the wily Themistocles, provided the heart of the naval forces.

The first confrontations between the Persians and the Greeks occurred at the pass of Thermopylae and in the waters off Artemisium, the northern tip of Euboea. At Thermopylae the Greek hoplites showed their mettle. Before the fighting began, a report came in that when the Persian archers shot their bows the arrows darkened the sky. One gruff Spartan replied merely, "Fine, then we'll fight in the shade." The Greeks at Thermopylae fought heroically, but the Persians took the position. In

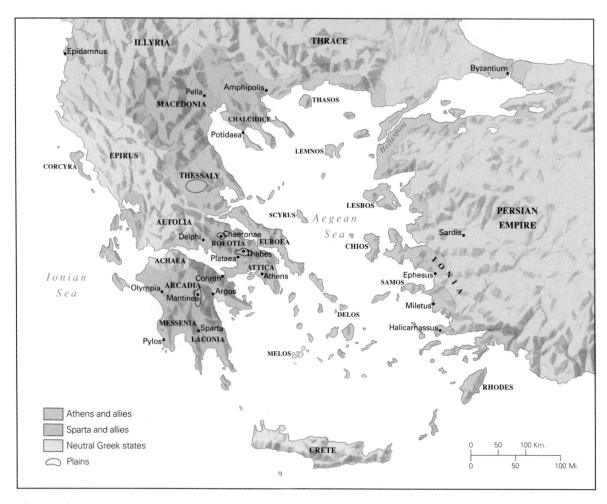

MAP 5.3 The Peloponnesian War This map shows the alignment of states during the Peloponnesian War and vividly illustrates the large scale of the war and its divisive impact.

480 B.C. the Greek fleet met the Persian armada at Salamis, an island just west of Athens. Though outnumbered by the Persians, the Greek navy won an overwhelming victory (see Listening to the Past). The remnants of the Persian fleet retired, and with them went all hope of Persian victory. In the following year, a coalition of Greek forces smashed the last Persian army at Plataea, a small polis in Boeotia. The Greeks remained free to develop their particular genius. These decisive victories meant that Greek political forms and intellectual concepts would be the heritage of the West.

In 478 B.C. the Athenians and their allies formed the Delian League, a grand naval alliance aimed at liberating Ionia from Persian rule. The Delian League was intended as a free alliance under the leadership of Athens. Athenians provided most of the warships and crews and determined how many ships or how much money each member of the league should contribute to the allied effort.

The Athenians, supported by the Delian League, carried the war against Persia. But Athenian success had a sinister side. While the Athenians drove the Persians out of the Aegean, they also became increasingly imperialistic, even to the point of turning the Delian League into an Athenian empire. Athens began reducing its allies to the status of subjects. Tribute was often collected by force, and the Athenians placed the economic resources of the Delian League under tighter and tighter control.

The expansion of Athenian power and the aggressiveness of Athenian rule alarmed Sparta and its allies. While relations between Athens and Sparta cooled, Pericles (ca 494–429 B.C.) became the leading statesman in Athens. Like the democracy he led, Pericles, an aristocrat of solid intellectual ability, was aggressive and imperialistic. At last, in 459 B.C., Sparta and Athens went to war over conflicts between Athens and some of Sparta's allies. The war ended in 445 B.C. with no serious damage to either side and nothing settled. But this war divided the Greek world between the two great powers.

During the 440s and 430s, Athens continued its severe policies toward its subject allies and came into conflict with Corinth, one of Sparta's leading supporters (see Map 5.3). In response the Spartans convened a meeting of their allies, whose complaints of Athenian aggression ended with a demand that Athens be stopped. Reluctantly the Spartans agreed to declare war. The real reason for war, according to the Athenian historian Thucydides, was very simple: "The truest explanation, though the one least mentioned, was the great growth of Athenian power and the fear it caused the Lacedaemonians [Spartans], which drove them to war."[7]

At the outbreak of this, the Peloponnesian War, a Spartan ambassador warned the Athenians: "This day will be the beginning of great evils for the Greeks." Few have ever spoken more prophetically. The Peloponnesian War lasted a generation (431–404 B.C.) and brought in its wake fearful plagues, famine, civil wars, widespread destruction, and huge loss of life. Thucydides described its cataclysmic effects:

For never had so many cities been captured and destroyed, whether by the barbarians or by the Greeks who were fighting each other. . . . Never had so many men been exiled or slaughtered, whether in the war or because of civil conflicts.[8]

As the war dragged on, older leaders like Pericles died and were replaced by men of the war generation. In Athens the most prominent of this new breed of politicians was Alcibiades (ca 450–404 B.C.), an aristocrat, a kinsman of Pericles, and a student of the philosopher Socrates (see page 140). Brilliant, handsome, charming, and popular with the people, Alcibiades was also self-seeking

The Persian Wars This vase dates to the early fifth century B.C. It depicts fighting between a heavily armed Greek hoplite on the left, carrying a shield and spear, and an Asian soldier who is less heavily armed. *(Source: The Metropolitan Museum of Art, Rogers Fund, 1906 [06.1021.117])*

FRIEZE   COFFERS   TYMPANUM

PEDIMENT
CYMATION
CORNICE
MUTULES
TRIGLYPHS
METOPES
GUTTAE
ARCHITRAVE
ABACUS
ECHINUS

STYLOBATE

Sectional View of the Parthenon This figure both indicates what the Parthenon looked like in antiquity and explains the complex nature of Greek temple building. The Parthenon's apparently simple façade is a work of great architectural sophistication. *(Source:* Guide to Sculptures of the Parthenon, *a British Museum publication)*

and egotistical and a shameless opportunist. His first thoughts were always for himself.

Alcibiades' schemes helped bring Athens down to defeat. Having planned an invasion of Sicily that ended in disaster, he deserted to the Spartans and plotted with the Persians, who had sided with Sparta, against his homeland. In the end, all of Alcibiades' intrigues failed. The Spartans defeated the Athenian fleet in the Aegean and blockaded Athens by land and sea. Finally, in 404 B.C. the Athenians surrendered and watched helplessly while the Spartans and their allies destroyed the walls of Athens to the music of flute girls. The

Peloponnesian War, which lasted twenty-seven years, dealt Greek civilization a serious blow.

The Birth of Historical Awareness

One positive development grew out of the Persian and Peloponnesian wars: the beginnings of historical writing. In his book *The Histories,* Herodotus (ca 485–425 B.C.), known as the father of history, chronicled the rise of the Persian Empire, sketched the background of Athens and Sparta, and described the land and customs of the Egyptians and the Scythians, who lived in the region of the mod-

The Athenian Acropolis This painting, though made in the nineteenth century, gives a vivid impression of what the buildings and their entire setting looked like in antiquity. It demonstrates the artistic appeal of these buildings and proves what Plutarch wrote of them: "Each of them is always in bloom, maintaining its appearance as though untouched by time, as though an ever-green breath and undecaying spirit had been mixed in its construction." *(Source: Neue Pinakothek, Munich)*

ern Crimea. The sheer scope of this work is awesome. Perhaps Herodotus's most striking characteristic was his curiosity. He diligently questioned everyone who could tell him anything about the Persian wars. The confrontation between East and West unfolds relentlessly in *The Histories.*

The outbreak of the Peloponnesian War prompted Thucydides (ca 460–ca 400 B.C.) to write an account of its course in the belief that it would be the greatest war in Greek history. An Athenian politician and general, Thucydides saw action in the war until he was exiled for a defeat. Exile gave him the time and opportunity to question eyewitnesses about the details of events and to visit battlefields.

Thucydides was intensely interested in human nature and how it manifested itself during the war. When a terrible plague struck Athens in 430 B.C., Thucydides described in the same clinical terms both the symptoms of the plague and the reactions of the Athenians. He portrayed the virtual breakdown of a society beset by war, disease, desperation, and despair.

Athenian Arts in the Age of Pericles

In the last half of the fifth century B.C., Pericles turned Athens into the showplace of Greece. He appropriated Delian League funds to pay for a huge building program, planning temples and other buildings to honor Athena, the patron goddess of the city, and to display to all Greeks the glory of the Athenian polis. Thus began the undertaking that turned the Acropolis into a monument for all time. Construction of the Parthenon began in 447 B.C., followed by the Propylaea, the temple of Athena Nike (Athena the Victorious), and the Erechtheum. Even today in their ruined state they still evoke awe.

The planning of the architects and the skill of the workmen who erected these buildings were very sophisticated. Visitors approaching the Acropolis first saw the Propylaea, the ceremonial gateway, a building of complicated layout and grand design whose Doric columns seemed to hold up the sky. On the right was the small temple of Athena Nike, built to commemorate the victory over the Persians. The Ionic frieze above its columns depicted the struggle between the Greeks and the Persians, a tribute to Athenian and Greek valor—and a reminder of Athens's part in the victory. To the left of the visitors, as they passed through the Propylaea, stood the Erechtheum, an Ionic temple that housed several ancient shrines. On its southern side was the famous Portico of the Caryatids, a porch whose roof was supported by statues of Athenian maidens.

As visitors walked on, they obtained a full view of the Parthenon, the chief monument to Athena and her city. The sculptures that adorned the temple portrayed the greatness of Athens and its goddess. The figures on the eastern pediment depicted Athena's birth, those on the west the victory of Athena over the god Poseidon in their struggle for the possession of Attica. Inside the Parthenon stood a huge statue of Athena, the masterpiece of the great sculptor, Phidias.

In many ways the Athenian Acropolis is the epitome of Greek art and its spirit. Although the buildings were dedicated to the gods and most of the sculptures portrayed gods, these works nonetheless express the Greek fascination with the human and the rational. Greek deities were anthropomorphic, and Greek artists portrayed them as human beings. The Acropolis also exhibits the rational side of Greek art. Greek artists portrayed action in a balanced, restrained, and sometimes even serene fashion, capturing the noblest aspects of human beings: their reason, dignity, and promise.

Other aspects of Athenian cultural life were as rooted in the life of the polis as were the architecture and sculpture of the Acropolis. The development of drama was tied to the religious festivals of the city. The polis sponsored the production of plays and required that wealthy citizens pay the expenses of their production. At the beginning of the year, dramatists submitted their plays to the archon. He chose those he considered best and assigned a theatrical troupe to each playwright. Many plays were highly controversial, but the archons neither suppressed nor censored them.

The Athenian dramatists were the first artists in European society to examine such basic questions as the rights of the individual, the demands of society on the individual, and the nature of good and evil. The dramatists used their art to portray, understand, and resolve life's basic conflicts.

Aeschylus (525–456 B.C.), the first of the great Athenian dramatists, was also the first to express the agony of the individual caught in conflict. In his trilogy of plays, *The Oresteia,* Aeschylus deals with the themes of betrayal, murder, and reconciliation, urging that reason and justice be applied to reconcile fundamental conflicts. The final play concludes with a prayer that civil dissension never be allowed to destroy the city and that the life of the city be one of harmony and grace.

Sophocles (496–406 B.C.) also dealt with matters personal and political. In *Antigone* he expressed the precedence of divine law over human defects and touched on the need for recognition of the law and adherence to it as a prerequisite for a tranquil state.

Sophocles' masterpieces have inspired generations of playwrights. Perhaps his most famous plays are *Oedipus the King* and its sequel, *Oedipus at Colonus. Oedipus the King* is the ironic story of a man doomed by the gods to kill his father and marry his mother. Try as he might to avoid his fate, Oedipus's every action brings him closer to its fulfillment. When at last he realizes that he has carried out the decree of the gods, Oedipus blinds himself and flees into exile. In *Oedipus at Colonus* Sophocles dramatizes the last days of the broken king, whose patient suffering and uncomplaining piety win him an exalted position. In the end the gods honor him for his virtue. The interpretation of these two plays has been hotly debated, but Sophocles seems to be saying that human beings should obey the will of the gods, even without fully understanding it, for the gods stand for justice and order.

Euripides (ca 480–406 B.C.), the last of the three great Greek tragic dramatists, also explored the theme of personal conflict within the polis and sounded the depths of the individual. With Euripides drama entered a new, in many ways more personal, phase. To him the gods were far less important than human beings. The essence of Euripides' tragedy is the flawed character—men and women who bring disaster on themselves and their loved ones because their passions overwhelm reason. Although Euripides' plays were less popular in his lifetime than were those of Aeschylus and Sophocles, Euripides was a dramatist of genius whose work later had a significant impact on Roman drama.

Writers of comedy treated the affairs of the polis bawdily and often coarsely. Even so, their plays, too, were performed at religious festivals. The comic playwrights dealt primarily with the political affairs of the polis and the conduct of its leading politicians. Best known are the comedies of Aristophanes (ca 445–386 B.C.), an ardent lover of his city and a merciless critic of cranks and quacks. He lampooned eminent generals, at times depicting them as morons. He commented snidely on Pericles, poked fun at Socrates, and hooted at Euripides. Like Aeschylus, Sophocles, and Euripides, Aristophanes used his art to dramatize his ideas on the right conduct of the citizen and the value of the polis.

Perhaps never were art and political life so intimately and congenially bound together as at Athens. Athenian art was the product of deep and

 "Procession of the Horsemen" from the Parthenon Frieze The great temple of Athena on the Acropolis, the Parthenon, was decorated by a band of sculpture depicting the religious procession to celebrate the festival of the payathena. Artists took their subjects from the actual procession. Here an Athenian artist has caught the young riders trying to restrain their unruly horses. The entire frieze blends idealism and realism in its depiction of human activity. *(Source: Courtesy of the Trustees of the British Museum)*

genuine love of the polis. It aimed at bettering the lives of the citizens and the quality of life in the state.

Daily Life in Periclean Athens

In sharp contrast with the rich intellectual and cultural life of Periclean Athens stands the simplicity of its material life. The Athenians—and in this respect they were typical of Greeks in general—lived very happily with comparatively few material possessions. In the first place, there were very few material goods to own. The thousands of machines, tools, and gadgets considered essential for modern life had no counterparts in Athenian life. The inventory of Alcibiades' goods, which the Athenians confiscated after his desertion, is enlightening. His household possessions consisted of chests, beds, couches, tables, screens, stools, baskets, and mats. Other common items of the Greek home included pottery, metal utensils for cooking, tools, luxury goods such as jewelry, and a few other things.

Like its furnishings, the Athenian house was rather simple. Whether large or small, the typical house consisted of a series of rooms built around a central courtyard, with doors opening onto the courtyard. Many houses had bedrooms on an upper floor. Artisans and craftsmen often set aside a room to use as a shop or work area. The two principal rooms were the men's dining room and the room where the women worked wool. Other rooms included the kitchen and bathroom.

In the courtyard were the well, a small altar, and a washbasin. If the family lived in the country, the stalls of the animals faced the courtyard. Even in the city, chickens and perhaps a goat or two roamed the courtyard together with dogs and cats.

Cooking, done over a hearth in the house, provided welcome warmth in the winter. Baking and roasting were done in ovens. Food consisted primarily of various grains, especially wheat and barley, as well as lentils, olives, figs, and grapes. Garlic and onion were popular garnishes, and wine was always on hand. These foods were stored at home in large jars; with them the Greek family sometimes ate fish, chicken, and vegetables. Women ground wheat into flour, baked it into bread, and on special occasions made honey or sesame cakes. The Greeks used olive oil for cooking, as families still do in modern Greece; they also used it as an unguent and as lamp fuel.

On special occasions, such as important religious festivals, a Greek family ate the animal sacrificed to the god and gave the god the exquisite delicacy of the thighbone wrapped in fat. A successful hunt for rabbits, deer, or wild boar could supplement the family's regular diet. The only Greeks who consistently ate meat were the Spartan warriors. They received a small portion of meat each day, together with the infamous Spartan black broth, a ghastly concoction of pork cooked in blood, vinegar, and salt. One Greek, after tasting the broth, commented that he could easily understand why the Spartans were so willing to die.

In the city a man might support himself as a craftsman—a potter, bronzesmith, sailmaker, or tanner—or he could contract with the polis to work on public buildings, such as the Parthenon and Erechtheum. Men without skills worked as paid laborers but competed with slaves for work. Slaves—usually foreigners, barbarian as well as Greek—were paid the same amount for their employment as were free men.

Slavery was commonplace in Greece, as it was throughout the rest of the ancient world. In its essentials Greek slavery resembled Mesopotamian slavery. Slaves received some protection under the law. Masters could mistreat or neglect their slaves, though killing them was illegal. In addition to doing skilled and unskilled labor, slaves served as domestics and performed light work around the house. Nurses for children, teachers of reading and writing, and guardians for young men were often slaves. The lives of these slaves were much like those of their owners.

The importance of slavery in Athens must not be exaggerated. Athenians did not own huge gangs of slaves as did Roman owners of large estates. Slave labor competed with free labor and kept wages down, but it never replaced the free labor that was the mainstay of the Athenian economy.

Most Athenians supported themselves by agriculture, but on most of the land it was difficult to reap a good crop from the soil. Many people must have consumed nearly everything they raised. Attic farmers were free and, though hardly prosperous, were by no means destitute. They could usually expect yields of five bushels of wheat and ten of barley per acre for every bushel of grain sown. A bad harvest meant a lean year. In many places farmers grew more barley than wheat because of the nature of the soil. Wherever possible, farmers also cultivated grape vines and olive trees.

The social condition of Athenian women has been the subject of much debate and little agreement. One of the difficulties is the fragmentary nature of the evidence. Most Greek historians of the time recounted primarily the political, diplomatic, and military events of the day, events in which women seldom played a notable part. Yet that does not mean that women were totally invisible in the life of the polis. Although women lacked official power, they played a vital role in shaping the society in which they lived. The same situation had existed in Hammurabi's Babylonia, and it would recur in the Hellenistic period.

The status of a free woman of the citizen class was strictly protected by law. Only her children, not those of foreigners or slaves, could be citizens. Only she was in charge of the household and the family's possessions. Yet the law protected her primarily to protect her husband's interests. Raping a free woman was a lesser crime than seducing her, because seduction involved the winning of her affections. This law was not concerned with the husband's feelings but with ensuring that he need not doubt the legitimacy of his children.

Women in Athens and elsewhere in Greece received a certain amount of social and legal protection from their dowries. Upon marriage, the bride's father gave the couple a gift of land or money, which the husband administered. However, the gift was never really his; and in the rare cases of divorce, it returned to the wife's domain. The same is often true in Greece today among the upper class.

Athenian women seem to have enjoyed a social circle of other women of their own class. They also attended public festivals, sacrifices, and funerals. Nonetheless, prosperous and respectable women probably spent much of their time in the house. A white complexion—a sign that a woman did not have to work in the fields—was valued highly.

Courtesans lived the freest lives of all Athenian women. Although some courtesans were simply prostitutes, others added intellectual accomplishments to physical beauty. In constant demand, cultured courtesans moved freely in male society. The most famous was Aspasia, mistress of Pericles and

Women Working The scene on this vase represents the women of the household at work. It shows how they produced woolen cloth, from the spinning of yarn to the completion of the cloth itself, here held by two women. *(Source: The Metropolitan Museum of Art, Fletcher Fund, 1931)*

supposedly a friend of Socrates. Under Pericles' roof, she participated in intellectual discussions equally with some of the most stimulating thinkers of the day. Yet her position, like that of most other courtesans, was precarious. After Pericles' death, Aspasia fended for herself, ending her days as the madam of a house of prostitution.

A woman's main functions were to raise the children, oversee the domestic slaves and hired labor, and together with her maids work wool into cloth. The woman of the household either did the cooking herself or directed her maids. In a sense, poor women lived freer lives than did wealthier women. They performed manual labor in the fields or sold goods in the agora, going about their affairs much as men did.

A distinctive feature of Athenian life and of Greek life in general was the belief that both homosexual and heterosexual practices were normal parts of life. No one has satisfactorily explained how the Greek attitude toward homosexual love developed or determined how common homosexual behavior was. Homosexuality was probably far more common among the aristocracy than among the lower classes. Even among the aristocracy, attitudes toward homosexuality were complex and sometimes conflicting. Most people saw homosexual love affairs among the young as a stage in the development of a mature heterosexual life. Warrior aristocracies generally emphasized the physical side of the relationship in the belief that warriors who were also lovers would fight all the harder to impress and to protect each other. Whatever their intellectual content, homosexual love affairs were overtly sexual.

One particularly important aspect of social life in Athens and elsewhere in Greece was religion. Yet the Greeks had no uniform faith or creed. Although the Greeks usually worshiped the same deities—Zeus, Hera, Apollo, Athena, and others—the cults of these gods and goddesses varied from polis to polis. Greek religion was often a matter more of ritual than of belief. Nor did cults impose an ethical code of conduct. Unlike the Egyptians and Hebrews, the Greeks lacked a priesthood as the modern world understands the term. In Greece priests and priestesses existed to care for temples and sacred property and to conduct the proper rituals, but not to make religious rules or doctrines, much less to enforce them. In short, there existed in Greece no central ecclesiastical authority and no organized creed.

Although temples to the gods were common, they were unlike modern churches or synagogues in that they were not normally places where a congregation met to worship as a spiritual community. Instead, the individual Greek either visited the temple occasionally on matters of private concern or walked in a procession to a particular temple to celebrate a particular festival. In Greek religion the altar, which stood outside the temple, was important. When the Greeks sought the favor of the gods, they offered them sacrifices. Greek religious observances were generally cheerful. Festivals and sacrifices were frequently times for people to meet together socially, times of high spirits and conviviality rather than of pious gloom.

Besides the Olympian gods, each polis had its own minor deities, each with his or her own local cult. The polis administered the cults and festivals, and all were expected to participate in this civic religion, regardless of whether they believed in the deities being worshiped. Participating unbelievers, who seem to have been a small minority, were not considered hypocrites. Rather, they were seen as patriotic, loyal citizens who in honoring the gods also honored the polis. If this attitude seems contradictory, an analogy may help. Before baseball games Americans stand at the playing of the national anthem, whether they are Democrats, Republicans, or neither, and whether they agree or disagree with the policies of the current administration. They honor their nation as represented by its flag. In somewhat the same way an ancient Greek honored the polis and demonstrated solidarity with it by participating in the state cults.

Some Greeks turned to mystery religions like those of the Eleusinian mysteries in Attica. These cults united individuals in an exclusive religious society with particular deities. Those who joined them went through a period of preparation in which they learned the essential beliefs of the cult and its necessary rituals. Once they had successfully undergone initiation, they were forbidden to reveal the secrets of the cult. In Classical Greece, relatively few except the wealthy could afford the luxuries of time and money to join the mystery religions.

For most Greeks religion was quite simple and close to nature. They believed in the supernatural and the primitive. The religion of the common people was a rich combination of myth, ritual, folklore, and cult. They believed in a world of deities who were all around them. The goddess Hestia oversaw the sanctity of the hearth; various nymphs resided at clear springs; and Pan, the lover of wild things and places, protected the herds and flocks. Deities and human beings shared their world so intimately that they could change places within it.

A single, very simple example can give an idea of the nature of this religion, its bond with nature, and its sense of ethics and propriety. Probably no one today thinks much about wading across a stream, unless it is too deep. That attitude would have horrified the Boeotian farmer and poet Hesiod, who would have considered it sacrilegious. Instead, he advises the traveler who encounters a stream:

Never cross the beautifully flowing water of an
   overflowing river on foot,
until having looked into the lovely stream and having
   washed your hands in the very lovely, clear waters,
you offer a prayer. Whoever crosses a river and
   with hands unwashed of evil,
to him the gods will wreak vengeance and will give
   him pain.[9]

This is an unaffected example of ritual purification, but no temple or sanctuary is needed for it.

Though Greek religion in general was individual or related to the polis, the Greeks also shared some Pan-Hellenic festivals, the chief of which were held at Olympia in honor of Zeus and at Delphi in honor of Apollo. The festivities at Olympia included athletic contests that have inspired the modern Olympic games. The Pythian games at Delphi also included musical and literary contests. Both the Olympic and the Pythian games were unifying factors in Greek life, bringing Greeks together culturally as well as religiously.

The Flowering of Philosophy

The myths and epics of the Mesopotamians are ample testimony that speculation about the origin of the universe and of mankind did not begin with the Greeks. The signal achievement of the Greeks was the willingness of some to treat these questions in rational rather than mythological terms. Although Greek philosophy did not fully flower until the Classical period, Ionian thinkers had already begun in the Lyric Age to ask what the universe was made of. These men are called the Pre-Socratics, for their work preceded the philosophical revolution begun by the Athenian Socrates.

The first of these Pre-Socratic thinkers, Thales (ca 600 B.C.), learned mathematics and astronomy from the Babylonians and geometry from the Egyptians. Yet there was an immense and fundamental difference between Near Eastern thought and the philosophy of Thales. The Near Eastern peoples considered events such as eclipses to be evil omens. Thales viewed them as natural phenomena that could be explained in natural terms. In short, he asked why things happened. He believed the basic element of the universe to be water. Although he was wrong, the way in which he had asked the question was momentous: it was the beginning of the scientific method.

Thales' follower Anaximander continued his work. He theorized that the basic element of the universe is the "boundless" or "endless"—something infinite and indestructible. Another Ionian, Heraclitus (ca 500 B.C.), declared the primal element to be fire. He also declared that the world

 Golden Chariot By the Classical period the Greeks had stopped using horse-drawn chariots in warfare. Yet they remained a symbol of aristocracy and a memory of the heroic past. Very few ancient artifacts capture that spirit as well as this chariot and its team, which is still trying to win the race. *(Source: Museum of Fine Arts, Boston)*

had neither beginning nor end: "This world, the world of all things, neither any god nor man made, but it always was and it is and it will be: an everlasting fire, measures kindling and measures going out."[10] The culmination of Pre-Socratic thought was the theory that four simple substances make up the universe: fire, air, earth, and water.

Not all of these early philosophers devoted their attention to pure philosophy or natural science. Aesop (d. 564 B.C.) devoted his attention to ethics, the rules of moral behavior. A slave endowed with a keen mind, Aesop made his points metaphorically, by using fables, which were as popular in antiquity as they are today. His tales, in which animals were often the main characters, spread throughout Greece, survived in medieval and modern Europe, and not only can still be enjoyed in books today but also form the plot line of some Bugs Bunny cartoons. They are a reservoir of good sense and simple patterns of behavior. In one fable Aesop tells of a hungry fox who encounters sun-ripened grapes in a vineyard. Try as he might, he cannot reach them. In disgust he leaves, muttering that they were probably sour and wormy anyway, whence comes the expression "sour grapes." The moral is that all fools can criticize what they cannot get. In another fable Aesop tells of a good-natured farmer whose dog falls into a well. The farmer climbs into the well to retrieve the dog, only to be bitten on the hand. Greatly angered, the farmer throws the dog back into the well. The moral again is simple: "Don't bite the hand that feeds you." Many people who never read the writings of philosophers learned from fables such as Aesop's something about life and ethics.

With this impressive heritage behind them, the philosophers of the Classical period ventured into new areas of speculation. This development was partly due to the work of Hippocrates (second half of the fifth century B.C.), the father of medicine. Like Thales, Hippocrates sought natural explanations for natural phenomena. Basing his opinions on empirical knowledge, not on religion or magic, he taught that natural means could be employed to fight disease. But Hippocrates broke away from the mainstream of Ionian speculation by declaring that medicine was a separate craft—just as ironworking was—that had its own principles.

The distinction between natural science and philosophy on which Hippocrates insisted was also promoted by the Sophists, who traveled the Greek world teaching young men. Despite differences of opinion on philosophical matters, the Sophists all agreed that human beings were the proper subject of study. They also believed that excellence could be taught, and they used philosophy and rhetoric to prepare young men for life in the polis. The Sophists laid great emphasis on logic and the meanings of words. They criticized traditional beliefs, religion, rituals, and myth and even questioned the laws of the polis. In essence, they argued that nothing is absolute, that everything is relative.

One of those whose contemporaries thought him a Sophist was Socrates (ca 470–399 B.C.), who sprang from the class of small artisans. Socrates spent his life in investigation and definition. Not, strictly speaking, a Sophist, because he never formally taught or collected fees from anyone, Socrates shared the Sophists' belief that human beings and their environment are the essential subjects of philosophical inquiry. His approach when posing ethical questions and defining concepts was to start with a general topic or problem and to narrow the matter to its essentials. He did so by continuous questioning, conducting a running dialogue with his listeners. Never did he lecture. Socrates thought that by constantly pursuing excellence, an essential part of which was knowledge, human beings could approach the supreme good and thus find true happiness. Yet in 399 B.C. Socrates was brought to trial, convicted, and executed on charges of corrupting the youth of the city and introducing new gods.

Socrates' student Plato (427–347 B.C.) carried on his master's search for the truth. Unlike Socrates, Plato wrote down his thoughts and theories and founded a philosophical school, the Academy. Most people rightly think of Plato as a philosopher. Yet his writings were also literary essays of great charm. They drew out characters, locales, and scenes from ordinary life that otherwise would have been lost to posterity. In addition, Plato used satire, irony, and comedy to relay his thoughts. Behind the elegance of his literary style, however, stand the profound thoughts of a brilliant mind grappling with the problems of his own day and the eternal realities of life. The destruction and chaos of the Peloponnesian War prompted him to ask new and different questions about the nature

PERIODS OF GREEK HISTORY

PERIOD	SIGNIFICANT EVENTS	MAJOR WRITERS
Bronze Age 2000–1100 B.C.	Arrival of the Greeks in Greece Rise and fall of the Mycenaean kingdoms	
Dark Age 1100–800 B.C.	Greek migrations within the Aegean basin Social and political recovery Evolution of the polis Rebirth of literacy	Homer Hesiod
Lyric Age 800–500 B.C.	Rise of Sparta and Athens Colonization of the Mediterranean basin Flowering of lyric poetry Development of philosophy and science in Ionia	Archilochus Sappho Tyrtaeus Solon Anaximander Heraclitus
Classical Period 500–338 B.C.	Persian wars Growth of Athenian empire Peloponnesian War Rise of drama and historical writing Flowering of Greek philosophy Spartan and Theban hegemonies Conquest of Greece by Philip of Macedon	Herodotus Thucydides Aeschylus Sophocles Euripides Aristophanes Plato Aristotle

of human society. He pondered where, why, and how the polis had gone wrong. He gave serious thought to the form that it should take. In these considerations Plato was not only a philosopher but a political scientist and a utopian.

Plato tried to show that a life of ignorance was wretched. From education, he believed, came the possibility of determining an all-comprising unity of virtues that would lead to an intelligent, moral, and ethical life. Plato concluded that only divine providence could guide people to virtue. In his opinion, divine providence was one intelligible and individualistic being. In short, he equated god with the concept of good.

Plato developed the theory that all visible, tangible things are unreal and temporary, copies of "forms" or "ideas" that are constant and indestructible. Only the mind, not the senses, can per-

ceive eternal forms. In Plato's view the highest form is the idea of good. He discussed these ideas in two works. In *The Republic* Plato applied his theory of forms to politics in an effort to describe the ideal polis. His perfect polis was utopian; it aimed at providing the greatest good and happiness to all its members. Plato thought that the ideal polis could exist only if its rulers were philosophers and were devoted to educating their people. He divided society into rulers, guardians of the polis, and workers. The role of individuals in each category would be decided by their education, wisdom, and ability. In Plato's republic men and women would be equal to one another, and women could become rulers. The utopian polis would be a balance, with each individual doing what he or she could to support the state and with each receiving from the state his or her just due. In

The Lion of Chaeronea   This stylized lion marks the mass grave of nearly three hundred elite Theban soldiers who died valiantly fighting the Macedonians at the Battle of Chaeronea. After the battle, when Philip viewed the bodies of these brave troops, he said: "May those who suppose that these men did or suffered anything dishonorable perish wretchedly." *(Source: Caroline Buckler)*

The Laws, however, Plato drew a more authoritarian picture of government and society, one not so very different from that of twentieth-century dictatorship.

A student of Plato, Aristotle (384–322 B.C.) went far beyond him in striving to understand the universe. The range of Aristotle's thought is staggering. Everything in human experience was fit subject for his inquiry. In *Politics* Aristotle followed Plato's lead by writing about the ideal polis, approaching the question more realistically than Plato had done. In *Politics* and elsewhere, Aristotle stressed moderation, concluding that the balance of the ideal state depended on people of talent and education who could avoid extremes.

Aristotle was both a philosopher and a scientist. He became increasingly interested in the observation and explanation of natural phenomena. He used logic as his method of scientific discussion, and he attempted to bridge the gap that Plato had created between abstract truth and concrete perception. He argued that the universe was finite, spherical, and eternal. He discussed an immaterial being that was his conception of god. Yet his god neither created the universe nor guided it. The inconsistencies of Aristotle on these matters are obvious. His god was without purpose. Yet for him scientific endeavor, the highest attainable form of living, reached the divine.

Aristotle expressed the heart of his philosophy in *Physics* and *Metaphysics.* In those masterful works he combined empiricism, or observation, and speculative method. In *Physics* he tried to explain how natural physical phenomena interact and how their interactions lead to the results that people see around them daily. He postulated four principles: matter, form, movement, and goal. A seed, for example, possesses both matter and an encoded form. Form determines whether a plant will be a rose or poison ivy. Growth represents movement, and the mature plant the goal of the seed. Although Aristotle considered nature impersonal, he felt that it had its own purposes. In a sense, this notion is a rudimentary ancestor of the concept of evolution.

In *On the Heaven* Aristotle took up the thread of Ionian speculation. His theory of cosmology added ether to air, fire, water, and earth as building blocks of the universe. He concluded that the universe revolves and that it is spherical and eternal. He wrongly thought that the earth is the center of the universe and that the stars and planets revolve around it.

Aristotle possessed one of history's keenest and most curious philosophical minds. While rethinking the old topics explored by the Pre-Socratics, he created whole new areas of study. In short, he tried to learn everything possible about the universe and everything in it.

The Final Act (404–338 B.C.)

Immediately after the Peloponnesian War, with Athens humbled, Sparta began striving for empire over the Greeks. The arrogance and imperialism of the Spartans turned their former allies against them. Even with Persian help Sparta could not maintain its hold on Greece. In 371 B.C. on the plain of Leuctra in Boeotia, a Theban army under the command of Epaminondas destroyed the flower of the Spartan army on a single summer day. But the Thebans were unable to bring peace to Greece. In 362 B.C. Epaminondas was killed in battle, and a period of stalemate set in. The Greek states were virtually exhausted.

The man who turned the situation to his advantage was Philip II, king of Macedonia (359–336 B.C.). Throughout most of Greek history Macedonia, which bordered Greece in the north (see Map 5.3), had been a backward, disunited kingdom, but Philip's genius and courage turned it into a major power. One of the ablest statesmen of antiquity, Philip united his powerful kingdom, built a redoubtable army, and pursued his ambition with drive and determination. His horizon was not limited to Macedonia, for he realized that he could turn the rivalry and exhaustion of the Greek states to his own purposes. By clever use of his wealth and superb army Philip won control of the northern Aegean and awakened fear in Athens, which had vital interests there. A comic playwright depicted one of Philip's ambassadors warning the Athenians:

Do you know that your battle will be with men
Who dine on sharpened swords,
And gulp burning firebrands for wine?
Then immediately after dinner the slave
Brings us desert—Cretan arrows
Or pieces or broken spears.
We have shields and breastplates for

Cushions and at our feet slings and arrows,
And we are crowned with catapults.[11]

In 338 B.C. a combined Theban-Athenian army met Philip's veterans at the Boeotian city of Chaeronea. Philip's army won a hard-fought victory: he had conquered Greece and put an end to Greek freedom. Because the Greeks could not put aside their quarrels, they fell to an invader.

SUMMARY

In a comparatively brief span of time the Greeks progressed from a primitive folk—backward and rude compared with their Near Eastern neighbors—to one of the most influential peoples of history. These originators of science and philosophy asked penetrating questions about the nature of life and society and came up with deathless responses to many of their own questions. Greek achievements range from the development of sophisticated political institutions to the creation of a stunningly rich literature. Brilliant but quarrelsome, they were their own worst enemies. As the Roman historian Pompeius Trogus later said of their fall:

The states of Greece, while each one wished to rule alone, all squandered sovereignty. Indeed, hastening without moderation to destroy one another in mutual ruin, they did not realize, until they were all crushed, that every one of them lost in the end.[12]

Nonetheless, their achievements outlived their political squabbles to become the cornerstone of all later Western development.

NOTES

1. K. J. Beloch, *Griechische Geschichte,* vol. 1, pt. 1 (Strassburg: K. J. Trübner, 1912), p. 49. Unless otherwise credited, all quotations from a foreign language in this chapter have been translated into English by John Buckler.
2. Hesiod, *Works and Days* 263–266.
3. F. Lasserre, *Archiloque* (Paris: Société d'Edition "Les Belles Lettres," 1958), frag. 9, p. 4.
4. W. Barnstable, *Sappho* (Garden City, N.Y.: Doubleday, 1965), frag. 24, p. 22.

5. Ibid., frag. 132, p. 106.
6. J. M. Edmonds, *Greek Elegy and Iambus* (Cambridge, Mass.: Harvard University Press, 1931), I.70, frag. 10.
7. Thucydides, *History of the Peloponnesian War* 1.23.
8. Ibid.
9. Hesiod, *Works and Days* 737–741.
10. E. Diels and W. Krantz, *Fragmente der Vorsokratiker,* 8th ed. (Berlin: Weidmannsche Verlagsbuchhandlung, 1960), Heraclitus frag. B30.
11. J. M. Edmonds, *The Fragments of Attic Comedy* (Leiden: E. J. Brill, 1971), 2.366–369, Mnesimachos frag. 7.
12. Justin 8.1.1–2.

SUGGESTED READING

Translations of the most important writings of the Greeks and Romans can be found in the volumes of the Loeb Classical Library published by Harvard University Press. Paperback editions of the major Greek and Latin authors are available as Penguin Classics. Recent translations of documents include C. Fornara, *Translated Documents of Greece and Rome,* vol. 1 (1977), and P. Harding, vol. 2 (1985).

Among the many general treatments of Greek history is that of H. Bengtson, *History of Greece* (English trans., 1988). Also good is J. Fine, *The Ancient Greeks* (1984).

A number of books on early Greece are available. A careful and learned synthesis can be found in Lord W. Taylour, *The Mycenaeans,* rev. ed. (1983). R. Castleton, *Minoans* (1993), uses archaeology, not always successfully, in an attempt to re-create the life of Bronze Age Crete. C. G. Thomas, *Myth Becomes History* (1993), is an excellent treatment of early Greece and modern historical attitudes toward it. R. Drews, *The Coming of the Greeks* (1988), puts the movement of the Greeks in the broader context of Indo-European migrations. No finer introduction to the Lyric Age can be found that A. R. Burn's *The Lyric Age* (1960). Its sequel, *Persia and the Greeks,* 2d ed. (1984), which is also unsurpassed, carries the history of Greece to the defeat of the Persians in 479 B.C. More recent is J. Boardman et al., *The Cambridge Ancient History,* 2d ed., vol. 4 (1988), but the coverage is very uneven. A. J. Graham, *Colony and Mother City in Ancient Greece,* rev. ed. (1984), gives a good but somewhat dated account of Greek colonization. R. Osborne, *Classical Landscape with Figures* (1985), looks at the relation of the polis to its surrounding landscape. R. A. Tomlinson, *From Mycenae to Con-*

stantinople (1992), is a broad study of the evolution of the city in the Greek and Roman world.

W. Burkert, *The Orientalizing Revolution* (1992), is a masterful discussion of Near Eastern influence on early Greek culture. A good survey of work on Sparta is P. Cartledge, *Sparta and Lakonia* (1979). J. F. Lazenby, *The Spartan Army* (1985), studies the evolution of the Spartan army and hoplite warfare. The Athenian democracy and the society that produced it continue to attract scholarly attention. Interesting and important are M. Ostwald, *From Popular Sovereignty to the Sovereignty of Law* (1986); M. H. Hansen, *The Athenian Assembly* (1987); and J. Ober, *Mass and Elite in Democratic Athens* (1989).

The history of the fifth century B.C. and the outbreak of the Peloponnesian War are treated in M. McGregor, *The Athenians and Their Empire* (1987); A. Ferrill, *The Origins of War* (1985), chap. 4; and E. Badian, *From Plataea to Potidaea* (1993), a collection of essays on major aspects of the period.

The fourth century B.C. has been one of the most fertile fields of recent research. G. Proietti, *Xenophon's Sparta* (1987), and P. Cartledge, *Agesilaos and the Crisis of Sparta* (1987), both treat Spartan government and society in its period of greatness and collapse. J. Buckler, *The Theban Hegemony, 371–362 B.C.* (1980), examines the period of Theban ascendancy, and his *Philip II and the Sacred War* (1989) studies the ways in which Philip of Macedonia used Greek politics to his own ends. J. Cargill, *The Second Athenian League* (1981), a significant study, traces Athenian policy during the fourth century B.C. G. Cawkwell, *Philip of Macedon* (1978), analyzes the career of the great conqueror, and R. M. Errington, *A History of Macedonia* (English trans., 1990), is the best general treatment of the topic published in recent years.

Greek social life has recently received a great deal of attention, constituting a theme of continuing interest among classical scholars. For a general study, see E. Fantham *et al,* eds. *Women in The Classical World* (1994) R. Just, *Women in Athenian Law and Life* (1988), explores such topics as daily life, the family, and women's role in society. N. Loraux, *The Children of Athena* (1993), examines Athenian myths to explore the ideas about citizenship and the status of women in Athenian life. M. Golden, *Children and Childhood in Ancient Athens* (1993), studies a neglected topic. D. Cohen, *Law, Sexuality, and Society* (1992), discusses what the Athenians thought was proper moral behavior and how they tried to enforce it. J. J. Winkler, *The Constraints of Desire* (1989), examines the anthropology of sex and gender in ancient Greece. S. Isager and J. E. Skydsgaard, *Ancient Greek Agriculture* (1992), endorses the theory that agriculture was the main source of wealth in ancient Greece. D. Sansone, *Greek Athletics and the Genesis of Sport* (1988), well illustrated, provides a good and far-ranging treatment of what athletics meant to the classical Greek world. The topic of slavery is addressed in Y. Garlan, *Slavery in Ancient Greece* (1988).

For Greek literature, culture, and science, see A. Lesky's classic *History of Greek Literature* (English trans., 1963), and for drama, H. C. Baldry, *The Greek Tragic Theater* (1971). Still unsurpassed on Greek philosophy is J. Burnet, *Greek Philosophy* (1914), and on science B. Farrington, *Greek Science*, 2 vols. (reprint, 1949). More recent is M. Clagett, *Greek Science in Antiquity* (1971). M. Ferejohn, *The Origins of Aristotelian Science* (1991), discusses earlier Greek scientific thought and Aristotle's response to it. Two new works explore medicine: M. D. Grmek, *Diseases in the Ancient Greek World* (1991), and J. Longrigg,

Greek Rational Medicine (1993), which emphasizes the importance of Greek physicians who concentrated on natural causes of illness and their cure rather than on magic and religion.

Studies of Greek religions and myth include J. D. Mikalson, *Athenian Popular Religion* (reprint, 1987), which opens a valuable avenue to the understanding of Greek popular religion in general. P. N. Hunt, ed., *Encyclopedia of Classical Mystery Religions* (1993), provides more than a thousand entries on mystery religions. It also discusses the later competition between them and Christianity. In general, W. Burkert, *Greek Religion* (1987), gives a masterful survey of ancient religious beliefs. K. Dowden, *The Uses of Greek Mythology* (1992), is a systematic study of the importance of mythology to Greek history, which explores its originality and its relation to Greek culture in general.

LISTENING TO THE
PAST

❋ ❋ ❋

A Veteran's Account of the Battle of Salamis

The battle of Salamis in 480 B.C. was the turning point in the Greek victory over the Persians. One man serving in the Greek fleet that day was the great Athenian dramatist Aeschylus. In his play The Persians *he gave a poetic account of the action. His was the first complete account of a major battle in Greek history, and his historical play was one of the earliest in Attic drama. Though giving few details of the naval maneuvers, which Herodotus recorded later, Aeschylus left a vivid sketch of the battle as seen through the eyes of a veteran.*

The Persian fleet was at sea to prevent the Greeks from escaping from the bay of Salamis (west of Athens), where they had anchored. At dawn the Greek ships lured the Persians into the bay, which became the scene of a furious naval battle.

Aeschylus produced The Persians *probably in 472 B.C., when most of those in the Greek audience could remember these events. The scene begins with a Persian herald reporting news of the battle to the queen, whose husband has not yet returned from the war. One of the remarkable aspects of this play is that Aeschylus uses a Persian in the royal court to praise Greek valor. The herald begins by describing the first movements of the Persian fleet, which expected the Greeks to flee.*

Herald: When the glare of sunlight died, and night
    Came on every [Persian] man was at his oar,
    Every man at arms who knew them.
    Rank encouraged rank, and long-boats sailed
    To stations each had been assigned.
    All night the captains kept the fleet awake;
    And night ran on. No Greek army set
    Secret sail; but when the steeds of day,
    White and luminous, began to cross
    The sky, a song-like, happy tumult sounded

From the Greeks, and island rocks returned
The high-pitched echo. Fear fell among us,
Deceived in hope; for they (and not as if to flee)
A solemn paean chanted, and to battle
    Rushed with fervent boldness: trumpets flared,
Putting every Greek aflame. At once
    Concordant strokes of oars in dissonance
Slapped the waters' depths: soon we saw
    Them all: first the right wing led in order,
Next advanced the whole fleet:
    A great concerted cry we heard: "O Greek
Sons, advance! Free your fathers' land,
Free your sons, your wives, the sanctuaries
Of paternal gods, the sepulchers
Of ancestors. Now the contest is drawn:
All is at stake!" And babel Persian tongues
Rose to meet it: no longer would the action
Loiter. Warships struck their brazen beaks
Together: a Greek man-of-war began
The charge, a Phoenician-ornamented stern
Was smashed; and another drove against another.
First the floods of Persians held the line,
But when the narrows choked them, and rescue hopeless,
Smitten by prows, their bronze jaws gaping,
Shattered entire was our fleet of oars.
The Greek warships, calculating, dashed
Round, and encircled us: ships showed their belly;
No longer could we see the water, charged
With ships' wrecks and men's blood.
Corpses glutted beaches and the rocks.
Every warship urged its own anarchic
Rout; and all who survived that expedition,
Like mackerel or some catch of fish,

Were stunned and slaughtered, boned with
  broken oars
And splintered wrecks: lamentations, cries,
Possessed the open sea, until the black
Eye of evening, closing, hushed them.
  The sum
Of troubles, even if I should rehearse them
For ten days, I could not exhaust. Rest
Content: never in a single day
So great a number died.

. . . .

Queen: Oh wretched am I alas! What doom
  Destroyed them?
Herald: There is an island fronting Salamis,
  Small, scarce an anchorage for ships,
  Where the dancer Pan rejoices on the
    shore;
  Whither Xerxes [the Persian king] sent
    those men to kill
  The shipwrecked enemies who sought the
    island
  As a refuge (easily, he thought, the Greek
    arms would be subdued);
  He also bid them rescue friends. He
    conned [studied]
  The future ill. For when a god gave Greeks
  The glory, that very day, fenced in bronze,
  They leaped ashore, and drew the circle
    tight
  At every point: mewed up, we could not
    turn.
  Many rattled to the ground, whom stones
  Had felled, and arrows, shot by bowstring,
  Others killed; and in a final rush,
  The end: they hacked, mangled their
    wretched limbs,
  Until the life of all was gone.
  Xerxes mourned, beholding the lowest
    depths
  Of woe, who, seated on a height that near
  The sea commanded all his host, his robes
  Destroying (and his lamentations shrill),
  Dispatched his regiments on land: they fled
  Orderless. Now you may lament their fate,
  Added to the others' summed before.

Bust of Aeschylus, from the Musei Capitolini, Rome. (*Source: Art Resource, NY*)

Questions for Analysis

1. Why did Aeschylus use a Persian herald to narrate the events of the battle at the Persian court?

2. What inspired the Greeks to mount a defense against the Persian invasion?

3. What was the Greek attitude toward the victory? Are there any religious overtones to the passage? If so, describe and explain them.

Source: *The Complete Greek Tragedies,* vol. 1, edited by D. Grene and R. Lattimore, Copyright (c) 1959 by University of Chicago Press. Reprinted by permission.

Hellenistic Diffusion

Wall-painting from
Pompeii of Pelias and his
daughters. *(Source:
Museo Nazionale Naples)*

Two years after his conquest of Greece, Philip of Macedon fell victim to an assassin's dagger. Philip's twenty-year-old son, historically known as Alexander the Great (r. 336–323 B.C.), assumed the Macedonian throne. This young man, one of the most remarkable personalities of all time, was to have a profound impact on history. By overthrowing the Persian Empire and by spreading *Hellenism*—Greek culture, language, thought, and the Greek way of life—as far as India, Alexander was instrumental in creating a new era, traditionally called Hellenistic to distinguish it from the Hellenic. As a result of Alexander's exploits, the individualistic and energetic culture of the Greeks came into intimate contact with the venerable older cultures of the Near East.

- What did the spread of Hellenism mean to the Greeks and the peoples of the East?
- What did the meeting of West and East hold for the development of economics, religion, philosophy, women's concerns, science, and medicine?

These are the questions we will explore in this chapter.

ALEXANDER AND THE GREAT CRUSADE

In 336 B.C. Alexander inherited not only Philip's crown but also his policies. After his victory at Chaeronea, Philip had organized the states of Greece into a huge league under his leadership and announced to the Greeks his plan to lead them and his Macedonians against the Persian Empire. Fully intending to carry out Philip's designs, Alexander proclaimed to the Greek world that the invasion of Persia was to be a great crusade, a mighty act of revenge for the Persian invasion of Greece in 480 B.C. Despite his youth, Alexander was well prepared to lead the attack. In 334 B.C. he led an army of Macedonians and Greeks into western Asia. In the next three years he won three major battles—at the Granicus River, at Issus, and at Gaugamela—victories that stand almost as road signs marking his march to the east (Map 6.1). Having overthrown the Persian Empire, he crossed the Indus

Bust of Alexander This Roman portrait of Alexander the Great is a copy of a Greek original. Alexander's youth and self-confidence are immediately apparent, yet the style is surprisingly simple for a bust of someone who had conquered the Persian Empire. The Greek inscription is equally simple: "Alexander, the son of Philip, Macedonian." *(Source: Louvre/Giraudon/Art Resource, NY)*

River in 326 B.C. and entered India, where he saw hard fighting. Finally, at the Hyphasis River his troops refused to go farther. Still eager to explore the limits of the world, Alexander turned south to the Indian Ocean and then turned west. In 324 B.C. a long, hard march brought him back to his camp at Susa. The great crusade was over, and Alexander himself died the next year in Babylon.

The political result of Alexander's premature death was chaos. Since several of the chief Macedonian officers aspired to Alexander's position as emperor and others opposed these ambitions, civil war lasting forty-three years tore Alexander's empire apart. By the end of this conflict, the most successful generals had carved out their own small and more or less stable monarchies.

Ptolemy immediately seized Egypt and transformed the native system of administration by appointing Greeks and Macedonians to the chief bureaucratic positions. Meanwhile, Seleucus won the bulk of Alexander's empire; his monarchy extended from western Asia to India. In the third century B.C., however, the eastern parts of Seleucus's monarchy gained their independence: The Parthians came to power in Iran, and the Greeks created a monarchy of their own in Bactria. Antigonus maintained control of the Macedonian monarchy in Europe. Until the arrival of the Romans in the eastern Mediterranean in the second century B.C., these great monarchies were often at war with one another, but without winning any significant political or military advantage. In that respect, the Hellenistic monarchy was no improvement on the Greek polis.

Despite the disintegration of his empire, Alexander was instrumental in changing the face of politics in the eastern Mediterranean. His campaign swept away the Persian Empire, which had ruled the East for over two hundred years. In its place he established a Macedonian monarchy. More important in the long run was his founding of new cities and military colonies, which scattered Greeks and Macedonians throughout the East. Thus the practical result of Alexander's campaign was to open the East to the tide of Hellenism.

 ## THE SPREAD OF HELLENISM

When the Greeks and Macedonians entered Asia Minor, Egypt, and the more remote East, they encountered civilizations older than their own. In some ways the Eastern cultures were more advanced than the Greek, in others less so. Thus this third great tide of Greek migration differed from

Alexander at the Battle of Issus At left, Alexander the Great, bareheaded and wearing a breastplate, charges King Darius, who is standing in a chariot. The moment marks the turning point of the battle, as Darius turns to flee from the attack. *(Source: National Museum, Naples/Alinari/Scala/Art Resource, NY)*

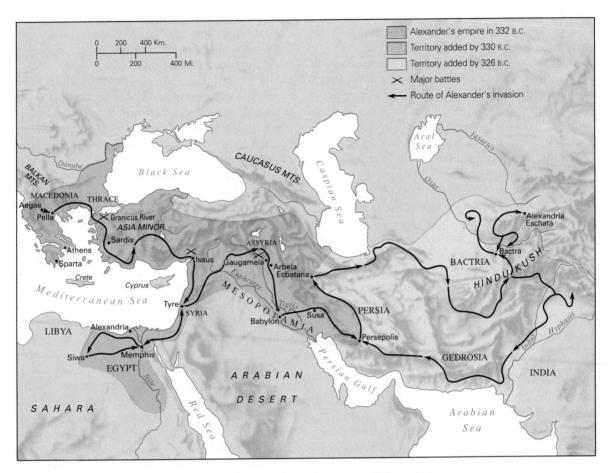

MAP 6.1 Alexander's Conquests This map shows the course of Alexander's invasion of the Persian Empire and the speed of his progress. More important than the success of his military campaigns was his founding of Hellenistic cities in the East.

preceding waves, which had spread over land that was uninhabited or inhabited by less-developed peoples.

How did Hellenism and the cultures of the East affect one another? What did the meeting of East and West entail for the history of the world?

Cities and Kingdoms

A major development of the Hellenistic kingdoms, the resurgence of monarchy had many repercussions. For most Greeks, monarchs were something out of the heroic past, something found in Homer's *Iliad* but not in daily life. Most Hellenistic

kingdoms encompassed numerous different peoples who had little in common. Hellenistic kings thus attempted to create a ruler cult that linked the king's authority with that of the gods and to establish an easily understandable symbol of political and religious unity within the kingdom.

Monarchy included royal women, who began to play an active part in political and diplomatic life (see Listening to the Past). Some of them did so in their own right, others by manipulating their husbands. Many Hellenistic queens have been depicted as willful or ruthless, especially in power struggles over the throne. In some cases those charges are accurate. Yet for the most part, queens served as examples that women were as capable of shouldering vast responsibilities and performing them successfully as men were.

Hellenistic kings needed large numbers of Greeks to run their kingdoms. Without them, royal business would have ground to a halt, and the conquerors would soon have been swallowed up by the far more numerous conquered population. Obviously, then, the kings had to encourage Greeks to immigrate and build new homes. Since Greek civilization was urban, the kings continued Alexander's policy of establishing cities throughout their kingdoms in order to entice Greeks to immigrate. Yet the creation of these cities posed a serious political problem that the Hellenistic kings failed to solve.

To the Greeks civilized life was unthinkable without the polis, which was far more than a mere city. The Greek polis was by definition sovereign. It was an independent, autonomous state run by its citizens, free of any outside power or restraint. Hellenistic kings, however, refused to grant sovereignty to their cities. They gave their cities all the external trappings of a polis. Each had an assembly of citizens, a council to prepare legislation, and a board of magistrates to conduct the city's political business. But these cities could not pursue their own foreign policy, wage their own wars, or govern their own affairs without interference from the king, who often placed his own officials in the cities to see that his decrees were followed. There were no constitutional links between city and king. The city was simply his possession. Its citizens had no voice in how the kingdom was run and no rights except for those the king granted.

In addition, the Hellenistic city was not homogeneous and could not spark the intensity of feeling that marked the polis. The Greek polis had enjoyed political and social unity even though it was normally composed of citizens, slaves, and resident aliens. The polis had one body of law and one set of customs. In contrast, in the Hellenistic city Greeks were an elite citizen class. Natives and non-Greek foreigners usually possessed lesser rights than Greeks and often had their own laws. In some instances this disparity spurred natives to assimilate Greek culture in order to rise politically and socially. Other peoples, such as many Jews, firmly resisted the essence of Hellenism.

In many respects the Hellenistic city resembled a modern city. It was a cultural center with theaters, temples, and libraries—a seat of learning and a place where people could find amusement. The Hellenistic city was also an economic center—a marketplace, a scene of trade and manufacturing. In short, the Hellenistic city offered cultural and economic opportunities but did not foster a sense of united, integrated enterprise.

Hellenistic kings tried to make the kingdom the political focus of citizens' allegiance. If the king could secure the frontiers of his kingdom, he could give it a geographical identity. He could then hope that his subjects would direct their primary loyalty to the kingdom rather than to a particular city. However, the kings' efforts to fix their borders led only to sustained warfare, and rule by force became the chief political principle of the Hellenistic world (Map 6.2).

Border wars were frequent and exhausting. The Seleucids and Ptolemies, for instance, waged five wars for the possession of southern Syria. Other kings followed Alexander's example and waged wars to reunify his empire under their own authority. By the third century B.C., a weary balance of power was reached, but only as the result of stalemate, not any political principle.

Though Hellenistic kings never built a true polis, that does not mean that their urban policy failed. The Hellenistic city remained the basic social and political unit in the Hellenistic East until the sixth century A.D. Cities were the chief agents of Hellenization, and their influence spread far beyond their walls. Roman rule in the Hellenistic East would later be based on this urban culture. In broad terms, Hellenistic cities were remarkably successful.

The Greeks and the Opening of the East

If the Hellenistic kings failed to satisfy the Greeks' political yearnings, they nonetheless succeeded in giving them unequaled economic and social opportunities. The ruling dynasties of the Hellenistic world were Macedonian, and Greeks filled all important political, military, and diplomatic positions. They constituted an upper class that sustained Hellenism. Besides building Greek cities, Hellenistic kings offered Greeks land and money as lures to further immigration.

The Hellenistic monarchy, unlike the Greek polis, did not depend solely on its citizens to fulfill its

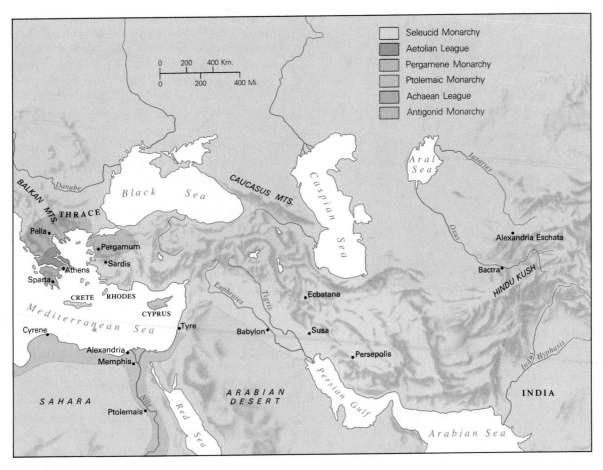

☐	Seleucid Monarchy
■	Aetolian League
■	Pergamene Monarchy
☐	Ptolemaic Monarchy
■	Achaean League
■	Antigonid Monarchy

❋ **MAP 6.2 The Hellenistic World**   After Alexander's death, no single commander could hold his vast conquests together, and his empire broke up into several kingdoms and leagues.

political needs. Talented Greeks could expect to rise quickly in the government bureaucracy. Appointed by the king, these administrators held their jobs year after year and had ample time to evolve new administrative techniques. The needs of the Hellenistic monarchy and the opportunities it offered thus gave rise to a professional corps of Greek administrators.

Greeks and Macedonians also found ready employment in the armies and navies of the Hellenistic monarchies. Alexander had proved the Greco-Macedonian style of warfare to be far superior to that of the Easterners, and Alexander's successors, themselves experienced officers, realized the importance of trained Greek and Macedonian soldiers. Moreover, Hellenistic kings were extremely reluctant to allow the native populations to serve in the army, fearing military rebellions among their conquered subjects. The result was the emergence of professional armies and navies consisting entirely of Greeks and Macedonians.

Greeks were able to dominate other professions as well. The kingdoms and cities recruited Greek writers and artists to bring Greek culture to Asian soil. Architects, engineers, and skilled craftsmen found their services in great demand. If Hellenistic kingdoms were to have Greek cities, those cities needed Greek buildings—temples, porticoes, gymnasia, theaters, fountains, and houses. Architects and engineers were sometimes commissioned to design and build whole cities, which they laid out in checkerboard fashion. An enormous wave of

✳ **Old Shepherdess**   Daily life for the poor and elderly was as hard in the Hellenistic period as in other times. Here a tough, old, scantily clothed shepherdess brings a sheep to market. Such scenes were common during the period; but art, not written sources, has preserved them for posterity. (*Source: Alinari/Art Resource, NY*)

construction took place under the Hellenistic monarchs.

New opportunities opened for women as well, owing in part to the examples of the queens. More women than ever before received educations that enabled them to enter medicine and other professions. Literacy among women increased dramatically, and their options expanded accordingly. Some won fame as poets, while others studied with philosophers and contributed to the intellectual life of the age. Women also began to participate in politics on a limited basis. They served in civil capacities, for which they often received public ac-

knowledgment. A few women received honorary citizenship from foreign cities because of aid given in times of crisis. As a rule, however, these developments touched only wealthy women, and not all of them. Although some poor women were literate, most were not.

The major reason for the new prominence of women was their increased participation in economic affairs. During the Hellenistic period some women took part in commercial transactions. They still lived under legal handicaps. In Egypt, for example, a Greek woman needed a male guardian to buy, sell, or lease land, to borrow money, and to represent her in other transactions. Yet often the guardian was present only to fulfill the letter of the law. The woman was the real agent and handled the business being transacted. In Hellenistic Sparta, women accumulated large fortunes and vast amounts of land. Spartan women, however, were exceptional. In most other areas, even women who were wealthy in their own right were formally under the protection of their male relatives.

Despite the opportunities they offered, the Hellenistic monarchies were hampered by their artificial origins. Their failure to win the political loyalty of their Greek subjects and their policy of wooing Greeks with lucrative positions encouraged a feeling of uprootedness and self-serving individualism among Greek immigrants. Once a Greek had left home to take service with, for instance, the army or the bureaucracy of the Ptolemies, he had no incentive beyond his pay and the comforts of life in Egypt to keep him there. If the Seleucid king offered him more money or a promotion, he might well accept it and take his talents to Asia Minor, where he could find the same sort of life and environment.

As long as Greeks continued to replenish their professional ranks, the Hellenistic kingdoms remained strong. In the process they drew an immense amount of talent from the Greek peninsula, draining the vitality of the Greek homeland. However, the Hellenistic monarchies could not keep recruiting Greeks forever, in spite of their wealth and willingness to spend lavishly. In time, the huge surge of immigration slowed greatly. Even then, the Hellenistic monarchs were reluctant to recruit Easterners to fill posts normally held by Greeks. The result was at first the stagnation of the Hellenistic world and finally, after 202 B.C., its collapse in the face of the young and vigorous Roman republic.

Greeks and Easterners

The Greeks in the East were a minority, but Hellenistic monarchies were remarkably successful in at least partially Hellenizing Easterners and spreading a uniform culture throughout the East. Indeed, the Near East had seen nothing comparable since the days when Mesopotamian culture had spread throughout the area. The spread of Greek culture, however, was wider than it was deep. At best it was a veneer, thicker in some places than in others. Hellenistic kingdoms were never entirely unified in language, customs, and thought. Greek culture took firmest hold along the shores of the Mediterranean, but in the Far East, in Persia and Bactria, it eventually gave way to Eastern cultures.

The Ptolemies in Egypt made no effort to spread Greek culture, and unlike other Hellenistic kings they were not city builders. Indeed, they founded only the city of Ptolemais near Thebes. At first the native Egyptian population, the descendants of the pharaoh's people, retained their traditional language, outlook, religion, and way of life. Initially untouched by Hellenism, the natives continued to be the foundation of the state: they fed it by their labor in the fields and financed its operations with their taxes.

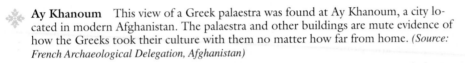

Ay Khanoum   This view of a Greek palaestra was found at Ay Khanoum, a city located in modern Afghanistan. The palaestra and other buildings are mute evidence of how the Greeks took their culture with them no matter how far from home. *(Source: French Archaeological Delegation, Afghanistan)*

The bureaucracy of the Ptolemies was ruthlessly efficient, and the native population was viciously and cruelly exploited. Even in times of hardship the king's taxes came first, although payment might mean starvation for the natives. Their desperation was summed up by one Egyptian, who scrawled the warning: "We are worn out; we will run away."[1]

Throughout the third century B.C., the Greek upper class in Egypt had little to do with the native population. But in the second century B.C., Greeks and native Egyptians began to intermarry and mingle their cultures and language. Some natives adopted Greek customs and language and began to play a role in the administration of the kingdom and even to serve in the army. While many Greeks and Egyptians remained aloof from each other, the overall result was the evolution of a widespread Greco-Egyptian culture.

Meanwhile, the Seleucid kings established many cities and military colonies in western Asia Minor and along the banks of the Tigris and Euphrates rivers in order to nurture a vigorous and large Greek population. The Seleucids had no elaborate plan for Hellenizing the native population, but the arrival of so many Greeks was bound to have an impact. Seleucid military colonies were generally founded near native villages, thus exposing Easterners to all aspects of Greek life. In Asia Minor and Syria, numerous native villages and towns developed along Greek lines, and some of them became Hellenized cities. Farther east, the Greek kings who replaced the Seleucids in the third century B.C. spread Greek culture to their neighbors, even into the Indian subcontinent.

For Easterners the prime advantage of Greek culture was its very pervasiveness. The Greek language became the common speech of the East. A common dialect called *koine* even influenced the speech of peninsular Greece itself. Greek became the speech of the royal court, bureaucracy, and army, and any Easterner who wanted to compete in business had to learn it. As early as the third century B.C., some Greek cities were giving citizenship to Hellenized natives.

The vast majority of Hellenized Easterners, however, took only the externals of Greek culture while retaining the essentials of their own way of life. A prime illustration is the impact of Greek culture on the Jews. Jews in Hellenistic cities were allowed to attend to their religious and internal affairs without interference from the Greek municipal government. They obeyed the king's commands, but there was virtually no royal interference with the Jewish religion. Indeed, the Greeks were always reluctant to tamper with anyone's religion.

Some Jews were given the right to become full citizens of Hellenistic cities, but few exercised that right. Citizenship would have obliged them to worship the gods of the city—a practice few Jews chose to follow. But Jews living in Hellenistic cities often embraced a good deal of Hellenism. So many Jews learned Greek, especially in Alexandria, that the Old Testament was translated into Greek. Yet no matter how much of Greek culture or its externals Jews borrowed, most remained attached to their religion. Thus, in spite of Hellenistic trappings, Hellenized Jews remained Jews at heart.

Though Greeks and Easterners adapted to each other's ways, there was never a true fusion of cultures. Nonetheless, each found useful things in the civilization of the other, and the two fertilized each other. This mingling of Greek and Eastern elements is what makes Hellenistic culture unique.

THE ECONOMIC SCOPE OF THE HELLENISTIC WORLD

The Hellenistic period did not see a revolution in the way people lived and worked. The material demands of Hellenistic society remained as simple as those of Athenian society in the fifth century B.C. Clothes and furniture were essentially unchanged, as were household goods, tools, and jewelry. Yet Alexander and his successors brought the East fully into the sphere of Greek economics, linking East and West in a broad commercial network. The spread of Greeks throughout the East created new markets and stimulated trade. The economic unity of the Hellenistic world, like its cultural bonds, would later prove valuable to the Romans.

Commerce

Alexander's conquest of the Persian Empire had immediate effects on trade. In the Persian capitals Alexander had found vast sums of gold, silver, and other treasure. This wealth financed the creation of new cities, the building of roads, and the develop-

Harbor and Warehouses of Delos During the Hellenistic period Delos became a thriving trading center. Shown here is the row of warehouses at water's edge. From Delos cargoes were shipped to virtually every part of the Mediterranean. *(Source: Adam Woolfitt/Woodfin Camp & Associates)*

ment of harbors. Most of the great monarchies coined their money on the Attic standard. Traders were less in need of moneychangers than in the days when each major power coined money on a different standard of value. As a result of Alexander's conquests, geographical knowledge of the East increased dramatically. The Greeks spread their law and methods of transacting business throughout the East. In bazaars, ports, and trading centers Greeks learned of Eastern customs and traditions while spreading knowledge of their own culture.

The Seleucid and Ptolemaic dynasties traded as far afield as India, Arabia, and sub-Saharan Africa. Overland trade with India and Arabia was conducted by caravan and was largely in the hands of Easterners. The caravan trade never dealt in bulk items or essential commodities; only luxury goods could be transported in this very expensive fashion. Once the goods reached the Hellenistic monarchies, Greek merchants took a hand in the trade.

In the early Hellenistic period, the Seleucids and Ptolemies ensured that the caravan trade proceeded efficiently. Later in the period—a time of increased war and confusion—they left the caravans unprotected. Taking advantage of this situation, Palmyra in the Syrian desert and Nabataean Petra in Arabia arose as caravan states. Such states protected the caravans from bandits and marauders and served as dispersal areas for caravan goods.

The Ptolemies discovered how to use monsoon winds to establish direct contact with India. One hardy merchant left a firsthand account of sailing this important maritime route:

Hippalos, the pilot, observing the position of the ports and the conditions of the sea, first discovered how to sail across the ocean. Concerning the winds of the ocean in this region, when with us the Etesian winds begin, in India a wind between southwest and south, named for Hippalos, sets in from the open sea. From then until now some mariners set forth from Kanes and some from the Cape of Spices. Those sailing to Dimurikes [in southern India] throw the bow of the ship farther out to sea. Those bound for Barygaza and the realm of the Sakas [in northern India] hold to the land no more than three days; and if the wind remains favorable, they hold the same course through the outer sea, and they sail along past the previously mentioned gulfs.[2]

Although this sea route never replaced overland caravan traffic, it kept direct relations between East and West alive, stimulating the exchange of ideas as well as goods.

More economically important than the exotic caravan trade were commercial dealings in essential commodities like raw materials, grain, and industrial products. The Hellenistic monarchies usually raised enough grain for their own needs as well as a surplus for export. For the cities of Greece and the Aegean this trade in grain was essential, because many of them could not grow enough.

The large-scale wars of the Hellenistic period often interrupted both the production and the distribution of grain. In addition, natural calamities, such as excessive rain or drought, frequently damaged harvests. Throughout the Hellenistic period, famine or severe food shortage remained a grim possibility.

The Greek cities paid for their grain by exporting olive oil and wine. Another significant commodity was fish, which for export was salted, pickled, or dried. This trade was doubly important because fish provided poor people with an essential element of their diet. Also important was the trade in honey, dried fruit, nuts, and vegetables. Of raw materials, wood was high in demand, but little trade occurred in manufactured goods.

Slaves were a staple of Hellenistic trade. The wars provided prisoners for the slave market; to a lesser extent, so did kidnapping and capture by pirates. The number of slaves involved cannot be estimated, but there is no doubt that slavery flourished. Both old Greek states and new Hellenistic kingdoms were ready slave markets, as was Rome

when it emerged triumphant from the Second Punic War (see page 181). Only the Ptolemies discouraged both the trade and slavery itself, and they did so only for economic reasons. Their system had no room for slaves, who would only have competed with free labor. Otherwise, slave labor was to be found in the cities and temples of the Hellenistic world, in the factories and fields, and in the homes of wealthy people. Slaves were vitally important to the Hellenistic economy.

Industry and Agriculture

Although demand for goods increased during the Hellenistic period, no new techniques of production appear to have developed. Manual labor, not machinery, continued to turn out the agricultural produce, raw materials, and few manufactured goods the Hellenistic world used. Nowhere was this truer than in mining.

Invariably miners were slaves, criminals, or forced laborers. The conditions under which they worked were frightful. The Ptolemies ran their gold mines along typically harsh lines. One historian gave a grim picture of the miners' lives:

The kings of Egypt condemn [to the mines] those found guilty of wrong-doing and those taken prisoner in war, those who were victims of false accusations and were put into jail because of royal anger. . . . The condemned—and they are very many—all of them are put in chains, and they work persistently and continually, both by day and throughout the night, getting no rest, and carefully cut off from escape.[3]

The Ptolemies even condemned women and children to work in the mines. The strongest men lived and died swinging iron sledgehammers to break up the gold-bearing quartz rock. Others worked underground, following the seams of quartz; laboring with lamps bound to their foreheads, they were whipped by overseers if they slacked off. Once the diggers had cut out blocks of quartz, young boys gathered up the blocks and carried them outside. All of them—men, women, and boys—worked until they died.

Apart from gold and silver, which were used primarily for coins and jewelry, iron was the most important metal and saw the most varied use. Even so, the method of its production never became very sophisticated.

Pottery remained an important commodity, and most of it was made locally. The pottery used in the kitchen, the coarse ware, did not change at all. Fancier pots and bowls, decorated with a shiny black glaze, came into use during the Hellenistic period. In the second century B.C. a red-glazed ware, often called Samian, burst on the market and soon dominated it. Despite the change in pottery styles, the method of production of all pottery, whether plain or fine, remained essentially unchanged.

Although new techniques of production and wider use of machinery did not develop, the volume of goods produced increased in the Hellenistic period. Small manufacturing establishments existed in nearly all parts of the Hellenistic world.

Just as all kings concerned themselves with trade and industry, they also paid special attention to agriculture. Much of their revenue was derived from the produce of royal lands, rents paid by the tenants of royal land, and taxation of agricultural land. Some Hellenistic kings even sought out and supported agricultural experts. The Ptolemies, who made the greatest strides in agriculture, sponsored experiments to improve seed grain. Hellenistic authors wrote handbooks discussing how farms and large estates could most profitably be run. Whether these efforts had any impact on the average farmer is difficult to determine.

The Ptolemies could decree what crops Egyptian farmers would plant and what animals would be raised. They recognized the need for well-planned and constant irrigation, and much native labor went into the digging and maintenance of canals and ditches. The Ptolemies also reclaimed a great deal of land from the desert. Nevertheless, it can be said that despite royal interest in agriculture and a more studied approach to it in the Hellenistic period, there is no evidence that agricultural productivity increased.

✤ RELIGION IN THE HELLENISTIC WORLD

In religion Hellenism gave Easterners far less than the East gave the Greeks. At first the Hellenistic period saw the spread of Greek religious cults throughout the East. When Hellenistic kings founded cities, they also built temples and established new cults and priesthoods for the old

Olympian gods. The new cults enjoyed the prestige of being the religion of the conquerors, and they were supported by public money. The most attractive aspects of the Greek cults were their rituals and festivities, including literary, musical, and athletic contests.

Despite various advantages, Greek cults suffered from some severe shortcomings. They were primarily concerned with ritual. Participation in the civic cults did not even require belief (see page 138). On the whole, the civic cults neither appealed to religious emotions nor embraced matters such as sin and redemption. Greek mystery religions helped fill this gap, but the centers of these religions were in old Greece. Although the new civic cults were lavish in pomp and display, they could not satisfy deep religious feelings or spiritual yearnings.

Even though the Greeks participated in the new cults for cultural reasons, they felt little genuine religious attachment to them and increasingly sought solace from other sources. Educated and thoughtful people turned to philosophy as a guide

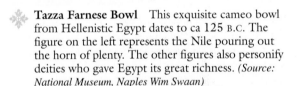

Tazza Farnese Bowl This exquisite cameo bowl from Hellenistic Egypt dates to ca 125 B.C. The figure on the left represents the Nile pouring out the horn of plenty. The other figures also personify deities who gave Egypt its great richness. *(Source: National Museum, Naples Wim Swaan)*

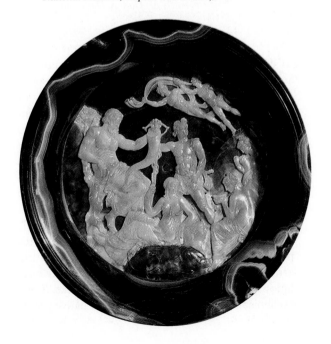

❀ Religious Syncretism   This relief was found at the Greek outpost of Dura-Europus, located on the Euphrates. In the center sits Zeus Olympius-Baalshamin, a combination of a Greek god and a Semitic god. The Eastern priest at the right is burning incense on an altar, while the figure on the left in Macedonian dress crowns the god. Both the religious sentiments and the style of art show the meeting of East and West. *(Source: Yale University Art Gallery, Dura-Europos Collection)*

to life. Others turned to superstition, magic, or astrology. Still others might shrug and speak of *Tyche,* which meant "Fate" or "Chance" or "Doom"—a capricious and sometimes malevolent force. In view of the decline of Greek religion, it is surprising the Eastern religions did not make more immediate headway among the Greeks. Only in the second century B.C., after a century of exposure to Eastern religions, did Greeks begin to adopt them.

Greek cults were attractive only to those socially aspiring Easterners who adopted Greek culture for personal advancement. Otherwise, Easterners were little affected by Greek religion. Nor did native religions suffer from the arrival of the Greeks. Some Hellenistic kings limited the power of native priest-

hoods, but they also subsidized some Eastern cults with public money. Alexander the Great actually reinstated several Eastern cults that the Persians had suppressed.

The only significant junction of Greek and Eastern religious traditions was the growth and spread of new "mystery religions," so called because they featured a body of ritual not to be divulged to anyone not initiated into the cult. The new mystery cults incorporated aspects of both Greek and Eastern religions and had broad appeal for both Greeks and Easterners who yearned for personal immortality. Since the Greeks were already familiar with old mystery cults, such as the Eleusinian mysteries in Attica, the new cults did not strike them as alien or barbarian. The new religions enjoyed one tremendous advantage over the old Greek mystery cults. Whereas old Greek mysteries were tied to particular places, such as Eleusis, the new religions spread throughout the Hellenistic world. People did not have to undertake long and expensive pilgrimages just to become members of the religion.

The mystery religions all claimed to save their adherents from the worst that fate could do and promised life for the soul after death. They all had a single concept in common: the belief that by means of the rites of initiation devotees became united with the god, who had himself died and risen from the dead. The sacrifice of the god and his victory over death saved the devotee from eternal death. Similarly, much like the old Greek mystery cults the Hellenistic mystery religions demanded a period of preparation in which the convert strove to become holy—that is, to live by the religion's precepts. Once aspirants had prepared themselves, they went through an initiation in which they learned the secrets of the religion. The initiation was usually a ritual of great emotional intensity, symbolizing the entry into a new life.

The Eastern mystery religions that took the Hellenistic world by storm were the Egyptian cults of Serapis and Isis. Serapis, who was invented by King Ptolemy, combined elements of the Egyptian god Osiris with aspects of the Greek gods Zeus, Pluto (prince of the underworld), and Asclepius (god of medicine). Serapis was believed to be the judge of souls, who rewarded virtuous and righteous people with eternal life. Like Asclepius, he was a god of healing. Serapis became an international god, and many Hellenistic Greeks thought of him as Zeus.

The cult of Isis enjoyed even wider appeal than that of Serapis. Isis, wife of Osiris, claimed to have conquered Tyche and promised to save any mortal who came to her. She became the most important goddess of the Hellenistic world, and her worship was very popular among women. She was the goddess of marriage, conception, and childbirth. Her priests claimed that she had bestowed on humanity the gift of civilization and had founded law and literature.

There was neither conflict between Greek and Eastern religions nor wholesale acceptance of one or the other. Greeks and Easterners noticed similarities among their respective deities and assumed that they were worshiping the same gods in different garb. These tendencies toward religious universalism and the desire for personal immortality would prove significant when the Hellenistic world came under the sway of Rome, for Hellenistic developments paved the way for the spread of Christianity.

Tyche This statue depicts Tyche as the city-goddess of Antioch, a new Hellenistic foundation of the Seleucid king Antiochus. Some Hellenistic Greeks worshiped Tyche in the hope that she would be kind to them. Philosophers tried to free people from her whimsies. Antiochus tried to win her favor by honoring her. *(Source: Photo Vatican Museums)*

❖ PHILOSOPHY AND THE PEOPLE

Philosophy during the Hellenic period was the exclusive province of the wealthy, for only they had leisure enough to pursue philosophical studies. During the Hellenistic period, however, philosophy reached out to touch the lives of more men and women than ever before. The reasons for this development were several. Since the ideal of the polis had declined, politics no longer offered people an intellectual outlet. Moreover, much of Hellenistic life, especially in the new cities of the East, seemed unstable and without venerable traditions. Many people in search of something permanent, something unchanging in a changing world, turned to philosophy. The decline of traditional religion and a growing belief in Tyche also led many Greeks to look to philosophy to protect against the worst that Tyche could do.

Philosophers themselves became much more numerous, and several new schools of philosophical thought emerged. There was a good deal of rivalry as philosophers tried to demonstrate the superiority of their views, but in spite of their differences the major branches of philosophy agreed on the necessity of making people self-sufficient. They all recognized the need to equip men and women to deal successfully with Tyche. The major schools of Hellenistic philosophy all taught that people could be truly happy only when they had turned their backs on the world and focused full attention on one enduring thing. They differed chiefly on what that enduring thing was.

Cynics

Undoubtedly the most unusual of the new philosophers were the Cynics, who urged a return to nature. They advised men and women to discard traditional customs and conventions (which were in decline anyway) and live simply. The Cynics believed that by rejecting material things people would become free and that nature would provide all necessities.

It was Diogenes of Sinope (ca 412–323 B.C.), one of the most colorful men of the period, who spread the philosophy of the Cynics. Diogenes came to Athens to study philosophy and soon evolved his own ideas on the ideal life. He came to the conclusion that happiness was possible only by living in accordance with nature and forgoing luxuries. He attacked social conventions because he considered them contrary to nature. Throughout Greece he gained fame for the rigorous way in which he put his beliefs into practice.

Diogenes' disdain for luxury and social pretense became legendary. Once, when he was living at Corinth, he was supposedly visited by Alexander the Great: "While Diogenes was sunning himself . . . Alexander stood over him and said: 'Ask me whatever gift you like.' In answer Diogenes said to him: 'Get out of my sunlight.'"[4] The story underlines the essence of Diogenes' teachings: even a great conqueror such as Alexander could give people nothing of any real value, for nature had already provided them with everything essential.

Diogenes did not establish a philosophical school in the manner of Plato and Aristotle. Instead, he and his followers took their teaching to the streets and marketplaces. More than any other philosophical group, the Cynics tried to reach the common people. As part of their return to nature, they often did without warm clothing, sufficient food, or adequate housing, which they considered unnecessary. The Cynics also tried to break down political barriers by declaring that people owed no allegiance to any city or monarchy. They said that all people are cosmopolitan—that is, citizens of the world. The Cynics reached across political boundaries to create a community of people sharing their humanity and living as close to nature as humanly possible. Although comparatively few men and women could follow such rigorous precepts, the Cynics influenced all the other major schools of philosophy.

Epicureans

Epicurus (340–270 B.C.), who founded his own school of philosophy at Athens, based his view of life on scientific theories and put forward a naturalistic theory of the universe. Although he did not deny the existence of the gods, he taught that they had no effect on human life. The essence of Epicurus's belief was that the principal good of human life is pleasure, which he defined as the absence of pain. He was not advocating drunken revels or sexual dissipation, which he thought actually caused pain. Instead, Epicurus concluded that any violent emotion is undesirable. Drawing on the teachings of the Cynics, he advocated mild self-discipline.

Even poverty he considered good, as long as people had enough food, clothing, and shelter. Epicurus also taught that individuals can most easily attain peace and serenity by ignoring the outside world and examining their personal feelings and reactions. Thus Epicureanism led to quietism.

Epicureans taught their followers to ignore politics and issues, for politics led to tumult, which would disturb the soul. Although Epicureans thought that the state originated through a social contract among individuals, they did not care about the political structure of the state, and they never speculated about the ideal state. Their ideals stood outside all political forms.

Stoics

Opposed to the passivity of the Epicureans, Zeno (335–262 B.C.), a philosopher from Citium in Cyprus, advanced a different concept of human beings and the universe. In Athens he formed his own school, the Stoa, named after the building where he preferred to teach.

Stoicism became the most popular Hellenistic philosophy and the one that later captured the mind of Rome. Zeno and his followers considered nature an expression of divine will; in their view, people could be happy only when living in accordance with nature. They stressed the unity of man and the universe, stating that all men were brothers and obliged to help one another.

Unlike the Epicureans, the Stoics taught that people should participate in politics and worldly affairs. Yet this idea never led to the belief that individuals should try to change the order of things. Time and again, the Stoics used the image of an actor in a play: the Stoic plays an assigned part and never tries to change the play. To the Stoics the important question was not whether they achieved anything but whether they lived virtuous lives. In that way they could triumph over Tyche, for Tyche could destroy achievements but not the nobility of their lives.

Like the Epicureans, the Stoics were indifferent to specific political forms. They believed that people should do their duty to the state in which they found themselves. The universal state they preached about was ethical, not political. The Stoics' most significant practical achievement was the creation of the concept of natural law. The Stoics concluded that as all men were brothers, partook

of divine reason, and were in harmony with the universe, one law—a part of the natural order of life—governed them all. The Stoic concept of a universal state governed by natural law is one of the finest heirlooms the Hellenistic world passed on to Rome.

 HELLENISTIC SCIENCE

The area in which Hellenistic culture achieved its greatest triumphs was science. Here, too, the ancient Near East made contributions to Greek thought. The patient observations of the Babylonians, who for generations had scanned the skies,

Tower of the Four Winds   This remarkable building, which still stands in Athens, was built by an astronomer to serve as a sundial, water-clock, and weather vane. It is one of the few examples of the application of Hellenistic science to daily life. (*Source: Ekdotike Athenon*)

provided the foundation of Hellenistic astronomy. The most notable of the Hellenistic astronomers was Aristarchus of Samos (ca 310–230 B.C.), who was educated in Aristotle's school. Aristarchus concluded that the sun is far larger than the earth and that the stars are exceedingly distant from the earth. He argued against Aristotle's view that the earth is the center of the universe. Instead, Aristarchus propounded the *heliocentric theory*—that the earth and planets revolve around the sun. His work is all the more impressive because he lacked even a rudimentary telescope.

Unfortunately Aristarchus's theories did not persuade the ancient world. In the second century A.D. Claudius Ptolemy, a mathematician and astronomer in Alexandria, accepted Aristotle's theory of the earth as the center of the universe, and their view prevailed for fourteen hundred years. Aristarchus's heliocentric theory lay dormant until resurrected in the sixteenth century by the brilliant Polish astronomer Nicolaus Copernicus.

In geometry Hellenistic thinkers discovered little that was new, but Euclid (ca 300 B.C.), a mathematician who lived in Alexandria, compiled a valuable textbook of existing knowledge. His book *The Elements of Geometry* has exerted immense influence on Western civilization, for it rapidly became the standard introduction to geometry. Generations of students, from the Hellenistic period to the present, have learned the essentials of geometry from it.

The greatest thinker of the Hellenistic period was Archimedes (ca 287–212 B.C.), who was a clever inventor as well. He lived in Syracuse in Sicily and watched Rome emerge as a power in the Mediterranean. When the Romans laid siege to Syracuse in the Second Punic War, Archimedes invented a number of machines to thwart the armed forces. His catapults threw rocks large enough to sink ships and disrupt battle lines. His grappling devices lifted ships out of the water. In a more peaceful vein, Archimedes invented the Archimedean screw and the compound pulley. Plutarch described Archimedes' dramatic demonstration of how easily his pulley could move huge weights with little effort:

A three-masted merchant ship of the royal fleet had been hauled on land by hard work and many hands. Archimedes put aboard her many men and the usual freight. He sat far away from her; without haste, but gently working a compound pulley with his hand, he drew her towards him smoothly and without faltering, just as though she were running on the surface of the sea.[5]

Archimedes was far more interested in pure mathematics than in practical inventions. His mathematical research, covering many fields, was his greatest contribution. In his book *On Plane Equilibriums* Archimedes dealt for the first time with the basic principles of mechanics, including the principle of the lever. He once said that if he were given a lever and a suitable place to stand, he could move the world. With his treatise *On Floating Bodies* Archimedes founded the science of hydrostatics. He concluded that whenever a solid floats in a liquid, the weight of the solid is equal to the weight of liquid displaced. The way he made his discovery has become famous:

When he was devoting his attention to this problem, he happened to go to a public bath. When he climbed down into the bathtub there, he noticed that water in the tub equal to the bulk of his body flowed out. Thus, when he observed this method of solving the problem, he did not wait. Instead, moved with joy, he sprang out of the tub, and rushing home naked he kept indicating in a loud voice that he had indeed discovered what he was seeking. For while running he was shouting repeatedly in Greek, "eureka, eureka" ("I have found it, I have found it.").[6]

Archimedes was willing to share his work with others, among them Eratosthenes (285–ca 204 B.C.), a native of Cyrene and a man of almost universal interests. Around 245 B.C. King Ptolemy invited Eratosthenes to Alexandria. The Ptolemies had done much to make Alexandria an intellectual, cultural, and scientific center. Eratosthenes came to Alexandria to become librarian of the royal library, a position of great prestige. While there, by letter, he struck up his friendship with Archimedes.

Eratosthenes used mathematics to further the geographical studies for which he is most famous. He calculated the circumference of the earth geometrically, estimating it as about 24,675 miles. (He was off by only 185 miles.) Eratosthenes also discussed the shapes and sizes of land and ocean and the irregularities of the earth's surface. He drew a map of the earth and used his own system to explain the divisions of the earth's landmass.

Using geographical information gained by Alexander the Great's scientists, Eratosthenes tried to fit the East into Greek geographical knowledge. He declared that a ship could sail from Spain either around Africa to India or directly westward to India. Not until the great days of Western exploration did sailors such as Vasco da Gama and Magellan actually prove Eratosthenes' theories. Like Eratosthenes, other Greek geographers also turned their attention southward to Africa. During this period the people of the Mediterranean learned of the climate and customs of Ethiopia and gleaned some scant information about equatorial Africa.

In the Hellenistic period the scientific study of botany had its origin. Aristotle's pupil Theophrastus (ca 372–288 B.C.) studied the botanical information made available by Alexander's penetration of the East. Theophrastus wrote two books on the subject, *History of Plants* and *Causes of Plants.* He carefully observed phenomena and based his conclusions on what he had actually seen. Theophrastus classified plants and accurately described their parts. He detected the process of germination and realized the importance of climate and soil to plants. Some of his work found its way into agricultural handbooks, but for the most part Hellenistic science did not carry the study of botany further.

Despite its undeniable brilliance, Hellenistic science suffered from a remarkable weakness almost impossible for practical-minded Americans to understand. Although scientists of this period invented such machines as the air gun, the water organ, and even the steam engine, they never used their discoveries as labor-saving devices. No one has satisfactorily explained why these scientists were so impractical, but one answer is quite possible: they and the rest of society saw no real need for machines. Slave labor was especially abundant and made labor-saving machinery superfluous. Science was applied only to war. Even so, later Hellenistic thinkers preserved the discoveries of Hellenistic science for the modern age.

The Celestial Globe In Greek mythology the god Atlas held the world on his strong shoulders, thereby preventing it from falling. Hellenistic scientists formed a very accurate idea of the shape and dimension of the earth. Here Atlas holds the globe, which rests on its axis and displays the skies, with figures representing constellations as well as the equator, tropics, and polar circles. *(Source: National Museum, Naples/Alinari/Art Resource, NY)*

❈ HELLENISTIC MEDICINE

The study of medicine flourished during the Hellenistic period, and Hellenistic physicians carried the work of Hippocrates into new areas. Herophilus, who lived in the first half of the third century B.C., worked at Alexandria and studied the writings of Hippocrates. He accepted Hippocrates' theory of the four humors and approached the study of medicine in a systematic, scientific fashion. He dissected dead bodies and measured what he observed. He discovered the nervous system and

SPREAD OF HELLENISM

338 B.C.	Battle of Chaeronea: Philip II of Macedonia conquers Greece
336 B.C.	Assassination of Philip II Alexander the Great inherits Macedonian crown
334–330 B.C.	Alexander overthrows the Persian Empire
334 B.C.	Battle of Granicus River
333 B.C.	Battle of Issus: Alexander conquers Asia Minor
331 B.C.	Battle of Gaugamela: Alexander conquers Mesopotamia
330 B.C.	Fall of Persepolis, principal Persian capital Fall of Ecbatana, last Persian capital
330–326 B.C.	Alexander conquers Bactria
326 B.C.	Alexander enters India; mutiny of his troops at the Hyphasis River
323 B.C.	Alexander dies in Babylon at the age of 32
323–275 B.C.	Alexander's empire divided into three monarchies; new dynasties founded by Ptolemy I (Egypt), Antigonus Gonatar (Macedonia, Asia Minor), and Seleucus I (Mesopotamia)
3d century B.C.	Development of the Hellenistic city
ca 300 B.C.	Euclid, *The Elements of Geometry*
ca 300–250 B.C.	Diffusion of philosophy; new schools founded by Epicurus (Epicureans) and Zeno (Stoics) Medical advantages by Herophilus, Erasistratus, Philinus, and Serapion
263 B.C.	Eumenes of Pergamum wins independence from the Seleucids, establishes the Pergamene monarchy
ca 250–200 B.C.	Scientific advances by Archimedes, Eratosthenes, and Aristarchus of Samos

concluded that two types of nerves, motor and sensory, exist. Herophilus also studied the brain, which he considered the center of intelligence. His younger contemporary, Erasistratus, also conducted research on the brain and nervous system and improved on Herophilus's work. He, too, followed in the tradition of Hippocrates and preferred to let the body heal itself by means of diet and air.

Both Herophilus and Erasistratus were members of the Dogmatic school of medicine at Alexandria. In this school speculation played an important part in research. So, too, did the study of anatomy, including dissection. Better knowledge of anatomy led to improvements in surgery. These advances enabled the Dogmatists to invent new surgical instruments and techniques.

In about 280 B.C. Philinus and Serapion, pupils of Herophilus, led a reaction against the Dogmatists. Believing that the Dogmatists had become too speculative, they founded the Empiric school of medicine at Alexandria. Claiming that the Dogmatists' emphasis on anatomy and physiology was misplaced, they concentrated instead on the observation and cure of illnesses. They also laid heavier stress on the use of drugs and medicine to treat illnesses. Heraclides of Tarentum (perhaps first century B.C.) discovered the benefits of opium and worked with other drugs that relieved pain. He also steadfastly rejected the relevance of magic to drugs and medicines.

Hellenistic medicine had its dark side, for many physicians were moneygrubbers, fools, and quacks. One of the angriest complaints comes from the days of the Roman Empire:

Of all men only a physician can kill a man with total impunity. Oh no, on the contrary, censure goes to him who dies and he is guilty of excess, and furthermore he is blamed. . . . Let me not accuse their [physicians'] avarice, their greedy deals with those whose fate hangs in the balance, their setting a price on pain, and their demands for down payment in case of death, and their secret doctrines.[7]

Abuses such as these existed already in the Hellenistic period. As is true today, many Hellenistic physicians did not take the Hippocratic oath very seriously.

Besides incompetent and greedy physicians, the Hellenistic world was plagued by people who claimed to cure illnesses through incantations and magic. Their potions included such concoctions as blood from the ear of an ass mixed with water to cure fever, or the liver of a cat killed when the moon was waning and preserved in salt. Broken bones could be cured by applying the ashes of a pig's jawbone to the break. The dung of a goat mixed with old wine was good for healing broken ribs. One charlatan claimed that he could cure epilepsy by making the patient drink spring water, drawn at night, from the skull of a man who had been killed but not cremated. These quacks even claimed that they could cure mental illness. The

 An Unsuccessful Delivery This funeral stele depicts a mother who has perhaps lost her own life as well as her baby's. Maternal and infant mortality was quite common in antiquity. A similar stele elsewhere bears the heartbreaking words attributed to the mother by her grieving family: "All my labor could not bring the child forth; he lies in my womb, among the dead." (*Source: National Museum, Athens*)

treatment for a person suffering from melancholy was calf dung boiled in wine. No doubt the patient became too sick to be depressed.

Quacks who prescribed such treatments were very popular but did untold harm to the sick and injured. They and greedy physicians also damaged the reputation of dedicated doctors who honestly and intelligently tried to heal and alleviate pain. Nonetheless, the work of men like Herophilus and Serapion made valuable contributions to the knowledge of medicine, and the fruits of their work were preserved and handed on to the world.

SUMMARY

Alexander established Macedonian and Greek colonies across western and central Asia for military reasons. They resulted in the spread of Hellenism as a side effect. In the Aegean and Near East the fusion of Greek and Eastern cultures laid the social, intellectual, and cultural foundations on which the Romans would later build. In the heart of the old Persian Empire, Hellenism was only another new influence that was absorbed by older ways of thought and life. Yet overall, in the exchange of ideas and the opportunity for different cultures to learn about one another, a new cosmopolitan society evolved. That society in turn made possible such diverse advances as a wider extent of trade and agriculture, the creation of religious and philosophical ideas that paved the way for Christianity, and greater freedom for women. People of the Hellenistic period also made remarkable advances in science and medicine. They not only built on the achievements of their predecessors, but they also produced one of the most creative intellectual eras of classical antiquity.

NOTES

1. Quoted in W. W. Tarn and G. T. Griffith, *Hellenistic Civilizations,* 3d ed. (Cleveland: Meridian Books, 1961), p. 199.
2. *Periplous of the Erythraian Sea* 57. Unless otherwise credited, all quotations from a foreign language in this chapter have been translated into English by John Buckler.
3. Diodorus 3.12.2–3.
4. Diogenes, *Laertius* 6.38.
5. Ibid., 14.13.
6. Vitruvius, *On Architecture* 9 Preface, 10.
7. Pliny the Elder, *Natural History* 29.8.18, 21.

SUGGESTED READING

General treatments of Hellenistic political, social, and economic history can be found in F. W. Walbank et al., *The Cambridge Ancient History,* 2d ed., vol. 7, pt. 1 (1984). Shorter is F. W. Walbank, *The Hellenistic World* (1981), a fresh appraisal by one of the foremost scholars in the field. The undisputed classic in this area is M. Rostovtzeff, *The Social and Economic History of the Hellenistic World,* 3 vols. (1941). R. M. Errington, *A History of Macedonia,* (English trans., 1990), places Macedonia clearly within a much broader Hellenistic context. Good selections of primary sources in accurate and readable translation can be found in M. M. Austin, *The Hellenistic World from Alexander to the Roman Conquest* (1981), and S. M. Burstein, *The Hellenistic Age from the Battle of Ipsos to the Death of Kleopatra III* (1985).

Each year brings a new crop of biographies of Alexander the Great. Still the best, however, is J. R. Hamilton, *Alexander the Great* (1973). Old but still useful is U. Wilcken, *Alexander the Great* (English trans., 1967), which has had a considerable impact on scholars and students alike. Although many historians have idealized Alexander the Great, recent scholarship has provided a more realistic and unflattering view of him. The foremost expert on Alexander is E. Badian, who gives a succinct account in *The Cambridge History of Iran,* vol. 2 (1985), chap. 8. Recent political studies of the Hellenistic period include A. B. Bosworth, *Conquest and Empire* (1988), which sets Alexander's career in a broad context, and F. L. Holt, *Alexander the Great and Bactria* (1988), which discusses the formation of a Greco-Macedonian frontier in central Asia.

A. K. Bowman, *Egypt After the Pharaohs* (1986), is a readable account of the impact of the Greeks and Macedonians on Egyptian society. The same topic is treated by N. Lewis, a major scholar in the field, in his *Greeks in Ptolemaic Egypt* (1986); and a brief, new study comes from the pen of another major scholar, A. E. Samuel, *The Shifting Sands of History: Interpretations of Ptolemaic Egypt* (1989), which deals with history and historiography. W. Heckel, *The Marshals of Alexander's Empire* (1992), treats the careers of the more than 130 men who were not actually Alexander's chief officers but nonetheless substantially shaped Hellenistic political history. S. Sherwin-White and A. Kuhrt, *From Samarkand to Sardis* (1992), offer a new study of the Seleucid Empire that puts it in an Asian rather than Greek perspective. J. D. Grainger, *Seleukos Nikator* (1990), examines how the Hellenistic king created his empire. R. A. Billows, *Antigone the One-Eyed and the Creation of the Hellenis-*

tic State (1990), examines the career of the one man who most nearly reunited Alexander's empire. E. V. Hansen, *The Attalids of Pergamon,* 2d ed. (1971), though dated, is still the best treatment of that kingdom. B. Bar-Kochva, *Judas Maccabaeus* (1988), treats the Jewish struggle against the Seleucids and Hellenistic influences. A good portrait of one of the busiest ports in the Hellenistic world can be found in R. Garland, *Piraeus* (1987).

Much new work has focused on the spread of Hellenism throughout the Near East. Very extensive is A. Kuhrt and S. Sherwin-White, eds., *Hellenism in the East* (1988), which touches on a broad range of topics, including biblical studies, Christianity, and Islam. A. E. Samuel, *The Promise of the West* (1988), studies the connections among Greek, Roman, and Jewish culture and thought and their significance for Western history. P. McKechnie, *Outsiders in the Greek Cities of the Fourth Century* (1989), provides an interesting study of the social dislocation of the Greeks in the time of Philip II and Alexander the Great.

No specific treatment of women in the Hellenistic world yet exists, but two recent studies shed light on certain aspects of the topic. N. L. Goodrich, *Priestesses* (1989), examines the importance of priestesses in cults from the Near East to Ireland.

Two general studies of religion in the Hellenistic world are F. Grant, *Hellenistic Religion: The Age of Syncretism* (1953), and H. J. Rose, *Religion in Greece and Rome* (1959). L. H. Feldman, *Jew and Gentile in the Ancient World* (1993), argues that the pagan response to Judaism within the Greco-Roman period was not as negative as often thought. R. van den Broek et al., eds., *Knowledge of God in the Graeco-Roman World* (1988), is a difficult but rewarding collection of essays that points out how similarly pagans, Hellenistic Jews, and Christians thought about human attempts to know God. R. E. Witt, *Isis in the Graeco-Roman World* (1971), an illustrated volume,

studies the origins and growth of the Isis cult; and more specifically, S. K. Heyob, *The Cult of Isis Among Women in the Graeco-Roman World* (1975), explores its popularity among women. The cult of Isis's consort Osiris is the subject of J. G. Griffiths, *The Origins of Osiris and His Cult* (1980); and for the mystery cults in general, see W. Burkert, *Ancient Mystery Cults* (1987), written by one of the finest scholars in the field.

Hellenistic philosophy and science have attracted the attention of a number of scholars, and the various philosophical schools are especially well covered. A general treatment can be recommended because it deals with the broader question of the role of the intellectual in the Classical period and Hellenistic world: F. L. Vatai, *Intellectuals in Politics in the Greek World from Early Times to the Hellenistic Age* (1984). Broader is S. Blundell's *The Origin of Civilization in Greek and Roman Thought* (1986), a survey of classical political and social theories through a period of ten centuries, from Aristotle to the Stoics and their Roman successors. A convenient survey of Hellenistic philosophy is A. A. Long, *Hellenistic Philosophy* (1974). F. Sayre, *The Greek Cynics* (1948), focuses on Diogenes' thought and manners. H. Jones, *The Epicurean Tradition* (1989), covers Epicurean philosophy from its inception to late Roman times. Three treatments of Stoicism are J. Rist, *Stoic Philosophy* (1969); F. H. Sandbach, *The Stoics* (1975); and M. L. Colish, *The Stoic Tradition from Antiquity to the Early Middle Ages,* 2 vols. (1985), which devotes a great deal of attention to the impact of Stoicism on Christianity. A good survey of Hellenistic science is G. E. R. Lloyd, *Greek Science After Aristotle* (1963), and specific studies of major figures can be found in T. L. Heath's solid work, *Aristarchos of Samos* (1920), still unsurpassed, and E. J. Dijksterhuis, *Archimedes,* rev. ed. (1987).

LISTENING TO THE
PAST

A Queen's Sacrifice for Her Society

During the Hellenistic period, women in the eastern Mediterranean became prominent in society and more obvious in their public roles. Hellenistic queens became role models for ordinary women. Nevertheless, even Hellenistic queens received criticism from men who felt that they had no business in public life, and they were often portrayed as vicious and vindictive. No one could ever say that of Queen Mother Cratesicleia of Sparta, however.

As described by the Greek biographer Plutarch, the political situation of Sparta at the time of this episode (ca 226 B.C.) was one of extreme danger. Shorn of its might first by the Thebans and later by the Macedonians, Sparta was too weak to compete successfully in the power struggles of the period. As a result, Sparta had to choose sides. When Cleomenes, king of Sparta, asked the help of the Egyptian king Ptolemy against the Macedonians, the cost was high.

Now, Ptolemy the king of Egypt promised him [Cleomenes] aid and assistance, but demanded his mother and his children as hostages. For a long time, therefore, he was ashamed to tell his mother, and though he often went to her and was at the very point of letting her know, he held his peace, so that she on her part became suspicious and enquired of his friends whether there was not something that he wished to tell her but hesitated to do so. Finally, when Cleomenes plucked up courage to speak of the matter, his mother burst into a hearty laugh and said: "Was this the thing that you were often of a mind to tell me but lost your courage? Make haste, put me on board a ship, and send this frail body wheresoever you think it will be of most use to Sparta, before old age destroys it sitting idly here."

Accordingly, when all things were ready, they came to Taenarus [a Spartan port] by land, while the army escorted them with the might of heavy-armed troops. And as Cratesicleia was about to embark, she drew Cleomenes aside by himself into the temple of Poseidon, and after embracing and kissing him in his anguish and deep trouble, said: "Come, O king of the Spartans, when we go forth let no one see us weeping or doing anything unworthy of Sparta. For this lies in our power, and this alone; but as for the issues of fortune, we shall have what the god may grant." After saying this, she composed her countenance and proceeded to the ship with her little grandson, and bade the captain put to sea with all speed.

When she arrived in Egypt, she learned that Sparta's enemies intended to use her and her grandson to pressure Cleomenes into surrender. Hostage though she was, she sent her son a message.

She sent word to him that he must do what was fitting and advantageous for Sparta, and not, because of one old woman and a little boy, be ever in fear of Ptolemy.

When Cleomenes was killed in a major battle, the alliance between Sparta and Ptolemy dissolved. Cleomenes' death sealed Cratesicleia's fate. Ptolemy ordered her execution. She was not at all dismayed and refused to grieve for herself. The words of Plutarch are a fitting tribute to her and other Spartan women.

So, then, Sparta, bringing her women's tragedy into emulous competition with that of her men, showed the world that in the last extremity Virtue cannot be outraged by Fortune.

Questions for Analysis

1. What does this episode tell us about the Spartan concept of duty and how it applies to men and women?

2. What does this episode convey about the importance of Cratesicleia, who held no actual political power?

3. What can be said of Plutarch's literary and historical portrayal of this incident? According to the words he gave Cratesicleia, Sparta would not suffer from the death of one old woman. What sort of model was she setting for others?

Coin depicting Queen Arsinoe II, wife of Ptolemy II, 265–246 B.C. *(Source: Ancient Art & Architecture Collection)*

Source: Slightly adapted and abbreviated from B. Perrin, trans., *Plutarch's Lives,* vol. 10 (Cambridge, Mass.: Harvard University Press, 1921), pp. 99–141.

The Glory of Rome

Etruscan soldiers carrying a slain comrade, from the lid of a fourth-century B.C. bronze container. *(Source: Scala/Art Resource, NY)*

"Who is so thoughtless and lazy that he does not want to know in what way and with what kind of government the Romans in less than 53 years conquered nearly the entire inhabited world and brought it under their rule—an achievement previously unheard of?"[1] This question was first asked by Polybius, a Greek historian who lived in the second century B.C. With keen awareness Polybius realized that the Romans were achieving something unique in world history.

What was that achievement? Rome was not the first to create a huge empire. The Persians and Alexander the Great had done the same thing. The Romans themselves admitted that in matters of art, literature, philosophy, and culture they learned from the Greeks. Rome's achievement lay in the ability of the Romans not only to conquer peoples but to incorporate them into the Roman system. Rome succeeded where the Greek polis had failed. Unlike the Greeks, who refused to share citizenship, the Romans extended their citizenship first to the Italians and later to the peoples of the provinces. With that citizenship went Roman government and law. Rome created a world state that embraced the entire Mediterranean area. For the first and second centuries A.D. the lot of the Mediterranean world was the Roman peace—the *pax Romana*, a period of security, order, harmony, flourishing culture, and expanding economy. It was a period that saw the wilds of Gaul, Spain, Germany, and eastern Europe introduced to Greco-Roman culture.

Nor was Rome's achievement limited to the ancient world. By the third century A.D., when the empire began to give way to the medieval world, the greatness of Rome and its culture had left an indelible mark on the ages to come. Rome's law, language, and administrative practices were a precious heritage to medieval and modern Europe.

- How did Rome rise to greatness?
- What effects did the conquest of the Mediterranean have on the Romans themselves?
- How did the Roman emperors govern the empire, and how did they spread Roman influence into northern Europe?
- Why did Christianity, originally a minor local religion, sweep across the Roman world to change it fundamentally?

- How did the Roman Empire meet the grim challenge of barbarian invasion and subsequent economic decline?

These are the questions we will answer in this chapter.

❖ THE LAND AND THE SEA

To the west of Greece the boot-shaped peninsula of Italy, with Sicily at its toe, occupies the center of the Mediterranean basin. As Map 7.1 shows, Italy and Sicily thrust southward toward Africa: the distance between southwestern Sicily and the northern African coast is at one point only about a hundred miles. Italy and Sicily literally divide the Mediterranean into two basins and form the focal point between the halves.

Like Greece and other Mediterranean lands, Italy enjoys a genial, almost subtropical climate. The winters are rainy, but the summer months are dry. Because of the climate the rivers of Italy usually carry little water during the summer, and some go entirely dry. Thus Italian rivers never became major thoroughfares for commerce and communications.

In the north of Italy the Apennine Mountains break off from the Alps and form a natural barrier. The Apennines hindered but did not prevent peoples from invading Italy from the north. North of the Apennines lies the Po Valley, an important part of modern Italy. In antiquity this valley did not become Roman territory until late in the history of the republic. From the north the Apennines run southward the entire length of the Italian boot; they virtually cut off access to the Adriatic Sea, inducing Italy to look west to Spain and Carthage rather than east to Greece.

Even though most of the land is mountainous, the hill country is not as inhospitable as are the Greek highlands. In antiquity the general fertility of the soil provided the basis for a large population. Nor did the mountains of Italy so carve up the land as to prevent the development of political unity. Geography proved kinder to Italy than to Greece.

In their southward course the Apennines leave two broad and fertile plains, those of Latium and Campania. These plains attracted settlers and

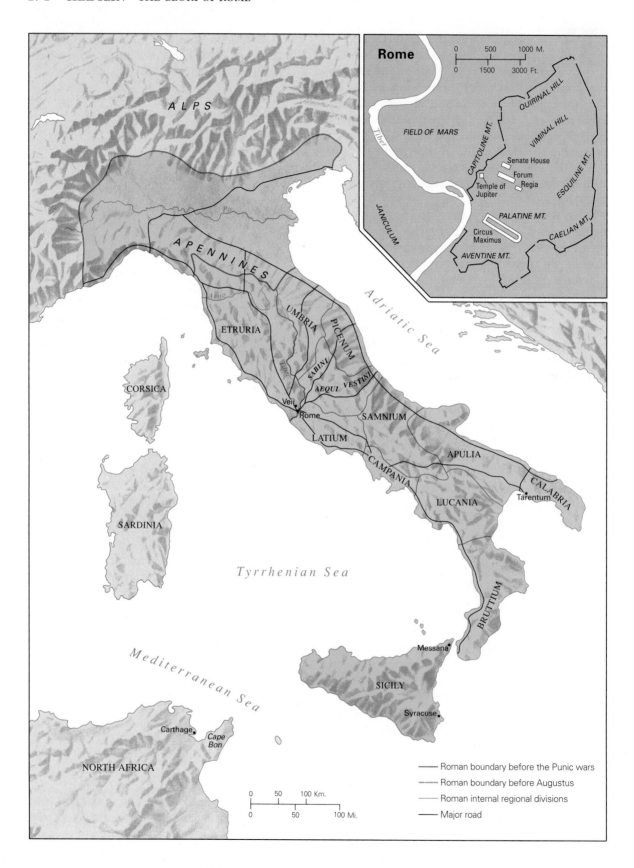

Rome

FIELD OF MARS

Tiber

JANICULUM

CAPITOLINE MT.

QUIRINAL HILL

VIMINAL HILL

Senate House

Forum

Temple of Jupiter

Regia

ESQUILINE MT.

PALATINE MT.

CAELIAN MT.

Circus Maximus

AVENTINE MT.

0   500   1000 M.

0   1500   3000 Ft.

ALPS

APENNINES

Po

Arno

UMBRIA

ETRURIA

PICENUM

Tiber

SABINI

AEQUI   VESTINI

Veii

Rome

SAMNIUM

LATIUM

CORSICA

Adriatic Sea

APULIA

CAMPANIA

CALABRIA

Tarentum

LUCANIA

SARDINIA

Tyrrhenian Sea

BRUTTIUM

Messana

Mediterranean Sea

SICILY

Syracuse

Carthage

Cape Bon

NORTH AFRICA

0   50   100 Km.

0   50   100 Mi.

——— Roman boundary before the Punic wars

- - - Roman boundary before Augustus

——— Roman internal regional divisions

——— Major road

invaders from the time when peoples began to move into Italy. Among these peoples were the Romans, who established their city on the Tiber River in Latium. The Tiber provided Rome with a constant source of water. Located at an easy crossing point on the Tiber, Rome stood astride the main avenue of communications between northern and southern Italy. The seven hills of Rome were defensible and safe from the floods of the Tiber. Rome was in an excellent position to develop the resources of Latium and maintain contact with the rest of Italy.

THE ETRUSCANS AND THE ROMAN CONQUEST OF ITALY (750–290 B.C.)

In recent years archaeologists have found traces of numerous early peoples in Italy. The origins of these cultures and their precise relations with one another are not yet well understood. In fact, no clear account of the prehistory of Italy is yet possible. Of the period before the appearance of the Etruscans (1200–750 B.C.), one fundamental fact is indisputable: peoples speaking Indo-European languages were moving into Italy from the north, probably in small groups. They were part of the awesome but imperfectly understood movement of peoples that spread the Indo-European family of languages from Spain to India.

Only with the coming of the Greeks does Italy enter the light of history. A great wave of Greek immigration swept into southern Italy and Sicily during the eighth century B.C. (see pages 123–124). The Greeks brought urban life to these regions, spreading cultural influence far beyond their city-states.

In the north the Greeks encountered the Etruscans, one of the truly mysterious peoples of antiquity. Who the Etruscans were and where they came from are unknown. Nonetheless, this fascinating people was to leave an indelible mark on the Romans. Skillful metalworkers, the Etruscans amassed extensive wealth by trading their manufactured

goods in Italy and beyond. The strength of their political and military institutions enabled them to form a loosely organized league of cities whose dominion extended as far north as the Po Valley and as far south as Latium and Campania (see Map 7.1). In Latium they founded cities and took over control of Rome. Like the Greeks, the Etruscans promoted urban life, and one of the places that benefited from Etruscan influence was Rome.

Early Roman history is an uneven mixture of fact and legend. Roman traditions often contain an important kernel of truth, but that does not make them history. In many cases they are significant because they illustrate the ethics, morals, and ideals that Roman society considered valuable. According to Roman legend, Romulus and Remus founded Rome in 753 B.C. During the years 753 to 509 B.C., the Romans embraced many Etruscan customs. They adopted the Etruscan alphabet, which the Etruscans themselves had adopted from the Greeks. The Romans later handed on this alphabet to medieval Europe and thence to the modern Western world. It was also thanks to the Etruscans that the Romans truly became urban dwellers.

Etruscan power and influence at Rome were so strong that Roman traditions preserved the memory of Etruscan kings who ruled the city. Under the Etruscans, Rome enjoyed contacts with the larger Mediterranean world, and the city began to grow. In the years 575 to 550 B.C., temples and public buildings began to grace the city. The Capitoline Hill became the religious center of the city when the temple of Jupiter Optimus Maximus (Jupiter the Best and Greatest) was built there. The Forum, located on the site of a former cemetery, began its history as a public meeting place, a development parallel to that of the Greek agora. Trade in metalwork became common, and the wealthier Roman classes began to import large numbers of fine Greek vases. The Etruscans had found Rome a collection of villages and made it a city.

According to Roman tradition, the Romans expelled the Etruscan king Tarquin the Proud from Rome in 509 B.C. and founded the republic. In the years that followed, the Romans fought numerous wars with their neighbors on the Italian peninsula. They became soldiers, and the grim fighting bred tenacity, a prominent Roman trait. At an early date the Romans also learned the value of alliances and

MAP 7.1 Italy and the City of Rome The geographical configuration of the Italian peninsula shows how Rome stood astride north-south communications and how the state that united Italy stood poised to move into Sicily and northern Africa.

❊ **Sarcophagus of Lartie Seianti** The woman portrayed on this lavish sarcophagus is the noble Etruscan Lartie Seianti. Although the sarcophagus is her place of burial, she is portrayed as in life, comfortable and at rest. The influence of Greek art on Etruscan is apparent on almost every feature of the sarcophagus. *(Source: Archaeological Museum, Florence/Nimatallah/Art Resource, NY)*

how to provide leadership for their allies. Alliances with the Latin towns around them provided them with a large reservoir of manpower. Their alliances involved the Romans in still other wars and took them farther afield in the Italian peninsula.

The growth of Roman power was slow but steady. Not until roughly a century after the founding of the republic did the Romans drive the Etruscans entirely out of Latium. Around 390 B.C. the Romans suffered a major setback when a new people, the Celts—or "Gauls," as the Romans called them—swept aside a Roman army and sacked Rome. More intent on loot than on land, they agreed to abandon Rome in return for a thousand pounds of gold.

During the century from 390 B.C. to 290 B.C., Romans rebuilt their city and recouped their losses. They also reorganized their army to create the mobile legion, a flexible unit capable of fighting on either broken or open terrain. The Romans finally brought Latium and their Latin allies fully under their control and conquered Etruria (see Map 7.1). In 343 B.C. they grappled with the Sam-nites in a series of bitter wars for the possession of Campania and southern Italy. The Samnites were a formidable enemy and inflicted serious losses on the Romans. But the superior organization, institutions, and manpower of the Romans won out in the end. Although Rome had yet to subdue the whole peninsula, for the first time in history the city stood unchallenged in Italy.

Rome's success in diplomacy and politics was as important as its military victories. Unlike the Greeks, the Romans did not simply conquer and dominate. Instead, they shared with other Italians both political power and degrees of Roman citizenship. With many of their oldest allies, such as the Latin cities, they shared full Roman citizenship. In other instances they granted citizenship without the franchise (*civitas sine suffragio*). Allies who held this status enjoyed all the rights of Roman citizenship except that they could not vote or hold Roman offices. They were subject to Roman taxes and calls for military service but ran their own local affairs. The Latin allies were able to acquire full Roman citizenship by moving to Rome.

✥ THE ROMAN REPUBLIC

By their willingness to extend their citizenship, the Romans took Italy into partnership. Rome proved itself superior to the Greek polis because it not only conquered but shared the fruits of conquest with the conquered. Rome could consolidate where Greece could only dominate. The unwillingness of the Greek polis to share its citizenship condemned it to a limited horizon. Not so with Rome. The extension of Roman citizenship strengthened the state, gave it additional manpower and wealth, and laid the foundation of the Roman Empire.

The Roman State and Social Conflict

The Romans summed up their political existence in a single phrase: *senatus populusque Romanus,* "the Roman senate and the people." The real genius of the Romans lay in the fields of politics and law. Unlike the Greeks, they did not often speculate on the ideal state or on political forms. Instead, they realistically met actual challenges and created institutions, magistracies, and legal concepts to deal with practical problems. Change was consequently commonplace in Roman political life; thus the constitution of 509 B.C. was far simpler than that of 27 B.C. Moreover, the Roman constitution was not a single written

✥ **The Roman Forum**   The Forum was the center of Roman political life. From simple beginnings it developed into the very symbol of Rome's imperial majesty. *(Source: Josephine Powell, Rome)*

document but a set of traditional beliefs, customs, and laws.

In the early republic, social divisions determined the shape of politics. Political power was in the hands of the aristocracy—the *patricians,* who were wealthy landowners. Patrician families formed clans, as did aristocrats in early Greece. They dominated the affairs of state, provided military leadership in time of war, and monopolized knowledge of law and legal procedure. The common people of Rome, the *plebeians,* had few of the patricians' advantages. Some plebeians formed their own clans and rivaled the patricians in wealth, but most plebeians were poor. They were the artisans, small farmers, and landless urban dwellers. The plebeians, rich and poor alike, were free citizens with a voice in politics. Nonetheless, they were overshadowed by the patricians.

Perhaps the greatest institution of the republic was the senate, which had originated under the Etruscans as a council of noble elders who advised the king. During the republic the senate advised the consuls and other magistrates. Because the senate sat year after year, while magistrates changed annually, it provided stability and continuity. It also served as a reservoir of experience and knowledge. Technically, the senate could not pass legislation; it could only offer its advice. But increasingly, because of the senate's prestige, its advice came to have the force of law.

The Romans created several assemblies through which the people elected magistrates and passed legislation. Patricians generally dominated, but in 471 B.C. the plebeians won the right to meet in an assembly of their own, the *concilium plebis,* and to pass ordinances.

The chief magistrates of the republic were two consuls, elected for one-year terms. At first the consulship was open only to patricians. The consuls commanded the army in battle, administered state business, and supervised financial affairs. In effect, they and the senate ran the state.

In 366 B.C. the Romans created the office of *praetor,* and in 227 B.C. the number of praetors was increased to four. When the consuls were away from Rome, the praetors could act in their place. The praetors dealt primarily with the administration of justice. When a praetor took office, he issued a proclamation declaring the principles by which he would interpret the law. These proclamations became very important because they usually covered areas where the law was vague and thus helped clarify the law.

After the age of overseas conquest (see pages 179–181), the Romans divided the Mediterranean area into provinces governed by former consuls and former praetors. Because of their experience in Roman politics, they were well suited to administer the affairs of the provincials and to fit Roman law and custom into new contexts.

The development of law was one of the Romans' most splendid achievements. Roman law began as a set of rules that regulated the lives and relations of citizens. This civil law, or *ius civile,* consisted of statutes, customs, and forms of procedure. Roman assemblies added to the body of law, and praetors interpreted it. The spirit of the law aimed at protecting the property, lives, and reputations of citizens, redressing wrongs, and giving satisfaction to victims of injustice.

As the Romans came into more frequent contact with foreigners, they had to devise laws to deal with disputes between Romans and foreigners and between foreigners living under Roman jurisdiction. In these instances, where there was no precedent to guide the Romans, the legal decisions of the praetors proved of immense importance. The praetors adopted aspects of other legal systems and resorted to the law of equity—what they thought was right and just to all parties. Free, in effect, to determine law, the praetors enjoyed a great deal of flexibility. This situation illustrates the practicality and the genius of the Romans. By addressing specific, actual circumstances the praetors developed a body of law, the *ius gentium,* "the law of peoples," that applied to Romans and foreigners and that laid the foundation for a universal conception of law. By the time of the late republic, Roman jurists were reaching decisions on the basis of the Stoic concept of *ius naturale,* "natural law," a universal law that could be applied to all societies.

Another important aspect of early Roman history was a great social conflict, usually known as the Struggle of the Orders, which developed between patricians and plebeians. What the plebeians wanted was real political representation and safeguards against patrician domination. The plebeians' efforts to obtain recognition of their rights is the crux of the Struggle of the Orders.

Rome's early wars gave the plebeians the leverage they needed: Rome's survival depended on the army, and the army needed the plebeians. The first showdown between plebeians and patricians came, according to tradition, in 494 B.C. To force the patricians to grant concessions, the plebeians seceded from the state; they literally walked out of Rome and refused to serve in the army. The plebeians' general strike worked. Because of it the patricians made important concessions. One of these was social. In 445 B.C. the patricians passed a law, the *lex Canuleia,* which for the first time allowed patricians and plebeians to marry one another. Furthermore, the patricians recognized the right of plebeians to elect their own officials, the *tribunes.* The tribunes in turn had the right to protect the plebeians from the arbitrary conduct of patrician magistrates. The tribunes brought plebeian grievances to the senate for resolution. The plebeians were not bent on undermining the state. Rather, they used their gains only to win full equality under the law.

The law itself was the plebeians' next target. Only the patricians knew what the law was, and only they could argue cases in court. All too often they had used the law for their own benefit. The plebeians wanted the law codified and published. The result of their agitation was the Law of the Twelve Tables. Later still, the plebeians forced the patricians to publish legal procedures as well. The plebeians had broken the patricians' legal monopoly and henceforth enjoyed full protection under the law.

The decisive plebeian victory came in 367 B.C. after rich plebeians joined the poor to mount a sweeping assault on patrician privilege. Wealthy plebeians demanded that the patricians allow them access to all the magistracies of the state. The senate did approve a law that stipulated that one of the two consuls had to be a plebeian. Though decisive, this victory did not automatically end the Struggle of the Orders. That happened only in 287 B.C. with the passage of a law, the *lex Hortensia,* that gave the resolutions of the concilium plebis the force of law for patricians and plebeians alike.

The Struggle of the Orders resulted in a Rome stronger and better united than before. It could have led to class warfare and anarchy, but again certain Roman traits triumphed. The values fostered by their social structure predisposed the Romans to compromise, especially in the face of common danger. Important, too, were Roman patience, tenacity, and a healthy sense of the practical. These qualities enabled both sides to keep working until they had resolved the crisis. The

Struggle of the Orders ended in 287 B.C. with a new concept of Roman citizenship. All citizens shared equally under the law. Theoretically, all could aspire to the highest political offices. Patrician or plebeian, rich or poor, Roman citizenship was equal for all.

The Age of Overseas Conquest (282–146 B.C.)

In 282 B.C. Rome embarked on a series of wars that left it the ruler of the Mediterranean world. There was nothing ideological about these wars. Unlike Napoleon or Hitler, the Romans did not map out grandiose strategies for world conquest. They had no idea of what lay before them. If they could have looked into the future, they would have stood amazed. In many instances the Romans did not even initiate action; they simply responded to situations as they arose. Though they sometimes declared war reluctantly, they nonetheless felt the need to dominate, to eliminate any state that could threaten them.

The Samnite wars had drawn the Romans into the political world of southern Italy. In 282 B.C., alarmed by the powerful newcomer, the Greek city of Tarentum in southern Italy called for help from Pyrrhus, king of Epirus in western Greece. A relative of Alexander the Great and an excellent general, Pyrrhus won two furious battles but suffered heavy casualties—thus the phrase "Pyrrhic victory" for a victory involving severe losses. Roman bravery and tenacity led him to comment: "If we win one more battle with the Romans, we'll be completely washed up." In 275 B.C. the Romans drove Pyrrhus from Italy and extended their sway over southern Italy. Once they did, the island of Sicily became a key for them to block Carthaginian expansion northward.

Pyrrhus once described Sicily as a future "wrestling ground for the Carthaginians and Romans." The Phoenician city of Carthage in North Africa (Map 7.2) had for centuries dominated the western Mediterranean. Sicily had long been a Carthaginian target. Since Sicily is the steppingstone to Italy, the Romans could not let it fall to an enemy. In 264 B.C. Carthage and Rome came to blows over the city of Messana, which commanded the strait between Sicily and Italy.

This conflict, the First Punic War, lasted for twenty-three years (264–241 B.C.). The Romans

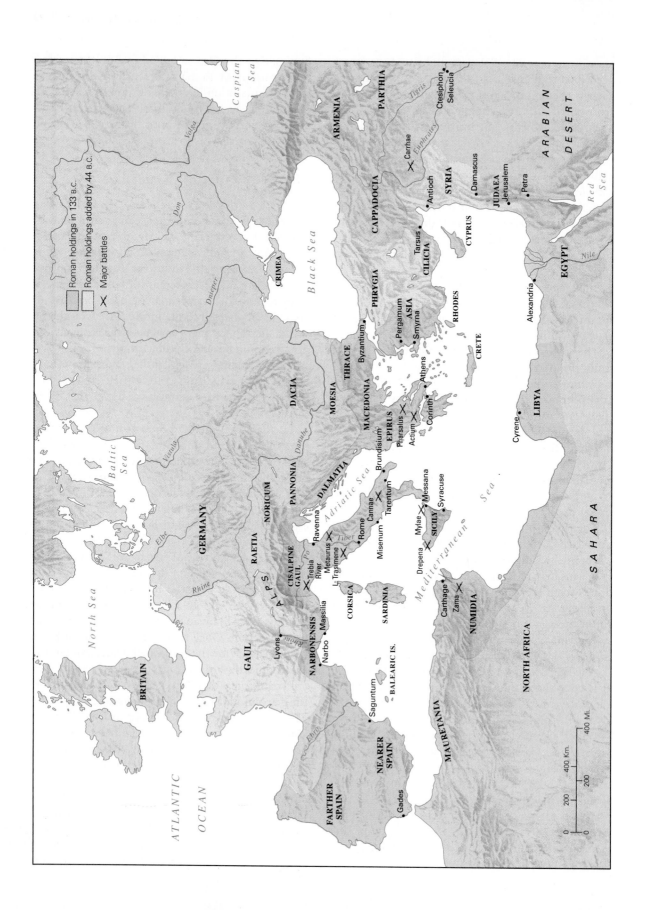

BRITAIN

GERMANY

North Sea

Baltic Sea

ATLANTIC OCEAN

GAUL

Lyons

Rhine

Rhône

RAETIA

NORICUM

ALPS

CISALPINE GAUL

PANNONIA

DACIA

MOESIA

THRACE

Black Sea

Caspian Sea

Volga

Don

Dnieper

Dniester

Vistula

Elbe

Danube

CRIMEA

ARMENIA

PARTHIA

CAPPADOCIA

✕ Carrhae

Tigris

Euphrates

Ctesiphon ● ● Seleucia

NARBONENSIS

Narbo ●

Massilia ●

CORSICA

SARDINIA

Saguntum ●

● BALEARIC IS.

NEARER SPAIN

FARTHER SPAIN

Gades ●

Ebro

Ravenna ●

Trebia River ✕

L. Trasimene ✕

Metaurus ✕

Rome ●

Tiber

Cannae ✕

Tarentum ●

Brundisium ●

DALMATIA

Adriatic Sea

EPIRUS

Pharsalus ✕

Actium ✕

MACEDONIA

Athens ●

Corinth ●

Byzantium ●

PHRYGIA

Pergamum ●

Smyrna ●

ASIA

CILICIA

Tarsus ●

RHODES

CRETE

CYPRUS

SYRIA

Antioch ●

● Damascus

JUDAEA

Jerusalem ●

● Petra

ARABIAN DESERT

Red Sea

EGYPT

Alexandria ●

Nile

LIBYA

Cyrene ●

Misenum ●

Drepana ✕

Mylae ✕

SICILY

Messana ●

Syracuse ●

Mediterranean Sea

Carthage ●

Zama ✕

NUMIDIA

NORTH AFRICA

MAURETANIA

SAHARA

Roman holdings in 133 B.C.

Roman holdings added by 44 B.C.

✕ Major battles

400 Mi.

0   200   400 Km.

0   200   400

quickly learned that they could not conquer Sicily unless they controlled the sea. Although they lacked a fleet and hated the sea as fervently as cats hate water, with grim resolution the Romans built a navy. They fought seven major naval battles with the Carthaginians, won six, and finally wore down the Carthaginians. In 241 B.C. the Romans took possession of Sicily, which became their first real province. Once again Rome's resources, manpower, and determination proved decisive.

The First Punic War was a beginning, not an end. Carthage was still a formidable enemy. After the war the Carthaginians expanded their power to Spain and turned the Iberian Peninsula into a rich field of operations. By 219 B.C. Carthage had found its avenger—Hannibal (ca 247–183 B.C.). In Spain, Hannibal learned how to lead armies and to wage war on a large scale. A brilliant general, he realized the advantages of swift mobile forces, and he was an innovator in tactics.

In 219 B.C. Hannibal defied the Romans by laying siege to the small city of Saguntum in Spain. When the Romans declared war the following year, he gathered his forces and led them on one of the most spectacular marches in ancient history. Hannibal carried the Second Punic War to the very gates of Rome. Starting in Spain, he led his troops—infantry, cavalry, and elephants—over the Alps and into Italy on a march of more than a thousand miles. Once in Italy, he defeated one Roman army at the Battle of Trebia (218 B.C.) and another at the Battle of Lake Trasimene (217 B.C.). At the Battle of Cannae in 216 B.C. Hannibal inflicted some forty thousand casualties on the Romans. He spread devastation throughout Italy but failed to crush Rome's iron circle of Latium, Etruria, and Samnium. The wisdom of Rome's political policy of extending rights and citizenship to its allies showed itself in these dark hours. Italy stood solidly with Rome against the invader. And Rome fought back.

The Roman general Scipio Africanus (ca 236–ca 183 B.C.) copied Hannibal's methods of mobile warfare. Scipio gave his new army combat experi-

ence in Spain, which he wrested from the Carthaginians. Meanwhile, the Roman fleet dominated the western Mediterranean and interfered with Carthaginian attempts to reinforce Hannibal. In 204 B.C. the Roman fleet landed Scipio in Africa, prompting the Carthaginians to recall Hannibal from Italy to defend the homeland. In 202 B.C., near the town of Zama (see Map 7.2), Scipio defeated Hannibal in one of the world's truly decisive battles. Scipio's victory meant that Rome's heritage would be passed on to the Western world.

The Second Punic War contained the seeds of still other wars. The Third Punic War ended in 146 B.C. when Scipio Aemilianus, grandson of Scipio Africanus, destroyed Carthage. As the Roman conqueror watched the death pangs of that great city, he turned to his friend Polybius with the words: "I fear and foresee that someday someone will give the same order about my fatherland." In 133 B.C., after years of brutal and ruthless warfare, Scipio Aemilianus finally conquered Spain.

In the civilized East, the world of Hellenistic states, Rome tried to avoid annexing territory. The East was already heavily populated, and those people would have become Rome's responsibility. New responsibilities meant new problems, and such headaches the Romans shunned. In the East the Romans preferred to be patrons rather than masters. Only when that policy failed did they directly annex land.

During the dark days of the Second Punic War, the king of Macedonia made an alliance with Hannibal against Rome. Even while engaged in the West, the Romans turned east to settle accounts. When the Romans intervened in the Hellenistic East, they went from triumph to triumph. The kingdom of Macedonia fell to the Roman legions, as did Greece and the Seleucid monarchy. By 146 B.C. the Romans stood unchallenged in the eastern Mediterranean and had turned many states and kingdoms into provinces. In 133 B.C. the king of Pergamum in Asia Minor left his kingdom to the Romans in his will. The Ptolemies of Egypt meekly obeyed Roman wishes. East and West, the Mediterranean had become *mare nostrum,* "our sea."

MAP 7.2 Roman Expansion During the Republic   The main spurt of Roman expansion occurred between 264 and 133 B.C., when most of the Mediterranean fell to Rome. The Roman conquest of Gaul and the eastern Mediterranean was achieved by 44 B.C.

Old Values and Greek Culture

Rome had conquered the Mediterranean world, but some Romans considered that victory a misfortune. The historian Sallust (86–34 B.C.), writing

❋ **Scene of the Life of a Child**   This scene depicts the life of Marcus Cornelius—his infancy, his playing with his ponies, and his death. The entire scene suggests a pleasant and loving, though brief, childhood. *(Source: Louvre/Bildarchiv Foto Marburg/Art Resource, NY)*

from hindsight, complained that the acquisition of an empire was the beginning of Rome's troubles:

But when through labor and justice our Republic grew powerful, great kings defeated in war, fierce nations and mighty peoples subdued by force, when Carthage the rival of the Roman people was wiped out root and branch, all the seas and lands lay open, then fortune began to be harsh and to throw everything into confusion. The Romans had easily borne labor, danger, uncertainty, and hardship. To them leisure, riches—otherwise desirable—proved to be burdens and torments. So at first money, then desire for power grew great. These things were a sort of cause of all evils.[2]

Sallust was not alone in his feelings. At the time, some senators had opposed the destruction of Carthage on the grounds that fear of their old rival would keep the Romans in check. In the second century B.C., Romans learned that they could not return to what they fondly considered a simple life. They were world rulers. The responsibilities they faced were complex and awesome. They had to change their institutions, social patterns, and way of thinking to meet the new era. They were in fact building the foundations of a great imperial system.

How did the Romans of the day meet these challenges? How did they lead their lives and cope with these momentous changes? Obviously there are as many answers to these questions as there were Romans. Yet two attitudes represent the major trends of the second century B.C. One was a

longing for the good old days and an idealized view of the traditional agrarian way of life. The other was an embracing of the new urban life, with its eager acceptance of Greek culture.

In Roman society ties within the family were very strong. The head of the family was the *paterfamilias,* a term that meant far more than merely "father." The paterfamilias was the oldest dominant male of the family. He held nearly absolute power over the lives of his wife and children as long as he lived. He could legally kill his wife for adultery or divorce her at will. He could kill his children or sell them into slavery. He could force them to marry against their will. Until the paterfamilias died, his sons could not legally own property. At his death, the wife and children of the paterfamilias inherited his property.

Despite his immense power, the paterfamilias did not necessarily act alone or arbitrarily. To deal with important family matters, he usually called a council of the adult males. In this way the leading members of the family aired their views. In these councils the women of the family had no formal part, but it can safely be assumed that they played an important role behind the scenes. Although the possibility of serious conflicts between a paterfamilias and his grown sons is obvious, no one in ancient Rome ever complained about the institution. Perhaps in practice the paterfamilias preferred to be lenient rather than absolute.

In the traditional Roman family, the wife was the matron of the family, a position of authority and respect. The virtues expected of a Roman matron were fidelity, chastity, modesty, and dedication to the family. She ran the household. She supervised the domestic slaves, planned the meals, and devoted a good deal of attention to her children. In wealthy homes during this period, the matron had begun to employ a slave as a wet nurse, but most ordinary Roman women nursed their babies and bathed and swaddled them daily. After the age of seven, sons—and in many wealthy households daughters too—began to undertake formal education.

The agricultural year followed the sun and the stars—the farmer's calendar. Farmers used oxen and donkeys to pull the plow, collecting the dung of the animals for fertilizer. The main money crops, at least for rich soils, were wheat and flax. Forage crops included clover, vetch, and alfalfa. Prosperous farmers raised olive trees chiefly for the oil. They also raised grapevines for the production of wine. Harvests varied depending on the soil, but farmers could usually expect yields of $5\frac{1}{2}$ bushels of wheat or $10\frac{1}{2}$ bushels of barley per acre.

An influx of slaves resulted from Rome's wars and conquests. Prisoners from Spain, Africa, and the Hellenistic East and even some blacks and other prisoners from Hannibal's army came to Rome as the spoils of war. The Roman attitude toward slaves and slavery had little in common with modern views. To the Romans slavery was a misfortune that befell some people, but it did not entail any racial theories. Races were not enslaved because the Romans thought them inferior. The black African slave was treated no worse—and no better—than the Spaniard. Indeed, some slaves were valued because of their physical distinctiveness: black Africans and blond Germans were particular favorites. For the talented slave, the Romans always held out the hope of eventual freedom. *Manumission*—the freeing of individual slaves by their masters—became so common that it had to be limited by law. Not even Christians questioned the institution of slavery. It was just a fact of life.

For most Romans, religion played an important part in life. Originally the Romans thought of the gods as invisible, shapeless natural forces. Only through Etruscan and Greek influence did Roman deities take on human form. Jupiter, the sky-god, and his wife, Juno, became equivalent to the Greek Zeus and Hera. Mars was the god of war but also guaranteed the fertility of the farm and protected it from danger. The gods of the Romans were not loving and personal. They were stern, powerful,

and aloof. But as long as the Romans honored the cults of their gods, they could expect divine favor.

In addition to the great gods, the Romans believed in spirits who haunted fields, forests, crossroads, and even the home itself. Some of the deities were hostile; only magic could ward them off (see Listening to the Past). The spirits of the dead, like ghosts in modern horror films, frequented places where they had lived. They, too,

 Vase Portrait of an Ethiopian Woman This vase, dating to ca 100 B.C., reflects Roman curiosity about different peoples. The portrait is realistic and not exaggerated. The silver inlay used for the whites of the eyes indicates that this was an expensive vase. *(Source: Courtesy of the Trustees of the British Museum)*

had to be placated but were ordinarily benign. As the poet Ovid (43 B.C.–A.D. 17) put it:

The spirits of the dead ask for little.
They are more grateful for piety than for an expensive
*   gift—*
Not greedy are the gods who haunt the Styx below.
A rooftile covered with a sacrificial crown,
Scattered kernels, a few grains of salt,
Bread dipped in wine, and loose violets—
These are enough.
Put them in a potsherd and leave them in the middle
*   of the road.*[3]

A good deal of Roman religion consisted of rituals such as those Ovid describes. These practices lived on long after the Romans had lost interest in the great gods. Even Christianity could not entirely wipe them out. Instead, Christianity was to incorporate many of these rituals into its own style of worship.

By the second century B.C. the ideals of traditional Roman society came into conflict with a new spirit of wealth and leisure. The conquest of the Mediterranean world and the spoils of war made Rome a great city. Roman life, especially in the cities, was changing and becoming less austere. The spoils of war went to build baths, theaters, and other places of amusement. Simultaneously, the new responsibilities of governing the world produced in Rome a sophisticated society. Romans developed new tastes and a liking for Greek culture and literature. They began to learn the Greek language. Hellenism dominated the cultural life of Rome. The poet Horace (64–8 B.C.) summed it up well: "Captive Greece captured her rough conqueror and introduced the arts into rustic Latium."

The new Rome produced a new Roman—imperial, cultured, and independent. In education and interests Romans began to break with the past. The new Hellenism profoundly stimulated the growth and development of Roman art and literature. The Roman conquest of the Hellenistic East resulted in wholesale confiscation of Greek paintings and sculpture to grace Roman temples, public buildings, and private homes. Roman artists copied many aspects of Greek art, but their emphasis on realistic portraiture carried on a native tradition.

Fabius Pictor (second half of the third century B.C.), a senator, wrote the first *History of Rome* in Greek. Other Romans translated Greek classics into Latin. Still others, such as the poet Ennius (239–169 B.C.), the father of Latin poetry, studied Greek philosophy, wrote comedies in Latin, and adapted many of Euripides' tragedies for the Roman stage. Ennius also wrote a history of Rome in Latin verse. Plautus (ca 254–184 B.C.) specialized in rough humor. He, too, decked out Greek plays in Roman dress but was no mere imitator. The Roman dramatist Terence (ca 195–159 B.C.) wrote comedies of refinement and grace that owed their essentials to Greek models. His plays lacked the energy and the slapstick of Plautus's rowdy plays. All of early Roman literature was derived from the Greeks, but it managed in time to speak in its own voice and to flourish because it had something of its own to say.

The conquest of the Mediterranean world brought the Romans leisure, and Hellenism influenced how they spent their free time. During the second century B.C. the Greek custom of bathing became a Roman passion and an important part of the day. In the early republic Romans had bathed infrequently, especially in the winter. Now large buildings containing pools and exercise rooms went up in great numbers, and the baths became an essential part of the Roman city. Architects built intricate systems of aqueducts to supply the bathing establishments with water. Conservatives railed at this Greek custom, calling it a waste of time and an encouragement to idleness. But the baths were socially important places where men and women went to see and be seen. Social climbers tried to talk to the "right people" and wangle invitations to dinner; politicians took advantage of the occasion to discuss the affairs of the day.

Did Hellenism and new social customs corrupt the Romans? Perhaps the best answer is this: the Roman state and the empire it ruled continued to exist for six more centuries. Rome did not collapse; the state continued to prosper. The golden age of Roman literature was still before it. The high tide of Roman prosperity still lay in the future. The Romans did not like change but took it in stride. That was part of their practical turn of mind and their strength.

The Late Republic (133–31 B.C.)

The wars of conquest created serious problems for the Romans. Some of the most pressing were political. The republican constitution had suited the needs of a simple city-state but was inadequate to meet the requirements of Rome's new position in international affairs (see Map 7.2). Sweeping changes and reforms were necessary to make it serve the demands of empire. A system of provincial administration had to be established. Armies had to be provided for defense, and a system of tax collection had to be created.

Other political problems were equally serious. During the wars Roman generals commanded huge numbers of troops for long periods of time. Men such as Scipio Aemilianus were on the point of becoming too mighty for the state to control. Although Rome's Italian allies had borne much of the burden of the fighting, they received fewer rewards than did Roman officers and soldiers. Italians began to agitate for full Roman citizenship and a voice in politics.

There were serious economic problems, too. Hannibal's operations and the warfare in Italy had left the countryside a shambles. The movements of numerous armies had disrupted agriculture. The prolonged fighting had also drawn untold numbers of Roman and Italian men away from their farms for long periods. The families of these soldiers could not keep the land under full cultivation. The people who defended Rome and conquered the world for Rome became impoverished for having done their duty. These problems, complex and explosive, largely account for the turmoil of the closing years of the republic.

When the legionaries returned to their farms in Italy, they encountered an appalling situation. All too often their farms looked like the farms of the people they had conquered. Many thus chose to sell their holdings. The wars of conquest had made some men astoundingly rich. These men bought up small farms to create huge estates, which the Romans called *latifundia*. Most landless veterans migrated to the cities, especially to Rome. Although some found work, most did not. Industry and small manufacturing were generally in the hands of slaves. Even when there was work, slave labor kept the wages of free men low. This trend held ominous consequences for the strength of Rome's armies. Landless men, even if they were Roman veterans and lived in Rome, could not be conscripted into the army. A large pool of experienced manpower was going to waste.

The landless former legionaries wanted a new start, and they were willing to support any leader who would provide it. One man who recognized the plight of Rome's peasant farmers and urban

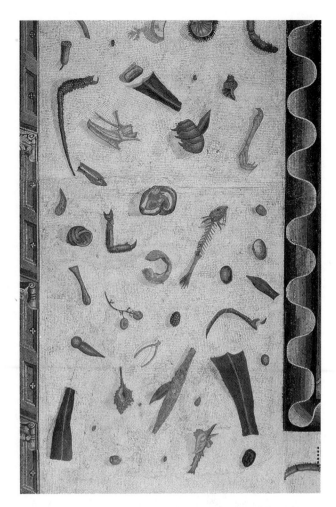

Roman Table Manners This mosaic is a floor that can never be swept clean. It whimsically suggests what a dining-room floor looked like after a lavish dinner, and it also tells something about the menu: a chicken head, a wishbone, remains of various seafoods, vegetables, and fruit are easily recognizable. *(Source: Museo Gregoria-Profano/Scala/Art Resource, NY)*

poor was an aristocrat, Tiberius Gracchus (163– 133 B.C.). Appalled by what he saw, Tiberius warned his countrymen that the legionaries were losing their land while fighting Rome's wars:

The wild beasts that roam over Italy have every one of them a cave or lair to lurk in. But the men who fight and die for Italy enjoy the common air and light, indeed, but nothing else. Houseless and homeless they wander about with their wives and children. And it is with lying lips that their generals exhort the soldiers in their battles to defend sepulchres and shrines from

THE ROMAN REPUBLIC

509 B.C.	Expulsion of the Etruscan king and founding of the Roman republic
471 B.C.	Plebeians win official recognition of their assembly, the *concilium plebis*
ca 450 B.C.	Law of the Twelve Tables
390 B.C.	The Gauls sack Rome
390–290 B.C.	Rebuilding of Rome Reorganization of the army Roman expansion in Italy
367 B.C.	Licinian-Sextian rogations
287 B.C.	Legislation of the *concilium plebis* made binding on entire population
282–146 B.C.	The era of overseas conquest
264–241 B.C.	First Punic War: Rome builds a navy, defeats Carthage, acquires Sicily
218–202 B.C.	Second Punic War: Scipio defeats Hannibal Rome dominates the western Mediterranean
200–148 B.C.	Rome conquers the Hellenistic east
149–146 B.C.	Third Punic War: savage destruction of Carthage
133–121 B.C.	The Gracchi introduce land reform Murder of the Gracchi by some senators
107 B.C.	Marius becomes consul and begins the professionalization of the army
91–88 B.C.	War with Rome's Italian allies
88 B.C.	Sulla marches on Rome and seizes dictatorship
79 B.C.	Sulla abdicates
78–27 B.C.	Era of civil war
60–49 B.C.	First Triumvirate: Pompey, Crassus, Julius Caesar
45 B.C.	Julius Caesar defeats Pompey's forces and becomes dictator
44 B.C.	Assassination of Julius Caesar
43–36 B.C.	Second Triumvirate: Marc Antony, Lepidus, Augustus
31 B.C.	Augustus defeats Antony and Cleopatra at Actium

the enemy, for not a man of them has an hereditary altar, not one of all these many Romans an ancestral tomb, but they fight and die to support others in luxury, and though they are styled masters of the world, they have not a single clod of earth that is their own.[4]

After his election as tribune of the people in 133 B.C., Tiberius proposed that public land be given to the poor in small lots. His was an easy and sensible plan, but it drew bitter resistance from many of the wealthy aristocrats who had usurped large tracts of public land for their own use. Violence broke out when a large body of senators killed Tiberius in cold blood. The death of Tiberius was the beginning of an era of political violence. In the end that violence would bring down the republic.

Although Tiberius was dead, his land bill became law. Furthermore, Tiberius's brother Gaius Gracchus (153–121 B.C.) took up the cause of reform. A veteran soldier with an enviable record and a fiery orator, Gaius also became tribune and demanded even more extensive reform than his brother. Gaius pushed legislation to provide the urban poor with cheap grain for bread. He proposed that Rome send many of its poor and propertyless people out to form colonies in southern Italy. The poor would have a new start and lead productive lives. As nonproductive families left for new opportunities abroad, Rome would be less crowded, sordid, and dangerous.

Gaius went a step further and urged that all Italians be granted full rights of Roman citizenship. This measure provoked a storm of opposition, and reactionary senators rose against Gaius Gracchus and murdered him and three thousand of his supporters. Once again the cause of reform had met with violence. Once again it was Rome's leading citizens who flouted the law.

In 107 B.C., Gaius Marius, an Italian "new man" (a politician not from the traditional Roman aristocracy), became consul. A man of fierce vigor and courage, Marius saw the army as the tool of his ambition. To prepare for war in North Africa against Jugurtha, a rebellious Numidian king, Marius reformed the Roman army. He took the unusual but not wholly unprecedented step of recruiting an army by permitting the landless to serve in the legions. Marius thus tapped Rome's vast reservoir of idle manpower. His volunteer army was a professional force, not a body of draftees, and in 106 B.C. it handily defeated Jugurtha.

There was, however, a disturbing side to Marius's reforms, one that later would haunt the republic. To encourage enlistments, Marius promised land to his volunteers after the war. Poor and landless veterans flocked to him, but when Marius proposed a bill to grant land to his veterans, the senate refused to act, in effect turning its back on the soldiers of Rome. This was a disastrous mistake. Henceforth, the legionaries expected their commanders—not the senate or the state—to protect their interests. By failing to reward the loyalty of Rome's troops, the senate set the stage for military rebellion and political anarchy.

Trouble was not long in coming. The senate's refusal to honor Marius's promises to his soldiers and a brief but bitter war between the Romans and their Italian allies over the issue of full citizenship (91–88 B.C.) set off serious political disturbances in Rome. In 88 B.C. the Roman general and conqueror Sulla (138–78 B.C.) marched on Rome with his army to put an end to the turmoil. Sulla made himself dictator, put his enemies to death, and confiscated their land. The constitution thus disrupted never was put back together effectively.

In 79 B.C. Sulla voluntarily abdicated his dictatorship and permitted the republican constitution to function once again. Yet dictatorship and civil war were to be the constant lot of Rome for the next fifty years. In the late republic the Romans were grappling with the simple and inescapable fact that their old city-state constitution was unequal to the demands of overseas possessions and the governing of provinces. Thus even Sulla's efforts to put the constitution back together proved hollow. Once the senate and other institutions of the Roman state had failed to come to grips with the needs of empire, once the authorities had lost control of their own generals and soldiers, and once the armies put their faith in commanders instead of in Rome, the republic was doomed.

The history of the late republic is the story of the power struggles of some of Rome's most famous figures: Julius Caesar and Pompey, Augustus and Marc Antony. One figure who stands apart is Cicero (106–43 B.C.), a practical politician whose greatest legacy to the Roman world and to Western civilization is his mass of political and oratorical writings.

Pompous, vain, and sometimes silly, Cicero was nonetheless one of the few men of the period to urge peace and public order. As consul in 63 B.C. he put down a conspiracy against the republic but

Julius Caesar This realistic bust of Caesar captures the power, intensity, and brilliance of the man. It is a study of determination and an excellent example of Roman portraiture. (*Source: Museo Nationale, Naples/Alinari/Art Resource, NY*)

sources, and both won the consulship. They dominated Roman politics until the rise of Julius Caesar, who became consul in 59 B.C. Together the three concluded a political alliance, the First Triumvirate, in which they agreed to advance one another's interests.

The man who cast the longest shadow over these troubled years was Julius Caesar (100–44 B.C.). More than a mere soldier, Caesar was a cultivated man. Born of a noble family, he received an excellent education, which he furthered by studying in Greece with some of the most eminent teachers of the day. He was also a shrewd politician of unbridled ambition. Since military service was an effective steppingstone to politics, Caesar launched his military career in Spain, where his courage won the respect and affection of his troops. Personally brave and tireless, Caesar was a military genius who knew how to win battles and turn victories into permanent gains. By 50 B.C. he had conquered all of Gaul (modern France). By 49 B.C. the First Triumvirate had fallen apart. Crassus had died in battle, and Caesar and Pompey, each suspecting the other of treachery, came to blows in a long and bloody civil war. Although Pompey enjoyed the official support of the government, Caesar finally defeated Pompey's forces in 45 B.C. He had overthrown the republic and made himself dictator.

Julius Caesar was not merely another victorious general. Politically brilliant, he was determined to make basic reforms, even at the expense of the old constitution. He took the first long step to break down the barriers between Italy and the provinces, extending citizenship to many of the provincials who had supported him. To cope with Rome's burgeoning population, Caesar sent his veterans and some eighty thousand of the poor and unemployed to colonies throughout the Mediterranean. Mostly located in Gaul, Spain, and North Africa, these colonies were important agents in spreading Roman culture in the western Mediterranean. A Roman empire composed of citizens, not subjects, was the result.

In 44 B.C. a group of conspirators assassinated Caesar and set off another round of civil war. Caesar had named his eighteen-year-old grandnephew, Octavian, as his heir. Octavian joined forces with two of Caesar's lieutenants, Marc Antony and Lepidus, in a pact known as the Second Triumvirate, and together they hunted down and defeated Caesar's murderers. In the process, however, Octavian

refused to use force to win political power. Instead, he developed the idea of "concord of the orders," an idealistic, probably unattainable balance among the elements that constituted the Roman state. Yet Cicero commanded no legions, and only legions commanded respect.

Sulla's real political heirs were Pompey and Julius Caesar. A man of boundless ambition, Pompey began his career as one of Sulla's lieutenants. After his army put down a rebellion in Spain, he himself threatened to rebel unless the senate allowed him to run for consul. He and another ambitious politician, Crassus, pooled political re-came into conflict with Antony, "boastful, arrogant, and full of empty exultation and capricious ambition."[5] Octavian painted lurid pictures of Antony lingering in the eastern Mediterranean, a romantic and foolish captive of the seductive Cleopatra, queen of Egypt and bitter enemy of Rome. In 31 B.C., with the might of Rome at his back, Octavian met and defeated the army and navy of Antony and Cleopatra at the Battle of Actium in Greece. Octavian's victory put an end to an age of civil war that had lasted since the days of Sulla. For this success, in 27 B.C. the senate voted Octavian the name *Augustus*.

THE PAX ROMANA

When Augustus put an end to the civil wars that had raged since 83 B.C., he faced monumental problems of reconstruction. He could easily have declared himself dictator, as Caesar had done, but the thought was repugnant to him. Augustus was neither an autocrat nor a revolutionary. His solution, as he put it, was to restore the republic. But was that possible? Some eighteen years of anarchy and civil war had shattered the republican constitution. From 29 to 23 B.C., Augustus toiled to heal Rome's wounds. The first problem facing him was to rebuild the constitution and the organs of government. Next he had to demobilize much of the army and care for the welfare of the provinces. Then he had to meet the danger of barbarians at Rome's European frontiers. Augustus was highly successful in meeting these challenges. His gift of peace to a war-torn world sowed the seeds of the empire's golden age.

Augustus's Settlement (31 B.C.–A.D. 14)

Augustus claimed that in restoring constitutional government he was also restoring the republic. Typically Roman, he preferred not to create anything new; he intended instead to modify republican forms and offices to meet new circumstances. Augustus expected the senate to administer some of the provinces, continue to be the chief deliberative body of the state, and act as a court of law. But he did not give the senate enough power to become his partner in government. As a result, the senate could not live up to the responsibilities that

Augustus assigned. Many of its prerogatives shifted by default to Augustus and his successors.

Augustus's own position in the restored republic was something of an anomaly. He could not simply surrender the reins of power, for someone else would have seized them. But how was he to fit into a republican constitution? Again Augustus had his own answer. He became *princeps civitatis,* the "first citizen of the state." This prestigious title carried no power; it indicated only that Augustus was the most distinguished of all Roman citizens. In effect, it designated Augustus as the first among

Augustus as Imperator Here Augustus, dressed in breastplate and uniform, emphasizes the imperial majesty of Rome and his role as *imperator.* The figures on his breastplate represent the restoration of peace, one of Augustus's greatest accomplishments and certainly one that he frequently stressed. *(Source: Alinari/Art Resource, NY)*

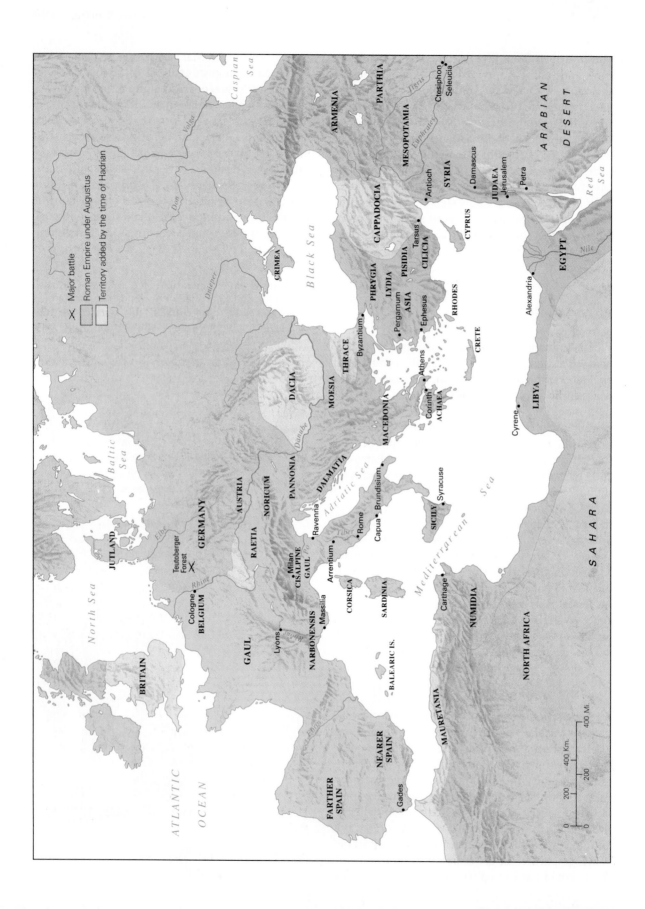

ATLANTIC OCEAN

North Sea

Baltic Sea

BRITAIN

JUTLAND

GERMANY

BELGIUM

Cologne

Teutoberger Forest ✕

GAUL

Lyons

NARBONENSIS

Massilia

NORICUM

RAETIA

AUSTRIA

PANNONIA

Milan

CISALPINE GAUL

Arrentium

Ravenna

Rome

Capua

DALMATIA

Adriatic Sea

Brundisium

Syracuse

SICILY

CORSICA

SARDINIA

BALEARIC IS.

Carthage

NUMIDIA

NORTH AFRICA

MAURETANIA

NEARER SPAIN

FARTHER SPAIN

Gades

Mediterranean Sea

SAHARA

DACIA

MOESIA

THRACE

Byzantium

MACEDONIA

Corinth

ACHAEA

Athens

Black Sea

CRIMEA

ARMENIA

PARTHIA

CAPPADOCIA

PHRYGIA

LYDIA

Pergamum

ASIA

Ephesus

PISIDIA

Tarsus

CILICIA

RHODES

CRETE

CYPRUS

MESOPOTAMIA

Ctesiphon

Seleucia

Antioch

SYRIA

Damascus

JUDAEA

Jerusalem

Petra

ARABIAN DESERT

Red Sea

EGYPT

Alexandria

LIBYA

Cyrene

Nile

Euphrates

Tigris

Volga

Don

Dnieper

Danube

Rhine

Elbe

Po

Tiber

Ebro

Caspian Sea

Legend:
✕ Major battle
Roman Empire under Augustus
Territory added by the time of Hadrian

400 Mi.

400 Km.

0 200 400

0 200

equals, a little "more equal" than anyone else in the state. His real power resided in the magistracies he held, in the powers granted him by the senate, and above all in his control of the army, which he turned into a permanent, standing organization.

What is to be made of Augustus's constitutional settlement? Despite his claims to the contrary, Augustus did not restore the republic. He created a constitutional monarchy, something completely new in Roman history. He was not exactly being a hypocrite, but he carefully kept his real military power in the background. As consul he had no more constitutional and legal power than his fellow consul. But in addition to the consulship, Augustus held many magistracies that his fellow consul did not hold. At first he held the consulship annually; then the senate voted him proconsular power on a regular basis. The senate also voted him *tribunicia potestas*—the "full power of the tribunes." Tribunician power gave Augustus the right to call the senate into session, present legislation to the people, and defend their rights. He held either high office or the powers of chief magistrate year in and year out. No other magistrate could do the same. Without specifically saying so, he had created the office of emperor, which included many traditional powers separated from their traditional offices.

Augustus's title as commander of the Roman army was *imperator,* with which Rome customarily honored a general after a major victory, and it came to mean "emperor" in the modern sense of the term. Augustus governed the provinces where troops were needed for defense. The frontiers were his special concern. There, Roman legionaries held the German barbarians at arm's length. Augustus made sure that Rome went to war only at his command. He controlled deployment of the Roman army and paid its wages. He granted it bonuses and gave veterans retirement benefits. To employ Rome's surplus of soldiers he also founded at least forty new colonies, which, like Julius Caesar's, were a significant tool in the spread of Roman culture. Thus he avoided the problems with the army

 MAP 7.3 Roman Expansion Under the Empire Augustus added vast tracts of Europe to the Roman Empire, which the emperor Hadrian later enlarged by assuming control over parts of central Europe, the Near East, and North Africa.

that the old senate had created for itself. Augustus never shared control of the army, and no Roman found it easy to defy him militarily.

Augustus, however, failed to solve a momentous problem. He never found a way to institutionalize his position with the army. The ties between the princeps and the army were always personal. The army was loyal to the princeps but not necessarily to the state. The Augustan principate worked well at first, but by the third century A.D. the army would make and break emperors at will. Nonetheless, it is a measure of Augustus's success that his settlement survived as long and as well as it did.

Administration and Expansion Under Augustus

To gain an accurate idea of the total population of the empire Augustus ordered a census to be taken in 28 B.C. In Augustus's day the population of the Roman Empire was between 70 million and 100 million people, fully 75 percent of whom lived in the provinces. In the areas under his immediate jurisdiction, Augustus put provincial administration on an orderly basis and improved its functioning. Believing that the cities of the empire should look after their own affairs, he encouraged local self-government and urbanism. Augustus respected local customs and ordered his governors to do the same.

As a spiritual bond between the provinces and Rome, Augustus encouraged the cult of Roma, goddess and guardian of the state. In the Hellenistic East, where king-worship was an established custom, the cult of *Roma et Augustus* (Rome and Augustus) grew and spread rapidly. Augustus then introduced it in the West. By the time of his death in A.D. 14, nearly every province in the empire could boast an altar or shrine to Roma et Augustus. In the West it was not the person of the emperor who was worshiped but his *genius*—his guardian spirit. In praying for the good health and welfare of the emperor, Romans and provincials were praying for the empire itself. The cult became a symbol of Roman unity.

For the history of Western civilization one of the most momentous aspects of Augustus's reign was Roman expansion into the wilderness of northern and western Europe (Map 7.3). Carrying on Caesar's work, Augustus pushed Rome's frontier into the region of modern Germany.

Augustus began his work in the west and north by completing the conquest of Spain. In Gaul, apart from minor campaigns, most of his work was peaceful. He founded twelve new towns, and the Roman road system linked new settlements with one another and with Italy. But the German frontier, along the Rhine River, was the scene of hard fighting. In 12 B.C. Augustus ordered a major invasion of Germany beyond the Rhine. In 9 A.D. Augustus's general Varus lost some twenty thousand troops at the Battle of the Teutoburger Forest. Thereafter the Rhine remained the Roman frontier.

Meanwhile, more successful generals extended the Roman standards as far as the Danube. Roman legions penetrated the area of modern Austria, southern Bavaria, and western Hungary. The regions of modern Serbia, Bulgaria, and Romania fell. Within this area the legionaries built fortified camps. Roads linked these camps with one another, and settlements grew up around the camps. Amid the vast expanse of forests, Roman towns, trade, language, and law began to exert a civilizing influence on the barbarians. Many military camps became towns, and many modern European cities owe their origins to the forts of the Roman army. For the first time, the barbarian north came into direct, immediate, and continuous contact with Mediterranean culture. The arrival of the Romans often provoked resistance from barbarian tribes that simply wanted to be left alone. In other cases, the prosperity and wealth of the new Roman towns lured barbarians eager for plunder. The Romans maintained peaceful relations with the barbarians whenever possible, but Roman legions remained on the frontier to repel hostile barbarians. The result was the evolution of a consistent, systematic frontier policy.

Literary Flowering

The Augustan settlement's gift of peace inspired a literary flowering unparalleled in Roman history. Augustus and many of his friends actively encouraged poets and writers. Horace, one of Rome's finest poets, offered his own opinion of Augustus and his era:

With Caesar Augustus the guardian of the state
Not civil rage nor violence shall drive out peace,
Nor wrath which forges swords
And turns unhappy cities against each other.[6]

To a generation that had known only vicious civil war, Augustus's settlement was an unbelievable blessing.

The tone and ideal of Roman literature, like that of the Greeks, was humanistic and worldly. Roman poets and prose writers celebrated the dignity of humanity and the range of its accomplishments. They stressed the physical and emotional joys of a comfortable, peaceful life. Their works were highly polished, elegant in style, and intellectual in conception. Roman poets referred to the gods often and treated mythological themes, but always the core of their work was human, not divine.

Virgil (70–19 B.C.), Rome's greatest poet, celebrated the new age in the *Georgics,* a poetic work on agriculture in four books. Virgil delighted in his own farm, and his poems sing of the pleasures of peaceful farm life. The poet also tells how to keep bees, grow grapes and olives, plow, and manage a farm. A sensitive man who delighted in simple things, Virgil left in his *Georgics* a charming picture of life in the Italian countryside during a period of peace.

Virgil's masterpiece is the *Aeneid,* an epic poem that is the Latin equivalent of the Greek *Iliad* and *Odyssey.* Virgil's account of the founding of Rome and the early years of the city gave final form to the legend of Aeneas, the Trojan hero who escaped to Italy at the fall of Troy. The principal Roman tradition held that Romulus was the founder of Rome, but the legend of Aeneas was known as early as the fifth century B.C. Virgil linked the legends of Aeneas and Romulus and preserved them both; in so doing, he connected Rome with Greece's heroic past. He also mythologized later aspects of Roman history. Recounting the story of Aeneas and Dido, the queen of Carthage, Virgil made their ill-fated love affair the cause of the Punic wars. But, above all, the *Aeneid* is the expression of Virgil's passionate belief in Rome's greatness. It is a vision of Rome as the protector of the good and noble against the forces of darkness and disruption.

The poet Ovid shared Virgil's views of the simple pleasures of life and also celebrated the popular culture of the day. In his *Fasti* (ca A.D. 8) he takes a personal approach to discuss and explain the ordinary festivals of the Roman year, festivals that most Romans took for granted. Without his work the modern world would be much the poorer in its knowledge of the popular religion of imperial Rome. For instance, he tells his readers that on a journey to Rome he encountered a white-robed

✿ **Ara Pacis**   This scene from the Ara Pacis, the Altar of Peace, celebrates Augustus's restoration of peace and the fruits of peace. Here Mother Earth is depicted with her children. The cow and the sheep under the goddess represent the prosperity brought by peace, especially the agricultural prosperity so highly cherished by Virgil. *(Source: Art Resource, NY)*

crowd in the middle of the road. A priest and farmers were performing an annual festival. Ovid stopped to ask the priest what was happening. The priest explained that they were sacrificing to Mildew, not a farmer's favorite goddess. By burning the offerings the priest and his friends asked the goddess to be so content with them that she would not attack the crops. He further asked her not to attack the farmer's tools but to be satisfied with swords and other weapons of iron. He reminded her that "there is no need for them; the world lives in peace."[6] In his poetry Ovid, like Virgil, celebrated the pax Romana, while giving a rare glimpse of ordinary Roman life.

In its own way Livy's history of Rome, entitled simply *Ab Urbe Condita (From the Founding of the City),* is the prose counterpart of the *Aeneid.* Livy (59 B.C.–A.D. 17) received training in Greek and Latin literature, rhetoric, and philosophy. He even

urged the future emperor Claudius to write history. Livy loved and admired the heroes and great deeds of the republic, but he was also a friend of Augustus and a supporter of the principate. He especially approved of Augustus's efforts to restore republican virtues.

The poet Horace (65–8 B.C.) rose from humble beginnings to friendship with Augustus. The son of a former slave and a tax collector, Horace nonetheless received an excellent education. He loved Greek literature and finished his education in Athens. After Augustus's victory he returned to Rome and became Virgil's friend. Horace happily turned his pen to celebrating Rome's newly won peace and prosperity. One of his finest odes commemorates Augustus's victory over Cleopatra at Actium in 31 B.C. Cleopatra is depicted as a frenzied queen, drunk with desire to destroy Rome. Horace saw in Augustus's victory the triumph of

West over East, of simplicity over excess. One of the truly moving aspects of Horace's poetry, like Virgil's and Ovid's, is his deep and abiding gratitude for the pax Romana.

For Rome, Augustus's age was one of hope and new beginnings. Augustus had put the empire on a new foundation. Constitutional monarchy was firmly established, and government was to all appearances a partnership between princeps and senate. The Augustan settlement was a delicate structure, and parts of it would in time be discarded. Nevertheless, it worked, and by building on it later emperors would carry on Augustus's work.

The solidity of Augustus's work became obvious at his death in A.D. 14. Since the principate was not technically an office, Augustus could not legally hand it to a successor. Augustus had recognized this problem and long before his death had found

a way to solve it. He shared his consular and tribunician powers with his adopted son, Tiberius, thus grooming him for the principate. In his will Augustus left most of his vast fortune to Tiberius, and the senate formally requested Tiberius to assume the burdens of the principate. Formalities apart, Augustus had succeeded in creating a dynasty.

 ## THE COMING OF CHRISTIANITY

During the reign of the emperor Tiberius (r. A.D. 14–37), perhaps in A.D. 29, Pontius Pilate, prefect of Judaea, the Roman province created out of the Jewish kingdom of Judah, condemned Jesus of Nazareth to death. Jesus lived in a troubled time,

Pontius Pilate and Jesus   This Byzantine mosaic from Ravenna illustrates a dramatic moment in Jesus' trial and crucifixion. Jesus stands accused before Pilate, and Pilate symbolically washes his hands of the whole affair. *(Source: Scala/Art Resource, NY)*

when Roman rule aroused hatred and unrest among the Jews. This climate of hostility formed the backdrop of Jesus' life and his ministry.

The entry of Rome into Jewish affairs was anything but peaceful. The civil wars that destroyed the republic wasted the prosperity of Judaea and the entire eastern Mediterranean world. Jewish leaders took sides in the fighting, and Judaea suffered its share of ravages and military confiscations. Peace brought little satisfaction to the Jews. Although Augustus treated Judaea generously, the Romans won no popularity by making Herod king of Judaea (ca 73–4 B.C.). King Herod gave Judaea prosperity and security, but the Jews hated his acceptance of Greek culture. He was also a bloodthirsty prince who murdered his own wife and sons. At his death the Jews broke out in revolt. For the next ten years Herod's successor waged almost constant war against the rebels. Added to the horrors of civil war were years of crop failure, which caused famine and plague.

At length the Romans intervened to restore order. Augustus put Judaea under the charge of a prefect answerable directly to the emperor. Religious matters and local affairs became the responsibility of the *Sanhedrin,* the highest Jewish judicial body. Although many prefects in Judaea tried to perform their duties scrupulously and conscientiously, many others were rapacious and indifferent to Jewish culture. Especially hated were the Roman tax collectors, called "publicans," many of whom pitilessly gouged the Jews. *Publicans* and *sinners*—the words became synonymous. Clashes between Roman troops and Jewish guerrillas inflamed the anger of both sides.

Among the Jews two movements spread. First was the rise of the Zealots, extremists who worked and fought to rid Judaea of the Romans. Resolute in their worship of Yahweh, they refused to pay any but the tax levied by the Jewish temple. Their battles with the Roman legionaries were marked by savagery on both sides. The second movement was the growth of militant apocalyptic sentiment—the belief that the coming of the Messiah was near. This belief was an old one among the Jews. But by the first century A.D. it had become more widespread and fervent than ever before. Typical was the Apocalypse of Baruch, which foretold the Messiah's appearance and the destruction of the Roman Empire, after which the Messiah would inaugurate a period of happiness and plenty for the Jews.

As the ravages of war became more widespread and conditions worsened, more and more people prophesied the imminent coming of the Messiah. One such was John the Baptist, "the voice of one crying in the wilderness, Prepare ye the way of the lord."[7] The sect described in the Dead Sea Scrolls readied itself for the end of the world. Its members were probably Essenes, who shared possessions, precisely as John the Baptist urged people to do. This sect also made military preparations for the day of the Messiah.

Jewish religious aspirations were only one part of the story, for Christianity was born into the pagan world of Rome and its empire. The term *pagans* refers to all those who believed in the Greco-Roman gods. Paganism at the time of Jesus' birth can be broadly divided into three types: the official state religion of Rome, the traditional Roman cults of hearth and countryside, and the new mystery religions that flowed from the Hellenistic East. The official state religion and its cults honored the traditional deities: Jupiter, Juno, Mars, and such newcomers as Isis (see page 161). This very formal religion of ritual and grand spectacle provided little emotional or spiritual comfort for the people. The state cults were a bond between the gods and the people, a religious contract to ensure the well-being of Rome.

For emotional and spiritual satisfaction, many Romans observed the old cults of home and countryside. These traditional cults brought the Romans back in touch with nature and with something elemental to Roman life. Particularly popular were rustic shrines—often a small building or a sacred tree in an enclosure—to honor the native spirit of the locality. Though familiar and simple, even this traditional religion was not enough for many. They wanted something more personal and immediate.

Many people in the Roman Empire found the answer to their need for emotionally satisfying religion and spiritual security in the various Hellenistic mystery cults (see pages 160–161). The appeal of the mystery religions was not simply that they provided emotional release. They gave their adherents what neither the traditional cults nor philosophy could—above all, security. But the mystery religions were by nature exclusive, and none was truly international, open to everyone.

Into this climate of Roman religious yearning, political severity, fanatical Zealotry, and messianic hope came Jesus of Nazareth (ca 5 B.C.–A.D. 29).

He was raised in Galilee, stronghold of the Zealots. Yet Jesus himself was a man of peace. Jesus urged his listeners to love God as their father and one another as God's children.

Jesus' teachings were Jewish. He declared that he would change not one jot of the Jewish law. His major deviation from orthodoxy was his insistence that he taught in his own name, not in the name of Yahweh. Was he then the Messiah? A small band of followers thought so, and Jesus claimed that he was. But Jesus had his own conception of the Messiah. Jesus would not destroy the Roman Empire. He told his disciples flatly that they were to "render unto Caesar the things that are Caesar's." Jesus would establish a spiritual kingdom, not an earthly one. Repeatedly he told his disciples that his kingdom was "not of this world," but one of eternal happiness in a life after death.

Of Jesus' life and teachings the prefect Pontius Pilate knew little and cared even less. All that concerned him was the maintenance of peace and order. The crowds following Jesus at the time of the Passover, a highly emotional time in the Jewish year, alarmed Pilate, who faced a volatile situation. Some Jews believed that Jesus was the long-awaited Messiah. Others were disappointed because he refused to preach rebellion against Rome. Still others hated and feared Jesus and wanted to be rid of him. The last thing Pilate wanted was a riot. These were the problems on Pilate's mind when Jesus stood before him. Jesus as king of the Jews did not worry him. The popular agitation surrounding Jesus did. To avert riot and bloodshed, Pilate condemned Jesus to death. It is a bitter historical irony that such a gentle man died such a cruel death. After being scourged, he was hung from a cross until he died in the sight of family, friends, enemies, and the merely curious.

Once Pilate's soldiers had carried out the sentence, the entire matter seemed to be closed. Then on the third day after Jesus' crucifixion, an odd rumor began to circulate in Jerusalem. Some of Jesus' followers were saying he had risen from the dead, while others accused them of having stolen his body. For the earliest Christians and for generations to come, the resurrection of Jesus became a central element of faith—and more than that, a promise: Jesus had triumphed over death, and his resurrection promised all Christians immortality.

In Jerusalem, meanwhile, the tumult subsided. Jesus' followers lived quietly and peacefully, unmolested by Roman or Jew. Pilate had no quarrel with them. Judaism already had many minor sects. Peter (d. A.D. 67?), the first of Jesus' followers, became the head of a sect that continued to observe Jewish law and religious customs. A man of traditional Jewish beliefs, Peter felt Jesus' teachings were meant exclusively for the Jews. Only in their practices of baptism and the Lord's Supper (the Eucharist) did the sect differ from normal Jewish custom.

Christianity might have remained a purely Jewish sect had it not been for Paul of Tarsus (A.D. 5?–67?). Questions about the conversion of Hellenized Jews and of Gentiles (non-Jews) to Christianity caused the sect grave problems. Were the Gentiles subject to the law of Moses? If not, was Christianity to have two sets of laws? The answer to these questions was Paul's momentous contribution to Christianity. Paul was unlike Jesus or Peter. Born in a thriving, busy city filled with Romans, Greeks, Jews, Syrians, and others, he was at home in the world of Greco-Roman culture. After his conversion to Christianity, he taught that his native Judaism was the preparation for the Messiah and that Jesus by his death and resurrection had fulfilled the prophecy of Judaism and initiated a new age. Paul taught that Jesus was the son of God, the giver of a new law, and he preached that Jesus' teachings were to be proclaimed to all, whether Jew or Gentile. Paul thus made a significant break with Judaism, Christianity's parent religion, for Judaism was exclusive and did not usually seek converts.

Paul's influence was far greater than that of any other early Christian. He traveled the length and breadth of the eastern Roman world, spreading his doctrine and preaching of Jesus. To little assemblies of believers in cities as distant as Rome and Corinth, he taught that Jesus had died to save all people. Paul's vision of Christianity won out over Peter's traditionalism. Christianity broke with Judaism and embarked on its own course.

What was Christianity's appeal to the Roman world? What did this obscure sect give people that other religions did not? Christianity possessed many different attractions. One of its appeals was its willingness to embrace both men and women, slaves and nobles. Many of the Eastern mystery religions with which Christianity competed were exclusive in one way or another, permitting only men or only Greeks and Romans to become devotees, for example.

Nevertheless, Christianity had many features in common with mystery religions (see pages 160–

161). Once people had prepared themselves for conversion by learning of Jesus' message and committing themselves to live by it, they were baptized. Like initiates in mystery religions, they entered a community of believers. The Christian community of believers was strengthened by the sacrament of the Eucharist, the communal celebration of the Lord's Supper. Like the mystery religions, Christianity had a priesthood to officiate at rituals, and offered adherents the promise of salvation. Christians believed that Jesus on the cross had defeated evil and that he would reward his followers with eternal life after death. Christianity also offered the possibility of forgiveness. Human nature was weak, and even the best Christians would fall into sin. But Jesus loved sinners and forgave those who repented. In its doctrine of salvation and forgiveness alone, Christianity had a powerful ability to give solace and strength to believers.

Christianity was attractive to many because it gave the Roman world a cause. Hellenistic philosophy had attempted to make men and women self-sufficient: people who became indifferent to the outside world could no longer be hurt by it. That goal alone ruled out any cause except the attainment of serenity. The Romans, never innovators in philosophy, merely elaborated this lonely and austere message. Instead of passivity, Christianity stressed the ideal of striving for a goal. Each and every Christian, no matter how poor or humble, supposedly worked to realize the triumph of Christianity on earth. This was God's will, a sacred duty for every Christian. By spreading the word of Christ, Christians played their part in God's plan. No matter how small, the part each Christian played was important. Since this duty was God's will, Christians believed that the goal would be achieved. The Christian was not discouraged by temporary setbacks, believing Christianity to be invincible.

Christianity gave its devotees a sense of community. No Christian was alone. All members of the Christian community strove toward the same goal of fulfilling God's plan. Each individual community was in turn a member of a greater community. And that community, the Church General, was indestructible.

So Christianity's attractions were many, from forgiveness of sin to an exalted purpose for each individual. Its insistence on the individual's importance gave solace and encouragement, especially to the poor and meek. Its claim to divine protection fed hope in the eventual success of the Christian community. Christianity made participation in the universal possible for everyone. The ultimate reward promised by Christianity was eternal bliss after death.

THE GOLDEN AGE

For fifty years after Augustus's death the dynasty that he established—known as the Julio-Claudians because they were all members of the Julian and Claudian clans—provided the emperors of Rome. Some of the Julio-Claudians, including Caligula and Nero, were weak and frivolous men who exercised their power stupidly and brought misery to the empire. But others, such as Tiberius and Claudius, were sound rulers and able administrators who were responsible for some notable achievements. During their reigns the empire largely prospered.

One of the most momentous achievements of the Julio-Claudians was Claudius's creation of an imperial bureaucracy composed of professional administrators. The numerous duties and immense responsibilities of the emperor prompted Claudius to delegate power. He began by giving the freedmen of his household official duties, especially in finances. It was a simple, workable system, and Claudius's innovations enabled the emperor to rule the empire more easily and efficiently.

In A.D. 68 Nero's inept rule led to military rebellion and his death, thus opening the way for widespread disruption. In A.D. 69, four men claimed the position of emperor. Roman armies in Gaul, on the Rhine, and in the East marched on Rome to make their commanders emperor. The man who emerged triumphant was Vespasian, commander of the eastern armies, who entered Rome in 70 and restored order.

By establishing the Flavian Dynasty (named after his clan), Vespasian turned the principate into an open and admitted monarchy. The Flavians (A.D. 69–96) carried on Augustus's work on the frontiers, gave the Roman world peace, and kept the legions in line. Their work paved the way for the era of the "five good emperors," the golden age of the empire (A.D. 96–180).

Beginning in the second century A.D., the era of the five good emperors was a period of almost unparalleled prosperity for the empire. Wars generally

✳ **Scene from Trajan's Column**   From 101 to 107 Trajan fought the barbarian tribes along the Danube. With remarkable realism, a feature of Roman art, this scene portrays Roman soldiers building fieldworks outside a city. *(Source: Ancient Art & Architecture Collection)*

ended in victories and were confined to the frontiers. The five good emperors—Nerva, Trajan, Hadrian, Antoninus Pius, and Marcus Aurelius—were among the noblest, most dedicated, ablest men in Roman history.

Under the Flavians the principate became a full-blown monarchy, and by the time of the five good emperors the principate was an office with definite rights, powers, and prerogatives. In the years between Augustus and the era of the five good emperors, the emperor had become an indispensable part of the imperial machinery. In short, without the emperor the empire would quickly have fallen to pieces. Augustus had been monarch in fact but not in theory; during their reigns, the five good emperors were monarchs in both.

The five good emperors were not power-hungry autocrats. The concentration of power was the result of empire. The easiest and most efficient way

to run the Roman Empire was to invest the emperor with vast powers. Furthermore, Roman emperors on the whole proved to be effective rulers and administrators. As capable and efficient emperors took on new tasks and functions, the emperor's hand was felt in more areas of life and government. The five good emperors were benevolent and exercised their power intelligently, but they were absolute kings all the same. Lesser men would later throw off the façade of constitutionality and use this same power in a despotic fashion.

One of the most significant changes in Roman government since Augustus's day was the enormous growth of the imperial bureaucracy created by Claudius. Hadrian, who became emperor in A.D. 117, reformed this system by putting the bureaucracy on an organized, official basis. He established imperial administrative departments to handle the work formerly done by imperial freedmen.

Hadrian also separated civil service from military service. Men with little talent or taste for the army could instead serve the state as administrators. Hadrian's bureaucracy demanded professionalism from its members. Administrators made a career of the civil service. These innovations made for more efficient running of the empire and increased the authority of the emperor—the ruling power of the bureaucracy.

The Roman army had also changed since Augustus's time. The Roman legion had once been a mobile unit, but its duties under the empire no longer called for mobility. The successors of Augustus generally called a halt to further conquests. The army was expected to defend what had already been won. Under the Flavian emperors (A.D. 69–96), the frontiers became firmly fixed. Forts and watch stations guarded the borders. Behind the forts the Romans built a system of roads that allowed the forts to be quickly supplied and reinforced in times of trouble. The army had evolved into a garrison force, with legions guarding specific areas for long periods.

The personnel of the legions was also changing. Italy could no longer supply all the recruits needed for the army. Increasingly, only the officers came from Italy and from the more Romanized provinces. The legionaries were mostly drawn from the less civilized provinces, especially the ones closest to the frontiers. In the third century A.D. the barbarization of the army would result in an army indifferent to Rome and its traditions. In the era of the five good emperors, however, the army was still a source of economic stability and a Romanizing agent. Men from the provinces and even barbarians joined the army to learn a trade and to gain Roman citizenship. Even so, the signs were ominous. Veterans from Julius Caesar's campaigns would hardly have recognized Hadrian's troops as Roman legionaries.

❖ LIFE IN THE GOLDEN AGE: IMPERIAL ROME AND THE PROVINCES

Many people, both ancient and modern, have considered these years one of the happiest epochs in Western history. But popular accounts have also portrayed Rome as already decadent by the time of the five good emperors. If Rome was decadent, who kept the empire running? For that matter, can life in Rome itself be taken as representative of life in other parts of the empire? Rome was unique and must be seen as such. Rome no more resembled a provincial city like Cologne than New York resembles Keokuk, Iowa. Only when the uniqueness of Rome is understood in its own right can one turn to the provinces to obtain a full and reasonable picture of the empire under the five good emperors.

Rome was truly an extraordinary city, especially by ancient standards. It was enormous, with a population somewhere between 500,000 and 750,000. Although it could boast of stately palaces, noble buildings, and beautiful residential areas, most people lived in jerrybuilt apartment houses. Fire and crime were perennial problems even after Augustus created fire and urban police forces. Streets were narrow, and drainage was inadequate. During the republic, sanitation had been a common problem. Numerous inscriptions record prohibitions against dumping human refuse and even cadavers on the grounds of sanctuaries and cemeteries. Under the empire this situation improved. By comparison with medieval and early modern European cities, Rome was a healthy enough place to live.

Rome was such a huge city that the surrounding countryside could not feed it. Because of the danger of starvation, the emperor, following republican practice, provided the citizen population with free grain for bread and, later, oil and wine. By feeding the citizenry, the emperor prevented bread riots caused by shortages and high prices. For the rest of the urban population who did not enjoy the rights of citizenship, the emperor provided grain at low prices. This measure was designed to prevent speculators from forcing up grain prices in times of crisis. By maintaining the grain supply, the emperor kept the favor of the people and ensured that Rome's poor and idle did not starve.

The emperor also entertained the Roman populace, often at vast expense. The most popular forms of public entertainment were gladiatorial contests and chariot racing. Gladiatorial fighting was originally an Etruscan funerary custom, a blood sacrifice for the dead. Many gladiators were criminals; some were the slaves of gladiatorial trainers; others were prisoners of war. Still others were free men who volunteered for the arena. Even women at times engaged in gladiatorial combat. Although some Romans protested gladiatorial fighting, most delighted in it. Not until the fifth century did Christianity put a stop to it.

The Romans were even more addicted to chariot racing than to gladiatorial shows. Under the empire, four permanent teams competed against one another. Each had its own color—red, white, green, or blue. Some Romans claimed that people cared more about their favorite team than about the race itself. Two-horse and four-horse chariots ran a course of seven laps, about five miles. A successful driver could be the hero of the hour. One charioteer, Gaius Appuleius Diocles, raced for twenty-four years. During that time he drove 4,257 starts and won 1,462 of them. His admirers honored him with an inscription that proclaimed him champion of all charioteers.

But people like the charioteer Diocles were no more typical of the common Roman than Babe Ruth is of the average American. Ordinary Romans left their mark in the inscriptions that grace their graves. They were proud of their work and accomplishments, affectionate toward their families and friends, and eager to be remembered after death. The funerary inscription of Paprius Vitalis to his wife is particularly engaging: "If there is anything good in the lower regions—I, however, finish a poor life without you—be happy there too, sweetest Thalassia . . . married to me for 40 years."[8]

The personal philosophies of typical Romans have come down from antiquity: "All we who are dead below have become bones and ashes, but nothing else."[9] "I was, I am not, I don't care." "To each his own tombstone." These Romans went about their lives as people have always done. Though fond of brutal spectacles, they also had their loves and dreams.

In the provinces and even on the frontiers, the era of the five good emperors was one of extensive prosperity, especially in western Europe. The Roman army had beaten back the barbarians and exposed them to the civilizing effects of Roman traders. The resulting peace and security opened Britain, Gaul, Germany, and the lands of the Danube to immigration. Agriculture flourished as large tracts of land came under cultivation. Most of this land was in the hands of free tenant farmers. From the time of Augustus slavery had declined in the empire, as had the growth of latifundia (see page 185). Augustus and his successors encouraged the rise of free farmers. Under the five good emperors this trend continued, and the holders of small parcels of land throve as never before. The emperors provided loans on easy terms to farmers, enabling them to rent land previously worked by slaves. They also permitted them to cultivate the new lands that were being opened up. Consequently, the small tenant farmer was becoming the backbone of Roman agriculture.

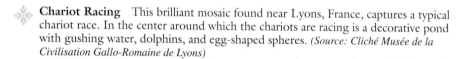

Chariot Racing   This brilliant mosaic found near Lyons, France, captures a typical chariot race. In the center around which the chariots are racing is a decorative pond with gushing water, dolphins, and egg-shaped spheres. (*Source: Cliché Musée de la Civilisation Gallo-Romaine de Lyons*)

In continental Europe the army was largely responsible for the new burst of expansion. The areas where legions were stationed readily became Romanized. When legionaries retired from the army, they often settled where they had served. Since they had usually learned a trade in the army, they brought essential skills to areas that badly needed trained men. These veterans took their retirement pay and used it to set themselves up in business.

The eastern part of the empire also participated in the boom. The Roman navy had swept the sea of pirates, and Eastern merchants traded throughout the Mediterranean. The flow of goods and produce in the East matched that of the West. Venerable cities like Corinth, Antioch, and Ephesus flourished as rarely before. The cities of the East built extensively, bedecking themselves with new amphitheaters, temples, fountains, and public buildings. For the East this age was the heyday of the city. Life there grew ever richer and more comfortable.

Trade among the provinces increased dramatically. Britain and Belgium became prime grain producers, much of their harvests going to the armies of the Rhine. Britain's wool industry probably got its start under the Romans. Italy and southern Gaul produced wine in huge quantities. Roman colonists had introduced the olive to southern Spain and northern Africa, an experiment so successful that these regions produced most of the oil consumed in the Western empire. In the East, Syrian farmers continued to cultivate the olive, and oil production reached an all-time high. Egypt was the prime grain producer of the East, and tons of Egyptian wheat went to feed the Roman populace. The Roman army in Mesopotamia consumed a high percentage of the raw materials and manufactured products of Syria and Asia Minor. The spread of trade meant the end of isolated and self-contained economies. By the time of the five good emperors, the empire had become an economic as well as a political reality (Map 7.4).

One of the most striking features of this period was the growth of industry in the provinces. Cities in Gaul and Germany eclipsed the old Mediterranean manufacturing centers. Italian cities were particularly hard hit by this development. Cities like Arretium and Capua had dominated the production of glass, pottery, and bronze ware. Yet in the second century A.D., Gaul and Germany took over the pottery market. Lyons in Gaul and later Cologne became the new center of the glassmaking industry. The cities of Gaul were nearly unrivaled in the manufacture of bronze and brass. For the first time in history, northern Europe was able to rival the Mediterranean as a producer of manufactured goods. Europe had entered fully into the economic and cultural life of the Mediterranean world.

The age of the five good emperors was generally one of peace, progress, and prosperity. The work of the Romans in northern and western Europe was a permanent contribution to the history of Western society. This period was also one of consolidation. Roads and secure sea lanes linked the empire in one vast web. The empire had become a commonwealth of cities, and urban life was its hallmark.

ROME AND THE EAST

Their march to empire and their growing interest in foreign peoples brought the Romans into contact with a world much larger than Europe and the Mediterranean. As early as the late republic, Roman commanders in the East encountered peoples who created order out of the chaos left by Alexander the Great and his Hellenistic successors. This meeting of West and East had two immediate effects. The first was a long military confrontation between the Romans and their Iranian neighbors. Second, Roman military expansion to the east coincided with Chinese expansion to the west, and the surprising result was a period when the major ancient civilizations of the world were in touch with one another. For the first time in history, peoples from the Greco-Roman civilization of the Mediterranean and peoples from central Asia, India, and China met one another and observed one another's cultures at first hand.

Romans Versus Iranians

When Roman armies moved into Mesopotamia in 92 B.C., they encountered the Parthians, a people who had entered the Iranian Plateau from central Asia in the time of the Persian kings. The disintegration of Alexander's eastern holdings enabled them to reap the harvest of his victory. They created an empire that once stretched from Armenia and Babylonia in the west to the Hellenistic kingdom of Bactria in the east (Map 7.5). They divided

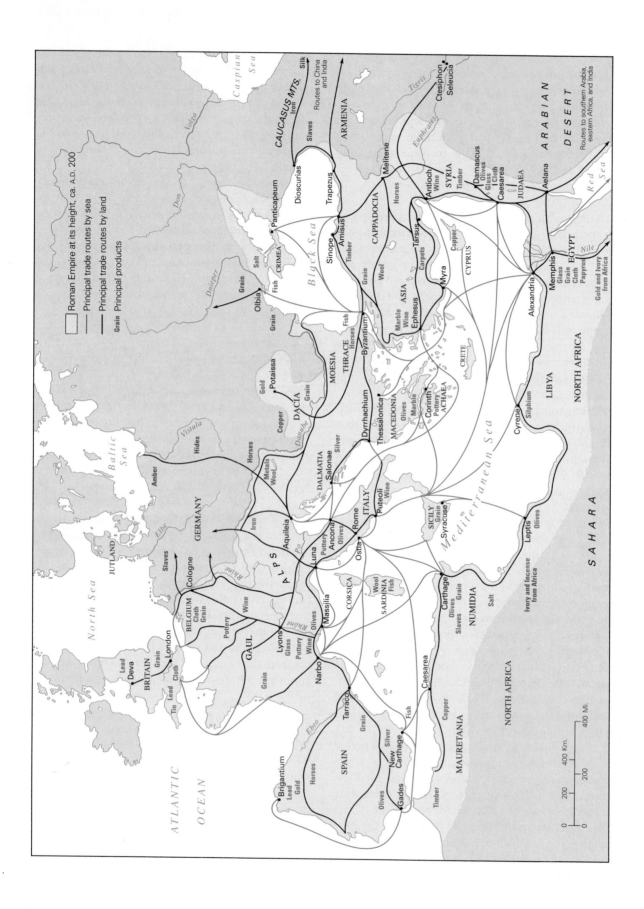

Roman Empire at its height, ca. A.D. 200

Principal trade routes by sea
Principal trade routes by land
Grain Principal products

their realm into large provinces, or *satrapies,* and created a flexible political organization to administer their holdings. Unlike China, however, Parthia never had a sophisticated bureaucracy. Nonetheless, the loose provincial organization enabled the Parthians to govern the many different peoples who inhabited their realm. The Romans marveled at Parthia's success, as the Greek geographer Strabo (ca 65 B.C.–A.D. 19) attests:

and now they rule so much territory and so many people that they have become in a way rivals of the Romans in the greatness of their empire.[10]

In the process the Parthians won their place in history as the heirs of the Persian Empire.

Although Augustus sought peace with the Parthians, later Roman emperors, beginning with Nero in A.D. 58, struggled to wrest Armenia and Mesopotamia from them. Until their downfall in 226, the Parthians met the Roman advance to the east with iron and courage.

The Romans found nothing to celebrate in the eclipse of the Parthians, for their place was immediately taken by the Sassanids, a people indigenous to southern Iran. As early as 230 the Sassanids launched a campaign to the west, which the Romans blunted. The setback was only temporary, for in 256 the great Persian king Shapur overran Mesopotamia and the Roman province of Syria. Four years later Shapur defeated the legions of the emperor Valerian, whom he took prisoner. Thereafter, the Romans and Sassanids fought long, bitter, and destructive wars in western Asia as the Romans battled to save their eastern provinces. Not until the reigns of Diocletian and Constantine was Roman rule again firmly established in western Asia.

Trade and Contact

Although warfare between Roman emperors and Iranian kings disrupted western Asia, it did not

prevent Iran from becoming a link between East and West. Iran's geographical position facilitated communications and trade between the Roman and Chinese empires, the two wealthiest and most commercially active realms in the ancient world. As the middlemen in this trade, the Parthians tried to keep the Chinese and Romans from making direct contact—and thus from learning how large a cut the Parthians took in commercial transactions.

An elaborate network of roads linked Parthia to China in the east, India in the south, and the Roman Empire in the west. The many branch roads even included routes to southern Russia. The most important of the overland routes was the Silk Road, named for the shipments of silk that passed from China through Parthia to the Roman Empire (see Map 7.5). Many other luxury items also passed along this route: the Parthians exported exotic fruits, rare birds, ostrich eggs, and other dainties to China in return for iron and delicacies like apricots. Other easily portable luxury goods included gems, gold, silver, spices, and perfumes. From the Roman Empire came glassware, statuettes, and slaves trained as jugglers and acrobats.

Rarely did a merchant travel the entire distance from China to Mesopotamia. Chinese merchants typically sold their wares to Parthians at the Stone Tower, located at modern Tashkurghan in Afghanistan. From there Parthian traders carried goods across the Iranian Plateau to Mesopotamia or Egypt. This overland trade fostered urban life in Parthia as cities arose and prospered along the caravan routes. In the process, the Parthians themselves became important consumers of goods, contributing to the volume of trade and reinforcing the commercial ties between East and West.

More than goods passed along these windswept roads. Ideas, religious lore, and artistic inspiration also traveled the entire route. A fine example of how ideas and artistic influences spread across long distances is a Parthian coin that caught the fancy of an artist in China. The coin bore an inscription—a practice the Parthians had adopted from the Greeks—and although the artist could not read it, he used the lettering as a motif on a bronze vessel. Similarly, thoughts, ideas, and literary works found ready audiences; Greek plays were performed at the court of the Parthian king. At a time when communication was difficult and often dangerous, trade routes were important avenues for the spread of knowledge about other societies.

✳ **MAP 7.4 The Economic Aspect of the Pax Romana** The Roman Empire was not only a political and military organization but also an intricate economic network through which goods from Armenia and Syria were traded for Western products from as far away as Spain and Britain.

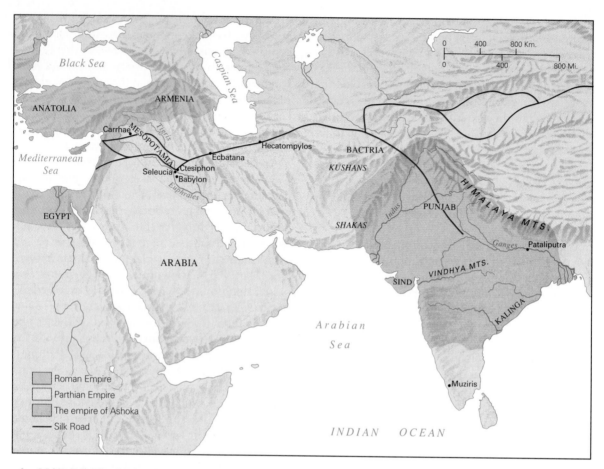

MAP 7.5 The Major Empires of Central and Southern Asia, ca 250 B.C. From Anatolia in the West to the Himalayas in the East, three great empires ruled western, central, and southern Asia. During these years, frontiers fluctuated, but the Silk Road served as a thread connecting them all.

This was also an era of exciting maritime exploration. Roman ships sailed from Egyptian ports to the mouth of the Indus River, where they traded local merchandise and wares imported by the Parthians. Merchants who made the voyage had to contend with wind, shoal waters, and pirates. Despite such dangers and discomforts, hardy mariners pushed into the Indian Ocean and beyond, reaching Malaya, Sumatra, and Java.

Direct maritime trade between China and the West began in the second century A.D. The period of this contact coincided with the era of Han greatness in China. It was the Han emperor Wu Ti who took the momentous step of opening the Silk Road to the Parthian Empire. Indeed, a later Han emperor sent an ambassador directly to the Roman Empire by sea. The ambassador, Kan Ying, sailed to the Roman province of Syria, where during the reign of the Roman emperor Nerva (96–98) he became the first Chinese official to have a firsthand look at the Greco-Roman world. Kan Ying enjoyed himself thoroughly, and in A.D. 97 delivered a fascinating report of his travels to his emperor:

The inhabitants of that country are tall and well-proportioned, somewhat like the Chinese, whence they are called Ta-ts'in. The country contains much gold, silver, and rare precious stones . . . corals, amber, glass . . . gold embroidered rugs and thin silk-cloth and asbestos cloth. All the rare gems of other foreign countries come from there. They make coins of gold and silver. Ten units of silver are worth one of gold. They traffic by sea with An-hsi (Parthia) and Tien-chu (India), the profit of which trade is ten-fold. They are honest in their transactions and there are no double prices. Cereals are always cheap. . . . Their kings always desired to send embassies to China, but the An-hsi (Parthians) wished to carry on trade with them in Chinese silks, and it is for this reason that they were cut off from communication.[11]

The sea route and to a lesser extent the Silk Road included India in this long web of communications that, once established, was never entirely broken.

THE EMPIRE IN CRISIS

The era of the five good emperors gave way to a period of chaos and stress. During the third century A.D. the Roman Empire was stunned by civil wars and barbarian invasions. By the time peace was restored, the economy was shattered, cities had shrunk in size, and agriculture was becoming manorial. In the disruption of the third century and the reconstruction of the fourth, the medieval world had its origins.

Civil Wars and Invasions in the Third Century

After the death of Marcus Aurelius, the last of the five good emperors, his son Commodus, a man totally unsuited to govern the empire, came to the throne. His misrule led to his murder and a renewal of civil war. After a brief but intense spasm of fighting, the African general Septimius Severus defeated other rival commanders and established the Severan Dynasty (A.D. 193–235). Although Septimius Severus was able to stabilize the empire, his successors proved incapable of disciplining the legions. When the last of the Severi was killed by one of his own soldiers, the empire plunged into still another grim, destructive, and this time prolonged round of civil war.

Over twenty different emperors ascended the throne in the forty-nine years between 235 and 284, and many rebels died in the attempt to seize power. So many military commanders seized rule that the middle of the third century has become known as the age of the barracks emperors. The Augustan principate had become a military monarchy, and that monarchy was nakedly autocratic.

The first and most disastrous result of the civil wars was trouble on the frontiers. It was Rome's misfortune that this era of anarchy coincided with immense movements of barbarian peoples, still another example of the effects of mass migrations in ancient history, this time against one of the best organized empires of antiquity. Historians still dispute the precise reason for these migrations, though their immediate cause was pressure from tribes moving westward across Asia. In the sixth century A.D., Jordanes, a Christianized Goth, preserved the memory of innumerable wars among the barbarians in his *History of the Goths*. Goths fought Vandals; Huns fought Goths. Steadily the defeated and displaced tribes moved toward the Roman frontiers. Finally, like "a swarm of bees"— to use Jordanes's image—the Goths, one such people, burst into Europe in A.D. 258.

When the barbarians reached the Rhine and Danube frontiers, they often found huge gaps in the Roman defenses. During much of the third century A.D., bands of Goths devastated the Balkans as far south as Greece. The Alamanni, a German people, at one point entered Italy and reached Milan before they were beaten back. Meanwhile, the Franks, still another German folk, invaded eastern and central Gaul and northeastern Spain. Saxons from Scandinavia sailed into the English Channel in search of loot. In the East the Sassanids overran Mesopotamia. If the Roman army had been guarding the borders instead of creating and destroying emperors, none of these invasions would have been possible. The barracks emperors should be credited with one accomplishment, however: they fought barbarians when they were not fighting one other. Only that kept the empire from total ruin.

Reconstruction Under Diocletian and Constantine (A.D. 284–337)

At the close of the third century A.D., the emperor Diocletian (r. 284–305) put an end to the period of turmoil. Repairing the damage done in the third century was the major work of the emperor Constantine (r. 306–337) in the fourth. But the price was high.

Under Diocletian, the princeps became *dominus*—"lord." The emperor claimed that he was "the elect of God"—that he ruled because of God's favor. Constantine even claimed to be the equal of Jesus' first twelve followers.

No mere soldier but rather an adroit administrator, Diocletian gave serious thought to the

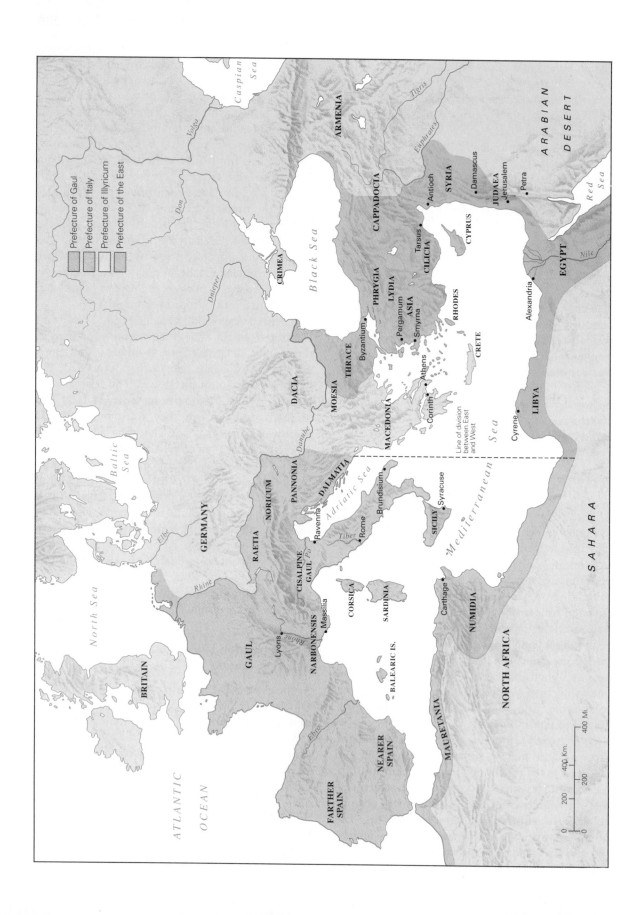

Prefecture of Gaul
Prefecture of Italy
Prefecture of Illyricum
Prefecture of the East

ATLANTIC OCEAN

North Sea

Baltic Sea

Caspian Sea

Black Sea

Mediterranean Sea

Adriatic Sea

Red Sea

BRITAIN

GERMANY

GAUL

NARBONENSIS
Lyons
Massilia

RAETIA

NORICUM

CISALPINE GAUL

PANNONIA

DALMATIA

Ravenna
Rome
Tiber

CORSICA

SARDINIA

BALEARIC IS.

FARTHER SPAIN

NEARER SPAIN

MAURETANIA

NORTH AFRICA

NUMIDIA

Carthage

SICILY
Syracuse
Brundisium

MACEDONIA

Corinth
Athens

MOESIA

DACIA

THRACE
Byzantium

CRIMEA

Volga

Don

Dnieper

Danube

Rhine

Elbe

Rhône

Ebro

Tiber

ARMENIA

CAPPADOCIA

PHRYGIA
LYDIA
ASIA
Pergamum
Smyrna

CILICIA
Tarsus

RHODES

CRETE

CYPRUS

Antioch
SYRIA
Damascus
JUDAEA
Jerusalem
Petra

ARABIAN DESERT

EGYPT
Alexandria
Nile

LIBYA
Cyrene

SAHARA

Euphrates

Tigris

Line of division between East and West

0   200   400 Km.
0   200   400 Mi.

empire's ailments. He recognized that the empire and its difficulties had become too great for one man to handle. He also realized that during the third century provincial governors had frequently used their positions to foment or participate in rebellions. To solve the first of these problems, Diocletian divided the empire into a western and an eastern half (Map 7.6). Diocletian assumed direct control of the eastern part; he gave the rule of the western part to a colleague, along with the title *augustus,* which had become synonymous with *emperor.* Diocletian and his fellow augustus further delegated power by appointing two men to assist them. Each man was given the title *caesar* to indicate his exalted rank. Although this system is known as the *Tetrarchy* because four men ruled the empire, Diocletian was clearly the senior partner and final source of authority.

Each half of the empire was further split into two prefectures, each governed by a prefect responsible to an augustus. Diocletian reduced the power of the old provincial governors by dividing provinces into smaller units. He organized the prefectures into small administrative units called *dioceses,* which were in turn subdivided into small provinces. Provincial governors were also deprived of their military power, retaining only their civil and administrative duties.

Diocletian's political reforms were a momentous step. The Tetrarchy soon failed, but Diocletian's division of the empire into two parts became permanent. Constantine and later emperors tried hard but unsuccessfully to keep the empire together. Throughout the fourth century A.D., the eastern and the western sections drifted apart. In later centuries the western part witnessed the fall of Roman government and the rise of barbarian kingdoms, while the eastern empire evolved into the majestic Byzantine Empire.

The most serious immediate matters confronting Diocletian and Constantine were economic, social, and religious. They needed additional revenues to support the army and the imperial court. Yet the wars and the barbarian invasions had caused widespread destruction and poverty. The fighting had struck a serious blow to Roman agriculture, which the emperors tried to revive. Christianity had become too strong either to ignore or to crush. The responses to these problems by Diocletian, Constantine, and their successors helped create the economic and social patterns that medieval Europe inherited.

The barracks emperors had dealt with economic hardship by depreciating the currency, cutting the silver content of coins until money was virtually worthless. As a result, the entire monetary system fell into ruin. In Egypt, governors had to order bankers to accept imperial money. The immediate result was crippling inflation throughout the empire.

The empire was less capable of recovery than in earlier times. Wars and invasions had disrupted normal commerce and the means of production and had hit the cities especially hard. Markets were disrupted, and travel became dangerous. Craftsmen, artisans, and traders rapidly left devastated regions. Cities were no longer places where trade and industry thrived. The devastation of the countryside increased the difficulty of feeding and supplying the cities. So extensive was the destruction that many wondered whether the ravages could be repaired at all.

The response of Diocletian and Constantine to these problems was marked by compulsion, rigidity, and loss of individual freedom. Diocletian's attempt to curb inflation illustrates the methods of absolute monarchy. In a move unprecedented in Roman history, he issued an edict that fixed maximum prices and wages throughout the empire. The measure proved a failure because it was unrealistic as well as unenforceable.

With the monetary system in ruins, most imperial taxes became payable in kind—that is, in goods or produce instead of money. The major drawback of payment in kind is its demands on transportation. Goods have to be moved from where they are grown or manufactured to where they are needed. Accordingly, the emperors locked into their occupations all people involved in the growing, preparation, and transportation of food and essential commodities. A baker or shipper could not go into any other business, and his son took up the trade at his death. The late Roman Empire had a place for everyone, and everyone had a place.

❄ **MAP 7.6 The Roman World Divided** Diocletian divided the Roman Empire into a western and an eastern half. This development foreshadowed the medieval division between the Latin West and the Byzantine East.

✤ **Diocletian's Tetrarchy** The emperor Diocletian's attempt to reform the Roman Empire by dividing rule among four men is represented in this sculpture, which in many features illustrates the transition from ancient to medieval art. The four tetrarchs demonstrate their solidarity by clasping one another on the shoulder. Nonetheless, each man has his other hand on his sword—a gesture that proved prophetic when Diocletian's reign ended and another struggle for power began. *(Source: Alinari/Art Resource, NY)*

The late Roman heritage to medieval Europe is most evident in agriculture. During the third century A.D., many free tenant farmers were killed or abandoned farms that had been ravaged in the fighting. Consequently, large tracts of land lay deserted. Great landlords with ample resources began to reclaim land and amass the huge estates that were the forerunners of medieval manors. In return for the protection and security that landlords could offer, free men and their families became the landlords' clients. To ensure a steady supply of labor for themselves, the landlords bound the free men to the soil. Henceforth they worked their patrons' land, not their own, and could not move elsewhere. Free men and women were in effect becoming serfs.

The Acceptance of Christianity

In religious affairs Constantine took the decisive step of recognizing Christianity as a legitimate religion. No longer would Christians suffer persecution for their beliefs as they had occasionally experienced earlier. Constantine himself died a Christian in 337. Why had the pagans persecuted Christians in the first place? Polytheism is by nature tolerant of new gods and accommodating in religious matters. Why was Christianity singled out for violence? These questions are still matters of scholarly debate, but some broad answers can be given.

A splendid approach to these problems has come from the eminent Italian scholar Marta Sordi.[12] Confronting a very complicated topic, she offers evidence that the Christians exaggerated the degree of pagan hostility to them and that most of the gory stories about the martyrs are fictitious. There were indeed some cases of pagan persecution of the Christians, but with few exceptions they were local and sporadic. Even Nero's notorious persecution was temporary and limited to Rome. No constant persecution of Christians occurred. Instead, pagans and Christians alike enjoyed long periods of tolerance and even friendship. Nonetheless, some pagans thought that Christians were atheists because they scorned the traditional pagan gods. Christians in fact either denied the existence of pagan gods or called them evil spirits. They went so far as to urge people not to worship pagan gods. In turn, pagans, who believed in their gods as fervently as the Christians believed in their one god, feared that the gods would withdraw their favor from the Roman Empire because of Christian blasphemy.

At first many pagans genuinely misunderstood Christian practices and rites. Even educated and cultured people like the historian Tacitus opposed Christianity because they saw it as a bizarre new sect. Tacitus believed that Christians hated the whole human race. As a rule, early Christians kept to themselves. Romans distrusted and feared their exclusiveness, which seemed unsociable and even subversive. They thought the Lord's Supper, at

ROMAN HISTORY AFTER AUGUSTUS

Period	Important Emperors	Significant Events
Julio-Claudians 27 B.C.–A.D. 68	Augustus, 27 B.C.–A.D. 14 Tiberius, 14–37 Caligula, 37–41 Claudius, 41–54 Nero, 54–68	Augustan settlement Beginning of the principate Birth and death of Jesus Expansion into northern and Western Europe Creation of the imperial bureaucracy
Year of the Four Emperors 68–69	Nero Galba Otho Vitellius	Civil war Major breakdown of the concept of the principate
Flavians 69–96	Vespasian, 69–79 Titus, 79–81 Domitian, 81–96	Growing trend toward the concept of monarchy Defense and further consolidation of the European frontiers
Antonines 96–192	Nerva, 96–98 Trajan, 98–117 Hadrian, 117–138 Antoninus Pius, 138–161 Marcus Aurelius, 161–180 Commodus, 180–192	The "golden age"—the era of the "five good emperors" Economic prosperity Trade and growth of cities in northern Europe Beginning of barbarian menace on the frontiers
Severi 193–235	Septimius Severus, 193–211 Caracalla, 211–217 Elagabalus, 218–222 Severus Alexander, 222–235	Military monarchy All free men within the empire given Roman citizenship
"Barracks Emperors" 235–284	Twenty-two emperors in forty-nine years	Civil war Breakdown of the empire Barbarian invasions Severe economic decline
Tetrarchy 284–337	Diocletian, 284–305 Constantine, 306–337	Political recovery Autocracy Legalization of Christianity Transition to the Middle Ages in the West Birth of the Byzantine Empire in the East

which Christians said that they ate and drank the body and blood of Jesus, was an act of cannibalism. Pagans also thought that Christians indulged in immoral and indecent rituals. They considered Christianity one of the worst of the Eastern mystery cults, for one of the hallmarks of many of those cults was disgusting rituals.

Another source of misunderstanding was that the pagans did not demand that Christians *believe* in pagan gods. Greek and Roman religion was never a matter of belief or ethics. It was purely a religion of ritual. One of the clearest statements of pagan theological attitudes comes from the Roman senator Symmachus in the later fourth century A.D.:

We watch the same stars; heaven is the same for us all; the same universe envelops us: what importance is it in what way anyone looks for truth? It is impossible to arrive by one route at such a great secret.[13]

Yet Roman religion was inseparable from the state. An attack on one was an attack on the other. The Romans were being no more fanatical or intolerant than the eighteenth-century English judge who declared the Christian religion part of the law of the land. All the pagans expected was performance of the ritual act, a small token of sacrifice. Those Christians who sacrificed went free, no matter what they personally believed.

As time went on, pagan hostility decreased. Pagans realized that Christians were not working to overthrow the state and that Jesus was no rival of Caesar. The emperor Trajan forbade his governors to hunt down Christians. Trajan admitted that he thought Christianity an abomination, but he preferred to leave Christians in peace.

The stress of the third century, however, seemed to some emperors the punishment of the gods. What else could account for such anarchy? With the empire threatened on every side, a few emperors thought that one way to appease the gods was by offering them the proper sacrifices. Such sacrifices would be a sign of loyalty to the empire, a show of Roman solidarity and religious piety. Consequently, a new wave of persecutions began out of desperation. Although the Christians depicted the emperor Diocletian as a fiend, he persecuted them in the hope that the gods would restore their blessings on Rome. Yet even these persecutions were never very widespread or long-lived; most pagans were not greatly sympathetic to the new round of persecutions. Pagan and Christian alike must have been relieved when Constantine legalized the Christian religion.

In time the Christian triumph would be complete. In 380 the emperor Theodosius made Christianity the official religion of the Roman Empire. At that point Christians began to persecute the pagans for their beliefs. History had come full circle.

The Construction of Constantinople

The triumph of Christianity was not the only event that made Constantine's reign a turning point in Roman history. Constantine took the bold step of building a new capital for the empire. Constantinople, the New Rome, was constructed on the site of Byzantium, an old Greek city on then Bosporus. Throughout the third century, emperors had found Rome and the West hard to defend. The eastern part of the empire was more easily defensible and escaped the worst of the barbarian devastation. It was wealthy and its urban life still vibrant. Moreover, Christianity was more widespread in the East than in the West, and the city of Constantinople was intended to be a Christian center.

SUMMARY

The Romans conquered the Mediterranean world only to find that conquest required them to change their way of life. Politically, their city-state constitution broke down and expired in the wars of the republic. Even so, men like Caesar and later Augustus sought new solutions to the problems confronting Rome. The result was a system of government capable of administering an empire with justice and fairness. Out of the failure of the republic arose the pax Romana of the empire.

The Roman Empire created by Augustus nearly collapsed before being restored by Diocletian and Constantine. Constantine's legalization and patronage of Christianity and his shift of the capital from Rome to Constantinople marked a new epoch in Western history as the ancient world gave way to the medieval. In the process the Roman Empire came into direct contact with its Asian neighbors, sometimes in anger but more often in peace. Never before in Western history and not again until modern times did one state govern so much territory for so long a time.

The true heritage of Rome is its long tradition of law and freedom. Under Roman law and government, the empire enjoyed relative peace and security for extensive periods of time. Through Rome the best of ancient thought and culture was preserved to make its contribution to modern life. Perhaps no better epitaph for Rome can be found than the words of Virgil:

While rivers shall run to the sea,
While shadows shall move across the valleys of
  mountains,
While the heavens shall nourish the stars,
Always shall your honor and your name and your
  fame endure.[14]

NOTES

1. Polybius, *The Histories* 1.1.5. Unless otherwise credited, all quotations from a foreign language in this chapter have been translated into English by John Buckler.
2. Sallust, *War with Catiline* 10.1–3.
3. Ovid, *Fasti* 2.535–539.
4. Plutarch, *Life of Tiberius Gracchus* 9.5–6.
5. Plutarch, *Life of Antony* 2.8.
6. Horace, *Odes* 4.15.
7. Matthew 3:3.
8. *Corpus Inscriptionum Latinarum,* vol. 6 (Berlin: G. Reimer, 1882), no. 9792.
9. Ibid., vol. 6, no. 14672.
10. Strabo, 11.9.2.
11. Quoted in W. H. Schoff, *The Periplus of the Erythraean Sea* (London: Longmans, Green, 1912), p. 276.
12. See M. Sordi, *The Christians and the Roman Empire,* trans. A. Bedini (Norman: University of Oklahoma Press, 1986).
13. Symmachus, *Relations* 3.10.
14. Virgil, *Aeneid* 1.607–609.

SUGGESTED READING

R. T. Ridley, *The History of Rome* (1989), is an undogmatic history of Rome, firmly based in the sources. The Etruscans have inspired a great deal of work, most notably M. Pallottino, *A History of Earliest Italy* (1991), which treats the entire period of early relations among peoples; E. Gabba, *Dionysius and the History of Archaic Rome* (1991), is the study of the origins of Rome. J. F. Gardner, *Being a Roman Citizen* (1993), is a broad work that includes material on former slaves, the lower classes, and much else. S. L. Dyson, *The Creation of the Roman Frontier* (1985), deals with the process by which the Romans established their frontiers. See also E. S. Gruen, *Culture and National Identity in Republican Rome* (1992).

A. M. Eckstein's *Senate and Generals* (1987) discusses how the decisions of individual generals affected both the senate and Roman foreign relations.

K. D. White, *Roman Farming* (1970), deals with agriculture. Work on Roman social history has advanced in several areas. A wealth of research on the Roman family and related topics has recently appeared, including K. R. Bradley, *Discovering the Roman Family* (1990), a series of essays on Roman social history; S. Dixon, *The Roman Family* (1992); S. Treggiari, *Roman Marriage* (1991); and R. A. Baumann, *Women and Politics in Ancient Rome* (1992). E. Eyben, *Restless Youth in Ancient Rome* (1993), explores the mores of youth of the upper class.

Some good general treatments of the empire include J. Wacher, ed., *The Roman World,* 2 vols. (1987), which attempts a comprehensive survey of the world of the Roman Empire.

R. MacMullen, *Enemies of the Roman Order* (1993), treats the ways in which the Romans dealt with alien and sometimes hostile behavior within the empire. V. Rudich, *Political Dissidence Under Nero* (1993), provides an unorthodox treatment of the subject that examines the reasons behind some popular rejections of official policy. D. J. Breeze and B. Dobson, *Roman Officers and Frontiers* (1993), analyze the careers of officers and how they defended the frontiers.

The commercial life of the empire is the subject of M. Rostovtzeff, *The Economic and Social History of the Roman Empire* (1957). J. Rich, *The City in Late Antiquity* (1992), traces the influence of late Roman cities on their medieval successors.

Social aspects of the empire are the subject of L. A. Thompson, *Romans and Blacks* (1989). J. Humphrey, *Roman Circuses and Chariot Racing* (1985), treats a topic very dear to the hearts of ancient Romans. C. A. Barton, *The Sorrows of the Ancient Romans* (1993), is an intriguing attempt to understand the Roman fascination with gladiatorial games. K. R. Bradley, *Slaves and Masters in the Roman Empire* (1988), discusses social controls in a slaveholding society.

Christianity, paganism, Judaism, and the ways in which they all met have received much attention of A. Chester, *The Social Context of Early Christianity* (1989). Jesus and the history of early Christianity are the subjects of much recent scholarship. In general, see J. T. Burtchaell, *From Synagogue to Church* (1992); related is J. Lieu, ed., *The Jews Among Pagans and Christians* (1992), which explores relations among all three sets of beliefs. More dramatic perhaps are J. D. Crossan, *The Historical Jesus* (1991); J. Meier, *A Marginal Jew* (1992); and *The Lost Gospel* (1993), which studies "The Book of Q" and its relation to Christian origins. F. R. Trombley, *Hellenic Religion and Christianization, c. 370–529,* 2 vols. (1993), is an excellent examination of how Greek religion influenced the development of Christianity in the eastern parts of the later Roman Empire.

New treatments of two of the most important Augustan poets are C. Kallendorf, ed., *Virgil* (1993), and W. S. Anderson, ed., *Ovid* (1993).

S. N. C. Lieu and M. Dodgeon, *Rome's Eastern Frontier, A.D. 226–363* (1988), rely primarily on documents to trace Rome's policy in the East during this difficult period. R. MacMullen, *Constantine* (1988), written by a leading scholar in the field, provides a broad and lucid interpretation of Constantine and the significance of his reign.

LISTENING TO THE
PAST

Popular Roman Views of Religion and Magic

Magic and enchantment have been constant factors wherever people have lived. Rome was no exception. A common aspect of Roman popular culture was the curse tablet. People who were particularly angry with someone often went to a professional sorcerer, who listened to their complaints and then wrote their curses on thin lead tablets and wrapped the tablets around nails. The curses were considered binding, and the various gods that were invoked were expected to carry them out. In return, the gods received payment for inflicting the curse.

People often called down the wrath of the gods on troublesome neighbors or commercial rivals. Many other curses involved love gone wrong. The first of the following three examples is one of them. For reasons that are left unstated, a woman calls down all sorts of catastrophes on her husband or lover, Plotius. The aggrieved party in this case makes it dramatically clear what she expects from Proserpina, the wife of Pluto, both gods of the underworld. The woman also invokes the help of Cerberus, the hound that guarded the gates of Hades. We do not know the fate of Plotius.

O wife of Pluto, good and beautiful Proserpina (unless I ought to call you Salvia), pray tear away from Plotius health, body, complexion, strength, faculties. Consign him to Pluto your husband. May he be unable to avoid this by devices of his. Consign that man to the fourth-day, the third-day, the every-day fever [malaria]. May they wrestle and wrestle it out with him, overcome and overwhelm him unceasingly until they tear away his life. So I consign him as victim to you Proserpina, unless, O Proserpina, unless I ought to call you Goddess of the Lower World. Send, I pray, someone to call up the three-headed dog [Cerberus] with request that he may tear out Plotius' heart. Promise Cerberus that you will give him three offerings—dates, dried figs,

and a black pig—if he has fulfilled his task before the month of March. All these, Proserpina Salvia, will I give you when you have made me master of my wish. I give you the head of Plotius, slave of Avonia. O Proserpina Salvia, I give you Plotius' forehead, Proserpina Salvia, I give you Plotius' eyebrows, Proserpina Salvia, I give you Plotius' eyelids. Proserpina Salvia, I give you Plotius' eye-pupils. Proserpina Salvia, I give you Plotius' nostrils, his ears, nose, and his tongue and teeth so that Plotius may not be able to utter what it is that gives him pain; his neck, shoulders, arms, fingers, so that he may not be able to help himself at all; his chest, liver, heart, lungs, so that he may not be able to feel what gives him pain; his abdomen, belly, navel, sides, so that he may not be able to sleep; his shoulder-blades, so that he may not be able to sleep well; his sacred part, so that he may not be able to make water; his buttocks, vent, thighs, knees, legs, shins, feet, ankles, soles, toes, nails, that he may not be able to stand by his own aid. Should there so exist any written curse, great or small—in what manner Plotius has, according to the laws of magic, composed any curse and entrusted it to writing, in such manner I consign, hand over to you, so that you may consign and hand over that fellow in the month of February. Blast him! damn him! blast him utterly! Hand him over, consign him, that he may not be able to behold, see, and contemplate any month further!

Curses and enchantments were not limited to love affairs. The following one concerns the next day's chariot race in Rome. The person invoking the curse was certainly not betting on Eucherius the charioteer and his horses.

I conjure you up, holy beings and holy names; join in aiding this spell, and bind, enchant, thwart, strike, overturn, conspire against, destroy, kill, break, Eucherius, the charioteer, and all his horses tomorrow in the circus at Rome. May he not leave the barriers well; may he not be quick in the contest; may he not outstrip anyone; may he not make the turns well; may he not win any prizes; and if he has pressed someone hard, may he not come off the victor; and if he follows some-one from behind, may he not overtake him; but may he meet with an accident; may he be bound; may he be broken; may he be dragged along by your power, in the morning and afternoon races. Now! Now! Quickly! Quickly!

The next curse is that of an outraged person who was the victim of a thief. The person calls on Hermes and other deities to catch the thief. The text is filled with unintelligible words—mumbo jumbo—that supposedly have magical powers.

I call you, Hermes, immortal god, who cuts a furrow down Olympus, and who [presides over] the sacred boat, O light-bringer Iao, the great ever-living, terrible to behold and terri-ble to hear, give up the thief whom I seek. Aberamentho oulerthe xenax sonelueothene-mareba. This spell is to be said twice at the purification. The spell of bread and cheese. Come to me, lisson maternamau, erte, prep-tektioun, intiki, ous, olokotous, periklusai, bring to me that which is lost, and make the thief manifest on this very day. And I invoke Hermes, the discoverer of thieves, and the sun and the eye-pupils of the sun, the two bringers-to-light of unlawful deeds, and Jus-tice, and Errinys, and Ammon, and Param-mon, to seize the throat of the thief and to manifest him this very day, at the present hour. The ceremony: the same spell [as that] pronounced at the purification. Take a flush-green vessel and put water in it and myrrh, and the herb cynocephalium, and dipping in it a branch of laurel, sprinkling each person with the water, take a tripod and place it upon an altar of earth. . . . Offer myrrh and frankin-cense and a frog's tongue, and taking some unsalted winter wheat and goat's cheese, give these to each, pronouncing the spell at length. "Lord Iao, light-bearer, give up the thief whom I seek." And if any of them does not swallow what was given him, that one is the thief.

❋ Curse tablet from the Roman temple at Uley in Gloucestershire, England. *(Source: Courtesy of the Trustees of the British Museum)*

Questions for Analysis

1. Given the many forms of curses and the common use of these tablets, what social functions did curse tablets serve in Roman society?

2. Does the fact that Romans resorted to these curses mean that they considered magic more powerful than formal religion? Why or why not?

3. What do the tablets tell us about the com-mon culture of the Romans?

Source: Slightly adapted from N. Lewis and M. Rein-hold, *Roman Civilization,* 2 vols. (New York: Harper & Row, 1966), vol. 1, pp. 479–480; vol. 2, pp. 569–570.

CHAPTER

8

The Making of Europe

Interior (view from the apse) of the Byzantine church San Vitale, Ravenna, 526–7 A.D. *(Source: Scala/Art Resource, NY)*

The five centuries between approximately 400 and 900 present a paradox. They witnessed the disintegration of the Western Roman Empire, which had been one of humanity's great political and cultural achievements. But they were also a creative and seminal period during which Europeans laid the foundations for medieval and modern Europe. It is not overstatement to say that this period saw the making of Europe.

The basic ingredients that went into the making of a distinctly European civilization were the cultural legacy of Greece and Rome, the customs and traditions of the Germanic peoples, and the Christian faith. The most important of these was Christianity. It absorbed and assimilated the other two. It reinterpreted the classics in a Christian sense. It instructed the Germanic peoples and gave them new ideals of living and social behavior. Christianity became the cement that held European society together.

During this period the Byzantine Empire, centered at Constantinople, served as a protective buffer between Europe and peoples to the east. The Byzantine Greeks and the Muslims (see Chapter 9) preserved the philosophical and scientific texts of the ancient world, which later formed the basis for study in science and medicine. The Byzantines also produced a great synthesis of Roman law, Justinian's *Code*. Living an urbane and sophisticated life at Constantinople, the Greeks set a standard far above the primitive existence of the West.

- How did the Greco-Roman heritage, Germanic traditions, and the Christian faith act on one another?
- How did they lead to the making of Europe?
- What influence did Byzantine culture have on the making of Europe?

This chapter will focus on these questions.

❋ THE GROWTH OF THE CHRISTIAN CHURCH

As we have seen, Christianity was a syncretic faith, absorbing and adapting many of the religious ideas of the eastern Mediterranean world. From Judaism came the concept, unique in the ancient world, of monotheism—belief in one God—together with the rich ethical and moral precepts of the Old Testament Scriptures. From Orphism, a set of sixth-century B.C. religious ideas, came the belief that the body is the prison of the soul. From Hellenistic thought came the notion of the superiority of spirit over matter. Likewise, scholars have noticed the similarity between the career of Jesus and that of the gods of Eastern mystery cults (see page 160).

While many elements of the Roman Empire disintegrated, the Christian church survived and grew. What is the church? Scriptural scholars tell us that the earliest use of the word *church* (in Greek, *ekklesia*) in the New Testament appears in Saint Paul's Letter to the Christians of Thessalonica in northern Greece, written about A.D. 51. By *ekklesia* Paul meant the local community of Christian believers. In Paul's later letters, the term *church* refers to the entire Mediterranean-wide assembly of Jesus' followers. After the legalization of Christianity by the emperor Constantine (see page 208) and the growth of institutional offices and officials, the word *church* was sometimes applied to those officials—much as the terms *the college* or *the university* are used today to refer to academic administrators. Then the bishops of Rome—known as popes from the Latin word *papa,* meaning "father"—claimed to speak and act as the source of unity for all Christians. The popes claimed to be the successors of Saint Peter and heirs to his authority as chief of the apostles, on the basis of Jesus' words:

You are Peter, and on this rock I will build my church, and the jaws of death shall not prevail against it. I will entrust to you the keys of the kingdom of heaven. Whatever you declare bound on earth shall be bound in heaven; whatever you declare loosed on earth shall be loosed in heaven.[1]

Roman bishops used this text, known as the Petrine Doctrine, to support their assertions of authority over other bishops in the church. Thus the popes maintained that they represented "the church." The word *church,* therefore, has several connotations. Modern Catholic theology frequently defines the church as "the people of God" and identifies it with local and international Christian communities, but in the Middle Ages the institutional and monarchial interpretations tended to be stressed.

Having gained the support of the fourth-century emperors, the church gradually adopted the Roman system of organization. Christianity had a dynamic missionary policy, and the church slowly succeeded in *assimilating*—that is, adapting—pagan peoples, both Germans and Romans, to Christian teaching. Moreover, the church possessed able administrators and leaders and highly literate and creative thinkers. These factors help to explain the survival and growth of the Christian church in the face of repeated Germanic invasions.

The Church and the Roman Emperors

The church benefited considerably from the emperors' support. In return, the emperors expected the support of the Christian church in maintaining order and unity. After legalizing its practice, Constantine encouraged Christianity throughout his reign. In 380 the emperor Theodosius went further than Constantine and made Christianity the official religion of the empire. Theodosius stripped Roman pagan temples of statues, made the practice of the old Roman state religion a treasonable offense, and persecuted Christians who dissented from orthodox doctrine. Most significant, he allowed the church to establish its own courts. Church courts began to develop their own body of law, called *canon law*. These courts, not the Roman government, had jurisdiction over the clergy and ecclesiastical disputes. At the death of Theodosius, the Christian church was considerably independent of the Roman state. The foundation for the medieval church's power had been laid.

In the fourth century, theological disputes frequently and sharply divided the Christian community. Some disagreements had to do with the nature of Christ. For example, Arianism, which originated with Arius (ca 250–336), a priest of Alexandria, denied that Christ was divine and co-eternal with God the Father—two propositions of orthodox Christian belief. Arius held that God the Father was by definition uncreated and unchangeable. Jesus, however, was born of Mary, grew in wisdom, and suffered punishment and death. Jesus was created by the will of the Father and thus was not co-eternal with the Father. Therefore, Arius reasoned, Jesus the Son must be less than or inferior to the Unbegotten Father, who is incapable of

suffering and did not die. This argument implies that Jesus stands somewhere between God the Creator and humanity in need of redemption. Orthodox theologians branded Arius's position a *heresy*—denial of a basic doctrine of faith.

Arianism enjoyed such popularity and provoked such controversy that Constantine, to whom religious disagreement meant civil disorder, interceded. In 325 he summoned a council of church leaders to Nicaea in Asia Minor and presided over it personally. The council produced the Nicene Creed, which defined the orthodox position that Christ is "eternally begotten of the Father" and of the same substance as the Father. Arius and those who refused to accept the creed were banished, the first case of civil punishment for heresy. This participation of the emperor in a theological dispute within the church paved the way for later emperors to claim that they could do the same.

So active was the emperor Theodosius's participation in church matters that he eventually came to loggerheads with Bishop Ambrose of Milan (339–397). Theodosius ordered Ambrose to hand over his cathedral church to the emperor. Ambrose's response had important consequences for the future:

At length came the command, "Deliver up the Basilica"; I reply, "It is not lawful for us to deliver it up, nor for your Majesty to receive it. . . . It is asserted that all things are lawful to the Emperor, that all things are his. But do not burden your conscience with the thought that you have any right as Emperor over sacred things. Exalt not yourself, but if you would reign the longer, be subject to God. It is written, God's to God and Caesar's to Caesar. The palace is the Emperor's, the Churches are the Bishop's. To you is committed jurisdiction over public, not over sacred buildings."[2]

Ambrose insisted that the church was independent of the state's jurisdiction. He insisted that, in matters relating to the faith or the church, the bishops were to be the judges of emperors, not the other way around. In a Christian society, harmony and peace depended on agreement between the bishop and the secular ruler. But if disagreement developed, Ambrose maintained, the church was ultimately the superior power because the church was responsible for the salvation of all (including the emperor). Throughout the Middle Ages, theologians, canonists, and propagandists repeatedly cited Ambrose's position as the basis of relations between the two powers.

Inspired Leadership

The early Christian church benefited from the brilliant administrative abilities of some church leaders and from identification of the authority and dignity of the bishop of Rome with the imperial traditions of the city. With the empire in decay, educated people joined and worked for the church in the belief that it was the one institution able to provide leadership. Bishop Ambrose, for example, the son of the Roman prefect of Gaul, was a trained lawyer and governor of a province. He is typical of those Roman aristocrats who held high public office, were converted to Christianity, and subsequently became bishops. Such men later provided social continuity from Roman to Germanic rule.

During the reign of Diocletian (284–305), the Roman Empire had been divided for administrative purposes into geographical units called *dioceses.* Gradually the church made use of this organizational structure. Christian bishops established their headquarters, or *sees,* in the urban centers of the old Roman dioceses. A bishop's jurisdiction extended throughout all parts of his diocese. The center of the bishop's authority was his cathedral (the word derives from the Latin *cathedra,* meaning "chair"). Thus church leaders capitalized on the Roman imperial method of organization and adapted it to ecclesiastical purposes.

After the removal of the imperial capital and the emperor to Constantinople (see page 210), the bishop of Rome exercised considerable influence in the West because he had no real competitor there. Successive bishops of Rome stressed the special importance of Rome in the framework of the old empire. They reminded Christians in other parts of the world that Rome was the burial place of Saint Peter and Saint Paul. Moreover, according to tradition, Saint Peter, the chief of Christ's first twelve followers, had lived and been executed in Rome. No other city in the world could make such claims.

In the fifth century the bishops of Rome began to stress their supremacy over other Christian communities and to urge other churches to appeal to Rome for the resolution of disputed doctrinal issues. Thus Pope Innocent I (r. 401–417) wrote to the bishops of north Africa:

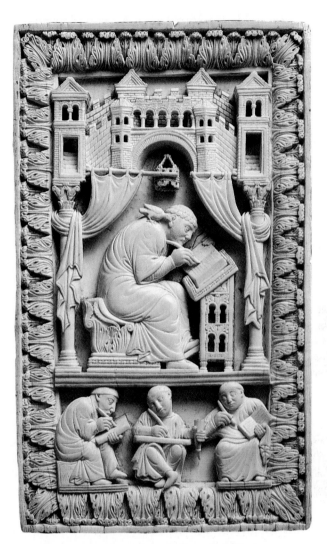

Pope Gregory I (r. 590–604) and Scribes   One of the four "Doctors" (or Learned Fathers) of the Latin church, Gregory is shown in this tenth-century ivory book cover writing at his desk while the Holy Spirit in the form of a dove whispers in his ear. Below, scribes copy Gregory's works. *(Source: Kunsthistorisches Museum, Vienna)*

We approve your action in following the principle that nothing which was done even in the most remote and distant provinces should be taken as finally settled unless it came to the notice of this See, that any just pronouncement might be confirmed by all the authority of this See, and that the other churches might from thence gather what they should teach.[3]

The prestige of Rome and the church as a whole was also enhanced by the courage and leadership of the Roman bishops. According to tradition, Pope Leo I (r. 440–461) met the advancing army of Attila the Hun in 452 and, through his power of persuasion, saved Rome from destruction. According to legend, three years later, Leo persuaded the Vandal leader Gaiseric not to burn the city, though the pope could not prevent a terrible sacking.

By the time Gregory I (r. 590–604) became pope, there was no civic authority left to handle the problems pressing the city. Flood, famine, plague, and invasion by the Lombards made for an almost disastrous situation. Pope Gregory concluded a peace with the Lombards, organized relief services that provided water and food for the citizens, and established hospitals for the sick and dying. The fact that it was Christian leaders, rather than imperial administrators, who responded to the city's dire needs could not help but increase the prestige and influence of the church.

Although Innocent I and Leo I strongly asserted the primacy of the Roman papacy, those assertions were not universally accepted. Local Christian communities and their leaders often exercised decisive authority over their local churches. Particular social and political conditions determined the actual power of the bishop of Rome in a given circumstance. The importance of arguments for the Roman primacy, holding the first place among Christian bishops, rests in the fact that they served as precedents for later appeals.

Missionary Activity

The word *catholic* derives from a Greek word meaning "general," "universal," or "worldwide." Christ had said that his teaching was for all peoples, and Christians sought to make their faith catholic—that is, believed everywhere. This could be accomplished only through missionary activity. As Saint Paul had written to the Christian community at Colossae in Asia Minor:

You have stripped off your old behavior with your old self, and you have put on a new self which will progress towards true knowledge the more it is renewed in the image of its creator; and in that image there is no room for distinction between Greek and Jew, between the circumcised or the uncircumcised, or between barbarian or Scythian, slave and free man. There is only Christ; he is everything and he is in everything.[4]

Paul urged Christians to bring the "good news" of Christ to all peoples. The Mediterranean served as the highway over which Christianity spread to the cities of the empire (Map 8.1).

Christian communities were scattered throughout Gaul and Britain during the Roman occupation. The effective beginnings of Christianity in Gaul can be traced to Saint Martin of Tours (ca 316–397), a Roman soldier who, after giving half of his cloak to a naked beggar, had a vision of Christ and was baptized. Martin founded the monastery of Ligugé, the first in Gaul; it became a center for the evangelization of the country districts. In 372 he became bishop of Tours and introduced a rudimentary parish system.

Tradition identifies the conversion of Ireland with Saint Patrick (ca 385–461), one of the most effective missionaries in history. Born in western England to a Christian family of Roman citizenship, Patrick was captured and enslaved by Irish raiders and taken to Ireland, where he worked for six years as a herdsman. He escaped and returned to England, where a vision urged him to Christianize Ireland. In preparation, Patrick studied in Gaul and in 432 was consecrated a bishop. He converted the Irish tribe by tribe, having first baptized each tribal chief.

In 445, with the approval of Pope Leo I, Patrick established his see in Armagh. Armagh was a monastery, and the monastery, rather than the diocese, served as the center of ecclesiastical organization in Ireland. Local tribes and the monastery were interdependent. The tribes supported the monastery economically, and the monastery provided religious and educational services for the tribes. Patrick also introduced the Roman alphabet and supported the codification of traditional laws. By the time of his death, the majority of the Irish people had received Christian baptism.

The Christianization of the English really began in 597, when Pope Gregory I sent a delegation of monks under the Roman Augustine to Britain to convert the English. Augustine's approach, like Patrick's, was to concentrate on converting the chief or king. When he succeeded in converting Ethelbert, king of Kent, the baptism of Ethelbert's people took place as a matter of course. Augustine established his see at Canterbury, the capital of Kent.

The conversion of the English had far-reaching consequences because Britain later served as a base

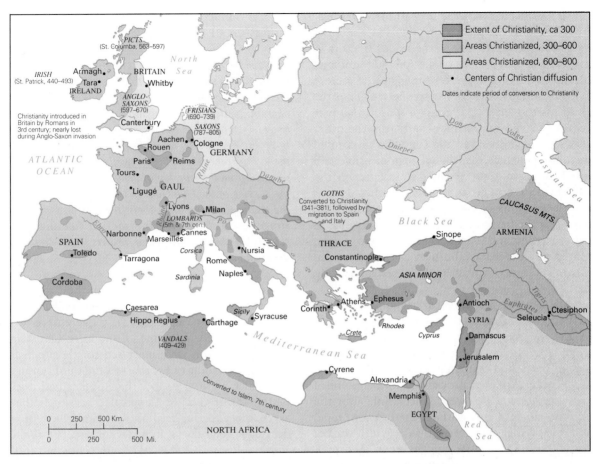

MAP 8.1 The Spread of Christianity   Originating in Judaea, the southern part of modern Israel and Jordan, Christianity spread throughout the Roman world. Roman sea lanes and Roman roads facilitated its expansion.

for the Christianization of the European continent (see Map 8.1). Between the fifth and tenth centuries, the great majority of peoples living on the European continent and the nearby islands accepted the Christian religion—that is, they received baptism, though baptism in itself did not automatically transform people into Christians.

Religion influenced all aspects of tribal life. All members of a tribe participated in religious observances because doing so was a social duty. Religion was not a private or individual matter; the religion of the chief or king determined the religion of the people. Thus Patrick, Augustine, and other missionaries concentrated their initial efforts on kings or tribal chieftains. According to custom, tribal chiefs negotiated with all foreign powers, including

the gods. Because the Christian missionaries represented a "foreign" power (the Christian God), the king dealt with them. Germanic kings accepted Christianity for various reasons: because they believed that the Christian God was more powerful than pagan gods and would deliver victory in battle; because Christianity taught obedience to (kingly) authority; or because Christian priests possessed knowledge and charisma that they associated with kingly power. Whatever the reason, if the ruler accepted Christian baptism, his people did so too. With the resulting mass baptism, however, the work of Christianization had only begun. Baptism meant either sprinkling the head or immersing the body in water. Conversion meant mental and heartfelt acceptance of the beliefs of Christianity.

The Germanic peoples were warriors who idealized the military virtues of physical strength, ferocity in battle, and loyalty to the leader. Victors in battle enjoyed the spoils of success and plundered the vanquished. The greater the fighter, the more trophies and material goods he collected. Thus the Germans had trouble accepting the Christian precepts of "love your enemies" and "turn the other cheek," and they found the Christian notions of sin and repentance virtually incomprehensible. Sin in Christian thought meant disobedience to the will of God as revealed in the Ten Commandments and the teaching of Christ. Good or "moral" behavior to the barbarians meant the observance of tribal customs and practices. In Germanic society, dishonorable behavior brought social ostracism. The inculcation of Christian ideals took a very long time.

How effective was Christian missionary activity? Between the fifth and tenth centuries most people in Europe received Christian baptism, learned something about the commandments and teachings of Jesus, and eventually identified themselves as Christian. So from a social and formal point of view the missionaries were "successful." But the chronic violence and warfare, theft, arson, rape, and pillage that characterized so much of society attest to the incomplete conversion of the European peoples and their unwillingness to follow Jesus' fundamental message to love God and one's neighbor.

Conversion and Assimilation

In Christian theology, conversion involves a turning toward God—that is, a conscious effort to live according to the Gospel message. How did missionaries and priests get masses of pagan and illiterate peoples to understand and live by Christian ideals and teachings? Through preaching, through assimilation, and through the penitential system.

Preaching aimed at instruction and edification. Instruction presented the basic teachings of Christianity. Edification was intended to strengthen the newly baptized in their faith through stories about the lives of Christ and the saints. Deeply ingrained pagan customs and practices, however, could not be stamped out by words alone or even by imperial edicts. Christian missionaries often pursued a policy of assimilation, easing the conversion of pagan men and women by stressing similarities between their customs and beliefs and those of Christianity.

A letter from Pope Gregory I to Augustine of Canterbury in 601 beautifully illustrates this policy:

we have been giving careful thought to the affairs of the English, and have come to the conclusion that the temples of the idols among that people should on no account be destroyed. The idols are to be destroyed, but the temples themselves are to be aspersed with holy water, altars set up in them, and relics deposited there. For if these temples are well-built, they must be purified from the worship of demons and dedicated to the service of the true God. In this way, we hope that the people, seeing that their temples are not destroyed, may abandon their error and, flocking more readily to their accustomed resorts, may come to know and adore the true God.[5]

How assimilation works is perhaps best appreciated through the example of a festival familiar to all Americans, Saint Valentine's Day. There were two Romans named Valentine. Both were Christian priests, and both were martyred for their beliefs around the middle of February in the third century A.D. Since about 150 B.C. the Romans had celebrated the festival of Lupercalia, at which they asked the gods for fertility for themselves, their fields, and their flocks, in mid-February, before the arrival of spring. Thus the early church "converted" the old festival of Lupercalia into Saint Valentine's Day. (Nothing in the lives of the two Christian martyrs connects them with lovers or the exchange of messages and gifts. That practice began in the later Middle Ages.)

In the early church confession meant that the sinner *publicly* acknowledged charges laid against him or her and *publicly* carried out the penitential works that the priest or bishop prescribed. For example, an adulterer might have to stand outside the church before services, wearing a sign naming his or her sin and asking for the prayers of everyone who entered. Beginning in the late sixth century, Irish and English missionaries brought the penitential system to continental Europe. The illiterate penitent knelt before the priest, who questioned the penitent about the sins he or she might have committed. The priest then imposed a penance. Penance usually meant fasting for a period of time on bread and water, which was intended as a medicine for the soul. Here is a section of the penitential prepared by Archbishop Theodore of Canterbury (668–690), which circulated widely at the time:

If anyone commits fornication with a virgin he shall do penance for one year. If with a married woman, he shall do penance for four years, two of these entire. . . .

A male who commits fornication with a male shall do penance for three years.

If a woman practices vice with a woman, she shall do penance for three years.

Whoever has often committed theft, seven years is his penance, or such a sentence as his priest shall determine, that is, according to what can be arranged with those whom he has wronged. . . .

If a layman slays another with malice aforethought, if he will not lay aside his arms, he shall do penance for seven years; without flesh and wine, three years.

He who defiles his neighbor's wife, deprived of his own wife, shall fast for three years two days a week and in the three forty-day periods.

Women who commit abortion before [the fetus] has life, shall do penance for one year or for the three forty-day periods or for forty days, according to the nature of the offense; and if later, that is, more than forty days after conception, they shall do penance as murderesses.[6]

As this sample suggests, writers of penitentials were preoccupied with sexual transgressions.

Penitentials provide an enormous amount of information about the ascetic ideals of early Christianity and about the crime-ridden realities of Celtic and Germanic societies. Penitentials also reveal the ecclesiastical foundations of some modern attitudes toward sex, birth control, and abortion. Unlike the earlier public penances, Celtic forms permitted the repeated reconciliation of the same

The Pantheon (Interior)   Originally a temple for the gods, the Pantheon later served as a Christian church. As such, it represents the adaptation of pagan elements to Christian purposes. *(Source: Alinari/Art Resource, NY)*

The Two Marys at the Sepulcher   This late-fourth-century ivory panel tells the story (Matthew 28:1–6) of Mary Magdalene and another woman named Mary, who went to Jesus' tomb. They discovered the stone at the entrance rolled away and an angel (lower panel, at left) sitting on it. The guards assigned to watch the tomb "trembled and became like dead men" (upper panel). The angel told the women that Jesus had risen. The blend of Roman artistic style—in spacing, drapery, men's hair fashion—and Christian subject matter shows the assimilation of classical form and Christian teaching. (*Source: Castello Sforzesco/Scala/Art Resource, NY*)

sinner in a *private* situation involving only the priest and penitent. We do not know whether these severe penances were actually enforced; some scholars believe they were not. In any case, the penitential system contributed to the growth of a different attitude toward religion: formerly public, corporate, and social, religious observances became private, personal, and individual.[7]

CHRISTIAN ATTITUDES TOWARD CLASSICAL CULTURE

Probably the major dilemma the early Christian church faced concerned Greco-Roman culture. In Greek philosophy, art, and architecture, in Roman law, literature, education, and engineering, the legacy of a great civilization continued. The Christian religion had begun and spread within this intellectual and psychological milieu. What was to be the attitude of Christians to the Greco-Roman world of ideas?

Adjustment

Christians in the first and second centuries believed that Christ would soon fulfill his promise to return and that the end of the world was near. Thus they considered knowledge useless and learning a waste of time, and they preached the duty of Christians to prepare for the Second Coming of the Lord. Good Christians who sought the Kingdom of Heaven by imitating Christ believed they had to disassociate themselves from the "filth" that Roman culture embodied.

Saint Paul (A.D. 5?–67?) had written, "The wisdom of the world is foolishness, we preach Christ crucified." And about a century and a half later, Tertullian (ca 160–220), an influential African Christian writer, condemned all secular literature as foolishness in the eyes of God. He called the Greek philosophers, such as Aristotle, "hucksters of eloquence" and compared them to "animals of self-glorification." "What has Athens to do with Jerusalem," he demanded, "the Academy with the Church? We have no need for curiosity since Jesus Christ, nor for inquiry since the gospel." Tertullian insisted that Christians would find in the Bible all the wisdom they needed.

Nevertheless, Christianity encouraged adjustment to the ideas and institutions of the Roman world. Specifically addressing Christians living among non-Christians in the hostile environment of Rome, for example, the author of the First Letter of Peter had written about the obligations of Christians toward civil authority:

For the sake of the Lord, accept the authority of every social institution: the emperor, as the supreme authority, and the governors as commissioned by him to punish criminals and praise good citizenship. God wants you to be good citizens. . . . Have respect for everyone and love for your community; fear God and honour the emperor.[8]

Christians really had little choice. Christianity did not emerge in a social or intellectual vacuum; Jewish and Roman cultures were the only cultures early Christians knew. Thus they had to adapt their Roman education to their Christian beliefs. Saint Paul himself believed there was a good deal of truth in pagan thought, as long as it was correctly interpreted and understood. The result was compromise.

Christians gradually came to terms with Greco-Roman culture. Saint Jerome (340–419), a distinguished theologian and linguist, remains famous for his translation of the Old and New Testament from Hebrew and Greek into the vernacular Latin. Called the Vulgate, his edition of the Bible served as the official translation until the sixteenth century; even today, scholars rely on it. Familiar with the writings of classical authors, Saint Jerome also believed that Christians should study the best of ancient thought because it would direct their minds to God. Christian attitudes toward women and toward homosexuality illustrate the ways early Christians adopted the views of their contemporary world.

Jesus, whom Christians accept as the Messiah, considered women the equal of men in his plan of salvation. He attributed no disreputable qualities to women, made no comment on the wiles of women, made no reference to them as inferior creatures. On the contrary, women were among his earliest and most faithful converts. He discussed his mission with them (John 4:21–25); he accepted the ministrations of a reformed prostitute; and women were the first persons to whom he revealed himself after his resurrection (Matthew 28:9–10). The influence of Jewish and Christian writers on the formation of medieval (and modern) attitudes toward women, however, was greater than Jesus' influence.

Jesus' message emphasized love for God and for one's fellow human beings. Later writers tended to stress Christianity as a religion of renunciation and asceticism, and they equated sexual activity with women. Their views derive from Platonic-Hellenistic ideas of the contemporary Mediterranean world. The Hellenistic Jewish philosopher Philo of Alexandria (ca 20 B.C.–ca 50 A.D.), for example, held that since the female represented sense perception and the male the higher, rational soul, the female was inferior to the male. Female beauty may come from God who created everything, the African church father Tertullian wrote, but it should be feared. Women should wear veils, he warned; otherwise, men will be endangered by the sight of them. Perhaps the most revolting image of women comes from Saint John Chrysostom (347–407), patriarch of Constantinople. This ruthless critic of contemporary morals characterized female beauty as "a white sepulchre; the parts within are full of so much uncleanliness."[9]

The church fathers acknowledged that God had established marriage for the generation of children, but they believed marriage was a concession to weak people who could not bear celibacy. Saint Augustine (see page 224) considered sexual intercourse a great threat to spiritual freedom. In daily life every act of intercourse was evil, he taught; every child was conceived by a sinful act and came into the world tainted with original sin. Celibacy was the highest good; intercourse little more than animal lust.

Women were considered incapable of writing on the subject, so we have none of their views. The church fathers, by definition, were men. Because many of them experienced physical desire when in the presence of women, misogyny (hatred of women) entered Christian thought. Although early Christian writers believed women the spiritual equals of men, and although Saint Melania, Saint Scholastica (see page 236), and some other women exercised influence as teachers and charismatic leaders, Christianity became a male-centered and sex-negative religion. "The Church Fathers regarded sex as at best something to be tolerated, an evil whose only good was procreation."[10] Until perhaps very recently, this attitude dominated Western thinking on human sexuality.

Toward homosexuality, according to a controversial study, Christians of the first three or four centuries simply imbibed the attitude of the world in which they lived. Many Romans indulged in homosexual activity, and contemporaries did not consider such behavior (or inclinations to it) immoral, bizarre, or harmful. Early Christians, too, considered homosexuality a conventional expression of physical desire and were no more susceptible to antihomosexual prejudices than pagans were. Some prominent Christians experienced loving same-gender relationships that probably had a sexual element. What eventually led to a change in public and Christian attitudes toward sexual behavior was the shift from the sophisticated urban culture of the Greco-Roman world to the rural culture of medieval Europe.[11]

Synthesis: Saint Augustine

The finest representative of the blending of classical and Christian ideas, and indeed one of the most brilliant thinkers in the history of the Western world, was Saint Augustine of Hippo (354–430). Aside from the scriptural writers, no one else has had a greater impact on Christian thought in succeeding centuries. Saint Augustine was born into an urban family in what is now Algeria in North Africa. His father was a pagan; his mother, Monica, a devout Christian. Because his family was poor—his father was a minor civil servant—the only avenue to success in a highly competitive world was a classical education.

Augustine received his basic education in the local school. By modern and even medieval standards, that education was extremely narrow: textual study of the writings of the poet Virgil, the orator-politician Cicero, the historian Sallust, and the playwright Terence. As in the Islamic and Chinese worlds (see pages 273 and 720), learning in the Christian West meant memorization. Education in the late Roman world aimed at appreciation of words, particularly those of renowned and eloquent orators.

At the age of seventeen, Augustine went to nearby Carthage to continue his education. There he took a mistress with whom he lived for fifteen years. At Carthage, Augustine began an intellectual and spiritual pilgrimage that led him through experiments with several philosophies and heretical Christian sects. In 383 he traveled to Rome, where he endured not only illness but also disappointment in his teaching: his students fled when their bills were due.

Finally, in Milan in 387, Augustine received Christian baptism. He later became bishop of the seacoast city of Hippo Regius in his native North Africa. He was a renowned preacher to Christians there, a vigorous defender of orthodox Christianity, and the author of over ninety-three books and treatises.

Augustine's autobiography, *The Confessions,* is a literary masterpiece and one of the most influential books in the history of Europe. Written in the form of a prayer, *The Confessions* describes Augustine's moral struggle: the conflict between his spiritual and intellectual aspirations and his sensual and material self.

The Confessions, written in the rhetorical style and language of late Roman antiquity, marks the synthesis of Greco-Roman forms and Christian thought. Many Greek and Roman philosophers had taught that knowledge and virtue are the same—that a person who really knows what is right will do what is right. Augustine rejected this idea. He believed that a person may know what is right but fail to act righteously because of the innate weakness of the human will. He pointed out that people do not always act on the basis of rational knowledge. A learned person can be corrupt and evil.

Augustine's ideas on sin, grace, and redemption became the foundation of all subsequent Christian theology, Protestant as well as Catholic. He wrote that the basic or dynamic force in any individual is the *will,* which he defined as "the power of the soul to hold on to or to obtain an object without constraint." The end or goal of the will determines the moral character of the individual. When Adam ate the fruit forbidden by God in the garden of Eden (Genesis 3:6), he committed "the original sin" and corrupted the will. By concupiscence or sexual desire, which all humans have, Adam's sin has been passed on by hereditary transmission through the flesh to all humanity. Original sin thus became a common social stain. Because Adam disobeyed God and fell, so all human beings have an innate tendency to sin: their will is weak. But, according to Augustine, God restores the strength of the will through grace (his love, assistance, support), which is transmitted through the sacraments, such as penance, or reconciliation, by the action of the Spirit.

Augustine also argued against the idea that the church consisted of a spiritual elite that was an alternative to society. Rather than seeing themselves as apart from society, Augustine said, Christians must live in and transform society. The notion of the church as a special spiritual elite, distinct from and superior to the rest of society, recurred many times in the Middle Ages. Each time it was branded a heresy, and Augustine's arguments were marshaled against it.

When the Visigothic chieftain Alaric conquered Rome in 410, horrified pagans blamed the disaster on the Christians. In response, Augustine wrote *City of God.* This profoundly original work contrasts Christianity with the secular society in which it existed. *City of God* presents a moral interpretation of the Roman government—in fact, of all history. Filled with references to ancient history and mythology, it remained for centuries the standard statement of the Christian philosophy of history.

According to Augustine, history is the account of God acting in time. Human history reveals that there are two kinds of people: those who live according to the flesh in the City of Babylon and those who live according to the spirit in the City of God. The former will endure eternal hellfire, the latter eternal bliss.

Augustine maintained that states came into existence as the result of Adam's fall and people's inclination to sin. The state is a necessary evil, but it can work for the good by providing the peace, justice, and order that Christians need in order to pursue their pilgrimage to the City of God. The particular form of government—whether monarchy, aristocracy, or democracy—is basically irrelevant. Any civil government that fails to provide justice is no more than a band of gangsters.

Although the state results from moral lapse—from sin—the church (the Christian community) is not entirely free from sin. The church is certainly not equivalent to the City of God. But the church, which is concerned with salvation, is responsible for everyone, including Christian rulers. Churches in the Middle Ages used Augustine's theory to defend their belief in the ultimate superiority of the spiritual power over the temporal. This remained the dominant political theory until the late thirteenth century.

✤ CHRISTIAN MONASTICISM

Christianity began and spread as a city religion. Since the first century, however, some especially pious Christians had felt that the only alternative to the decadence of urban life was complete separation from the world. The fourth century witnessed a significant change in the relationship between Christianity and the broader society. Until Constantine's legalization of Christianity, Christians were a persecuted minority. Some were tortured and killed. Christians greatly revered these *martyrs* who, like Jesus, suffered and died for their faith. When Christianity was legalized and the persecutions ended, a new problem arose.

Where Christians had been a suffering minority, now they came to be identified with the state: non-Christians could not advance in the imperial service. But if Christianity had triumphed, so had "the world," for secular attitudes and values pervaded the church. The church of martyrs no longer existed. Some scholars believe the monasteries provided a way of life for those Christians who wanted to make a total response to Christ's teachings—people who wanted more than a lukewarm Christianity. The monks became the new martyrs. Saint Anthony of Egypt (d. 356), the first monk for whom there is concrete evidence and the person later considered the father of monasticism, went to Alexandria during the last persecution in the hope of gaining martyrdom. Christians believed that monks, like the martyrs before them, could speak to God and that their prayers had special influence with him.

Western Monasticism

Monasticism began in Egypt in the third century. At first individuals and small groups withdrew from cities and organized society to seek God through prayer in caves and shelters in the desert or mountains. Gradually large colonies of monks emerged in the deserts of upper Egypt. They were called hermits from the Greek word *eremos,* meaning "desert." Many devout women also were attracted to the monastic life. Although monks (and nuns) led isolated lives and the monastic movement represented the antithesis of the ancient ideal of an urban social existence, ordinary people soon recognized the monks and nuns as holy people and sought them as spiritual guides.

When monasticism spread to western Europe, several factors worked against the continuation of the eremitical form. The cold, snow, ice, and fog that covered much of northern Europe for many months of the year discouraged isolated living. Dense forests filled with wild animals and wandering Germanic tribes presented obvious dangers.

Saint Benedict Holding his *Rule* in his left hand, the seated and cowled patriarch of Western monasticism blesses a monk with his right hand. His monastery, Monte Cassino, is in the background. *(Source: Biblioteca Apostolica Vaticana)*

Moreover, church leaders did not really approve of eremitical life. Hermits sometimes claimed to have mystical experiences—direct communications with God. If hermits could communicate directly with the Lord, what need had they for the priest and the institutional church? The scholarly bishop Basil of Caesarea in Cappadocia in Asia Minor argued that the eremitical life posed the danger of excessive concern with the self and did not provide the opportunity for the exercise of charity, the first virtue of any Christian. Saint Basil and the church hierarchy encouraged *coenobitic monasticism,* communal living in monasteries, which provided an environment for training the aspirant in the virtues of charity, poverty, and freedom from self-deception.

In the fourth, fifth, and sixth centuries, many experiments in communal monasticism were made in Gaul, Italy, Spain, Anglo-Saxon England, and Ireland. While at Rome, Saint Jerome attracted a group of aristocratic women whom he instructed in Scripture and the ideals of ascetic life. After studying both eremitical and coenobitic monasticism in Egypt and Syria, John Cassian established two monasteries near Marseilles in Gaul around 415. The abbey or monastery of Lérins on the Mediterranean Sea near Cannes (ca 410) encouraged the severely penitential and extremely ascetic behavior common in the East, such as long hours of prayer, fasting, and self-flagellation. It was this tradition of harsh self-mortification that the

Roman-British monk Saint Patrick carried from Lérins to Ireland in the fifth century. Church organization in Ireland became closely associated with the monasteries, and Irish monastic life followed the ascetic Eastern form.

Around 540 the former Roman senator Cassiodorus established a monastery, the Vivarium, on his estate in Italy. Cassiodorus enlisted highly educated and sophisticated men to copy both sacred and secular manuscripts, intending this to be their sole occupation. Cassiodorus started the association of monasticism with scholarship and learning. This developed into a great tradition in the medieval and modern worlds. The fifth and sixth centuries witnessed the appearance of many other monastic lifestyles.

The Rule of Benedict

In 529 Benedict of Nursia (480–543), who had experimented with both the eremitical and the communal forms of monastic life, wrote a brief set of regulations for the monks who had gathered around him at Monte Cassino between Rome and Naples. Benedict's *Rule* derives from a longer, repetitious, and sometimes turgid document called *The Rule of the Master*. Benedict's guide for monastic life proved more adaptable and slowly replaced all others. *The Rule of Saint Benedict* has influenced all forms of organized religious life in the Roman church.

Saint Benedict conceived of his *Rule* as a simple code for ordinary men. It outlined a monastic life of regularity, discipline, and moderation. Each monk had ample food and adequate sleep. Self-destructive acts of mortification were forbidden. In an atmosphere of silence, the monk spent part of the day in formal prayer, which Benedict called the "Work of God." This consisted of chanting psalms and other prayers from the Bible. The rest of the day was passed in study and manual labor. After a year of probation, the monk made three vows.

First, the monk vowed stability: he promised to live his entire life in the monastery of his profession. The object of this vow was to prevent the wandering so common in Saint Benedict's day. Second, the monk vowed conversion of manners— that is, to strive to improve himself and to come closer to God. Third, he promised obedience to the *abbot,* or head of the monastery.

The Rule of Saint Benedict expresses the assimilation of the Roman spirit into Western monasticism. It reveals the logical mind of its creator and the Roman concern for order, organization, and respect for law. Its spirit of moderation and flexibility is reflected in the patience, wisdom, and understanding with which the abbot is to govern and, indeed, with which life is to be led.

Saint Benedict's *Rule* implies that a person who wants to become a monk or nun need have no previous ascetic experience or even a particularly strong bent toward the religious life. Thus it allowed for the admission of newcomers with different backgrounds and personalities. From Chapter 59, "The Offering of Sons by Nobles or by the Poor," and from Benedict's advice to the abbot— "The abbot should avoid all favoritism in the monastery. . . . A man born free is not to be given higher rank than a slave who becomes a monk" (Chapter 2)—we know that men of different social classes belonged to his monastery. This flexibility helps to explain the attractiveness of Benedictine monasticism throughout the centuries.

The Rule of Saint Benedict had one fundamental purpose. The exercises of the monastic life were designed to draw the individual slowly but steadily away from attachment to the world and love of self and toward the love of God. But the monastic life as conceived by Saint Benedict did not lean too heavily in any one direction. With its division of the day into prayer, study, and manual labor, it struck a balance between asceticism and idleness. It thus provided opportunities for persons of entirely different abilities and talents—from mechanics to gardeners to literary scholars. Benedict's *Rule* contrasts sharply with Cassiodorus's narrow concept of the monastery as a place for aristocratic scholars and bibliophiles.

Benedictine monasticism also suited the social circumstances of early medieval society. The Germanic invasions had fragmented European life: the self-sufficient rural estate replaced the city as the basic unit of civilization. A monastery, too, had to be economically self-sufficient. It was supposed to produce from its lands and properties all that was needed for food, clothing, shelter, and liturgical service of the altar. The monastery fitted in—indeed, represented—the trend toward localism. The Benedictine form of religious life also proved congenial to women. Five miles from Monte Cassino at Plombariola, Benedict's twin sister Scholastica

(480–543) adapted the *Rule* for the use of her community of nuns. Many other convents for nuns were established in the early Middle Ages.

Benedictine monasticism also succeeded partly because it was so materially successful. In the seventh and eighth centuries, monasteries pushed back forest and wasteland, drained swamps, and experimented with crop rotation. The abbey of Jumièges, in the diocese of Rouen, followed this pattern. Such Benedictine houses made a significant contribution to the agricultural development of Europe, earning immense wealth in the process. The communal nature of their organization, whereby property was held in common and profits were pooled and reinvested, made this contribution possible.

Finally, monasteries conducted schools for local young people. Some learned about prescriptions and herbal remedies and went on to provide medical treatment for their localities. A few copied manuscripts and wrote books. This training did not go unappreciated in a society desperately in need of it. Local and royal governments drew on the services of the literate men and able administrators the monasteries produced.

❀ THE MIGRATION OF THE GERMANIC PEOPLES

The migration of peoples from one area to another has been a dominant and continuing feature of world history. The causes of early migrations varied and are not thoroughly understood by scholars. But there is no question that they profoundly affected both the regions to which peoples moved and the regions they left behind.

The *Völkerwanderungen,* or migrations of the Germanic peoples, were important in the decline of the Western Roman Empire and in the making of European civilization. Since about 150, Germanic tribes from the regions of the northern Rhine, Elbe, and Oder rivers had pressed along the Rhine-Danube frontier of the Roman Empire. Some tribes, such as the Visigoths and Ostrogoths, led a settled existence, engaged in agriculture and trade, and accepted Arian Christianity. Other tribes, such as the Angles, Saxons, and Huns, led a nomadic life unaffected by Roman influences. Scholars do not know exactly when the Mongolian tribe called the Huns began to move westward

from China, but about 370 they pressured the Goths along the Rhine-Danube frontier.

Why did the Germans migrate? Although many twentieth-century scholars have tried to answer this question, the answer is not known. Perhaps overpopulation and the resulting food shortages caused migration. Perhaps victorious tribes forced the vanquished to move southward. Probably "the primary stimulus for this gradual migration was the Roman frontier, which increasingly offered service in the army and work for pay around the camps."[12]

By the late third century, a large percentage of military recruits came from the Germanic peoples. Besides army recruits, several types of barbarian peoples entered the empire and became affiliated with Roman government. The *laeti,* refugees or prisoners of war, were settled with their families in areas of Gaul and Italy under the supervision of Roman prefects and landowners. Generally isolated from the local Roman population, the laeti farmed regions depopulated by plague. The men had to serve in the Roman army.

Free barbarian units called *foederati,* stationed near major provincial cities, were a second type of affiliated barbarian group. Research has suggested that rather than giving them land, the Romans assigned the foederati shares of the tax revenues from the region.[13] Living close to Roman communities, the foederati quickly assimilated into Roman culture. In fact, in the fourth century, some foederati rose to the highest ranks of the army and moved in the most cultured and aristocratic circles.

The arrival of the Huns in the West in 376 precipitated the entry of entire peoples, the *gentes,* into the Roman Empire. Pressured by defeat in battle, starvation, or the movement of other peoples, tribes such as the Ostrogoths and Visigoths entered in large numbers, perhaps as many as twenty thousand men, women, and children.[14] Once the Visigoths were inside the empire, Roman authorities exploited their hunger by forcing them to sell their own people in exchange for dogflesh: "the going rate was one dog for one Goth." The bitterness of those enslaved was aggravated by the arrival of the Ostrogoths. A huge rebellion erupted, and the Goths crushed the Roman army at Adrianople on August 9, 378.[15] This date marks the beginning of massive Germanic invasions into the empire (Map 8.2).

Except for the Lombards, whose conquests of Italy persisted into the mid-eighth century, the movements of Germanic peoples on the European

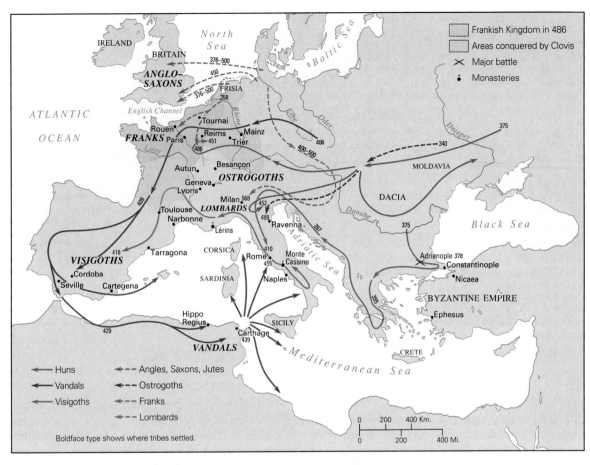

MAP 8.2 The Germanic Migrations The Germanic tribes infiltrated and settled in all parts of western Europe. The Huns, who were Mongolian, not Germanic, originated in central Asia. Their victory over the Ostrogoths led the emperor to allow the Visigoths to settle within the empire, a decision that proved disastrous for Rome.

continent ended about 600. Between 450 and 565 the Germans established a number of kingdoms, but none except the Frankish kingdom lasted very long. Unlike modern nation-states, the Germanic kingdoms did not have definite geographical boundaries. The Visigoths overran much of southwestern Gaul. Establishing their headquarters at Toulouse, they exercised a weak domination over Spain until a great Muslim victory at Guadalete in 711 ended Visigothic rule. The Vandals, whose destructive ways are commemorated in the word *vandal,* settled in North Africa. In northern and western Europe in the sixth century, the Burgundians established rule over lands roughly circumscribed by old Roman army camps at Lyons, Besançon, Geneva, and Autun.

In northern Italy the Ostrogothic king Theodoric (r. 471–526) established his capital at Ravenna and gradually won control of all Italy, Sicily, and the territory north and east of the upper Adriatic. Though attached to the customs of his people, Theodoric pursued a policy of assimilation between Germans and Romans. He maintained close relations with the emperor at Constantinople and attracted to his administration able scholars such as Cassiodorus (see page 227). Theodoric's accomplishments were not insignificant, but after his death his administration fell apart.

The most enduring Germanic kingdom was established by the Frankish chieftain Clovis (r. 481–511). Originally only a petty chieftain in northwestern Gaul (modern Belgium), Clovis began to

 **Helmet of King Agiluf** Germanic chieftains wanted to be portrayed as Roman-style rulers in order to convey Roman ideals of power. On this plaque for the helmet of the Lombard king Agiluf, the king sits enthroned in majesty flanked by body-guards while subject cities bring tribute. *(Source: Scala/Art Resource, NY)*

expand his territories in 486. His Catholic wife Clothilde worked to convert her husband and supported the founding of churches and monasteries. Clothilde is representative of the role women played in the Christianization and Romanization of the Germanic kingdoms (see Listening to the Past). Clovis's conversion to orthodox Christianity in 496 won him the crucial support of the papacy and the bishops of Gaul. As the defender of Roman Catholicism against heretical Germanic tribes, Clovis went on to conquer the Visigoths, extending his domain as far as the Pyrenees and making Paris his headquarters. Because he was descended from the half-legendary chieftain Merovech, the dynasty that Clovis founded has been called Merovingian (see pages 345–346).

The island of Britain, conquered by Rome during the reign of Claudius, shared fully in the life of the Roman Empire during the first four centuries of the Christian era. A military aristocracy governed, and the official religion was the cult of the emperor. Towns were planned in the Roman fashion, with temples, public baths, theaters, and amphitheaters. In the countryside, large manors controlled the surrounding lands. Roman merchants brought Eastern luxury goods and Eastern religions—including Christianity—into Britain. The native Britons, a peaceful Celtic people, became thoroughly Romanized. Their language was Latin. Their lifestyle was Roman.

After the Visigothic defeat of the Roman emperor at Adrianople, however, Roman troops were withdrawn from Britain, leaving it unprotected. The savage Picts from Scotland harassed the north. Teutonic tribes from modern-day Norway, Sweden, and Denmark—the Angles, Saxons, and Jutes — stepped up their assaults. Germans took over the best lands and humbled the Britons. The sporadic raids continued for over a century and led to Germanic control of most of Britain. Historians have labeled the period from 500 to 1066 "Anglo-Saxon." Germanic tribes never subdued Scotland, where the Picts remained strong, or Wales, where the Celts and native Britons continued to put up stubborn resistance.

GERMANIC SOCIETY

After the Germans replaced the Romans, Germanic customs and traditions shaped European society for centuries. What sorts of social, political, and economic life did the Germans have? Scholars are hampered in answering such questions because the Germans did not write and thus kept no written records before their conversion to Christianity. The earliest information about them comes from moralistic accounts by Romans such as the historian Tacitus, who was acquainted only with the tribes living closest to the borders of the Roman Empire and imposed Greco-Roman categories of tribes and nations on the Germanic peoples he described. Tacitus's ethnographic classifications dominated scholarly writing until fairly recently. Only in the past few decades have anthropologists begun to study early Germanic society on its own terms.

Kinship, Class, and Law

The Germans had no notion of the state as we in the twentieth century use the term; they thought in social, not political, terms. The basic Germanic social unit was the tribe, or *folk*. Members of the folk believed that they were all descended from a common ancestor. Blood united them. Kinship protected them. Law was custom—unwritten and handed down by word of mouth from generation to generation. Custom regulated everything. Members were subject to their tribe's customary law wherever they went, and friendly tribes respected one another's laws.

Germanic tribes were led by kings or tribal chieftains. The chief, recognized as the strongest and bravest in battle, was elected from among the male members of the strongest family. He led the tribe in war, settled disputes among its members, conducted negotiations with outside powers, and offered sacrifices to the gods.

Closely associated with the chief in some southern tribes was the *comitatus,* or "war band." Writing at the end of the first century, Tacitus described the war band as the bravest young men in the tribe. They swore loyalty to the chief, fought with him in battle, and were not supposed to leave the battlefield without him; to do so implied cowardice and disloyalty and resulted in social disgrace. Social egalitarianism existed among members of the war band.

During the migrations of the third and fourth centuries, and as a result of constant warfare, the war band was transformed into a system of stratified ranks. Armbands, first obtained through contact with the Romans, came to be coveted as marks of rank, especially the gold ones reserved for the "royal families." During the Ostrogothic conquest of Italy under Theodoric, warrior nobles also

sought to acquire land, both as a mark of prestige and as a means to power. As land and wealth came into the hands of a small elite class, social inequalities emerged and gradually grew stronger.[16] These inequalities help to explain the origins of the European noble class (see pages 349–350).

King Lhodari of the Alemanni The Alemanni occupied territory in southwestern Germany and Switzerland in the fifth century but did not accept Christianity until the late seventh or early eighth century. King Lhodari had Alemanni law (hitherto transmitted orally) written down in Latin. (In French speech the name *Allemands* came to signify all Germans.) Here the ninth-century artist portrays Lhodari in Roman military garb. (*Source: Bibliothèque Nationale, Paris*)

As long as custom determined all behavior, the early Germans had no need for written law. Beginning in the late sixth century, however, German tribal chieftains began to collect, write, and publish lists of their customs. Why then? The Christian missionaries who were slowly converting the Germans to Christianity wanted to read about German ways in order to assimilate the tribes to Christianity, and they encouraged German rulers to write their customs down. Moreover, by the sixth century the Germanic rulers needed regulations that applied to the Romans under their jurisdiction as well as to their own people.

Today, if a person holds up a bank, American law maintains that the robber attacks both the bank and the state in which it exists—a sophisticated notion involving the abstract idea of the state. In early Germanic law, all crimes were regarded as crimes against a person.

According to the code of the Salian Franks, every person had a particular monetary value to the tribe. This value was called the *wergeld*, which literally means "man-money" or "money to buy off the spear." Men of fighting age had the highest wergeld, then women of childbearing age, then children, and finally the aged. If a person accused of a crime agreed to pay the wergeld and if the victim and his or her family accepted the payment, there was peace. If the accused refused to pay the wergeld or if the victim's family refused to accept it, a blood feud ensued. Individuals depended on their kin for protection, and kinship served as a force of social control.

The early law codes are patchwork affairs studded with additions made in later centuries. Yet much historical information can be gleaned from them. The law code of the Salian Franks issued by Clovis offers a general picture of Germanic life and problems in the early Middle Ages and is typical of the law codes of other tribes. The Salic Law lists the money fines to be paid to the victim or the family for injuries such as theft, rape, assault, arson, and murder. It is not really a code of law at all but a list of tariffs or fines for particular offenses.

If any person strike another on the head so that the brain appears, and the three bones which lie above the brain shall project, he shall be sentenced to 1200 denars, which make 300 shillings. . . .

If any one have killed a free woman after she has begun bearing children, he shall be sentenced to 2400 denars, which make 600 shillings. . . .

If any one shall have drawn a harrow through another's harvest after it has sprouted, or shall have gone through it with a wagon where there was no road, he shall be sentenced to 120 denars, which make 30 shillings. . . .[17]

Germanic law aimed at the prevention or reduction of violence. It was not concerned with abstract justice.

As Germanic kings accepted Christianity and as Romans and Germans increasingly intermarried, the distinction between Germanic and Roman law blurred and, in the course of the seventh and eighth centuries, disappeared. The result would be the new feudal law.

Germanic Life

The Germans usually resided in small villages. Climate and geography determined the basic patterns of agricultural and pastoral life. In the flat or open coastal regions, men engaged in animal husbandry, especially cattle raising. Many tribes lived in small settlements on the edges of clearings where they raised barley, wheat, oats, peas, and beans. They tilled their fields with a simple wooden scratch plow and harvested their grains with a small iron sickle. Women ground the kernels of grain with a grindstone and made the resulting flour into a dough that they shaped into flat cakes and baked on clay trays. Much of the grain was fermented into a strong, thick beer. Women performed the heavy work of raising, grinding, and preserving cereals, a mark, some scholars believe, of their low status in a male-dominated society. Women were also responsible for weaving and spinning.

Within the small villages there were great differences in wealth and status. Free men constituted the largest class. The number of cattle a man possessed indicated his wealth and determined his social status. "Cattle were so much the quintessential indicator of wealth in traditional society that the modern English term 'fee' (meaning cost of goods or services), which developed from the medieval term 'fief,' had its origin in the Germanic term *fihu* . . . , meaning cattle, chattels, and hence, in general, wealth."[18] Free men also shared in tribal warfare. Slaves (prisoners of war) worked as farm laborers, herdsmen, or household servants.

Germanic society was patriarchal: within each household the father had authority over his wives, children, and slaves. The Germans practiced

Vandal Landowner   The adoption of Roman dress—short tunic, cloak, and sandals—reflects the way the Germanic tribes accepted Roman lifestyles. Likewise both the mosaic art form and the man's stylized appearance show the Germans' assimilation of Roman influences. Notice that the rider has a saddle but no stirrups. (*Source: Courtesy of the Trustees of the British Museum*)

polygamy, and men who could afford them had more than one wife.

Did the Germans produce goods for trade and exchange? Ironworking was the most advanced craft of the Germanic peoples. Much of northern Europe had iron deposits at or near the earth's surface, and the dense forests provided wood for charcoal. Most villages had an oven and smiths who produced agricultural tools and instruments of war—one-edged swords, arrowheads, and shields. In the first two centuries A.D., the quantity and quality of German goods increased dramatically, and the first steel swords were superior to the weapons of Roman troops. Germanic goods, however, were produced for war and the subsistence economy, not for trade. Goods were also used for gift giving, a social custom that conferred status on

the giver. Gift giving showed the higher (economic) status of the giver, cemented friendship, and placed the receiver in the giver's debt.[19] Goods that could not be produced in the village were acquired by raiding and warfare rather than by commercial exchanges. Raids between tribes brought the victors booty; captured cattle and slaves were traded or given as gifts. Warfare determined the economy and the individual's status within Germanic society.

What was the position of women in Germanic society? Did they have, as some scholars contend, a higher status than they were to have later in the Middle Ages? The law codes provide the best evidence. The codes show societies that regarded women as family property. A marriageable daughter went to the highest bidder. A woman of childbearing years had a very high wergeld. The codes also protected the virtue of women. For example, the Salic Law of the Franks fined a man a large amount if he pressed the hand of a woman and even more if he touched her above the elbow. But heavy fines did not stop injury, rape, or abduction. Widows were sometimes seized on the battlefields where their dead husbands lay and were forced to marry the victors.

A few slaves and peasant women used their beauty and their intelligence to advance their positions. The slave Fredegunda, for whom King Chilperic murdered his Visigothic wife, became a queen and held her position after her husband's death. Another slave, Balthilda, became the wife of Clovis II. During her sons' minority she worked to alleviate the evils of the slave trade.[20]

✤ THE BYZANTINE EAST (CA 400–788)

Constantine (r. 306–337) and later emperors tried to maintain the unity of the Roman Empire, but during the fifth and sixth centuries the western and eastern halves drifted apart. Justinian (r. 527–565) waged long and hard-fought wars against the Ostrogoths and temporarily regained Italy and North Africa. But his conquests had disastrous consequences. Justinian's wars exhausted the resources of the Byzantine state, destroyed Italy's economy, and killed a large part of Italy's population. The wars paved the way for the easy conquest of Italy by the Lombards shortly after Justinian's death. In the late sixth century, the territory of the Western Roman Empire came under Germanic sway, while in the East the Byzantine Empire continued the traditions and institutions of the caesars.

Latin Christian culture was only one legacy the Roman Empire bequeathed to the Western world. The Byzantine culture centered at Constantinople—Constantine's "new Rome"—was another. The Byzantine Empire maintained a high standard of living, and for centuries the Greeks were the most civilized people in the Western world. The Byzantine Empire held at bay, or at least hindered, barbarian peoples who otherwise could have wreaked additional devastation on western Europe, retarding its development. Most important, however, is the role of Byzantines, together with the Muslims (see pages 272–276), as preservers of the wisdom of the ancient world. Throughout the long years when barbarians in western Europe trampled down the old and then painfully built something new, Byzantium protected and then handed on to the West the intellectual heritage of Greco-Roman civilization.

Byzantine East and Germanic West

As imperial authority disintegrated in the West during the fifth century, civic functions were performed first by church leaders and then by Germanic chieftains. Meanwhile, in the East, the Byzantines preserved the forms and traditions of the old Roman Empire and even called themselves Romans. Byzantine emperors traced their lines back past Constantine to the emperor Augustus. The senate that sat in Constantinople carried on the traditions and preserved the glory of the old Roman senate. The army that defended the empire was the direct descendant of the old Roman legions. Even the chariot factions of the Roman Empire lived on under the Greeks, who cheered their favorites as enthusiastically as had the Romans of Hadrian's day.

The position of the church differed considerably in the Byzantine East and the Germanic West. The fourth-century emperors Constantine and Theodosius had wanted the church to act as a unifying force within the empire, but the Germanic invasions made that impossible. The bishops of Rome repeatedly called on the emperors at Constantinople for military support against the invaders, but rarely could the emperors send it. The church in the West steadily grew away from the empire and became involved in social and political affairs. Nevertheless, until the eighth century, the popes, who were often selected by the clergy of Rome, continued to send announcements of their election to the emperors at Constantinople—a sign that the Roman popes long thought of themselves as bishops of the Roman Empire.

The popes were preoccupied with conversion of the Germans, the Christian attitude toward classical culture, and relations with Germanic rulers. Because the Western church concentrated on its missionary function, it took centuries for the clergy to be organized. Most church theology in the West came from the East, and the overwhelming majority of popes were of Eastern origin.

Tensions occasionally developed between church officials and secular authorities in the West. Pope Gelasius I (r. 492–496) insisted that bishops, not civil authorities, were responsible for the administration of the church. Gelasius maintained that two powers governed the world: the sacred authority of popes and the royal power of kings. And, he insisted, the sacred power was the greater, because priests had to answer to God even for the actions of kings.

Such an assertion was virtually unheard-of in the East, where the emperor's jurisdiction over the church was fully acknowledged. The emperor in Constantinople nominated the *patriarch,* as the highest prelate of the Eastern church was called. The Eastern emperor looked on religion as a branch of the state. Religion was such a vital aspect of the social life of the people that the emperor devoted considerable attention to it. He considered it his duty to protect the faith, not only against heathen enemies but also against heretics within the empire. In case of doctrinal disputes, the emperor, following Constantine's example at Nicaea, summoned councils of bishops and theologians to settle problems.

The steady separation of the Byzantine East and the Germanic West reflects differences in the ways Christianity and classical culture were received in the two parts of the Roman Empire. In the West, Christians at first were a small, alien minority within the broad Roman culture. They kept apart from the rest of society, condemning, avoiding, and demystifying Roman society and classical culture. In Byzantium, by contrast, most Greeks were Christian. Greek *apologists,* or defenders, of Christianity insisted on harmony between Christianity and classical culture: they used Greek philosophy to buttress Christian tenets.

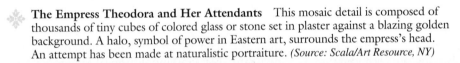

The Empress Theodora and Her Attendants   This mosaic detail is composed of thousands of tiny cubes of colored glass or stone set in plaster against a blazing golden background. A halo, symbol of power in Eastern art, surrounds the empress's head. An attempt has been made at naturalistic portraiture. *(Source: Scala/Art Resource, NY)*

Eastern Monasticism

From Egypt, Christian monasticism had spread to the Greek provinces of Syria and Palestine and to Byzantium itself. Saint Basil composed a rule that influenced all Eastern monasticism—the *Long Rules*. Basil recommended the establishment of communities of economically self-sufficient monks (or nuns) living lives of moderation. He discouraged the severe asceticism (flagellation of the body, excessive fasting, lengthy vigils with little sleep) that was so common in Egypt. Basil also supported the establishment of urban monasteries.

With the financial assistance of the emperor Justinian I (r. 527–565) and that of wealthy noble men and women, monasteries soon spread throughout the Eastern empire. Seventy abbeys were erected in Constantinople alone. Beginning in the tenth century, the monasteries acquired fields, pastures, livestock, mills, saltworks, and urban rental properties, as well as cash and precious liturgical vessels. The exemption of Byzantine monasteries from state taxes also served to increase monastic wealth.

What did the monasteries do with their revenues? Did the Greek monasteries have an impact on the broader society? Implementing Saint Basil's belief that *philanthropia,* active love for humankind, was a central part of the monastic vocation, monasteries performed important social services: they distributed food, clothing, and money to the poor and needy. Many monasteries contained within their compounds hospitals for the sick (see page 240); homes for the destitute elderly staffed by monks or nuns; and inns for travelers where the food and lodging were free. Orphans, cripples, the mentally ill, and battered women also found temporary or permanent refuge in the monasteries of monks or nuns. The Byzantine scholar Norman Baynes has written, "The Byzantine in his hour of need turned instinctively to the ascete (monk) in the full assurance of his sympathy and succor." A few monks undertook evangelical work. For example, Saint Nikon (c. 930–1000) reconverted the peoples of Crete after the Muslim occupation and preached among the pagan Slavs of the Peloponnesus. The Christian East, however, never regarded missionary or charitable work as the primary work of monasticism.

The main duty of the monk or nun was to pray. Monks and nuns served the world not so much by what they *did* as by what they *were:* people of prayer, of holiness. The monastery was the scene of the daily and continuous ritual of the divine office. The monks spent heavily on the sacred vestments and vessels used in their liturgies, which in the course of the centuries became famous for their elaborateness and splendor. The holy and charismatic *elder* (or *starets* in Slavonic) became a characteristic figure in Eastern monasticism: he or she was the spiritually mature physician capable of guiding others and healing their souls. Thus Saint Melania (383–439), abbess of a community of nuns at the Mount of Olives in Jerusalem, guided Evagrius of Pontus (ca 345–ca 399), a Syrian who later served as the spiritual father of many of the Egyptian monks at Nitria and Kellia in upper Egypt.

Monasticism in the Greek world differed in fundamental ways from the monasticism that evolved in western Europe. First, while *The Rule of Saint Benedict* gradually became the universal guide or constitution for all European monasteries, each individual house in the Byzantine world developed its own *typikon,* or set of rules for organization and behavior. The *typika* contain regulations about novitiate, diet, clothing, liturgical functions, commemorative services for benefactors, and the election of officials, such as the *hegoumenos,* or superior of the house. Second, while stability in the monastery eventually characterized Western monasticism (see page 227), many Eastern monks, especially those with a reputation for holiness, "moved frequently from one monastery to another or alternated between a coenobitic monastery and a hermit's kellion"[21] (cell). Finally, unlike the case in the West, where monasteries often established schools for the youth of the neighborhood, education never became a central feature of the Greek monasteries. Children destined for the monastic life were taught to read and write in some monasteries where monks or nuns devoted themselves to study and writing. But those houses were very few, and no monastery assumed responsibility for the general training of the local young. Since bishops and patriarchs of the Greek church were recruited only from the monasteries, Greek monasteries did exercise a cultural influence.

External Threats and Internal Conflicts

The wars of Justinian's reign left the Byzantine Empire economically and demographically weakened. Over the next two centuries, two additional troubles threatened its very survival: foreign invasion and internal theological disputes.

Beginning around 560, the Avars, a mounted Asiatic nomad group, and the Slavs, an Indo-European people probably originating in Galicia (southeastern Poland and western Ukraine), burst into the Balkan Peninsula. In the meantime, the Sassanid Persians threatened the eastern provinces. By 602 both the northern and the eastern frontiers of the Byzantine Empire had collapsed. In 626 a combined force of Persians and Avars attacked Constantinople itself. Only Byzantine control of the sea and the superhuman exertions of the emperor Heraclius (r. 610–641) saved the empire. But this effort so thoroughly exhausted both the Persians and the Greeks that they proved no match for the Arabs, who overran the eastern provinces of the empire between 632 and 640 (see pages 251–252).

Constantinople again faced sieges between 674 and 678 and from 717 to 718. Again Byzantine naval supremacy and the use of "Greek fire" (see page 239) saved the day. The Balkans, however, were lost to the Slavs; the eastern provinces, to the Arabs.

From all of these military disruptions certain benefits did result. First, the territories lost to the empire contained peoples of very diverse ethnic origins, languages, and religions. The territories that continued under imperial authority gradually achieved a strong cultural unity. They were Greek in culture and administration, orthodox in religion.

Second, foreign invasions created the need for internal reorganization. Heraclius and his successors militarized the administration. The empire was divided into *themes*, or military districts, governed by *strategoi*, or generals, who held both civil and military authority. The strategoi were directly responsible to the emperor. This reorganization brought into being a new peasant army. Foreign invasion had broken up the great landed estates of the empire, and the estate land was distributed to peasant soldiers, who equipped and supported themselves from the profits of the land. Formerly the Byzantine state had relied on foreign mercenaries. Now each theme had an army of native soldiers with a permanent (landed) interest in the preservation of the empire. The government saved the costs of hiring troops and was assured the loyalty of native soldiers. The elevation of peasants to military status revitalized the social structure.

In addition, some scholars maintain that the military disasters of the period led to an increase in popular piety and devotion to *icons*—images or representations in painting, bas-relief, or mosaic of God the Father, Jesus, the Virgin, or the saints. Since the third century, the church had allowed people to venerate icons. Although all prayer had to be directed to God the Father, Christian teaching held that icons representing the saints fostered reverence and that Jesus and the saints could most effectively plead a cause to God the Father. *Iconoclasts,* those who favored the destruction of icons, argued that people were worshiping the image itself rather than what it signified. This, they claimed, constituted *idolatry,* a violation of the Mosaic prohibition of graven images in the Ten Commandments.

The result of the controversy over icons was a terrible theological conflict that split the Byzantine world for a century. In 730 the emperor Leo III (r. 717–741) ordered the destruction of the images. The removal of icons from Byzantine churches provoked a violent reaction: entire provinces revolted, and the empire and Roman papacy severed relations. Since Eastern monasteries were the fiercest defenders of icons, Leo's son Constantine V (r. 741–775), nicknamed "Copronymous" ("Dung-name") by his enemies, took the war to the monasteries. He seized their properties, executed some of the monks, and forced others into the army. Theological disputes and civil disorder over the icons continued intermittently until 843, when the icons were restored.

The implications of the iconoclastic controversy extended far beyond strictly theological issues. Iconoclasm raised the question of the right of the emperor to intervene in religious disputes—a central problem in the relations of church and state. Iconoclasm antagonized the pope and served to encourage him in his quest for an alliance with the Frankish monarchy (see page 346). Iconoclasm thus contributed to the end of Byzantine political influence in central Italy. Arab control of the Mediterranean in the seventh and eighth centuries furthered the separation of the Roman and Byzantine churches by dividing the two parts of Christendom. Separation bred isolation. Isolation, combined with prejudice on both sides, bred hostility.

In 1054 a theological disagreement led the bishop of Rome and the patriarch of Constantinople to excommunicate each other. The outcome was a continuing *schism,* or split, between the Roman Catholic and the Greek Orthodox churches. The bitterness generated by iconoclasm contributed to that schism. Finally, the acceptance of icons profoundly influenced subsequent religious art. That art rejected the Judaic and Islamic prohibition of figural representation and continued in the Greco-Roman tradition of human representation.

Despite religious differences, the Byzantine Empire served as a bulwark for the West, protecting it against invasions from the East. The Greeks stopped the Persians and blunted Arab attacks, and they fought courageously against Turkish invaders until the fifteenth century, when they were finally overwhelmed. Byzantine Greeks slowed the impetus of Slavic incursions in the Balkans and held the Russians at arm's length.

Turning from war to peace, the Byzantines set about civilizing the Slavs, both in the Balkans and in Russia. Byzantine missionaries spread the word of Christ, and one of their triumphs was the conversion of the Russians in the tenth century. The Byzantine missionary Cyril invented a Slavic alphabet using Greek characters, and this script (called the Cyrillic alphabet) is still in use today. Cyrillic script made possible the birth of Russian literature. Similarly, Byzantine art and architecture became the basis and inspiration of Russian forms. The Byzantines were so successful that the Russians claimed to be the successors of the Byzantine Empire. For a time, Moscow was even known as the "Third Rome" (the second Rome being Constantinople).

The Law Code of Justinian

One of the most splendid achievements of the Byzantine emperors was the preservation of Roman law for the medieval and modern worlds. Roman law had developed from many sources—decisions by judges, edicts of the emperors, legislation passed by the senate, and the opinions of jurists expert in the theory and practice of law. By the fourth century, Roman law had become a huge, bewildering mass. Its sheer bulk made it almost unusable. Some laws had become outdated; some repeated or contradicted others.

The emperor Justinian appointed a committee of eminent jurists to sort through and organize the laws. The result was the *Code,* which distilled the legal genius of the Romans into a coherent whole, eliminated outmoded laws and contradictions, and clarified the law itself.

Justinian next set about bringing order to the equally huge body of Roman *jurisprudence,* the science or philosophy of law. To harmonize the often differing opinions of Roman jurists, Justinian directed his jurists to clear up disputed points and to issue definitive rulings. Accordingly, in 533 his lawyers published the *Digest,* which codified Roman legal thought. Then Justinian's lawyers compiled a handbook of civil law, the *Institutes.*

These three works—the *Code, Digest,* and *Institutes*—are the backbone of the *corpus juris civilis,* the "body of civil law," which is the foundation of law for nearly every modern European nation. The following excerpts on marriage and adultery provide valuable information on the status of women in Roman and Byzantine law:

Roman citizens unite in legal marriage when they are joined according to the precepts of the law, and males have attained the age of puberty and the females are capable of childbirth, whether they are the heads of families or the children of families, if the latter have also the consent of the relatives under whose authority they may be, for this should be obtained and both civil and natural law require that it should be secured.

The lex Julia ("Julian law," dating from 18 B.C.) declares that wives have no right to bring criminal accusations for adultery against their husbands, even though they may desire to complain of the violation of the marriage vow, for while the law grants this privilege to men it does not concede it to women. . . .

The right is granted to the father to kill a man who commits adultery with his daughter while she is under his control.[22]

Byzantine Intellectual Life

Among the Byzantines, education was highly prized, and because of them many masterpieces of ancient Greek literature survived to influence the intellectual life of the modern world. The literature of the Byzantine Empire was predominately Greek, although Latin was long spoken by top politicians, scholars, and lawyers. Among members of the large reading public, history was a favorite subject. Generations of Byzantines read the historical works of Herodotus, Thucydides, and others. Some Byzantine historians condensed long histories, such as those of Polybius; others wrote detailed narratives of their own days.

The most remarkable Byzantine historian was Procopius (ca 500–ca 562), who left a rousing account praising Justinian's reconquest of North Africa and Italy. Procopius's *Secret History,* however, is a vicious and uproarious attack on Justinian and his wife, the empress Theodora. The Byzantines are often depicted as dull and lifeless, but such opinions are hard to defend in the face of Procopius's description of Justinian's character:

For he was at once villainous and amenable; as people say colloquially, a moron. He was never truthful with anyone, but always guileful in what he said and did, yet easily hoodwinked by any who wanted to deceive him. His nature was an unnatural mixture of folly and wickedness.[23]

How much of this is true, how much the hostility of a sanctimonious hypocrite relishing the gossip he spreads, we will never know. Certainly *The Secret History* is robust reading.

Later Byzantine historians chronicled the victories of their emperors and the progress of their barbarian foes. Like Herodotus before them, they were curious about foreigners and left striking descriptions of the Turks, who eventually overwhelmed Byzantium. They sometimes painted unflattering pictures of the uncouth and grasping princes of France and England, whom they encountered on the Crusades.

In mathematics and geometry the Byzantines discovered little that was new. Yet they were exceptionally important as catalysts, for they passed Greco-Roman learning on to the Arabs, who assimilated it and made remarkable advances with it. The Byzantines were equally uncreative in astronomy and natural science, but at least they faithfully learned what the ancients had to teach.

Only when science could be put to military use did the Byzantines make advances. The best-known Byzantine scientific discovery was chemical—"Greek fire" or "liquid fire," an explosive compound made of crude oil mixed with resin and sulphur, which was heated and propelled by a pump through a bronze tube. As the liquid jet left the tube, it was ignited. The Byzantines zealously guarded details of Greek fire's composition. The equivalent of a modern flamethrower, it saved Constantinople from Arab assault in 678. In me-

Woman Carrying Pitcher   This detail from a floor mosaic in the Great Palace at Constantinople shows a woman balancing a huge water ewer on her shoulder, which suggests part of her daily work. Notice the large earrings and the coiffured hair. *(Source: Scala/Art Resource, NY)*

chanics the Byzantines continued the work of Hellenistic and Roman inventors of artillery and siege machinery.

The Byzantines devoted a great deal of attention to medicine, and the general level of medical competence was far higher in the Byzantine Empire than it was in the medieval West. The Byzantines assimilated the discoveries of Hellenic and Hellenistic medicine but added very few of their own. The basis of their medical theory was Hippocrates' concept of the four humors (see page 140). Byzantine physicians emphasized the importance of diet and rest and relied heavily on herbal drugs. Perhaps their chief weakness was excessive use of bleeding and burning, which often succeeded only in further weakening an already feeble patient.

Greek medical science, however, could not cope with the terrible disease, often called "the Justinian plague," that swept through the Byzantine Empire, Italy, southern France, Iberia, and the Rhine Valley between 541 and approximately 700. Probably originating in northwestern India and carried to the Mediterranean region by ships, the disease was similar to modern forms of bubonic plague. Characterized by high fevers, chills, delirium, and enlarged lymph nodes, or by inflammation of the lungs that caused hemorrhages of black blood, the plague carried off tens of thousands of people. It reappeared in eight- or twelve-year cycles (558–561, 580–582, 599–600, and so on) but killed fewer people each time.

The epidemic had profound political as well as social consequences. It weakened Justinian's military resources, thus hampering his efforts to restore unity to the Mediterranean world (see page 181). Demographic disasters resulting from the plague also prevented Byzantine and Persian forces from offering more than token opposition to the Muslim armies when the Arabs swarmed out of Arabia in 634[24] (see page 252).

Still, by the ninth or tenth century, most major Greek cities had hospitals for the care of the sick. The hospital operated by the Pantokrator monastery in Constantinople possessed fifty beds divided into five wards for different illnesses. A female gynecologist practiced in the women's ward. The hospital staff also included an ophthalmologist (specialist in the functions and diseases of the eye), a surgeon who performed hernia repairs, two general practitioners, two surgeons who worked an outpatient clinic, and an attendant responsible for keeping instruments clean. The imperial Byzantine government, more caring than some twentieth-century ones, bore the costs of this hospital and others.

Constantinople: The Second Rome

In the tenth century Constantinople was the greatest city in the Christian world: the seat of the imperial court and administration, a large population center, and the pivot of an extensive volume of international trade. As a natural geographical entrepôt between East and West, the city's markets offered goods from many parts of the world. About 1060 the Spanish Jew Benjamin of Tudela reported that Constantinople had merchant communities from Babylon, Canaan, Egypt, Hungary, Persia, Russia, Sennar (in the Sudan), and Spain, plus two thousand Jews.

But Constantinople did not enjoy constant political stability. Between the accession of Heraclius in 610 and the fall of the city to Western Crusaders in 1204 (see page 371), four separate dynasties ruled at Constantinople. Imperial government involved such intricate court intrigue, assassinations, and military revolts that the word *byzantine* is sometimes used in English to mean extremely entangled and complicated politics. For example, in 963 the emperor Nicephorus I Phocas married Theophano, the widow of the emperor Romanus II. In 969 Nicephorus was murdered and replaced by his nephew John I Tzimisces, Theophano's lover and an exceptionally able general.

In commerce, Jewish, Muslim (see pages 269–271), and Italian merchants controlled most foreign trade. Beginning in the eleventh century, the Venetians acquired important commercial concessions in Byzantium, thereby laying the foundations for future Venetian prosperity (see pages 360, 467). Among the Greeks, commerce faced ancient prejudices, and aristocrats and monasteries usually invested their wealth in real estate, which involved little risk but brought little gain. As in the medieval West and early modern China, rural ideals permeated Byzantine society. The landed aristocracy always held the dominant social position in the empire. Greek merchants and craftsmen, even when they acquired considerable wealth, never won social prominence.

Behind the public life of the imperial court with its assassinations and complicated politics, beyond the noise and bustle of the marketplaces thronged with Venetian and Eastern merchants, and behind the monastery walls enclosing the sophisticated theological debates of the monks, what do we know of the private life of the Constantinopolitan Greeks? Recent research has revealed a fair amount about the Byzantine *oikos*, or household. The Greek household included family members and servants, some of whom were slaves. Artisans lived and worked in their shops. Clerks, civil servants, minor officials, business people—those who today would be called middle class—commonly dwelled in multistory buildings perhaps comparable to the apartment complexes of modern American cities. Wealthy aristocrats resided in free-standing mansions that frequently included interior courts, galleries, large reception halls, small sleeping rooms, reading and writing rooms, baths, and *oratories,* chapels where all members of the household met for religious services. A complicated system of locks protected most houses from intrusion.

In the homes of the upper classes, the segregation of women seems to have been the first principle of interior design. Private houses contained a *gynaikonitis,* or women's apartment, where women were kept strictly separated from the outside world (the Muslim harem, discussed on page 269, probably derives from this Greek institution). The fundamental reason for this segregation was the family's honor: "An unchaste daughter is guilty of harming not only herself but also her parents and relatives. That is why you should keep your daughters under lock and key, as if proven guilty or imprudent, in order to avoid venomous bites," as an eleventh-century Byzantine writer put it.[25] Women did not receive outside guests, at least in theory. Although they were allowed at family banquets, they could not attend if wine was served or questionable entertainment was given. To do so gave a husband grounds for divorce.

Marriage served as part of a family's strategy for social advancement. The family and the entire kinship group participated in the selection of brides and grooms. Wealth and social connections were the chief qualities sought in potential candidates. Weddings could take place at home, in the oratory of the bride's house, or in the local church.

Scholars know a great deal about the sleeping arrangements of the imperial couples. The emperor Romanus III (r. 1028–1034), for example, shared the bed of his wife, the empress Zoe; she shared the bed of her lover, later the emperor Michael IV (r. 1034–1041). The domestic arrangements of Byzantine rulers, however, were hardly typical, and little is known about the sleeping and sexual practices of lesser mortals. The church prescribed periods of abstinence, especially during Lent (the forty days before Easter) and on Saturday and Sunday. How closely practice conformed to precept is not known. The availability of relatively good medical attention suggests that those who could afford a physician secured his services. Women delivered children seated or standing up.

SUMMARY

Saint Augustine died in 430 as the Vandals approached the coastal city of Hippo. Scholars have sometimes described Augustine as standing with one foot in the ancient world and one in the Middle Ages. Indeed, Augustine represents the end of ancient culture and the birth of what has been called the Middle Ages. A new and different kind of society was gestating in the mid-fifth century.

The world of the Middle Ages combined Germanic practices and institutions, classical ideas and patterns of thought, Christianity, and a significant dash of Islam (see Chapter 9). Christianity, because it creatively and energetically fashioned the Germanic and classical legacies, was the most powerful agent in the making of Europe. Saint Augustine of Hippo, dogmatic thinker and Christian bishop, embodied the coming world-view. In the Byzantine Empire a vigorous intellectual life, which preserved Greek scientific and medical knowledge and Roman law, flourished.

NOTES

1. Matthew 16:18–19.
2. R. C. Petry, ed., *A History of Christianity: Readings in the History of Early and Medieval Christianity* (Englewood Cliffs, N.J.: Prentice-Hall, 1962), p. 70.
3. H. Bettenson, ed., *Documents of the Christian Church* (Oxford: Oxford University Press, 1947), p. 113.
4. Colossians 3:9–11.
5. L. Sherley-Price, trans., *Bede: A History of the English Church and People* (Baltimore: Penguin Books, 1962), pp. 86–87.
6. J. T. McNeill and H. Gamer, trans., *Medieval Handbooks of Penance* (New York: Octagon Books, 1965), pp. 184–197.
7. L. White, "The Life of the Silent Majority," in *Life and Thought in the Early Middle Ages,* ed. R. S. Hoyt (Minneapolis: University of Minnesota Press, 1967), p. 100.
8. 1 Peter 2:11–20.
9. Quoted in V. L. Bullough, *The Subordinate Sex: A History of Attitudes Toward Women* (Urbana: University of Illinois Press, 1973), p. 114.
10. Ibid., pp. 118–119.
11. See J. Boswell, *Christianity, Social Tolerance, and Homosexuality: Gay People in Western Europe from the Beginning of the Christian Era to the Fourteenth Century* (Chicago: University of

Chicago Press, 1980), Chs. 3 and 5, esp. pp. 87, 127–131.

12. T. Burns, *A History of the Ostrogoths* (Bloomington: Indiana University Press, 1984), pp. 18, 21.

13. See W. Goffart, *Barbarians and Romans: The Techniques of Accommodation* (Princeton, N.J.: Princeton University Press, 1980), Ch. 3, and esp. Conclusion, pp. 211–230.

14. See P. J. Geary, *Before France and Germany: The Creation and Transformation of the Merovingian World* (New York: Oxford University Press, 1988), pp. 18–25.

15. Ibid., p. 24.

16. Ibid., pp. 108–112.

17. E. F. Henderson, ed., *Select Historical Documents of the Middle Ages* (London: G. Bell & Sons, 1912), pp. 176–189.

18. Geary, *Before France and Germany*, p. 46.

19. Ibid., p. 50.

20. See S. F. Wemple, "Sanctity and Power: The Dual Pursuit of Early Medieval Women," in *Becoming Visible: Women in European History*, 2d ed., ed. R. Bridenthal et al. (Boston: Houghton Mifflin, 1987), pp. 133–136.

21. A.-M. Talbot, "Monasteries," in *The Oxford Dictionary of Byzantium*, vol. 2, ed. A. Kazhdan (New York: Oxford University Press, 1991), p. 1393.

22. Quoted in E. Amt, ed., *Women's Lives in Medieval Europe: A Sourcebook* (New York: Routledge, 1993), pp. 34–35.

23. R. Atwater, trans., *Procopius: The Secret History* (Ann Arbor: University of Michigan Press, 1963), bk. 8.

24. W. H. McNeill, *Plagues and Peoples* (New York: Doubleday, 1976), pp. 127–128.

25. Quoted in E. Patlagean, "Byzantium in the Tenth and Eleventh Centuries," in *A History of Private Life: From Pagan Rome to Byzantium*, ed. P. Ariès and G. Duby (Cambridge, Mass.: Harvard University Press, 1987), p. 573.

SUGGESTED READING

Students seeking information on the early Christian church will find sound material in these reference works: *Encyclopedia of the Early Church,* ed. Angelo Di Berardino, trans. A. Walford, 2 vols. (1992); J. F. Kelly, *The Concise Dictionary of Early Christianity* (1992); *The Oxford Illustrated History of Christianity,* ed. J. McManners (1990); and *The Oxford Dictionary of Byzantium,* ed. A. Kazhdan (1991), which is cited in the Notes.

J. Herrin's *The Formation of Christendom* (1987) is unquestionably the best recent synthesis of the history of the early Middle Ages; it also contains an excellent discussion of Byzantine, Muslim, and Western art. In addition to the other studies listed in the Notes, students may consult the following works for a more detailed treatment of the early Middle Ages. Both M. Grant, *The Dawn of the Middle Ages* (1981), which emphasizes innovation and development, and P. Brown, *The World of Late Antiquity, A.D. 150–750,* rev. ed. (1989), which stresses social and cultural change, are lavishly illustrated and lucidly written introductions to the entire period. Grant has especially valuable material on the Germanic kingdoms, Byzantium, and eastern Europe. J. Pelikan, *The Excellent Empire: The Fall of Rome and the Triumph of the Church* (1987), describes how interpretations of the fall of Rome have influenced our understanding of Western culture. *The Cambridge Illustrated History of the Middle Ages, 350–950,* ed. R. Fossier, trans. J. Sondheimer (1989), contains some of the best recent French research on the period, though the style is often abstruse.

There is a rich literature on the Christian church and its role in the transition from ancient to medieval civilization. J. Pelikan, *Jesus Through the Centuries: His Place in the History of Culture* (1985), discusses the image of Jesus held by various cultures over the centuries and its function in the development of these cultures. F. Oakley, *The Medieval Experience: Foundations of Western Cultural Singularity* (1974), emphasizes the Christian roots of Western cultural uniqueness. W. Meeks, *The First Urban Christians: The Social World of the Apostle Paul* (1983), provides fascinating material on the early Christians and shows that they came from all social classes. For a solid appreciation of Christian life in a non-Christian society, see M. Mullin, *Called to Be Saints: Christian Living in First Century Rome* (1992). J. Richards, *Consul of God: The Life and Times of Gregory the Great* (1980), is the first significant study in seventy years of this watershed pontificate. P. Brown, *The Cult of the Saints: Its Rise and Function in Latin Christianity* (1982), describes the significance of the saints in popular religion. Students seeking to understand early Christian attitudes on sexuality and how they replaced Roman ones should consult the magisterial work of P. Brown, *The Body and Society: Men, Women, and Sexual Renunciation in Early Christianity* (1988); the profound study of J. Cohen, *"Be Fertile and Increase, Fill the Earth and Master It": The Ancient and Medieval Career of a Biblical Text* (1992), gives a lucid analysis of the church fathers' commentaries on the biblical text implied in the title and thus their views on marriage.

For the synthesis of classical and Christian cultures, see C. N. Cochrane, *Christianity and Classical Culture*

(1957), a deeply learned monograph. The best biography of Saint Augustine is P. Brown, *Augustine of Hippo* (1967), which treats him as a symbol of change. J. B. Russell, *Dissent and Order in the Middle Ages: The Search for Legitimate Authority* (1992), offers a provocative discussion of religious orthodoxy and heresy in the church.

For the Germans see, in addition to Burns's work cited in the Notes, J. M. Wallace-Hadrill, *The Barbarian West: The Early Middle Ages, A.D. 400–1000* (1962), and A. Lewis, *Emerging Europe, A.D. 400–1000* (1967), both of which describe Germanic customs and society and the Germanic impact on the Roman Empire. A rich but difficult study is H. Wolfram, *History of the Goths,* trans. T. J. Dunlop (1988), which explores Germanic tribal formation and places Gothic history within the context of late Roman society and institutions. F. Lot, *The End of the Ancient World* (1965), emphasizes the economic and social causes of Rome's decline. G. Le Bras, "The Sociology of the Church in the Early Middle Ages," in S. L. Thrupp, ed., *Early Medieval Society* (1967), discusses the Christianization of the barbarians. E. Amt, ed., *Women's Lives in Medieval Europe: A Sourcebook* (1993), is perhaps the best available collection of primary materials on women from biblical times through the thirteenth century.

The phenomenon of monasticism has attracted interest throughout the centuries. The best modern edition of the document is T. Fry et al., eds., *RB 1980: The Rule of St. Benedict in Latin and English with Notes* (1981), which contains a history of Western monasticism and a scholarly commentary on the *Rule*.

L. Eberle, trans., *The Rule of the Master* (1977), offers the text of and a commentary on Benedict's major source. Especially useful for students is O. Chadwick, *The Making of the Benedictine Ideal* (1981), a short but profound essay that emphasizes the personality of Saint Benedict in the development of the Benedictine ideal. G. Constable, *Medieval Monasticism: A Select Bibliography* (1976), is a useful research tool. Two beautifully illustrated syntheses by leading authorities are D. Knowles, *Christian Monasticism* (1969), which sketches monastic history through the middle of the twentieth century, and G. Zarnecki, *The Monastic Achievement* (1972), which focuses on the medieval centuries. L. J. Daly, *Benedictine Monasticism* (1965), stresses day-to-day living; H. W. Workman, *The Evolution of the Monastic Ideal* (1962), shows the impact of the monastic ideal on later religious orders. For women in monastic life, see S. F. Wemple, *Women in Frankish Society: Marriage and the Cloister, 500–900* (1981), an important book with a good bibliography.

For Byzantium, see J. J. Norwich, *Byzantium: The Early Centuries* (1989), an elegantly written sketch; E. Patlagean, "Byzantium in the Tenth and Eleventh Centuries," in *A History of Private Life*, vol. 1, *From Pagan Rome to Byzantium* (1987); J. Hussey, *The Byzantine World* (1961); S. Runciman, *Byzantine Civilization* (1956); and A. Bridge, *Theodora: Portrait in a Byzantine Landscape* (1984), a romantic and amusing biography of the courtesan who became empress. A. Harvey, *Economic Expansion in the Byzantine Empire, 900–1200* (1989), should prove useful for research on social and economic change.

The Conversion of Clovis

Modern Christian doctrine holds that conversion is a process, the gradual turning toward Jesus and the teachings of the Christian Gospels. But in the early medieval world, conversion was perceived more as a onetime event determined by the tribal chieftain. If he accepted baptism, the mass conversion of his people followed. The selection here about the Frankish king Clovis is from the History of the Franks *by Gregory, bishop of Tours (ca 540–594), written about a century after the events it describes.*

The first child which Clotild bore for Clovis was a son. She wanted to have her baby baptized, and she kept urging her husband to agree to this. "The gods who you worship are no good," she would say. "They haven't even been able to help themselves, let alone others. . . . Take your Saturn, for example, who ran away from his own son to avoid being exiled from his kingdom, or so they say; and Jupiter, that obscene perpetrator of all sorts of mucky deeds, who couldn't keep his hands off other men, who had his fun with all his female relatives and couldn't even refrain from intercourse with his own sister. . . .

"You ought instead to worship Him who created at a word and out of nothing heaven, and earth, the sea and all that therein is, who made the sun to shine, who lit the sky with stars, who peopled the water with fish, the earth with beasts, the sky with flying creatures, by whose hand the race of man was made, by whose gift all creation is constrained to serve in deference and devotion the man He made." However often the Queen said this, the King came no nearer to belief. . . .

The Queen, who was true to her faith, brought her son to be baptized. . . . The child was baptized; he was given the name Ingomer; but no sooner had he received baptism than he died in his white robes. Clovis was extremely angry. He began immediately

to reproach his Queen. "If he had been dedicated in the name of my gods," he said, "he would have lived without question; but now that he has been baptized in the name of your God he has not been able to live a single day!" "I give thanks to Almighty God," replied Clotild, "the Creator of all things who has not found me completely unworthy, for He has deigned to welcome into his Kingdom a child conceived in my womb. . . ."

Some time later Clotild bore a second son. He was baptized Chlodomer. He began to ail and Clovis said, "What else do you expect? It will happen to him as it happened to his brother: no sooner is he baptized in the name of your Christ than he will die!" Clotild prayed to the Lord and at His commands the baby recovered.

Queen Clotild continued to pray that her husband might recognize the true God and give up his idol-worship. Nothing could persuade him to accept Christianity. Finally war broke out against the Alamanni and in this conflict he was forced by necessity to accept what he had refused of his own free will. It so turned out that when the two armies met on the battlefield there was a great slaughter and the troops of Clovis were rapidly being annihilated. He raised his eyes to heaven when he saw this, felt compunction in his heart and was moved to tears. "Jesus Christ," he said, "you who Clotild maintains to be the Son of the living God, you who deign to give help to those in travail and victory to those who trust in you, in faith I beg the glory of your help. If you will give me victory over my enemies, and if I may have evidence to that miraculous power which the people dedicated to your name say that they have experienced, then I will believe in you and I will be baptized in your name. I have called upon my own gods, but, as I see only too clearly, they have no intention of helping me. I therefore cannot believe that they possess any power for they do not come to the assistance of those who trust them. I now call upon you. I want to believe in you, but I must first be saved from my enemies." Even as he said this the Alamanni turned their backs and began to run away. As soon as they saw that their King was killed, they submitted to Clovis. "We beg you," they said, "to put an end to this slaughter. We are prepared to obey you." Clovis stopped the war. He made a speech in which he called for peace. Then he went home. He told the Queen how he had won a victory by calling on the name of Christ. This happened in the fifteenth year of his reign (496).

The Queen then ordered Saint Remigius, Bishop of the town of Rheims, to be summoned in secret. She begged him to impart the word of salvation to the King. The Bishop asked Clovis to meet him in private and began to urge him to believe in the true God, Maker of heaven and earth, and to forsake his idols, which were powerless to help him or anyone else. The King replied: "I have listened to you willingly, holy father. There remains one obstacle. The people under my command will not agree to forsake their gods. I will go and put to them what you have said to me." He arranged a meeting with this people, but God in his power had preceded him, and before he could say a word all those present shouted in unison: "We will give up worshipping our mortal gods, pious King, and we are prepared to follow the immortal God about whom Remigius preaches." This news was reported to the Bishop. He was greatly pleased and he ordered the baptismal pool to be made ready. . . . The baptistry was prepared, sticks of incense gave off clouds of perfume, sweet-smelling candles gleamed bright and the holy place of baptism was filled with divine fragrance. God filled the hearts of all present with such grace that they imagined themselves to have been transported to some perfumed paradise. King Clovis asked that he might be baptized first by the Bishop. Like some new Constantine he stepped forward to the baptismal pool, ready to wash away the sores of his old leprosy and to be cleansed in flowing water from the sordid stains which he had borne so long.

King Clovis confessed his belief in God Almighty, three in one. He was baptized in the name of the Father, the Son and the Holy

Ninth-century ivory carving showing Clovis being baptized by Saint Remi. (*Source: Musée Condé, Chantilly/Laurie Platt Winfrey, Inc.*)

Ghost, and marked in holy chrism [an anointing oil] with the sign of the Cross of Christ. More than three thousand of his army were baptized at the same time.

Questions for Analysis

1. Who took the initiative in urging Clovis's conversion? What can we deduce from that?

2. According to this account, why did Clovis ultimately accept Christianity?

3. For the Salian Franks, what was the best proof of divine power?

4. On the basis of this selection, do you consider the *History of the Franks* reliable history? Why or why not?

Source: L. Thorpe, trans., *The History of the Franks by Gregory of Tours* (Harmondsworth, Eng.: Penguin, 1974), p. 159; and P. J. Geary, ed., *Readings in Medieval History* (Peterborough, Ont.: Broadview Press, 1991), pp. 165–166.

The Islamic World,
ca 600–1400

Arch before the *mihrab* (small niche) in the beautiful mosque of Cordova, which was begun by Abd er Rahman I in 795. *(Source: MAS Barcelona)*

Around 610, in the important commercial city of Mecca in what is now Saudi Arabia, a merchant called Muhammad began to have religious visions. By the time he died in 632, most of Arabia had accepted his creed. A century later, his followers controlled Syria, Palestine, Egypt, Iraq, Persia (present-day Iran), northern India, North Africa, Spain, and part of France. Within another century Muhammad's beliefs had been carried across central Asia to the borders of China. In the ninth, tenth, and eleventh centuries the Muslims created a brilliant civilization centered at Baghdad in Iraq, a culture that profoundly influenced the development of both Eastern and Western civilizations.

- Who were the Arabs?
- What are the main tenets of the Muslim faith?
- What factors account for the remarkable spread of Islam?
- How did the Muslims govern the vast territories they conquered?
- Why did the Shi'ite Muslim tradition arise, and how did the split between Shi'ites and Sunnis affect the course of Islam?
- What position did women hold in Muslim society?
- What features characterized the societies of the great Muslim cities of Baghdad and Cordoba?
- How did the Muslims view Western society and culture?

This chapter explores those questions.

THE ARABS BEFORE ISLAM

The Arabian peninsula, perhaps a third of the size of Europe or the United States, covers about a million square miles. Ancient Greek geographers named the peninsula *Arabian* after the Bedouin Arabs, nomads who grazed their animals in the sparse patches of grass that dotted the vast, semi-arid land. Thus *Arab* originally meant a native of Arabia. After Islam spread and peoples of various ethnic backgrounds attached themselves to or intermarried with the Arabs, they assumed an Arab identity. Today, the term *Arab* refers to an ethnic identity; *Arabic* means a linguistic and cultural heritage.

In the sixth century A.D. most Arabs were not nomads; most led a settled existence. In the southwestern mountain valleys of the Arabian peninsula, plentiful rainfall and sophisticated irrigation techniques resulted in highly productive agriculture that supported fairly dense population settlements. In other areas scattered throughout the peninsula, oasis towns based on the cultivation of date palms grew up around wells. Some oasis towns sustained sizable populations including artisans, merchants, and religious leaders. Some, such as Mecca, served as important trading outposts. The presence of the Ka'ba, a temple containing a black stone thought to be a god's dwelling place, also attracted pilgrims and enabled Mecca to become the metropolis of western Arabia. Mecca served economic and religious/cultic functions.

Thinly spread over the entire peninsula, the nomadic Bedouins migrated from place to place, grazing their sheep, goats, and camels. Though always small in number, Bedouins were the most important political and military force in the region because of their toughness, solidarity, fighting traditions, and ability to control trade and lines of communication. Between the peoples settled in oasis towns and the Bedouin nomads were seminomads. As the agricultural conditions around them fluctuated, they practiced either settled agriculture or nomadic pastoralism.

For all Arabs the basic social unit was the tribe—a group of blood relations that descended in the male line. The tribe provided protection and support and in turn received members' total loyalty. Like the Germanic peoples in the age of their migrations (see pages 228–229), Arab tribes were not static entities but continually evolving groups. A particular tribe might include both nomadic and sedentary members.

Strong economic links joined all Arab peoples. Nomads and seminomads depended on the agriculturally productive communities for food they could not produce, cloth, metal products, and weapons. Nomads paid for these goods with the livestock, milk and milk products, hides, and hair wanted by oasis towns. Nomads acquired income by serving as desert guides and as guards for caravans. Plundering caravans and extorting protection money also yielded funds.

In northern and central Arabia, tribal confederations dominated by a warrior aristocracy characterized Arab political organization. The warrior aristocrats possessed several assets that help to explain their power. They had tremendous physical toughness, and they had a few horses, which though difficult to maintain in desert conditions gave them speed and mobility. They paid tribute to no one and claimed blood descent from some great chief. Within a confederation, tribes competed for preeminence.

In the southern parts of the peninsula in the early seventh century, religious aristocracies tended to hold political power. Many oasis or market towns contained members of one holy family who claimed to be servants or priests of the deity who resided in the town, and they served as guardians of the deity's shrine, or *haram*. The family imposed rules for behavior at the shrine. Murder was forbidden at the shrine, and a tribesman knew that even his bitterest enemy would not attack him there. At the haram, a *mansib*, or cultic leader, adjudicated disputes and tried to get agreements among warrior tribes. All Arabs respected the harams because they feared retribution if the gods' shrines were desecrated and because the harams served as neutral places for arbitration among warring tribes.

The power of the northern warrior aristocracy rested on its fighting skills. The southern religious aristocracy, by contrast, depended on its cultic and economic power. Located in agricultural areas that were also commercial centers, the religious aristocracy had a stronger economic base than the warrior aristocrats. Scholarship has shown that the arbitrator role of the mansib marks a step toward a society governed by law.[1] The political genius of Muhammad was to bind together these different tribal groups into a strong unified state.

✳ MUHAMMAD AND THE FAITH OF ISLAM

A fair amount is known about Jesus after he began his public ministry at about age thirty, but little is known about his early life. Similarly, a good deal is known about Muhammad after his "call" as God's messenger at age forty, but little is known about him before then. Except for a few vague remarks in the Qur'an, the sacred book of Islam, no contemporary account of Muhammad's life (ca 570–632) survives. Arabic tradition accepts as historically true some of the sacred legends that developed about him, but those legends were not written down until about a century after his death. (Similarly, the earliest accounts of the life of Jesus, the Christian Gospels, were not written down until forty or fifty years after his death.)

Orphaned at the age of six, Muhammad was brought up by his paternal uncle. As a young man he became a merchant in the caravan trade. Later he entered the service of a wealthy widow, Khadija, and their subsequent marriage brought him financial security while she lived. Muhammad apparently was extremely pious, self-disciplined, and devoted to contemplation. At about forty, in a cave in the hills near Mecca where he was accustomed to pray, Muhammad had a profound religious experience. In a vision an angelic being (whom Muhammad later interpreted to be Gabriel, God's messenger) commanded him to preach the revelations that God would be sending him. Muhammad began to preach to the people of Mecca, urging them to give up their idols and submit to the one indivisible God. During his lifetime Muhammad's followers jotted down his revelations haphazardly. After his death scribes organized the revelations into chapters. In 651 they published the version of them that Muslims consider authoritative, the Qur'an (from an Arabic word meaning "reading" or "recitation"). Muslims revere the Qur'an for its sacred message and for the beauty of its Arabic language.

Islam, the strict monotheistic faith that is based on the teachings of Muhammad, rests on the principle of the absolute unity and omnipotence of Allah, God. The word *Islam* means "submission to God," and *Muslim* means "a person who submits." Thus the community of Muslims consists of people who have submitted to God by accepting his teachings as revealed by Muhammad, the Prophet. Muslims believe that Muhammad was the last of the prophets, completing the work begun by Abraham, Moses, and Jesus. According to the Qur'an, both Jewish and Christian authorities acknowledged the coming of a final prophet. The Jewish rabbi Kab al-Ahbar, an early convert to Islam and the source of much of the Jewish material in the early Islamic tradition, asserted "the disciples of Jesus asked, O Spirit of God, will there be another religious community after us?" And, the rabbi re-

Qur'an with Kufic Script Kufic takes its name from the town of Kufa, south of Baghdad in Iraq, at one time a major center of Muslim learning. The script relates to the angular form of the Arabic alphabet used in producing fine copies of the Qur'an. *(Source: Mashed Shrine Library, Iran/Robert Harding Picture Library)*

ported, Jesus said: "Yes, the community of Ahmad [that is Muhammad]. It will comprise people who are wise, knowing, devout, and pious."[2]

Muslims believe that they worship the same God as Jews and Christians. Islam's uncompromising monotheism—belief in the oneness of God—

spelled the end of paganism everywhere that Islam was accepted.

Monotheism, however, had flourished in Middle Eastern Semitic and Persian cultures for centuries before Muhammad. According to one scholar, "Muhammad was not the founder of Islam; he did not start a new religion." Instead, like the Old Testament prophets, Muhammad came as a reformer. In Jewish, Christian, and Muslim theology, a prophet is not someone who predicts the future; a prophet speaks the word of God. Muhammad insisted that he was not preaching a new message; rather, he was calling people back to the one true God, urging his contemporaries to reform their lives, to return to the faith of Abraham, the first monotheist.[3]

Muhammad's social and political views are inseparable from his religious ideas. Muhammad displayed genius as both political strategist and religious teacher. He gave Arabs the idea of a unique and unified *umma,* or community, which consisted of all those whose primary identity and bond was a common religious faith and commitment, not a tribal tie. The umma was to be a religious and political community led by Muhammad for the achievement of God's will on earth.

In the early seventh century the southern Arab tribal confederations, which centered around sacred enclaves, lacked cohesiveness and unity and were constantly warring; they recognized no single higher authority. The Islamic notion of an absolute higher authority transcended the boundaries of individual tribal units and fostered the political consolidation of the tribal confederations. Islam teaches that God is not only all-powerful and all-knowing but has set forth a law against which *all* human actions are measured. The fundamental tenet of Islam, to which any believer must subscribe, is "There is no God but God, and Muhammad is his Prophet." If one accepts the idea of

Jonah and the Whale The story of Jonah in the Old Testament describes a prophet who tried to avoid his responsibilities and is swallowed by a whale; it is a parable of divine mercy, urging people to repent and seek forgiveness. The Chinese artist who executed this superb painting had never seen a whale, but he possessed imagination, delicacy, and mastery of movement. *(Source: Edinburgh University Library)*

God's oneness and Muhammad's claim to be his Prophet, then it follows that all authority comes from God *through Muhammad*. Within the umma, the law of God was discerned and applied through Muhammad. Thus, in the seventh century, Islam centralized authority, both political and religious, in Muhammad's hands.[4]

The Qur'an is much holier to Muslims than the Torah and the Gospels are to Jews and Christians. The Qur'an prescribes a strict code of moral behavior. A Muslim must recite the profession of faith in God and in Muhammad as his prophet: "There is no God but God, and Muhammad is his Prophet." A believer must also pray five times a day, fast and pray during the sacred month of Ramadan, make a pilgrimage to the holy city of Mecca once during his or her lifetime, and give alms to the Muslim poor. The Qur'an forbids alcoholic beverages and gambling. It condemns *usury* in business—that is, lending money and charging the borrower interest—and taking advantage of market demand for products by charging high prices. Some foods, such as pork, are forbidden, a dietary regulation perhaps adopted from the Mosaic law of the Hebrews.

Compared with earlier Arab standards, the Qur'an sets forth an austere sexual code. Muslim jurisprudence condemned licentious behavior by both men and women, and the status of women improved. About marriage, illicit intercourse, and inheritance, the Qur'an states:

Of . . . women who seem good in your eyes, marry but two, three, or four; and if ye still fear that ye shall not act equitably, then only one. . . .

The whore and the fornicator: whip each of them a hundred times. . . .

The fornicator shall not marry other than a whore; and the whore shall not marry other than a fornicator. . . .

Men who die and leave wives behind shall bequeath to them a year's maintenance. . . . And your wives shall have a fourth part of what you leave, if you have no issue; but if you have issue, then they shall have an eighth part.

With regard to your children, God commands you to give the male the portion of two females; and if there be more than two females, then they shall have two-thirds of what their father leaves; but if there be one daughter only, she shall have the half.[5]

By contrast, Western law has tended to punish prostitutes, not their clients.

With respect to matters of property in the seventh and eighth centuries, Muslim women were more emancipated than Western women. Islamic law gave a woman control of all the property she brought to her marriage, except for the dowry. Half of the dowry went to the husband; the other half remained hers in case the marriage failed. A Muslim woman could dispose of her property in any way she wished. A Western woman had no such power.

Islam warns about the Last Judgment and the importance of the life to come. The Islamic Last Judgment bears striking resemblance to the Christian one: on that day God will separate the saved and the damned. The Qur'an describes in detail the frightful tortures with which God will punish the damned: scourgings, beatings with iron clubs, burnings, and forced drinking of boiling water. Muhammad's account of the heavenly rewards of the saved and the blessed are equally graphic but are different in kind from those of Christian theology. The Muslim vision of heaven features lush green gardens surrounded by refreshing streams. There, the saved, clothed in rich silks, lounge on brocaded couches, nibbling ripe fruits, sipping delicious beverages, and enjoying the companionship of physically attractive people.

How do the Muslim faithful merit the rewards of heaven? Salvation is by God's grace and choice alone. Because God is all-powerful, he knows from the moment of conception whether a person will be saved. But predestination does not mean that believers have no reason to try to achieve heaven. Muslims who suffer and die for the faith in battle are ensured the rewards of heaven. For others, the Qur'anic precepts mark the path to salvation.

THE EXPANSION OF ISLAM

Muhammad's preaching at first did not appeal to many people. Legend has it that for the first three years he attracted only fourteen believers. Muhammad's teaching constituted social revolution. He preached a revelation that opposed the undue accumulation of wealth and social stratification and that held all men as brothers within a social order ordained by God. Moreover, he urged the destruction of the idols in the Ka'ba at Mecca, a site that drew thousands of devout Arabs annually and thus brought important revenue to the city. The bankers and merchants of Mecca fought him. The townspeople turned against him, and he and his followers were forced to flee to Medina. This *hijra*, or emigration, occurred in 622, and Muslims later dated the beginning of their era from that event. At Medina, Muhammad attracted increasing numbers of believers, and his teachings began to have an impact.

Expansion to the West

By the time Muhammad died in 632, he had welded together all the Bedouin tribes. The crescent of Islam, the Muslim symbol, controlled most of the Arabian peninsula. In the next hundred years, one rich province of the old Roman Empire after another came under Muslim domination— first Syria, then Egypt, then all of North Africa (Map 9.1).

In 711 a Muslim force crossed the Strait of Gibraltar and at the Guadalete River easily defeated the weak Visigothic kingdom in Spain. A few Christian princes supported by the Frankish rulers held out in the Pyrenees Mountains, but the Muslims controlled most of Spain until the twelfth century. The political history of Christian Spain in the Middle Ages is the history of the *reconquista*, the Christian reconquest of that country.

In 719 the Muslims pushed beyond the Pyrenees into the kingdom of the Franks. At the Battle of Tours in 733, the Frankish chieftain Charles Martel defeated the Arabs and halted their northern expansion. The Muslims had greatly overextended their forces. Ultimately, Charlemagne expelled them from France.

Expansion to the East

Between 632 and 640, the Arabs surged to the east into the Sassanid kingdom of Persia (see page 55). When they defeated the Persians at Nihawand in 651, Muslim control of the Persian Empire was completed. The wealth seized at the Persian capital, Ctesiphon, astounded the victorious, uneducated Bedouin tribesmen, who according to one modern scholar did not understand what they had won:

Some of the warriors, unfamiliar with gold pieces, were willing to exchange them for silver ones. Others, who had never seen camphor before, took it for salt and used it in cooking. When blamed at Hira for selling an aristocratic woman who had fallen as his share of booty for only a thousand silver pieces, an Arabian replied that he never thought there was a number higher than ten hundred.[6]

The government headquarters of the vast new empire was transferred from Medina to Damascus in Syria. A contemporary proverb speaks of the Mediterranean as a Muslim lake.

The Muslims continued their drive eastward. In the mid-seventh century, they occupied the province of Khorasan, where the city of Merv became the center of Muslim control over eastern Persia (Map 9.2) and the base for campaigns farther east. By 700 the Muslims had crossed the Oxus River and swept toward Kabul, today the capital of Afghanistan. They penetrated Kazakhstan and then seized Tashkent, one of the oldest cities in central Asia. The clash of Muslim horsemen with a Chinese army at the Talas River in 751 seems to mark the farthest Islamic penetration into central Asia.

From Makran in southern Persia a Muslim force marched into the Indus Valley in northern India and in 713 founded an Islamic community at Multan. Beginning in the eleventh century, Muslim dynasties from Ghazni in Afghanistan carried Islam deeper into the Indian subcontinent.

Reasons for the Spread of Islam

By the beginning of the eleventh century the crescent of Islam flew from the Iberian heartlands to northern India. How can this rapid and remarkable expansion be explained? Muslim historians attribute Islamic victories to God's support for the Muslim faith. True, the Arabs won their military successes because they possessed a religious fervor and loyalty that their enemies could not equal. They were convinced of the necessity of the *jihad*, or holy war. The Qur'an does not explicitly mention this subject, but because the Qur'an does suggest that God sent the Prophet to establish justice on earth, it follows that justice will take effect only where Islam triumphs. Just as Christians have the

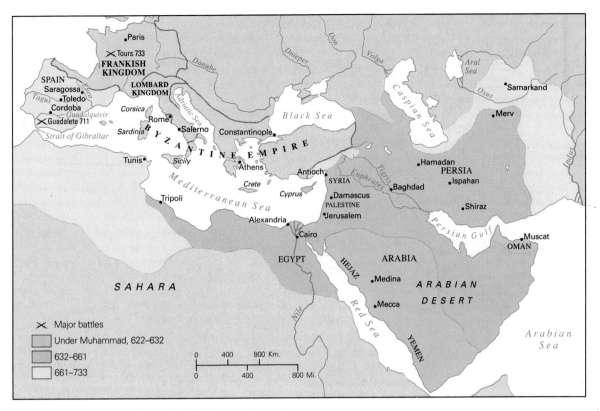

MAP 9.1 Expansion of Islam to 733 Political weaknesses in the territories they conquered, as well as superior fighting skills, help explain the speed with which the Muslims expanded.

missionary obligation to spread their faith, so Muslims have the obligation, as individuals and as a community, and to extend Islam. *Jihad* also came to mean the struggle to defend Islam. Those who waged it were assured happiness in the world to come.

The Muslim outburst from Arabia and subsequent successes had strong economic, political, and military, as well as religious, causes. The Arab surge reflects the economic needs of a tough people squeezed into a semibarren, overpopulated area and the desire to share in the rich life of the Fertile Crescent. Arab expansion in the seventh and eighth centuries was another phase of the infiltration that had taken the ancient Hebrews to the other end of the Fertile Crescent (see Map 1.1, page 9). Also, recent conflicts between the Byzantine and Sassanid empires had left both weak and divided.

In the Byzantine provinces of Egypt and Syria, moreover, theological squabbles and factional divisions helped the Muslim advance. Groups alienated from Byzantine rule expressed their dissatisfaction by quickly capitulating to the Arabs in return for promises of religious freedom and the protection of their property. In the period between 642 and 643, an Arab army officer recorded his pledges to the people of Qum, in Persia:

In the name of God, the Merciful and the Compassionate. This is what Suwayd ibn Muqarrin gave to the inhabitants of Qumis and those who are dependent on them, concerning safe-conduct for themselves, their religions and their property, on condition that they pay the jizya [a poll tax] from the hand of every adult male, according to his capacity, that they show goodwill and do not deceive, that they guide the Muslim traveler, and that they accommodate Muslims who

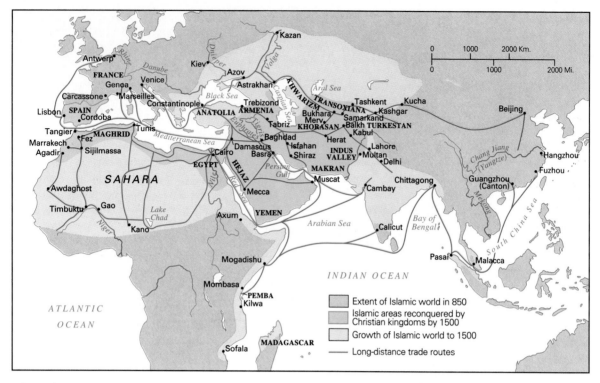

MAP 9.2 Expansion of Islam to 1500   Islam spread along the commercial arteries that extended from the eastern Mediterranean all the way to China, Southeast Asia, and Malaysia.

make a halt with them for a day and a night with their average food. If they change this or make light of their obligations, the pact [dhimma] with them is void.[7]

The Muslim conquest of Syria provides an example of the combination of motives—economic, religious, and political—that propelled early Muslim expansion. Situated to the north of the Arabian peninsula, Syria had been under Byzantine-Christian (or Roman) rule for centuries. Arab caravans knew the market towns of southern Syria and the rich commercial centers of the north, such as Edessa, Aleppo, and Damascus. Syria's economic prosperity attracted the Muslims, and perhaps Muhammad saw the lands as a potential means of support for the poor who flooded Medina. Syria also contained sites important to the Muslim faith: Jerusalem, where Jesus and other prophets mentioned in the Qur'an had lived and preached; and Hebron, the traditional burial place of Abraham, the father of monotheism. Finally, a practical polit-

ical reason encouraged expansion. The centralization of the Islamic state depended on the control of the nomadic tribes of the Arabian and Syrian deserts. In the 630s the Byzantine state, barely recovering from a long war with the Sassanid empire of Persia over Syria, was trying to forge alliances with the nomadic tribes. From the Muslim perspective, the Islamic state had to win over these peoples before the Byzantines did so. Expansion in Syria, therefore, was absolutely essential.[8]

Military organization also helps account for the Muslims' rapid success. The leadership maintained a cohesive hold on the troops, and internal conflicts did not arise to slow their initial advances. The military elite solved the problem of recruitment for the army. Fixed salaries, regular pay, and the lure of battlefield booty attracted the rugged tribesmen. In the later campaigns to the east, many recruits were recent converts to Islam from Christian, Persian, and Berber backgrounds. The assurance of army wages secured the loyalty of these very diverse men. Here is an eleventh-century description of the Egyptian army (medieval numbers were always greatly exaggerated):

Each corps has its own name and designation. One group are called Kitamis [a Berber tribe]. These came from Qayrawan in the service of al-Mu'izz li-Din Allah. They are said to number 20,000 horsemen. . . . Another group is called Masmudis. They are blacks from the land of the Masmudis and said to number 20,000 men. Another group are called the Easterners, consisting of Turks and Persians. They are so-called because they are not of Arab origin. Though most of them were born in Egypt, their name derives from their origin. They are said to number 10,000 powerfully built men. Another group are called the slaves by purchase. . . . They are slaves bought for money and are said to number 30,000 men. Another group are called Bedouin. They are from the Hijaz [Hejaz] and are all armed with spears. They are said to number 50,000 horsemen. Another group are called Ustads. These are servants [eunuchs], black and white, bought for service. They number 30,000 horsemen.[9]

In classical Islam, ethnicity and concepts of nation, country, and political sovereignty played a very small role in defining political power and authority in territorial terms. For Muslims, religion was the core of identity. They divided the world into two fundamental sections: the House of Islam, which consisted of all those regions where the law of Islam prevailed, and the House of War, which was the rest of the world. "As there is one God in heaven, so there can be only one ruler on earth." By the logic of Islamic law, no political entity outside of Islam can exist permanently. Every Muslim, accordingly, has the religious duty of the jihad—carrying out the war of conversion. Consequently, a state of war exists permanently between

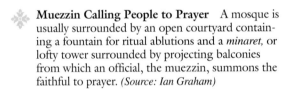

Muezzin Calling People to Prayer   A mosque is usually surrounded by an open courtyard containing a fountain for ritual ablutions and a *minaret,* or lofty tower surrounded by projecting balconies from which an official, the muezzin, summons the faithful to prayer. *(Source: Ian Graham)*

the House of Islam and the House of War. With the conversion or conquest of all humankind, the war will end.

In practice, of course, Muslims did recognize divisions among unbelievers. The most basic distinction was between those who possessed revealed religions—Jews and Christians, whose faiths are based on the revelations in the Scriptures—and those who did not. Jews and Christians who submitted to Islam enjoyed the protection of the state. They were known as *dhimmis,* or "protected people." Islam also accommodated Zoroastrians, Hindus, Buddhists, and other polytheists. Europeans regarded Muslims as "heretics" or "infidels" who when conquered had to choose between conversion and death.[10] There were, of course, many exceptions, but in general the Christian attitude toward Islam was far more bigoted and intolerant than was the attitude of Islam toward Christianity (see page 380).

What was the fate of Jews living under Islam? How does their experience compare with that of Jews living in Christian Europe? Recent scholarship shows that in Europe, Jews were first marginalized in the Christian social order, then completely expelled from it (see pages 379–380). In Islam, though marginalized, Jews participated fully in commercial and professional activities, some attaining an economic equality with their Muslim counterparts. Why? The 17th Sur (chapter) of the Qur'an, entitled Bani Isra'il, "The Children of Israel," accords to the Jews a special respect because they were "the people of the Book." Scriptural admonitions of the Qur'an carried over into social and political legislation, and "the relative stability over time of the basic law regarding their (Jews') legal status assured them a considerable degree of continuity."[11] In contrast, Western Christian legislation about the Jews fluctuated, making their legal position more ambiguous, tenuous, and insecure. Also, Islamic culture was an urban and commercial culture that gave the merchant considerable respect; medieval Christian culture was basically rural and agricultural; it did not revere the business person.

Finally, the Muslim practice of establishing camp cities in newly conquered territories facilitated expansion. New military towns, such as Al-Fustat in Egypt and Basra in Iraq, became sites from which future conquests were planned and directed. They safeguarded Muslim identity and prevented the Muslim conquerors, at first a small minority, from being assimilated into the larger indigenous population. As the subject peoples became Muslim, the army towns became major centers for the spread of Islamic culture.

CONSOLIDATION OF THE ISLAMIC STATE

Although centered in towns, Islam arose within a tribal society that lacked stable governing institutions. When Muhammad died in 632, he left a large Muslim umma, but this community stood in danger of disintegrating into separate tribal groups. Some tribespeople even attempted to elect new chiefs. What provisions did Muhammad make for the religious and political organization of his followers? How was the vast and hastily acquired empire that came into existence within one hundred years of his death to be governed?

The Caliphate

Muhammad fulfilled his prophetic mission, but his religious work remained. The Muslim umma had to be maintained and Islam carried to the rest of the world. To achieve these goals, political and military power had to be exercised. But neither the Qur'an nor the Sunna, the account of the Prophet's sayings and conduct in particular situations, offered guidance for the succession (see page 248).

In this crisis, a group of Muhammad's ablest followers elected Abu Bakr (573–634), a close supporter of the Prophet, and hailed him as *khalifa,* or caliph, an Arabic term combining the ideas of leader, successor, and deputy (of the Prophet). This election marked the decisive victory of the concept of a universal community of Muslim believers. The goals of the Muslim umma were set down in the Qur'an to make the faith revealed to Muhammad the cornerstone of Muslim law, government, and personal behavior.

Because the law of the Qur'an was to guide the community, there had to be an authority to enforce the law. Muslim teaching held that the law was paramount. God is the sole source of the law, and the ruler is bound to obey the law. Government exists not to make law but to enforce it. Muslim teaching also maintained that there is no distinction between the temporal and spiritual domains: social law is a basic strand in the fabric of comprehensive religious law. Thus religious belief and political power are inextricably intertwined: the first sanctifies the second, and the second sustains the first.[12] The creation of Islamic law in an institutional sense took three or four centuries and is one of the great achievements of medieval Islam.

In the two years of his rule (632–634), Abu Bakr governed on the basis of his personal prestige within the Muslim umma. He sent out military expeditions, collected taxes, dealt with tribes on behalf of the entire community, and led the community in prayer. Gradually, under Abu Bakr's first three successors, Umar (r. 634–644), Uthman (r. 644–656), and Ali (r. 656–661), the caliphate emerged as an institution. Umar succeeded in ex-

erting his authority over the Bedouin tribes involved in ongoing conquests. Uthman asserted the right of the caliph to protect the economic interests of the entire umma. Uthman's publication of the definitive text of the Qur'an showed his concern for the unity of the umma. But Uthman's enemies accused him of nepotism—of using his position to put his family in powerful and lucrative jobs—and of unnecessary cruelty. Opposition coalesced around Ali, and when Uthman was assassinated in 656, Ali was chosen to succeed him.

The issue of responsibility for Uthman's murder raised the question of whether Ali's accession was legitimate. Uthman's cousin Mu'awiya, a member of the Umayyad family, who had built a power base as governor of Syria, refused to recognize Ali as caliph. In the ensuing civil war, Ali was assassinated, and Mu'awiya (r. 661–680) assumed the caliphate. Mu'awiya founded the Umayyad Dynasty

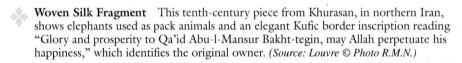

Woven Silk Fragment   This tenth-century piece from Khurasan, in northern Iran, shows elephants used as pack animals and an elegant Kufic border inscription reading "Glory and prosperity to Qa'id Abu-l-Mansur Bakht-tegin, may Allah perpetuate his happiness," which identifies the original owner. *(Source: Louvre © Photo R.M.N.)*

and shifted the capital of the Islamic state from Medina to Damascus in Syria. From 661 to 750 Damascus served as the center of the Muslim government bureaucracy.

The first four caliphs were elected by their peers, and the theory of an elected caliphate remained the Islamic legal ideal. Three of the four "patriarchs," as they were called, were murdered, however, and civil war ended the elective caliphate. Beginning with Mu'awiya, the office of caliph was in fact, but never in theory, dynastic. Two successive dynasties, the Umayyad (661–750) and the Abbasid (750–1258), held the caliphate.

From its inception with Abu Bakr, the caliphate rested on the principle that Muslim political and religious unity transcended tribalism. Mu'awiya sought to enhance the power of the caliphate by making the tribal leaders dependent on him for concessions and special benefits. At the same time, his control of a loyal and well-disciplined army enabled him to develop the caliphate in an authoritarian direction. Through intimidation he forced the tribal leaders to accept his son Yazid as his heir—thereby establishing the dynastic principle of succession. By distancing himself from a simple life within the umma and withdrawing into the palace that he built at Damascus, and by surrounding himself with symbols and ceremony, Mu'awiya laid the foundations for an elaborate caliphal court. Many of Mu'awiya's innovations were designed to protect him from assassination. A new official, the *hajib,* or chamberlain, restricted access to the caliph, who received visitors seated on a throne surrounded by bodyguards. Beginning with Mu'awiya, the Umayyad caliphs developed court ritual into a grand spectacle.

The assassination of Ali and the assumption of the caliphate by Mu'awiya had another profound consequence. It gave rise to a fundamental division in the umma and in Muslim theology. Ali had claimed the caliphate on the basis of family ties—he was Muhammad's cousin and son-in-law. When Ali was murdered, his followers argued—partly because of the blood tie, partly because Muhammad had designated Ali *imam,* or leader in community prayer—that Ali had been the Prophet's designated successor. These supporters of Ali were called *Shi'ites,* or *Shi'at Ali,* or simply *Shi'a*—Arabic terms all meaning "supporters" or "partisans" of Ali. In succeeding generations, opponents of the

Umayyad Dynasty emphasized their blood descent from Ali and claimed to possess divine knowledge that Muhammad had given them as his heirs.

Other Muslims adhered to the practice and beliefs of the umma, based on the precedents of the Prophet. They were called *Sunnis,* which derived from *Sunna.* When a situation arose for which the Qur'an offered no solution, Sunnite scholars searched for a precedent in the Sunna, which gained an authority comparable to the Qur'an itself.

What basically distinguished Sunni and Shi'ite Muslims was the Shi'ite doctrine of the *imamate.* According to the Sunnites, the caliph, the elected successor of the Prophet, possessed political and military leadership but not Muhammad's religious authority. In contrast, according to the Shi'ites, the imam (leader) is directly descended from the Prophet and is the sinless, divinely inspired political leader and religious guide of the community. Put another way, both Sunnites and Shi'ites maintain that authority within Islam lies first in the Qur'an and then in the Sunna. Who interprets these sources? Shi'ites claim that the imam does, for he is invested with divine grace and insight. Sunnites insist that interpretation comes from the consensus of the *ulema,* a group of religious scholars.

The Umayyad caliphs were Sunnis, and throughout the Umayyad period the Shi'ites constituted a major source of discontent. Shi'ite rebellions expressed religious opposition in political terms. The Shi'ites condemned the Umayyads as worldly and sensual rulers, in contrast to the pious and true "successors" of Muhammad.

The Abbasid clan, which based its claim to the caliphate on the descent of Abbas, Muhammad's uncle, exploited the situation. The Abbasids agitated the Shi'ites, encouraged dissension among tribal factions, and contrasted Abbasid piety with the pleasure-loving style of the Umayyads. Through open rebellion in 747, the Abbasids overthrew the Umayyads. In 750 the Abbasids won recognition as caliphs and later set up their capital at Baghdad in Iraq. The Abbasid Dynasty lasted until 1258, but its real power began to disintegrate in the mid-ninth century.

Scholars agree that the Abbasid revolution established a basis for rule and citizenship more cosmopolitan and Islamic than the narrow, elitist,

THE ISLAMIC WORLD, CA 600–1258

610	Muhammad preaches reform, monotheism
610–733	Spread of Islam across Arabia, southern Europe, North Africa, and Asia as far as India
622	The hijra—Muhammad and his followers emigrate to Medina
632	Muhammad dies
632–661	Caliphate emerges as an institution
642	Muslims' victory at Nihawand signals their control of the Persian Empire
651	Publication of the Qur'an, the sacred book of Islam
661–750	The Umayyad Dynasty
661	Umayyads move Muslim capital from Medina to Damascus
713	Spread of Islam to India, with the founding of a Muslim community at Multan
733	Charles Martel defeats Arabs at Battle of Tours, halting spread of Islam in northwestern Europe
750–1258	The Abbasid Dynasty
751	Battle at Talas River slows Islamic penetration of central Asia
762	Abbasids move Muslim capital from Damascus to Baghdad
945	Buyids occupy Baghdad
946	Blinding of Caliph al-Mustakfi signals the practical end of the Abbasid Dynasty
1055	Baghdad falls to the Seljuk Turks
1258	Mongols destroy Baghdad and kill the last of the Abbasid caliphs

and Arab basis that had characterized Umayyad government. Moreover, under the Umayyads the Muslim state had been governed by one ruler; during the Abbasid caliphate, steady disintegration occurred as provincial governors gradually won independent power. Although at first Muslims represented only a small minority of the conquered peoples, Abbasid rule provided the political and re-ligious milieu in which Islam gained, over the centuries, the allegiance of the vast majority of the population from Spain to Afghanistan.

Administration of the Islamic State

The Islamic conquests brought into being a new imperial system that dominated southwestern Asia and North Africa. The Muslims adopted the patterns of administration used by the Byzantines in Egypt and Syria and by the Sassanids in Persia. Arab *emirs,* or governors, were appointed and given overall responsibility for good order, the maintenance of the armed forces, and tax collecting. Below them, experienced native officials—Greeks, Syrians, Copts (Egyptian Christians)—remained in office. Thus there was continuity with previous administrations.

The Arab conquerors developed devices to meet the changing needs of their empire. Tradition holds that the second caliph, Umar, established the *diwan,* or financial bureau. This agency recorded the names of soldiers, together with their salaries from state revenues. The diwan converted payments in kind to monetary equivalents and dispersed sums to tribal chieftains for distribution to their followers. All later departments of Muslim administration derive from this core.

The Umayyad caliphate witnessed the further development of the imperial administration. At the head stood the caliph, who led the holy war against unbelievers. Theoretically, he had the ultimate responsibility for the interpretation of the sacred law. In practice, the ulema interpreted the law as revealed in the Qur'an and in the Sunna. In the course of time the ulema's interpretations constituted a rich body of law, the *shari'a,* which covered social, criminal, political, commercial, and ritualistic matters. The ulema enjoyed great prestige in the Muslim community and was consulted by the caliph on difficult legal and spiritual matters. The *qadis,* or judges, who were well versed in the sacred law, carried out the judicial functions of the state. Nevertheless, Muslim law prescribed that all people have access to the caliph, and he set aside special times for hearing petitions and for the direct redress of grievances.

The central administrative organ was the *diwan al-kharaj,* which collected the taxes that paid soldiers' salaries and financed charitable and public works that the caliph undertook, such as aid to the poor (as the Qur'an prescribed), and construction of mosques, irrigation works, and public baths.

As Arab conquests extended into Spain, central Asia, and Afghanistan, lines of communication had to be kept open. Emirs and other officials, remote from the capital at Damascus and later Baghdad, might revolt. Thus a relay network known as the *barid* was established to convey letters and intelligence reports between the capital and the various outposts. The barid employed a special technical vocabulary, as similar networks used by the Byzantine and Sassanid empires had done.

The early Abbasid period witnessed considerable economic expansion and population growth, so the work of government became more complicated. New and specialized departments emerged, each with a hierarchy of officials. The most important new official was the *vizier,* a position that the Abbasids adopted from the Persians. Initially, the vizier was the caliph's chief assistant. The vizier advised the caliph on matters of general policy, supervised the bureaucratic administration, and, under the caliph, superintended the army, the provincial governors, and relations with foreign governments. As the caliphs withdrew from leading Friday prayers and other routine functions, the viziers gradually assumed power. But the authority and power of the vizier usually depended on the caliph's personality and direct involvement in state affairs. Many viziers used their offices for personal gain and wealth. Although some careers ended with the vizier's execution, there were always candidates seeking the job.

The vizier al-Fustat (d. 924) set down some of his reflections on government. They sound more like cynical aphorisms than serious policy principles:

The basis of government is trickery; if it succeeds and endures, it becomes policy.

It is better to keep the affairs of government moving on the wrong path than to stand still on the right one.[13]

In theory, the caliph and his central administration governed the whole empire. In practice, the many parts of the empire enjoyed considerable local independence; and as long as public order was maintained and taxes were forwarded to the diwan al-kharaj, the central government rarely interfered. In theory, Muslim towns did not possess the chartered self-governing status of the towns and cities of medieval Europe (see pages 381–382). In practice, although a capable governor kept a careful eye on municipal activities, wealthy merchants and property owners had broad local autonomy.

❖ DECENTRALIZATION OF THE ISLAMIC STATE

The Umayyad state virtually coincided with all Islamic states. Under the Abbasids, decentralization began nearly from the start of the dynasty. In 755 a Umayyad prince who had escaped death at the hands of the triumphant Abbasids and fled to Spain set up an independent regime at Cordoba (see Map 9.2). In 800, the emir in Tunisia in North Africa set himself up as an independent ruler and refused to place the caliph's name on the local coinage. In 820, Tahir, the son of a slave, was rewarded with the governorship of Khorasan because he had supported the caliphate. Once there, Tahir ruled independently of Baghdad, not even mentioning the caliph's name in the traditional Friday prayers in recognition of caliphal authority.

This sort of decentralization occurred all over the Muslim world. The enormous distance separating many provinces from the imperial capital enabled the provinces to throw off the caliph's jurisdiction. Particularism and ethnic or tribal tendencies, combined with strength and fierce ambition, led to the creation of local dynasties. Incompetent or immature caliphs at Baghdad were unable to enforce their authority over distant and strong local rulers. This pattern led to the decline of the Abbasids and invasion by foreign powers.

Decline of the Abbasids

In the later ninth century, rebellions shook Arabia, Syria, and Persia, and a slave revolt devastated Iraq. These disorders hurt agricultural productivity and in turn cut tax receipts. Having severely taxed the urban mercantile groups, the caliphate had already alienated the commercial classes. Disorder and disintegration threatened the Muslim state.

In the meantime, the luxury and extravagance of the caliphal court imposed a terrible financial burden. In the caliph's palace complexes, maintained by staffs numbering in the tens of thousands, an important visitor would be conducted through elaborate rituals and confronted with indications of the caliph's majesty and power: rank upon rank of

❖ **Embassy to the Court of Ethiopia** Describing an event that happened centuries before, a fourteenth-century artist depicts a Muslim embassy to the king of Ethiopia to arrange for the extradition of early converts to Islam who had fled to Ethiopia. The easy movement of the figures suggests the influence of Chinese artists who immigrated to Baghdad and Persia during the Mongol period. Both Chinese and Muslim artists believed the blacks dressed very simply. *(Source: Edinburgh University Library)*

lavishly appointed guards, pages, servants, slaves, and other retainers; lush parks full of exotic wild beasts; fantastic arrays of gold and silver objects, ornamented furniture, precious carpets and tapestries, pools of mercury, and ingenious mechanical devices. The most famous of the mechanical devices was a gold and silver tree with leaves that rustled, branches that swayed, and mechanical birds that sang as the breezes blew.[14]

Some caliphs in the early tenth century worked to halt the process of decay. But in 945, the Buyids, a Shi'ite clan originating in Daylam, the mountainous region on the southern shores of the Caspian Sea, overran Iraq and occupied Baghdad. The caliph, al-Mustakfi, was forced to recognize the Buyid leader Mu'izz al-Dawla as *amir al-umara,* emir of emirs, and to allow the celebration of Shi'ite festivals—though the caliph and most of the people were Sunnites. A year later the caliph was accused of plotting against his new masters. He was snatched from his throne, dragged through the streets to Mu'izz al-Dawla's palace, and blinded. Blinding was a practice that the Buyids adopted from the Byzantines as a way of rendering a ruler incapable of carrying out his duties. This incident marks the practical collapse of the Abbasid caliphate, although the caliphs remained as puppets of the Buyids and symbols of Muslim unity until the Mongols killed the last of them in 1258.

The Assault of the Turks and Mongols

In the mid-tenth century, the Seljuk Turks began to besiege the Islamic world. Originating in Turkestan in central Asia and displaying great physical endurance and mobility, the Turks surged westward. They accepted Sunnite Islam near Bukhara (then a great Persian commercial and intellectual center), swarmed over the rest of Persia, and pushed through Iraq and Syria. Baghdad fell to them on December 18, 1055, and the caliph became a puppet of the Turkish *sultan*—literally, "he with authority." The sultans replaced the Buyids as masters of the Abbasid caliphate. The Turks did not acquire all of the former Abbasid state. To the west, the Shi'ite Fatimids, so-called because they claimed descent from Muhammad's daughter Fatima, had conquered present-day central Algeria, Sicily, and, in 969, Egypt.

Thus by the middle of the eleventh century, there were three centers of Muslim power: Cordoba in Spain, Cairo in Egypt, and Baghdad in Iraq. Within the Baghdad caliphate the construction of mosques, schools, canals, and roads for commerce and pilgrimages by Nizam al-Mulk (1018–1092), the vizier of three sultans, signaled new intellectual and spiritual vitality. A Turkish sultan ruled in a Muslim state.

Into this world in the early thirteenth century exploded the Mongols, a people descended from an ethnic group that originated in the area that is present-day Siberia. The Mongols adhered to shamanism, a religion in which unseen gods, demons, and ancestral spirits are thought to be responsive only to *shamans,* or priests. In 1206 their leader Jenghiz Khan (1162–1227), having welded the Mongols and related Turkish tribes into a strong confederation, swept westward.

Whether the Mongols were driven by economic or military pressures, or were attracted by the sophisticated life to the west, scholars do not know. With perhaps sixty thousand highly disciplined soldiers, the Mongols left a trail of blood and destruction. They used terror as a weapon, and out of fear the rich commercial centers of central Asia—Khwarizm, Bukhara (whose mosques were turned into stables), Herat, Samarkand, Baikal (whose peoples were all slaughtered or enslaved)—fell before them. When Jenghiz Khan died, his empire stretched from northern China and Korea to the Caspian Sea and from the Danube River to the Arctic. In 1242 the Mongols sacked Kiev. By 1250 they controlled all of southern Russia under the title "Khanate of the Golden Horde," and they ruled it for two hundred years.

Under Jenghiz Khan's grandsons, Hulagu (1217–1265) and Kublai Khan (1216–1294), the Mongol Empire expanded farther. In the west, Hulagu sacked and burned Baghdad and killed the last Abbasid caliph (1258). His hordes captured Damascus in 1260, and only a major defeat at Ayn Jalut in Syria saved Egypt and the Muslim lands in North Africa and perhaps Spain. In the east, meanwhile, Kublai Khan campaigned in China. His defeat of the Song (Sung) Dynasty and establishment of the Yuan Dynasty marked the greatest territorial extent of the Mongol Empire.

Hulagu tried to eradicate Muslim culture, but his descendant Ghazan embraced Islam in 1295 and worked for the revival of Muslim culture. As the Turks had done earlier, so did the Mongols, once converted, inject new vigor into the faith and spirit of Islam. In the Middle East the Mongols governed through Persian viziers and native financial officials.

❖ THE LIFE OF THE PEOPLE

When the Prophet appeared, Arab society consisted of independent Bedouin tribal groups loosely held together by loyalty to a strong leader and by the belief that all members of a tribe were descended from a common ancestor. Heads of families elected the *sheik,* or tribal chief. He was usually chosen from among aristocratic warrior families whose members had a strong sense of their superiority. Birth determined aristocracy.

According to the Qur'an, however, birth counted for nothing; zeal for Islam was the only criterion for honor: "O ye folk, verily we have created you male and female. . . . Verily the most honourable of you in the sight of God is the most pious of you."[15] The idea of social equality founded on piety was a basic Muslim doctrine. As a thirteenth-century commentator explained:

We have created everyone of you by means of a father and mother. All are equal in this and there is no reason therefore for boasting of one's lineage (the old Arab view being that in lineage lay honour). Through piety are souls brought to perfection and persons may compete for excellence in it; and let him who desires honour seek it in piety.[16]

When Muhammad defined social equality, he was thinking about equality among Muslims alone. But even among Muslims a sense of pride in ancestry could not be destroyed by a stroke of the pen. Claims of birth remained strong among the first Muslims; and after Islam spread outside of Arabia, full-blooded Bedouin tribesmen regarded themselves as superior to foreign converts.

The Classes of Society

In the Umayyad period, Muslim society consisted of four classes. At the top were the caliph's household and the ruling Arab Muslims. Descended from Bedouin tribespeople and composed of warriors, veterans, governing officials, and town settlers, this class constituted the aristocracy. Because birth continued to determine membership, it was more a caste than a class. It was also a relatively small group, greatly outnumbered by villagers and country people.

Converts constituted the second class in Islamic society. Converts to Islam had to attach themselves to one of the Arab tribes as clients. For economic, social, and cultural reasons they greatly resented having to do this. They believed they represented a culture superior to the culture of the Arab tribespeople. From the Muslim converts eventually came the members of the commercial and learned professions—merchants, traders, teachers, doctors, artists, and interpreters of the shari'a. Second-class citizenship led some Muslim converts to adopt Shi'ism (see page 258) and other unorthodox doctrines inimical to the state. Over the centuries, Berber, Copt, Persian, Aramaean, and other converts to Islam intermarried with their Muslim conquerors. Gradually assimilation united peoples of various ethnic and "national" backgrounds. However, in the words of one scholar, "an Arabian remained a native of the peninsula, but an Arab became one who professed Islam and spoke Arabic, regardless of national origin."[17]

Dhimmis, or "protected peoples"—Jews, Christians, and Zoroastrians—formed the third class. They were allowed to practice their religions, maintain their houses of worship, and conduct their business affairs, as long as they gave unequivocal recognition to Muslim political supremacy. Here is a formula drawn up in the ninth century as a pact between Muslims and their nonbelieving subjects:

I accord to you and to the Christians of the city of so-and-so that which is accorded to the dhimmis . . . safe-conduct . . . namely:

You will be subject to the authority of Islam and to no contrary authority. You will not refuse to carry out any obligation which we think fit to impose upon you by virtue of this authority.

If any one of you speaks improperly of Muhammed, may God bless and save him, the Book of God, or of His religion, he forfeits the protection [dhimma] of God, of the Commander of the Faithful, and of all the

Lustre Dish: Prince Khusraw Discovers Shirin Bathing Major Persian pottery centers at Ravy and Kashan produced ceramic masterpieces often in styles influenced by Chinese artists or by imported Chinese porcelains. The subjects derived from Persian literature. *(Source: Courtesy of the Freer Gallery of Art, Smithsonian Institution, Washington, D.C.)*

Muslims; his property and his life are at the disposal of the Commander of the Faithful. . . .

If any one of them commits fornication with a Muslim woman or goes through a form of marriage with her or robs a Muslim on the highway or subverts a Muslim from his religion or aids those who made war against the Muslims by fighting with them or by showing them the weak points of the Muslims, or by harboring their spies, he has contravened his pact . . . and his life and his property are at the disposal of the Muslims. . . .

You may not display crosses in Muslim cities, nor proclaim polytheism, nor build churches or meeting places for your prayers . . . nor proclaim your polytheistic beliefs on the subject of Jesus [beliefs relating to the Trinity]. . . .

Every adult male of sound mind among you shall have to pay a poll tax [jizya] of one dinar, in good coin, at the beginning of each year.[18]

Restrictions placed on Christians and Jews were not severe, and both groups seem to have thrived under Muslim rule. Rare outbursts of violence against Christians and Jews occurred only when Muslims felt that the dhimmis had stepped out of line and broken the agreement. The social position of the "protected peoples" deteriorated during the Crusades (see pages 369–370) and the Mongol invasions, when there was a general rise of religious loyalties. At those times Muslims suspected the dhimmis, often rightly, of collaborating with the enemies of Islam.

At the bottom of the social scale were slaves. The Qur'an's acceptance of slavery parallels that of the Old and New Testaments. The Qur'an forbids the enslavement of Muslims or "protected peoples," and Muhammad had recommended the hu-

mane treatment of slaves. Emancipation was a meritorious act, but the Qur'an did not grant freedom to slaves who accepted Islam.

The Muslim duty of the holy war ensured a steady flow of slaves. Prisoners of war or people captured in raids or purchased in the slave markets, slaves constituted very large numbers in the Muslim world. The great Muslim commander Musa ibn Nusayr, the son of a Christian enslaved in Iraq, is reputed to have taken 300,000 prisoners of war in his North African campaigns (708–718) and 30,000 virgins from the Visigothic nobility of Spain (these numbers are surely greatly inflated). Every soldier, from general to private, had a share of slaves from the captured prisoners. In the slave

❈ **Muslim Slave Market**   Slaves of several races were available at this thirteenth-century market at Zabid in Yemen. Women and children were wanted more than men: boys for military or administrative service, attractive women for the harem. Emancipation or the attainment of high political or military positions worked against the growth of class consciousness among slaves. (*Source: Bibliothèque Nationale, Paris*)

markets of Damascus and Baghdad in the tenth and eleventh centuries, a buyer could select from white slaves brought from Spain, Sicily, and southeastern Europe, yellow slaves from central Asia, brown slaves from India, and black slaves from sub-Saharan Africa.

Most slaves in the Islamic world went into the army or worked as household servants. Some were entrusted with business or administrative responsibilities. Few performed the kinds of agricultural labor commonly associated with slavery in the Western Hemisphere. Islamic law declared the children of a female slave to be slaves, but the offspring of a free male and a slave woman were free because lineage was in the paternal line. Many Muslims took slave women as concubines; the children belonged to the father and were free. In classical Islamic civilization, slaves played a large and sometimes distinguished role in the military, politics, religion, and the arts and sciences. Many caliphs were the emancipated sons of Turkish, Greek, and black slave women.

By the beginning of the tenth century, Islamic society had undergone significant change. The courtier al-Fadl b. Yahya, writing in 903, divided humankind into four classes:

Firstly, rulers elevated to office by their deserts; secondly, viziers, distinguished by their wisdom and understanding; thirdly, the upper classes, elevated by their wealth; and fourthly, the middle classes to which belong men marked by their culture. The remainder are filthy refuse, a torrent of scum, base cattle, none of whom thinks of anything but his food and sleep.[19]

The last category hardly reflects compassion for the poor and unfortunate. However, it is clear that birth as a sign of social distinction had yielded to wealth and talent.

Women in Classical Islamic Society

Arab tribal law gave women virtually no legal status. According to tribal law, at birth girls could be buried alive by their fathers. They were sold into marriage by their guardians for a price. Their husband could terminate the union at will. And women had virtually no property or succession rights. The Qur'an sought to improve the social position of women.

The Qur'an, like the religious writings of all traditions, represents moral precept rather than social practice, and the texts are open to different interpretations. Yet modern scholars tend to agree that the Islamic sacred book intended women as the spiritual and sexual equals of men and gave women considerable economic rights. In the early Umayyad period, moreover, women played an active role in the religious, economic, and political life of the community. They owned property. They had freedom of movement and traveled widely. They participated in the politics of the caliphal succession. Women participated with men in the public religious rituals and observances. But this Islamic ideal of women and men of equal value to the community did not last.[20] As Islamic society changed, the precepts of the Qur'an were interpreted to meet different circumstances.

In the later Umayyad period, the status of women declined. The rapid conquest of vast territories led to the influx of large numbers of slave women. As wealth replaced birth as the criterion of social status, men more and more viewed women as possessions, as a form of wealth. The increasingly inferior status of women is revealed in three ways: in the relationship of women to their husbands, in the practice of veiling women, and in the seclusion of women in harems.

On the rights and duties of a husband to his wife, the Qur'an states that "men are in charge of women because Allah hath made the one to excel the other, and because they (men) spend of their property (for the support of women). So good women are obedient, guarding in secret that which Allah hath guarded."[21] A tenth-century interpreter, Abu Ja'far Muhammad ibn-Jarir al-Tabari, commented on that passage in this way:

Men are in charge of their women with respect to disciplining (or chastising) them, and to providing them with restrictive guidance concerning their duties toward God and themselves (i.e., the men), by virtue of that by which God has given excellence (or preference) to the men over their wives: i.e., the payment of their dowers to them, spending of their wealth on them, and providing for them in full.[22]

A thirteenth-century commentator on the same Qur'anic passage goes into more detail and argues that women are incapable of and unfit for any public duties, such as participating in religious rites, giving evidence in the law courts, or being involved in any public political decisions.[23] Muslim

✴ **Birth of Prince Rustaw** Childbirth in the Islamic world, as in medieval Europe, was a process entirely in the hands of midwives. The presence of a male physician as here suggests a very difficult birth: the doctor has performed a caesarean section. This manuscript painting was executed in Egypt ca 1510 as an illustration of the Persian hero Rustaw. *(Source: Topkapi Saray Museum, Istanbul)*

society fully accepted this view, and later interpreters further categorized the ways in which men were superior to women.

The Sunni aphorism "There shall be no monkery Islam" captures the importance of marriage in Muslim culture and the Muslim belief that a sexually frustrated person was dangerous to the community. Islam vehemently discouraged sexual abstinence. Islam expected that every man and woman, unless physically incapable or financially unable, would marry: marriage was a safeguard of chastity, essential to the stability both of the family and of society. Marriage in Muslim society was a sacred contract between two families.

As in medieval Europe (see pages 428–429) and in Ming China (pages 719–720), marriage was considered too important an undertaking to be left to the romantic emotions of the young. Families or guardians, not the prospective bride and groom, identified suitable partners and finalized the contract. The official wedding ceremony consisted of an offer and its acceptance by representatives of the bride and groom's parents at a meeting before witnesses. A wedding banquet followed at which men and women feasted separately; the quality of the celebration, of the gifts, and of the food depended on the relative wealth of the two families. Because it was absolutely essential that the bride be a virgin, marriages were arranged shortly after the onset of the girl's menarche at age twelve or thirteen. Youthful marriages ensured a long period of fertility.

A wife's responsibilities depended on the financial status of her husband. A farmer's wife helped in the fields, ground the corn, carried water, prepared food, and did the myriad of tasks necessary in rural life. Shopkeepers' wives in the cities often helped in business. In an upper-class household, the lady supervised servants, looked after all domestic arrangements, and did whatever was needed for her husband's comfort.

In every case, children were the wife's special domain. A mother exercised authority over her children and enjoyed their respect. A Muslim tradition asserts that "Paradise is at the mother's feet." Thus, as in Chinese culture, the prestige of the young wife depended on the production of children—especially sons—as rapidly as possible. A wife's failure to have children was one of the main reasons for a man to take a second wife or to divorce his wife entirely.

Like the Jewish tradition, Muslim law permitted divorce, but the Qur'an seeks to preserve the union and to protect a possible child's paternity. The law prescribed that if a man intended to divorce his wife, he should avoid hasty action and not have intercourse with her for four months; hopefully, they would reconcile. If the woman became pregnant during that period, the father could be identified:

Women who are divorced have to wait for three monthly periods (before remarriage), and if they believe in God and the Last Day, they must not hide unlawfully what God has formed within their wombs. Their (ex)husbands would do well to take them back in that period, if they wish to be reconciled. Women also have recognized rights as men have, though men are over them in rank.[24]

Some interpreters of the Islamic traditions on divorce show a marked similarity to the Christian attitude. For example, some Pharisees asked Jesus whether it was permissible for a man to divorce his wife. When the Pharisees quoted the Mosaic law as allowing divorce, Jesus discussed the Mosaic law as

a concession to human weakness, arguing that what God has joined together no one should separate. In other words, Jesus held that divorce is wrong, whatever the law does to regulate it (Mark 10:2–9). Likewise, the commentator Ibn Urnan reported the Prophet as saying, "The lawful thing which God hates most is divorce."[25]

Interpretations of the Qur'an's statements on polygamy give an example of the declining status of women. The Qur'an permitted a man to have four wives, provided "that all are treated justly. . . . Marry of the women who seem good to you, two or three or four; and if ye fear that you cannot do justice (to so many) then one (only) or the captives that your right hand possess."[26] Where the Qur'an permitted polygamy, Muslim jurists interpreted the statement as having legal force. The Prophet's emphasis on justice to the several wives, however, was understood as a mere recommendation.[27] Although the Qur'an allowed polygamy, only very wealthy men could afford several wives. The vast majority of Muslim males were monogamous because women could not earn money and men had difficulty enough supporting one wife.

In contrast to the Christian view of sexual activity as something inherently shameful and even within marriage only a cure for sexual desire, Islam maintained a healthy acceptance of sexual pleasure for both males and females. Islam held that sexual satisfaction for both partners in marriage was necessary to prevent extramarital activity. Men, however, were entitled to as many as four legal partners. Women had to be content with one. Because satisfaction of the sexual impulse for males allowed polygamy,

one can speculate that fear of its inverse—one woman with four husbands—might explain the assumption of women's insatiability, which is at the core of the Muslim concept of female sexuality. Since Islam assumed that a sexually frustrated individual is a very problematic believer and a troublesome citizen, . . . the distrust of women is even greater.[28]

Modern sociologists contend that polygamy affects individuals' sense of identity. It supports men's self-images as primarily sexual beings. And, by emphasizing wives' inability to satisfy their husbands, it undermines women's confidence in their sexuality. The function of polygamy as a device to humiliate women is evident in an aphorism from Moroccan folklore: "Debase a woman by bringing in (the house) another one."[29]

In many present-day Muslim cultures, few issues are more sensitive than those of the veiling and the seclusion of women. These practices have their roots in pre-Islamic times, and they took firm hold in classical Islamic society. The head veil seems to have been the mark of free-born urban women; wearing the veil distinguished free women from slave women. Country and desert women did not wear veils because they interfered with work. Probably of Byzantine or Persian origin, the veil indicated respectability and modesty. As the Arab conquerors subjugated various peoples, they adopted some of the vanquished peoples' customs, one of which was veiling. The Qur'an contains no specific rule about the veil, but its few vague references have been interpreted as sanctioning the practice. Gradually, all parts of a woman's body were considered *pudendal* (shameful because they were capable of arousing sexual desire) and were not allowed to be seen in public.

Even more restrictive of the freedom of women than veiling was the practice of *purdah,* literally seclusion behind a screen or curtain—the harem system. The English word *harem* comes from the Arabic *haram,* meaning "forbidden" or "sacrosanct," which the women's quarters of a house or palace were considered to be. The practice of secluding women in a harem also derives from Arabic contacts with other Eastern cultures. Scholars do not know precisely when the harem system began, but within "one-and-a-half centuries after the death of the Prophet, the (harem) system was fully established. . . . Amongst the richer classes, the women were shut off from the rest of the household."[30] The harem became another symbol of male prestige and prosperity, as well as a way to distinguish and set apart upper-class women from peasants.

Trade and Commerce

Islam had a highly positive disposition toward profit-making enterprises. In the period from 1000 to 1500, there was less ideological resistance to the striving for profit in trade and commerce than there was in the Christian West. Christianity tended to condemn the acquisition of wealth beyond one's basic needs. "For Islam, the stress is laid rather upon the good use to be made of one's possessions, the merit that lies in expending them intelligently and distributing them with generosity—an attitude more favourable to economic expansion than that of the Christian theologians."[31]

Since Muslim theology and law were fully compatible with profitable economic activity, trade and commerce played a prominent role in the Islamic world. Muhammad had earned his living in business as a representative of the city of Mecca, which carried on a brisk trade from southern Palestine to southwestern Arabia. Although Bedouin nomads were among the first converts to Islam, Islam arose in a mercantile, not an agricultural, setting. The merchant had a respectable place in Muslim society. According to the sayings of the Prophet:

The honest, truthful Muslim merchant will stand with the martyrs on the Day of Judgment.

I commend the merchants to you, for they are the couriers of the horizons and God's trusted servants on earth.[32]

In contrast to the social values of the medieval West and of Confucian China, Muslims tended to look with disdain on agricultural labor and to hold trade in esteem. The Qur'an, moreover, had no prohibition against trade with Christians or other unbelievers.

Western scholars have tended to focus attention on the Mediterranean Sea as the source of Islamic mercantile influence on Europe in the Middle Ages. From the broad perspective of Muslim commerce, however, the Mediterranean held a position much subordinate to other waterways: the Black Sea; the Caspian Sea and the Volga River, which gave access deep into Russia; the Aral Sea, from which region caravans departed for China; the Gulf of Aden; and the Arabian Sea and the Indian Ocean, which linked the Arabian gulf region with eastern Africa, the Indian subcontinent, and eventually Indonesia and the Philippines. These served as the main commercial seaways of the Islamic world.

By land Muslim traders pushed south from North Africa across the Sahara into west-central Africa (see Map 9.2). By the tenth century they

Muslim Dhow   Hundreds of these lateen-rigged Arab vessels gave Islam mastery of the Indian Ocean. The Muslim fleet in the Mediterranean never equaled the one in the Indian Ocean, a circumstance that helps to explain Venetian and Genoese power in the Mediterranean in the thirteenth century. *(Source: Bibliothèque Nationale, Paris)*

had penetrated as far east as China and possibly Korea. They were pursuing silk, which was the earliest Chinese gift to the world. Travelers called the land route going through Samarkand, Bukhara, and other Turkestan towns the "great silk way," and along that way caravans collected the merchandise of Transoxiana and Turkestan. A private ninth-century list mentions a great variety of commodities transported into and through the Islamic world by land and by sea:

Imported from India: tigers, leopards, elephants, leopard skins, red rubies, white sandalwood, ebony, and coconuts

From China: aromatics, silk, porcelain, paper, ink, peacocks, fiery horses, saddles, felts, cinnamon

From the Byzantines: silver and gold vessels, embroidered cloths, fiery horses, slave girls, rare articles in red copper, strong locks, lyres, water engineers, specialists in plowing and cultivation, marble workers, and eunuchs

From Arabia: Arab horses, ostriches, thoroughbred she-camels, and tanned hides

From Barbary and Maghrib (the Arabic name for northwest Africa, an area that included Morocco, Algeria, and Tunisia): leopards, acacia, felts, and black falcons

From Egypt: ambling donkeys, fine cloths, papyrus, balsam oil, and, from its mines, high-quality topaz

From the Khazars (a people living on the northern shore of the Black Sea): slaves, slave women, armor, helmets, and hoods of mail

From Samarkand: paper

From Ahwaz (a city in southwestern Persia): sugar, silk brocades, castanet players and dancing girls, kinds of dates, grape molasses, and candy.[33]

Camels made long-distance land transportation possible. Stupid and vicious, camels nevertheless proved more efficient for desert transportation than horses or oxen. The use of the camel to carry heavy and bulky freight facilitated the development of world commerce.

Between the eighth and twelfth centuries, the Islamic world functioned virtually as a free-trade area in which goods circulated freely. The Muslims developed a number of business techniques that facilitated the expansion of trade. For example, they originated the concept of the bill of exchange, which made the financing of trade more flexible. The Muslims also seem to have come up with the idea of the joint stock company—an arrangement that lets a group of people invest in a venture and share in its profits and losses in proportion to the amount each has invested. Also, many financial and business terms—check, coffer, cipher, nadir, zenith, zero, and risk—entered the English language from Arabic.

Vigorous long-distance trade had significant consequences. Commodities produced in one part of the world became available in many other places, providing a uniformity of consumer goods among diverse peoples living over a vast area. Trade promoted scientific advances in navigation, shipbuilding, and cartography. For example, from the Chinese, Arabic sailors seem to have learned about the compass, an instrument that mariners used to determine directions on the earth's surface by means of a magnetic needle. Muslims carried the compass to Europe, and in the twelfth century it came into wide navigational use. Muslim mariners also developed the astrolabe, an instrument used to determine latitude and the time of day.

Long-distance trade brought some merchants fabulous wealth. A jeweler in Baghdad remained rich even after the caliph al-Muqtadir (r. 908–937) had seized 16 million dinars of his property. Many merchants in Siraf owned homes worth 30,000 dinars and had fortunes of 4 million dinars.[34] To appreciate the value of these sums in terms of present-day buying power, more information about the cost of living in tenth- and eleventh-century Muslim cities is needed. Nevertheless, it can be said that the sums represent very great riches.

Did Muslim economic activity amount to a kind of capitalism? If by capitalism is meant private (not state) ownership of the means of production, the production of goods for market sale, profit as the main motive for economic activity, competition, a money economy, and the lending of money at interest, then, unquestionably, the medieval Muslim economy had capitalistic features. Students of Muslim economic life have not made a systematic and thorough investigation of Muslims' industries, businesses, and seaports, but the impressionistic evidence is overwhelming: "Not only did the Muslim world know a capitalist sector, but this sector was apparently the most extensive in history before the establishment of the world market created by the Western European bourgeoisie, and this did not outstrip it in importance until the sixteenth century."[35]

Urban Centers

Long-distance trade provided the wealth that made possible a gracious and sophisticated culture in the cities of the Muslim world. Although cities and mercantile centers dotted the entire Islamic empire, the cities of Baghdad and Cordoba at their peak in the tenth century stand out as the finest examples of cosmopolitan Muslim civilization. Baghdad was founded in 762 by the second Abbasid caliph, al-Mansur, on the Tigris River, astride the major overland highways. It became the administrative, strategic, and commercial capital of the Muslim world. The presence of the caliph and his court and administration, caliphal patronage of learning and the arts, and Baghdad's enormous commercial advantages gave the city international prestige. On its streets thronged a kaleidoscope of races, creeds, costumes, and cultures, an almost infinite variety of peoples: returning travelers, administrative officials, slaves, visitors, merchants from Asia, Africa, and Europe. Shops and marketplaces offered the rich and extravagant a dazzling and exotic array of goods from all over the world.

The caliph Harun al-Rashid (r. 786–809) presided over a glamorous court. His vast palace with hundreds of officials, his harems with thousands of slave girls, his magnificent banquets, receptions, and ceremonies—all astounded foreign visitors. Harun al-Rashid invited writers, dancers, musicians, poets, and artists to live in Baghdad, and he is reputed to have rewarded one singer with a hundred thousand silver pieces for a single song. This brilliant era provided the background for the tales that appear in *A Thousand and One Nights,* the great folk classic of Arabic literature.

The central plot of the fictional tales involves the efforts of Scheherazade to keep her husband, Schariar, legendary king of Samarkand, from killing her. She entertains him with one tale a night for 1,001 nights. The best-known tales are "Aladdin and His Lamp," "Sinbad the Sailor," and "Ali Baba and the Forty Thieves." Also known as *The Arabian Nights,* this book offers a sumptuous collection of caliphs, viziers, and genies, varieties of sexual experiences, and fabulous happenings. *The Arabian Nights,* though folklore, has provided many of the images that Europeans have used since the eighteenth century to describe the Islamic world.

Cordoba in southern Spain competed with Baghdad for the cultural leadership of the Islamic world. In the tenth century, no city in Asia or Europe could equal dazzling Cordoba. Its streets were well paved and lighted, and the city had an abundant supply of fresh water. With a population of about 1 million, Cordoba contained 1,600 mosques, 900 public baths, 213,177 houses for ordinary people, and 60,000 mansions for generals, officials, and the wealthy. In its 80,455 shops, 13,000 weavers produced silks, woolens, and brocades that were internationally famous. The English language has memorialized the city's leather with the word *cordovan.* Cordoba invented the process of manufacturing crystal. Cordoba was a great educational center with 27 free schools and a library containing 400,000 volumes. (By contrast, the great Benedictine abbey of Saint-Gall in Switzerland had about 600 books. The use of paper—whose manufacture the Muslims had learned from the Chinese—instead of vellum, gave rise to this great disparity.) Through Iran and Cordoba the Indian game of chess entered western Europe.

Cordoba's scholars made contributions in chemistry, medicine and surgery, music, philosophy, and mathematics. Cordoba's fame was so great it is no wonder that the contemporary Saxon nun Hroshwita of Gandersheim (d. 1000) could describe the city as the "ornament of the world."[36]

Education and Intellectual Life

Urban and sophisticated Muslim culture possessed a strong educational foundation. Recent scholarly research provides exciting information about medieval Muslim education. Muslim culture placed extraordinary emphasis on knowledge, especially religious knowledge; indeed, knowledge and learning were esteemed above every other human activity. Knowledge provided the guidelines by which men and women should live. What kinds of educational institutions existed in the Muslim world? What was the method of instruction? What social or practical purposes did Muslim education serve?

Islam is a religion of the law, and the institution for instruction in Muslim jurisprudence was the *madrasa,* the school for the study of Muslim law and religious science. The Arabic noun *madrasa* derives from a verb meaning "to study." The first madrasas were probably established in Khurasan in northeastern Persia. By 1193, thirty madrasas existed in Damascus; between 1200 and 1250, sixty more were established there. Aleppo, Jerusalem, Alexandria, and above all Cairo also witnessed the foundation of madrasas. Schools were urban phenomena.

Wealthy merchants endowed these schools, providing salaries for the teachers, stipends for students, and living accommodations for both (see Listening to the Past). The *shaykh,* or teacher, served as a guide to the correct path of living. All Islamic higher education rested on a close relationship between teacher and students, so in selecting a teacher, the student (or his father) considered the character and intellectual reputation of the shaykh, not that of any institution. Students built their subsequent careers on the reputation of their teachers.

Learning depended heavily on memorization. In primary school, which was often attached to the institution of higher learning, a boy began his education by memorizing the entire Qur'an. Normally, he achieved this feat by the time he was seven or eight! In adolescence students learned by

Public Library at Hulwan near Baghdad   In this scene from everyday life, the teacher, second from left with open book, instructs students by commenting on the text. Library books rest on the shelves in the background. *(Source: Bibliothèque Nationale, Paris)*

heart an introductory work in one of the branches of knowledge, such as jurisprudence or grammar. Later he analyzed the texts in detail. Because the hadith—traditions containing the sayings, commands of, or stories about the Prophet and his companions—laid great stress on memory, students learned the entire texts through memory and will-power. Memorizing from 400 to 500 lines a day was considered outstanding. Every class day, the shaykh examined the student on the previous

day's learning and determined whether the student fully understood what he had memorized. Students of course learned to write, for they had to write down the teacher's commentary on a particular text. But the overwhelming emphasis was on the oral transmission of knowledge.

Because Islamic education focused on particular books or texts, when the student had mastered that text to his teacher's satisfaction, the teacher issued the student a *ijaza,* or license, certifying that he had studied a book or collection of traditions with his teacher. The ijaza allowed the student to transmit on the authority of his teacher a text to the next generation. The ijaza legalized the transmission of sacred knowledge.[37]

Apart from the fundamental goal of preparing men to live wisely and in accordance with God's law, Muslim higher education aimed at preparing men to perform religious and legal functions in the umma, or community: as Qur'an- or hadith-readers, as preachers in the mosques, as professors, educators, copyists, and especially as judges. Judges issued *ifta,* or legal opinions, in the public courts; their training was in the Qur'an, hadith, or some text forming part of the shar'ia. Islam did not know the division between religious and secular knowledge characteristic of the modern Western world.

What about women—what educational opportunities were available to them? "The seeking of knowledge is a duty of every Muslim," Muhammad had said, but Islamic culture was ambivalent on the issue of female education. Because of the basic Islamic principle that "Men are the guardians of women, because God has set the one over the other," the law excluded women from participation in the legal, religious, or civic occupations for which the madrasa prepared young men. Moreover, educational theorists insisted that men should study in a sexually isolated environment because feminine allure would distract male students. Rich evidence shows that no woman studied or held a professorship in the schools of Cairo, for example. Nevertheless, many young women received substantial educations from their parents or family members; the initiative invariably rested with their fathers or older brothers. The daughter of Ali ibn Muhammad al-Diruti al Mahalli, for example, memorized the Qur'an, learned to write, and received instruction in several sacred works. One biographical dictionary containing the lives of 1,075 women reveals that 411 had memorized the Qur'an, studied with a particular teacher, and received the ijaza. After marriage, responsibility for a woman's education belonged to her husband.[38]

How does Islamic higher education compare with that available in medieval Europe (see page 395) or Ming China (see pages 720–721)? There are some striking similarities and some major differences. In the Christian West and in China, primary and higher education was institutional. The church operated schools and universities in Europe. Local villages or towns ran schools in China. In contrast, in the Islamic world the transmission of knowledge depended overwhelmingly on the personal relationship of teacher and student: though dispensed through the madrasa, education was not institutional. In Europe the reward for satisfactory completion of a course of study was a degree granted by the university. In Muslim culture, it was not the school but the individual teacher who granted the ijaza. In China, the imperial civil service examination tested candidates' knowledge and rewarded achievement with appointments in the state bureaucracy.

In all three cultures education rested heavily on the study of basic religious, legal, or philosophical texts: the Old and New Testaments or the Justinian Code in Europe; the ethical writings of Confucian philosophy in China; the Qur'an, hadith, and legal texts deriving from these in the Muslim world. In all three cultures memorization played a large role in the acquisition and transmission of information. In the European university, however, the professor lectured on biblical text or passages of the Code, and in the Muslim madrasa the shaykh commented on a section of the Qur'an or hadith. Both professors and shaykhs sometimes disagreed fiercely about the correct interpretations of a particular text, forcing students to question, to think critically, to choose between divergent opinions. Such does not appear to be the case in China; there, critical thinking and individual imagination were discouraged.

Finally, educated people in each culture shared the same broad literary and religious or ethical culture, giving that culture cohesion and stability. Just as a man who took a degree at Cambridge University in England shared the Latin language and general philosophical outlook of someone with a degree from Montpellier in France or Naples in Italy, so a Muslim gentleman from Cairo spoke and read the same Arabic and knew the same hadith as a man from Baghdad or Samarkand. Such education as women received in Christian Europe, the Islamic world, or Ming China began and usually ended in the home and with the family.

The cosmopolitan nature of the Muslim world gave rise to a period of intellectual vitality. In spite of schism, warfare, and dynastic conflicts, the sacred Arabic language and dedication to scholarship and learning combined Semitic, Hellenic, and Persian knowledge. "A scholar might publish in Samarkand the definitive work on arithmetic used in the religious schools of Cairo. Or, in a dialogue with colleagues in Baghdad and Hamadan, he could claim to have recovered the unalloyed teachings of Aristotle in the libraries of Fez and Cordoba."[39] Modern scholars consider Muslim creativity and vitality from about 900 to 1200 one of the most brilliant periods in the world's history.

The Persian scholar al-Khwarizmi (d. ca 850) harmonized Greek and Indian findings to produce astronomical tables that formed the basis for later Eastern and Western research. Al-Khwarizmi also studied mathematics, and his textbook on algebra (from the Arabic *al-Jabr*) was the first work in which the word *algebra* is used to mean the "transposing of negative terms in an equation to the opposite side."

Muslim medical knowledge far surpassed that of the West. The Baghdad physician al-Razi (865–925) produced an encyclopedic treatise on medicine that was translated into Latin and circulated widely in the West. Al-Razi was the first physician to make the clinical distinction between measles and smallpox. The great surgeon of Cordoba, al-Zahrawi (d. 1013), produced an important work in which he discussed the cauterization of wounds (searing with a branding iron) and the crushing of stones in the bladder. In Ibn Sina of Bukhara (980–1037), known in the West as Avicenna, Muslim science reached its peak. His *al-Qanun* codified all Greco-Arabic medical thought, described the contagious nature of tuberculosis and the spreading of diseases, and listed 760 pharmaceutical drugs. Muslim scholars also wrote works on geography and jurisprudence.

Man Bitten by a Dog   Alert to the dangers of rabies and other diseases transmitted by animals, the author of this text discusses pharmaceutical remedies. Medical manuscripts were greatly valued. *(Source: Courtesy of the Freer Gallery of Art, Smithsonian Institution, Washington, DC)*

Likewise, in philosophy the Muslims made significant contributions. The Arabs understood philosophy not as a separate and distinct discipline but as a branch of theology related, like theology, to the study of the Qur'an. The Abbasid caliph al-Ma'mun (r. 813–833) established at Baghdad in 830 the House of Wisdom, a center for research and translation. Under the direction of Humayn ibn-Ishaq (d. 873), the House of Wisdom made a systematic effort to acquire and translate the chief works of ancient Greek philosophy and science. Humayn supervised the translation of almost all of Aristotle's works and the complete medical writings of Hippocrates. At the same research center al-Kindi (d. ca 870) was the first Muslim thinker to try to harmonize Greek philosophy and the religious precepts of the Qur'an. Al-Kindi sought to integrate Islamic concepts of human beings and their relations to God and the universe with the principles of ethical and social conduct discussed by Plato and Aristotle.

Inspired by Plato's *Republic* and Aristotle's *Politics,* the distinguished philosopher al-Farabi (d. 950) wrote a political treatise describing an ideal city whose ruler is morally and intellectually perfect and who has as his goal the citizens' complete happiness. Avicenna maintained that the truths found by human reason cannot conflict with the truths of revelation as given in the Qur'an. Ibn Rushid, or Averroës (1126–1198), of Cordoba, a judge in Seville and later royal court physician, paraphrased and commented on the works of Aristotle. He insisted on the right to subject all knowledge, except the dogmas of faith, to the test of reason.

Through Latin translations of these Muslim philosophers, Arabic and Hebrew writings and Greek philosophy were transmitted to the European West (see page 396). Scholasticism, the leading philosophical system of medieval Europe (see page 396), leaned heavily on Aristotelian thought. Europeans gained their knowledge of Aristotle primarily from Muslim translators and commentators.

Sufism

In the ninth and tenth centuries, in Arabia, Syria, Egypt, and Iraq, a popular religious movement arose within Islam. Some especially devout individuals within the community rejected what they considered the increasing materialism of Muslim life and sought a return to the simplicity of the Prophet's time. Called *Sufis* from the simple coarse woolen *(suf)* garments they wore, these men and women followed an ascetic lifestyle, dedicating themselves to fasting, prayer, and meditation on the Qur'an. Through asceticism and a deep love of God, Sufis sought a direct or mystical union with God. Sufi ideals—careful following of the Qur'an, the avoidance of sin, and a humble yearning toward God—were embodied in the word *zuhd,* renunciation.

The woman mystic Rabia (d. 801) epitomizes this combination of renunciation and devotionalism. An attractive woman who refused marriage so that nothing would distract her from a total commitment to God, Rabia attracted followers, whom she served as a spiritual guide. Her poem in the form of prayer captures her deep devotion:

O my lord, if I worship thee from fear of hell, and if I worship thee in hope of paradise, exclude me thence, but if I worship thee for thine own sake, then withhold not from me thine eternal beauty.

Sufism grew into a mass movement that drew people from all social classes. Though its sources were the Qur'an and the Sunna, Sufism accepted ideas from Christian and Buddhist monasticism and from Hindu devotionalism. Consequently, the ulema, the religious scholars who interpreted the Qur'an and Muslim law, looked on Sufism as a heretical movement and an unnecessary deviation from orthodoxy. The ulema also felt that the Sufis challenged their religious authority. Just as ecclesiastical authorities in Europe looked on Christian mystics with suspicion because the direct mystical union with God denied the need for the institutional church, so the Muslim ulema condemned and persecuted extreme Sufis for their rejection of religious formalism.

The Muslim View of the West

Europeans and Muslims of the Middle East were geographical neighbors. The two peoples shared a common cultural heritage from the Judeo-Christian past. But a thick psychological iron curtain restricted contact between them. The Muslim assault on Christian Europe in the eighth and ninth centuries—villages were burned, monasteries sacked,

✳ **Sufi Collective Ritual**   Collective or group rituals, in which Sufis tried through ec-
static experiences to come closer to God, have always fascinated outsiders, including
non-Sufi Muslims. Here the sixteenth-century Persian painter Sultan Muhammad illustrates the writing of the fourteenth-century lyric poet Hafiz. Just as Hafiz's poetry
moved back and forth between profane and mystical themes, so it is difficult to determine whether the ecstasy achieved here is alcoholic or spiritual. Many figures seem
to enjoy wine. Notice the various musical instruments and the delicate floral patterns
so characteristic of Persian art. *(Source: Courtesy of The Arthur M. Sackler Museum, Harvard University)*

and Christians sold into slavery (see page 357)—left a legacy of bitter hostility. Europeans' fierce intolerance also helped buttress the barrier between the two peoples. Christians felt threatened by a faith that acknowledged God as creator of the universe but denied the doctrine of the Trinity; that accepted Christ as a prophet but denied his divinity; that believed in the Last Judgment but seemed to make sex heaven's greatest reward. Popes preached against the Muslims; theologians penned tracts against them; and church councils condemned them. Europeans' perception of Islam as a menace helped inspire the Crusades of the eleventh through thirteenth centuries (see pages 368–372). The knightly class believed that it had a sacred obligation to fight the Muslims. As a popular song during the Second Crusade put it:

God has brought before you his suit against the Turks and Saracens [Crusaders' hostile term for Muslims], who have done him great despite [injury]. They have seized his fiefs, where God was first served [that is, the holy places in Palestine] and recognized as Lord.[40]

During the Crusades, Europeans imposed Christianity on any lands they conquered from Islam, and they compelled Muslims to choose among conversion, exile, and death. By the thirteenth century, Western literature, such as the Florentine poet Dante's *Divine Comedy,* portrayed the Muslims as the most dreadful of Europe's enemies, guilty of every kind of crime.

Muslims had a strong aversion to travel in Europe. They were quite willing to trade with Europeans, but they rejected European culture. Medieval Europe had no resident Muslim communities where a traveler could find the mosques, food, or other things needed for the Muslim way of life. Muslims generally had a horror of going among those they perceived as infidels, and often when compelled to make diplomatic or business contacts, they preferred to send Jewish or Christian intermediaries, the dhimmis. Commercially, from the Muslim perspective, Europe had very little to offer, apart from fine English woolens, which the Muslims admired. There was only a trickle of slaves from central and southeastern Europe.

Did Western culture have any impact on Islam? Muslims considered Christianity to be a flawed religion superseded by Islam. "For the Muslim, Christ was a precursor, for the Christian Muhammad was an impostor. For the Muslim, Christianity was an early, incomplete, and obsolete form of the true religion."[41] Religion dominated the Islamic perception of Europe. Muslims understood Europe not as Western, European, or white but as Christian. And the fact that European culture was Christian immediately discredited it in Muslim eyes. Christians were presumed to be hostile to Islam and were thought to be culturally inferior. Thus Muslims had no interest in them.

An enormous quantity of Muslim historical writing survives from the period between about 800 and 1600. Although the material reflects some knowledge of European geography, it shows an almost total lack of interest among Muslim scholars in European languages, life, and culture. Before the nineteenth century, not a single grammar book or dictionary of any Western language existed in the Muslim world. By contrast, Western scholarship on the Middle East steadily advanced. By the early seventeenth century, a curious European student could find an extensive literature on the history, religion, and culture of the Muslim peoples. In 1633, a professorship in Arabic studies was founded at Cambridge University in England.[42]

As in language and literature, so in science, engineering, and medicine: the medieval West had no influence on the Muslim world. Muslims had only contempt for Western science. Here is a twelfth-century account of a Muslim's impression of European medical practice:

The Lord of Munaytira (a Crusading Baron) wrote to my uncle asking him to send a physician to treat one of his companions who was sick. He sent him a . . . physician called Thabit. He had hardly been away for ten days, when he returned, and we said to him: "How quickly you have healed the sick!" and he replied, "They brought me two patients, a knight with an abscess on his leg, and a woman afflicted with a mental disorder. I made the knight a poultice, and the abscess burst and he felt better. I put the woman on a diet and kept her humour moist. Then a Frankish physician came to them and said to them: 'This man knows nothing about how to treat them!' Then he said to the knight: 'Which do you prefer, to live with one leg or to die with two?' and the knight said: 'To live with one.' Then the physician said: 'Bring me a strong knight and an ax,' and they brought them. Meanwhile I stood by. Then he put the sick man's leg on a wooden block and said to the knight: 'Strike his leg with the ax and cut it off with one blow!' Then, while I watched, he struck one blow, but the leg was not severed; then he struck a second blow, and the marrow of the leg spurted out, and the man died at once.

"The physician then turned to the woman, and said: 'This woman has a devil in her head who has fallen in love with her. Shave her hair off.' So they shaved her head, and she began once again to eat their usual diet, with garlic and mustard and such like. Her disorder got worse, and he said:

"'The devil has entered her head.' Then he took a razor, incised a cross on her head and pulled off the skin in the middle until the bone of the skull appeared; this he rubbed with salt, and the woman died forthwith.

"Then I said to them: 'Have you any further need of me?' and they said no and so I came home, having learned things about their medical practice which I did not know before."[43]

Only in the art of warfare did Muslims show an interest in European knowledge. During the Crusades, the Muslims adopted Frankish weapons and methods of fortification. Overall, though, medieval Muslims considered Christian Europe a backward land and almost always described Europeans as "ignorant infidels."[44]

SUMMARY

Islam is an extraordinary phenomenon in world history. Its universal monotheistic creed helps to explain its initial attractiveness to Bedouin tribes. Driven by the religious zeal of the jihad, Muslims carried their faith from the Arabian peninsula through the Middle East to North Africa, Spain, and southern France in the west and to the borders of China and northern India in the east—within the short span of one hundred years. Economic need, the political weaknesses of their enemies, strong military organization, and the practice of establishing army cities in newly conquered territories account for their expansion.

Two successive dynasties—the Umayyad, centered at Damascus in Syria, and the Abbasid, located at Baghdad in Iraq—governed the Islamic state. A large imperial bureaucracy headed by a vizier supervised the administration of the state.

All government agencies evolved from the diwan. As provincial governors acquired independent power, which the caliphs could not check, centralized authority within the Islamic state disintegrated.

Commerce and trade also spread the faith of Muhammad. Although its first adherents were nomads, Islam developed and flourished in a mercantile milieu. By land and sea, Muslim merchants transported a rich variety of goods across Asia, the Middle East, Africa, and western Europe. Muslim business procedures and terminology have greatly influenced the West.

On the basis of the wealth that trade generated, a gracious, sophisticated, and cosmopolitan culture developed with centers at Baghdad and Cordoba. In the tenth and eleventh centuries, the Islamic world witnessed enormous intellectual vitality and creativity. Muslim scholars produced important work in many disciplines, especially mathematics, medicine, and philosophy. Muslim civilization in the Middle Ages was far in advance of that of Christian Europe, and Muslims, with some justification, looked on Europeans as ignorant barbarians.

NOTES

1. See F. McG. Donner, *The Early Islamic Conquests* (Princeton, N.J.: Princeton University Press, 1981), pp. 14–37.
2. Quoted in F. E. Peters, *A Reader on Classical Islam* (Princeton, N.J.: Princeton University Press, 1994), p. 47.
3. J. L. Esposito, *Islam: The Straight Path* (New York: Oxford University Press, 1988), pp. 6–17; the quotation is on p. 15.
4. Donner, *The Early Islamic Conquests*, pp. 57–60.
5. Quoted in J. O'Faolain and L. Martines, eds., *Not in God's Image: Women in History from the Greeks to the Victorians* (New York: Harper & Row, 1973), pp. 108–115.
6. Quoted in P. K. Hitti, *The Near East in History* (Princeton, N.J.: Van Nostrand, 1961), p. 211.
7. B. Lewis, ed. and trans., *Islam: From the Prophet Muhammad to the Capture of Constantinople, vol. 1, Politics and War* (New York: Harper & Row, 1974), p. 239.
8. Donner, *The Early Islamic Conquests*, pp. 92–101.
9. Quoted ibid., p. 217.

10. See B. Lewis, *The Muslim Discovery of Europe* (New York: Norton, 1982), pp. 59–63. Discussion herein is based heavily on this important work by Lewis.

11. See M. R. Cohen, *Under Crescent and Cross: The Jews in the Middle Ages* (Princeton, N.J.: Princeton University Press, 1994), Ch. 4; the quotation is on p. 74.

12. See G. E. von Grunebaum, *Medieval Islam: A Study in Cultural Orientation* (Chicago: University of Chicago Press, 1954), pp. 142–150.

13. Quoted in Lewis, *Politics and War,* p. 201.

14. L. I. Conrad, "Caliphate," in *Dictionary of the Middle Ages,* vol. 3, ed. J. R. Strayer (New York: Scribner's, 1983), p. 45.

15. Quoted in R. Levy, *The Social Structure of Islam,* 2d ed. (Cambridge: Cambridge University Press, 1957), p. 55.

16. Ibid.

17. Hitti, *The Near East in History,* p. 229.

18. B. Lewis, ed. and trans., *Islam: From the Prophet Muhammad to the Capture of Constantinople, vol. 2, Religion and Society* (New York: Harper & Row, 1975), pp. 219–221.

19. Quoted in Levy, *The Social Structure of Islam,* p. 67.

20. N. Coulson and D. Hinchcliffe, "Women and Law Reform in Contemporary Islam," in *Women in the Muslim World,* ed. L. Beck and N. Keddie (Cambridge, Mass.: Harvard University Press, 1982), p. 37.

21. Quoted in B. F. Stowasser, "The Status of Women in Early Islam," in *Muslim Women,* ed. F. Hussain (New York: St. Martin's Press, 1984), p. 25.

22. Quoted ibid., pp. 25–26.

23. Quoted ibid., p. 26.

24. Peters, *A Reader on Classical Islam,* pp. 249–250; the quotation is on p. 250.

25. Ibid.

26. Quoted ibid., p. 16.

27. G. Nashat, "Women in Pre-Revolutionary Iran: A Historical Overview," in *Women and Revolution in Iran,* ed. G. Nashat (Boulder, Colo.: Westview Press, 1983), pp. 47–48.

28. F. Mernissi, *Beyond the Veil: Male-Female Dynamics in Modern Muslim Society* (New York: Schenkman, 1975), p. 16.

29. Ibid.

30. Quoted in D. J. Gerner, "Roles in Transition: The Evolving Position of Women in Arab Islamic Countries," in Hussain, *Muslim Women,* p. 73.

31. Quoted in Cohen, *Under Crescent and Cross,* p. 90.

32. Lewis, *Religion and Society,* pp. 126–127.

33. Adapted from Lewis, ibid., pp. 154–157.

34. Hitti, *The Near East in History,* p. 278.

35. M. Rodinson, *Islam and Capitalism,* trans. Brian Pearce (Austin: University of Texas Press, 1981), p. 56.

36. R. Hillenbrand, "Cordoba," in Strayer, *Dictionary of the Middle Ages,* vol. 3, pp. 597–601.

37. I have leaned heavily here on the important study of J. Berkey, *The Transmission of Knowledge in Medieval Cairo. A Social History of Islamic Education* (Princeton, N.J.: Princeton University Press, 1992), pp. 22–43.

38. Ibid., pp. 161–181; the quotation is on p. 161.

39. P. Brown, "Understanding Islam," *New York Review of Books,* February 22, 1979, pp. 30–33.

40. Quoted in R. W. Southern, *The Making of the Middle Ages* (New Haven, Conn.: Yale University Press, 1961), p. 55.

41. Lewis, *The Muslim Discovery of Europe,* p. 297.

42. Ibid., pp. 296–297.

43. Quoted ibid., p. 222.

44. Ibid.

Suggested Reading

The titles by F. E. Peters and M. R. Cohen cited in the Notes are especially useful: Peters for its rich collection of documents on many facets of the culture of classical Islam, Cohen for the study of Jews and Christians living in Muslim societies. C. Lindholm, *The Anthropology of Islam* (1995), argues that Islam is the most egalitarian of the Middle Eastern religions. Perhaps the best introduction to Shi'ism is Y. Richard, *Shi'ite Islam* (1994). For the social, commercial, and political significance of the obligatory Muslim pilgrimage to Mecca, see F. E. Peters, *The Hajj: The Muslim Pilgrimage to Mecca and the Holy Places* (1994). For general surveys, the curious student may consult A. Hourani, *A History of the Arab Peoples* (1991), a readable and important synthesis, and S. Fisher and W. Ochsenwald, *The Middle East: A History* (1990), which has helpful bibliographical material. The older studies of H. A. R. Gibb, *Mohammedanism: An Historical Survey,* 2d. ed. (1970), and J. J. Saunders, *A History of Medieval Islam* (1965), are still useful. For the Prophet, see W. M. Watt, *Muhammad at Mecca* (1953) and *Muhammad at Medina* (1956), and M. Rodinson, *Mohammed,* trans. A. Carter (1971). M. G. S. Hodgson, *The Classical Age of Islam,* vol. 1 of *The Venture of Islam* (1964), is comprehensive but for the specialist. K. Cragg and R. M. G. Speight, eds., *Islam from Within: Anthology of a*

Religion (1980), offers a fine collection of primary materials on the beginnings of Islam. For the cultural impact of Islam, G. E. von Grunebaum, *Classical Islam: A History 600–1258,* trans. K. Watson, (1970), remains valuable.

The best recent study of Muslim expansion is F. M. Donner, *The Early Islamic Conquests* (1986). For law and religious authority, see, in addition to the title by J. Berkey cited in the Notes, N. J. Coulson, *A History of Islamic Law* (1964); J. N. D. Anderson, *Islamic Law in the Modern World* (1959); R. P. Mottahedeh, *Loyalty and Leadership in Early Islamic Society* (1986); and S. D. Gottein, *Studies in Islamic History and Institutions* (1966).

For Muslim commercial practices, see A. L. Udovitch, *Partnership and Profit in Medieval Islam* (1970), but its thesis should be compared with the work by Rodinson cited in the Notes. For agricultural practices, see A. M. Watson, *Agricultural Innovation in the Early Islamic World* (1983), and the fascinating material in T. F. Glick, *Islamic and Christian Spain in the Early Middle Ages* (1979). For slavery in the Arab world, see B. Lewis, *Race and Slavery in the Middle East* (1990), which demythologizes the Western view of the Middle East as free of racial prejudice, and G. Murray, *Slavery in the Arab World* (1989), which explains the persistence of slavery in Muslim societies in sexual, not economic, terms. W. M. Watson, *Islam and the Integration of Society* (1961), provides an important sociological interpretation of factors that led to the unity of very diverse peoples.

In the avalanche of material that has recently appeared on women and gender in Islamic societies, J. Tucker, *Gender and Islamic History* (1993), which offers a broad sketch and an excellent introduction to the many problems in the study of gender, is especially recommended. B. F. Stowasser, *Women in the Qur'an, Traditions, and Interpretation* (1994), gives a fine analysis of the Qur'an's statement on women. The following studies contain fascinating and important discussions: L. Ahmed, *Women and Gender in Islam: Historical Roots of a Modern Debate* (1992); D. Kandiyoti, "Islam and Patriarchy: A Comparative Perspective," in *Women in Middle Eastern History,* ed. B. Baron and N. Keddie (1991), pp. 23–42; J. F. Tucker, "The Arab Family in History: 'Otherness' and the Study of the Family," in *Arab Women: Old Boundaries, New Frontiers,* ed. J. F. Tucker (1993), which although focusing on the period since 1800 will interest students of any period; N. Hijab, *Womanpower* (1988); and G. Nashat, "Women in the Middle East, 8000 B.C.–A.D. 1800," in *Restoring Women to History* (1988).

For Islamic art, see the stunning achievement of S. S. Blair and J. M. Bloom, *The Art and Architecture of Islam, 1250–1800* (1994), which authoritatively treats the trends in Islamic art and discusses virtually all masterpieces in Islamic lands. The older studies of O. Grabar, *The Formation of Islamic Art* (1987), and D. Talbot Rice, *Islamic Art,* rev. ed. (1985), provide valuable material.

On the Mongols, see P. Ratchnevsky, *Genghis Khan* (1993), which is based on Chinese, Mongol, and Persian sources, as well as European ones, to give a balanced account of the great world conqueror; M. Rossabi, *Khubilai Khan: His Life and Times* (1988); and D. Morgan, *The Mongols* (1986), an especially readable study. R. E. Dunn, *The Adventures of Ibn Battuta: A Muslim Traveler of the Fourteenth Century* (1987), gives a fascinating account of Asian and African societies by a Muslim world-traveler.

The Endowment of a Madrasa

In classical Islam, learning was considered an act of piety, a way of worshiping God. The emphasis Muslims place on learning inspired wealthy people to establish and endow madrasas, schools for the study of Muslim jurisprudence. The patron or benefactor shared in the good that the school did. This inscription (1339) from a marble tablet on a mosque in Tlemcen (modern northwest Algeria) served as a memorial to the donors and as a legal record.

In the name of God, the Merciful and the Compassionate: May God bless our Lord and our Master Muḥammad and his family and save them. Praise be to God the Lord of the Worlds, and a good end for the pious [Qur'ān, vii, 128].

The building of this blessed mosque, with the college [*madrasa*] attached to it on the western side, was ordered by our master the very just Sultan, the amir of the Muslims, the fighter in the Holy War [*mujāhid*] for the sake of the Lord of the Worlds, Abu'l-Ḥasan, the son of our master, the amir of the Muslims, the fighter in the Holy War for the sake of the Lord of the Worlds Abū Sa'īd, the son of our master the amir of the Muslims, the fighter in the Holy War for the sake of the Lord of the Worlds Abū Yūsuf ibn 'Abd al-Ḥaqq, may God support his rule and perpetuate his memory by good works. He showed his sincerity toward God by his pious works, both private and public, and he consecrated the said college for the benefit of students of the noble science and for its teaching. He consecrated the following, from his royal bounty, to the said mosque and the said college, may God enable them to profit from it:

The whole of the garden of al-Quṣayr, situated in upper al-'Ubbād, bought from the two children of 'Abd al-Wāḥid al-Quṣayr. . . .

The whole of the large garden and the house adjoining it on the western side known by the name of Dāwūd ibn 'Alī, bought from his heirs, situated in the lowest part of a lower al-'Ubbād. . . .

The whole of the garden known as the garden of al-Bādisī, also inherited from him, bought from Yaḥyā the son of the said Dāwūd, situated in the lowest part of lower al-'Ubbād.

The whole of the garden called Ibn Qar'ūsh, near the said garden of al-Bādisī, also inherited from him and bought from the son of 'Abd al-Wāḥid and 'Isā.

The whole of four orchards of which the highest is known by the name of Ibn Makkiyya, the second, of Muḥammad ibn al-Sarrāj, the third, of Faraj al-Madlisī, and the fourth, of Ibn al-Qudā Qā'isa, also inherited from him and bought from all the heirs.

The whole of his two houses which are to the north of the mosque of lower al-'Ubbād, bought from them likewise.

A half-share of the garden of al-Zuhrī, with the whole of two mills built nearby, in the direction of al-Warīṭ.

The whole of two mills also built at Qal'at Banī Mu'allā, outside the Kashūṭ gate of Tlemcen, may God guard it.

The whole of the bathhouse known as the bathhouse of al-'Āliya,[1] which is inside the

---

1. Few private houses had bathing facilities. Thus, following the practice of ancient Roman cities, most Muslim cities had public bathhouses (segregated for the two sexes) where people could cleanse themselves for a cheap price. Bathhouses were a source of revenue for their owners.

said city in the neighborhood of the iron gate, with its two adjoining shops to the right as one goes out by the southern gate, the small house adjoining it on the inner side and the upper chamber above the vestibule.

A half-share of the old bathhouse inside the city of al-Manṣūra, may God protect it.

A piece of plough-land, of the size of 20 yokes, at Tīman Yubīn in Zīdūr in the territory of Tlemcen, to provide foodstuffs for the convent of al-Ubbād, may God cause it to flourish, for the poor and for pilgrims, resident and transient.

Another piece of land of 10 yokes in the said place for those who lodge in the said college at the rate of 15 ṣāʿ per student per month. . . .

The rest of the square adjoining the said mosque, being the remainder of the garden on which the mosque was built, bought from the heirs of Muḥammad ibn ʿAbd al-Wāḥid, from the heirs of his father, his mother, and of their maternal aunt Maymūna, so that the heirs retain no claim or right of any kind.

Manuscript Illustration of teacher and pupil. (*Source: Bibliothèque Nationale, Paris*)

Questions for Analysis

1. What were the donors' motives in the foundation and endowment of the madrasa? Why were all the donors listed in the inscription?

2. What kinds of gifts were given, and why were the gifts and their locations described in such detail?

3. How would you compare the endowment of this Muslim school and the endowment of your college of university?

Source: *Repertoire chronologique d'epigraphie arabe,* vol. 15, pp. 103–107, no. 5764. Reprinted from *Islam: From the Prophet Muhammad to the Capture of Constantinople,* vol. 2, *Religion and Society,* ed. and trans. Bernard Lewis (New York: Oxford University Press, 1987), pp. 16–18.

10

Africa Before European Intrusion, ca 400–1500

This painting from a later fourteenth-century manuscript from the monastery of Gunda Gundie in Ethiopia, depicts Elija on a red horse, and below his disciple Elisha who grasps his master's cloak. On the right are Enoch and Esdras, completing this group of authors of apocalyptic visions. *(Source: From* Ethiopian Painting *by Jules Leroy (Frederick A. Praeger, Publishers). Reproduced with permission.)*

etween about 400 and 1500, Africa witnessed the development of highly sophisticated civilizations alongside a spectrum of more simply organized societies. Until fairly recently, ethnocentrism, Eurocentrism, and white racism have limited what Asians, Europeans, and Americans have known about Africa. The more that historians, sociologists, and anthropologists have learned about early African civilizations, the more they have come to appreciate the richness, diversity, and dynamism of those cultures.

- What patterns of social and political organization prevailed among the peoples of Africa?
- What types of agriculture and commerce did Africans engage in?
- What values do Africans' art, architecture, and religions express?

In a discussion of the major civilizations of Africa before 1500, these are the questions this chapter explores.

❖ THE LAND AND PEOPLES OF AFRICA

Africa is immense. The world's second largest continent (after Asia), it is three times as big as Europe and covers 20 percent of the earth's land surface. The coastal regions of Africa felt the impact of other cultures, and African peoples in turn have influenced European, Middle Eastern, and Asian societies. African peoples have never been isolated from other peoples. Five climatic zones roughly divide the continent (Map 10.1). Fertile land with unpredictable rainfall borders parts of the Mediterranean coast in the north and the southwestern coast of the Cape of Good Hope in the south. Inland from these areas lies dry steppe country with little plant life. The southern fringe of this area is called the Sahel. The steppes gradually give way to Africa's great deserts: the Sahara in the north and the Namib and Kalahari in the south. The vast Sahara—3.5 million square miles—takes its name from the Arabic word for "tan," the color of the desert. (Folk etymology ascribes the word *Sahara* to an ancient Arabic word that sounds like a parched man's gasp for water.) Savanna—flat grasslands—extends in a swath across the widest part of the continent, as well as across parts of south-central Africa and along the eastern coast. One of the richest habitats in the world and comprising perhaps 55 percent of the African continent, the savanna has always invited migration and cultural contacts. Thus it is the most important region of West Africa historically. Dense, humid, tropical rain forests stretch along coastal West Africa and on both sides of the equator in central Africa until they are stopped by volcanic mountains two-thirds of the way across the continent.

The climate in most of Africa is tropical. Subtropical climates are limited to the northern and southern coasts and to regions of high elevation. Rainfall is seasonal in most parts of the continent and is very sparse in desert and semidesert areas.

Geography and climate have shaped the economic development of the peoples of Africa just as they have shaped the lives of people everywhere else. In the eastern African plains, the earliest humans hunted wild animals. The drier steppe regions favored the development of herding. Wetter savanna regions, like the Nile Valley, encouraged the rise of grain-based agriculture. The tropical forests favored hunting and gathering and, later, root-based agriculture. Regions around rivers and lakes supported economies based on fishing.

The peoples of Africa are as diverse as the topography of the continent. In North Africa, contacts with Asian and European civilizations date back to the ancient Phoenicians, Greeks, and Romans. The native Berbers, who lived along the Mediterranean, intermingled with many different peoples—with Muslim Arabs, who first conquered the region of North Africa in the seventh and eighth centuries A.D.; with Spanish Muslims and Jews, many of whom settled in North Africa after their expulsion from Spain in 1492 (see pages 484–485); and with sub-Saharan blacks.[1] The peoples living along the east, or Swahili, coast developed a maritime civilization and had rich commercial contacts with India, China, and the Malay Archipelago.

Historians and sociologists today vigorously dispute the racial classification of the Egyptians in this period. Genetically, Egyptians were Arabian, Greek, and sub-Saharan African in origin. Some scholars prefer to explain the Egyptians as a cultural, rather than a racial, group. In any case, geography tended to isolate Egypt from the rest of the continent and brought Egypt more into contact with Mediterranean civilizations.

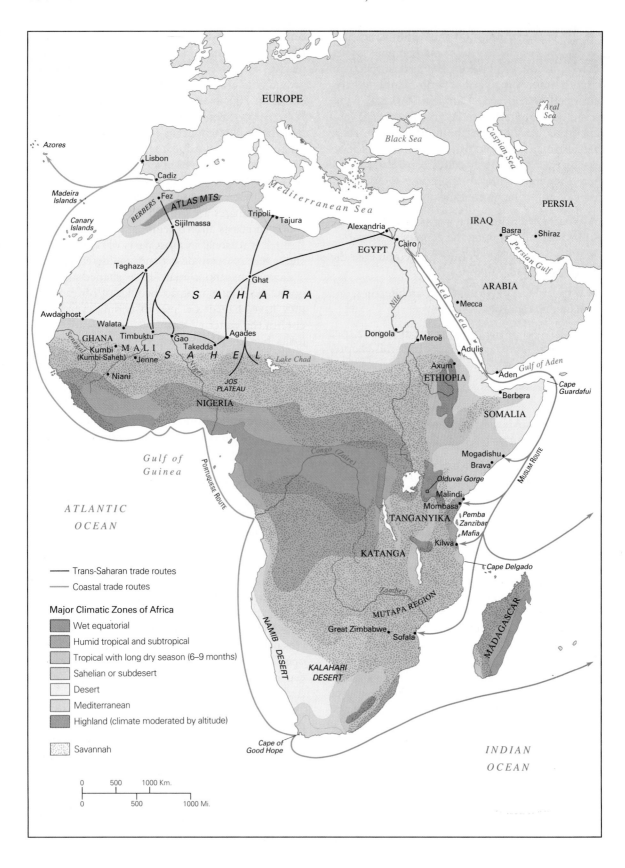

Trans-Saharan trade routes

Coastal trade routes

Major Climatic Zones of Africa

Wet equatorial

Humid tropical and subtropical

Tropical with long dry season (6–9 months)

Sahelian or subdesert

Desert

Mediterranean

Highland (climate moderated by altitude)

Savannah

 Tassili Rock Painting   This scene of cattle grazing near the group of huts (represented on the left by stylized white ovals) reflects the domestication of animals and the development of settled pastoral agriculture. Women and children seem to perform most of the domestic chores. Tassili is a mountainous region in the Sahara. *(Source: Henri Lhote, Montrichard, France)*

Black Africans inhabited the region south of the Sahara, an area of savanna and rain forest. In describing them, the ancient Greeks used the term *Ethiopians,* which meant "people with burnt faces." The Berbers coined the term *Akal-n-Iquinawen,* which survives today as *Guinea.* The Arabs introduced another term, *Bilad al-Sudan,* which survives as *Sudan.* The Berber and Arab words both mean the "land of the blacks." Short-statured peoples sometimes called Pygmies inhabited the equatorial rain forests. South of those forests, in the southern third of the continent, lived the Khoisan, a small people of yellow-brown skin color who primarily were hunters.

EARLY AFRICAN SOCIETIES

Africa was one of the sites where agriculture began. Archaeological investigations suggest that knowledge of cultivation moved west from ancient Judaea (southern Palestine) and arrived in the Nile Delta in Egypt about the fifth millennium before Christ. Settled agriculture then traveled down the Nile Valley and moved west across the southern

 MAP 10.1 Africa Before 1500   For centuries trade linked West Africa with Mediterranean and Asian societies. Note the various climatic zones, the trans-Saharan trade routes, and the trade routes along the coast of East Africa.

edge of the Sahara to the central and western Sudan. By the first century B.C. settled agriculture existed in West Africa. From there it spread to the equatorial forests. African farmers learned to domesticate plants, including millet, sorghum, and yams. Cereal-growing people probably taught forest people to plant regular fields. Gradually African farmers also learned to clear land by burning. They evolved a sedentary way of life: living in villages, clearing fields, relying on root crops, and fishing.

Nok Woman   Hundreds of terra-cotta sculptures such as the head of this woman survive from the Nok culture, which originated in the central plateau of northern Nigeria in the first millennium B.C. *(Source: National Museum, Lagos, Nigeria/Werner Forman Archive/Art Resource, NY)*

Between 1500 and 1000 B.C. settled agriculture also spread southward from Ethiopia along the Rift Valley of present-day Kenya and Tanzania. Archaeological evidence reveals that the peoples of this region grew cereals, raised cattle, and used tools made of wood and stone. Cattle raising spread more quickly than did planting. Early African peoples prized cattle highly. Many trading agreements, marriage alliances, political compacts, and treaties were negotiated in terms of cattle.

Cereals such as millet and sorghum are indigenous to Africa. Scholars speculate that traders brought bananas, taros (a type of yam), sugar cane, and coconut palms to Africa from Southeast Asia. Because tropical forest conditions were ideal for banana trees, their cultivation spread rapidly; they were easier to raise than cereal grains. Donkeys, pigs, chickens, geese, and ducks were also domesticated.

The evolution to a settled life had profound effects. In contrast to nomadic conditions, settled societies made shared or common needs more apparent, and those needs strengthened ties among extended families. Population also increased:

The change from a hunter-gatherer economy to a settled farming economy affected population numbers. . . . What remains uncertain is whether in the agricultural economy there were more people, better fed, or more people, less well fed. . . . In precolonial Africa agricultural and pastoral populations may not have increased steadily over time, but fluctuated cyclically, growing and declining, though overall slowly growing.[2]

Scholars dispute the route by which ironworking spread to sub-Saharan Africa. Some believe that the Phoenicians brought the technique for smelting iron to northwestern Africa and that from the north it spread southward. Others insist that it spread from the Meroe region on the Nile westward. Most of West Africa had acquired knowledge of ironworking by 250 B.C. and archaeologists believe that Meroe achieved pre-eminence as an iron-smelting center only in the first century B.C. Thus a stronger case can probably be made for the Phoenicians. The great African overland trade routes may have carried knowledge of ironworking southward; in any case, by about A.D. 600 it was widely understood in sub-Saharan Africa. Ancient iron tools found at the village of Nok on the Jos

Plateau in present-day Nigeria seem to prove a knowledge of ironworking in West Africa. Nok culture (ca 800 B.C.–A.D. 200) enjoys enduring fame for its fine terra-cotta (baked clay) sculptures.

Around the time of Christ, Bantu-speakers—a small group of people who had long occupied modern-day Nigeria on Africa's west coast—began to move southeastward, settling for a time in central Africa, south of the equatorial rain forests. Because much of central Africa is a plateau, its topsoil is thin and ground water is scarce. These conditions promote migratory rather than settled agriculture. The Bantu continued to move gradually south and east, reaching present-day Zimbabwe by the eighth century and the southeastern coast by the sixteenth century. Knowledge of ironworking gave the Bantu a distinct advantage over hunters and gatherers such as the Khoisan people they encountered, whom they absorbed and displaced.

Describing the village life of Bantu people in the nineteenth century, the Scottish missionary explorer David Livingstone (1813–1873) wrote,

Food abounds, and very little labor is required for its cultivation. . . . When a garden becomes too poor for good crops . . . the owner removes a little farther into the forest, applies fire round the roots of the larger trees to kill them, cuts down the smaller, and a new, rich garden is ready for the seed.[3]

Livingstone's evaluation aside, farming always requires considerable skill and labor—and even more effort if performed by women, as much of it was in Africa.

❧ AFRICAN KINGDOMS IN THE WESTERN SUDAN (CA 1000 B.C.–A.D. 200)

The region bounded on the north by the Sahara, on the south by the Gulf of Guinea, on the west by the Atlantic Ocean, and on the east by the mountains of Ethiopia is known as the Sudan. In the savanna lands of the western Sudan—where the Bantu migrations originated—a series of dynamic kingdoms emerged in the millennium before European intrusion.

Between 1000 B.C. and A.D. 200, the peoples of the western Sudan made the momentous shift from nomadic hunting to settled agriculture. The rich savanna proved ideally suited to the production of cereals, especially rice, millet, and sorghum, and people situated near the Senegal River and Lake Chad supplemented their diet with fish. Food supply tends to affect population, and the peoples of the region—known as the Mande-speakers and the Chadic-speakers, or Sao—increased dramatically in number. By A.D. 400 the entire savanna, particularly the areas around Lake Chad, the Niger River bend, and present-day central Nigeria (see Map 10.1), had a large population.

Families and clans affiliated by blood kinship lived together in villages or small city-states. The basic social unit was the extended family. A chief, in consultation with a council of elders, governed a village. Some villages seem to have formed kingdoms. Village chiefs were responsible to regional heads, who answered to provincial governors, who in turn were responsible to a king. The chiefs and their families formed an aristocracy.

Kingship in the Sudan may have emerged from the priesthood, whose members were believed to make rain and to have contact with spirit powers. African kings always had religious sanction or support for their authority and were often considered divine. In this respect, early African kingship bears a strong resemblance to Germanic kingship of the same period: the authority of the king rested in part on the ruler's ability to negotiate with outside powers, such as the gods.

African religions were animistic and polytheistic. Most people believed that a supreme being had created the universe and was the source of all life. The supreme being breathed spirit into all living things, and the *anima,* or spirit, residing in such things as trees, water, and earth had to be appeased. In the cycle of the agricultural year, for example, all the spirits had to be propitiated from the time of clearing the land through sowing the seed to the final harvest. Because special ceremonies were necessary to satisfy the spirits, special priests with the knowledge and power to communicate with them through sacred rituals were needed. Thus the heads of families and villages were likely to be priests. The head of each family was responsible for maintaining the family ritual cults—ceremonies honoring the dead and living members of the family.[4]

In sum, the most prominent feature of early African society was a strong sense of community, based on the blood relationship and on religion.

Extended families made up the villages that collectively formed small kingdoms. What spurred the expansion of these small kingdoms into formidable powers controlling sizable territory was the development of long-distance trade. And what made long-distance or trans-Saharan trade possible was the camel.

The Trans-Saharan Trade

The expression "trans-Saharan trade" refers to the north-south trade across the Sahara (see Map 10.1). The camel had an impact on this trade comparable to the impact of the horse on European agriculture (see page 403). Although scholars dispute exactly when the camel was introduced from central Asia—first into North Africa, then into the Sahara and the Sudan—they agree that it was before A.D. 200. Camels can carry about 500 pounds as far as 25 miles a day and can go for days without drinking, living on the water stored in their stomachs. Sometimes stupid and vicious, camels had to be loaded on a daily, sometimes twice-daily, basis. And much of the cargo for a long trip was provisions for the journey itself. Nevertheless, camels proved more efficient for desert transportation than horses or oxen, and the use of this beast to carry heavy and bulky freight not only brought economic and social change to Africa but affected the development of world commerce.

Sometime in the fifth century the North African Berbers fashioned a saddle for use on the camel. This saddle had no direct effect on commercial operations, for a merchant usually walked and guided the camel on foot. But the saddle gave the Berbers and later the Arabian inhabitants of the region maneuverability on the animal and thus a powerful political and military advantage: they came to dominate the desert and to create lucrative routes across it. The Berbers determined who could enter the desert, and they extracted large sums of protection money from merchant caravans in exchange for a safe trip.

Between A.D. 700 and 900 the Berbers developed a network of caravan routes between the Mediterranean coast and the Sudan (see Map 10.1). The Morocco-Niger route ran from Fez to Sijilmassa on the edge of the desert and then south by way of Taghaza and Walata and back to Fez. Another route originated at Sijilmassa and extended due south to Timbuktu with a stop at Taghaza. A third route ran south from Tripoli to Lake Chad. A fourth ran from Egypt to Gao by way of the Saharan oases of Ghat and Agades and then on to Takedda.

The long expedition across the Sahara testifies to the spirit of the traders and to their passion for wealth. Because of the blistering sun and daytime temperatures of 110 degrees, the caravan drivers preferred to travel at night, when the temperature might drop to the low 20s. Ibn Battuta, an Arab traveler who made the journey in the fourteenth century when trans-Saharan traffic was at its height, wrote an account of the experience.

Nomadic raiders, the Tuareg Berbers, posed a serious threat. The Tuaregs lived in the desert uplands and preyed on the caravans as a way of life. Thus merchants made safe-conduct agreements with them and selected guides from among them. Caravans of twelve thousand camels were reported in the fourteenth century. Large numbers of merchants crossed the desert together to discourage attack. Blinding sandstorms often isolated part of a line of camels and on at least one occasion buried alive some camels and drivers. Water was the biggest problem. The Tuaregs sometimes poisoned wells to wipe out caravans and steal their goods. To satisfy normal thirst and to compensate for constant sweating, a gallon of water a day per person was required. Desperate thirst sometimes forced the traders to kill camels and drink the foul, brackish water in their stomachs. It took Ibn Battuta twenty-five days to travel from Sijilmassa to the oasis of Taghaza and another sixty-five days to travel from Taghaza to the important market town of Walata.

The Arab-Berber merchants from North Africa who controlled the caravan trade carried manufactured goods—silk and cotton cloth, beads, mirrors—as well as dates and salt (essential in tropical climates to replace the loss from perspiration) from the Saharan oases and mines to the Sudan. These products were exchanged for the much-coveted commodities of the West African savanna—gold, ivory, gum, kola nuts (eaten as a stimulant), and captive slaves.

The steady growth of trans-Saharan trade had three important effects on West African society.

The trade stimulated gold mining and the search for slaves. Parts of modern-day Senegal, Nigeria, and Ghana contained rich veins of gold. Both sexes shared in mining it. Men sank the shafts and hacked out gold-bearing rocks and crushed them, separating the gold from the soil. Women washed the gold in gourds. Alluvial gold (mixed with soil, sand, or gravel) was separated from the soil by panning. Scholars estimate that by the eleventh century nine tons were exported to Europe annually— a prodigious amount for the time, since even with modern machinery and sophisticated techniques the total gold exports from the same region in 1937 amounted to only twenty-one tons. A large percentage of this metal went to Egypt. From there it was transported down the Red Sea and eventually to India (see Map 10.3) to pay for the spices and silks demanded by Mediterranean commerce. West African gold proved "absolutely vital for the monetization of the medieval Mediterranean economy and for the maintenance of its balance of payments with South Asia."[5] African gold linked the entire world, exclusive of the Western Hemisphere.

Slaves were West Africa's second most valuable export (after gold). African slaves, like their early European and Asian counterparts, seem to have been peoples captured in war. In the Muslim cities of North Africa, southern Europe, and southwestern Asia, the demand for household slaves was high among the elite. Slaves were also needed to work the gold and salt mines. Recent research suggests, moreover, that large numbers of black slaves were recruited through the trans-Saharan trade for Muslim military service. High death rates from disease, manumission, and the assimilation of some blacks into Muslim society meant that the demand for slaves remained high for centuries. Table 10.1 shows one scholar's tentative conclusions, based on many kinds of evidence, about the scope of the trans-Saharan slave trade. The total number of blacks enslaved over an 850-year period may be tentatively estimated at over 4 million.[6]

Slavery in Muslim societies, as in European and Asian countries before the fifteenth century, was not based strictly on skin color. Muslims also enslaved Caucasians who had been purchased, seized in war, or kidnapped from Europe. The households of wealthy Muslims in Cordoba, Alexandria, or Tunis often included slaves of a number of

Bust of Man from Jenne   Founded in the eighth century on the Bani River in Mali, and by the thirteenth a thriving entrepôt for gold, slaves, and salt, Jenne must have been an important artistic center, since many terra-cotta figures have been discovered there. The beautiful stole suggests the figure was a ruler or member of the elite. *(Source: Detroit Institute of Arts, Eleanor Clay Ford Fund. Acc. #78.32)*

TABLE 10.1 ESTIMATED MAGNITUDE OF TRANS-SAHARAN SLAVE TRADE, 650–1500

Years	Annual Average of Slaves Traded	Total
650–800	1,000	150,000
800–900	3,000	300,000
900–1100	8,700	1,740,000
1100–1400	5,500	1,650,000
1400–1500	4,300	430,000

Source: From R. A. Austen, "The Trans-Saharan Slave Trade: A Tentative Census," in The Uncommon Market: Essays in the Economic History of the Atlantic Slave Trade, *ed. H. A. Gemery and J. S. Hogendorn (New York: Academic Press, 1979). Used with permission.*

races, all of whom had been completely cut off from their cultural roots. Likewise, West African kings who sold blacks to traders from the north also bought a few white slaves—Slavic, British, and Turkish—for their domestic needs. Race had little to do with the phenomenon of slavery.[7]

The trans-Saharan trade also stimulated the development of vigorous urban centers in West Africa. Scholars date the growth of African cities from around the beginning of the ninth century. Families that had profited from trade tended to congregate in the border zones between the savanna and the Sahara. They acted as middlemen between the miners to the south and Muslim merchants from the north. By the early thirteenth century, these families had become powerful black merchant dynasties. Muslim traders from the Mediterranean settled permanently in the trading depots, from which they organized the trans-Saharan caravans. The concentration of people stimulated agriculture and the craft industries. Gradually cities of sizable population emerged. Jenne, Gao, and Timbuktu, which enjoyed commanding positions on the Niger River bend, became centers of the export-import trade. Sijilmassa grew into a thriving market center. Kumbi, with between 15,000 and 20,000 inhabitants, was probably the largest city in the western Sudan in the twelfth century. (By European standards Kumbi was a metropolis; London and Paris achieved its size only in the late thirteenth century.) Between 1100 and 1400 these cities played a dynamic role in the commercial life of West Africa and Europe and became centers of intellectual creativity.

Perhaps the most influential consequence of the trans-Saharan trade was the introduction of Islam to West African society. Muslim expansion began soon after Muhammad's death in 632 (see pages 251–252). By the tenth century, Muslim Berbers controlled the north-south trade routes to the savanna. By the eleventh century, African rulers of Gao and Timbuktu had accepted Islam. The king of Ghana was also influenced by Islam. Muslims quickly became integral to West African government and society.

Conversion to Islam introduced West Africans to a rich and sophisticated culture. By the late eleventh century, Muslims were guiding the ruler of Ghana in the operation of his administrative machinery. The king of Ghana adopted the Muslim diwan, the agency for keeping financial records (see page 260). Because efficient government depends on the preservation of records, the arrival of Islam in West Africa marked the advent of written documents there. Arab Muslims also taught the rulers of Ghana how to manufacture bricks, and royal palaces and mosques began to be built of brick. African rulers corresponded with Muslim architects, theologians, and other intellectuals, who advised them on statecraft and religion. Islam accelerated the development of the African empires of the ninth through fifteenth centuries.

AFRICAN KINGDOMS AND EMPIRES (CA 800–1450)

All African societies shared one basic feature: a close relationship between political and social organization. Ethnic or blood ties bound clan members together. What scholars call "stateless societies" were culturally homogeneous ethnic societies. The smallest ones numbered fewer than a hundred people and were nomadic hunting groups. Larger stateless societies of perhaps several thousand people lived a settled and often agricultural or herding life.

The period from about 800 to 1450 witnessed the flowering of several powerful African states. In the western Sudan, the large empires of Ghana and Mali developed, complete with massive royal bureaucracies. On the east coast emerged powerful city-states based on sophisticated mercantile activities and, like Sudan, very much influenced by Islam. In Ethiopia, in central East Africa, kings relied on the Christian faith of their people to strengthen political authority. In South Africa the empire of Great Zimbabwe, built on the gold trade with the east coast, flourished.

The Kingdom of Ghana (ca 900–1100)

So remarkable was the kingdom of Ghana during the age of Africa's great empires that writers throughout the medieval world, such as the fourteenth-century Muslim historian Ibn Khaldun, praised it as a model for other rulers. Medieval Ghana also holds a central place in the historical consciousness of the modern state of Ghana. Since this former British colony attained independence in 1957, its political leaders have hailed the medieval period as a glorious heritage. The name of the modern republic of Ghana—which in fact lies far from the site of the old kingdom—was selected to signify the rebirth of an age of gold in black Africa.

The nucleus of the territory that became the kingdom of Ghana was inhabited by Soninke people who called their ruler *ghana,* or war chief. By the late eighth century Muslim traders and other foreigners applied the word to the region where the Soninke lived, the black kingdom south of the Sahara. The Soninke themselves called their land "Aoukar" or "Awkar," by which they meant the region north of the Senegal and Niger Rivers. Only the southern part of Aoukar received enough rainfall to be agriculturally productive, and it was in this area that the civilization of Ghana developed. Skillful farming and an efficient system of irrigation led to the production of abundant crops, which eventually supported a population of as many as 200,000.

The Soninke name for their king—war chief—aptly describes the king's major preoccupation in the tenth century. In 992 Ghana captured the Berber town of Awdaghost, strategically situated on the trans-Saharan trade route (see Map 10.1). Thereafter Ghana controlled the southern portion of a major caravan route. Before the year 1000 the rulers of Ghana had extended their influence almost to the Atlantic coast and had captured a number of small kingdoms in the south and east. By the beginning of the eleventh century, the king exercised sway over a territory approximately the size of Texas. No other power in the West African region could successfully challenge him.

Throughout this vast West African area, all authority sprang from the king. Religious ceremonies and court rituals emphasized the king's sacredness and were intended to strengthen his authority. The king's position was hereditary in the matrilineal line—that is, the heir of the ruling king was one of the king's sister's sons (presumably the eldest or fittest for battle). According to the eleventh-century Spanish Muslim geographer al-Bakri (1040?–1094): "This is their custom . . . the kingdom is inherited only by the son of the king's sister. He the king has no doubt that his successor is a son of his sister, while he is not certain that his son is in fact his own."[8]

A council of ministers assisted the king in the work of government, and from the ninth century on, most of these ministers were Muslims. Detailed evidence about the early Ghanaian bureaucracy has not survived, but scholars suspect that separate agencies were responsible for taxation, royal property, foreigners, forests, and the army. The royal administration was well served by Muslim ideas, skills, and especially literacy. The king and his people, however, clung to their ancestral religion, and the basic political institutions of Ghana remained African.

The king of Ghana held his court in Kumbi. Al-Bakri provides a valuable picture of the city in the eleventh century:

The city of Ghana consists of two towns lying on a plain, one of which is inhabited by Muslims and is large, possessing twelve mosques—one of which is a congregational mosque for Friday prayer; each has its imam, its muezzin and paid reciters of the Quran. The town possesses a large number of jurisconsults and learned men.[9]

Benin Queen Mother Queens wore a specially woven crown with a high forward-pointing peak, called a "chicken's beak" that symbolized rank. This projection, known as an *ede,* was believed to possess spiritual powers. Notice the roped necklace, probably made of strands of woven gold. *(Source: British Museum/Michael Holford)*

Either for their own protection or to preserve their special identity, the Muslims lived separate from the African artisans and tradespeople. The Muslim community in Ghana must have been large and prosperous to have supported twelve mosques. The *imam* was the religious leader who conducted the ritual worship, especially the main prayer ser-

vice on Fridays. The *muezzin* led the prayer responses after the imam; he needed a strong voice so that those at a distance and the women in the harem, or enclosure, could hear. Muslim religious leaders exercised civil authority over their coreligionists. Their presence and that of other learned Muslims also suggests vigorous intellectual activity.

Al-Bakri describes the town where the king lived and the royal court:

The town inhabited by the king is six miles from the Muslim one and is called Al Ghana. . . . The residence of the king consists of a palace and a number of dome-shaped dwellings, all of them surrounded by a strong enclosure, like a city wall. In the town . . . is a mosque, where Muslims who come on diplomatic missions to the king pray. The town where the king lives is surrounded by domed huts, woods, and copses where priest-magicians live; in these woods also are the religious idols and tombs of the kings. Special guards protect this area and prevent anyone from entering it so that no foreigners know what is inside. Here also are the king's prisons, and if anyone is imprisoned there, nothing more is heard of him.[10]

The king adorns himself, as do the women here, with necklaces and bracelets; on their heads they wear caps decorated with gold, sewn on material of fine cotton stuffing. When he holds court in order to hear the people's complaints and to do justice, he sits in a pavilion around which stand ten horses wearing golden trappings; behind him ten pages stand, holding shields and swords decorated with gold; at his right are the sons of the chiefs of the country, splendidly dressed and with their hair sprinkled with gold. The governor of the city sits on the ground in front of the king with other officials likewise sitting around him. Excellently pedigreed dogs guard the door of the pavilion. . . . The noise of a sort-of drum, called a daba, and made from a long hollow log, announces the start of the royal audience. When the king's coreligionists appear before him, they fall on their knees and toss dust on their heads—this is their way of greeting their sovereign. Muslims show respect by clapping their hands.[11]

What sort of juridical system did Ghana have? How was the guilt or innocence of an accused person determined? Justice derived from the king, who heard cases at court or on his travels throughout his kingdom. As al-Bakri recounts:

When a man is accused of denying a debt or of having shed blood or some other crime, a headman (village chief) takes a thin piece of wood, which is sour and bitter to taste, and pours upon it some water which he then gives to the defendant to drink. If the man vomits, his innocence is recognized and he is congratulated. If he does not vomit and the drink remains in his stomach, the accusation is accepted as justified.[12]

This appeal to the supernatural for judgment was very similar to the justice by ordeal that prevailed among the Germanic peoples of western Europe at the same time. Complicated cases in Ghana seem to have been appealed to the king, who often relied on the advice of Muslim legal experts.

The king's elaborate court, the administrative machinery he built, and the extensive territories he governed were all expensive. The king of Ghana needed a lot of money, and he apparently had four main sources of support. The royal estates—some hereditary, others conquered in war—produced annual revenue, mostly in the form of foodstuffs for the royal household. The king also received tribute annually from subordinate chieftains (lack of evidence prevents an estimate of the value of this tax). Customs duties on goods entering and leaving the country generated revenues. Salt was the largest import. Berber merchants paid a tax to the king on the cloth, metalwork, weapons, and other goods that they brought into the country from North Africa; in return these traders received royal protection from bandits. African traders bringing gold into Ghana from the south also paid the customs duty.

Finally, the royal treasury held a monopoly on the export of gold. The gold industry was undoubtedly the king's largest source of income. It was on gold that the fame of medieval Ghana rested. The ninth century geographer al-Ya-qubi wrote, "its king is mighty, and in his lands are gold mines. Under his authority are various other kingdoms—and in all this region there is gold."[13]

The governing aristocracy—the king, his court, and Muslim administrators—occupied the highest rung on the Ghanaian social ladder. On the next rung stood the merchant class. Considerably below the merchants stood the farmers, cattle breeders, supervisors of the gold mines, and skilled craftsmen and weavers—what today might be called the middle class. Some merchants and miners must have enjoyed great wealth, but, as in all aristocratic

societies, money alone did not suffice. High status was based on blood and royal service. At the bottom of the social ladder were slaves, who worked in households, on farms, and in the mines. As in Asian and European societies of the time, slaves accounted for only a small percentage of the population.

Apart from these social classes stood the army. According to al-Bakri, "the king of Ghana can put 200,000 warriors in the field, more than 40,000 being armed with bow and arrow."[14] Like most medieval estimates, this is probably a gross exaggeration. Even a modern industrialized state with

 Oni Obalufon   African masks always had religious significance. Some were intended as a disguise, some filled a ritual function in religious festivals, and some served as funerary representations of the deceased. This fourteenth-century copper mask was made for Oni (king) Obalufon. *(Source: Ife Museum/National Commission for Museums and Monuments, Lagos, Nigeria)*

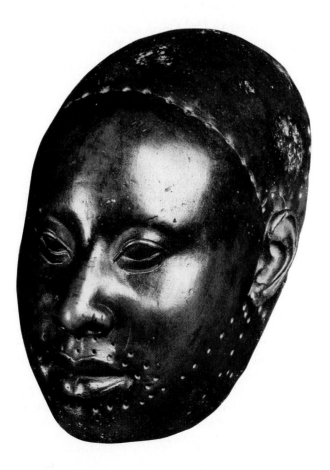

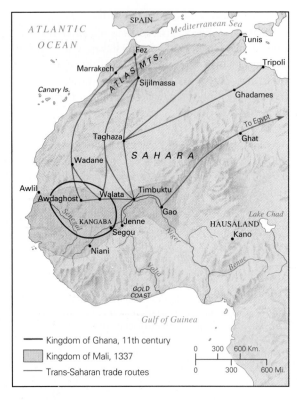

MAP 10.2 The Kingdom of Mali The economic strength of the kingdom of Mali rested heavily on the trans-Saharan trade.

The Kingdom of Mali (ca 1200–1450)

During the century after the collapse of Kumbi, a cloud of obscurity hung over the western Sudan. The kingdom of Ghana split into several small kingdoms that feuded among themselves. One people, the Mandinke, lived in the kingdom of Kangaba on the upper Niger River. The Mandinke had long been part of the Ghanaian empire, and the Mandinke and Soninke belonged to the same language group. Kangaba formed the core of the new empire of Mali. Building on Ghanaian foundations, Mali developed into a better-organized and more powerful state than Ghana.

The kingdom of Mali (Map 10.2) owed its greatness to two fundamental assets. First, its strong agricultural and commercial base provided for a large population and enormous wealth. Second, Mali had two rulers, Sundiata and Mansa Musa, who combined military success with exceptionally creative personalities.

The earliest surviving evidence about the Mandinke, dating from the early eleventh century, indicates that they were extremely successful at agriculture. Consistently large harvests throughout the twelfth and thirteenth centuries meant a plentiful supply of food, which encouraged steady population growth. The geographical location of Kangaba also placed the Mandinke in an ideal position in West African trade. Earlier, during the period of Ghanaian hegemony, the Mandinke had acted as middlemen in the gold and salt traffic flowing north and south. In the thirteenth century Mandinke traders formed companies, traveled widely, and gradually became a major force in the entire West African trade.

Sundiata (r. ca 1230–1255) set up his capital at Niani, transforming the city into an important financial and trading center. He then embarked on a policy of imperial expansion. Through a series of military victories, Sundiata and his successors absorbed into Mali other territories of the former kingdom of Ghana and established hegemony over the trading cities of Gao, Jenne, and Walata.

These expansionist policies were continued in the fourteenth century by Sundiata's descendant Mansa Musa (r. ca 1312–1337), early Africa's most famous ruler. In the language of the Mandinke, *mansa* means "emperor." Mansa Musa fought many campaigns and checked every attempt at re-

sophisticated means of transportation, communication, and supply lines would have enormous difficulty mobilizing so many men for battle. The king of Ghana, however, was not called "war chief" for nothing. He maintained at his palace a crack standing force of a thousand men, comparable to the Roman Praetorian Guard. These thoroughly disciplined, well-armed, totally loyal troops protected the king and the royal court. They lived in special compounds, enjoyed the favor of the king, and sometimes acted as his personal ambassadors to subordinate rulers. In wartime, this regular army was augmented by levies of soldiers from conquered peoples and by the use of slaves and free reserves. The force that the king could field was sizable, if not as huge as al-Bakri estimated.

Timbuktu   Begun as a Tuareg seasonal camp in the eleventh century, Timbuktu emerged as a great commercial entrepôt in the fourteenth century and as an important Muslim educational center in the sixteenth. A strong agricultural base, watered by the nearby Niger River, supported a sizable population. *(Source: Library of Congress)*

bellion. Ultimately his influence extended northward to several Berber cities in the Sahara, eastward to Timbuktu and Gao, and westward as far as the Atlantic Ocean. Throughout his territories he maintained strict royal control over the rich trans-Saharan trade. Thus this empire, roughly twice the size of the Ghanaian kingdom and containing perhaps 8 million people, brought Mansa Musa fabulous wealth.

Mansa Musa built on the foundations of his predecessors. The stratified aristocratic structure of Malian society perpetuated the pattern set in Ghana, as did the system of provincial administration and annual tribute. The emperor took responsibility for the territories that formed the heart of the empire and appointed governors to rule the outlying provinces or dependent kingdoms. But Mansa Musa made a significant innovation: in a practice strikingly similar to a system used in both China and France at that time, he appointed members of the royal family as provincial governors. He could count on their loyalty, and they received valuable experience in the work of government.

In another aspect of administration, Mansa Musa also differed from his predecessors. He became a devout Muslim. Although most of the Mandinke clung to their ancestral animism, Islamic practices and influences in Mali multiplied.

The most celebrated event of Mansa Musa's reign was his pilgrimage to Mecca in 1324–1325, during which he paid a state visit to the sultan of Egypt. Mansa Musa's entrance into Cairo was magnificent. Preceded by five hundred slaves, each carrying a six-pound staff of gold, he followed with a huge host of retainers including one hundred elephants each bearing one hundred pounds of gold. The emperor lavished his wealth on the citizens of the Egyptian capital. Writing twelve years later, al-Omari, one of the sultan's officials, recounts:

This man Mansa Musa spread upon Cairo the flood of his generosity: there was no person, officer of the court, or holder of any office of the Sultanate who did not receive a sum of gold from him. The people of Cairo earned incalculable sums from him, whether by buying and selling or by gifts. So much gold was current in Cairo that it ruined the value of money.[15]

Mansa Musa's gold brought about terrible inflation throughout Egypt. For the first time, the Mediterranean world gained concrete knowledge of the wealth and power of the black kingdom of Mali, and it began to be known as one of the great empires of the world. Mali retained this international reputation into the fifteenth century.

Musa's pilgrimage also had significant consequences within Mali. He gained some understanding of the Mediterranean countries and opened diplomatic relations with the Muslim rulers of Morocco and Egypt. His zeal for the Muslim faith and Islamic culture increased. Musa brought back from Arabia the distinguished architect al-Saheli, whom he commissioned to build new mosques at Timbuktu and other cities. These mosques served as centers for the conversion of Africans. Musa employed Muslim engineers to build in brick. He also encouraged Malian merchants and traders to wear the distinctive flowing robes and turbans of Muslim males.

Timbuktu began as a campsite for desert nomads. Under Mansa Musa it grew into a thriving entrepôt, attracting merchants and traders from North Africa and all parts of the Mediterranean world. These people brought with them cosmopolitan attitudes and ideas. In the fifteenth century Timbuktu developed into a great center for scholarship and learning. Architects, astronomers, poets, lawyers, mathematicians, and theologians flocked there. One hundred fifty schools were devoted to the study of the Qur'an. The school of

Islamic law enjoyed a distinction in Africa comparable to the prestige of the school at Cairo (see page 272). A vigorous trade in books flourished in Timbuktu. Leo Africanus, a sixteenth-century Muslim traveler and writer who later converted to Christianity, recounts that around 1500 Timbuktu had a

great store of doctors, judges, priests, and other learned men that are bountifully maintained at the king's cost and charges. And hitherto are brought diverse manuscripts or written books out of Barbarie the north African states, from Egypt to the Atlantic Ocean which are sold for more money than any other merchandise.

It is easy to understand why the university at Timbuktu was called by a contemporary writer "the Queen of the Sudan." Timbuktu's tradition and reputation for African scholarship lasted until the eighteenth century.

Moreover, in the fourteenth and fifteenth centuries many Muslim intellectuals and Arabic traders married native African women. These unions brought into being a group of racially mixed people. The necessity of living together harmoniously, the traditional awareness of diverse cultures, and the cosmopolitan atmosphere of Timbuktu all contributed to a rare degree of racial toleration and understanding. After visiting the court of Mansa Musa's successor in 1352–1353, Ibn Battuta observed that

the Negroes possess some admirable qualities. They are seldom unjust, and have a greater abhorrence of injustice than any other people. Their sultan shows no mercy to anyone who is guilty of the least act of it. There is complete security in their country. Neither traveler nor inhabitant in it has anything to fear from robbers. . . . They do not confiscate the property of any white man who dies in their country, even if it be uncounted wealth. On the contrary, they give it into the charge of some trustworthy person among the whites, until the rightful heir takes possession of it.[16]

Ethiopia: The Christian Kingdom of Axum

Egyptian culture exerted a profound influence on the sub-Saharan kingdom of Nubia in northeastern Africa (Map 10.3). Nubia's capital was at Meroe; thus the country is often referred to as the Nubian

AFRICAN KINGDOMS AND EMPIRES (CA 800–1450) **299**

❖ **Church of Saint George, Lalibela** Shortly before A.D. 1100 the political capital of Ethiopia was moved south from Axum to Lalibela. Legend holds that Saint George, the third-century Christian martyr, ordered villagers here to construct a church in his honor. They carved it from a hillside of volcanic rock. Worshipers entered through the subterranean trench to the left of the building. Concentric Greek crosses, formed of four equal arms and symbolizing the universal Christian Church, made up the roof. *(Source: Kal Muller/Woodfin Camp & Associates)*

kingdom of Meroe. As part of the Roman Empire, Egypt was naturally subject to Hellenistic and Roman cultural forces, and it became an early center of Christianity. Nubia, however, was never part of the Roman Empire; its people clung to ancient Egyptian religious ideas. Christian missionaries went to the upper Nile region and succeeded in converting the Nubian rulers around A.D. 600. By that time there were three separate Nubian states, of which the kingdom of Nobatia, centered at

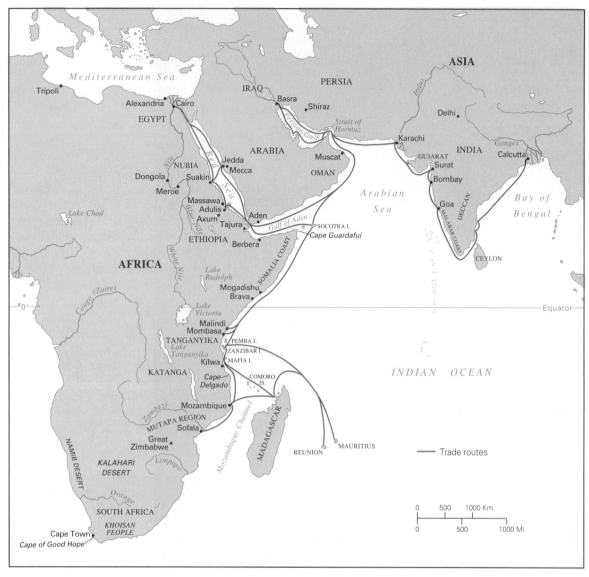

MAP 10.3 Trade Routes Between East Africa and India The Indian Ocean, controlled by the Muslim merchant fleet until the arrival of the Portuguese in the late fifteenth century, was of far greater importance for world trade than the Mediterranean. Gold from Great Zimbabwe passed through the cities on the East African coast before shipment north to the Middle East and east to India and China.

Dongola, was the strongest. The Christian rulers of Nobatia had close ties with Ethiopia.

The kingdom of Ethiopia, centered at Axum (see Map 10.3), had had important commercial contacts with the Roman world. Perhaps partly for that reason, Axum officially adopted Christianity in A.D. 350, just a short time after Christianity be-

came legal within the Roman Empire itself. Ethiopia adopted the Egyptian or Coptic form of Christianity. According to its Monophysitic doctrine, Christ has only one, divine, nature. Orthodox teaching holds that Christ's nature is both human and divine. The Egyptian partriarch of Alexandria appointed the first bishop of Axum, an appointment that led to close religious ties between Egypt and Ethiopia. At the time Axum was a powerful cosmopolitan center whose mercantile activities played a major part in international commerce and whose military and political power was the dominant influence in East Africa.

The expansion of Islam in the eighth century severed Axum's commercial contacts with the Byzantine Empire and ended its control of the Red Sea routes. The kingdom declined as a major power. Ethiopia's high mountains encouraged an inward concentration of attention and hindered access from the outside. Twelfth-century Crusaders returning from the Middle East told of a powerful Christian ruler, Prester John, whose lands lay behind Muslim lines and who was eager to help restore the Holy Land to Christian control. Europeans identified that kingdom with Ethiopia. In the later thirteenth century, the dynasty of the Solomonid kings witnessed a literary and artistic renaissance particularly notable for works of hagiography (biographies of saints), biblical exegesis, and manuscript illumination. The most striking feature of Ethiopian society in the period from 500 to 1500 was the close relationship between the church and the state. Coptic Christianity inspired a fierce devotion and tended to equate doctrinal heresy with political rebellion, thus reinforcing central monarchial power.

The East African City-States

In the first century A.D., a merchant-seaman from Alexandria in Egypt sailed down the Red Sea and out into the Indian Ocean. Along the coasts of East Africa and India he found seaports. He took careful notes on all he observed, and the result, *Periplus of the Erythraean Sea* (as the Greeks called the Indian Ocean), is the earliest surviving literary evidence of the city-states of the East African coast. Although primarily preoccupied with geography and navigation, the *Periplus* includes accounts of the local peoples and their commercial activities. Even in the days of the Roman emperors, the *Periplus* testifies, the East African coast had strong commercial links with India and the Mediterranean.

Greco-Roman ships traveled from Adulis on the Red Sea around the tip of the Gulf of Aden and down the African coast that the Greeks called "Azania," in modern-day Kenya and Tanzania (see Map 10.3). These ships carried manufactured goods—cotton cloth, copper and brass, iron tools, and gold and silver plate. At the African coastal emporiums, Mediterranean merchants exchanged these goods for cinnamon, myrrh and frankincense, captive slaves, and animal byproducts such as ivory, rhinoceros horns, and tortoise shells. Somewhere around Cape Guardafui on the Horn of Africa, the ships caught the monsoon winds eastward to India, where ivory was in great demand.

An omission in the *Periplus* has created a debate over the racial characteristics of the native peoples in East Africa and the dates of Bantu migrations into the area. The author, writing in the first century, did not describe the natives; apparently he did not find their skin color striking enough to comment on. Yet in the fifth century, there are references to these peoples as "Ethiopians." Could this mean that migrating black Bantu-speakers reached the east coast between the first and the fifth centuries? Possibly. The distinguished archaeologist Neville Chittick, however, thinks not: "The writer of the *Periplus* made few comments on the physical nature of the inhabitants of the countries which he described . . . therefore nothing can be based on the mere omission of any mention of skin color."[17]

In the first few centuries of the Christian era, many merchants and seamen from the Mediterranean settled in East African coastal towns. Succeeding centuries saw the arrival of more traders. The great emigration from Arabia after the death of Muhammad accelerated Muslim penetration of the area, which the Arabs called the *Zanj*, "land of the blacks." Arabic Muslims established along the coast small trading colonies whose local peoples were ruled by kings and practiced various animistic religions. Eventually—whether through Muslim political hegemony or gradual assimilation—the coastal peoples slowly converted to Islam. Indigenous African religions, however, remained strong in the interior of the continent.

Beginning in the late twelfth century, fresh waves of Arabs and of Persians from Shiraz poured down the coast, first settling at Mogadishu, then pressing southward to Kilwa (see Map 10.3). Everywhere they landed, they introduced Islamic culture to the indigenous population. Similarly, from the earliest Christian centuries through the Middle Ages, Indonesians crossed the Indian

Ocean and settled on the African coast and on the large island of Madagascar, or Malagasy, an Indonesian word. All these immigrants intermarried with Africans, and the resulting society combined Asian, African, and especially Islamic traits. The East African coastal culture was called Swahili, after a Bantu language whose vocabulary and poetic forms exhibit a strong Arabic influence. The thirteenth-century Muslim mosque at Mogadishu and the fiercely Muslim populations of Mombasa and Kilwa in the fourteenth century attest to strong Muslim influence.

By the late thirteenth century Kilwa had become the most powerful city on the coast, exercising political hegemony as far north as Pemba and as far south as Sofala (see Map 10.3). In the fourteenth and fifteenth centuries the coastal cities were great commercial empires comparable to Venice and

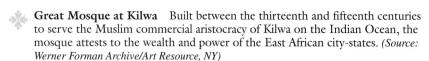

Great Mosque at Kilwa   Built between the thirteenth and fifteenth centuries to serve the Muslim commercial aristocracy of Kilwa on the Indian Ocean, the mosque attests to the wealth and power of the East African city-states. *(Source: Werner Forman Archive/Art Resource, NY)*

Genoa (see page 385). Like those Italian city-states, Kilwa, Mombasa, and Mafia were situated on offshore islands. The tidal currents that isolated them from the mainland also protected them from landside attack.

Much current knowledge about life in the East African trading societies rests on the account of Ibn Battuta. When he arrived at Kilwa, he found, in the words of a modern historian,

the city large and elegant, its buildings, as was typical along the coast, constructed of stone and coral rag [roofing slate]. Houses were generally single storied, consisting of a number of small rooms separated by thick walls supporting heavy stone roofing slabs laid across mangrove poles. Some of the more formidable structures contained second and third stories, and many were embellished with cut stone decorative borders framing the entranceways. Tapestries and ornamental niches covered the walls and the floors were carpeted. Of course, such appointments were only for the wealthy; the poorer classes occupied the timeless mud and straw huts of Africa, their robes a simple loincloth, their dinner a millet porridge.[18]

On the mainland were fields and orchards of rice, millet, oranges, mangoes, and bananas, and pastures and yards for cattle, sheep, and poultry. Yields were apparently high; Ibn Battuta noted that the rich enjoyed three enormous meals a day and were very fat.

From among the rich mercantile families that controlled the coastal cities arose a ruler who by the fourteenth century had taken the Arabic title *sheik*. The sheik governed both the island city and the nearby mainland. Farther inland, tribal chiefs ruled with the advice of councils of elders.

The Portuguese, approaching the East African coastal cities in the late fifteenth century, were astounded at their enormous wealth and prosperity. This wealth rested on monopolistic control of all trade in the area. Some coastal cities manufactured goods for export: Mogadishu produced a cloth for the Egyptian market; Mombasa and Malindi processed iron tools; and Sofala made Cambay cottons for the interior trade. The bulk of the cities' exports, however, consisted of animal products—leopard skins, tortoise shell, ambergris, ivory—and gold. The gold originated in the Mutapa region south of the Zambezi River, where the Bantu

mined it. As in tenth-century Ghana, gold was a royal monopoly in the fourteenth-century coastal city-states. The Mutapa kings received it as annual tribute, prohibited outsiders from entering the mines or participating in the trade, and controlled shipments down the Zambezi to the coastal markets. The prosperity of Kilwa rested on its traffic in gold.

African goods satisfied the widespread aristocratic demand for luxury goods. In Arabia, leopard skins were made into saddles, shells were made into combs, and ambergris was used in the manufacture of perfumes. Because the tusks of African elephants were larger and more durable than the tusks of Indian elephants, African ivory was in great demand in India for sword and dagger handles, carved decorative objects, and the ceremonial bangles used in Hindu marriage rituals. In China, the wealthy valued African ivory for use in the construction of sedan chairs.

In exchange for these natural products, the Swahili cities bought pottery, glassware and beads, and many varieties of cloth. Swahili kings imposed enormous duties on imports, perhaps more than 80 percent of the value of the goods themselves. Even so, traders who came to Africa made fabulous profits.

Slaves were another export from the East African coast. Reports of slave trading began with the *Periplus*. The trade accelerated with the establishment of Muslim settlements in the eighth century and continued down to the arrival of the Portuguese in the late fifteenth century. In fact, the East African coastal trade in slaves persisted at least to the beginning of the twentieth century.

As in West Africa, traders obtained slaves primarily through raids and kidnapping. As early as the tenth century, Arabs from Oman enticed hungry children with dates. When the children accepted the sweet fruits, they were abducted and enslaved. Profit was the traders' motive.

The Arabs called the northern Somalia coast *Ras Assir* ("Cape of Slaves"). From there, Arab traders transported slaves northward up the Red Sea to the markets of Arabia, Persia, and Iraq. Muslim dealers also shipped blacks from the region of Zanzibar across the Indian Ocean to markets in India. Rulers of the Deccan Plateau in central India used large numbers of black soldier-slaves in their military campaigns. Slaves also worked on the

AFRICA, CA 400–1500

ca 1st century A.D.	Beginning of Bantu migrations
ca A.D. 200	First use of the camel for trans-Saharan transportation
4th century	Ethiopia accepts Christianity
600–1500	Extensive slave trade from sub-Saharan Africa to the Mediterranean
6th and 7th centuries	Political and commercial ascendancy of Ethiopia
9th century	Decline of Ethiopia
11th century	Islam penetrates sub-Saharan Africa Height of the kingdom of Ghana
13th and 14th centuries	Kingdom of Mali
ca 1312–1337	The reign of Mansa Musa, medieval Africa's most famous ruler
14th and 15th centuries	Height of the Swahili (East African) city-states

docks and *dhows* (typical Arab lateen-rigged ships) in the Muslim-controlled Indian Ocean and as domestic servants and concubines throughout South and East Asia.

As early as the tenth century, sources mention persons with "lacquer-black bodies" in the possession of wealthy families in Song (Sung) China.[19] In 1178 a Chinese official noted in a memorial to the emperor that Arab traders were shipping thousands of blacks from East Africa to the Chinese port of Guangzhou (Canton) by way of the Malay Archipelago. The Chinese employed these slaves as household servants, as musicians, and, because East Africans were often expert swimmers, as divers to caulk the leaky seams of ships below the water line.

By the thirteenth century, Africans living in many parts of South and East Asia had made significant economic and cultural contributions to their societies. Neither Asian nor Western scholars have adequately explored this subject. It appears, however, that in Indian, Chinese, and East African markets, slaves were never as valuable a commodity as ivory. Thus the volume of the eastern slave trade did not approach that of the trans-Saharan trade.[20]

South Africa

South Africa, the region bordered on the northwest by tropical grasslands and on the northeast by the Zambezi River (see Map 10.3), enjoys a mild and temperate climate. Desert conditions prevail along the Atlantic coast, which gets less than five inches of annual rainfall. Eastward, rainfall increases, though some areas receive less than twenty inches a year. Although the Limpopo Valley in the east is very dry, temperate grasslands characterize the highlands to the north and northwest (the region of the modern Orange Free State, the Transvaal, and Zimbabwe). Considerable variations in climate occur throughout much of South Africa from year to year.

Located at the southern extremity of the Afro-Eurasian landmass, South Africa has a history that is very different from the histories of West Africa, the Nile Valley, and the east coast. Over the centuries, North and West Africa felt the influences of Phoenician, Greek, Roman, and Muslim cultures; the Nile Valley experienced the impact of major Egyptian, Assyrian, Persian, and Muslim civilizations; and the coast of East Africa had important contacts across the Indian Ocean with southern and eastern Asia and across the Red Sea with Arabia and Persia. South Africa, however, remained far removed from the outside world until the arrival of the Portuguese in the late fifteenth century—with one important exception. Bantu-speaking people reached South Africa in the eighth century. They brought with them skills in ironworking and mixed farming (settled crop production plus cattle and sheep raising) and an immunity to the kinds of diseases that later decimated the Amerindians of South America (see pages 524–525).

The earliest residents of South Africa were hunters and gatherers. In the first millennium after the birth of Christ, new farming techniques from the north arrived. A lack of water and timber (which were needed to produce the charcoal used in iron smelting) slowed the spread of iron technology and tools and thus of crop production in western South Africa. These advances, however, reached the western coastal region by 1500. By that date Khoisan-speakers were farming in the arid western regions. To the east, descendants of Bantu immigrants grew sorghum, raised sheep and cattle, and fought with iron-headed spears. They practiced polygamy and traced their descent in the male line.

In 1871 a German explorer discovered the ruined city of Great Zimbabwe southeast of the modern Rhodesian town of Fort Victoria. Archaeologists consider Great Zimbabwe the most

Ruins of Great Zimbabwe   Considered the most impressive monument in the African interior south of the Ethiopian highlands, these ruins of Great Zimbabwe consist of two complexes of dry-stone buildings, some surrounded by a massive serpentine wall 32 feet high and 17 feet thick at its maximum. Great Zimbabwe was the center of a state whose wealth rested on gold. *(Source: Robert Aberman/Barbara Heller Archive/Art Resource, NY)*

powerful monument in Africa south of the Nile Valley and the Ethiopian highlands. The ruins consist of two vast complexes of dry-stone buildings, a fortress, and an elliptically shaped enclosure commonly called the Temple. Stone carvings, gold and copper ornaments, and Asian ceramics once decorated the buildings. The ruins extend over sixty acres and are encircled by a massive wall. The entire city was built from local granite between the eleventh and fifteenth centuries without any outside influence.

These ruins tell a remarkable story. Great Zimbabwe was the political and religious capital of a vast empire. During the first millennium A.D., settled crop cultivation, cattle raising, and work in metal led to a steady buildup in population in the Zambezi-Limpopo region. The area also contained a rich gold-bearing belt. Gold ore lay near the surface; alluvial gold lay in the Zambezi River tributaries. In the tenth century the inhabitants collected the alluvial gold by panning and washing; after the year 1000 the gold was worked in open mines with iron picks. Traders shipped the gold eastward to Sofala (see Map 10.3). The wealth and power of Great Zimbabwe rested on this gold trade.[21]

Great Zimbabwe declined in the fifteenth century, perhaps because the area had become agriculturally exhausted and could no longer support the large population. Some people migrated northward and settled in the valley of the Mazoe River, a tributary of the Zambezi. This region also contained gold, and there the settlers built a new empire in the tradition of Great Zimbabwe. Rulers of this empire were called "Mwene Mutapa," and their power too was based on the gold trade carried on by means of the Zambezi River and Indian Ocean ports. It was this gold that the Portuguese sought when they arrived on the East African coast in the late fifteenth century.

SUMMARY

In the fifteenth century, the African continent contained a number of very different societies and civilizations. In West Africa, Mali continued the brisk trade in gold, salt, and slaves that had originated many centuries earlier. Islam, which had spread to sub-Saharan Africa through the caravan trade, had

tremendous influence on the peoples of the western Sudan, their administrative forms, and their cities. The impact of the Islamic faith was also felt in East Africa, whose bustling port cities were in touch with the cultures of the Mediterranean and the Indian Ocean. While the city-states of the eastern coast conducted complicated mercantile activities with foreign powers, the Christian kingdom of Ethiopia led an isolated, inward-looking existence. In South Africa, the vast empire of Great Zimbabwe was giving way to yet another kingdom whose power was based on precious gold.

NOTES

1. See J. Hiernaux, *The People of Africa* (New York: Scribner's, 1975), pp. 46–48.
2. "African Historical Demography" (proceedings of a seminar held in the Centre of African Studies, University of Edinburgh, April 29–30, 1977), p. 3.
3. Quoted in R. W. July, *Precolonial Africa: An Economic and Social History* (New York: Scribner's, 1975), p. 135.
4. J. S. Trimingham, *Islam in West Africa* (Oxford: Oxford University Press, 1959), pp. 6–9.
5. R. A. Austen, *Africa in Economic History* (London: James Currey/Heinemann, 1987), p. 36.
6. R. A. Austen, "The Trans-Saharan Slave Trade: A Tentative Census," in *The Uncommon Market: Essays in the Economic History of the Atlantic Slave Trade*, ed. H. A. Gemery and J. S. Hogendorn (New York: Academic Press, 1979), pp. 1–71, esp. p. 66.
7. July, *Precolonial Africa*, pp. 124–129.
8. Quoted in J. O. Hunwick, "Islam in West Africa, A.D. 1000–1800," in *A Thousand Years of West African History*, ed. J. F. Ade Ajayi and I. Espie (New York: Humanities Press, 1972), pp. 244–245.
9. Quoted in A. A. Boahen, "Kingdoms of West Africa, c. A.D. 500–1600," in *The Horizon History of Africa* (New York: American Heritage, 1971), p. 183.
10. Al-Bakri, *Kitab al-mughrib fdhikr bilad Ifriqiya wa'l-Maghrib (Description de l'Afrique Septentrionale)*, trans. De Shane (Paris: Adrien-Maisonneuve, 1965), pp. 328–329.
11. Quoted in R. Oliver and C. Oliver, eds., *Africa in the Days of Exploration* (Englewood Cliffs, N.J.: Prentice-Hall, 1965), p. 10.
12. Quoted in Boahen, "Kingdoms of West Africa, c. A.D. 500–1600," p. 184.

13. Quoted in E. J. Murphy, *History of African Civilization* (New York: Delta, 1972), p. 109.

14. Quoted ibid., p. 111.

15. Quoted ibid., p. 120.

16. Quoted in Oliver and Oliver, *Africa in the Days of Exploration,* p. 18.

17. H. N. Chittick, "The Peopling of the East African Coast," in *East Africa and the Orient: Cultural Syntheses in Pre-Colonial Times,* ed. H. N. Chittick and R. I. Rotberg (New York: Africana Publishing, 1975), p. 19.

18. July, *Precolonial Africa,* p. 209.

19. See Austen, "The Trans-Saharan Slave Trade," p. 65; J. H. Harris, *The African Presence in Asia* (Evanston, Ill.: Northwestern University Press, 1971), pp. 3–6, 27–30; and P. Wheatley, "Analecta Sino-Africana Recensa," in Chittick and Rotberg, *East Africa and the Orient,* p. 109.

20. See I. Hrbek, ed., *Africa from the Seventh to the Eleventh Century, General History of Africa,* vol. 3 (Berkeley: University of California Press; New York: UNESCO, 1991), pp. 294–295, 346–347.

21. P. Curtin et al., *African History,* rev. ed. (New York: Longman, 1984), pp. 284–287.

SUGGESTED READING

The titles by Austen, Chittick, Curtin et al., Hiernaux, Hrbek, and Wheatley listed in the Notes represent some of the most reliable scholarship on early African history, and they are especially recommended. Most contain useful bibliographies. The enterprising student should also see B. Davidson, *African Civilization Revisited* (1991), a useful collection of primary documents with material on all parts of Africa; R. O. Collins, ed., *Problems in African History: The Precolonial Centuries* (1993), another collection of sources; and V. B. Khapoya, *The African Experience* (1994), and R. Oliver, *The African Experience* (1991), both of which offer broad interpretations.

For specific topics in early African history, see, in addition to the topics in the Notes, J. Suret-Canale, "The Traditional Societies in Tropical Africa and the Concept of the 'Asiatic Production,'" in J. Suret-Canale, *Essays on African History* (1988), which explores a Marxist understanding of pre-colonial African societies. For the east coast, see J. de Vere Allen, *Swahili Origins* (1993), a study of the problem of Swahili identity; R. Oliver and G. Mathews, eds., *History of East Africa* (1963), perhaps still the standard general work on this part of the continent; and G. S. P. Freeman-Grenville, *The East African Coast: Select Documents from the First to the Earlier Nineteenth Century* (1962), which has valuable material from Arabic, Chinese, and Portuguese perspectives. The works of J. S. Trimingham, *A History of Islam in West Africa* (1970) and *Islam in East Africa* (1974), remain standard studies on the important issue of Islam. J. Kritzeck and W. H. Lewis, eds., *Islam in Africa* (1969), and M. Lombard, *The Golden Age of Islam* (1975), are also helpful. For the importance of the camel to African trade, R. W. Bulliet, *The Camel and the Wheel* (1975), is basic.

Students interested in the art of early Africa will find the following titles provocative and attractively produced: K. Ezra, *Royal Art of Benin* (1992); E. Eyo and F. Willett, *Treasures of Ancient Nigeria* (1980); and P. Ben-Amos, *The Art of Benin* (1980), which describes the political, social, and religious significance of Benin art through beautiful illustrations.

LISTENING TO THE
PAST

The Epic of Old Mali

Just as the Greek epic poems the Iliad *and the* Odyssey *serve as essential sources for the early history of ancient Greece, so the testimony of African griots provide information about early West African societies. There were three classes of griots. Musician-entertainers in the service of nobles formed the lowest group. In the middle group were griots who acted as praise-singers of kings and as their advisers. "Traditionalists" who were attached to a royal household and whose function was to recite from memory in sung poems the royal family's historic traditions and to stress the family's rights and precedence constituted the highest-ranking griots. The Mandinke griot Djeli Mamadou Kouyate was a member of this third group. This selection is from the beginning of his account of old Mali, which is an important source for the early history of the kingdom of Mali.*

I am a griot. It is I, Djeli Mamadou Kouyate, son of Bintou Kouyate and Djeli Kediane Kouyate, master in the art of eloquence. Since time immemorial the Kouyates have been in the service of the Keita princes of Mali; we are vessels of speech, we are the repositories which harbor secrets many centuries old. The art of eloquence has no secrets for us; without us the names of kings would vanish into oblivion, we are the memory of mankind; by the spoken word we bring to life the deeds and exploits of kings for younger generations. . . . I know the list of all the sovereigns who succeeded to the throne of Mali. . . . I teach kings the history of their ancestors so that the lives of the ancients might serve them as an example, for the world is old, but the future springs from the past. . . . Listen to my word, you who want to know; by my mouth you will learn the history of Mali. . . . Listen to the story of the Buffalo. I am going to tell you of Maghan Sundiata, of Mari-Djata, of Sogolon Djata, of Nare Maghan Djata: the man of many names against whom sorcery could avail nothing. . . . Listen then, sons of Mali, children of the black people, listen to my word, for I am going to tell you of Sundiata, the father of the Bright Country, of the savanna land, the ancestor of those who draw the bow, the master of a hundred vanished kings.

Questions for Analysis

1. How did Djeli Mamadou Kouyate secure his position as a griot?

2. What did Kouyate understand his social function to be?

3. According to Kouyate, what purpose did history serve among the Mali? Does this purpose resemble that among any other people you have studied, such as the Christians, Muslims, or Chinese?

4. Consider the value of oral history for the modern historian.

Source: B. Davidson, *African Civilization Revisited* (Trenton, N.J.: Africa World Press, 1991), p. 90.

✤ A griot retells the history of his people. *(Source: Bibliothèque Nationale, Paris)*

11

Tradition and Change in Asia, ca 320–1400

Tai-tsung receiving Tibetan Envoy, by Yen Li-pên (d. 673); ink and color on silk. *(Source: The Palace Museum Beijing. Photo: Wan-go Weng)*

Between approximately 320 and 1400 the various societies of Asia continued to evolve their own distinct social, political, and religious institutions. These years saw momentous changes sweep across Asia. The tide of change surged back and forth between East and West. In the first half of the period Arab conquerors and their new Muslim faith reached the Indian subcontinent and Afghanistan. In central Asia they met the Turks moving westward from the borders of China. The result of this contact was widespread conversion of the Turks to Islam. Muslim Turks then spread their new religion to northern India, which they conquered. Others continued westward, settling in Anatolia and sinking the ethnic and cultural roots of modern Turkey. Meanwhile, Japan emerged into the light of history. Although affected by Chinese culture, philosophy, and religion, the Japanese adapted these influences to their way of life.

In the second half of the period the Mongols swept from their homeland north of China. They conquered China and unsuccessfully hurled two vast fleets at Japan. Toward the end of the period, the travels of the Venetian merchant Marco Polo to Beijing (Peking) gave promise of a new era of East-West contact.

- What effect did these great movements of peoples have on the traditional societies of Asia?
- How were new religious and cultural ideas received by the long-established cultures of the East?
- What political and economic effects did these events have on newcomer and native alike?

This chapter explores these three questions.

❖ INDIA, FROM TRIUMPH TO INVASION (CA 320–1400)

Under the Gupta kings, India enjoyed one of the most magnificent cultural flowerings in its long history. By about 800 the caste system (see pages 71–72) had fully evolved, dividing Indian society into thousands of self-contained subcastes. The incursion of the Muslim Turks—the second permanent foreign influence on India—introduced a new religion that also accelerated the decline of Buddhism in India.

The Gupta Empire (ca 320–480)

For years after the end of Mauryan power, India suffered fragmentation and foreign domination, though even political turmoil did not interrupt the evolution of Indian culture. Not until about 320 did another line of Indian kings, the Guptas, extend their authority over much of the subcontinent. Founded by Chandragupta—unrelated to the founder of the Mauryan Empire by the same name—the Guptas' original home was in the area of modern Bihar in the Ganges Valley (Map 11.1). The Guptas consciously modeled their rule after that of the Mauryan Empire. Although the Guptas failed to restore Ashoka's empire, they united northern India and received tribute from states in Nepal and the Indus Valley. They also gave large parts of India a period of peace and political unity.

The real creator of the Gupta Empire was Chandragupta's son Samudragupta (ca 335–375), who defeated many of the rulers of southern India and then restored them to their thrones as his subjects. With frontier states he made alliances, and over them he extended his protection. By means of military conquest and political shrewdness, Samudragupta brought much of India from the Himalayas in the north to the Vindhya Mountains in the south under his government.

Samudragupta boasted of his accomplishments:

His far-reaching fame, deep-rooted in peace, emanated from the restoration of the sovereignty of many fallen royal families. . . . He, who had no equal in power in the world, eclipsed the fame of the other kings by the radiance of his versatile virtues, adorned by innumerable good actions. He, who was enigmatic, was the real force that generated good and destroyed the evil. Having a compassionate heart, he could easily be won over by faithfulness, loyalty, and homage.[1]

In fact, Samudragupta had reason to boast of his accomplishments. By putting an end to weakness and fragmentation, he laid the foundations of India's golden age.

Under Samudragupta's son Chandragupta II (ca 375–415), the glory of the Guptas reached its height. Perhaps Chandragupta's most significant exploit was the overthrow of the Shakas (invaders from the borders of China) in western India. As a result, the busy maritime trade between western India and the Middle East and China came under

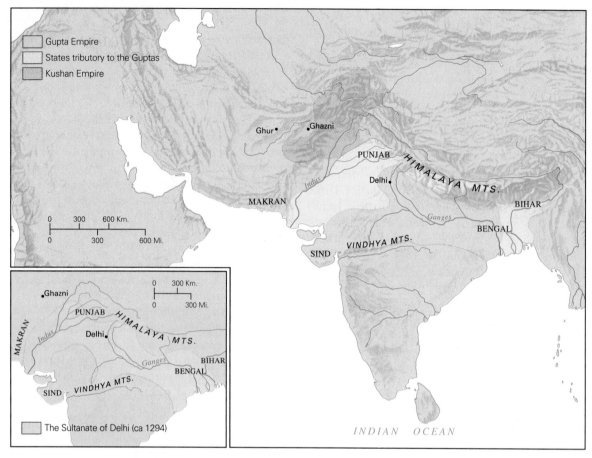

✻ **MAP 11.1 Political Map of India from ca 400 to ca 1294**   This map and inset show the political face of India from the time of the imperial Guptas to the arrival of Muslim invaders. They also demonstrate the importance of the Indus and Ganges river valleys, perhaps the most coveted area in India.

the protection of the Guptas, and the Indian people were once again in direct touch with the wider world.

The great crisis of the Gupta Empire was the invasion of the Huns. The migration of these nomads from central Asia shook the known world. By at least 450 a group of them known as the White Huns thundered into India. Mustering his full might, the ruler Skandagupta (ca 455–467) threw back the invaders. Although the Huns failed to uproot the Gupta Empire, they dealt the dynasty a fatal blow. By 500 the glory of the Gupta kings was past. Soon the country once again reverted to a pattern of local kingdoms in constant conflict.

Even though the Guptas failed to unite India permanently, they saved India for a period from political fragmentation, foreign domination, and

confusion. The peace they established released cultural and intellectual energies that shaped one of the sunniest epochs in India's long history. A prominent feature was interest in the literature of the Aryans, written in Sanskrit, which was the spoken language of India. Sanskrit masterpieces were preserved, and traditional epic poems and verses on mythological themes were reworked and polished. The Gupta period also saw the rise of Indian drama. India's greatest poet, Kalidasa (ca 380–450), like Shakespeare, melded poetry and drama. Poets composed epics for the courts of the Gupta kings, and other writers experimented with prose romances and popular tales.

The Guptas also made a lasting impact on Indian religion. For political purposes they promoted Hinduism to the detriment of Buddhism. In effect,

The Mriga Jataka   The Buddhist caves at Ajanta contain the most important surviving collection of wall paintings from the Gupta period. Religious in inspiration, they are also spontaneous and unrestrained, as this detail of a royal servant holding an energetic dog on a leash reflects. *(Source: Satish Pavashav/Dinodia Picture Agency)*

they pushed Buddhism into decline. By the time that Islam reached India, Buddhism had virtually disappeared. In the future, India would be divided between Muslim and Hindu.

In science, too, the Gupta period could boast of impressive intellectual achievements. Science never appealed to the Indians as much as religion, but Indian mathematicians arrived at the concept of zero, which is necessary for higher mathematics. Other scientific thinkers wrestled with the concept of gravitation centuries before Sir Isaac Newton (1642–1727).

Daily Life in India

The first reliable and abundant information about the daily life of the Indian people dates from the period of the Gupta Empire. One of the most instructive and, to modern minds, amazing characteristics of Indian society is its remarkable stability and veneration for its age-old customs and traditions. Indian society changed slowly, so it is possible to take a look at daily life and social customs in the millennium between the fourth and fourteenth centuries.

Although Indian agriculture ranged from subsistence farming to the working of huge estates, agricultural life ordinarily meant village life. The average farmer worked a small plot of land outside the village, aided by the efforts of the extended family. All the family members pooled their resources—human, animal, and material—under the direction of the head of the family. Shared work, shared sacrifice, and joint confrontation of hazards strengthened family ties. The Indian farming family usually lived close to the bone: bad weather and heavy taxes frequently condemned its members to a lean year of poverty and hardship.

To all Indian farmers, rich and poor, water supply was crucial. India's great scourge is merciless droughts, which cause plants to wither, the earth to crack, and famine to stalk the countryside. Indian farmers quickly learned to drill deep into the ground to tap permanent sources of water. They also irrigated their fields by diverting rivers and digging reservoirs and canals. As in Hammurabi's Mesopotamia, maintenance of waterworks demanded constant effort, and disputes over water rights often led to local quarrels.

The agricultural year began with spring plowing. The ancient plow, drawn by two oxen wearing yokes and collars, had an iron-tipped share and a handle with which the farmer guided it. Similar plows are still used in parts of India. Once plowed and sown, the land yielded a rich variety of crops. Rice, the most important and popular grain, was sown at the beginning of the long rainy season. Beans, lentils, and peas were the farmer's friends, for they grew during the cold season and were harvested in the spring when fresh food was scarce. Cereal crops like wheat, barley, and millet provided carbohydrates and other nutrients. Large estates grew sugar cane. Some families cultivated vegetables, spices, and flowers in their gardens. Village orchards kept people supplied with fruit, and the inhabitants of well-situated villages could eat their fill of fresh and dried fruit and sell the surplus at a nearby town.

Indian farmers raised and bred livestock. Most highly valued were cattle. They were used for plowing and esteemed for their milk. Their hides and horns were precious raw materials, as were the fleeces of sheep. All the animals of the community were in the hands of the village cowherd or shepherd, who led them to and from pasture and protected them from wild animals and thieves.

Farmers fortunate enough to raise surpluses found ready markets in towns and cities. There they came into contact with merchants and traders, some of whom dealt in local commodities and others in East-West trade. Like their Muslim counterparts, Indian merchants enjoyed a respectable place in society. There were huge profits to be made in foreign commerce. Daring Indian sailors founded new trading centers along the coasts of Southeast Asia and in the process spread Indian culture. Other Indian merchants specialized in the caravan trade that continued to link China, Iran, India, and the West.

Local craftsmen and tradesmen lived and worked in specific parts of a town or village. Their shops were open to the street; the family lived on the floor above. The busiest tradesmen dealt in milk and cheese, oil, spices, and perfumes. Equally prominent but disreputable were tavernkeepers. Indian taverns were haunts of criminals and con artists, and in the worst of them fighting was as common as drinking. In addition to these tradesmen and merchants a host of peddlers shuffled through towns and villages selling everything from bath salts to fresh-cut flowers.

Leatherworkers were economically important but were considered *outcastes* (those without places in the traditional social structure). Indian religious and social customs condemned those who made a living handling the skins of dead animals. Masons, carpenters, and brickmakers were more highly respected. As in all agricultural societies, blacksmiths were essential. Pottery was used in all households, but Indian potters, unlike their counterparts in the ancient Near East and the Greco-Roman world, neither baked their wares in kilns nor decorated them. The economic life of the village, then, consisted of a harmonious balance of agriculture and small business.

What of the village itself—its people and its daily sights? Encircled by walls, the typical village was divided into quarters by two main streets that intersected at the center of the village. The streets were unpaved, and the rainy season turned them into a muddy soup. Cattle and sheep roamed as freely as people. The villagers shared their simple houses with such household pets as cats, parrots, and geese. Half-wild mongooses served as effective protection against snakes. The pond outside the village served as its main source of water and also as a spawning ground for fish, birds, and mosquitoes. Women drawing water frequently encountered water buffaloes wallowing in the shallows. After the farmers returned from the fields in the evening, the village gates were closed until morning.

The period following the fall of the Guptas saw the slow proliferation and hardening of the caste system. Early Indian society was divided into four major groups: priests (*Brahman*), warriors (*Kshatriya*), peasants (*Vaishya*) and serfs (*Shudra*) (see page 72). Further subdivisions arose, reflecting differences in trade or profession, tribal or racial affiliation, religious belief, and place of residence. By about 800 these distinctions had solidified into an approximation of the caste system as it is known today. Eventually Indian society comprised perhaps as many as three thousand castes. Each caste had its own governing body, which enforced the rules of the caste. Those incapable of living up to the rules were expelled, becoming outcastes. These unfortunates lived hard lives, performing tasks that others considered unclean or lowly.

For all members of Indian society, regardless of caste, marriage and the family were the focus of life. Once again, far more is known about the upper levels of society than about the lower levels. As in earlier eras, the Indian family of this period was an extended family: grandparents, uncles and aunts, cousins, and nieces and nephews all lived together in the same house or compound. The joint family was under the authority of the eldest male, who might even take several wives. The family affirmed its solidarity by the religious ritual of honoring its dead ancestors—a ritual that linked the living and the dead.

Special attention was devoted to the raising of sons, but all children were pampered. The great poet Kalidasa depicts children as the greatest joy of their father's life:

With their teeth half-shown in causeless laughter,
and their efforts at talking so sweetly uncertain,
when children ask to sit on his lap
a man is blessed, even by the dirt on their bodies.[2]

Children in poor households worked as soon as they were able. Children in wealthier households faced the age-old irritations of reading, writing, and arithmetic. Less attention was paid to daughters, though in the most prosperous families they were usually literate.

Boys of the three upper castes underwent a religious initiation symbolizing a second birth. Ideally, they then entered into a period of asceticism and religious training at the hands of *gurus*, Brahman teachers with whom the boys boarded. In reality,

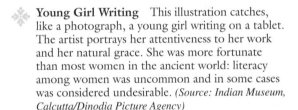

Young Girl Writing   This illustration catches, like a photograph, a young girl writing on a tablet. The artist portrays her attentiveness to her work and her natural grace. She was more fortunate than most women in the ancient world: literacy among women was uncommon and in some cases was considered undesirable. *(Source: Indian Museum, Calcutta/Dinodia Picture Agency)*

relatively few went through this expensive education. Having completed their education, young men were ready to lead adult lives, the first and foremost step in which was marriage.

Child-marriage, unknown in earlier periods, later became customary. Indians considered child-marriage desirable, in part because of their attitudes toward women. Girls were thought to be unusually fascinated by sex. Lawgivers feared that young girls left to their own whims would take lovers as soon as they reached puberty and become pregnant before they were married. Girls who had lost their virginity could seldom hope to find good husbands; most became financial burdens and social disgraces to their families. Daughters were customarily betrothed before their first menstrual period, often to men whom they had never seen. The wedding and consummation of the marriage did not take place until after a girl had reached puberty and could start a family.

After an elaborate wedding ceremony, a newly married couple set up quarters in the house or compound of the bridegroom's father. In contrast to ancient Jewish practice, newlyweds were not expected to consummate their marriage on the first night. Indian custom delicately acknowledged that two strangers, though married, might need some time to adjust to their new mode of life.

An Indian wife had two main duties: to manage the house and to produce children, preferably sons. Her husband was her master, to whom she owed obedience. Indian women spent their entire lives, from childhood to old age, under the authority of men. Indian law was blunt:

A woman is not independent, the males are her masters. . . . Their fathers protect them in childhood, their husbands protect them in youth, and their sons protect them in age; a woman is never fit for independence.[3]

Denied a significant role in life outside the home, wives made the household their domain. All domestic affairs were under their control. As a rule, women rarely left the house, and then only with a chaperone. Among one stratum of high-caste Hindus, the Kshatriyas, wives' bonds with their husbands were so strong that it was felt a wife should have no life apart from her husband. A widow was expected to perform the act of *sati*, throwing herself on his funeral pyre. Yet there is reason to think that this custom did not become common practice.

Within the home, the position of a wife often depended chiefly on her own intelligence and strength of character. In the best of cases a wife was considered a part of her husband, his friend and comforter as well as his wife. Wives were traditionally supposed to be humble, cheerful, and diligent even toward worthless husbands. In reality, some women, far from being docile, ruled the roost. An Indian verse paints a vivid picture of what a henpecked husband could expect:

But when she has him in her clutches
  it's all housework and errands!
"Fetch a knife to cut this gourd!"
  "Get me some fresh fruit!"

"We want wood to boil the greens,
  and for a fire in the evening!"
"Now paint my feet!"
  "Come and massage my back!"

So . . . resist the wiles of women,
  avoid their friendship and company.
The little pleasure you get from them
  will only lead you into trouble![4]

Most women, however, were frankly and unashamedly subservient to their husbands. Nevertheless, despite the severe limitations of her society, the typical wife lived her days honored, cherished, and loved by her husband and family.

The most eagerly desired event was the birth of children. Marriage had no other purpose. Before consummating their marriage, the newlyweds repeated traditional prayers for the wife to become pregnant immediately. While pregnant, the wife was treated like a queen, nearly suffocated with affection and attention, and rigorously circumscribed by religious ritual. At labor and birth, while the women of the household prepared for the birth, the husband performed rituals intended to guarantee an easy delivery and a healthy child. After the birth, the parents performed rituals intended to bring the baby happiness, prosperity, and desirable intellectual, physical, and moral qualities. Infants were pampered until they reached the age of schooling and preparation for the adult world.

India and Southeast Asia

Between about 650 and 1250, Indian merchants and missionaries disseminated Indian culture throughout Southeast Asia. The earlier history of the area is the product of archaeological studies. So far the evidence has allowed scholars to trace the movements of numerous peoples without being able to tell very much about them. It is known that Indian penetration of Southeast Asia changed things considerably, and Sanskrit gave peoples a common mode of written expression. The demands of trade frequently led to small Indian settlements, generally located on the coast, stretching from modern Thailand in the west to the Mekong Delta of modern Vietnam (Map 11.2). In these trading posts Indians met natives, and the result was often intermarriage and the creation of a cul-ture fertilized by both. The greatest influence of India on Southeast Asian societies came in the courts of local rulers, who often adopted Indian customs and values, embraced Hinduism and Buddhism, and learned Sanskrit.

Although there is no denying Indian influence on Southeast Asia, its strength should not be exaggerated. Outside the courts of the rulers, native societies maintained their own cultural identity even when they assimilated various Indian customs. Perhaps two examples can illustrate the process. Taking up the *Ramayana,* an Indian epic poem describing the deeds of the Vedic heroes, the Javanese retained the essentials of the Indian narrative but added to it native Javanese legends, thus creating a work that did not belong solely to either culture. So, too, with religion. Early peoples in the region of Cambodia and in Tibet adapted Buddhism to

MAP 11.2 States of Southeast Asia from ca 650 to ca 1250   This map illustrates the greatest extent of several major Southeast Asian states. The boundaries are somewhat approximate, for states gained and lost territory several times during this long period.

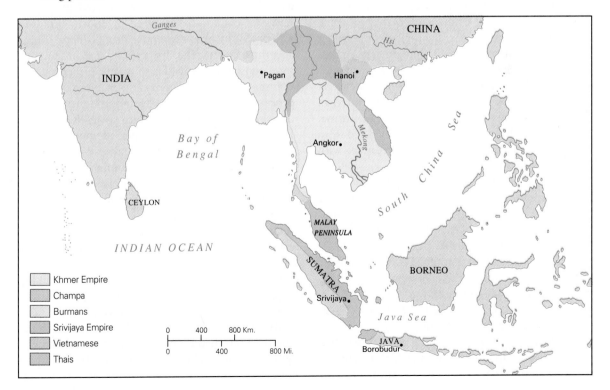

their own values, attitudes, and customs. In both cases local tradition shaped Buddhism in its own likeness.

When the Indians entered Southeast Asia, they encountered both indigenous peoples and newcomers moving southward from the frontiers of China. Their relations with these peoples varied greatly. Contact with the vigorous tribes moving into the southern areas of the mainland was generally peaceful. But commercial rivalry sometimes led to active warfare with the native states in the Malay Peninsula and the islands of the Indian Ocean. Although many of the events of these years are imperfectly known, a fairly clear picture has emerged of the situation in the region (see Map 11.2).

On the mainland three major groups of newcomers pushed southward toward the Indian Ocean from the southern borders of China. Their movements entailed prolonged fighting. As in other such extensive migrations, the newcomers fought one another as often as they fought the native populations. The Vietnamese, the group least influenced by Indian culture, established themselves on the eastern coast of the mainland. In 939 they became independent of China and extended their power southward along the coast of present-day Vietnam. The Thais lived to the west in what is today southwestern China and northern Burma. In the eighth century the Thai tribes united in a confederacy and even expanded northward against Tang China; like China, however, the Thai confederacy fell to the Mongols in 1253. Still farther west another tribal people, the Burmans, migrated in the eighth century to the area of modern Burma. They too established a state, which they ruled from their capital, Pagan, and came into contact with India and Ceylon.

The most important mainland state was the Khmer Empire of Cambodia, which controlled the heart of the region. The Khmers were indigenous to the area, and by around 400 they had created an independent state. Founded in 802, their empire eventually extended its southern borders to the sea and the northeastern Malay Peninsula. Generally successful in a long series of wars with the Vietnamese, the Khmers reached the peak of their power in 1219 and then declined.

Far different from these land-based states was the maritime empire of Srivijaya, which originated as a city-state on the island of Sumatra. Like the Khmers, the people of Srivijaya were indigenous.

Their wealth was based on seaborne trade and on tolls that they exacted from ships passing through their waters. Their navy ruled the waters around Sumatra, Borneo, and Java. Though long predominant in the area, Srivijaya suffered a stunning blow in 1025: a commercial rival in southern India launched a large naval raid that succeeded in capturing the king and capital of the empire. Unable to hold their gains, the Indians retreated, but the Srivijaya Empire never recovered its former vigor. By the mid-thirteenth century the arrival of Chinese traders further weakened the empire, and eventually it fell to local rivals.

Although the political histories of all these peoples varied, their responses to Indian culture were similar. The coastal states, influenced by the presence of trading stations, were the first to adopt and adapt Indian ways. The very concept of kingship came from India. Local rulers and their elites, like good Indian kings, began to observe *dharma* (the moral law) and to govern their peoples by its precepts. Sanskrit, both the Indian language and the script in which it was written, surmounted the barriers raised by the many different native languages of the region. Indian mythology took hold, as did Indian architecture and sculpture. Some of the world's greatest edifices were erected in central Java and Cambodia, inspired by Indian building principles, techniques, and cultural ideals. Kings and their courts, the first to embrace Indian culture, consciously spread it to their subjects.

Indian religion was also instrumental in this process. Certain aspects of Hinduism proved popular, but Buddhism took Southeast Asia by storm. Buddhism emphasized the value of popular education, and its temples, monasteries, and missionaries helped bring education to the common people. Especially influential was the Buddhist concept of the *bodhisattva,* a buddha-in-becoming (see page 80). Inspired by this ideal, many kings and local rulers strove to give their subjects good and humane government. Buddhist missionaries from India played a prominent role in these developments. Local converts continued the process by making pilgrimages to India and Sri Lanka to worship and to observe Indian life for themselves.

By the twelfth century, Indian culture, secular and religious, had found a permanent new home in Southeast Asia. The process was for the most part peaceful; unlike the case with Western newcomers in modern times, no truly forced colonization

✿ **Angkor Wat**   This aerial view of Angkor Wat illustrates the great artistic achievements of the Khmers, who planned and built this architectural monument. The temple also reflects Indian influence, for the god chiefly honored here is Vishnu. *(Source: Photography Collection, Harry Ransom Humanities Research Center, the University of Texas at Austin)*

seems to have occurred. Chinese influence flourished more strongly among the Vietnamese, and Islam would later rival Buddhism; but Indian culture persisted, especially in the southern part of the region. Seldom has the world seen such a protracted and pervasive cultural diffusion. It stands as a monument to the vitality and magnetism of Indian civilization.

India Under Siege

Between roughly 650 and 1400 India experienced turmoil and invasion as wave after wave of foreign armies moved into the subcontinent. Arabs, Turks, and Mongols all swept into India. Particularly during the six centuries from 636 to 1296, invaders

beat against India and its neighbors. This complex and imperfectly understood phenomenon had four distinct phases. The Muslim Arabs' attack on the Sind area (636–713) was followed by the battle for Afghanistan (643–870). Muslims next pushed into the Punjab (870–1030) and finally conquered the valley of the Ganges (1175–1206). Between onslaughts, conflict persisted between newcomer and native.

Arabs under the leadership of Muhammad ibn-Qasim reached the western coast of modern Pakistan in 636 and pushed on into the Sind and the Indus Valley (see Map 11.1). But the Islamic conquest of northern India came at the hands of Turkish converts to Islam. While huge numbers of Turks advanced on the Byzantine Empire and won

INDIA, CA 320–CA 1400

ca 320–480	Gupta Empire
ca 380–450	Kalidasa, India's greatest poet
636–1206	Muslim invasions of India
ca 1193	Destruction of Buddhism in India
1290–1320	Sultanate of Delhi
1398	Timur conquers the Punjab and Delhi

control of Asia Minor, others remained in the East. In 986 Sabuktigin, a Turkish chieftain in Afghanistan and a devout Muslim, launched his initial raid into the Punjab. Once again, India suffered its age-old fate: invasion by a strong and confident power through the northwestern corridor. Sabuktigin's son Mahmud stepped up the frequency and intensity of the raids until he had won the Punjab. Then, like other invaders before him, he began pushing toward the Ganges. Mahmud systematically looted secular palaces and Hindu shrines, and he destroyed Indian statues as infidel idols. Even the Arab conquerors of the Sind fell to him. The Indus Valley, the Punjab, and the rest of northwestern India were in the grip of the invader.

Mahmud's death gave India roughly a century and a half of fitful peace marred by local conflicts. Then a new line of Turkish rulers that had arisen in Afghanistan, with its capital at Ghur (see Map 11.1), renewed Muslim attacks on India. After conquering Mahmud's Indian holdings, Muhammad of Ghur struck eastward toward the Ganges in 1192. Muhammad's generals captured Delhi and extended their control nearly throughout northern India. Like Mahmud, Muhammad and his generals considered Hindu and Buddhist religious statues nothing more than idols; Muslim troops destroyed them in vast numbers. Buddhist centers of worship and learning suffered grievously. In 1193 a Turkish raiding party destroyed the great Buddhist university at Nalanda in Bihar. Most Buddhists took refuge from this dual military and religious assault in Tibet and places farther east. Buddhism, which

had thrived so long in peaceful and friendly competition with Hinduism, was pushed out of its native soil by the invaders.

When Muhammad of Ghur fell to an assassin in 1206, one of his generals, the former slave Qutb-ud-din, seized the reins of power and made his capital at Delhi. To prevent assimilation by the far more numerous Indians, the Muslims recruited Turks and Iranians from outside India, many of whom were fleeing the widespread Mongol devastation of Iran and the Middle East. Under the sultanate of Delhi, Iranian influences deeply affected Hindu art and architecture. Iranians introduced the minaret—an essential architectural feature of the mosque—as well as the arch and the dome. So great was the impact of Iranian Muslims that Urdu, the official language of modern Pakistan, evolved as a mixture of Persian with Arabic and Hindi.

The most lasting impact of the invader was religious. Islam replaced Hinduism and Buddhism in the Indus Valley (modern Pakistan) and in Bengal at the mouth of the Ganges (modern Bangladesh). Elsewhere in India, where Muslim influence was far less powerful, Hinduism resisted the newcomers and their religion. Most Indians looked on the successful invaders simply as a new ruling caste, capable of governing and taxing them but otherwise peripheral to their lives. The myriad castes largely governed themselves, isolating the newcomers.

Hinduism enjoyed profound devotion from the Indian people. The years of war and invasion had not hindered the development of a pious, devotional Hinduism called Bhakti. Bhakti emphasized personal reverence for and worship of a Hindu deity such as Krishna, Shiva, or Rama. Bhakti nourished impassioned love of the Hindu gods among ordinary folk. There was a certain amount of mutual borrowing between Islam and Hindu tradition. But in general, Hinduism's beliefs and social organization had a strong hold over the people of India; roughly 75 percent remained Hindu.

By about 1400 India was as politically divided as it had been before the Gupta Empire. Yet the events of the preceding millennium had had more than political and military significance. The march of armies had brought Islam into India and driven out Buddhism. Meanwhile, Hinduism had flourished. These developments were to be critically important for the future of the entire region, for in them lie the origins of the modern nations of India, Pakistan, and Bangladesh.

❧ CHINA'S GOLDEN AGE (580–CA 1400)

The years between the fall of the Han Dynasty in the third century and the rise of the Ming in the fourteenth brought some of China's brightest days and some of its darkest. During this period the Chinese absorbed foreign influences, notably Buddhism, that fundamentally shaped their society. Chinese cultural traditions, especially Confucianism, drew new strength and vitality from abroad. This was a golden era of enormous intellectual and artistic creativity in Chinese history.

Sui, Tang, and Song (Sung) emperors and statesmen reunited the empire, repaired the foundations of national strength, and once again made China one of the world's unrivaled states. Even later political disruption, particularly the invasion of the Mongols, could not undo the achievements of those who shaped the history of these years. The Mongols were the first foreigners ever to rule all of China, but their domination lasted only ninety-seven years, until the Ming emperors once again united the land under a native dynasty.

Buddhism Flourishes in China

Buddhism reached China from the west before the Han Dynasty, but it flourished between the fall of the Han in 220 and the rise of the Sui in 581. Buddhism reached China by means of merchants and travelers from India. It initially won a place for itself in China because it offered a refreshing and novel solution to social disruption and political chaos (see pages 80–81). It was ultimately successful in China because it had powerful appeal for many different segments of society.

To Chinese scholars, the Buddhist concepts of transmigration of souls, karma, and nirvana posed a stimulating intellectual challenge. For rulers the Buddhist church was a source of magical power and a political tool. Because it was neither barbarian nor Chinese, this foreign faith could embrace both groups equally. To the middle and lower classes, Buddhism's egalitarianism came as a breath of fresh air. The lower orders of society had as much chance as the elites to live according to Buddha's precepts. Simple faith and devotion alone could win enlightenment and salvation. For many, regardless of social status, Buddhism's promise of eternal bliss as the reward for a just and upright life was deeply comforting. In a rough and tumultuous age, moreover, Buddhism's emphasis on kindness, charity, and the value of human life offered hope of a better life on earth.

If Buddhism changed Chinese life, China likewise changed Buddhism. Mahayana Buddhism, the more flexible and widespread of Buddhism's two schools (see pages 79–80), gave rise to several new sects responsive to specific Chinese needs. The Tian-tai sect, which later gave rise to the Tendai sect in Japan (see page 336), was favored by Chinese scholars, who attempted to resolve the numerous intellectual problems in Buddhism and to organize its doctrines in keeping with traditional Chinese thought. Most popular was the Pure Land sect. It too would later have a vast impact on Japanese society. Like its Indian counterpart, this sect was very lenient. Instead of following Buddha's Eightfold Path, people had only to declare their sincere faith in Buddha to reach paradise, the "pure land." Many simple and uneducated people found in the Pure Land sect a comforting route to joy scarcely attainable on earth.

The True Word sect, which won more popularity in Japan than in China, promised adherents immortality through magic, rituals, and chants. The Chan sect, the forerunner of Zen Buddhism in Japan, combined elements of Daoism and Buddhism. Like Doaoism itself, Chan dreamed of a return to nature and simplicity. Chan emphasized

Buddhism Reaches China This scene illustrates the spread of Buddhism from India to China. The writing at the left, printed in Chinese characters, is a translation of a Buddhist text originally written in Sanskrit. This scene of Buddha addressing a follower is the earliest dated example of block-printing. *(Source: The British Library)*

meditation and preached that individuals were responsible for their own ultimate enlightenment. In this respect Chan was quite similar to Buddha's teaching that each person must tread the path of enlightenment alone. One of the prime reasons for Buddhism's success in China was its extraordinary ability to accommodate itself to local thought, beliefs, and conditions.

Buddhist monks from abroad introduced monasticism to China, and the resulting monasteries became more than merely centers for religious practice and study. Like their Christian counterparts in medieval Europe, Buddhist monasteries played an active role in social, economic, and political life. Buddhist missionary monks traveled the trade routes with Buddhist merchants, who gave

the newly formed monasteries a secular function: increasingly, they entrusted their money and wares to the monasteries for safekeeping, in effect transforming the monasteries into banks and warehouses. Buddhist merchants often endowed monks with money or land to support temples and monasteries. The monks, who thus became powerful landlords, hired peasants to work the monastic and temple lands, and the tenants in turn became ready converts to Buddhism. Formidable in wealth and numbers, monasteries became influential participants in politics, rivaling the power of the traditional Chinese landlords. The monasteries' prosperity and political power further protected converts from local Chinese lords and reinforced the spread of Buddhism.

Buddhism also had a profound impact on the artistic life of China. Buddhist art, like the faith's religious message, first reached China along the Silk Road. At Tun-huang in northwestern China, thousands of artists worked for centuries to transform a mile-long stretch of hillside into a monumental shrine. The life of Buddha offered Chinese painters and sculptors a wealth of new themes. From the fourth century on, Buddha and his life became inseparable from Chinese art.

Thus Buddhism's appeal to the Chinese was religious, social, and artistic. Its message struck a sympathetic chord among nobles and peasants alike. It endowed China with a new view of human dignity, the promise of personal salvation, and a compelling vision of peace.

The Tang Dynasty (618–907)

The Tang emperors rose to greatness on the shoulders of their predecessors, the Sui Dynasty (581–618). Sui land reforms helped to restore prosperity to a storm-tossed land, and Sui waterworks strengthened ties between northern and southern China. The crowning achievement of the Sui was the Grand Canal, connecting the eastern reaches of the Yellow River to the eastern waters of the Huai and Yangtze Rivers (Map 11.3). The canal facilitated the shipping of tax grain from the recently developed Yangtze Delta to the centers of political and military power in northern China. Henceforth the rice-growing Yangtze Valley and southern China generally played an ever more influential role in the country's economic and political life, strengthening China's internal cohesion.

Though successful as reformers, the Sui emperors fell prey to a grim combination of military defeat and massive peasant uprisings. From these unlikely conditions rose the Tang Dynasty (618–907), probably the greatest dynasty in Chinese history. Its founder, who took the imperial name Tai Zong, was an able general and astute politician. He was also an educated and far-sighted administrator who followed conscientiously the lessons of Chinese history. Having seen the results of oppression, Tai Zong avoided extravagance and continued Sui reforms.

Tai Zong tried first to alleviate the poverty of the peasants. Building on the Sui system, he ordered that land be divided among the peasants as equally as possible and that imperial officials safe-

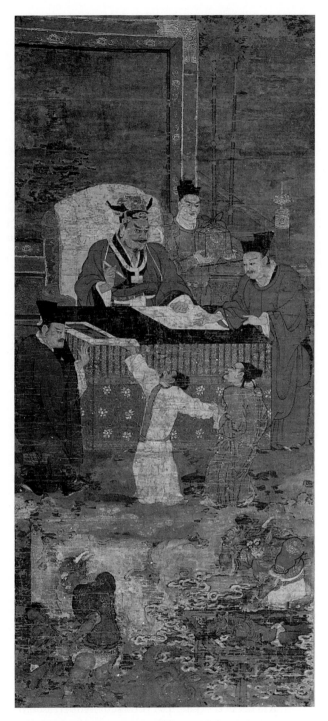

Justice in Court   This picture gives an idealized look at the system of law, but that does not mean that it is misleading. A council of judges review the law, examine the testimony, and deliver a verdict. This is a fine example of the mandarin scholar-official serving the state. *(Source: Courtesy, Museum of Fine Arts, Boston. Denman Waldo Ross Collection, Acc. no. 06.317)*

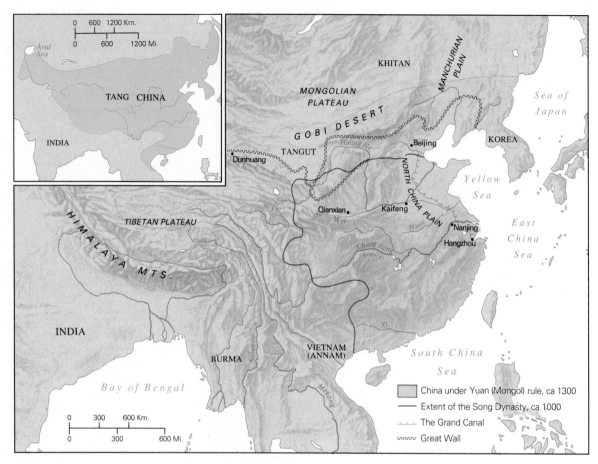

✳ **MAP 11.3 Political Divisions of China from the Tang to the Yuan Dynasty, 618–1368** This map and inset illustrate how the Tang Dynasty and its successors were able to sustain the expanded frontiers of the Han Dynasty, although their hold in the west was always somewhat tenuous.

guard the peasants' holdings. A prosperous peasantry, in Tai Zong's view, would provide a secure and steady base of income for the empire. In practice, the attempt to equalize landholdings quickly broke down, and by 780 the law was revoked. Even so, Tai Zong's efforts were not entirely in vain: he had done enough to give agriculture a much-needed boost, and productivity increased in both grain and livestock. Not since the Han Dynasty had the peasants been so well off.

In the civil sphere, Tang accomplishments far outstripped anything known in Europe until the growth of national states in the seventeenth century. Tang emperors subdivided the administration of the empire into departments, much like the nu-

merous agencies of modern governments. Tang departments oversaw military organization, maintenance and supply of the armies, foreign affairs, administration of justice, finance, building and transportation, education, and much else. During this period no other state on earth was as politically sophisticated as the Tang Empire.

A bureaucracy of this scope demanded huge numbers of educated and trained personnel. Tang emperors revived and expanded the Han method of hiring and promoting government officials on the basis of education, ability, and merit. This process reinforced Confucian values, ethics, and emphasis on scholarship. Candidates for official positions were expected to learn the Confucian classics, to master the rules of poetry, and to discuss practical administrative and political matters. Universities were founded to train able and dedicated young men. Graduates passed a demanding battery of oral and written examinations to prove their ability. Training was hard and long; although students did not endure the physical discipline of Mesopotamian scribes, they sacrificed much to achieve success.

Mandarin scholar-officials also played an important cultural role. Since much of an official's training involved the study of literature, history, and politics, China's literary heritage became integral to contemporary life. Because nearly any literate man in the empire could take the examinations, centers for study sprouted throughout China. Knowledge of the classics spread throughout the empire, fostering cultural unity. The mandarin system became an institution in which people from every part of China could meet on a common ground.

In foreign affairs the Tang turned their attention first to the Turks, who had spread their power from the northern borders of China to the Byzantine Empire in Asia Minor. By Tai Zong's death in 649, Chinese armies had conquered all of Turkestan in the west.

Chinese influence in Tibet came somewhat more peacefully, despite some Sino-Tibetan rivalries and wars. For years the Tibetans had lived a partly nomadic and partly agricultural life on China's western border. Then in the early seventh century one of their chieftains unified the Tibetan tribes and sought a marriage alliance with Tai Zong. The emperor sent his daughter to Tibet with musicians, craftsmen, and technicians to introduce new tools and techniques, along with books on Chinese agricultural methods. The Tibetans modeled their culture partially on the Tang. The Koreans and Japanese adopted Chinese culture more enthusiastically. China's script and literature, Buddhism, crafts, and political ideas and techniques spread widely, making Chinese culture dominant throughout eastern Asia.

The Song Dynasty (960–1279)

In the middle of the eighth century, Tang foreign policy collapsed in rout and rebellion. The defeat of Chinese armies in central Asia and on the south-

Head of the Dragon   Just as the Greeks built their Tower of the Four Winds for astronomical functions, so did the astronomer Guo Shoujing. His calculation of the length of the solar year was accurate to within twenty seconds. Like the Greeks, he produced an architectural masterpiece. *(Source: Patrick Lui & Associates)*

western border undercut the emperor's authority. Beginning in 755 powerful generals revolted in response to imperial malfeasance. The Tang Dynasty ended in a conflagration of military rebellions, peasant uprisings, and barbarian invasions. The period from 907 to 960, known as the Era of the Five Dynasties, resembled the age of the barracks emperors of the Roman Empire (see page 205). Weak and distracted, China presented an easy target to the barbarians, and one group of nomads, known as the Khitan, captured Beijing and most of northeastern China and Manchuria.

The founder of the Song Dynasty, the northern general Zhao Kuangyin, made his bid for empire in 960. Against great odds and with great effort Zhou Kuangyin—known as Emperor Song Tai Zu—stabilized northern China and extended control over the south, not only in China but as far as Indonesia.

Despite sporadic warfare, the early Song period enjoyed broad-based economic prosperity for a variety of demographic and economic reasons. The population had increased to an unprecedented 100 million. Rapidly increasing urbanization went hand in hand with greatly expanded agricultural productivity. Advances in the technology and production of coal and iron also played a significant part, as did improvements in communications. Efficient water transport fostered the development of a national market for domestic products. The tea trade boomed. In the Han period tea had been a luxury item, but during the Tang period tea became immensely popular throughout China. Trade was brisk in other commodities as well. Porcelain continued to be a prime export and domestic product. Salt continued to be a state monopoly.

The political and economic success of the Song permitted the technological innovations of the Tang period to reach full growth. Foremost among them was the invention of printing, which changed the history of China and the entire world. Tang craftsmen developed the art of carving words and pictures onto wooden blocks, inking them, and then pressing the blocks onto paper. Each block consisted of an entire page of text and illustrations. Such whole-page blocks were being printed as early as the middle of the ninth century, and in the eleventh century movable type was invented. Movable type was never widely used in China, but when this Chinese invention reached Europe in the fifteenth century, it revolutionized the communication of ideas. In China as well as in Europe, the invention and spread of printing dramatically increased the availability of books and lowered their price. Scholarship flourished, and literacy spread rapidly among the general population.

The Tang also invented gunpowder, originally for use in fireworks. By the early Song period people were using gunpowder to propel arrows—in effect, the first rockets. Later, projectiles were given a gunpowder charge so that they exploded on impact.

In this period the abacus, perhaps already introduced by the Han period, saw broader use. Inventions included the combination of the water wheel and the bellows that enabled smelters to increase the output of pig iron. Under the Song, government-operated spinning and weaving mills produced cheap, durable, and comfortable cotton clothing.

Economic vitality and the consolidation of Song rule gave a great impetus to urbanization. City dwellers were becoming economically more important than the landed gentry. Rich urbanites indulged in increasingly costly dress and food. Well-to-do urban women, however, suffered a severe decline in social standing. The most obvious sign of their changed status was the custom of footbinding, which made a woman's feet nearly useless. As long as women's labor was needed to help keep starvation from the door, women possessed a certain status, albeit lowly. But in prosperous urban households, women no longer fulfilled an economic function and, in effect, became ornaments. To show the world that their men were prosperous enough to support them, women bound the feet of their infant daughters until the arches broke and the foot healed to half its normal growth. Not until the twentieth century was this custom abandoned.

In international affairs, the Song used diplomacy to avoid war and play off one state against the other. In 1114, however, the Jurchen, a people from the northeastern frontier, marched against the Song. In 1126 they sacked the Song capital and drove the remnants of the imperial court to the southern city of Hangzhou (Hangchow).

The Song emperors who governed from Hangzhou, commonly known as the Southern Song Dynasty, held on to the area below the Yangtze River from 1127 to 1279. The Southern Song resisted the northerners but established a stable border with them. Although there never was genuine peace between the two, fighting was usually limited to border areas. For 152 years the Southern Song flourished, despite the annual tribute they paid to the northerners.

The Southern Song period is especially notable for a great increase in the volume of maritime trade, both oceanic and coastal. Chinese shipwrights built large, stable junks with huge cargo capacity. These ships enabled Chinese merchants to sail directly to Korea and Japan, which became

CHINA, CA 320–CA 1400

220–589	Buddhism flourishes in China
581–618	Sui Dynasty and restoration of public order
618–907	Tang Dynasty: economic, political, and artistic flowering
907–960	Era of the Five Dynasties: warfare and revolt
960–1279	Song Dynasty and Neo-Confucian thought
1021–1086	Wang Anshi, author and political reformer
1215–1279	Mongol conquest of China
ca 1300	Marco Polo travels in China

eager importers of Chinese goods. Ocean voyages were rendered considerably easier and safer by the Chinese invention of the magnetic compass, which was widely used in China at least two centuries earlier than in the rest of the world. The shipping of Chinese goods to the West was mostly in the hands of Arabs. Thus southern China under the Song entered fully and prosperously into a commercial network that stretched from Japan all the way to the Mediterranean.

The invention of printing and the increased volume of trade led to two momentous innovations: the use of paper money and the development of banking. Paper money originated under the Song as notes of deposit—documents certifying that a person had deposited a specific amount of copper coinage with the government. Notes of deposit rapidly gave way to true paper money, which anyone could cash in for copper coins. The legendary Venetian merchant and adventurer Marco Polo (ca 1254–1342) wrote one of the earliest descriptions of how Chinese paper money was issued:

The coinage of this paper money is authenticated with as much form and ceremony as if it were actually of pure gold or silver; for to each note a number of officers, specially appointed, not only subscribe their names, but affix their signets also; and when this has been regularly done by the whole of them, the principal officer . . . having dipped into vermillion the royal seal committed to his custody, stamps with it the piece of paper, so that the form of the seal tinged with the vermillion remains impressed upon it.[5]

To this day American paper money carries the signatures of federal officials, the seals of the Federal Reserve Bank, and the Great Seal of the United States; only the vermillion is absent.

The popularity of the convenient and portable paper money also gave rise to the new profession of counterfeiting; Chinese counterfeiters risked their heads, for those inept or unlucky enough to be caught were decapitated. Paper money in turn gave rise to a system of credit and banking that enabled merchants to deposit money, take out loans, and invest in commercial ventures. Facilitated by the new monetary and banking systems, trade burgeoned so much that the Song government derived more revenue from trade and taxes on trade than from the traditional land tax.

Cultural Blossoming of the Tang and Song

The economic reforms, political stability, and military successes of the Tang and Song nourished a splendid era in the history of Chinese culture. Although the Tang period is best known for its poetry, many forms of art flourished during these years. Potters produced porcelain of extraordinarily high quality and delicate balance. Porcelain of

✳ **Song Baby Pillow**   This imaginative piece of art was surely more decorative than practical. It represents an uncomfortable-looking pillow for the head, supported by the form of a sleeping, plump infant. During the Song period children became a popular motif in art. *(Source: The Avery Brundage Collection/Laurie Platt Winfrey, Inc.)*

uniformly high quality became a major item of export to western Asia and Europe.

Within the past seventeen years the excavations of Tang imperial tombs at Qianxian in Shaanxi province have shed welcome light on the sculpture and painting of this vibrant period. At Qianxian scores of life-size statues of horses and warriors guard the tombs of emperors while rows of statues of dignitaries, lions, and sheep stand in silent audience. Inside the tombs, ceramic statuettes of ceremonial troops serve as guardians.

The royal tombs display Tang painting at its best. The walls are graced with the painted figures of respectful mandarins, court ladies, and warrior guards. Scenes of hunting and polo lend an air of energy and vivacity. Mythological creatures ward off evil spirits. Realistic and graceful in form, the paintings exhibit a sophisticated sense of perspective. The total effect is joyous, even gay. Tang painters captured life accurately and with a deft touch.

The glory of Tang literature was poetry, which achieved unmatched elegance and brilliance. Tang poetry was sophisticated, urbane, and learned. Thoroughly familiar with earlier poetry and with history, Tang poets were also influenced by Chinese and foreign folk songs. They were consummate masters of meter and rhythm, their poems often gemlike. Though formal and rigorous in composition, Tang poetry expresses genuine emotion, frequently with humor and sensitivity. Some poets strung songs together to accompany drama, in effect creating Chinese opera. Tang poets created new vehicles for verse, and they themselves became the models for their Song successors and all later Chinese poets (see Listening to the Past).

One of the most delightful of the Tang poets was Li Bo (701–762), whose poetry is polished, learned, and good-natured. Unlike most Tang poets, Li Bo was never a mandarin official, although he was familiar with the cultivated life of the imperial court. He was a member in good standing of the literary circle known as the Eight Immortals of the Wine Cup, and his poems allude often to his love of wine. Even banishment from the court did not dampen his spirits, for Li Bo loved his wine, his art, and all of nature too much ever to become morose. One of his most famous poems describes an evening of drinking with only the moon and his shadow for company:

A cup of wine, under the flowering trees;
I drink alone, for no friend is near.
Raising my cup I beckon the bright moon,
For he, with my shadow, will make three men.
The moon, alas, is no drinker of wine;
Listless, my shadow creeps about at my side.

. . . .

Now we are drunk, each goes his way.
May we long share our odd, inanimate feast,
And we meet at last on the cloudy River of the sky.[6]

Another poem captures a moment of joy that the poet experienced while walking in the mountains on a summer day:

Gently I stir a white feather fan,
With open shirt sitting in a green wood.
I take off my cap and hang it on a jutting stone;
A wind from the pine-trees trickles on my bare head.[7]

Li Bo is said to have died one night in the company of his old friend the moon.

Chinese River Festival   The beauty and delicacy of Chinese painting are obvious in this lively scene of people enjoying a river festival. Like the great poets, Chinese painters delighted in scenes from daily life. *(Source: The Metropolitan Museum of Art, Fletcher Fund, 1947, A. W. Bahr Collection)*

Less cheerful but no less talented was Bo Juyi (772–846), whose poems often reflect the concerns of a scholar-official. He felt the weight of his responsibilities as governor of several small provinces and sympathized with the people whom he governed. At times Bo Juyi worried about whether he was doing his job justly and well:

From my high castle I look at the town below
Where the natives of Pa cluster like a swarm of flies.
How can I govern these people and lead them aright?
I cannot even understand what they say.

But at least I am glad, now that the taxes are in,
To learn that in my province there is no discontent.[8]

Watching the reapers in the fields, he described their work and wondered about their fate and his:

Tillers of the soil have few idle months;
. . . .
Suddenly the hill is covered with yellow corn.
Wives and daughters shoulder baskets of rice;
Youths and boys carry the flasks of wine.
Following after they bring a wage of meat
To the strong reapers toiling on the southern hill,
Whose feet are burned by the hot earth they tread,
Whose backs are scorched by flames of the shining sky.
. . . .
And I to-day . . . by virtue of what right
Have I never once tended field or tree?
. . . .
Thinking of this, secretly I grew ashamed;
And all day the thought lingered in my head.[9]

Though a high official, he enjoyed such simple things as the pine trees growing around his house and a river babbling over its stony bed. At age seventy-four he died of a stroke, comforted by his wine and poetry.

The artists and thinkers of the Song period brought to fulfillment what the Tang had so brilliantly begun. Buoyed by political stability and economic prosperity, the Song explosion of learning and thought was a direct result of the invention of printing. The availability of books enabled scholars to amass their own libraries and thus to pursue their studies more easily and deeply. Song scholars formed circles to discuss their interests and ideas and to share their work with others. Song publishers printed the classics of Chinese literature in huge

editions to satisfy scholarly appetites. Works on philosophy, science, and medicine were also consumed avidly. Han and Tang poetry and historical works became the models for Song writers' own work. One popular literary innovation was the encyclopedia, which first appeared in the Song period, at least five centuries before publication of a European encyclopedia.

One of the most influential Song schools of thought (which gave rise to an intellectual trend known as Neo-Confucianism) was that of Wang Anshi (1021–1086), whose interests embraced economics, politics, literary style, and the classics of Chinese literature. As a Song minister of state, Wang Anshi launched a series of political and economic innovations with his "New Laws." The "Young Shoots" law extended low-interest loans to poor farmers, as some governments do today. Another law substituted a graduated tax for forced labor on state work projects. Like the Roman emperor Diocletian (see page 207), Wang Anshi introduced official price controls and limitations on profits; he went further than Diocletian by coupling this measure with a plan to equalize the land tax. Though marked by realism and good sense, Wang Anshi's innovations ultimately failed against bureaucratic infighting among officials and serious opposition from wealthy merchants and great landowners.

Other schools of Neo-Confucian thought confronted purely intellectual problems and left a more enduring imprint. The Cheng-Zu school achieved one of the greatest intellectual feats of a great age by adding a metaphysical dimension to traditional Confucianism's secular approach to human life and the universe. Metaphysics—the theoretical philosophy of being—gave Confucianism an intellectual depth and sophistication that equipped it to challenge what had long been a Buddhist monopoly of ultimate truth.

Neo-Confucians mined Confucian, Buddhist, and Daoist thought to create this new metaphysics. Meanwhile, one of the finest minds of the age, Zu Xi (1120–1200), addressed himself to the metaphysical problem of evil. He was primarily responsible for formulating Rational Neo-Confucianism. He read the commentaries of other scholars and then sought to explain them in his own terms. He concluded that people are born with principle (*li*) and matter (*Ch'i*). Purity of matter allows people clearly to appreciate principle. Impurity of matter means that people improperly realize principle and leads to various degrees of evil behavior. People can correct this imbalance, Zu Xi taught, through Confucian study and Buddhist meditation. In effect, Zu Xi explained not only how evil develops in the world but how it can be corrected.

Zu Xi wrote learned commentaries on the classics of Chinese literature. He was also the premier historian of his day. In striving for a unified view of life and the universe, he interpreted history and literature in support of his philosophical ideas. Unparalleled among the works of Neo-Confucians, Zu Xi's writings became classics; they have been read, revered, and imitated for centuries. He and other intellectuals breathed new life into Confucianism to meet the challenge of Buddhism.

Song poets and painters matched the greatness of their Tang predecessors. The Song particularly excelled at painting. Two dramatically dissimilar approaches to art arose. Some painters, like Li Longmian (ca 1040–1106), stressed exact realism. Others, like Mi Fei (ca 1051–1107), pursued a mystical romanticism in which space and natural elements were suggested with a few brush strokes.

The culture of the Tang and Song periods is remarkable for its breadth and variety, as well as its brilliance. From painting to poetry, from philosophy to history, these years gave rise to exquisite masterpieces. Yet despite cultural brilliance and political and economic success, the Southern Song emperors lived in the twilight of a great era. In the north a new and unforeseen danger, the Mongols, was on the verge of shaking the world from China to Hungary.

The Mongol Conquest (1215–1368)

In 1215 the Southern Song and their northern neighbors felt the first tremor of what was to be among the most remarkable movements of people in all history. Jenghiz Khan (1162–1227) and his huge band of Mongols, Tatars, and Turks burst into northern China. Marco Polo left a vivid description of their endurance and military skill:

They are brave in battle, almost to desperation, setting little value upon their lives, and exposing themselves without hesitation to all manner of danger.

Their disposition is cruel. They are capable of supporting every kind of privation, and when there is a necessity for it, can live for a month on the milk of their mares, and upon such wild animals as they may chance to catch. The men are habituated to remain on horseback during two days and two nights, without dismounting, sleeping in that situation whilst their horses graze. No people on earth can surpass them in fortitude under difficulties, nor show greater patience under wants of every kind.[10]

In 1215 the Mongols overwhelmed the Jurchens in the north and captured Beijing. All of northern China fell in 1234. The Southern Song held on tenaciously against the invaders, but Jenghiz Khan's grandson Kublai Khan (1216–1294) extinguished the dynasty and annexed all of southern China by 1279 (see Map 11.3). For the first time in history, all of China was ruled by foreigners. By 1271 Kublai Khan (also known as the Great Khan) had proclaimed himself emperor of China and founder of the Yuan Dynasty (1271–1368).

The Mongols distrusted the traditional mandarin class yet needed the mandarin's bureaucratic system. They compromised by assigning foreigners—Turks, Muslims from central Asia, and even a handful of European adventurers—to the highest administrative posts and allowing Chinese to hold lower offices. The Mongol conquest did not hinder China's trade: the expansion begun under the Song continued. By establishing his capital at Beijing, Kublai Khan helped reunite northern and southern China commercially: the wealth of the south flowed north to sustain the capital.

A conquering minority, the Mongols proclaimed repressive laws against the far more numerous Chinese. The northern Chinese, who were conquered first, had broader political and legal rights than the southerners but bore a far heavier burden of taxes and services. The Mongols disarmed the Chinese people and forbade them to assemble in large numbers and even to travel by night. The Chinese were captives in their own country.

The Mongols linked their internal policy with their dealings with the outside world. Some scholars argue that the Mongols provided a climate of peace and tolerance that facilitated friendly relations with those involved in long-distance trade. A realistic or even cynical view is that it served the Mongols, who were outsiders, very handsomely to

The Silk Road The Mongol conquest at least secured the safety of merchants traveling the Silk Road. There were few inns or hostels along the route, except in the cities. Most merchants, like those shown here, pitched camp each night by their camels. (*Source: National Palace Museum, Taiwan*)

seek outside economic support for their rule, all the while keeping the Chinese in their place.

Into this world wandered Marco Polo with his father and uncle. The three Polos had journeyed by land across Asia to the court of Kublai Khan, who received them with warmth and curiosity. Adept in four Asian languages, Marco Polo was uniquely equipped to collect accurate information about China. Although he visited South China, he probably seldom traveled far from Beijing. Instead, he seems to have drawn heavily on Chinese accounts for his information. He trained his insatiable curiosity on the land of China, its people and their customs, and everything likely to stimulate commerce. After seventeen years in China, the Polos returned to Italy, where Marco wrote a vivid ac-

count of their travels. At first considered sheer fantasy, his book was widely read and contributed enormously to familiarizing Europeans with Asia.

Mongol repression bred bitter resentment throughout China. By the middle of the fourteenth century, moreover, the Mongol hold on East Asia was weakening. Struggles among claimants to the Yuan throne seriously compromised the Great Khan's power and prestige, and Kublai Khan's successors proved weak and incompetent. In this atmosphere of crisis, some Chinese formed secret societies dedicated to overthrowing the oppressor. The most effective secret society, known as the Red Turbans, consisted of peasants and artisans, who had suffered the most from Mongol rule. Their rebellion in 1351 caught the Mongols totally off-guard. One of the rebels was a poor peasant and former monk best known to history as Hong Wu.

In 1356 Hong Wu and his followers stormed the important city of Nanjing (Nanking). Securing control over southern and central China, they pushed the Mongols northward, and by 1368 the Chinese had driven the Mongols completely out of China. Hung Wu established the Ming Dynasty (1368–1644). Once again China was united under one of its sons. In the following years Ming emperors would continue to push the Mongols north. They also rebuilt the Chinese economy by reclaiming abandoned farmland, by repairing neglected dikes and canals that were essential to fruitful agriculture, and by reforesting the countryside. As a result, under Ming rule China again prospered.

✤ JAPAN, DAWN OF THE RISING SUN

Japan entered the light of history late, and Japanese historical writing originated even later. The earliest reliable information on Japan comes from sporadic notices in Chinese histories; the first of them dates from A.D. 57. The Japanese people, by the time of their first appearance in history, had already had extensive exposure to Chinese culture. The Japanese derived much from the Chinese, but they molded their borrowings to suit their special needs. Early Japan saw the growth of an indigenous culture that the Chinese influenced but never overwhelmed.

The Japanese Islands

The heart of Japan is four major islands (Map 11.4). The largest and most important is Honshu. Honshu and the two southern islands surround the Inland Sea, a narrow stretch of water dotted with smaller islands. All four major islands are mountainous, with craggy interiors and some active volcanoes. Rugged terrain divides the land into numerous small valleys watered by streams. There is little flat land, and only 16 percent of the total area is arable. Japan's climate ranges from subtropical in the south, which the Pacific bathes in warm currents, to a region of cold winters in the north. Rainfall is abundant, favoring rice production. Yet nature can be harsh: Japan is a land buffeted by earthquakes, typhoons, and tidal waves.

✤ **Creation of Japan** This Japanese painting portrays two deities standing in the clouds above the Pacific Ocean. The god, sword at his side, stirs the waters with a lance and thereby creates the home islands of Japan. *(Source: Courtesy, Museum of Fine Arts, Boston, William Sturgis Bigelow Collection, Acc. no. 11.7972)*

MAP 11.4 The Islands of Japan, ca 1185
This map illustrates the importance of the island of
Honshu and the Inland Sea in the development
of early Japanese society.

Despite occasional rages, the sea provides a rich
harvest, and the Japanese have traditionally been
fishermen and mariners. Since the land is rugged
and lacking in navigable waterways, the Inland Sea,
like the Aegean in Greece, was the readiest avenue
of communication. Hence the land bordering the
Inland Sea developed as the political and cultural
center of early Japan. Geography also blessed Japan
with a moat—the Korea Strait and the Sea of
Japan. Consequently, the Japanese for long periods
were free to develop their way of life without external interference. Continuity has been a hallmark
of Japanese history.

Early Japan and the Yamato State

The beginnings of Japanese history are lost in the
mists of legend. The Chinese historian Wei Zhi

wrote one of the earliest reliable descriptions of
Japanese life in A.D. 297:

*The land of Wa [Japan] is warm and mild. In winter
as in summer the people live on raw vegetables and
go barefooted. They live in houses; father and mother,
elder and younger, sleep separately. They smear their
bodies with pink and scarlet, just as the Chinese use
powder. They serve food on bamboo and wooden
trays, helping themselves with their fingers.*[11]

The society that Wei Zhi and other Chinese
sources portray was based on agriculture and dominated by a warrior aristocracy. Clad in helmet and
armor, these warriors wielded swords and battle-
axes and often the bow. Some of them rode into
battle on horseback. Social stratification was rigid.
Peasants served at the command of nobles. At the
bottom of the social scale were slaves—usually
house servants. Slaves may have accounted for
about 5 percent of the total population.

Early Japan was divided into numerous political
units, although by about 513 their number had
been greatly reduced. Each pocket of local authority was under the rule of a particular clan—a large
group of families that claimed descent from a common ancestor and worshiped a common deity.
Each clan had its own chieftain, who marshaled
clan forces for battle and served as clan chief priest.
In Japan as in many other ancient societies, political power was a function of family strength, organization, and cohesion.

By the third century A.D. the Yamato clan had
seized the fertile area south of Kyoto, near Osaka
Bay (see Map 11.4). At the center of the Yamato
holdings was a rich plain, which constituted the
chief economic resource of the clan. Gradually the
Yamato clan, which traced its descent from the
sun-goddess, subordinated a huge number of
other clans to create the Yamato state. The chieftain of the Yamato clan proclaimed himself emperor and ruler over the other chieftains. Clans
that recognized Yamato dominion continued to
exercise local authority, and some clans were given
specific military or religious functions to fulfill. In
an effort to centralize further the administration of
the state, the emperor created a council of chieftains, whose members were treated as though they
were appointed officials.

The Yamato also used their religion to subordinate the gods of their supporters, much as Ham-

murabi had used Marduk (see page 20). Creating a hierarchy of gods under the authority of their sun-goddess, the Yamato established her chief shrine in eastern Honshu, where she could catch the first rays of the rising sun. Around the shrine there grew up local clan cults, giving rise to a native religion known as Shinto, the Way of the Gods. Shinto was a unifying force: the chief deity of Shinto, the sun-goddess, became the nation's protector. Shinto also stressed the worship of ancestors, thus strengthening the link between the present and the past. Much of its appeal rose from the fact that it was a happy religion. Its rituals celebrated the beauty of nature instead of invoking the hazards of fate or divine wrath. Shinto emphasized ritual cleanliness, and its festivals were marked by wine, song, and good cheer.

By the sixth century the powerful Yamato state was struggling to dominate Korea. From the dawn of their history the Japanese had held parts of Korea, but by 562 the Koreans had driven them out. Much more important was Korea's role as the avenue through which Chinese influence reached Japan. The Japanese adapted the Chinese systems of writing and record keeping, which allowed for bureaucratic administration along Chinese lines and set the stage for literature, philosophy, and written history.

Another influence of lasting importance to the Japanese was Buddhism. In 538 a Korean king sent the Yamato court Buddhist images and scriptures. The new religion immediately became a political football. One faction of the ruling clan favored its official adoption, and other factions opposed it. The resulting turmoil, both religious and political, ended only in 587, when members of the pro-Buddhist group defeated their opponents on the battlefield. Buddhism proved important to Japanese life for three broad reasons. First, it was a new and sophisticated but appealing religion that met needs not envisaged by Shinto. Second, it served as an influential carrier of Chinese culture. Finally, its acceptance by Japan's rulers enabled it to play an influential role in politics.

The victorious pro-Buddhist faction undertook a sweeping reform of the state, partly to strengthen Yamato rule and partly to introduce Chinese political and bureaucratic concepts. The architect of this effort was Prince Shotoku (574–622), the author of the "Seventeen Article Constitution," a triumph of Buddhist ethical and Confucian political thought. Issued in 604, the constitution was not a blueprint for government but a list of moral and ethical Buddhist precepts stressing righteous political conduct. It upheld the rights of the ruler and commanded his subjects to obey him. The constitution recommended an intricate bureaucracy like China's and admonished the nobility to avoid strife and opposition. Although the "Seventeen Article Constitution" never became the law of the entire land, it spelled out what Shotoku considered the proper goals of government and pointed the way to future reform.

Prince Shotoku   The author of the "Seventeen Article Constitution" is shown here with many of the attributes of a Chinese mandarin official. His sword shows that he was more than a mere administrator and was ready to resist those who opposed his reforms. (*Source: Imperial Household Collection, Kyoto*)

The death of Prince Shotoku in 622 set off some twenty years of political chaos. Finally in 645 supporters of his policies overthrew the government. The following year they proclaimed the Taika Reforms, a bold effort to create a complete imperial and bureaucratic system like that of the Tang Empire. For all their hopes, the Taika Reforms failed to make Japan a small-scale copy of Tang China. Nonetheless, the reformers created a nation with all the political trappings of its neighbors. The symbol of this new political awareness was the establishment in 710 of Japan's first true capital and first city, at Nara, just north of modern Osaka.

Nara, which was modeled on the Tang capital, gave its name to an era that lasted until 794, an era characterized by the continued importation of Chinese ideas and methods. Buddhism triumphed both religiously and politically. The Buddhist monasteries that ringed the capital were both religious centers and wealthy landlords, and the monks were active in the political life of the capital. In the Nara era, Buddhism and the imperial court were hand in glove.

The Heian Era (794–1185)

Buddhist influence at Nara showed its dark side in 765 when a Buddhist monk usurped the throne. He deposed the emperor but five years later lost power and was banished. The results were twofold. The imperial family moved the capital to Heian—modern Kyoto—where it remained until 1867. And a strong reaction against Buddhism and Chinese culture soon set in, strikingly symbolized by the severance of relations with China after 838. Thereafter the Japanese assimilated and adapted what they had imported. In a sense their intellectual and cultural childhood had come to an end, and they were ready to go their own way.

Though under a cloud, Buddhism not only survived the reaction but actually made gains. Before closing the door on China, the Japanese admitted two new Buddhist cults that gradually became integral parts of Japanese life. In 805 a Japanese monk introduced the Tendai (Chinese Tiantai) sect (see page 321). Though a complex product of China's high culture, Tendai proved popular because it held out the possibility of salvation to all. In addition to its religious message, Tendai preached the Confucian ideal of service to the state. The Shingon (True Word) sect arrived in 806 on the heels of Tendai. Like its Chinese precursor, this Japanese sect promised salvation through ritual, magical incantations, and masses for the dead.

Patronized initially by the nobility, both sects held the seeds of popular appeal. The common people cared nothing for Tendai and Shingon as metaphysical and intellectual systems but were strongly attracted by their magic and by the prospect of personal salvation. As Tendai and Shingon spread Buddhism throughout Japan, they were gradually transformed into distinctively Japanese religions. Furthermore, Buddhist art had an aesthetic appeal to the Japanese people.

Only later, during the Kamakura Shogunate (1185–1333), did Buddhism begin a vigorous proselytizing campaign. The emphasis on equality and salvation that was the hallmark of both Tendai and Shingon prepared the way for two sects that promised their followers sure and immediate salvation. The Pure Land sect (see page 321) preached that paradise could be reached through simple faith in Buddha. Neither philosophical understanding of Buddhist scriptures nor devotion to rituals was necessary. The second sect, an offshoot of the first, was the Lotus Sutra sect of Nichiren (1222–1281), a fiery and intolerant preacher. To be saved, according to Nichiren, people only had to invoke sincerely the Lotus Sutra, not the Buddha himself. Nichiren wanted to create a national faith, one that opposed Pure Land Buddhism (which called on Amida Buddha) and all other Buddhist sects but his own. Stripped of its intellectual top-weight, Buddhism made greater headway in the countryside than ever before.

The eclipse of Chinese influence liberated Japanese artistic and cultural impulses. The Japanese continued to draw on Chinese models but forged new paths of their own. They made great strides in writing. To express themselves more easily and clearly, Japanese scholars modified the Chinese script that they had adopted during the Yamato period. For the first time it became possible to write the Japanese language using the native syntax.

The reform of their written language unshackled Japanese writers. No longer bound in the straitjacket of Chinese, they created their own literary style and modes of expression. The writing of history, which had begun in the Nara era, received a huge boost, as did poetry. Completely original was the birth of the novel. One of the finest novels is

The Tale of Genji, by the court lady Murasaki Shikibu (978–ca 1016). This ageless work treats court life, paying minute attention to dialogue and exploring personalities. Not merely a novelist, Murasaki wrote about the mission of the novelist and the purpose of the novel. Other writers also produced novels. Sei Shonagon's *Pillow Book* is another masterpiece. These works bore no resemblance to any works in Chinese literature. The Japanese had launched their own independent and fertile literary tradition.

Politically, the Heian era saw aristocrats striving to free themselves from imperial control. The aristocrats quickly won out over the emperors. The biggest winners were the Fujiwara family. In the ninth century members of this family had regularly served as regents for the emperors and had married and connived their way into almost complete domination of the imperial line of rulers. As other families rose to prominence, setting the stage for intrigue and infighting at court, the effectiveness of the imperial government was further diminished.

In 1156, fed by declining central power, feuds among the great families, and the ambitions of local lords, open rebellion and civil war erupted. The two most powerful contenders in the struggle were the Taira and Minamoto clans, who quickly outstripped both the emperor and the Fujiwara. Both clans relied on *samurai*, skilled warriors who were rapidly consolidating as a new social class. By 1192 the Minamoto had vanquished all opposition, and their leader Yoritomo (1147–1199) became *shogun*, or general-in-chief. With him began the Kamakura Shogunate, which lasted until 1333.

The Land and the Samurai

The twelfth-century events that culminated in the Kamakura Shogunate involved a new relation between the samurai and the land. That relation eventually led to a fusion of the military, civil, and judicial aspects of government into a single authority. The Japanese samurai were a very important part of a larger system. Without an independent income of their own, the samurai needed the economic support of others. They depended economically on the *shoen*, a private domain outside imperial control. The shoen typically consisted of a village and its farmland, normally land capable of growing rice. Land was essential to the maintenance of the samurai.

Five-Story Pagoda   This pagoda is a splendid example of Japanese architecture of the Heian period. Such buildings were intended to complement their natural surroundings. (*Source: Courtesy, Horyuji Temple*)

Both samurai and shoen owed their origins directly to the gradual breakdown of central authority in the Heian era. The shoen had its roots in the ninth century, when local lords began escaping imperial taxes and control by formally giving their land to a Buddhist monastery, which was exempt from taxes, or to a court official who could get special privileges from the emperor. The local lord then received his land back as a tenant and paid his protector a nominal rent. The monastery or official received a steady income from the land, and the tenant was thereafter free of imperial taxes and jurisdiction. In spite of his legal status as a tenant, the local lord continued to exercise actual authority over the land—all the more so, in fact, since imperial officials could no longer touch him.

The many other people who were economically, politically, and legally dependent on the shoen, and who had various functions within it, enjoyed the rights of the *shiki,* a share of the produce of the land. The shoen was cultivated by independent farmers *(myoshu)* who owned specific fields, by dependent farmers, or, typically, by a combination of both. Unlike peasants in medieval Europe, dependent farmers never became serfs.

To keep order on the shoen and to protect it from harm, lords organized private armies. As the central government weakened, local lords and their armies of professional soldiers—the samurai—grew stronger. They were the only source of law and order in the countryside. The samurai and his lord had a double bond. The lord extended his authority over the samurai in return for the latter's loyalty and service. The samurai originally received from his lord only shiki rights to produce. Later the samurai received grants of land for their service. Each samurai entered into his lord's service in a formal ceremony that included a religious element.

The samurai had their own military and social code of conduct, later called *Bushido,* or "Way of the Warrior." The bedrock of the samurai code was loyalty to the lord, to which everything else was secondary. Preferring death to dishonor, the samurai showed complete dedication in the act of *seppuku* (sometimes incorrectly called *harakiri*), ritual suicide by disemboweling oneself. Yoritomo founded the Kamakura Shogunate on the samurai and their code. Attitudes that blossomed in Yoritomo's lifetime long outlasted the political system he built.

By the end of the twelfth century the samurai constituted the ruling class at the local level; they were warrior aristocrats who were close to the land and to those who worked it. Their code of conduct embraced religion, personal conduct, and practical affairs. According to the *Bushido,* samurai were expected to respect the gods, keep honorable company, be fair and even generous to others, and be sympathetic to the weak and helpless.

The symbols of the samurai were their swords, with which they were expected to be expert, and the cherry blossom, which falls with the spring wind, signifying the way in which samurai gave their lives for their lords. Like knights, samurai went into battle in armor and often on horseback. Like the ancient Spartans, samurai were expected to make do with little and like it. Physical hardship became routine, and soft living was despised as weak and unworthy. Although the full-blown samurai code did not take final shape until the later Ashikaga Shogunate, by the end of the twelfth century the samurai had left their mark on Japanese cultural life as well as on military affairs.

The Kamakura Shogunate (1185–1333)

The Kamakura Shogunate derives its name from Kamakura, the seat both of the Minamoto clan and of Yoritomo's shogunate. Yoritomo's victory meant that the emperor was still an ornament, honored and esteemed but mostly powerless.

Based on the loyalty of his followers, Yoritomo's rule was an extension of the way in which he ran his own estate. Having established his *bakufu* (tent government) at Kamakura, Yoritomo created three bodies, staffed by his retainers, to handle political and legal matters. His administrative board drafted government policy. Another board regulated lords and samurai, and a board of inquiry served as the court of the land.

For administration at the local level, Yoritomo created two groups of officials: military land stewards and military governors. The military land stewards were responsible for the collection of taxes. Charged with governing most estates, they saw to the estates' proper operation and maintained law and order in return for a share of the produce. The military governors oversaw the military and police protection of the provinces. They supervised the conduct of the military land stewards in peacetime and commanded the provincial samurai in war.

Yoritomo's successors did not inherit his ability, and in 1219 the Hojo family, a powerful vassal, reduced the shogun to a figurehead. Until 1333, the Hojo family held the reins of power by serving as regents of the shogun. The shogun had joined the emperor as a political ornament.

Internal affairs continued unchanged during the Hojo Regency, but a formidable challenge appeared from abroad. A massive seaborne invasion rudely interrupted Japan's self-imposed isolation in the thirteenth century. Its lingering effects weakened the Hojo Regency and eventually led to the

JAPAN, CA 320–CA 1400

3d century A.D.	Creation of the Yamato state
538	Introduction of Buddhism
604	Shotoku's "Seventeen Article Constitution"
646	Taika Reforms
710	Establishment of Nara as Japan's first capital and first city
710–794	Nara era
794–1185	Heian era and literary flowering
1185–1333	Kamakura Shogunate and Japanese feudalism
1274 and 1281	Unsuccessful Mongol invasions of Japan

downfall of the Kamakura Shogunate. The Mongol leader Kublai Khan, having overrun China and Korea, turned his eyes toward Japan. In 1274 and again in 1281 he sent huge numbers of ships and men to storm the islands. On both occasions the Mongols managed to land but were beaten back by samurai. What proved decisive, however, were two fierce storms that destroyed the Mongol fleets. Marco Polo recounted what he heard about one invasion force:

It happened, after some time, that a north wind began to blow with great force, and the ships of the Tartars, which lay near the shore of the island, were driven foul of each other. . . . The gale, however, increased to so violent a degree that a number of vessels foundered. The people belonging to them, by floating upon the pieces of the wreck, saved themselves upon an island lying about four miles from the coast of Zipangu [Japan].[12]

The Japanese claimed that they were saved by the *kamikaze,* the Divine Wind—which lent its name to the thousands of Japanese aviators who tried to become a sort of divine wind in World War II by crashing their airplanes onto American warships.

The Hojo regents successfully defended Japan but were unable to reward their vassals satisfacto-rily because little booty was found among the wreckage of the Mongol fleets. Discontent grew among the samurai, and by the fourteenth century the entire political system was breaking down. Both the imperial and the shogunate families were divided among themselves. Because the land could not support more samurai, who were rapidly growing in number, many samurai families became impoverished. Poverty created a pool of warriors ready for plunder, and the samurai shifted their loyalty to local officials who could offer them adequate maintenance.

The combination of factional disputes among Japan's leading families and among the samurai remained explosive until 1331, when the emperor Go-Daigo tried to recapture real power. His attempt sparked an uprising by the great families, local lords, samurai, and even Buddhist monasteries, which commanded the allegiance of thousands of samurai. Go-Daigo destroyed the Kamakura Shogunate in 1333 but lost the loyalty of his followers. By 1338 one of his most important military leaders, Ashikaga Takauji, had defeated the emperor and established the Ashikaga Shogunate, which lasted until 1573. Takauji's victory was also a victory for the samurai, who took over civil authority throughout Japan. The day of the samurai had fully dawned.

SUMMARY

By about 1400, traditional religious, social, and intellectual values had been challenged and fertilized by new peoples and new ideas throughout Asia. Most of India clung to Hinduism while Islam took root in modern Pakistan and Bangladesh. China incorporated and distilled Buddhism, which won a place next to Confucianism in Chinese life. Japan imported much of Chinese culture only to mold it into something distinctly Japanese. Finally, firm economic and cultural links made it virtually impossible for any Asian people to continue to develop in isolation.

NOTES

1. O. P. Singh Bhatia, trans., *The Imperial Guptas* (New Delhi: New India Press, 1962), p. 79.

2. A. L. Basham, trans., *The Wonder That Was India* (New York: Grove Press, 2nd ed., 1959), p. 161.

3. *Vasishtha* 4.5.1–2, trans. G. Bühler, in *The Sacred Laws of the Aryas,* part 2, *Vasishtha and Baudhayana* (Oxford: Clarendon Press, 1882), p. 31.

4. *Sutrakritanga* 1.4.2, quoted in Basham, *The Wonder That Was India,* pp. 459–460.

5. *The Travels of Marco Polo, the Venetian* (London: J. M. Dent and Sons, 1908), p. 203.

6. A. Waley, trans., *More Translations from the Chinese* (New York: Knopf, 1919), p. 27.

7. Ibid., p. 29.

8. Ibid., p. 71.

9. Ibid., p. 41.

10. *The Travels of Marco Polo,* p. 128.

11. R. Tsunoda et al., *Sources of the Japanese Tradition* (New York: Columbia University Press, 1958), p. 6.

12. *The Travels of Marco Polo,* pp. 325–326.

SUGGESTED READING

K. N. Chaudhuri, *Asia Before Europe* (1990), discusses the economy and civilization of cultures within the basin of the Indian Ocean. P. B. Golden, *An Introduction to the History of the Turkic Peoples* (1992), is a broad survey that covers the spread of Turks through central Asia and the Middle East. D. Simon, ed., *The Cambridge History of Early Inner Asia* (1990), is an ambitious and successful collection that ranges in time from prehistory to the early thirteenth century A.D. and in space from the Near East to India. A. Wink, Al-Hind, *The Making of the Indo-Islamic World,* vol. 1 (1990), is a massive and often difficult volume that examines economic expansion in India and its links to the Middle East. The reign of the Guptas is especially well documented. O. P. Singh Bhatia, trans., *The Imperial Guptas* (1962), treats the entire dynasty. In a series of works S. K. Maity covers many facets of the period: *Gupta Civilization: A Study* (1974), *The Imperial Guptas and Their Times* (1975), and *Economic Life in North India in the Gupta Period* (1975). Good treatments of Indian society and daily life can be found in A. L. Basham, *The Wonder That Was India,* 2nd ed. (1959), Ch. 6, and J. Auboyer, *Daily Life in Ancient India from 200 B.C. to A.D. 700* (1965).

Broad in scope are two books by H. G. Q. Wales: *The Indianization of China and of South-East Asia* (1967) and *The Making of Greater India,* 3d ed. (1974). H. Akira, *A History of Indian Buddhism* (1990), studies Buddhist influence on commerce, which so facilitated the spread of Buddhism beyond India.

An extensive survey of the Islamic invasions of India is J. F. Richards, "The Islamic Frontier in the East: Expansion into South Asia," *South Asia* 4 (1974): 90–109, in which Richards makes the point that many Indian princes put up stiff resistance to the invaders. A good treatment of early Islam in India is K. A. Nizami, *Some Aspects of Religion and Politics in India During the Thirteenth Century* (repr. 1970). In two books, *Islam in the Indian Subcontinent* (1980) and *Islam in India and Pakistan* (1982), A. Schimmel surveys many aspects of Islam, including architecture, life, art, and traditions in the subcontinent. G. S. Pomerantz, "The Decline of Buddhism in India," *Diogenes* 96 (1976): 38–66, treats the demise of Buddhism on its native soil.

Two works concentrate on the sultanate of Delhi: M. Habib and K. A. Nizami, eds., *Comprehensive History of India,* vol. 5, *Delhi Sultanate* (1970), and P. Hardy, "The Growth of Authority over a Conquered Political Elite: The Early Delhi Sultanate as a Possible Case Study," in J. F. Richards, ed., *Kingship and Authority in South Asia* (1978).

The standard work on the arrival of Buddhism in China is E. Zürcher, *The Buddhist Conquest of China,* 2 vols. (1959) C. W. Ernst, *Eternal Garden* (1992), is a far-ranging study of the mysticism, history, and politics at a major religious center, enlightening because of its emphasis on the relations between Muslim religion and politics. V. Hansen, *Changing Gods in Medieval China, 1127–1276* (1990), studies the social history of popular religion. Also good on the intellectual climate of the time are E. Balazs, *Chinese Civilization and Bureaucracy* (1964), and H. Welch and A. Seidel, eds., *Facets of Taoism* (1979). L. Kohn, *Taoist Mystical Philosophy* (1991), discusses Daoist mysticism in connection with controversies in Buddhist thought. Shorter and more popular is A. Wright, *Buddhism in Chinese History* (1959). Two books by K. Ch'en, *Buddhism in China* (1964) and *The Chinese Transformation of Buddhism* (1973), cover the early evolution of Buddhism in China. B. Gray, *Buddhist Cave Paintings at Tunhuang* (1959), is the place to begin study of the artistic impact of Buddhism on China.

Political events from the time of the Sui to the Song Dynasty are particularly well covered. A. F. Wright, *The Sui Dynasty* (1978), has become the standard work on this important dynasty. Though old, W. Bingham, *The Founding of the T'ang Dynasty: The Fall of Sui and Rise of T'ang* (1941), is still useful. C. P. Fitzgerald, *Son of Heaven: A Biography of Li Shih-min, Founder of the T'ang Dynasty* (1933), is likewise an old treatment of the first Tang emperor. Newer and broader is J. Perry and B. Smith, eds., *Essays on T'ang Society* (1976). The career of An Lu-shan is admirably discussed by E. G. Pullyblank, *The Background of the Rebellion of An Lu-shan* (1955). The difficult Era of the Five Dynasties is well covered by G. Wang, *The Structure of Power in North China During the Five Dynasties* (1963). Various aspects of Song developments receive attention in J. T. C. Liu and P. Golas, eds., *Changes in Sung China* (1969), and E. A. Kracke, Jr., *Civil Service in Early Sung China (960–1067)* (1953).

A brief treatment of the Tang tombs at Jianxian, well illustrated with color plates, is N. H. Dupree, "T'ang Tombs in Chien County, China," *Archaeology* 32, no. 4 (1979): 34–44. Students interested in further discussion of the great poets of the period can find no better place to start than the work of A. Waley, a gifted translator: *The Life and Times of Po Chü-i* (1949) and *The Poetry and Career of Li Po, 701–762* (1950). Wang Anshi still generates controversy, and a variety of views can be found in J. T. C. Liu, *Reform in Sung China: Wang An-shih (1021–1086) and His New Policies* (1959), and in J. Meskill, ed., *Wang An-shih— Practical Reformer?* (1963).

For the Mongols in their native setting, see L. Kwanten, *Imperial Nomads: A History of Central Asia, 500–1500 A.D.* (1979), a comprehensive picture of central Asian developments. H. D. Martin, *The Rise of Chinghis Khan and His Conquest of North China* (1950), studies the rise of the Mongols to greatness. J. Dardess's "From Mongol Empire to Yuan Dynasty: Changing Forms of Imperial Rule in Mongolia and Central Asia," *Monumenta Serica* 30 (1972–1973): 117–165, traces the evolution of Mongol government. His *Conquerors and Confucians: Aspects of Political Change in Late Yuan China* (1973) continues the study for a somewhat later period. Dardess's "The Transformations of Messianic Revolt and the Founding of the Ming Dynasty," *Journal of Asian Studies* 29 (1970): 539–558, treats some of the factors behind the overthrow of the Yuan Dynasty.

Among the many fine general works on Japan, the following are especially recommended in addition to those cited in the Notes: G. Trewartha, *Japan: A Geography* (1965); and E. O. Reischauer and J. K. Fairbank, *East Asia: The Great Tradition* (1960). More recent works include C. Schirokauer, *A Brief History of Chinese and Japanese Civilizations*, 2d ed. (1989); J. K. Fairbank, E. O. Reischauer, and A. Craig, *East Asia: Tradition and Transformation*, rev. ed. (1989); C. Totman, *Japan Before Perry* (1981); and A. Tiedmann, ed., *An Introduction to Japanese Civilization* (1974).

For early Japanese history, W. G. Aston, trans., *Nihongi: Chronicles of Japan from Earliest Times to A.D. 697* (1896, repr. 1990), despite its age, is still the only English translation of the earliest historical chronicle. J. P. Maas, *Antiquity and Anachronism in Japanese History* (1992), makes the bold suggestion that an exaggerated history of antiquity led to a distorted perception of the past. G. J. Groot, *The Prehistory of Japan* (1951), is still useful though rapidly becoming dated. The same is true of J. E. Kidder, *Japan Before Buddhism* (1959). Newer and quite readable is Kidder, *Early Buddhist Japan* (1972), which is well illustrated. J. M. Kitagawa, *Religion in Japanese History* (1966), discusses both Shinto and Buddhism.

Early Japanese literary flowering has attracted much attention. I. Morris, *The World of the Shining Prince: Court Life in Ancient Japan* (1964), provides a general treatment of the climate in which early Japanese artists lived. Murasaki Shikibu, *The Tale of Genji*, has been recently translated by R. Bowring (1988); I. Morris translated *The Pillow Book of Sei Shonagon*, 2 vols. (1967).

Japanese feudalism, like its medieval European counterpart, continues to excite discussion and disagreement. Some provocative works include P. Duus, *Feudalism in Japan*, 2d ed. (1976); E. O. Reischauer, "Japanese Feudalism," in R. Coulborn, ed., *Feudalism in History* (1956), pp. 26–48, and T. Keirstead, *The Geography of Power in Medieval Japan* (1992), which attempts to determine the cultural framework of the existence and development of the shoen system. For military affairs, see W. W. Farris, *Heavenly Warriors* (1992), which studies the early development of military organization and methods of warfare, and K. F. Friday, *Hired Swords* (1992), which treats the evolution of state military development in connection with the emergence of the samurai.

Women in Chinese Society

Women seldom made their voices heard in antiquity. Literature, like politics, was mostly a male preserve. Two moving exceptions to the norm are the poems reprinted here.

In the first, a woman has been divorced by her husband. She has lived her adult life in a region far from her home. She will return to the land of her brothers, who hold no sympathy for her plight. Her lament is poignant but without bitterness. This work is a striking example of popular culture. The situation that it described was surely not unique but one that happened all too often.

The mulberry leaves have fallen
All yellow and seared.
Since I came to you,
Three years I have eaten poverty.
The waters of the Ch'i were in flood;
They wetted the curtains of the carriage.
It was not I who was at fault;
It is you who have altered your ways,
It is you who are unfaithful,
Whose favours are cast this way and that.

Three years I was your wife.
I never neglected my work.
I rose early and went to bed late;
Never did I idle.
First you took to finding fault with me,
Then you became rough with me.
My brothers disowned me;
'Ho, ho,' they laughed.
And when I think calmly over it,
I see that it was I who brought all this upon
    myself.

I swore to grow old along with you;
I am old, and have got nothing from you but
    trouble.
The Ch'i has its banks,

The swamp has its sides;
With hair looped and ribboned
How gaily you talked and laughed,
And how solemnly you swore to be true,
So that I never thought there could be a
    change.
No, of a change I never thought;
and that *this* should be the end!

The next poem is the lament of a widow who has lost her husband in war. To describe the nature of her marriage, she uses the analogy of plants that bind themselves together. At the end of the poem, she looks forward to the day when she will join her husband at the end of her life.

The cloth-plant grew till it covered the thorn
    bush;
The bindweed spread over the wilds.
My lovely one is here no more.
With whom? No, I sit alone.

The cloth-plant grew till it covered the
    brambles;
The bindweed spread across the borders of
    the field.
My lovely one is here no more.
With whom? No, I lie down alone.

The horn pillow so beautiful,
The worked coverlet so bright!
My lovely one is here no more.
With whom? No, alone I watch till dawn.

Summer days, winter nights—
Year after year of them must pass
Till I go to him where he dwells.
Winter nights, summer days—
Year after year of them must pass
Till I go to his home.

Questions for Analysis

1. What does the first poem tell about the social status of women? What rights did they have, what powers, what means of protection?

2. Why do the brothers laugh at the woman in the first poem rather than showing sympathy for her misfortunes?

3. Does the widow in the second poem face the same situation as the one in the first? What are the differences between the two women, and how can we account for them?

Source: A. Waley, trans., *The Book of Songs.* Copyright 1937 Houghton Mifflin Company. Reprinted by permission.

Ch'ing dynasty painting of woman peeking from behind baton door. *(Source: By courtesy of the Trustees of the Victoria & Albert Museum)*

12

Europe in the Early and Central Middle Ages

Cover of *Codex Aureus* of Saint Emmeram, ca 870 A.D. *(Source: Bayerische Staatsbibliothek)*

The Frankish chieftain Charles Martel defeated Muslim invaders in 733 at the Battle of Tours in central France.[1] Muslims and Christians have interpreted the battle differently. Muslims considered it a minor skirmish and attributed the Frankish victory to Muslim difficulties in maintaining supply lines over long distances and to ethnic conflicts and unrest in Islamic Spain. Christians considered the Frankish victory one of the great battles of history because it halted Muslim expansion in Europe. A century later, in 843, Charles Martel's three great-great-grandsons, after a bitter war, concluded the Treaty of Verdun, which divided the European continent among themselves. Civil disorder and foreign invasion then wracked Europe for about the next 150 years.

Between 733 and 843, a distinctly European society emerged. A new kind of social and political organization, later called feudalism, appeared. And for the first time since the collapse of the Roman Empire, most of western Europe was united under one government, which reached its peak under Charles Martel's grandson, Charlemagne. Christian missionary activity among the Germanic peoples continued, and strong ties were forged with the Roman papacy. A revival of study and learning—the Carolingian Renaissance—occurred during the reign of Charlemagne.

By the last quarter of the tenth century, after a long and bitter winter of discontent, signs of a European spring appeared. That spring lasted from the early eleventh to the end of the thirteenth century. The period from about 1050 to 1300, the central Middle Ages, was a time of creativity and vitality between two eras of crisis. During the central Middle Ages, European society experienced demographic growth, religious reform, increasing political stability, and enormous economic development.

- How did Charlemagne acquire and govern his vast empire, and what was the Carolingian Renaissance?
- What was feudalism, and how did it come about?
- What factors contributed to the disintegration of the Carolingian Empire, and what were the ingredients of the revival of Europe?
- How did the Christian church and civil government develop and influence one another during the early and central Middle Ages?
- How did medieval rulers work to solve their problems of government, thereby laying the foundations of the modern state?
- How did medieval towns originate, and how do they reveal the beginnings of radical change in medieval society?

These are the questions this chapter will explore.

THE CAROLINGIAN ERA

The Frankish kingdom that had emerged under Clovis by the early sixth century included most of what is now France and a large section of southwestern Germany. Clovis's baptism into orthodox Christianity won him church support against other Germanic tribes. Clovis died in 511, and the Merovingian Dynasty went on to rule for two centuries.

Rule is, of course, too strong a verb. Conquering the vast territories proved easier for the Merovingians than governing them, given their inadequate political institutions. When he died, Clovis divided his kingdom among his four sons, according to Frankish custom. Because of the vast size of the kingdom, the division made sense. Practically, however, Clovis's decision was disastrous, because it led to civil war. The four Merovingian heirs hated each other, and each one fought to deprive his relatives of their portions of the kingdom. Thus in 558 Clovis's youngest son, Lothair, acquired the whole kingdom after he had murdered two of his nephews and eliminated one rebellious brother by burning him and his family alive. After Lothair died, the two remaining sons of Clovis continued the civil war until just one of them survived.

In this domestic violence the remarkable Queen Brunhilda (d. 631), wife of King Sigebert of the East Frankish kingdom, played an important role. Chilperic, ruler of the West Frankish kingdom, murdered his wife Galswintha so that he could marry his mistress Fredegunda. Galswintha and Brunhilda were sisters, and Brunhilda promptly instigated war between the East and West Frankish kingdoms. Hatred of Fredegunda led her to continue the war even after the deaths of both Sigebert and Chilperic. During the reigns of her son and grandson, Brunhilda actually ruled the East Frankish kingdom, displaying considerable political skill and a merciless use of violence in pursuit of royal goals.

The long period of civil war in the Frankish kingdom may have provided the opportunity for the emergence of a distinct aristocratic class. Research in Frankish family history has revealed that a noble ruling class existed before the mid-sixth century. Members of this class belonged to families of high reputation, who gradually intermarried with members of the old Gallo-Roman senatorial class. They possessed wealth and great villas and led an aristocratic lifestyle. They exercised rights of lordship over their lands and tenants, dispensing local customary, not royal, law. From these families came almost all the bishops of the church. Because they had a political distinction from the rest of society, they constituted a noble class.[2]

The Rise of the Carolingian Dynasty

The rise of the Carolingians—their name derives from the Latin *Carolus,* for "Charles"—was partly due to papal support. In the early eighth century, missionaries supported Charles Martel and his son Pippin III as they attempted to bring the various Germanic tribes under their jurisdiction. The Anglo-Saxon missionary Wynfrith, or Boniface (680–754), as he was later called, was the most important. Boniface's achievements were remarkable. He helped shape the structure of the German church. He established *The Rule of Saint Benedict* in all the monasteries he founded or reformed, thus promoting monastic unity. And, with the support of the king, he held councils to reform the church in the Frankish kingdom.

Saint Boniface preached throughout Germany against divorce, polygamous unions, and incest. On these matters German custom and ecclesiastical law completely disagreed. The Germans allowed divorce: a man simply repudiated his wife (divorce did not require her consent). The Germanic peoples also practiced polygamy and incest—sexual relations between brothers and sisters or parents and children—on a wide scale. Church councils and theologians stressed that marriage, validly entered into—that is, freely consented to—could not be ended.

Boniface's preaching was not without impact. Some fifty years later, in 802, Charles Martel's grandson Charlemagne would prohibit incest. Charlemagne also would decree that a husband might separate from an adulterous wife, that the woman could be punished, and that the man could not remarry in her lifetime. Charlemagne would also encourage severe punishment for adulterous men. The publication of laws does not usually or instantly end deeply rooted social practices, but Charlemagne's efforts brought new dignity to marriage and to women.

Charles Martel had been king of the Franks in fact but not in title. His son Pippin III (r. 751–768) made himself king in title as well as in fact. According to Germanic custom, which had the force of law, the kingship had to pass to someone of royal blood. Pippin did not want to murder the ineffectual Merovingian king, but he did want the kingship. So he consulted the pope, who tacitly supported the deposition of the last Merovingian king and recognized the Carolingians. The Merovingian ruler was removed and forced to become a monk.

Pippin was the first ruler to be anointed by the pope with the sacred oils and acknowledged as *rex et sacerdos* ("king and priest"). Anointment, rather than royal blood, set the Christian king apart. Pippin also cleverly eliminated possible threats to the Frankish throne, and the pope promised him support in the future. When Pippin died, his son Charlemagne succeeded him.

The Empire of Charlemagne

Charles the Great (r. 768–814), generally known as Charlemagne, built on the military and diplomatic foundations of his ancestors. Einhard, his secretary and biographer, wrote a lengthy idealization of the warrior-ruler. It has serious flaws but is the earliest medieval biography of a layman, and historians consider it generally accurate:

Charles was large and strong, and of lofty stature, though not disproportionately tall . . . the upper part of his head was round, his eyes very large and animated, nose a little long, hair fair, and face laughing and merry. Thus his appearance was always stately and dignified . . . although his neck was thick and somewhat short, and his belly rather prominent; but the symmetry of the rest of his body concealed these defects. His health was excellent, except during the four years preceding his death.[3]

Though crude and brutal, Charlemagne was a man of enormous intelligence. He appreciated good literature, such as Saint Augustine's *City of God,* and Einhard considered him an unusually effective speaker. Recent scholarship disputes Ein-

Merovingian Army   This sixth- or seventh-century ivory depicts a nobleman in civilian dress followed by seven warriors. Notice that the mounted men do not have stirrups and seem to have fought with spears and bows and arrows. The power of the Frankish aristocracy rested on these private armies. *(Source: Landesmuseum, Trier)*

hard's claim that Charlemagne could not write. Charlemagne had four legal wives and six concubines and even after the age of sixty-five continued to sire children. Three of his sons reached adulthood, but only one outlived him. Four surviving grandsons, however, ensured perpetuation of the family.

Charlemagne's most striking characteristic was his phenomenal energy, which helps to explain his great military achievements.[4] Continuing the expansionist policies of his ancestors, Charlemagne fought more than fifty campaigns and became the greatest warrior of the early Middle Ages. He subdued all of the north of modern France and, in the course of a thirty-year war against the semibarbaric Saxons, added most of the northwestern German tribes to the Frankish kingdom. Because of repeated rebellions by the Saxons, Charlemagne, according to Einhard, ordered more than four thousand Saxons slaughtered in one day.

To the south, he also achieved spectacular results. In 773–774 the Lombards in northern Italy were threatening the papacy. Charlemagne marched south, overran fortresses at Pavia and Spoleto, and incorporated Lombardy into the Frankish king-

dom and to his title as king of the Franks he added king of the Lombards. He successfully fought the Byzantine Empire for Venetia (excluding the city of Venice), Istria, and Dalmatia and temporarily annexed those areas to his kingdom.

In the west, Charlemagne tried to occupy Basque territory in northwestern Spain. When his long siege of Saragossa proved unsuccessful and the Saxons on his northeastern borders rebelled, Charlemagne decided to withdraw. At Roncesvalles in 778, the Basques annihilated his rear guard, which was under the command of Count Roland. This attack was Charlemagne's only defeat, and he forbade people to talk about it. The expedition, however, inspired the great medieval epic *The Song of Roland,* written down around 1100, which portrays Roland as the ideal chivalric knight and Charlemagne as exercising a sacred kind of kingship. Although many of the epic's details differ from the historical evidence, *The Song of Roland* is important because it reveals the popular image of Charlemagne in later centuries.

By around 805, the Frankish kingdom included all of continental Europe except Spain, Scandinavia, southern Italy, and the Slavic fringes of the

✤ **MAP 12.1 The Carolingian World** The extent of Charlemagne's nominal jurisdiction was extraordinary: it was not equaled until the nineteenth century.

East (Map 12.1). The Muslims in northeastern Spain were checked by the establishment of strongly fortified areas known both as *marches* and as *marks*. Not since the third century A.D. had any ruler controlled so much of the Western world.

Charlemagne ruled a vast rural world dotted with isolated estates and characterized by constant petty violence. His empire was not a state as people today understand that term; it was a collection of primitive peoples and semibarbaric tribes. Apart from a small class of warrior aristocrats and clergy, almost everyone engaged in agriculture. Trade and commerce played only a small part in the economy. Cities served as the headquarters of bishops and as ecclesiastical centers.

By constant travel, personal appearances, and the sheer force of his personality, Charlemagne sought to awe conquered peoples with his fierce presence and terrible justice. By confiscating the estates of great territorial magnates, he acquired lands and goods with which to gain the support of lesser lords, further expanding the territory under his control.

The political power of the Carolingians rested on the cooperation of the dominant social class, the Frankish aristocracy. By the seventh century, through mutual cooperation and frequent marriage alliances, these families exercised great power that did not derive from the Merovingian kings. The Carolingians themselves had emerged from this aristocracy, and their military and political success depended on the support of the nobility. The lands and booty with which Charles Martel and Charlemagne rewarded their followers in these noble families enabled the nobles to improve their economic position. In short, Carolingian success was a matter of reciprocal help and reward.[5]

Two or three hundred counts from this imperial aristocracy governed at the local level. They had full military and judicial power and held their offices for life but could be removed by the emperor for misconduct. As a link between local authorities and the central government, Charlemagne appointed officials called *missi dominici,* "agents of the lord king." The empire was divided into visitorial districts. Each year, beginning in 802, two missi, usually a count and a bishop or abbot, visited assigned districts. They held courts and investigated their districts' judicial, financial, and clerical activities. They held commissions to regulate crime, moral conduct, the clergy, education, the poor, and many other matters. The missi checked up on the counts and worked to prevent the counts' positions from becoming hereditary: strong counts with hereditary estates would have weakened Charlemagne's power. In the marks—especially in unstable areas—officials called margraves had extensive powers to govern.

A modern state has institutions of government such as a civil service, courts of law, financial agencies for collecting and apportioning taxes, and police and military powers. These did not exist in Charlemagne's empire. Instead, dependent relationships cemented by oaths promising faith and loyalty held society together. Nevertheless, although the empire lacked viable institutions, some Carolingians involved in governing did have vigorous political ideas. The abbots and bishops who served as Charlemagne's advisers worked out what was for their time a sophisticated political ideology.

In letters and treatises, churchmen set before their ruler high standards of behavior and of government. They wrote that although a ruler holds power from God the ruler is obliged to respect the law just as all subjects of the empire were required to obey the ruler. The abbots and bishops envisioned a unified Christian society presided over by a king who was responsible for maintaining peace, law, and order and dispensing justice, without which, they pointed out, neither the ruler nor the kingdom had any justification. These views derived largely from Saint Augustine's theories of kingship. Inevitably, they could not be realized in an illiterate, preindustrial society. But they were the seeds from which medieval and even modern ideas of government were to develop.

In the autumn of the year 800, Charlemagne paid a momentous visit to Rome. Einhard gave his account of what happened:

His last journey there [to Rome] was due to another factor, namely that the Romans, having inflicted many injuries on Pope Leo—plucking out his eyes and tearing out his tongue, he had been compelled to beg the assistance of the king. Accordingly, coming to Rome in order that he might set in order those things which had exceedingly disturbed the condition of the Church, he remained there the whole winter. It was at the time that he accepted the name of Emperor and Augustus. At first he was so much opposed to this that he insisted that although that day was a great [Christian] feast, he would not have entered the Church if he had known beforehand the pope's intention. But he bore very patiently the jealousy of the Roman Emperors [that is, the Byzantine rulers] who were indignant when he received these titles. He overcame their arrogant haughtiness with magnanimity, a virtue in which he was considerably superior to them, by sending frequent ambassadors to them and in his letters addressing them as brothers.[6]

For centuries scholars have debated the significance of the imperial coronation of Charlemagne by the pope. Did Charles plan the ceremony in

Saint Peter's on Christmas Day, or did he merely accept the title of emperor? What did he have to gain from it?

Three points seem certain. First, Charlemagne gained the imperial *title* "Holy Roman emperor" and considered himself a Christian king ruling a Christian people. His motto, *Renovatio romani imperi* ("Revival of the Roman Empire"), reinforces the notion that Charles was consciously perpetuating old Roman imperial notions while at the same time identifying with the new Rome of the Christian church. Charlemagne and his government represented a combination of Frankish practices and Christian ideals—the two basic elements of medieval European society. Second, later German rulers were anxious to gain the imperial title and to associate themselves with the legends of Charlemagne and ancient Rome. Third, ecclesiastical authorities continually cited the event as proof that the dignity of the imperial crown could be granted only by the pope. The imperial coronation of Charlemagne, whether planned by the Carolingian court or by the papacy, was to have a profound effect on the course of German history and on the later history of Europe.

The Carolingian Intellectual Revival

It is ironic that Charlemagne's most enduring legacy was the stimulus he gave to scholarship and learning. Barely literate, preoccupied with the control of vast territories, much more a warrior than a thinker, Charlemagne nevertheless set in motion a cultural revival that had widespread and long-lasting consequences.

The revival of learning associated with Charlemagne and his court at Aachen drew its greatest inspiration from seventh- and eighth-century intellectual developments in the Anglo-Saxon kingdom of Northumbria, situated at the northernmost tip of the old Roman world (see Map 12.1). Northumbrian monasteries produced scores of religious books, commentaries on the Scriptures, illuminated manuscripts, law codes, and collections of letters and sermons. The finest product of Northumbrian art is probably the Gospel book produced at Lindisfarne around 700. The incredible expense involved in the publication of such a book—for vellum (calfskin or lambskin specially prepared for writing), coloring, and gold leaf—represents in part an aristocratic display of wealth.

In Gaul and Anglo-Saxon England, women shared with men in the work of evangelization and in the new Christian learning. Kings and nobles, seeking suitable occupations for daughters who did not or would not marry, founded monasteries for nuns. Some were *double monasteries,* housing both men and women in two adjoining establishments and governed by a woman—the *abbess.* Double monasteries provided women of the ruling class with something to rule. Nuns and monks worked together. Nuns looked after the children given to the monastery as *oblates* ("offerings"), the elderly who retired at the monastery, and travelers who needed hospitality. Monks provided protection, for

Lindisfarne Gospels "In the beginning was the Word" (John 1:1), and the crucial texts for the preservation and spread of the Christian faith were the Gospels. Bishop Eadfrith of Lindisfarne (ca 690) produced this carpet, or cover page, for a Gospel book. Reflecting the Celtic tradition of interlaced ornaments and figurative imagery, this work is a superb example of Northumbrian culture. The style became celebrated throughout Christian Europe. *(Source: The British Library)*

in a violent age an isolated house of women invited attack. The monks also did the heavy work on the land. Perhaps the most famous abbess of the Anglo-Saxon period was Saint Hilda (d. 680). A noblewoman of considerable learning and administrative ability, she ruled the double monastery of Whitby on the Northumbrian coast, advised kings and princes, hosted a synod in 664, and encouraged scholars and poets. Several generations after Hilda, Saint Boniface wrote many letters to Whitby and to other houses of nuns, pleading for copies of books.[7]

The finest representative of Northumbrian and indeed all Anglo-Saxon scholarship is the Venerable Bede (ca 673–735). At the age of seven he was given by his parents as an oblate to Abbot Benet Biscop's monastery at Wearmouth. Later he was sent to the new monastery at Jarrow, five miles away. There, surrounded by the books that Benet Biscop had brought from Italy, Bede spent the rest of his life.

The author of learned commentaries on the Scriptures, Bede also devoted himself to other scholarly fields. Modern scholars praise him for his *Ecclesiastical History of the English Nation,* which is the chief source of information about early Britain. Bede searched far and wide for his information, discussed the validity of his evidence, compared various sources, and exercised a rare critical judgment. For these reasons, he has been called "the first scientific intellect among the Germanic peoples of Europe."[8]

At about the time that monks at Lindisfarne were producing their Gospel book and Bede at Jarrow was writing his *History,* another Northumbrian monk was at work on a nonreligious epic poem that provides considerable information about the society that produced it. In contrast to the works of Bede, which were written in Latin, the poem *Beowulf* was written in the vernacular Anglo-Saxon. Although *Beowulf* is the only native English heroic epic, all the events of the tale take place in Denmark and Sweden, suggesting the close relationship between England and Scandinavia in the eighth century. Scholars have hailed it as a masterpiece of Western literature.[9]

The physical circumstances of life in the seventh and eighth centuries make Northumbrian cultural achievements all the more remarkable. Learning was pursued under terribly difficult circumstances. Monasteries such as Jarrow and Lindisfarne stood on the very fringes of the European world (see

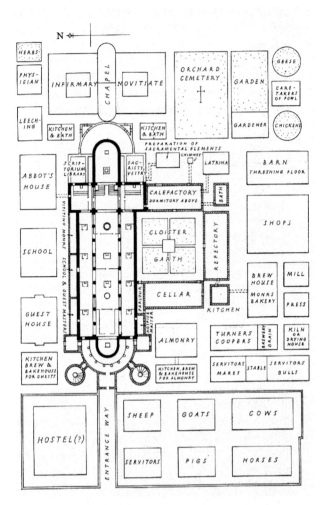

Plan for an Ideal Monastery This is a ninth-century architectural design for a self-supporting monastic community of 270 members. The primary focus of the monks' lives was the church and the cloister, which appropriately appear in the center of the plan. Notice the herb garden close to the physician's quarters. The western entrance for visitors was surrounded by the hostel for poor guests and pens for farm animals—with all the inevitable smells. (*Source: Kenneth John Conant, Carolingian and Romanesque Architecture, 800–1200. Pelican History of Art, 2d rev. ed. New York: Pelican, 1978, p. 57*)

Map 12.1). The barbarian Picts, just an afternoon's walk from Jarrow, were likely to attack at any time. Winter could be extremely harsh. In 664, for example, deep snow was hardened by frost from early winter until mid-spring. When it melted away, many animals, trees, and plants were found dead. To make matters worse, disease could take terrible tolls. Bede described events in the year 664:

In the same year of our Lord 664 . . . a sudden pestilence first depopulated the southern parts of Britain and then attacked the kingdom of the Northumbrians as well. Raging far and wide for a long time with *cruel devastation it struck down a great multitude of men. . . . This same plague oppressed the island of Ireland with equal destruction.*[10]

Damp cold with bitter winds blowing across the North Sea must have pierced everything, even stone monasteries. Inside, only one room, the *calefactory*, or "warming room," had a fire. Scribes in the *scriptorium*, or "writing room," had to stop frequently to rub circulation back into their numb hands. These monk-artists and monk-writers paid a high physical price for what they gave to posterity.

If Northumbrian cultural achievements had remained entirely insular, they would have been of slight significance. As it happened, an Englishman from Northumbria played a decisive role in the transmission of English learning to the Carolingian Empire and continental Europe, where Charlemagne promoted a revival that later scholars named the Carolingian Renaissance. The support Charlemagne gave to education and learning preserved the writings of the ancients and laid the foundations for all subsequent medieval culture.

At his court at Aachen, Charlemagne assembled learned men from all over Europe. The most important scholar and the leader of the palace school was the Northumbrian Alcuin (ca 735–804). From 781 until his death, Alcuin was the emperor's chief adviser on religious and educational matters. An unusually prolific scholar, Alcuin prepared some of the emperor's official documents and wrote many moral *exempla*, or "models," which set high standards for royal behavior and constitute a treatise on kingship. Alcuin's letters to Charlemagne set forth political theories on the authority, power, and responsibilities of a Christian ruler.

Aside from Alcuin's literary efforts, scholars at Charlemagne's court copied books and manuscripts and built up libraries. They used the beautifully clear handwriting now known as Carolingian minuscule, from which modern Roman type is derived. This script is called "minuscule" because it has lower-case as well as capital letters; the script that the Romans used had only capitals. Because lower-case letters are smaller than capitals, scribes using Carolingian minuscule could put more words on each sheet of vellum and could increase the number of texts they copied.

The development of Carolingian minuscule illustrates the way a seemingly small technological change can have broad cultural consequences.

Saint Luke from the Ada Gospels   After the cross, the most famous early Christian symbols were representations of the four evangelists: Matthew (man), Mark (lion), Luke (a winged ox), and John (eagle), based on the text in Revelation 4:7. The Ada School of painting, attached to the court of Charlemagne, gets its name from Ada, Charlemagne's sister, who commissioned some of the school's work. In this lavishly illuminated painting dating from the late eighth or early ninth century, a statuesque Saint Luke sits enthroned, his draperies falling in nervous folds reminiscent of Byzantine art, and surrounded by an elaborate architectural framework. This is a splendid example of Carolingian Renaissance art. *(Source: Municipal Library, Trier)*

Scholars established schools all across Europe, attaching them to monasteries and cathedrals. They placed great emphasis on the education of priests, trying to make all priests at least able to read, write, and do simple arithmetic. The greatest contribution of the scholars at Aachen was not so much the originality of their ideas as their hard work of salvaging and preserving the thought and writings of the ancients. The Carolingian Renaissance was a rebirth of interest in, study of, and preservation of the language, ideas, and achievements of classical Greece and Rome.

Although the scholars worked with Latin, the common people spoke their vernacular languages. The Bretons, for example, retained the local dialect of Britanny; and the Saxons and Bavarians, despite their geographical closeness, could not understand each other (see Map 12.1). Communication among the diverse peoples of the Carolingian Empire was possible only through the medium of Latin.

Once basic literacy was established, monastic and other scholars went on to more difficult work. By the middle years of the ninth century, there was a great outpouring of more sophisticated books. Ecclesiastical writers, imbued with the legal ideas of ancient Rome and the theocratic ideals of Saint Augustine, instructed the semibarbaric rulers of the West. And it is no accident that medical study in the West began, at Salerno in southern Italy, in the late ninth century, *after* the Carolingian Renaissance.

Alcuin completed the work of his countryman Boniface—the Christianization of northern Europe. Latin Christian attitudes penetrated deeply into the consciousness of European peoples. By the tenth century, the patterns of thought and lifestyles of educated western Europeans were those of Rome and Latin Christianity. Even the violence and destruction of the great invasions of the late ninth and tenth centuries could not destroy the strong foundations laid by Alcuin and his colleagues.

❈ DIVISION AND DISINTEGRATION OF THE CAROLINGIAN EMPIRE (814–987)

Charlemagne left his vast empire to his only surviving son, Louis the Pious (814–840), who was crowned emperor in his father's lifetime. Deeply religious and well educated, Louis was no soldier,

and he could not retain the respect and loyalty of the warrior aristocracy on whom he depended for troops and for administration of his territories. The disintegration that had begun in Charlemagne's last years accelerated as soon as he died.

The basic reason for the collapse of the Carolingian Empire is that it was too big. Bad roads swarming with thugs and rivers infested with pirates made communication within the empire very difficult. In Charlemagne's lifetime the empire was held together by the sheer force of his personality and driving energy. After his death, it began to fall apart. The empire lacked a bureaucracy like that of the Roman Empire—the administrative machinery necessary for strong and enduring government. It was a collection of tribes held together at the pleasure of warrior aristocrats, men most interested in strengthening their own local positions and ensuring that they could pass on to their sons the offices and estates they had amassed. Why should counts, abbots, and bishops obey the unimpressive, distant Louis the Pious, who represented a centralizing power that threatened their local interests? What counted was strength in one's own region and the preservation of family holdings.

The Frankish custom of dividing estates among all male heirs hastened the empire's disintegration. Between 817 and his death in 840, Louis the Pious made several divisions of the empire. Dissatisfied with their portions and anxious to gain the imperial title, Louis's three sons—Lothair, Louis the German, and Charles the Bald—fought bitterly among themselves. Finally, in the Treaty of Verdun of 843, the brothers agreed to partition the empire (Map 12.2).

Lothair, the eldest, received the title "emperor," still a source of prestige, and the so-called middle kingdom, an area extending diagonally across Europe from Flanders to Lombardy. Almost immediately, this kingdom broke up into many petty principalities. From the tenth century to the twelfth and thirteenth centuries, when French and German monarchs were trying to build strong central governments, the "middle kingdom" was constantly contested among them.

The eastern and most Germanic part of the Carolingian Empire passed to Louis the German. The western kingdom went to Charles the Bald; it included the provinces of Aquitaine and Gascony and formed the basis of medieval and modern France. The descendants of Charles the Bald held on in the west until 987, when the leading

MAP 12.2 Division of the Carolingian Empire, 843 The Treaty of Verdun (843), which divided the empire among Charlemagne's grandsons, is frequently taken as the start of the separate development of Germany, France, and Italy. The "middle kingdom" of Lothair, however, lacked defensive borders and any political or linguistic unity and quickly broke up into numerous small territories.

magnates elected Hugh Capet as king. The heirs of Louis the German ruled the eastern kingdom until 911, but real power was in the hands of local chieftains. Everywhere in the tenth century, fratricidal warfare among the descendants of Charlemagne accelerated the spread of feudalism.

Feudalism and Manorialism

Feudalism, which emerged in western Europe in the ninth century, was a type of government "in which political power was treated as a private possession and was divided among a large number of lords."[11] This kind of government characterized most parts of western Europe from about 900 to 1300. Feudalism actually existed at two social levels: (1) at the level of armed retainers who became knights and (2) at the level of counts and other royal officials who ruled great feudal principalities. A wide and deep gap in social standing and political function separated these social levels.

In the early eighth century, the Carolingian kings and other powerful men needed bodyguards and retainers—armed men who could fight. Charles Martel, using techniques common among his Merovingian predecessors, purchased the support and loyalty of his followers with grants of land or estates taken from churchmen or laymen or with movable wealth such as weapons or jewelry captured in battle.[12] Charles and other powerful men bound their retainers by oaths of loyalty and ceremonies of homage. Personal ties of loyalty cemented the relationship between lord and retainer. These retainers became known as *vassals,* from a Celtic term meaning "servant." Since knights were not involved in any government activity, and since only men who exercised political power were considered noble, knights were not part of the noble class. Down to the eleventh century, political power was concentrated in a small group of counts.

Counts, descended from the old Frankish aristocracy (see page 349), constituted the second level of feudalism. Under Charles Martel and his heirs, counts monopolized the high offices in the Carolingian Empire. At the local level, they had full judicial, military, and financial power. They held courts that dispensed justice, collected taxes, and waged wars. For most ordinary people, the counts were the government. Charlemagne regularly sent missi to inspect the activities of the counts, but there was slight chance of a corrupt or wicked count being removed from office.

Countships were not hereditary in the eighth century, but they tended to remain within the same family. In the eighth and early ninth centuries, regional concentrations of power depended on family connections and political influence at the king's court. The disintegration of the Carolingian Empire, however, served to increase the power of regional authorities. Civil wars and the great invasions of the ninth century (see pages 355–358) weakened the power and prestige of kings because they could do little about domestic violence. Common people turned for protection to the strongest local power, the counts, whom they considered their rightful rulers. Thus, in the ninth and tenth centuries, great aristocratic families governed virtually independent territories in which distant and weak kings could not interfere. "Political power had become a private, heritable property for great counts and lords."[13] This is what is meant by feudalism as a form of government.

Because feudal society was a military society, men held the dominant positions in it. A high premium was put on physical strength, fighting skill, and bravery. The legal and social position of women was not as insignificant as might be expected, however. Charters recording gifts to the church indicate that women held land in many areas. Women frequently endowed monasteries, churches, and other religious establishments. The possession of land obviously meant economic power. Moreover, women inherited *fiefs,* or landed estates. In southern France and Catalonia in Spain, women inherited feudal property as early as the tenth century. Other evidence also attests to women's status. In parts of northern France, children sometimes identified themselves in legal documents by their mother's name rather than their father's, indicating that the mother's social position in the community was higher than the father's.

In a treatise he wrote in 822 on the organization of the royal household, Archbishop Hincmar of Reims placed the queen directly above the treasurer. She was responsible for giving the knights their annual salaries. She supervised the manorial accounts. Thus, in the management of large households with many knights to oversee and complicated manorial records to supervise, the lady of the manor was likely to have highly important responsibilities. With such responsibility went power and influence.[14]

Feudalism concerned the rights, powers, and lifestyle of the military elite. *Manorialism* involved the services and obligations of the peasant classes who worked on the landed estates of the warring class. Feudalism and manorialism were inextricably linked. Peasants needed protection, and lords demanded something in return for providing that protection. Free farmers surrendered themselves and their lands to the lord's jurisdiction. The land was given back to them to farm, but they became tied to the land by various kinds of payments and services. In France, England, Germany, and Italy, local custom determined precisely what those services were, but certain practices became common everywhere. The peasant was obliged to turn over to the lord a percentage of the annual harvest, usually in produce, sometimes in cash. The peasant paid a fee to marry someone from outside the

lord's estate. To inherit property, the peasant paid a fine—often the best sheep or cow the person owned. Most significant, the peasant became a *serf*—part of the lord's permanent labor force, bound to the land and not allowed to leave it without the lord's permission. With vast stretches of uncultivated virgin land and a tiny labor population, the most profitable form of capital was not land but laborers.

The transition from freedom to serfdom was slow; its speed was closely related to the degree of political order in a given region. Even in the late eighth century, there were still many free peasants. And within the legal category of serfdom there were many economic levels, ranging from the highly prosperous to the desperately poor. Nevertheless, a social and legal revolution was taking place. By the year 800, perhaps 60 percent of the population of western Europe—completely free a century before—had been reduced to serfdom. The ninth-century Viking assaults on Europe created extremely unstable conditions and individual insecurity, leading to additional loss of personal freedom.

❖ GREAT INVASIONS OF THE NINTH CENTURY

After the Treaty of Verdun and the division of Charlemagne's empire among his grandsons, continental Europe presented an easy target for foreign invaders. All three kingdoms were torn by domestic dissension and disorder. No European political power was strong enough to put up effective resistance to external attacks.

Assaults on Western Europe

From the moors of Scotland to the mountains of Sicily, there arose in the ninth century the Christian prayer, "Save us, O God, from the violence of the Northmen." The Northmen, also known as Normans or Vikings, were pagan Germanic peoples from Norway, Sweden, and Denmark who had remained beyond the sway of the Christianizing and civilizing influences of the Carolingian Empire. Some scholars believe that the name Viking derives from the Old Norse word *vik,* meaning "creek." A *Viking,* then, was a pirate who waited in a creek or bay to attack passing vessels.

✦ **Vikings Invade Britain** In this twelfth-century representation of the Viking invasions, warriors appear to be armed with helmets, spears, and shields. Rowing their open boats across the rough North Sea and English Channel, they had great courage. *(Source: The Pierpont Morgan Library/Art Resource, NY)*

Viking assaults began around 787, and by the mid-tenth century the Vikings had brought large sections of continental Europe and Britain under their sway (Map 12.3). In the east they pierced the rivers of Russia as far as the Black Sea. In the west they sailed as far as Iceland, Greenland, and even the coast of North America, perhaps as far south as Long Island Sound, New York.

The Vikings were superb seamen with advanced methods of boatbuilding. Propelled either by oars or by sails, deckless, and about 65 feet long, a Viking ship could carry between forty and sixty men—quite enough to harass an isolated monastery or village. Against these ships navigated by thoroughly experienced and utterly fearless sailors, the Carolingian Empire, with no navy, was helpless. The Vikings moved swiftly, attacked, and escaped to return again.

Scholars disagree about the reasons for Viking attacks and migrations. Some maintain that overpopulation forced the Vikings to emigrate. Others argue that climatic conditions and crop failures forced migration. Still others insist that the Vikings were looking for trade and new commercial contacts, along with targets for plunder. Plunder they did. Viking attacks were savage. At first they attacked and sailed off laden with booty. Later, on returning, they settled down and colonized the areas they had conquered (Map 12.4). Between 876 and 954, Viking control extended from Dublin across the Irish Sea to Britain, then across northern Britain and the North Sea to the Vikings' Scandinavian homelands. These invaders also overran a large part of northwestern France and called the territory Norsemanland, from which the word *Normandy* derives.

Scarcely had the savagery of the Viking assaults begun to subside when Europe was hit from the east and south. Beginning about 890, Magyar tribes crossed the Danube and pushed steadily westward. (People thought of them as returning Huns, so the Magyars came to be known as Hungarians.) They subdued northern Italy, compelled Bavaria and Saxony to pay tribute, and penetrated even into the Rhineland and Burgundy. These roving bandits attacked isolated villages and monasteries, taking prisoners and selling them in the Eastern slave markets. The Magyars were not colonizers; their sole object was booty and plunder.

The Vikings and Magyars depended on fear. In their initial attacks on isolated settlements, they put many people to the sword. The Vikings also seized thousands of captives as slaves. From the British Isles and from territories along the Baltic, the Vikings took *thralls* (slaves) to be sold in the markets of Magdeburg on the Elbe River and Regensburg in Bavaria on the Danube and to supply the huge demand for slaves in the Muslim world. The slave trade represented an important part of Viking commerce. The Icelander Hoskuld Dala-Kolsson of Laxardal paid three marks of silver—three times the price of a common concubine—for

To Greenland
and North America

ICELAND

874

Faeroe Is.
800

Shetland Is.
700

VIKINGS

Novgorod
820

ATLANTIC

OCEAN

SCOTLAND
Iona
North
Sea

RUSSIA

Volga

Lindisfarne
Jarrow
859–878

Durrow
IRELAND
839

York

841–884

SAXONY

Saint Wandrille
Jumièges Rouen
St. Denis
NORMANDY
Loire

Aachen Fulda
Echternach

Elbe

Oder

Vistula

882

Dnieper

843–882

Santiago

896–911
Bordeaux

Garonne

Reichenau
BURGUNDY
917
Saint Gall

Rhine

BAVARIA

MAGYARS

895

883

941

Seine

900

895

907

Lisbon
844

Tagus

844

859–861

Barcelona

Balearic Is.

PROVENCE
Marseilles Lérins

Corsica

Sardinia

Rome
846

899

LOMBARDY

Danube

Black Sea

866

Monte
Cassino

Constantinople

Ob

842

MUSLIMS

827
Sicily

840–886

Mediterranean Sea

Monastery

Vikings

Magyars

Muslims

0   200   400 Km.

0   200   400 Mi.

❈ MAP 12.3 The Great Invasions of the Ninth Century Note the Vikings' penetration of eastern Europe and their probable expeditions to North America. What
impact did their various invasions have on European society?

a pretty Irish girl; she was one of twelve offered by
a Viking trader.

From the south the Muslims also began new encroachments, concentrating on the two southern
peninsulas, Italy and Spain. Seventh- and early-
eighth-century Islamic movements had been for

conquest and colonization, but the goal of ninth-
and tenth-century incursions was plunder. In Italy
the Muslims drove northward and sacked Rome in
846. Most of Spain had remained under their
domination since the eighth century. Expert seamen, they sailed around the Iberian Peninsula and

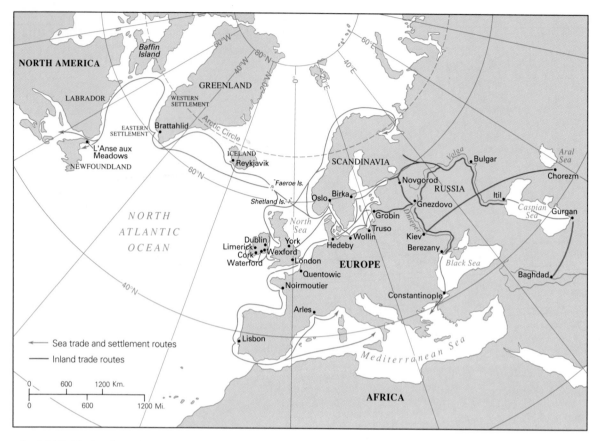

MAP 12.4 Viking Settlement and Trade Routes Viking trade and settlements extended from Newfoundland and Greenland to deep into Russia.

braved the dangerous shoals and winds of the Atlantic coast. They also attacked Mediterranean settlements along the coast of Provence. But Muslim attacks on the European continent in the ninth and tenth centuries were less destructive than the assaults of the more primitive Vikings and Magyars.

What was the effect of these invasions on the structure of European society? Viking, Magyar, and Muslim attacks accelerated the development of feudalism. Lords capable of rallying fighting men, supporting them, and putting up resistance to the invaders did so. They also assumed political power in their territories. Weak and defenseless people sought the protection of local strongmen. Free peasants sank to the level of serfs. Consequently, European society became further fragmented. Public power became increasingly decentralized.

The ninth-century invaders left significant traces of their own cultures. The Muslims made an important contribution to European agriculture, primarily through their influence in Spain. The

Vikings, too, made positive contributions to the areas they settled. They carried everywhere their unrivaled knowledge of shipbuilding and seamanship. The northeastern and central parts of England where the Vikings settled became known as the Danelaw because Danish law and customs, not English, prevailed there. York in northern England, once a Roman army camp and then an Anglo-Saxon town, became a thriving center of Viking trade with Scandinavia (see Map 12.4). At Dublin on the east coast of Ireland, Viking iron and steel workers and comb makers established a center for trade with the Hebrides, Iceland, and Norway. The Irish cities of Limerick, Cork, Wexford, and Waterford trace their origins to Viking trading centers.

The Vikings and the Kievan Principality

In antiquity the Slavs lived as a single people in central Europe. With the start of the mass migrations of the late Roman Empire, the Slavs moved in different directions and split into three groups. Between the fifth and ninth centuries, the eastern Slavs, from whom the Ukrainians, the Russians, and the White Russians descend, moved into the vast and practically uninhabited area of present-day European Russia and the Ukraine.

In the ninth century, the Vikings appeared in the lands of the eastern Slavs. Called Varangians in the old Russian chronicles, the Vikings were interested primarily in international trade. Moving up and down the rivers, the Vikings soon linked Scandinavia and northern Europe to the Black Sea and to the Byzantine Empire with its capital at Constantinople (see Map 12.4). They built a few strategic forts along the rivers, from which they raided the neighboring Slavic tribes and collected tribute. Slaves were the most important article of tribute, and *Slav* even became the word for "slave" in several European languages.

To increase and protect their international commerce, the Vikings declared themselves the rulers of the eastern Slavs. According to tradition, the semilegendary chieftain Ruirik founded the princely dynasty about 860. In any event, the Varangian ruler Oleg (r. 878–912) established his residence at Kiev. He and his successors ruled over a loosely united confederation of Slavic territories—the Kievan principality—until 1054. The Viking prince and his clansmen quickly became assimilated into the Slavic population, taking local wives and emerging as the noble class.

Assimilation and loss of Scandinavian ethnic identity was speeded up by the conversion of the Vikings and local Slavs to Eastern Orthodox Christianity by missionaries of the Byzantine Empire. The written language of these missionaries, an early form of Slavic now known as Old Church Slavonic, was subsequently used in all religious and nonreligious documents in the Kievan state. Thus the rapidly Slavified Vikings left two important legacies: they created a loose unification of Slavic territories under a single ruling prince and a single ruling dynasty, and they imposed a basic religious unity by accepting Orthodox Christianity (as opposed to Roman Catholicism) for themselves and the eastern Slavs.

Even at its height under Great Prince Iaroslav the Wise (r. 1019–1054), the unity of the Kievan principality was extremely tenuous. Trade, rather than government, was the main concern of the rulers. Moreover, the Slavified Vikings failed to find a way of peacefully transferring power from one generation to the next. In medieval western Europe this fundamental problem of government was increasingly resolved by resort to the principle of *primogeniture:* the king's eldest son received the crown as his rightful inheritance when his father died. In early Kiev, however, there were apparently no fixed rules, and much strife accompanied each succession. Between 1054 and 1237, Kiev disintegrated into more and more competing units, each ruled by a prince claiming to be a descendant of Ruirik. Even when only one prince was claiming to be the great prince, the whole situation was very unsettled.

A given prince owned a certain number of farms or landed estates and had them worked directly by his people, mainly slaves, called *kholops* in Russian. Outside of these estates, the prince exercised only very limited authority in his principality. Excluding the clergy, two kinds of people lived there: the noble *boyars* and the commoner peasants. The boyars were the descendants of the original Viking warriors, and they also held their lands as free and clear private property. Although the boyars normally fought in princely armies, the customary law declared that they could serve any prince they wished. The ordinary peasants were also truly free. They could move at will wherever opportunities were greatest. In the touching phrase of the times, theirs was "a clean road, without boundaries."[15] In short, fragmented princely power, private property, and personal freedom all went together.

REVIVAL AND RECOVERY

The eleventh century witnessed the beginnings of political stability in western Europe. Foreign invasions gradually declined, and domestic disorder subsided. This development gave people security in their persons and property. Political order and security provided the foundation for economic recovery and contributed to a slow increase in population.

The Decline of Invasion and Civil Disorder

In the tenth century Charlemagne's descendants continued to hold the royal title in the West Frankish kingdom, but they exercised no effective control over the great feudal lords. Research on medieval France has focused on regions and principalities, emphasizing the diversity of languages and cultures, the differences in social structure, and the division of public authority. Northern French society, for example, had strong feudal elements, but in the south the fief and vassalage were almost unknown. The southern territories used Roman law, but the northern counties and duchies relied on unwritten customary law that was not codified until the thirteenth century. The kings of France in the eleventh century were kings in name but petty barons in fact; no ruler exercised wide jurisdiction. Broad generalizations about France are difficult to make.[16]

Normandy gradually emerged as the strongest territory with the greatest relative level of peace. At Saint-Clair-sûr-Epte in Normandy in 911 the West Frankish ruler Charles the Simple, unable to oust the Vikings, officially recognized their leader Rollo and later invested him with more lands. In return, Rollo gave allegiance to Charles and agreed to hold the region as a barrier against future Viking attacks. Rollo and his men were baptized as Christians and supported the West Frankish ruler when he needed their help. Additional Northmen arrived but were easily pacified. The late tenth and early eleventh centuries saw the assimilation of Norman and French. Major assaults on France had ended.

After the death of the last Carolingian ruler in 987, an assembly of nobles met to choose a successor. The nobles selected Hugh Capet, who was *dux Francorum*—duke, or leader, of the Franks—and head of a powerful clan in the West Frankish kingdom. The history of France as a separate kingdom starts with the selection of Hugh Capet as king. The first Capetian kings (so called from the *côpe,* or cloak, that Hugh Capet wore as abbot of Saint-Denis) were weak in comparison with the duke of Normandy; but by hanging on to what they had, they laid the foundations for later political stability.

In Anglo-Saxon England recovery followed a different pattern. The Vikings had made a concerted effort to conquer and rule the whole island, and probably no part of Europe suffered more. The victory of the remarkable Alfred, king of the West Saxons, over Guthrun the Dane at Edington in 878 inaugurated a great political revival. Alfred and his immediate successors built a system of local defenses and slowly extended royal rule beyond Wessex (the area controlled by the West Saxons) to other Anglo-Saxon peoples until one law—royal law—replaced local custom. Alfred and his successors also laid the foundations for an efficient system of local government responsible directly to the king. Under the pressure of the Vikings, the seven kingdoms of England were gradually united under one ruler.

In the east, the German king Otto I (r. 936–973) inflicted a crushing defeat on the Hungarians at the banks of the Lech River in 955. This battle halted the Magyars' westward expansion and threat to Germany and made Otto a great hero to the Germans. It also signified the revival of the German monarchy and demonstrated that Otto was a worthy successor to Charlemagne.

When chosen king, Otto had selected Aachen as the site of his coronation to symbolize his intention to continue the tradition of Charlemagne. The basis of his power was to be alliance with and control of the church. Otto asserted the right to control ecclesiastical appointments. Before receiving religious consecration, bishops and abbots had to perform feudal homage for the lands that accompanied the church office. This practice, later known as investiture, was to create a grave crisis in the eleventh century (see pages 364–368).

Some of our knowledge of Otto derives from *The Deeds of Otto,* a history of his reign in heroic verse written by a nun, Hrotswitha of Gandersheim (ca 935–ca 1003). A learned poet, she also produced six verse plays and is considered the first dramatist after the fall of the ancient classical theater.

Otto's coronation by the pope in 962 revived the imperial dignity and laid the foundation for what was later called the Holy Roman Empire. Having the support of the church in Germany and Italy, Otto filled a power vacuum in northern Italy and brought peace among the great aristocratic families. Peace and political stability in turn promoted the revival of Venice and other northern Italian cities.

Although plague, climatic deterioration (which reduced agricultural productivity), and invasions had drastically reduced population throughout Italy, most of the northern Italian city-states survived the disorders of the early Middle Ages. By the ninth century, some Italian cities showed considerable economic dynamism, in particular Venice. Venice won privileged access to Byzantine markets; imported silk, textiles, cosmetics, and Crimean slaves; and sold these to Padua and other cities. By the eleventh century Venetian commerce had stimulated economic growth in the Lombard cities such as Milan and Cremona. Those cities and Sicily supplied Venice with food in exchange for luxury goods from the East. The rising economic importance of Venice and later of Genoa, Pisa, and other Italian cities became a central factor in the struggle between the papacy and the German empire.

Population, Climate, and Mechanization

A steady growth of population also contributed to Europe's general recovery. The decline of foreign invasions and internal civil disorder reduced the number of people killed and maimed. Feudal armies in the eleventh through thirteenth centuries continued their destruction, but they were small by modern standards and fought few pitched battles. Most medieval conflicts consisted of sieges directed at castles or fortifications. As few as twelve men with sufficient food and water could defend a castle for a long time. The survival of more young people—those most often involved in war and usually the most sexually active—meant a population rise.

The weather cooperated with the revival. Meteorologists believe that a significant warming trend occurred from the ninth century until about 1200. In the century between 1080 and 1180, England, France, and Germany experienced exceptionally mild winters and dry summers. Good weather helps to explain advances in population growth, land reclamation, and agricultural yield. Increased agricultural output profoundly affected Europeans' health, commerce, industry, and general lifestyle. A better diet had an enormous impact on women's lives: a better diet meant increased body fat and increased fertility; more iron in the diet meant that women were less anemic and less subject to opportunistic diseases. Some students believe that it was in the central Middle Ages that Western women began to outlive men.

The tenth and eleventh centuries also witnessed a remarkable spurt in mechanization, especially in

Arabic Water Mill   Irrigation, essential to the growth of an agricultural economy, was greatly advanced by Arab inventions such as this *noria,* or water wheel, which harnessed the power of moving water. *(Source: Biblioteca Apostolica Vaticana)*

the use of energy. The increase in the number of water mills was spectacular. The abundance of slave labor in the ancient world had retarded the development of mills, but by the mid-ninth century, on the lands of the abbey of Saint-Germain-des-Prés near Paris, there were 59 mills powered by water. Succeeding generations saw a continued increase. *Domesday Book,* William the Conqueror's great survey of English economic resources in the late eleventh century (see page 373), recorded 5,624 water mills. One scholar has calculated that on average each mill supplied fifty households. Besides grinding wheat or other grains to produce flour, water mills became essential in fulling—the process of scouring, cleansing, and thickening cloth. In the past, to clean and increase the bulk and weight of cloth, men or women had trampled the cloth in a trough. Now, wooden hammers were raised and dropped on the cloth by means of a revolving drum connected to the spindle of a water wheel. Water mills revolutionized grinding and fulling by using natural, rather than human, energy.

Successful at adapting waterpower to human needs, medieval engineers soon harnessed windpower. They replaced the wheels driven by water with sails. Unlike water, which always flows in the same direction, wind can blow from many directions. Windmill engineers solved this problem very ingeniously by mounting the framed wooden body, which contained the machinery and carried the sails, on a massive upright post free to turn with the wind.[17]

❧ REVIVAL AND REFORM IN THE CHRISTIAN CHURCH

The eleventh century witnessed the beginnings of a remarkable religious revival. Monasteries, always the leaders in ecclesiastical reform, remodeled themselves under the leadership of the Burgundian abbey of Cluny. Subsequently, new religious orders, such as the Cistercians, were founded and became a broad spiritual movement.

The papacy itself, after a century of corruption and decadence, was cleaned up. The popes worked to clarify church doctrine and codify church law. They and their officials sought to communicate with all the clergy and peoples of Europe through a clearly defined, obedient hierarchy of bishops. Pope Gregory VII's strong assertion of papal

power led to profound changes and serious conflict with secular authorities. The revival of the church manifested itself in the crusading movement.

Monastic Revival

The Viking, Magyar, and Muslim invaders attacked and ransacked many monasteries across Europe. Some religious communities fled and dispersed. In the period of political disorder that followed the disintegration of the Carolingian Empire, many religious houses fell under the control and domination of local feudal lords. Powerful laymen appointed themselves as abbots but kept their wives or mistresses. They took for themselves the lands and goods of monasteries, spending monastic revenues and selling monastic offices. All over Europe, temporal powers dominated the monasteries. The level of spiritual observance and intellectual activity declined.

In 909 William the Pious, duke of Aquitaine, established the abbey of Cluny near Macon in Burgundy. In his charter of endowment, Duke William declared that Cluny was to enjoy complete independence from all feudal (or secular) and episcopal lordship. The new monastery was to be subordinate only to the authority of Saints Peter and Paul as represented by the pope.

This monastery and its foundation charter came to exert vast religious influence. The first two abbots of Cluny, Berno (910–927) and Odo (927–942), set very high standards of religious behavior and stressed strict observance of *The Rule of Saint Benedict.* Cluny gradually came to stand for clerical celibacy and the suppression of *simony* (the sale of church offices). In the eleventh century, a series of highly able abbots ruled Cluny for a long time. These abbots paid careful attention to sound economic management. In a disorderly world, Cluny represented religious and political stability. Lay persons placed lands under Cluny's custody and monastic houses under its jurisdiction for reform. Benefactors wanted to be associated with Cluniac piety. Moreover, properties and monasteries under Cluny's jurisdiction enjoyed special protection, at least theoretically, from violence.[18] In this way hundreds of monasteries, primarily in France and Spain, came under Cluny's authority. Cluny was not the only center of monastic reform. The abbey of Gorze in Lotharingia (modern Lorraine) exercised a correcting influence on German

Consecration of the Church of Cluny   Pope Urban II surrounded by mitred bishops appears on the left, Abbot Hugh of Cluny with cowled monks on the right. A French nobleman who had been a monk of Cluny, Urban coined the term *curia* as the official designation of the central government of the church. (*Source: Bibliothèque Nationale, Paris*)

religious houses and directed a massive reform of monasteries in central Europe.

Deeply impressed lay people showered gifts on monasteries with good reputations. Jewelry, rich vestments, elaborately carved sacred vessels, and even lands and properties poured into some houses. But with this wealth came lay influence. And as the monasteries became richer, the lifestyle of the monks grew increasingly luxurious, monastic observance and spiritual fervor declined. Soon fresh demands for reform were heard. The result was the founding of new religious orders in the late eleventh and early twelfth centuries. The best representatives of the new reforming spirit were the Cistercians.

In 1098 a group of monks left the rich abbey of Molesmes in Burgundy and founded a new house in the swampy forest of Cîteaux, planning to avoid all involvement with secular feudal society. They decided to accept only uncultivated lands far from regular habitation. They intended to refuse all gifts of mills, serfs, tithes, ovens—the traditional manorial sources of income. The early Cistercians determined to avoid elaborate liturgy and ceremony and to keep their chant simple. And they refused to allow the presence of powerful lay people in their monasteries, because they knew that such influence was usually harmful to careful observance.

The first monks at Cîteaux experienced sickness, a dearth of recruits, and terrible privation, but their sincerity and idealism attracted attention. In 1112 a twenty-three-year-old nobleman called Bernard joined the community at Cîteaux, together with thirty of his aristocratic companions. Thereafter, this reforming movement gained impetus. Cîteaux founded 525 new monasteries in the course of the twelfth century, and its influence on European society was profound. Unavoidably, however, Cistercian success brought wealth, and wealth brought power, both of which by the later twelfth century had begun to compromise Cistercian ideals.

Reform of the Papacy

Some scholars believe that the monastic revival spreading from Cluny influenced reform of the Roman papacy and eventually the reform of the entire Christian church. Important figures in this reform movement, such as Pope Gregory VII (r. 1073–1085) had spent some time at Cluny. And the man who consolidated the reform movement and strengthened the medieval papal monarchy, Pope Urban II (r. 1088–1099), had been a monk and prior at Cluny. But the precise degree of Cluny's impact on the reform movement cannot be measured. The broad goals of the Cluniac movement and those of the Roman papacy, however, were the same.

In the tenth century the papacy provided little leadership to the Christian peoples of western Europe. Factions in Rome sought to control the papacy for their own material gain. Popes were appointed to advance the political ambitions of their families—the great aristocratic families of Rome—and not because of special spiritual qualifications.

At the local parish level there were many married priests. Taking Christ as the model for the priestly life, the Roman church had always encouraged clerical celibacy, and it had been an obligation for ordination since the fourth century. But in the tenth and eleventh centuries, probably a majority of European priests were married or living with a woman.

Serious efforts at reform began under Pope Leo IX (r. 1049–1054). Leo traveled widely and held councils at Pavia, Reims, and Mainz that issued decrees against simony, clerical marriage, and violence. His representatives held church councils across Europe, pressing for moral reform. They urged those who could not secure justice at home to appeal to the pope, the ultimate source of justice. By his character and actions, Leo set high moral standards for the West.

During the short reign of Nicholas II (r. 1058–1061), a council held in the ancient church of Saint John Lateran at Rome in 1059 devised a new method of electing the pope to remove the in-

fluence of Roman aristocratic factions from papal elections. Since the eighth century, the priests of the major churches in and around Rome had constituted a special group, called a "college," that advised the pope when he summoned them to meetings. These chief priests were called "cardinals" from the Latin *cardo*, meaning "hinge." The cardinals were the hinges on which the church turned. The Lateran Synod of 1059 decreed that the authority and power to elect the pope rested solely in this college of cardinals. The college retains that power today.

When the office of pope was vacant, the cardinals were responsible for governing the church. (In the Middle Ages the college of cardinals numbered around twenty-five or thirty, most of them from Italy. In 1586 the figure was set at seventy. In the 1960s Pope Paul VI virtually doubled that number, appointing men from all parts of the globe to reflect the international character of the church.) By 1073 the progress of reform in the Christian church was well advanced. The election of Cardinal Hildebrand as Pope Gregory VII in 1073 changed the direction of reform from a moral to a political one.

Cardinal Hildebrand had received a good education at Rome and spent some time at Cluny, where his strict views of clerical life were strengthened. He believed that the pope, as the successor of Saint Peter, was the Vicar of God on earth and that papal orders were the orders of God. Once Hildebrand became pope, he and his assistants began to insist on the "freedom of the church." By this they meant the freedom of churchmen to obey canon law and their freedom from control and interference by lay people.

"Freedom of the church" pointed to the end of *lay investiture*—the selection and appointment of church officials by secular authorities. Bishops and abbots were invested with a staff representing pastoral jurisdiction and a ring signifying union with the diocese or monastic community. When laymen gave these symbols, they appeared to be distributing spiritual authority. Ecclesiastical opposition to lay investiture was not new in the eleventh century. It, too, had been part of church theory for centuries. But Gregory's attempt to put theory into practice was a radical departure from long usage. Since feudal monarchs depended on the literacy and administrative knowledge of churchmen for the operation of their governments, Gregory's program seemed to spell disaster for stable royal administration. It provoked a terrible crisis.

The Controversy over Lay Investiture

In February 1075 Pope Gregory held a council at Rome that published a decree against lay investiture:

If anyone henceforth shall receive a bishopric or abbey from the hands of a lay person, he shall not be considered as among the number of bishops and abbots. . . . Likewise if any emperor, king . . . or any one at all of the secular powers, shall presume to perform investiture with bishoprics or with any other ecclesiastical dignity . . . he shall feel the divine displeasure as well with regard to his body as to his other belongings.[19]

In short, clerics who accepted investiture from laymen were to be deposed, and laymen who invested clerics were to be *excommunicated*—cut off from the sacraments and the Christian community.

The church's penalty of excommunication relied for its effectiveness on public opinion. Gregory believed the strong support he enjoyed for his moral reform would carry over to his political reforms; he thought that excommunication would compel rulers to abide by his changes. Immediately, however, Henry IV in the Holy Roman Empire, William the Conqueror in England, and Philip I in France protested.

The strongest reaction came from Germany and Henry IV. In two basic ways, the relationship of the German kings to the papacy differed from that of other monarchs: the pope crowned the German emperor, and both the empire and the papal states claimed northern Italy. Since the time of Charlemagne the emperor had controlled some territory and bishops in Italy.

In addition to the subject of lay investiture, a more fundamental issue was at stake. Gregory's decree raised the question of the proper role of the monarch in a Christian society. Did a king have ultimate jurisdiction over all his subjects, including the clergy? For centuries, tradition had answered this question in favor of the ruler, so it is no wonder that Henry protested the papal assertions about investiture. Indirectly, they undermined imperial power and sought to make papal authority supreme.

An increasingly bitter exchange of letters ensued. Gregory accused Henry of lack of respect for the papacy and insisted that disobedience to the pope was disobedience to God. Henry protested in a letter beginning, "Henry King not by usurpation, but by the pious ordination of God, to Hildebrand, now not Pope, but false monk."

Within the empire, in January 1076, the German bishops who had been invested by Henry withdrew their allegiance from the pope. Gregory replied by excommunicating them and suspending Henry from the kingship. The lay nobility delighted in the bind the emperor had been put in: with Henry IV excommunicated and cast outside the Christian fold, they did not have to obey him and could advance their own interests. Gregory hastened to support them. The Christmas season of 1076 witnessed an ironic situation in Germany: the clergy supported the emperor, and the great nobility favored the pope.

Henry outwitted Gregory. Crossing the Alps in January 1077, he approached the pope's residence at Canossa in northern Italy. According to legend, Henry stood for three days in the snow seeking forgiveness. As a priest, Pope Gregory was obliged to grant absolution and to readmit the emperor to the Christian community. Although the emperor, the most powerful ruler in Europe, bowed before the pope, Henry actually scored only a temporary victory. When the sentence of excommunication was lifted, he regained the kingship and authority over his rebellious subjects. But for the next two hundred years, in Germany and elsewhere, secular rulers were reluctant to pose a serious challenge to the papacy.

For Germany the incident at Canossa settled nothing. The controversy over lay investiture and the position of the king in Christian society continued. Finally, in 1122, at a conference held at Worms, a compromise settled the issue. Bishops were to be chosen according to canon law—that is, by the clergy—in the presence of the emperor or his delegate. The emperor surrendered the right to invest bishops with the ring and staff. The papacy achieved technical success, because rulers could not longer invest. But lay rulers still possessed an effective veto over ecclesiastical appointments, because they were permitted to be present at ecclesiastical elections and to accept or refuse feudal homage from the new prelates. Papal power was enhanced, but neither side won a clear victory.

William the Conqueror of England and Philip I of France were just as guilty of lay investiture as the German emperor, and both quarreled openly with Gregory. However, Rome's conflict with the western rulers never reached the proportions of the dispute with the German emperor. Gregory VII and his successors had the diplomatic sense to avoid creating three enemies at once.

The long controversy had tremendous social and political consequences in Germany. For half a century, between 1075 and 1125, civil war was chronic in the empire. Preoccupied with Italy and the quarrel with the papacy, the German emperors could do little about it. The lengthy struggle between papacy and emperor allowed emerging noble dynasties, such as the Zähringer of Swabia, to enhance their position. By the eleventh century these great German families had achieved a definite sense of themselves as noble.[20] To control their lands, the great lords built castles, which were both military strongholds and centers of administration for the surrounding territories. The German aristocracy subordinated the knights and reinforced their dependency with strong feudal ties. They reduced free men and serfs to an extremely servile position. Henry IV and Henry V were compelled to surrender rights and privileges to the nobility. When the papal-imperial conflict ended in 1122, the nobility held the balance of power in Germany, and later German kings, such as Frederick Barbarossa (see page 375), would fail in their efforts to strengthen the monarchy against the princely families. For these reasons, particularism, localism, and feudal independence characterized the Holy Roman Empire in the central Middle Ages. The investiture controversy had a catastrophic effect there, severely retarding development of a strong centralized monarchy.

In the late eleventh century and throughout the twelfth, the papacy pressed Gregory's campaign for reform of the church. Pope Urban II laid the foundations for the papal monarchy by reorganizing the central government of the Roman church. He recognized the college of cardinals as a definite consultative body. This agency, together with the papal chapel, constituted the papal court, or *curia Romana*—the papacy's administrative and financial bureaucracy and its court of law. The papal court, though not fully developed until the mid-twelfth century, was the first well-organized institution of monarchial authority in medieval Europe.

The Roman curia had its greatest impact as a court of law. As the highest ecclesiastical tribunal, it formulated canon law for all of Christendom. It was the instrument with which the popes pressed the goals of reform and centralized the church. The curia sent legates to hold councils in various parts of Europe. Councils published decrees and sought to enforce the law. When individuals in any part of Christian Europe felt they were being denied justice in their local church courts, they could appeal to Rome. Slowly but surely, in the central Middle Ages the papal curia developed into the court of final appeal for all of Christian Europe. The majority of cases that came to the Roman curia related to disputes over church property or ecclesiastical elections and, especially, to questions of marriage and annulment. Since the fourth century, Christian values had influenced the administration of the law, and bishops frequently sat in civil courts that heard marriage cases. In the tenth and eleventh centuries, church officials began to claim that they had exclusive jurisdiction over marriage. Appeals to an ecclesiastical tribunal, rather than to a civil court, or appeals from a civil court to a church court, implied the acceptance of a church court's jurisdiction.

Most of the popes in the twelfth and thirteenth centuries were canon lawyers who recognized the authority of church courts. The most famous of them, the man whose pontificate represented the height of medieval papal power, was Innocent III (r. 1198–1216). Innocent judged a vast number of cases. He compelled King Philip Augustus of France to take back his wife, Ingeborg of Denmark. He arbitrated the rival claims of two disputants to the imperial crown of Germany. He forced King John of England to accept as archbishop of Canterbury a man John did not really want.

By the early thirteenth century, papal efforts at reform begun more than a century before had attained phenomenal success. The popes themselves were men of high principles and strict moral behavior. The frequency of clerical marriage and the level of violence had declined considerably. The practice of simony was much more the exception than the rule. Yet the seeds of future difficulties were being planted. As the volume of appeals to Rome multiplied, so did the size of the papal bureaucracy. As the number of lawyers increased, so did concern for legal niceties and technicalities,

EUROPE IN THE MIDDLE AGES

ca 700	Publication of the Lindisfarne Gospel book, Bede's *Ecclesiastical History of the English Nation,* and *Beowulf*
ca 710–750	Missionary work of Wynfrith (Boniface) supports the efforts of Charles Martel and Pippin III to assimilate Germanic tribes
733	Charles Martel defeats Muslims at Battle of Tours
751	Pippin III elected king by Frankish magnates
754	The pope anoints Pippin III king at Paris, establishing an important alliance between the Christian church and the Frankish ruler
756	Pippin III donates the Papal States to the papacy
768	Charlemagne succeeds to the Frankish throne
768–805	Charlemagne conquers all of continental Europe except Spain, Scandinavia, southern Italy, and Slavic fringes of the East
781	Alcuin enters Charlemagne's court at Aachen as chief adviser on religious and educational matters
ca 787	Viking raids of Carolingian territories begin
800	Imperial coronation of Charlemagne
814	Louis the Pious succeeds to Charlemagne's empire
843	Treaty of Verdun: Charlemagne's empire divided among his grandsons Lothair, Louis the German, and Charles the Bald
ca 845–900	Viking, Magyar, and Muslim invasions complete the disintegration of the Carolingian Empire
878	King Alfred's victory over Guthrun inaugurates political recovery in Anglo-Saxon England
909	Founding of the abbey of Cluny—first step in the revival of monasticism and reform of the church
955	Otto I's victory at Lech River ends Magyar incursions in Germany
962	Otto's coronation lays the foundation for the Holy Roman Empire
987	Election of Hugh Capet as king of the West Frankish kingdom
1049	Pope Leo IX begins serious reform of the church
1059	Lateran Synod gives power of papal election to the college of cardinals
1073	Cardinal Hildebrand becomes Pope Gregory VII
1075	Church issues decree against lay investiture that leads to conflict between the pope and the rulers of Germany, England, and France
1096–1099	The First Crusade
1098	Founding of the Cistercian order
1122	Compromise at Worms removes power of investiture from lay rulers but grants them effective veto over ecclesiastical appointments
1202–1204	The Fourth Crusade; sacking of Constantinople cements the split between Eastern and Western churches

fees, and church offices. As early as the mid-twelfth century, John of Salisbury, an Englishman working in the papal curia, had written that the people condemned the curia for its greed and indifference to human suffering. Nevertheless, the power of the curia continued to grow, as did its bureaucracy.

Thirteenth-century popes devoted their attention to the bureaucracy and their conflicts with the German emperor Frederick II. Some, like Gregory IX (r. 1227–1241), abused their prerogatives to such an extent that their moral impact was seriously weakened. Even worse, Innocent IV (r. 1243–1254) used secular weapons, including military force, to maintain his leadership. These popes badly damaged papal prestige and influence. By the early fourteenth century, the seeds of disorder would grow into a vast and sprawling tree, and once again cries for reform would be heard.

The Crusades

The Crusades of the eleventh and twelfth centuries were the most obvious manifestation of the papal claim to the leadership of Christian society. The enormous popular response to papal calls for crusading reveals the influence of the reformed papacy. The Crusades also reflect the church's new understanding of the noble warrior class. As a distinguished scholar of the Crusades wrote, "just as rulership earlier had been Christianized . . . , so now was the military profession; it acquired a direct ecclesiastical purpose, for war in the service of the church or for the weak came to be regarded as holy and was declared to be a religious duty not only for the king but also for every individual knight."21

Crusades in the late eleventh and early twelfth centuries were holy wars sponsored by the papacy for the recovery of the Holy Land from the Muslim Arabs or the Turks. They grew out of the long conflict between Christians and Muslims in Spain, where by about 1250 Christian kings had regained roughly 90 percent of the peninsula. Although people of all ages and classes participated in the Crusades, so many knights did so that crusading became a distinctive feature of the upper-class lifestyle. In an aristocratic, military society, men coveted reputations as Crusaders; the Crusades manifested the religious and chivalric ideals— as well as the tremendous vitality—of medieval society.

The Roman papacy supported the holy war in Spain and by the late eleventh century, amid the bitter struggle over investiture with the German emperors, had strong reasons for wanting to launch an expedition against Muslim infidels in the Middle East as well. If the pope could muster a large army against the enemies of Christianity, his claim to be leader of Christian society in the West would be strengthened. Moreover, in 1054 a serious theological disagreement had split the Greek church of Byzantium and the Roman church of the West. The pope believed that a crusade would lead to strong Roman influence in Greek territories and eventually the reunion of the two churches.

In 1071 at Manzikert in eastern Anatolia, Turkish soldiers in the pay of the Arabs defeated a Greek army and occupied much of Asia Minor (Map 12.5). The emperor at Constantinople appealed to the West for support. Shortly afterward, the holy city of Jerusalem fell to the Turks, and the papacy claimed to be outraged that the holy city was in the hands of unbelievers. Since the Muslims had held Palestine since the eighth century, what the papacy actually feared was that the Seljuk Turks would be less accommodating to Christian pilgrims than the Muslims had been.

In 1095 Pope Urban II journeyed to Clermont in France and called for a great Christian holy war against the infidels. He urged Christian knights who had been fighting one another to direct their energies against the true enemies of God, the Muslims. Urban proclaimed an *indulgence,* or remission of the temporal penalties imposed by the church for sin, to those who would fight for and regain the holy city of Jerusalem.

Few speeches in history have had such a dramatic effect as Urban's call at Clermont for the First Crusade. Godfrey of Bouillon, Geoffrey of Lorraine, and many other great lords from northern France immediately had the cross of the Crusader sewn on their tunics. Encouraged by popular preachers, thousands of people of all classes joined the crusade. Although most of the Crusaders were French, pilgrims from many regions streamed southward from the Rhineland, through Germany and the Balkans. Of all of the developments of the central Middle Ages, none better reveals Europeans' religious and emotional fervor and the influence of the reformed papacy than the extraordinary outpouring of support for the First Crusade.

Religious convictions inspired many, but mundane motives were also involved. For the curious

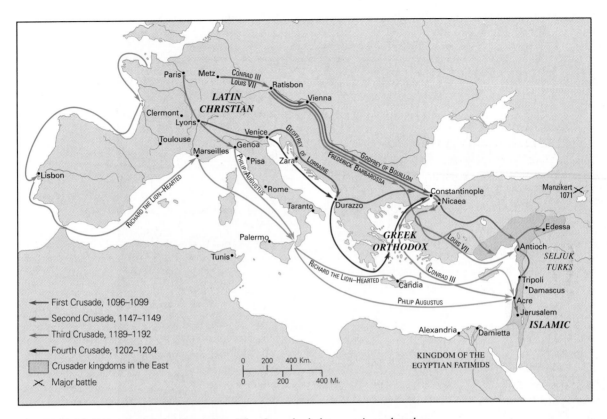

MAP 12.5 Routes of the Crusades   The Crusades led to a major cultural encounter between Muslim and Christian values. What significant intellectual and economic effects resulted?

and the adventurous, the crusade offered foreign travel and excitement. It provided kings, who were trying to establish order and build states, the perfect opportunity to get rid of troublemaking knights. It gave land-hungry younger sons a chance to acquire fiefs in the Middle East.

The Crusades brought to the surface latent Christian prejudice against the Jews. Between the sixth and tenth centuries, descendants of Sephardic (from the modern Hebrew word *Separaddi*, meaning "Spaniard") Jews had settled along the trade routes of western Europe. In the eleventh century, they played a major role in the international trade between the Muslim Middle East and the West. Jews also lent money to peasants, townspeople, and nobles. Because the Jews performed these useful economic services, kings and lords protected them. When the First Crusade was launched, many poor knights had to borrow from Jews to equip themselves for the expedition. Debt bred resentment against Jews. Christian preachers often focused their remarks on Jerusalem, blaming the

Jews there for Jesus' crucifixion. They conveniently ignored the fact that Jesus had forgiven all his executioners—Luke 22:34. With the atmosphere thus poisoned, as crusading armies passed through the Rhineland in May and June 1096, they directed assaults on Jewish communities in Speyer, Worms, Mainz, Cologne, Trier, and Metz. The resulting massacres testify to the general ignorance, bigotry, and lack of concentrated strategy that characterized the entire crusading movement.

The First Crusade was successful mostly because of the enthusiasm of the participants. The Crusaders had little more than religious zeal. They knew nothing about the geography, climate, or culture of the Middle East. Although there were several counts with military experience among the throng, the Crusaders could never agree on a leader, and the entire expedition was marked by disputes among the great lords. Lines of supply were never set up. Starvation and disease wracked the army, and the Turks slaughtered hundreds of noncombatants. Nevertheless, convinced that

The Capture of Jerusalem in 1099   As engines hurl stones to breach the walls, Crusaders enter on scaling ladders. Scenes from Christ's Passion (above) identify the city as Jerusalem. *(Source: Bibliothèque Nationale, Paris)*

"God wills it"—the war cry of the Crusaders—the army pressed on and in 1099 captured Jerusalem. Although the Crusaders fought bravely, Arab disunity was a chief reason for their victory. At Jerusalem, Edessa, Tripoli, and Antioch, Crusader kingdoms were founded on the Western feudal model.

Between 1096 and 1270, the crusading ideal was expressed in eight papally approved expedi-

tions to the East. Despite the success of the First Crusade, none of the later ones accomplished very much. The Third Crusade (1189–1192) was precipitated by the recapture of Jerusalem by the sultan Saladin in 1187. Frederick Barbarossa of the Holy Roman Empire, Richard (Lion-Heart) of England, and Philip Augustus of France participated, and the Third Crusade was better financed than previous ones. But disputes among the leaders and strategic problems prevented any lasting results.

During the Fourth Crusade (1202–1204), careless preparation and inadequate financing had disastrous consequences for Latin-Byzantine relations. When the Crusaders could not pay the Venetians the money promised for transport to the Holy Land, the Venetians agreed to postpone the debt if the Crusaders attacked Zara, a *Christian* city on the Dalmatian coast (the Dalmatian forests were the source of the oak that the Venetians used for shipbuilding). The Crusaders took Zara on November 24, 1202. At Zara, envoys from the dethroned Byzantine emperor Isaac II and his son Alexius promised reunification of the Greek and Latin churches, large payments to the Venetians, and Byzantine support for the expedition to the Holy Land. Thus in April 1204, the Crusaders and Venetians stormed Constantinople, sacked the city destroying its magnificent library, and grabbed thousands of relics that were later sold in Europe. From this destruction the Byzantine Empire as a political unit never recovered. Moreover, the assault of one Christian people on another—when one of the goals of the Fourth Crusade was reunion of Greek and Latin churches—made the split between the Greek and Latin churches permanent. It also helped to discredit the entire crusading movement.

In 1208, two expeditions of children set out on a crusade to the Holy Land. One contingent turned back; the other was captured and sold into slavery. Two later crusades against the Muslims were undertaken by King Louis IX of France and added to his prestige as a pious ruler. Apart from that, the last of the official crusades accomplished nothing at all.

Crusades were also mounted against groups perceived as Christendom's social enemies. In 1208 Pope Innocent III proclaimed a crusade against the Albigensians, a heretical sect concentrated in southern France that rejected orthodox doctrine on the relationship of God and man, on the sacraments, and on the clerical hierarchy. Fearing that religious division would lead to civil disorder, the French monarchy joined the crusade and inflicted a savage defeat on the Albigensians at Muret in 1213. Fearful of encirclement by imperial territories, the popes also promoted crusades against Emperor Frederick II in 1227 and 1239. This use of force against a Christian ruler backfired, damaging the credibility of the papacy as the sponsor of peace.

What impact did the Crusades have on women? That is a difficult question. Fewer women than men directly participated (societies usually perceive war as a masculine enterprise). Given the aristocratic bias of the chroniclers, we have more information about royal and noble ladies who went to the Holy Land than about middle-class and peasant women, though the latter groups contributed the greater numbers. Eleanor of Aquitaine (1122?–1204) accompanied her husband King Louis VII on the Second Crusade (1147–1149), and the thirteenth-century English chronicler Matthew Paris says that large numbers of women went on the Seventh Crusade (1248–1254) so that they could obtain the crusading indulgence. The Crusades illustrate that women in feudal society exercised considerable power. Women who stayed home assumed their husbands' responsibilities in the management of estates, the dispensation of justice to vassals and serfs, and the protection of property from attack. Since Crusaders frequently could finance the expedition only by borrowing, it fell to their wives to repay the loans. These heavy responsibilities brought women a degree of power. The many women who operated inns and shops in the towns through which crusading armies passed profited from the rental of lodgings and the sale of foodstuffs, clothing, arms, and fodder for animals. For prostitutes, also, crusading armies offered business opportunities.

The Crusades introduced some Europeans to Eastern luxury goods, but the Crusades' overall cultural impact on the West remains debatable. By the late eleventh century, strong economic and intellectual ties with the East had already been made. The Crusades testify to the religious enthusiasm of the central Middle Ages. But, as Steven Runciman, a distinguished scholar of the Crusades, concluded in his three-volume history: "The triumphs of the Crusade were the triumphs of faith. But faith without wisdom is a dangerous thing. . . . In the long sequence of interaction and fusion between Orient and Occident out of which our civilization has grown, the Crusades were a tragic and destructive episode."[22]

In addition to the feudal states that the Crusaders set up along the Syrian and Palestinian coasts, which managed to survive for about two centuries before the Muslims reconquered them, the Crusaders left in the Middle East two legacies that continue to resonate. First, the long struggle between Islam and Christendom and the example of persecution set by Christian kings and prelates left an inheritance of deep bitterness; relations between Muslims and their Christian and Jewish subjects worsened. Second, European merchants, primarily Italians, had established communities in the Crusader states. After those kingdoms collapsed, Muslim rulers still encouraged trade with European businessmen. Commerce with the West benefited both Muslims and Europeans, and it continued to flourish.[23]

MEDIEVAL ORIGINS OF THE MODERN STATE

Rome's great legacy to Western civilization had been the concepts of the state and the law. But for almost five hundred years after the disintegration of the Roman Empire in the West, the state as a reality did not exist. Political authority was completely decentralized. Power was spread among many feudal lords, who gave their localities such protection and security as their strength allowed and whose laws affected a relative few. In the mid-eleventh century, many overlapping layers of authority—earls, counts, barons, knights—existed between a king and the ordinary people.

In these circumstances, medieval rulers had common goals. To increase public order, they wanted to establish an effective means of communication with all peoples. They also wanted more revenue and efficient bureaucracies. The solutions they found to these problems laid the foundations for modern national states.

The modern state is an organized territory with definite geographical boundaries that are recognized by other states. It has a body of law and institutions of government. If the state claims to govern according to law, it is guided in its actions by the law. The modern national state counts on the loyalty of its citizens, or at least of a majority of them. In return, it provides order so that citizens can go about their daily work and other activities. It protects its citizens in their persons and property. The state tries to prevent violence and to ap-

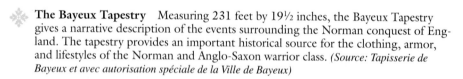

The Bayeux Tapestry   Measuring 231 feet by 19½ inches, the Bayeux Tapestry gives a narrative description of the events surrounding the Norman conquest of England. The tapestry provides an important historical source for the clothing, armor, and lifestyles of the Norman and Anglo-Saxon warrior class. *(Source: Tapisserie de Bayeux et avec autorisation spéciale de la Ville de Bayeux)*

prehend and punish those who commit it. It supplies a currency or medium of exchange that permits financial and commercial transactions. The state conducts relations with foreign governments. In order to accomplish even these minimal functions, the state must have officials, bureaucracies, laws, courts of law, soldiers, information, and money. States with these attributes are relatively recent developments.

Unification and Communication

Political developments in England, France, and Germany provide good examples of the beginnings of the national state in the central Middle Ages. Under the pressure of the Viking invasions of the ninth and tenth centuries, the seven kingdoms of Anglo-Saxon England united under one king. At the same time, for reasons historians still cannot fully explain, England was divided into local *shires,* or counties, each under the jurisdiction of a sheriff appointed by the king. The kingdom of England, therefore, had a political head start on the rest of Europe.

When Edward the Confessor (r. 1042–1066) died, his cousin Duke William of Normandy—known in English history as William the Conqueror—claimed the English throne and in 1066 defeated the Anglo-Saxon claimant on the battlefield of Hastings. As William subdued the rest of the country, he distributed lands to his Norman followers and required all feudal lords to swear an oath of allegiance to him as king.

William the Conqueror (r. 1066–1087) preserved the Anglo-Saxon institution of sheriffs representing the king at the local level but replaced Anglo-Saxon sheriffs with Normans. A sheriff had heavy duties. He maintained order in the shire. He caught criminals and had them tried in the shire court over which his deputy, the undersheriff, presided. He collected taxes and, when the king ordered him to do so, raised an army of foot soldiers. For all his efforts, the sheriff received no pay. This system, whereby unpaid officials governed the county, served as the basic pattern of English local government for many centuries. It cost the Crown nothing, but it restricted opportunities for public service to the well-to-do.

William also retained another Anglo-Saxon device, the *writ.* This brief administrative order, written in the vernacular (Anglo-Saxon) by a government clerk, was the means by which the central government communicated with people at the local level. Sheriffs were empowered to issue writs relating to matters in their counties.

At his Christmas court in 1085, William decided to conduct a systematic investigation of the entire country to determine how much wealth there was in his new kingdom and who held what land. Groups of royal officials or judges were sent to every part of England. In every village and farm, the priest and six local people were put under oath to answer the questions of the king's commissioners truthfully. In the words of a contemporary chronicler:

He sent his men over all England into every shire and had them find out how many hundred hides there were in the shire [a hide was a measure of land large enough to support one family], or what land and cattle the king himself had, or what dues he ought to have in twelve months from the shire. Also . . . what or how much everybody had who was occupying land in England, in land or cattle, and how much money it was worth. So very narrowly did he have it investigated, that there was no single hide nor yard of land, nor indeed . . . one ox nor one cow nor one pig was there left out, and not put down in his record: and all these records were brought to him afterwards.[24]

The resulting record, called *Domesday Book* from the Anglo-Saxon word *doom* meaning "judgment," provided William and his descendants with information vital for the exploitation and government of the country. Knowing the amount of wealth every area possessed, the king could tax accordingly. Knowing the amount of land his vassals had, he could allot knight service fairly.

In 1128 the Conqueror's granddaughter Matilda was married to Geoffrey of Anjou. Their son, who became Henry II of England and inaugurated the Angevin (from Anjou) Dynasty, inherited the French provinces of Normandy, Anjou, Maine, and Touraine in northwestern France (Map 12.6). When Henry married the great heiress Eleanor of Aquitaine in 1152, he claimed lordships over Aquitaine, Poitou, and Gascony in southwestern France. The so-called Angevin empire included most of the British Isles and half of France. The histories of England and France in the central Middle Ages were thus closely intertwined.

In the early twelfth century, France consisted of a number of virtually independent provinces, each

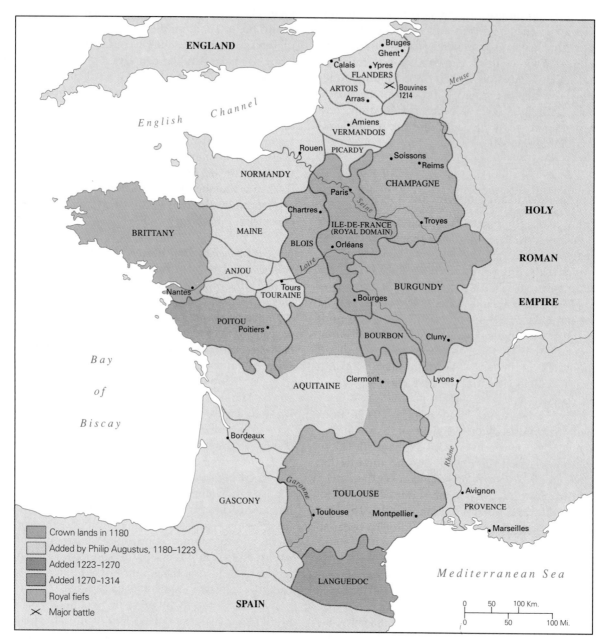

ENGLAND

• Bruges
Ghent •
Calais • • Ypres
FLANDERS
ARTOIS   × Bouvines
Arras •   1214
                                        Meuse

• Amiens
VERMANDOIS

Rouen • PICARDY
NORMANDY   • Soissons
                • Reims
                CHAMPAGNE

Paris •
Chartres •   Seine

BRITTANY   ÎLE-DE-FRANCE
                (ROYAL DOMAIN)
MAINE   • Troyes

BLOIS
        • Orléans
ANJOU   BURGUNDY

Nantes •   Tours •
        TOURAINE   • Bourges

POITOU   BOURBON
Poitiers •   • Cluny

HOLY

ROMAN

EMPIRE

English *Channel*

Bay

of

Biscay

AQUITAINE   Clermont •   • Lyons

• Bordeaux

        Garonne

GASCONY   TOULOUSE   • Avignon
                        PROVENCE
        • Toulouse   Montpellier •
                                • Marseilles

SPAIN   LANGUEDOC

Mediterranean *Sea*

Loire   Rhône

	Crown lands in 1180
	Added by Philip Augustus, 1180–1223
	Added 1223–1270
	Added 1270–1314
	Royal fiefs
×	Major battle

0   50   100 Km.
0   50   100 Mi.

MAP 12.6 Growth of the Kingdom of France   Some scholars believe that Philip II received the title "Augustus" (from a Latin word meaning "to increase") because he vastly expanded the territories of the kingdom of France.

governed by its local ruler. Unlike the king of England, the king of France had jurisdiction over a very small area. Chroniclers called King Louis VI (r. 1108–1137) *roi de Saint-Denis,* king of Saint-Denis, because the territory he controlled was limited to Paris and the Saint-Denis area surrounding the city. This region, the Île-de-France or royal domain, became the nucleus of the French state. The clear goal of the medieval French king was to increase the royal domain and extend his authority.

The work of unifying France began under Louis VI's grandson Philip II (r. 1180–1223). Rigord, Philip's biographer, gave him the title "Augustus" (from a Latin word meaning "to increase") because he vastly enlarged the territory of the king-dom of France (see Map 12.6). By defeating a ba-ronial plot against the Crown, Philip Augustus ac-quired the northern counties of Artois and Vermandois. The rich province of Normandy, held by King John of England, who was Philip's vassal, fell to the French in 1204. Within two years Philip also gained the farmlands of Maine, Touraine, and Anjou. By the end of his reign Philip was effec-tively master of northern France.

In the thirteenth century, Philip Augustus's de-scendants acquired important holdings in the south, and by the end of the thirteenth century, most of the provinces of modern France had been added to the royal domain through diplomacy, marriage, war, and inheritance. The king of France was stronger than any group of nobles who might try to challenge his authority.

Philip Augustus devised a method of governing the provinces and providing for communication between the central government in Paris and local communities. He decided that each province would retain its own institutions and laws. But royal agents, called *baillis* in the north and *seneschals* in the south, were sent from Paris into the provinces as the king's official representatives with authority to act for him. The baillis and seneschals were appointed by, paid by, and respon-sible to the king. Unlike the English sheriffs, they were never natives of the provinces to which they were assigned, and they could not own land there. This policy reflected the fundamental principle of French administration that royal interests super-seded local interests. But although France was ad-ministered by a centralized professional royal bu-reaucracy, the French system was characterized by a great variety of customs, laws, and provincial in-stitutions at the local level. Although it sometimes fell into disrepair, although one scholar has called it decrepit from the start, the basic system that Philip Augustus created lasted until the Revolution of 1789.

The political problems of Germany differed from those of France and England. The eleventh-century investiture controversy between the Ger-man emperor and the Roman papacy had left Ger-many shattered and divided (see pages 364–365). In the twelfth and thirteenth centuries, Germany was split into hundreds of independent provinces, principalities, bishoprics, duchies, and free cities.

There were several barriers to the development of a strong central government. Unlike the French kings, the German rulers lacked a strong royal do-main to use as a source of revenue and a base from which to expand royal power. No accepted princi-ple of succession to the throne existed; as a result, the death of the Holy Roman emperor was often followed by disputes, civil war, and anarchy. More-over, German rulers were continually attracted south by the wealth of the northern Italian cities or by dreams of restoring the imperial glory of Charlemagne. Time after time the German kings got involved in Italian affairs, and in turn the pa-pacy, fearful of a strong German power in northern Italy, interfered in German affairs. German princes took bribes from whichever authority—the em-peror or the pope—best supported their own par-ticular ambitions. Consequently, in contrast to France and England, the German empire witnessed little royal centralization.

Frederick Barbarossa (r. 1152–1190) of the House of Hohenstaufen tried valiantly to unify the empire. Just as the French rulers branched out from the Île-de-France, Frederick tried to use his family duchy of Swabia in southwestern Germany as a power base (Map 12.7). Like William the Conqueror, Frederick required all his vassals to take an oath of allegiance to him as emperor.

Outside Swabia, Frederick tried to make feudal-ism work as a system of government. He made al-liances with the great lay princes: they acknowl-edged that their lands were fiefs of the emperor, and he in turn recognized their military and politi-cal jurisdiction over their territories. Frederick also compelled the great churchmen to become his vas-sals, so that when they died he could control their estates. In 1158 Frederick forbade private warfare and ordered severe penalties for violations of the peace.

Unfortunately, Frederick Barbarossa did not concentrate his efforts and resources in one area. He, too, became embroiled in the affairs of Italy. In the eleventh and twelfth centuries, the northern Italian cities had grown rich on trade, and Freder-ick believed that if he could gain the imperial crown, he could cash in on Italian wealth.

Between 1154 and 1188, Frederick made six expeditions into Italy. His scorched-earth policy was successful at first, resulting in significant con-quests in the north. The brutality of his methods, however, provoked revolts, and the Italian cities formed an alliance with the papacy. In 1176 Fred-erick suffered a defeat at Legnano (see Map 12.7). This battle marked the first time a feudal cavalry of

0 100 200 300 Km.

0 100 200 300 Mi.

Lübeck

HOLSTEIN

POMERANIA

Bremen

BRANDENBURG

FRISIA

SAXONY

Brandenburg

LUSATIA

POLAND

Goslar

LOWER
LORRAINE

Cologne

THURINGIA

MEISSEN

Aix-la-Chapelle

FRANCONIA

Prague

Trier

Mainz

BOHEMIA

MORAVIA

Worms

Verdun

UPPER
LORRAINE

AUSTRIA

Toul

Augsburg

BAVARIA

Salzburg

SWABIA

STYRIA

FRANCE

Besançon

CARINTHIA

BURGUNDY-
ARLES

CARNIOLA

VERONA

HUNGARY

✕ Legnano 1176

LOMBARDY

Milan

Venice

Pavia

Roncaglia

REPUBLIC OF VENICE

Avignon

Arles

Florence

Marseilles

TUSCANY

PAPAL
STATES

CORSICA

Rome

Capua

APULIA

Naples

Salerno

SARDINIA

KINGDOM OF SICILY

Messina

✕ Major battle

Palermo

Holy Roman Empire, ca 1200

SICILY

Kingdom of Sicily

Republic of Venice

armed knights was decisively defeated by bourgeois infantrymen. Frederick was forced to recognize the municipal autonomy of the northern Italian cities. Germany and Italy remained separate and followed separate courses of development.

Frederick Barbarossa's Italian ventures contributed nothing to the unification of the German states. Because the empire lacked a stable bureaucratic system of government, his presence was essential for the maintenance of peace. During Frederick's absences, the fires of independence and disorder spread, and the princes and magnates consolidated their power. By 1187 Frederick had to accept again the reality of private warfare. The power of the princes cost the growth of a centralized monarchy.

Law and Justice

Throughout Europe in the twelfth and thirteenth centuries, the law was a hodgepodge of Germanic customs, feudal rights, and provincial practices. Kings wanted to blend these elements into a uniform system of rules acceptable and applicable to all their peoples. In France and England, kings successfully contributed to the development of national states through the administration of their laws.

The French king Louis IX (r. 1226–1270) was famous in his time for his concern for justice. Each French province, even after being made part of the kingdom of France, retained its unique laws and procedures, but Louis IX created a royal judicial system. He established the Parlement of Paris, a kind of supreme court that welcomed appeals from local administrators and from the courts of feudal lords throughout France. By the very act of appealing the decisions of feudal courts to the Parlement of Paris, French people in far-flung provinces were recognizing the superiority of royal justice.

Louis was the first French monarch to publish laws for the entire kingdom. The Parlement of Paris registered (or announced) these laws, which forbade private warfare, judicial duels, gambling, blaspheming, and prostitution. Louis sought to identify justice with the kingship, and gradually royal justice touched all parts of the kingdom.

Under Henry II (r. 1154–1189), England developed and extended *common law*—a law common to and accepted by the entire country. No other country in medieval Europe did so. Each year Henry sent out *circuit judges* (royal officials who traveled in a given circuit or district) to hear civil and criminal cases. Wherever the king's judges sat, there sat the king's court. Slowly, the king's court gained jurisdiction over all property disputes and criminal actions.

An accused person formally charged with a crime did *not* undergo trial by jury, however. He or she was tried by ordeal. The accused was tied hand and foot and dropped in a lake or river. People believed that water was a pure substance and would reject anything foul or unclean. Thus a person who sank was considered innocent, and a person who floated was considered guilty. Although the community decided whether the accused had sunk or floated, people believed that God determined innocence or guilt. Thus a priest had to be present to bless the water.

Henry II and others considered this ancient Germanic method irrational and disliked community control of the process. But Henry had no alternative. Then in 1215, the Fourth Lateran Council of the church forbade the presence of priests at trials by ordeal and thus effectively abolished them. Gradually, in the course of the thirteenth century, the king's judges adopted the practice of calling upon twelve people (other than the accusing jury) to consider the question of innocence or guilt. This became the jury of trial, but it was very slowly accepted because medieval people had more confidence in the judgment of God than in the judgment of twelve ordinary people.

One aspect of Henry's judicial reforms encountered stiff resistance from an unexpected source: Thomas Becket, a friend and former chief adviser whom Henry had made archbishop of Canterbury. When Henry wanted to bring all persons in the kingdom under the jurisdiction of the royal courts, Thomas Becket's opposition led to another dramatic conflict between temporal and spiritual powers.

In the 1160s many literate people accused of crimes claimed "benefit of clergy" even though they were not clerics and often had no intention of being ordained. Benefit of clergy gave the accused

✤ **MAP 12.7 The Holy Roman Empire, ca 1200** Frederick Barbarossa tried to use the feudal bond to tie the various provinces, principalities, bishop-rics, duchies, and free cities to the imperial monarchy.

Limoges Casket   The principal city of Limousin in west-central France, Limoges was famous for the superb work of its enamelers and goldsmiths. This casket, or chest, showing Thomas Becket's execution (lower panel) and burial (upper panel) was used to preserve relics of Becket. The two scenes are done on gilded copper plaques nailed over wood. *(Source: British Rail Pension Fund)*

the right to be tried in church courts, which meted out mild punishments. A person found guilty in the king's court might suffer mutilation—loss of a hand, loss of a foot, castration—or even death. Ecclesiastical punishments, in contrast, tended to be an obligation to say certain prayers or to make a pilgrimage. In 1164 Henry II insisted that everyone, including clerics, be subject to the royal courts. Becket vigorously protested that church law required clerics to be subject to church courts. The disagreement between the king and the archbishop dragged on for years. The king grew increasingly bitter that his appointment of Becket had proved to be such a mistake. Late in December 1170, in a fit of rage, Henry expressed the wish that Becket be destroyed. Four knights took the king at his word, went to Canterbury, and killed the archbishop in his cathedral as he was leaving evening services.

What Thomas Becket could not achieve in life, he gained in death. The assassination of an archbishop in his own church during the Christmas season turned public opinion in England and throughout western Europe against the king. Within months, miracles were recorded at Becket's tomb, and in a short time Canterbury Cathedral became a major pilgrimage and tourist site. Henry had to back down. He did public penance for the murder and gave up his attempts to bring clerics under the authority of the royal court.

Henry II's son John (r. 1199–1216) inherited a heavy debt from his father and from his brother, Richard I (r. 1189–1199), whose crusading zeal had cost the country dearly. While returning from the Holy Land, Richard had been captured by the duke of Austria, with whom he had quarreled, and England had paid an enormous ransom to secure his release. Between 1180 and 1220, England experienced severe inflation, which drove prices up. In 1204 John lost the rich province of Normandy to Philip Augustus of France and then spent the rest of his reign trying to get it back. To finance that war, he got in deeper and deeper trouble with his barons. John squeezed as much money as possible from his position as feudal lord. He forced widows to pay exorbitant fines to avoid unwanted marriages. He sold young girls who were his feudal wards to the highest bidder. These actions antagonized the nobility.

John also alienated the church and the English townspeople. He rejected Pope Innocent III's nominee to the see of Canterbury. And he infuriated the burghers of the towns by extorting money from them and threatening to revoke the towns' charters of self-government.

All the money John raised did not bring him success. In July 1214, John's coalition of Flemish, German, and English cavalry suffered a severe defeat at the hands of Philip Augustus of France at Bouvines in Flanders. This battle ended English hopes for the recovery of territories from France and also strengthened the barons' opposition to John. On top of his heavy taxation, his ineptitude as a soldier in a society that idealized military glory was the final straw. Rebellion begun by northern barons eventually grew to involve many of the English nobility, including the archbishop of Canterbury and the earl of Pembroke, respectively the leading ecclesiastical and lay peers. After lengthy negotiations, John met the barons at Runnymede, a meadow along the Thames River. There he was forced to approve and to attach his seal to Magna Carta, the treaty that became the cornerstone of English justice and law.

Magna Carta—the Great Charter—signifies the principle that the king and the government shall be under the law, that everyone—including the king—must obey the law. It defends the interests of widows, orphans, townspeople, free men, and the church. Some clauses contain the germ of the ideas of due process of law and the right to a fair and speedy trial. Every English king in the Middle Ages reissued Magna Carta as evidence of his promise to observe the law. Because it was reissued frequently and because later generations appealed to Magna Carta as a written statement of English liberties, it acquired an almost sacred importance as a guarantee of law and justice.

In the later Middle Ages, English common law developed features that differed strikingly from the system of Roman law operative in continental Europe. Common law relied on precedents: a decision in an important case served as an authority for deciding similar cases. By contrast, continental judges, trained in Roman law, used the fixed legal maxims of the sixth century text known as the Justinian *Code* to decide their cases. Thus the common-law system evolved and reflected the changing experience of the people, while the Roman-law tradition tended toward an absolutist approach. In countries influenced by common law, such as Canada and the United States, the court is open to the public; in countries with Roman-law traditions, such as France and the Latin American nations, courts need not be public. Under common law, people accused in criminal cases have a right to see the evidence against them; under the other system, they do not. Common law urges judges to be impartial; in the Roman-law system, judges interfere freely in activities in their courtrooms. Finally, whereas torture is foreign to the common-law tradition, it was once widely used in the Roman legal system.

The extension of law and justice led to a phenomenal amount of legal codification all over Europe. Legal texts and encyclopedias exalted royal authority, consolidated royal power, and emphasized political and social uniformity. The pressure for social conformity in turn contributed to a rising hostility toward minorities, Jews, and homosexuals.

By the late eleventh century, many towns in western Europe had small Jewish populations. The laws of most countries forbade Jews to own land, though they could hold land pledged to them for debts. By the twelfth century, many Jews were usurers: they lent to consumers but primarily to new or growing business enterprises. New towns and underdeveloped areas where cash was scarce welcomed Jewish settlers. Like other business people, the Jews preferred to live near their work; they also settled close to their synagogue or school. Thus originated the Jews' street or quarter or ghetto. Such neighborhoods gradually became legally defined sections where Jews were required to live.

Jews had been generally tolerated and had become important parts of the urban economies through trade and finance. Some Jews had risen to positions of power and prominence. Through the twelfth century, for example, Jews managed the papal household. The later twelfth and entire thirteenth centuries, however, witnessed increasingly ugly anti-Semitism. Why? Present scholarship does not provide completely satisfactory answers, but we have some clues. Shifting agricultural and economic patterns aggravated social tensions. The indebtedness of peasants and nobles to Jews in an increasingly cash-based economy; the xenophobia that accompanied and followed the Crusades; Christian merchants' and financiers' resentment of Jewish business competition; the spread of vicious accusations of ritual murders or sacrileges against Christian property and persons; royal and papal legislation aimed at social conformity—these factors all contributed to rising anti-Semitism. Philip Augustus of France used hostility to Jews as an excuse to imprison them and then to demand heavy ransom for their release. The Fourth Lateran Council of 1215 forbade Jews to hold public office, restricted their financial activities, and required them to wear distinctive clothing. In 1290 Edward I of England capitalized on mercantile and other resentment of Jews to expel them from the country in return for a large financial grant. In 1302 Philip IV of France followed suit and confiscated their property. Fear, ignorance, greed, stupidity, and the pressure for social conformity all played a part in anti-Semitism of the central Middle Ages.

Early Christians displayed no special prejudice against homosexuals. Some of the church fathers, such as Saint John Chrysostom (347–407), preached against them, but a general indifference to homosexual activity prevailed throughout the early Middle Ages. In the early twelfth century, a large homosexual literature circulated. Publicly known homosexuals—for example, Ralph, archbishop of Tours (1087–1118), and King Richard I of England—held high ecclesiastical and political positions.

Beginning in the late twelfth century, however, a profound change occurred in public attitudes toward homosexual behavior. Scholars have only begun to investigate why this occurred, and the root cause of intolerance rarely yields to easy analysis. In the thirteenth century, a fear of foreigners, especially Muslims, became associated with the crusading movement. Heretics were the most despised minority in an age that stressed religious and social uniformity. The notion spread that both Muslims and heretics, the great foreign and domestic menaces to the security of Christian Europe, were inclined to homosexual relations. In addition, the systematization of law and the rising strength of the state made any religious or sexual distinctiveness increasingly unacceptable. Whatever the precise cause, "between 1250 and 1300 homosexual activity passed from being completely legal in most of Europe to incurring the death penalty in all but a few legal compilations."[25] Spain, France, England, Norway, and several Italian city-states adopted laws condemning homosexual acts. Most of these laws remained on statute books until the twentieth century. Anti-Semitism and hostility to homosexuals were at odds with the general creativity and vitality of the period.

✤ **A Jewish Expulsion** Subject to ancient and irrational prejudices and lacking legal rights, Jewish people lived and worked in an area according to the pleasure of kings and lords. The increasing anti-Semitism of the thirteenth century led to their expulsion from many places. *(Source: Bibliothèque royale Albert 1er, Brussels/ms 5 fol. 265 recto)*

✤ ECONOMIC REVIVAL

A salient manifestation of Europe's recovery after the tenth-century disorders and of the vitality of the central Middle Ages was the rise of towns and the growth of a new business and commercial class.

These developments were to lay the foundations for Europe's transformation, centuries later, from a rural agricultural society into an industrial urban society—a change with global implications.

Why and how did these developments occur when they did? Part of the answer has already been given. Without increased agricultural output, there would not have been an adequate food supply for new town dwellers. Without a rise in population, there would have been no one to people the towns. Without a minimum of peace and political stability, merchants could not have transported and sold goods.

The Rise of Towns

Early medieval society was traditional, agricultural, and rural. The emergence of a new class that was none of these constituted a social revolution. The new class—artisans and merchants—came from the peasantry. They were landless younger sons of large families, driven away by land shortage. Or they were forced by war and famine to seek new possibilities. Or they were unusually enterprising and adventurous, curious and willing to take a chance.

Few towns of the tenth and eleventh centuries were "new" in the sense that they had been carved out of forest and wilderness. Some medieval towns that had become flourishing centers of trade by the mid-twelfth century had originally been Roman army camps, or perhaps forts erected during the ninth-century Viking invasions. York in northern England, Bordeaux in west-central France, and Cologne in west-central Germany are good examples of ancient towns that underwent revitalization in the eleventh century. Great cathedrals and monasteries, which represented a demand for goods and services, also attracted concentrations of people. Italian seaport cities such as Venice, Pisa, and Genoa had been centers of shipping and commerce in earlier times. Muslim attacks and domestic squabbles had cut their populations and drastically reduced the volume of their trade in the early Middle Ages, but trade with Constantinople and the East had never stopped entirely. The restoration of order and political stability promoted rebirth and new development. Medieval towns had a few characteristics in common. Walls enclosed the town. (The terms *burgher* and *bourgeois* derive from the Old English and Old German words

burg, burgh, borg, and *borough* for "a walled or fortified place.") The town had a marketplace. It often had a mint for the coining of money and a court to settle disputes.

In each town, many people inhabited a small, cramped area. As population increased, towns rebuilt their walls, expanding the living space to accommodate growing numbers. Through an archaeological investigation of the amount of land gradually enclosed by walls, historians have gained a rough estimate of medieval town populations. For example, the walled area of the German city of Cologne equaled 100 hectares in the tenth century (1 hectare = 2.471 acres), about 185 hectares in 1106, about 320 in 1180, and 397 in the fourteenth century. In 1180 Cologne's population was at least 32,000; in the mid-fourteenth century, perhaps 40,000.[26] The concentration of the textile industry in the Low Countries brought into being the most populous cluster of cities in western Europe: Ghent with about 56,000 people, Bruges with 27,000, Tournai and Brussels each with perhaps 20,000.[27] Paris, together with Milan, Venice, and Florence, each with about 80,000, led all Europe in population.

The aristocratic nobility glanced down with contempt and derision at the moneygrubbing townspeople but were not above borrowing from them. The rural peasantry peered up with suspicion and fear at the town dwellers. Some farmers fled to the towns seeking wealth and freedom. But most farmers wondered what was the point of making money. They believed that only land had real permanence. Nor did the new commercial class make much sense initially to churchmen. The immediate goal of the middle class was obviously not salvation. It would be a long while before churchmen developed a theological justification for the new class.

Town Liberties and Town Life

The history of towns in the eleventh through thirteenth centuries consists largely of merchants' efforts to acquire liberties. In the Middle Ages, *liberties* meant special privileges. For the town dweller, liberties included the privilege of living and trading on the lord's land. The most important privilege a medieval townsperson could gain was personal freedom. It gradually developed that an individual who lived in a town for a year and a day, and was accepted by the townspeople, was free of servile obligations and servile status. More than anything else, perhaps, the personal freedom that came with residence in a town contributed to the emancipation of the serfs in the central Middle Ages. Liberty meant citizenship, and, unlike foreigners and outsiders of any kind, a full citizen of a town did not have to pay taxes and tolls in the market. Obviously, this exemption increased profits.

In the twelfth and thirteenth centuries, towns fought for, and slowly gained, legal and political rights. Gradually, towns across Europe acquired the right to hold municipal courts that alone could judge members of the town. In effect, this right gave them judicial independence.[28]

In the acquisition of full rights of self-government, the *merchant guilds* played a large role. Medieval people were long accustomed to communal enterprises. In the late tenth and early eleventh centuries, those who were engaged in foreign trade joined together in merchant guilds; united enterprise provided them greater security and less risk of losses than did individual action. At about the same time, the artisans and craftsmen of particular trades formed their own guilds. These were the butchers, bakers, and candlestick makers. Members of the *craft guilds* determined the quality, quantity, and price of the goods produced and the number of apprentices and journeymen affiliated with the guild.

Research indicates that, by the fifteenth century, women composed the majority of the adult urban population. Many women were heads of households.[29] They engaged in every kind of urban commercial activity, both as helpmates to their husbands and independently. In many manufacturing trades women predominated, and in some places women were a large percentage of the labor force. In fourteenth-century Frankfurt, for example, about 33 percent of the crafts and trades were entirely female, about 40 percent wholly male, and the remaining crafts roughly divided between the sexes. Craft guilds provided greater opportunity for women than did merchant guilds. Most members of the Paris silk and woolen trades were women, and some achieved the mastership. Widows frequently followed their late husbands' professions, but if they remarried outside the craft, they lost the mastership. Between 1254 and 1271, the chief magistrate of Paris drew up the following regulations for the silk industry:

Any woman who wishes to be a silk spinster [woman who spins] on large spindles in the city of Paris . . . may freely do so, provided she observe the following customs and usages of the crafts:

No spinster on large spindles may have more than three apprentices, unless they be her own or her husband's children born in true wedlock; nor may she contract with them for an apprenticeship of less than seven years. . . . If a working woman comes from outside Paris and wishes to practice the said craft in the city, she must swear before the guardians of the craft that she will practice it well and loyally and conform to its customs and usages.[30]

Guild records show that women received lower wages than men for the same work, on the grounds that they needed less income.

Recent research demonstrates that women with ready access to cash—such as female innkeepers, alewives, and women in trade—"extended credit on purchases, gave cash advances to good customers or accepted articles on pawn . . . and many widows supplemented their earnings from their late husbands' businesses or homesteads by putting out cash at interest." Likewise, Christian noblewomen, nuns, and Jewish businesswomen participated in money lending. Wherever Jews lived, Jewish women were active moneylenders—for example, in northern France (where in the thirteenth century Jewish women constituted a third of all Jewish lenders), the German-speaking parts of Europe, Navarre, Catalonia, and throughout Italy. Loans made by all women tended to be very small (in comparison to those extended by men), for domestic consumption (to tide over a household in some emergency, in contrast to productive loans such as those to repair or replace a piece of farm equipment), and for short terms (a few weeks or a month).[31]

By the late eleventh century, especially in the towns of the Low Countries and northern Italy, the leaders of the merchant guilds were quite rich and powerful. They constituted an oligarchy in their towns, controlling economic life and bargaining with kings and lords for political independence. Full rights of self-government included the right to hold a town court, the right to select the mayor and other municipal officials, and the right to tax and collect taxes.

A charter that King Henry II of England granted to the merchants of Lincoln around 1157 nicely illustrates the town's rights. The passages quoted clearly suggest that the merchant guild had been the governing body in the city for almost a century and that anyone who lived in Lincoln for a year and a day was considered free:

Henry, by the grace of God, etc. . . . Know that I have granted to my citizens of Lincoln all their liberties and customs and laws which they had in the time of Edward [King Edward the Confessor] and William and Henry, kings of England. And I have granted them their gild-merchant, comprising men of the city and other merchants of the shire, as well and freely as they had it in the time of our aforesaid predecessors. . . . I also confirm to them that if anyone has lived in Lincoln for a year and a day without dispute from any claimant, and has paid the customs [tax levied by the king] . . . then let the defendant remain in peace in my city of Lincoln as my citizen, without [having to defend his] right.[32]

Kings and lords discovered that towns attracted increasing numbers of people—people whom the lords could tax. Moreover, when burghers bargained for a town's political independence, they offered sizable amounts of ready cash. Consequently, feudal lords ultimately agreed to self-government.

Gates pierced the town walls, and visitors waited at the gates to gain entrance to the town. When the gates were opened early in the morning, guards inspected the quantity and quality of the goods brought in, and they collected the customary taxes. Part of the taxes went to the lord on whose land the town stood, part to the town council for civic purposes. Constant repair of the walls was usually the town's greatest expense.

Medieval cities served, above all else, as markets. In some respects the entire city was a marketplace. The place where a product was made and sold was

Hammering Cobblestones Laborers pave the highway leading from the walled city of Bavay in France. The original roadbed was loose earth. Upkeep of the roads and walls was often a town's greatest expense. *(Source: Bibliothèque royale Albert 1ᵉʳ, Brussels/ms 9242, fol. 48 verso)*

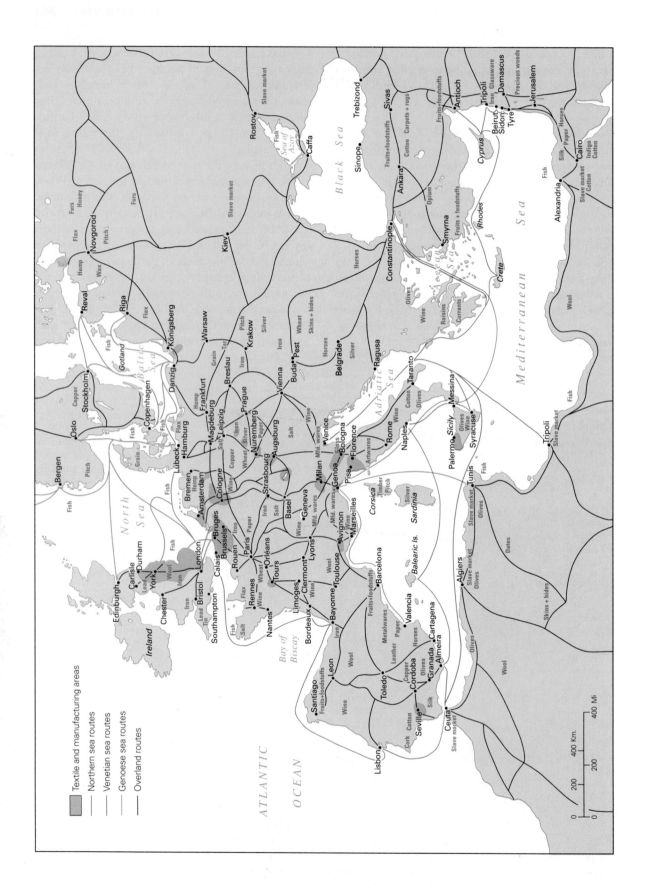

also typically the merchant's residence. Usually the ground floor was the scene of production. A window or door opened from the main workroom directly onto the street, and passersby could look in and see the goods being produced. The merchant's family lived above the business on the second or third floor. As the business and the family expanded, the merchant built additional stories on top of the house.

Because space within the town walls was limited, expansion occurred upward. Second and third stories were built jutting out over the ground floor and thus over the street. Since the streets were narrow to begin with, houses lacked fresh air and light. Initially, houses were made of wood and thatched with straw. Fire was a constant danger and spread rapidly. Municipal governments consequently urged construction in stone or brick.

Most medieval cities developed haphazardly. There was little town planning. As the population increased, space became more and more limited. Air and water pollution presented serious problems. Many families raised pigs for household consumption in sties next to the house. Horses and oxen, the chief means of transportation and power, dropped tons of dung on the streets every year. It was universal practice in the early towns to dump household waste, both animal and human, into the road in front of one's house. The stench must have been abominable. Lack of space, air pollution, and sanitation problems bedeviled urban people in medieval times, as they do today. Still, people wanted to get into medieval cities because they represented opportunities for economic advancement, social mobility, and improvement in legal status.

The Revival of Long-Distance Trade

The eleventh century witnessed a remarkable revival of trade, as artisans and craftsmen manufactured goods for local and foreign consumption (Map 12.8). Most trade centered in towns and was controlled by professional traders. The transportation of goods involved serious risks. Shipwrecks were common. Pirates infested the sea lanes, and

MAP 12.8 Trade and Manufacturing in Medieval Europe Notice the number of cities and the sources of silver, iron, copper, lead, paper, wool, carpets and rugs, and slaves.

robbers and thieves roamed virtually all of the land routes. Since the risks were so great, merchants preferred to share them. A group of people would thus pool some of their capital to finance an expedition to a distant place. When the ship or caravan returned and the goods brought back were sold, the investors would share the profits. If disaster struck the caravan, an investor's loss was limited to the amount of that individual's investment.

What goods were exchanged? What towns took the lead in medieval international trade? The Italian cities, especially Venice, led the West in trade in general and completely dominated the Asian market. Ships carried salt from the Venetian lagoon, pepper and other spices from North Africa, slaves and silks and purple textiles from the East to northern and western Europe. Lombard and Tuscan merchants exchanged those goods at the town markets and regional fairs of France, Flanders, and England. (Fairs were periodic gatherings that attracted buyers, sellers, and goods from all over Europe.) Flanders controlled the cloth industry: the towns of Bruges, Ghent, and Ypres built up a vast industry in the manufacture of cloth. Italian merchants exchanged their products for Flemish tapestries, fine broadcloth, and other textiles.

Two circumstances help to explain the lead Venice and the Flemish towns gained in long-distance trade. Both enjoyed a high degree of peace and political stability, but geographical factors were equally, if not more, important (see Map 12.8). Venice was ideally located at the northwestern end of the Adriatic Sea, with easy access to the transalpine land routes as well as the Adriatic and Mediterranean sea lanes. The markets of North Africa, Byzantium, and Russia and the great fairs of Ghent in Flanders and Champagne in France provided commercial opportunities that Venice quickly seized. The geographical situation of Flanders also offered unusual possibilities. Just across the Channel from England, Flanders had easy access to English wool. Indeed, Flanders and England developed a very close economic relationship.

Wool was the cornerstone of the English medieval economy. Scholars have estimated that, by the end of the twelfth century, roughly 6 million sheep grazed on the English moors and downs.[33] Population growth in the twelfth century and the success of the Flemish and Italian textile industries created foreign demand for English wool. The production of English wool stimulated Flemish manufacturing, and the expansion of the Flemish cloth industry in turn spurred the production of English wool. The availability of raw wool also encouraged the development of domestic cloth manufacture within England. The port cities of London, Hull, Boston, and Bristol thrived on the wool trade. In the thirteenth century, commercial families in these towns grew fabulously rich.

The Commercial Revolution

A steadily expanding volume of international trade from the late eleventh through the thirteenth centuries was a sign of the great economic surge, but it was not the only one. In cities all across Europe, trading and transportation firms opened branch offices. Credit was widely extended, considerably facilitating exchange. Merchants devised the letter of credit, which made unnecessary the slow and dangerous shipment of coin for payment.

A new capitalistic spirit developed. Professional merchants were always on the lookout for new markets and opportunities. They invested surplus capital in new enterprises. They became involved in a wide variety of operations. The typical prosperous merchant in the later thirteenth century might well be involved in buying and selling, shipping, lending some capital at interest, and other types of banking. Medieval merchants were fiercely competitive. Some scholars consider capitalism a modern phenomenon, beginning in the fifteenth or sixteenth century. But in their use of capital to make more money, in their speculative pursuits and willingness to gamble, in their competitive spirit, and in the variety of their interests and operations, medieval businessmen displayed the traits of capitalists.

The ventures of the German Hanseatic League illustrate these impulses. The Hanseatic League was a mercantile association of towns formed to achieve mutual security and exclusive trading rights. During the thirteenth century, perhaps two hundred cities from Holland to Poland joined the league, but Lübeck always remained the dominant member. From the thirteenth to the sixteenth century, the Hanseatic League controlled trade over a Novgorod-Reval-Lübeck-Hamburg-Bruges-London axis—that is, the trade of northern Europe (see Map 12.8). In the fourteenth century, Hanseatic merchants branched out into southern Germany and Italy by land and into French, Spanish, and Portuguese ports by sea.

The ships of league cities carried furs, wax, copper, fish, grain, timber, and wine. These goods were exchanged for finished products, mainly cloth and salt, from western cities. At cities such as Bruges and London, Hanseatic merchants secured special trading concessions exempting them from all tolls and allowing them to trade at local fairs. Hanseatic merchants established foreign trading centers called "factories." The most famous was the London Steelyard, a walled community with warehouses, offices, a church, and residential quarters for company representatives.[34]

By the late thirteenth century, Hanseatic merchants had developed an important business tool, the business register. Merchants publicly recorded their debts and contracts and received a league guarantee for them. This device proved a decisive factor in the later development of credit and commerce in northern Europe.[35] These activities required capital, risk taking, and aggressive pursuit of opportunities—the essential ingredients of capitalism. They also yielded fat profits.

These developments added up to what one modern scholar has called "a commercial revolution, . . . probably the greatest turning point in the history of our civilization."[36] This is not a wildly extravagant statement. In the long run, the commercial revolution of the central Middle Ages brought about radical change in European society. One remarkable aspect of this change is that the commercial classes did not constitute a large part of the total population—never more than 10 percent. They exercised an influence far in excess of their numbers.

The commercial revolution created a great deal of new wealth. Wealth meant a higher standard of living. The new availability of something as simple as spices, for example, allowed for variety in food. Dietary habits gradually changed. Tastes became more sophisticated. Contact with Eastern civilizations introduced Europeans to eating utensils, and table manners improved. Nobles learned to eat with forks and knives instead of tearing the meat from a roast with their fingers. They began to use napkins instead of wiping their greasy fingers on the dogs lying under the table.

The existence of wealth did not escape the attention of kings and other rulers. Wealth could be taxed, and through taxation kings could create strong and centralized states. In the years to come, alliances with the middle classes were to enable kings to defeat feudal powers and aristocratic interests and to build the states that came to be called "modern."

The commercial revolution also provided the opportunity for thousands of serfs to improve their social position. The slow but steady transformation of European society from almost completely rural and isolated to a relatively more sophisticated one constituted the greatest effect of the commercial revolution that began in the eleventh century.

Still, most towns remained small. The castle, the manorial village, and the monastery dominated the landscape. The feudal nobility and churchmen determined the prevailing social attitudes, values, and patterns of thought and behavior. The commercial changes of the eleventh through thirteenth centuries did, however, lay the economic foundations for the later development of urban life and culture.

SUMMARY

The culture that emerged in Europe between 733 and 843 has justifiably been called the "first" European civilization. That civilization had definite characteristics: it was Christian, feudal, and infused with Latin ideas and models. Almost all people were baptized Christians. Latin was the common language—written as well as spoken—of educated people everywhere. This culture resulted from the mutual cooperation of civil and ecclesiastical authorities. Kings and church leaders supported each other's goals and utilized each other's prestige and power. Kings encouraged preaching and publicized church doctrines, such as the stress on monogamous marriage. In return, church officials urged obedience to royal authority. The support that Charlemagne gave to education and learning, the intellectual movement known as the Carolingian Renaissance, proved his most enduring legacy.

The enormous size of Charlemagne's empire, its lack of viable administrative institutions, the domestic squabbles among his descendants, and the invasions of the Vikings, Magyars, and Muslims—these factors all contributed to the empire's disintegration. As the empire broke down, a new form of decentralized government, later known as feudalism, emerged. In a feudal society public and political power was held by a small group of military leaders. No civil or religious authority could maintain stable government over a very wide area. Local strongmen provided what little security existed.

Commerce and long-distance trade were drastically reduced. Because of their agricultural and commercial impact, the Viking and Muslim invaders were the most dynamic and creative forces of the period.

In the year 1000, having enough to eat was the rare privilege of a few nobles, priests, and monks. By the eleventh century, however, manorial communities were slowly improving their agricultural output through increased mechanization, especially the use of waterpower and windpower; these advances, aided by warmer weather, meant more food and increasing population.

In the eleventh century, rulers and local authorities gradually imposed some degree of order within their territories. Peace and domestic security contributed to the rise in population, bringing larger crops for the peasants and improving trading conditions for the townspeople. The church overthrew the domination of lay influences, and the spread of the Cluniac and Cistercian orders marked the ascendancy of monasticism. The Gregorian reform movement with its stress on the "freedom of the church" led to a grave conflict with kings over lay investiture. The papacy achieved a technical success on the religious issue, but in Germany the greatly increased power of the nobility, at the expense of the emperor, represents the significant social consequence. Having put its own house in order, the Roman papacy in the twelfth and thirteenth centuries built the first strong government bureaucracy. In the central Middle Ages, the church exercised general leadership of European society. The Crusades exhibit that leadership, though their consequences for Byzantine-Western and for Christian-Muslim relations proved disastrous.

Through the instruments of justice and finance, the kings of England and France attacked feudal rights and provincial practices, built centralized bureaucracies, and gradually came in contact with all their subjects. In so doing, these rulers laid the foundations for modern national states. The German emperors, preoccupied with Italian affairs and with a quest for the imperial crown, allowed feudal and local interests to triumph. Medieval cities recruited people from the countryside and brought into being a new social class: the middle class. Cities provided economic opportunity, which, together with the revival of long-distance trade and a new capitalistic spirit, led to greater wealth, a higher standard of living, and upward social mobility.

NOTES

1. For the date of this battle, October 17, 733, see L. White, *Medieval Technology and Social Change* (Oxford: Clarendon Press, 1962), p. 3 n. 3 and p. 12.

2. See F. Irsigler, "On the Aristocratic Character of Early Frankish Society," in *The Medieval Nobility: Studies on the Ruling Class of France and Germany from the Sixth to the Twelfth Century,* ed. and trans. T. Reuter (New York: North-Holland, 1978), pp. 105–136, esp. p. 123.

3. Einhard, *The Life of Charlemagne,* with a Foreword by S. Painter (Ann Arbor: University of Michigan Press, 1960), pp. 50–51.

4. P. Stafford, *Queens, Concubines, and Dowagers: The King's Wife in the Early Middle Ages* (Athens: University of Georgia Press, 1983), pp. 60–62.

5. See K. F. Werner, "Important Noble Families in the Kingdom of Charlemagne," in Reuter, *The Medieval Nobility,* pp. 174–184.

6. Quoted in B. D. Hill, ed., *Church and State in the Middle Ages* (New York: Wiley, 1970), pp. 46–47.

7. J. Nicholson, "Feminae Gloriosae: Women in the Age of Bede," in *Medieval Women,* ed. D. Baker (Oxford: Basil Blackwell, 1978), pp. 15–31, esp. p. 19, and C. Fell, *Women in Anglo-Saxon England and the Impact of 1066* (Bloomington: Indiana University Press, 1984), p. 109.

8. R. W. Southern, *Medieval Humanism and Other Studies* (Oxford: Basil Blackwell, 1970), p. 3.

9. D. Wright, trans., *Beowulf* (Baltimore: Penguin Books, 1957), pp. 9–19.

10. L. Sherley-Price, trans., *Bede: A History of the English Church and People* (Baltimore: Penguin Books, 1962), bk. 3, chap. 27, p. 191.

11. J. R. Strayer, "The Two Levels of Feudalism," in *Medieval Statecraft and the Perspectives of History* (Princeton, N.J.: Princeton University Press, 1971), p. 63. This section leans heavily on this seminal study.

12. See B. S. Bachrach, "Charles Martel, Mounted Shock Combat, the Stirrup, and Feudalism," in *Studies in Medieval and Renaissance History,* vol. 7 (1970), pp. 49–75, esp. pp. 66–75.

13. Strayer, "The Two Levels of Feudalism," pp. 65–76, esp. p. 71.

14. See D. Herlihy, "Land, Family, and Women in Continental Europe, 701–1200," in *Women in Medieval Society,* ed. S. M. Stuard (Philadelphia: University of Pennsylvania Press, 1976), pp. 13–45.

15. Quoted in R. Pipes, *Russia Under the Old Regime* (New York: Charles Scribner's Sons, 1974), p. 48.

16. See E. M. Hallam, *Capetian France, 987–1328* (New York: Longman, 1980), pp. 12–43.

17. J. Gimpel, *The Medieval Machine: The Industrial Revolution of the Middle Ages* (New York: Penguin Books, 1976), pp. 7, 10–15.

18. See B. Rosenwein, *Rhinoceros Bound: Cluny in the Tenth Century* (Philadelphia: University of Pennsylvania Press, 1982), Ch. 2.

19. Quoted in Hill, ed., *Church and State in the Middle Ages,* p. 68.

20. See J. B. Freed, *The Counts of Falkenstein: Noble Self-consciousness in Twelfth-Century Germany,* Transactions of the American Philosophical Society, vol. 74, pt. 6 (Philadelphia, 1984), pp. 9–11.

21. C. Erdmann, *The Origin of the Idea of the Crusade,* trans. M. Baldwin and W. Goffart (Princeton, N.J.: Princeton University Press, 1977), p. 57.

22. S. Runciman, *A History of the Crusades,* vol. 3, *The Kingdom of Acre* (Cambridge: Cambridge University Press, 1955), p. 480.

23. Cited ibid., pp. 23–25.

24. Quoted in D. C. Douglas and G. E. Greenaway, eds., *English Historical Documents,* vol. 2 (London: Eyre & Spottiswoode, 1961), p. 853.

25. J. Boswell, *Christianity, Social Tolerance, and Homosexuality: Gay People in Western Europe from the Beginning of the Christian Era to the Fourteenth Century* (Chicago: University of Chicago Press, 1980), pp. 270–293; the quotation is from p. 293. For alternative interpretations, see K. Thomas, "Rescuing Homosexual History," *New York Review of Books,* December 4, 1980, pp. 26ff.; and J. DuQ. Adams, *Speculum* 56 (April 1981): 350ff. For the French monarchy's persecution of the Jews, see J. W. Baldwin, *The Government of Philip Augustus: Foundations of French Royal Power in the Middle Ages* (Berkeley: University of California Press, 1986), pp. 51–52, and W. C. Jordan, *The French Monarchy and the Jews* (Philadelphia: University of Pennsylvania Press, 1989).

26. J. C. Russell, *Medieval Regions and Their Cities* (Bloomington: University of Indiana Press, 1972), p. 91.

27. Ibid., pp. 113–117.

28. H. Pirenne, *Economic and Social History of Medieval Europe* (New York: Harcourt, Brace, 1956), p. 53.

29. See D. Herlihy, *Medieval and Renaissance Pistoia: The Social History of an Italian Town, 1200–1430* (New Haven, Conn.: Yale University Press, 1967), p. 257.

30. Quoted in J. O'Faolain and L. Martines, eds., *Not in God's Image: Women in History from the*

Greeks to the Victorians (New York: Harper & Row, 1973), pp. 155–156.

31. W. C. Jordan, *Women and Credit in Pre-Industrial and Developing Societies* (Philadelphia: University of Pennsylvania Press, 1993), pp. 20ff.

32. Quoted in Douglas and Greenaway, *English Historical Documents,* pp. 969–970.

33. M. M. Postan, *The Medieval Economy and Society: An Economic History of Britain in the Middle Ages* (Baltimore: Penguin Books, 1975), pp. 213–214.

34. See P. Dollinger, *The German Hansa,* trans. and ed. D. S. Ault and S. H. Steinberg (Stanford, Calif.: Stanford University Press, 1970).

35. C. M. Cipolla, *Before the Industrial Revolution: European Society and Economy, 1000–1700,* 2d ed. (New York: Norton, 1980), p. 197.

36. R. S. Lopez, "The Trade of Medieval Europe: The South," in *The Cambridge Economic History of Europe,* vol. 2, ed. M. M. Postan and E. E. Rich (Cambridge: Cambridge University Press, 1952), p. 289.

SUGGESTED READING

The best general treatment of the Carolingian world is R. McKitterick, *The Frankish Kingdom Under the Carolingians, 751–987* (1983). The same author's *The Carolingians and the Written Word* (1989) will prove essential for many aspects of the Carolingian Renaissance, as will her edited *The Uses of Literacy in Early Medieval Europe* (1990), which includes articles on Ireland, Anglo-Saxon England, Merovingian Gaul, Muslim Spain, and Byzantium.

Einhard's *Life of Charlemagne,* cited in the Notes, is a good starting point for study of the great chieftain. The best general biography of Charlemagne is D. Bullough, *The Age of Charlemagne* (1965). P. Riche, *Daily Life in the World of Charlemagne,* trans. J. McNamara (1978), is a richly detailed study of many facets of Carolingian society by a distinguished authority. The same scholar's *Education and Culture in the Barbarian West: From the Sixth Through the Eighth Century,* trans. J. J. Contreni (1976), provides an excellent though technical treatment of Carolingian intellectual activity. For agricultural and economic life, G. Duby, *The Early Growth of the European Economy: Warriors and Peasants from the Seventh to the Twelfth Century* (1978), relates economic behavior to other aspects of human experience in a thoroughly readable style. The importance of technological developments in the Carolingian period is described by L. White, *Medieval Technology and Social Change* (1962), now a classic work.

In addition to the references to Bede and *Beowulf* in the Notes, D. L. Sayers, trans., *The Song of Roland* (1957), provides an excellent key, in epic form, to the values and lifestyles of the feudal classes, and the beautifully written evocation by P. H. Blair, *Northumbria in the Days of Bede* (1976), is highly recommended.

For the Christian church, its development as an institution, and its impact on pagan Germanic peoples, see the monumental work of F. Kempf et al., *The Church in the Age of Feudalism,* trans. A. Biggs (1980), vol. 3 of the *History of the Church* series edited by H. Jedin and J. Dolan. The scope of G. Tellenbach, *The Church in Western Europe from the Tenth to the Early Twelfth Century,* trans. T. Reuter (1993), is indicated by its title, but see also C. Morris, *The Papal Monarchy: The Western Church, 1050–1250* (1989). F. Paxton, *Christianizing Death: The Creation of Ritual Process in Early Medieval Europe* (1990), and T. Head, *Hagiography and the Cult of the Saints* (1990), are valuable books dealing with specialized topics.

For feudalism and manorialism, see, in addition to the references given in the Notes, S. Reynolds, *Fiefs and Vassals* (1994); F. L. Ganshof, *Feudalism* (1961); and J. R. Strayer, "Feudalism in Western Europe," in *Feudalism in History,* ed. R. Coulborn (1956). M. Bloch, *Feudal Society,* trans. L. A. Manyon (1961), remains important. The best broad treatment of peasant life and conditions is G. Duby, *Rural Economy and Country Life in the Medieval West,* trans. C. Postan (1968).

J. Brondsted, *The Vikings* (1960), is an excellently illustrated study of many facets of Viking culture. G. Jones, *A History of the Vikings,* rev. ed. (1984), provides a comprehensive survey of the Viking world based on the latest archaeological findings and numismatic evidence; P. H. Sawyer, *Kings and Vikings: Scandinavia and Europe, A.D. 700–1100* (1983), relies heavily on the literary evidence.

R. Bartlett, *The Making of Europe: Conquest, Colonization and Cultural Change, 950–1350* (1993), is a superb synthesis emphasizing expansion. Two broad surveys, D. Nicholas, *The Evolution of the Medieval World: Society, Government and Thought in Europe, 312–1500* (1992), and G. Holmes, ed., *The Oxford History of Medieval Europe* (1992), contain useful, up-to-date material. D. Bates, *Normandy Before 1066* (1982), traces the history of the region from the earliest Viking settlement to the time of ducal government and presents important material on social history. For Spain, R. Fletcher, *The Quest for El Cid* (1990), provides an excellent introduction to Spanish social and political conditions through a study of Rodrigo Dias, the eleventh-century soldier of fortune who became the Spanish national hero. Fletcher's *Moorish Spain* (1992) provides a highly readable

LISTENING TO THE
PAST

An Arab View of the Crusades

The Crusaders helped shape the understanding that Arabs and Europeans had of each other and all subsequent relations between the Christian West and the Arab world. To medieval Christians, the crusades were papally approved military expeditions for the recovery of holy places in Palestine; to the Arabs, these campaigns were "Frankish wars" or "Frankish invasions" for the acquisition of territory.

Early in the thirteenth century, Ibn Al-Athir (1160–1223), a native of Mosul, an important economic and cultural center in northern Mesopotamia (modern Iraq), wrote a history of the First Crusade. He relied on Arab sources for the events he described. Here is his account of the Crusaders' capture of Antioch:

The power of the Franks first became apparent when in the year 478/1085–86[1] they invaded the territories of Islam and took Toledo and other parts of Andalusia. Then in 484/1091 they attacked and conquered the island of Sicily and turned their attention to the African coast. Certain of their conquests there were won back again but they had other successes, as you will see.

In 490/1097 the Franks attacked Syria. This how it all began: Baldwin, their King, a kinsman of Roger the Frank who had conquered Sicily, assembled a great army and sent word to Roger saying: "I have assembled a great army and now I am on my way to you, to use your bases for my conquest of the African coast. Thus you and I shall become neighbors."

Roger called together his companions and consulted them about these proposals. "This will be a fine thing for them and for us!" they declared, "for by this means these lands will be converted to the Faith!" At this Roger raised one leg and farted loudly, and swore

that it was of more use than their advice. "Why?" "Because if this army comes here it will need quantities of provisions and fleets of ships to transport it to Africa, as well as reinforcements from my own troops. Then, if the Franks succeed in conquering this territory they will take it over and will need provisioning from Sicily. This will cost me my annual profit from the harvest. If they fail they will return here and be an embarrassment to me here in my own domain." . . .

He summoned Baldwin's messenger and said to him: "If you have decided to make war on the Muslims your best course will be to free Jerusalem from their rule and thereby win great honor. I am bound by certain promises and treaties of allegiance with the ruler of Africa." So the Franks made ready to set out to attack Syria.

Another story is that the Fatimids of Egypt were afraid when they saw the Seljuqids extending their empire through Syria as far as Gaza, until they reached the Egyptian border and Atsiz invaded Egypt itself. They therefore sent to invite the Franks to invade Syria and so protect Egypt from the Muslims.[2] But God knows best.

When the Franks decided to attack Syria they marched east to Constantinople, so that they could cross the straits and advance into Muslim territory by the easier, land route. When they reached Constantinople, the Emperor of the East refused them permission to pass through his domains. He said: "Unless you first promise me Antioch, I shall not allow you to cross into the Muslim empire." His real intention was to incite them to attack the Muslims, for he was convinced that the Turks, whose invincible control over Asia Minor he had observed, would exterminate every one of them. They accepted his conditions and in 490/1097 they crossed the Bosphorus at

Constantinople. . . . They . . . reached Antioch, which they besieged.

When Yaghi Siyan, the ruler of Antioch, heard of their approach, he was not sure how the Christian people of the city would react, so he made the Muslims go outside the city on their own to dig trenches, and the next day sent the Christians out alone to continue the task. When they were ready to return home at the end of the day he refused to allow them. "Antioch is yours," he said, "but you will have to leave it to me until I see what happens between us and the Franks." Who will protect our children and our wives?" they said. "I shall look after them for you." So they resigned themselves, to their fate, and lived in the Frankish camp for nine months, while the city was under siege.

Yaghi Siyan showed unparalleled courage and wisdom, strength and judgment. If all the Franks who died had survived they would have overrun all the lands of Islam. He protected the families of the Christians in Antioch and would not allow a hair of their heads to be touched.

After the siege had been going on for a long time the Franks made a deal with . . . a cuirass-maker called Ruzbih whom they bribed with a fortune in money and lands. He worked in the tower that stood over the riverbed, where the river flowed out of the city into the valley. The Franks sealed their pact with the cuirass-maker, God damn him! and made their way to the water-gate. They opened it and entered the city. Another gang of them climbed the tower with their ropes. At dawn, when more than 500 of them were in the city and the defenders were worn out after the night watch, they sounded their trumpets. . . . Panic seized Yaghi Siyan and he opened the city gates and fled in terror, with an escort of thirty pages. His army commander arrived, but when he discovered on enquiry that Yaghi Siyan had fled, he made his escape by another gate. This was of great help to the Franks, for if he had stood firm for an hour, they would have been wiped out. They entered the city by the gates and sacked it, slaughtering all the Muslims they found there. This happened in jumada I (491/April/May 1098). . . .

It was the discord between the Muslim princes . . . that enabled the Franks to overrun the country.

✳ Miniature showing lightly clad Muslims.
(Source: Bibliothèque Nationale, Paris)

Questions for Analysis

1. From the Arab perspective, when did the Crusade begin?

2. How did Ibn Al-Athir explain the Crusaders' expedition to Syria?

3. Why did Antioch fall to the Crusaders?

4. The use of dialogue in historical narrative is a very old device dating from the Greek historian Thucydides (fifth century B.C.). Assess the value of Ibn Al-Athir's dialogues for the modern historian.

Notes: 1. Muslims traditionally date events from Muhammad's hegira, or emigration, to Medina which occurred in 622 according to the Christian calendar. 2. Although Muslims, Fatimids were related doctrinally to the Shi'ites, and the dominant Sunni Muslims therefore considered the Fatimids heretics.

(Sources: P. J. Geary, ed., *Readings in Medieval History* (Peterborough, Ontario: Broadview Press, 1991), pp. 443–444; E. J. Costello, trans., *Arab Historians of the Crusades* (Berkeley and Los Angeles: University of California Press, 1969).

sketch of the history of Islamic Spain from the eighth to the seventeenth century. For the developing social and economic importance of the Flemish towns, see D. Nicholas, *Medieval Flanders* (1992).

The relationship of the monks to the ecclesiastical crisis of the late eleventh century is discussed by N. F. Cantor, "The Crisis of Western Monasticism," *American Historical Review* 66 (1960), but see also the essential analysis of J. Van Engen, "The 'Crisis of Cenobitism' Reconsidered: Benedictine Monasticism in the Years 1050–1150," *Speculum* 61 (1986): 269–304, as well as H. E. J. Cowdrey, *The Cluniacs and the Gregorian Reform* (1970), an impressive but difficult study. Cowdrey's *The Age of Abbot Desiderius: Monte Cassino, the Papacy, and the Normans in the Eleventh and Early Twelfth Centuries* (1983) focuses on Monte Cassino, the oldest black monk monastery. The advanced student will benefit considerably from the works by C. Erdmann, J. B. Freed, and B. Rosenwein that are cited in the Notes. I. S. Robinson, *The Papacy, 1073–1198: Continuity and Innovation* (1990), explores the changing role of the papacy in the eleventh and twelfth centuries and the development of the new model of papal government.

The following studies provide exciting and highly readable general accounts of the Crusades: J. Riley-Smith, *What Were the Crusades?* (1977), and R. C. Finucane, *Soldiers of the Faith: Crusaders and Muslims at War* (1983). There are excellent articles on many facets of the Crusades, including "The Children's Crusade," "Crusade Propaganda," "Crusader Art and Architecture," and "The Political Crusades"—all written by authorities—in J. R. Strayer, ed., *The Dictionary of the Middle Ages,* vol. 4 (1984). For the Fourth Crusade, see the excellent study of D. E. Queller, *The Fourth Crusade: The Capture of Constantinople* (1977), which gives an important revisionist interpretation. B. Lewis, *The Muslim Discovery of Europe* (1982), gives the Muslim view of the Crusades. Serious students will eventually want to consult the multivolume work of K. M. Setton, gen. ed., *A History of the Crusades* (1955–1977). C. Tyerman, *England and the Crusades, 1095–1588* (1988), treats the central topics of financing and the impact of the Crusades on economic, political, and social life.

G. O. Sayles, *The Medieval Foundations of England* (1961), traces political and social conditions to the end of the twelfth century. H. G. Richardson and G. O. Sayles, *The Governance of Medieval England from the Conquest to Magna Carta* (1963), focuses on administrative developments. For the Becket controversy, see F. Barlow, *Thomas Becket* (1986), the best recent study, and D. Knowles, *Thomas Becket* (1970). J. C. Holt, *Magna Carta* (1969), remains the best modern treatment of the document.

For France, both E. Hallam, *The Capetian Kings of France, 987–1328* (1980), and R. Fawtier, *The Capetian Kings of France* (1962), are readable introductions. Advanced students of medieval French administrative history should see J. Baldwin, *The Government of Philip Augustus: Foundations of French Royal Power in the Middle Ages* (1986), and J. R. Strayer, *The Reign of Philip the Fair* (1980). On Germany, H. Furhman, *Germany in the High Middle Ages,* trans. T. Reuther (1986), and G. Barraclough, *The Origins of Modern Germany* (1963), provide an excellent explanation of the problems and peculiarities of the Holy Roman Empire; the latter is a fine example of the Marxist interpretation of medieval history. M. Pacaut, *Frederick Barbarossa,* trans. A. J. Pomerans (1980), is perhaps the best one-volume treatment of that important ruler.

For the economic revival of Europe, see in addition to the titles by Dollinger, Herlihy, Postan, and Russell given in the Notes, T. H. Lloyd, *England and the German Hanse, 1157–1611: A Study in Their Trade and Commercial Diplomacy* (1992), which is essential for northern European commercial development. See also C. M. Cipolla, *Before the Industrial Revolution of the Middle Ages* (1976). The effect of climate on population and economic growth is discussed in the remarkable work of E. L. Ladurie, *Times of Feast, Times of Famine: A History of Climate Since the Year 1000,* trans. B. Bray (1971).

For women, see S. F. Wemple, *Women in Frankish Society: Marriage and the Cloister, 500 to 900* (1981), a basic work; C. Klapisch-Zuber, ed., *A History of Women,* vol. 2, *Silences of the Middle Ages* (1992), which contains useful essays on many aspects of women's lives and status; and S. Shahar, *The Fourth Estate: Women in the Middle Ages* (1983), a provocative work. J. M. Bennett, *Women in the Medieval English Countryside: Gender and Household in Brigstock Before the Plague* (1987), is a fascinating case study. E. Amt, ed., *Women's Lives in Medieval Europe: A Sourcebook* (1993), has fresh primary material on many aspects of the lives of noble, business, and peasant women.

Those interested in the origins of medieval towns and cities will learn how historians use the evidence of coins, archaeology, tax records, geography, and laws in J. F. Benton, ed., *Town Origins: The Evidence of Medieval England* (1968). S. Reynolds, *An Introduction to the History of English Medieval Towns* (1982), explores the social structure, political organization, and economic livelihood of English towns. R. H. Hilton, *English and French Towns in Feudal Society* (1992), is an exciting comparative study. C. Platt's well-illustrated *The English Medieval Town* (1979) makes excellent use of archaeological data and contains detailed information on the wool and cloth trades.

13

Creativity and Crisis in the Central and Later Middle Ages

Miniature of King Charles VII presiding at the trial of the Duc d'Alençon. *(Source: Bayerische Staatsbibliothek, Munich)*

The central Middle Ages witnessed some of the most remarkable achievements in the history of the Western world. Europeans displayed tremendous creativity in many facets of culture. The university, a unique Western contribution to civilization, came into being. The Gothic cathedral manifested medieval people's deep Christian faith, their sense of community, and their appreciation of the worlds of nature, humanity, and God.

In the medieval world, the nobility fought, the clergy prayed, and the peasantry worked to produce the food on which all depended. The lives of the vast majority of ordinary people continued to be conditioned by their local geography, climate, religion, and parish. For the peasantry, considerable social mobility existed in the central Middle Ages. Then, between 1300 and 1450, Europeans experienced a series of frightful shocks: economic dislocation, plague, war, and social upheaval. The last book of the New Testament—the Book of Revelation, dealing with visions of the end of the world, disease, war, famine, and death—inspired thousands of sermons and religious tracts. Death and preoccupation with death make the fourteenth century one of the most wrenching periods of Western civilization.

The progression from the vitality and creativity of the central Middle Ages to the crises of the later Middle Ages brings to mind a number of questions:

- How did the universities, the Gothic cathedrals, and troubadour poetry evolve, and what do they reveal about medieval ideals and society?
- How did people actually live, and what were their major preoccupations and lifestyles?
- What were the social and psychological effects of economic difficulties, disease, and war in the later Middle Ages?
- What impact did schism in the Christian church have on the lives of ordinary people?
- What political and social factors were reflected in the development of national literatures and in the expansion of literacy?

These are among the questions this chapter will explore.

❖ MEDIEVAL UNIVERSITIES

Just as the first strong secular states emerged in the thirteenth century, so did the first universities. This was no coincidence. The new bureaucratic states and the church needed educated administrators, and universities were a response to this need.

Since the time of the Carolingian Empire, monasteries and cathedral schools had offered the only formal instruction available. Monasteries were geared to religious concerns. They wished to maintain an atmosphere of seclusion and silence and were unwilling to accept large numbers of noisy lay students. In contrast, schools attached to cathedrals and run by the bishop and his clergy were frequently situated in bustling cities, and in the eleventh century in Bologna and other Italian cities wealthy businessmen established municipal schools. Inhabited by peoples of many backgrounds and "nationalities," cities stimulated the growth and exchange of ideas. In the course of the twelfth century, cathedral schools in France and municipal schools in Italy developed into universities.

The growth of the University of Bologna coincided with a revival of interest in Roman law. The study of Roman law as embodied in Justinian's *Code* had never completely died out in the West, but this sudden burst of interest seems to have been inspired by Irnerius (d. 1125), a great teacher at Bologna. His fame attracted students from all over Europe. Irnerius not only explained the Roman law of Justinian's *Code* but applied it to difficult practical situations. An important school of civil law was founded at Montpellier in France, but Bologna remained the greatest law school throughout the Middle Ages.

At Salerno, interest in medicine had persisted for centuries. Greek and Muslim physicians there had studied the use of herbs as cures and experimented with surgery. The twelfth century ushered in a new interest in Greek medical texts and in the work of Arab and Greek doctors. Students of medicine poured into Salerno and soon attracted royal attention. In 1140, when King Roger II (r. 1130–1154) of Sicily took the practice of medicine under royal control, his ordinance stated:

Who, from now on, wishes to practice medicine, has to present himself before our officials and examiners, in order to pass their judgment. Should he be bold enough to disregard this, he will be punished by imprisonment and confiscation of his entire property. In this way we are taking care that our subjects are not endangered by the inexperience of the physicians.[1]

In the first decades of the twelfth century, students converged on Paris. They crowded into the cathedral school of Notre Dame and spilled over into the area later called the Latin Quarter—whose name probably reflects the Italian origin of many of the students. The cathedral school's international reputation had already drawn to Paris scholars from all over Europe. One of the most famous of them was Peter Abélard.

The son of a minor Breton knight, Peter Abélard (1079–1142) studied in Paris, quickly absorbed a large amount of material, and set himself up as a teacher. Fascinated by logic, which he believed could be used to solve most problems, Abélard used a method of systematic doubting in his writing and teaching. As he put it, "By doubting we come to questioning, and by questioning we perceive the truth." Other scholars merely asserted theological principles; Abélard discussed and analyzed them.

The influx of students eager for learning and the presence of dedicated and imaginative teachers created the atmosphere in which universities grew. In northern Europe—at Paris and later at Oxford and Cambridge in England—associations or guilds of professors organized universities. They established the curriculum, set the length of time for study, and determined the form and content of examinations. University faculties grouped themselves according to academic disciplines, or schools—law, medicine, arts, and theology. The professors, known as "Schoolmen" or "Scholastics," developed a method of thinking, reasoning, and writing in which questions were raised and authorities cited on both sides of a question. The goal of the Scholastic method was to arrive at definitive answers and to provide a rational explanation for what was believed on faith.

The Scholastic approach rested on the recovery of classical philosophical texts and on ancient Greek and Arabic texts that had entered Europe in the early twelfth century. Thirteenth-century philosophers relied on Latin translations of these texts, especially translations of Aristotle. The Scholastics reinterpreted Aristotelian texts in a Christian sense.

In exploration of the natural world, Aristotle's axioms were not precisely followed. Medieval scientists argued from authority, such as the Bible, Justinian's *Code,* or ancient scientific treatises, rather than from direct observation and experimentation, as modern scientists do. Thus the conclusions of medieval scientists were often wrong. Nevertheless, natural science gradually emerged as a discipline distinct from philosophy.

Many of the problems that Scholastic philosophers raised dealt with theological issues. For example, they addressed the question that interested all Christians, educated and uneducated: How is a person saved? Saint Augustine's thesis—that, as a result of Adam's fall, human beings have a propensity to sin—had become a central feature of medieval church doctrine. The church taught that it possessed the means to forgive the sinful: grace conveyed through the sacraments. The Scholastics held that one must also *decide* to use the grace received. In other words, a person must use his or her reason to advance to God.

Thirteenth-century Scholastics devoted an enormous amount of time to collecting and organizing knowledge on all topics. These collections were published as *summa,* or reference books. There were summa on law, philosophy, vegetation, animal life, and theology. Saint Thomas Aquinas (1225–1274), a professor at Paris, produced the most famous collection, the *Summa Theologica,* which deals with a vast number of theological questions.

Aquinas drew an important distinction between faith and reason. He maintained that, although reason can demonstrate many basic Christian principles such as the existence of God, other fundamental teachings such as the Trinity and original sin cannot be proved by logic. That reason cannot establish them does not, however, mean they are contrary to reason. Rather, people understand such doctrines through revelation embodied in Scripture. Scripture cannot contradict reason, nor reason Scripture:

The light of faith that is freely infused into us does not destroy the light of natural knowledge [reason] implanted in us naturally. For although the natural light of the human mind is insufficient to show us these things made manifest by faith, it is nevertheless impossible that these things which the divine principle gives us by faith are contrary to these implanted in us by nature [reason]. Indeed, were that the case, one or the other would have to be false, and, since both are given to us by God, God would have to be the author of untruth, which is impossible.[2]

Thomas Aquinas and all medieval intellectuals held that the end of both faith and reason was the knowledge of, and union with, God. His work later became the fundamental text of Roman Catholic doctrine.

At all universities, the standard method of teaching was the *lecture*—that is, a reading. The professor read a passage from the Bible, Justinian's *Code,* or one of Aristotle's treatises. He then explained and interpreted the passage; his interpretation was called a *gloss.* Students wrote down everything. Because books had to be copied by hand, they were extremely expensive, and few students could afford them. Students therefore depended for study on their own or on friends' notes accumulated over a period of years. Examinations were given after three, four, or five years of study, when the student applied for a degree. The professors determined the amount of material students had to know for each degree, and students frequently insisted that the professors specify precisely what that material was. Examinations were oral and very difficult. If the candidate passed, he was awarded the first, or bachelor's, degree. Further study, about as long, arduous, and expensive as it is today, enabled the graduate to try for the master's and doctor's degrees. Degrees were technically licenses to teach. Most students, however, did not become teachers. They staffed the expanding royal and papal administrations.

FROM ROMANESQUE GLOOM TO "UNINTERRUPTED LIGHT"

It is difficult for twentieth-century people to appreciate the extraordinary amounts of energy, imagination, and money involved in building medieval churches. Between 1180 and 1270 in France alone, eighty cathedrals, about five hundred abbey churches, and tens of thousands of parish churches were constructed. This construction represents a remarkable investment for a country of scarcely 18 million people. More stone was quarried for churches in medieval France than had been mined in ancient Egypt, where the Great Pyramid alone consumed 40.5 million cubic feet of stone. All these churches displayed a new architectual style. Fifteenth-century critics called the new style

Gothic because they mistakenly believed the fifth-century Goths had invented it. It actually developed partly in reaction to the earlier Romanesque style, which resembled ancient Roman architecture.

The manner in which a society spends its wealth expresses its values. Cathedrals, abbeys, and village churches testify to the deep religious faith and piety of medieval people. If the dominant aspect of medieval culture had not been the Christian faith, the builder's imagination and the merchant's money would have been used in other ways.

Interior of La Sainte Chapelle, Paris   The central features of the Gothic style—pointed arch, ribbed vaulting, and flying buttress—made possible the construction of churches higher than ever before and the use of stained glass to replace stone walls. King Louis IX built this church to house the crown of thorns and other relics that he brought back from the Crusades. The result is a building of breathtaking beauty, a jeweled reliquary. *(Source: Art Resource, NY)*

In the ninth and tenth centuries, the Vikings and Magyars had burned hundreds of wooden churches. In the eleventh century, the abbots wanted to rebuild in a more permanent fashion, and after the year 1000, church building increased on a wide scale. Because fireproofing was essential, ceilings had to be made of stone. Therefore, builders replaced wooden roofs with arched stone ceilings called vaults. The stone ceilings were heavy; only thick walls would support them. Because the walls were so thick, the windows were small, allowing little light into the interior of the church. In northern Europe, twin bell towers often crowned these Romanesque churches, giving them a powerful, fortresslike appearance. Built primarily by monasteries, Romanesque churches reflect the quasi-military, aristocratic, and pre-urban society that built them.

The inspiration for the Gothic style originated in the brain of one monk, Suger, abbot of Saint-Denis (1122–1151). When Suger became abbot, he decided to reconstruct the old Carolingian abbey church at Saint-Denis. Work began in 1137. On June 11, 1144, King Louis VII and a large crowd of bishops, dignitaries, and common people witnessed the solemn consecration of the first Gothic church in France.

Not unknown before 1137, the basic features of Gothic architecture—the pointed arch, the ribbed vault, and the flying buttress—allowed unprecedented interior lightness. Since the ceiling of a Gothic church weighed less than that of a Romanesque church, the walls could be thinner. Stained-glass windows were cut into the stone, flooding the church with light. The interior, Suger exulted, "would shine with the wonderful and uninterrupted light of most sacred windows, pervading the interior beauty."[3]

Begun in the Île-de-France, Gothic architecture spread throughout France with the expansion of royal power. French architects were soon invited to design and supervise the construction of churches in other parts of Europe, and the new style traveled rapidly.

The construction of a Gothic cathedral represented a gigantic investment of time, money, and corporate effort. The bishop and the clergy of the cathedral made the decision to build, but they depended on the support of all social classes. Bishops raised revenue from contributions by people in their dioceses, and the clergy appealed to the king and the nobility. Above all, the church relied on the financial help of those with the greatest amount of ready cash, the commercial classes.

Money was not the only need. A great number of craftsmen had to be assembled: quarrymen, sculptors, stonecutters, masons, mortar makers, carpenters, blacksmiths, glassmakers, roofers. Unskilled laborers had to be recruited for the heavy work. The construction of a large cathedral was rarely completed in one lifetime; many cathedrals were never finished at all. Because generation after generation added to the building, many Gothic churches show the architectural influences of two or even three centuries.

Towns competed to build the largest and most splendid church. In northern France in the late twelfth and early thirteenth centuries, cathedrals grew progressively taller. The people of Beauvais exceeded everyone: their church, started in 1247, reached 157 feet. Unfortunately, the weight imposed on the vaults was too great, and the building collapsed in 1284. Medieval people built cathedrals to glorify God—and if mortals were impressed, so much the better.[4]

Cathedrals served secular as well as religious purposes. The sanctuary containing the altar and the bishop's chair belonged to the clergy, but the rest of the church belonged to the people. In addition to marriages, baptisms, and funerals, there were scores of feast days on which the entire town gathered in the cathedral for festivities. Local guilds met in the cathedrals to arrange business deals, plan recreational events and the support of disabled members. Magistrates and municipal officials held political meetings there. Pilgrims slept there, lovers courted there, and traveling actors staged plays there. The cathedral belonged to all.

First and foremost, however, the cathedral was intended to teach the people the doctrines of Christian faith through visual images. Architecture became the servant of theology. The west front of the cathedral faced the setting sun, and its wall was usually devoted to the scenes of the Last Judgment. The north side, which received the least sunlight, displayed events from the Old Testament. The south side, washed in warm sunshine for much of the day, depicted scenes from the New Testament. This symbolism implied that the Jewish people of the Old Testament lived in darkness and that the Gospel brought by Christ illuminated the world. Every piece of sculpture, furniture, and stained glass had some religious or social significance.

Stained glass beautifully reflects the creative energy of the central Middle Ages. It is both an integral part of Gothic architecture and a distinct form of painting. The glassmaker "painted" the picture with small fragments of glass held together with strips of lead. As Gothic churches became more skeletal and had more windows, stained glass replaced manuscript illumination as the leading kind of painting. Thousands of scenes in the cathedral celebrate nature, country life, and the activities of ordinary people. All members of medieval society had a place in the City of God, which the Gothic cathedral represented.

The drama, derived from the church's liturgy, emerged as a distinct art form during the same period. For centuries, skits based on Christ's Nativity and Resurrection had been performed in monasteries and cathedrals. Beginning in the thirteenth century, plays based on these and other biblical themes and on the lives of the saints were performed in the towns. Guilds financed these "mystery plays"—so called because they were based on the mysteries of the Christian faith. Performed first at the cathedral altar, then in the church square, and later in the town marketplace, mystery plays enjoyed great popularity. By combining comical farce based on ordinary life with serious religious scenes, they allowed the common people to understand and identify with religious figures and the mysteries of their faith.

❋ TROUBADOUR POETRY

In the twelfth and thirteenth centuries a remarkable literary culture blossomed in southern France. The word *troubadour* comes from the Provençal word *trobar*, which in turn derives from the Arabic *taraba*, meaning "to sing" or "to sing poetry." A troubadour was a poet of Provence who wrote lyric verse in his or her native language and sang it at one of the noble courts. Troubadour songs had a variety of themes. Men sang about "courtly love," the pure love a knight felt for his lady, whom he sought to win by military prowess and patience; about the love a knight felt for the wife of his feudal lord; or about carnal desires seeking satisfac-

tion. Women troubadours *(trobairitz)* focused on their emotions, their intimate feelings, or their experiences with men. Some poems exalted the married state, and others idealized adulterous relationships; some were earthy and bawdy, and others advised young girls to remain chaste in preparation for marriage. Many poems celebrate the beauties of nature; a few speak of the sexual frustrations of nuns. The married Countess Beatrice of Dia (1150–1200?) expresses the hurt she feels after being jilted by a young knight:

I've suffered great distress
From a knight whom I once owned.
Now, for all time, be it known:
I loved him-yes, to excess.
His jilting I've regretted,
Yet his love I never really returned.
Now for my sin I can only burn:
Dressed, or in my bed.

O if I had that knight to caress
Naked all night in my arms,
He'd be ravished by the charm
Of using, for cushion, my breast.
His love I more deeply prize
Than Floris did Blancheflor's
Take that love, my core,
My sense, my life, my eyes!

Lovely lover, gracious, kind,
When will I overcome your fight?
O if I could lie with you one night!
Feel those loving lips on mine!
Listen, one thing sets me afire:
Here in my husband's place I want you,
If you'll just keep your promise true:
Give me everything I desire.[5]

Because of its varied and contradictory themes, courtly love has been one of the most hotly debated topics in all medieval studies. One scholar concludes that it was at once "a literary movement, an ideology, an ethical system, an expression of the play element in culture, which arose in an aristocratic Christian environment exposed to Hispano-Arabic influences."[6] Another scholar insists there is no evidence for the practice of courtly love. If, however, the knight's love represented the respect of a vassal for his lady, a respect that inspired him to noble deeds, then perhaps courtly love contributed to an improvement in the status of women.

Troubadours certainly felt Hispano-Arabic influences. In the eleventh century, Christians of southern France were in intimate contact with the Arabized world of Andalusia, where reverence for the lady in a "courtly" tradition had long existed. In 1064 the Provençal lord Guillaume de Montreuil captured Barbastro and, according to legend, took a thousand slave girls from Andalusia back to Provence. Even if this figure is an exaggeration, those women who came to southern France would have been familiar with the Arabic tradition of sung poetry and continued it in their new land. Troubadour poetry thus represents another facet of the strong Muslim influence on European culture and life.[7]

The romantic motifs of the troubadours also influenced the northern French *trouvères,* who wrote adventure-romances in the form of epic poems. At the court of his patron Marie of Champagne, Chrétien de Troyes (ca 1135–1183) used the legends of the fifth-century British king Arthur to discuss contemporary chivalric ideals and their moral implications. Such poems as *Lancelot, Percival and the Holy Grail,* and *Tristan and Isolde* reveal Chrétien as the founding father of the Western romantic genre. The theme of these romances centers on the knight-errant who seeks adventures and who, when faced with crises usually precipitated by love, acquires new values and grows in wisdom.

The songs of the troubadours and trouvères were widely imitated in Italy, England, and Germany, and they spurred the development of vernacular languages (see pages 432–433). Most of the troubadours and trouvères came from and wrote for the aristocratic classes, and their poetry suggests the interests and values of noble culture in the central Middle Ages.

✤ LIFE IN CHRISTIAN EUROPE IN THE CENTRAL MIDDLE AGES

In the late ninth century, medieval intellectuals described Christian society as composed of those who pray (the monks), those who fight (the nobles), and those who work (the peasants). According to this image of social structure, function determined social classification.[8] Reality, however, was somewhat different. In the eleventh and twelfth centuries, most clerics and monks descended from the noble class and retained aristocratic attitudes and values, and the lay brothers who did most of the agricultural labor on monastic estates came from the peasant classes. The division of society into fighters, monks, and peasants also presents too static a view of a world in which there was considerable social mobility. Moreover, such a social scheme does not take into consideration townspeople and the emerging commercial classes. That omission, however, is easy to understand. Traders and other city dwellers were not typical members of medieval society. Medieval people were usually contemptuous (at least officially) of profit-making activities, and even after the appearance of urban commercial groups, the ideological view of medieval Christian society remained the one formulated in the ninth century: the three-part division among peasants, nobles, and monks.

Those Who Work

According to one modern scholar, "Peasants were rural dwellers who possess (if they do not own) the means of agricultural production."[9] Some peasants worked continuously on the land. Others supplemented their ordinary work as brewers, carpenters, tailors, or housemaids with wage labor in the field. In either case, all peasants supported lords, clergy, townspeople, as well as themselves. The men and women who worked the land in the twelfth and thirteenth centuries made up the overwhelming majority of the population, probably more than 90 percent. Yet it is difficult to form a coherent picture of them. The records that serve as historical sources were written by and for the aristocratic classes.

It is important to remember that peasants' conditions varied widely across Europe and that geography and climate as much as human initiative and local custom determined the peculiar quality of rural life.[10] The problems that faced the farmer in Yorkshire, England, where the soil was rocky and the weather rainy, were very different from those of the Italian peasant in the sun-drenched Po Valley.

Another obstacle to the creation of a coherent picture of the peasants has been historians' tendency to group all peasants into one social class. Although medieval theologians lumped everyone who worked the land into the "those who work" category, there were many kinds of peasants—ranging from complete slaves to free and very rich

⚜ **The Three Classes** Medieval people believed that their society was divided among clerics, warriors, and workers, here represented by a monk, a knight, and a peasant. The new commercial class had no recognized place in the agrarian military world. *(Source: The British Library)*

farmers. The status of the peasantry fluctuated widely all across Europe. The period from 1050 to 1250 was one of considerable social mobility.

Slaves were found in western Europe in the central Middle Ages, but in steadily declining numbers. That the word *slave* derives from *Slav* attests to the widespread trade in men and women from the Slavic areas in the Middle Ages. Around the year 1200, there were in aristocratic and upper-middle-class households in Provence, Catalonia, Italy, and Germany a few slaves—blond Slavs from the Baltic, olive-skinned Syrians, and blacks from Africa. Legal language differed considerably from place to place,

and the distinction between slave and serf was not always clear. Both lacked freedom—the power to do as one wished—and both were subject to the arbitrary will of one person, the lord. A serf, however, could not be bought and sold like an animal or an inanimate object, as the slave could.

The serf was required to perform labor services on the lord's land. The number of workdays varied, but it was usually three days a week except in the planting or harvest seasons, when it increased. Serfs frequently had to pay arbitrary levies, as for marriage or inheritance (see page 355). The precise amounts of tax paid to the lord depended on local custom and tradition. A free person had to do none of these things. For his or her landholding, rent had to be paid to the lord, and that was often the sole obligation. A free person could move and live as he or she wished.

Serfs were tied to the land, and serfdom was a hereditary condition. A person born a serf was likely to die a serf, though many did secure their freedom. About 1187 Glanvill, an official of King Henry II and an expert on English law, described how *villeins* (literally, "inhabitants of small villages")—as English serfs were called—could be made free:

A person of villein status can be made free in several ways. For example, his lord, wishing him to achieve freedom from the villeinage by which he is subject to him, may quit-claim [release] him from himself and his heirs; or he may give or sell him to another with intent to free him. . . . No person of villein status can seek his freedom with his own money, . . . because all the chattels of a villein are deemed to be the property of his lord that he cannot redeem himself from villeinage with his own money, as against his lord. If, however, a third party provides the money and buys the villein in order to free him, then he can maintain himself for ever in a state of freedom as against his lord who sold him. . . . If any villein stays peaceably for a year and a day in a privileged town and is admitted as a citizen into their commune, that is to say, their gild, he is thereby freed from villeinage.[11]

Thus, with the advent of a money economy, serfs could save money and, through a third-person intermediary, buy their freedom.

The economic revival that began in the eleventh century (see pages 380–386) advanced the cause of individual liberty. Hundreds of new towns arose in Ireland, in Mecklenburg and Pomerania in northeastern Germany, and in reconquest Spain; their settlers often came from long distances. Some colonial towns were the offspring of colonial traders. For example, Venetian and Genoese merchants founded in the Crimean region trading posts that served as entrepôts on the routes to China. The thirteenth century witnessed enormous immigration to many parts of Europe that previously had been sparsely settled. Immigration and colonization provided the opportunity for freedom and social mobility.[12]

Another opportunity for increased personal freedom, or at least for a reduction in traditional manorial obligations and dues, was provided by the reclamation of waste and forest land in the eleventh and twelfth centuries. Marshes and fens were drained and slowly made arable. This type of agricultural advancement frequently improved the peasants' social and legal condition. A serf could clear a patch of fen or forest land, make it productive, and, through prudent saving, buy more land and eventually purchase freedom. Settlers on the lowlands of the abbey of Bourbourg in Flanders, who had erected dikes and extended the arable land, possessed hereditary tenures by 1159. They secured personal liberty and owed their overlord only small payments.

In the thirteenth century, the noble class frequently needed money to finance crusading, building, or other projects. For example, in 1240 when Geoffrey de Montigny became abbot of Saint-Pierre-le-Vif in the Senonais region of France, he found the abbey church in bad disrepair and needed revenues to rebuild it. Geoffrey also discovered that the descendants of families who had once owed the abbey servile obligations now refused to recognize their bondage. Some of these peasants had grown wealthy. When the abbot determined to reclaim these peasants in order to get the revenues to rebuild his church, a legal struggle ensued. In 1257 a compromise was worked out whereby Geoffrey manumitted 366 persons who in turn agreed to pay him £500 a year over a twelve-year period.[13]

In the central Middle Ages, most European peasants, free and unfree, lived on a *manor,* the estate of a lord. The manor was the basic unit of medieval rural organization and the center of rural life. All other generalizations about manors and manorial life have to be limited by variations in the quality of the soil, local climatic conditions, and methods of cultivation. Manors varied from several thousand acres to as little as 120 acres. Recent archaeological evidence suggests that a manor might include several villages, one village whose produce was divided among several lords, or an isolated homestead.

The arable land of the manor was divided into two sections. The *demesne,* or home farm, was cultivated by the peasants for the lord. The other, usually larger section was held by the peasantry. All the arable land, both the lord's and the peasants', was divided into strips, and the strips belonging to any given individual were scattered throughout the manor. All peasants cooperated in the cultivation of the land, working it as a group. All shared in any disaster as well as in any large harvest.

A manor usually held pasture or meadowland for the grazing of cattle, sheep, and sometimes goats. Often the manor had some forest land as well. Forests had enormous economic importance. They were the source of wood for building and fuel, resin for lighting, ash for candles, and ash and lime for fertilizers and all sorts of sterilizing products. The forests were used for feeding pigs, cattle, and domestic animals on nuts, roots, and wild berries.

The fundamental objective of all medieval agriculture was the production of an adequate food supply. Using the method that historians have called the *open-field system,* peasants divided the arable land of a manor into two or three fields without hedges or fences to mark the individual holdings of the lord, serfs, and freemen. Beginning in the eleventh century in parts of France, England, and Germany, peasants divided all the arable land into three large fields. In any one year, two of the fields were cultivated and one lay fallow. One part of the land was sown with winter cereals such as rye and wheat, the other with spring crops such as peas, beans, and barley. Each year the crop was rotated. Local needs, the fertility of the soil, and dietary customs determined what was planted and the method of crop rotation.

In the early twelfth century, the production of iron increased greatly. In the thirteenth century, the wooden plow continued to be the basic instrument of agricultural production, but its edge was strengthened with iron. Only after the start of the fourteenth century, when lists of manorial equipment began to be kept, is there evidence for pitchforks, spades, axes, and harrows.

The plow and the harrow (a cultivating instrument with heavy teeth that breaks up and smoothes the soil) were increasingly drawn by horses. The development of the padded horse collar, resting on the horse's shoulders and attached to the load by shafts, led to an agricultural revolution. The horse collar let the animal put its entire weight into the task of pulling. In the twelfth century, the use of horses, rather than oxen, spread because horses' greater strength brought greater efficiency to farming. Horses, however, were an enormous investment, perhaps comparable to a modern tractor. They had to be shod (another indication of increased iron production), and the oats they ate were costly. Although horses represent a crucial element in the improvement of husbandry, students of medieval agriculture are not sure whether the greater use of horses increased crop yields.

The thirteenth century witnessed a tremendous spurt in the use of horses to haul carts to market. Large and small farmers increasingly relied on horses to pull wagons because they could travel much faster than oxen. Consequently, goods

 Boarstall Manor, Buckinghamshire   In 1440, Edmund Rede, lord of this estate, had a map made showing his ancestor receiving the title from King Edward I (lower field). Notice the manor house, church, and peasants' cottages along the central road. In the common fields, divided by hedges, peasants cultivated on a three-year rotation cycle—winter wheat, spring oats, and fallow. Peasants' pigs grazed freely in the woods, indicated by trees. We don't know whether the peasants could hunt the deer. *(Source: Buckinghamshire Record Office, Aylesbury)*

reached a market faster, and the number of markets within an area to which the peasant had access increased. The opportunities and temptations for consumer spending on nonagricultural goods multiplied.[14]

Agricultural yields varied widely from place to place and from year to year. By twentieth-century standards, they were very low. Inadequate soil preparation, poor seed selection, lack of manure— all made low yields virtually inevitable. And, like farmers of all times and places, medieval peasants were at the mercy of the weather. Yet there was striking improvement over time. Researchers have tentatively concluded that between the ninth and early thirteenth centuries, yields of cereals approximately doubled, and on the best-managed estates farmers harvested five bushels of grain for every bushel of seed planted. Grain yields were probably greatest on large manorial estates, where there was more professional management.

A modern Illinois farmer expects to get 40 bushels of soybeans, 150 bushels of corn, and 50 bushels of wheat for every bushel of seeds planted. Of course, modern costs of production in labor, seed, and fertilizer are quite high, but this yield is at least ten times that of the farmer's medieval ancestor. Some manors may have achieved a yield of 12 or even 15 to 1, but the *average* manor probably got a yield of only 5 to 1 in the thirteenth century.[15]

Life on the Manor For most people in medieval Europe, life meant country life. A person's horizons were not likely to extend beyond the manor on which he or she was born. True, peasants who colonized sparsely settled regions such as eastern Germany must have traveled long distances. But most people rarely traveled more than twenty-five miles beyond their villages. Their world was small, narrow, and provincial in the original sense of the

Late Medieval Wheelless Plow The sharp-pointed colter of this plow cut the earth while the attached moldboard lifted, turned, and pulverized the soil. As the man steers the plow, his wife prods the oxen. The caption reads, "God speed the plow, and send us corn [wheat] enough." (*Source: Trinity College Library, Cambridge*)

word: limited by the boundaries of the province. This way of life did not have entirely unfortunate results. A farmer had a strong sense of family and the certainty of its support and help in time of trouble. People knew what their life's work would be—the same as their mother's or father's. They had a sense of place, and pride in that place was reflected in adornment of the village church. Religion and the village gave people a sure sense of identity and with it psychological peace. Modern people—urban, isolated, industrialized, rootless, and thoroughly secularized—have lost many of these reinforcements.

But, even aside from the unending physical labor, life on the manor was dull. Medieval men and women must have had a crushing sense of frustration. Often they sought escape in heavy drinking. English judicial records of the thirteenth century reveal a surprisingly large number of "accidental" deaths. Strong, robust, commonsensical farmers do not ordinarily fall on their knives and stab themselves, or slip out of boats and drown, or get lost in the woods on a winter's night. They were probably drunk. Many of these accidents occurred, as the court records say, "coming from an ale." Brawls and violent fights were frequent at taverns.

Scholars have recently spent much energy investigating the structure of medieval peasant households. Because little concrete evidence survives, conclusions are very tentative. It appears, however, that a peasant household consisted of a simple nuclear family: a married couple alone, a couple of children, or a widow or widower with children. Peasant households were *not* extended families containing grandparents or married sons and daughters and their children. The simple family predominated in thirteenth-century England, in northern France in the fourteenth century, and in fifteenth-century Tuscany. Before the first appearance of the Black Death (see pages 419–421), perhaps 94 percent of peasant farmers married, and both bride and groom were in their early twenties. The typical household numbered about five people—the parents and three children.[16]

Women played a significant role in the agricultural life of medieval Europe. Historians often overlook this obvious fact. Women worked with men in wheat and grain cultivation, in the vineyards, and in the harvest and preparation of crops needed by the textile industry—flax and plants used for dyeing cloth, such as madder (which produces shades of red) and woad (which yields blue dye). Especially at harvest time women shared with their fathers and husbands the backbreaking labor in the fields, work that was especially difficult for them because of weaker muscular development and frequent pregnancies. Lords of great estates commonly hired female day laborers to shear sheep, pick hops (used in the manufacture of beer and ale), tend gardens, as well as do household chores such as cleaning, laundry, and baking. Servant girls in the country considered their hired status as temporary, until they married. Thrifty farm wives contributed to the family income by selling for cash the produce of their gardens or kitchen: butter, cheese, eggs, fruit, soap, mustard, cucumbers. In a year of crisis, careful management was often all that separated a household from starvation. And starvation was a very real danger to the peasantry down to the eighteenth century.

Women managed the house. The size and quality of peasants' houses varied according to their relative prosperity, and usually depended on the amount of land held. The poorest peasants lived in windowless cottages built of wood and clay or wattle and thatched with straw. These cottages consisted of one large room that served as the kitchen and living quarters for all. Everyone slept there. The house had an earthen floor and a fireplace. The lack of windows meant that the room was very sooty. A trestle table, several stools, one or two beds, and a chest for storing clothes constituted the furniture. A shed attached to the house provided storage for tools and shelter for animals. Prosperous peasants added rooms and furniture as they could be afforded, and some wealthy peasants in the early fourteenth century had two-story houses with separate bedrooms for parents and children.

Every house had a small garden and an outbuilding. Onions, garlic, turnips, and carrots were grown and stored through the winter. Cabbage was raised and pickled almost everywhere. Preserving and storing other foods were the basic responsibility of the women and children.

Women dominated in the production of ale for the community market. They had to know how to mix the correct proportions of barley, water, yeast, and hops in 12-gallon vats of hot liquid. Brewing was hard and dangerous work. Records of the English coroners' courts reveal that 5 percent of women who died lost their lives in brewing accidents, falling into the vats of boiling liquid.[17] Ale was the universal drink of the common people in northern Europe. By modern American standards the rate of consumption was heroic. Each monk of Abingdon Abbey in twelfth-century England was allotted 3 gallons a day, and a man working in the fields for ten hours probably drank much more.[18]

The mainstay of the diet for peasants everywhere—and for all other classes—was bread. It was a hard, black substance made of barley, millet, and oats, rarely of expensive wheat flour. The housewife usually baked the household supply once a week. If sheep, cows, or goats were raised, she also made cheese.

The diet of those living in an area with access to a river, lake, or stream was supplemented with fish, which could be preserved by salting. In many places there were severe laws against hunting and trapping in the forests. Deer, wild boars, and other game were strictly reserved for the king and nobility. These laws were flagrantly violated, however, and stolen rabbits and wild game often found their way to the peasants' tables.

Lists of peasant obligations and services to the lord, such as the following from Battle Abbey, commonly included the payment of chickens and eggs:

John of Coyworth holds a house and thirty acres of land, and owes yearly 2 p at Easter and Michaelmas; and he owes a cock and two hens at Christmas, of the value of 4 d.[19]

Except for the rare chicken or illegally caught wild game, meat appeared on the table only on the great feast days of the Christian year: Christmas, Easter, and Pentecost. Then the meat was likely to be pork from the pig slaughtered in the fall and salted for the rest of the year. Some scholars believe that, by the mid-thirteenth century, there was a great increase in the consumption of meat generally. If so, this improvement in diet is further evidence of an improved standard of living.

Breakfast, eaten at dawn before people departed for their farmwork, might well consist of bread, an onion (easily stored through the winter months), and a piece of cheese, washed down with milk or ale. Farmers, then as now, ate their main meal around noon. This was often soup—a thick *potage* of boiled cabbage, onions, turnips, and peas, seasoned with a bone or perhaps a sliver of meat. The

evening meal, taken at sunset, consisted of leftovers from the noon meal, perhaps with bread, cheese, milk, or ale.

Once children were able to walk, they helped their parents in the hundreds of chores that had to be done. Small children were set to collecting eggs, if the family had chickens, or gathering twigs and sticks for firewood. As they grew older, children had more responsible tasks, such as weeding the family vegetable garden, shearing the sheep, helping with the planting or harvesting, and assisting their mothers in the endless tasks of baking, cooking, and preserving. Because of poor diet, terrible sanitation, and lack of medical care, the death rate among children was phenomenally high.

Health Care What medical attention was available to the sick person in Western Europe between 1050 and 1300? Scholars are only beginning to explore this question, and there are many aspects of public health that we know little about. The steady rise in population in these centuries is usually attributed to the beginnings of political stability, the reduction of violence, and the increases in cultivated land and food supply. It may also be ascribed partly to better health care. Survival to adulthood probably meant a tough people. A recent study of skeletal remains in the village of Brandes in Orisans in Burgundy showed that peasants enjoyed very good health: they were well built, they had excellent teeth, and their bones revealed no signs of chronic disease. This evidence comes from only one village, but preliminary research confirms the impression that is given by romantic literature: in the prime of life the average person had an innocent raw vitality that enabled him or her to eat, drink, and make love with great gusto.[20]

In recent years scholars have produced some exciting information relating to the natural processes of pregnancy and childbirth. But the acquisition of information has not been easy. Because modesty forbade the presence of men at the birth of a child, very few men could write about it, and there was general illiteracy among women. One woman who wrote extensively, the twelfth-century physician Trotula of Salerno, tended to explain problems of gynecology (women's health) and obstetrics (pregnancy and childbirth) in terms of the relative degree of heat and cold and moisture and dryness within the female body. On the potential difficulty of childbirth she wrote

There are, however, certain women so narrow in the function of childbearing that scarcely ever or never do they succeed. . . . Sometimes external heat comes up around the internal organs and they are straightened in the act of giving birth. Sometimes the exit from the womb is small, the woman is too fat, or the foetus is dead, not helping nature by its own movements. This often happens to a woman giving birth in winter. If she has by nature a tight opening of the womb, the coldness of the season constricts the womb still more. Sometimes the heat all goes out of the woman herself and she is left without strength to help herself in childbearing. . . . Let her sides, abdomen, hips, and flanks be rubbed with oil of roses or oil of violets.[21]

Trotula believed that sneezing, which forced the woman to push her inner organs downward, should be induced. Her general knowledge cannot be called scientific.

Midwives learned their work through a practical apprenticeship, not through any sort of professional study. Most could not read, and even if they could, few medical texts existed. Because the first pregnancy of many women ended fatally, women of all social classes had a great fear of childbirth. Trotula, Hildegard of Bingen, and other writers on obstetrics urged pregnant women to pray that Christ would grant them a safe childbed.[22]

In the thirteenth century midwives began the practice of delivery by caesarean section—birth by an incision through the abdominal wall and uterus—so called from the traditional belief that the Roman statesman Julius Caesar had been born by means of this operation. Caesarean sections were performed only if the mother had died in labor; the purpose of the operation was the baptism of the child to assure its salvation.

Caesarean sections posed serious ethical problems. Who was to decide whether the mother was

A Caesarean Birth The midwife lifts a male child from the abdominal opening in the mother's dead body. Her helper prepares a tub of water to bathe the child. Since few infants survived the procedure, midwives needed witnesses to assert that they had not bungled the birth or deliberately killed the infant. *(Source: The British Library)*

dead? (The stethoscope was not invented until 1819.) Who could decide whether the fetus was alive after the mother's death? In a very difficult birth should the life of the mother be sacrificed for the sake of the child? An Old English translation of Trotula's advice to midwives states that "whan the woman is feble and the chylde may noght comyn out, then it is better that the chylde is slayne than that the moder of the child also dye." The greatest theologian of the age, Saint Thomas Aquinas in his treatise on baptism is also explicit: "Evil should not be done that good may come. Therefore one should not kill the mother in order to baptize the child; if, however, the child be still alive in the womb after the mother has died, the mother should be opened in order to baptize the child."[23] Since caesarean sections were performed only after the mother was dead, the choice of the mother's life or the child's never arose.[24] About 1400, male surgeons, motivated by professional, scientific, and probably financial interests, began to perform caesarean sections. Thus through caesarean births men entered the field of obstetrics.[25]

Childhood diseases, poor hygiene, tooth decay, wounds received in fighting, and the myriad ail-ments and afflictions for which even modern medical science has no cure—from cancer to the common cold—must have caused considerable suffering. For the sick what care existed?

As in all ages, the sick everywhere depended above all on the private nursing care of relatives and friends. For public health, English sources provide the largest evidence to date. In the British Isles the twelfth century witnessed a momentous breakthrough in the establishment of institutional care in hospitals. In addition to the infirmaries run by monks and nuns, there were at least 113 hospitals in England with possibly as many as 3,494 beds. Medieval hospitals were built by the royal family, the clergy, barons, and ordinary people to alleviate the suffering of the sick, not just to house them. Hospitals attracted considerable popular support, and in their charitable contributions women played an especially strong role in the endowment of hospitals.[26]

As in the developed modern world, persons living in or near a town or city had a better chance of receiving some form of professional attention than did those in remote rural areas. English documents label at least ninety practitioners as *medicus,* mean-

Saint Maurus, Healing A rich body of legend developed around Maurus, a nobleman's son given as an oblate to Saint Benedict. In the eleventh century, Maurus had a reputation, unsupported by evidence, for medical knowledge and curative powers. Here he is depicted giving a patient some kind of pharmaceutical preparation. *(Source: Bibliothèque municipale de Troyes)*

ing physician, surgeon, or medical man, but that is a pitifully small number in a population of perhaps 2 million. With so few doctors, only the largest cities—such as London, York, Winchester, and Canterbury, which all catered to pilgrims and travelers—had resident physicians. At other hospitals, physician consultants were brought in as the occasion required. Most people, of course, did not live in or near large towns. They relied for assistance on the chance presence of a local monk or nun with herb and pharmaceutical knowledge, a local person skilled in setting broken bones, or the wise village person experienced in treating diseases.

Since public morality and ancient tradition forbade the examination of female patients by men, women could practice obstetrics and gynecology. But although women played active roles as healers and in the general care of the sick, male doctors jealously guarded their status and admitted very few women to university medical schools when they were founded; "Francesca Romano, who was licensed as a surgeon in 1321 by Duke Carl of Calabria is the exception that proves the rule."[27] The medical faculty at the University of Paris in the fourteenth century penalized women who practiced medicine because they lacked a degree—which they were not allowed to get.

Popular Religion   Apart from the land, the weather, and the peculiar conditions that existed on each manor, the Christian religion had the greatest impact on the daily lives of ordinary people in the central Middle Ages. Religious practices varied widely from country to country and even from province to province. But nowhere was religion a one-hour-on-Sunday or High Holy Days affair. Christian practices and attitudes permeated virtually all aspects of everyday life.

As the Germanic and Celtic peoples were Christianized, their new religion became a fusion of Jewish, pagan, Roman, and Christian practices. In the central Middle Ages, all people shared as a natural and public duty in the religious life of the community.

The village church was the center of community life—social, political, and economic as well as religious. Most of the important events in a person's life took place in or around the church. A person was baptized there, within hours of birth. Men and women confessed their sins to the village priest there and received, usually at Easter and Christmas, the sacrament of the Eucharist. In front of the church, the bishop reached down from his horse and confirmed a person as a Christian by placing his hands over the candidate's head and making the sign of the cross on the forehead. (Bishops Thomas Becket of Canterbury and Hugh of Lincoln were considered especially holy men because they got down from their horses to confirm.) Young people courted in the churchyard and, so the sermons of the priests complained, made love in the church cemetery. Priests urged couples to marry publicly in the church, but many married privately, without witnesses (see page 429).

In the church, women and men could pray to the Virgin and the local saints. The stone in the church altar contained relics of the saints, often a local saint to whom the church itself had been dedicated. The saints had once lived on earth and thus, people believed, understood human problems. They could be helpful intercessors with Christ or with God the Father. They could perform miracles. The saint became the special property of the locality where his or her relics rested. Thus to secure the saint's support and to guarantee the region's prosperity, a busy traffic in relics developed—bones, articles of clothing, the saint's tears or saliva, even dust from the saint's tomb. The understanding that existed between the saint and the peasants rested on the customary medieval relationship of mutual fidelity and aid: peasants would offer the saint prayers, loyalty, and gifts to the shrine or church in return for the saint's healing and support. When saints failed to receive the attention they felt they deserved, they sometimes took offense and were vindictive. An English knight whose broken arm was healed by Saint James forgot to thank the saint at his shrine at Reading, whereupon the saint punished the knight by breaking his other arm.

What had been the saints' social background when alive? "The initiative in creating a cult (of a saint) always belonged to believers"[28] (ordinary people). Although papal authorities insisted that they had the exclusive right to examine the lives and activities of candidates for sainthood in a formal "trial," popular opinion declared people saints. Between 1185 and 1431, only seventy official investigations were held at Rome, but hundreds of new persons across Europe were venerated as saints. Church officials and educated clergy evaluated candidates according to the "heroic virtue" of their lives, but lay people judged solely by the candidates' miracles.

Modern research suggests a connection between the models of holiness and the social structures in different parts of Europe. Northern Europeans and southern Europeans chose saints of different social backgrounds or classes. In France and Germany, saints were primarily men and women of the nobility. In Italy and Mediterranean lands, saints tended to be *popolani*—non-nobles, nonaristocrats. The cult of the saints, which developed in a rural environment among uneducated people, is a central feature of popular culture in the Middle Ages.[29]

Popular religion consisted largely of rituals heavy with symbolism. Before slicing a loaf of bread, the good wife tapped the sign of the cross on the loaf with her knife. Before the planting, the village priest customarily went out and sprinkled the fields with water, symbolizing refreshment and life. Shortly after a woman had successfully delivered a child, she was "churched." Churching was a ceremony of thanksgiving based on the Jewish rite of purification. When a child was baptized, a few grains of salt were dropped on its tongue. Salt had been the symbol of purity, strength, and incorruptibility for the ancient Hebrews, and the Romans had used it in their sacrifices. It was used in Christian baptism to drive away demons and to strengthen the infant in its new faith.

The entire calendar was designed with reference to Christmas, Easter, and Pentecost. Saints' days were legion. Everyone participated in village processions. The colored vestments the priests wore at Mass gave the villagers a sense of the changing seasons of the church's liturgical year. The signs and symbols of Christianity were visible everywhere.

What did people actually *believe*? It is difficult to say, partly because medieval peasants left few written records of their thoughts, partly because in any age there is often a great disparity between what people profess to believe and their conduct or the ways they act on their beliefs. Peasants accepted what family custom and the clergy taught them. Recent research has shown that in the central Middle Ages a new religious understanding emerged. "Whereas early Christianity looked to holy men and women and early medieval society turned to saints to effect the connection between God and humankind through prayers of intercession," in the twelfth century a sacramental system developed. The seven sacraments—Baptism, Penance, Eucharist, Confirmation, Marriage, Holy Orders,

Extreme Unction—brought grace, the divine assistance or help needed to lead a good Christian life and to merit salvation. At the center of the sacramental system stood the Eucharist, the small piece of bread that through the words of priestly consecration at the Mass, became the living body of Christ and, when worthily consumed, became a channel of Christ's grace. The ritual of consecration, repeated at every altar of Christendom, became a unifying symbol in a complex world.[30]

The Mass was in Latin, but the priest delivered sermons on the Gospel in the vernacular—or he was supposed to. An almost universal criticism of the parish clergy in the twelfth and thirteenth centuries was that they were incapable of explaining basic Christian teaching to their parishioners. The growth of the universities did not improve the situation, because few diocesan clerics attended them and those who did obtain degrees secured administrative positions. The only parish priest to be canonized in the entire Middle Ages, the Breton lawyer and priest Saint Yves (d. 1303), had resigned a position as a diocesan judge to serve rural parishioners. At the trial for his canonization, laypeople stressed not only that he led a simple and frugal life but that he put his forensic skills to the service of preaching the Christian gospels. Saint Yves is the great exception that proves the rule that the medieval parish clergy were generally incapable of preaching in a rural milieu. Parish priests celebrated the liturgy and administered the sacraments, but they had other shortcomings. A thirteenth-century Alsatian chronicler said that the peasants of the region did not complain that their pastors lived in concubinage, because that made them less fearful for the virtue of their daughters.[31]

Christians had long had special reverence and affection for the Virgin Mary as the Mother of Christ. In the eleventh century, theologians began to emphasize the depiction of Mary at the crucifixion in the Gospel of John (19:25–27):

But standing by the cross of Jesus were his mother, and his mother's sister, Mary the wife of Clopas, and Mary Magdalene. When Jesus saw his mother and the disciple whom he loved standing near, he said to his mother, "Woman, behold, your son!" Then he said to the disciple, "Behold, your mother!"

Medieval scholars interpreted this passage as expressing Christ's compassionate concern for all humanity and Mary's spiritual motherhood of all Christians. The huge outpouring of popular devotions to Mary concentrated on her role as Queen of Heaven and, because of her special relationship to Christ, as all-powerful intercessor with him. Masses on Saturdays specially commemorated her, sermons focused on her unique influence with Christ, and hymns and prayers to her multiplied.

Those Who Fight

The nobility, though a small fraction of the total population, strongly influenced all aspects of medieval culture—political, economic, religious, educational, and artistic. For that reason, European society in the twelfth and thirteenth centuries may be termed aristocratic.

Members of the nobility enjoyed a special legal status. A nobleman was free personally and in his possessions. He was limited only by his military obligation to king, duke, or prince. As the result of his liberty, he had certain rights and responsibilities. He raised troops and commanded them in the field. He held courts that dispensed a sort of justice. Sometimes he coined money for use within his territories. As lord of the people who settled on his lands, he made political decisions affecting them, resolved disputes among them, and protected them in time of attack. The liberty and privileges of the noble were inheritable, perpetuated by blood and not by wealth alone.

The nobleman was a professional fighter. His social function, as churchmen described it, was to protect the weak, the poor, and the churches by arms. He possessed a horse and a sword. These, and the leisure time in which to learn how to use them in combat, were the visible signs of his nobility. He was encouraged to display chivalric virtues—courtesy, loyalty to his commander, and generosity. All nobles were knights, but not all knights were noble.[32]

Those who aspired to the aristocracy desired a castle, the symbol of feudal independence and military lifestyle. Through military valor, a fortunate marriage, or outstanding service to king or lord, poor knights could and did achieve positions in the upper nobility of France and England. Not so in Germany, where a large class of unfree knights, or *ministerials,* fought as warriors or served as stewards who managed nobles' estates or households. In the twelfth century, ministerials sometimes ac-

quired fiefs and wealth. The most important ministerials served the German kings and had significant responsibilities. Legally, however, they remained of servile status: they were not noble.[33]

Infancy, Childhood, and Youth   The rate of infant mortality (the number of babies who died before their first birthday) in the central Middle Ages must have been staggering. The limited information indicates that midwives had surely contributed to the death rate of both the newborn and the mother. Natural causes—disease and poor or insufficient food—also resulted in many deaths. Infanticide, however, which was common in the ancient world, seems to have declined in the central Middle Ages. Ecclesiastical pressure worked steadily against it. Infanticide in medieval Europe is another indication of the slow and very imperfect Christianization of European peoples.

On the other hand, the abandonment of infant children seems to have been the most favored form of family limitation, widely practiced throughout the entire Middle Ages. Abandonment was "the voluntary relinquishing of control over children by their natal parents or guardians, whether by leaving them somewhere, selling them, or legally consigning authority to some other person or institution."[34] Why did parents do this? What became of the children? What was the rate of abandonment? What attitudes did medieval society have toward this practice?

Poverty or local natural disaster led some parents to abandon their children because they could not support them. Thus Saint Patrick wrote that, in times of famine, fathers would sell their sons and daughters so that the children could be fed. Parents sometimes gave children away because they were illegitimate or the result of incestuous unions.

Sometimes parents believed that someone of greater means or status might find the child and bring it up in better circumstances than the natal parents could provide. Disappointment in the sex of the child or its physical weakness or deformity might also lead parents to abandon it. Finally, some parents were indifferent—they "simply could not be bothered" with the responsibilities of parenthood.[35]

The Christian Middle Ages witnessed a significant development in the disposal of superfluous children: they were given to monasteries as *oblates,* or "offerings." Boys and girls were given to

Children Given to Creditors　Ecclesiastical laws against lending money at interest were widely flouted, and many nobles, having borrowed beyond their ability to repay, fell heavily into debt. The selling or giving of children to creditors, illustrated here, was one solution to indebtedness. (*Source: The Bodleian Library, Oxford*)

monasteries or convents as permanent gifts. By the seventh century, church councils and civil codes had defined the practice: "Parents of any social status could donate a child, of either sex, at least up to the age of ten." Contemporaries considered oblation a religious act, for the child was offered to God often in recompense for parental sin. But oblation also served social and economic functions. The monastery nurtured and educated the child in a familial atmosphere, and it provided career opportunities for the mature monk or nun despite his or her humble origins.[36] In the twelfth and thirteenth centuries, the incidence of noble parents giving their younger sons and daughters to religious houses increased dramatically; nobles wanted to preserve the estate intact for the eldest son. In

the early thirteenth century, the bishop of Paris observed that children were "cast into the cloister by parents and relatives just as if they were kittens or piglets whom their mothers could not nourish; so that they may die to the world not spiritually but . . . civilly, that is—so that they may be deprived of their hereditary position and that it may devolve on those who remain in the world." The abandonment of children remained a socially acceptable institution. Ecclesiastical and civil authorities never legislated against it.[37]

For children of aristocratic birth, the years from infancy to around the age of seven or eight were primarily years of play. Infants had their rattles, as the twelfth-century monk Guibert of Nogent reports, and young children their special toys. Guibert of Nogent speaks in several places in his autobiography of "the tender years of childhood"—the years from six to twelve. Describing the severity of the tutor whom his mother assigned to him, Guibert wrote:

Placed under him, . . . I was kept from ordinary games and never allowed to leave my master's company, or to eat anywhere else than at home, in everything I had to show self-control in word, look, and deed, so that he seemed to require of me the conduct of a monk rather than a clerk. While others of my age wandered everywhere at will and were unchecked in the indulgence of such inclinations as were natural at their age, I, hedged in with constant restraints and dressed in my clerical garb, would sit and look at the troops of players like a beast awaiting sacrifice. Even on Sundays and saints' days I had to submit to the severity of school exercises.[38]

Guibert's mother had intended him for the church. At about the age of seven, a boy of the noble class who was not intended for the church was placed in the household of one of his father's friends or relatives. There he became a servant to the lord and received his formal training in arms. He was expected to serve the lord at the table, to assist him as a private valet when called on to do so, and, as he gained experience, to care for the lord's horses and equipment. The boy might have a great deal of work to do, depending on the size of the household and the personality of the lord. The work that children did, medieval people believed, gave them experience and preparation for later life.

Training was in the arts of war. The boy learned to ride and to manage a horse. He had to acquire skill in wielding a sword, which sometimes weighed as much as twenty-five pounds. He had to be able to hurl a lance, shoot with a bow and arrow, and care for armor and other equipment. Increasingly, in the eleventh and twelfth centuries, noble youths learned to read and write some Latin. Still, on thousands of charters from that period, nobles signed with a cross (+) or some other mark. Literacy for the nobility became more common in the thirteenth century. Formal training was concluded around the age of twenty-one with the ceremony of knighthood. The custom of knighting, though never universal, seems to have been widespread in France and England but not in Germany. Once knighted, a young man was supposed to be courteous, generous, and, if possible, handsome and rich. Above all, he was to be loyal to his lord and brave in battle. In a society lacking strong institutions of government, loyalty was the cement that held aristocratic society together. The greatest crime was called a *felony*, which meant treachery to one's lord.

Parents often wanted to settle daughters' futures as soon as possible. Men tended to prefer young brides. A woman in her late twenties or thirties had relatively few years in which to produce children; thus aristocratic girls in the central Middle Ages were married at around the age of sixteen.

The future of many young women was not enviable. For a girl of sixteen, marriage to a man in his thirties was not the most attractive prospect, and marriage to a widower in his forties and fifties was even less so. If there were a large number of marriageable young girls in a particular locality, their "market value" was reduced. In the early Middle Ages, it had been the custom for the groom to present a dowry to the bride and her family, but by the late twelfth century the process was reversed. Thereafter, the size of the marriage portions that brides and their families offered to prospective husbands rose higher and higher.

What was a young woman unhappily married to a much older man to do? The literature of courtly love is filled with stories of young bachelors in love with young married women. How hopeless their love was is not known. The cuckolded husband is a stock figure in masterpieces such as *The Romance of Tristan and Isolde*, Chaucer's *The Merchant's Tale*, and Boccaccio's *Fiammetta's Tale.*

Power and Responsibility   The responsibilities of a noble in the central Middle Ages depended on the size and extent of his estates, the number of his dependents, and his position in his territory relative to others of his class and to the king. As a vassal a noble was required to fight for his lord or for the king when called on to do so. By the mid-twelfth century, this service was limited in most parts of western Europe to forty days a year. The noble was obliged to attend his lord's court on important occasions when the lord wanted to put on great displays, such as at Easter, Pentecost, and Christmas. When the lord knighted his eldest son or married off his eldest daughter, he called his vassals to his court. They were expected to attend and to present a contribution known as a "gracious aid."

Until the late thirteenth century, when royal authority intervened, a noble in France or England had great power over the knights and peasants on his estates. He maintained order among them and dispensed justice to them. The quality of justice varied widely: some lords were vicious tyrants who exploited and persecuted their peasants; others were reasonable and evenhanded. In any case, the quality of life on the manor and its productivity were related in no small way to the temperament and decency of the lord—and his lady.

Women played a large and important role in the functioning of the estate (see Listening to the Past). They were responsible for the practical management of the household's "inner economy"— cooking, brewing, spinning, weaving, caring for yard animals. The lifestyle of the medieval warrior nobles required constant travel, both for purposes of war and for the supervision of distant properties. Frequent pregnancies and the reluctance to expose women to hostile conditions kept the lady at home and therefore able to assume supervision of the family's fixed properties. When the lord was away for long periods—on crusade, for instance, the lord could be gone from two to five years, if he returned at all—his wife often became the sole manager of the family properties. Between 1060 and 1080, the lady Hersendis was the sole manager of her family's properties in northern France while her husband was on crusade in the Holy Land.

Women Defending Castle Women shared with men the difficulties and dangers of defending castles. Armed with rocks and bows and arrows, and not hesitating to poke a finger through a chain-mail helmet and into the eye of a knight scaling the walls on a ladder, these noble ladies try to fight off attackers. *(Source: Bibliothèque royale Albert 1er, Brussels)*

Nor were women's activities confined to managing households and estates in their husbands' absence. Medieval warfare was largely a matter of brief skirmishes, and few men were killed in any single encounter. But altogether the number slain ran high, and there were many widows. Aristocratic widows frequently controlled family properties and fortunes and exercised great authority. Although the evidence is scattered and sketchy, there are indications that women performed many of the functions of men. In Spain, France, and Germany they bought, sold, and otherwise transferred property. Gertrude, labeled "Saxony's almighty widow" by the chronicler Ekkehard of Aura, took a leading role in conspiracies against the emperor Henry V.

Those Who Pray

Monasticism represented some of the finest aspirations of medieval civilization. The monasteries were devoted to prayer, and their standards of Christian behavior influenced the entire church. The monasteries produced the educated elite that was continually drawn into the administrative service of kings and great lords. Monks kept alive the remains of classical culture and experimented with new styles of architecture and art. They introduced new techniques of estate management and land reclamation. Although relatively few in number in the central Middle Ages, the monks played a significant role in medieval society.

Toward the end of his *Ecclesiastical History of England and Normandy,* when he was well into his sixties, Orderic Vitalis, a monk of the Norman abbey of Saint Evroul, interrupted his narrative to explain movingly how he happened to become a monk:

And so, O glorious God, you didst inspire my father Odeleric to renounce me utterly and submit me in all things to thy governance. So, weeping, he gave me, a weeping child, into the care of the monk Reginald, and sent me away into exile for love of thee, and never saw me again. And I, a mere boy, did not presume to oppose my father's wishes, but obeyed him in all things, for he promised me for his part that if I became a monk I should taste of the joys of Heaven with the Innocents after my death. . . . And so, a boy of ten, I crossed the English channel and came into Normandy as an exile, unknown to all, knowing no one.[39]

Orderic Vitalis (ca 1075–ca 1140) was one of the leading scholars of his time. As such, he is not a representative figure or even a typical monk. Intellectuals, those who earn their living or spend most of their time working with ideas, are never typical figures of their times. In one respect, however, Orderic was quite representative of the monks of the central Middle Ages: although he had no doubt that God wanted him to be a monk, the decision was actually made by his parents. Orderic was the third son of a knight who held lands in western England. Concern for the provision of his two older sons probably led the knight to give his youngest boy to the monastery.

Medieval monasteries were religious institutions whose organization and structure fulfilled the social needs of the feudal nobility. The monasteries provided noble children with both an honorable and aristocratic life and opportunities for ecclesiastical careers.[40] As medieval society changed economically, and as European society ever so slowly developed middle-class traits, the monasteries almost inevitably drew their manpower, when they were able, from the middle classes. Until that time, they were preserves of the aristocratic nobility.

Through the Middle Ages, social class also defined the kinds of religious life open to women. Kings and nobles usually established convents for their daughters, sisters, aunts, or aging mothers. Entrance was restricted to women of the founder's class. Since a well-born lady could not honorably be apprenticed to a tradesperson or do any kind of manual labor, the sole alternative to life at home was the religious life.

The founder's endowment and support greatly influenced the later social, economic, and political status of the convent. A few convents received large endowments and could accept many women. Amesbury Priory in Wiltshire, England, for example, received handsome endowments from King Henry II and his successors. In 1256 Amesbury supported a prioress and 76 nuns, 7 priests, and 16 lay brothers. The convent raised £100 in annual rents and £40 from the wool clip—very large sums at the time. By 1317 Amesbury had 177 nuns.[41] Most houses of women, however, possessed limited resources and remained small in numbers.

The office of abbess or prioress, the house's superior, customarily went to a nun of considerable social standing. Since an abbess or prioress had responsibility for governing her community and

Synagogue Hildegard of Bingen, the first major German mystic, developed a rich theology on the basis of her visions. Here Synagogue is portrayed as a tall woman commanded by God to prepare humanity for the coming of Christ. In her arms Moses holds up the stone tablets of the Ten Commandments; in her lap are the patriarchs and prophets who foretold the birth of Christ. The headband symbolizes the Virgin Mary: because Mary gave the world the savior, Hildegard makes Synagogue the Mother of the Incarnation. *(Source: Rheinische Bildarchiv)*

for representing it in any business with the outside world, she was a woman of local, sometimes national, power and importance. Although the level of intellectual life in the women's houses varied widely, the career of Hildegard of Bingen suggests the activities of some nuns in the central Middle Ages. The tenth child of a lesser noble family, Hildegard (1098–1179) was given when eight years old as an oblate to an abbey in the Rhineland, where she learned Latin and received a good education. In 1147 Hildegard founded the convent of Rupertsberg near Bingen. There she produced a body of writings including the *Scivias (Know the Ways)*, a record of her mystical visions that incorporates vast theological learning; the *Physica (On the Physical Elements)*, a classification of the natural elements, such as plants, animals, metals, and the movements of the heavenly bodies; a mystery play; and a medical work that led a distinguished twentieth-century historian of science to describe Hildegard as "one of the most original writers of the Latin West in the twelfth century." At the same time, she carried on a vast correspondence with scholars, prelates, and ordinary people and had such a reputation for wisdom that a recent writer has called her "the Dear Abby of the twelfth century to whom everyone came or wrote for advice or comfort."[42] An exceptionally gifted person, Hildegard represents the Benedictine ideal of great learning combined with a devoted monastic life. Like intellectual monks, however, intellectual nuns were not typical of the era.

In medieval Europe the monasteries of men greatly outnumbered those of women. The pattern of life within individual monasteries varied widely from house to house and from region to region. One central activity, however—the work of God— was performed everywhere. Daily life centered around the liturgy.

Seven times a day and once during the night, the monks went to choir to chant the psalms and other prayers prescribed by Saint Benedict. Prayers were offered for peace, rain, good harvests, the civil authorities, the monks' families, and their benefactors. Monastic patrons in turn lavished gifts on the monasteries, which often became very wealthy. Through their prayers the monks performed a valuable service for the rest of society.

Prayer justified the monks' spending a large percentage of their income on splendid objects to enhance the liturgy; monks praised God, they believed, not only in prayer but in everything connected with prayer. They sought to accumulate priestly vestments of the finest silks, velvets, and embroideries, as well as sacred vessels of embossed silver and gold and ornamented and bejeweled Gospel books. Every monastery tried to acquire the relics of its patron saint, which necessitated the production of a beautiful reliquary to house the relics. The liturgy, then, inspired a great deal of art, and the monasteries became the crucibles of art in Western Christendom.

The monks fulfilled their social responsibility by praying. It was generally agreed that they could best carry out this duty if they were not distracted by worldly needs. Thus great and lesser lords gave the monasteries lands that would supply the community with necessities.

The usual method of economic organization was the manor. Many monastic manors were small enough and close enough to the abbey to be supervised directly by the abbot. But if a monastery held and farmed vast estates, the properties were divided into administrative units under the supervision of one of the monks of the house.

The Cistercians, whose constitution insisted that they accept lands far from human habitation, were ideally suited to the agricultural needs and trends

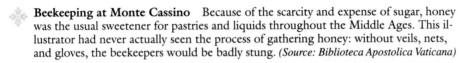

Beekeeping at Monte Cassino   Because of the scarcity and expense of sugar, honey was the usual sweetener for pastries and liquids throughout the Middle Ages. This illustrator had never actually seen the process of gathering honey: without veils, nets, and gloves, the beekeepers would be badly stung. *(Source: Biblioteca Apostolica Vaticana)*

of their times. In the Low Countries they built dikes to hold back the sea, and the reclaimed land was put to the production of cereals. In the eastern parts of Germany they took the lead in draining swamps and cultivating wasteland. As a result of their efforts, the rich, rolling land of French Burgundy was turned into lush vineyards, and the rocky soil and damp downs of northern and central England were turned into sheep runs.

Some monasteries lent their surplus revenues to the local nobility and peasantry. In the twelfth century the abbey of Savigny in Normandy, for example, acted as a banking house, providing loans at interest to many noble families of Normandy and Brittany. Although church law opposed usury—lending at interest—one reliable scholar has recently written that "it was clerics and ecclesiastical institutions (monasteries and nunneries) that constituted the main providers of credit."[43]

Whatever work particular monks did and whatever economic activities individual monasteries were involved in, monks also performed social services and exerted an influence for the good. In addition to running schools and "hospitals," monasteries like Saint Albans, situated north of London on a busy thoroughfare, served as hotels and resting places for travelers. In short, monasteries performed a variety of social services in an age when there was no "state" and no conception of social welfare as a public responsibility.

✤ CRISES OF THE LATER MIDDLE AGES

In the later years of the thirteenth century, Europeans seemed to run out of steam. The crusading movement gradually fizzled out. Few new cathedrals were constructed, and if a cathedral had not been completed by 1300, the chances were high that it never would be. The strong rulers of England and France, building on the foundations of their predecessors, increased their authority and gained the loyalty of all their subjects. The vigor of those kings, however, did not pass to their immediate descendants. Meanwhile, the church, which for two centuries had guided Christian society, began to face grave difficulties. A violent dispute between the papacy and the kings of England and France badly damaged the prestige of the pope.

But religious struggle was only one of the crises that would face European society in the fourteenth century.

A Challenge to Religious Authority

In 1294, King Edward I of England and Philip the Fair of France declared war on each other. To finance this war, both kings laid taxes on the clergy. Kings had been taxing the church for decades. Pope Boniface VIII (r. 1294–1303), arguing from precedent, insisted that kings gain papal consent for taxation of the clergy and forbade churchmen to pay the taxes. But Edward and Philip refused to accept this decree, partly because it hurt royal finances and partly because the papal order threatened royal authority within their countries. Edward immediately denied the clergy the protection of the law, an action that meant its members could be attacked with impunity. Philip halted the shipment of all ecclesiastical revenue to Rome. Boniface had to back down.

Philip the Fair and his ministers continued their attack on all powers in France outside royal authority. Philip arrested a French bishop who was also the papal legate. When Boniface defended the ecclesiastical status and diplomatic immunity of the bishop, Philip replied with the trumped-up charge that the pope was a heretic. The papacy and the French monarchy waged a bitter war of propaganda. Finally, in 1302, in a letter entitled *Unam Sanctam* (because its opening sentence spoke of one holy Catholic church), Boniface insisted that all Christians, including kings, are subject to the pope. Philip's university-trained advisers, with an argument drawn from Roman law, maintained that the king of France was completely sovereign in his kingdom and responsible to God alone. French mercenary troops went to Italy and arrested the aged pope at Anagni. Although Boniface was soon freed, he died shortly afterward.

The Black Death

Economic difficulties originating in the later thirteenth century were fully manifest by the start of the fourteenth. In the first decade, the countries of northern Europe experienced considerable price inflation. The costs of grain, livestock, and dairy products rose sharply. Severe weather, which historical geographers label "the Little Ice Age," made a serious situation frightful. An unusual number of storms brought torrential rains, ruining the wheat, oat, and hay crops on which people and animals depended almost everywhere. Population had steadily increased in the twelfth and thirteenth centuries, and large amounts of land had been put under cultivation. The amount of food yielded, however, did not match the level of population growth. Bad weather had disastrous results. Poor harvests—one in four was likely to be poor—led to scarcity and starvation. Almost all of northern Europe suffered a terrible famine in the years 1315 to 1317. Then in 1318 disease hit cattle and sheep, drastically reducing the herds and flocks. Another bad harvest in 1321 brought famine, starvation, and death. The undernourished population was ripe for the Grim Reaper, who appeared in 1348 in the form of the Black Death.

In October 1347, Genoese ships traveling from the Crimea in southern Russia brought the bubonic plague to Messina, from where it spread across Sicily and up into Italy. By late spring of 1348, southern Germany was attacked. Frightened French authorities chased a galley bearing the disease from the port of Marseilles, but not before plague had infected the city. In June 1348 two ships entered the Bristol Channel and introduced it into England. All Europe felt the scourge of this horrible disease (Map 13.1).

The bacillus that causes the plague, *Pasteurella pestis,* likes to live in the bloodstream of an animal or, ideally, in the stomach of a flea. The flea in turn resides in the hair of a rodent, sometimes a squirrel but preferably the hardy, nimble, and vagabond black rat. In the fourteenth century, the host black rat traveled by ship, where it could feast for months on a cargo of grain or live snugly among bales of cloth. Fleas bearing the bacillus also had no trouble nesting in saddlebags.[44] Comfortable, well fed, and often having greatly multiplied, the black rats ended their ocean voyage and descended on the great cities of Europe.

The plague took two forms—bubonic and pneumonic. The rat was the transmitter of the bubonic form of the disease. The pneumonic form was communicated directly from one person to another.

Although by the fourteenth century urban authorities from London to Paris to Rome had begun to try to achieve a primitive level of sanitation, urban conditions remained ideal for the spread of disease. Narrow streets filled with mud, refuse, and human excrement were as much cesspools as thoroughfares. Dead animals and sore-covered beggars greeted the traveler. Houses whose upper stories

 Saint Dominic and the Inquisition The fifteenth-century court painter to the Spanish rulers Ferdinand and Isabella, Pedro Berruguete (d. 1504) here portrays an event from the life of Saint Dominic. Dominic presides at the trial of Count Raymond of Toulouse, who had supported the Albigensian heretics. Raymond, helmeted and on horseback, repented and was pardoned; his companions, who would not repent, were burned. Smoke from the fire has put one of the judges to sleep, and other officials, impervious to the human tragedy, chat among themselves. *(Source: Museo del Prado, Madrid)*

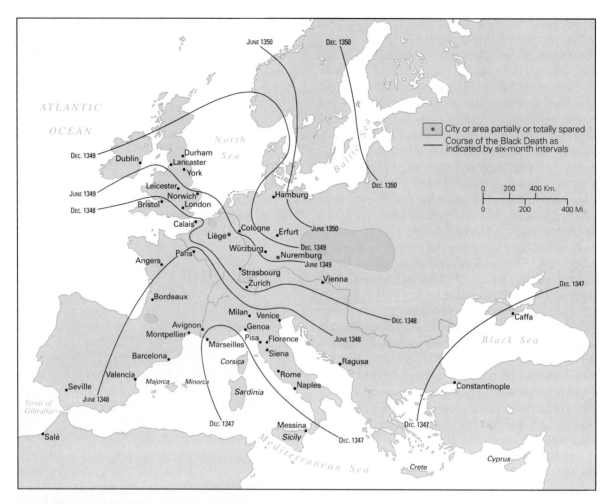

✳ **MAP 13.1 The Course of the Black Death in Fourteenth-Century Europe**
Notice the routes that the bubonic plague took across Europe. How do you account
for the fact that several regions were spared the "dreadful death"?

projected over the lower ones eliminated light
and air. And extreme overcrowding was commonplace. When all members of an aristocratic family
lived and slept in one room, it should not be surprising that six or eight persons in a middle-class
or poor household slept in one bed—if they had
one.

Standards of personal hygiene remained fright-
fully low. Fleas and body lice were universal afflictions: everyone from peasants to archbishops had
them. One more bite did not cause much alarm.
But if that nibble came from a bacillus-bearing flea,
an entire household or area was doomed.

The symptoms of the bubonic plague started
with a growth the size of a nut or an apple in the
armpit, in the groin, or on the neck. This was the
boil, or *buba,* that gave the disease its name and
caused agonizing pain. If the buba was lanced and
the pus thoroughly drained, the victim had a
chance of recovery. The secondary stage was the
appearance of black spots or blotches caused by
bleeding under the skin. Finally, the victim began
to cough violently and spit blood. This stage, indicating the presence of thousands of bacilli in the
bloodstream, signaled the end, and death followed
in two or three days. Rather than evoking compassion for the victim, a French scientist has written,
everything about the bubonic plague provoked
horror and disgust: "All the matter which exuded
from their bodies let off an unbearable stench;

sweat, excrement, spittle, breath, so fetid as to be overpowering; urine turbid, thick, black or red."[45]

Fourteenth-century medical literature indicates that physicians had no rational explanation for the disease, could sometimes ease the pain, but had no cure. Most people—lay, scholarly, and medical—believed that the Black Death was caused by some "vicious property in the air" that carried the disease from place to place. When ignorance was joined to fear and ancient bigotry, savage cruelty sometimes resulted. Many people believed that the Jews had poisoned the wells of Christian communities and thereby infected the drinking water. This charge led to the murder of thousands of Jews across Europe. According to one chronicler, sixteen thousand were killed at the imperial city of Strasbourg alone in 1349. That sixteen thousand is probably a typically medieval numerical exaggeration does not lessen the horror of the massacre.

The Italian writer Giovanni Boccaccio (1313–1375), describing the course of the disease in Florence in the preface to his book of tales, *The Decameron*, pinpointed the cause of the spread:

Moreover, the virulence of the pest was the greater by reason that intercourse was apt to convey it from the sick to the whole, just as fire devours things dry or greasy when they are brought close to it. Nay, the evil went yet further, for not merely by speech or association with the sick was the malady communicated to the healthy with consequent peril of common death, but any that touched the clothes of the sick or aught else that had been touched or used by them, seemed thereby to contract the disease.[46]

The highly infectious nature of the plague, especially in areas of high population density, was recognized by a few sophisticated Arabs. When the disease struck the town of Salé in Morocco, Ibu Abu Madyan shut in his household with sufficient food and water and allowed no one to enter or leave until the plague had passed. Madyan was entirely successful. The rat that carried the disease-bearing flea avoided travel outside the cities. Thus the countryside was relatively safe. City dwellers who could afford to move fled to the country districts.

Because population figures for the period before the arrival of the plague do not exist for most countries and cities, only educated guesses can be made about mortality rates. Of a total English population of perhaps 4.2 million, probably 1.4 million died of the Black Death in its several visits.[47] Densely populated Italian cities endured incredible losses. Florence lost between half and two-thirds of its 1347 population of 85,000 when the plague visited in 1348. The disease recurred intermittently in the 1360s and 1370s and reappeared many times down to 1700. Population losses in Bohemia and Poland seem to have been much less. Historians of medicine have recently postulated that people with blood type O are immune to the bubonic disease; since this blood type predominated in Hungary, that region would have been slightly affected. No estimates of population losses have ever been attempted for Russia and the Balkans.

Economic historians and demographers sharply dispute the impact of the plague on the economy in the late fourteenth century. The traditional view that the plague had a disastrous effect has been greatly modified. The clearest evidence comes from England, where the agrarian economy showed remarkable resilience. Although the severity of the disease varied from region to region, it appears that by about 1375 most landlords enjoyed revenues near those of the pre-plague years. By the early fifteenth century seigneurial prosperity reached a medieval peak. Why? The answer appears to lie in the fact that England and many parts of Europe suffered from overpopulation in the early fourteenth century. Population losses caused by the Black Death "led to increased productivity by restoring a more efficient balance between labour, land, and capital."[48] Population decline meant a sharp increase in per capita wealth. Increased demand for labor meant greater mobility among peasant and working classes. Wages rose, providing better distribution of income. The shortage of labor and steady requests for higher wages put landlords on the defensive. Some places, such as Florence, experienced economic prosperity as a long-term consequence of the plague.

Even more significant than the social effects were the psychological consequences. The knowledge that the disease meant almost certain death provoked the most profound pessimism. Imagine an entire society in the grip of the belief that it was at the mercy of a frightful affliction about which nothing could be done, a disgusting disease from which family and friends would flee, leaving one to die alone and in agony. It is not surprising that

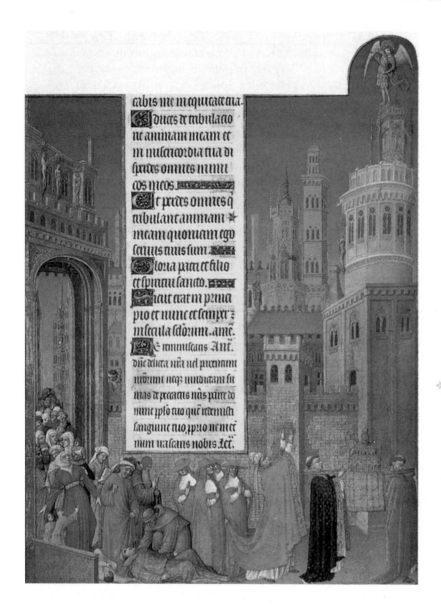

Procession of Saint Gregory According to the *Golden Legend,* a thirteenth-century collection of saints' lives, in 590 when plague ravaged Rome, Pope Gregory I ordered a procession around the city to beg heaven to end the epidemic. As the people circle the walls, a deacon falls victim, and Pope Gregory sees an angel on top of Hadrian's tomb (thereafter called Castel Sant'Angelo), which Gregory interprets to mean the plague is ending. *(Source: Musée Condé, Chantilly/The Bridgeman Art Library, London)*

some sought release in orgies and gross sensuality while others turned to the severest forms of asceticism and frenzied religious fervor. Some extremists joined groups of *flagellants,* men and women who whipped and scourged themselves as penance for their and society's sins, in the belief that the Black Death was God's punishment for humanity's wickedness.

The literature and art of the fourteenth century reveal a terribly morbid concern with death. One highly popular artistic motif, the Dance of Death, depicted a dancing skeleton leading away a living person. No wonder survivors experienced a sort of shell shock and a terrible crisis of faith. Lack of confidence in the leaders of society, lack of hope for the future, defeatism, and malaise wreaked enormous anguish and contributed to the decline of the Middle Ages. A long international war added further misery to the frightful disasters of the plague.

The Hundred Years' War (ca 1337–1453)

Another phase of the centuries-old struggle between the English and French monarchies, the Hundred Years' War was fought intermittently from 1337 to 1453. Its causes were both distant and immediate. The English claimed Aquitaine as an ancient feudal inheritance. In 1329 England's King Edward III (r. 1327–1377) paid homage to Philip VI (r. 1328–1350) for Aquitaine. French policy, however, was strongly expansionist, and in 1337 Philip, determined to exercise full jurisdiction there, confiscated the duchy. This action was the immediate cause of the war. Edward III maintained that the only way he could exercise his rightful sovereignty over Aquitaine was by assuming the title of king of France.[49] As the grandson and eldest surviving male descendant of Philip the Fair, he believed he could rightfully make this claim.

For centuries, economic factors involving the wool trade and the control of Flemish towns had served as justifications for war between France and England. The wool trade between England and Flanders was the cornerstone of both countries' economies; they were closely interdependent. Flanders was a fief of the French crown, and the Flemish aristocracy was highly sympathetic to the monarchy in Paris. But the wealth of Flemish merchants and cloth manufacturers depended on English wool, and Flemish burghers strongly supported the claims of Edward III.

The governments of both England and France manipulated public opinion to support the war. Edward III issued letters to the sheriffs describing in graphic terms the evil deeds of the French and listing royal needs. Kings in both countries instructed the clergy to deliver sermons filled with patriotic sentiment. The royal courts sensationalized the wickedness of the other side and stressed the great fortunes to be made from the war. Philip VI sent agents to warn communities about the dangers of invasion and to stress the French crown's revenue needs to meet the attack.[50]

The Hundred Years' War was popular because it presented unusual opportunities for wealth and advancement. Poor knights and knights who were unemployed were promised regular wages. Criminals who enlisted were granted pardons. The great nobles expected to be rewarded with estates. Royal exhortations to the troops before battles repeatedly stressed that, if victorious, the men might keep whatever they seized. The French chronicler Jean Froissart wrote that, at the time of Edward III's expedition of 1359, men of all ranks flocked to the English king's banner. Some came to acquire honor, but many came in order "to loot and pillage the fair and plenteous land of France."[51]

The period of the Hundred Years' War witnessed the final flowering of the aristocratic code of medieval chivalry. Indeed, the enthusiastic participation of the nobility in both France and England was in response primarily to the opportunity the war provided to display chivalric behavior. War was considered an ennobling experience: there was something elevating, manly, fine, and beautiful about it. Describing the French army before the Battle of Poitiers (1356), a contemporary said:

Then you might see banners and pennons unfurled to the wind, whereon fine gold and azure shone, purple, gules and ermine. Trumpets, horns and clarions—you might hear sounding through the camp; the Dauphin's [title borne by the eldest son of the king of France] great battle made the earth ring.[52]

This romantic and "marvelous" view of war holds little appeal for modern men and women, who are more conscious of the slaughter, brutality, dirt, and blood that war inevitably involves. Also, modern thinkers are usually conscious of the broad mass of people, while the chivalric code applied only to the aristocratic military elite. When English knights fought French ones, they were social equals fighting according to a mutually accepted code of behavior. The infantry troops were looked on as inferior beings. When a peasant force at Longueil destroyed a contingent of English knights, their comrades mourned them because "it was too much that so many good fighters had been killed by mere peasants."[53]

The war was fought almost entirely in France and the Low Countries (Map 13.2). It consisted mainly of a series of random sieges and cavalry raids. During the war's early stages, England was highly successful. At Crécy in northern France in 1346, English longbowmen scored a great victory over French knights and crossbowmen. Although the fire of the longbow was not very accurate, it allowed for rapid reloading, and English archers could send off three arrows to the French crossbowmen's one. The result was a blinding shower of arrows that unhorsed the French knights and caused mass confusion. The firing of cannon— probably the first use of artillery in the West—created further panic. Thereupon the English horsemen charged and butchered the French.

1337
(before the Battle of Crécy)

Held by the kings
of England

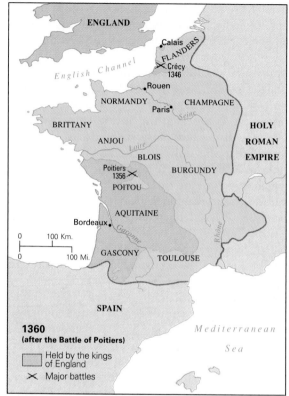

1360
(after the Battle of Poitiers)

Held by the kings
of England

✕ Major battles

ca 1429
(after the siege of Orléans)

Held by the kings
of England

✕ Major battle

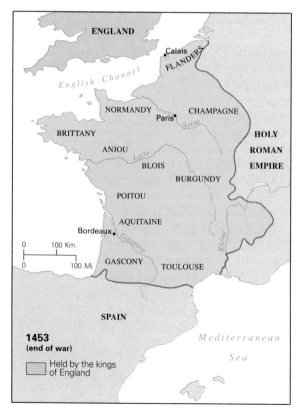

1453
(end of war)

Held by the kings
of England

The Battle of Crécy, 1346 Pitched battles were unusual in the Hundred Years' War. At Crécy, the English scored a spectacular victory. The longbow proved a more effective weapon than the French crossbow, but characteristically the artist concentrated on the aristocratic knights. (*Source: Bibliothèque Nationale, Paris*)

Ten years later, Edward the Black Prince, using the same tactics as at Crécy, smashed the French at Poitiers, captured the French king, and held him for ransom. Again, at Agincourt near Arras in 1415, the chivalric English soldier-king Henry V (r. 1413–1422) gained the field over vastly superior numbers. By 1419 the English had advanced to the walls of Paris. But the French cause was not lost. Though England scored the initial victories, France won the war.

The ultimate French success rests heavily on the actions of an obscure French peasant girl, Joan of Arc, whose vision and work revived French fortunes and led to victory. Born in 1412 to well-to-do peasants in the village of Domrémy in

MAP 13.2 English Holdings in France During the Hundred Years' War The year 1429 marked the greatest extent of English holdings in France. Why was it unlikely that England could have held these territories permanently?

Champagne, Joan of Arc grew up in a religious household. During adolescence she began to hear voices, which she later said belonged to Saint Michael, Saint Catherine, and Saint Margaret. In 1428 these voices spoke to her with great urgency, telling her that the dauphin (the uncrowned King Charles VII) had to be crowned and the English expelled from France. Joan went to the French court, persuaded the king to reject the rumor that he was illegitimate, and secured his support for her relief of the besieged city of Orléans (see Map 13.2).

Joan arrived before Orléans on April 28, 1429. Seventeen years old, she knew little of warfare and believed that if she could keep the French troops from swearing and frequenting brothels, victory would be theirs. On May 8 the English, weakened by disease and lack of supplies, withdrew from Orléans. Ten days later, Charles VII was crowned king at Reims. These two events marked the turning point in the war.

In 1430 England's allies, the Burgundians, captured Joan and sold her to the English. When the English handed her over to the ecclesiastical authorities for trial, the French court did not intervene. The English wanted Joan eliminated for obvious political reasons, but sorcery (witchcraft) was the charge at her trial. Witch persecution was increasing in the fifteenth century, and Joan's wearing of men's clothes appeared not only aberrant but indicative of contact with the Devil. In 1431 the court condemned her as a heretic. Her claim of direct inspiration from God, thereby denying the authority of church officials, constituted heresy. She was burned at the stake in the marketplace at Rouen. A new trial in 1456 rehabilitated her name. In 1920 she was canonized and declared a holy maiden, and today she is revered as the second patron saint of France.

The relief of Orléans stimulated French pride and rallied French resources. As the war dragged on, loss of life mounted, and money appeared to be flowing into a bottomless pit, demands for an end increased in England. The clergy and intellectuals pressed for peace. Parliamentary opposition to additional war grants stiffened. Slowly the French reconquered Normandy and finally ejected the English from Aquitaine. At the war's end in 1453, only the town of Calais remained in English hands (see Map 13.2).

For both France and England, the war proved a disaster. In France the English had slaughtered thousands of soldiers and civilians. In the years after the sweep of the Black Death, this additional killing meant a grave loss of population. The English had laid waste to hundreds of thousands of acres of rich farmland, leaving the rural economy of many parts of France a shambles. The war had disrupted trade and the great fairs, resulting in the drastic reduction of French participation in international commerce. Defeat in battle and heavy taxation contributed to widespread dissatisfaction and aggravated peasant grievances.

The costs of the war were tremendous. England spent over £5 million on the war effort, a huge sum in the fourteenth and fifteenth centuries. Manpower losses had greater social consequences. The knights who ordinarily handled the work of local government as sheriffs, coroners, jurymen, and justices of the peace were abroad, and their absence contributed to the breakdown of order at the local level. The English government attempted to finance the war effort by raising taxes on the wool crop. Because of steadily increasing costs, the Flemish and Italian buyers could not afford English wool. Consequently, raw wool exports slumped drastically between 1350 and 1450.[54]

The long war also had a profound impact on the political and cultural lives of the two countries. Most notably, it stimulated the development of the English Parliament. Between 1250 and 1450, representative assemblies from several classes of society flourished in many European countries. In the English Parliaments, French Estates, German Diets, and Spanish Cortes, deliberative practices developed that laid the foundations for the representative institutions of modern liberal-democratic nations. Representative assemblies declined in most countries after the fifteenth century, but the English Parliament endured. Edward III's constant need for money to pay for the war compelled him to summon not only the great barons and bishops but knights of the shires and burgesses from the towns as well. Between the outbreak of the war in 1337 and the king's death in 1377, parliamentary assemblies met twenty-seven times. Parliament met in thirty-seven of the fifty years of Edward's reign.[55]

In England theoretical consent to taxation and legislation was given in one assembly for the entire country. France had no such single assembly; instead, there were many regional or provincial assemblies. Why did a national representative assembly fail to develop in France? The initiative for convening assemblies rested with the king, who needed revenue almost as much as the English ruler.

No one in France wanted a national assembly. Linguistic, geographic, economic, legal, and political differences were very strong. People tended to think of themselves as Breton, Norman, Burgundian, or whatever, rather than French. Through much of the fourteenth and early fifteenth centuries, weak monarchs lacked the power to call a national assembly. Provincial assemblies, highly jealous of their independence, did not want a national assembly. The costs of sending delegates to it would be high, and the result was likely to be increased taxation. Finally, the Hundred Years' War itself hindered the growth of a representative body of government. Possible violence on dangerous roads discouraged people from travel.

In both countries, however, the war did promote *nationalism*—the feeling of unity and identity that binds together a people who speak the same language, have a common ancestry and customs, and live in the same area. In the fourteenth century, nationalism largely took the form of hostility toward foreigners. Both Philip VI and Edward III drummed up support for the war by portraying the enemy as an alien, evil people. Edward III sought to justify his personal dynastic quarrel by linking it with England's national interests. As the Parliament Roll of 1348 states:

The Knights of the shires and the others of the Commons were told that they should withdraw together and take good counsel as to how, for withstanding the malice of the said enemy and for the salvation of our said lord the King and his Kingdom of England . . . the King could be aided.[56]

After victories, each country experienced a surge of pride in its military strength. Just as English patriotism ran strong after Crécy and Poitiers, so French national confidence rose after Orléans. French national feeling demanded the expulsion of the enemy not merely from Normandy and Aquitaine but from French soil. Perhaps no one expressed this national consciousness better than Joan of Arc, when she exulted that the enemy had been "driven out of *France.*"

Religious Crisis

In times of crisis or disaster, people of all faiths have sought the consolation of religion. In the fourteenth century, however, the official Christian church offered very little solace. In fact, the leaders of the church added to the sorrow and misery of the times.

From 1309 to 1376, the popes lived in the city of Avignon in southeastern France. In order to control the church and its policies, Philip the Fair of France pressured Pope Clement V to settle in Avignon. Critically ill with cancer, Clement lacked the will to resist Philip. This period in church history is often called the Babylonian Captivity (referring to the seventy years the ancient Hebrews were held captive in Mesopotamian Babylon).

The Babylonian Captivity badly damaged papal prestige. The Avignon papacy reformed its financial administration and centralized its government. But the seven popes at Avignon concentrated on bureaucratic matters to the exclusion of spiritual objectives. In 1377 Pope Gregory XI (r. 1370–

1378) brought the papal court back to Rome. Unfortunately, he died shortly after the return. At Gregory's death, Roman citizens demanded an Italian pope who would remain in Rome.

Urban VI (r. 1378–1389), Gregory's successor, had excellent intentions for church reform. He wanted to abolish simony, pluralism (holding several church offices at the same time), absenteeism, clerical extravagance, and ostentation, but he went about the work of reform in a tactless, arrogant, and bullheaded manner. He delivered blistering attacks on cardinals and threatened to excommunicate some of them. When he was advised that such excommunications would not be lawful unless the guilty had been warned three times, he shouted, "I can do anything, if it be my will and judgment."[57] Urban's quick temper and irrational behavior have led scholars to question his sanity. His actions brought disaster.

The cardinals slipped away from Rome, met at Anagni, and declared Urban's election invalid because it had come about under threats from the Roman mob. The cardinals then proceeded to elect Cardinal Robert of Geneva, the cousin of King Charles V of France, as pope. Cardinal Robert took the name Clement VII (r. 1378–1394) and set himself up at Avignon in opposition to the legally elected Urban. So began the Great Schism, which divided Western Christendom until 1417.

The powers of Europe aligned themselves with Urban or Clement along strictly political lines. France recognized the Frenchman, Clement; England, France's historic enemy, recognized Urban. The scandal provoked horror and vigorous cries for reform. The common people—hard-pressed by inflation, wars, and plague—were thoroughly confused about which pope was legitimate. The schism weakened the religious faith of many Christians and gave rise to instability and religious excesses. At a time when ordinary Christians needed the consolation of religion and confidence in religious leaders, church officials were fighting among themselves for power.

The English scholar and theologian John Wyclif (1329–1384) wrote that papal claims of temporal power had no foundation in the Scriptures and that the Scriptures alone should be the standard of Christian belief and practice. He urged the abolition of such practices as the veneration of saints, pilgrimages, pluralism, and absenteeism. Sincere Christians, Wyclif said, should read the Bible for themselves. Wyclif's views had broad social and economic significance. He urged that the church be stripped of its property. His idea that every Christian free of mortal sin possessed lordship was seized on by peasants in England during a revolt in 1381 and used to justify their goals.

Although Wyclif's ideas were vigorously condemned by ecclesiastical authorities, they were widely disseminated by humble clerics and enjoyed great popularity in the early fifteenth century. The teachings of Wyclif's followers, called Lollards, allowed women to preach and to consecrate the Eucharist. Women, some well educated, played a significant role in the movement. After Anne, sister of Wenceslaus, king of Germany and Bohemia, married Richard II of England, members of Queen Anne's household carried Lollard principles back to Bohemia, where they were spread by John Hus, rector of the University of Prague.

In response to continued calls throughout Europe for a council, the two colleges of cardinals—one at Rome, the other at Avignon—summoned a council at Pisa in 1409. A distinguished gathering of prelates and theologians deposed both popes and selected another. Neither the Avignon pope nor the Roman pope would resign, however, and the appalling result was the creation of a threefold schism.

Finally, because of the pressure of the German emperor Sigismund, a great council met at the imperial city of Constance (1414–1418). It had three objectives: to end the schism, to reform the church "in head and members" (from top to bottom), and to wipe out heresy. The council condemned the Lollard ideas of John Hus, and he was burned at the stake. The council eventually deposed the three schismatic popes and elected a new leader, the Roman cardinal Colonna, who took the name Martin V (1417–1431).

Martin proceeded to dissolve the council. Nothing was done about reform. The schism was over, and though councils subsequently met at Basel and at Ferrara-Florence, in 1450 the papacy held a jubilee, celebrating its triumph over the conciliar movement. In the later fifteenth century, the papacy concentrated on Italian problems to the exclusion of universal Christian interests. The schism and the conciliar movement, however, had exposed the crying need for ecclesiastical reform, thus laying the foundations for the great reform efforts of the sixteenth century.

 ## MARRIAGE AND THE PARISH IN THE LATER MIDDLE AGES

Marriage and the local parish church continued to be the center of the lives of most people. Scholars long believed that because peasants were illiterate and left very few statements about their marriages, generalizations could not be made about them. Recent research in English manorial, ecclesiastical, and coroners' records, however, has uncovered fascinating material. Evidence abounds of teenage flirtations, and many young people had sexual contacts—some leading to conception. Premarital pregnancy may have been deliberate: because children were economically important, the couple wanted to be sure of fertility before entering marriage.

"Whether rich or poor, male or female, the most important rite de passage for peasant youth was marriage."[58] Did they select their own spouses or accept their parents' choices? Church law stressed that for a marriage to be valid both partners had to freely consent to it. Nevertheless, the evidence overwhelmingly shows, above all where land or other property accompanied the union, that parents took the lead in arranging their children's marriages. Parents might have to depend on a son- or daughter-in-law for care in old age. Marriage determined the life partner, the economic circumstances in which the couple would live, and the son-in-law who might take on the family land. Most marriages were between men and women of the same village; where the name and residence of a husband are known, perhaps 41 percent were outsiders. Once the prospective bride or groom had been decided on, parents paid the lord's fee. To allow for objections to the union, parents saw that the parish priest published on three successive Sundays the banns—public announcements that the couple planned to marry. And parents made the financial settlement. The couple then proceeded to the church door. There they made the vows, rings were blessed and exchanged, and the ceremony concluded with some kind of festivity.[59]

The general pattern in late medieval Europe was marriage between men in their middle or late twenties and women under twenty.[60] Poor peasants and wage laborers, both men and women, did not marry until their mid or late twenties. In the later Middle Ages, as earlier—indeed, until the late nineteenth century—economic factors rather than romantic love or physical attraction determined whom and when a person married. The young agricultural laborer on the manor had to wait until he had sufficient land. Thus most men had to wait until their fathers died or yielded the holding. The late age of marriage affected the number of children a couple had. The journeyman craftsman in the urban guild faced the same material difficulties. Prudent young men selected (or their parents selected for them) girls who would bring the most land or money to the union.

With marriage for men postponed, was there any socially accepted sexual outlet? Municipal authorities in many European towns set up legal houses of prostitution or red-light districts either outside the city walls or away from respectable neighborhoods. For example, authorities in Montpellier set aside Hot Street for prostitution, required public women to live there, and forbade anyone to molest them. Prostitution thus passed from being a private concern to a social matter requiring public supervision.[61] Publicly owned brothels were more easily policed and supervised than privately run ones.

Prostitution was an urban phenomenon because only populous towns had large numbers of unmarried young men, communities of transient merchants, and a culture accustomed to a cash exchange. Although the risk of disease limited the number of years a woman could practice this profession, many women prospered. Some acquired sizable incomes. In 1361 Françoise of Florence, a prostitute working in a brothel in Marseilles, made a will in which she made legacies to various charities and left a large sum as a dowry for a poor girl to marry. Legalized prostitution suggests that public officials believed the prostitute could make a positive contribution to the society; it does not mean the prostitute was respected. Rather, she was scorned and distrusted. Legalized brothels also reflect a greater tolerance for male than for female sexuality.[62]

Once a couple married, the union ended only with the death of one partner. Deep emotional bonds knit members of medieval families. Most parents delighted in their children, and the church encouraged a cult of paternal care. Divorce did not exist. The church held that a marriage validly entered into, with mutual oral consent or promise of two parties, could not be dissolved. Annulments were granted in extraordinary circumstances, such

Shepherds Dancing   As in all ages, young people (and some not so young) enjoyed dancing, and the marriage or baptismal feast or harvest celebration provided an opportunity, perhaps accompanied by singing or the music of someone talented on the harmonica or as seen here (lower right) on a bagpipe. (*Source: Bibliothèque Nationale, Paris*)

as male impotence, on the grounds that a lawful marriage had never existed.[63]

Theologians of the day urged that the couple's union be celebrated and witnessed in a church ceremony and blessed by a priest. A great number of couples, however, treated marriage as a private act. They made the promise and spoke the words of marriage to each other without witnesses and then proceeded to enjoy the sexual pleasures of marriage. This practice led to a great number of disputes, because one or the other of the two parties could later deny having made a marriage agreement. The records of the ecclesiastical courts reveal evidence of marriages contracted in a garden, in a blacksmith's shop, at a tavern, and, predictably, in a bed.

Marriage and collective work on the land remained the focus of life for the European peasantry in the thirteenth century. Craft guilds, however, provided the small minority of men and women living in towns and cities with the psychological satisfaction of involvement in the manufacture of a superior product. The guild member also had economic security. The guilds looked after the sick, the poor, the widowed, and the orphaned. Masters and employees worked side by side.

In the fourteenth century, those ideal conditions began to change. The fundamental objective of the craft guild was to maintain a monopoly on its product, and to do so recruitment and promotion were carefully restricted. Some guilds required a high entrance fee for apprentices; others admitted only relatives of members. Restrictions limited the number of apprentices and journeymen to match the anticipated openings for masters. Women experienced the same exclusion. A careful study of the records of forty-two craft guilds in Cologne, for example, shows that in the fifteenth century all but six became virtual male preserves.[64] The decreasing number of openings created serious frustrations. Strikes and riots occurred in the Flemish towns, in France, and in England.

The recreation of all classes reflected the fact that late medieval society was organized for war and that violence was common. The aristocracy engaged in tournaments or jousts; archery and wrestling had great popularity among ordinary people. Everyone enjoyed the cruel sports of bullbaiting and bearbaiting. The hangings and mutilations of criminals were exciting and well-attended events, with all the festivity of a university town before a Saturday football game. Chroniclers exulted in describing executions, murders, and massacres. Here a monk gleefully describes the gory execution of William Wallace in 1305:

Wilielmus Waleis, a robber given to sacrilege, arson and homicide . . . was condemned to most cruel but justly deserved death. He was drawn through the streets of London at the tails of horses, until he reached a gallows of unusual height, there he was suspended by a halter; but taken down while yet alive, he was mutilated, his bowels torn out and burned in a fire, his head then cut off, his body divided into four, and his quarters transmitted to four principal parts of Scotland.[65]

Violence was as English as roast beef and plum pudding, as French as bread, cheese, and *potage.*

 ## PEASANT REVOLTS

In the fourteenth century, economic and political difficulties, disease, and war profoundly affected the lives of European peoples. Decades of slaughter and destruction, punctuated by the decimating visits of the Black Death, made a grave economic situation virtually disastrous. In many parts of France and the Low Countries, fields lay in ruin or untilled for lack of labor power. In England, as taxes increased, criticisms of government policy and mismanagement multiplied.

Peasant revolts occurred often in the Middle Ages. Early in the thirteenth century, the French preacher Jacques de Vitry asked rhetorically, "How many serfs have killed their lords or burnt their castles?"[66] And in the fourteenth and fifteenth centuries, social and economic conditions caused a great increase in peasant uprisings.

In 1358, when French taxation for the Hundred Years' War fell heavily on the poor, the frustrations of the French peasantry exploded in a massive uprising called the *Jacquerie,* after a supposedly happy agricultural laborer, Jacques Bonhomme (Good Fellow). Two years earlier, the English had captured the French king John and many nobles and held them for ransom. The peasants resented paying for their lords' release. Recently hit by plague, experiencing famine in some areas, and harassed by fur-collar criminals, peasants erupted in anger and frustration in Picardy, Champagne, and the area around Paris. Crowds swept through the countryside slashing the throats of nobles, burning their castles, raping their wives and daughters, killing or maiming their horses and cattle. Artisans, small merchants, and parish priests joined the peasants. Urban and rural groups committed terrible destruction, and for several weeks the nobles were on the defensive. Then the upper class united to repress the revolt with merciless ferocity. Thousands of the "Jacques," innocent as well as guilty, were cut down.

The Peasants' Revolt in England in 1381, involving perhaps a hundred thousand people, was probably the largest single uprising of the entire Middle Ages. The causes of the rebellion were complex and varied from place to place. In general, though, the thirteenth century had witnessed the steady commutation of labor services for cash rents, and the Black Death had drastically cut the labor supply. As a result, peasants demanded higher wages and fewer manorial obligations. Thirty years earlier the parliamentary Statute of Laborers of 1351 had declared:

Whereas to curb the malice of servants who after the pestilence were idle and unwilling to serve without securing excessive wages, it was recently ordained . . . that such servants, both men and women, shall be bound to serve in return for salaries and wages that were customary . . . five or six years earlier.[67]

This attempt by landlords to freeze wages and social mobility could not be enforced. As a matter of fact, the condition of the English peasantry steadily improved in the course of the fourteenth century. Why then was the outburst in 1381 so serious? It was provoked by a crisis of rising expectations.

The relative prosperity of the laboring classes led to demands that the upper classes were unwilling to grant. Unable to climb higher, the peasants found release for their economic frustrations in revolt. But economic grievances combined with other factors. The south of England, where the revolt broke out, had been subjected to frequent and destructive French raids. The English government did little to protect the south, and villages grew increasingly scared and insecure. Moreover, decades of aristocratic violence, much of it perpetrated against the weak peasantry, had bred hostility and bitterness. In France frustration over the lack of permanent victory increased. In England the social and religious agitation of the popular preacher John Ball fanned the embers of discontent. Sayings such as Ball's famous couplet "When Adam delved and Eve span; Who was then the gentleman?" reflect real revolutionary sentiment.

The straw that broke the camel's back in England was the reimposition of a head tax on all adult males. Beginning with assaults on the tax collectors, the uprising in England followed much the same course as had the Jacquerie in France. Castles and manors were sacked; manorial records were destroyed. Many nobles, including the archbishop of Canterbury, who had ordered the collection of the tax, were murdered. Urban discontent merged with rural violence. Apprentices and journeymen, frustrated because the highest positions in the guilds were closed to them, rioted.

The boy-king Richard II (r. 1377–1399) met the leaders of the revolt, agreed to charters ensuring peasants' freedom, tricked them with false promises, and then proceeded to crush the uprising with terrible ferocity. Although the nobility tried to restore ancient duties of serfdom, virtually a century of freedom had elapsed, and the

John Ball   Outdoors after Mass the priest from Kent preached his radical egalitarianism: "matters goeth not well . . . in England nor shall (they) till everything be common and . . . there be no villains (serfs) nor gentlemen . . . What have we deserved, or why should we be kept thus in servage (servitude)?" All contemporary writers blamed Ball for fomenting the rebellion of 1381. But the evidence shows that peasant demands were limited and local: hunting rights in the woods, freedom from miscellaneous payments, exemption from special work on the lord's bridges or parks. *(Source: Private Collection)*

commutation of manorial services continued. Rural serfdom had disappeared in England by 1550.

Conditions in England and France were not unique. In Florence in 1378, the *ciompi,* the poor propertyless workers, revolted. Serious social trouble occurred in Lübeck, Brunswick, and other German cities. In Spain in 1391, massive uprisings in Seville and Barcelona took the form of vicious attacks on Jewish communities. Rebellions and uprisings everywhere reveal deep peasant and working-class frustration and the general socioeconomic crisis of the time.

❧ VERNACULAR LITERATURE IN THE LATER MIDDLE AGES

Few developments express the emergence of national consciousness more vividly than the emergence of national literatures. Across Europe people spoke the language and dialect of their particular locality and class. In England, for example, the common people spoke regional English dialects, and the upper classes conversed in French. Official documents and works of literature were written in Latin or French. Beginning in the fourteenth century, however, national languages—the vernacular—came into widespread use not only in verbal communication but in literature as well. Two masterpieces of European culture, Dante's *Divine Comedy* (1310–1320), and Chaucer's *Canterbury Tales* (1387–1400), brilliantly manifest this new national pride.

Dante Alighieri (1265–1321) descended from an aristocratic family in Florence, where he held several positions in the city government. Dante called his work a "comedy" because he wrote it in Italian and in a different style from the "tragic" Latin; a later generation added the adjective "divine," referring both to its sacred subject and to Dante's artistry. Each of the *Divine Comedy*'s three parts describes one of the three realms of the next world—Hell, Purgatory, and Paradise. Dante recounts his imaginary journey through these regions toward God. The Roman poet Virgil, representing reason, leads Dante through Hell, where he observes the torments of the damned and denounces the disorders of his own time, especially ecclesiastical ambition and corruption. Passing up into Purgatory, Virgil shows the poet how souls are purified of their disordered inclinations. From Purgatory, Beatrice, a woman Dante once loved and the symbol of divine revelation in the poem, leads Dante to Paradise. In Paradise, home of the angels and saints, Saint Bernard—representing mystic contemplation—leads Dante to the Virgin Mary. Through her intercession he at last attains a vision of God.

The *Divine Comedy* portrays contemporary and historical figures, comments on secular and ecclesiastical affairs, and draws on Scholastic philosophy. Within the framework of a symbolic pilgrimage to the City of God, the *Divine Comedy* embodies the psychological tensions of the age. A profoundly Christian poem, it also contains bitter criticism of some church authorities. In its symmetrical structure and use of figures from the ancient world, such as Virgil, the poem perpetuates the classical tradition. But as the first major work of literature in the Italian vernacular, it is distinctly modern.

Geoffrey Chaucer (1340–1400), the son of a London wine merchant, was an official in the administrations of the English kings Edward III and Richard II and wrote poetry as an avocation. Chaucer's *Canterbury Tales* is a collection of stories in lengthy, rhymed narrative. On a pilgrimage to the shrine of Saint Thomas Becket at Canterbury (see page 378), thirty people of various social backgrounds each tell a tale. The Prologue sets the scene and describes the pilgrims, whose characters are further revealed in the story each one tells. For example, the gentle Christian Knight relates a chivalric romance; the gross Miller tells a vulgar story about a deceived husband; the earthy Wife of Bath, who has buried five husbands, sketches a fable about the selection of a spouse. In depicting the interests and behavior of all types of people, Chaucer presents a rich panorama of English social life in the fourteenth century. Like the *Divine Comedy, Canterbury Tales* reflects the cultural tensions of the times. Ostensibly Christian, many of the pilgrims are also materialistic, sensual, and worldly, suggesting the ambivalence of the broader society's concern for the next world and frank enjoyment of this one.

Perhaps the most versatile and prolific French writer of the later Middle Ages was Christine de Pisan (1363?–1434?). The daughter of a professor of astrology, Christine had acquired a broad knowledge of Greek, Latin, French, and Italian literature. The deaths of her father and husband left her with three small children and her mother to support, and she resolved to earn her living with her pen. In addition to poems and books on love, religion, and morality, Christine produced major historical works and many letters. *The City of Ladies* (1404) lists the great women of history and their contributions to society, and *The Book of Three Virtues* provides prudent and practical advice on household management for women of all social classes and at all stages of life. Christine de Pisan's wisdom and wit are illustrated in her autobiographical *Avison-Christine*. She records that a man told her that an educated woman is unattractive because there are so few, to which she responded that an ignorant man was even less attractive because there are so many.

From the fifth through the thirteenth century, the overwhelming majority of people who could read and write were priests, monks, and nuns. Beginning in the fourteenth century, a variety of evidence attests to the increasing literacy of laypeople. In England, as one scholar has recently shown, the number of schools in the diocese of York quadrupled between 1350 and 1500; information from the Flemish and German towns is similar: children were sent to schools and received the fundamentals of reading, writing, and arithmetic. The penetration of laymen into the higher positions of government administration, long the preserve of clerics, indicates the rising lay literacy.

The spread of literacy represents a response to the needs of an increasingly complex society. Trade, commerce, and expanding government bureaucracies required more and more literate people. Late medieval culture remained an oral culture in which most people received information by word of mouth. But by the mid-fifteenth century, even before the printing press was turning out large quantities of reading materials, the evolution toward a literary culture is already perceptible.[68]

The Wife of Bath The fame of medieval England's greatest poet, Geoffrey Chaucer, rests on *The Canterbury Tales,* consisting of a Prologue and the stories of twenty-four pilgrims on their way to Canterbury. The earthy, vivacious Wife of Bath, having had five husbands "not counting other company in youth," is very blunt about her charms and her power:

> *In wyfhode I wol use myn instrument*
> *As freely as my Maker hath it sent.*

Faithful to Chaucer's description, the artist shows her with wide-brimmed hat, hair in a net, and riding astride, not sidesaddle as ladies were expected to do. *(Source: Reproduced by permission of The Huntington Library, San Marino, California)*

SUMMARY

Universities—institutions of higher learning unique to the West—emerged from cathedral and municipal schools and provided trained officials for the new government bureaucracies. The soaring Gothic cathedrals that medieval towns erected demonstrate civic pride, deep religious faith, and economic vitality.

The performance of agricultural services and the payment of rents preoccupied peasants throughout the Middle Ages. Though peasants led hard lives, the reclamation of waste and forest lands, migra-

tion to frontier territory, or flight to a town offered means of social mobility. The Christian faith, though perhaps not understood at an intellectual level, provided a strong emotional and spiritual solace.

By 1100 the nobility possessed a strong class consciousness. Aristocratic values and attitudes shaded all aspects of medieval culture. Trained for war, nobles often devoted considerable time to fighting, and intergenerational squabbles were common. Yet a noble might shoulder heavy judicial, political, and economic responsibilities, depending on the size of his estates.

The monks and nuns exercised a profound influence on matters of the spirit. In their prayers, monks and nuns battled for the Lord, just as the chivalrous knights clashed on the battlefield. In their chant and rich ceremonial, in their architecture and literary productions, and in the example of many monks' lives, the monasteries inspired Christian peoples to an incalculable degree. As the crucibles of sacred art, the monasteries became the cultural centers of Christian Europe.

Late medieval preachers likened the crises of their times to the Four Horsemen of the Apocalypse in the Book of Revelation, who brought famine, war, disease, and death. The crises of the fourteenth and fifteenth centuries were acids that burned deeply into the fabric of traditional medieval European society. Bad weather—beyond human control—brought poor harvests, which contributed to the international economic depression. Disease, fostered widespread depression and dissatisfaction. Population losses caused by the Black Death and the Hundred Years' War encouraged the working classes to try to profit from the labor shortage by selling their services higher. When peasant frustrations exploded in uprisings, the frightened nobility and upper middle class joined to crush the revolts. But events had heightened social consciousness among the poor.

The increasing number of schools leading to the growth of lay literacy represents a positive achievement of the later Middle Ages. So also does the development of national literatures. The first sign of a literary culture appeared.

Religion held society together. European culture was a Christian culture. But the Great Schism weakened the prestige of the church and people's faith in papal authority. The conciliar movement, by denying the church's universal sovereignty, strengthened the claims of secular governments to jurisdiction over all their peoples. The later Middle Ages witnessed a steady shift of loyalty away from the church and toward the emerging national states.

NOTES

1. Quoted in H. E. Sigerist, *Civilization and Disease* (Chicago: University of Chicago Press, 1943), p. 102.

2. Quoted in J. H. Mundy, *Europe in the High Middle Ages, 1150–1309* (New York: Basic Books, 1973), pp. 474–475.

3. E. Panofsky, trans. and ed., *Abbot Suger on the Abbey Church of St.-Denis and Its Art Treasures* (Princeton, N.J.: Princeton University Press, 1946), p. 101.

4. See J. Gimpel, *The Cathedral Builders* (New York: Grove Press, 1961), pp. 42–49.

5. Quoted in J. J. Wilhelm, ed., *Lyrics of the Middle Ages: An Anthology* (New York: Garland Publishers, 1993), pp. 94–95.

6. R. Boase, *The Origin and Meaning of Courtly Love* (Manchester, Eng.: 1977), pp. 129–130.

7. I have leaned on the very persuasive interpretation of M. R. Menocal, *The Arabic Role in Medieval Literary History* (Philadelphia: University of Pennsylvania Press, 1990), pp. ix–xv and 27–33.

8. G. Duby, *The Chivalrous Society,* trans. C. Postan (Berkeley: University of California Press, 1977), pp. 90–93.

9. B. A. Hanawalt, *The Ties That Bound: Peasant Families in Medieval England* (New York: Oxford University Press, 1986), p. 5.

10. E. Power, "Peasant Life and Rural Conditions," in J. R. Tanner et al., *The Cambridge Medieval History,* vol. 7 (Cambridge: Cambridge University Press, 1958), p. 716.

11. Glanvill, "De Legibus Angliae," bk. 5, chap. 5, in *Social Life in Britain from the Conquest to the Reformation,* ed. G. G. Coulton (London: Cambridge University Press, 1956), pp. 338–339.

12. See R. Bartlett, "Colonial Towns and Colonial Traders," in *The Making of Europe: Conquest, Colonization, and Cultural Change, 950–1350* (Princeton, N.J.: Princeton University Press, 1993), pp. 167–196.

13. See W. C. Jordan, *From Servitude to Freedom: Manumission in the Senonais in the Thirteenth Century* (Philadelphia: University of Pennsylvania Press, 1986), esp. Ch. 3, pp. 37–58.

14. See John L. Langdon, *Horses, Oxen, and Technological Innovation: The Use of Draught Animals in English Farming, 1066–1500* (New York: Cambridge University Press, 1986), esp. pp. 254–270.

15. G. Duby, *The Early Growth of the European Economy: Warriors and Peasants from the Seventh to the Twelfth Century* (Ithaca, N.Y.: Cornell University Press, 1978), pp. 213–219.

16. See Hanawalt, *The Ties That Bound,* pp. 90–100.

17. Ibid., p. 149.

18. On this quantity and medieval measurements, see D. Knowles, "The Measures of Monastic

Beverages," in *The Monastic Order in England* (Cambridge: Cambridge University Press, 1962), p. 717.

19. S. R. Scargill-Bird, ed., *Custumals of Battle Abbey in the Reigns of Edward I and Edward II* (London: Camden Society, 1887), pp. 213–219.

20. G. Duby, ed., *A History of Private Life,* vol. 2, *Revelations of the Middle Ages* (Cambridge, Mass.: Harvard University Press, 1988), p. 585.

21. Quoted in E. Amt, ed., *Women's Lives in the Middle Ages: A Sourcebook* (New York: Routledge, 1992), pp. 103–104.

22. See C. Klapisch-Zuber, ed., *A History of Women,* vol. 2, *Silences of the Middle Ages* (Cambridge, Mass.: Harvard University Press, 1992), p. 289 et seq.

23. See R. Blumenfeld-Kosinski, *Not of Woman Born: Representations of Caesarian Birth in Medieval and Renaissance Culture* (Ithaca, N.Y.: Cornell University Press, 1990), p. 27.

24. Ibid.

25. Ibid., p. 47.

26. E. J. Kealey, *Medieval Medicus: A Social History of Anglo-Norman Medicine* (Baltimore: Johns Hopkins University Press, 1981), p. 102.

27. Klapisch-Zuber, *Silences of the Middle Ages,* p. 299.

28. See A. Gurevich, *Medieval Popular Culture: Problems of Belief and Perception,* trans. J. M. Bak and P. A. Hollingsworth (New York: Cambridge University Press, 1990), Ch. 2, pp. 39–77, esp. p. 76.

29. Ibid.

30. See M. Rubin, *Corpus Christi: The Eucharist in Late Medieval Culture* (New York: Cambridge University Press, 1992), p. 13 et seq.

31. A. Vauchez, *The Laity in the Middle Ages: Religious Beliefs and Devotional Practices,* ed. D. E. Bornstein, trans. M. J. Schneider (Notre Dame, Ind.: University of Notre Dame Press, 1993), pp. 99–102.

32. Duby, *The Chivalrous Society,* p. 98.

33. J. B. Freed, "The Origins of the European Nobility: The Problem of the Ministerials," *Viator* 7 (1976): 214.

34. J. Boswell, *The Kindness of Strangers: The Abandonment of Children in Western Europe from Late Antiquity to the Renaissance* (New York: Pantheon Books, 1989), p. 24. This section relies heavily on this important work.

35. Ibid., pp. 428–429.

36. Ibid., pp. 238–239.

37. Ibid., pp. 297, 299, and the Conclusion.

38. J. F. Benton, ed. and trans., *Self and Society in Medieval France: The Memoirs of Abbot Guibert of Nogent* (New York: Harper & Row, 1970), p. 46.

39. M. Chibnall, ed. and trans., *The Ecclesiastical History of Orderic Vitalis* (Oxford: Oxford University Press, 1972), 2.xiii.

40. R. W. Southern, *Western Society and the Church in the Middle Ages* (Baltimore: Penguin Books, 1970), pp. 224–230, esp. p. 228.

41. See M. W. Labarge, *A Small Sound of the Trumpet: Women in Medieval Life* (Boston: Beacon Press, 1986), pp. 104–105.

42. J. M. Ferrante, "The Education of Women in the Middle Ages in Theory, Fact, and Fantasy," in *Beyond Their Sex: Learned Women of the European Past,* ed. P. H. Labalme (New York: New York University Press, 1980), pp. 22–24.

43. W. C. Jordan, *Women and Credit in Pre-Industrial and Developing Societies* (Philadelphia: University of Pennsylvania Press, 1993), p. 61.

44. W. H. McNeill, *Plagues and Peoples* (New York: Doubleday, 1976), pp. 151–168.

45. Quoted in P. Ziegler, *The Black Death* (Harmondsworth, Eng.: Pelican Books, 1969), p. 20.

46. J. M. Rigg, trans., *The Decameron of Giovanni Boccaccio* (London: J. M. Dent & Sons, 1903), p. 6.

47. Ziegler, *The Black Death,* pp. 232–239.

48. J. Hatcher, *Plague, Population and the English Economy, 1348–1530* (London: Macmillan Education, 1986), p. 33.

49. See G. P. Cuttino, "Historical Revision: The Causes of the Hundred Years' War," *Speculum* 31 (July 1956): 463–472.

50. J. Barnie, *War in Medieval English Society: Social Values and the Hundred Years' War* (Ithaca, N.Y.: Cornell University Press, 1974), p. 6.

51. Quoted ibid., p. 34.

52. Quoted ibid., p. 73.

53. Ibid., pp. 72–73.

54. M. M. Postan, "The Costs of the Hundred Years' War," *Past and Present* 27 (April 1964): 34–53.

55. See G. O. Sayles, *The King's Parliament of England* (New York: Norton, 1974), app., pp. 137–141.

56. C. Stephenson and G. F. Marcham, eds., *Sources of English Constitutional History,* rev. ed. (New York: Harper & Row, 1972), p. 217.

57. Quoted in J. H. Smith, *The Great Schism 1378: The Disintegration of the Medieval Papacy* (New York: Weybright & Talley, 1970), p. 141.

58. Hanawalt, *The Ties That Bound,* p. 197. This section leans heavily on Hanawalt's important work.

59. Ibid., pp. 194–204.

60. See D. Herlihy, *Medieval Households* (Cam-

bridge, Mass.: Harvard University Press, 1985), pp. 103–111.

61. L. L. Otis, *Prostitution in Medieval Society: The History of an Urban Institution in Languedoc* (Chicago: University of Chicago Press, 1987), p. 2.

62. Ibid., pp. 118–130.

63. See R. H. Helmholz, *Marriage Litigation in Medieval England* (Cambridge: Cambridge University Press, 1974), pp. 28–29 and passim.

64. See M. C. Howell, *Women, Production, and Patriarchy in Late Medieval Cities* (Chicago: University of Chicago Press, 1986), pp. 134–135.

65. A. F. Scott, ed., *Everyone a Witness: The Plantagenet Age* (New York: Thomas Y. Crowell, 1976), p. 263.

66. Quoted in M. Bloch, *French Rural History,* trans. J. Sondeimer (Berkeley: University of California Press, 1966), p. 169.

67. Stephenson and Marcham, *Sources of English Constitutional History,* p. 225.

68. See M. Keen, *English Society in the Later Middle Ages, 1348–1500* (New York: Penguin Books, 1990), pp. 219–239.

SUGGESTED READING

The achievements of the central and later Middle Ages have attracted considerable scholarly attention, and the curious student will have no difficulty finding exciting material. Three general surveys of the period 1050 to 1300 are especially recommended: D. Nicholas, *The Evolution of the Medieval World* (1992), explores the major themes of the age in depth; G. Holmes, ed., *The Oxford History of Medieval Europe* (1992), discusses the creativity of the period in a series of essays; and J. R. Strayer, *Western Europe in the Middle Ages* (1955), is a masterful synthesis.

N. Orme, *Education and Society in Medieval and Renaissance England* (1989), focuses on early education, schools, and literacy in English medieval society. J. Leclercq, *The Love of Learning and the Desire of God* (1974), discusses monastic literary culture. For the development of literacy among laypeople and the formation of a literate mentality, the advanced student should see M. T. Clanchy, *From Memory to Written Record: England, 1066–1307* (1979).

For the new currents of thought in the central Middle Ages, see C. Brooke, *The Twelfth Century Renaissance* (1970), a splendidly illustrated book with copious quotations from the sources; E. Gilson, *Héloïse and Abélard* (1960), which treats the medieval origins of modern humanism against the background of Abélard the teacher; D. W. Robertson, Jr., *Abélard and Héloïse* (1972), which is highly readable, com-

monsensical, and probably the best recent study of Abélard and the love affair he supposedly had; C. H. Haskins, *The Renaissance of the Twelfth Century* (1971), a classic; and C. W. Hollister, ed., *The Twelfth Century Renaissance* (1969), a well-constructed anthology with source materials on many aspects of twelfth-century culture.

On the medieval universities, C. H. Haskins, *The Rise of the Universities* (1959), is a good introduction. H. De Ridder-Symoens, ed., *A History of the University in Europe,* vol. 1, *Universities in the Middle Ages* (1991) offers up-to-date interpretations by leading scholars. H. Rashdall, *The Universities of Europe in the Middle Ages* (1936), is the standard scholarly work. G. Leff, *Paris and Oxford Universities in the Thirteenth and Fourteenth Centuries* (1968), gives a fascinating sketch and includes a useful bibliography.

F. and J. Gies, *Cathedral, Forge, and Waterwheel* (1993), provides an exciting and illustrated survey of medieval technological achievements. The following studies are all valuable for the evolution and development of the Gothic style: P. Frankl, *The Gothic* (1960); O. von Simson, *The Gothic Cathedral* (1973); and J. Bony, *French Gothic Architecture of the 12th and 13th Centuries* (1983). H. Kraus, *Gold Was the Mortar: The Economics of Cathedral Building* (1979), describes how the cathedrals were financed. D. Grivot and G. Zarnecki, *Gislebertus, Sculptor of Autun* (1961), is the finest appreciation of Romanesque architecture written in English. For the actual work of building, see D. Macaulay, *Cathedral: The Story of Its Construction* (1961), which explores the engineering problems involved in cathedral building and places the subject within its social context. For the most important cathedrals in France, architecturally and politically, see A. Temko, *Notre Dame of Paris: The Biography of a Cathedral* (1968); G. Henderson, *Chartres* (1968); and A. Katzenellengoben, *The Sculptural Programs of Chartres Cathedral* (1959), by a distinguished art historian. E. Panofsky, *Abbot Suger on the Abbey Church of St.-Denis and Its Art Treasures* (1946), provides a contemporary background account of the first Gothic building. C. A. Bruzelius, *The Thirteenth-Century Church at St.-Denis* (1985), traces later reconstruction. J. Gimpel, *The Medieval Machine: The Industrial Revolution of the Middle Ages* (1977), an extremely useful book, discusses the mechanical and scientific problems involved in early industrialization and shows how construction affected the medieval environment.

On troubadour poetry, see, in addition to the titles by R. Boase and J. J. Wilhelm cited in Notes, M. Bogin, *The Women Troubadours* (1980).

For the Black Death, see P. Ziegler, *The Black Death* (1969), a fascinating and highly readable study. For the social implications of disease, see W. H. Mc-

Neill, *Plagues and Peoples* (1976); F. F. Cartwright, *Disease and History* (1972); and H. E. Sigerist, *Civilization and Disease* (1970). For the economic effects of the plague, see J. Hatcher, *Plague, Population, and the English Economy, 1348–1550* (1977).

The standard study of the long military conflicts of the fourteenth and fifteenth centuries remains E. Perroy, *The Hundred Years' War* (1959). J. Barnie's *War in Medieval English Society* treats the attitudes of patriots, intellectuals, and the general public. D. Seward, *The Hundred Years' War: The English in France, 1337–1453* (1981), tells an exciting story, and J. Keegan, *The Face of Battle* (1977), Ch. 2, "Agincourt," describes what war meant to the ordinary soldier. B. Tuchman, *A Distant Mirror: The Calamitous Fourteenth Century* (1980), gives a vivid picture of many facets of fourteenth-century life while concentrating on the war. The best treatment of the financial costs of the war is probably M. M. Postan, "The Costs of the Hundred Years' War," cited in the Notes. E. Searle and R. Burghart, "The Defense of England and the Peasants' Revolt," *Viator* 3 (1972), is a fascinating study of the peasants' changing social attitudes. R. Barber, *The Knight and Chivalry* (1982), and M. Keen, *Chivalry* (1984), give fresh interpretations of the cultural importance of chivalry.

For political and social conditions in the fourteenth and fifteenth centuries, see the works by Sayles, Bloch, Hanawalt, and Helmholz cited in the Notes. The following studies are also useful: P. S. Lewis, *Later Medieval France: The Polity* (1968); L. Romier, *A History of France* (1962); A. R. Meyers, *Parliaments and Estates in Europe to 1789* (1975); R. G. Davies and J. H. Denton, eds., *The English Parliament in the Middle Ages* (1981); I. Kershaw, "The Great Famine and Agrarian Crisis in England, 1315–1322," *Past and Present* (May 1973); K. Thomas, "Work and Leisure in Pre-industrial Society," *Past and Present* 29 (December 1964); R. Hilton, *Bond Men Made Free: Medieval Peasant Movements and the English Rising of 1381* (1973), a comparative study; M. Keen, *The Outlaws of Medieval Legend* (1961) and "Robin Hood—Peasant or Gentleman?" *Past and Present* 19 (April 1961): 7–18; and P. Wolff, "The 1391 Pogrom in Spain: Social Crisis or Not?" *Past and Present* 50 (February 1971): 4–18. Students are especially encouraged to consult the brilliant achievement of E. L.

Ladurie, *The Peasants of Languedoc,* trans. J. Day (1976). R. H. Hilton, ed., *Peasants, Knights, and Heretics: Studies in Medieval English Social History* (1976), contains a number of valuable articles primarily on the social implications of agricultural change. J. C. Holt, *Robin Hood* (1982), is a soundly researched and highly readable study of the famous outlaw.

For women's economic status in the late medieval period, see the important study of M. C. Howell, *Women, Production, and Patriarchy in Late Medieval Cities* (1986). B. Hanawalt, *The Ties That Bind,* cited in the Notes, gives a living picture of the family lives of ordinary people in rural communities. D. Nicholas, *The Domestic Life of a Medieval City: Women, Children, and the Family in Fourteenth-Century Ghent* (1985), focuses on an urban society. C. Klapisch-Zuber, ed., *A History of Women,* vol. 2, *Silences of the Middle Ages* (1992), contains useful essays on many aspects of women's lives and status. S. Shahar, *The Fourth Estate: Women in the Middle Ages* (1983), is a provocative work. J. M. Bennett, *Women in the Medieval English Countryside: Gender and Household in Brigstock Before the Plague* (1987), is a fascinating case study. E. Amt, ed., *Women's Lives in Medieval Europe: A Sourcebook* (1993), has fresh primary material on many aspects of the lives of noble, business, and peasant women.

The poetry of Dante and Chaucer may be read in the following editions: D. Sayers, trans., *Dante: The Divine Comedy,* 3 vols. (1963); and N. Coghill, trans., *Chaucer's Canterbury Tales* (1977). The social setting of *Canterbury Tales* is brilliantly evoked in D. W. Robertson, Jr., *Chaucer's London* (1968).

For the religious history of the period, F. Oakley, *The Western Church in the Later Middle Ages* (1979), is an excellent introduction. R. N. Swanson, *Church and Society in Late Medieval England* (1989), provides a good synthesis of English conditions. S. Ozment, *The Age of Reform, 1250–1550* (1980), discusses the Great Schism and the conciliar movement in the intellectual context of the ecclesio-political tradition of the Middle Ages. Students seeking a highly detailed and comprehensive work should consult H. Beck et al., *From the High Middle Ages to the Eve of the Reformation,* trans. A. Biggs, vol. 14 in the History of the Church series, ed. H. Jedin and J. Dolan (1980).

A Medieval Noblewoman

In 1115 Guibert (ca 1064?–1124), descendant of a noble family and abbot of Noyon in Picardy, wrote an autobiography, one of the rare examples in the Middle Ages of this literary genre. Cast in the form of a prayer to God, like Saint Augustine's Confessions, *on which it was modeled, Guibert's autobiography includes a sketch of his mother's life. Guibert deeply loved his mother, was dependent on her, and seems to have concentrated on her virtues. He thus gives us an informed, if perhaps idealized, picture of a twelfth-century French noblewoman.*

First and above all, therefore, I render thanks to Thee for that Thou didst bestow on me a mother fair, yet chaste, modest and most devout. . . .

Almost the whole of Good Friday had my mother passed in excessive pain of travail. . . . Racked, therefore, by pains long-endured, and her tortures increasing as her hour drew near, when she thought I had at last in a natural course come to the birth, instead I was returned within the womb. By this time my father, friends, and kinsfolk were crushed with dismal sorrowing for both of us, for whilst the child was hastening the death of the mother, and she her child's in denying him deliverance, all had reason for compassion. . . . So they ask[ed] counsel in their need and [fled] for help to the altar of the Lady Mary, and to her . . . this vow was made and in the place of an offering this gift laid upon the Gracious Lady's altar: that should a male child come to the birth, he should be given up to the service of God and of herself in the ministry, but if one of the weaker sex, she should be handed over to the corresponding calling. At once was born a weak little being, almost an abortion, and at that timely birth there was rejoicing only for my mother's deliverance, the child being such a miserable object. . . . On

that same day . . . I was put into the cleansing water [baptized, for fear of death]. . . .

Once I had been beaten in school—the school being no other than the dining-hall in our house, for he had given up the charge of others to take me alone, my mother having wisely required him to do this for a higher emolument and a better position. When, therefore, at a certain hour in the evening, my studies, such as they were, had come to an end, I went to my mother's knees after a more severe beating than I had deserved. And when she, as she was wont, began to ask me repeatedly whether I had been whipped that day, I, not to appear a tell-tale, entirely denied it. Then she, whether I liked it or not, threw off the inner garments which they call a vest or shirt, and saw my little arms blackened and the skin of my back everywhere puffed up with the cuts from the twigs. And being grieved to the heart by the very savage punishment inflicted on my tender body, troubled, agitated and weeping with sorrow, she said: "You shall never become a clerk, nor any more suffer so much to get learning." At that I, looking at her with what reproach I could, replied: "If I had to die on the spot, I would not give up learning my book and becoming a clerk." Now she had promised that if I wished to become a knight, when [I] reached the age for it, she would give me the arms and equipment.

She, when hardly of marriageable age, was given to my father, a mere youth, by provision of my grandfather. . . . Now it so happened that at the very beginning of that lawful union conjugal intercourse was made ineffective through the bewitchments of certain persons. For it was said that their marriage drew upon them the envy of a step-mother, who, having nieces of great beauty and nobility, was plotting to entangle one of them with my father.

Meeting with no success in her designs, she is said to have used magical arts to prevent entirely the consummation of the marriage. His wife's virginity thus remaining intact for three years, during which he endured his great misfortune in silence, at last, driven to it by his kinsfolk, my father was the first to reveal the facts. Imagine how my kinsmen tried hard in every way to bring about a divorce, and their constant pressure upon my father, young and raw, to become a monk. . . . This, however, was not done for his soul's good, but with the purpose of getting possession of his property. But when their suggestion produced no effect, they began to hound the girl herself, far away as she was from her kinsfolk and harassed by the violence of strangers, into voluntary flight out of sheer exhaustion under their insults, and without waiting for divorce. Meanwhile she endured all this, bearing with calmness the abuse that was aimed at her, and, if out of this rose any strife, pretending ignorance of it. Besides certain rich men perceiving that she was not in fact a wife, began to assail the heart of the young girl; but Thou, O lord, the builder of inward chastity, didst inspire her with purity stronger than her nature or her youth. . . .

In plainness of living there was nothing that she could do, for her delicacy and her sumptuous rearing did not admit of a meagre diet. In other matters no one knew what self-denial she practised. With these eyes I have seen and made certain by touch that whereas over all she wore garments of rich material, next to her skin she was covered with the roughest haircloth, which she wore not only in the daytime, but, what was a great hardship for a delicate body, she even slept in it at night.

The night offices she hardly ever missed, being as regular at the services attended by all God's people in holy seasons; in such fashion that scarcely ever in her house was there rest from the singing of God's praises by her chaplains. . . . A few years before her death she conceived a strong desire to take the sacred veil. When I tried to dissuade her, putting forward as authority the passage where it is written, "Let no prelate attempt to veil widows," saying that her most chaste life would be sufficient without the external veil . . . yet so

Medieval noblewoman at work, from a fifteenth-century manuscript. *(Source: The British Library)*

much more was she inflamed and by no reasoning could be driven from her resolve. So she prevailed, and when taking the veil in the presence of John, the Abbot of that place, gave satisfactory reasons for this act, and in the end she proved that . . . her consecration was invited by signs from heaven.

Questions for Analysis

1. What values shaped Guibert's representation of his mother?

2. How did her marriage come about, and how would you describe her married life?

3. What is the value of this picture of a noblewoman for a present-day historian?

Source: C. C. Swinton Bland, trans., *The Autobiography of Guibert of Nogentsous-Coucy* (New York, 1925); and E. Amt, ed., *Women's Lives in Medieval Europe* (New York: Routledge, 1993), pp. 142–149.

14

The Americas Before European Intrusion, ca 400–1500

This plate from the *Codex Mendoza* dipicts the Aztec legend of the founding of Mexico-Tenochtitlan on the spot where an eagle— an incarnation of Huitzilopochtli— perched on a cactus. *(Source: The Bodleian Library, Oxford)*

Between approximately A.D. 300 and 1500, sophisticated civilizations developed in the Western Hemisphere. But unlike most other societies in the world, which felt the influences of other cultures—sub-Saharan Africa, for example, experienced the impact of Muslims, Asians, and Europeans—Amerian societies grew in almost total isolation from other peoples. Then, in 1501–1502, the Florentine explorer Amerigo Vespucci (1451–1512) sailed down the eastern coast of South America to Brazil. Convinced that he had found a new world, Vespucci published an account of his voyage. Shortly thereafter the German geographer Martin Waldseemüller proposed that this new world be called "America" to preserve Vespucci's memory. Initially applied only to South America, by the end of the sixteenth century the term *America* was used for both continents in the Western Hemisphere.

To the peoples of the Americas, the notion of discovery meant nothing. They did not write about it, and most of the information we have about the Americas derives from European sources. Thus the "new world" was in a very real sense a European invention. Even for Europeans the concept of discovery presented problems. In matters of geography, as in other branches of knowledge, medieval Europeans believed that all human knowledge was contained in the Scriptures, the writings of the church fathers, and the Greek and Roman authors, none of whom mentioned a new world. The adventurous explorers of the fifteenth and sixteenth centuries sailed west searching for Asia and Africa because Europeans believed that those continents and Europe composed the only world that existed. They did not expect to find new continents. Long before the arrival of Europeans, however, sophisticated civilizations were flourishing in Central and South America.

- What is the geography of the Americas, and how did it shape the lives of the peoples?

- What patterns of social and political organization did Amerindian peoples display before the European intrusion?

- What are the significant cultural achievements of the Maya, the Aztecs, and the Incas?

This chapter considers these questions.

THE GEOGRAPHY AND PEOPLES OF THE AMERICAS

The distance from the Bering Strait, which separates Asia from North America, to the southern tip of South America is about eleven thousand miles. A mountain range extends all the way from Alaska to the tip of South America, crossing Central America from northwest to southeast and making for rugged country along virtually the entire western coast of both continents.

Scholars use the term *Mesoamerica* to designate the area of present-day Mexico and Central America. Mexico is dominated by high plateaus bounded by coastal plains. Geographers have labeled the plateau regions "cold lands," the valleys between the plateaus "temperate lands," and the Gulf and Pacific coastal regions "hot lands." The Caribbean coast of Central America—modern Belize, Guatemala, Honduras, Nicaragua, El Salvador, Costa Rica, and Panama—is characterized by thick jungle lowlands, heavy rainfall, and torrid heat; it is an area generally unhealthy for humans. Central America's western uplands, with their more temperate climate and good agricultural land, support the densest population in the region.

Like Africa, South America is a continent of extremely varied terrain (see Map 14.3). The entire western coast is edged by the Andes, the highest mountain range in the Western Hemisphere. On the east coast another mountain range—the Brazilian Highlands—accounts for one-fourth of the area of modern-day Brazil. Three-fourths of South America—almost the entire interior of the continent—is lowland plains. The Amazon River, at 4,000 miles the second longest river in the world, bisects the north-central part of the continent, draining 2.7 million square miles of land. Tropical lowland rain forests with dense growth and annual rainfall in excess of 80 inches extend from the Amazon and Orinoco river basins northward all the way to southern Mexico.

Most scholars believe that people began crossing the Bering Strait from Russian Siberia between fifty thousand and twenty thousand years ago, when the strait was narrower than it is today. Skeletal finds indicate that these immigrants belonged to several ethnic groups now known collectively as American Indians, or Amerindians. Amerindians were nomadic and technologically

✤ **Colossal Head Monument from San Lorenzo** Measuring 9 feet, 4 inches in height, and over 10 tons in weight, this basalt head is a superb example of Olmec sculpture intended as architecture. The facial features have led some scholars to suggest African influences, but that hypothesis has not been proven. *(Source: National Tarn/Photo Researchers, Inc.)*

primitive people who lived by hunting small animals, fishing, and gathering wild fruits. As soon as an area had been exploited and a group had grown too large for the land to support, some families broke off from the group and moved on, usually southward. Gradually the newcomers spread throughout the Americas, losing contact with one another.

At the time the Europeans arrived, most of the peoples of North America and the huge Amazon basin were Neolithic hunters and farmers, some migratory and some living in villages. Hunters of big game (bison, elk, boar) armed with heavy stone missiles, traveled in small groups. Sizable groups of people who had learned to cultivate the soil lived a more settled life. Archaeological excavations indicate that corn was grown in Mexico City around 2500 B.C. Before 2300 B.C. the

Amerindians also were raising beans, squash, pumpkins, and, in the area of modern Peru, white potatoes.

Amerindians in central Mexico built *chinampas,* floating gardens. They dredged soil from the bottom of a lake or pond, placed the soil on mats of woven twigs, and then planted crops in the soil. Chinampas were enormously productive, yielding up to three harvests a year. So extensive was this method of agriculture that central Mexico became known as the chinampas region. In Peru, meanwhile, people terraced the slopes of the Andes with stone retaining walls to keep the hillsides from sliding. Both chinampas and terraced slopes required the large labor force that became available with stable settlement.

Agricultural advancement had definitive social and political consequences. Careful cultivation of the land brought a reliable and steady food supply, which contributed to a relatively high fertility rate and in turn to a population boom. Because corn and potatoes require much less labor than does grain, Amerindian civilizations had a large pool of people who were not involved in agriculture and thus were available to construct religious and political buildings and serve in standing armies.[1]

MESOAMERICAN CIVILIZATIONS FROM THE OLMECS TO THE TOLTECS

Several American civilizations arose between roughly 1500 B.C. and A.D. 900: the civilizations of the Olmecs, the Maya, Teotihuacán, and the Toltecs. Archaeological investigations of these civilizations are under way, and more questions than answers about them remain, but scholars generally accept a few basic conclusions about them.

Scholars believe that Olmec civilization is the oldest of the early advanced Amerindian civilizations. Olmec culture, based on agriculture, spread over regions in central Mexico that lie thousands of miles apart. The Olmec practice of building scattered ceremonial centers found its highest cultural expression in the civilization of the Maya. The Maya occupied the area of present-day Yucatán, the highland crescent of eastern Chiapas in Mexico, and much of Guatemala and western Honduras. In the central plateau of Mexico an "empire" centered at Teotihuacán arose. Scholars hotly debate whether the Teotihuacán territory constituted an empire, but they agree that Teotihuacán society was heavily stratified and that it exercised military, religious, and political power over a wide area. The Toltecs, whose culture adopted many features of Teotihuacán and Olmec civilizations, was the last advanced Amerindian civilization before the rise of the Aztecs.

The Olmecs

Population growth in the region of southern Veracruz and Tabasco (see Map 14.2) led to the development of the first distinct Mesoamerican civilization: the Olmec. Scholars estimate that the Olmecs thrived from approximately 1500 B.C. to A.D. 300. All subsequent Mesoamerican cultures derive from their culture. At present-day San Lorenzo, the center of Olmec society, were groups of large stone buildings where the political elite and the priestly hierarchy resided with their retainers. Peasant farmers inhabited the surrounding countryside. From careful study of the surviving architectural structures and their richly carved jade sculptures, scholars have learned that a small hereditary elite governed the mass of workers and that the clustered buildings served as sites for religious ceremonies and as marketplaces for the exchange of agricultural produce and manufactured goods. The Olmecs also possessed a form of writing.

Around 900 B.C. San Lorenzo was destroyed, probably by migrating peoples from the north, and power passed to La Venta in Tabasco. Archaeological excavation at La Venta has uncovered a huge volcano-shaped pyramid. Standing 110 feet high at an inaccessible site on an island in the Tonala River, the so-called Great Pyramid was the center of the Olmec religion. The upward thrust of this monument, like that of the cathedrals of medieval Europe, may have represented the human effort to get closer to the gods. Built of huge stone slabs, the Great Pyramid required, scholars estimated, some 800,000 man-hours of labor. It testifies to the region's bumper harvests, which were able to support a labor force large enough to build such a monument. Around 300 B.C., La Venta fell, and Tres Zapotes, 100 miles to the northwest, became the leading Olmec site.

Olmec ceremonialism, magnificent sculpture, skillful stone work, social organization, and writing were important cultural advances that paved the way for the developments of the Classic period (A.D. 300–900), the golden age of Mesoamerican civilization.

The Maya of Central America

In the Classic period the Maya attained a level of intellectual and artistic achievement equaled by no other Amerindian people and by few peoples anywhere. The Maya developed a sophisticated system of writing, perhaps derived partly from the Olmec. They invented a calendar more accurate than the European Gregorian calendar. And they made advances in mathematics that Europeans did not match for several centuries.

Who were the Maya, and where did they come from? What was the basis of their culture? What is the significance of their intellectual and artistic achievement? The word *Maya* seems to derive from

Zamna, the name of a Maya god. Linguistic evidence leads scholars to believe that the first Maya were a small North American Indian group that emigrated from southern Oregon and northern California to the western highlands of Guatemala. Between the third and second millennia B.C. various groups, including the Cholans and Tzeltalans, broke away from the parent group and moved north and east into the Yucatán peninsula. The Cholan-speaking Maya, who occupied the area during the time of great cultural achievement, apparently created the culture.

Maya culture rested on agriculture. The staple crop in Mesoamerica was maize (corn). In 1972, a geographer and an aerial photographer studying the Campeche region of the Yucatán peninsula (Map 14.1) proved that the Maya practiced intensive agriculture in raised narrow rectangular plots that they built above the low-lying, seasonally flooded land bordering rivers. Because of poor soil caused by heavy tropical rainfall and the fierce sun, farmers may also have relied on *milpa* for growing maize. Using this method, farmers cut down the trees in a patch of forest and set the wood and brush afire. They then used a stick to poke holes through the ash and planted maize seed in the holes. A milpa (the word refers to both the area and the method) produced for only two years, after which it had to lie fallow for between four and seven years. Throughout the Yucatán Peninsula, the method of burning and planting in the fertile ashes, known as *swidden agriculture,* remains the typical farming practice today.

In addition to maize, the Maya grew beans, squash, chili peppers, some root crops, and fruit trees. Turkeys were domesticated, but barkless

Cylindrical Vessel Because the Maya suffered a high death rate from warfare, sacrificial ritual, and natural causes, the subject of death preoccupied them. Many art objects depict death as a journey into Xibalba, the Maya hell, and to rebirth for the Maya in children and grandchildren who replace them. Here three Xibalbans receive a sacrificial head on a drum. The scrawny torso of one has the look of starvation, and the excrement implies a revolting smell. The next figure, with a skeletal head, insect wings, and a distended stomach, suggests a parasitic disease. A common if nauseating scene. *(Source: © Justin Kerr 1985. Courtesy Houston Art Museum)*

dogs that were fattened on corn seem to have been the main source of protein. In the Yucatán, men trapped fish along the shores. The discovery of rich Maya textiles all over Mesoamerica indicates that cotton was widely exported.

The raised-field and milpa systems of intensive agriculture yielded food sufficient to support large population centers. The entire Maya region could have had as many as 14 million inhabitants. At Uxmal, Uaxactún, Copán, Piedras Negras, Tikal, Palenque, and Chichén Itzá (see Map 14.1), archaeologists have uncovered the palaces of nobles, elaborate pyramids where nobles were buried, engraved steles (stone-slab monuments), masonry temples, altars, sophisticated polychrome pottery, and courts for games played with a rubber ball. The largest site, Tikal, may have had 40,000 people. Since these centers lacked industrial activities, scholars avoid calling them cities. Rather they were religious and ceremonial centers.

Public fairs accompanying important religious festivals in population centers seem to have been the major Maya economic institutions. Jade, obsidian, beads of red spiny oyster shell, lengths of cloth, and cacao (chocolate) beans—all in high demand in the Mesoamerican world—served as the medium of exchange. The extensive trade among Maya communities, plus a common language, promoted the union of the peoples of the region and gave them a common sense of identity. Merchants trading beyond Maya regions, such as with the Mije-speaking peoples of the Pacific coast, the post-Olmec people of the Gulf coast, the Zapotecs of the Valley of Oaxaca, and the Teotihuacanos of the central valley of Mexico were considered state ambassadors bearing "gifts" to royal neighbors who reciprocated with their own "gifts." Since this long-distance trade played an important part in international relations, merchants conducting it were high nobles or even members of the royal family.

The Maya were a Stone Age people. Lacking iron tools until a few centuries before the Spanish conquest and beasts of burden until after the conquest, how were goods transported to distant regions? The extensive networks of rivers and swamps were the main arteries of transportation; over them large canoes carved out of hardwood trees carried cargoes of cloth and maize. Wide roads also linked Maya centers; on the roads merchants and lords were borne in litters, goods and produce on human backs. Trade produced considerable wealth that seems to have been concen-

MAP 14.1 The Maya World, a.d. 300–900
Archaeologists have discovered the ruins of dozens of Mayan city-states. Only the largest of them are shown here. Called the "Greeks of the New World," the Maya perfected the only written language in the Western Hemisphere, developed a sophisticated political system and a flourishing trade network, and created elegant art.

trated in a noble class, for the Maya had no distinctly mercantile class. They did have a sharply defined hierarchical society. A hereditary elite owned private land, defended society, carried on commercial activities, exercised political power, and directed religious rituals. The intellectual class also belonged to the ruling nobility. The rest of the people were free workers, serfs, and slaves.

The Maya developed a system of hieroglyphic writing with 850 characters and used it to record chronology, religion, and astronomy in books made of bark paper and deerskin. The recent deciphering of this writing has demonstrated that inscriptions on steles are actually historical documents recording the births, accessions, marriages, wars, and deaths of Maya kings. An understanding of the civilization's dynastic history allows scholars to interpret more accurately Maya pictorial imagery and to detect patterns in Maya art. They are

❋ **Palace Doorway Lintel at Yaxchi-lan, Mexico** Lady Xoc, principal wife of King Shield-Jaguar, who holds a torch over her, pulls a thorn-lined rope through her tongue to sanctify with her blood the birth of a younger wife's child—reflecting the importance of blood sacrifice in Maya culture. The elaborate headdresses and clothes of the royal couple show their royal status. *(Source: © Justin Kerr 1985)*

finding that the imagery explicitly portrays the text in pictorial scenes and on stelar carvings.[2]

In the sixteenth century, Spanish friars taught Maya students to write their language in the Roman script so that the friars could understand Maya culture. Maya deities and sacrificial customs, however, provoked Spanish outrage. To hasten Maya conversion to Christianity, the priests tried to extirpate all native religion by destroying Maya sculpture and books. Only one Maya hieroglyphic book survived: the *Popul Vuh,* or Book of Council, which was written in European script by a young Quiche noble. Scholars call this document the Maya "Bible," meaning that like the Judeo-Christian scriptures the *Popul Vuh* gives the Maya view of the creation of the world, concepts of good and

evil, and the entire nature and purpose of the living experience.

A method of measuring and recording time to arrange and commemorate events in the life of a society and to plan the agricultural and ceremonial year is a basic feature of all advanced societies. From careful observation of the earth's movements around the sun, the Maya invented a calendar of eighteen 20-day months and one 5-day month, for a total of 365 days. Using a system of bars (— = 5) and dots ($\circ$ = 1), the Maya devised a form of mathematics based on the vigesimal (20) rather than the decimal (10) system. They proved themselves masters of abstract knowledge—notably in astronomy, mathematics, calendric development, and the recording of history.

Maya civilization lasted about a thousand years, reaching its peak between approximately A.D. 600 and 900, the period when the Tang Dynasty was flourishing in China, Islam was spreading in the Middle East, and Carolingian rulers were extending their sway in Europe. Between the eighth and tenth centuries, the Maya abandoned their cultural and ceremonial centers, and Maya civilization collapsed. Archaeologists and historians attribute the collapse to some combination of foreign invasions led by peoples attracted to the wealth of the great Maya centers, domestic revolts of subject peoples, disease, overpopulation resulting from crop failures, and the acquisition of so much territory by expansionist kings that rulers could not govern effectively. Just as scholars give no single reason for the decline and fall of the Roman Empire in Europe, so current scholarship holds that many factors were responsible for the fall of Maya civilization. The Maya, however, were not totally vanquished. Having resisted Indian invaders and the encroachments of Spanish American civilization, about 2 million Maya survive today on the Yucatán peninsula.

Teotihuacán and Toltec Civilizations

During the Classic period the Teotihuacán Valley in central Mexico witnessed the flowering of a remarkable civilization built by a new people from regions east and south of the Valley of Mexico. The city of Teotihuacán had a population of over 200,000—larger than any European city at the time. The inhabitants were stratified into distinct social classes. The rich and powerful resided in a special precinct, in houses of palatial splendor. Ordinary working people, tradespeople, artisans, and obsidian craftsmen lived in apartment compounds, or *barrios,* on the edge of the city. The inhabitants of the barrios seem to have been very poor and related by kinship ties and perhaps by shared common ritual interests. Agricultural laborers lived outside the city. Teotihuacán was a great commercial center, the entrepôt for trade and culture for all of Mesoamerica. It was also the ceremonial center of an entire society, a capital filled with artworks, a mecca that attracted thousands of pilgrims a year.

In the center of the city stood the Pyramids of the Sun and the Moon. The Pyramid of the Sun was built of sun-dried bricks and faced with stone. Each of its sides is 700 feet long and 200 feet high.

The smaller Pyramid of the Moon is similar in construction. In lesser temples, natives and outlanders worshiped the rain-god and the feathered serpent later called Quetzalcoatl. These gods were associated with the production of corn, the staple of the people's diet.

Although Teotihuacán dominated Mesoamerican civilization during the Classic period, other centers also flourished. In the isolated valley of Oaxaca at modern-day Monte Albán (see Map 14.2), for example, Zapotecan-speaking peoples established a great religious center whose temples and elaborately decorated tombs testify to the wealth of the nobility. The art—and probably the entire culture—of Monte Albán and other centers derived from Teotihuacán.

As had happened to San Lorenzo and La Venta, Teotihuacán collapsed before invaders. Around A.D. 700 semibarbarian hordes from the southwest burned Teotihuacán; Monte Albán fell shortly afterward. By 900 the golden age of Mesoamerica had ended. There followed an interregnum known as the "Time of Troubles" (ca A.D. 800–1000), characterized by disorder and extreme militarism. Whereas nature gods and their priests seem to have governed the great cities of the earlier period, militant gods and warriors dominated the petty states that now arose. Among these states, the most powerful heir to Teotihuacán was the Toltec confederation, a weak union of strong states. The Toltecs admired the culture of their predecessors and sought to absorb and preserve it. Through intermarriage, they assimilated with the Teotihuacán people. In fact, every new Mesoamerican confederation became the cultural successor of earlier confederations.

Under Toliptzin (ca 980–1000), the Toltecs extended their hegemony over most of central Mexico. Toliptzin established his capital at Tula. Its splendor and power became legendary during his reign. Apparently he took the name "Quetzalcoatl," signifying his position as high priest of the Teotihuacán god worshiped by the Toltecs. According to the "Song of Quetzalcoatl," a long Aztec glorification of Toliptzin,

he was very rich and had everything necessary to eat and drink, and the corn under his reign was in abundance, and the squash very fat, an arm's length around, and the ears of corn were so tall that they were carried with both arms. . . . And more than that the said Quetzalcoatl had all the wealth of the world, gold and silver and green stones jade and other precious things and a great abundance of coca trees in different colors, and the said vassals of the said Quetzalcoatl were very rich and lacked nothing. . . . Nor did they lack corn, nor did they eat the small ears but rather they used them like firewood to heat up their baths.[3]

Later, Aztec legends described a powerful struggle between the Toltecs' original tribal god, Tezcatlipoca, who required human sacrifices, and the newer Toltec-Teotihuacán god Quetzalcoatl, who gave his people bumper corn crops, fostered learning and the arts, and asked only the sacrifice of animals like butterflies and snakes. Tezcatlipoca won

❈ **Tezcatlipoca and Quetzalcoatl** The Aztecs were deeply concerned with the passage of time, and like the Maya they had a solar year of 365 days divided into 18 months of 20 days each. The Aztec *tonalamatl*, or sacred "book of days," included a ritual calendar that portrayed thirteen Lords of the Day and nine Lords of the Night, each of them associated with a particular bird. This early-sixteenth-century illustration of a book of days shows Tezcatlipoca and Quetzalcoatl, who were major Lords of the Day. *(Source: Bibliothèque de l'Assemblée, Paris)*

this battle, and the priest-king Toliptzin-Quetzal-coatl was driven into exile. As he departed, he promised to return and regain his kingdom.

Whatever reality lies behind this legend, it became a cornerstone of Aztec tradition. It also played a profound role in Mexican history: by a remarkable coincidence, Quetzalcoatl promised to return in the year that happened to be 1519, the year in which the Spanish explorer Hernando Cortés landed in Mexico. Belief in the Quetzalcoatl legend helps explain the Aztec emperor Montezuma's indecisiveness about the Spanish adventurers and his ultimate fate (see pages 522–523).

After the departure of Toliptzin-Quetzalcoatl, troubles beset the Toltec state. Drought led to crop failure. Northern barbarian peoples, the Chichimec, attacked the borders in waves. Weak, incompetent rulers could not quell domestic uprisings. When the last Toltec king committed suicide in 1174, the Toltec state collapsed. In 1224 the Chichimec captured Tula.

The last of the Chichimec to arrive in central Mexico were the Aztecs. As before, the vanquished strongly influenced the victors: the Aztecs absorbed the cultural achievements of the Toltecs. The Aztecs—building on Olmec, Maya, Teotihuacán, and Toltec antecedents—created the last unifying civilization in Mexico before the arrival of the Europeans.

✤ AZTEC SOCIETY: RELIGION AND WAR

Although the terms *Aztec* and *Mexica* are used interchangeably here, *Mexica* is actually the more accurate word because it is a pre-Columbian term designating the dominant ethnic people of the island capital of Tenochtitlán-Tlalelolco. Aztec derives from *Aztlan,* the legendary homeland of the Mexica people before their migration into the Valley of Mexico, is *not* a pre-Columbian word, and was popularized by nineteenth-century historians.[4]

The Aztecs who appeared in the Valley of Mexico spoke the same Nahuatl language as the Toltecs but otherwise had nothing in common with them. Poor, unwelcome, looked on as foreign barbarians, the Aztecs had to settle on a few swampy islands in Lake Texcoco. From these unpromising beginnings they rapidly assimilated the culture of the

Toltecs and in 1428 embarked on a policy of territorial expansion. By the time Cortés arrived in 1519, the Aztec confederation encompassed all of central Mexico from the Gulf of Mexico to the Pacific Ocean as far south as Guatemala (Map 14.2). Thirty-eight subordinate provinces paid tribute to the Aztec king.

The growth of a strong mercantile class led to an influx of tropical wares and luxury goods: cotton, feathers, cocoa, skins, turquoise jewelry, and gold. The upper classes enjoyed an elegant and extravagant lifestyle; the court of Emperor Montezuma II (r. 1502–1520) was more magnificent than anything in western Europe. How, in less than two hundred years, had the Mexicans (from the Aztec word *mizquitl,* meaning "desolate land," or from *Mixitli,* the Aztec god of war) grown from an insignificant tribe of wandering nomads to a people of vast power and fabulous wealth?

The Aztecs' pictorial records attribute their success to the power of their war-god Huitzilopochtli and to their own drive and willpower. Will and determination they unquestionably had, but there is another explanation for their success: the Aztec state was geared for war. In the course of the fifteenth century, the primitive tribesmen who had arrived in the Valley of Mexico in 1325 transformed themselves into professional soldiers. Military campaigns continued; warriors were constantly subduing new states and crushing rebellions. A strong standing army was the backbone of the Aztec state, and war became the central feature of Mexica culture.

Warfare was a formal stylized ritual conducted according to rules whose goal was the capture, not the execution, of the enemy. Warriors hurled projectiles into their massed foes, intending to demoralize, not to kill. Then, a crippling blow with his obsidian "sword" to a foe's knees or to one of the muscles in the back of the thigh enabled the Aztec warrior to bring him to the ground. Once subdued, men with ropes tied the captive and took him to the rear of the battlefield.[5]

Religion and Culture

In Mexica society, religion was the dynamic factor that transformed other aspects of the culture: economic security, social mobility, education, and especially war. War was an article of religious faith. The state religion of the Aztecs initially gave them powerful advantages over other groups in central

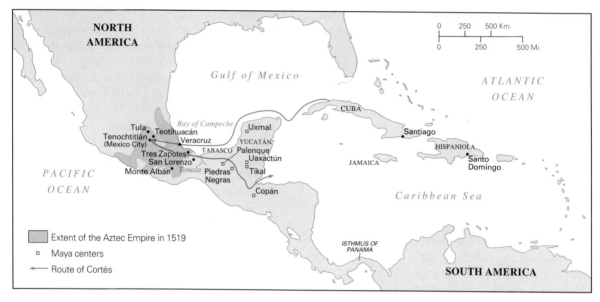

MAP 14.2 The Aztec Empire, 1519 Aztecs controlled much of central Mexico. The Maya survived in the Yucatán Peninsula and some of present-day Guatemala. Notice the number of cities.

Mexico; it inspired them to conquer vast territories in a remarkably short time.[6] But that religion also created economic and political stresses that could not easily be resolved and that ultimately contributed heavily to the society's collapse.

Chief among the Aztecs' many gods was Huitzilopochtli, who symbolized the sun blazing at high noon. The sun, the source of all life, had to be kept moving in its orbit if darkness was not to overtake the world. To keep it moving, Aztecs believed, the sun had to be fed frequently precious fluids—that is, human blood. Human sacrifice was a sacred duty, essential for the preservation and prosperity of humankind. Black-robed priests carried out the ritual:

The victim was stretched out on his back on a slightly convex stone with his arms and legs held by four priests, while a fifth ripped him open with a flint knife and tore out his heart. The sacrifice also often took place in a manner which the Spanish described as gladiatorio: the captive was tied to a huge disk of stone . . . by a rope that left him free to move; he was armed with wooden weapons, and he had to fight several normally-armed Aztec warriors in turn. If, by an extraordinary chance, he did not succumb to their attacks, he was spared; but nearly always the "gladia-

tor" fell, gravely wounded, and a few moments later he died on the stone, with his body opened by the black-robed, long-haired priests.[7]

Mass sacrifice was also practiced:

Mass sacrifices involving hundreds and thousands of victims could be carried out to commemorate special events. The Spanish chroniclers were told, for example, that at the dedication in 1487, of the great pyramid of Tenochtitlán four lines of prisoners of war stretching for two miles each were sacrificed by a team of executioners who worked night and day for four days. Allotting two minutes for sacrifice, the demographer and historian Sherbourne Cook estimated that the number of victims associated with that single event was 14,100. The scale of these rituals could be dismissed as exaggerations were it not for the encounters of Spanish explorers with . . . rows of human skulls in the plazas of the Aztec cities. . . . In the plaza of Xocotlan "there were . . . more than one hundred thousand of them."[8]

The Mexica did not invent human sacrifice; it seems to have been practiced by many Mesoamerican peoples. The Maya, for example, dedicated their temples with the blood of freshly executed victims. Anthropologists have proposed several explanations—none of them completely satisfactory—for the Aztecs' practice of human sacrifice and the cannibalism that often accompanied it. Some suggest that human sacrifice served to regulate population growth. Yet ritual slaughter had been practiced by earlier peoples—the Olmecs, the Maya, the dwellers of Teotihuacán, and the Toltecs—in all likelihood before population density had reached the point of threatening the food supply. Moreover, since almost all the victims were men—warriors captured in battle—population growth could still have exceeded the death rate. Executing women of child-bearing age would have had more effect on population growth.

According to a second hypothesis, the ordinary people were given victims' bodies as a source of protein.[9] These people lived on a diet of corn, beans, squash, tomatoes, and peppers. Wildlife was scarce, and dog meat, chicken, turkey, and fish were virtually restricted to the upper classes. The testimony of modern nutritionists that beans supply ample protein, and the evidence that, in an area teeming with wild game, the Huron Indians of North America ritually executed captives and feasted on their stewed bodies, weaken the validity of this theory.

A third, more plausible, theory holds that ritual human sacrifice was an instrument of state terrorism—that the Aztec rulers crushed dissent with terror. The Aztecs controlled a large confederation of city-states by sacrificing prisoners seized in battle; by taking hostages from among defeated peoples as ransom against future revolt; and by demanding from subject states an annual tribute of people to be sacrificed to Huitzilopochtli. Unsuccessful generals, corrupt judges, and careless public officials, even people who accidentally entered forbidden precincts of the royal palaces, were routinely sacrificed. When the supply of such victims ran out, slaves, plebeians, and even infants torn from their mothers suffered ritual execution. The emperor Montezuma II, who celebrated his coronation with the sacrifice of fifty-one hundred people, could be said to have ruled by holocaust. Trumpets blasted and drums beat all day long announcing the sacrifice of yet another victim. Blood poured down the steps of the pyramids. Death and fear stalked everywhere. Ordinary people appear to have endured this living nightmare by escaping into intoxicating drink and drugs.[10] Even this interpretation, however, does not put the practice of human sacrifice in its full cultural context.

The Mexica state religion required constant warfare for two basic reasons. One was to meet the gods' needs for human sacrifice; and, secondly, warriors for the next phase of imperial expansion. ". . . the sacred campaigns of Huitzilopochtli were synchronized with the political and economic needs of the Mexica nation as a whole."[11] Nobles, warriors, and commoners who secured captives on the battlefield shared in the booty, lands, and the

 The Goddess Tlazolteotl The Aztecs believed that Tlazolteotl (sometimes called "Mother of the Gods"), by eating refuse, consumed the sins of humankind. As the goddess of childbirth, Tlazolteotl was extensively worshiped. Notice the squatting position for childbirth, then common all over the world. *(Source: Dumbarton Oaks Research Library and Collections, Washington, D.C.)*

emperor's rich rewards of gold and silver jewelry, feathered costumes, and other articles of distinctive dress—depending on the number of captives they won. Nobles could grow wealthier, and the ordinary soldier could be promoted to the nobility. Social status, especially in the early period of Aztec expansion, depended on military performance. Warfare, therefore, offered the powerful incentive of upward social mobility. Moreover, defeated peoples had to pay tribute in foodstuffs to support rulers, nobles, warriors, and the imperial bureaucracy. The vanquished supplied laborers for agriculture, the economic basis of Mexica society. Likewise, conquered peoples had to produce workers for the construction and maintenance of the entire Aztec infrastructure—roads, dike systems, aqueducts, causeways, and the royal palaces. Finally, merchants also benefited, for war opened new markets for traders' goods in subject territories.

When the Spaniards under Hernando Cortés (1485–1547) arrived in central Mexico in 1519, the sacred cult of Huitzilopochtli had created a combination of interrelated problems for the emperor Montezuma II. The thirty-eight provinces of the empire, never really assimilated into the Mexica state and usually governed by members of the defeated dynasty, seethed with rebellion. Population increases at the capital Tenochtitlán had forced the emperor to lay increasingly heavier tribute on conquered provinces, which in turn, murdered the tribute collectors. Invasion and reconquest followed. "The provinces were being crushed beneath a cycle of imperial oppression: increases in tribute, revolt, reconquest, retribution, higher tribute, resentment, and repeated revolt."[12] By causing the death in battle and by sacrifice of thousands of food producers, Mexica religion destroyed the very economic basis of the empire.

Faced with grave crisis, Montezuma attempted to solve the problem by freezing social positions. He purged the court of many officials, drastically modified the dress and behavior of the merchant class, and severely limited the honors given to low-born warriors and all but the highest nobility. These reforms provoked great resentment, reduced incentive, and virtually ended social mobility. Scholars have traditionally portrayed Montezuma as weak-willed and indecisive when faced by the Spaniards. But recent research has shown that he was a very determined, even autocratic ruler. Terrible domestic problems whose roots lay in a religious cult requiring appalling human slaughter offer the fundamental explanation for the Mexica collapse.[13]

The Life of the People

A wealth of information has survived about fifteenth- and sixteenth-century Mexico. The Aztecs were deeply interested in their own past, and in their pictographic script they wrote many books recounting their history, geography, and religious practices. They loved making speeches, and every public or social occasion gave rise to lengthy orations, which scribes copied down. The Aztecs also preserved records of their legal disputes, which alone amounted to vast files. The Spanish conquerors subsequently destroyed much of this material. But enough documents remain to construct a picture of the Mexica people at the time of the Spanish intrusion.

No sharp social distinctions existed among the Aztecs during their early migrations. All were equally poor. The head of a family was both provider and warrior, and a sort of tribal democracy prevailed in which all adult males participated in important decision making. By the early sixteenth century, however, Aztec society had changed. A stratified social structure had come into being, and the warrior aristocracy exercised great authority.

Scholars do not yet understand precisely how this change evolved. According to Aztec legend, the Mexicans admired the Toltecs and chose their first king, Acamapichti, from among them. The many children he fathered with Mexica women formed the nucleus of the noble class. At the time of the Spanish intrusion into Mexico, men who had distinguished themselves in war occupied the highest military and social positions in the state. Generals, judges, and governors of provinces were appointed by the emperor from among his servants who had earned reputations as war heroes. These great lords, or *tecuhtli,* dressed luxuriously and lived in palaces. Like feudal lords, the provincial governors exercised full political, judicial, and military authority on the emperor's behalf. In their territories they maintained order, settled disputes, and judged legal cases; oversaw the cultivation of land; and made sure that tribute—in food or gold—was paid. The governors also led troops in wartime. These functions resembled those of feudal lords in western Europe during the Middle

Ages (see pages 413–414). Just as only nobles of France and England could wear fur and carry a sword, just as gold jewelry and elaborate hairstyles for women distinguished royal and noble classes in African kingdoms, so in Mexica societies only the *tecuhtli* could wear jewelry and embroidered cloaks.

Beneath the great nobility of soldiers and imperial officials was the class of warriors. Theoretically every freeman could be a warrior, and parents dedicated their male children to war, burying a male child's umbilical cord with some arrows and a shield on the day of his birth. In actuality the sons of nobles enjoyed advantages deriving from their fathers' position and influence in the state. At the age of six, boys entered a school that trained them for war. Future warriors were taught to fight with a *macana,* a paddle-shaped wooden club edged with bits of obsidian (a volcanic rock similar to granite but as sharp as glass). This weapon could be brutally effective: during the Spanish invasion, Aztec warriors armed with macanas slashed off horses' heads with one blow. Youths were also trained in the use of spears, bows and arrows, and lances fitted with obsidian points. They learned to live on little food and sleep and to accept pain without complaint. At about age eighteen a warrior fought his first campaign. If he captured a prisoner for ritual sacrifice, he acquired the title *iyac,* or warrior. If in later campaigns he succeeded in killing or capturing four of the enemy, he became a *tequiua*—one who shared in the booty and thus was a member of the nobility. Warriors enjoyed a privileged position in Mexica society because they provided the state with the victims necessary for its survival. If a young man failed in several campaigns to capture the required four prisoners, he joined the *maceualtin,* the plebeian or working class.

The maceualtin were the ordinary citizens—the backbone of Aztec society and the vast majority of the population. The word *maceualti* means "worker" and implied boorish speech and vulgar behavior. Members of this class performed all sorts of agricultural, military, and domestic services and carried heavy public burdens not required of noble warriors. Government officials assigned the maceualtin work on the temples, roads, and bridges. Army officers called them up for military duty, but Mexicans considered this an honor and a religious rite, not a burden. Unlike nobles, priests, orphans, and slaves, maceualtin paid taxes. Maceualtin in the capital, however, possessed certain rights: they

✳ **Coronation Stone of Montezuma**   Originally located within the ritual center at Tenochtitlán, this quadrangular stone, carved with hieroglyphics in the Nahual language of the Aztecs, commemorates the start of Montezuma's reign, July 15, 1503, the date of his coronation. The sculpture associates his rule with the cycle of birth, death, and renewal. *(Source: Art Institute of Chicago, Major Acquisitions Centennial Endowment)*

held their plots of land for life, and they received a small share of the tribute paid by the provinces to the emperor.

Beneath the maceualtin were the *thalmaitl,* the landless workers or serfs. Some social historians speculate that this class originated during the "Time of Troubles," a period of migrations and upheavals in which weak and defenseless people placed themselves under the protection of strong warriors. The thalmaitl provided agricultural labor at times of planting and harvesting, paid rents in kind, and were bound to the soil—they could not move off the land. The thalmaitl resembled in many ways the serfs of western Europe, but unlike serfs they performed military service when called on to do so. They enjoyed some rights as citizens and generally were accorded more respect than slaves.

Slaves were the lowest social class. Like Asian, European, and African slaves, most were prisoners captured in war or kidnapped from enemy tribes.

But Aztecs who stole from a temple or private house or plotted against the emperor could also be enslaved, and people in serious debt sometimes voluntarily sold themselves into slavery. Female slaves often became their masters' concubines. Mexican slaves, however, differed fundamentally from European ones: "Tlatlocotin slaves could possess goods, save money, buy land and houses and even slaves for their own service."[14] Slaves could purchase their freedom. If a male slave married a free woman, their offspring were free, and a slave who escaped and managed to enter the emperor's palace was automatically free. Most slaves eventually gained their freedom. Mexican slavery, therefore, had humane qualities, in marked contrast with the slavery that the Spanish later introduced into South America and that the English imposed in North America.

Women of all social classes played important roles in Mexica society, but those roles were restricted entirely to the domestic sphere. As the little hands of the new-born male child were closed around a tiny bow and arrow indicating his warrior destiny, so the infant female's hands were wrapped around miniature weaving instruments and a small broom: weaving was a sacred and exclusively female art; the broom signalled a female's responsibility for the household shrines and for keeping the household swept and free of contamination. Almost all of the Mexica people married, a man at about twenty when he had secured one or two captives, a woman a couple years earlier. As in premodern Asian and European societies, parents selected their children's spouse, using neighborhood women as go-betweens. Save for the few women vowed to the service of the temple, marriage and the household was woman's fate; marriage represented social maturity for both sexes. Pregnancy became the occasion for family and neighborhood feasts, and a successful birth launched celebrations lasting from ten to twenty days. The rich foods available, such as frogs stewed with green chilis or gophers with sauce, as well as the many varieites of tamales, suggest that women had a sophisticated knowledge of food preparation. Women also had the care of small children.

Women took no part in public affairs—with a few notable exceptions. As the bearing of children was both a social duty and a sacred act, midwives enjoyed great respect. The number of midwives at a confinement indicated rank: a noblewoman often had two or three midwives. As in the medieval European West, in a very difficult birth midwives sacrificed the life of the child for that of the mother. Mexica society also awarded high status and authority to female physicians and herbalists. They treated men as well as women, setting broken bones and prescribing herbal remedies for a variety of ailments. The sources, though limited, imply that a few women skilled at market trading achieved economic independence. The woman weaver capable of executing complicated designs also had the community's esteem. Prostitutes in the state brothels, not local Mexica but tribute girls from the provinces given to successful warriors as part of their rewards, probably did not enjoy esteem.[15]

Alongside the secular social classes stood the temple priests. Huitzilopochtli and each of the numerous lesser gods had many priests to oversee the upkeep of the temple, assist at religious ceremonies, and perform ritual sacrifices. The priests also did a brisk business in foretelling the future from signs and omens. Aztecs consulted priests on the selection of wives and husbands, on the future careers of newborn babies, and before leaving on journeys or for war. Temples possessed enormous wealth in gold and silver ceremonial vessels, statues, buildings, and land. Fifteen provincial villages had to provide food for the temple at Texcoco and wood for its eternal fires. The priests who had custody of all this property did not marry and were expected to live moral and upright lives. From the temple revenues and resources, the priests supported schools, aided the poor, and maintained hospitals. The chief priests had the ear of the emperor and often exercised great power and influence.

At the peak of the social pyramid stood the emperor. The various Aztec historians contradict one another about the origin of the imperial dynasty, but modern scholars tend to accept the verdict of one sixteenth-century authority that the "custom has always been preserved among the Mexicans (that) the sons of kings have not ruled by right of inheritance, but by election."[16] A small oligarchy of the chief priests, warriors, and state officials made the selection. If none of the sons proved satisfactory, a brother or nephew of the emperor was chosen, but election was always restricted to the royal family.

The Aztec emperor was expected to be a great warrior. He led Mexican and allied armies into battle. All his other duties pertained to the welfare of his people. It was up to the emperor to see that justice was done—he was the final court of appeal. He also held ultimate responsibility for ensuring an adequate food supply. The emperor Montezuma I (r. 1440–1467) distributed twenty thousand loads of stockpiled grain when a flood hit Tenochtitlán. The records show that the Aztec emperors took their public duties seriously.

The Cities of the Aztecs

When the Spanish entered Tenochtitlán (which they called "Mexico City") in November 1519, they could not believe their eyes. According to Bernal Díaz, one of Cortés's companions,

when we saw all those cities and villages built in the water, and other great towns on dry land, and that straight and level causeway leading to Mexico, we were astounded. These great towns and cues (temples)

and buildings rising from the water, all made of stone, seemed like an enchanted vision. . . . Indeed, some of our soldiers asked whether it was not all a dream.[17]

Tenochtitlán had about 60,000 households. The upper class practiced polygamy and had many children, and many households included servants and slaves. The total population probably numbered around 250,000. At the time, no European city and few Asian ones could boast a population even half that size. The total Aztec Empire has been estimated at around 5 million inhabitants.

Originally built on salt marshes, Tenochtitlán was approached by four great highways that connected it with the mainland. Wide straight streets and canals crisscrossed the city. Boats and canoes plied the canals. Lining the roads and canals stood thousands of rectangular one-story houses of mortar faced with stucco. Although space was limited, many small gardens and parks were alive with the

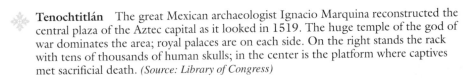

Tenochtitlán   The great Mexican archaeologist Ignacio Marquina reconstructed the central plaza of the Aztec capital as it looked in 1519. The huge temple of the god of war dominates the area; royal palaces are on each side. On the right stands the rack with tens of thousands of human skulls; in the center is the platform where captives met sacrificial death. *(Source: Library of Congress)*

colors and scents of flowers. The Mexicans loved flowers and used them in ritual ceremonies.

A large aqueduct whose sophisticated engineering astounded Cortés carried pure water from distant springs and supplied fountains in the parks. Streets and canals opened onto public squares and marketplaces. Tradespeople offered every kind of merchandise. Butchers hawked turkeys, ducks, chickens, rabbits, and deer; grocers sold kidney beans, squash, avocados, corn, and all kinds of peppers. Artisans sold intricately designed gold, silver, and feathered jewelry. Seamstresses offered sandals, loincloths and cloaks for men, and blouses and long skirts for women—the clothing customarily worn by ordinary people—and embroidered robes and cloaks for the rich. Slaves for domestic service, wood for building, herbs for seasoning and medicine, honey and sweets, knives, jars, smoking tobacco, even human excrement used to cure animal skins—all these wares made a dazzling spectacle.

At one side of the central square of Tenochtitlán stood the great temple of Huitzilopochtli. Built as a pyramid and approached by three flights of 120 steps each, the temple was about 100 feet high and dominated the city's skyline. According to Cortés it was

so large that within the precincts, which are surrounded by a very high wall, a town of some five hundred inhabitants could easily be built. All round inside this wall there are very elegant quarters with very large rooms and corridors where their priests live.[18]

Describing the Aztec way of life for the emperor Charles V, Cortés concluded: "considering that they are barbarous and so far from the knowledge of God and cut off from all civilized nations, it is truly remarkable to see what they have achieved in all things."[19] Certainly Cortés's views reflect his own culture and outlook, but it is undeniable that Mexica culture was remarkable.

❖ **MAP 14.3 The Inca Empire, 1463–1532** South America, which extends 4,750 miles in length and 3,300 miles from east to west at its widest point, contains every climatic zone and probably the richest variety of vegetation on earth. Roads built by the Incas linked most of the Andean region.

❖ THE INCAS OF PERU

In the late 1980s archaeologists working in the river valleys on the west coast of present-day Peru uncovered stunning evidence of complex societies that flourished between 5,000 and 3,000 years ago—roughly the same period as the great pyramids of Egypt. In spite of the altitude and dryness of the semidesert region, scores of settlements existed (Map 14.3). Perhaps the most spectacular was the one at Pampa de las Llamas-Moxeke in the Casma Valley. Stepped pyramids and U-shaped buildings, some more than ten stories high, dominated these settlements. Were these structures warehouses for storing food or cultic temples? Were these settlements connected in some sort of political association? Was there sufficient commercial activity to justify calling them cities? Why did these peoples, who lived on a diet of fish, sweet potatoes, beans, and peanuts, suddenly abandon their settlements and move into the Andean highlands? Scholars have only begun to process these vast remains, but radio carbon dating has already demonstrated that the settlements are older than the Maya and Aztec structures.[20]

Another archaeological discovery is providing scholars with rich information about pre-Columbian society. For some time, the villagers of Sipán in northern Peru supplemented their meager incomes by plundering ancient cemeteries and pyramids. One night in 1987 while digging deep in a pyramid, they broke into one of the richest funerary chambers ever located, and they filled their sacks with ceramic, gold, and silver objects. A dispute about the distribution of the loot led one dissatisfied thief to go to the police. When archaeologists from Lima and the United States arrived, they ranked the discoveries at Sipán with those at Tutankhamen's tomb in Egypt and the terra-cotta statues of the Qin Dynasty warriors near Xian, China.

The treasures from the royal tombs at Sipán derive from the Moche civilization, which flourished along a 250-mile stretch of Peru's northern coast between A.D. 100 and 800. Rivers that flowed out of the Andes Mountains into the valleys allowed the Moche people to develop complex irrigation systems for agricultural development. Each Moche valley contained a large ceremonial center with palaces and pyramids surrounded by settlements of up to 10,000 people. The dazzling gold and silver artifacts, elaborate hairdresses, and ceramic vessels display a remarkable skill in metalwork. Much of later Inca technology seems clearly based on the work of the Moche.[21]

The Aztec civilization of Mexico had already passed its peak when the Spanish landed in America. So too had a greater culture to the south, that of the Incas of Peru. Like the Aztecs, the Incas were "a small militaristic group that came to power late, conquered surrounding groups, and established one of the most extraordinary empires in the world."[22] Gradually, Inca culture spread throughout Peru. Modern knowledge of the Incas is concentrated on the last century before Spanish intrusion (1438–1532); today's scholars know far less about earlier developments.

In the center of Peru rise the cold highlands of the Andes Mountains. Six valleys of fertile and wooded land at altitudes ranging from 8,000 to 11,000 feet punctuate highland Peru. The largest of these valleys are Huaylas, Cuzco, and Titicaca. It was there that Inca civilization developed and flourished.

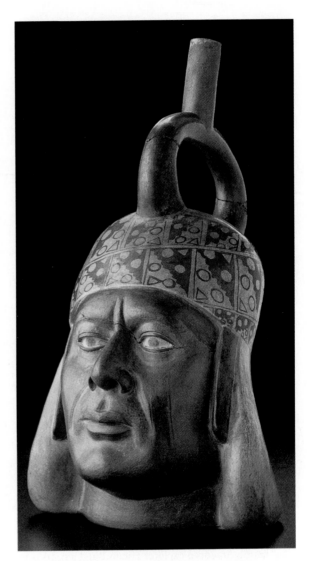

Portrait Vessel of a Ruler   Artisans of the Moche culture on the northern coast of Peru produced objects representing many aspects of their world, including this flat-bottomed stirrup-spout jar with a ruler's face. The commanding expression conveys a strong sense of power, as does the elaborate headdress with the geometric designs of Moche textiles worn only by elite persons. *(Source: Art Institute of Chicago. Kate S. Buckingham Endowment, 1955.2338)*

Archaeologists still do not understand how people of the Andean region acquired a knowledge of agriculture. Around 2500 B.C. they were relying on fish and mussels for food. Early agriculture seems to have involved cultivating cotton for ordinary clothing, ceremonial dress, and fish nets. Beautifully dyed cotton textiles, swatches of which

✳ **Machu Picchu** The citadel of Machu Picchu, surrounded by mountains in the clouds, clings to a spectacular crag in upland Peru. It was discovered in 1911 by the young American explorer Hiram Bingham. Its origin and the reason for its abandonment remain unknown. *(Source: Photo Researchers)*

have been found in ancient gravesites, may also have served as articles for trade. The central highland region of the Andes is much less well suited to agriculture than is Mesoamerica; in the Andes arable land is scarce. Yet between A.D. 600 and 1000, remarkable agricultural progress was made.

The Incas constructed great terraces along the mountain slopes and shored them up with walls to retain moisture. With only a foot plow, bronze hoe, and *guano* (the dried excrement of sea birds) as fertilizer, the Amerindians of Peru produced bumper crops of white potatoes. Potatoes ordinarily cannot be stored for long periods, but the Inca

of the Andean highlands developed a product called *chuñu,* freeze-dried potatoes made by subjecting potatoes alternately to nightly frosts and daily sun. Chuñu will keep unspoiled for several years. The construction of irrigation channels also facilitated the cultivation of corn. Potatoes and corn required far less labor and time than did the cultivation of wheat in Europe or rice in China.

By the fifteenth century, enough corn, beans, chili peppers, squash, tomatoes, sweet potatoes, peanuts, avocados, and white potatoes were harvested to feed not only the farmers themselves but also massive armies and administrative bureaucracies and thousands of industrial workers. Wild animals had become almost extinct in the region and were the exclusive preserve of the nobility. Common people rarely ate any meat other than guinea pigs, which most families raised. Chicha, a beer fermented from corn, was the staple drink.

Inca Imperialism

Who were the Incas? *Inca* was originally the name of the governing family of an Amerindian group that settled in the basin of Cuzco (see Map 14.3). From that family, the name was gradually extended to all people living in the Andes valleys. The Incas themselves used the word to identify their chief or emperor. Here the term is used for both the ruler and the people.

As with the Aztecs, so with the Incas: religious ideology was the force that transformed the culture. Religious concepts created pressure for imperialist expansion—with fatal consequences.

The Incas believed their ruler descended from the sun-god and that the health and prosperity of the state depended on him. Dead rulers were thought to link the people to the sun-god. When the ruler died, his corpse was preserved as a mummy in elaborate clothing and housed in a sacred and magnificent chamber. The mummy was brought in procession to all important state ceremonies, his advice was sought in time of crisis, and hundreds of human beings were sacrificed to him. In ordinary times, the dead ruler was carried to visit his friends, and his heirs and relatives came to dine with him. Some scholars call this behavior the "cult of the royal mummies" because it was a kind of ancestor worship.

The mummies were not only the holiest objects in the Inca world, but also a powerful dynamic force in Inca society. According to the principle of the "split inheritance," when an Inca ruler died, the imperial office, insignia, and rights and duties of the monarchy passed to the new king. The dead ruler, however, retained full and complete ownership of all his estates and properties. His royal descendants as a group managed his lands and sources of income for him and used the revenues to care for his mummy and to maintain his cult. Thus a new ruler came to the throne land- or property-poor. In order to live in the royal style, strengthen his administration, and reward his supporters, he had to win his own possessions by means of war and imperial expansion.[23]

Around A.D. 1000 the Incas were one of many small groups fighting among themselves for land and water. As they began to conquer their neighbors, a body of religious lore came into being that ascribed divine origin to their earliest king, Manco Capac (ca 1200) and promised warriors the gods' favor and protection. Strong historical evidence, however, dates only from the reign of Pachacuti Inca (1438–1471), who launched the imperialist phase of Inca civilization.

If the cult of ancestor or mummy worship satisfied some Inca social needs, in time it also created serious problems. The desire for conquest provided incentives for courageous (or ambitious) nobles: those who were victorious in battle and gained new territories for the state could expect lands, additional wives, servants, herds of llamas, gold, silver, fine clothes, and other symbols of high status. And even common soldiers who distinguished themselves in battle could be rewarded with booty and raised to noble status. The imperial interests of the emperor paralleled those of other social groups. Thus, under Pachacuti Inca and his successors Topa Inca (1471–1493) and Huayna Capac (1493–1525), Inca domination was gradually extended by warfare to the frontier of present-day Ecuador and Colombia in the north and to the Maule River in present-day Chile in the south (see Map 14.3), an area of about 350,000 square miles. Eighty provinces, scores of ethnic groups, and 16 million people came under Inca control. A remarkable system of roads held the empire together.

Before Inca civilization, each group that entered the Andes valleys had its own distinct language. These languages were not written and have become extinct. Scholars will probably never understand the linguistic condition of Peru before the fifteenth century when Pachacuti made Quechua (pronounced "keshwa") the official language of his people and administration. Conquered peoples were forced to adopt the language, and Quechua spread the Inca way of life throughout the Andes. Though not written until the Spanish in Peru adopted it as a second official language, Quechua had replaced local languages by the seventeenth and eighteenth centuries and is still spoken by most Peruvians today.

Whereas the Aztecs controlled their subject peoples through terror, the Incas governed by means of imperial unification. They imposed not only their language but their entire panoply of gods: the sun-god, divine ancestor of the royal family; his wife the moon-god; and the thunder-god, who brought life-giving rain. Magnificent temples scattered throughout the expanding empire housed idols of these gods and the state-appointed priests who attended them. Priests led prayers and elaborate rituals, and, on such occasions as a terrible natural disaster or a great military victory, they sacrificed human beings to the gods. Subject peoples were required to worship the state gods. Imperial unification was also achieved through the forced participation of local chieftains in the central bureaucracy and through a policy of colonization called *mitima*. To prevent rebellion in newly conquered territories, Pachacuti transferred all their inhabitants to other parts of the empire, replacing them with workers who had lived longer under Inca rule and whose independent spirit had been broken.[24] An excellent system of roads—averaging three feet in width, some paved and others not—facilitated the transportation of armies and the rapid communication of royal orders by runners. The roads followed straight lines wherever possible but also crossed pontoon bridges and tunneled through hills. This great feat of Inca engineering bears striking comparison with ancient Roman roads, which also linked an empire.

Rapid Inca expansion, however, produced stresses. Although the pressure for growth remained unabated, in the reign of Topa Inca open lands began to be scarce. Topa Inca had some success in attacks on the eastern slopes of the Andes, but his attempts to penetrate the tropical Amazon forest east of the Andes led to repeated military disasters. The Incas waged wars with highly trained armies drawn up in massed formation and fought pitched battles on level ground, often engaging in hand-to-hand combat, or they launched formal assaults on fortresses. But in dense jungles, the troops could not maneuver or maintain order against enemies using guerrilla tactics and sniping at them with deadly blowguns. Another source of stress was discontent among subject peoples in conquered territories. Many revolted. It took Huayna Capac several years to put down a revolt in Ecuador. Even the system of roads and trained runners eventually caused administrative problems. The average runner could cover about 50 leagues or 175 miles per day—a remarkable feat of physical endurance, especially at high altitude—but the larger the empire became, the greater the distances to be covered. The round trip from the capital at Cuzco to Quito in Ecuador, for example,

took from 10 to 12 days, so that an emperor might have to base urgent decisions on incomplete or out-of-date information. The empire was overextended. "In short, the cult of the royal mummies helped to drive the Inca expansion, but it also linked economic stress, administrative problems, and political instabilities in a cyclical relationship."[25]

In 1525 the Inca Huayna Capac died of plague while campaigning in Ecuador. Between that date and the arrival of the Spanish conquistador Francisco Pizarro in 1532, the Inca throne was bitterly contested by two of Huayna's sons, the half-brothers Huascar and Atauhualpa. Inca law called for a dying emperor to assign the throne to his most competent son by his principal wife, who had to be the ruler's full sister. Huascar, unlike Atauhualpa, was the result of such an incestuous union and thus had a legitimate claim to the throne. Atauhualpa, who had fought with Huayna Capac in his last campaign, tried to convince Huascar that their father had divided the kingdom and had given him (Atauhualpa) the northern part. Huascar bitterly rejected his half-brother's claim.

When Huascar came to the throne, the problems facing the Inca Empire had become critical: the dead rulers controlled too much of Peru's land and resources. Huascar proposed a radical solution:

annoyed one day with these dead (his ancestors), [he] said that he ought to order them all buried and take from them all that they had, and that there should not be dead men but living ones, because (the dead) had all that was best in the country.[26]

Although Atauhualpa had the grave liability of being born of a nonincestuous union, to the great nobility responsible for the cult of the royal mummies, Huascar's proposal represented a far graver threat to the established order: Huascar intended to insult the mummies who linked the Inca people to the gods, and if his proposals were enacted, the anger of the mummies would ensure a disastrous future. (The nobility did not say the obvious—that if Huascar buried the dead and took their vast properties, the nobles would be deprived of wealth and power.) Not surprisingly, the nobles threw their support behind Atauhualpa.

In the civil war that began in 1532, Atauhualpa's veteran warriors easily defeated Huascar's green recruits. On his way to his coronation at Cuzco,

THE AMERICAS, CA 400–1500

ca 20,000 b.c.	Migration across the Bering Strait to the Americas
ca 1500 b.c.–a.d. 300	Rise of Olmec culture
ca a.d. 400–600	Height of Teotihuacán civilization
ca 600–900	Peak of Maya civilization
ca 800–1000	"Time of Troubles" in Mesoamerica
ca 980–1000	Toltec hegemony
ca 1000	Beginning of Inca expansion
ca 1325	Arrival of the Aztecs in the Valley of Mexico
mid-15th century	Height of Aztec culture
1438–1493	Great Age of Inca imperialism
1519	Arrival of the Spanish
1521	Collapse of the Aztecs
1532	Spanish execution of the Inca king and decline of Inca Empire

Atauhualpa encountered Pizzaro and 168 Spaniards who had recently entered the kingdom. The Spaniards quickly became the real victors in the Inca kingdom (see pages 523–524). The cult of the royal mummies had brought, or at least contributed heavily to, Inca collapse.

Inca Society

The fundamental unit of early Inca society was the *ayllu,* or clan, whose members were all those who claimed a common male ancestor. A village typically consisted of several ayllus. Each had its own farmland and woodland, which all members tended. The chief, or *curacas,* of an ayllu, to whom all members owed allegiance, conducted relations with outsiders.

In the fifteenth century, Pachacuti Inca and Topa Inca superimposed imperial institutions on those of kinship. They ordered allegiance to be paid to the ruler at Cuzco rather than to the curacas. They drafted local men for distant wars and relocated the entire populations of certain regions through the mitima system. Entirely new ayllus were formed, based on residence rather than kinship.

The emperors sometimes gave newly acquired lands to victorious generals, distinguished civil servants, and favorite nobles. These lords subsequently exercised authority previously held by the native curacas. Whether long-time residents or new colonists, common people had the status of peasant farmers, which entailed heavy agricultural or other obligations. Just as in medieval Europe peasants worked several days each week on their lord's lands, so the Inca people had to work on state lands (that is, the emperor's lands) or on lands assigned to the temple. Peasants also labored on roads and bridges; terraced and irrigated new arable land; served on construction crews for royal palaces, temples, and public buildings such as fortresses; acted as runners on the post roads; and excavated in the imperial gold, silver, and copper mines. The imperial government annually determined the number of laborers needed for these various undertakings, and each district had to supply an assigned quota. The government also made an ayllu responsible for the state-owned granaries and for the production of cloth for army uniforms.

The state required everyone to marry and even decided when and sometimes whom a person should marry. Men married around the age of twenty, women a little younger. A young man who wanted a certain girl hung around her father's house and shared in the work. The Incas did not especially prize virginity; premarital sex was common. The marriage ceremony consisted of the joining of hands and the exchange of a pair of sandals. This ritual was followed by a large wedding feast, at which the state presented the bride and groom with two complete sets of clothing, one for everyday wear and one for festive occasions. If a man or woman did not find a satisfactory mate, the provincial governor selected one for him or her. Travel was forbidden, so couples necessarily came from the same region. Like most warring societies with high male death rates, the Incas practiced polygamy, though the cost of supporting many wives restricted it largely to the upper classes.

In many aspects of daily life, the common people were regimented, denied both choice and initiative. The Incas, however, took care of the poor and aged who could not look after themselves, distributed grain in time of shortage and famine, and supplied assistance in natural disasters. Scholars have debated whether Inca society was socialistic, totalitarian, or a forerunner of the welfare state; it may be merely a matter of definition. Although the Inca economy was strictly regulated, there certainly was not an equal distribution of wealth. Everything above and beyond the masses' basic needs went to the emperor and the nobility.

The backbreaking labor of ordinary people in the fields and mines made possible the luxurious lifestyle of the great Inca nobility. The nobles—called *Orejones,* or "Big Ears," by the Spanish because they pierced their ears and distended the lobes with heavy jewelry—were the ruling Inca's kinsmen. Lesser nobles included the curacas, royal household servants, public officials, and entertainers. As the empire expanded in the fifteenth century, there arose a noble class of warriors, governors, and local officials, whose support the ruling Inca secured with gifts of land, precious metals, and llamas and alpacas (llamas were used as beasts of burden; alpacas were raised for their long fine wool). The nobility was exempt from agricultural work and from other kinds of public service.

SUMMARY

Several strong Amerindian civilizations flourished in the Western Hemisphere in the years between 400 and 1500. The Maya are justly renowned for their art and their accomplishments in abstract thought, especially mathematics. The Aztecs built a unified culture based heavily on the Toltec heritage and distinguished by achievements in engineering, sculpture, and architecture. The Incas revealed a genius for organization, and their state was virtually unique in its time for assuming responsibility for all its people. In both the Mexica and the Inca societies religious ideology shaped other facets of the culture. The Mexica cult of war and human sacrifice and the Inca cult of the royal mummies proved fatal weaknesses and contributed to the decline of those societies.

Inca culture did not die with the Spaniard Pizarro's strangulation of Atauhualpa (p. 524). In May 1536 his successor Inca Mancu Yupanki led a massive revolt against the Spanish and then led his people to Machu Picchu deep in the Valcahamba range of the Andes. Inca military resistance to Spanish domination continued throughout the sixteenth to eighteenth centuries. In 1780 Jose Gabriel Kunturkanki, a highly educated businessman and landowner, proclaimed himself Inca Tupac Amaru II and launched a native independence movement that the Spanish put down with the greatest difficulty (p. 919).

NOTES

1. See F. Braudel, *The Structures of Everyday Life: Civilization and Capitalism, 15th–18th Century,* vol. 1, trans. S. Reynolds (New York: Harper & Row, 1981), pp. 160–161.

2. See L. Schele and M. E. Miller, *The Blood of Kings: Dynasty and Ritual in Maya Art* (New York: Braziller, 1986), pp. 14–15, passim.

3. Quoted in I. Bernal, *Mexico Before Cortez: Art, History, and Legend,* rev. ed., trans. Willis Barnstone (New York: Anchor Books, 1975), p. 68.

4. G. W. Conrad and A. A. Demarest, *Religion and Empire: The Dynamics of Aztec and Inca Expansionism* (New York: Cambridge University Press, 1993), p. 71.

5. See I. Clendinnen, *Aztecs: An Interpretation* (New York: Cambridge University Press, 1992), pp. 115–117.

6. J. Soustelle, *Daily Life of the Aztecs on the Eve of the Spanish Conquest,* trans. P. O'Brian (Stan-

ford, Calif.: Stanford University Press, 1970), p. 97.

7. See M. Harris, *Cannibals and Kings* (New York: Random House, 1977), pp. 99–110; the quotation is from p. 106.

8. Ibid., pp. 109–110.

9. See R. Padden, *The Hummingbird and the Hawk* (Columbus: Ohio State University Press, 1967), pp. 76–99.

10. I am relying heavily here on Conrad and Demarest, *Religion and Empire*, pp. 37–44.

11. Ibid., p. 49.

12. Ibid., p. 57.

13. Ibid., pp. 66–70.

14. Soustelle, *Daily Life of the Aztecs*, p. 74.

15. See Clendinnen, pp. 153–173.

16. Quoted in Soustelle, p. 89.

17. B. Díaz, *The Conquest of New Spain*, trans. J. M. Cohen (New York: Penguin Books, 1978), p. 214.

18. Quoted in J. H. Perry, *The Discovery of South America* (New York: Taplinger, 1979), pp. 161–163.

19. Quoted ibid., p. 163.

20. William K. Stevens, "Andean Culture Found to Be as Old as the Great Pyramids," *New York Times*, October 3, 1989, p. C1.

21. John Noble Wilford, "Lost Civilization Yields Its Riches as Thieves Fall Out," *New York Times*, July 29, 1994, pp. C1, C28.

22. J. A. Mason, *The Ancient Civilizations of Peru* (New York: Penguin Books, 1978), p. 108.

23. Conrad and Demarest, *Religion and Empire*, pp. 91–94.

24. Mason, *The Ancient Civilization of Peru*, p. 123.

25. Ibid., p. 132.

26. Ibid., p. 136.

SUGGESTED READING

The titles by Clendinnen, Conrad and Demarest, and Schele and Miller, cited in the Notes, represent some of the most exciting recent research on pre-Columbian Mesoamerican societies. For the Maya, students should also see L. Schele and D. Freidel, *A Forest of Kings: The Untold Story of the Ancient Maya* (1990), a splendidly illustrated work, providing expert treatment of many facets of the Maya world; R. Wright, *Time Among the Maya* (1989), which gives a highly readable account of the important Maya agricultural and religious calendars; M. D. Coe, *The Maya*, 4th ed. (1987), a sound and well-illustrated survey. For the Aztecs, R. F. Townsend, *The Aztecs* (1992), discusses the various classes of Mexica society, as well as expansion, education, and religious ritual in a clearly illustrated study. M. León-Portilla, *The Aztec Image of Self and Society: An Introduction to Nahua Culture* (1992), is perhaps the best appreciation of Aztec religious ritual and symbolism. For warfare, R. Hassig, *Aztec Warfare: Imperial Expansion and Political Control* (1988), is probably the standard work.

Students desiring books exploring the entire hemisphere before the arrival of Columbus might see B. Fagan, *Kingdoms of Gold, Kingdoms of Jade* (1991), a fine work in comparative anthropology, and *America in 1492*, ed. A. M. Josephy (1992), an interesting collection of essays, many written by leading scholars. For the impact of the Spanish on Mesoamerican peoples, see I. Clendinnen, *Ambivalent Conquests: Maya and Spanish in Yucatan, 1517–1570* (1987), a profoundly sensitive, learned, and important study; R. Wright, *Stolen Continents: The Americas through Indian Eyes since 1492* (1992), which emphasizes the persistence and survival of native American cultures and peoples; and *In the Wake of Contact: Biological Responses to Conquest*, ed. C. S. Larsen and G. Milner (1994), a useful collection of articles dealing with many parts of the world.

The following older studies may also prove helpful for particular topics: S. Masuda, I. Shimada, and C. Morris, eds., *Andean Ecology and Civilization* (1985) and E. R. Wolfe, ed., *The Valley of Mexico: Studies in Pre-Hispanic Ecology and Society* (1976), are important for environmental research; L. Baudin, *A Socialist Empire: The Incas of Peru* (1961), which gives a provocative interpretation of the Incas, while V. W. Van Hagen, *Realm of the Incas* (1961), offers a popular account; and F. Katz, *The Ancient American Civilisations* (1972), a standard anthropological work that surveys all the major Mesoamerican cultures, and T. Todorov, *The Conquest of America*, trans. R. Howard (1984), an important, but difficult, study in cross-cultural perceptions.

LISTENING TO THE
PAST

The Installation of the Inca

All societies have special ceremonies in which the head of state, ruler, or king is officially constituted or consecrated. These rites, often involving religious ritual, set the head of state apart from all others.

In 1653 the Spanish Jesuit Bernabe Cobo (1580–1657) completed his Historia del Nuevo Mundi *(History of the New World), a major Spanish source for Inca history and institutions. Cobo's work is not based on firsthand observation. Modern scholars believe it rests on lost sixteenth-century manuscripts, but, taking into account Cobo's period and prejudices, they consider it highly reliable. Here is Cobo's account of an Inca's installation, his majesty and splendor.*

. . . The prince was not crowned until the funeral rites of his father were concluded, and after this, all of the great lords and gentlemen who resided in the court and whoever could comfortably come from all over the kingdom gathered in the plaza of Cuzco for the installation and coronation. . . . The Inca took possession of the kingdom when he put the fringe on his forehead, which was like the royal crown, and after it, he put on the rest of the insignias that the Peruvian kings used; besides the fringe there was the *sunturpaucar*, the *champi*, the rainbow and two serpents, and the other emblems that each one picked out.

The way his vassals installed him and swore allegiance to him is as follows. Once all the lords were together in the plaza and the king was seated in the middle on his *duho*,[1] one by one the lords stood up, first the *orejones*[2] and after them the caciques and lords in charge of the most towns. In their hands they had some little feathers called *tocto* from certain birds . . . . They stood barefooted before the Inca and turned the palms of their hands toward him, showing their reverence. They also swore allegiance by the Sun, raising their faces toward

it, and by the earth, to be loyal to the Inca and serve him in whatever he ordered them to do.

The king was dressed and adorned in the same clothing as the Inca nobles and *orejones*. The king was distinguished only by having larger holes pierced in his ears and larger and more lavish earplugs, by having his hair cut short to the breadth of one or two fingers, and by his *lluato* [headband] which was many-colored. The braided headbands worn by other members of the Inca lineage were of a single color. The Inca wore a cloak and a shirt, with *ojotas* on his feet; in this respect he followed the custom of the common people, but his clothing was . . . made of the finest wool and the best cloth that was woven in his whole kingdom, with more brilliant colors and finer-quality weaving. The *mamaconas*[3] made his clothing for him, and most of it was made from vicuña wool, which is almost as fine as silk. . . .

The fringe (royal insignia that they always wore in place of a crown or diadem) was called *maxcapaycha;* it was made of very fine red wool. They had it sewn to the *llauto* and hanging in the middle of their forehead, and it reached down to their eyebrows. . . . The *sunturpaucar* and the *champi* were two of the king's other insignias, besides the royal standard. The *sunturpaucar* was a staff, a little shorter than a pike, all covered and adorned from top to bottom with short feathers of various colors. . . . The *champi*[4] was a certain kind of weapon with which they fought in wars. In front of the Inca, at the sides of the royal standard, two *champis* on two long staves were held and the Inca himself, instead of a scepter, carried a short *champi*, like a baton with a golden head. The royal banner or standard was a small, square pennant, about ten or twelve palms around the edge, made of cotton or wool cloth; it was fixed on the end of a long pole so as to stand out stiffly and not wave in the wind. Each king had his arms and emblems painted on it. . . .

The Incas made a majestic display both in their personal style of life and adornment and in the pomp and splendor that accompanied them and with which they were served inside and outside of their homes. The multitude of servants that they had in their palace was incredible. Many of these servants were the children of caciques and noblemen. These youngsters were raised in the royal house so that they would learn civil customs. The Incas felt that it was a sign of grandeur to support many servants and have many wives and concubines. They were served all the exquisite, precious, and rare things that the land produced, and they had these things brought for their pleasure from the most distant corners of their empire. . . . Serving women brought him all of his food on gold, silver, and pottery plates and set them before him on some very thin, small green rushes.

Wherever he went, and many times within a town, the Inca was carried on the shoulders of bearers supporting a splendid litter covered on the inside with gold; carrying this litter was a special favor and honor. When the Inca traveled, he had a large following of *orejones*; these were the nobles and military men, who added security as well as authority to the Inca's group.

The riches of these barbarian kings were so immense that it is not easy to describe. They never found that their wealth was insufficient, nor were they ever worried about finding a way to remedy their needs, because they never had any; rather they had peace of mind and abundance of everything, for they were more concerned about how to divest themselves of what was left over from their large income than in seeking new ways to obtain and keep treasures. This was due to the fact that whatever their vassals produced or acquired was at their service and disposal. . . .
The riches that were collected and gathered together just in the city of Cuzco, as the capital and court of the empire, were incredible; in it there were many important houses of the dead kings with all the treasure that each one had accumulated in his life. Since the one who ascended to the throne did not touch his predecessor's property and riches, which were given over to the *guaca* and service of the deceased, the new king had his own house built and acquired silver and gold and all the rest; thus the treasure in the city was immense. . . .

So Cuzco was the richest city that has been found in this New World, and the reason why

Painting of Inca chief (Pretender) Lloque Yupanqui, ca. 1615. (*Source: Collection Musée de l'Homme, Paris*)

it had such a great amount of wealth in silver and gold and precious stones was because the caciques and governors made presents of all of these things to the Inca when they visited him in his court and when he passed through their lands as he was visiting his kingdom. . . .

Questions for Analysis

1. What symbols were used in the installation of the Inca, and what do they represent?

2. Why did the Inca travel by litter? What does this method of conveyance tell us about Inca society and technology?

3. Compare the lifestyle of the Inca and the Chinese emperor K'ang-hsi or the French king Louis XIV. What do they all have in common? How does religious ideology support the rule of each?

4. Why does Cobo dwell on the wealth and riches of the Inca?

Source: *History of the Inca Empire by Father Bernabe Cobo,* trans. and ed. R. Hamilton (Austin: University of Texas Press, 1979), pp. 244–49.

Notes: 1. A low stool or bench, the symbol of the Inca's high office. 2. Nobles distinguished by their big ears, from which heavy jewelry extended. 3. Cloistered women who were dedicated to the service of the Inca gods and who also trained all royal household servants. 4. Similar to a mace and carried by the Inca, in war; like the scepter carried by European monarchs, the *champi* was an emblem of authority and of the Inca's duty to defend his people and extend his empire.

15

European Society in the Age of the Renaissance and Reformation

Michelangelo painted the entire Sistine Chapel ceiling by himself, 1508–1512. *(Source: Nippon Television Network Corporation, Tokyo, 1994)*

While the Four Horsemen of the Apocalypse were carrying war, plague, famine, and death across the continent of Europe, a new culture was emerging in southern Europe. The fourteenth century witnessed the beginnings of remarkable changes in many aspects of Italian society. In the fifteenth century, these phenomena spread beyond Italy and gradually influenced society in northern Europe. These cultural changes have collectively been labeled the Renaissance.

The idea of reform is as old as Christianity itself: the need for reform of the individual Christian and of the institutional church is central to the Christian faith. The Christian humanists of the late fifteenth and early sixteenth centuries called for reform of the church on the pattern of the early church, primarily through educational and social change. These cries for reformation were not new. Men and women of every period believed the early Christian church represented a golden age. What was new were the criticisms of educated lay people whose religious needs were not being met. In the sixteenth century, demands for religious reform became so strong that they became enmeshed with social, political, and economic factors.

- What does the term *Renaissance* mean?
- How did the Renaissance manifest itself in politics, government, art, and social organization?
- Why did the theological ideas of Martin Luther trigger political, social, and economic reactions?
- What response did the Catholic church make to the movements for reform?

This chapter explores these questions.

Economic and Political Origins of the Italian Renaissance

The period extending roughly from 1050 to 1300 witnessed phenomenal commercial and financial development, the growing political power of self-governing cities in northern Italy, and great population expansion. The period from the late thirteenth to the late sixteenth century was characterized by an amazing flowering of artistic energies.[1] Scholars commonly use the term *Renaissance* to describe the cultural achievements of the fourteenth through sixteenth centuries. Those achievements rest on the economic and political developments of earlier centuries.

In the great commercial revival of the eleventh century, northern Italian cities led the way. By the middle of the twelfth century, Venice, supported by a huge merchant marine, had grown enormously rich from overseas trade. It profited tremendously from the diversion of the Fourth Crusade to Constantinople (see page 371). Genoa and Milan enjoyed the benefits of a large volume of trade with the Middle East and northern Europe. These cities fully exploited their geographical positions as natural crossroads for mercantile exchange between the East and West.

Florence too possessed enormous wealth despite geographical constraints. It was an inland city without easy access to water transportation. But toward the end of the thirteenth century, Florentine merchants and bankers acquired control of papal banking. From their position as tax collectors for the papacy, Florentine mercantile families began to dominate European banking on both sides of the Alps. The profits from loans, investments, and money exchanges that poured back to Florence were pumped into urban industries, such as the Florentine wool industry, which was the major factor in the city's financial expansion and population increase. Florence purchased the best-quality wool from England and Spain, developed remarkable techniques for its manufacture into cloth, and employed thousands of workers in the manufacturing process. Florentine woolen cloth brought the highest prices in the fairs, markets, and bazaars of Europe, Asia, and Africa. Scholars tend to agree that the first artistic and literary manifestations of the Italian Renaissance appeared in Florence.

In the course of the twelfth century, Milan, Florence, Genoa, Siena, and Pisa fought for and won political and economic independence from surrounding feudal nobles. The nobles, attracted by the opportunities of long-distance and maritime trade, the rising value of urban real estate, the new public offices available in the expanding cities, and the chances for advantageous marriages into rich commercial families, frequently settled within the cities. Marriage vows often sealed business contracts between the rural nobility and the mercantile aristocracy. This merger of the northern Italian feudal nobility and the commercial aristocracy brought into being a new social class—an urban nobility.

This new class made citizenship and political participation in the city-states dependent on a property qualification, years of residence within the city, and social connections. Only a tiny percentage of the male population possessed these qualifications. A new group, called the *pòpolo,* disenfranchised and heavily taxed, bitterly resented its exclusion from power. Throughout most of the thirteenth century, in city after city, the pòpolo used armed force and violence to take over the city governments. Members of the pòpolo could not establish civil order within their cities, however. Consequently, these movements for republican government—government in which political power theoretically resides in the people and is exercised by their chosen representatives—failed. By the year 1300 *signori* (despots, or one-man rulers) or *oligarchies* (the rule of merchant aristocracies) had triumphed everywhere.[2]

For the next two centuries, the Italian city-states were ruled by signori or by constitutional oligarchies. In the signories, despots pretended to observe the law while actually manipulating it to conceal their basic illegality. Oligarchic regimes possessed constitutions, but through a variety of schemes a small, restricted class of wealthy merchants exercised the judicial, executive, and legislative functions of government. Thus in 1422 Venice had a population of 84,000, but 200 men held all power; and Florence had about 40,000 people, but 600 men ruled. Oligarchic regimes maintained only a façade of republican government. Nostalgia for the Roman form of government, combined with calculating shrewdness, prompted the leaders of Venice, Milan, and Florence to use the old forms.

In the fifteenth century, political power and elite culture centered at the princely courts of despots and oligarchs. "A court was the space and personnel around a prince as he made laws, received ambassadors, made appointments, took his meals, and proceeded through the streets."[3] The princely court afforded the despot or oligarchs the opportunity to display and assert their wealth and power. They flaunted their patronage of learning and the arts by munificent gifts to writers, philosophers, and artists, and they promoted occasions for magnificent pageantry and elaborate ritual—all designed to assert their wealth and power. The rulers of the city-states governed as monarchs. They crushed urban revolts, levied taxes, and killed their enemies. And they used massive building programs to employ, and the arts to overawe, the masses.

Renaissance Italians had a passionate attachment to their individual city-states. This intensity of local feeling perpetuated the dozens of small states and hindered the development of a unified Italian state.

In the fifteenth century, five powers dominated the Italian peninsula: Venice, Milan, Florence, the Papal States, and the kingdom of Naples. Venice had a sophisticated constitution and was a republic in name, but an oligarchy of merchant-aristocrats actually ran the city. Milan was also called a republic, but despots of the Sforza family ruled harshly and dominated the smaller cities of the north. Likewise in Florence the form of government was republican, but between 1434 and 1494 power in Florence was held by the great Medici banking family. Though not public officers, Cosimo de' Medici (1434–1464) and Lorenzo de' Medici (1469–1492) ruled from behind the scenes. Central Italy consisted mainly of the Papal States, which during the Babylonian Captivity (see page 427) had come under the sway of important Roman families. Pope Alexander VI (r. 1492–1503), aided militarily and politically by his son Cesare Borgia, reasserted papal authority in the papal lands. Cesare Borgia, the inspiration of Machiavelli's *The Prince* (see page 478), began the work of uniting the peninsula by ruthlessly conquering and exacting total obedience from the principalities making up the Papal States. South of the Papal States, the kingdom of Naples had long been disputed by the Aragonese and by the French. In 1435 it passed to Aragon.

The five major Italian city-states competed furiously among themselves for territory. They used diplomacy, spies, paid informers, and any other means to advance their ambitions. While the states of northern Europe were moving toward centralization and consolidation, the world of Italian politics resembled a jungle where the powerful dominated the weak.

In one significant respect, however, the Italian city-states anticipated future relations among competing European states after 1500. Whenever one Italian state appeared to gain a dominant position on the peninsula, the other states joined forces to establish a *balance of power* against the major threat. In forming these shifting alliances, Renaissance Italians invented the machinery of modern diplomacy: permanent embassies with resident ambassadors in capitals where political relations and commercial ties needed continual monitoring. The

✤ **A Bank Scene, Florence**   Originally a "bank" was just a counter; if covered with a carpet like this Ottoman geometric rug with a kufic border, it became a bank of distinction. Moneychangers who sat behind the counter became "bankers," exchanging different currencies and holding deposits for merchants and business people. *(Source: Prato, San Francesco/Scala/Art Resource, NY)*

resident ambassador is one of the great achievements of the Italian Renaissance.

At the end of the fifteenth century, Venice, Florence, Milan, and the Papal States possessed great wealth and represented high cultural achievement. However, their imperialistic ambitions at one another's expense, and their resulting inability to form a common alliance against potential foreign enemies, made Italy an inviting target for invasion. When Florence and Naples entered into an agreement to acquire Milanese territories, Milan called on France for support.

In Florence a Dominican friar, Girolamo Savonarola (1452–1498), had been predicting an invasion by France. In a number of fiery sermons between 1491 and 1494, Savonarola attacked what he considered the paganism and moral vice of the city, the undemocratic government of Lorenzo de' Medici, and the corruption of Pope Alexander VI. For a time he enjoyed wide support among the ordinary people; he became the religious leader of

Florence and as such contributed to the fall of the Medicis. Savonarola stands as proof that the common people did not share the worldly outlook of the commercial and intellectual elite. Eventually, however, people wearied of his moral denunciations, and he was excommunicated by the pope and executed.

The invasion of Italy in 1494 by the French king Charles VIII (r. 1483–1498) inaugurated a new period in Italian and European power politics. Italy became the focus of international ambitions and the battleground of foreign armies. Charles swept the peninsula with little opposition. Florence, Rome, and Naples soon bowed before him. When Piero de' Medici, Lorenzo's son, went to the French camp seeking peace, the Florentines exiled the Medicis and restored republican government.

In the sixteenth century, the political and social life of Italy was upset by the relentless competition for dominance between France and the Holy Roman Empire. In 1519 Charles V succeeded his grandfather Maximilian as Holy Roman emperor. When the French returned to Italy in 1521, there began a series of conflicts called the Habsburg-Valois Wars (named for the German and French dynasties), whose battlefield was often Italy. The Italian cities suffered severely from the continual warfare, especially in the frightful sack of Rome in 1527 by imperial forces under Charles V. Thus the failure of the Italian city-states to form a common alliance against foreign enemies led to the continuation of the centuries-old subjection of the Italian peninsula by outside invaders.

❉ INTELLECTUAL HALLMARKS OF THE RENAISSANCE

Some Italians in the fourteenth and fifteenth centuries believed that they were living in a new era. The realization that something new and unique was happening first came to men of letters in the fourteenth century, especially to poet and humanist Francesco Petrarch (1304–1374). Petrarch thought that the Germanic invasions had caused a sharp cultural break with the glories of Rome and had ushered in what he called the "Dark Ages." Medieval people had recognized no cultural division between the world of the Roman emperors and their own times, but in the opinion of Petrarch and many of his contemporaries, the thousand-year period between the fourth and the fourteenth centuries constituted a barbarian, or Gothic, or "middle" age (hence historians' use of the expression "Middle Ages"). The sculptors, painters, and writers of the Renaissance spoke contemptuously of their medieval predecessors and identified themselves with the thinkers and artists of Greco-Roman civilization. Petrarch believed he was witnessing a new golden age of intellectual achievement—a rebirth or, to use the French word that came into English, a *renaissance.*

The division of historical time into periods is often arbitrary and done by historians for their own convenience. In terms of the way most people lived and thought, no sharp division existed between the Middle Ages and the Renaissance. The guild and the parish, for example, continued to provide strong support for the individual and to exercise great social influence. Renaissance intellectuals, however, developed a new sense of historical distance and some important poets, writers, and artists believed they were living in a new age.

The Renaissance also manifested itself in new attitudes towards individuals, learning, and the world at large. There was a renewal of belief in the importance of the individual, a rebirth of interest in the Latin classics and in antique lifestyles, and a restoration of interest in the material world.

Individualism

Though the Middle Ages had seen the appearance of remarkable individuals, recognition of such persons was limited. Saint Augustine in the fifth century and Peter Abélard and Guibert of Nogent in the twelfth—men who perceived themselves as unique and produced autobiographical statements—stand out, for Christian humility discouraged self-absorption. In the fourteenth and fifteenth centuries, however, a large literature presenting a distinctly Renaissance individualism emerged.

Many distinctive individuals gloried in their uniqueness. Italians of unusual abilities were self-consciously aware of their singularity and unafraid to be different from their neighbors; they had enormous confidence in their ability to achieve great things. Leon Battista Alberti (1404–1474), a writer, architect, and mathematician, remarked, "Men can do all things if they will."[4] The Florentine goldsmith and sculptor Benvenuto Cellini (1500–1574) prefaced his *Autobiography* with a sonnet that declares:

My cruel fate hath warr'd with me in vain:
Life, glory, worth, and all unmeasur'd skill,
Beauty and grace, themselves in me fulfill
That many I surpass, and to the best attain.[5]

Certain of his genius, Cellini wrote so that the whole world might appreciate it.

Individualism stressed personality, genius, uniqueness, and the fullest development of capabilities and talents. Artist, athlete, painter, scholar, sculptor, whatever—a person's abilities should be stretched until fully realized. Thirst for fame, a driving ambition, a burning desire for success drove such people to achieve their potential. The quest for glory was a central component of Renaissance individualism.

Humanism

In the cities of Italy, especially Rome, civic leaders and the wealthy populace showed great archaeological zeal for the recovery of manuscripts, statues, and monuments. The Vatican Library, planned in the fifteenth century to house the nine thousand manuscripts collected by Pope Nicholas V (r. 1447–1455), remains one of the richest repositories of ancient and medieval documents. Patrician Italians consciously copied the lifestyle of the ancients and tried to trace their genealogies back to ancient Rome.

The revival of interest in antiquity was also apparent in the serious study of the Latin classics. This feature of the Renaissance became known as the "new learning," or simply "humanism," the term used by the Florentine rhetorician and historian Leonardo Bruni (1370–1444). The words *humanism* and *humanist* derived from the Latin *humanitas,* which Cicero used to refer to the literary culture needed by anyone who wanted to be considered educated and civilized. Humanism focused on human beings—their achievements, interests, and capabilities. Although churchmen supported the new learning, by the later fifteenth century Italian humanism was increasingly a lay phenomenon.

Appreciation of the literary culture of the Romans had never died in the West. Bede and John of Salisbury (see page 368), for example, had studied and imitated the writings of the ancients. But medieval writers had accepted pagan and classical authors uncritically. Renaissance humanists, in contrast, were skeptical of their authority, conscious of the historical distance separating themselves from the ancients, and fully aware that classical writers often disagreed among themselves. Medieval writers looked to the classics to reveal God. Renaissance humanists studied the classics to understand human nature, though from a strongly Christian perspective. For example, in a remarkable essay, *On the Dignity of Man,* the Florentine writer Pico della Mirandola (1463–1494) stressed that man possesses great dignity because he was made as Adam in the image of God before the Fall and as Christ after the Resurrection. According to Pico, man's place in the universe is somewhere between the beasts and the angels, but, because of the divine image planted in him, there are no limits to what man can accomplish. Humanists rejected classical ideas that were opposed to Christianity. Or they sought through reinterpretation an underlying harmony between the pagan and secular and the Christian faith. The fundamental difference between medieval humanists and Renaissance ones is that the latter were more self-conscious about what

they were doing and stressed the realization of human potential.[6]

The leading humanists of the early Renaissance were rhetoricians, seeking effective and eloquent communication, both oral and written. They loved the language of the classics and scorned the corrupt, "barbaric" Latin of the medieval schoolmen. Literary humanists of the fourteenth century wrote each other highly stylized letters imitating ancient authors, and they held witty philosophical dialogues in conscious imitation of Plato's Academy of the fourth century B.C. Renaissance writers were very excited by the purity of ancient Latin. Eventually, however, they became concerned more about form than about content, more about the way an idea was expressed than about the significance and validity of the idea.

Secular Spirit

Secularism is a basic concern with the material world instead of with eternal and spiritual matters. A secular way of thinking tends to find the ultimate explanation of everything and the final end of human beings within the limits of what the senses can discover. Medieval business people ruthlessly pursued profits while medieval monks fought fiercely over property. But medieval society was religious, not secular: the dominant ideals focused on the otherworldly, on life after death. Renaissance people often held strong and deep spiritual beliefs. But Renaissance society was secular: attention is concentrated on the here and now, often on the acquisition of material things. The fourteenth and fifteenth centuries witnessed the slow but steady growth of secularism in Italy.

The economic changes and rising prosperity of the Italian cities in the thirteenth century worked a fundamental change in social and intellectual attitudes and values. Worries about shifting rates of interest, shipping routes, personnel costs, and employee relations did not leave much time for thoughts about penance and purgatory. Wealth made possible greater material pleasures, a more comfortable life, the leisure time to appreciate and patronize the arts. Money could buy many sensual gratifications, and the rich, social-climbing bankers and merchants of the Italian cities came to see life more as an opportunity to be enjoyed than as a painful pilgrimage to the City of God.

In *On Pleasure,* the humanist Lorenzo Valla (1406–1457) defended the pleasures of the senses as the highest good. Scholars praise Valla as a father of modern historical criticism. His study *On the False Donation of Constantine* (1444) demonstrated by careful textual examination that an anonymous eighth-century document supposedly giving the papacy jurisdiction over vast territories in western Europe was a forgery. Medieval people had accepted the Donation of Constantine as valid, and the proof that it was a forgery weakened the foundations of papal claims to temporal authority. Lorenzo Valla's work exemplifies the application of critical scholarship to old and almost-sacred writings, as well as the new secular spirit of the Renaissance.

The tales in *The Decameron* (1353), by the Florentine Giovanni Boccaccio (1313–1375), describe ambitious merchants, lecherous friars, and cuckolded husbands and portray a frankly acquisitive, sensual, and worldly society. Historians, however, must be cautious in basing conclusions solely on literature. Boccaccio's figures were stock literary characters not unknown in the Middle Ages, and writers draw on their imagination as well as on social experience. Nevertheless, *The Decameron* contains none of the "contempt of the world" theme so pervasive in medieval literature.

Renaissance writers justified the accumulation and enjoyment of wealth with references to ancient authors, and church leaders did little to combat the new secular spirit. In the fifteenth and early sixteenth centuries, the papal court and the households of the cardinals were just as worldly as those of great urban patricians. Renaissance popes beautified the city of Rome, patronized artists and men of letters, and expended enormous enthusiasm and huge sums of money. A new papal chancellery, begun in 1483 and finished in 1511, stands as one of the architectural masterpieces of the High Renaissance. Pope Julius II (r. 1503–1513) tore down the old Saint Peter's Basilica and began work on the present structure in 1506. Michelangelo's dome for Saint Peter's is still considered his greatest work.

Although papal interests fostered the new worldly attitude, the broad mass of the people and the intellectuals and leaders of society remained faithful to the Christian church. Few questioned the basic tenets of the Christian religion. The thousands of pious paintings, sculptures, processions, and pilgrimages of the Renaissance period prove that strong religious feeling persisted.

Art and the Artist

No feature of the Renaissance evokes greater admiration than its artistic masterpieces. The 1400s (called *quattrocento* in Italian) and 1500s (*cinquecento*) bore witness to a dazzling creativity in painting, architecture, and sculpture. In all the arts, the city of Florence first led the way. In the period art historians describe as the High Renaissance (1500–1527) Rome took the lead. The main characteristics of High Renaissance art—classical balance, harmony, and restraint—are revealed in the masterpieces of Leonardo da Vinci (1452–1519), Raphael (1483–1520), and Michelangelo (1475–1564), all of whom worked in Rome.

In early Renaissance Italy, art manifested corporate power. Powerful urban groups such as guilds and religious confraternities commissioned works of art. The Florentine cloth merchants, for example, delegated Filippo Brunelleschi (1377–1446) to build the magnificent dome on the cathedral of Florence and selected Lorenzo Ghiberti (1378–1455) to design the bronze doors of the baptistry. These works were signs of the merchants' dominant influence in the community. Corporate patronage is also reflected in the Florentine government's decision to hire Michelangelo to create a sculpture of David, the great Hebrew hero and king. The subject matter of art through the early fifteenth century, as in the Middle Ages, remained overwhelmingly religious.

Increasingly in the later quattrocento, individuals and oligarchs, rather than corporate groups, sponsored works of art. Merchants, bankers, popes, and princes supported the arts as a means of glorifying themselves, their families, and their power. Vast sums were spent on family chapels, frescoes, religious panels, and tombs. Writing about 1470, the Florentine oligarch Lorenzo de' Medici declared that over the past thirty-five years his family had spent the astronomical sum of 663,755 gold florins for artistic and architectural commissions. And, he said, "I think it casts a brilliant light on our estate [public reputation] and it seems to me that the monies were well spent and I am very pleased with this."[7]

As the fifteenth century advanced, the subject matter of art became steadily more secular. Religious topics, such as the Annunciation of the Virgin, remained popular among both patrons and artists, but classical themes and motifs, such as the lives and loves of pagan gods and goddesses, figured increasingly in painting and sculpture. The individual portrait emerged as a distinct artistic genre. People were conscious of their physical uniqueness and wanted their individuality immortalized. In the fifteenth century, members of the newly rich middle class often had themselves painted in a scene of romantic chivalry or in courtly society. Rather than reflecting a spiritual ideal, as medieval painting and sculpture tended to do, Renaissance portraits mirrored reality.

The Florentine painter Giotto (1276–1337) led the way in the use of realism; his treatment of the human body and face replaced the formal stiffness and artificiality that had for so long characterized the representation of the human body. The sculptor Donatello (1386–1466) probably exerted the greatest influence of any Florentine artist before Michelangelo. His many statues express an appreciation of the incredible variety of human nature. Medieval artists had depicted the nude body only in a spiritualized and moralizing context. Donatello revived the classical figure with its balance and self-awareness. The short-lived Florentine Masaccio (1401–1428), sometimes called the father of modern painting, inspired a new style characterized by great realism, narrative power, and effective use of light and dark.

Narrative artists depicted the body in a more scientific and natural manner. The female figure is voluptuous and sensual. The male body, as in Michelangelo's *David* (1501–1504) and *The Last Judgment* (1534–1541), is strong and heroic. This glorification of the human body is a sign of the secular spirit of the age. Brunelleschi and Piero della Francesca (1420–1492) seem to have pioneered *perspective* in painting—the linear representation of distance and space on a flat surface. *The Last Supper* (ca 1495–1498) of Leonardo da Vinci, with its stress on the tension between Christ and the disciples, is a subtle psychological interpretation.

As important as realism was the new "international style," so called because of the wandering careers of influential artists, the close communications and rivalry of princely courts, and the increased trade in works of art. Rich color, decorative detail, curvilinear rhythms, and swaying forms characterized the international style. As the term *international* implies, this style was European, not merely Italian.

The growing secular influences on art are reflected in the improved social status of the artist in the Renaissance. The lower-middle-class medieval master mason had been viewed in the same light as a mechanic. The artist in the Renaissance was considered a free intellectual worker. Artists did not produce unsolicited pictures or statues for the general public; that could mean loss of status. They usually worked on commission from a powerful prince. The artist's reputation depended on the support of powerful patrons, and through them some artists and architects achieved not only economic security but great wealth. All aspiring artists received a practical (not theoretical) education in a recognized master's workshop. For example, Michelangelo was apprenticed at age thirteen to the artist Ghirlandaio (1449–1494), although he later denied that fact to make it appear he never had any formal training. The more famous an artist was, the more he attracted assistants or apprentices.

Renaissance society respected and rewarded the distinguished artist. At a time when a person could live in a princely fashion on 300 ducats a year, Leonardo da Vinci was making 2,000 ducats annually. Michelangelo was paid 3,000 ducats for painting the ceiling of the Sistine Chapel. When he agreed to work on Saint Peter's Basilica, he refused a salary; he was already a wealthy man.[8] In 1537 the prolific letter writer, humanist, and satirizer of princes Pietro Aretino (1492–1556) wrote to Michelangelo while he was painting the Sistine Chapel:

To the Divine Michelangelo:
Sir, just as it is disgraceful and sinful to be unmindful of God so it is reprehensible and dishonourable for any man of discerning judgement not to honour you as a brilliant and venerable artist whom the very stars use as a target at which to shoot the rival arrows of their favour. You are so accomplished, therefore, that hidden in your hands lives the idea of a new king of creation. . . . And it is surely my duty to honour you with this salutation, since the world has many kings but only one Michelangelo.[9]

The Renaissance witnessed the birth of the concept of the artist as genius. In the Middle Ages, people believed that only God created, albeit through individuals; the medieval conception recognized no particular value in artistic originality. Boastful Renaissance artists and humanists came to think that a work of art was the deliberate creation of a unique personality, of an individual who transcended traditions, rules, and theories. A genius had a peculiar gift, which ordinary laws should not inhibit. Cosimo de' Medici described a painter, because of his genius, as "divine," implying that the artist shared in the powers of God. Aretino and others applied the word *divine* to Michelangelo.

But the student must remember that Italian Renaissance culture was that of a small mercantile elite, a business patriciate with aristocratic pretensions. Renaissance culture did not directly affect the broad middle classes, let alone the vast urban proletariat. Renaissance humanists were a smaller and narrower group than the medieval clergy had ever been. In the Middle Ages, high churchmen had commissioned the construction of the Gothic cathedrals, but, once finished, the buildings were for all to enjoy. Nothing comparable was built in the Renaissance. A small, highly educated group of literary humanists and artists created the culture of and for an exclusive elite. They cared little for ordinary people.[10]

The Renaissance in the North

In the last quarter of the fifteenth century, Italian Renaissance thought and ideals penetrated north-

Benozzo Gozzoli: Journey of the Magi   Few Renaissance paintings better illustrate art in the service of the princely court, in this case the Medici. Commissioned by Piero de' Medici to adorn his palace chapel, everything in this fresco—the large crowd, the feathers and diamonds adorning many of the personages, the black servant in front—serve to flaunt the power and wealth of the House of Medici. There is nothing especially religious about it; the painting could more appropriately be called "Journey of the Medici." *(Source: Scala/Art Resource, NY)*

ern Europe. Students from the Low Countries, France, Germany, and England flocked to Italy, imbibed the "new learning," and carried it back to their countries. However, cultural traditions of northern Europe tended to remain more distinctly Christian, or at least pietistic, than those of Italy. Italian humanists certainly were strongly Christian, as the example of Pico della Mirandola shows. But in Italy secular and pagan themes and Greco-Roman motifs received more humanistic attention than they received north of the Alps. The Renaissance in northern Europe had a distinctly religious character, and what fundamentally distinguished Italian humanists from northern ones is that the latter had a program for broad social reform based on Christian ideals.

Christian humanists in northern Europe were interested in the development of an ethical way of life. To achieve it, they believed, the best elements of classical and Christian cultures should be combined. For example, the classical ideals of calmness, stoical patience, and broad-mindedness should be joined in human conduct with the Christian virtues of love, faith, and hope. Northern humanists also stressed the use of reason, rather than acceptance of dogma, as the foundation for an ethical way of life. Like the Italians, they were impatient with Scholastic philosophy. Christian humanists had a profound faith in the power of human intellect to bring about moral and institutional reform. They believed that human nature had been corrupted by sin but nevertheless was fundamentally good and capable of improvement through education, which would lead to piety and an ethical way of life.

The Englishman Thomas More (1478–1535) towers above other figures in sixteenth-century English social and intellectual history. More's political stance and his resulting fate later, at the time of the Reformation (see page 501), have tended to obscure his contribution to Christian humanism. More, who practiced law, was deeply interested in the classics; his household served as a model of warm Christian family life and as a mecca for foreign and English humanists. He entered government service during the reign of Henry VIII and was sent as ambassador to Flanders. There More found the time to write *Utopia* (1516), which presented a revolutionary view of society.

Utopia, which literally means "nowhere," describes an ideal socialistic community on an island somewhere off the mainland of the New World. All its children receive a good education, and since the goal of all education is to develop rational faculties, adults divide their days equally between manual labor or business pursuits and various intellectual activities. The profits from business and property are held strictly in common, so there is absolute social equality. The Utopians use gold and silver both to make chamber pots and to prevent wars by buying off their enemies. By this casual use of precious metals, More meant to suggest that the basic problems in society were caused by greed. Utopian law exalts mercy above justice. Citizens of Utopia lead a nearly perfect existence because they live by reason. More punned on the word *Utopia,* which he termed "a good place. A good place which is no place."

More's ideas were profoundly original in the sixteenth century. The long-prevailing view was that vice and violence exist because women and men are basically corrupt. But More maintained that acquisitiveness and private property promote all sorts of vices and civil disorders and that because society protects private property, *society's* flawed institutions are responsible for corruption and war. Today people take this view so much for granted that it is difficult to appreciate how radical it was in the sixteenth century. According to More, the key to improvement and reform of the individual was reform of the social institutions that mold the individual.

Better known by contemporaries than Thomas More was the Dutch humanist Desiderius Erasmus of Rotterdam (1466?–1536), whose life work became the application of the best humanistic learning to the study and explanation of the Bible. As a mature scholar with an international reputation stretching from Cracow to London, a fame that rested largely on his exceptional knowledge of Greek, Erasmus could boast with truth, "I brought it about that humanism, which among the Italians . . . savored of nothing but pure paganism, began nobly to celebrate Christ."[11]

Erasmus's long list of publications includes *The Adages* (1500), a list of Greek and Latin precepts on ethical behavior; *The Education of a Christian Prince* (1504), which combines idealistic and practical suggestions for the formation of a ruler's character; *The Praise of Folly* (1509), a satire of worldly wisdom and a plea for the simple and spontaneous Christian faith of children; and, most important of all, a critical edition of the Greek New Testament (1516). In the preface to the New

Testament, Erasmus explained the purpose of his great work:

Only bring a pious and open heart, imbued above all things with a pure and simple faith. . . . For I utterly dissent from those who are unwilling that the sacred Scriptures should be read by the unlearned translated into their vulgar tongue, as though Christ had taught such subtleties that they can scarcely be understood even by a few theologians. . . . Christ wished his mysteries to be published as openly as possible. I wish that even the weakest woman should read the Gospel—should read the epistles of Paul. And I wish these were translated into all languages, so that they might be read and understood, not only by Scots and Irishmen, but also by Turks and Saracens. . . . Why do we prefer to study the wisdom of Christ in men's writings rather than in the writing of Christ himself?[12]

Two fundamental themes run through all of Erasmus's scholarly work. First, education—study of the Bible and the classics—is the means to reform, the key to moral and intellectual improvement. Second, the essence of Erasmus's thought is, in his own phrase, "the philosophy of Christ." By this Erasmus meant that Christianity is an inner attitude of the heart or spirit. Christianity is not formalism, special ceremonies, or law; Christianity is Christ—his life and what he said and did, not what theologians have written about him.

Whereas the writings of Erasmus and More have strong Christian themes and have drawn the attention primarily of scholars, the stories of the French humanist François Rabelais (1490?–1553) possess a distinctly secular flavor and have attracted broad readership. The most roguishly entertaining Renaissance writer, Rabelais was convinced that "laughter is the essence of manhood." Rabelais's *Gargantua* and *Pantagruel* (serialized between 1532 and 1552) belong among the great comic masterpieces of world literature. These stories' gross and robust humor introduced the adjective *Rabelaisian* into the language.

In *Gargantua* and *Pantagruel* the reader enters a world of Renaissance vitality, ribald joviality, and intellectual curiosity. On his travels Gargantua meets various absurd characters, and within their hilarious exchanges there occur serious discussions on religion, politics, philosophy, and education. Rabelais had received an excellent humanistic education in a monastery, and Gargantua discusses the disorders of contemporary religious and secular

life. Like Erasmus, Rabelais satirized hypocritical monks, pedantic academics, and pompous lawyers. But unlike Erasmus, Rabelais applied wild and gross humor. Like Thomas More, Rabelais believed that institutions molded individuals and that education was the key to a moral and healthy life. The aristocratic residents of Rabelais's Thélèma, the abbey that Gargantua establishes, live for the full gratification of their physical instincts and rational curiosity. Thélèma, whose motto is "Do as Thou Wilt," admits women *and* men; allows all to eat, drink, sleep, and work when they choose; provides excellent facilities for swimming, tennis, and football; and encourages sexual experimentation and marriage. Rabelais believed profoundly in the basic goodness of human beings and the rightness of instinct.

The distinctly religious orientation of the literary works of the Renaissance in the north also characterized northern art and architecture. Some Flemish painters, notably Rogier van der Weyden (1399/1400–1464) and Jan van Eyck (1366–1441), were considered the artistic equals of Italian painters, were much admired in Italy, and worked a generation before Leonardo and Michelangelo. One of the earliest artists successfully to use oil-based paints, van Eyck, in paintings such as *Ghent Altarpiece* and the portrait *Giovanni Arnolfini and His Bride,* shows the Flemish love for detail; the effect is great realism and remarkable attention to human personality.

Another Flemish painter, Hieronymous Bosch (ca 1450–1516), frequently used religious themes, but in combination with grotesque fantasies, colorful imagery, and peasant folk legends. Many of Bosch's paintings reflect the confusion and anguish often associated with the end of the Middle Ages. In *Death and the Miser,* Bosch's dramatic treatment of the Dance of Death theme, the miser's gold, increased by usury, is ultimately controlled by diabolical rats and toads, and his guardian angel urges him to choose the crucifix.

A quasi-spiritual aura likewise infuses architectural monuments in the north. The city halls of wealthy Flemish towns such as Bruges, Brussels, Louvain, and Ghent strike the viewer more as shrines to house the bones of saints than as settings for the mundane decisions of politicians and business people. Northern architecture was little influenced by the classical revival so obvious in Renaissance Rome and Florence.

 **Jan van Eyck: Madonna of Chancellor Rodin**   The tough and shrewd chancellor who ordered this rich painting visits the Virgin and Christ-Child (though they seem to be visiting him). An angel holds the crown of heaven over the Virgin's head while Jesus, the proclaimed savior of the world, holds it in his left hand and raises his right hand in blessing. Through the colonnade, sculpted with scenes from Genesis, is the city of Bruges. Van Eyck's achievement in portraiture is extraordinary; his treatment of space and figures and his ability to capture the infinitely small and the very large prompted art historian Erwin Panofsky to write that "his eye was at one and the same time a microscope and a telescope." *(Source: © Louvre/Photo R.M.N.)*

SOCIAL CHANGE DURING THE RENAISSANCE

The Renaissance changed many aspects of Italian and, subsequently, European society. The new developments brought about real breaks with the medieval past in education and political thought, through new printing technology, and in the experience of women and blacks.

Education and Political Thought

Education and moral behavior were central preoccupations of the humanists. Humanists poured out treatises, often in the form of letters, on the structure and goals of education and the training of rulers. In one of the earliest systematic programs for the young, Peter Paul Vergerio (1370–1444) wrote Ubertinus, the ruler of Carrara:

For the education of children is a matter of more than private interest; it concerns the State, which indeed regards the right training of the young as, in certain aspects, within its proper sphere. . . . Above all, respect for Divine ordinances is of the deepest importance; it should be inculcated from the earliest years.

Reverence towards elders and parents is an obligation closely akin.

We call those studies liberal which are worthy of a free man; those studies by which we attain and practice virtue and wisdom; that education which calls forth, trains and develops those highest gifts of body and of mind which ennoble men, and which are rightly judged to rank next in dignity to virtue only.[13]

Part of Vergerio's treatise specifies subjects for the instruction of young men in public life: history teaches virtue by examples from the past; ethics focuses on virtue itself; and rhetoric, or public speaking, trains for eloquence.

No book on education had broader influence than Baldassare Castiglione's *The Courtier* (1528). This treatise sought to train, discipline, and fashion the young man into the courtly ideal, the gentleman. According to Castiglione (1478–1529), the educated man of the upper class should have a broad background in many academic subjects, and his spiritual and physical, as well as intellectual, capabilities should be trained. The courtier should have easy familiarity with dance, music, and the arts. Castiglione envisioned a man who could compose a sonnet, wrestle, sing a song and accompany himself on an instrument, ride expertly, solve diffi-cult mathematical problems, and above all speak and write eloquently (see Listening to the Past). In the sixteenth and seventeenth centuries, the courtier envisioned by Castiglione became the model of the European gentleman.

No Renaissance book on any topic has been more widely read and studied in all the centuries since its publication in 1513 than the short politi-cal treatise *The Prince*, by Niccolò Machiavelli (1469–1527). Some political scientists maintain that Machiavelli was describing the actual competi-tive framework of the Italian states with which he was familiar. Other thinkers praise *The Prince* be-cause it revolutionized political theory and de-stroyed medieval views of the nature of the state. Still other scholars consider this work a classic be-cause it deals with eternal problems of government and society.

Born to a modestly wealthy Tuscan family, Machiavelli received a good education in the Latin classics. He entered the civil service of the Floren-tine government and served on thirty diplomatic missions. When the exiled Medicis returned to power in Florence in 1512, they expelled Machi-avelli from his position as an officer of the city gov-ernment. In exile he wrote *The Prince*.

The subject of *The Prince* is political power: how the ruler should gain, maintain, and increase it. A good humanist, Machiavelli explores the problems of human nature and concludes that human beings are selfish and out to advance their own interests. This pessimistic view of humanity leads him to maintain that the prince may have to manipulate the people in any way he finds necessary:

For a man who, in all respects, will carry out only his professions of good, will be apt to be ruined amongst so many who are evil. A prince therefore who desires to maintain himself must learn to be not always good, but to be so or not as necessity may require.[14]

The prince should combine the cunning of a fox with the ferocity of a lion to achieve his goals. Pon-dering the question of whether it is better for a ruler to be loved or feared, Machiavelli wrote:

It will naturally be answered that it would be desir-able to be both the one and the other; but as it is diffi-cult to be both at the same time, it is much more safe to be feared than to be loved, when you have to choose between the two. For it may be said of men in

general that they are ungrateful and fickle, dissem-blers, avoiders of danger, and greedy of gain. So long as you shower benefits upon them, they are all yours.[15]

Medieval political theorists and theologians had stressed the way government *ought* to be. They had set high moral and Christian standards for the ruler's conduct. In their opinion, the test of good government was whether it provided justice, law, and order. Machiavelli maintained that the ruler should be concerned not with the way things ought to be but with the way things actually are. The sole test of whether a government was "good" was whether it was effective, whether the ruler in-creased his power. Machiavelli believed that politi-cal action cannot be restricted by moral considera-tions, but he did not advocate amoral behavior. In the *Discourses of the Ten Books of Titus Livy*, he even showed his strong commitment to republican gov-ernment. Nevertheless, on the basis of a simplistic interpretation of *The Prince*, the adjective *Machi-avellian* entered the language as a synonym for de-vious, corrupt, and crafty politics in which the end justifies the means. Machiavelli's ultimate signifi-cance rests on two ideas: that one permanent social order reflecting God's will cannot be established and that politics has its own laws and ought to be considered a science.[16]

Movable Type and the Spread of Literacy

Sometime in the thirteenth century, paper money and playing cards from China reached the West. They were *block-printed*—that is, each word, phrase, or picture was carved on a separate wooden block to be inked and used for printing. This method of reproduction was extraordinarily expen-sive and slow. By the middle of the fifteenth cen-tury, Europeans had mastered paper manufacture, which also originated in China and was introduced by the Arabs to the West in the twelfth century. Then around 1455, probably through the com-bined efforts of three men—Johann Gutenberg, Johann Fust, and Peter Schöffer, all experimenting at Mainz—movable type came into being in the West. The mirror image of each letter (rather than entire words or phrases) was carved in relief on a small block. Individual letters, easily movable, were put together to form words in lines of type that made up a page. An infinite variety of texts could be printed by reusing and rearranging pieces of type.

The effects of the invention of movable-type printing were not obvious overnight. But within a half-century of the publication of Gutenberg's Bible of 1456, printing from movable type brought about radical changes. It transformed both the private and the public lives of Europeans. Governments that "had employed the cumbersome methods of manuscripts to communicate with their subjects switched quickly to print to announce declarations of war, publish battle accounts, promulgate treaties or argue disputed points in pamphlet form. Theirs was an effort 'to win the psychological war.'" Printing made propaganda possible, emphasizing differences between opposing groups such as Crown and nobility, church and state. These differences laid the basis for the formation of distinct political parties.

Printing also stimulated the literacy of lay people and eventually came to have a deep effect on their private lives. Although most of the earliest books and pamphlets dealt with religious subjects, students, housewives, businessmen, and upper- and middle-class people sought books on all subjects. Printers responded with moralizing, medical, practical, and travel manuals. Pornography as well as piety assumed new forms. For example, the satirist Pietro Aretino used the shock of sex in pornography as a vehicle to criticize: his *Sonnetti lussuriosi* (1527) and *Ragionamenti* (1534–1536), sonnets accompanying sixteen engravings of as many sexual positions, attacked princely court life, humanist education, and false clerical piety.[17] Broadsides and flysheets allowed great public festivals, religious ceremonies, and political events to be experienced vicariously by the stay-at-home. Since books and other printed materials were read aloud to illiterate listeners, print bridged the gap between written and oral cultures.[18]

Women in Renaissance Society

How did women experience the Renaissance? Did they participate in the intellectual and artistic changes of the period? How did the status of women in the fourteenth to sixteenth centuries compare with that of women in the eleventh to thirteenth centuries?

During the Renaissance the status of upper-class women declined. If women in the High Middle Ages are compared with those of fifteenth- and sixteenth-century Italy with respect to the kind of work they performed, their access to property and political power, and their role in shaping the outlook of their society, it is clear that ladies in the Renaissance ruling classes generally had less power than comparable ladies in the feudal age.

In the cities of Renaissance Italy, well-to-do girls received an education similar to boys'. Young ladies learned their letters and studied the classics. Many read Greek as well as Latin, knew the poetry of Ovid and Virgil, and could speak one or two "modern" languages, such as French or Spanish. In this respect, Renaissance humanism represented a real educational advance for women. Some women, though a small minority among humanists, acquired great learning and fame. Some Italian women published books, and Sofonisba Anguissola (1530–1625) achieved international renown for her paintings.

Laura Cereta (1469–1499) illustrates the successes and failures of educated Renaissance women. Educated by her father, who was a member of the governing elite of Brescia in Lombardy, she learned languages, philosophy, theology, and mathematics. She also gained self-confidence and a healthy respect for her own potential. By the age of fifteen, when she married, her literary career was already launched, as her letters to several cardinals attest. For Laura Cereta, however, as for all educated women of the period, the question of marriage forced the issue: she could choose a husband, family, and full participation in social life or else study and withdrawal from the world. Cereta chose marriage but was widowed at eighteen and was able to spend the remaining twelve years of her life in study. Responding to the envy of other women and the hostility of men who felt threatened, Laura Cereta criticized "empty women, who strive for no good but exist to adorn themselves . . . these women of majestic pride, fantastic coiffures, outlandish ornament, and necks bound with gold or pearls [which] bear the glittering symbols of their captivity to men." She believed that women's inferior status derived not from the divine order of things but from the choices women were making: "For knowledge is not given as a gift, but through study. . . . The free mind, not afraid of labor, presses on to attain the good."[19] Despite Laura Cereta's faith in women's potential, most men believed that a woman who became learned violated nature and thus ceased to be a woman. Brilliant women such as Laura Cereta were severely attacked by men who feared threats to male dominance in the intellectual realm.

Sofonisba Anguissola: The Artist's Sister Minerva A nobleman's daughter and one of the first Italian women to become a recognized artist, Sofonisba did portraits of her five sisters and of prominent people. The coiffure, elegant gown, necklaces, and rings depict aristocratic dress in the mid-sixteenth century. *(Source: Milwaukee Art Museum)*

Laura Cereta was a prodigy. Ordinary girls of the urban upper middle class received some training in painting, music, and dance, in addition to a classical education. What were they to do with this training? They were to be gracious, affable, charming—in short, decorative. Renaissance women were better educated than their medieval counterparts. But whereas education trained a young man to participate in the public affairs of the city, it prepared a woman for the social functions of the home. An educated lady was supposed to know how to attract artists and literati to her husband's court and how to grace her husband's household. An educated man was supposed to know how to rule and participate in public affairs.

With respect to love and sex, the Renaissance witnessed a downward shift in women's status. In the medieval literature of courtly love—the etiquette books and romances—manners shaped the man to please the woman. According to *The Courtier,* Castiglione's manual on courtesy and good behavior, the woman was to make herself pleasing to the man. In contrast to the medieval tradition of relative sexual equality, Renaissance humanists laid the foundations for the bourgeois double standard. Men, and men alone, operated in the public sphere; women belonged in the home. Castiglione, the foremost spokesman of Renaissance love and manners, completely separated love from sexuality. For women, sex was restricted entirely to marriage. Ladies were bound to chastity, to the roles of wife and mother in a politically arranged marriage. Men, however, could pursue sensual indulgence outside marriage.[20]

Did the Renaissance have an impact on the lives of ordinary women? Women, of course, continued to perform economic functions in the expanding industries. Rural women assisted husbands and fathers in agricultural tasks. Urban women helped in the shops and were heavily involved in the Florentine textile industry, weaving cloth and reeling and winding silk. In the Venetian Arsenal, the state-controlled dock and ship construction area—the largest single industrial plant in Europe—women made sails. Widows frequently ran their husbands' businesses, and in Italy and France some became full members of guilds.

Educational opportunities being severely limited, few girls received an education. Women may have taken civic pride in the new monuments and art works in their localities, as far as they could understand them. But apart from that, the literary and art works of the Renaissance had no effect on ordinary women—or men. Many scholars believe the period of the Renaissance witnessed the emergence of the irreversible divide between an educated elite that participates in a "high culture" of art, music, literature, and learning, and the broad mass whose "popular culture" involves tools, houses, and the man-made environment.[21]

Official attitudes toward rape provide another index of the status of women in the Renaissance. A careful study of the legal evidence from Venice from 1338 to 1358 shows that rape was not considered a particularly serious crime against either the victim or society. The rape of a young girl of marriageable age or a child under twelve was considered a graver crime than the rape of a married woman. Still, the punishment for rape of a noble, marriageable girl was only a fine or about six months' imprisonment. In an age when theft and robbery were punished by mutilation, and forgery and sodomy by burning, this penalty was very mild indeed. In the eleventh century, William the Conqueror had decreed that rapists be castrated, implicitly according women protection and a modicum of respect. But in the early Renaissance, Venetian laws and their enforcement show that the governing oligarchy believed that rape damaged, but only slightly, men's property—women.[22]

Evidence from Florence in the fifteenth century also sheds light on infanticide, which historians are only now beginning to study in the Middle Ages and Renaissance. Early medieval penitentials and church councils legislated against abortion and infanticide. Nevertheless, Pope Innocent III (r. 1198–1216) was moved to establish an orphanage "because so many women were throwing their children into the Tiber."[23] In the fourteenth and early fifteenth centuries, a considerable number of children died in Florence under suspicious circumstances such as exposure or suffocation. These deaths occurred too frequently to have all been accidental, and far more girls than boys died, thus reflecting societal discrimination against girl children as inferior and less useful than boys. Dire poverty led some parents to do away with unwanted children.

The gravity of the problem of infanticide, which violated both the canon law of the church and the civil law of the state, forced the Florentine government to build the Foundling Hospital. Supporters of the institution maintained that, without public responsibility, "many children would soon be found dead in the rivers, sewers, and ditches, unbaptized."[24] The large size of the hospital suggests that great numbers of children were abandoned.

Blacks in Renaissance Society

Ever since the time of the Roman republic, a few black people had lived in western Europe. They had come, along with white slaves, as the spoils of war. Even after the collapse of the Roman Empire, Muslim and Christian merchants continued to import them. The evidence of medieval art attests to the presence of Africans in the West and Europeans' awareness of them. In the twelfth and thirteenth centuries, a large cult surrounded Saint Maurice, who was portrayed as a black knight martyred in the fourth century for refusing to renounce his Christian faith. Saint Maurice received the special veneration of the nobility.

Until the fifteenth century, the number of blacks living in western Europe was small. Then, in the fifteenth century, sizable numbers of black slaves began to enter Europe. Portuguese explorers imported perhaps a thousand a year and sold them at the markets of Seville, Barcelona, Marseilles, and Genoa. By the mid-sixteenth century, blacks, slave and free, constituted about 10 percent of the populations of the Portuguese cities of Lisbon and Évora; other cities had smaller percentages. In all, blacks made up roughly 3 percent of the Portuguese population. The Venetians specialized in the import of white slaves, but blacks were so greatly in demand at the Renaissance courts of northern Italy that the Venetians defied papal threats of excommunication to secure them.

What roles did blacks play in Renaissance society? What image did Europeans have of Africans? The medieval interest in curiosities, the exotic, and the marvelous continued into the Renaissance. Because of their rarity, black servants were highly prized and a symbol of wealth. In the late fifteenth century, Isabella, the wife of Gian Galazzo Sforza, took pride in the fact that she had ten black servants. In 1491 Isabella of Este, duchess of Mantua, instructed her agent to secure a black girl between four and eight years old, "shapely and as black as possible." The duchess saw the child as a source of entertainment: "we shall make her very happy and shall have great fun with her." She hoped that the little girl would become "the best buffoon in the world."[25] The cruel ancient tradition of retaining a professional "fool" for the amusement of a noble family persisted through the Renaissance—and even down to the twentieth century.

Adult black slaves filled a variety of positions. Many served as maids, valets, and domestic servants. The Venetians employed blacks—slave and free—as gondoliers and stevedores on the docks. In Portugal, they supplemented the labor force in virtually all occupations.[26] In Renaissance Spain and Italy, blacks performed as dancers, as actors and actresses in courtly dramas, and as musicians, sometimes making up full orchestras.[27] Slavery during the Renaissance foreshadowed the American, especially the later Brazilian, pattern.

Before the sixteenth-century "discoveries" of the non-European world, Europeans had little concrete knowledge of Africans and their cultures. Europeans knew little about them beyond biblical accounts and their attitude toward Africans was ambivalent.[28] On the one hand, Europeans perceived Africa as a remote place, the home of strange people isolated by heresy and Islam from supposedly superior European civilization. They believed that contact with Christian Europeans could only "improve" black Africans, even slaves. Theologians taught that God was light, and blackness, the opposite of light, was believed to represent the hostile forces of evil, sin, and the devil. Thus in medieval and early Renaissance art the devil was commonly represented as a black man. On the other hand, blackness was also associated with certain positive qualities. It symbolized the emptiness of worldly goods and the humility of the monastic way of life. Black vestments and funeral trappings indicated grief, and Christ had said that those who mourn are blessed. Thus in Renaissance society blacks—like women—were signs of wealth; both were used for display.

POLITICS AND THE STATE IN THE RENAISSANCE (CA 1450–1521)

The High Middle Ages witnessed the beginnings of many of the basic institutions of the modern state. Sheriffs, inquests, juries, circuit judges, professional bureaucracies, and representative assemblies all trace their origins to the twelfth and thirteenth centuries (see pages 375, 377). The linchpin for the development of states, however, was strong monarchy, and during the period of the Hundred Years' War, no ruler in western Europe was able to provide effective leadership. The resurgent power of feudal nobilities weakened the centralizing work begun earlier.

Beginning in the fifteenth century, rulers utilized the aggressive methods implied by Renaissance political ideas to rebuild their governments. First in Italy (see pages 468–469), then in France, England, and Spain, rulers began the work of reducing violence, curbing unruly nobles and troublesome elements, and establishing domestic order. The Holy Roman Empire of Germany, however, remained divided into scores of independent principalities.

The despots and oligarchs of the Italian city-states, together with Louis XI of France, Henry VII of England, and Ferdinand of Aragon, were tough, cynical, calculating rulers. In their ruthless push for power and strong governments, they sub-ordinated morality to hard results. They preferred to be secure and feared rather than loved. They could not have read Machiavelli's *The Prince,* but their actions were in harmony with its ideas.

Some historians have called Louis XI (r. 1461–1483), Henry VII (r. 1485–1509), and Ferdinand and Isabella in Spain (r. 1474–1516) "new monarchs" because they invested kingship with a strong sense of royal authority and national purpose. They stressed that the monarchy was the one institution that linked all classes and peoples within definite territorial boundaries. They insisted on the respect and loyalty of all subjects and ruthlessly suppressed opposition and rebellion, especially from the nobility. And they loved the business of kingship and worked hard at it.

In other respects, however, the methods of these rulers, which varied from country to country, were not so new. They reasserted long-standing ideas and practices of strong monarchs in the Middle Ages. To advance their authority, they seized on the maxim of the Justinian *Code*: "What pleases the prince has the force of law." Like medieval rulers, Renaissance rulers tended to rely on middle-class civil servants. Using tax revenues, medieval rulers had built armies to crush feudal anarchy. Renaissance townspeople with commercial and business interests wanted a reduction of violence and usually they were willing to pay taxes in order to achieve it.

France

The Hundred Years' War left France badly divided, drastically depopulated, commercially ruined, and agriculturally weak. Nonetheless, the ruler whom Joan of Arc had seen crowned at Reims, Charles VII (r. 1422–1461), revived the monarchy and France. He seemed an unlikely person to do so. Frail, indecisive, and burdened with questions about his paternity (his father was deranged, his mother notoriously promiscuous), Charles VII nevertheless began France's long recovery.

Charles reorganized the royal council, giving increased influence to the middle-class men, and strengthened royal finances through such taxes as the *gabelle* (on salt) and the *taille* (on land). By establishing regular companies of cavalry and archers—recruited, paid, and inspected by the state—Charles created the first permanent royal army. In 1438 he published the Pragmatic Sanction of Bourges, giving the French crown major control over the appointment of bishops, and depriving the pope of French ecclesiastical revenues. The Pragmatic Sanction established the Gallican (or French) liberties because it affirmed the special rights of the French crown over the French church. Greater control over the church and the army helped to consolidate the authority of the French crown.

Charles's son Louis XI (r. 1461–1483), called the "Spider King" by his subjects because of his treacherous and cruel character, was very much a Renaissance prince. Facing the perpetual French problems of unification of the realm and reduction of feudal disorder, he saw money as the answer. Louis promoted new industries, such as silk weaving at Lyons and Tours, and entered into commercial treaties with other countries. The revenues raised through these economic activities and severe taxation were used to improve the army. With the army Louis stopped aristocratic brigandage and slowly cut into urban independence. He was also able to gain territory that furthered his goal of expanding royal authority and unifying the kingdom. Some scholars have credited Louis XI with laying the foundations for later French royal absolutism. Indeed, he worked tirelessly to remodel the government after the disorders of the fourteenth and early fifteenth centuries. In his reliance on finances supplied by the middle classes to fight the feudal nobility, Louis was thought to be typical of the new monarchs.

England

English society suffered severely from the disorders of the fifteenth century. The aristocracy dominated the government and indulged in mischievous violence at the local level. Population, decimated by the Black Death, continued to decline. Then between 1455 and 1471, supporters of the ducal houses of York and Lancaster waged civil war, commonly called the Wars of the Roses because the symbol of the Yorkists was a white rose and that of the Lancastrians a red one. The chronic disorder hurt trade, agriculture, and domestic industry, and the authority of the monarchy sank lower than it had been in centuries.

The Yorkist Edward IV (r. 1461–1483) began re-establishing domestic tranquillity. He defeated the Lancastrian forces and after 1471 began to reconstruct the monarchy and consolidate royal power. Henry VII (r. 1485–1509) of the Welsh house of Tudor advanced the work of restoring royal prestige by crushing the power of the nobility and establishing order and law at the local level.

The Hundred Years' War had cost the nation dearly, and the money to finance it had been raised by Parliament, the arena where the nobility exerted its power. As long as the monarchy was dependent on the Lords and the Commons for revenue, the king had to call Parliament. Thus Edward IV, and subsequently the Tudors except for Henry VIII, conducted foreign policy by means of diplomacy and avoided expensive wars. Unlike the continental countries of Spain and France, England had no standing army or professional civil service bureaucracy. The Tudors relied on the support of unpaid local justices of the peace—influential landowners in the shires—to handle the work of local government. From the royal point of view, they were an inexpensive method of government. Thus for a time the English monarchy did not depend on Parliament for money, and the Crown undercut that source of aristocratic influence.

Henry VII did summon several meetings of Parliament in the early years of his reign, primarily to confirm laws, but the center of royal authority while he was king was the royal council, which governed at the national level. The royal council handled any business the king put before it—executive, legislative, judicial. It also dealt with real or potential aristocratic threats through a judicial offshoot, the Court of Star Chamber, so called because of the stars painted on the ceiling of the room in which it met. The court applied principles of Roman law, a system that exalted the power of the Crown as the embodiment of the state. The court's methods were sometimes terrifying: evidence and proceedings were secret, torture could be applied, and juries were not called. These procedures ran directly counter to English common-law precedents, but they effectively reduced aristocratic troublemaking.

The Tudors won the support of the influential upper middle class because the Crown linked government policy with the interests of that class. A commercial or agricultural upper class fears and dislikes few things more than disorder and violence. Grave, secretive, cautious, and always thrify, Henry VII promoted peace and social order, and the gentry did not object to arbitrary methods, like those used by the Court of Star Chamber, because the government had ended the long period of anarchy. At the same time both English exports of wool and the royal export tax on that wool steadily increased. When Henry VII died in 1509, he left a country at peace both domestically and internationally, a substantially augmented treasury, and the dignity and role of the royal majesty much enhanced.

Spain

Political development in Spain followed a pattern different from that of France and England. The central theme in the history of medieval Spain's separate kingdoms was disunity and plurality. Different languages, laws, and religious communities made for a rich cultural diversity shaped by Hispanic, Roman, Visigothic, Muslim, and Jewish traditions.

By the middle of the fifteenth century, the centuries-long *reconquista*—the attempts of the northern Christian kingdoms to control the entire peninsula—was nearing completion. The kingdoms of Castile and Aragon dominated weaker kingdoms, and with the exception of Granada, the Iberian Peninsula had been won for Christianity. The wedding in 1469 of the dynamic and aggressive Isabella, heiress of Castile, and the crafty and persistent Ferdinand, heir of Aragon, was the final major step in the unification and Christianization of Spain.

Ferdinand and Isabella pursued a common foreign policy. Under their rule Spain remained a loose confederation of separate states, but they determined to strengthen royal authority. To curb rebellious and warring aristocrats, they revived an old medieval institution. In the towns, popular groups called *hermandades,* or brotherhoods, were given the authority to act both as local police forces and as judicial tribunals. The hermandades repressed violence with such savage punishments that by 1498 they could be disbanded. The decisive step that Ferdinand and Isabella took to curb aristocratic power was the restructuring of the royal council. The king and queen appointed to the council only people of middle-class background; they rigorously excluded aristocrats and great territorial magnates. The council and various government boards recruited men trained in Roman law.

In the extension of royal authority and the consolidation of the territories of Spain, the church was the linchpin. Through a diplomatic alliance with the Spanish pope Alexander VI, the Spanish monarchs secured the right to appoint bishops in Spain and in the Hispanic territories in America. This power enabled the "Most Catholic Kings of Spain," a title that the pope granted to Ferdinand and Isabella, to establish, in effect, a national church.[29] Revenues from ecclesiastical estates provided the means to raise an army to continue the reconquista. The victorious entry of Ferdinand and Isabella into Granada on January 6, 1492, signaled the conclusion of eight centuries of Spanish struggle against the Arabs in southern Spain. In 1512 Ferdinand conquered Navarre in the north.

Although the Muslims had been defeated, there still remained a sizable and, in the view of the Catholic sovereigns, potentially dangerous minority, the Jews. Since ancient times, Christian governments had usually suppressed religious faiths that differed from the official state religion, considering them politically dangerous. France and England had expelled their Jewish populations in the Middle Ages, but in Spain Jews had been tolerated and had played a decisive role in the economic and intellectual life of the several Spanish kingdoms. Then, in the late fourteenth century, anti-Semitic riots and pogroms led many Spanish Jews to convert to Christianity; such people were called *conversos.*

By the middle of the fifteenth century, many conversos held high positions in Spanish society as financiers, physicians, merchants, tax collectors, and even officials of the church hierarchy. Numbering perhaps 200,000 in a total population of about 7.5 million, Jews exercised an influence quite disproportionate to their numbers. Aristocratic grandees who borrowed heavily from Jews resented their financial dependence, and churchmen questioned the sincerity of Jewish conversions. At first, Isabella and Ferdinand continued the policy of royal toleration—Ferdinand himself had inherited Jewish blood from his mother. But many conversos apparently reverted to the faith of their ancestors, prompting Ferdinand and Isabella in 1478 to secure Rome's permission to revive the Inquisition, a medieval judicial procedure for the punishment of heretics.

Although the Inquisition was a religious institution established to safeguard the Catholic faith, in Spain it was controlled by the Crown and served primarily as a political unifying force. Because the Spanish Inquisition commonly applied torture to extract confessions, first from lapsed conversos, then from Muslims, and later from Protestants, it

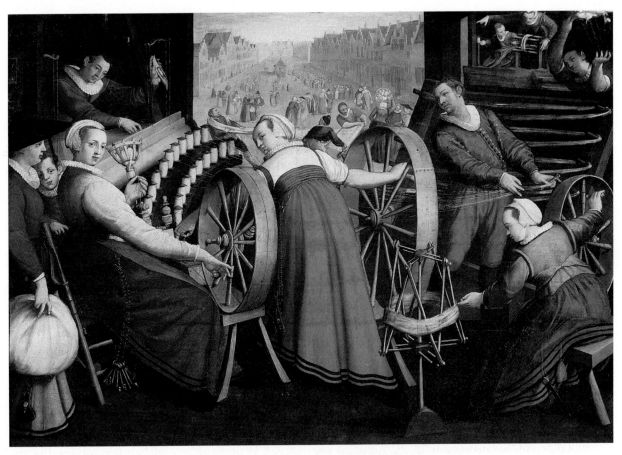

✳ **van Schwanenburgh: The Spinners**   In the late sixteenth century, the prosperity of Leyden in Holland rested on the textile industry, which in turn depended on the import of merino wool from Spain. In this lush scene three large spinning wheels are operated simultaneously. Women composed 30 percent of the work force but earned much less than men. *(Source: Stedelijk Museum, "De Lakenhal," Leiden, Holland)*

gained a notorious reputation. Thus the word *inquisition,* meaning "any judicial inquiry conducted with ruthless severity," came into the English language.

In 1492, Isabella and Ferdinand took a further dire and drastic step against backsliding conversos. They issued an edict expelling all practicing Jews from Spain. Of the community of perhaps 200,000 Jews, 150,000 fled. (Efforts were made, through last-minute conversions, to retain good Jewish physicians.) Absolute religious orthodoxy and purity of blood (untainted by Jews or Muslims) became the theoretical foundation of the Spanish national state.

The diplomacy of the Catholic rulers of Spain achieved a success they never anticipated. Partly out of hatred for the French and partly to gain international recognition for their new dynasty, Ferdinand and Isabella in 1496 married their second daughter, Joanna, heiress to Castile, to the archduke Philip, heir through his mother to the Burgundian Netherlands and through his father to the Holy Roman Empire.

Germany and the Habsburg Dynasty

The marriage in 1477 of Maximilian I of the house of Habsburg and Mary of Burgundy was a decisive event in early modern European history. Burgundy consisted of two parts: the French duchy with its capital at Dijon, and the Burgundian Netherlands with its capital at Brussels. Through this union with the rich and powerful duchy of Burgundy, the Austrian House of Habsburg, the strongest ruling family in the empire, started to become an international power.

In the fifteenth and sixteenth centuries, as in the Middle Ages, relations among states continued to be greatly affected by the connections of royal families. Marriage often determined the diplomatic status of states. The Habsburg-Burgundian marriage angered the French, who considered Burgundy part of French territory. Within the empire, German principalities that resented Austria's preeminence began to see that they shared interests with France. The marriage of Maximilian and Mary inaugurated centuries of conflict between the Austrian House of Habsburg and the kings of France. Germany was to be the chief arena of the struggle.

"Other nations wage war; you, Austria, marry." Historians dispute the origins of the adage, but no one questions its accuracy. The heir of Mary and Maximilian, Philip of Burgundy, married Joanna of Castile, daughter of Ferdinand and Isabella of Spain. Philip and Joanna's son Charles V (1500–1558) fell heir to a vast conglomeration of territories. Through a series of accidents and unexpected deaths, Charles inherited Spain from his mother, together with her possessions in the Americas and the Spanish dominions in Italy, Sicily, Sardinia, and Naples. From his father he inherited the Habsburg lands in Austria, southern Germany, the Low Countries, and Franche-Comté in east-central France.

Charles's inheritance was an incredibly diverse collection of states and peoples, each governed in a different manner and held together only by the person of the emperor (Map 15.1). Charles's Italian adviser, the grand chancellor Gattinara, told the young ruler: "God has set you on the path toward world monarchy." Charles not only believed this; he was convinced that it was his duty to maintain the political and religious unity of Western Christendom. In this respect Charles V was the last medieval emperor.

Charles needed and in 1519 secured the imperial title from the electors. Forward-thinking Germans proposed government reforms. They urged placing the administration in the hands of an imperial council whose president, the emperor's appointee, would have ultimate executive power. They also recommended reforms of the imperial finances, the army, and the judiciary. Such ideas did not interest the young emperor at all. When he finally arrived in Germany from Spain and opened his first Diet (assembly of the estates of the empire) at Worms in January 1521, he naively announced that "the empire from of old has had not many masters, but one, and it is our intention to be that one." Charles went on to say that he was to be treated as of greater account than his predecessors because he was more powerful than they had been. In view of the long history of aristocratic power in the Holy Roman Empire, Charles's notions were pure fantasy.

Charles continued the Burgundian policy of his grandfather Maximilian. German revenues and German troops were subordinated to the needs of other parts of the empire, first Burgundy and then Spain. Habsburg international interests came before the need for reform in Germany.

Two years before the electors chose as emperor the nineteen-year-old Charles, Martin Luther had launched a movement to reform the church.

✤ THE CONDITION OF THE CHURCH (CA 1400–1517)

The papal conflict with the German emperor Frederick II in the thirteenth century, followed by the Babylonian Captivity and then the Great Schism (see pages 427–428), badly damaged the prestige of church leaders. In the fourteenth and fifteenth centuries, leaders of the conciliar movement reflected educated public opinion when they called for the reform of the church "in head and members" (see page 428). The humanists of Italy and the Christian humanists of northern Europe denounced corruption in the church. As Machiavelli put it, "We Italians are irreligious and corrupt above others, because the Church and her representatives set us the worst example."[30] In *The Praise of Folly,* Erasmus condemned the absurd superstitions of the parish clergy and the excessive rituals of the monks. The records of episcopal visitations of parishes, civil court records, and even such literary masterpieces as Chaucer's *Canterbury Tales* and Boccaccio's *The Decameron* tend to confirm the perceptions of corruption.

Signs of Disorder

In the early sixteenth century, critics of the church concentrated their attacks on three disorders: cleri-

MAP 15.1 The European Empire of Charles V   Charles V exercised theoretical jurisdiction over more territory than anyone since Charlemagne. This map does not show his Latin American and Asian possessions.

Legend:
- Lands inherited by Charles V
- Lands gained by Charles V, 1519–1556
- States favorable to Charles V
- Enemies of Charles V
- Boundary of Holy Roman Empire

cal immorality, clerical ignorance, and clerical pluralism. There was little pressure for doctrinal change; the emphasis was on moral and administrative reform.

Since the fourth century, church law had required candidates for the priesthood to accept absolute celibacy. The requirement had always been difficult to enforce. Many priests, especially those ministering to country people, had concubines, and reports of neglect of the rule of celibacy were common. Immorality, of course, included more than sexual transgressions. Clerical drunkenness, gambling, and indulgence in fancy dress were frequent charges. There is no way of knowing how many priests were guilty of such behavior. But because such conduct was so much at odds with the church's rules and moral standards, it scandalized the educated faithful.

The bishops enforced regulations regarding the education of priests casually. As a result, standards for ordination were shockingly low. The evidence points consistently to the low quality of the Italian clergy. In northern Europe—in England, for ex-

ample—recent research shows an improvement in clerical educational standards in the early sixteenth century. Nevertheless, parish priests throughout Europe were not as educated as the educated laity. Predictably, Christian humanists, with their concern for learning, condemned the ignorance or low educational level of the clergy. Many priests could barely read and write, and critics laughed at the illiterate priest mumbling Latin words to the Mass that he could not understand.

Pluralism and absenteeism constituted the third major abuse. Many clerics, especially higher ecclesiastics, held several *benefices,* or offices, simultaneously but seldom visited them, let alone performed the spiritual responsibilities those offices entailed.

The Folly of Indulgences This woodcut viciously satirizes the church's sale of indulgences. With one foot in the holy water symbolizing the rite of purification (Psalm 50) and the other foot resting on the coins paid for indulgences, the church, portrayed as a rapacious eagle with its right hand stretched out for offerings, writes out an indulgence with excrement—which represents its worth. Fools with a false sense of security sit in the animal's gaping mouth, representing hell, to which a devil delivers the pope wearing a three-tiered crown and holding the keys to heaven originally given to Saint Peter. (*Source: Kunstsammlungen der Veste Coburg*)

Instead, they collected revenues from each benefice and paid a poor priest a fraction of the income to fulfill the spiritual duties of a particular local church. The French king Louis XII's diplomat Antoine du Prat is perhaps the most notorious example of absenteeism. He was archbishop of Sens, but the first time he entered his cathedral was in his own funeral procession.

Critics condemned pluralism, absenteeism, and the way money seemed to change hands when a bishop entered into his office. Although royal governments strengthened their positions and consolidated their territories in the fifteenth and sixteenth centuries, rulers lacked sufficient revenues to pay and reward able civil servants. The Christian church, with its dioceses and abbeys, possessed a large proportion of the wealth of the countries of Europe. What better way for a ruler to reward government officials, who were usually clerics, than with bishoprics and other high church offices? The practice was sanctioned by centuries of tradition. Thus churchmen who served as royal councilors, diplomats, treasury officials, chancellors, viceroys, and judges were paid by the church for their services to the state. It is astonishing that so many conscientiously tried to carry out their religious duties on top of their public burdens.

In most countries except England, members of the nobility occupied the highest church positions. The spectacle of proud, aristocratic prelates living in magnificent splendor contrasted very unfavorably with the simple fishermen who were Christ's disciples. Nor did the popes of the period 1450 to 1550 set much of an example. They lived like secular Renaissance princes, supporting artists and undertaking building projects, often making the papal court a model of luxury and scandal. Some popes used papal power and wealth to advance the material interests of their own families.

The court of the Spanish pope Rodrigo Borgia, Alexander VI (r. 1492–1503), who publicly acknowledged his mistress and children, reached new heights of impropriety. Because of the prevalence of intrigue, sexual promiscuity, and supposed poisonings, the name Borgia became a synonym for moral corruption. Pope Julius II (r. 1503–1513) donned military armor and personally led papal troops against the French invaders of Italy in 1506. After him, Giovanni de' Medici, the son of Lorenzo de' Medici, carried on as Pope Leo X (r. 1513–1521) the Medicean tradition of being a great patron of the arts.

Signs of Vitality

Calls for reform testify to the spiritual vitality of the church as well as to its problems. In the late fifteenth and early sixteenth centuries, both individuals and groups within the church were working actively for reform. In Spain, for example, Cardinal Francisco Jiménez (1436–1517) visited religious houses, encouraged the monks and friars to obey their rules and constitutions, and set high standards for the training of the diocesan clergy.

In Holland, beginning in the late fourteenth century, a group of pious lay people called Brethren of the Common Life sought to make religion a personal, inner experience. They lived in stark simplicity while daily carrying out the Gospel teaching of feeding the hungry, clothing the naked, and visiting the sick. The Brethren also taught in local schools to prepare devout candidates for the priesthood and the monastic life. The spirituality of the Brethren of the Common Life found its finest expression in the classic *The Imitation of Christ* by Thomas à Kempis, which urges Christians to take Christ as their model and seek perfection in a simple way of life. As Protestants would do later, the Brethren stressed the centrality of Scripture in the spiritual life.[31] In the mid-fifteenth century, the movement had houses in the Netherlands, in central Germany, and in the Rhineland; it was a true religious revival.

If external religious observances are a measure of depth of heartfelt conviction, Europeans in the early sixteenth century remained deeply pious and loyal to the Roman Catholic church. Villagers participated in processions honoring the local saints. Middle-class people made pilgrimages to the great shrines such as Saint Peter's in Rome. The upper classes continued to remember the church in their wills.

The papacy also expressed concern for reform. Pope Julius II summoned an ecumenical, or universal, council, which met in the church of Saint John Lateran in Rome from 1512 to 1517. Most of the bishops were Italian and did not represent a broad cross section of international opinion, so the designation *ecumenical* was not really appropriate. Nevertheless, the bishops and theologians who attended the Lateran Council strove earnestly to reform the church. The council recommended higher standards for education of the clergy and instruction of the common people. The bishops placed the responsibility for eliminating

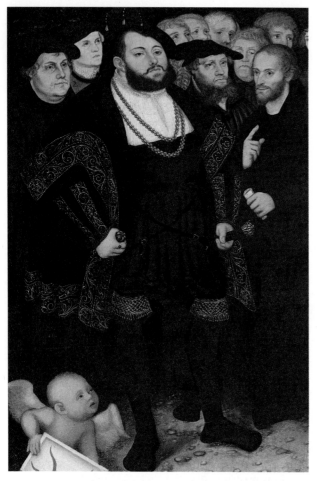

✦ **Lucas Cranach the Younger: Luther and the Wittenberg Reformers** The massive figure of John Frederick, elector of Saxony, who protected and supported Luther, dominates this group portrait. Luther is on the far left, his associate Philip Melancthon far right in the front. Luther's face shows a quiet determination. *(Source: The Toledo Museum of Art, Toledo, Ohio; Gift of Edward Drummond Libbey)*

bureaucratic corruption squarely on the papacy and suggested significant doctrinal reforms. But many obstacles stood in the way of ecclesiastical change. Nor did the actions of an obscure German friar immediately force the issue.

✦ MARTIN LUTHER AND THE BIRTH OF PROTESTANTISM

As a result of a personal religious struggle, a German Augustinian friar, Martin Luther (1483–1546) launched the Protestant Reformation of the sixteenth century. Luther articulated the widespread desire for reform of the Christian church and the deep yearning for salvation that were typical of his time.

Martin Luther was born at Eisleben in Saxony, the second son of a copper miner who later became a mine owner. At considerable sacrifice, his father sent him to school and then to the University of Erfurt. Hans Luther intended his son to study law and have a legal career, which for centuries had been the steppingstone to public office and material success. Badly frightened during a thunderstorm, however, young Luther vowed to become a friar. Without consulting his father, he entered a monastery at Erfurt in 1505. Luther was ordained a priest in 1507 and after additional study earned the doctorate of theology. From 1512 until his death, he served as professor of Scripture at the new University of Wittenberg.

Martin Luther was exceedingly scrupulous in his monastic observances and was devoted to prayer, penances, and fasting; but the doubts and conflicts that trouble any sensitive young person who has just taken a grave step were especially intense in young Luther. He had terrible anxieties about sin, and he worried continually about his salvation. Luther intensified his monastic observances but still found no peace of mind.

Luther's wise and kindly confessor, Staupitz, directed him to the study of Saint Paul's letters. Gradually, Luther arrived at a new understanding of the Pauline letters and of all Christian doctrine. He came to believe that salvation comes not through external observances and penances but through a simple faith in Christ. Faith is the means by which God sends humanity his grace, and faith is a free gift that cannot be earned.

The Ninety-five Theses

An incident illustrative of the condition of the church in the early sixteenth century propelled Martin Luther onto the stage of history and brought about the Reformation in Germany. The University of Wittenberg lay within the archdiocese of Magdeburg. The archbishop of Magdeburg, Albert, held two other high ecclesiastical offices. To hold all three offices simultaneously— blatant pluralism—required papal dispensation. Archbishop Albert borrowed money from the Fuggers, a wealthy banking family of Augsburg, to pay Pope Leo X for the dispensation (the pope wanted the money to complete work on Saint Peter's Basilica). Leo X then authorized Archbishop Albert to sell indulgences in Germany to repay the Fuggers.

Wittenberg was in the political jurisdiction of the elector Frederick of Saxony. When Frederick forbade the sale of indulgences within his duchy, people of Wittenberg, including some of Professor Luther's students, streamed across the border from Saxony into Jütenborg in Thuringia to buy them.

What exactly was an *indulgence*? According to Catholic theology, individuals who sin alienate themselves from God and his love. In order to be reconciled to God, the sinner must confess his or her sins to a priest and do the penance that the priest assigns. The doctrine of indulgence rested on three principles. First, God is merciful, but he is also just. Second, Christ and the saints, through their infinite virtue, established a "treasury of merits" on which the church, because of its special relationship with Christ and the saints, can draw. Third, the church has the authority to grant sinners the spiritual benefits of those merits. Originally an indulgence was a remission of the temporal (priest-imposed) penalties for sin. Beginning in the twelfth century, the papacy and bishops had given Crusaders such indulgences. By the later Middle Ages people widely believed that an indulgence secured total remission of penalties for sin—on earth or in purgatory—and ensured swift entry into heaven.

Archbishop Albert hired the Dominican friar John Tetzel to sell the indulgences. Tetzel mounted an advertising blitz. One of his slogans—"As soon as coin in coffer rings, the soul from purgatory springs"—brought phenomenal success. Men and women bought indulgences not only for themselves but for deceased parents, relatives, or friends.

Luther was severely troubled that ignorant people believed they had no further need for repentance once they had purchased an indulgence. Thus, according to historical tradition, in the academic fashion of the times, on the eve of All Saints' Day (October 31), 1517, he attached to the door of the church at Wittenberg Castle a list of ninety-five theses (or propositions) on indulgences. By this act Luther intended only to start a theological discussion of the subject and to defend the theses publicly.

Luther's theses were soon translated from Latin into German, printed, and read throughout the empire. Immediately, broad theological issues were raised. When questioned, Luther rested his fundamental argument on the principle that there was no biblical basis for indulgences. But, replied Luther's opponents, to deny the legality of indulgences was to deny the authority of the pope who had authorized them. The issue was drawn: where did authority lie in the Christian church?

The papacy responded with a letter condemning some of Luther's propositions, ordering that his books be burned, and giving him two months to recant or be excommunicated. Luther retaliated by publicly burning the letter. By January 3, 1521, when the excommunication was supposed to become final, the controversy involved more than theological issues. The papal legate wrote, "All Germany is in revolution. Nine-tenths shout 'Luther' as their warcry; and the other tenth cares nothing about Luther, and cries 'Death to the court of Rome.'"[32]

In this highly charged atmosphere the twenty-one-year-old emperor Charles V held his first Diet at Worms and summoned Luther to appear before it. When ordered to recant, Luther replied in language that rang all over Europe:

Unless I am convinced by the evidence of Scripture or by plain reason—for I do not accept the authority of the Pope or the councils alone, since it is established that they have often erred and contradicted themselves—I am bound by the Scriptures I have cited and my conscience is captive to the Word of God. I cannot and will not recant anything, for it is neither safe nor right to go against conscience. God help me. Amen.[33]

The emperor declared Luther an outlaw of the empire and denied him legal protection. Duke Frederick of Saxony, however, protected him.

Protestant Thought

Between 1520 and 1530, Luther worked out the basic theological tenets that became the articles of faith for his new church and subsequently for all Protestant groups. At first the word *Protestant* meant "Lutheran," but with the appearance of many protesting sects it became a general term applied to all non-Catholic Christians. Ernst Troeltsch, a German student of the sociology of religion, has defined *Protestantism* as a "modification of Catholicism, in which the Catholic formulation of questions was retained, while a different answer was given to them." Luther provided new answers to four old, basic theological issues.[34]

First, how is a person to be saved? Traditional Catholic teaching held that salvation was achieved by both faith *and* good works. Luther held that salvation comes by faith alone. Women and men are saved, said Luther, by the arbitrary decision of God, irrespective of good works or the sacraments. God, not people, initiates salvation.

Second, where does religious authority reside? Christian doctrine had long maintained that authority rests both in the Bible and in the traditional teaching of the church. Luther maintained that authority rests in the Word of God as revealed in the Bible alone and as interpreted by an individual's conscience. He urged that each person read and reflect on the Scriptures.

Third, what is the church? Medieval churchmen had tended to identify the church with the clergy. Luther re-emphasized the Catholic teaching that the church consists of the entire community of Christian believers.

Finally, what is the highest form of Christian life? The medieval church had stressed the superiority of the monastic and religious life over the secular. Luther argued that all vocations, whether ecclesiastical or secular, have equal merit and that every person should serve God according to his or her individual calling. Protestantism, in sum, represented a reformulation of the Christian heritage.

The Social Impact of Luther's Beliefs

As early as 1521, Luther had a vast following. By the time of his death in 1546, people of all social classes had become Lutheran. What was the immense appeal of Luther's religious ideas?

Historical research on the German towns has shown that two significant late medieval developments prepared the way for Luther's ideas. First, since the fifteenth century, city governments had expressed resentment at clerical privileges and immunities. Religious orders frequently held large amounts of urban property, but priests, monks, and nuns paid no taxes and were exempt from civic responsibilities such as defending the city. City governments were determined to integrate the clergy into civic life by reducing their privileges and giving them public responsibilities.

Second, critics of the late medieval church, especially informed and intelligent townspeople, had condemned the irregularity and poor quality of sermons. As a result, prosperous burghers in many towns had established preacherships. Preachers were men of superior education who were required to deliver about a hundred sermons a year, each lasting about forty-five minutes. Luther's ideas attracted many preachers, and in Stuttgart, Reutlingen, and other towns, preachers became Protestant

Hans Holbein the Younger: Christ as the Man of Sorrows The scriptural basis of this concept is Isaiah 53:3–5: "He was pierced for our offenses, crushed by our sins. Upon him was the chastisement that makes us whole; by his stripes we were healed." Using a theme characteristic of early-sixteenth-century German piety, and placing the subject within a Renaissance architectural structure, Holbein produced this devotional painting in 1520 for the private use of the donor. *(Source: Öffentliche Kunstsammlung Basel)*

leaders. Preacherships also encouraged the Protestant form of worship, in which the sermon, not the Eucharist, was the central part of the service.[35]

In the countryside the attraction of the German peasants to Lutheran beliefs was almost predictable. Luther himself came from a peasant background and admired the peasants' ceaseless toil. Peasants respected Luther's defiance of church authority. Moreover, they thrilled to the words Luther used in his treatise *On Christian Liberty* (1520): "A Christian man is the most free lord of all and subject to none." Taken out of context, these words easily stirred social unrest.

Fifteenth-century Germany had witnessed several peasant revolts. In the early sixteenth century, the economic condition of the peasantry varied from place to place but was generally worse than it had been in the fifteenth century and was deteriorating. Crop failures in 1523 and 1524 aggravated an explosive situation. In 1525 representatives of the Swabian peasants met at the city of Memmingen and drew up twelve articles that expressed their grievances. The peasants complained that nobles had seized village common lands, which traditionally had been used by all; that nobles had imposed new rents and services on the peasants working properties; and that nobles had forced poor peasants to pay unjust death duties in the form of their best horses or cows. Wealthy, socially mobile peasants especially resented these burdens, which, they maintained, were new.[36] The peasants believed their demands conformed to Scripture and cited Luther as a theologian who could prove that they did.

Luther wanted to prevent rebellion. At first he sided with the peasants and in his tract *An Admonition to Peace* blasted the nobles:

We have no one on earth to thank for this mischievous rebellion, except you lords and princes, especially you blind bishops and mad priests and monks. . . . In your government you do nothing but flay and rob your subjects in order that you may lead a life of splendor and pride, until the poor common folk can bear it no longer.[37]

But nothing justified the use of armed force, he warned: "The fact that rulers are unjust and wicked does not excuse tumult and rebellion; to punish wickedness does not belong to everybody, but to the worldly rulers who bear the sword."[38] As for biblical support for the peasants' demands, he maintained that Scripture had nothing to do with earthly justice or material gain.

Massive revolts first broke out near the Swiss frontier and then swept through Swabia, Thuringia, the Rhineland, and Saxony. The crowds' slogans came directly from Luther's writings. "God's righteousness" and the "Word of God" were invoked in the effort to secure social and economic justice. The peasants who expected Luther's support were soon disillusioned. He had written of the "freedom" of the Christian, but he had meant the freedom to obey the Word of God, for in sin men and women lose their freedom and break their relationship with God. To Luther, freedom meant independence from the authority of the Roman church; it did *not* mean opposition to legally established secular powers. Firmly convinced that rebellion hastened the end of civilized society, he wrote a tract *Against the Murderous, Thieving Hordes of the Peasants:* "Let everyone who can smite, slay, and stab [the peasants], secretly and openly, remembering that nothing can be more poisonous, hurtful or devilish than a rebel."[39] The nobility ferociously crushed the revolt. Historians estimate that over seventy-five thousand peasants were killed in 1525.

Luther took literally these words in Saint Paul's Letter to the Romans: "Let every soul be subject to the higher powers. For there is no power but of God: the powers that be are established by God. Whosoever resists the power, resists the ordinance of God: and they that resist shall receive to themselves damnation."[40] As it developed, Lutheran theology exalted the state, subordinated the church to the state, and everywhere championed "the powers that be." The revolt of 1525 strengthened the authority of lay rulers. Peasant economic conditions, however, moderately improved. For example, in many parts of Germany, enclosed fields, meadows, and forests were returned to common use.

Like the peasants, educated people and humanists were much attracted by Luther's words. He advocated a simpler, personal religion based on faith and the Scriptures, a return to the spirit of the early church, the abolition of elaborate ceremonial—precisely the reforms the northern humanists had been calling for. Ulrich Zwingli (1484–1531), for example, a humanist of Zurich, was strongly influenced by Luther's bold stand. It stimulated Zwingli's reforms in the Swiss city of Zurich and later in Bern.

Luther's linguistic skill, together with his translation of the New Testament in 1523, led to the acceptance of his dialect of German as the standard version of German. His insistence that everyone should read and reflect on the Scriptures attracted the literate and thoughtful middle classes partly because he appealed to their intelligence. Moreover, the business classes, preoccupied with making money, envied the church's wealth, disapproved of the luxurious lifestyle of some churchmen, and resented tithes and ecclesiastical taxation. Luther's doctrines of salvation by faith and the priesthood of all believers not only raised the religious status of the commercial classes but protected their pocketbooks as well.

Hymns, psalms, and Luther's two catechisms (1529)—compendiums of basic religious knowledge—also show the power of language in spreading the ideals of the Reformation. The reformers knew "that rhyme, meter, and melodies could forcefully impress minds and affect sensibilities." Lutheran hymns such as "A Mighty Fortress Is Our God" expressed deep feelings, were easily remembered, and imprinted on the mind central points of doctrine. Luther's *Larger Catechism* contained brief sermons on the main articles of faith; his *Shorter Catechism* gave concise explanations of doctrine in question-and-answer form. Both catechisms stressed the importance of the Ten Commandments, the Lord's Prayer, the Apostle's Creed, and the sacraments for the believing Christian. Though originally intended for the instruction of pastors, these catechisms became powerful tools for the indoctrination of men and women of all ages, especially the young.[41]

What appeal did Luther's message have for women? Luther's argument that all vocations have equal merit in the sight of God gave dignity to those who performed ordinary, routine, domestic tasks. The abolition of monasticism in Protestant territories led to the exaltation of the home, which Luther and other reformers stressed as the special domain of the wife. The Christian home, in contrast to the place of business, became the place for the exercise of the gentler virtues—love, tenderness, reconciliation, the carrying of one another's burdens. The Protestant abolition of private confession to a priest freed women from embarrassing explorations of their sexual lives. Protestants established schools where girls, as well as boys, became literate in the catechism and the Bible. The reformers stressed marriage as the cure for clerical concupiscence. Protestantism thus proved attractive to the many women who had been priests' concubines and mistresses: they became legal and honorable wives.[42]

For his time, Luther held enlightened views on matters of sexuality and marriage. He wrote to a young man, "Dear lad, be not ashamed that you desire a girl, nor you my maid, the boy. Just let it lead you into matrimony and not into promiscuity, and it is no more cause for shame than eating and drinking."[43] Luther was confident that God took delight in the sexual act and denied that original sin affected the goodness of creation. He believed, however, that marriage was a woman's career. A student recorded Luther as saying, early in his public ministry, "Let them bear children until they are dead of it; that is what they are for." A happy marriage to the former nun Katharine von Bora mellowed him, and another student later quoted him as saying, "Next to God's Word there is no more precious treasure than holy matrimony. God's highest gift on earth is a pious, cheerful, God-fearing, home-keeping wife, with whom you may live peacefully, to whom you may entrust your goods, and body and life."[44] Though Luther deeply loved his "dear Katie," he believed that women's principal concerns were children, the kitchen, and the church.

GERMANY AND THE PROTESTANT REFORMATION

The history of the Holy Roman Empire in the later Middle Ages is a story of dissension, disintegration, and debility. Unlike Spain, France, and England, the empire lacked a strong central power. In 1356 the Golden Bull legalized what had long existed—government by an aristocratic federation. Each of seven electors gained virtual sovereignty in his own territory. The agreement ended disputed elections in the empire; it also reduced the central authority of the Holy Roman emperor. The empire was characterized by weak borders, localism, and chronic disorder. The nobility strengthened their territories, while imperial power declined.

The Political Impact of Luther's Beliefs

In the sixteenth century, the practice of religion remained a public matter. Everyone participated in the religious life of the community, just as almost everyone shared in the local agricultural work.

Peasants Sack the Abbey of Weissenau   Convinced that the monks lived idle, luxurious lives on money squeezed from the poor, peasants sacked the abbeys during the great revolt of 1525. *(Source: Château de Waldburg, Archives/Schneiders/Artephot)*

Whatever spiritual convictions individuals held in the privacy of their consciences, the emperor, king, prince, magistrate, or other civil authority determined the official form of religious practice within his jurisdiction. Almost everyone believed that the presence of a faith different from that of the majority represented a political threat to the security of the state. Only a tiny minority, and certainly none of the princes, believed in religious liberty.

Against this background, the religious storm launched by Martin Luther swept across Germany. Several elements in his religious reformation stirred patriotic feelings. Anti-Roman sentiment ran high. Humanists lent eloquent intellectual support. And Luther's translation of the New Testament into German evoked national pride.

For decades devout lay people and churchmen had called on the German princes to reform the church. In 1520 Luther took up the cry in his *Appeal to the Christian Nobility of the German Nation.* Unless the princes destroyed papal power in Germany, Luther argued, reform was impossible. He urged the princes to confiscate ecclesiastical wealth and to abolish indulgences, dispensations, pardons, and clerical celibacy. He told them that it was their public duty to bring about the moral reform of the church. Luther based his argument in part on the papacy's financial exploitation of Germany:

How comes it that we Germans must put up with such robbery and such extortion of our property at the hands of the pope? Why do we Germans let them make such fools and apes of us? It would all be more bearable if in this way they only stole our property; but they lay waste the churches and rob Christ's sheep of their pious shepherds, and destroy the worship and the Word of God.[45]

These words fell on welcome ears and itchy fingers. Luther's appeal to German patriotism gained him strong support, and national feeling influenced many princes otherwise confused by or indifferent to the complexities of the religious issues.

The church in Germany possessed great wealth. And, unlike other countries, Germany had no strong central government to check the flow of gold to Rome. Rejection of Roman Catholicism and adoption of Protestantism would mean the legal confiscation of lush farmlands, rich monasteries, and wealthy shrines. Some German princes were sincerely attracted to Lutheranism, but many civil authorities realized that they had a great deal to gain by embracing the new faith. A steady stream of duchies, margraviates, free cities, and bishoprics did so and secularized church property. The decision reached at Worms in 1521 to condemn Luther and his teaching was not enforced because the German princes did not want to enforce it.

Many princes used the religious issue to extend their financial and political independence. The results were unfortunate for the improvement of German government. The Protestant movement ultimately proved a political disaster for Germany.

Charles V must share blame with the German princes for the disintegration of imperial authority in the empire. He neither understood nor took an interest in the constitutional problems of Germany, and he lacked the material resources to oppose Protestantism effectively there. Throughout his reign he was preoccupied with his Flemish, Spanish, Italian, and American territories. Moreover, the Turkish threat prevented him from acting effectively against the Protestants; Charles's brother Ferdinand needed Protestant support against the Turks who besieged Vienna in 1529.

Five times between 1521 and 1555, Charles V went to war with the Valois kings of France. The issue each time was the Habsburg lands acquired by the marriage of Maximilian and Mary of Burgundy. Much of the fighting occurred in Germany. The cornerstone of French foreign policy in the sixteenth and seventeenth centuries was the desire to keep the German states divided. Thus Europe witnessed the paradox of the Catholic king of France supporting the Lutheran princes in their challenge to his fellow Catholic, Charles V. Habsburg-Valois Wars advanced the cause of Protestantism and promoted the political fragmentation of the German empire.

Finally, in 1555, Charles agreed to the Peace of Augsburg, which, in accepting the status quo, officially recognized Lutheranism. Each prince was permitted to determine the religion of his territory. Most of northern and central Germany became Lutheran; the south remained Roman Catholic. There was no freedom of religion, however.

Princes or town councils established state churches to which all subjects of the area had to belong. Dissidents, whether Lutheran or Catholic, had to convert or leave. The political difficulties Germany inherited from the Middle Ages had been compounded by the religious crisis of the sixteenth century.

❖ THE GROWTH OF THE PROTESTANT REFORMATION

By 1555 much of northern Europe had broken with the Roman Catholic church. All of Scandinavia, England (except during the reign of Mary Tudor), Scotland, and large parts of Switzerland, Germany, and France had rejected the religious authority of Rome and adopted new faiths. Because a common religious faith had been the one element uniting all of Europe for almost a thousand years, the fragmentation of belief led to profound changes in European life and society. The most significant new form of Protestantism was Calvinism, of which the Peace of Augsburg had made no mention at all.

Calvinism

In 1509, while Luther was studying for the doctorate at Wittenberg, John Calvin (1509–1564) was born in Noyon in northwestern France. Luther inadvertently launched the Protestant Reformation. Calvin, however, had the greater impact on future generations. In 1533 he experienced a religious crisis, as a result of which he converted to Protestantism. His theological writings profoundly influenced the social thought and attitudes of Europeans and English-speaking peoples all over the world, especially in Canada and the United States.

Convinced that God selects certain people to do his work, Calvin believed that God had specifically called him to reform the church. Accordingly, he accepted an invitation to assist in the reformation of the city of Geneva. There, beginning in 1541, Calvin worked assiduously to establish a Christian society ruled by God through civil magistrates and reformed ministers. Geneva, "a city that was a Church," became the model of a Christian community for sixteenth-century Protestant reformers.

To understand Calvin's Geneva, it is necessary to understand Calvin's ideas. These he embodied in *The Institutes of the Christian Religion,* first published in 1536 and definitively issued in 1559. The cornerstone of Calvin's theology was his belief in the absolute sovereignty and omnipotence of God and the total weakness of humanity. Before the infinite power of God, he asserted, men and women are as insignificant as grains of sand.

Calvin did not ascribe free will to human beings, because that would detract from the sovereignty of God. Men and women cannot actively work to achieve salvation; rather, God in his infinite wisdom decided at the beginning of time who would be saved and who damned. This viewpoint constitutes the theological principle called *predestination*:

Predestination we call the eternal decree of God, by which he has determined in himself, what he would have become of every individual of mankind. . . . God has once for all determined, both whom he would admit to salvation, and whom he would condemn to destruction. We affirm that this counsel, as far as concerns the elect, is founded on his gratuitous mercy, totally irrespective of human merit; but that to those whom he devotes to condemnation, the gate of life is closed by a just and irreprehensible, but incomprehensible, judgment. How exceedingly presumptuous it is only to inquire into the causes of the Divine will; which is in fact, and is justly entitled to be, the cause of everything that exists. . . . For the will of God is the highest justice; so that what he wills must be considered just, for this very reason, because he wills it.[46]

Many people have found the doctrine of predestination, which dates back to Saint Augustine and Saint Paul, a pessimistic view of the nature of God, who, they feel, revealed himself in the Old and New Testaments as merciful as well as just. But "this terrible decree," as even Calvin called it, did not lead to pessimism or fatalism. Rather, the Calvinist believed in the redemptive work of Christ and was confident that God had elected (saved) him or her. Predestination served as an energizing dynamic, forcing a person to undergo hardships in the constant struggle against evil.

Calvin aroused Genevans to a high standard of morality. Using his sermons and a program of religious education, God's laws and man's were enforced in Geneva. Using his *Genevan Catechism*, published in 1541, children and adults memorized set questions and answers and acquired a summary of their faith and a guide for daily living. Calvin's sermons and his *Catechism* gave a whole generation of Genevans thorough instruction in the reformed religion.[47]

In the reformation of the city, the Genevan Consistory also exercised a powerful role. This body consisted of twelve laymen, plus the Company of Pastors, of which Calvin was the permanent moderator (presider). The duties of the Consistory were "to keep watch over every man's life [and] to admonish amiably those whom they see leading a disorderly life." Calvin emphasized that the Consistory's activities should be thorough and "its eyes may be everywhere," but corrections were only "medicine to turn sinners to the Lord."[48]

Although all municipal governments in early modern Europe regulated citizens' conduct, none did so with the severity of Geneva's Consistory under Calvin's leadership. Nor did it make any distinction between what we would consider crimes against society and simple unchristian conduct. The Consistory investigated and punished absence from sermons, criticism of ministers, dancing, playing cards, family quarrels, and heavy drinking. The civil authorities handled serious crimes and heresy and, with the Consistory's approval, sometimes used torture to extract confessions. Between 1542 and 1546 alone seventy-six persons were banished from Geneva and fifty-eight executed for heresy, adultery, blasphemy, and witchcraft.

Calvin reserved his harshest condemnation for religious dissenters, declaring them "dogs and swine":

God makes plain that the false prophet is to be stoned without mercy. We are to crush beneath our heel all affections of nature when His honor is concerned. The father should not spare his child, nor brother his brother, nor husband his own wife or the friend who is dearer to him than life. No human relationship is more than animal unless it be grounded in God.[49]

Calvin translated his words into action. He made an example of the Spanish humanist Michael Servetus, who, persecuted by the Spanish Inquisition, escaped to Geneva. In addition to denying the Trinity—which identifies God as three divine persons, Father, Son, and Holy Spirit—Servetus insisted that a person under twenty cannot commit a mortal sin. The city fathers considered this idea dangerous to public morality, "especially in these days when the young are so corrupted." Servetus was burned at the stake.

To many sixteenth-century Europeans, Calvin's Geneva seemed "the most perfect school of Christ since the days of the Apostles." Religious refugees from France, England, Spain, Scotland, and Italy

THE LATER MIDDLE AGES, RENAISSANCE, AND PROTESTANT AND CATHOLIC REFORMATIONS, 1300–1600

1309–1376	Babylonian Captivity of the papacy
1310–1320	Dante, *The Divine Comedy*
1337–1453	Hundred Years' War
1347–1351	The Black Death (returned intermittently until ca 1700)
1356	Golden Bull transforms the Holy Roman Empire into an aristocratic confederation
ca 1376	John Wyclif attacks the church's temporal power and asserts the supremacy of the Scriptures
1378–1417	The Great Schism
1381	Peasants' revolt in England
1387–1400	Chaucer, *Canterbury Tales*
1404	Christine de Pisan, *The City of Ladies*
1414–1418	Council of Constance ends the schism, postpones reform, executes John Hus
1453	Capture of Constantinople by the Ottoman Turks, ending the Byzantine Empire
1455–1471	Wars of the Roses in England
1456	Gutenberg Bible
1492	Unification of Spain under Ferdinand and Isabela; expulsion of Jews and Muslims from Spain Columbus reaches the Americas
1494	France invades Italy, inaugurating sixty years of war on Italian soil
1513	Machiavelli, *The Prince*
1517	Martin Luther publishes the Ninety-five Theses
1523	Luther's translation of the New Testament into German
1525	Peasants' revolt in Germany
1533	Act in Restraint of Appeals inaugurates the English Reformation
1536	Calvin, *The Institutes of the Christian Religion*
1540	Loyola founds the Society of Jesus (Jesuits)
1541	Calvin establishes a theocracy in Geneva
1543	Copernicus, *On the Revolutions of the Heavenly Spheres*
1545–1563	Council of Trent
1555	Peace of Augsburg officially recognized
1588	Spanish Armada
1603	Shakespeare, *Hamlet*
1611	Authorized or King James Version of the Bible

✿ **Calvinist Worship**   A converted house in Lyons, France, serves as a church for the simple Calvinist service. Although Calvin's followers believed in equality and elected officials administered the church, here men and women are segregated, and some people sit on hard benches while others sit in upholstered pews. Beside the pulpit an hourglass hangs to time the preacher's sermon. (Could the dog sit still for that long?) (*Source: Bibliothèque publique et universitaire, Geneva*)

visited the city. Subsequently, the Reformed church of Calvin served as the model for the Presbyterian church in Scotland, the Huguenot church in France, and the Puritan churches in England and New England. The Calvinist provision for congregational participation and vernacular liturgy helped to satisfy women's desire to belong to and participate in a meaningful church organization. The Calvinist ethic of the "calling" dignified all work with a religious aspect: hard work, well done, was said to be pleasing to God. This doctrine encouraged an aggressive, vigorous activism. In the *Institutes* Calvin provided a systematic theology for Protestantism. The Reformed church of Calvin had a strong and well-organized machinery of government. These factors, together with the social

and economic applications of Calvin's theology, made Calvinism the most dynamic force in sixteenth- and seventeenth-century Protestantism.

The Anabaptists

The name *Anabaptist* derives from a Greek word meaning "to baptize again." The Anabaptists, sometimes described as the left wing of the Reformation, believed that only adults could make a free choice about religious faith, baptism, and entry into the Christian community. Thus they considered the practice of baptizing infants and children preposterous and wanted to rebaptize believers who had been baptized as children. Anabaptists took the Gospel and, at first, Luther's teachings absolutely literally and favored a return to the kind of church that had existed among the earliest Christians—a voluntary association of believers who had experienced an inner light.

Anabaptists maintained that only a few people would receive the inner light. This position meant that the Christian community and the Christian state were not identical. In other words, Anabaptists believed in the separation of church and state and in religious tolerance. They almost never tried to force their values on others. In an age that believed in the necessity of state-established churches, Anabaptist views on religious liberty were thought to undermine that concept.

Each Anabaptist community or church was entirely independent; it selected its own ministers and ran its own affairs. In 1534 the community at Münster in Germany, for example, established a legal code that decreed the death penalty for insubordinate wives. Moreover, the Münster community also practiced polygamy and forced all women under a certain age to marry or face expulsion or execution.

Anabaptists admitted women to the ministry. They shared goods as the early Christians had done, refused all public offices, and would not serve in the armed forces. In fact, they laid great stress on pacifism. A favorite Anabaptist scriptural quotation was "By their fruits you shall know them," suggesting that if Christianity was a religion of peace, the Christian should not fight. With such beliefs Anabaptists were inevitably a minority. Anabaptism later attracted the poor, the unemployed, the uneducated. Geographically, Anabaptists drew their members from depressed urban areas.

Ideas such as absolute pacifism and the distinction between the Christian community and the state brought down on these unfortunate people fanatical hatred and bitter persecution. Zwingli, Luther, Calvin, and Catholics all saw—quite correctly—the separation of church and state as leading ultimately to the complete secularization of society. The powerful rulers of Swiss and German society immediately feared that the combination of religious differences and economic grievances would lead to civil disturbances. In Saxony, in Strasbourg, and in the Swiss cities, Anabaptists were either banished or executed by burning, beating, or drowning. Their community spirit and the edifying example of their lives, however, contributed to the survival of Anabaptist ideas.

The Quakers with their gentle pacifism, the Baptists with their emphasis on an inner spiritual light, the Congregationalists with their democratic church organization, and, in 1787, the authors of the U.S. Constitution with their concern for the separation of church and state—all trace their origins in part to the Anabaptists of the sixteenth century.

The English Reformation

As on the continent of Europe, the Reformation in England had social and economic causes as well as religious ones. As elsewhere, too, Christian humanists had for decades been calling for the purification of the church. When the personal matter of the divorce of King Henry VIII (r. 1509–1547) became enmeshed with political issues, a complete break with Rome resulted.

Demands for ecclesiastical reform dated back at least to the fourteenth century. The Lollards (see page 428) had been driven underground in the fifteenth century but survived in parts of southern England and the Midlands. Working-class people, especially cloth workers, were attracted to their ideas. The Lollards stressed the individual's reading and interpretation of the Bible, which they considered the only standard of Christian faith and holiness. They put no stock in the value of the sacraments and were vigorously anticlerical. Lollards opposed ecclesiastical wealth, the veneration of the saints, prayers for the dead, and all war. Although they had no notion of justification by faith, like Luther they insisted on the individual soul's direct responsibility to God.

Still, traditional Catholicism exerted an enormously strong, diverse, and vigorous hold over the imagination and loyalty of the people. The teachings of Christianity were graphically represented in the liturgy, constantly reiterated in sermons, enacted in plays, and carved and printed on walls, screens, and the windows of parish churches. A zealous clergy, increasingly better educated, engaged in a "massive catechetical enterprise." No substantial gulf existed between the religion of the clergy and educated elite and the broad mass of the English people.[50] The Reformation in England was an act of state, initiated by the king's emotional life.

In 1527, having fallen in love with Anne Boleyn, Henry wanted his marriage to Catherine of Aragon annulled. Catherine had failed to bear a boy child, and Henry claimed that only a male heir to the throne could prevent a disputed succession. He thus petitioned Pope Clement VII (r. 1523–1534) for an annulment. When Henry had married Catherine, he had secured a dispensation from Pope Julius II eliminating all legal technicalities about Catherine's previous union with Henry's late brother, Arthur. Henry now argued that Pope Julius's dispensation had contradicted the law of God—that a man may not marry his brother's widow. The English king's request reached Rome at the very time that Luther was widely publishing tracts condemning the papacy. If Clement had granted Henry's annulment and thereby admitted that Julius II had erred, Clement would have given support to the Lutheran assertion that popes substitute their own evil judgments for the law of God. This Clement could not do, so he delayed acting on Henry's request.[51] The capture and sack of Rome in 1527 by mercenaries working for the emperor Charles V, Queen Catherine's nephew, thoroughly tied the pope's hands.

Since Rome appeared to be thwarting Henry's matrimonial plans, he decided to remove the English church from papal jurisdiction. Henry used Parliament to legalize the Reformation in England. The Act in Restraint of Appeals (1533) declared the king to be the supreme sovereign in England and forbade judicial appeals to the papacy, thus establishing the Crown as the highest legal authority in the land. The Act for the Submission of the Clergy (1534) required churchmen to submit to the king and forbade the publication of ecclesiastical laws without royal permission. The Supremacy Act of 1534 declared the king the supreme head of the Church of England.

An authority on the Reformation Parliament has written that probably only a small number of those who voted for the Restraint of Appeals actually knew they were voting for a permanent break with Rome.[52] Some opposed the king. John Fisher, the bishop of Rochester, a distinguished scholar and humanist, lashed the clergy with scorn for their cowardice. Thomas More, who had written *Utopia* nearly two years before (see page 475), resigned the chancellorship rather than acknowledge the rejection of papal authority. Fisher, More, and other dissenters were beheaded for treason in 1535.

When Anne Boleyn failed twice to produce a male child, Henry VIII charged her with adulterous incest and in 1536 had her beheaded. His third wife, Jane Seymour, gave Henry the desired

son, Edward, but died in childbirth. Henry went on to three more wives before he passed to his reward in 1547.

Between 1535 and 1539, under the influence of his chief minister, Thomas Cromwell, Henry decided to dissolve the English monasteries because he wanted their wealth. The king ended nine hundred years of English monastic life, dispersed the monks and nuns, and confiscated their lands. Hundreds of properties were sold to the middle and upper classes and the proceeds spent on war. The closing of the monasteries did not achieve a more equitable distribution of land and wealth. Rather, the "bare ruined choirs where late the sweet birds sang"—as Shakespeare's Sonnet 73 describes the desolate religious houses—testified to the loss of a valuable cultural force in English life. The redistribution of land, however, strengthened the upper classes and tied them to the Tudor Dynasty.

Henry retained such traditional Catholic practices and doctrines as auricular confession, clerical celibacy, and *transubstantiation* (the doctrine that the bread and wine of the Eucharist are transformed into the body and blood of Christ although their appearance does not change). But Protestant literature circulated, and Henry approved the selection of men of Protestant sympathies as tutors for his son.

Did the religious changes have broad popular support? Recent scholarship has emphasized that the English Reformation came from above. The surviving evidence does not allow us to gauge the degree of opposition to (or support for) Henry's break with Rome. Certainly, many lay people wrote to the king, begging him to spare the monasteries. "Most laypeople acquiesced in the Reformation because they hardly knew what was going on, were understandably reluctant to jeopardise life or limb, a career or the family's good name."[53] But not all quietly acquiesced. In 1536 popular opposition in the north to the religious changes led to the Pilgrimage of Grace, a massive multiclass rebellion that proved the largest in English history. In 1546 serious rebellions in East Anglia and in the west, despite possessing economic and Protestant components, reflected considerable public opposition to the state-ordered religious changes.[54]

After Henry's death, the English church shifted left and right. In the short reign of Henry's sickly son Edward VI (r. 1547–1553), strongly Protestant ideas exerted a significant influence on the

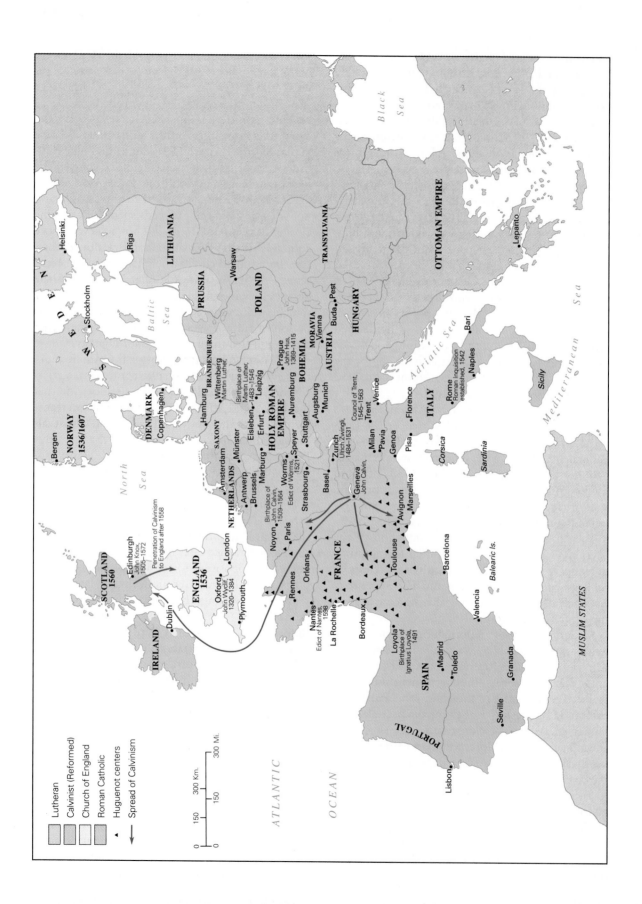

Lutheran

Calvinist (Reformed)

Church of England

Roman Catholic

◄ Huguenot centers

→ Spread of Calvinism

0   150   300 Km.

0   150   300 Mi.

ATLANTIC

OCEAN

North Sea

IRELAND

Dublin

SCOTLAND 1560

Edinburgh
John Knox,
1505–1572

Penetration of Calvinism
to England after 1558

ENGLAND 1536

London

Oxford
John Wyclif,
1320–1384

Plymouth

NORWAY 1536/1607

Bergen

S W E D E N

Stockholm

Helsinki

Riga

Baltic Sea

LITHUANIA

Warsaw

PRUSSIA

POLAND

DENMARK

Copenhagen

Hamburg

BRANDENBURG

Wittenberg
Martin Luther

Birthplace of
Martin Luther,
1483–1546

Eisleben

Leipzig

NETHERLANDS

Amsterdam

Münster

SAXONY

Antwerp

Brussels

Marburg

Birthplace of
John Calvin,
1509–1564

Noyon

Erfurt

HOLY ROMAN EMPIRE

Worms

Edict of Worms,
1521

Speyer

Nuremberg

Augsburg

Munich

Stuttgart

Prague

John Hus,
1369–1415

BOHEMIA

MORAVIA

AUSTRIA

Vienna

Buda

Pest

HUNGARY

TRANSYLVANIA

OTTOMAN EMPIRE

Black Sea

Lepanto

Adriatic Sea

Bari

Naples

Mediterranean Sea

Rome
Roman Inquisition
established, 1542

ITALY

Florence

Venice

Trent

Council of Trent,
1545–1563

Milan

Pavia

Genoa

Pisa

Corsica

Sardinia

Sicily

Paris

Strasbourg

Basel

Zurich
Ulrich Zwingli,
1484–1531

Geneva
John Calvin,

Avignon

Marseilles

Rennes

Orléans

FRANCE

Toulouse

Bordeaux

Nantes
Edict of Nantes,
1598

La Rochelle

Loyola
Birthplace of
Ignatius Loyola,
1491

Barcelona

Valencia

Balearic Is.

SPAIN

Madrid

Toledo

Granada

Seville

PORTUGAL

Lisbon

MUSLIM STATES

religious life of the country. Archbishop Thomas Cranmer simplified the liturgy, invited Protestant theologians to England, and prepared the first *Book of Common Prayer* (1549). In stately and dignified English, the *Book of Common Prayer* included, together with the Psalter, the order for all services of the Church of England.

The equally brief reign of Mary Tudor (r. 1553–1558) witnessed a sharp move back to Catholicism. The devoutly Catholic daughter of Catherine of Aragon and Henry, Mary rescinded the Reformation legislation of her father's reign and fully restored Roman Catholicism. Mary's marriage to her cousin Philip of Spain, son of the emperor Charles V, proved highly unpopular in England, and her persecution and execution of several hundred Protestants further alienated her subjects. Mary's death raised to the throne her sister Elizabeth (r. 1558–1603) and inaugurated the beginnings of religious stability.

Elizabeth had been raised a Protestant, but at the start of her reign sharp differences existed in England. Catholics wanted a Roman Catholic ruler, but a vocal number of returning exiles wanted all Catholic elements in the Church of England eliminated. Members of the latter group were called Puritans because they wanted to "purify" the church. Probably one of the shrewdest politicians in English history, Elizabeth chose a middle course between Catholic and Puritan extremes. She insisted on dignity in church services and political order in the land. She did not care what people believed as long as they kept quiet about it. Avoiding precise doctrinal definitions, Elizabeth had herself styled "Supreme Governor of the Church of England, Etc.," and left it to her subjects to decide what the "Etc." meant.

The parliamentary legislation of the early years of Elizabeth's reign—laws sometimes labeled the "Elizabethan Settlement"—required outward conformity to the Church of England and uniformity in all ceremonies. Everyone had to attend Church of England services; those who refused were fined. During Elizabeth's reign, the Anglican church

 **MAP 15.2 The Protestant and the Catholic Reformations** The reformations shattered the religious unity of Western Christendom. What common cultural traits predominated in regions where a particular branch of the Christian faith was maintained or took root?

(from the Latin *Ecclesia Anglicana*), as the Church of England was called, moved in a moderately Protestant direction. Services were conducted in English, monasteries were not re-established, and the clergy were allowed to marry. But the bishops remained as church officials, and apart from language, the services were quite traditional.

THE CATHOLIC AND THE COUNTER-REFORMATIONS

Between 1517 and 1547, the reformed versions of Christianity known as Protestantism made remarkable advances. All of England, Scandinavia, much of Scotland and Germany, and sizable parts of France and Switzerland adopted the creeds of Luther, Calvin, and other reformers. Still, the Roman Catholic church made a significant comeback. After about 1540, no new large areas of Europe, except for the Netherlands, accepted Protestant beliefs (Map 15.2).

Historians distinguish between two types of reform within the Catholic church in the sixteenth and seventeenth centuries. The Catholic Reformation began before 1517 and sought renewal basically through the stimulation of a new spiritual fervor. The Counter-Reformation started in the 1540s as a reaction to the rise and spread of Protestantism. The Counter-Reformation was a Catholic effort to convince or coerce dissidents or heretics to return to the church.

The Renaissance princes who sat on the throne of Saint Peter were not blind to the evils that existed. Modest reform efforts had begun with the Lateran Council that Pope Julius II called in 1512. The Dutch pope Adrian VI (r. 1522–1523) instructed his legate in Germany "to say that we frankly confess that God permits this [Lutheran] persecution of his church on account of the sins of men, especially those of the priests and prelates."[55]

Overall, why did the popes, spiritual leaders of the Western church, move so slowly? The answers lie in the personalities of the popes themselves, in their preoccupation with political affairs in Italy, and in the awesome difficulty of reforming so complicated a bureaucracy as the Roman curia. Clement VII, a true Medici, was far more interested in elegant tapestries and Michelangelo's painting of the Last Judgment than in theological disputes in barbaric Germany or far-off England.

In the Habsburg-Valois conflicts in Italy Clement first backed the emperor Charles. He then switched to the French ruler. Shortly afterward, the emperor's Spanish and German mercenaries sacked and looted Rome and took him captive.

The idea of reform was closely linked to the idea of a general council representing the entire church. Popes such as Clement VII, remembering fifteenth-century conciliar attempts to limit papal authority, resisted calls for a council, fearing loss of power, revenue, and prestige.

The Council of Trent

In the papal conclave that followed the death of Clement VII, Cardinal Alexander Farnese promised two German cardinals that if he were elected pope he would summon a council. He won the election and ruled as Pope Paul III (r. 1534–1549). This Roman aristocrat, humanist, and astrologer, who immediately made his teenage grandsons cardinals, seemed an unlikely person to undertake serious reform. Yet Paul III appointed as cardinals several learned and reform-minded men; established the Inquisition in the Papal States; and called a council, which finally met at Trent, an imperial city close to Italy (see Map 15.2).

The Council of Trent met intermittently from 1545 to 1563. It was called not only to reform the church but to secure reconciliation with the Protestants. Lutherans and Calvinists were invited to participate, but their insistence that the Scriptures be the sole basis for discussion made reconciliation impossible. International politics repeatedly cast a shadow over the theological debates. Charles V opposed discussions on any matter that might further alienate his Lutheran subjects. The French kings worked against any reconciliation of Roman Catholicism and Lutheranism, wanting the German states to remain divided. Portugal, Poland, Hungary, and Ireland sent representatives, but very few German bishops attended.

Another problem was the persistence of the conciliar theory of church government. Some bishops wanted a concrete statement asserting the supremacy of a church council over the papacy. The adoption of the conciliar principle could have led to a divided church. The bishops had a provincial and national outlook; only the papacy possessed an international religious perspective. The centralizing tenet was established that all acts of the council required papal approval.

In spite of the obstacles, the achievements of the Council of Trent are impressive. It dealt with both doctrinal and disciplinary matters. The council gave equal validity to the Scriptures and to tradition as sources of religious truth and authority. It reaffirmed the seven sacraments and the traditional Catholic teaching on transubstantiation, rejecting Lutheran and Calvinist positions.

The council tackled the problems arising from ancient abuses by strengthening ecclesiastical discipline. Tridentine (from *Tridentum,* the Latin word for "Trent") decrees required bishops to reside in their own dioceses, suppressed pluralism and simony, and forbade the sale of indulgences. Clerics who kept concubines were to give them up. In a highly original canon, the council required every diocese to establish a seminary for the education and training of the clergy and insisted that preference for admission be given to sons of the poor. Seminary professors were to determine whether candidates for ordination had *vocations*—genuine callings as evidenced by purity of life, detachment from the broader secular culture, and a steady inclination toward the priesthood. This was a novel idea, since from the time of the early church, parents had determined their sons' (and daughters') religious careers. Also, great emphasis was laid on preaching and instructing the laity, especially the uneducated.

One decision had especially important social consequences for lay people. Since the time of the Roman Empire, many couples had treated marriage as a completely personal matter, exchanged vows privately without witnesses, and thus formed clandestine (secret) unions. This widespread practice frequently led later to denials by one party that a marriage had taken place, to conflicts over property, and to disputes in the ecclesiastical courts that had jurisdiction over marriage. The Tridentine decree *Tametsi* (1563) stipulated that for a marriage to be valid, consent (the essence of marriage) as expressed in the vows had to be given publicly before witnesses, one of whom had to be the parish priest. Trent thereby ended secret marriages in Catholic countries.

The Council of Trent did not bring about reform immediately. But the Tridentine decrees laid a solid basis for the spiritual renewal of the church and for the enforcement of correction. For four centuries, the doctrinal and disciplinary legislation of Trent served as the basis for Roman Catholic faith, organization, and practice.

New Religious Orders and the Inquisition

The establishment of new religious orders within the church reveals a central feature of the Catholic Reformation. These new orders developed in response to the need to raise the moral and intellectual level of the clergy and people. Education was a major goal of them all.

The Ursuline order of nuns, founded by Angela Merici (1474–1540), attained enormous prestige for the education of women. The daughter of a country gentleman, Angela Merici worked for many years among the poor, sick, and uneducated around her native Brescia in northern Italy. In 1535 she established the Ursuline order to combat heresy through Christian education of young girls. The Ursulines sought to re-Christianize society by training future wives and mothers. Approved as a religious community by Paul III in 1544, the Ursulines rapidly grew and spread to France and the New World. Their schools in North America, stretching from Quebec to New Orleans, provided superior education for young women and inculcated the spiritual ideals of the Catholic Reformation.

The Society of Jesus, founded by Ignatius Loyola (1491–1556), a former Spanish soldier, played a powerful international role in resisting the spread of Protestantism, converting Asians and Latin American Indians to Catholicism, and spreading Christian education all over Europe. While recuperating from a severe battle wound to his legs, Loyola studied a life of Christ and other religious books and decided to give up his military career and become a soldier of Christ. His great classic, *Spiritual Exercises,* directed the individual imagination and will to the reform of life and a new spiritual piety.

Loyola was apparently a man of considerable personal magnetism. After study at the universities

Juan de Valdes Leal: Pope Paul III Approves the Jesuit Constitutions Although Paul III devoted considerable energy to advancing the interests of his (Farnese) family, he also tried to meet the challenge of Protestantism—by means of the Council of Trent and new religious orders. When the Jesuit constitutions were read to him, Paul III supposedly murmured, "There is the finger of God." The portrait of Ignatius Loyola (holding the paper) is a reasonable likeness; that of the pope is an idealization: in 1540 he was a very old man. (*Source: MAS, Barcelona*)

in Salamanca and Paris, he gathered a group of six companions and in 1540 secured papal approval of the new Society of Jesus, whose members were called Jesuits. The first Jesuits were recruited primarily from the wealthy merchant and professional classes. They saw the Reformation as a pastoral problem, its causes and cures related not to doctrinal issues but to people's spiritual condition. Reform of the church as Luther and Calvin understood the word *reform* played no role in the future the Jesuits planned for themselves. Their goal was "to help souls." Loyola also possessed a gift for leadership that consisted in spotting talent and "in the ability to see how at a given juncture change is more consistent with one's scope than staying the course."[56]

The Society of Jesus developed into a highly centralized, tightly knit organization. Candidates underwent a two-year novitiate, in contrast to the usual one-year probation required by older religious orders. In addition to the traditional vows of poverty, chastity, and obedience, professed members vowed "special obedience to the sovereign pontiff regarding missions."[57] Thus, as stability—the promise to live one's life in the monastery—was what made a monk, so mobility—the commitment to go anywhere for the help of souls—was the defining characteristic of a Jesuit. Flexibility and the willingness to respond to the needs of time and circumstance formed the Jesuit tradition. In this respect they were very modern, and they attracted many recruits.

The Society of Jesus achieved phenomenal success for the papacy and the reformed Catholic church. Jesuit schools adopted the modern humanist curricula and methods. They first concentrated on the children of the poor but soon were educating the sons of the nobility. As confessors and spiritual directors to kings, Jesuits exerted great political influence. Operating on the principle that the end sometimes justifies the means, they were not above spying. Indifferent to physical comfort and personal safety, they carried Christianity to India and Japan before 1550 and to Brazil, North America, and the Congo in the seventeenth century. Within Europe, the Jesuits brought southern Germany and much of eastern Europe back to Catholicism.

In 1542 Pope Paul III established the Sacred Congregation of the Holy Office with jurisdiction over the Roman Inquisition, a powerful instrument of the Counter-Reformation. A committee of six cardinals, the Roman Inquisition had judicial authority over all Catholics and the power to arrest, imprison, and execute. Under the fanatical Cardinal Caraffa, it vigorously attacked heresy. The Roman Inquisition operated under the principles of Roman law. It accepted hearsay evidence, was not obliged to inform the accused of charges against them, and sometimes used torture. Echoing one of Calvin's remarks about heresy, Cardinal Caraffa wrote, "No man is to lower himself by showing toleration towards any sort of heretic, least of all a Calvinist."[58] The Holy Office published the *Index of Prohibited Books,* a catalogue of forbidden reading.

Within the Papal States, the Roman Inquisition effectively destroyed heresy (and some heretics). Outside the papal territories, its influence was slight. Governments had their own judicial systems for the suppression of treasonable activities, as religious heresy was then considered.[59]

SUMMARY

From about 1050 to 1300, a new economy emerged in Italy, based on Venetian and Genoese shipping and long-distance trade and on Florentine banking and cloth manufacture. The combination of these commercial activities and the struggle of urban communities for political independence from surrounding feudal lords led to the appearance of a new wealthy aristocratic class. With this foundation, Italy was the scene of a remarkable intellectual and artistic flowering. Based on renewed interest in the Greco-Roman world, the Renaissance had a classicizing influence on many facets of culture. Despots or oligarchs ruled the city-states of fifteenth- and sixteenth-century Italy and manipulated Renaissance culture to enhance their personal power. Moving beyond Italy, the individualism, humanism, and secular spirit characteristic of the Italian Renaissance affected the culture of all Europe.

In northern Europe, city merchants and rural gentry allied with rising monarchies. Using taxes provided by business people, kings provided a greater degree of domestic peace and order, conditions essential for trade. In Spain, France, and England, rulers also emphasized royal dignity and authority. Except in the Holy Roman Empire, feudal monarchies gradually evolved in the direction of nation-states.

In the sixteenth century and through most of the seventeenth, religion and religious issues continued to play a major role in the lives of individuals and in the policies and actions of governments. The age of the Reformation presents very real paradoxes. The break with Rome and the rise of Lutheran, Anglican, Calvinist, and other faiths destroyed the unity of Europe as an organic Christian society. The strength of religious convictions caused political fragmentation, and religion, whether Protestant or Catholic, decisively influenced the growth of national states. Although most reformers rejected religious toleration, they helped pave the way for it.

Scholars have maintained that the sixteenth century witnessed the beginnings of the modern world. They are both right and wrong. The sixteenth-century revolt from the church laid the groundwork for the eighteenth-century revolt from the Christian God, one of the strongest supports of life in Western culture. In this respect, the Reformation marks the beginning of the modern world, with its secularism and rootlessness. At the same time, it can be argued that the sixteenth century represents the culmination of the Middle Ages. Martin Luther's anxieties about salvation show him to be very much a medieval man. His concerns had deeply troubled serious individuals since the time of Saint Augustine. Modern people tend to be less troubled by them.

NOTES

1. See L. Martines, *Power and Imagination: City-States in Renaissance Italy* (New York: Vintage Books, 1980), esp. pp. 332–333.

2. Ibid., pp. 22–61.

3. Ibid., pp. 221–237, esp. p. 221.

4. Quoted in J. Burckhardt, *The Civilization of the Renaissance in Italy* (London: Phaidon Books, 1951), p. 89.

5. *Memoirs of Benvenuto Cellini; A Florentine Artist; Written by Himself* (London: J. M. Dent & Sons, 1927), p. 2.

6. See C. Trinkaus, *In Our Image and Likeness: Humanity and Divinity in Italian Humanist Thought,* vol. 2 (London: Constable, 1970), pp. 505–529.

7. See Martines, *Power and Imagination,* Ch. 13, esp. pp. 241, 243.

8. See A. Hauser, *The Social History of Art,* vol. 2 (New York: Vintage Books, 1959), Ch. 3, esp. pp. 60, 68.

9. G. Bull, trans., *Aretino: Selected Letters* (Baltimore: Penguin Books, 1976), p. 109.

10. Hauser, *The Social History of Art,* pp. 48–49.

11. Quoted in E. H. Harbison, *The Christian Scholar and His Calling in the Age of the Reformation* (New York: Charles Scribner's Sons, 1956), p. 109.

12. Quoted in F. Seebohm, *The Oxford Reformers* (London: J. M. Dent & Sons, 1867), p. 256.

13. Quoted in W. H. Woodward, *Vittorino da Feltre and Other Humanist Educators* (Cambridge: Cambridge University Press, 1897), pp. 96–97.

14. C. E. Detmold, trans., *The Historical, Political and Diplomatic Writings of Niccolò Machiavelli* (Boston: J. R. Osgood, 1882), pp. 51–52.

15. Ibid., pp. 54–55.

16. See F. Gilbert, *Machiavelli and Guicciardini: Politics and History in Sixteenth Century Florence* (New York: Norton, 1984), pp. 197–200.

17. See L. Hunt, *The Invention of Pornography: Obscenity and the Origins of Modernity, 1500–1800* (New York: Zone Books, 1993), pp. 10, 93–95.

18. Quoted in E. L. Eisenstein, *The Printing Press as an Agent of Change: Communications and Cultural Transformations in Early Modern Europe,* vol. 1 (New York: Cambridge University Press, 1979), p. 135; for an overall discussion, see pp. 126–159.

19. M. L. King, "Book-lined Cells: Women and Humanism in the Early Italian Renaissance," in *Beyond Their Sex: Learned Women of the European Past,* ed. P. H. Labalme (New York: New York University Press, 1980), pp. 66–81, esp. p. 73.

20. This account rests on J. Kelly-Gadol, "Did Women Have a Renaissance?" in *Becoming Visible: Women in European History,* ed. R. Bridenthal and C. Koontz (Boston: Houghton Mifflin, 1977), pp. 137–161, esp. p. 161.

21. See Peter Burke, "What Is the History of Popular Culture," in *What Is History Today?* ed. J. Gardiner (Atlantic Highlands, N.J.: Humanities Press, 1989), pp. 121–123.

22. G. Ruggerio, "Sexual Criminality in Early Renaissance Venice, 1338–1358," *Journal of Social History* 8 (Spring 1975): 18–31.

23. Quoted in R. C. Trexler, "Infanticide in Florence: New Sources and First Results," *History of Childhood Quarterly* 1 (Summer 1973): 99.

24. Ibid., p. 100.

25. J. Devisse and M. Mollat, *The Image of the Black in Western Art,* trans. W. G. Ryan, vol. 2 (New York: Morrow, 1979), pt. 2, pp. 187–188.

26. See C. M. Saunders, *A Social History of Black Slaves and Freedmen in Portugal, 1441–1555* (New York: Cambridge University Press, 1982), pp. 59, 62–88, 176–179.

27. Ibid., pp. 190–194.

28. Ibid., pp. 255–258.

29. See J. H. Elliott, *Imperial Spain, 1469–1716* (New York: Mentor Books, 1963), esp. pp. 75, 97–108.

30. Quoted in Burckhardt, *The Civilization of the Renaissance in Italy,* p. 262.

31. See R. R. Post, *The Modern Devotion: Confrontation with Reformation and Humanism* (Leiden: E. J. Brill, 1968), esp. pp. 237–238, 255, 323–348.

32. Quoted in O. Chadwick, *The Reformation* (Baltimore: Penguin Books, 1976), p. 55.

33. Quoted in E. H. Harbison, *The Age of Reformation* (Ithaca, N.Y.: Cornell University Press, 1963), p. 52.

34. This discussion is based heavily on Harbison, *The Age of Reformation,* pp. 52–55.

35. See S. E. Ozment, *The Reformation in the Cities: The Appeal of Protestantism to Sixteenth-Century Germany and Switzerland* (New Haven, Conn.: Yale University Press, 1975), pp. 32–45.

36. See S. E. Ozment, *The Age of Reform, 1250–1550: An Intellectual and Religious History of Late Medieval and Reformation Europe* (New Haven, Conn.: Yale University Press, 1980), pp. 273–279.

37. Quoted ibid., p. 280.

38. Quoted ibid., p. 281.

39. Quoted ibid., p. 284.

40. Romans 13:1–2.

41. G. Strauss, *Luther's House of Learning: Indoctrination of the Young in the German Reformation* (Baltimore: Johns Hopkins University Press, 1978), esp. pp. 159–162, 231–233.

42. See R. H. Bainton, *Women of the Reformation in Germany and Italy* (Minneapolis: Augsburg, 1971), pp. 9–10; and Ozment, *The Reformation in the Cities,* pp. 53–54, 171–172.

43. Quoted in H. G. Haile, *Luther: An Experiment in Biography* (Garden City, N.Y.: Doubleday, 1980), p. 272.

44. Quoted in J. Atkinson, *Martin Luther and the Birth of Protestantism* (Baltimore: Penguin Books, 1968), pp. 247–248.

45. *Martin Luther: Three Treatises* (Philadelphia: Muhlenberg Press, 1947), pp. 28–31.

46. J. Allen, trans., *John Calvin: The Institutes of the Christian Religion* (Philadelphia: Westminster Press, 1930), bk. 3, chap. 21, paras. 5, 7.

47. E. W. Monter, *Calvin's Geneva* (New York: Wiley, 1967), pp. 98–108.

48. Ibid., p. 137.

49. Quoted in Bainton, *Women of the Reformation in Germany and Italy,* pp. 69–70.

50. E. Duffy, *The Stripping of the Altars: Traditional Religion in England, 1400–1580* (New Haven, Conn.: Yale University Press, 1992), pp. 2–6, and passim.

51. See R. Marius, *Thomas More: A Biography* (New York: Knopf, 1984), pp. 215–216.

52. See S. E. Lehmberg, *The Reformation Parliament 1529–1536* (Cambridge: Cambridge University Press, 1970), pp. 174–176, 204–205.

53. J. J. Scarisbrick, *The Reformation and the English People* (Oxford: Basil Blackwell, 1984), pp. 81–84, esp. p. 81.

54. Ibid.

55. Quoted in P. Smith, *The Age of the Reformation,* rev. ed. (New York: Henry Holt, 1951), p. 346.

56. See J. W. O'Malley, *The First Jesuits* (Cambridge, Mass.: Harvard University Press, 1993), p. 376.

57. Ibid., p. 298.

58. Quoted in Chadwick, *The Reformation,* p. 270.

59. See P. Grendler, *The Roman Inquisition and the Venetian Press, 1540–1605* (Princeton, N.J.: Princeton University Press, 1977).

SUGGESTED READING

Scores of exciting studies are available on virtually all aspects of the Renaissance. In addition to the titles given in the Notes, the curious student should see P. Burke, *The Italian Renaissance: Culture and Society in Italy* (1986), an important sociological interpretation relating culture and society, and J. H. Plumb, *The Italian Renaissance* (1965), a superbly written book. P. Burke, *The Historical Anthropology of Early Modern Italy* (1987), contains many useful essays on Italian cultural history in a comparative European framework. J. R. Hale, *Renaissance Europe: The Individual and Society, 1480–1520* (1978), is an excellent treatment of individualism by a distinguished authority. Hale's magisterial achievement, *The Civilization of Europe in the Renaissance* (1994) reveals how the very idea of "Europe" crystallized. For Renaissance humanism and education, see P. F. Grendler, *Schooling in Renaissance Italy: Literacy and Learning, 1300–1600* (1989); J. H. Moran, *The Growth of English Schooling, 1340–1548: Learning, Literacy, and Laicization in Pre-Reformation York Diocese* (1985); and J. F. D'Amico, *Renaissance Humanism in Papal Rome: Humanists and Churchmen on the Eve of the Reformation* (1983), which are all highly readable works of outstanding scholarship. For the city where much of it originated, G. A. Brucker, *Renaissance Florence* (1969), gives a good description of Florentine economic, political, social, and cultural history. Learned, provocative, and beautifully written, and a work on which this chapter leans heavily, L. Martines, *Power and Imagination: City-States in Renaissance Italy* (1980), is probably the best broad appreciation of the period produced in several decades. For the Renaissance court, see the splendid achievement of G. Lubkin, *A Renaissance Court: Milan Under Galeazzo Maria Sforza* (1994).

J. R. Hale, *Machiavelli and Renaissance Italy* (1966), is a sound short biography, but advanced students may want to consult the sophisticated intellectual biography of S. de Grazia, *Machiavelli in Hell* (1989). F. Gilbert, *Machiavelli and Guicciardini,* mentioned in the Notes, places the two thinkers in their intellectual and social context.

The best introduction to the Renaissance in northern Europe and a book that has greatly influenced twentieth-century scholarship is J. Huizinga, *The Waning of the Middle Ages: A Study of the Forms of Life, Thought, and Art in France and the Netherlands in the Dawn of the Renaissance* (1954). This book challenges the whole idea of a Renaissance. R. J. Knecht, *Renaissance Warrior and Patron: The Reign of Francis I* (1994), is the standard study of that important French ruler. W. Blockman and W. Prevenier, *The Burgundian Netherlands* (1986) is essential for the culture of the Burgundy. The leading northern humanist is sensitively treated in M. M. Phillips, *Erasmus and the Northern Renaissance* (1956), and J. Huizinga, *Erasmus of Rotterdam* (1952). R. Marius, *Thomas More: A Biography* (1984), is an original study of the great English humanist and statesman. J. Leclercq, trans., *The Complete Works of Rabelais* (1963), is easily available.

The following titles should prove useful for various aspects of Renaissance social history: G. Ruggerio, *Violence in Early Renaissance Venice* (1980), a pioneering study of crime and punishment in a stable society; J. C. Brown, *Immodest Acts: The Life of a Lesbian Nun in Renaissance Italy* (1985), which is helpful for an understanding of the role and status of women; and I. Maclean, *The Renaissance Notion of Women* (1980). The student who wishes to study blacks in medieval and early modern European society should see the rich and original achievement of J. Devisse and M. Mollat, *The Image of the Black in Western Art,* cited in the Notes.

Renaissance art has inspired vast research. M. Baxandall, *Painting and Experience in Fifteenth Century Italy* (1988), is essential, and A. Martindale, *The Rise of the Artist in the Middle Ages and Early Renaissance* (1972), is a splendidly illustrated introduction. One of the finest appreciations of Renaissance art, written by one of the greatest art historians of this century, is E. Panofsky, *Meaning in the Visual Arts* (1955). Both Italian and northern painting are treated in the brilliant study of M. Meiss, *The Painter's Choice: Problems in the Interpretation of Renaissance Art* (1976), a collection of essays dealing with Renaissance style, form, and meaning. L. Steinberg, *The Sexuality of Christ in Renaissance Art and in Modern Oblivion*

(1983), is a brilliant work that relates Christ's sexuality to incarnational theology. J. M. Saslow, *Ganymede in the Renaissance* (1986), which uses images of Ganymede as a metaphor for emotional and sexual relations between men and youths, provides information on social attitudes toward homosexuality. R. Jones and N. Penny, *Raphael* (1983), celebrates the achievements of that great master.

Students interested in the city of Rome might consult P. Partner, *Renaissance Rome, 1500–1559: A Portrait of a Society* (1979), and the elegantly illustrated study of C. Hibbert, *Rome: The Biography of a City* (1985). Da Vinci's scientific and naturalist ideas and drawings are available in I. A. Richter, ed., *The Notebooks of Leonardo da Vinci* (1985). The magisterial achievement of J. Pope-Hennessy, *Cellini* (1985), is a superb evocation of that artist's life and work.

The following works not only are useful for the political and economic history of the Renaissance but also contain valuable bibliographical information: A. J. Slavin, ed., *The "New Monarchies" and Representative Assemblies* (1965), a collection of interpretations, and R. Lockyer, *Henry VII* (1972), a biography with documents illustrative of the king's reign. For Spain, see P. Liss, *Isabel the Queen: Life and Times* (1992); N. Rubin, *Isabella of Castile: The First Renaissance Queen* (1991); J. S. Gerber, *The Jews of Spain: A History of the Sephardic Experience* (1992); H. Kamen, *Inquisition and Society in Spain in the Sixteenth and Seventeenth Centuries* (1985); B. Bennasar, *The Spanish Character: Attitudes and Mentalities from the Sixteenth to the Nineteenth Century,* trans. B. Keen (1979). For the Florentine business classes, see I. Origo, *The Merchant of Prato* (1957); G. Brucker, *Two Memoirs of Renaissance Florence: The Diaries of Buonaccorso Pitti and Gregorio Dati,* trans. J. Martines (1967); and Paul Grendler, ed., *An Italian Renaissance Reader* (1987).

There are many easily accessible and lucidly written general studies of the religious reformations of the sixteenth century. P. Chaunu, ed., *The Reformation* (1989), is a lavishly illustrated anthology of articles by an international team of scholars, a fine appreciation of both theological and historical developments with an up-to-date bibliography. E. Cameron, *The European Reformation* (1991), provides a comprehensive survey based on recent research. A. Pettegree, ed., *The Early Reformation in Europe* (1992), explores the Reformation as an international movement and compares developments in different parts of Europe. L. W. Spitz, *The Protestant Reformation, 1517–1559* (1985), provides a comprehensive survey. For the recent trend in scholarship, interpreting the Reformation against the background of fifteenth-century reforming developments, see the excellent study of J. F. D'Amico, cited above, and J. H. Overfield, *Humanism and Scholasticism in Late Medieval Germany* (1984), which portrays the intellectual life of the

A Universal Man

Some people of the Renaissance believed in the ideal of universality, the achievement of distinction in many different skills and branches of knowledge. As one humanist put it, "A man is able to learn many things and make himself universal in many excellent arts." (Not everyone thought this: while Michelangelo was painting the Sistine Chapel, he complained to his father that "painting is not my profession.") Leon Battista Alberti (1404–1474), the illegitimate son of a family exiled from Florence, strongly believed he could be a universal man. A scholar-humanist, mathematician, and musician, he wrote treatises on domestic morality, the physical remains of antiquity, painting, and architecture. Here is a section of Alberti's autobiography.

And finally he embraced with zeal and forethought everything which pertained to fame. To omit the rest, he strove so hard to attain a name in modeling and painting that he wished to neglect nothing by which he might gain the approbation of good men. His genius was so versatile that you might almost judge all the fine arts to be his. . . .

He played ball, hurled the javelin, ran, leaped, wrestled, and above all delighted in the steep ascent of mountains; he applied himself to all these things for the sake of health rather than sport or pleasure. As a youth he excelled in warlike games. With his feet together, he could leap over the shoulders of men standing by; he had almost no equal among those hurling the lance. An arrow shot by his hand from his chest could pierce the strongest iron breastplate. . . . On horseback, holding in his hand one end of a long wand, while the other was firmly fixed to his foot, he could ride his horse violently in all directions for hours at a time as he wished, and the wand would remain completely immobile. Strange and marvelous! that the most spirited horses and those most impatient of riders would, when he first mounted them, tremble vio-

lently and shudder as if in great fear. He learned music without teachers, and his compositions were approved by learned musicians. He sang throughout his whole life, but in private, or alone. . . . He delighted in the organ and was considered an expert among the leading musicians.

When he had begun to mature in years, neglecting everything else, he devoted himself entirely to the study of letters, and spent some years of labour on canon and civil law. Finally after so many nightly vigils and such great constancy, he fell gravely ill from the exertion of his studies. Since his relatives were neither kind nor humane to him in his illness, by way of consoling himself between his convalescence and cure he wrote the play *Philodoxeos*, putting aside his legal studies—this when he was only twenty years old. And as soon as his health permitted, he resumed his studies, intending to complete the law, but again he was seized by a grave illness. . . .

At length, on the orders of his doctors, he desisted from those studies which were most fatiguing to the memory, just when they were about to flourish. But in truth, because he could not live without letters, at the age of twenty-four he turned to physics and the mathematical arts. . . .

Although he was affable, gentle, and harmful to no one, nevertheless he felt the animosity of many evil men, and hidden enmities, both annoying and very burdensome; in particular the harsh injuries and intolerable insults from his own relatives. He lived among the envious and malevolent with such modesty and equanimity that none of his detractors or rivals, although very hostile towards him, dared to utter a word about him in the presence of good and worthy men unless it was full of praise and admiration. . . .

When he heard that a learned man of any kind had arrived, he would at once work his way into a position of familiarity with him and thus from any source whatsoever he began to learn what he was ignorant of. From craftsmen, architects, shipbuilders, and even from cobblers he sought information to see if by chance they preserved anything rare or unusual or special in their arts; and he would then communicate such things to those citizens who wished to know them. He pretended to be ignorant in many things so that he might observe the talents and habits and skill of others. And so he was a zealous observer of whatsoever pertained to inborn talent of the arts.

He wholly despised the pursuit of material gain. He gave his money and goods to his friends to take care of and to enjoy. Among those by whom he believed himself loved, he was not only outgoing about his affairs and his habits but even about his secrets. He never betrayed the secrets of another but remained silent forever. . . .

He was by nature prone to wrath and bitter in spirit, but he could repress his rising indignation immediately by taking thought. Sometimes he deliberately fled from the verbose and the headstrong because with them he could not subdue his wrath. At other times he voluntarily submitted to the bold, in order to grow in patience. . . .

He wrote some books entitled *On Painting*, and in this very art of painting he created works unheard of and unbelievable to those who saw them. . . .

He had within himself a ray by which he could sense the good or evil intentions of men towards himself. Simply by looking at them, he could discover most of the defects of anyone in his presence. He used all kinds of reasoning and great effort, but in vain, to make more gentle towards himself those whom he had learned at one glance would be inimical. . . .

He could endure pain and cold and heat. When, not yet fifteen, he received a serious wound in the foot, and the physician, according to his custom and skill, drew together the broken parts of the foot and sewed them through the skin with a needle, he scarcely uttered a sound of pain. With his own hands, though in such great pain, he even aided the ministering doctor and treated his own wound though he was burning with fever. . . . By some defect in his nature he loathed garlic and also honey, and the mere sight of them, if by chance they were offered to him, brought on vomiting. But he conquered himself by

Bronze medallion of Leon Battista Alberti, by Matteo di Andrea de' Pasti. *(Source: Alinari/Art Resource, NY)*

force of looking at and handling the disagreeable objects, so that they came to offend him less, thus showing by example that men can do anything with themselves if they will.

He took extraordinary and peculiar pleasure in looking at things in which there was any mark of beauty or adornment. He never ceased to wonder at old men who were endowed with dignity of countenance, and unimpaired and vigorous, and he proclaimed that he honoured them as "delights of nature." He declared that quadrupeds, birds, and other living things of outstanding beauty were worthy of benevolence because by the very distinction of their nature they deserved favour. When his favorite dog died he wrote a funeral oration for him.

Questions for Analysis

1. What distinctively Renaissance traits did Alberti show?

2. According to his own assessment, what personal or human qualities did Alberti possess?

3. Did Alberti appear to have any psychological complexes or difficulties? How would you explain them?

Source: "Self-Portrait of a Universal Man" by Leon Battista Alberti from *The Portable Renaissance Reader*, edited by J. B. Ross and M. M. McLaughlin. Copyright 1968 by Penguin USA.

German universities, the milieu from which the Protestant Reformation emerged. For the condition of the church in the late fifteenth and early sixteenth centuries, see D. Hay, *The Church in Italy in the Fifteenth Century* (1977), and P. Heath, *The English Parish Clergy on the Eve of the Reformation* (1969).

For the central figure of the early Reformation, Martin Luther, students should see the works by Atkinson and Haile mentioned in the Notes, as well as E. Erikson, *Young Man Luther: A Study in Psychoanalysis and History* (1962); G. Brendler, *Martin Luther: Theology and Revolution* (1991), a response to the Marxist interpretation of Luther as the tool of the aristocracy who sold out the peasantry; and H. Boehmer, *Martin Luther: Road to Reformation* (1960), a well-balanced work treating Luther's formative years.

The best study of John Calvin is W. J. Bouwsma, *John Calvin: A Sixteenth-Century Portrait* (1988), an authoritative study that places Calvin within Renaissance culture. R. T. Kendall, *Calvinism and English Calvinism to 1649* (1981), presents English conditions. R. M. Mitchell, *Calvin and the Puritan's View of the Protestant Ethic* (1979), interprets the socioeconomic implications of Calvin's thought. Students interested in the left wing of the Reformation should see the profound though difficult work of G. H. Williams, *The Radical Reformers* (1962). For reform in other parts of Switzerland, see T. Brady, *Turning Swiss* (1990), and L. P. Wendel, *Always Among Us: Images of the Poor in Zwingli's Zurich* (1990).

For various aspects of the social history of the period, see in addition to the titles by Bainton and Ozment cited in the Notes, S. E. Ozment, *Magdalena and Balthasar* (1987), which reveals many features of social life through the letters of a Nuremburg couple; and K. von Greyerz, ed., *Religion and Society in Early Modern Europe, 1500–1800* (1984), both of which contain interesting essays on religion, society, and popular culture. For women, see M. E. Wiesner, *Women and Gender in Early Modern Europe* (1993); L. Roper, *The Holy Household: Women and Morals in Reformation Augsburg* (1991), an important study in local religious history as well as the history of gender; M. Wiesner, *Women in the Sixteenth Century: A Bibliography* (1983), a useful reference tool; and S. M. Wyntjes, "Women in the Reformation Era," in *Becoming Visible: Women in European History,* ed. R. Bridenthal and C. Koonz (1977), an interesting general survey. The best recent treatment of marriage and the family is S. E. Ozment, *When Fathers Ruled: Family Life in Reformation Europe* (1983). Ozment's

edition of *Reformation Europe: A Guide to Research* (1982) contains not only helpful references but valuable articles on such topics as "The German Peasants," "The Anabaptists," and "The Confessional Age: The Late Reformation in Germany." For Servetus, see R. H. Bainton, *Hunted Heretic: The Life and Death of Michael Servetus* (1953), which remains valuable.

For England, in addition to the fundamental work by Duffy cited in the Notes, see A. G. Dickens, *The English Reformation* (1964). K. Thomas, *Religion and the Decline of Magic* (1971), provides a useful treatment of pre-Reformation popular religion. S. J. Gunn and P. G. Lindley, eds., *Cardinal Wolsey: Church, State and Art* (1991), is a useful study of that important prelate. The marital trials of Henry VIII are treated in both the sympathetic study of G. Mattingly, *Catherine of Aragon* (1949), and A. Fraser, *The Wives of Henry VIII* (1992). The legal implications of Henry VIII's divorces have been thoroughly analyzed in J. J. Scarisbrick, *Henry VIII* (1968), an almost definitive biography. On the dissolution of the English monasteries, see D. Knowles, *The Religious Orders in England,* vol. 3 (1959), one of the finest examples of historical prose in English written in the twentieth century. Knowles's *Bare Ruined Choirs* (1976) is an attractively illustrated abridgment of *The Religious Orders in England.* G. R. Elton, *The Tudor Revolution in Government* (1959), discusses the modernization of English government under Thomas Cromwell; the same author's *Reform and Reformation: England, 1509–1558* (1977) combines political and social history in a broad study. Many aspects of English social history are discussed in J. Youings, *Sixteenth Century England* (1984), a beautifully written work that is highly recommended.

P. Janelle, *The Catholic Reformation* (1951), is a comprehensive treatment of the Catholic Reformation from a Catholic point of view, and A. G. Dickens, *The Counter Reformation* (1969), gives the Protestant standpoint in a beautifully illustrated book. The definitive study of the Council of Trent was written by H. Jedin, *A History of the Council of Trent,* 3 vols. (1957–1961). For the Jesuits, see W. W. Meissner, *Ignatius of Loyola: The Psychology of a Saint* (1993), and J. W. O'Malley, *The First Jesuits* (1993); these books are basic not only for the beginnings of the Society of Jesus but for the refutation of many myths about the Jesuits. Perhaps the best recent work on the Spanish Inquisition is W. Monter, Frontiers of Heresy: *The Spanish Inquisition from the Basque Lands to Sicily* (1990).

The Age of European Expansion and Religious Wars

❖

A detail from an early 17th-century Flemish painting depiction maps, illustrated travel books, a globe, a compass, and an astrolabe. *(Source: Reproduced by courtesy of the Trustees, The National Gallery, London)*

Between 1450 and 1650 two developments dramatically altered the world: Europeans' overseas expansion and the reformations of the Christian church. Europeans carried their cultures to other parts of the globe. Overseas expansion brought them into confrontation with ancient civilizations in Africa, Asia, and the Americas. These confrontations led first to conquest, then to exploitation, and finally to profound social changes in both Europe and the conquered territories. Likewise, the Renaissance and the religious reformations drastically changed intellectual, political, religious, and social life in Europe. War and religious issues dominated the politics of European states. Although religion was commonly used to rationalize international conflict, wars were fought for power and territory.

- Why, in the sixteenth and seventeenth centuries, did a relatively small number of people living on the edge of the Eurasian landmass gain control of the major sea lanes of the world and establish political and economic hegemony on distant continents?

- How were a few Spaniards, fighting far from home, able to overcome the powerful Aztec and Inca Empires in America?

- What effect did overseas expansion have on Europe and on conquered societies?

- What were the causes and consequences of the religious wars in France, the Netherlands, and Germany?

- How did the religious crises of this period affect the status of women?

- How and why did African slave labor become the dominant form of labor organization in the New World?

- What religious and intellectual developments led to the growth of skepticism?

- What literary masterpieces of the English-speaking world did this period produce?

This chapter addresses these questions.

DISCOVERY, RECONNAISSANCE, AND EXPANSION

Historians of Europe have called the period from 1450 to 1650 the "Age of Discovery," "Age of Reconnaissance," and "Age of Expansion." All three labels are appropriate. "Age of Discovery" refers to the era's phenomenal advances in geographical knowledge and technology, often achieved through trial and error. In 1350 it took as long to sail from the eastern end of the Mediterranean to the western end as it had taken a thousand years earlier. Even in the fifteenth century, Europeans knew little more about the earth's surface than the Romans had known. By 1650, however, Europeans had made an extensive reconnaissance—or preliminary exploration—and had sketched fairly accurately the physical outline of the whole earth. Much of the geographical information they had gathered was tentative and not fully understood—hence the appropriateness of "Age of Reconnaissance."

The designation "Age of Expansion" refers to the migration of Europeans to other parts of the world. This colonization resulted in political control of much of South and North America; coastal regions of Africa, India, China, and Japan; and many Pacific islands. Political hegemony was accompanied by economic exploitation, religious domination, and the introduction of European patterns of social and intellectual life. The sixteenth-century expansion of European society launched a new age in world history. None of the three "Age" labels reflects the experiences of non-European peoples. Africans, Asians, and native Americans had known the geographies of their regions for centuries. They made no "discoveries" and undertook no reconnaissance, and they experienced "expansion" only as forced slave laborers.

Overseas Exploration and Conquest

The outward expansion of Europe began with the Viking voyages across the Atlantic in the ninth and tenth centuries. Under Eric the Red and Leif Ericson, the Vikings discovered Greenland and the eastern coast of North America. They made permanent settlements in, and a legal imprint on, Iceland, Ireland, England, Normandy, and Sicily. The Crusades of the eleventh through thirteenth centuries were another phase in Europe's attempt to explore and exploit peoples on the periphery of the continent. But the lack of a strong territorial base, superior Muslim military strength, and sheer misrule combined to make the Crusader kingdoms short-lived. In the mid-fifteenth century, Europe seemed ill prepared for further international

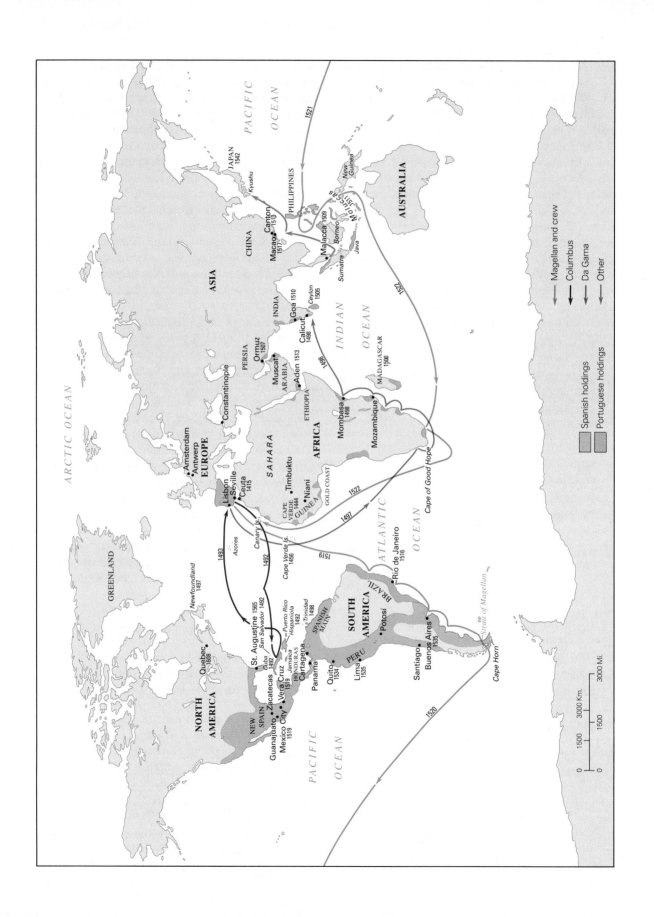

ARCTIC OCEAN

PACIFIC OCEAN

GREENLAND

Newfoundland
1497

NORTH
AMERICA

NEW
SPAIN

Quebec
1608

St. Augustine 1565
Cuba
San Salvador 1492
Puerto Rico 1493
Hispaniola
1492
Jamaica
Trinidad
1498

Guanajuato
Zacatecas
Mexico City Vera Cruz
1519   1519
HONDURAS
Cartagena
Panama
Quito
1534

SPANISH
MAIN

PERU

Lima
1535

Santiago

Buenos Aires
1535

Potosí

BRAZIL

SOUTH
AMERICA

Rio de Janeiro
1516

Strait of Magellan

Cape Horn

1520

PACIFIC
OCEAN

ATLANTIC
OCEAN

1493

1492

1519

1497

1522

Azores

Canary Is.

Cape Verde Is.
1456

EUROPE
Amsterdam
Antwerp

Lisbon
Seville

Ceuta
1415

Constantinople

SAHARA

CAPE
VERDE
GUINEA
Timbuktu
Niani
1444
GOLD COAST

AFRICA

ETHIOPIA

Cape of Good Hope

Mombasa
1498

Mozambique

MADAGASCAR
1500

INDIAN
OCEAN

ARABIA
Adén 1513
Muscat
1507
Ormuz
PERSIA

INDIA
Calicut
1498
Goa 1510
Ceylon
1505

ASIA

CHINA

Macao
1517
Canton
1513

JAPAN
1542
Kyushu

PHILIPPINES

1521

Majacca 1509
Borneo
Sumatra
Java

New
Guinea

AUSTRALIA

1520

PACIFIC
OCEAN

0   1500   3000 Km.

0   1500   3000 Mi.

Magellan and crew
Columbus
Da Gama
Other

Spanish holdings

Portuguese holdings

ventures. By 1450 a grave new threat had appeared in the East: the Ottoman Turks.

Combining excellent military strategy with efficient administration of their conquered territories, the Turks had subdued most of Asia Minor and begun to settle on the western side of the Bosporus. The Muslim Ottoman Turks under Sultan Mohammed II (r. 1451–1481) captured Constantinople in 1453, pressed northwest into the Balkans, and by the early sixteenth century controlled the eastern Mediterranean. The Turkish menace badly frightened Europeans. In France in the fifteenth and sixteenth centuries, twice as many books were printed about the Turkish threat as about the American discoveries. Yet the fifteenth and sixteenth centuries witnessed a fantastic continuation, on a global scale, of European expansion.

Political centralization in Spain, France, and England helps to explain those countries' outward push. In the fifteenth century, Isabella and Ferdinand had consolidated their several kingdoms to achieve a more united Spain. The Catholic rulers revamped the Spanish bureaucracy and humbled dissident elements, notably the Muslims and the Jews. The Spanish monarchy was stronger than ever before and in a position to support foreign ventures; it could bear the costs and dangers of exploration. But Portugal, situated on the extreme southwestern edge of the European continent, got the start on the rest of Europe. Still insignificant as a European land power despite its recently secured frontiers, Portugal sought greatness in the unknown world overseas.

Portugal's taking of Ceuta, an Arab city in northern Morocco, in 1415 marked the beginning of European exploration and control of overseas territory (Map 16.1). The objectives of Portuguese policy included the historic Iberian crusade to Christianize Muslims and the search for gold, for an overseas route to the spice markets of India, and for the mythical Christian ruler of Ethiopia, Prester John.

In the early phases of Portuguese exploration, Prince Henry (1394–1460), called "the Naviga-

tor" because of the annual expeditions he sent down the western coast of Africa, played the leading role. In the fifteenth century, most of the gold that reached Europe came from the Sudan in West Africa and from the Akan peoples living near the area of present-day Ghana. Muslim caravans brought the gold from the African cities of Niani and Timbuktu and carried it north across the Sahara to Mediterranean ports. Then the Portuguese muscled in on this commerce in gold. Prince Henry's carefully planned expeditions succeeded in reaching Guinea, and under King John II (r. 1481–1495) the Portuguese established trading posts and forts on the Guinea coast and penetrated into the continent all the way to Timbuktu (see Map 16.1). Portuguese ships transported gold to Lisbon, and by 1500 Portugal controlled the flow of gold to Europe. The golden century of Portuguese prosperity had begun.

The spices Europeans wanted, however, came from South Asia and the Moluccan islands, not from African kingdoms. Thus the Portuguese pushed farther south down the west coast of Africa. In 1487 Bartholomew Diaz rounded the Cape of Good Hope at the southern tip, but storms and a threatened mutiny forced him to turn back. On a second expedition (1497–1499), the Portuguese mariner Vasco da Gama reached India and returned to Lisbon loaded with samples of Indian wares. King Manuel (r. 1495–1521) promptly dispatched thirteen ships under the command of Pedro Alvares Cabral, assisted by Diaz, to set up trading posts in India. On April 22, 1500, the coast of Brazil in South America was sighted and claimed for the crown of Portugal. Cabral then proceeded south and east around the Cape of Good Hope and reached India. Half of the fleet was lost on the return voyage, but the six spice-laden vessels that dropped anchor in Lisbon harbor in July 1501 more than paid for the entire expedition. Thereafter, convoys were sent out every March. Lisbon became the entrance port for Asian goods into Europe—but not without a fight.

For centuries the Muslims had controlled the rich spice trade of the Indian Ocean, and they did not surrender it willingly. Portuguese commercial activities were accompanied by the destruction or seizure of strategic Muslim coastal forts, which later served Portugal as both trading posts and military bases. Alfonso de Albuquerque, whom the Portuguese crown appointed as governor of India

❧ **MAP 16.1 Overseas Exploration and Conquest in the Fifteenth and Sixteenth Centuries** The voyages of discovery marked another phase in the centuries-old migrations of European peoples. Consider the major contemporary significance of each of the three voyages depicted on this map.

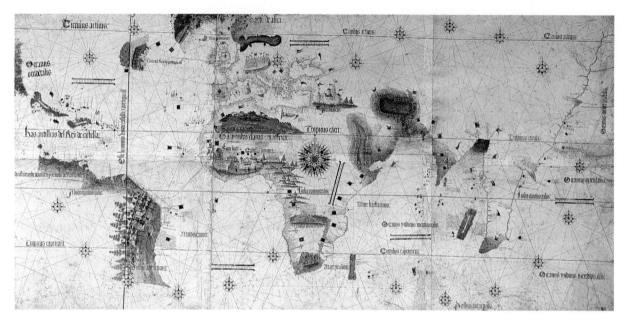

The Cantino Map   This map (1502) is named for the agent secretly commissioned to design it in Lisbon for the duke of Ferrara, an avid Italian map collector. It reveals such good knowledge of the African continent, of the islands of the West Indies, and of the shoreline of present-day Venezuela, Guiana, and Brazil in South America that modern scholars suspect there may have been clandestine voyages to the Americas shortly after Columbus's. *(Source: Biblioteca Estense Universitaria, Modena)*

(1509–1515), decided that these bases and not inland territories should control the Indian Ocean. Accordingly, his cannon blasted open the ports of Calicut, Ormuz, Goa, and Malacca, the vital centers of Arab domination of south Asian spice trade (see Map 16.1). This bombardment laid the foundation for Portuguese imperialism in the sixteenth and seventeenth centuries—a strange way to bring Christianity to "those who were in darkness." As one scholar wrote about the opening of China to the West, "while Buddha came to China on white elephants, Christ was borne on cannon balls."[1]

In March 1493, between the voyages of Diaz and da Gama, Spanish ships entered Lisbon harbor bearing a triumphant Italian explorer in the service of the Spanish monarchy. Christopher Columbus (1451–1506), a Genoese mariner, had secured Spanish support for an expedition to the East (see Listening to the Past). He sailed from Palos, Spain, to the Canary Islands and crossed the Atlantic to the Bahamas, landing in October 1492 on an island that he named San Salvador and believed to be the coast of India.

Technological Stimuli to Exploration

Technological developments were the key to Europe's remarkable outreach. By 1350 cannon made of iron or bronze and able to fire iron or stone balls had been fully developed in western Europe. This artillery emitted frightening noises and great flashes of fire and could batter down fortresses and even city walls. Sultan Mohammed II's siege of Constantinople in 1453 provides a classic illustration of the effectiveness of cannon fire.

Constantinople had very strong walled fortifications. The sultan secured the services of a Western technician, who built fifty-six small cannon and a gigantic gun that could hurl stone balls weighing about eight hundred pounds. The gun had to be moved by several hundred oxen and could be loaded and fired only by about a hundred men working together. Reloading took two hours. This awkward but powerful weapon breached the walls of Constantinople before it cracked on the second day of the bombardment. Lesser cannon finished the job.

Although early cannon posed serious technical difficulties for land warfare, they could be used at sea. The mounting of cannon on ships and improved techniques of shipbuilding gave impetus to European expansion. Since ancient times, most seagoing vessels had been narrow, open boats called *galleys,* propelled largely by oarsmen: slaves or convicts who had been sentenced to the galleys manned the oars of the cargo and war ships that sailed the Mediterranean (both types of ship carried soldiers for defense). Well suited to the calm and thoroughly explored waters of the Mediterranean, galleys could not withstand the rough winds and uncharted shoals of the Atlantic. The need for sturdier craft, as well as population losses caused by the Black Death, forced the development of a new style of ship that did not require soldiers for defense or a large crew of oarsmen.

In the course of the fifteenth century, the Portuguese developed the *caravel,* a small, light, three-masted sailing ship. Though somewhat slower than the galley, the caravel held more cargo and was highly maneuverable. When fitted with cannon, it could dominate larger vessels, such as the round ships commonly used in commerce. The substitution of windpower for manpower, and artillery fire for soldiers, signaled a great technological advance and gave Europeans navigational and fighting ascendancy over the rest of the world.[2]

Other fifteenth-century developments in navigation helped make possible the conquest of the Atlantic. The magnetic compass enabled sailors to determine their direction and position at sea. The astrolabe, an instrument developed by Muslim navigators in the twelfth century and used to determine the altitude of the sun and other celestial bodies, permitted mariners to plot their latitude, or position north or south of the equator. Steadily improved maps and sea charts provided information about distances, sea depths, and geography.

The Explorers' Motives

The expansion of Europe was not motivated by demographic pressures. The Black Death had caused serious population losses from which Europe had not recovered in 1500. Few Europeans emigrated to North or South America in the sixteenth century. Half of those who did sail to begin a new life in America died en route; half of those who reached what they regarded as the New World eventually returned to their homeland. Why, then, did explorers brave the Atlantic and Pacific Oceans, risking their lives to discover new continents and spread European culture?

The reasons are varied and complex. People of the sixteenth century were still basically medieval: their attitudes and values were shaped by religion and expressed in religious terms. In the late fifteenth century, crusading fervor remained a basic part of the Portuguese and Spanish national ideal. The desire to Christianize Muslims and pagan peoples played a central role in European expansion. Queen Isabella of Spain, for example, showed a fanatical zeal for converting the Muslims to Christianity and concentrated her efforts on the Muslims in Granada. But after the abortive crusading attempts of the thirteenth century, Isabella and other rulers realized full well that they lacked the material resources to mount the full-scale assault on Islam necessary for victory. Crusading impulses thus shifted from the Muslims to the pagan peoples of Africa and the Americas.

Moreover, after the *reconquista*—the Christian reconquest of Muslim areas—enterprising young men of the Spanish upper classes found economic and political opportunities severely limited. As a study of the Castilian city Ciudad Real shows, the traditional aristocracy controlled the best agricultural land and monopolized urban administrative posts. Great merchants and a few nobles (surprisingly, since Spanish law forbade noble participation in commercial ventures) dominated the textile and leather-glove manufacturing industries. Thus many ambitious men emigrated to the Americas to seek their fortunes.[3]

Government sponsorship and encouragement of exploration also help to account for the results of the various voyages. Individual mariners and explorers could not afford the massive sums needed to explore mysterious oceans and to control remote continents. The strong financial support of Prince Henry the Navigator led to Portugal's phenomenal success in the spice trade. Even the grudging and modest assistance of Isabella and Ferdinand eventually brought untold riches—and complicated problems—to Spain. The Dutch in the seventeenth century, through such government-sponsored trading companies as the Dutch East India Company, reaped enormous wealth, and although the Netherlands was a small country in size, it dominated the European economy in 1650.

Scholars have frequently described the European discoveries as a manifestation of Renaissance curiosity about the physical universe—the desire to know more about the geography and peoples of the world. There is truth to this explanation. Cosmography, natural history, and geography aroused enormous interest among educated people in the fifteenth and sixteenth centuries. Just as science fiction and speculation about life on other planets excite readers today, quasi-scientific literature about Africa, Asia, and the Americas captured the imaginations of Europeans. Oviedo's *General History of the Indies* (1547), a detailed eyewitness account of plants, animals, and peoples, was widely read.

Spices were another important incentive to voyages of discovery. Introduced into western Europe by the Crusaders in the twelfth century, nutmeg, mace, ginger, cinnamon, and pepper added flavor and variety to the monotonous diet of Europeans. Spices were also used in the preparation of medicinal drugs and incense for religious ceremonies. In the late thirteenth century, the Venetian Marco Polo (1254?–1324?), the greatest of medieval travelers, had visited the court of the Chinese emperor. The widely publicized account of his travels in the *Book of Various Experiences* stimulated the trade in spices between Asia and Italy. The Venetians came to hold a monopoly of trade in western Europe.

Spices were grown in India and China, shipped across the Indian Ocean to ports on the Persian Gulf, and then transported by Arabs across the Arabian Desert to Mediterranean ports. But the rise of the Ming Dynasty in China in the late fourteenth century resulted in the expulsion of foreigners. And the steady penetration of the Ottoman Turks into the eastern Mediterranean and of Muslims across North Africa forced Europeans to seek a new route to the Asian spice markets.

The basic reason for European exploration and expansion, however, was the quest for material profit. Mariners and explorers frankly admitted this. As Bartholomew Diaz put it, his motives were "to serve God and His Majesty, to give light to those who were in darkness and to grow rich as all men desire to do." When Vasco da Gama reached the port of Calicut, India, in 1498, a native asked what the Portuguese wanted. Da Gama replied, "Christians and spices."[4] The bluntest of the Spanish conquistadors, Hernando Cortés, announced as he prepared to conquer Mexico, "I have come to win gold, not to plow the fields like a peasant."[5]

A sixteenth-century diplomat, Ogier Gheselin de Busbecq, summed up explorers' paradoxical attitude: in expeditions to the Indies and the Antipodes, he said, "religion supplies the pretext and gold the motive."[6]

The Problem of Christopher Columbus

The year 1992, which marked the quincentenary of Columbus's first voyages to the Americas, spawned an enormous amount of discussion about the significance of his voyages. Journalists, scholars, amateurs, and polemicists debated Columbus's accomplishments and failures. Until the 1980s most writers generally would have agreed with the Harvard historian Samuel Eliot Morison in his 1942 biography of Columbus:

The whole history of the Americas stems from the Four Voyages of Columbus; and as the Greek city-states looked back to the deathless gods as their founders, so today a score of independent nations and dominions unite in homage to Columbus, the stout-hearted son of Genoa, who carried Christian civilization across the Ocean Sea.[7]

In 1942, we must remember, the Western Powers believed they were engaged in a life-and-death struggle to defend "Christian civilization" against the evil forces of fascism. As the five hundredth anniversary of his famous voyage approached, however, Columbus underwent severe criticism.

Critics charged that he enslaved and sometimes killed the Indians and was a cruel and ineffective governor of Spain's Caribbean colony. Moreover, they said, he did not discover a previously unknown continent: Africans and other Europeans had been to the Western Hemisphere before him. And not only did he not discover a "new" continent, he not not realize what he had found. In short, according to his harshest critics, he was a fool who didn't know what was going on around him. Some claim that he was the originator of European exploitation of the non-European world and destroyed the paradise that had been the New World.[8]

Because those judgments rest on social and ethical standards that did not exist in Columbus's world, responsible scholars consider them ahistorical. Instead, using the evidence of his journal (sea log) and letters, let us ask three basic questions: (1) What kind of man was Columbus, and what forces or influences shaped him? (2) In sailing westward from Europe, what were his goals? (3) Did he achieve his goals, and what did he make of his discoveries?

�֎ **Pepper Harvest**   To break the monotony of their bland diet, Europeans had a passion for pepper, which—along with cinnamon, cloves, nutmeg, and ginger—was the main object of the Asian trade. Since one kilo of pepper cost 2 grams of silver at the place of production in the East Indies and from 10 to 14 grams of silver in Alexandria, 14 to 18 grams in Venice, and 20 to 30 grams at the markets of northern Europe, we can appreciate the fifteenth-century expression "As dear as pepper." Here natives fill vats, and the dealer tastes a peppercorn for pungency. *(Source: Bibliothèque Nationale, Paris)*

The central feature in the character of Christopher Columbus is that he was a deeply religious man. He began the *Journal* of his voyage to the Americas, written as a letter to Ferdinand and Isabella of Spain, with this recollection:

On 2 January in the year 1492, when your Highnesses had concluded their war with the Moors who reigned in Europe, I saw your Highnesses' banners victoriously raised on the towers of the Alhambra, the citadel of the city, and the Moorish king come out of the city gates and kiss the hands of your Highnesses and the prince, My Lord. And later in that same month, on the grounds of information I had given your Highnesses concerning the lands of India . . . your Highnesses decided to send me, Christopher Columbus, to see these parts of India and the princes and peoples of those lands and consider the best means for their conversion.[9]

He had witnessed the Spanish reconquest of Granada and shared fully in the religious and nationalistic fervor surrounding that event. Just seven months separated Isabella and Ferdinand's entry

into Granada on January 6 and Columbus's departure westward on August 3, 1492. In his mind, the two events were clearly linked. Long after Europeans knew something of Columbus's discoveries in the Caribbean, they considered the restoration of Muslim Granada to Christian hands as Ferdinand and Isabella's greatest achievements; for the conquest, in 1494 the Spanish pope Alexander VI (r. 1492–1503) rewarded them with the title of "Most Catholic Kings." Like the Spanish rulers and most Europeans of his age, Columbus understood Christianity as a missionary religion that should be carried to places and peoples where it did not exist. Although Columbus's character certainly included material and secular qualities, first and foremost, as he wrote in 1498, he believed he was a divine agent:

God made me the messenger of the new heaven and the new earth of which he spoke in the Apocalypse of St. John after having spoken of it through the mouth of the prophet Isaiah; and he showed me the post where to find it.[10]

A second and fundamental facet of Columbus the man is that he was very knowledgeable about the sea. He was familiar with fifteenth-century Portuguese navigational aids such as portolans—written descriptions of routes showing bays, coves, capes, ports, and the distances between these places—and the magnetic compass. He had spent years consulting geographers, mapmakers, and navigators. And, as he implies in his *Journal,* he had acquired not only theoretical but practical experience:

I have spent twenty-three years at sea and have not left it for any length of time worth mentioning, and I have seen everything from east to west [meaning he had been to England] and I have been to Guinea" [North and West Africa].[11]

Some of Columbus's calculations, such as his measurement of the distance from Portugal to Japan as 2,760 miles (it is actually 12,000), proved inaccurate. But his successful thirty-three-day voyage to the Caribbean owed a great deal to his seamanship and his knowledge and skillful use of instruments.

What was the object of his first voyage? What did Columbus set out to do? He gives the answer in the very title of the expedition, "The Enterprise of the Indies." He wanted to find a direct ocean route to Asia, which would provide the opportunity for a greatly expanded trade, a trade in which the European economy, and especially Spain, would participate. Two scholars have recently written, "If Columbus had not sailed westward in search of Asia, someone else would have done so. The time was right for such a bold undertaking."[12] Someone else might have done so, but the fact remains that Columbus, displaying a characteristic Renaissance curiosity and restless drive, actually accepted the challenge.

How did Columbus interpret what he had found, and did he think he had achieved what he set out to do? His mind had been formed by the Bible and the geographical writings of classical authors, as were the minds of most educated people of his time. Thus, as people in every age have often done, Columbus ignored the evidence of his eyes; he described what he saw in the Caribbean as an idyllic paradise, a peaceful garden of Eden. When accounts of his travels were published, Europeans' immediate fascination with this image of the New World meant that Columbus's propaganda created an instant myth. But when he sensed that he had not found the spice markets and bazaars of Asia,

his goal changed from establishing trade with the (East) Indians and Chinese to establishing the kind of trade the Portuguese were then conducting with Africa and with Cape Verde and other islands in the Atlantic (see Map 16.1). That meant setting up some form of government in the Caribbean islands, even though Columbus had little interest in, or capacity for, governing. In 1496, he forcibly subjugated the island of Hispaniola, enslaved the Indians, and laid the basis for a system of land grants tied to the Indians' labor service. Borrowing practices and institutions from reconquest Spain and the Canary Islands, Columbus laid the foundation for Spanish imperial administration. In all of this, Columbus was very much a man of his times. He never understood, however, that the scale of his discoveries created problems of trade, settlers, relations with the Indians, and, above all, government bureaucracy.[13]

The Conquest of Aztec Mexico and Inca Peru

Technological development also helps to explain the Spanish conquest of Aztec Mexico and Inca Peru.

The strange end of the Aztec nation remains one of the most fascinating events in the annals of human societies. The Spanish adventurer Hernando Cortés (1485–1547) landed at Vera Cruz in February 1519. In November he entered Tenochtitlán (Mexico City) and soon had the emperor Montezuma II (r. 1502–1520) in custody. In less than two years Cortés destroyed the monarchy, gained complete control of the Mexican capital, and extended his jurisdiction over much of the Aztec Empire. Why did a strong people defending its own territory succumb so quickly to a handful of Spaniards fighting in dangerous and completely unfamiliar circumstances? How indeed, since Montezuma's scouts sent him detailed reports of the Spaniards' movements? The answers to these questions lie in the fact that at the time of the Spanish arrival the Aztec and Inca Empires faced grave internal difficulties brought on by their religious ideologies; by the Spaniards' boldness, timing, and technology; and by Aztec and Incan psychology and attitudes toward war.

The Spaniards arrived in late summer, when the Aztecs were preoccupied with harvesting their crops and not thinking of war. From the Spaniards' perspective, their timing was ideal. A series of natural phenomena, signs, and portents seemed to augur disaster for the Aztecs. A comet was seen in daytime, a column of fire had appeared every midnight for a year, and two temples were suddenly destroyed, one by lightning unaccompanied by thunder. These and other apparently inexplicable events seemed to presage the return of the Aztec god Quetzalcoatl and had an unnerving effect on the Aztecs. They looked on the Europeans riding "wild beasts" as extraterrestrial forces coming to establish a new social order. Defeatism swept the nation and paralyzed its will.

The Aztec state religion, the sacred cult of Huitzilopochtli, necessitated constant warfare against neighboring peoples to secure captives for religious sacrifice and laborers for agricultural and infrastructural work. Lacking an effective method of governing subject peoples, the Aztecs controlled thirty-eight provinces in central Mexico through terror. When Cortés landed, the provinces were being crushed under a cycle of imperial oppression: increases in tribute provoked revolt, which led to reconquest, retribution, and demands for higher tribute, which in turn sparked greater resentment and fresh revolt. When the Spaniards appeared, the Totonacs greeted them as liberators, and other subject peoples joined them against the Aztecs. Even before the coming of the Spaniards, Montezuma's attempts to resolve the problem of constant warfare by freezing social positions—thereby ending the social mobility that war provided—aroused the resentment of his elite, mercantile, and lowborn classes. Montezuma faced terrible external and internal difficulties.[14]

Montezuma refrained from attacking the Spaniards as they advanced toward his capital and welcomed Cortés and his men into Tenochtitlán. Historians have often condemned the Aztec ruler for vacillation and weakness. But he relied on the advice of his state council, itself divided, and on the dubious loyalty of tributary communities. When Cortés—with incredible boldness—took Montezuma hostage, the emperor's influence over his people crumbled.

The major explanation for the collapse of the Aztec Empire to six hundred Spaniards lies in the Aztecs' notion of warfare and their level of technology. Forced to leave Tenochtitlán to settle a conflict elsewhere, Cortés placed his lieutenant, Alvarado, in charge. Alvarado's harsh rule drove the Aztecs to revolt, and they almost succeeded in destroying the Spanish garrison. When Cortés re-

turned just in time, the Aztecs allowed his reinforcements to join Alvarado's besieged force. No threatened European or Asian state would have conceived of doing such a thing: dividing an enemy's army and destroying the separate parts was basic to their military tactics. But for the Aztecs warfare was a ceremonial act in which "divide and conquer" had no place.

Having allowed the Spanish forces to reunite, the entire population of Tenochtitlán attacked the invaders. The Aztecs killed many Spaniards. In retaliation, the Spaniards executed Montezuma. The Spaniards escaped from the city and inflicted a crushing defeat on the Aztec army at Otumba near Lake Texcoco on July 7, 1520. The Spaniards won because "the simple Indian methods of mass warfare were of little avail against the manoeuvring of a well-drilled force."[15] Aztec weapons proved no match for the terrifyingly noisy and lethal Spanish cannon, muskets, crossbows, and steel swords. European technology decided the battle. Cortés began the systematic conquest of Mexico.

From 1493 to 1527 the Inca Huayna Capac ruled as a benevolent despot (the word *Inca* refers both to the ruler of the Amerindians who lived in the valleys of the Andes Mountains in present-day Peru and to the people themselves). His power was limited only by custom. His millions of subjects considered him a god, firm but just to his people, merciless to his enemies. Only a few of the Inca's closest relatives dared look at his divine face. Nobles approached him on their knees, and the masses kissed the dirt as he rode by in his litter. The borders of his vast empire were well fortified and threatened by no foreign invaders. Grain was plentiful, and apart from an outbreak of smallpox in a distant province—introduced by the Spaniards—no natural disaster upset the general peace. An army of fifty thousand loyal troops stood at the Inca's disposal. Why did this powerful empire fall so easily to Francisco Pizarro and his band of 175 men armed with one small, ineffective cannon?

The Incas were totally isolated. They had no contact with other Amerindian cultures and knew nothing at all of Aztec civilization or its collapse to the Spaniards in 1521. Since about the year 1500, Inca scouts had reported "floating houses" on the seas, manned by white men with beards. Tradesmen told of strange large animals with feet of silver (as horseshoes appeared in the brilliant sunshine). Having observed a border skirmish between Indians and white men, intelligence sources advised

Huayna Capac that the Europeans' swords were as harmless as women's weaving battens. A coastal chieftain had poured chicha, the native beer, down the barrel of a gun to appease the god of thunder. These incidents suggest that Inca culture provided no basis for understanding the Spaniards and the significance of their arrival. Moreover, even if the strange pale men planned war, there were very few of them, and the Incas believed that they could not be reinforced from the sea.[16]

At first the Incas did not think that the strangers intended trouble. They believed the old Inca legend that the creator-god Virocha—who had brought civilization to them, become displeased, and sailed away promising to return someday—had indeed returned. Belief in a legend prevented the Incas, like the Aztecs, from taking prompt action.

Religious ideology contributed to grave domestic crisis within the empire. When the ruler died, his corpse was preserved as a mummy. The mummy was both a holy object and a dynamic force in Inca society. It was housed in a sacred chamber and dressed in fine clothing. It was carried in procession to state ceremonies and was asked for advice in times of trouble. This cult of the royal mummies left a new Inca (ruler) with the title and insignia of his office but little else. Because each dead Inca retained possession of the estates and properties he had held in life, each new Inca lacked land. Thus, to strengthen his administration, secure the means to live in the royal style, and reward his supporters, a new Inca had to engage in warfare to acquire land.

In 1525, Huascar succeeded his father Huayna Capac as Inca and was crowned at Cuzco, the Incas' capital city, with the fringed headband symbolizing his imperial office. By this time, the dead rulers controlled most of Peru's land and resources. The nobility managed the estates of the dead Inca rulers. Needing land and other possessions, Huascar proposed burying the mummies of all of the dead Incas and using the profits from their estates for the living.

According to Inca law, the successor of a dead Inca had to be a son by the ruler's principal wife, who had to be the ruler's full sister. Huascar was the result of such an incestuous union. His half-brother Atauhualpa was not. Atauhualpa tried to persuade Huascar to split the kingdom with him, claiming that their father's dying wish was for both sons to rule. Huascar rejected this claim. The great nobles responsible for the cult of the royal mummies, however, were alarmed and outraged by Huascar's proposal to bury the mummies. Not only would Huascar be insulting the dead mummies and thus provoke their anger and retaliation, but the nobility would be deprived of the wealth and power they enjoyed as custodians of the cult. Willing to ignore the fact that Atauhualpa had not been born of an incestuous union, the nobles supported Atauhualpa's claim to rule. Civil war ensued, and Atauhualpa emerged victorious.[17] The five-year struggle may have exhausted him and damaged his judgment.

Francisco Pizarro (ca 1475–1541) landed on the northern coast of Peru on May 13, 1532, the very day Atauhualpa won the decisive battle against his brother. The Spaniard soon learned about the war and its outcome. As Pizarro advanced across the steep Andes toward Cuzco, Atauhualpa was proceeding to the capital for his coronation. Atauhualpa stopped at the provincial town of Cajamarca. He, like Montezuma in Mexico, was kept fully informed of the Spaniards' movements. His plan was to lure the Spaniards into a trap, seize their horses and ablest men for his army, and execute the rest. What had the Inca, surrounded by his thousands of troops, to fear? Atauhualpa thus accepted Pizarro's invitation to meet in the central plaza of Cajamarca with his bodyguards "unarmed so as not to give offense." He rode right into the Spaniard's trap. Pizarro knew that if he could capture that Inca, from whom all power devolved, he would have the "Kingdom of Gold" for which he had come to the New World.

The Inca's litter arrived in the ominously quiet town square. One cannon blast terrified the Indians. The Spaniards rushed out of hiding and slaughtered them. Atauhualpa's fringed headband was instantly torn from his head. He offered to purchase his freedom with a roomful of gold. Pizarro agreed to this ransom, and an appropriate document was drawn up and signed. But after the gold had been gathered from all parts of the empire to fill the room—its dimensions were 17 feet by 22 feet by 9 feet—the Spaniards trumped up charges against Atauhualpa and strangled him. The Inca Empire lay at Pizarro's feet.

The South American Holocaust

In the sixteenth century, about 200,000 Spaniards emigrated to the New World. Soldiers demobilized from the Spanish and Italian campaigns, adventurers and drifters unable to find work in Spain, they did not intend to work in the New World. After assisting in the conquest of the Aztecs and the subjugation of the Incas, these drifters wanted to settle down and become a ruling class. In temperate grazing areas they carved out vast estates and imported Spanish sheep, cattle, and horses for the kinds of ranching with which they were familiar. In the coastal tropics, unsuited for grazing, the Spanish erected huge sugar plantations. Columbus had introduced sugar into the West Indies; Cortés had introduced it into Mexico. Sugar was a great luxury in Europe, and demand for it was high. Around 1550 the discovery of silver at Zacatecas and Guanajuato in Mexico and Potosí in present-day Bolivia stimulated silver rushes. How were the cattle ranches, sugar plantations, and silver mines to be worked? Obviously, by the Indians.

The Spanish quickly established the *encomienda* system, whereby the Crown granted the conquerors the right to employ groups of Indians in a town or area as agricultural or mining laborers or as tribute-payers. Theoretically, the Spanish were forbidden to enslave the Indian natives; in actuality, the encomiendas were a legalized form of slavery. The European demand for sugar, tobacco, and silver prompted the colonists to exploit the Indians mercilessly. Unaccustomed to forced labor, especially in the blistering heat of tropical cane fields or the dark, dank, and dangerous mines, Indians died like flies. Recently scholars have tried to reckon the death rate of the Amerindians in the sixteenth century. Some historians maintain that the Indian population of Peru fell from 1.3 million in 1570 to 600,000 in 1620; central Mexico had 25.3 million Indians in 1519 and 1 million in 1605.[18] Some demographers dispute these figures, but all agree that the decline of the native Indian population in all of Spanish-occupied America amounted to a catastrophe greater in scale than any that has occurred even in the twentieth century.

What were the causes of this devastating slump in population? Students of the history of medicine have suggested the best explanation: disease. The

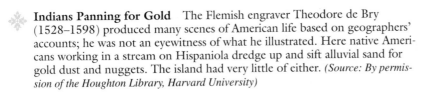

Indians Panning for Gold   The Flemish engraver Theodore de Bry (1528–1598) produced many scenes of American life based on geographers' accounts; he was not an eyewitness of what he illustrated. Here native Americans working in a stream on Hispaniola dredge up and sift alluvial sand for gold dust and nuggets. The island had very little of either. *(Source: By permission of the Houghton Library, Harvard University)*

major cause of widespread epidemics is migration, and those peoples isolated longest from other societies suffer most. Contact with disease builds up bodily resistance. At the beginning of the sixteenth century, Amerindians probably had the unfortunate distinction of longer isolation from the rest of humankind than any other people on earth. Crowded concentrations of laborers in the mining camps bred infection, which the miners carried to their home villages. With little or no resistance to diseases brought from the Old World, the inhabitants of the highlands of Mexico and Peru, especially, fell victim to smallpox. According to one expert, smallpox caused "in all likelihood the most severe single loss of aboriginal population that ever occurred."[19]

Although disease was the prime cause of the Indian holocaust, the Spaniards themselves contributed heavily to the Indians' death rate.[20] According to the Franciscan missionary Bartolomé de Las Casas (1474–1566), the Spanish maliciously murdered thousands:

This infinite multitude of people [the Indians] was . . . without fraud, without subtilty or malice . . . toward the Spaniards whom they serve, patient, meek and peaceful. . . .

To these quiet Lambs . . . came the Spaniards like most c(r)uel Tygres, Wolves and Lions, enrag'd with a sharp and tedious hunger; for these forty years past, minding nothing else but the slaughter of these unfortunate wretches, whom with divers kinds of torments neither seen nor heard of before, they have so cruelly and inhumanely butchered, that of three millions of people which Hispaniola it self did contain, there are left remaining alive scarce three hundred persons.[21]

Las Casas's remarks concentrate on the tropical lowlands, but the death rate in the highlands was also staggering.

The Christian missionaries who accompanied the conquistadors and settlers—Franciscans, Dominicans, and Jesuits—played an important role in converting the Indians to Christianity, teaching them European methods of agriculture, and inculcating loyalty to the Spanish crown. In terms of numbers of people baptized, missionaries enjoyed phenomenal success, though the depth of the Indians' understanding of Christianity remains debatable. Missionaries, especially Las Casas, asserted that the Indians had human rights, and through Las Casas's persistent pressure the emperor Charles

V in 1531 abolished the worst abuses of the encomienda system.

Some scholars offer a psychological explanation for the colossal death rate of the Indians, suggesting that they simply lost the will to survive because their gods appeared to have abandoned them to a world over which they had no control. Hopelessness, combined with abusive treatment and overwork, pushed many men to suicide, many women to abortion or infanticide.

Whatever its precise causes, the astronomically high death rate created a severe labor shortage in Spanish America. As early as 1511, King Ferdinand of Spain observed that the Indians seemed to be "very frail" and that "one black could do the work of four Indians."[22] Thus was born an absurd myth and the massive importation of black slaves from Africa (see pages 665–674).

Colonial Administration

Having seized the great Indian ceremonial centers in Mexico and Peru, the Spanish conquistadors proceeded to subdue the main areas of native American civilization in the New World. Columbus, Cortés, and Pizarro claimed the lands they had "discovered" for the crown of Spain. How were these lands to be governed?

According to the Spanish theory of absolutism, the Crown was entitled to exercise full authority over all imperial lands. In the sixteenth century the Crown divided Spain's New World territories into four *viceroyalties,* or administrative divisions. New Spain, with its capital at Mexico City, consisted of Mexico, Central America, and present-day California, Arizona, New Mexico, and Texas. Peru, with its viceregal seat at Lima, originally consisted of all the lands in continental South America but later was reduced to the territory of modern Peru, Chile, Bolivia, and Ecuador. New Granada, with Bogotá as its administrative center, included present-day Venezuela, Colombia, Panama, and, after 1739, Ecuador. La Plata, with Buenos Aires as its capital, consisted of Argentina, Uruguay, and Paraguay. Within each territory a *viceroy,* or imperial governor, had broad military and civil authority as the Spanish sovereign's direct representative. The viceroy presided over the *audiencia,* twelve to fifteen judges who served as advisory council and as the highest judicial body.

From the early sixteenth century to the beginning of the nineteenth, the Spanish monarchy acted on the mercantilist principle that the colonies existed for the financial benefit of the mother country. The mining of gold and silver was always the most important industry in the colonies. The Crown claimed the *quinto,* one-fifth of all precious metals mined in the Americas. Gold and silver yielded the Spanish monarchy 25 percent of its total income. In return, Spain shipped manufactured goods to the New World and discouraged the development of native industries.

The Portuguese governed their colony of Brazil in a similar manner. After the union of the crowns of Portugal and Spain in 1580, Spanish administrative forms were introduced. Local officials called *corregidores* held judicial and military powers. Mercantilist policies placed severe restrictions on Brazilian industries that might compete with those of Portugal. In the seventeenth century the use of black slave labor made possible the cultivation of coffee, cotton, and sugar. In the eighteenth century Brazil led the world in the production of sugar. The unique feature of colonial Brazil's culture and society was its thoroughgoing mixture of Indians, whites, and blacks.

The Economic Effects of Spain's Discoveries on Europe

The sixteenth century has often been called Spain's golden century. The influence of Spanish armies, Spanish Catholicism, and Spanish wealth was felt all over Europe. This greatness rested largely on the influx of precious metals from the Americas.

The mines at Zacatecas, Guanajuato, and Potosí in Peru poured out huge quantities of precious metals. To protect this treasure from French and English pirates, armed convoys transported it each year to Spain. Between 1503 and 1650, 16 million kilograms of silver and 185,000 kilograms of gold entered Seville's port. Spanish predominance, however, proved temporary.

In the sixteenth century, Spain experienced a steady population increase, creating a sharp rise in the demand for food and goods. Spanish colonies in the Americas also represented a demand for products. Since Spain had expelled some of the best farmers and businessmen—the Muslims and Jews—in the fifteenth century, the Spanish economy was suffering and could not meet the new demands. Prices rose. Because the cost of manufacturing cloth and other goods increased, Spanish products could not compete in the international market with cheaper products made elsewhere. The textile industry was badly hurt. Prices spiraled upward faster than the government could levy taxes to dampen the economy. (Higher taxes would have cut the public's buying power; with fewer goods sold, prices would have come down.)

Did the flood of silver bullion from America cause the inflation? Prices rose most steeply before 1565, but bullion imports reached their peak between 1580 and 1620. Thus there is no direct correlation between silver imports and the inflation rate. Did the substantial population growth accelerate the inflation rate? It may have done so. After 1600, when the population pressure declined, prices gradually stabilized. One fact is certain: the price revolution severely strained government budgets. Several times between 1557 and 1647, Spain's king Philip II and his successors repudiated the state debt, thereby undermining confidence in the government and leading the economy into shambles.

As Philip II paid his armies and foreign debts with silver bullion, Spanish inflation was transmitted to the rest of Europe. Between 1560 and 1600, much of Europe experienced large price increases. Prices doubled and in some cases quadrupled. Spain suffered most severely, but all European countries were affected. People who lived on fixed incomes, such as the continental nobles, were badly hurt because their money bought less. Those who owed fixed sums of money, such as the middle class, prospered: in a time of rising prices, debts had less value each year. Food costs rose most sharply, and the poor fared worst of all.

Seaborne Trading Empires

By 1550, European overseas reconnaissance had led to the first global seaborne trade. For centuries the Muslims had controlled the rich spice trade of the Indian Ocean; Muslim expeditions had been across Asian and African land routes. The Europeans' discovery of the Americas and their exploration of the Pacific for the first time linked the entire world by intercontinental seaborne trade. That trade brought into being three successive commercial empires: the Portuguese, the Spanish, and the Dutch.

In the sixteenth century, naval power and shipborne artillery gave Portugal hegemony over the sea route to India. To Lisbon the Portuguese fleet brought spices, which the Portuguese paid for with

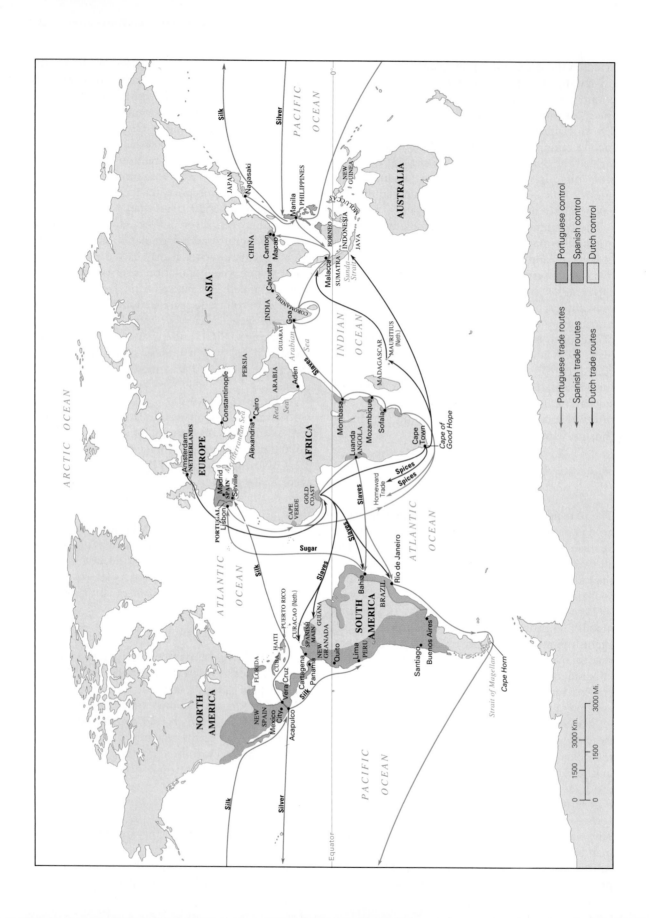

textiles produced at Gujarat and Coromandel in India and with gold and ivory from East Africa (Map 16.2). From their fortified bases at Goa on the Arabian Sea and at Malacca on the Malay Peninsula, ships of Malabar teak carried goods to the Portuguese settlement at Macao in the South China Sea. From Macao, loaded with Chinese silks and porcelains, Portuguese ships sailed to the Japanese port of Nagasaki and to the Philippine port of Manila, where Chinese goods were exchanged for Spanish (that is, Latin American) silver. Throughout Asia, the Portuguese traded in slaves—black Africans, Chinese, and Japanese. The Portuguese imported to India horses from Mesopotamia and copper from Arabia; from India they exported hawks and peacocks for the Chinese and Japanese markets.

Across the Atlantic, Portuguese Brazil provided most of the sugar consumed in Europe in the sixteenth and early seventeenth centuries. African slave labor produced the sugar on the plantations of Brazil, and Portuguese merchants, some of them Jewish, controlled both the slave trade between West Africa and Brazil (see pages 545–546) and the commerce in sugar between Brazil and Portugal. The Portuguese were the first worldwide traders, and Portuguese was the language of the Asian maritime trade.

Spanish possessions in the New World constituted basically a land empire and, as already described, in the sixteenth century the Spaniards devised a method of governing that empire. But across the Pacific the Spaniards also built a seaborne empire, centered at Manila in the Philippines, which had been "discovered" by Ferdinand Magellan in 1521. Between 1564 and 1571, the Spanish navigator Miguel Lopez de Legazpi sailed from Mexico and through a swift and almost bloodless conquest took over the Philippine Islands. Legazpi founded Manila, which served as the trans-Pacific bridge between Spanish America and the extreme Eastern trade.

Chinese silk, sold by the Portuguese in Manila for American silver, was transported to Acapulco in Mexico, from which it was carried overland to Vera Cruz for re-export to Spain. Because hostile Pacific winds prohibited direct passage from the Philippines to Peru, large shipments of silk also went south from Acapulco to Peru (see Map 16.2). Spanish merchants could never satisfy the European demand for silk, so huge amounts of bullion went from Acapulco to Manila. For example, in 1597, 12 million pesos of silver, almost the total value of the transatlantic trade, crossed the Pacific. After about 1640, the Spanish silk trade declined because it could not compete with Dutch imports.

In the latter half of the seventeenth century, the worldwide Dutch seaborne trade predominated. The Dutch Empire was built on spices. In 1599 a Dutch fleet returned to Amsterdam carrying 600,000 pounds of pepper and 250,000 pounds of cloves and nutmeg. Those who had invested in the expedition received a 100 percent profit. The voyage led to the establishment in 1602 of the Dutch East India Company, founded with the stated intention of capturing the spice trade from the Portuguese.

The Dutch fleet, sailing from the Cape of Good Hope and avoiding the Portuguese forts in India, steered directly for the Sunda Strait in Indonesia (see Map 16.2). The Dutch wanted direct access to and control of the Indonesian sources of spices. In return for assisting Indonesian princes in local squabbles and disputes with the Portuguese, the Dutch won broad commercial concessions. Through agreements, seizures, and outright war, they gained control of the western access to the Indonesian archipelago. Gradually, they acquired political domination over the archipelago itself. Exchanging European manufactured goods—armor, firearms, linens, and toys—the Dutch soon had a monopoly on the very lucrative spice trade.[23]

The seaborne empires profited from the geographical reconnaissance and technological developments of the sixteenth century. The empires of Portugal, Spain, and Holland had strong commercial ambitions. They also paved the way for the eighteenth-century mercantilist empires of France and Great Britain.

The Chinese and Japanese Discovery of the West

The desire to Christianize pagan peoples was a major motive in Europeans' overseas expansion. The Indians of Central and South America, the

✳ **MAP 16.2 Seaborne Trading Empires in the Sixteenth and Seventeenth Centuries** In the sixteenth century, for the first time, the entire globe was linked by seaborne trade. In the seventeenth century American silver paid for Asian silks and spices, and African slaves in Latin America produced sugar for the tables of Europe.

Muslims and polytheistic peoples of the Pacific, and the Confucian, Buddhist, and Shinto peoples of China and Japan became objects of Christianizing efforts. In this missionary activity the new Jesuit Order was dominant and energetic.

In 1582 the Jesuit Matteo Ricci (1552–1610) settled at Macao on the mouth of the Canton River. Like the Christian monks who had converted the Germanic tribes of early medieval Europe, Ricci sought first to convert the emperor and elite groups and then, through gradual assimilation, to win the throngs of Chinese. He tried to present Christianity to the Chinese in Chinese terms. He understood the Chinese respect for learning and worked to win converts among the scholarly class. When Ricci was admitted to the Imperial City at Beijing (Peking), he addressed the emperor Wan-li:

Li Ma-tou [Ricci's name transliterated into Chinese], your Majesty's servant, comes from the Far West, addresses himself to Your Majesty with respect, in order to offer gifts from his country. Despite the distance, fame told me of the remarkable teaching and fine institutions with which the imperial court has endowed all its peoples. I desired to share these advantages and live out my life as one of Your Majesty's subjects, hoping in return to be of some small use.[24]

Ricci presented the emperor with two clocks, one of them decorated with dragons and eagles in the Chinese style. The emperor's growing fascination with clocks gave Ricci the opportunity to display other examples of Western technology. He instructed court scholars about astronomical equipment and the manufacture of cannon and drew for them a map of the world—with China at its center. These inventions greatly impressed the Chinese intelligentsia. Over a century later a Jesuit wrote, "The Imperial Palace is stuffed with clocks, . . . watches, carillons, repeaters, organs, spheres, and astronomical clocks of all kinds—there are more than four thousand pieces from the best masters of Paris and London."[25] The Chinese first learned about Europe from the Jesuits.

But the Christians and the Chinese did not understand one another. Because the Jesuits served the imperial court as mathematicians, astronomers, and cartographers, the Chinese emperors allowed them to remain in Beijing. The Jesuits, however, were primarily interested in converting the Chinese to Christianity. The missionaries thought that

by showing the pre-eminence of Western science, they were demonstrating the superiority of Western religion. This was a relationship that the Chinese did not acknowledge. They could not accept a religion that required total commitment and taught the existence of an absolute. Only a small number of the highly educated, convinced of a link between ancient Chinese tradition and Christianity, became Christians. Most Chinese were hostile to the Western faith. They accused Christians of corrupting Chinese morals because they forbade people to honor their ancestors—and corruption of morals translated into disturbing the public order. They also accused Christians of destroying Chinese sanctuaries, of revering a man (Christ) who had been executed as a public criminal, and of spying on behalf of the Japanese.

The "Rites Controversy," a dispute over ritual between the Jesuits and other Roman Catholic religious orders, sparked a crisis. The Jesuits supported the celebration of the Mass in Chinese and the performance of other ceremonies in terms understandable to the Chinese. The Franciscans and other missionaries felt that the Jesuits had sold out the essentials of the Christian faith in order to win converts.

One burning issue was whether Chinese reverence for ancestors was homage to the good that the dead had done during their lives or an act of worship. The Franciscans secured the support of Roman authorities who considered themselves authorities on Chinese culture and decided against the Jesuits. In 1704 and again in 1742 Rome decreed that Roman ceremonial practice in Latin (not in Chinese) was to be the law for Chinese missions. (This decision continued to govern Roman Catholic missionary activity until the Second Vatican Council in 1962.) Papal letters also forbade Chinese Christians from participating in the rites of ancestor worship. The emperor in turn banned Christianity in China, and the missionaries were forced to flee.

The Christian West and the Chinese world learned a great deal from each other. The Jesuits probably were "responsible for the rebirth of Chinese mathematics in the seventeenth and eighteenth centuries," and Western contributions stimulated the Chinese development of other sciences.[26] From the Chinese, Europeans got the idea of building bridges suspended by chains. The first Western experiments in electrostatics and magnetism in the seventeenth century derived from

Chinese models. Travel accounts about Chinese society and customs had a profound impact on Europeans, making them more sensitive to the beautiful diversity of peoples and manners, as the essays of Montaigne (see pages 546–547) and other Western thinkers reveal.

Initial Japanese contacts with Europeans paralleled those of the Chinese. In 1542, Portuguese merchants arrived in Japan and quickly won large profits carrying goods between China and Japan. Dutch and English ships followed, also enjoying the rewards of the East Asian trade. The Portuguese merchants vigorously supported Christian missionary activity, and in 1547 the Jesuit missionary Saint Francis Xavier landed at Kagoshima, preached widely, and in two years won many converts. From the beginning, however, the Japanese government feared that native converts might have conflicting political loyalties. Divided allegiance could encourage European invasion of the islands—the Japanese authorities had the example of the Philippines, where Spanish conquest followed missionary activity.

Convinced that European merchants and missionaries had contributed to the general civil disorder, which the regime was trying to eradicate, the Japanese government decided to expel the Spanish and Portuguese and to close Japan to all foreign influence. A decree of 1635 was directed at the commissioners of the port of Nagasaki, a center of Japanese Christianity:

If there is any place where the teachings of the padres (Catholic priests) is practiced, the two of you must order a thorough investigation. . . . If there are any Southern Barbarians (Westerners) who propagate the teachings of the padres, or otherwise commit crimes, they may be incarcerated in the prison.[27]

In 1639, an imperial memorandum decreed: "hereafter entry by the Portuguese galeota [galleon or large oceangoing warship] is forbidden. If they insist on coming [to Japan], the ships must be destroyed and anyone aboard those ships must be beheaded.[28]

When tens of thousands of Japanese Christians made a stand on the peninsula of Shimabara, the Dutch lent the Japanese government cannon. The Protestant Dutch hated Catholicism, and as businessmen they hated the Portuguese, their great commercial rivals. Convinced that the Dutch had come only for trade and did not want to proselytize, the imperial government allowed the Dutch to remain. But Japanese authorities ordered them to remove their factory-station from Hirado on the western tip of Kyushu to the tiny island of Deshima, which covered just 2,100 square feet. The government limited Dutch trade to one ship a year, watched the Dutch very closely, and required Dutch officials to pay an annual visit to the capital to renew their loyalty. The Japanese also compelled the Dutch merchants to perform servile acts that other Europeans considered humiliating.

Long after Christianity ceased to be a potential threat to the Japanese government, the fear of Christianity sustained a policy of banning Western books on science or religion. Until well into the eighteenth century, Japanese intellectuals were effectively cut off from Western developments. The Japanese opinion of Westerners was not high. What little the Japanese knew derived from the few Dutch businessmen at Deshima. Very few Japanese people ever saw Europeans. If they did, they considered them "a special variety of goblin that bore only a superficial resemblance to a normal human being." The widespread rumor was that when Dutchmen urinated they raised one leg like dogs.[29]

✦ POLITICS, RELIGION, AND WAR

In 1559 France and Spain signed the Treaty of Cateau-Cambrésis, which ended the long conflict known as the Habsburg-Valois Wars. This event marks a watershed in early modern European history. Spain (the Habsburg side) was the victor. France, exhausted by the struggle, had to acknowledge Spanish dominance in Italy, where much of the war had been fought. Spanish governors ruled in Sicily, Naples, and Milan, and Spanish influence was strong in the Papal States and Tuscany. The Treaty of Cateau-Cambrésis ended an era of strictly dynastic wars and initiated a period of conflicts in which politics and religion played the dominant roles.

The wars of the late sixteenth century differed considerably from earlier wars. Sixteenth- and seventeenth-century armies were bigger than medieval ones; some forces numbered as many as fifty thousand men. Because large armies were expensive, governments had to reorganize their administrations to finance them. The use of gunpowder altered both the nature of warfare and popular attitudes toward it. Guns and cannon killed and wounded from a distance, indiscriminately. Writers scorned gunpowder as a coward's weapon that allowed a common soldier to kill a gentleman. Gunpowder weakened the notion, common during the Hundred Years' War (1337–1453), that warfare was an ennobling experience. Governments utilized propaganda, pulpits, and the printing press to arouse public opinion to support war.[30]

Late sixteenth-century conflicts fundamentally tested the medieval ideal of a unified Christian society governed by one political ruler—the emperor—to whom all rulers were theoretically subordinate, and one church, to which all people belonged. The Protestant Reformation had killed this ideal, but few people recognized it as dead. Catholics continued to believe that Calvinists and Lutherans could be reconverted; Protestants persisted in thinking that the Roman church should be destroyed. Most people believed that a state could survive only if its members shared the same faith. The settlement finally achieved in 1648, known as the Peace of Westphalia, signaled the end of the medieval ideal.

The Origins of Difficulties in France (1515–1559)

In the first half of the sixteenth century, France continued the recovery begun during the reign of Louis XI (r. 1461–1483). The population losses caused by the plague and the disorders accompanying the Hundred Years' War had created such a labor shortage that serfdom virtually disappeared. Cash rents replaced feudal rents and servile obligations. This development clearly benefited the peasantry. Meanwhile, the declining buying power of money hurt the nobility. Domestic and foreign trade picked up; mercantile centers expanded.

The charming and cultivated Francis I (r. 1515–1547) and his athletic, emotional son Henry II (r. 1547–1559) governed through a small, efficient council. In 1539 Francis issued an ordinance that placed the whole of France under the jurisdiction of the royal law courts and made French the language of those courts. This act had a powerful centralizing impact. The *taille,* a tax on land, provided what strength the monarchy had and supported a strong standing army. Unfortunately, the tax base was too narrow to support France's extravagant promotion of the arts and ambitious foreign policy.

Deliberately imitating the Italian Renaissance princes, the Valois monarchs lavished money on a vast building program and on Italian artists. Francis I commissioned the Paris architect Pierre Lescot to rebuild the palace of the Louvre and Michelangelo's star pupil, Il Rosso, to decorate the wing of the Fontainebleau chateau. After acquiring Leonardo da Vinci's painting *Mona Lisa,* Francis brought Leonardo himself to France. Whatever praise Francis I and Henry II deserve for importing Italian Renaissance art and architecture to France, they spent far more than they could afford.

The Habsburg-Valois Wars, which had begun in 1522, also cost more than the government could afford. In addition to the time-honored practices of increasing taxes and heavy borrowing, Francis I tried two new devices to raise revenue: the sale of public offices and a treaty with the papacy. The former proved to be only a temporary source of money. The offices sold tended to become hereditary within a family, and once a man bought an office he and his heirs were tax-exempt. The sale of public offices thus created a tax-exempt class known as the "nobility of the robe."

The treaty with the papacy was the Concordat of Bologna (1516), in which Francis agreed to recognize the supremacy of the papacy over a universal council, thereby accepting a monarchial, rather than a conciliar view of church government. In return, the French crown gained the right to appoint all French bishops and abbots. This understanding gave the monarchy a rich supplement of money and offices and power over ecclesiastical organization that lasted until the Revolution of 1789. The Concordat of Bologna helps to explain why France did not later become Protestant: in effect, it established Catholicism as the state religion. The Concordat, however, perpetuated disorders within the French church. The government used ecclesiastical offices to pay and reward civil servants, who were likely to be worldly priests who possessed few special spiritual qualifications and were not inclined to work to elevate the intellectual and moral standards of the parish clergy. Thus the teachings of Luther and Calvin, spread far and wide because of the invention of printing from movable type some sixty years before, found a receptive audience.

After the publication of Calvin's *Institutes of the Christian Religion* in 1536, sizable numbers of French people were attracted to the "reformed religion," as Calvinism was called. Because Calvin wrote in French rather than Latin, his ideas gained wide circulation. At first, Calvinism drew converts from among reform-minded members of the

❖ **Rossi and Primaticcio: The Gallery of Francis I**   Flat paintings alternating with rich sculpture provide a rhythm that directs the eye down the long gallery at Fontainebleau, constructed between 1530 and 1540. Francis I sought to re-create in France the elegant Renaissance lifestyle found in Italy. *(Source: Art Resource, NY)*

Catholic clergy, the industrious middle classes, and artisan groups. Most Calvinists lived in Paris, Lyons, Meaux, Grenoble, and other major cities.

In spite of condemnation by the universities, government bans, and massive burnings at the stake, the numbers of Protestants in France grew steadily. When Henry II died in 1559, perhaps one-tenth of the population had become Calvinist.

Religious Riots and Civil War in France (1559–1589)

For thirty years, from 1559 to 1589, violence and civil war divided and shattered France. The feebleness of the monarchy was the seed from which the weeds of civil violence germinated. The three weak sons of Henry II could not provide the necessary leadership, and the French nobility took advantage of this monarchial weakness. In the second half of the sixteenth century, between two-fifths and one-half of the nobility at one time or another became Calvinist, frequently adopting the "reformed religion" as a religious cloak for their independence from the monarchy. Armed clashes between Catholic royalist lords and Calvinist antimonarchial lords occurred in many parts of France.

Among the upper classes, the fundamental object of the struggle was power. At lower social levels, however, religious concerns were paramount.

Working-class crowds composed of skilled craftsmen and the poor wreaked terrible violence on people and property. Both Calvinists and Catholics believed that the others' books, services, and ministers polluted the community. Preachers incited violence, and ceremonies like baptisms, marriages, and funerals triggered it. Protestant pastors encouraged their followers to destroy statues and liturgical objects in Catholic churches. Catholic priests urged their flocks to shed the blood of the Calvinist heretics.

In the fourteenth and fifteenth centuries, crowd action—attacks on great nobles and rich prelates—had expressed economic grievances. In contrast, religious rioters of the sixteenth century believed that they could assume the power of public magistrates and rid the community of corruption. Municipal officials criticized the crowds' actions, but the participation of pastors and priests in these riots lent them some legitimacy.[31]

A savage Catholic attack on Calvinists in Paris on August 24, 1572 (Saint Bartholomew's Day), followed the usual pattern. The occasion was a religious ceremony—the marriage of the king's sister Margaret of Valois to the Protestant Henry of Navarre—that was intended to help reconcile Catholics and Huguenots, as French Calvinists were called. The night before the wedding, the leader of the Catholic aristocracy, Henry of Guise, had Gaspard de Coligny, leader of the Huguenot party, attacked. Rioting and slaughter followed. The Huguenot gentry in Paris was massacred, and religious violence spread to the provinces. Between August 25 and October 3, perhaps twelve thousand Huguenots perished at Meaux, Lyons, Orléans, and Paris.

The Saint Bartholomew's Day massacre led to the War of the Three Henrys, a civil conflict among factions led by the Protestant Henry of Navarre, by King Henry III (who succeeded the tubercular Charles IX), and by the Catholic Henry of Guise. The Guises wanted not only to destroy Calvinism but to replace Henry III with a member of the Guise family. France suffered fifteen more years of religious rioting and domestic anarchy. Agriculture in many areas was destroyed; commercial life declined severely; starvation and death haunted the land.

What ultimately saved France was a small group of Catholic moderates called *politiques*. They believed that no religious creed was worth the incessant disorder and destruction and that only the restoration of a strong monarchy could reverse the trend toward collapse. The death of Queen Catherine de' Medici, followed by the assassinations of Henry of Guise and King Henry III, paved the way for the accession of the politique and Protestant Henry of Navarre, who ascended the throne as Henry IV (r. 1589–1610).

This glamorous prince, "who knew how to fight, to make love, and to drink," as a contemporary remarked, knew that the majority of the French were Roman Catholics. Declaring "Paris is worth a Mass," Henry knelt before the archbishop of Bourges and was received into the Roman Catholic church. Henry's willingness to sacrifice religious principles in the interest of a strong monarchy saved France. The Edict of Nantes, which Henry published in 1598, granted to Huguenots liberty of conscience and liberty of public worship in two hundred fortified towns, such as La Rochelle. The reign of Henry IV and the Edict of Nantes prepared the way for French absolutism in the seventeenth century (see page 558) by helping to restore internal peace in France.

The Revolt of the Netherlands and the Spanish Armada

In the last quarter of the sixteenth century, the political stability of England, the international pres-

tige of Spain, and the moral influence of the Roman papacy all became mixed up with a religious crisis in the Low Countries. By this time, the Netherlands was the pivot around which European money, diplomacy, and war revolved. What began as a movement for the reformation of the Catholic church developed into a struggle for Dutch independence from Spanish rule.

The Habsburg emperor Charles V (r. 1519–1556) had inherited the seventeen provinces that compose present-day Belgium and Holland. The French-speaking southern towns produced fine linens and woolens; the wealth of the Dutch-speaking northern cities rested on fishing, shipping, and international banking. In the cities of both regions of the Low Countries, trade and commerce had produced a vibrant cosmopolitan atmosphere.

Each of the seventeen provinces of the Netherlands was self-governing and enjoyed the right to make its own laws and collect its own taxes. Only economic connections and the recognition of a common ruler in the person of the emperor Charles V united the provinces. Delegates from each province met together in the Estates General, but important decisions had to be referred back to each provincial Estate for approval. In the middle of the sixteenth century, the provinces of the Netherlands had a limited sense of federation.

In the Low Countries, as elsewhere, corruption in the Roman church and the critical spirit of the Renaissance provoked pressure for reform. Lutheran tracts and Dutch translations of the Bible flooded the seventeen provinces in the 1520s and 1530s, and Protestant ideas circulated freely in the cosmopolitan atmosphere of the commercial centers. But Charles's Flemish loyalty checked the spread of Lutheranism. Charles had been born in Ghent and raised in the Netherlands; he was Flemish in language and culture. He identified with the Flemish and they with him.

In 1556, however, Charles V abdicated and divided his territories. His younger brother Ferdinand received Austria and the Holy Roman Empire and ruled as Ferdinand I (r. 1558–1564). His son Philip inherited Spain, the Low Countries, Milan and the kingdom of Sicily, and the Spanish possessions in America and ruled as Philip II (r. 1556–1598).

Lutheranism posed no serious threat to Spanish rule in the Low Countries; it was the spread of Calvinism that upset the applecart. By the 1560s,

✳ **To Purify the Church**   The destruction of pictures and statues representing biblical events, Christian doctrine, or sacred figures was a central feature of the Protestant Reformation. Here Dutch Protestant soldiers destroy what they consider idols in the belief that they are purifying the church. *(Source: Fotomas Index)*

there was a strong, militant minority of Calvinists to whom Calvinism appealed because of its intellectual seriousness, moral gravity, and approval of any form of labor well done. Many working-class people converted because Calvinist employers would hire only fellow Calvinists. Well organized and with the backing of rich merchants, Calvinists quickly gained a wide following, and the Calvinist reformed religion tended in the 1570s to encourage opposition to "illegal" civil authorities.

In August of 1566, a year of very high grain prices, fanatical Calvinists, primarily of the poorest classes, embarked on a rampage of frightful destruction. As in France, Calvinist destruction in the Low Countries was incited by popular preaching, and attacks were aimed at religious images as symbols of false doctrines, not at people. The cathedral of Notre Dame at Antwerp was the first target. Begun in 1124 and finished only in 1518, this church stood as a monument to the commercial prosperity of Flanders, the piety of the business classes, and the artistic genius of centuries. On six successive summer evenings, crowds swept through the nave, attacking the greatest concentration of artworks in northern Europe: altars, paintings, books, tombs, ecclesiastical vestments, missals, manuscripts, ornaments, stained-glass windows, and sculptures. Before the havoc was over, thirty more churches had been sacked and irreplaceable libraries burned. From Antwerp the destruction spread to Brussels and Ghent and north to the provinces of Holland and Zeeland.

From Madrid, Philip II sent twenty thousand Spanish troops led by the duke of Alva to pacify the Low Countries. Alva interpreted "pacification" to mean the ruthless extermination of religious and political dissidents. His repressive measures and heavy taxation triggered widespread revolt.

For ten years, between 1568 and 1578, civil war raged in the Netherlands between Catholics and Protestants and between the seventeen provinces and Spain. Spanish generals could not halt the fighting. In 1576 the seventeen provinces united under the leadership of Prince William of Orange,

CHAPTER 16 THE AGE OF EUROPEAN EXPANSION AND RELIGIOUS WARS

called "the Silent" because of his remarkable discretion. In 1578 Philip II sent his nephew Alexander Farnese, duke of Parma, with an army of German mercenaries to crush the revolt once and for all. Avoiding pitched battles, Farnese fought by patient sieges. One by one the cities of the south fell and finally Antwerp, the financial capital of northern Europe.

Antwerp marked the farthest extent of Spanish jurisdiction and ultimately the religious division of the Netherlands. The ten southern provinces, the Spanish Netherlands (the future Belgium), remained Catholic and under the control of the Spanish Habsburgs. The seven northern provinces were Protestant and, led by Holland, formed the Union of Utrecht and in 1581 declared their independence from Spain. Thus was born the United Provinces of the Netherlands (Map 16.3).

Geography and sociopolitical structure differentiated the two countries. The northern provinces were ribboned with sluices and canals and therefore were highly defensible. Several times the Dutch had broken the dikes and flooded the countryside to halt the advancing Farnese. In the southern provinces the Ardennes Mountains interrupt the otherwise flat terrain. In the north the commercial aristocracy possessed the predominant power; in the south the landed nobility had the greater influence. The north was Protestant; the south remained Catholic.

Philip II and Alexander Farnese did not accept the division of the Low Countries, and the strug-

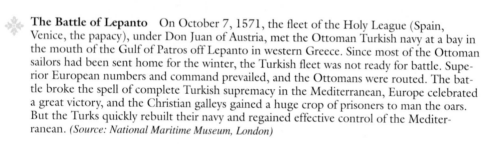

The Battle of Lepanto   On October 7, 1571, the fleet of the Holy League (Spain, Venice, the papacy), under Don Juan of Austria, met the Ottoman Turkish navy at a bay in the mouth of the Gulf of Patros off Lepanto in western Greece. Since most of the Ottoman sailors had been sent home for the winter, the Turkish fleet was not ready for battle. Superior European numbers and command prevailed, and the Ottomans were routed. The battle broke the spell of complete Turkish supremacy in the Mediterranean, Europe celebrated a great victory, and the Christian galleys gained a huge crop of prisoners to man the oars. But the Turks quickly rebuilt their navy and regained effective control of the Mediterranean. *(Source: National Maritime Museum, London)*

gle continued after 1581. The Protestant United Provinces repeatedly asked the Protestant Queen Elizabeth of England for assistance. But she was reluctant to antagonize Philip II by supporting the Dutch against the Spanish. The Spanish king had the steady flow of silver from the Americas at his disposal, and Elizabeth, lacking such treasure, wanted to avoid war. She realized, however, that if she did not help the Protestant Netherlands and they were crushed by Farnese, the Spanish were likely to invade England.

Three developments forced Elizabeth's hand. First, the wars in the Low Countries—the chief market for English woolens—badly hurt the English economy. When wool was not exported, the Crown lost valuable customs revenues. Second, the murder of William the Silent in July 1584 eliminated not only a great Protestant leader but the chief military check on the Farnese advance. Third, the collapse of Antwerp appeared to signal a Catholic sweep through the Netherlands. The next step, the English feared, would be a Spanish invasion of their island. For these reasons, Elizabeth pumped £250,000 and two thousand troops into the Protestant cause in the Low Countries between 1585 and 1587. Increasingly fearful of plots orchestrated by the Catholic Mary, Queen of Scots, Elizabeth's cousin and probable heir, Elizabeth finally signed her death warrant. Mary was beheaded on February 18, 1587. Sometime between March 24 and 30, the news of Mary's death reached Philip II.

Philip of Spain considered himself the international defender of Catholicism and heir to the medieval imperial power. When Pope Sixtus V (r. 1585–1590) heard of the death of the Queen of Scots, he promised to pay Philip a million gold ducats the moment Spanish troops landed in England. Alexander Farnese had repeatedly warned that, to subdue the Dutch, he would have to conquer England and cut off the source of Dutch support.

In these circumstances Philip prepared a vast fleet to sail from Lisbon to Flanders, fight off Elizabeth's navy *if* it attacked, rendezvous with Farnese, and escort his barges across the English Channel. The expedition's purpose was to transport the Flemish army for a cross-Channel assault. Philip expected to receive the support of English Catholics and anticipated a great victory for Spain.

On May 9, 1588, *la felicissima armada*—"the most fortunate fleet" of 130 vessels as it was called in official documents—sailed from Lisbon harbor.

MAP 16.3 The Netherlands, 1578–1609 Though small in geographical size, the Netherlands held a strategic position in the religious struggles of the sixteenth century.

An English fleet of about 150 ships—smaller, faster, and more maneuverable than the Spanish ships, and many having greater firepower—met the Spanish fleet in the Channel. A combination of storms and squalls, spoiled food and rank water aboard the Spanish ships, inadequate Spanish ammunition, and, to a lesser extent, English fire ships that caused the Spanish to scatter gave England the victory. Many Spanish ships sank on the journey home around Ireland; perhaps 65 managed to reach home ports.

The battle in the Channel had mixed consequences. Spain soon rebuilt its navy, and after 1588 the quality of the Spanish fleet improved. More silver reached Spain from the New World between 1588 and 1603 than in any other fifteen-year period. The war between England and Spain dragged on for years.

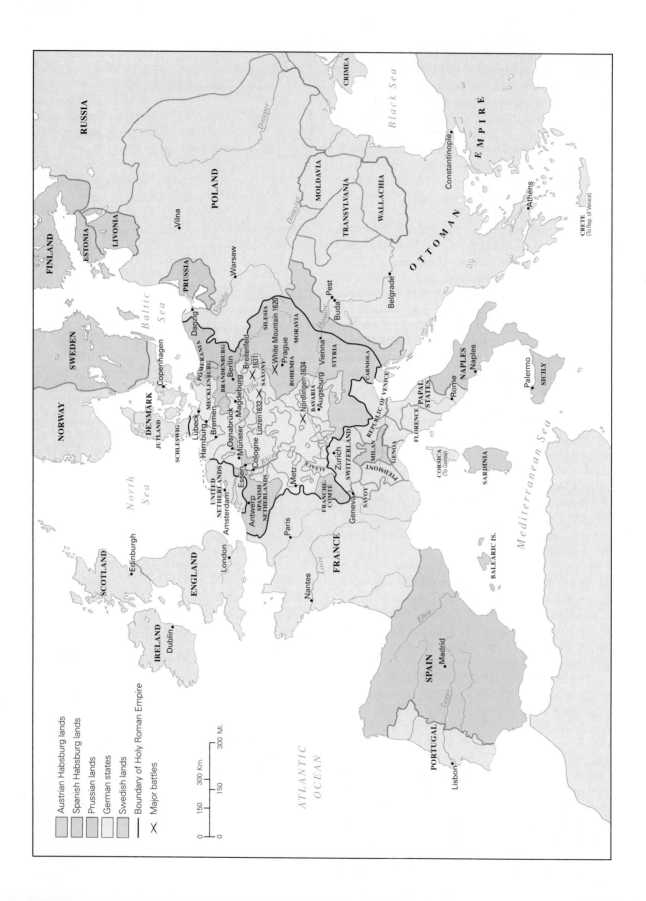

RUSSIA

Black Sea

OTTOMAN EMPIRE

CRIMEA

Constantinople

Athens

CRETE
(To Rep. of Venice)

POLAND

Vilna

MOLDAVIA

TRANSYLVANIA

WALLACHIA

Belgrade

Buda

Pest

Dnieper

Dniester

FINLAND

SWEDEN

NORWAY

Baltic Sea

ESTONIA

LIVONIA

PRUSSIA

Danzig

Warsaw

Vistula

SILESIA

MORAVIA

White Mountain 1620

Prague

BOHEMIA

SAXONY

1631

Breitenfeld

Berlin

BRANDENBURG

POMERANIA

MECKLENBURG

Copenhagen

DENMARK

JUTLAND

SCHLESWIG

Lübeck

Hamburg

Bremen

Osnabrück

Münster

Magdeburg

Lützen 1632

Elbe

Nördlingen 1634

Vienna

STYRIA

CARNIOLA

Augsburg

BAVARIA

REPUBLIC OF VENICE

Rome

PAPAL STATES

FLORENCE

NAPLES

Naples

Palermo

SICILY

GENOA

MILAN

PIEDMONT

SAVOY

Zurich

SWITZERLAND

Geneva

ALSACE

FRANCHE-COMTÉ

Metz

Rhine

Cologne

Essen

UNITED NETHERLANDS

Amsterdam

Antwerp

SPANISH NETHERLANDS

Paris

FRANCE

Nantes

Loire

North Sea

ENGLAND

London

SCOTLAND

Edinburgh

IRELAND

Dublin

ATLANTIC OCEAN

SPAIN

Madrid

PORTUGAL

Lisbon

Tagus

Ebro

BALEARIC IS.

CORSICA
(To Genoa)

SARDINIA

Mediterranean Sea

CORSICA

Vienna

Legend:

Austrian Habsburg lands

Spanish Habsburg lands

Prussian lands

German states

Swedish lands

Boundary of Holy Roman Empire

✗ Major battles

0   150   300 Km.

0   150   300 Mi.

The defeat of the Spanish Armada was decisive, however, in the sense that it prevented Philip II from reimposing unity on western Europe by force. He did not conquer England, and Elizabeth continued her financial and military support of the Dutch. In the Netherlands neither side gained significant territory. The borders of 1581 tended to become permanent. In 1609 Philip III of Spain (r. 1598–1621) agreed to a truce, in effect recognizing the independence of the United Provinces. In seventeenth-century Spain the memory of the defeat of the Armada contributed to a spirit of defeatism. In England the victory gave rise to a David and Goliath legend that enhanced English national sentiment.

The Thirty Years' War (1618–1648)

Meanwhile, the political-religious situation in central Europe deteriorated. An uneasy truce had prevailed in the Holy Roman Empire since the Peace of Augsburg of 1555. The Augsburg settlement, recognizing the independent power of the German princes, had undermined the authority of the central government. According to the Augsburg settlement, the faith of the prince determined the religion of his subjects. There was no freedom of religion. If a prince was Lutheran, his subjects would be Lutheran. If a prince was Catholic, his subjects would be too. Dissidents had to convert or move to an area where their religion was recognized. Later in the century, Catholics grew alarmed because Lutherans, in violation of the Peace of Augsburg, were steadily acquiring German bishoprics. And Protestants were not pleased by militant Jesuits' success in reconverting several Lutheran princes to Catholicism. The spread of Calvinism further confused the issue. Lutherans feared that Catholic and Calvinist gains would totally undermine the Augsburg principles. In an increasingly tense situation, Lutheran princes formed the Protestant Union (1608). Catholics retaliated with the Catholic League (1609). The Holy Roman Empire was divided into two armed camps.

MAP 16.4 Europe in 1648   Which country emerged from the Thirty Years' War as the strongest European power? What dynastic house was that country's major rival in the early modern period?

Dynastic interests were also at stake. The Spanish Habsburgs strongly supported the goals of the Austrian Habsburgs: the unity of the empire under Habsburg rule and the preservation of Catholicism within the empire.

Violence erupted first in Bohemia (Map 16.4). The Bohemians were Czech and German in nationality, and Lutheran, Calvinist, Catholic, and Hussite in religion; all these faiths enjoyed a fair degree of religious freedom in Bohemia. In 1617 Ferdinand of Styria, the new Catholic king of Bohemia, closed some Protestant churches. In retaliation, on May 23, 1618, Protestants hurled two of Ferdinand's officials from a castle window in Prague. They fell 70 feet but survived: Catholics claimed that angels had caught them; Protestants said the officials fell on a heap of soft horse manure. Called the "defenestration of Prague," this event marked the beginning of the Thirty Years' War (1618–1648).

Historians traditionally divide the war into four phases. The first, or Bohemian, phase (1618–1625) was characterized by civil war in Bohemia, as Bohemians fought for religious liberty and independence from Austrian Habsburg rule. In 1620 Ferdinand, newly elected Holy Roman Emperor Ferdinand II (r. 1619–1637), totally defeated Protestant forces at the Battle of the White Mountain and followed up his victories by wiping out Protestantism in Bohemia.

The second, or Danish, phase of the war (1625–1629)—so called because of the participation of King Christian IV of Denmark (r. 1588–1648), the ineffective leader of the Protestant cause—witnessed additional Catholic victories. The year 1629 marked the peak of Habsburg power. The Jesuits persuaded Ferdinand to issue the Edict of Restitution. It specified that all Catholic properties lost to Protestantism since 1552 were to be restored and only Catholics and Lutherans (*not* Calvinists, Hussites, or other sects) were to be allowed to practice their faiths. Ferdinand appeared to be embarked on a policy to unify the empire. Protestants throughout Europe feared collapse of the balance of power in north-central Europe.

The third, or Swedish, phase of the war (1630–1635) began when Swedish king Gustavus Adolphus (1594–1632) intervened to support the Protestant cause within the empire. In 1631, with French support, Gustavus Adolphus won a brilliant victory at Breitenfeld (see Map 16.4). Again in

1632 he was victorious at Lützen, though he was fatally wounded in the battle. The participation of the Swedes in the Thirty Years' War proved decisive for the future of Protestantism and later German history. The Swedish victories ended the Habsburg ambition of uniting all the German states under imperial authority.

The death of Gustavus Adolphus, followed by the defeat of the Swedes at the Battle of Nördlingen in 1634, prompted the French to enter the war on the side of the Protestants. Thus began the French, or international, phase of the Thirty Years' War (1635–1648). For almost a century, French foreign policy had been based on opposition to the Habsburgs, because a weak Holy Roman Empire enhanced France's international stature. Now, in 1635, France declared war on Spain and again sent financial and military assistance to the Swedes and the German Protestant princes. The war dragged on; neither side had the resources to win a quick, decisive victory. French, Dutch, and Swedes, supported by Scots, Finns, and German mercenaries, burned, looted, and destroyed German agriculture and commerce.

Finally, in October 1648, peace was achieved. The treaties signed at Münster and Osnabrück— the Peace of Westphalia—mark a turning point in European political, religious, and social history. The treaties recognized the sovereign, independent authority of the German princes. Each ruler could govern his particular territory and make war and peace as well. With power in the hands of more than three hundred princes, with no central government, courts, or means of controlling unruly rulers, the Holy Roman Empire as a real state was effectively destroyed.

The independence of the United Provinces of the Netherlands was acknowledged. The political divisions within the empire, and the acquisition of the province of Alsace increased France's size and prestige, and the treaties allowed France to intervene at will in German affairs. Sweden achieved a powerful presence in northeastern Germany (see Map 16.4). The treaties also denied the papacy the right to participate in German religious affairs— a restriction symbolizing the reduced role of the church in European politics.

The Westphalian treaties stipulated that the Augsburg religious agreement of 1555 should stand permanently. The sole modification made Calvinism, along with Catholicism and Lutheranism, a legally permissible creed. In practice, the north German states remained Protestant, the south German states Catholic.

The Thirty Years' War settled little but was a disaster for the German economy and society—probably the most destructive event in German history before the twentieth century. Population losses were frightful. Perhaps one-third of the urban residents and two-fifths of the inhabitants of rural areas died. Entire areas of Germany were depopulated, partly by military actions, partly by disease— typhus, dysentery, bubonic plague, and syphilis (brought to Europe from the Americas) accompanied the movements of armies—and partly by the thousands of refugees who fled to safer areas.

In Germany the European-wide economic crisis caused primarily by the influx of silver from South America was badly aggravated by the war. Scholars still cannot estimate the value of losses in agricultural land and livestock, in trade and commerce. Those losses, compounded by the flood of Spanish silver, brought on severe price increases. Inflation was worse in Germany than anywhere else in Europe.

The population decline caused a rise in the value of labor. Owners of great estates had to pay more for agricultural workers. Farmers who needed only small amounts of capital to restore their lands started over again. Many small farmers, however, lacked the revenue to rework their holdings and became day laborers. Nobles and landlords were able to buy up many small holdings and amass great estates. In some parts of Germany, especially east of the Elbe River in areas like Mecklenburg and Pomerania, peasants' loss of land led to a new serfdom.[32] The Thirty Years' War contributed to the legal and economic decline of the largest segment of German society.

❖ CHANGING ATTITUDES

What were the cultural consequences of the religious wars and of the worldwide discoveries? What impact did the discoveries and wars have on Europeans' attitudes? The clash of traditional religious and geographical beliefs with the new knowledge provided by explorers—combined with decades of devastation and disorder within Europe—bred confusion, uncertainty, and insecurity. Geographical evidence based on verifiable scientific proofs contradicted the evidence of the Scriptures and of the classical authors.

The Horrors of War   Following Richelieu's invasion of Lorraine in 1633, the French engraver Jacques Callot (1592/3–1635) produced a series of etchings collectively titled *The Great Miseries of War,* depicting the theft, rape, and brutality for which soldiers of the Thirty Years' War gained an enduring reputation. *(Source: Courtesy of the Trustees of the British Museum)*

The age of religious wars revealed extreme and violent contrasts. It was a deeply religious period in which men fought passionately for their beliefs; 70 percent of the books printed dealt with religious subjects. Yet the times saw the beginnings of religious skepticism. Europeans explored new continents, partly with the missionary aim of Christianizing the peoples they encountered. Yet the Spanish, Portuguese, Dutch, and English proceeded to dominate and enslave the Indians and blacks they encountered. While Europeans indulged in gross sensuality, the social status of women declined. The exploration of new continents reflects deep curiosity and broad intelligence. Yet Europeans believed in witches and burned thousands at the stake. Sexism, racism, and skepticism had all originated in ancient times. But late in the sixteenth century they began to take on their familiar modern forms.

The Status of Women

Did new ideas about women appear in this period? Theological and popular literature on marriage published in Reformation Europe helps to answer this question. Manuals emphasized the qualities expected of each partner. A husband was obliged to provide for the material welfare of his wife and children, to protect his family while remaining steady and self-controlled. He was to rule his household firmly but justly; he was not to behave like a tyrant—a guideline that counselors repeated frequently. A wife was to be mature, a good household manager, and subservient and faithful to her spouse. The husband also owed fidelity. Both Protestant and Catholic moralists rejected the double standard of sexual morality, considering it a threat to family unity. Counselors believed that marriage should be based on mutual respect and trust. Although they discouraged impersonal unions arranged by parents, they did not think romantic attachments—based on physical attraction and love—a sound basis for an enduring relationship.

A woman might assist in her own or her husband's business and do charitable work. But moralists held that involvement in social or public activities was inappropriate because it distracted the wife from her primary responsibility: her household. If a woman suffered under her husband's yoke, writers explained, her submission, like the pain of childbearing, was a punishment inherited from Eve, penance for man's fall. Moreover, they said, a woman's lot was no worse than a man's: he had to earn the family's bread by the sweat of his brow.[33]

Catholics viewed marriage as a sacramental union; validly entered into, it could not be dissolved. Protestants stressed the contractual nature of marriage: each partner promised the other support, companionship, and the sharing of mutual property. Protestants recognized the right of both parties to divorce and remarry for various reasons, including adultery and irreparable breakdown.[34]

Society in the early modern period was patriarchal. Women neither lost their identity nor lacked meaningful work, but the all-pervasive assumption was that men ruled. Leading students of the Lutherans, Catholics, French Calvinists, and English Puritans tend to agree that there was no improvement in women's long-standing subordinate status.

Artists' drawings of plump, voluptuous women and massive, muscular men reveal the contemporary standards of physical beauty. It was a sensual age that gloried in the delights of the flesh. Some people, such as the humanist poet Pietro Aretino (1492–1556), found sexual satisfaction with people of either sex. Reformers and public officials simultaneously condemned and condoned sexual "sins."

Prostitution was common because desperate poverty forced women and young men into it. Since the later Middle Ages, licensed houses of prostitution had been common in urban centers. When in 1566 Pope Pius IV (r. 1559–1565) expelled all the prostitutes from Rome, so many people left and the city suffered such a loss of revenue that in less than a month the pope was forced to rescind the order. Scholars debated Saint Augustine's notion that prostitutes serve a useful social function by preventing worse sins. Civil authorities in both Catholic and Protestant countries licensed houses of public prostitution. These establishments were intended for the convenience of single men, and some Protestant cities, such as Geneva and Zurich, installed officials in the brothels with the express purpose of preventing married men from patronizing them.

Single women of the middle and working classes in the sixteenth and seventeenth centuries worked in many occupations and professions—as butchers, shopkeepers, nurses, goldsmiths, and midwives and in the weaving and printing industries. Most women who were married assisted in their husbands' businesses. What became of the thousands of women who left convents and nunneries during the Reformation? This question pertains primarily to women of the upper classes, who formed the dominant social group in the religious houses of late medieval Europe. Luther and the Protestant reformers believed that celibacy had no scriptural

basis and that young girls were forced by their parents into convents and, once there, were bullied by men into staying. Therefore, reformers favored the suppression of women's religious houses and encouraged former nuns to marry. Marriage, the reformers maintained, not only gave women emotional and sexual satisfaction but freed them from clerical domination, cultural deprivation, and sexual repression.[35] It appears that these women passed from clerical domination to subservience to husbands.

Some nuns in the Middle Ages probably did lack a genuine religious vocation, and some religious houses did witness financial mismanagement and moral laxness. Nevertheless, convents had provided women of the upper classes with an outlet for their literary, artistic, medical, or administrative talents if they could not or would not marry. When the convents were closed, marriage became virtually the only occupation available to upper-class Protestant women.

The great European witch scare reveals more about contemporary attitudes toward women.

The Great European Witch-Hunt

The period of the religious wars witnessed a startling increase in the phenomenon of witch-hunting, whose prior history was long but sporadic. "A witch," according to Chief Justice Edward Coke of England (1552–1634), "was a person who hath conference with the Devil to consult with him or to do some act." This definition by the highest legal authority in England demonstrates that educated people, as well as the ignorant, believed in witches. Witches were thought to be individuals who could mysteriously injure other people or animals—by causing a person to become blind or impotent, for instance, or by preventing a cow from giving milk.

Belief in witches dates back to the dawn of time. For centuries, tales had circulated about old women who made nocturnal travels on greased broomsticks to *sabbats,* or assemblies of witches, where they participated in sexual orgies and feasted on the flesh of infants. In the popular imagination witches had definite characteristics. The vast majority were married women or widows between fifty and seventy years old, crippled or bent with age, with pockmarked skin. They often practiced midwifery or folk medicine, and most had sharp tongues and were quick to scold.

Religious reformers' extreme notions of the Devil's powers and the insecurity created by the religious wars contributed to the growth of belief in witches. The idea developed that witches made pacts with the Devil in return for the power to work mischief on their enemies. Since pacts with the Devil meant the renunciation of God, witchcraft was considered heresy, and persecution for it had actually begun in the later fourteenth century when it was so declared. Persecution reached its most virulent stage in the late sixteenth and seventeenth centuries.

Fear of witches took a terrible toll of innocent lives in several parts of Europe. In southwestern Germany, 3,229 witches were executed between 1561 and 1670, most by burning. The communities of the Swiss Confederation in central Europe tried 8,888 persons between 1470 and 1700 and executed 5,417 of them as witches. In all the centuries before 1500, witches in England had been suspected of causing perhaps "three deaths, a broken leg, several destructive storms and some bewitched genitals." Yet between 1559 and 1736, almost 1,000 witches were executed in England.[36]

Historians and anthropologists have offered a variety of explanations for the great European witch-hunt. Some scholars maintain that charges of witchcraft were a means of accounting for inexplicable misfortunes. The English in the fifteenth century had blamed their military failures in France on Joan of Arc's witchcraft. In the seventeenth century the English Royal College of Physicians attributed undiagnosable illnesses to witchcraft. Some scholars think that in small communities, which typically insisted on strict social conformity, charges of witchcraft were a means of attacking and eliminating the nonconformist; witches, in other words, served the collective need for scapegoats. The evidence of witches' trials, some writers suggest, shows that women were not accused because they harmed or threatened their neighbors; rather, people believed such women worshiped the Devil, engaged in wild sexual activities with him, and ate infants. Other scholars argue the exact opposite: that people were tried and executed as witches because their neighbors feared their evil powers. According to still another theory, the unbridled sexuality attributed to witches was a figment of their accusers' imagination—a psychological projection by their accusers resulting from Christianity's repression of sexuality.

✦ **Witches Worshiping the Devil**   In medieval Christian art, a goat symbolizes the damned at the Last Judgment, following Christ's statement that the Son of Man would separate believers from nonbelievers as a shepherd separates the sheep from the goats (Matthew 25:31–32). In this manuscript illustration, a witch arrives at a sabbat and prepares to venerate the Devil in the shape of a goat by kissing its anus. (*Source: The Bodleian Library, Oxford*)

Despite an abundance of hypotheses, scholars cannot fully understand the phenomenon. Specific reasons for the persecution of women as witches probably varied from place to place. Nevertheless, given the broad strand of misogyny (hostility to women) in Western religion, the ancient belief in the susceptibility of women (the so-called weaker vessels) to the Devil's allurements, and the pervasive seventeenth-century belief about women's multiple and demanding orgasms and thus their sexual insatiability, it is not difficult to understand why women were accused of all sorts of mischief and witchcraft. Charges of witchcraft provided a legal basis for the execution of tens of thousands of women. The most important capital crime for women in early modern times, witchcraft has considerable significance for the history and status of women.[37]

African Slave and Indian Woman A black slave approaches an Indian prostitute. Unable to explain what he wants, he points with his finger; she eagerly grasps for the coin. The Spanish caption above moralizes on the black man using stolen money—yet the Spaniards ruthlessly expropriated all South American mineral wealth. (*Source: New York Public Library*)

European Slavery and the Origins of American Racism

Except for the Aborigines of Australia, almost all peoples in the world have engaged in the enslavement of other human beings at some time in their histories. Since ancient times, victors in battle have enslaved conquered peoples. In the later Middle Ages slavery was deeply entrenched in southern Italy, Sicily, Crete, and Mediterranean Spain. The bubonic plague, famines, and other epidemics created a severe shortage of agricultural and domestic workers throughout Europe, encouraging Italian merchants to buy slaves from the Balkans, Thrace,

southern Russia, and central Anatolia for sale in the West. In 1364 the Florentine government allowed the unlimited importation of slaves as long as they were not Catholics. Between 1414 and 1423, at least ten thousand slaves were sold in Venice alone. The slave trade was a lucrative business enterprise in Italy during the Renaissance. Where profits were high, papal threats of excommunication completely failed to stop it. Genoese slave traders set up colonial stations in the Crimea and along the Black Sea, and according to an international authority on slavery, these outposts were "virtual laboratories" for the development of slave plantation agriculture in the New World.[38] This form of slavery had nothing to do with race; almost all of these slaves were white. How, then, did black African slavery enter the European picture and take root in the New World?

The capture of Constantinople by the Ottoman Turks in 1453 halted the flow of white slaves from the Black Sea region and the Balkans. Mediterranean Europe, cut off from its traditional source of slaves, had no alternative source for slave labor but sub-Saharan Africa. The centuries-old trans-Saharan trade in slaves was greatly stimulated by the existence of a ready market for slaves in the vineyards and sugar plantations of Sicily and Majorca. By the later fifteenth century, before the discovery of America, the Mediterranean had developed an "American" form of slavery.

Meanwhile, the Genoese and other Italians had colonized the Canary Islands in the western Atlantic. And sailors working for Portugal's Prince Henry the Navigator (see page 517) discovered the Madeira Islands and made settlements there. In this stage of European expansion, "the history of slavery became inextricably tied up with the history of sugar."[39] Population increases and monetary expansion in the fifteenth century led to an increasing demand for sugar even though it was an expensive luxury that only the affluent could afford. Between 1490 and 1530, between 300 and 2,000 black slaves arrived annually at the port of Lisbon (Map 16.5). From Lisbon, where African slaves performed most of the manual labor and constituted 10 percent of the city's population, slaves were transported to the sugar plantations of Madeira, the Azores, the Cape Verde Islands, and then Brazil. Sugar and those small Atlantic islands gave slavery in the Americas its distinctive shape. Columbus himself spent a decade in Madeira and took sugar plants on his voyages to "the Indies."

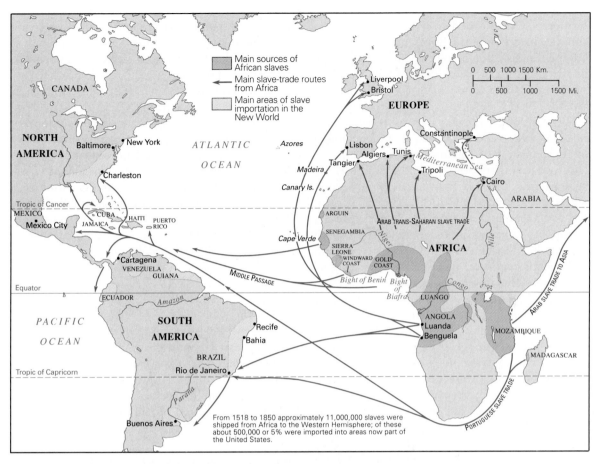

Main sources of African slaves
Main slave-trade routes from Africa
Main areas of slave importation in the New World

From 1518 to 1850 approximately 11,000,000 slaves were shipped from Africa to the Western Hemisphere; of these about 500,000 or 5% were imported into areas now part of the United States.

MAP 16.5 The African Slave Trade   Decades before the discovery of America, Greek, Russian, Bulgarian, Armenian, and then black slaves worked the plantation economies of southern Italy, Sicily, Portugal, and Mediterranean Spain—thereby serving as models for the American form of slavery.

As European economic exploitation of the Americas proceeded, the major problem settlers faced was a shortage of labor. As early as 1495, the Spanish solved the problem by enslaving the native Indians. In the next two centuries, the Portuguese, Dutch, and English followed suit.

Unaccustomed to any form of forced labor, certainly not to panning gold for more than twelve hours a day in the broiling sun, the Indians died "like fish in a bucket," as one Spanish settler reported.[40] In 1515 the Spanish missionary Bartolomé de Las Casas (see page 526), who had seen the evils of Indian slavery, urged the future emperor Charles V to end Indian slavery in his American dominions. Las Casas recommended the importation of blacks from Africa, both because church law did not strictly forbid black slavery and

because he thought blacks could better survive under South American conditions. Charles agreed, and in 1518 the African slave trade began. (When the blacks arrived, Las Casas immediately regretted his suggestion.) Columbus's introduction of sugar plants, moreover, stimulated the need for black slaves, and the experience and model of plantation slavery in Portugal and on the Atlantic islands encouraged the establishment of a similar agricultural pattern in the New World.

Several European nations participated in the African slave trade. Portugal brought the first slaves to Brazil; by 1600, 4,000 were being imported annually. After its founding in 1621, the Dutch West India Company, with the full support of the government of the United Provinces, transported thousands of Africans to Brazil and the

Caribbean. Only in the late seventeenth century, with the chartering of the Royal African Company, did the English get involved. Thereafter, large numbers of African blacks poured into the West Indies and North America. In 1790 there were 757,181 blacks in a total U.S. population of 3,929,625. When the first census was taken in Brazil in 1798, blacks numbered about 2 million in a total population of 3.25 million.

European settlers brought to the Americas the racial attitudes they had absorbed in Europe. Their beliefs and attitudes toward blacks derived from two basic sources: Christian theological speculation about the nature of God (light) and the Devil (black), and Muslim ideas. In the sixteenth and seventeenth centuries, the English, for example, were extremely curious about Africans' lives and customs, and slavers' accounts were extraordinarily popular. Travel literature depicted Africans as savages because of their eating habits, morals, clothing, and social customs; as barbarians because of their language and methods of war; and as heathens because they were not Christian. English people saw similarities between apes and Africans; thus the terms *bestial* and *beastly* were frequently applied to Africans. Africans were believed to possess a potent sexuality. One seventeenth-century observer considered Africans "very lustful and impudent, . . . their members' extraordinary greatness is a token of their lust." African women were considered sexually aggressive with a "temper hot and lascivious."[41]

"At the time when Columbus sailed to the New World, Islam was the largest world religion, and the only world religion that showed itself capable of expanding rapidly in areas as far apart and as different from each other as Senegal [in northwest Africa], Bosnia [in the Balkans], Java, and the Philippines."[42] Medieval Arabic literature emphasized blacks' physical repulsiveness, mental inferiority, and primitivism. In contrast to civilized peoples from the Mediterranean to China, some Muslim writers claimed, sub-Saharan blacks were the only peoples who had produced no sciences or stable states. The fourteenth-century Arab historian Ibn Khaldun (1332–1406) wrote that "the only people who accept slavery are the Negroes, owing to their low degree of humanity and their proximity to the animal stage." Though black kings, Khaldun alleged, sold their subjects without even a pretext of crime or war, the victims bore no resentment because they gave no thought to the

future and had "by nature few cares and worries; dancing and rhythm are for them inborn."[43] It is easy to see how such absurd images developed into the classic stereotypes used to justify black slavery in South and North America in the seventeenth, eighteenth, and nineteenth centuries. Medieval Christians and Muslims had similar notions of blacks as inferior and primitive people ideally suited to enslavement. Perhaps centuries of commercial contacts between Muslim and Mediterranean peoples had familiarized the latter with Muslim racial attitudes. The racial beliefs that the Portuguese, Spanish, Dutch, and English brought to the New World, however, derive primarily from Christian theological speculation.

❖ LITERATURE AND ART

The age of religious wars and overseas expansion also witnessed extraordinary intellectual and artistic ferment. This effervescence can be seen in prose, poetry, and drama, in art, and in music. In many ways, the literature, visual arts, music, and drama of the period mirrored the social and cultural conditions that gave rise to them.

The Essay: Michel de Montaigne

Decades of religious fanaticism brought famine, civil anarchy, and death and led both Catholics and Protestants to doubt that any one faith contained absolute truth. The late sixteenth and seventeenth centuries witnessed the beginning of modern *skepticism,* a school of thought founded on doubt that total certainty or definitive knowledge is ever attainable. The skeptic is cautious and critical and suspends judgment. Perhaps the finest representative of early modern skepticism is the Frenchman Michel de Montaigne (1533–1592).

Montaigne came from a bourgeois family that had made a fortune selling salted herring and wine and in 1477 had purchased the title and property of Montaigne in Gascony; his mother descended from a Jewish family that had been forced to flee Spain. Montaigne received a classical education before studying law and securing a judicial appointment in 1554. At the age of thirty-eight, Montaigne resigned his judicial post, retired to his estate, and devoted the rest of his life to study, contemplation, and the effort to understand himself. His wealth provided him the leisure time to do so. Like the Greeks, he believed that the object of life was to "know thyself," for self-knowledge teaches men and women how to live in accordance with nature and God.

Montaigne developed a new literary genre, the essay—from the French word *essayer,* meaning "to test or try"—to express his thoughts and ideas. His *Essays* provide insight into the mind of a remarkably humane, tolerant, and civilized man. Montaigne was a humanist; he loved the Greek and Roman writers and was always eager to learn from them. From the ancient authors, especially the Roman Stoic Seneca, he acquired a sense of calm, inner peace, and patience and broad-mindedness.

Montaigne grew up during the French civil wars—a period when religious ideology had set family against family, even brother against brother. He wrote:

In this controversy . . . France is at present agitated by civil wars. . . . [Even] among the good men . . . we see many whom passion drives outside the bounds of reason, and makes them sometimes adopt unjust, violent, and even reckless courses.[44]

Though he remained a Catholic, Montaigne possessed a detachment and a willingness to look at all sides of a question:

I listen with attention to the judgment of all men; but so far as I can remember, I have followed none but my own. Though I set little value upon my own opinion, I set no more on the opinions of others.

In the book-lined tower where he passed his days, Montaigne became a deeply learned man. Yet he was not ignorant of the world of affairs, and he criticized scholars and bookworms who ignored the life around them. His essay "On Cannibals" reflects the impact of overseas discoveries on Europeans' consciousness. His tolerant mind rejected the notion that one culture is superior to another:

I long had a man in my house that lived ten or twelve years in the New World, discovered in these latter days, and in that part of it where Villegaignon landed [Brazil]. . . .

I find that there is nothing barbarous and savage in [that] nation, by anything that I can gather, excepting, that every one gives the title of barbarism to everything that is not in use in his own country. As, indeed, we have no other level of truth and reason, than the example and idea of the opinions and customs of the place wherein we live.[45]

In his belief in the nobility of human beings in the state of nature, uncorrupted by organized society, and in his cosmopolitan attitude toward different civilizations, Montaigne anticipated many eighteenth-century thinkers.

The thought of Michel de Montaigne marks a sharp break with the past. Faith and religious certainty had characterized the intellectual attitudes of Western society for a millennium. Montaigne's rejection of any kind of dogmatism, his secularism, and his skepticism thus represent a basic change. In his own time and throughout the seventeenth century, few would have agreed with him. Montaigne inaugurated an era of doubt. "Wonder," he said, "is the foundation of all philosophy, research is the means of all learning, and ignorance is the end."[46]

Elizabethan and Jacobean Literature

In addition to the development of the essay as a literary genre, the period fostered remarkable creativity in other branches of literature. England, especially in the latter part of Elizabeth's reign and in the first years of her successor James I (r. 1603–1625), witnessed unparalleled brilliance. The terms *Elizabethan* and *Jacobean* (the latter refers to the reign of James) are used to designate the English music, poetry, prose, and drama of this period. The poetry of Sir Philip Sidney (1554–1586), such as *Astrophel and Stella,* strongly influenced later poetic writing. *The Faerie Queene* of Edmund Spenser (1552–1599) endures as one of the greatest moral epics in any language. Above all, the immortal dramas of Shakespeare and the stately prose of the Authorized or King James Version of the Bible mark the Elizabethan and Jacobean periods as the golden age of English literature.

William Shakespeare (1564–1616), the son of a successful glove manufacturer who rose to the highest municipal office in the Warwickshire town of Stratford-on-Avon, chose a career on the London stage. By 1592 he had gained recognition as an actor and playwright. Between 1599 and 1603, Shakespeare performed in the Lord Chamberlain's Company and became co-owner of the Globe Theatre, which after 1603 presented his plays.

Shakespeare's genius lies in the originality of his characterizations, the diversity of his plots, his understanding of human psychology, and his unexcelled gift for language. Shakespeare was a Renaissance man in his deep appreciation for classical culture, individualism, and humanism. Such plays as *Julius Caesar, Pericles,* and *Antony and Cleopatra* deal with classical subjects and figures. Several of his comedies have Italian Renaissance settings. The nine history plays, including *Richard II, Richard III,* and *Henry IV,* enjoyed the greatest popularity among Shakespeare's contemporaries. Written during the decade after the defeat of the Spanish Armada, the history plays express English national consciousness. Lines such as these from *Richard II* reflect this sense of national greatness with unparalleled eloquence:

This royal Throne of Kings, this sceptre'd Isle,
This earth of Majesty, this seat of Mars,
This other Eden, demi-paradise,
This fortress built by Nature for herself,
Against infection and the hand of war:
This happy breed of men, this little world,
This precious stone, set in the silver sea,
Which serves it in the office of a wall,
Or as a moat defensive to a house,
Against the envy of less happier Lands,
This blessed plot, this earth, this Realm, this
    England.

Shakespeare's later plays, above all the tragedies *Hamlet, Othello,* and *Macbeth,* explore an enormous range of human problems and are open to an almost infinite variety of interpretations. *Othello,* which the nineteenth-century historian Thomas Macaulay called "perhaps the greatest work in the world," portrays an honorable man destroyed by a flaw in his own character and the satanic evil of his supposed friend Iago. The central figure in *Hamlet,* a play suffused with individuality, wrestles with moral problems connected with revenge and with man's relationship to life and death. The soliloquy in which Hamlet debates suicide is perhaps the most widely quoted passage in English literature:

To be, or not to be: that is the question:
Whether 'tis nobler in the mind to suffer
The slings and arrows of outrageous fortune,
Or to take arms against a sea of troubles,
And by opposing end them?

Hamlet's sad cry, "There is nothing either good or bad but thinking makes it so," expresses the anguish and uncertainty of modern man. *Hamlet* has always enjoyed great popularity, because in his many-faceted personality people have seen an aspect of themselves.

In 1929, in lectures at Oxford University, the novelist Virginia Woolf created an imaginary situation. What would have happened, she wondered, if Shakespeare had had a gifted sister who wanted to be an actress and to write poetry or plays? Unlike her brother, she would not have been sent to grammar school. If on her own she learned to read and write and occasionally picked up a book, her parents soon would have interrupted and told her to mend the stockings or mind the stew. Before she was out of her teens, her parents, loving though they were, would have selected a husband for her. If the force of her gift for learning and the stage was strong enough, she would have the choice of obeying her parents or leaving their home. If she succeeded in getting to London, she would discover that the theater did not hire women. Dependent on the kindness of strangers even for food, she probably would have found herself pregnant. And then "who shall measure the heat and violence of the poet's heart when caught and tangled in a woman's body?—she kills herself." Woolf concludes her story:

This may be true or it may be false—who can say?—but what is true in it, so it seemed to me, reviewing the story of Shakespeare's sister as I have made it, is that any woman born with a great gift in the sixteenth century would certainly have gone crazed, shot herself, or ended her days in some lonely cottage outside the village, half witch, half wizard, feared and mocked at.[47]

Unlike her contemporary Montaigne, Shakespeare's sister would not have had "a room of her own"—that is, the financial means to study and to write, even apart from the social and cultural barriers against a woman doing so.

The other great masterpiece of the Jacobean period was the Authorized or King James Version of the Bible (1611). Based on the best scriptural research of the time and divided into chapters and verses, the Authorized Version is actually a revision of earlier versions of the Bible rather than an original work. Yet it provides a superb expression of the mature English vernacular in the early seventeenth century. Thus Psalm 37:

Fret not thy selfe because of evill doers, neither bee
    thou envious against the workers of iniquitie.
For they shall soone be cut downe like the grasse;
    and wither as the greene herbe.

*Trust in the Lord, and do good, so shalt thou dwell in
the land, and verely thou shalt be fed.*

*Delight thy selfe also in the Lord; and he shall give
thee the desires of thine heart.*

*Commit thy way unto the Lord: trust also in him, and
he shall bring it to passe.*

*And he shall bring forth thy righteousness as the
light, and thy judgement as the noone day.*

The Authorized Version, so called because it was
produced under royal sponsorship—it had no official ecclesiastical endorsement—represented the
Anglican and Puritan desire to encourage lay people to read the Scriptures. It quickly achieved great
popularity and displaced all earlier versions. British
settlers carried this Bible to the North American
colonies, where it became known as the "King
James Bible." For centuries this version of the
Bible has had a profound influence on the language and lives of English-speaking peoples.

Baroque Art and Music

Throughout European history, the cultural tastes
of one age have often seemed quite unsatisfactory
to the next. So it was with the baroque. The term
baroque may have come from a Portuguese word

for an "odd-shaped, imperfect pearl." Late-eight-
eenth-century art critics used it as an expression of
scorn for what they considered an overblown, un-
balanced style. The hostility of these critics has
long since passed, and modern specialists agree
that the triumphs of the baroque mark one of the
high points in the history of Western culture.

The early development of the baroque is complex. Most scholars stress the influence of Rome
and the revitalized Catholic church of the later sixteenth century. The papacy and the Jesuits encouraged the growth of an intensely emotional, exuber-
ant art. These patrons wanted artists to go beyond
the Renaissance focus on pleasing a small, wealthy
cultural elite. They wanted artists to appeal to the
senses and thereby touch the souls and kindle the
faith of ordinary churchgoers while proclaiming
the power and confidence of the reformed Catholic church. In addition to this underlying religious emotionalism, the baroque drew its sense of
drama, motion, and ceaseless striving from the
Catholic Reformation. The interior of the famous
Jesuit Church of Jesus in Rome—the Gesù—combined all these characteristics in its lavish, shimmer-
ing, wildly active decorations and frescoes.

Taking definite shape in Italy after 1600, the
baroque style in the visual arts developed with

Veronese: Feast in the House of Levi   Using the story in Mark 2:15, which says
that many tax collectors and sinners joined Jesus at dinner, the Venetian painter celebrated patrician wealth and luxury in Venice's golden age. The black servants,
dwarfs, and colonnades all contribute to the sumptuous setting. *(Source: Gallerie
dell'Accademia/Archivio Cameraphoto Venezia/Art Resource, NY)*

Velázquez: Juan de Pareja   This portrait (1650) of the Spanish painter Velázquez's one-time assistant, a black man of obvious intellectual and sensual power and himself a renowned religious painter, suggests the integration of some blacks in seventeenth-century society. The elegant lace collar attests to his middle-class status. *(Source: The Metropolitan Museum of Art)*

exceptional vigor in Catholic countries—in Spain and Latin America, Austria, southern Germany, and Poland. Yet baroque art was more than just "Catholic art" in the seventeenth century and the first half of the eighteenth. True, neither Protestant England nor the Netherlands ever came fully under the spell of the baroque, but neither did Catholic France. And Protestants accounted for some of the finest examples of baroque style, especially in music. The baroque style spread partly because its tension and bombast spoke to an agitated age, which was experiencing great violence and controversy in politics and religion.

In painting, the baroque reached maturity early in the work of Peter Paul Rubens (1577–1640), the most outstanding and representative of baroque painters. Studying in his native Flanders and in Italy, where he was influenced by such masters as Michelangelo, Rubens developed his own rich,

sensuous, colorful style, characterized by animated figures, melodramatic contrasts, and monumental size. Rubens excelled in glorifying monarchs such as Queen Mother Marie de' Medici of France. He was a devout Catholic—nearly half of his pictures treat Christian subjects—yet among his trademarks are the fleshy, sensual nudes who populate his canvases as Roman goddesses, water nymphs, and remarkably voluptuous saints and angels.

In music, the baroque style reached its culmination almost a century later in the dynamic, soaring lines of the endlessly inventive Johann Sebastian Bach (1685–1750), one of the greatest composers of the Western world. Organist and choirmaster of several Lutheran churches across Germany, Bach was equally at home writing secular concertos and sublime religious cantatas. Bach's organ music, the greatest ever written, combines the baroque spirit of invention, tension, and emotion in an unforgettable striving toward the infinite. Unlike Rubens, Bach was not fully appreciated in his lifetime, but since the early nineteenth century his reputation has grown steadily.

SUMMARY

In the sixteenth and seventeenth centuries, Europeans for the first time gained access to large parts of the globe. European peoples had the intellectual curiosity, driving ambition, and scientific technology to attempt feats that were as difficult and expensive then as going to the moon is today. Exploration and exploitation contributed to a more sophisticated standard of living in the form of spices and Asian luxury goods and to a terrible international inflation resulting from the influx of South American silver and gold. Governments, the upper classes, and especially the peasantry were badly hurt by the inflation. Meanwhile, the middle class of bankers, shippers, financiers, and manufacturers prospered for much of the seventeenth century.

Europeans' technological development contributed to their conquest of Aztec Mexico and Inca Peru. Along with technology, Europeans brought disease to the New World and thereby caused a holocaust among the Indians. Overseas reconnaissance led to the first global seaborne commercial empires of the Portuguese, the Spanish, and the Dutch.

European expansion and colonization took place against a background of religious conflict and rising national consciousness. The sixteenth and seventeenth centuries were by no means a secular period. Although the medieval religious framework had broken down, people still thought largely in religious terms. Europeans used religious doctrine to explain what they did politically and economically. Religious ideology served as a justification for a variety of conflicts: the French nobles' opposition to the Crown, the Dutch struggle for political and economic independence from Spain. In Germany, religious pluralism and foreign ambitions added to political difficulties. After 1648 the divisions between Protestants and Catholics tended to become permanent. Sexism, racism, and religious skepticism were harbingers of developments to come.

NOTES

1. Quoted in C. M. Cipolla, *Guns, Sails, and Empires: Technological Innovation and the Early Phases of European Expansion, 1400–1700* (New York: Minerva Press, 1965), pp. 115–116.
2. J. H. Parry, *The Age of Reconnaissance* (New York: Mentor Books, 1963), Chs. 3 and 5.
3. See C. R. Phillips, *Ciudad Real, 1500–1750: Growth, Crisis, and Readjustment in the Spanish Economy* (Cambridge, Mass.: Harvard University Press, 1979), pp. 103–104, 115.
4. Quoted in Cipolla, *Guns, Sails, and Empires,* p. 132.
5. Quoted in F. H. Littell, *The Macmillan Atlas History of Christianity* (New York: Macmillan, 1976), p. 75.
6. Quoted in Cipolla, *Guns, Sails, and Empires,* p. 133.
7. Quoted in S. E. Morison, *Admiral of the Ocean Sea: A Life of Christopher Columbus* (Boston: Little, Brown, 1942), p. 339.
8. T. K. Rabb, "Columbus: Villain or Hero," *Princeton Alumni Weekly,* October 14, 1992, pp. 12–17.
9. J. M. Cohen, ed. and trans., *The Four Voyages of Christopher Columbus* (New York: Penguin Books, 1969), p. 37.
10. Quoted in R. L. Kagan, "The Spain of Ferdinand and Isabella," in *Circa 1492: Art in the Age of Exploration,* ed. J. A. Levenson (Washington, D.C.: National Gallery of Art, 1991), p. 60.
11. Quoted in F. Maddison, "Tradition and Innovation: Columbus' First Voyage and Portuguese Navigation in the Fifteenth Century," ibid., p. 69.
12. W. D. Phillips and C. R. Phillips, *The Worlds of Christopher Columbus* (Cambridge: Cambridge University Press, 1992), p. 273.
13. See ibid.
14. See G. W. Conrad and A. A. Demarest, *Religion and Empire: The Dynamics of Aztec and Inca Expansionism* (New York: Cambridge University Press, 1993), pp. 67–69.
15. G. C. Vaillant, *Aztecs of Mexico* (New York: Penguin Books, 1979), p. 241. Chapter 15, on which this section leans, is fascinating.
16. V. W. Von Hagen, *Realm of the Incas* (New York: New American Library, 1961), pp. 204–207.
17. Conrad and Demarest, *Religion and Empire,* pp. 135–139.
18. N. Sanchez-Albornoz, *The Population of Latin America: A History,* trans. W. A. R. Richardson (Berkeley: University of California Press, 1974), p. 41.
19. Quoted in A. W. Crosby, *The Columbian Exchange: Biological and Cultural Consequences of 1492* (Westport, Conn.: Greenwood, 1972), p. 39.
20. Ibid., pp. 35–59.
21. Quoted in C. Gibson, ed., *The Black Legend: Anti-Spanish Attitudes in the Old World and the New* (New York: Knopf, 1971), pp. 74–75.
22. Quoted in L. B. Rout, Jr., *The African Experience in Spanish America* (New York: Cambridge University Press, 1976), p. 23.
23. See Parry, *The Age of Reconnaissance,* Chs. 12, 14, and 15.
24. Quoted in S. Neill, *A History of Christian Missions* (New York: Penguin Books, 1977), p. 163.
25. Quoted in C. M. Cipolla, *Clocks and Culture: 1300–1700* (New York: Norton, 1978), p. 86.
26. J. Gernet, *A History of Chinese Civilization* (New York: Cambridge University Press, 1982), p. 458.
27. Quoted in A. J. Andrea and J. H. Overfield, *The Human Record,* vol. 1 (Boston: Houghton Mifflin, 1990), pp. 406–407.
28. Ibid., p. 408.
29. See D. Keene, *The Japanese Discovery of Europe,* rev. ed. (Stanford, Calif.: Stanford University Press, 1969), pp. 1–17. The quotation is on page 16.
30. See J. Hale, "War and Public Opinion in the Fifteenth and Sixteenth Centuries," *Past and Present* 22 (July 1962): 29.
31. See N. Z. Davis, "The Rites of Violence: Religious Riot in Sixteenth Century France," *Past and Present* 59 (May 1973): 51–91.
32. H. Kamen, "The Economic and Social Consequences of the Thirty Years' War," *Past and Present* 39 (April 1968): 44–61.
33. This passage is based heavily on S. E. Ozment, *When Fathers Ruled: Family Life in Reformation*

Europe (Cambridge, Mass.: Harvard University Press, 1983), pp. 50–99.

34. Ibid., pp. 85–92.

35. Ibid., pp. 9–14.

36. N. Cohn, *Europe's Inner Demons: An Enquiry Inspired by the Great Witch-Hunt* (New York: Basic Books, 1975), pp. 253–254; K. Thomas, *Religion and the Decline of Magic* (New York: Charles Scribner's Sons, 1971), pp. 450–455.

37. See E. W. Monter, "The Pedestal and the Stake: Courtly Love and Witchcraft," in *Becoming Visible: Women in European History,* ed. R. Bridenthal and C. Koonz (Boston: Houghton Mifflin, 1977), pp. 132–135; and A. Fraser, *The Weaker Vessel* (New York: Random House, 1985), pp. 100–103.

38. C. Verlinden, *The Beginnings of Modern Colonization,* trans. Y. Freccero (Ithaca, N.Y.: Cornell University Press, 1970), pp. 5–6, 80–97.

39. This section leans heavily on D. B. Davis, *Slavery and Human Progress* (New York: Oxford University Press, 1984), pp. 54–62.

40. Quoted in D. P. Mannix with M. Cowley, *Black Cargoes: A History of the Atlantic Slave Trade* (New York: Viking Press, 1968), p. 5.

41. Ibid., p. 19.

42. See P. Brown, "Understanding Islam," *New York Review of Books,* February 22, 1979, pp. 30–33.

43. Davis, *Slavery and Human Progress,* pp. 43–44.

44. D. M. Frame, trans., *The Complete Works of Montaigne* (Stanford, Calif.: Stanford University Press, 1958), pp. 175–176.

45. C. Cotton, trans., *The Essays of Michel de Montaigne* (New York: A. L. Burt, 1893), pp. 207, 210.

46. Ibid., p. 523.

47. V. Woolf, *A Room of One's Own* (New York: Harcourt, Brace & World, 1957), p. 51.

SUGGESTED READING

Perhaps the best starting point for the study of European society in the age of exploration is Parry's *Age of Reconnaissance,* cited in the Notes, which treats the causes and consequences of the voyages of discovery. Parry's splendidly illustrated *The Discovery of South America* (1979) examines Europeans' reactions to the maritime discoveries and treats the entire concept of new discoveries. For the earliest British reaction to the Japanese, see *A World Elsewhere: Europe's Encounter with Japan in the Sixteenth and Seventeenth Centuries* (1990). The urbane studies of C. M. Cipolla present fascinating material on technological

and sociological developments written in a lucid style. In addition to the titles cited in the Notes, see *Cristofano and the Plague: A Study in the History of Public Health in the Age of Galileo* (1973) and *Public Health and the Medical Profession in the Renaissance* (1976). Morison's *Admiral of the Ocean Sea,* also listed in the Notes, is the standard biography of Columbus. The advanced student should consult F. Braudel, *Civilization and Capitalism, 15th–18th Century,* trans. S. Reynolds, vol. 1, *The Structures of Everyday Life* (1981); vol. 2, *The Wheels of Commerce* (1982); and vol. 3, *The Perspective of the World* (1984). These three fat volumes combine vast erudition, a global perspective, and remarkable illustrations. For the political ideas that formed the background of the first Spanish overseas empire, see A. Pagden, *Spanish Imperialism and the Political Imagination* (1990).

For the religious wars, in addition to the references cited in the Notes to this chapter, see J. H. M. Salmon, *Society in Crisis: France in the Sixteenth Century* (1975), which traces the fate of French institutions during the civil wars. A. N. Galpern, *The Religions of the People in Sixteenth-Century Champagne* (1976), is a useful case study in religious anthropology, and W. A. Christian, Jr., *Local Religion in Sixteenth Century Spain* (1981), traces the attitudes and practices of ordinary people.

A cleverly illustrated introduction to the Low Countries is K. H. D. Kaley, *The Dutch in the Seventeenth Century* (1972). The study by J. L. Motley, *The Rise of the Dutch Republic,* vol. 1 (1898), still provides a good comprehensive treatment and is fascinating reading. For Spanish military operations in the Low Countries, see G. Parker, *The Army of Flanders and the Spanish Road, 1567–1659: The Logistics of Spanish Victory and Defeat in the Low Countries' Wars* (1972). The same author's *Spain and the Netherlands, 1559–1659: Ten Studies* (1979), contains useful essays, of which students may especially want to consult "Why Did the Dutch Revolt Last So Long?" For the later phases of the Dutch-Spanish conflict, see J. I. Israel, *The Dutch Republic and the Hispanic World, 1606–1661* (1982), which treats the struggle in global perspective.

Of the many biographies of Elizabeth of England, W. T. MacCaffrey, *Queen Elizabeth and the Making of Policy, 1572–1588* (1981), examines the problems posed by the Reformation and how Elizabeth solved them. J. E. Neale, *Queen Elizabeth I* (1957), remains valuable, and L. B. Smith, *The Elizabethan Epic* (1966), is a splendid evocation of the age of Shakespeare with Elizabeth at the center. The best recent biography is C. Erickson, *The First Elizabeth* (1983), a fine, psychologically resonant portrait.

Nineteenth- and early-twentieth-century historians described the defeat of the Spanish Armada as a great victory for Protestantism, democracy, and capitalism, which those scholars tended to link together. Recent historians have focused on its contemporary significance. For a sympathetic but judicious portrait of the man who launched the Armada, see G. Parker, *Philip II* (1978). The best recent study of the leader of the Armada is P. Pierson, *Commander of the Armada: The Seventh Duke of Medina Sidonia* (1989). D. Howarth, *The Voyage of the Armada* (1982), discusses the expedition largely in terms of the individuals involved, and G. Mattingly, *The Armada* (1959), gives the diplomatic and political background; both Howarth and Mattingly tell very exciting tales. M. Lewis, *The Spanish Armada* (1972), also tells a good story, but strictly from the English perspective. Significant aspects of Portuguese culture are treated in A. Hower and R. Preto-Rodas, eds., *Empire in Transition: The Portuguese World in the Time of Camões* (1985).

C. V. Wedgwood, *The Thirty Years' War* (1961), must be qualified in light of recent research on the social and economic effects of the war, but it is still a good (though detailed) starting point on a difficult period. Various opinions on the causes and results of the war are given in T. K. Rabb's anthology, *The Thirty Years' War* (1981). In addition to the articles by Hale and Kamen cited in the Notes, the following articles, both of which appear in the scholarly journal *Past and Present*, provide some of the latest important findings: J. V. Polisensky, "The Thirty Years' War and the Crises and Revolutions of Sixteenth Century Europe," 39 (1968), and M. Roberts, "Queen Christina and the General Crisis of the Seventeenth Century," 22 (1962).

As background to the intellectual changes instigated by the Reformation, D. C. Wilcox, *In Search of God and Self: Renaissance and Reformation Thought* (1975), contains a perceptive analysis, and T. Ashton, ed., *Crisis in Europe, 1560–1660* (1967), is fundamental. For women, marriage, and the family, see L. Stone, *The Family, Sex, and Marriage in England, 1500–1800* (1977), an important but controversial work; D. Underdown, "The Taming of the Scold," and S. Amussen, "Gender, Family, and the Social Order," in *Order and Disorder in Early Modern England,* ed. A. Fletcher and J. Stevenson (1985); A. Macfarlane, *Marriage and Love in England: Modes of Reproduction, 1300–1848* (1986); C. R. Boxer, *Women in Iberian Expansion Overseas, 1415–1815* (1975), an invaluable study of women's role in overseas immigration; and S. M. Wyntjes, "Women in the Reformation Era," a quick survey of conditions in different countries, in Bridenthal and Koonz's *Becoming Visible.* Ozment's *When Fathers Ruled,* cited in the Notes, is a seminal study concentrating on Germany and Switzerland.

On witches and witchcraft see, in addition to the titles by Cohn and Thomas in the Notes, J. B. Russell, *Witchcraft in the Middle Ages* (1976) and *Lucifer: The Devil in the Middle Ages* (1984); M. Summers, *The History of Witchcraft and Demonology* (1973); and H. R. Trevor-Roper, *The European Witch-Craze of the Sixteenth and Seventeenth Centuries* (1967), an important collection of essays.

As background to slavery and racism in North and South America, students should see J. L. Watson, ed., *Asian and African Systems of Slavery* (1980), a valuable collection of essays. Davis's *Slavery and Human Progress,* cited in the Notes, shows how slavery was viewed as a progressive force in the expansion of the Western world. For North American conditions, interested students should consult W. D. Jordan, *The White Man's Burden: Historical Origins of Racism in the United States* (1974), and the title by Mannix listed in the Notes, a hideously fascinating account. For Caribbean and South American developments, see F. P. Bowser, *The African Slave in Colonial Peru* (1974); J. S. Handler and F. W. Lange, *Plantation Slavery in Barbados: An Archeological and Historical Investigation* (1978); and R. E. Conrad, *Children of God's Fire: A Documentary History of Black Slavery in Brazil* (1983).

The leading authority on Montaigne is D. M. Frame. In addition to his translation of Montaigne's works cited in the Notes, see his *Montaigne's Discovery of Man* (1955).

LISTENING TO THE
PAST

Columbus Describes His First Voyage

On his return voyage to Spain in January 1493, Christopher Columbus composed a letter intended for wide circulation and had copies of it sent ahead to Isabella and Ferdinand and others when the ship docked at Lisbon. Because the letter sums up Columbus's understanding of his achievements, it is considered the most important document of his first voyage. Remember that his knowledge of Asia rested heavily on Marco Polo's Travels, *published around 1298.*

Since I know that you will be pleased at the great success with which the Lord has crowned my voyage, I write to inform you how in thirty-three days I crossed from the Canary Islands to the Indies, with the fleet which our most illustrious sovereigns gave me. I found very many islands with large populations and took possession of them all for their Highnesses; this I did by proclamation and unfurled the royal standard. No opposition was offered.

I named the first island that I found 'San Salvador,' in honour of our Lord and Saviour who has granted me this miracle. . . . When I reached Cuba, I followed its north coast westwards, and found it so extensive that I thought this must be the mainland, the province of Cathay.[1] . . . From there I saw another island eighteen leagues eastwards which I then named 'Hispaniola.'[2] . . .

Hispaniola is a wonder. The mountains and hills, the plains and meadow lands are both fertile and beautiful. They are most suitable for planting crops and for raising cattle of all kinds, and there are good sites for building towns and villages. The harbours are incredibly fine and there are many great rivers with broad channels and the majority contain gold.[3] The trees, fruits and plants are very different from those of Cuba. In Hispaniola there are many spices and large mines of gold and other metals. . . .[4]

The inhabitants of this island, and all the rest that I discovered or heard of, go naked, as their mothers bore them, men and women alike. A few of the women, however, cover a single place with a leaf of a plant or piece of cotton which they weave for the purpose. They have no iron or steel or arms and are not capable of using them, not because they are not strong and well built but because they are amazingly timid. All the weapons they have are canes cut at seeding time, at the end of which they fix a sharpened stick, but they have not the courage to make use of these, for very often when I have sent two or three men to a village to have conversation with them a great number of them have come out. But as soon as they saw my men all fled immediately, a father not even waiting for his son. And this is not because we have harmed any of them; on the contrary, wherever I have gone and been able to have conversation with them, I have given them some of the various things I had, a cloth and other articles, and received nothing in exchange. But they have still remained incurably timid. True, when they have been reassured and lost their fear, they are so ingenuous and so liberal with all their possessions that no one who has not seen them would believe it. If one asks for anything they have they never say no. On the contrary, they offer a share to anyone with demonstrations of heartfelt affection, and they are immediately content with any small thing, valuable or valueless, that is given them. I forbade the men to give them bits of broken crockery, fragments of glass or tags of laces, though if they could get them they fancied them the finest jewels in the world.

I hoped to win them to the love and service of their Highnesses and of the whole Spanish nation and to persuade them to collect and give us of the things which they possessed in abundance and which we needed. They have no religion and are not idolaters; but all believe that power and goodness dwell in the sky and they are firmly convinced that I have come from the sky with these ships and people. In this belief they gave me a good reception everywhere, once they had overcome their fear; and this is not because they are stupid—far from it, they are men of great intelligence, for they navigate all those seas, and give a marvellously good account of everything—but because they have never before seen men clothed or ships like these. . . .

In all these islands the men are seemingly content with one woman, but their chief or king is allowed more than twenty. The women appear to work more than the men and I have not been able to find out if they have private property. As far as I could see whatever a man had was shared among all the rest and this particularly applies to food. . . . In another island, which I am told is larger than Hispaniola, the people have no hair. Here there is a vast quantity of gold, and from here and the other islands I bring Indians as evidence.

In conclusion, to speak only of the results of this very hasty voyage, their Highnesses can see that I will give them as much gold as they require, if they will render me some very slight assistance; also I will give them all the spices and cotton they want . . . I will also bring them as much aloes as they ask and as many slaves, who will be taken from the idolaters. I believe also that I have found rhubarb and cinnamon and there will be countless other things in addition . . .

So all Christendom will be delighted that our Redeemer has given victory to our most illustrious King and Queen and their renowned kingdoms, in this great matter. They should hold great celebrations and render solemn thanks to the Holy Trinity with many solemn prayers, for the great triumph which they will have, by the conversion of so many peoples to our holy faith and for the temporal benefits which will follow, for not only Spain, but all Christendom will receive encouragement and profit.

This is a brief account of the facts.
Written in the caravel off the Canary Islands.[5]

15 February 1493

At your orders
THE ADMIRAL

Questions for Analysis

1. How did Columbus explain the success of his voyage?

German woodcut depicting Columbus's landing at San Salvador. *(Source: John Carter Brown Library)*

2. What was Columbus's view of the native Americans he met?

3. Evaluate Columbus's statements that the Caribbean islands possessed gold, cotton, and spices.

4. Why did Columbus cling to the idea that he had reached Asia?

Source: J. M. Cohen, ed. and trans., *The Four Voyages of Christopher Columbus.* Copyright © 1969 Penguin Books Ltd.

1. Cathay is the old name for China. In the logbook and later in this letter Columbus accepts the native story that Cuba is an island which they can circumnavigate in something more than twenty-one days, yet he insists here and later, during the second voyage, that it is in fact part of the Asiatic mainland. 2. Hispaniola is the second largest island of the West Indies; Haiti occupies the western third of the island, the Dominican Republic the rest. 3. This did not prove to be true. 4. These statements are also inaccurate. 5. Actually Columbus was off Santa Maria in the Azores.

Absolutism and Constitutionalism in Europe, ca 1589–1725

The Queen's Staircase is among the grandest of the surviving parts of Louis XIV's palace at Versailles. *(Source: © Photo R.M.N.)*

The seventeenth century in Europe was an age of intense conflict and crisis. The crisis had many causes, but the era's almost continuous savage warfare was probably the most important factor. War drove governments to build enormous armies and levy ever higher taxes on an already hard-pressed, predominately peasant population. Deteriorating economic conditions also played a major role. Europe as a whole experienced an unusually cold and wet climate over many years—a "little ice age" that brought small harvests, periodic food shortages, and even starvation. Not least, the combination of war, increased taxation, and economic suffering triggered social unrest and widespread peasant revolts, which were both a cause and an effect of profound dislocation.

The many-sided crisis of the seventeenth century posed a grave challenge to European governments: how were they to maintain order? The most common response of monarchial governments was to seek more power to deal with the problems and the threats that they perceived. Indeed, European rulers in this period generally sought to attain *absolute,* or complete, power and build absolutist states. Thus monarchs regulated religious sects, and they abolished the liberties long held by certain areas, groups, or provinces. Absolutist rulers also created new state bureaucracies to enhance their power and to direct the economic life of the country in the interest of the monarch. Above all, monarchs fought to free themselves from the restrictions of custom, competing institutions, and powerful social groups. In doing so, they sought freedom from the nobility and from traditional representative bodies—most commonly known as Estates or Parliament—that were usually dominated by the nobility.

The monarchial demand for freedom of action upset the status quo and led to bitter political battles. Nobles and townspeople sought to maintain their traditional rights, claiming that monarchs could not rule at will but rather had to respect representative bodies and follow established constitutional practices. Thus opponents of absolutism argued for *constitutionalism*—the limitation of the state by law. In seventeenth-century Europe, however, advocates of constitutionalism generally lost out and would-be absolutists triumphed in most countries.

There were important national variations in the development of absolutism. The most spectacular example occurred in western Europe, where Louis XIV built on the heritage of a well-developed monarchy and a strong royal bureaucracy. Moreover, when Louis XIV came to the throne, the powers of the nobility were already somewhat limited, the French middle class was relatively strong, and the peasants were generally free from serfdom. In eastern Europe and Russia, absolutism emerged out of a very different social reality: a powerful nobility, a weak middle class, and an oppressed peasantry composed of serfs. Eastern monarchs generally had to compromise with their nobilities as they fashioned absolutist states. Finally, in Holland and England, royal absolutism did not triumph. In England especially, the opponents of unrestrained monarchial authority succeeded in firmly establishing a constitutional state, which guaranteed that henceforth Parliament and the monarch would share power.

Thus in the period between roughly 1589 and 1725, two basic patterns of government emerged in Europe: absolute monarchy and the constitutional state. Almost all subsequent governments in the West have been modeled on one of these patterns, which have also influenced greatly the rest of the world in the last three centuries.

- How and why did Louis XIV of France lead the way in forging the absolute state?

- How did Austrian, Prussian, and Russian rulers in eastern Europe build absolute monarchies—monarchies that proved even more durable than that of Louis XIV?

- How did the absolute monarchs' interaction with artists, architects, and writers contribute to the splendid cultural achievements of both western and eastern Europe in this period?

- How and why did the constitutional state triumph in Holland and England?

This chapter explores these questions.

❖ FRANCE: THE MODEL OF ABSOLUTE MONARCHY

France had a long history of unifying and centralizing monarchy, although the actual power and effectiveness of the French kings had varied enormously over time. Passing through a time of troubles and civil war after the death of Henry II in

1559, both France and the monarchy recovered under Henry IV and Cardinal Richelieu in the early seventeenth century. They laid the foundations for fully developed French absolutism under the "Great Monarch," Louis XIV. Providing inspiration for rulers all across Europe, Louis XIV and the mighty machine he fashioned deserve special attention

The Foundations of French Absolutism

Henry IV, the ingenious Huguenot-turned-Catholic, ended the French religious wars with the Edict of Nantes in 1598 (see page 534). The first of the Bourbon dynasty, Henry IV and his great minister Maximilian de Béthune, duke of Sully (1560–1641), then laid the foundations of later French absolutism.

Henry denied influence on the royal council to the nobility, which had harassed the countryside for half a century. Maintaining that "if we are without compassion for the people, they must succumb and we all perish with them," Henry also lowered taxes paid by the overburdened peasantry. Sully reduced the crushing royal debt accumulated during the era of religious conflict, encouraged French trade, and started a countrywide highway system. Within twelve years, Henry IV and his minister had restored public order in France and laid the foundation for economic prosperity. Unfortunately, the murder of Henry IV in 1610 by a crazed fanatic led to a severe crisis.

After the death of Henry IV, the queen-regent Marie de' Medici led the government for the child-king Louis XIII (r. 1610–1643), but feudal nobles and princes of the blood dominated the political scene. In 1624 Marie de' Medici secured the appointment of Armand Jean du Plessis—Cardinal Richelieu (1585–1642)—to the council of ministers. It was a remarkable appointment. The next year Richelieu became president of the council, and after 1628 he was first minister of the French crown. Richelieu used his strong influence over King Louis XIII to exalt the French monarchy as the embodiment of the French state.

Richelieu's policy was the total subordination of all groups and institutions to the French monarchy. The French nobility, with its selfish and independent interests, had long constituted the foremost threat to the centralizing goals of the Crown and to a strong national state. Now Richelieu crushed aristocratic conspiracies with quick executions, and he never called a session of the Estates General—the ancient representative body of the medieval orders that was primarily a representative of the nobility.

The genius of Cardinal Richelieu was reflected in the administrative system he established. He extended the use of the royal commissioners called *intendants,* each of whom held authority in one of France's thirty-two *généralités* (districts). The intendants were authorized "to decide, order and execute all that they see good to do." Usually members of the upper middle class or minor nobility, the intendants were appointed directly by the monarch, to whom they were solely responsible. They recruited men for the army, supervised the collection of taxes, presided over the administration of local law, checked up on the local nobility, and regulated economic activities—commerce, trade, the guilds, marketplaces—in their districts. As the intendants' power grew during Richelieu's administration, so did the power of the centralized state.

The cardinal perceived that Protestantism often served as a cloak for the political intrigues of ambitious lords. When the Huguenots revolted in 1625, Richelieu personally supervised the siege of their walled city, La Rochelle, and forced it to surrender. Thereafter, fortified cities were abolished. Huguenots were allowed to practice their faith, but they no longer possessed armed strongholds or the means to be an independent party in the state.

French foreign policy under Richelieu was aimed at the destruction of the fence of Habsburg territories that surrounded France. Consequently, in the Thirty Years' War Richelieu supported the Habsburgs' enemies, like the Lutheran king Gustavus Adolphus (see page 539). French influence became an important factor in the political future of the German Empire.

These new policies, especially war, cost money. Richelieu fully realized the need for greater revenues through increased taxation. But seventeenth-century France remained "a collection of local economies and local societies dominated by local elites." The government's power to tax was limited by the rights of assemblies in some provinces (such as Brittany) to vote their own taxes, the hereditary exemption from taxation of many wealthy members of the nobility and the middle class, and the royal pension system. Therefore, Richelieu—and later Louis XIV—temporarily solved their financial problems by securing the cooperation of local elites. Even in France royal absolutism was restrained by its need to compromise with the financial interests of well-entrenched groups.[1]

In building the French state, Richelieu believed that he had to take drastic measures against persons and groups within France and conduct a tough anti-Habsburg foreign policy. He knew that his actions sometimes seemed to contradict traditional Christian teaching. As a priest and bishop, how did he justify his policies? He developed his own *raison d'état* (reason of state): "What is done for the state is done for God, who is the basis and foundation of it." This being so, Richelieu maintained that, "Where the interests of the state are concerned, God absolves actions which, if privately committed, would be a crime."[2]

Richelieu persuaded Louis XIII to appoint his protégé Jules Mazarin (1602–1661) as his successor. Governing for the child-king Louis XIV, Mazarin became the dominant power in the government. He continued the centralizing policies of Richelieu, but in 1648 his unpopular attempts to increase royal revenues and expand the state bureaucracy resulted in a widespread rebellion known as the Fronde. Bitter civil war ensued between the monarchy and the opposition, led by the nobility and middle class. Riots and turmoil wracked Paris and the nation. Violence continued intermittently for the next twelve years.

Conflicts during the Fronde had a traumatic effect on the young Louis XIV. The king and his mother were frequently threatened and sometimes treated as prisoners by aristocratic factions. This period formed the cornerstone of Louis's political education and of his conviction that the sole alternative to anarchy was to concentrate as much power as possible in his own hands. Yet Louis XIV also realized that he would have to compromise with the bureaucrats and social elites who controlled local institutions and constituted the state bureaucracy. And he did so.

The Monarchy of Louis XIV

In the reign of Louis XIV (r. 1643–1715), the longest in European history, the French monarchy reached the peak of its absolutist development. In the magnificence of his court, in his absolute power, in the brilliance of the culture over which he presided and which permeated all of Europe, and in his remarkably long life, the "Sun King"

Philippe de Champaigne: Cardinal Richelieu This portrait, with its penetrating eyes, expression of haughty and imperturbable cynicism, and dramatic sweep of red robes, suggests the authority, grandeur, and power that Richelieu wished to convey as first minister of France. *(Source: Reproduced by courtesy of the Trustees, The National Gallery, London)*

dominated his age. It was said that when Louis sneezed, all Europe caught cold.

Born in 1638, king at the age of five, Louis entered into personal, or independent, rule in 1661. Always a devout Catholic, Louis believed that God had established kings as his rulers on earth. The royal coronation consecrated Louis to God's service, and he was certain that although kings were a race apart, they had to obey God's laws and rule for the good of the people.

Louis's education was more practical than formal. He learned statecraft by direct experience.

❄ **Louis XIV**   A skilled horseman and an enthusiastic hunter, Louis XIV rode with his armies on their many campaigns. This painting of Louis as a Roman general by Mignard Pierre (1612–1695) captures the king's enormous physical energy and proud self-confidence. *(Source: Galleria Sabauda, Turin/Scala/Art Resource, NY)*

hundreds of candles illuminated the domed ceiling, where allegorical paintings celebrated the king's victories. Louis skillfully used the art and architecture of Versailles to overawe his subjects and visitors and reinforce his power. Many monarchs subsequently imitated Louis XIV's example, and French became the language of diplomatic exchange and of royal courts all across Europe.

Historians have often said that Louis XIV was able to control completely the nobility, which historically had opposed the centralizing goals of the French monarchy. The duke of Saint-Simon, a high-ranking noble and fierce critic of the king, wrote in his memoirs, that Louis XIV

reduced everyone to subjection, and brought to his court those very persons he cared least about. Whoever was old enough to serve did not dare demur. It was still another device to ruin the nobles by accustoming them to equality and forcing them to mingle with everyone indiscriminately. . . .

Upon rising, at bedtime, during meals, in his apartments, in the gardens of Versailles, everywhere the courtiers had a right to follow, he would glance right and left to see who was there; he saw and noted everyone; he missed no one, even those who were hoping they would not be seen. . . .

Louis XIV took great pains to inform himself on what was happening everywhere, in public places, private homes, and even on the international scene. . . . Spies and informers of all kinds were numberless.[3]

The misery he suffered during the Fronde gave him an eternal distrust of the nobility and a profound sense of his own isolation. Accordingly, silence, caution, and secrecy became political tools for the achievement of his goals. His characteristic answer to requests of all kinds became the enigmatic "Je verrai" ("I shall see").

Louis XIV installed his royal court at Versailles, an old hunting lodge ten miles from Paris. His architects, Le Nôtre and Le Vau, turned what the duke of Saint-Simon called "the most dismal and thankless of sights" into a veritable paradise. Louis XIV required all the great nobility of France—at the peril of social, political, and sometimes economic disaster—to live at Versailles for at least part of the year. Versailles became a model of rational order, the center of France, and the perfect symbol of the king's power. In the gigantic Hall of Mirrors

As Saint-Simon suggests, the king did use court ceremonial to curb the great nobility. By excluding the highest nobles from his councils, he also weakened their ancient right to advise the king and to participate in government. They became mere instruments of policy, their time and attention occupied with operas, balls, gossip, and trivia.

Recent research, however, has demonstrated that Louis XIV actually secured the active collaboration of the nobility. Thus Louis XIV separated power from status and grandeur at Versailles: he secured the nobles' cooperation, and the nobility enjoyed their status and the grandeur in which they lived. The nobility agreed to participate in projects that both exalted the monarchy and reinforced their own ancient aristocratic prestige. Thus French government in the seventeenth century rested on a social and political structure in which the nobility continued to exercise great influence.[4]

In day-to-day government Louis utilized several councils of state, which he personally attended, and the intendants, who acted for the councils throughout France. A stream of questions and instructions flowed between local districts and Versailles, and under Louis XIV a uniform and centralized administration was imposed on the country. The councilors of state came from the upper middle class or from the recently ennobled, who were popularly known as "nobility of the robe" (because of the long judicial robes many of them wore). These ambitious professional bureaucrats served the state in the person of the king.

Throughout Louis's long reign and despite increasing financial problems, he never called a meeting of the Estates General. Thus his critics had no means of united action. French government remained highly structured, bureaucratic, centered at Versailles, and responsible to Louis XIV.

Economic Management and Religious Policy

Louis XIV's bureaucracy, court, and army cost a great amount of money, and the French method of collecting taxes consistently failed to produce the necessary revenue. An old agreement between the Crown and the nobility permitted the king to tax the common people if he did not tax the nobles. Because many among the rich and prosperous classes were exempt, the tax burden fell heavily on those least able to pay: the poor peasants.

The king named Jean-Baptiste Colbert (1619–1683), the son of a wealthy merchant-financier, as controller-general of finances. Colbert came to manage the entire royal administration and proved himself a financial genius. His central principle was that the French economy should serve the state, and he rigorously applied to France the system called mercantilism.

Hall of Mirrors, Versailles   The grandeur and elegance of the Sun King's reign are reflected in the Hall of Mirrors at the Versailles palace. The king's victories were celebrated in paintings on the domed ceiling. Hundreds of candles lit up the dome. *(Source: Giraudon/Art Resource, NY)*

Mercantilism is a collection of government policies for the regulation of economic activities, especially commercial activities, by and for the state. In the seventeenth and eighteenth centuries, a nation's international power was thought to be based on its wealth—specifically on the gold so necessary for fighting wars. To accumulate gold, economic theory suggested, a country should always sell more goods abroad than it bought. Colbert insisted that France should be self-sufficient, able to produce within its borders everything needed by the subjects of the French king. If France were self-sufficient, the outflow of gold would be halted, debtor states would pay in bullion, and, with the wealth of the nation increased, France's power and prestige would be enhanced.

Colbert attempted to accomplish self-sufficiency through state support for both old industries and newly created ones. New factories in Paris manufactured mirrors to replace Venetian imports, for example. To ensure a high-quality finished product, Colbert set up a system of state inspection and regulation. He compelled all craftsmen to organize into guilds, and he encouraged skilled foreign craftsmen and manufacturers to immigrate to France. To improve communications, he built roads and canals. To protect French products, he placed high tariffs on foreign goods. His most important accomplishment was the creation of a powerful merchant marine to transport French goods. Colbert tried to organize and regulate the entire French economy for the glory of the French state as embodied in the king.

Colbert's achievement in the development of manufacturing was prodigious. The commercial classes prospered, and between 1660 and 1700 their position steadily improved. The national economy, however, rested on agriculture. Although French peasants were not serfs, as were the peasants of eastern Europe, they were mercilessly taxed. After 1685 other hardships afflicted them: savage warfare, poor harvests, continuing deflation of the currency, and fluctuation in the price of grain. Many peasants emigrated. A totally inadequate tax base and heavy expenditure for war in the later years of Louis's reign made Colbert's goals unattainable.

Economic policy was complicated in 1685 by Louis XIV's revocation of the Edict of Nantes. The new law ordered the destruction of churches, the closing of schools, the Catholic baptism of Huguenots, and the exile of Huguenot pastors

who refused to renounce their faith. Why did Louis, by revoking the edict, persecute some of his most loyal and industrially skilled subjects?

Recent scholarship has convincingly shown that Louis XIV was basically tolerant. He insisted on religious unity not for religious but for political reasons. His goal was "one king, one law, one faith." He hated division within the realm and insisted that religious unity was essential to his royal dignity and to the security of the state. Thus after permitting religious liberty in the early years of his reign, Louis finally decided to crack down on Protestants.

Although France's large Catholic majority applauded Louis XIV, writers in the eighteenth century and later damned him for intolerance and for the adverse impact that revocation had on the economy and foreign affairs. They claimed that tens of thousands of Huguenot craftsmen, soldiers, and business people emigrated, depriving France of their skills and tax revenues and carrying their bitterness to Holland, England, and Prussia. Although the claims of economic damage were exaggerated, the revocation of the Edict of Nantes certainly aggravated Protestant hatred for Louis and for his armies.

French Classicism

Scholars characterize French art and literature during the age of Louis XIV as "French classicism." French artists and writers of the late seventeenth century deliberately imitated the subject matter and style of classical antiquity; their work resembled that of Renaissance Italy. French art possessed the classical qualities of discipline, balance, and restraint. Classicism was the official style of Louis's court.

After Louis's accession to power, the principles of absolutism molded the ideals of French classicism. Individualism was not allowed, and artists glorified the state as personified by the king. Precise rules governed all aspects of culture. Formal and restrained perfection was the goal.

Contemporaries said that Louis XIV never ceased playing the role of grand monarch on the stage of his court, and he used music and theater as a backdrop for court ceremonial. Among composers Louis favored Jean-Baptiste Lully (1632–1687), whose orchestral works and court ballets combine lively animation with the restrained austerity typical of French classicism. His operatic productions were a powerful influence throughout Europe. Louis also supported François Couperin (1668–1733), whose harpsichord and organ works possess the grandeur the king loved, and Marc-Antoine Charpentier (1634–1704), whose solemn religious music entertained him at meals.

Louis XIV loved the stage, and in the plays of Molière and Racine his court witnessed the finest achievements of the French theater. Playwright, stage manager, director, and actor, Molière produced comedies that exposed the hypocrisies and follies of society through brilliant caricature. *Tartuffe* satirized the religious hypocrite; *Les Femmes Savantes (The Learned Women)* mocked the fashionable pseudointellectuals of the day. Molière made the bourgeoisie the butt of his ridicule; he stopped short of criticizing the nobility, thus reflecting the policy of his royal patron.

While Molière dissected social mores, his contemporary Jean Racine (1639–1699) analyzed the power of love. Racine based his tragic dramas on Greek and Roman legends, and his persistent theme is the conflict of good and evil. Several of his plays—*Andromaque, Bérénice, Iphigénie,* and *Phèdre*—bear the names of women and deal with the power of passion in women. For simplicity of language, symmetrical structure, and calm restraint, the plays of Racine represent the finest examples of French classicism.

Jean-Baptiste Poquelin, also known as Molière This is an elegant, sensuous, and romantic portrait of the playwright whose works set the moral tone of Louis's court. Louis basked in Molière's admiration, approved his social criticism, and amply rewarded him. *(Source: Musée de Versailles/Photographie Bulloz)*

The Wars of Louis XIV

Visualizing himself as a great military hero, Louis XIV used almost endless war to exalt himself above the other rulers of Europe. Military glory was his aim. In 1666 Louis appointed François le Tellier (later marquis of Louvois) secretary of war. Louvois created a professional army, which was modern in the sense that the French state, rather than private nobles, employed the soldiers.

A commissariat was established to feed the troops, taking the place of the usual practice of living off the countryside. Uniforms and weapons were standardized. A rational system of recruitment, training, discipline, and promotion was imposed. With this new military machine, one national state, France, was able to dominate the politics of Europe for the first time.

Louis continued on a broader scale the expansionist policy begun by Cardinal Richelieu. In 1667, using a dynastic excuse, he invaded Flanders, part of the Spanish Netherlands, and

Franche-Comté. He thus acquired twelve towns, including the important commercial centers of Lille and Tournai (Map 17.1). Five years later, Louis personally led an army of over a hundred thousand men into Holland. The Dutch ultimately saved themselves only by opening the dikes and flooding the countryside. This war, which lasted six years and eventually involved the Holy Roman Empire and Spain, was concluded by the Treaty of Nijmegen (1678). Louis gained additional Flemish towns and all of Franche-Comté.

Encouraged by his successes, by the weakness of the German Empire, and by divisions among the other European powers, Louis continued his aggression. In 1681 he seized the city of Strasbourg and three years later sent his armies into the province of Lorraine. At that moment the king seemed invincible. In fact, Louis had reached the limit of his expansion at Nijmegen. The wars of the

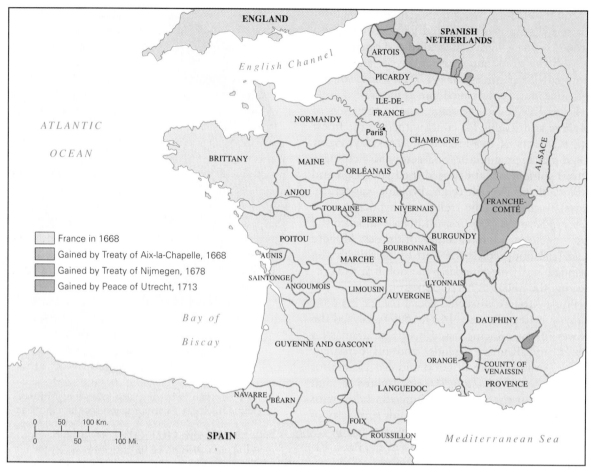

❈ **MAP 17.1 Acquisitions of Louis XIV, 1668–1713**   The desire for glory and the weakness of his German neighbors encouraged Louis's expansionist policy. But he paid a high price for his acquisitions.

1680s and 1690s brought him no additional territories. In 1689 the Dutch prince William of Orange, a bitter foe, became king of England. William joined the League of Augsburg—which included the Habsburg emperor, the kings of Spain and Sweden, and the electors of Bavaria, Saxony, and the Palatinate—adding British resources and men to the alliance. Neither the French nor the league won any decisive victories. France lacked the means to win; it was financially exhausted.

At the same time a series of bad harvests between 1688 and 1694 brought catastrophe. Cold, wet summers reduced the harvests by an estimated one-third to two-thirds, and in many provinces the death rate rose to several times the normal figure. Rising grain prices, new taxes, a slump in manufac-

turing, and the constant nuisance of pillaging troops—all these meant great suffering for the French people. France wanted peace at any price. Louis XIV granted a respite for five years while he prepared for the conflict later known as the War of the Spanish Succession.

This struggle (1701–1713) involved the dynastic question of the succession to the Spanish throne. When Charles I (r. 1665–1700) died in 1700, his will left the Spanish crown and the worldwide Spanish Empire to Philip of Anjou, Louis XIV's grandson. By accepting this will, Louis obviously would gain power in Spain; he would also be reneging on an earlier treaty to divide the vast Spanish possessions between himself and the Holy Roman emperor. He accepted the will, thereby provoking a great war.

The Dutch and the English would not accept French acquisition of the Spanish Netherlands and of the rich trade with the Spanish colonies, which would make France too strong in Europe and in North America. Thus in 1701 they joined with the Austrians and Prussians in the Grand Alliance. In the ensuing series of conflicts, Louis suffered major defeats and finally sued for peace.

The war was concluded at Utrecht in 1713, where the principle of partition was applied. Louis's grandson Philip remained the first Bourbon king of Spain on the understanding that the French and Spanish crowns would never be united. France surrendered Newfoundland, Nova Scotia, and the Hudson Bay territory to England, which also acquired Gibraltar, Minorca, and control of the African slave trade from Spain. The Dutch gained little because Austria received the former Spanish Netherlands (Map 17.2).

The Peace of Utrecht represented the balance-of-power principle in operation, setting limits on the extent to which any one power, in this case France, could expand. The treaty completed the decline of Spain as a great power. It vastly expanded the British Empire. The Peace of Utrecht also marked the end of French expansionist policy. In Louis's thirty-five-year quest for military glory, his main territorial acquisition after 1678 was Strasbourg. Even revisionist historians sympathetic to Louis acknowledge "that the widespread misery in France during the period was in part due to royal policies, especially the incessant wars."[5] The news of Louis's death in 1715 brought rejoicing throughout France.

THE DECLINE OF ABSOLUTIST SPAIN IN THE SEVENTEENTH CENTURY

Spanish absolutism and greatness had preceded that of the French. In the sixteenth century, Spain (or, more precisely, the kingdom of Castile) had developed the standard features of absolute monarchy: a permanent professional bureaucracy, a standing army, and national taxes that fell most heavily on the poor. Spain developed its mighty international absolutism on the basis of silver bullion from Peru. But by the 1590s the seeds of disaster were sprouting, and in the seventeenth century Spain experienced a steady decline. The lack of a strong middle class (largely the result of the expul-

sion of the Jews and Moors), agricultural crisis and population decline, failure to invest in productive enterprises, intellectual isolation and psychological malaise—by 1715 all combined to reduce Spain to a second-rate power.

The fabulous flow of silver from Mexico and Peru had led Philip II to assume the role of defender of Roman Catholicism in Europe (see pages 534–539). But when the "Invincible Armada" went down in 1588, a century of Spanish pride and power went with it. After 1590 a spirit of defeatism and disillusionment crippled most reform efforts.

Philip II's Catholic crusade had been financed by the revenues of the Spanish-Atlantic economy. In the early seventeenth century, the Dutch and English began to trade with the Spanish colonies, and Mexico and Peru developed local industries. Between 1610 and 1650, Spanish trade with the colonies fell 60 percent, and the American silver lodes started to run dry. Yet in Madrid royal expenditures remained high. The result was chronic deficits and frequent cancellations of Spain's national debt. These brutal cancellations—a form of bankruptcy—shook public confidence in the state.

Spain, in contrast to the other countries of western Europe, developed only a tiny middle class. Public opinion, taking its cue from the aristocracy, condemned moneymaking as vulgar and undignified. Those with influence or connections sought titles of nobility and social prestige, or they became priests, monks, and nuns. The flood of gold and silver had produced severe inflation, and many businessmen found so many obstacles in the way of profitable enterprise that they simply gave up.

Spanish aristocrats, attempting to maintain an extravagant lifestyle that they could no longer afford, increased the rents on their estates. High rents and heavy taxes in turn drove the peasants from the land. Agricultural production suffered, and the peasants departed for the large cities, where they swelled the ranks of beggars.

Their most Catholic majesties, the kings of Spain, had no solutions to these dire problems. Philip IV (r. 1622–1665) left the management of his several kingdoms to Count Olivares. An able administrator, the count devised new sources of revenue, but he clung to the grandiose belief that the solution to Spain's difficulties rested in a return to the imperial tradition. Unfortunately, the imperial tradition demanded the revival of war with the Dutch in 1622 and a long war with France over Mantua (1628–1659). These conflicts, on top of

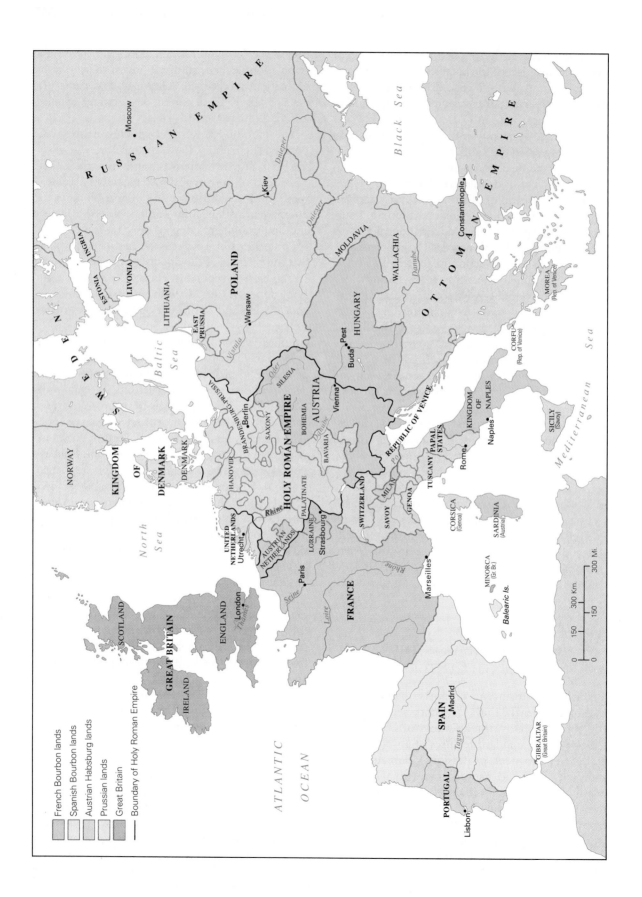

RUSSIAN EMPIRE

Moscow

Black Sea

OTTOMAN EMPIRE

Dnieper

Kiev

Dniester

MOLDAVIA

POLAND

WALLACHIA

Danube

Constantinople

HUNGARY

Warsaw

Pest

MOREA
(Rep. of Venice)

Mediterranean Sea

Buda

Vienna

CORFU
(Rep. of Venice)

SILESIA

AUSTRIA

Oder

REPUBLIC OF VENICE

KINGDOM
OF
NAPLES

BRANDENBURG-PRUSSIA

Berlin

SAXONY

BOHEMIA

HOLY ROMAN EMPIRE

Danube

Naples

SICILY
(Savoy)

EAST
PRUSSIA

LITHUANIA

Vistula

NORWAY

KINGDOM

OF

DENMARK

DENMARK

HANOVER

BAVARIA

SWITZERLAND

MILAN

SAVOY

GENOA

PALATINATE

Rhine

UNITED
NETHERLANDS

Utrecht

AUSTRIAN
NETHERLANDS

LORRAINE

Strasbourg

TUSCANY

PAPAL
STATES

Rome

Po

CORSICA
(Genoa)

SARDINIA
(Austria)

North
Sea

Baltic
Sea

SWEDEN

FINLAND

ESTONIA

LIVONIA

SCOTLAND

GREAT BRITAIN

ENGLAND

London

Thames

IRELAND

Paris

Seine

Loire

FRANCE

Rhône

Marseilles

MINORCA
(Gr Br)

Balearic Is.

ATLANTIC

OCEAN

SPAIN

Madrid

Tagus

GIBRALTAR
(Great Britain)

PORTUGAL

Lisbon

French Bourbon lands
Spanish Bourbon lands
Austrian Habsburg lands
Prussian lands
Great Britain
Boundary of Holy Roman Empire

300 Mi.

300 Km.

150

150

0

0

an empty treasury, brought disaster. The Treaty of the Pyrenees of 1659, which ended the French-Spanish wars, compelled Spain to surrender extensive territories to France. After this treaty, Spain's decline as a great power became irreversible.

Seventeenth-century Spain was the victim of its past. It could not forget the grandeur of the sixteenth century and look to the future. The most cherished Spanish ideals were military glory and strong Roman Catholic faith. In the seventeenth century, Spain lacked the finances and the manpower to fight long, expensive wars. Spain also ignored the new mercantile ideas and scientific methods because they came from heretical nations, Holland and England.

In the brilliant novel *Don Quixote,* the Spanish writer Miguel de Cervantes (1547–1616) produced one of the masterpieces of world literature. *Don Quixote* delineates the whole fabric of sixteenth-century Spanish society. The main character, Don Quixote, lives in a dream world, traveling about the countryside seeking military glory. A leading scholar wrote, "The Spaniard convinced himself that reality was what he felt, believed, imagined. He filled the world with heroic reverberations. Don Quixote was born and grew."[6]

❈ ABSOLUTISM IN EASTERN EUROPE: AUSTRIA, PRUSSIA, AND RUSSIA

The rulers of eastern Europe also labored to build strong absolutist states in the seventeenth century. But they built on social and economic foundations different from those in western Europe. These foundations were laid between 1400 and 1650,

❈ **MAP 17.2 Europe in 1715** The Peace of Utrecht ended the War of the Spanish Succession and redrew the map of Europe. A French Bourbon king succeeded to the Spanish throne on the understanding that the French would not attempt to unite the French and Spanish crowns. France surrendered to Austria the Spanish Netherlands (later Belgium), then in French hands; and France recognized the Hohenzollern rulers of Prussia. Spain ceded Gibraltar to Great Britain, for which it has been a strategic naval station ever since. Spain also granted to Britain the *asiento,* the contract for supplying African slaves to America.

when the princes and the landed nobility of eastern Europe rolled back the gains made by the peasantry during the High Middle Ages and reimposed serfdom on the rural masses. The nobility also enhanced its power as the primary social force by reducing the importance of the towns and the middle classes.

Despite the strength of the nobility, strong kings did begin to emerge in many eastern European lands in the course of the seventeenth century. There were endless wars, and in this atmosphere of continuous military emergency monarchs found ways to reduce the political power of the landlord nobility. Cautiously leaving the nobles the unchallenged masters of their peasants, eastern monarchs gradually monopolized political power in three key areas. They imposed and collected permanent taxes without consent. They maintained permanent standing armies, which policed their subjects in addition to fighting abroad. And they conducted relations with other states as they pleased.

There were important variations on the absolutist theme in eastern Europe. The royal absolutism created in Prussia was stronger and more effective than that established in Austria. This advantage gave Prussia a thin edge over Austria in the struggle for power in east-central Europe in the eighteenth century, and it prepared the way for Prussia's unification of the German people in the nineteenth century. As for Russia, it developed its own form of autocratic government at an early date, and its political absolutism was quite different from that of France or even Prussia.

Lords and Peasants

Lords and peasants were the basic social groups in eastern Europe, a vast region including Bohemia, Silesia, Hungary, eastern Germany, Poland, Lithuania, and Russia. Peasants in eastern Europe had done relatively well in the period from roughly 1050 to 1300, a time of gradual economic expansion and population growth. Eager to attract German settlers to their sparsely populated lands, the rulers and nobles of eastern Europe had offered potential newcomers economic and legal incentives. Large numbers of incoming settlers had obtained land on excellent terms and gained much personal freedom. These benefits were gradually extended to the local Slavic populations, even

THE RISE OF WESTERN ABSOLUTISM AND CONSTITUTIONALISM

1581	Formation of the Republic of the United Provinces of the Netherlands
1588	Defeat of the Spanish Armada
1589–1610	Reign of Henry IV of France; economic reforms help to restore public order, lay foundation for absolutist rule
1598	Edict of Nantes: Henry IV ends the French wars of religion
1610–1650	Spanish trade with the New World falls by 60 percent
1618–1648	Thirty Years' War
1624–1642	Richelieu dominates French government
1625	Huguenot revolt in France; siege of La Rochelle
1629–1640	Charles I attempts to rule England without Parliament
1640–1660	Long Parliament in England
1642–1649	English civil war
1643–1715	Reign of Louis XIV
1648–1660	The Fronde: French nobility opposes centralizing efforts of monarchy
1648	Peace of Westphalia confirms Dutch independence from Spain
1649	Execution of Charles I; beginning of the Interregnum in England
1653–1658	Cromwell rules England as military dictator
1659	Treaty of the Pyrenees forces Spain to cede extensive territories to France
1660	Restoration of the English monarchy: Charles II returns from exile
1661	Louis XIV enters into independent rule
ca 1663–1683	Colbert directs Louis XIV's mercantilist economic policy
1667	France invades Holland
1673	Test Act excludes Roman Catholics from public office in England
1685	Louis XIV revokes the Edict of Nantes
1685–1688	James II rules England, attempts to restore Roman Catholicism as state religion
1688	The Glorious Revolution establishes a constitutional monarchy in England under Mary and William III
1689	Enactment of the Bill of Rights in England
1701–1713	War of the Spanish Succession
1713	Peace of Utrecht ends French territorial acquisitions, expands the British Empire, completes decline of Spain as a great power

THE RISE OF ABSOLUTISM IN EASTERN EUROPE

1050–1300	Increasing economic development in eastern Europe encourages decline in serfdom
1054	Death of Prince Iaroslav the Wise, under whom the Kievan state reached its highest development
1054–1237	Kiev is divided into numerous territories ruled by competing princes
1237–1242	Mongol invasion and conquest of Russia
1252	Alexander Nevsky, prince of Moscow, recognizes Mongol overlordship
1327–1328	Suppression of the Tver revolt; Mongol khan recognizes Ivan I as great prince
1400–1650	The nobility reimposes serfdom in eastern Europe
ca 1480	Ivan III rejects Mongol overlordship and begins to use the title of tsar
1533–1584	Rule of Tsar Ivan IV (the Terrible): defeat of the khanates of Kazan and Astrakhan; subjugation of the boyar aristocracy
1598–1613	Time of Troubles in Russia
1613	Election of Michael Romanov as tsar: re-establishment of autocracy
1640–1688	Rule of Frederick William, the Great Elector, in Brandenburg-Prussia
1652	Patriarch Nikon's reforms split the Russian Orthodox church
1670–1671	Cossack revolt of Stenka Razin in Russia
1683	Siege of Vienna by the Ottoman Turks
1682–1725	Rule of Tsar Peter the Great
1683–1699	Habsburg conquest of Hungary and Transylvania
1703	Founding of St. Petersburg
1713–1740	Rule of King Frederick William I in Prussia

those of central Russia. Thus by 1300 serfdom had all but disappeared in eastern Europe. Peasants were able to bargain freely with their landlords and move about as they pleased.

After about 1300, however, as Europe's population and economy declined grievously, mainly because of the Black Death, noble landlords sought to solve their tough economic problems by more heavily exploiting the peasantry. In western Europe this attempt generally failed, but in the vast region east of the Elbe River in Germany the landlords were successful in degrading peasants. By 1500 eastern peasants were on their way to becoming serfs again.

Eastern lords triumphed because they made their kings and princes issue laws that restricted the right of their peasants to move to take advantage of better opportunities elsewhere. In Prussian territories by 1500, the law required that runaway peasants be hunted down and returned to their lords, and a runaway servant was to be nailed to a post by one ear and given a knife to cut himself loose. Moreover, lords steadily took more and more of their peasants' land and arbitrarily imposed heavier and heavier labor obligations. By the early 1500s, lords in many territories could command their peasants to work for them without pay for as many as six days a week.

Punishing Serfs This seventeenth-century illustration from Adam Olearius's *Travels in Moscovy* suggests what eastern serfdom really meant. The scene is eastern Poland. There, according to Olearius, a common command of the lord was, "Beat him till the skin falls from the flesh." Selections from Olearius's book are found in this chapter's Listening to the Past. *(Source: University of Illinois Library, Champaign)*

The gradual erosion of the peasantry's economic position was bound up with manipulation of the legal system. The local lord was also the local prosecutor, judge, and jailer. There were no independent royal officials to provide justice or uphold the common law.

Between 1500 and 1650, the social, legal, and economic conditions of peasants in eastern Europe continued to decline. In Poland, for example, nobles gained complete control over their peasants in 1574. In Russia the right of peasants to move from a given estate was abolished in 1603. In 1649 a new law code completed the legal re-establishment of permanent hereditary serfdom. The common fate of peasants in eastern Europe by the middle of the seventeenth century was serfdom.

The consolidation of serfdom between 1500 and 1650 was accompanied by the growth of estate agriculture, particularly in Poland and eastern Germany. In the sixteenth century, European economic expansion and population growth resumed after the great declines of the late Middle Ages. Eastern lords had powerful economic incentives to increase the production of their estates, and they did so. Generally, the estates were inefficient and technically backward, but they nevertheless succeeded in squeezing sizable surpluses out of the impoverished peasants. These surpluses were sold to foreign merchants, who exported them to the growing cities of wealthier western Europe.

The re-emergence of serfdom in eastern Europe in the early modern period was a momentous human development. Above all, it reflected the fact that eastern lords enjoyed much greater political power than their western counterparts. In the late Middle Ages, when much of eastern Europe was experiencing innumerable wars and general political chaos, the noble landlord class had greatly increased its political power at the expense of the ruling monarchs. Moreover, the western concept and reality of sovereignty, as embodied in a king who protected the interests of all his people, was not well developed in eastern Europe before 1650.

Finally, with the approval of weak kings, the landlords systematically undermined the medieval privileges of the towns and the power of the urban classes. For example, instead of selling their products to local merchants in the towns, as required in the Middle Ages, the landlords often sold directly to foreign capitalists. Eastern towns also lost their medieval right of refuge and were compelled to return runaways to their lords. The population of the towns and the urban middle classes declined greatly. This development both reflected and promoted the supremacy of noble landlords in most of eastern Europe in the sixteenth century.

Austria and the Ottoman Turks

The Habsburgs of Austria emerged from the Thirty Years' War (see pages 539–540) impoverished and exhausted. The effort to root out Protestantism in the German lands had failed utterly, and the authority of the Holy Roman Empire and its Habsburg emperors had declined almost to the vanishing point. Yet defeat in central Europe also opened new vistas. The Habsburg monarchs were forced to turn inward and eastward in an attempt to fuse their diverse holdings into a strong, unified state.

An important step in this direction had actually been taken in Bohemia during the Thirty Years' War. Protestantism had been strong among the Czechs, a Slavic people concentrated in Bohemia. In 1618 the Czech nobles who controlled the Bohemian Estates—the representative body of the different legal orders—had risen up against their Habsburg king. This revolt was crushed, and then the Czech nobility was totally restructured to ensure its loyalty to the monarchy. With the help of this new nobility, the Habsburgs established strong direct rule over reconquered Bohemia. The condition of the enserfed peasantry worsened. Protestantism was also stamped out, and religious unity began to emerge. The reorganization of Bohemia was a giant step toward royal absolutism.

After the Thirty Years' War, Ferdinand III (r. 1637–1657) centralized the government in the hereditary German-speaking provinces, most notably Austria, Styria, and the Tyrol. The king created a permanent standing army ready to put down any internal opposition. The Habsburg monarchy was then ready to turn toward the vast plains of Hungary, in opposition to the Ottoman Turks.

The Ottomans had come out of Anatolia, in present-day Turkey, to create one of history's greatest military empires. Their armies had almost captured Vienna in 1529, and for more than 150 years

thereafter the Ottomans ruled all of the Balkan territories, almost all of Hungary, and part of southern Russia. In the late seventeenth century, under vigorous reforming leadership, the Ottoman Empire succeeded in marshaling its forces for one last mighty blow at Christian Europe. A huge Turkish army surrounded Vienna and laid siege to it in 1683. After holding out against great odds for two months, the city was relieved at the last minute, and the Ottomans were forced to retreat. As their Russian and Venetian allies attacked on other fronts, the Habsburgs conquered all of Hungary and Transylvania (part of present-day Romania) by 1699 (Map 17.3).

The Turkish wars and this great expansion strengthened the Habsburg army and promoted some sense of unity in the Habsburg lands. But Habsburg efforts to create a fully developed, highly centralized, absolutist state were only partly successful. The Habsburg state remained a composite of three separate and distinct territories: the old "hereditary provinces" of Austria, the kingdom of Bohemia, and the kingdom of Hungary. Each part had its own laws and political life, for the three noble-dominated Estates continued to exist, though with reduced powers. Above all, the Hungarian nobility effectively thwarted the full development of Habsburg absolutism. Time and again throughout the seventeenth century, Hungarian nobles rose in revolt against the attempts of Vienna to impose absolute rule. They never triumphed decisively, but neither were they ever crushed.

Hungarians resisted because many of them were Protestants, especially in the area long ruled by the more tolerant Turks, and they hated the heavy-handed attempts of the conquering Habsburgs to re-Catholicize everyone. Moreover, the lords of Hungary and even part of the Hungarian peasantry had become attached to a national ideal long before most of the other European peoples. They were determined to maintain as much independence and local control as possible. Thus when the Habsburgs were bogged down in the War of the Spanish Succession (see page 564), the Hungarians rose in one last patriotic rebellion under Prince Francis Rákóczy in 1703. Rákóczy and his forces were eventually defeated, but this time the Habsburgs had to accept many of the traditional privileges of the Hungarian aristocracy in return for Hungarian acceptance of hereditary Habsburg rule. Thus Hungary, unlike Austria or Bohemia,

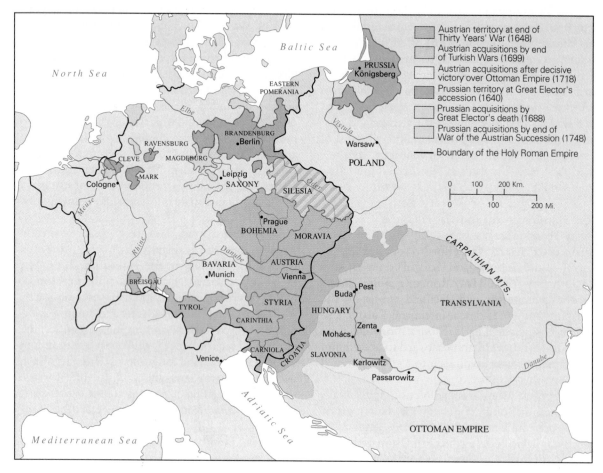

MAP 17.3 Growth of Austria and Brandenburg-Prussia to 1748   Austria expanded to the southwest into Hungary and Transylvania at the expense of the Ottoman Empire. It was unable to hold the rich German province of Silesia, however, which was conquered by Brandenburg-Prussia.

never came close to being fully integrated into a centralized, absolute Habsburg state.

The Emergence of Prussia

As the status of east German peasants declined steadily after 1400, local princes lost political power, and a revitalized landed nobility became the undisputed ruling class. The Hohenzollern family, which ruled through different branches as the electors of Brandenburg and the dukes of Prussia, were little more than the largest landowners in a landlord society. Nothing suggested that the Hohenzollerns and their territories would ever play an important role in European or even German affairs.

Brandenburg was a helpless spectator in the Thirty Years' War, its territory alternately ravaged by Swedish and Habsburg armies. Yet the country's devastation prepared the way for Hohenzollern absolutism, because foreign armies dramatically weakened the political power of the Estates—the representative assemblies of the realm. The weakening of the Estates helped the very talented young elector Frederick William (r. 1640–1688), later known as the "Great Elector," to ride roughshod over traditional constitutional liberties and to take a giant step toward royal absolutism.

When Frederick William came to power in 1640, the twenty-year-old ruler was determined to unify his three quite separate provinces and to add to them by diplomacy and war. These provinces were Brandenburg itself, the area around Berlin; Prussia, inherited in 1618 when the junior branch of the Hohenzollern family died out; and scattered holdings along the Rhine in western Germany (see Map 17.3). Each province was inhabited by Germans; but each had its own Estates, dominated by the nobility and the landowning classes.

The struggle between the Great Elector and the provincial Estates was long, complicated, and intense. After the Thirty Years' War, the representatives of the nobility zealously reasserted the right of the Estates to vote taxes, a right the Swedish armies of occupation had simply ignored. Yet first in Brandenburg and then in Prussia, the Great Elector eventually had his way. To pay for the permanent standing army that he first established in 1660, Frederick William forced the Estates to accept the introduction of permanent taxation without consent. The soldiers doubled as tax collectors and policemen, becoming the core of the expanding state bureaucracy. The power of the Estates declined rapidly thereafter, and the Great Elector turned the screws of taxation. State revenue tripled and the size of the army leaped about tenfold during his reign.

In accounting for the Great Elector's fateful triumph, two factors appear central. First, as in the formation of every absolutist state, war was a decisive factor. The ongoing struggle between Sweden and Poland for control of the Baltic after 1648 and the wars of Louis XIV in western Europe created an atmosphere of permanent crisis. It was no accident that, except in commercially minded Holland, constitutionalism won out only in England, the only major country to escape devastating foreign invasions in the seventeenth century.

Second, the nobility had long dominated the government through the Estates but only for its own narrow self-interest. When, therefore, the Great Elector reconfirmed the nobility's freedom from taxation and its unlimited control over the peasants in 1653 and after, the nobility accepted a self-serving compromise. While Frederick William reduced the nobility's political power, the bulk of the Great Elector's new taxes fell on towns, and royal authority stopped at the landlords' gates.

By the time of his death in 1688, the Great Elector had created a single state out of scattered principalities. But his new creation was still small and fragile. It was Frederick William I, "the Soldiers' King" (r. 1713–1740), who truly established

❉ **A Prussian Giant Grenadier**   Frederick William I wanted tall, handsome soldiers. He dressed them in tight, bright uniforms to distinguish them from the peasant population from which most soldiers came. He also ordered several portraits of his favorites from his court painter, J. C. Merk. Grenadiers wore the distinctive mitre cap instead of an ordinary hat so that they could hurl their heavy hand grenades unimpeded by a broad brim. *(Source: Copyright reserved to Her Majesty Queen Elizabeth II)*

Prussian absolutism and gave it its unique character. A dangerous psychoneurotic as well as a talented reformer, Frederick William I created the best army in Europe, for its size, and he infused military values into a whole society.

Frederick William's attachment to the army and military life was intensely emotional. He had, for example, a bizarre, almost pathological love for tall soldiers, whom he credited with superior strength and endurance. Like some fanatical modern-day basketball coach in search of a championship team, he sent his agents throughout both Prussia and all of Europe, tricking, buying, and kidnapping top recruits. Neighboring princes sent him their giants as gifts to win his gratitude. Prussian mothers told their sons: "Stop growing or the recruiting agents will get you."[7] Frederick William's love of the army was also based on a hardheaded conception of the struggle for power and a dog-eat-dog view of international politics. Throughout his long reign he never wavered in his conviction that the welfare of king and state depended above all else on the army.

As in France, the cult of military power provided the rationale for a great expansion of royal absolutism. As the ruthless king himself put it: "I must be served with life and limb, with house and wealth, with honour and conscience, everything must be committed except eternal salvation—that belongs to God, but all else is mine."[8] To make good these extraordinary demands, Frederick William created a strong and exceptionally honest bureaucracy, which administered the country and tried to develop it economically. The last traces of the parliamentary Estates and local self-government vanished.

The king's grab for power brought him into considerable conflict with the noble landowners, the Junkers. In the end the Prussian nobility responded to a combination of threats and opportunities and became the officer caste. By 1739 all but 5 of 245 officers with the rank of major or above were aristocrats. A new compromise had been worked out: the nobility imperiously commanded the peasantry in the army as well as on its estates.

Coarse and crude, penny-pinching and hard working, Frederick William achieved results. Above all, he built a first-rate army out of third-rate resources. Twelfth in Europe in population, Prussia had the fourth largest army by 1740, behind France, Russia, and Austria. Soldier for soldier, the Prussian army became the best in Europe, astonishing foreign observers with its precision,

skill, and discipline. Curiously, the king loved his "blue boys" so much that he hated to "spend" them. This most militaristic of kings was, paradoxically, almost always at peace.

Nevertheless, the Prussian people paid a heavy and lasting price for the obsessions of the royal drillmaster. Civil society became rigid and highly disciplined. Prussia became the "Sparta of the North"; unquestioning obedience was the highest virtue. As a Prussian minister later summed up, "To keep quiet is the first civic duty."[9] Thus the absolutism of Frederick William I combined with harsh peasant bondage and Junker tyranny to lay the foundations for probably the most militaristic country of modern times.

The Rise of Moscow

In the ninth century, the Vikings, those fearless warriors from Scandinavia, appeared in the lands of the eastern Slavs. Called "Varangians" in the old Russian chronicles, the Vikings were interested primarily in international trade. In order to increase and protect their international commerce, they declared themselves the rulers of the eastern Slavs. The Varangian ruler Oleg (r. 878–912) established his residence at Kiev. He and his successors ruled over a loosely united confederation of Slavic territories—the Kievan state—which reached its height under Prince Iaroslav the Wise (r. 1019–1054).

After Iaroslav's death in 1054, Kiev disintegrated into more and more competing units, each ruled by a prince. A given prince owned a certain number of farms or landed estates and had them worked directly by his people, mainly slaves, called *kholops* in Russian. Outside of these estates, the prince exercised limited authority in his principality. Excluding the clergy, two kinds of people lived there: the noble boyars and the commoner peasants.

Like the Germans and the Italians, the eastern Slavs might have emerged from the Middle Ages weak and politically divided had it not been for the Mongol conquest of the Kievan state. Wild nomadic tribes from present-day Mongolia, the Mongols were temporarily unified in the thirteenth century by Jenghiz Khan (1162–1227), one of history's greatest conquerors. In five years his armies subdued all of China. His successors then wheeled westward, smashing everything in their path and reaching the plains of Hungary victorious before they pulled back in 1242. The Mongol army—the

Golden Horde—was savage in the extreme, often slaughtering entire populations of cities before burning them to the ground.

Having devastated and conquered, the Mongols ruled the eastern Slavs for more than two hundred years. They forced all the bickering Slavic princes to submit to their rule and to give them tribute and slaves. If the conquered peoples rebelled, the Mongols were quick to punish with death and destruction. Thus the Mongols unified the eastern Slavs, for the Mongol khan was acknowledged by all as the supreme ruler.

Beginning with Alexander Nevsky in 1252, the previously insignificant princes of Moscow became particularly adept at serving the Mongols. They loyally put down popular uprisings and collected the khan's harsh taxes. By way of reward, the princes of Moscow emerged as hereditary great princes. Eventually the Muscovite princes were able to destroy their princely rivals and even to replace the khan as supreme ruler.

One of the more important Muscovite princes was Ivan I (r. 1328–1341), popularly known as "Ivan the Moneybag." Extremely stingy, Ivan I built up a large personal fortune and increased his influence by loaning money to less frugal princes to pay their Mongol taxes. Ivan's most serious rival was the prince of Tver, who joined his people in 1327 in a revolt against Mongol oppression. Appointed commander of a large Russian-Mongol army, Ivan laid waste to Tver and its lands. For this proof of devotion, the Mongols made Ivan the general tax collector for all the Slavic lands they had subjugated and named him great prince. Ivan also convinced the metropolitan of Kiev, the leading churchman of all eastern Slavs, to settle in Moscow. Ivan I thus gained greater prestige.

In the next hundred-odd years, the great princes of Moscow significantly increased their holdings. Then, in the reign of Ivan III (r. 1462–1505), the process of gathering in the territories around Moscow was largely completed. Of the principalities that Ivan III purchased and conquered, Novgorod with its lands extending almost to the Baltic Sea was most crucial (Map 17.4). Thus the princes of Moscow defeated all rivals to win complete princely authority.

Not only was the prince of Moscow the *unique* ruler, he was the *absolute* ruler, the autocrat, the *tsar*—the Slavic contraction for "caesar," with all its connotations. This imperious conception of absolute power was powerfully reinforced by two de-velopments. First, about 1480 Ivan III stopped acknowledging the khan as his supreme ruler. There is good evidence to suggest that Ivan and his successors saw themselves as khans. Certainly they assimilated the Mongol concept of kingship as the exercise of unrestrained and unpredictable power.

Second, after the fall of Constantinople to the Turks in 1453, the tsars saw themselves as the heirs of both the caesars and Orthodox Christianity, the one true faith. All the other kings of Europe were heretics: only the tsars were rightful and holy rulers. This idea was promoted by Orthodox churchmen, who spoke of "holy Russia" as the "Third Rome." Ivan's marriage to the daughter of the last Byzantine emperor further enhanced the aura of an imperial inheritance for Moscow. Worthy successor to the mighty khan and the true Christian emperor, the Muscovite tsar was a king claiming unrestricted power as his God-given right. The Mongol inheritance weighed heavily on Russia.

As peasants had begun losing their freedom of movement in the fifteenth century, so had the noble boyars begun losing power and influence. For example, when Ivan III conquered the principality of Novgorod in the 1480s, he confiscated fully 80 percent of the land, executing the previous owners or resettling them nearer Moscow. He then kept more than half of the confiscated land for himself and distributed the remainder to members of a newly emerging service nobility, who held the tsar's land on the explicit condition that they serve in the tsar's army. Moreover, Ivan III began to require boyars outside Novgorod to serve him if they wished to retain their lands.

The rise of the new service nobility accelerated under Ivan IV (r. 1533–1584), the famous "Ivan the Terrible." Having ascended the throne at age three, Ivan suffered insults and neglect at the hands of the haughty boyars after his mother died. But at age sixteen he suddenly pushed aside his hated boyar advisers and crowned himself. Selecting the beautiful and kind Anastasia of the popular Romanov family for his wife and queen, the young tsar soon declared war on the remnants of Mongol power. He defeated the faltering khanates of Kazan and Astrakhan between 1552 and 1556, adding vast new territories to Russia. In the course of these wars, Ivan virtually abolished the old distinction between hereditary boyar private property and land granted temporarily for service. All nobles, old and new, had to serve the tsar in order to hold any land.

Principality of Moscow, ca 1300

Acquisitions by Ivan III's accession (1462)

Acquisitions under Ivan III (1462–1505)

Acquisitions by death of Ivan the Terrible (1584)

Acquisitions by Peter the Great's accession (1689)

Acquisitions under Peter the Great (1689–1725)

✕ Major battles

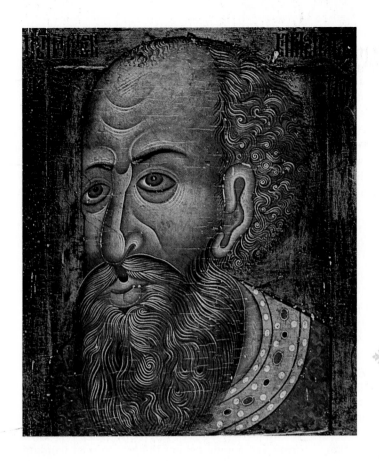

Ivan the Terrible Ivan IV, the first to take the title Tsar of Russia, executed many Muscovite boyars and their peasants and servants. His control of all land, trade, and industry restricted Russian social and economic development. *(Source: National Museum, Copenhagen, Denmark)*

The transformation of the entire nobility into a service nobility was completed in the second part of Ivan the Terrible's reign. In 1557 Ivan turned westward, and for the next twenty-five years Muscovy waged an exhausting, unsuccessful war primarily with the large Polish-Lithuanian state, which controlled not only Poland but much of the Ukraine in the sixteenth century. Quarreling with the boyars over the war and blaming them for the sudden death of his beloved Anastasia in 1560, the increasingly cruel and demented Ivan turned to strike down all who stood in his way.

Above all, he reduced the ancient Muscovite boyar families with a reign of terror. Leading boyars, their relatives, and even their peasants were executed en masse by a special corps of unquestioning servants. Dressed in black and riding black horses, they were forerunners of the modern dictator's secret police. Large estates were confiscated, broken up, and reapportioned to the lower service nobility, which was totally dependent on the autocrat.

Ivan also took giant strides toward making all commoners servants of the tsar. As the service nobles demanded more from their peasants, more and more peasants fled toward the wild, recently conquered territories to the east and south. There they formed free groups and outlaw armies known as Cossacks. The Cossacks maintained a precarious independence beyond the reach of the oppressive landholders and the tsar's hated officials. The solution to this problem was to complete the tying of the peasants to the land, making them serfs perpetually bound to serve the noble landholders, who were bound in turn to serve the tsar.

In the time of Ivan the Terrible, urban traders and artisans were also bound to their towns and

MAP 17.4 Expansion of Russia to 1725 After the disintegration of the Kievan state and the Mongol conquest, the princes of Moscow and their descendants gradually extended their rule over an enormous territory.

jobs so that the tsar could tax them more heavily. The urban classes had no security in their work or property and remained weak and divided. Even the wealthiest merchants were basically dependent agents of the tsar.

As has so often occurred in Russia, the death of an iron-fisted tyrant—in this case, Ivan the Terrible in 1584—ushered in an era of confusion and violent struggles for power. Events were particularly chaotic after Ivan's son Theodore died in 1598 without an heir. The years 1598 to 1613 are aptly called the Time of Troubles.

Close relatives of the deceased tsar intrigued against and murdered each other, alternately fighting and welcoming the invading Swedes and Poles, who even occupied Moscow. Most serious for the cause of autocracy, there was a great social upheaval as Cossacks marched northward, rallying peasants and slaughtering nobles and officials. This social explosion from below, which combined with a belated surge of patriotic opposition to the Polish invaders, brought the nobles to their senses. In 1613 they elected Ivan's sixteen-year-old grand-nephew, Michael Romanov, the new hereditary tsar and rallied around him in the face of common internal and external threats.

Michael's reign saw the gradual re-establishment of tsarist autocracy (see Listening to the Past). The recently rebellious peasants were ground down further, while Ivan's heavy military obligations on the nobility were relaxed considerably, a trend that continued after his death. The result was a second round of mass upheaval and protest.

In the mid-seventeenth century, the unity of the Russian Orthodox church was torn apart by the religious reforms of the patriarch Nikon, a dogmatic purist who wished to bring "corrupted" Russian practices of worship into line with the Greek Orthodox model. The self-serving church hierarchy quickly went along, but the intensely religious common people resisted. Great numbers left the church and formed illegal communities of "Old Believers," who were hunted down and persecuted. After the great split, the Russian masses were alienated from the established church, which became totally dependent on the state for its authority.

Again the Cossacks revolted against the state, which was doggedly trying to catch up with them on the frontiers and reduce them to serfdom. Under the leadership of Stenka Razin they moved up the Volga River in 1670 and 1671, attracting a great undisciplined army of peasants, murdering landlords, and high church officials, and proclaiming freedom from oppression. In response to this rebellion, finally defeated by the government, the thoroughly scared upper classes tightened the screws of serfdom even further.

The Reforms of Peter the Great

It is now possible to understand the reforms of Peter the Great (r. 1682–1725) and his kind of monarchial absolutism. Contrary to some historians' assertions, Peter was interested primarily in military power and not in some grandiose westernization plan. A giant for his time, at six feet seven inches, and possessing enormous energy and determination, Peter was determined to increase Russia's power and to continue the territorial expansion that had gained a large part of the Ukraine in 1667 and had completed the conquest of Siberia in the seventeenth century. Little wonder that the forty-three years of Peter's rule knew only one year of peace.

When Peter took full control in 1689, the heart of his part-time army still consisted of cavalry made up of boyars and service nobility. The Russian army was lagging behind the professional standing armies being formed in Europe in the seventeenth century. The core of such armies was a highly disciplined infantry—an infantry that fired and refired rifles as it fearlessly advanced, before charging with fixed bayonets. Such a large, permanent army was enormously expensive. Given the desire to conquer more territory, Peter's military problem was serious.

Peter's solution was, in essence, to tighten up Muscovy's old service system and really make it work. He put the nobility back in harness with a vengeance. Every nobleman, great or small, was once again required to serve in the army or in the civil administration—for life. Since a more modern army and government required skilled technicians and experts, Peter created schools and even universities. One of his most hated reforms required five years of compulsory education away from home for every young nobleman. Peter established a merit-based military-civilian bureaucracy in which some people of non-noble origin rose to high positions. He also searched out talented foreigners—twice in his reign he went abroad to study and observe—and placed them in his service. These measures combined to make the army and government more powerful and efficient.

Peter also greatly increased the service requirements of the commoners. He established a regular standing army of more than 200,000 soldiers. In addition, special forces of Cossacks and foreigners numbered more than 100,000. The departure of a drafted peasant boy was regarded by his family and village as almost like a funeral, as indeed it was, since the recruit was drafted for life. The peasantry also served with its taxes, which increased threefold during Peter's reign. Serfs were arbitrarily assigned to work in the growing number of factories and mines.

The constant warfare of Peter's reign consumed from 80 to 85 percent of all revenues but brought only modest territorial expansion. Yet after initial losses in the Great Northern War with Sweden, which lasted from 1700 to 1721, Peter's new war machine crushed Sweden's smaller army in the Ukraine at Poltava in 1709, one of the most significant battles in Russian history. Sweden never really regained the offensive. Annexing Estonia and much of present-day Latvia (see Map 17.4), Russia became the dominant power on the Baltic Sea and very much a European Great Power. If victory or defeat is the ultimate historical criterion, Peter's reforms were a success.

There were other important consequences of Peter's reign. Because of his feverish desire to use modern technology to strengthen the army, many Westerners and Western ideas flowed into Russia for the first time. A new class of educated Russians began to emerge. At the same time, vast numbers of Russians, especially among the poor and weak, hated Peter's massive changes. The split between the enserfed peasantry and the educated nobility thus widened, even though all were caught up in the endless demands of the sovereign.

A new idea of state interest, distinct from the tsar's personal interests, began to take hold. Peter claimed to act for the common good, and he attached explanations to his decrees in an attempt to gain the support of the populace. Yet, as before, the tsar alone decided what the common good was.

In sum, Peter built on the service obligations of old Muscovy. His monarchial absolutism was truly the culmination of the long development of a unique Russian civilization. Yet the creation of a more modern army and state introduced much that was new and Western to that civilization. This development paved the way for Russia to move much closer to the European mainstream in its thought and institutions during the Enlightenment under Catherine the Great.

Absolutism and the Baroque

The rise of royal absolutism in eastern Europe had major cultural consequences. Inspired in part by Louis XIV of France, the great and not-so-great rulers called on the artistic talent of the age to glorify their power and magnificence. This exaltation of despotic rule was particularly striking in architecture and city planning.

As soaring Gothic cathedrals expressed the idealized spirit of the High Middle Ages, so dramatic baroque palaces symbolized the age of absolutist power. By 1700 palace building had become an obsession for the rulers of central and eastern Europe. Their baroque palaces were clearly intended to overawe the people with the monarch's strength. One such palace was Schönbrunn, an enormous Viennese Versailles begun in 1695 by Emperor Leopold I to celebrate Austrian military victories and Habsburg might.

Petty princes also contributed mightily to the mania of palace building. The not-very-important elector-archbishop of Mainz, the ruling prince of that city, confessed apologetically that "building is a craze which costs much, but every fool likes his own hat."[10] The archbishop of Mainz's own "hat" was an architectural gem, like that of another churchly ruler, the prince-bishop of Würzburg. In central and eastern Europe, the favorite noble servants of royalty became extremely rich and powerful, and they, too, built grandiose palaces in the capital cities. These palaces were in part an extension of the monarch, for they surpassed the buildings of less favored nobles.

Palaces like Schönbrunn and Würzburg were magnificent examples of the baroque style. They expressed the baroque delight in bold, sweeping statements intended to provide a dramatic emotional experience. To create this experience, baroque masters dissolved the traditional artistic frontiers: the architect permitted the painter and the artisan to cover the undulating surfaces with wildly colorful paintings, graceful sculptures, and fanciful carvings. Space was used in a highly original way, to blend everything together in a total environment.

Not content with fashioning ostentatious palaces, absolute monarchs and baroque architects remodeled existing capital cities or built new ones to

✤ **Würzburg, the Prince-Bishop's Palace** The baroque style brought architects, painters, and sculptors together in harmonious, even playful partnership. This magnificent monumental staircase, designed by Johann Balthasar Neumann in 1735, merges into the vibrant ceiling frescoes by Giovanni Battista Tiepolo. A man is stepping out of the picture, and a painted dog resembles a marble statue. *(Source: Erich Lessing/Art Resource, NY)*

reflect royal magnificence and the centralization of political power. Karlsruhe, founded in 1715 as the capital city of a small German principality, is one extreme example. There, broad, straight avenues radiated out from the palace, so that all roads—like all power—were focused on the ruler. More typically, the monarch's architects added new urban areas alongside the old city, and these areas became the real heart of the expanding capital.

The distinctive features of the new additions were their broad avenues, their imposing government buildings, and their rigorous mathematical layout. Along major thoroughfares the nobles built elaborate townhouses; stables and servants' quarters were built on the alleys behind. Under arcades along the avenues appeared smart and expensive shops, the first department stores, with plate-glass windows and fancy displays. The additions brought reckless speed to the European city. Whereas everyone had walked through the narrow, twisting streets of the medieval town, the high and mighty raced down the broad boulevards in elegant carriages. A social gap opened between the wealthy riders and the gaping, dodging pedestrians.

No city illustrates better than St. Petersburg the close ties among politics, architecture, and urban development in this period. In 1702 Peter the Great's armies seized a desolate Swedish fortress on one of the water-logged islands at the mouth of the Neva River on the Baltic Sea. Within a year the tsar had decided to build a new city there and to make it, rather than ancient Moscow, his capital. The land was swampy and inhospitable. But for Peter it was a future metropolis gloriously bearing his name. After the decisive Russian victory at Poltava in 1709, he moved into high gear. In one imperious decree after another, he ordered his people to build a new city, his "window on Europe."

Peter believed that it would be easier to reform the country militarily and administratively from such a city than from Moscow, and his political goals were reflected in his architectural ideas. First Peter wanted a comfortable, "modern" city. Modernity meant broad, straight, stone-paved avenues, houses built in a uniform line, large parks, canals for drainage, stone bridges, and street lighting. Second, all building had to conform strictly to detailed architectural regulations set down by the government. Finally, each social group—the nobility, the merchants, the artisans, and so on—was to live in a certain section of town. In short, the city

and its population were to conform to a carefully defined urban plan of the baroque type.

Peter used the methods of Russian autocracy to build his modern capital. The creation of St. Petersburg was just one of the heavy obligations he dictatorially imposed on all social groups in Russia. The peasants bore the heaviest burdens. Just as the government drafted peasants for the army, it also drafted from 25,000 to 40,000 men each summer to labor in St. Petersburg for three months, without pay. Peasants hated forced labor in the capital, and each year from one-fourth to one-third of those sent risked brutal punishment and ran away. Many peasant construction workers died each summer from hunger, sickness, and accidents. Beautiful St. Petersburg was built on the shoveling, carting, and paving of a mass of conscripted serfs.

Peter also drafted more privileged groups to his city, but on a permanent basis. Nobles were sum-

St. Petersburg, ca 1760 Rastrelli's remodeled Winter Palace, which housed the royal family until the Russian Revolution of 1917, stands on the left along the Neva River. The Navy Office with its golden spire and other government office buildings are nearby and across the river. Russia became a naval power and St. Petersburg a great port. *(Source: Michael Holford)*

marily ordered to build costly stone houses and palaces in St. Petersburg and to live in them most of the year. Merchants and artisans were also commanded to settle and build in St. Petersburg. These nobles and merchants were then required to pay for the city's avenues, parks, canals, embankments, pilings, and bridges. The building of St. Petersburg was, in truth, an enormous direct tax levied on the wealthy, who in turn forced the peasantry to do most of the work. No wonder so many Russians hated Peter's new city.

Yet the tsar had his way. By the time of his death in 1725, there were at least six thousand houses and numerous impressive government buildings in St. Petersburg. Under the remarkable women who ruled Russia throughout most of the eighteenth century, St. Petersburg blossomed as a majestic and well-organized city, at least in its wealthy showpiece sections. Chief architect Bartolomeo Rastrelli combined Italian and Russian traditions into a unique, wildly colorful St. Petersburg style in many noble palaces and government buildings. All the while St. Petersburg grew rapidly, and its almost 300,000 inhabitants in 1782 made it one of the world's largest cities. A magnificent and harmonious royal city, St. Petersburg proclaimed the power of Russia's rulers and the creative potential of the absolutist state.

✤ ENGLAND: THE TRIUMPH OF CONSTITUTIONAL MONARCHY

In 1588 Queen Elizabeth I of England exercised great personal power, but by 1689 the power of the English monarchy was severely limited. Change in England was anything but orderly. Seventeenth-century England displayed little political stability. It executed one king, experienced a bloody civil war, experimented with military dictatorship, then restored the son of the murdered king, and finally, after a bloodless revolution, established constitutional monarchy. Political stability came only in the 1690s. Yet out of this tumultuous century England built the foundations for a strong and enduring constitutional monarchy.

In the middle years of the seventeenth century, the problem of sovereignty was vigorously debated. In *Leviathan,* the English philosopher and political theorist Thomas Hobbes (1588–1679) maintained that sovereignty is ultimately derived from the people, who transfer it to the monarchy by implicit contract. The power of the ruler is absolute, Hobbes said, but kings do not hold their power by divine right. This abstract theory pleased no one in the seventeenth century, but it did stimulate fruitful thinking about England's great seventeenth-century problem—the problem of order and political power.

The Decline of Absolutism in England (1603–1660)

Elizabeth I's extraordinary success was the result of her political shrewdness and flexibility, her careful management of finances, her wise selection of ministers, her clever manipulation of Parliament, and her sense of royal dignity and devotion to hard work. After her Scottish cousin James Stuart succeeded her as James I (r. 1603–1625), Elizabeth's strengths seemed even greater.

King James was learned and, with thirty-five years' experience as king of Scotland, politically shrewd. But he was not as interested in displaying the majesty and mystique of monarchy as Elizabeth had been, and he lacked the common touch. Moreover, James was a dogmatic proponent of the theory of divine right of kings. "There are no privileges and immunities," said James, "which can stand against a divinely appointed King." This typically absolutist notion implied total royal jurisdiction over the liberties, persons, and properties of English men and women. Such a view ran directly counter to many long-standing English ideas, including the belief that a person's property could not be taken away without due process of law. And in the House of Commons the English had a strong representative body to question these absolutist pretensions.

The House of Commons guarded the state's pocketbook, and James and later Stuart kings badly needed to open that pocketbook. James I looked on all revenues as a windfall to be squandered on a lavish court and favorite courtiers. The extravagance displayed in James's court, as well as the public flaunting of his male lovers, weakened respect for the monarchy. These actions also stimulated the knights and burgesses who sat in the House of Commons at Westminster to press for a thorough discussion of royal expenditures, religious reform, and foreign affairs. In short, the Commons aspired to sovereignty—the ultimate political power in the realm.

During the reigns of James I and his son Charles I (r. 1625–1649) the English House of Commons was very different from the assembly that Henry VIII had manipulated into passing his Reformation legislation. The class that dominated the Commons during the Stuarts' reign wanted political power corresponding to its economic strength. A social revolution had brought about this change. The dissolution of the monasteries and the sale of monastic land had enriched many people. Agricultural techniques like the draining of wasteland had improved the land and increased its yield. In the seventeenth century old manorial common land was enclosed and profitably turned into sheep runs. Many invested in commercial ventures at home, such as the expanding cloth industry, and in foreign trade. Many also made prudent marriages. These developments increased social mobility. The typical pattern was for the commercially successful to set themselves up as country gentry. This elite group possessed a far greater proportion of the land and of the nation's wealth in 1640 than in 1540. Increased wealth resulted in a better-educated and more articulate House of Commons.

In England, unlike France, no social stigma was attached to paying taxes. Members of the House of Commons were willing to tax themselves provided they had some say in state spending and state policies. The Stuart kings, however, considered such ambitions intolerable presumption and a threat to their divine-right prerogative. Consequently, at every Parliament between 1603 and 1640, bitter squabbles erupted between Crown and Commons. Like the Great Elector in Prussia, Charles I tried to govern without Parliament (1629–1640) and to finance his government by arbitrary levies. And as in Prussia these absolutist measures brought intense political conflict.

Religion was another source of conflict. In the early seventeenth century, increasing numbers of English people felt dissatisfied with the Church of England established by Henry VIII and reformed by Elizabeth. Many Puritans (see page 535) remained committed to "purifying" the Anglican church of Roman Catholic elements—elaborate vestments and ceremonies, the position of the altar in the church, even the giving and wearing of wedding rings.

Many Puritans were also attracted by the socioeconomic implications of John Calvin's theology. Calvinism emphasized hard work, sobriety, thrift, competition, and postponement of pleasure, and it

tended to link sin and poverty with weakness and moral corruption. These attitudes, which have frequently been called the "Protestant ethic," "middle-class ethic," or "capitalist ethic," fit in precisely with the economic approaches and practices of many (successful) business people and farmers. These "Protestant virtues" represented the prevailing values of members of the House of Commons.

James I and Charles I both gave the impression of being highly sympathetic to Roman Catholicism. Charles supported the policies of Archbishop of Canterbury William Laud (1573–1645), who tried to impose elaborate ritual and rich ceremonial on all churches. People believed that the country was being led back to Roman Catholicism. In 1637 Laud attempted to impose two new elements on the church organization in Scotland: a new prayer book, modeled on the Anglican Book of Common Prayer, and bishoprics, which the Presbyterian Scots firmly rejected. The Scots revolted. To finance an army to put down the Scots, King Charles was compelled to summon Parliament in November 1640. It was a fatal decision.

For eleven years Charles I had ruled without Parliament, financing his government through extraordinary stopgap levies considered illegal by most English people. Most members of Parliament believed that such taxation without consent amounted to absolutist despotism. Thus they were not willing to trust the king with an army. Accordingly, the Parliament summoned in November 1640 (commonly called the Long Parliament because it sat from 1640 to 1660) enacted legislation that limited the power of the monarch and made arbitrary government impossible.

In 1641 the Commons passed the Triennial Act, which compelled the king to summon Parliament every three years. The Commons impeached Archbishop Laud and abolished the House of Lords and the ecclesiastical Court of High Commission. King Charles reluctantly accepted these measures. But understanding and peace were not achieved, and an uprising in Ireland precipitated civil war.

Ever since Henry II had conquered Ireland in 1171, English governors had mercilessly ruled the land, and English landlords had ruthlessly exploited the Irish people. The English Reformation had made a bad situation worse: because the Irish remained Catholic, religious differences united with economic and political oppression. Without an army, Charles I could neither come to terms with the Scots nor put down the Irish rebellion, and the Long Parliament remained unwilling to place an army under a king it did not trust. Charles thus recruited an army drawn from the nobility and the nobility's cavalry staff, the rural gentry, and mercenaries. The parliamentary army that rose in opposition was composed of the militia of the city of London, country squires with business connections, and men with a firm belief that serving was their spiritual duty.

The English civil war (1642–1649) tested whether ultimate political power in England was to

✤ **Periodical Sheet on the English Civil War** Single sheets or broadsides spread the positions of the opposing sides to the nonliterate public. *Mercurius Rusticus,* intended for country people, conveyed the royalist argument. *(Source: The British Library)*

reside in the king or in Parliament. The civil war did not resolve that problem, although it ended in 1649 with the execution of King Charles on the charge of high treason and thus dealt a severe blow to the theory of divine-right, absolute monarchy in England. Kingship was abolished in England, and a *commonwealth,* or republican form of government, was proclaimed.

In fact, the army that had defeated the royal forces controlled the government, and Oliver Cromwell controlled the army. Indeed, the period from 1649 to 1660, known as the Interregnum because it separated two monarchial periods, was a transitional time of military dictatorship, and for most of that time Cromwell was head of state.

Oliver Cromwell (1599–1658) came from the country gentry, the class that dominated the House of Commons in the early seventeenth century. He was a member of the Long Parliament. Cromwell rose in the parliamentary army and achieved nationwide fame by infusing the army with his Puritan convictions and molding it into the highly effective military machine, called the New Model Army, that defeated the royalist forces. The army prepared a constitution, the Instrument of Government (1653), that invested executive power in a lord protector (Cromwell) and a council of state. The instrument provided for triennial parliaments and gave Parliament the sole power to raise taxes. But after repeated disputes, Cromwell tore up the document and proclaimed quasi-martial law.

On the issue of religion, Cromwell favored broad toleration, and the Instrument of Government gave all Christians, except Roman Catholics, the right to practice their faith. Cromwell welcomed the immigration of Jews, because of their skills, and they began to return to England after four centuries of absence. As for Irish Catholicism, Cromwell identified it with sedition. In 1649 he crushed rebellion in Ireland with merciless savagery, leaving a legacy of Irish hatred for England. He also rigorously censored the press, forbade sports, and kept the theaters closed in England.

Cromwell pursued mercantilist economic policies similar to those that Colbert established in France. He enforced a navigation act requiring that English goods be transported on English ships. The navigation act was a great boost to the development of an English merchant marine and brought about a short but successful war with the commercially threatened Dutch.

Military government collapsed when Cromwell died in 1658. Fed up with military rule, the English longed for a return to civilian government, restoration of the common law, and social and religious stability. Moreover, the strain of creating a community of puritanical saints proved too psychologically exhausting. Government by military dictatorship was an experiment in absolutism that the English never forgot or repeated. By 1660 they were ready to try a restoration of monarchy.

The Restoration of the English Monarchy

The Restoration of 1660 re-established the monarchy in the person of Charles II (r. 1660–1685), eldest son of Charles I. At the same time both houses of Parliament were also restored, together with the established Anglican church. The Restoration failed to resolve two serious problems. What was to be the attitude of the state toward Puritans, Catholics, and dissenters from the established church? And what was to be the constitutional relationship between the king and Parliament?

Charles II, a relaxed, easygoing, and sensual man, was basically not much interested in religious issues. But the new members of Parliament were, and they proceeded to enact a body of laws that sought to compel religious uniformity. Those who refused to receive the sacrament of the Church of England could not vote, hold public office, preach, teach, attend the universities, or even assemble for meetings, according to the Test Act of 1673.

In politics, Charles II was at first determined to get along with Parliament and share power with it. His method for doing so had profound importance for later constitutional development. The king appointed a council of five men who served both as his major advisers and as members of Parliament, thus acting as liaison agents between the executive and the legislature. It gradually came to be accepted that the council of five was answerable in Parliament for the decisions of the king.

Harmony between the Crown and Parliament rested on the understanding that Charles would summon Parliament frequently and Parliament would vote him sufficient revenues. However, although Parliament believed that Charles should have large powers, it did not grant him an adequate income. Accordingly, in 1670 Charles entered into a secret agreement with Louis XIV. The French king would give Charles £200,000 annually. In return Charles would relax the laws against

Catholics, gradually re-Catholicize England, support French policy against the Dutch, and convert to Catholicism himself.

When the details of this secret treaty leaked out, a wave of anti-Catholic fear swept England. Charles had produced only bastards, and therefore it appeared that his brother and heir, James, duke of York, who had publicly acknowledged his Catholicism, would inaugurate a Catholic dynasty. The combination of hatred for the French absolutism embodied in Louis XIV and hostility to Roman Catholicism led the Commons to pass an exclusion bill denying the succession to a Roman Catholic. But Charles quickly dissolved Parliament, and the bill never became law.

James II (r. 1685–1688) succeeded his brother. Almost at once the worst English anti-Catholic fears, already aroused by Louis XIV's recent revocation of the Edict of Nantes, were realized. In direct violation of the Test Act, James appointed Roman Catholics to positions in the army, the universities, and local government. The king was suspending the law at will and appeared to be reviving the absolutism of his father (Charles I) and grandfather (James I). He went further. Attempting to broaden his base of support with Protestant dissenters and nonconformists, James issued a declaration of indulgence granting religious freedom to all.

Two events gave the signals for revolution. First, seven bishops of the Church of England petitioned the king that they not be forced to read the declaration of indulgence because of their belief that it was an illegal act. They were imprisoned in the Tower of London but subsequently acquitted amid great public enthusiasm. Second, in June 1688 James's second wife produced a male heir. A Catholic dynasty seemed assured. The fear of a Roman Catholic monarchy, supported by France and ruling outside the law, prompted a group of eminent persons to offer the English throne to James's Protestant daughter, Mary, and her Dutch husband, Prince William of Orange. In December 1688 James II, his queen, and their infant son fled to France and became pensioners of Louis XIV. Early in 1689, William and Mary were crowned king and queen of England.

The English call the events of 1688 to 1689 the "Glorious Revolution." The revolution was indeed glorious in the sense that it replaced one king with another with a minimum of bloodshed. It also represented the destruction, once and for all, of the idea of divine-right absolutism in England. William and Mary accepted the English throne from Parliament and in so doing explicitly recognized the supremacy of Parliament.

The men who brought about the revolution quickly framed their intentions in the Bill of Rights, the cornerstone of the modern British constitution. The basic principles of the Bill of Rights were formulated in direct response to Stuart absolutism. Law was to be made in Parliament; once made, it could not be suspended by the Crown. Parliament had to be called at least every three years. Both elections to and debate in Parliament were to be free, in the sense that the Crown was not to interfere in them. Judges would hold their offices "during good behavior," a provision that assured judicial independence.

In striking contrast to the states of continental Europe, there was to be no standing army that could be used against the English population in peacetime. Moreover, the Bill of Rights granted Protestants the right to possess firearms. Additional legislation granted freedom of worship to Protestant dissenters and nonconformists and required that the English monarch always be Protestant.

The Glorious Revolution found its best defense in John Locke's *Second Treatise of Civil Government* (1690). The political philosopher Locke (1632–1704) maintained that people set up civil governments in order to protect life, liberty, and property. A government that oversteps its proper function—protecting the natural rights of life, liberty, and property—becomes a tyranny. (By "natural" rights, Locke meant rights basic to all men because all have the ability to reason.) Under a tyrannical government, the people have the natural right to rebellion. Recognizing the close relationship between economic and political freedom, Locke linked economic liberty and private property with political freedom.

Locke served as the great spokesman for the liberal English revolution of 1688 to 1689 and for representative government. His idea, inherited from ancient Greece and Rome, that there are natural or universal rights equally valid for all peoples and societies, played a powerful role in eighteenth-century Enlightenment thought. His ideas on liberty and tyranny were especially popular in colonial America.

The events of 1688 to 1689 did not constitute a *democratic* revolution. The revolution formalized Parliament's great power, and Parliament represented the upper classes. The great majority of English people had little say in their government. The English revolution established a constitutional monarchy; it also inaugurated an age of aristocratic government.

In the course of the eighteenth century, the cabinet system of government evolved out of Charles II's old council-of-five system. The term *cabinet* derives from the small private room in which English rulers consulted their chief ministers. In a cabinet system, the leading ministers formulate common policy and conduct the business of the country. During the administration of one royal minister, Sir Robert Walpole, who led the cabinet from 1721 to 1742, the idea developed that the cabinet was responsible to the House of Commons. Walpole enjoyed the favor of the monarchy and of the House of Commons and came to be called the king's first, or "prime," minister. In the English cabinet system, both legislative and executive power are held by the leading ministers, who form the government.

The Dutch Republic in the Seventeenth Century

In the late sixteenth century, the seven northern provinces of the Netherlands, of which Holland and Zeeland were the most prosperous, had thrown off Spanish domination (see pages 534–539). The seventeenth century then witnessed an unparalleled flowering of Dutch scientific, artistic, and literary achievement. In this period, often called the golden age of the Netherlands, Dutch ideas and attitudes played a profound role in shaping a new and modern world-view.

The Republic of the United Provinces of the Netherlands represents a variation in the development of the modern constitutional state. Within each province an oligarchy of wealthy merchants called regents handled domestic affairs in the local Estates. The provincial Estates held virtually all the power. A federal assembly, or States General, handled matters of foreign affairs, such as war, but all issues had to be referred back to the local Estates for approval. The regents in each province jealously guarded local independence and resisted efforts at centralization. Nevertheless, Holland, which had the largest navy and the most wealth, dominated the republic and the States General.

The government of the United Provinces conforms to none of the standard categories of seventeenth-century political organization. The Dutch were not monarchial but fiercely republican. The government was controlled by wealthy merchants and financiers. Though rich, their values were not aristocratic but strongly middle class. The political success of the Dutch rested on the phenomenal commercial prosperity of the Netherlands. The moral and ethical bases of that commercial wealth were thrift, hard work, and simplicity in living.

John Calvin had written, "From where do the merchant's profits come except from his own diligence and industry." This attitude undoubtedly encouraged a sturdy people who had waged a centuries-old struggle against the sea. Louis XIV's hatred of the Dutch was proverbial. They represented all that he despised—middle-class values, religious toleration, and independent political institutions.

Alone of all European peoples in the seventeenth century, the Dutch practiced religious toleration. Peoples of all faiths were welcome within their borders. Jews enjoyed a level of acceptance and absorption in Dutch business and general culture unique in early modern Europe. It is a testimony to the urbanity of Dutch society that in a century when patriotism was closely identified with religious uniformity, the Calvinist province of Holland allowed its highest official, Jan van Oldenbarneveldt, to continue to practice his Roman Catholic faith. As long as business people conducted their religion in private, the government did not interfere with them.

Toleration paid off. It attracted a great amount of foreign capital and business expertise. The Bank of Amsterdam became Europe's best source of cheap credit and commercial intelligence and the main clearing-house for bills of exchange. People of all races and creeds traded in Amsterdam, at whose docks on the Amstel River five thousand ships were berthed. Joost van den Vondel, the poet of Dutch imperialism, exulted:

Rembrandt: The Jewish Bride   Holland's greatest painter, Rembrandt (1606–1669) combined an expressive mastery of technique, emotional depth, psychological penetration, and enormous range—religious scenes, still lifes, portraits. The so-called Jewish Bride (ca 1665), perhaps a wedding portrait of two wealthy people, reveals the artist's unsurpassed handling of light, so characteristic of his later work. *(Source: Rijksmuseum-Stichting)*

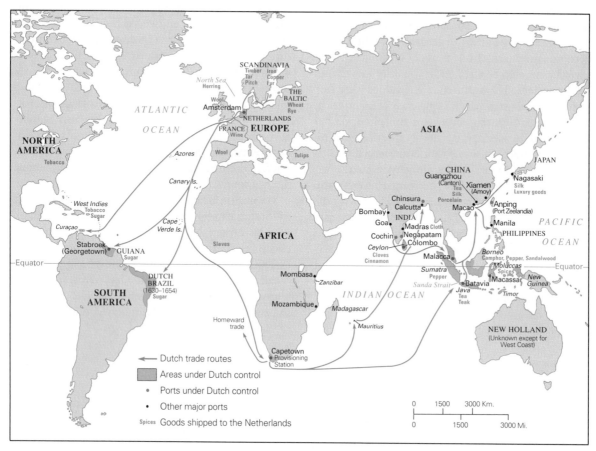

MAP 17.5 Seventeenth-Century Dutch Commerce Dutch wealth rested on commerce, and commerce depended on the huge Dutch merchant marine, manned by perhaps forty-eight thousand sailors. The fleet carried goods from all parts of the globe to the port of Amsterdam.

God, God, the Lord of Amstel cried, hold every
*   conscience free;*
And Liberty ride, on Holland's tide, with billowing
*   sails to sea,*
And run our Amstel out and in; let freedom gird the
*   bold,*
And merchant in his counting house stand elbow deep
*   in gold.*[11]

The fishing industry was a cornerstone of the Dutch economy. For half of the year, from June to December, fishing fleets combed the dangerous English coast and the North Sea, raking in tiny herring. Profits from herring stimulated shipbuilding, and even before 1600 the Dutch were offering the lowest shipping rates in Europe. In 1650 the Dutch merchant marine was the largest in Europe,

comprising roughly half of the European total. All the wood for these ships had to be imported: the Dutch bought whole forests from Norway. They controlled the Baltic grain trade, buying entire wheat and rye crops in Poland, east Prussia, and Swedish Pomerania. Foreign merchants coming to Amsterdam could buy anything from precision lenses for the newly invented microscope to muskets for an army of five thousand.

In 1602 a group of the regents of Holland formed the Dutch East India Company, a joint stock company. Each investor received a percentage of the profits proportional to the amount of money he had put in. Within a half-century, the Dutch East India Company had cut heavily into Portuguese trading in East Asia. The Dutch seized the Cape of Good Hope, Ceylon, and Malacca and established trading posts in each place. In the 1630s the Dutch East India Company was paying its investors about a 35 percent annual return on their investments. The Dutch West India Company, founded in 1621, traded extensively with Latin America and Africa (Map 17.5).

Trade and commerce brought the Dutch prodigious wealth. In the seventeenth century, the Dutch enjoyed the highest standard of living in Europe, perhaps in the world. Amsterdam and Rotterdam built massive granaries where the surplus of one year could be stored against possible shortages the next. Thus food prices fluctuated very little, except during the 1650s when several bad harvests reduced supplies. By the standards of Cologne, Paris, or London, salaries were high for all workers, except women. All classes of society, including unskilled laborers, ate well. The low price of bread meant that, compared with other places in Europe, a higher percentage of a worker's income could be spent on fish, cheese, butter, vegetables, even meat. A scholar recently described the Netherlands as "an island of plenty in a sea of want."[12]

Dutch economic leadership was eventually sapped by wars, beginning with those with France and England in the 1670s. The long War of the Spanish Succession, in which the Dutch supported England against France, was a costly drain on Dutch manpower and financial resources. The peace signed in 1713 to end that war marked the beginning of Dutch economic decline.

SUMMARY

War, religious strife, economic depression, and peasant revolts were all aspects of a deep crisis in seventeenth-century Europe. Rulers responded by aggressively seeking to expand their power, which they claimed was essential to meet emergencies and quell disorders. Claiming also that they ruled by divine right, monarchs sought the freedom to wage war, levy taxes, and generally make law as they saw fit. Although they were limited by technology and inadequate financial resources, monarchial governments on the European continent succeeded to a large extent, overpowering organized opposition and curbing the power of the nobility and the traditional representative institutions.

The France of Louis XIV led the way to royal absolutism. France developed a centralized bureaucracy, a professional army, a state-directed economy, all of which Louis personally supervised. The king saw himself as the representative of God on earth and accountable to no one here below. His majestic bearing and sumptuous court dazzled contemporaries. Yet behind the grand façade of unchallenged personal rule and obedient bureaucrats working his will there stood major limitations on Louis XIV's power. Most notable were the financial independence of some provinces and the nobility's traditional freedom from taxation, which Louis himself was compelled to reaffirm.

Within a framework of resurgent serfdom and entrenched nobility, Austrian and Prussian monarchs also fashioned absolutist states in the seventeenth and early eighteenth centuries. These monarchs won absolutist control over standing armies, permanent taxes, and legislative bodies. But they did not question the underlying social and economic relationships. Indeed, they enhanced the privileges of the nobility, which furnished the leading servitors for enlarged armies and growing government bureaucracies.

In Russia, social and economic trends were similar to those in Austria and Prussia. Unlike those two states, however, Russia had a long history of powerful princes. Tsar Peter the Great succeeded in tightening up Russia's traditional absolutism and modernizing it by reforming the army, the bureaucracy, and the defense industry. In Russia and throughout eastern Europe, war and the needs of the state in time of war weighed heavily in the triumph of absolutism.

Triumphant absolutism interacted spectacularly with the arts. It molded the ideals of French classicism, which glorified the state as personified by Louis XIV. Baroque art, which had grown out of the Catholic Reformation's desire to move the faithful and exalt the faith, admirably suited the secular aspirations of eastern European rulers. Thus baroque art attained magnificent heights in eastern Europe, symbolizing the ideal and harmonizing with the reality of imperious royal absolutism.

Holland and England defied the general trend toward absolute monarchy. While Holland prospered under a unique republican confederation that placed most power in the hands of the different provinces, England—fortunately shielded from continental armies and military emergencies by its navy and the English Channel—evolved into the first modern constitutional state. The bitter conflicts between Parliament and the first two Stuart rulers, James I and Charles I, tested where supreme power would rest in the state. The resulting civil war deposed the king, but it did not settle the question. A revival of absolutist tendencies under James II brought on the Glorious Revolution of 1688, and the people who made that revolution settled three basic issues. Power was divided between king and Parliament, with Parliament enjoying the greater share. Government was to be based on the rule of law. And the liberties of English people were to be made explicit in written form, in the Bill of Rights. This constitutional settlement marked an important milestone in world history, although the framers left to later generations the task of making constitutional government work.

NOTES

1. J. B. Collins, *Fiscal Limits of Absolutism: Direct Taxation in Early Seventeenth Century France* (Berkeley: University of California Press, 1988), pp. 1, 3–4, 215–222.
2. Quoted in J. H. Elliot, *Richelieu and Olivares* (Cambridge: Cambridge University Press, 1984), p. 135; and in W. F. Church, *Richelieu and Reason of State* (Princeton, N.J.: Princeton University Press, 1972), p. 507.
3. S. de Gramont, ed., *The Age of Magnificence: Memoirs of the Court of Louis XIV by the Duc de Saint Simon* (New York: Capricorn Books, 1964), pp. 141–145.
4. See W. Beik, *Absolutism and Society in Seventeenth Century France: State Power and Provincial Aristocracy in Languedoc* (Cambridge: Cambridge University Press, 1985), pp. 279–302.
5. W. F. Church, *Louis XIV in Historical Thought: From Voltaire to the Annales School* (New York: Norton, 1976), p. 92.
6. B. Bennassar, *The Spanish Character: Attitudes and Mentalities from the Sixteenth to the Nineteenth Century,* trans. B. Keen (Berkeley: University of California Press, 1979), p. 125.
7. Quoted in R. Ergang, *The Potsdam Fuhrer: Frederick William I, Father of Prussian Militarism* (New York: Octagon Books, 1972), pp. 85, 87.
8. Quoted in R. A. Dorwart, *The Administrative Reforms of Frederick William I of Prussia* (Cambridge, Mass.: Harvard University Press, 1953), p. 226.
9. Quoted in H. Rosenberg, *Bureaucracy, Aristocracy, and Autocracy: The Prussian Experience,* *1660–1815* (Boston: Beacon Press, 1966), p. 38.
10. Quoted in J. Summerson, in *The Eighteenth Century: Europe in the Age of Enlightenment,* ed. A. Cobban (New York: McGraw-Hill, 1969), p. 80.
11. Quoted in D. Maland, *Europe in the Seventeenth Century* (New York: Macmillan, 1967), pp. 198–199.
12. S. Schama, *The Embarrassment of Riches: An Interpretation of Dutch Culture in the Golden Age* (New York: Knopf, 1987), pp. 165–170.

SUGGESTED READING

Students who wish to explore the problems presented in this chapter will find a rich and exciting literature. G. Parker, *Europe in Crisis, 1598–1618* (1980), provides a sound introduction to the social, economic, and religious tensions of the period, as does R. S. Dunn, *The Age of Religious Wars, 1559–1715,* 2d ed. (1979). T. Aston, ed., *Crisis in Europe, 1560–1660* (1967), contains essays by leading historians. P. Anderson, *Lineages of the Absolutist State* (1974), is a stimulating Marxist interpretation of absolutism in western and eastern Europe.

Louis XIV and his age have attracted the attention of many scholars. J. Wolf, *Louis XIV* (1968), remains the best available biography. Two works of W. H. Lewis, *The Splendid Century* (1957) and *The Sunset of the Splendid Century* (1963), make delightful light reading. The advanced student will want to consult the excellent historiographical analysis by W. F. Church mentioned in the Notes, *Louis XIV in Historical Thought.* Perhaps the best works of the Annales school on the period are P. Goubert, *Louis XIV and Twenty Million Frenchmen* (1972), and Goubert's heavily detailed *The Ancien Régime: French Society, 1600–1750,* 2 vols. (1969–1973), which contains invaluable material on the lives and work of ordinary people. R. Bonney, *The King's Debts: Finance and Politics in France, 1589–1661* (1981), and A. Trout, *Jean-Baptiste Colbert* (1978), consider economy and financial conditions. R. Hatton, *Europe in the Age of Louis XIV* (1979), is a splendidly illustrated survey of many aspects of seventeenth-century European culture.

For Spain, M. Defourneaux, *Daily Life in Spain in the Golden Age* (1976), is extremely useful. See also C. R. Phillips, *Ciudad Real, 1500–1750: Growth, Crisis, and Readjustment in the Spanish Economy* (1979), a significant case study. V. L. Tapie, *The Age of Grandeur: Baroque Art and Architecture* (1960), emphasizes the relationship between art and politics with excellent illustrations. Art and architecture are also treated admirably in E. Hempel, *Baroque Art and Architecture in Central Europe* (1965), and G. Hamilton, *The Art and Architecture of Russia* (1954).

The best study on early Prussian history is still F. L. Carsten, *The Origin of Prussia* (1954). Rosenberg, *Bureaucracy, Aristocracy, and Autocracy,* cited in the Notes, is a masterful analysis of the social context of Prussian absolutism. Ergang, *The Potsdam Fuhrer,* also cited in the Notes, is an exciting and critical biography of ramrod Frederick William I. G. Craig, *The Politics of the Prussian Army, 1640–1945* (1964), expertly traces the great influence of the military on the Prussian state over three hundred years. R. J. Evans, *The Making of the Habsburg Empire, 1550–1770* (1979), analyzes the development of absolutism in Austria, as does A. Wandruszka, *The House of Habsburg* (1964). D. McKay and H. Scott, *The Rise of the Great Powers, 1648–1815* (1983), is a good general account. R. Vierhaus, *Germany in the Age of Absolutism* (1988), offers a thorough survey of the different German states.

On eastern European peasants and serfdom, D. Chirot, ed., *The Origins of Backwardness in Eastern Europe: Economics and Politics from the Middle Ages Until the Twentieth Century* (1989), is a wide-ranging introduction. E. Levin, *Sex and Society in the World of the Orthodox Slavs, 900–1700* (1989), carries family history to eastern Europe. J. Blum, *Lord and Peasant in Russia from the Ninth to the Nineteenth Century* (1961), provides a good look at conditions in rural Russia, and P. Avrich, *Russian Rebels, 1600–1800* (1972), treats some of the violent peasant upheavals that those conditions produced. R. Hellie, *Enserfment and Military Change in Muscovy* (1971), is outstanding. In addition to the fine survey by N. V. Riasanovsky, *A History of Russia* (1963), J. Billington, *The Icon and the Axe* (1970), is a stimulating history of early Russian intellectual and cultural developments. B. H. Sumner, *Peter the Great and the Emergence of Russia* (1962), is a good brief introduction, which may be compared with N. V. Riasanovsky, *The Image of Peter the Great in Russian History and Thought* (1985).

English political and social issues of the seventeenth century are considered by M. Ashley, *The House of Stuart: Its Rise and Fall* (1980); C. Hill, *A Century of Revolution* (1961); and K. Wrightson, *English Society, 1580–1680* (1982). Comprehensive treatments of Parliament include C. Russell's *Crisis of Parliaments, 1509–1660* (1971), and *Parliaments and English Politics, 1621–1629* (1979). L. Stone, *The Causes of the English Revolution* (1972), and B. Manning, *The English People and the English Revolution* (1976), are recommended. D. Underdown, *Revel, Riot, and Rebellion* (1985), discusses the extent of popular involvement. For English intellectual currents, see J. O. Appleby, *Economic Thought and Ideology in Seventeenth Century England* (1978). Other recommended works include P. Collinson, *The Religion of Protestants* (1982); R. Thompson, *Women in Stuart England and America* (1974); and A. Fraser, *The Weaker Vessel* (1985). For Cromwell and the Interregnum, A. Fraser, *Cromwell, the Lord Protector* (1973), is valuable. C. Hill, *The World Turned Upside Down* (1972), discusses radical thought during the period. For the Restoration and the Glorious Revolution, see R. Hutton, *Charles II: King of England, Scotland and Ireland* (1989); J. Childs, *The Army, James II, and the Glorious Revolution* (1980); and L. G. Schwoerer, *The Declaration of Rights, 1689* (1981), a fine assessment of that fundamental document. The ideas of John Locke are analyzed by J. P. Kenyon, *Revolution Principles: The Politics of Party, 1689–1720* (1977).

On Holland, K. H. D. Haley, *The Dutch Republic in the Seventeenth Century* (1972), is a splendidly illustrated appreciation of Dutch commercial and artistic achievements, and Schama, *The Embarrassment of Riches,* cited in the Notes, is a lively recent synthesis. R. Boxer, *The Dutch Seaborne Empire* (1980), is useful for Dutch overseas expansion. V. Barbour, *Capitalism in Amsterdam in the Seventeenth Century* (1950), and D. Regin, *Traders, Artists, Burghers: A Cultural History of Amsterdam in the Seventeenth Century* (1977), focus on the leading Dutch city. The leading statesmen of the period may be studied in these biographies: H. H. Rowen, *John de Witt, Grand Pensionary of Holland, 1625–1672* (1978); S. B. Baxter, *William the III and the Defense of European Liberty, 1650–1702* (1966); and J. den Tex, *Oldenbarnevelt,* 2 vols. (1973).

LISTENING TO THE
PAST

A Foreign Traveler in Russia

Russia in the seventeenth century remained a remote and mysterious land for western and even central Europeans, who had few direct contacts with the tsar's dominion. Knowledge of Russia came mainly from occasional travelers who had visited Muscovy and sometimes wrote accounts of what they had seen.

The most famous of these accounts was by the German Adam Olearius (ca 1599–1671), who was send to Moscow by the duke of Holstein on three diplomatic missions in the 1630s. These missions ultimately proved unsuccessful, but they provided Olearius with a rich store of information for his Travels in Moscovy, *from which the following excerpts are taken. Published in German in 1647 and soon translated into several languages (but not Russian), Olearius's unflattering but well-informed study played a major role in shaping European ideas about Russia.*

The government of the Russians is what political theorists call a "dominating and despotic monarchy," where the sovereign, that is, the tsar or the grand prince who has obtained the crown by right of succession, rules the entire land alone, and all the people are his subjects, and where the nobles and princes no less than the common folk—townspeople and peasants—are his serfs and slaves, whom he rules and treats as a master treats his servants. . . .

If the Russians be considered in respect to their character, customs, and way of life, they are justly to be counted among the barbarians. . . . The vice of drunkenness is so common in this nation, among people of every station, clergy and laity, high and low, men and women, old and young, that when they are seen now and then lying about in the streets, wallowing in the mud, no attention is paid to it, as something habitual. If a cart driver comes upon such a drunken pig whom he happens to know, he shoves him onto his cart and drives him home, where he is paid his fare. No one ever refuses an opportunity to drink and to get drunk, at any time and in any place, and usually it is done with vodka. . . .

The Russians being naturally tough and born, as it were, for slavery, they must be kept under a harsh and strict yoke and must be driven to do their work with clubs and whips, which they suffer without impatience, because such is their station, and they are accustomed to it. Young and half-grown fellows sometimes come together on certain days and train themselves in fisticuffs, to accustom themselves to receiving blows, and, since habit is second nature, this makes blows given as punishment easier to bear. Each and all, they are slaves and serfs. . . .

Because of slavery and their rough and hard life, the Russians accept war readily and are well suited to it. On certain occasions, if need be, they reveal themselves as courageous and daring soldiers. . . .

Although the Russians, especially the common populace, living as slaves under a harsh yoke, can bear and endure a great deal out of love for their masters, yet if the pressure is beyond measure, then it can be said of them: "Patience, often wounded, finally turned into fury." A dangerous indignation results, turned not so much against their sovereign as against the lower authorities, especially if the people have been much oppressed by them and by their supporters and have not been protected by the higher authorities. And once they are aroused and enraged, it is not easy to appease them. Then, disregarding all dangers that may ensue, they resort to every kind of violence and behave like madmen. . . . They own little; most of them have no feather beds; they lie on cushions, straw, mats, or their clothes; they sleep on benches and, in winter, like the non-Germans [i.e., natives] in Livonia, upon the oven, which serves them for cooking and is flat on the top; here husband, wife, children, servants, and maids huddle together. In some houses in the countryside we saw chickens and pigs under the benches and the ovens. . . .

Russians are not used to delicate food and dainties; their daily food consists of porridge, turnips, cabbage, and cucumbers, fresh and pickled, and in Moscow mostly of big salt fish which stink badly, because of the thrifty use of salt, yet are eaten with relish. . . .

The Russians can endure extreme heat. In the bathhouse they stretch out on benches and let themselves be beaten and rubbed with bunches of birch twigs and wisps of bast (which I could not stand); and when they are hot and red all over and so exhausted that they can bear it no longer in the bathhouse, men and women rush outdoors naked and pour cold water over their bodies; in winter they even wallow in the snow and rub their skin with it as if it were soap; then they go back into the hot bathhouse. And since bathhouses are usually near rivers and brooks, they can throw themselves straight from the hot into the cold bath. . . .

Generally noble families, even the small nobility, rear their daughters in secluded chambers, keeping them hidden from outsiders; and a bridegroom is not allowed to have a look at his bride until he receives her in the bridal chamber. Therefore some happen to be deceived, being given a misshapen and sickly one instead of a fair one, and sometimes a kinswoman or even a maidservant instead of a daughter; of which there have been examples even among the highborn. No wonder therefore that often they live together like cats and dogs and that wife-beating is so common among Russians. . . .

In the Kremlin and in the city there are a great many churches, chapels, and monasteries, both within and without the city walls, over two thousand in all. This is so because every nobleman who has some fortune has a chapel built for himself, and most of them are of stone. The stone churches are round and vaulted inside. . . . They allow neither organs nor any other musical instruments in their churches, saying: Instruments that have neither souls nor life cannot praise God. . . .

In their churches there hang many bells, sometimes five or six, the largest not over two hundredweights. They ring these bells to

V. Vasnetsou (1848–1926), Red Square in the late seventeenth century. (*Source: Sovfoto/Eastfoto*)

summon people to church, and also when the priest during mass raises the chalice. In Moscow, because of the multitude of churches and chapels, there are several thousand bells, which during the divine service create such a clang and din that one unaccustomed to it listens in amazement.

Questions for Analysis

1. In what ways were all social groups in Russia similar, according to Olearius?

2. How did Olearius characterize the Russians in general? What supporting evidence did he offer for his judgment?

3. Did Olearius find any positive or admirable traits in the Russian people? What were they?

4. On the basis of these representative passages, why do you think Olearius's book was so popular and influential in central and western Europe?

Source: G. Vernadsky and R. T. Fisher Jr., eds., *A Source Book for Russian History*. Copyright © 1972 by Yale University Press. Reprinted by permission.

A History of World Societies: A Brief Overview

Period (CA 10,000–CA 400 B.C.)	Africa and the Middle East	The Americas
10,000 B.C.	New Stone Age culture, ca 10,000–3500	Migration into Americas begins, ca 11,000
5000 B.C.	"Agricultural revolution" originates in Tigris-Euphrates and Nile River Valleys, ca 6000 First writing in Sumeria; Sumerian city-states emerge, ca 3500 Egypt unified under Narmer, 3100–2660 Metalworking in Caucasus, 3000	Maize domesticated in Mexico, ca 5000
2500 B.C.	Old Kingdom in Egypt; construction of the pyramids, 2660–2180 Akkadian Empire, 2370–2150 Middle Kingdom in Egypt, 2080–1640 Hyksos "invade" Egypt, 1640–1570 Hammurabi, 1792–1750 Hebrew monotheism, ca 1700	First pottery in Americas, Ecuador, ca 3000 First metalworking in Peru, ca 2000
1500 B.C.	Hittite Empire, ca 1450–1200 Akhenaten institutes worship of Aton, ca 1360 New Kingdom in Egypt; creation of Egyptian Empire, ca 1570–1075 Moses leads Hebrews out of Egypt, ca 1300–1200	Olmec civilization, Mexico, ca 1500 B.C.–A.D. 300
1000 B.C.	Political fragmentation of Egypt; rise of small kingdoms, ca 1100–700 United Hebrew kingdom, 1020–922: Saul, David, Solomon Ironworking spreads throughout Africa, ca 1000 B.C.–A.D. 300 Divided Hebrew kingdom: Israel (922–721), Judah (922–586) Assyrian Empire, 745–612 Zoroaster, ca 600	Olmec center at San Lorenzo destroyed, ca 900; power passes to La Venta in Tabasco Chavin civilization in Andes, ca 1000–200 B.C.
500 B.C.	Babylonian captivity of the Hebrews, 586–539 Cyrus the Great founds Persian Empire, 550 Persians conquer Egypt, 525 Darius and Xerxes complete Persian conquest of Middle East, 521–464	Olmec civilization, ca 1500 B.C.–A.D. 300 Fall of La Venta; Tres Zapotes becomes leading Olmec site
400 B.C.	Spartan Hegemony in Greece 399–371 B.C. Theban Hegemony in Greece 371–362 B.C. Philip of Macedon's Conquest of Greece, 338 B.C.	

East Asia	India and Southeast Asia	Europe
"Agricultural revolution" originates in Yellow River Valley, ca 4000		
Horse domesticated in China, ca 2500	Indus River Valley civilization, ca 2500–1500; capitals at Mohenjo-daro and Harappa	Greek Bronze Age, 2000–1100 Arrival of Greeks in peninsular Greece
Shang Dynasty, first writing in China, ca 1523–ca 1027	Aryans arrive in India; Early Vedic Age, ca 1500–1000 Vedas, oldest Hindu sacred texts	Height of Minoan culture, 1700–1450 Mycenaeans conquer Minoan Crete, ca 1450 Mycenaean Age, 1450–1200
Zhou Dynasty, promulgation of the Mandate of Heaven, ca 1027–221	Later Vedic Age; solidification of caste system, ca 1000–500 Upanishads; foundation of Hinduism, 800–600	Trojan War, ca 1180 Fall of the Mycenaean kingdom, 1100 Greek Dark Age, ca 1100–800 Roman Republic founded, 509 Origin of Greek polis, ca 700 Greek Lyric Age; rise of Sparta and Athens, 800–500
Confucius, 551–479 First written reference to iron, ca 521	Siddhartha Gautama (Buddha), 563–483	Persian Wars, 499–479 Growth of Athenian Empire; flowering of Greek drama, philosophy, and history, 5th century Peloponnesian War, 431–404 Plato, 426–347

Period (CA 300 B.C.–AD 500)	Africa and the Middle East	The Americas
300 B.C.	Alexander the Great extends empire, 334–331 Death of Alexander (323): Ptolemy conquers Egypt, Seleucus rules Asia	
200 B.C.	Scipio Africanus defeats Hannibal at Zama, 202	
100 B.C.	Dead Sea Scrolls Pompey conquers Syria and Palestine, 63	
A.D 100	Jesus Christ, ca 4 B.C.–A.D. 30 Paul, d. ca 65 Bantu migrations begin Jews revolt from Rome, Romans destroy Hebrew temple in Jerusalem: end of the ancient Hebrew state, 70	
A.D 200	Camel first used for trans-Saharan transport, ca 200 Expansion of Bantu peoples, ca 200–900 Axum (Ethiopia) controls Red Sea trade, ca 250	Classic Age of the Maya, ca 300–900 Olmec civilization, ca 1500 B.C.–A.D. 300
A.D 300	Axum accepts Christianity, ca 4th century	Maya civilization in Central America, ca 300–1500 Classic period of Teotihuacán civilization in Mexico, ca 300–900
A.D 500	Political and commercial ascendancy of Axum, ca 6th–7th centuries Muhammad, 570–632; the *hijra,* 622 Extensive slave trade from sub-Saharan Africa to Mediterranean, ca 600–1500 Umayyad Dynasty, 661–750, with capital at Damascus; continued expansion of Islam	Tiahuanaco civilization in South America, ca 600–1000

East Asia	India and Southeast Asia	Europe
Lao-tzu and development of Taoism, 4th century Han Fei-tzu and Li Ssu and development of Legalism, ca 250–208	Alexander invades India, 327–326 Chandragupta founds Mauryan Dynasty, 322–ca 185 Ashoka, 273–232 King Arsaces of Parthia defeats Seleucid monarchy and begins conquest of Persia, ca 250–137	Peloponnesian War, 431–404 Plato, 426–347 Gauls sack Rome, ca 390 Roman expansion, 390–146 Sparton Hegemony in Greece, 399–371 B.C. Theban Hegemony in Greece, 371–362 B.C. Philip of Macedon's Conquest of Greece, 338 B.C. Conquests of Alexander the Great, 334–323 Punic Wars, destruction of Carthage, 264–146
Qin Dynasty and unification of China; construction of the Great Wall, destruction of Confucian literature, 221–210 Han Dynasty, 202 B.C.–A.D. 220	Greeks invade India, ca 183–145 Mithridates creates Parthian Empire, ca 171–131	Late Roman Republic, 133–27
Chinese expansion to South China Sea and Vietnam, ca 111 Silk Road opens to Parthian and Roman Empires; Buddhism enters China, ca 104	First Chinese ambassadors to India and Parthia, ca 140 Bhagavad Gita, ca 100 B.C.–A.D. 100	Formation of First Triumvirate (Caesar, Crassus, Pompey), 60 Julius Caesar killed, 44 Formation of Second Triumvirate, (Octavian, Antony, Lepidus), 43 Octavian seizes power, 31
First written reference (Chinese) to Japan, A.D. 45 Chinese invent paper, 105 Emperor Wu, 140–186	Shakas and Kushans invade eastern Parthia and India, 1st century A.D. Roman attacks on Parthian Empire, 115–211	Octavian rules imperial Rome as Augustus, 27 B.C.–A.D. 14 Roman Empire at greatest extent, 117
Creation of Yamato state in Japan, ca 3d century Buddhism gains popularity in China and Japan, ca 220–590 Fall of Han Dynasty, 220 Three Kingdoms era in China, 221–280	Kushan rule in northwestern India, A.D. 2d–3d centuries Fall of the Parthian Empire, rise of the Sassanids, ca 225	Breakdown of the pax Romana, ca 180–284; civil wars, economic decline, invasions Reforms by Diocletian, 284–305
Barbarian invasions, 4th–5th centuries	Chandragupta I founds Gupta Dynasty in India, ca 320–500 Chandragupta II conquers western India, establishes trade with Middle East and China, ca 400 Huns invade India, ca 450	Reign of Constantine, 306–337; Edict of Milan, 313; founding of Constantinople, 324; Council of Nicaea, 325 Theodosius recognizes Christianity as official state religion, 380 Germanic raids of western Europe, 5th century Clovis unites Franks and rules Gauls, 481–511
Sui Dynasty in China, 580–618; restoration of public order "Constitution" of Shotoku in Japan, 604 Tang Dynasty, 618–907; cultural flowering	Sanskrit drama, ca 600–1000 Muslim invasions of India, ca 636–1206	Saint Benedict publishes his *Rule*, 529 Law Code of Justinian, 529 Synod of Whitby, 664

Period (CA 700–1500)	Africa and the Middle East	The Americas
700	Abbasid Dynasty, 750–1258; Islamic capital moved to Baghdad Decline of Ethiopia, ca 9th century Golden age of Muslim learning, ca 900–1100 Kingdom of Ghana, ca 900–1100 Mahmud of Ghazna, 998–1030	"Time of Troubles" in Mesoamerica, 800–1000
1000	Islam penetrates sub-Saharan Africa, ca 11th century Kingdom of Benin, ca 1100–1897 Kingdom of Mali, middle Niger region, ca 1200–1450 Mongol invasion of Middle East, ca 1220	Inca civilization in South America, ca 1000–1500 Toltec hegemony, ca 1000–1300 Aztecs arrive in Valley of Mexica, ca 1325
1200	Kingdom of Mali, ca 1200–1450 Mongols conquer Baghdad, 1258; fall of Abbasid Dynasty	Maya civilization in Central America, ca 300–1500 Inca civilization in South America, ca 1000–1500 Toltec hegemony, ca 1000–1300
1300	Rise of Yoruba states, West Africa, ca 1300 Height of Swahili (East African) city-states, ca 1300–1500 Mansa Musa rules Mali, 1312–1337	Tenochtitlán (Mexico City) founded by Aztecs, 1325
1400	Zara Yakob rules Ethiopia, 1434–1468 Arrival of Portugese in Benin, ca 1440 Songhay Empire, West Africa, ca 1450–1591 Atlantic slave trade, ca 1450–1850 Ottoman Empire, 1453–1918 Vasco da Gama arrives on East African coast, 1498	Height of Inca Empire, 1438–1493 Reign of Montezuma I, 1440–1468; height of Aztec culture Columbus reaches the Americas, 1492
1500	Portugal dominates East Africa, ca 1500–1650 Safavid Empire in Persia, 1501–1722 Peak of Ottoman power under Suleiman the Magnificent, 1520–1566 Height of Kanem-Bornu under Idris Alooma, 1571–1603 Portuguese found Angola, 1571 Battle of Lepanto, 1571, signals Ottoman naval weakness in the eastern Mediterranean Height of Safavid power under Shah Abbas, 1587–1629	South American holocaust, ca 1500–1600 First African slaves, ca 1510 Cortés arrives in Mexico, 1519; Aztec Empire falls, 1521 Pizarro reaches Peru, 1531; conquers Incas Spanish conquer the Philippines, 1571

East Asia	India and Southeast Asia	Europe
Taika Reform Edict in Japan, 655 Nara era, creation of Japan's first capital, 710–784 Heian era in Japan, 794–1185; literary flowering Era of the Five Dynasties in China, 907–960; warfare, revolt Song Dynasty, 960–1279	Khmer Empire (Kampuchea) founded, 802	Charles Martel defeats Muslims at Tours, 733 Charles the Great (Charlemagne), 768–814 Invasions of Carolingian Empire, 9th–10th centuries Treaty of Verdun divides Carolingian Empire, 843 Cluny monastery founded, 910
Vietnam gains independence from China, ca 1000 China divided between empires of Song (south) and Jin (north), 1127 Kamakura Shogunate, 1185–1333 Mongol conquest of China, 1215–1368	Construction of Angkor Wat, ca 1100–1150 Muslim conquerors end Buddhism in India, 1192 Peak of Khmer Empire in southeast Asia, ca 1200 Turkish sultanate at Delhi, 1206–1526; Indian culture divided into Hindu and Muslim	Yaroslav the Wise, 1019–1054; peak of Kievan Russia Schism between Latin and Greek churches, 1054 Norman Conquest of England, 1066 Investiture struggle, 1073–1122 The Crusades, 1096–1270 Growth of trade and towns, 12th–13th centuries Frederick Barbarossa invades Italy, 1154–1158
Kamakura Shogunate, 1185–1333 Unsuccessful Mongol invasions of Japan, 1274, 1281 Yuan (Mongol) Dynasty, 1279–1368	Peak of Khmer Empire in southeast Asia, ca 1200 Turkish sultanate at Delhi, 1206–1526; Indian culture divided into Hindu and Muslim	Magna Carta, 1215 Thomas Aquinas, *Summa Theologica*, 1253 Prince Alexander Nevsky recognizes Mongol overlordship of Moscow, 1252
Marco Polo arrives at Kublai Khan's court, ca 1275 Ashikaga Shogunate, 1336–1408 Hung Wu drives Mongols from China, 1368; founds Ming Dynasty, 1368–1644	Mongol chieftain Timur the Lame (Tamerlane) conquers the Punjab, 1398	Babylonian Captivity of the papacy, 1309–1376 Tver revolt in Russia, 1327–1328 Hundred Years' War, 1337–1453 Bubonic plague, 1347–1700 Ottoman Turks invade Europe, 1356 Peasants' Revolt in England, 1381
Early Ming policy encourages foreign trade, ca 15th century Ming maritime expeditions to India, Middle East, Africa, 1405–1433	Sultan Mehmed II, 1451–1481 Pasha Sinon, Ottoman architect, 1491–1588 Vasco da Gama reaches India, 1498	Beginnings of representative government, ca 1350–1500 Italian Renaissance, ca 1400–1530 Voyages of discovery, ca 1450–1600 Ottomans capture Constantinople, 1453; end of Byzantine Empire War of the Roses in England, 1455–1485 Unification of Spain completed, 1492
Portuguese trade monopoly in East Asia, ca 16th century Christian missionaries active in China and Japan, ca 1550–1650 Unification of Japan, 1568–1600	Barbur defeats Delhi sultanate, 1526–1527; founds Mughal Empire Akbar expands Mughal Empire, 1556–1605	Martin Luther, Ninety-five Theses, 1517 Charles V elected Holy Roman emperor, 1519 Henry VIII leads English Reformation, 1534 Council of Trent, 1545–1563 Dutch United Provinces declare independence, 1581 Spanish Armada, 1588

Period (CA 1600–1900)	Africa and the Middle East	The Americas
1600	Dutch West India Co. supplants Portuguese in West Africa, ca 1630 Dutch settle Cape Town, 1651 Rise of Ashanti Empire, founded on Gold Coast trade, ca 1700–1750	British settle Jamestown, 1607 Champlain founds Quebec, 1608 Dutch found New Amsterdam, 1624 Black labor allows tenfold increase in production of Carolinian rice and Virginian tobacco, ca 1730–1760 Silver production quadruples in Mexico and Peru, ca 1700–1800
1700	Approximately 11 million slaves shipped from Africa, ca 1450–1850 Dutch found Cape Colony, 1657 Rise of the Ashanti, West Africa, ca 1700 Decline of the Safavid Empire under Nadir Shah, 1737–1747	Spain's defeat in War of the Spanish Succession, 1701–1714, prompts trade reform, leading to colonial dependence on Spanish goods, 18th century
1750	Sultan Selim III introduces administrative and military reforms, 1761–1808 British seize Cape Town, 1795 Napoleon's campaign in Egypt, 1798	"French and Indian Wars," 1756–1763 Quebec Act, 1774 American Revolution, 1775–1783 Comunero revolution, New Granada, 1781
1800	Muhammad Ali founds dynasty in Egypt, 1805–1848 Slavery abolished in British Empire, 1807 Peak year of African transatlantic slave trade, 1820	Latin American wars of independence from Spain, 1806–1825 Brazil wins independence from Portugal, 1822 Monroe Doctrine, 1823 Political instability in most Latin American countries, 1825–1870 Mexican War, 1846–1848
1850	Crimean War, 1853–1856 Suez Canal opens, 1869 Europeans intensify "scramble for Africa," 1880–1900 Battle of Omdurman, 1898 Boer War, 1899–1902	American Civil War, 1861–1865 British North America Act, 1867, for Canada Porfirio Diaz controls Mexico, 1876–1911 United States practices "dollar diplomacy" in Latin America, 1890–1920s Spanish-American War, 1898; United States gains Philippines
1900	Union of South Africa formed, 1910 French annex Morocco, 1912 Ottoman Empire enters World War One on Germany's side Treaty of Sèvres dissolves Ottoman Empire, 1919; Mustafa Kemal mounts nationalist struggle in Turkey	Massive immigration from Europe and Asia to the Americas, 1880–1914 Mexican Revolution, 1910 Panama Canal opens, 1914 United States enters World War One, 1917 Mexico adopts constitution, 1917

East Asia	India and Southeast Asia	Europe
Tokugawa Shogunate, 1600–1867 Japan expels all Europeans, 1637 Manchus establish Qing Dynasty, 1644 Height of Qing Dynasty under K'ang-hsi, 1662–1722 Height of Edo urban culture in Japan, ca 1700	Height of Mughal Empire under Shah Jahan, 1628–1658 British found Calcutta, 1690 Decline of Mughal Empire, ca 1700–1800 Persian invaders sack Delhi, 1739	Romanov Dynasty in Russia, 1613 Thirty Years' War, 1618–1648 Brandenburg-Prussia unified, 1640–1688 English Civil War, 1642–1646 Louis XIV, king of France, 1643–1715 Ottoman Turks besiege Vienna, 1683 Revocation of Edict of Nantes, 1685 The Glorious Revolution in England, 1688 War of Spanish Succession, 1701–1713 Treaty of Utrecht, 1713
Tokugawa regime in Japan, characterized by political stability and economic growth, 1600–1867 Manchus establish Qing Dynasty, 1644–1911 Height of Qing Dynasty under Emperor Ch'ien-lung, 1736–1799	Mughal power contested by Hindus and Muslims, 18th century Persian invaders defeat Mughal army, loot Delhi, 1739 French and British fight for control of India, 1740–1763	Growth of absolutism in central and eastern Europe, ca 1680–1790 The Enlightenment, ca 1680–1800 Development of Cabinet system in England, 1714–1742 Height of land enclosure in England, ca 1760–1810
Maximum extent of Qing Empire, 1759	Battle of Plassey, 1757 Treaty of Paris, 1763; French colonies to Britain Cook in Australia, 1768–1771; first British prisoners to Australia, 1788 East India Act, 1784	Englishman James Watt produces first steam engine, 1769 Louis XVI of France, 1774–1792 Outbreak of French Revolution, 1789 National Convention declares France a republic, 1792
Java War, 1825–1830 Anglo-Chinese Opium War, 1839–1842 Treaty of Nanjing, 1842: Manchus surrender Hong Kong to British	British found Singapore, 1819 British defeat last independent native state in India, 1848	Napoleonic Empire, 1804–1814 Congress of Vienna, 1814–1815 European economic penetration of non-Western countries, ca 1816–1880 Greece wins independence from Ottoman Empire, 1829 Revolutions in France, Prussia, Italy, and Austria, 1848–1849
Taiping Rebellion, 1850–1864 Perry's arrival opens Japan to United States and Europe, 1853 Meiji Restoration in Japan, 1867 Adoption of constitution in Japan, 1890 Sino-Japanese War, 1894–1895 "Hundred Days of Reform" in China, 1898	Great Rebellion in India, 1857–1858 French seize Saigon, 1859 Indian National Congress formed, 1885 French acquire Indochina, 1893	Second Empire and Third Republic in France, 1852–1914 Unification of Italy, 1859–1870 Otto von Bismarck's reign of power in German affairs, 1862–1890 Franco-Prussian War, 1870–1871; foundation of the German Empire Parliamentary Reform Bill, Great Britain, 1867 Second Socialist International, 1889–1914
Boxer Rebellion in China, 1900–1903 Russo-Japanese War, 1904–1905 Chinese Revolution; fall of Qing Dynasty, 1911 Chinese Republic, 1912–1949	Commonwealth of Australia, 1900 Muslim League formed, 1906 Radicals make first calls for Indian independence, 1907 Amritsar massacre in India, 1919 Intensification of Indian nationalism, 1919–1947	Revolution in Russia; Tsar Nicholas II forced to issue October Manifesto, 1905 Triple Entente (Britain, Russia, France), 1914–1918 World War One, 1914–1918 Treaty of Versailles, 1919

Period (CA 1920–1990)	Africa and the Middle East	The Americas
1920	Cultural nationalism in Africa, 1920s Treaty of Lausanne recognizes Turkish Republic, 1923 Reza Shah leads Iran, 1925–1941	U.S. "consumer revolution," 1920s Stock market crash in United States; Great Depression begins, 1929
1930	African farmers organize first "cocoa holdups," 1930–1931 Iraq gains independence, 1932 Syrian-French friendship treaty, 1936	Revolutions in six South American countries, 1930 New Deal begins in United States, 1933
1940	Civil war between Arabs and Jews in Palestine; state of Israel is created, 1948 Apartheid system in South Africa, 1948–1991 Libya gains independence, 1949	Surprise attack by Japan on Pearl Harbor, 1941 United Nations established, 1945 Perón regime in Argentina, 1946–1953
1950	Egypt declared a republic; Nasser named premier, 1954 Morocco, Tunisia, Sudan, and Ghana gain independence, 1956–1957 French-British Suez invasion, 1956	Fidel Castro takes power in Cuba, 1959
1960	Mali, Nigeria, and the Congo gain independence, 1960 Biafra declares independence from Nigeria, 1967 Arab-Israeli Six-Day War, 1967	Cuban missile crisis, 1962 Military dictatorship in Brazil, 1964–1985 United States escalates war in Vietnam, 1964
1970	"Yom Kippur War," 1973 Islamic revolution in Iran, 1979 Camp David Accords, 1979	Military coup in Chile, 1973 U.S. Watergate scandal, 1974 Revolutions in Nicaragua and El Salvador, 1979
1980	Iran-Iraq War, 1980–1988 Reforms in South Africa, 1989 to present	U.S. military buildup, 1980–1988 Argentina restores civilian rule, 1983
1990	Growth of Islamic fundamentalism, 1990 to present Iraq driven from Kuwait by United States and allies, 1991 Israel and Palestinians sign peace agreement, 1993 Nelson Mandela elected president of South Africa, 1994	Canada, Mexico, and United States form free-trade area (NAFTA), 1994 Haiti establishes democratic government, 1994 Permanent extension of Treaty on the Non-Proliferation of Nuclear Weapons, 1995

East Asia	India and Southeast Asia	Europe
Kita Ikki advocates ultranationalism in Japan, 1923 Jiang Jieshi unites China, 1928	Mohandas "Mahatma" Gandhi launches nonviolent resistance campaign, 1920	Mussolini seizes power in Italy, 1922 Stalin takes power in U.S.S.R., 1927 Depths of Great Depression, 1929–1933
Japan invades China, 1931 Mao Zedong's Long March, 1934 Sino-Japanese War, 1937–1945	Mahatma Gandhi's Salt March, 1930 Japanese conquer empire in southeast Asia, 1939–1942	Hitler gains dictatorial power, 1933 Civil War in Spain, 1936–1939 Germany invades Poland, 1939 World War Two, 1939–1945
United States drops atomic bombs on Hiroshima and Nagasaki, 1945 Chinese civil war, 1945–1949; Communists win	Philippines gain independence, 1946 India (Hindu) and Pakistan (Muslim) gain independence, 1947	Yalta Conference, 1945 Marshall Plan, 1947 NATO alliance, 1949 Soviet Union and Red China sign 30-year alliance treaty, 1949
Korean War, 1950–1953 Japan begins long period of rapid economic growth, 1950 Mao Zedong announces Great Leap Forward, 1958	Vietnamese nationalists defeat French; Vietnam divided, 1954 Islamic Republic of Pakistan declared, 1956	Death of Stalin, 1953 Warsaw Pact, 1955 Revolution in Hungary, 1956 Creation of the Common Market, 1957
Sino-Soviet split becomes apparent, 1960 Great Proletarian Cultural Revolution in China, 1965–1969	Indira Gandhi prime minister of India, 1966–1977, 1980–1984	Student revolution in France, 1968 Soviet invasion of Czechoslovakia, 1968
Communist victory in Vietnam War, 1975 China pursues modernization, 1976 to present	India-Pakistan war, 1971 Chinese invade Vietnam, 1979	German Chancellor Willy Brandt's Ostpolitik, 1969–1973 Soviet invasion of Afghanistan, 1979
Japanese foreign investment surge, 1980–1992 China crushes democracy movement, 1989	Sikh nationalism in India, 1984 to present Corazón Aquino takes power in Philippines, 1986	Soviet reform under Mikhail Gorbachev, 1985–1991 Anticommunist revolutions sweep eastern Europe, 1989
Birthrates keep falling Economic growth and political repression in China, 1990 to present Japan and United States reach auto agreement, 1995	Vietnam embraces foreign investment, 1990 to present U.S. military bases closed in Philippines, 1991	Continued high unemployment, 1990 to present Soviet Union ceases to exist, 1991 Civil war in Bosnia, 1991 to present

Index

Merk, J. C., 573 (illus.)

Meroe, Nubian capital of, 298–299

Merovech, Clovis descent from, 230

Merovingian Dynasty, 230, 345; end of, 346; army of, 347 (illus.)

Mesoamerica, 441; Olmecs in, 443; cultures in, 443–462; "Time of Troubles" in, 447; Teotihuacán and Toltec civilizations in, 447–449; Aztecs in, 449–456. See also Americas; Latin America; New World; South America; Spanish America

Mesopotamia, 9 (map); rivers in, 11; civilization in, 13–18; Sumerian writing in, 15–16, 15 (illus.); thought and religion in, 16–18; spread of culture, 18–23; in Persian Empire, 58; deities of, 72; ancient India and, 81; trade of, 201; Nero and, 203. See also Babylon

Messana, Rome and, 179

Messenia (Greece), 121, 126

Messiah: Jews and, 195; Jesus as, 196, 223

Metals and metallurgy: working with, 12; in ancient China, 110

Metaphysics, in China, 330

Metaphysics (Aristotle), 142

Mexico, 441; Maya and, 445; Cortés in, 449; Aztecs in, 449–456, 450 (map); European conquest of, 522–523; Spanish trade with, 565. See also Latin America; Mesoamerica; Spanish America

Mexico City, 455; corn in, 442. See also Tenochtitlán

Meyer, Eduard, 56

Michael IV (emperor), 241

Michael Romanov (Russia), 578

Michelangelo, 472; Sistine Chapel painting by, 466 (illus.), 472, 473. See also Renaissance

Middle Ages: Muslim education in, 272–276; Islamic, European, and Chinese education in, 274; Europe in early and central, 344–392; Crusades during, 368–372; origins of modern state in, 372–381; anti-Semitism in, 379–380; economic revival in, 380–387; commercial revolution in, 386–387; central, 395; social mobility in, 395; universities during, 395–397; cathedral architecture during, 398–399; troubador poetry in, 399–400; life in Christian Europe during, 400–418; health care in, 406–409; popular religion in, 409–411; nobility in, 411–415; monasteries in, 415–418; royal authority asserted during, 418; Black Death during, 418–422; crises of later, 418–432; Hundred Years' War during, 422–427; religious

crisis in, 427–428; marriage and parish in, 428–430; peasant revolts in, 430–432; French noblewomen in, 438–439 and illus.; and use of term, 470. See also Christianity

Middle class: in Kingdom of Ghana, 295; commercial revolution and, 386–387; in France, 482; lack of, in Spain, 565. See also Commercial class

Middle East: use of term, 14; ancient Israel in, 40–48; Minoan trade with, 120; Mongol government in, 262–263; First Crusade in, 369–370. See also Arabs; Near East; Muslim society; Palestine

Midwives, 267 (illus.), 407–408. See also Childbirth; Gynecology; Women

Mi Fei, 331

Migration(s): Mesopotamian, 27; of Hyksos, 27–28; in East, 39; of Medes and Persians, 53–55; Germanic, 228–231, 229 (map); of Bedouins, 247; Viking invasions as, 356. See also Expansion; Immigrants and immigration; Movement

Mije-speaking peoples, 445

Milan, Italy, 381; Renaissance and, 467; oligarchy in, 468; power of, 468

Military: in Sparta, 127; service in ancient Rome, 199; Islamic organization of, 254–255; Islamic towns established by, 256; slaves of Muslim soldiers, 265–266; in Kingdom of Ghana, 296; Charlemagne and, 347–349; of Martel, Charles, 354; in feudal society, 354–355; Crusades and, 368; nobility and, 411; Aztec, 449; under Frederick William I, 573 (illus.), 573–574. See also Armed forces; Infantry; Wars and warfare

Military districts, in Byzantine Empire, 237

Military government, in England, 584–585

Minamoto clan, 338

Minaret, in India, 320. See also Architecture

Minerals: in ancient Egypt, 24; in Persian Empire, 54; in Hellenistic Greece, 158

Ming Dynasty (China), 333; spice trade and, 520

Mining, African trade and, 290–291. See also Minerals

Ministerials, knights as, 411

Minoans, 117–120; navy of, 119 (illus.); Mycenaean contact with, 120

Minorca, surrender to England, 565

Misogyny, 223

Missing link, 6

Missionaries, 218–220; Indian, 317; Chinese Buddhist, 322; contact with

China and Japan, 529–531. See also Christianity; Roman Catholic Church

Moche civilization, 457 and illus.

Mohammed II (Ottoman Turk), 517; cannon of, 518

Mohenjo-daro, 67 (illus.), 67–70, 68 (illus.); decline of, 69–70

Molesmes, abbey of, 363

Molière, 563 and illus.

Moluccan islands, Portuguese trade with, 517

Mombasa, 302, 303

Monarchies, 123; in Hellenistic Greece, 151–152, 154; in Germany, 366; absolute, 557; in 17th century Europe, 557; in England, 582–586; restoration in England, 585–586. See also Absolutism

Monasteries: in Gaul, 218; in Eastern empire, 236; in Japan, 337; women in double, 350–351; plan for, 351 (illus.); civilization and, 351–352; at Cluny, 362; revival of, 362–364; Cîteaux, 363–364; schools in, 395; dissolution of English, 501. See also Monasticism

Monasticism, 225–228, 414–418; in western Europe, 225–226; Benedictine, 227–228; in East, 236; in China, 322; convents and, 415. See also Monasteries

Monastic manors, 417–418

Money, wergeld as, 232

Money economy, serfs and, 402

Moneylending: Crusades and, 369; in Middle Ages, 382. See also Usury Mongol

Mongolia and Mongolians: Toba people, 112; migration of Huns and, 228

Mongolian Plateau, 91

Mongols: Empire of, 262; attack on Russia, 262; Jenghiz Khan and, 262; Kublai Khan and, 262; assault on Islamic world, 262–263; attacks on India, 319; in China, 321; trade and, 331–332; conquest of China by, 331–333; impact on China, 331–333; defeat by Chinese, 333; Hong Wu attack on, 333; attack on Japan, 339; conquest of Russia by, 574–575

Monks, 350–351, 416–417; Buddhist, 79, 322; as martyrs, 225; duties of, 236. See also Christianity; Monasteries; Monasticism

Monogamy, in ancient Israel, 46

Monophysic doctrine, 300

Monotheism, 215; in ancient Egypt, 29; Islam and, 248, 249–250. See also Jews and Judaism

Montaigne, Michel de, 531, 546–547

Monte Albán, 447